HAVE YOU THOUGHT ABOUT
Customizing THIS BOOK?

The Prentice Hall Just-In-Time Program In Decision Science

You can combine chapters from this book with chapters from any of the Prentice Hall titles listed on the following page to create a text tailored to your specific course needs. You can add your own material or cases from our extensive case collection. By taking a few minutes to look at what is sitting on your bookshelf and the content available on our Web site, you can create your ideal textbook.

The Just-In-Time program offers:

➡ **Quality of Material to Choose From**—In addition to the books listed, you also have the option to include any of the cases from Prentice Hall Custom Business Resources, which gives you access to cases (and teaching notes where available) from Darden, Harvard, Ivey, NACRA, and Thunderbird. Most cases can be viewed online at our Web site.

➡ **Flexibility**—Choose only that material you want, either from one title or several titles (plus cases) and sequence it in whatever way you wish.

➡ **Instructional Support**—You have access to the text-specific CD-ROM that accompanies the traditional textbook and desk copies of your JIT book.

➡ **Outside Materials**—There is also the option to include up to 20% of the text from materials outside of Prentice Hall Custom Business Resources.

➡ **Cost Savings**—Students pay only for material you choose. The base price is $6.00, plus $2.00 for case material, plus $.09 per page. The text can be shrink-wrapped with other Pearson textbooks for a 10% discount. Outside material is priced at $.10 per page plus permission fees.

➡ **Quality of Finished Product**—Custom cover and title page—including your name, school, department, course title, and section number. Paperback, perfect bound, black-and-white printed text. Customized table of contents. Sequential pagination throughout the text.

Visit our Web site at www.prenhall.com/custombusiness and create your custom text

on our bookbuildsite or download order forms online.

THE PRENTICE HALL
JUST-IN-TIME PROGRAM

You can customize your textbook with chapters from any of the following Prentice Hall titles:*

Business Statistics

⟹ Berenson/Levine/Krehbiel, BASIC BUSINESS STATISTICS, 10/e
⟹ Groebner/Shannon/Fry/Smith, BUSINESS STATISTICS: A DECISION-MAKING APPROACH, 7/e
⟹ Levine/Stephan/Krehbiel/Berenson, STATISTICS FOR MANAGERS USING MICROSOFT EXCEL, 5/e
⟹ Levine/Krehbiel/Berenson, BUSINESS STATISTICS: A FIRST COURSE, 4/e
⟹ Newbold/Carlson/Thorne, STATISTICS FOR BUSINESS AND ECONOMICS, 5/e
⟹ Groebner/Shannon/Fry/Smith, A COURSE IN BUSINESS STATISTICS, 4/e

Operations Management

⟹ Anupindi/Chopra/Deshmukh/Van Mieghem/Zemel, MANAGING BUSINESS PROCESS FLOWS, 2/e
⟹ Bozarth/Handfield, INTRODUCTION TO OPERATIONS AND SUPPLY CHAIN MANAGEMENT
⟹ Chopra/Meindl, SUPPLY CHAIN MANAGEMENT, 2e
⟹ Foster, MANAGING QUALITY, 2/e
⟹ Handfield/Nichols, Jr., SUPPLY CHAIN MANAGEMENT
⟹ Heineke/Meile, GAMES AND EXERCISES FOR OPERATIONS MANAGEMENT
⟹ Heizer/Render, OPERATIONS MANAGEMENT, 9/e
⟹ Heizer/Render, PRINCIPLES OF OPERATIONS MANAGEMENT, 7/e
⟹ Krajewski/Ritzman/Malhotra, OPERATIONS MANAGEMENT, 8/e
⟹ Latona/Nathan, CASES AND READINGS IN PRODUCTION AND OPERATIONS MANAGEMENT
⟹ Ritzman/Krajewski, FOUNDATIONS OF OPERATIONS MANAGEMENT
⟹ Schmenner, PLANT AND SERVICE TOURS IN OPERATIONS MANAGEMENT, 5/e

Management Science/Spreadsheet Modeling

⟹ Balakrishnan/Render/Stair, MANAGERIAL DECISION MODELING WITH SPREADSHEETS, 2/e
⟹ Eppen/Gould/Schmidt/Moore/Weatherford, INTRODUCTORY MANAGEMENT SCIENCE, 5/e
⟹ Render/Stair/Hanna, QUANTITATIVE ANALYSIS FOR MANAGEMENT, 9/e
⟹ Render/Greenberg/Stair, CASES AND READINGS IN MANAGEMENT SCIENCE, 2e
⟹ Taylor, INTRODUCTION TO MANAGEMENT SCIENCE, 9/e

For more information, or to speak to a customer service representative, contact us at 1-800-777-6872.

www.prenhall.com/custombusiness

* Selection of titles on the JIT program is subject to change.

OPERATIONS MANAGEMENT

Ninth Edition

Jay Heizer

Jesse H. Jones Professor of Business Administration
Texas Lutheran University

Barry Render

Charles Harwood Professor of Operations Management
Crummer Graduate School of Business
Rollins College

PEARSON

Prentice
Hall

Upper Saddle River, New Jersey 07458

Library of Congress Cataloging-in-Publication Data
Heizer, Jay H.
    Operations management / Jay Heizer, Barry Render.—9th ed.
      p. cm.
    Includes bibliographical references and index.
    ISBN-13: 978-0-13-234271-1
    ISBN-10: 0-13-234271-5
1. Production management.   I. Render, Barry. II. Title.
    TS155.H3726 2006
    658.5—dc22

                                                                    2007031675

AVP/Editor in Chief: Eric Svendsen
AVP/Executive Editor: Mark Pfaltzgraff
Product Development Manager: Ashley Santora
Project Manager: Susan Abraham
Editorial Assistant: Vanessa Bain
Media Project Manager: Ashley Lulling
Marketing Manager: Anne Howard
Marketing Assistant: Susan Osterlitz
Senior Managing Editor: Judy Leale
Project Manager, Production: Suzanne Grappi
Permissions Project Manager: Charles Morris
Operations Specialist: Michelle Klein
Art Director: Steven Frim
Interior Design: Christy Mahon
Cover Design: Steven Frim
Cover Illustration/Photo:
Illustration (Interior): Precision Graphics
Director, Image Resource Center: Melinda Patelli
Manager, Rights and Permissions: Zina Arabia
Manager, Visual Research: Beth Brenzel
Manager, Cover Visual Research & Permissions: Karen Sanatar
Image Permission Coordinator: Annette Linder
Composition: GGS Book Services
Full-Service Project Management: GGS Book Services
Printer/Binder: RR Donnelley/Willard
Typeface: 10/12 Times

Credits and acknowledgments borrowed from other sources and reproduced, with permission, in this textbook appear on appropriate page within text.

Microsoft® and Windows® are registered trademarks of the Microsoft Corporation in the U.S.A. and other countries. Screen shots and icons reprinted with permission from the Microsoft Corporation. This book is not sponsored or endorsed by or affiliated with the Microsoft Corporation.

Pearson Education LTD.
Pearson Education Singapore, Pte. Ltd
Pearson Education, Canada, Ltd
Pearson Education–Japan

Pearson Education Australia PTY, Limited
Pearson Education North Asia Ltd
Pearson Educación de Mexico, S.A. de C.V.
Pearson Education Malaysia, Pte. Ltd

10 9 8 7 6 5 4 3 2 1
ISBN-13: 978-0-13-234271-1
ISBN-10: 0-13-234271-5

Jay Heizer holds the Jesse H. Jones Chair of Business Administration at Texas Lutheran University in Seguin, Texas. He received his B.B.A. and M.B.A. from the University of North Texas and his Ph.D. in Management and Statistics from Arizona State University (1969). He was previously a member of the faculty at the University of Memphis, the University of Oklahoma, Virginia Commonwealth University, and the University of Richmond. He has also held visiting positions at Boston University, George Mason University, the Czech Management Center, and the Otto-Von-Guericka University Magdeburg.

Dr. Heizer's industrial experience is extensive. He learned the practical side of operations management as a machinist apprentice at Foringer and Company, production planner for Westinghouse Airbrake, and at General Dynamics, where he worked in engineering administration. Additionally, he has been actively involved in consulting in the OM and MIS areas for a variety of organizations including Philip Morris, Firestone, Dixie Container Corporation, Columbia Industries, and Tenneco. He holds the CPIM certification from APICS—the Association for Operations Management.

Professor Heizer has co-authored five books and has published over thirty articles on a variety of management topics. His papers have appeared in the *Academy of Management Journal, Journal of Purchasing, Personnel Psychology, Production & Inventory Control Management, APICS-The Performance Advantage, Journal of Management History, IIE Solutions* and *Engineering Management*, among others. He has taught operations management courses in undergraduate, graduate, and executive programs.

Barry Render holds the Charles Harwood Professorship in Operations Management at the Crummer Graduate School of Business at Rollins College, in Winter Park, Florida. He received his B.S. in Mathematics and Physics at Roosevelt University, and his M.S. in Operations Research and Ph.D. in Quantitative Analysis at the University of Cincinnati. He previously taught at George Washington University, University of New Orleans, Boston University, and George Mason University, where he held the Mason Foundation Professorship in Decision Sciences and was Chair of the Decision Science Department. Dr. Render has also worked in the aerospace industry for General Electric, McDonnell Douglas, and NASA.

Professor Render has co-authored ten textbooks with Prentice Hall, including *Managerial Decision Modeling with Spreadsheets, Quantitative Analysis for Management, Service Management, Introduction to Management Science*, and *Cases and Readings in Management Science. Quantitative Analysis for Management* is now in its 10th edition and is a leading text in that discipline in the U.S. and globally. His more than one hundred articles on a variety of management topics have appeared in *Decision Sciences, Production and Operations Management, Interfaces, Information and Management, Journal of Management Information Systems, Socio-Economic Planning Sciences, IIE Solutions*, and *Operations Management Review*, among others.

Dr. Render has also been honored as an AACSB Fellow and was twice named as a Senior Fullbright Scholar. He was vice-president of the Decision Science Institute Southwest Region and served as Software Review Editor for *Decision Line* for 6 years. He has also served as Editor of the *New York Times* Operations Management special issues from 1996 to 2001. From 1984 to 1993, Dr. Render was President of Management Service Associates of Virginia, Inc., whose technology clients included FBI, U.S. Navy, Fairfax County, Virginia, and C&P Telephone.

He teaches operations management courses in Rollins College's MBA and Executive MBA programs. He has received that school's Welsh Award as Professor of the Year, and was selected by Roosevelt University as the 1996 recipient of the St. Claire Drake Award for Outstanding Scholarship. In 2005, Dr. Render received the Rollins MBA Student Award for Best Overall Course.

BRIEF CONTENTS

CONTENTS

PART TWO
Designing Operations 155

CD-ROM Tutorials

Darden Restaurants has a rich history, growing from one Red Lobster restaurant in 1968 to nearly 1,400 Red Lobster, Olive Garden, Bahama Breeze, and Seasons 52 restaurants serving 325 million guests annually. Today, we are a multibrand restaurant growth company with more than 155,000 employees, bound together by common operating practices and a unifying culture. In fact, we believe that building and maintaining a strong culture is the single most important reason we've enjoyed nearly 40 years of success as a company.

While a lot of things go into it, we believe there are three elements in particular that have made and continue to make the culture at Darden a strong, winning one. First, as an organization, we have a clear and motivating core purpose—to make a positive difference in the lives of others—which we describe as our commitment to "nourishing and delighting everyone we serve."

As a restaurant company, we certainly want to nourish people in the literal sense with delicious, high-quality meals that sustain them. But we also want to nourish the *spirits* of our guests—to delight them with service and ambiance that enables them to re-energize or to connect with family and friends over a great meal. We want to nourish and delight our employees by contributing to their well-being and to their personal and professional growth. And we want to nourish and delight our partners, which include our suppliers, the communities where we live and work, and our investors.

The second key feature of our culture, our commitment to diversity, is critical to achieving our core purpose. We are convinced that we learn and grow together as people and as a business by bringing meaningful differences to the table.

The third key element of our culture is making sure that as an organization, we are constantly dreaming big dreams. We consistently envision and communicate a fundamentally new reality. By providing ourselves with a compelling vision, we are inspired to do better with the basics of our jobs, so that we and the organization are steadily improving.

So how does all of this relate to this textbook and your study of operations management? As our founding chairman, Joe Lee, once stated, "Operations is our strategy." We are a world leader in restaurant operations and international supply chains. Accordingly, we are pleased to be a contributor to the leading textbook in operations. I believe that the Darden video case studies provide valuable business insight. However, I hope that by defining our culture, I have given you the context to fully understand what we collectively aspire to do. Our mission is to be a truly great and long-lasting company, the best in casual dining now and for generations.

CLARENCE OTIS, JR.
Chairman and CEO
Darden Restaurants Inc.

Welcome to your operations management (OM) course. In this book, we present a state-of-the-art view of the activities of the operations function. Operations is an exciting area of management that has a profound effect on the productivity of both manufacturing and services. Indeed, few activities have as much impact on the quality of our lives. The goal of this text is to present a broad introduction to the field of operations in a realistic, practical manner. Operations management includes a blend of topics from accounting, industrial engineering, management, management science, and statistics. Even if you are not planning on a career in the operations area, you will likely be working with people who are. Therefore, having a solid understanding of the role of operations in an organization is of substantial benefit to you. This book will also help you understand how OM affects society and your life. Certainly, you will better understand what goes on behind the scenes when you buy a meal at an Olive Garden, a Red Lobster, or a Hard Rock Cafe, place an order through Amazon.com, buy a customized Dell computer over the Internet, or enter Arnold Palmer Hospital for medical care.

Although many of our readers are not OM majors, we know that marketing, finance, accounting, and MIS students will find the material both interesting and useful as we develop a fundamental working knowledge of the operation side of the firm. Over a half-million readers of our earlier editions seem to have endorsed this premise.

THREE VERSIONS ARE AVAILABLE

This text is available in the three versions: *Operations Management*, Ninth Edition, which is hardcover, *Principles of Operations Management*, Seventh Edition, a paperback, and *Operations Management*, Flexible Edition, a package of a paperback text and a unique Student Lecture Guide. All three books include the identical core chapters 1–17. However, *Operations Management*, Ninth Edition and Flexible Edition also include six quantitative modules in Part IV.

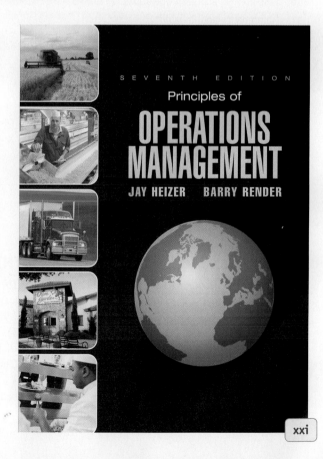

OPERATIONS MANAGEMENT, NINTH EDITION
ISBN: 0-13-234271-5

PART I INTRODUCTION

1. Operations and Productivity
2. Operations Strategy in a Global Environment
3. Project Management
4. Forecasting

PART II DESIGNING OPERATIONS

5. Design of Goods and Services
6. Managing Quality
S6. Statistical Process Control
7. Process Strategy
S7. Capacity Planning
8. Location Strategies
9. Layout Strategies
10. Human Resources and Job Design
S10. Work Measurement

PART III MANAGING OPERATIONS

11. Supply Chain Management
S11. Outsourcing as a Supply Chain Strategy
12. Inventory Management
13. Aggregate Planning
14. Material Requirements Planning (MRP) and ERP
15. Short-Term Scheduling
16. Just-in-Time and Lean Operations
17. Maintenance and Reliability

PART IV QUANTITATIVE MODULES

A. Decision-Making Tools
B. Linear Programming
C. Transportation Models
D. Waiting-Line Models
E. Learning Curves
F. Simulation

PRINCIPLES OF OPERATIONS MANAGEMENT, SEVENTH EDITION
ISBN: 0-13-234328-2

PART I INTRODUCTION

1. Operations and Productivity
2. Operations Strategy in a Global Environment
3. Project Management
4. Forecasting

PART II DESIGNING OPERATIONS

5. Design of Goods and Services
6. Managing Quality
S6. Statistical Process Control
7. Process Strategy
S7. Capacity Planning
8. Location Strategies
9. Layout Strategies
10. Human Resources and Job Design
S10. Work Measurement

PART III MANAGING OPERATIONS

11. Supply Chain Management
S11. Outsourcing as a Supply Chain Strategy
12. Inventory Management
13. Aggregate Planning
14. Material Requirements Planning (MRP) and ERP
15. Short-Term Scheduling
16. Just-in-Time and Lean Operations
17. Maintenance and Reliability

NEW FEATURES IN THIS EDITION

Service Integration with Video Case Studies on Darden Restaurant's Olive Garden and Red Lobster Chains In this edition, we take you behind the scenes at Darden Restaurants, with four new video case studies, photos, examples, problems, and a Global Company Profile (Chapter 11). This multi-billion-dollar restaurant chain has opened its doors so we could examine its use of statistical quality control (Supplement 6), location selection (Chapter 8), supply chains (Chapter 11), and global outsourcing (Supplement 11) in a series of 10- to 14-minute videos.

Our prior editions focused on Arnold Palmer Hospital, Hard Rock Cafe, Wheeled Coach Ambulances, and Regal Marine. All of these videos and cases appear in this edition, along with the new ones from Darden.

Darden's Global Supply Chains

Video Case

Darden Restaurants (subject of the *Global Company Profile* at the beginning of this chapter), owner of popular brands such as Olive Garden and Red Lobster, requires unique supply chains to serve more than 300 million meals annually. Darden's strategy is operations excellence, and Senior VP Jim Lawrence's task is to ensure competitive advantage via Darden's supply chains. For a firm with purchases exceeding $1.5 billion, managing the supply chains is a complex and challenging task.

Darden, like other casual dining restaurants, has unique supply chains that reflect its menu options. Darden's supply chains are rather shallow, often having just one tier of suppliers. But it has four distinct supply chains.

First, "smallware" is a restaurant industry term for items such as linens, dishes, tableware and kitchenware, and silverware. These are purchased, with Darden taking title as they are received at the Darden Direct Distribution (DDD) warehouse in Orlando, Florida. From this single warehouse, smallware items are shipped via common carrier (trucking companies) to Olive Garden, Red Lobster, Bahama Breeze, and Seasons 52 restaurants.

Second, frozen, dry, and canned food products are handled economically by Darden's 11 distribution centers in North America, which are managed by major U.S. food distributors, such as MBM, Maines, and Sygma. This is Darden's second supply line.

Third, the fresh food supply chain (not frozen and not canned), where life is measured in days, includes dairy products, produce, and meat. This supply chain is B2B, where restaurant managers directly place orders with a preselected group of independent suppliers.

Fourth, Darden's worldwide seafood supply chain is the final link. Here Darden has developed independent suppliers of salmon, shrimp, tilapia, scallops, and other fresh fish that are source inspected by Darden's overseas representatives to ensure quality. These fresh products are flown to the U.S. and shipped to 16 distributors, with 22 locations, for quick delivery to the restaurants. With suppliers in 35 countries, Darden must be on the cutting edge when it comes to collaboration, partnering, communication, and food safety. It does this with heavy travel schedules for purchasing and quality control personnel, native-speaking employees onsite, and aggressive communication. Communication is a critical element; Darden tries to develop as much forecasting transparency as possible. "Point of sale (POS) terminals," says Lawrence, "feed actual sales every night to suppliers."

Discussion Questions*

1. What are the advantages of each of Darden's four supply chains?
2. What are the complications of having four supply chains?
3. Where would you expect ownership/title to change in each of Darden's four supply chains?
4. How do Darden's four supply chains compare with those of other firms, such as Dell or an automobile manufacturer? Why do the differences exist, and how are they addressed?

*You may wish to view this video on your DVD before answering these questions.

Source: Written by Professors Barry Render (Rollins College), Jay Heizer (Texas Lutheran University), and Beverly Amer (Northern Arizona University).

A New Way to Teach OM Problem Solving

Without question, the boxed quantitative examples throughout the book are critical to the students learnin g process. These examples now apply a new technique to bring the topic to life and help students prepare for homework and exams. We think that our expanded pedagogical approach that walks the reader through each example is a huge improvement in this edition. As you can see in the sample below, we (1) state the problem; (2) describe the approach to take in solving it; (3) develop the complete and detailed solution; (4) provide insight as to why this solution has relevance; (5) give a learning exercise with the answer—so the reader can make a change in the problem and resolve it just to make sure the technique is clear; and (6) note which homework problems relate to this example.

EXAMPLE 8

A production order quantity model

Nathan Manufacturing, Inc., makes and sells specialty hubcaps for the retail automobile aftermarket. Nathan's forecast for its wire-wheel hubcap is 1,000 units next year, with an average daily demand of 4 units. However, the production process is most efficient at 8 units per day. So the company produces 8 per day but uses only 4 per day. The company wants to solve for the optimum number of units per order. (*Note:* This plant schedules production of this hubcap only as needed, during the 250 days per year the shop operates.)

Approach: Gather the cost data and apply Equation (12-7):

$$\text{Annual demand} = D = 1{,}000 \text{ units}$$
$$\text{Setup costs} = S = \$10$$
$$\text{Holding cost} = H = \$0.50 \text{ per unit per year}$$
$$\text{Daily production rate} = p = 8 \text{ units daily}$$
$$\text{Daily demand rate} = d = 4 \text{ units daily}$$

Solution:

$$Q_p^* = \sqrt{\frac{2DS}{H[1-(d/p)]}}$$

$$Q_p^* = \sqrt{\frac{2(1{,}000)(10)}{0.50[1-(4/8)]}}$$

$$= \sqrt{\frac{20{,}000}{0.50(1/2)}} = \sqrt{80{,}000}$$

$$= 282.8 \text{ hubcaps, or } 283 \text{ hubcaps}$$

Insight: The difference between the production order quantity model and the basic EOQ model is the annual holding cost, which is reduced in the production order quantity model.

Learning exercise: If Nathan can increase its daily production rate from 8 to 10, how does Q_p^* change? [Answer: $Q_p^* = 258$.]

Related problems: 12.16, 12.17, 12.18, 12.37

Expanded Material on Supply Chain Management Our treatment of this timely topic has been expanded. (Details are listed under Chapter 11 in the next section.) We also offer the first major discussion in any OM text of outsourcing as a supply chain strategy as our new Supplement 11.

Self-Tests At the end of each chapter, we have added self-tests to help students review the material they have just learned. Answers appear in Appendix IV.

Self-Test

- *Before taking the self-test*, refer to the learning objectives listed at the beginning of the chapter and the key terms listed at the end of the chapter.
- *Use the key at the back of the text to **correct** your answers.*
- *Restudy pages that correspond to any questions you answered incorrectly or material you feel uncertain about.*

1. In this chapter, *quality* is defined as:
  a) the degree of excellence at an acceptable price and the control of variability at an acceptable cost
  b) how well a product fits patterns of consumer preferences
  c) the totality or features and characteristics of a product or service that bears on its ability to satisfy stated or implied needs
  d) even though it cannot be defined, you know what it is

2. 100% inspection:
  a) will always catch all of the defective parts
  b) means that only good parts will be shipped to a customer
  c) is practical and generally a good idea
  d) means that every part is checked to see whether or not it is defective

3. The seven basic concepts of TQM are _____, _____, _____, _____, _____, _____, and _____.

4. ISO 14000 is an EC standard to address _____.

5. The seven tools of total quality management are _____, _____, _____, _____, _____, _____, and _____.

6. Cause-and-effect diagrams are also known as:
  a) quality loss charts
  b) target specification graphs
  c) fish-bone charts
  d) Ishikawa diagrams
  e) a and b
  f) c and d

7. The Taguchi method includes all except which of the following major concepts:
  a) employee involvement
  b) remove the effects of adverse conditions
  c) quality loss function
  d) target specifications

8. Quality cannot be _____ into a product.

Overlays Help Teach Critical Path Method and House of Quality To help students follow the multi-step processes of finding a project's critical path (Chapter 3) or building a house of quality (Chapter 5), we have created innovative colorful clear overlays to expand and bring these topics to life.

Virtual Office Hours for All Solved Problems in the Text In the back of each book, students will find both a CD-ROM and a DVD. The CD-ROM contains our helpful homework software, Excel OM and POM for Windows, self-study quizzes, practice problems, and more. The DVD, a new feature, includes video cases, video clips, and an exciting new tool to help students solve problems. We call the new tool *Virtual Office Hours*. This feature opens the authors' office doors to students 24 hours a day. The authors walk the students through every one of the Solved Problems in the text. Detailed explanations as to how to tackle each Solved Problem take from 4 minutes to 20 minutes, depending on complexity. Using our 70 years of teaching experience, we are able to explain, in simple terms, why each problem is important and what steps to follow to reach the answer.

CHAPTER-BY-CHAPTER CHANGES

To highlight the extent of the revision from our previous edition, here are a few of the changes, on a chapter-by-chapter basis. We have added new material on the subject of supply chain management, with a major revision of Chapter 11, "Supply Chain Management" and the addition of Supplement 11, "Outsourcing as a Supply Chain Strategy." A new Self-Test has been added in every chapter. Examples (which are boxed to set them off from text) now all follow a new pedagogical style, described earlier in the Preface.

Chapter 1, "Operations and Productivity" New figures on the growth of services, a new *OM in Action* box on productivity at Starbucks, and three new homework problems have been added.

Chapter 2, "Operations Strategy in a Global Environment" The chapter contains revised material on global trade, a new *OM in Action* box on banking giant Wachovia, and a new section on core competencies.

Chapter 3, "Project Management" The chapter includes an updated *Global Company Profile* featuring Bechtel's work in Iraq, a new *OM in Action* box on rebuilding the Pentagon after 9/11, a new illustration of critical path analysis using transparency overlays, and three new homework problems.

Chapter 4, "Forecasting" We begin this chapter with a new *Global Company Profile* featuring forecasting at Disney World, followed by new *OM in Action* boxes on Olive Garden/Red Lobster and FedEx. We have also added eight new homework problems.

Chapter 5, "Design of Goods and Services" A striking change in this chapter is the use of transparency overlays to build a house of quality. We have also added updated material on new product development and time-based competition, a new *OM in Action* box, and two new homework problems.

Chapter 6, "Managing Quality" A new *OM in Action* box on quality issues at Mercedes, new material on Six Sigma, benchmarking, and process improvement with flowcharts (Example 2), plus three new homework problems appear in this chapter.

Supplement 6, "Statistical Process Control" We have added a new *OM in Action* box on Frito-Lay's use of SPC, material on Darden's SPC charts, five new homework problems, and a new video case study, "Farm to Fork—Quality at Darden Restaurants."

Chapter 7, "Process Strategy" We have enhanced material on process selection, updated and expanded the section on mass customization, added a new example on value stream mapping, expanded the RFID discussion, and added two new homework problems.

Supplement 7, "Capacity Planning" We have added new material on build-for-change as well as two new complementary *OM in Action* boxes, "Too Much Capacity at GM and Ford" and "Too Little Capacity at Dalrymple Bay." The chapter also contains new material on capacity management, a new solved problem, three new homework problems, and a revision of the video case study on Arnold Palmer Hospital.

Chapter 8, "Location Strategies" The material on geographic information systems has been revised and expanded, there are three new homework problems, and we have added a new video case study, "Locating the Next Red Lobster Restaurant."

Chapter 9, "Layout Strategies" The *Global Company Profile* on McDonald's has been completely rewritten, we have expanded coverage of ASRS and cross-docking, revised coverage of process layout in Example 1 and Solved Problem 9.1, revised the *OM in Action* box on auto disassembly lines, added six new homework problems, and revised the video case study on Arnold Palmer Hospital.

Chapter 10, "Human Resources and Job Design" We begin the chapter with an exciting new Global Company Profile featuring Rusty Wallace's NASCAR racing team. A new *OM in Action* box on traffic jams in the operating room, a new solved problem tied to the Rusty Wallace team is in place, and two new homework problems are included in the changes to the chapter.

Chapter 11, "Supply Chain Management" In keeping with the growing importance of supply chains as an OM topic, we have rewritten and expanded this chapter in many ways. For example, we begin with a new *Global Company Profile* featuring Darden Restaurants and close with a new video case study called "Darden's Global Supply Chains." There is a major new section on e-procurement, expanded coverage of logistics, and a new section called "Measuring Supply Chain Performance," which includes three example boxes that use actual data from Home Depot, Pepsi, and Coke. We have also added a new solved problem and four homework problems, and we have rewritten the "Dell's Value Chain" case study.

Supplement 11, "Outsourcing as a Supply Chain Strategy" This all-new supplement is a first for OM texts and reflects the importance of outsourcing in our global economy. We define several terms that relate to outsourcing, discuss strategic planning and core competencies, and look at trends, risks, and ethical issues. Quantitative techniques to help make rational outsourcing decisions and audits/metrics for evaluating performance are both treated. Three *OM in Action* boxes, nine homework problems, a case study dealing with India's Tata Consultancy, and the video case study "Outsourcing Offshore at Darden" complete the supplement.

Chapter 12, "Inventory Management" We have strengthened the quantitative pedagogy in this chapter with three additional solved problems and seven new homework problems.

Chapter 13, "Aggregate Planning" There is expanded coverage of planning tasks/responsibilities, a new *OM in Action* box, "Building the Plan at Snapper," a new view of how the aggregate plan relates to other OM topics, more material on yield management, and an additional homework problem.

Chapter 14, "Material Requirements Planning and ERP" We have added new material and an example of order splitting, as well as two new homework problems.

Chapter 15, "Short-Term Scheduling" We have added more coverage of service scheduling, including a new *OM in Action* box on scheduling call center employees, added six new homework problems, and added a new case study, "Old Oregon Wood Store."

Chapter 16, "JIT and Lean Operations" This new chapter title reflects our expanded view of lean operations and Toyota Production System (TPS). There is a new *Global Company Profile* on Toyota Motor Corp.'s use of JIT and TPS in San Antonio, more coverage of variability, throughput, and JIT partnerships, and new sections on TPS and lean operations. A new *OM in Action* box describes how Louis Vuitton is going lean.

Chapter 17, "Maintenance and Reliability" We have added a new *OM in Action* box on Flight 548's deadly crash and two new homework problems.

Module A, "Decision-Making Tools" In this module, we have revised our treatment of EVPI, added a solved problem on that topic, and added five new homework problems.

Module B, "Linear Programming" The company example we follow through this chapter has new products: x-pods and BlueBerrys, and we have added five new homework problems.

Module C, "Transportation Models" This module has three new homework problems.

Module D, "Waiting-Line Models" We have added a new *OM in Action* box on emergency room management to the module, as well as five new homework problems.

Module E, "Learning Curves" There are two new homework problems in this module.

Module F, "Simulation" There are two new homework problems for this edition.

FREE STUDENT CD-ROM AND DVD WITH EVERY NEW TEXT

Packaged free with every new copy of the text are a student CD-ROM and a student DVD that contain exciting resources to liven up the course and help students learn the content material.

- **Virtual Office Hours** Professors Heizer and Render appear on the DVD, walking students through each of the chapter Solved Problems.

- **PowerPoint lecture notes** Based on an extensive set of over 1,000 newly revamped PowerPoint slides, these lecture notes provide reinforcement to the main points of each chapter and allow students to review chapter material. A link to the text's Companion Web site allows students to access the PowerPoint slides by chapter.

- **Twenty-six exciting video cases** These video cases feature real companies (Darden Restaurants, Regal Marine, Hard Rock Cafe, Ritz Carlton, Wheeled Coach, and Arnold Palmer Hospital) and allow students to watch short video clips, read about the key topics, answer questions, and then e-mail their answers to their instructors. These case studies can also be assigned without using class time to show the videos. Each of these was developed and written by the text authors to specifically supplement the book's content (on the DVD).

- **DVD video clips** Another expanded feature on the student CD-ROM is thirty-four 1- to 2-minute videos, which appear throughout the book and are noted in the margins. These video clips illustrate chapter-related topics with videos at Harley-Davidson, Ritz Carlton, Hard Rock Cafe, Olive Garden, and other firms.

- **Active models** The 28 active models appear in files on the student CD-ROM. Samples of the models appear in most text chapters.

- **Practice problems** These problems provide problem-solving experience. They supplement the examples and solved problems found in each chapter and are located on the CD-ROM.

- **Self-study quizzes** For each chapter, a link is provided to our text's companion Web site, where these quizzes allow students to test their understanding of each topic. Plant tours can also be accessed through this link.

- **POM for Windows software** POM for Windows is a powerful tool for easily solving OM problems. Its 24 modules can be used to solve most of the homework problems in the text (CD-ROM).

- **Problem-solving software** Excel OM is our exclusive user-friendly Excel add-in. Excel OM automatically creates worksheets to model and solve problems. Users select a topic from the pull-down menu, fill in the data, and then Excel will display and graph (where appropriate) the results. This software is great for student homework, what-if analysis, or classroom demonstrations (CD-ROM). This edition includes a new version of Excel OM that's compatible with Microsoft Excel 2007 as well as earlier versions of Excel (CD-ROM).

- **Excel OM data files** Examples in the text that can be solved with Excel OM appear on data files on the CD-ROM. They are identified by an icon in the margin of the text.

- **Tutorial chapters** *Statistical Tools for Managers, Acceptance Sampling, The Simplex Method of Linear Programming, The MODI and VAM Methods of Solving Transportation Problems,* and *Vehicle Routing and Scheduling* are provided as additional material on the CD-ROM.

- **Microsoft Project** Microsoft Project, the most popular and powerful project management package, is now available on an additional (Value-Pack) student CD-ROM. This version is documented in Chapter 3 and is activated to work for 120 days.

INSTRUCTOR'S RESOURCES

Test Item File The test item file, extensively updated by Professor Charles Munson, contains a variety of true/false, multiple-choice, fill-in-the-blank, short-answer, problem- and topic-integrating questions for each chapter. The test item file can also be downloaded by instructors from Prentice Hall's companion Web site at **www.prenhall.com/heizer**.

New TestGen Software The print Test Banks are designed for use with the TestGen test-generating software. This computerized package allows instructors to custom design, save, and generate classroom tests. The test program permits instructors to edit, add, or delete questions from the test banks; edit existing graphics and create new graphics; analyze test results; and organize a database of tests and student results. This new software allows for greater flexibility and ease of use. It provides many options for organizing and displaying tests, along with a search and sort feature.

Instructor's Solutions Manual The Instructor's Solutions Manual, written by the authors (and extensively proofed by Professor Annie Puciloski), contains the answers to all of the discussion questions, ethical dilemmas, active models, and cases in the text, as well as worked-out solutions to all of the end-of-chapter problems, and internet cases. The Instructor's Solutions Manual can also be downloaded by instructors from Prentice Hall's companion Web site, at **www.prenhall.com/heizer**.

PowerPoint Presentations An extensive set of PowerPoint presentations, created by Professor Jeff Heyl of Lincoln University, is available for each chapter. Comprising well over 2,000 slides, Professor Heyl has created this set with excellent color and clarity. These slides can also be downloaded from Prentice Hall's companion Web site, at **www.prenhall.com/heizer**.

Instructor's Resource Manual The Instructor's Resource Manual, updated by Professor Pedro Reyes, contains many useful resources for the instructor—course outlines, video notes, Internet exercises, additional teaching resources, and faculty notes. It also provides a snapshot of the 2,000 PowerPoint lecture slides. The Instructor's Resource Manual can also be downloaded by instructors from Prentice Hall's companion Web site, at **www.prenhall.com/heizer**.

PH GradeAssist PH GradeAssist is a powerful online homework/exam system for instructors and students. Using PH GradeAssist, instructors can assign many of the homework problems from the text and/or problems/questions from the Test Item File for their students to take online at any time frame determined by the instructor. With many options for randomizing the sequence, timing, and scoring, PH GradeAssist makes giving and grading homework and exams easy. Many end-of-chapter problems have been converted by the authors to an algorithmic form, meaning that there are numerous versions of each problem with different data for each student. Solutions to each problem and its data set are provided, if instructors wish, to the students immediately after they complete the assignment. Grades are recorded by the program into the instructor's grade book.

Instructor's Resource CD-ROM The Instructor's Resource CD-ROM provides the electronic files for the entire Instructor's Solutions Manual (in Microsoft Word), PowerPoint presentations (in PowerPoint), Test Item File (in Microsoft Word), and computerized test bank (TestGen). These files can also be downloaded from the Instructor Catalog page.

Video Package Designed specifically for the Heizer/Render texts, the video package contains the following 36 videos:

- Operations Management at Hard Rock (Ch. 1)
- A Plant Tour of Winnebago Industries (Ch. 1)
- Regal Marine: Operations Strategy (Ch. 2)
- Hard Rock Cafe's Global Strategy (Ch. 2)
- Overview of OM and Strategy at Whirlpool (Ch. 2)
- Project Management at Arnold Palmer Hospital (Ch. 3)
- Managing Hard Rock's Rockfest (Ch. 3)
- Forecasting at Hard Rock Cafe (Ch. 4)
- Regal Marine: Product Design (Ch. 5)
- Product Design and Supplier Partnerships at Motorola (Ch. 5)
- The Culture of Quality at Arnold Palmer Hospital (Ch. 6)
- Ritz Carlton: Quality (Ch. 6)
- Competitiveness and Continuous Improvement at Xerox (Ch. 6)
- Service Quality and Design at Marriott (Ch. 6)
- SPC and Quality at Darden Restaurants (Supp. 6)
- Statistical Process Control at Kurt Manufacturing (Supp. 6)
- Wheeled Coach: Process Strategy (Ch. 7)
- Process Analysis at Arnold Palmer Hospital (Ch. 7)
- Process Strategy and Selection (Ch. 7)
- Technology and Manufacturing: Flexible Manufacturing Systems (Ch. 7)
- Capacity Planning at Arnold Palmer Hospital (Supp. 7)
- Locating the Next Red Lobster (Ch. 8)
- Where to Place Hard Rock's Cafe (Ch. 8)
- Wheeled Coach: Facility Layout (Ch. 9)
- Laying Out Arnold Palmer Hospital's New Facility (Ch. 9)
- Hard Rock Cafe's Human Resource Strategy (Ch. 10)
- Teams and Employee Involvement at Hewlett-Packard (Ch. 10)
- Darden's Global Supply Chains (Ch. 11)
- Regal Marine: Supply Chain Management (Ch. 11)
- Arnold Palmer Hospital's Supply Chain (Ch. 11)
- E-Commerce and Teva Sports Sandals (Ch. 11)
- Darden's Global Outsourcing (Supp. 11)
- Wheeled Coach: Inventory Control (Ch. 12)
- Wheeled Coach: Materials Requirements Planning (Ch. 14)
- Scheduling at Hard Rock Cafe (Ch. 15)
- JIT at Arnold Palmer Hospital (Ch. 16)

COMPANION WEB SITE

Visit our companion Web site, at **www.prenhall.com/heizer**, to find text-specific resources for students and faculty. Some of the resources you will find include:

For Students:

Self-Study Quizzes These extensive quizzes contain a broad assortment of questions, 20–25 per chapter, which include multiple choice, true or false, and Internet essay questions. The quiz questions are graded and can be transmitted to the instructor for extra credit or serve as practice exams.

Virtual Tours These company tours provide direct links to companies ranging from a hospital to an auto manufacturer that practice key concepts. After touring each Web site, students are asked questions directly related to the concepts discussed in the chapter.

Internet Case Studies Assign additional free case study material from this Web site. Detailed solutions appear in the Solutions Manual.

For Faculty:

Instructor support materials can be downloaded from the Prentice Hall online catalog at www.prenhall.com. This password-protected area provides faculty with the most current and advanced support materials available: Instructor's Solutions Manual, Instructor's Resource Manual, PowerPoint slides, and Test Questions.

ACKNOWLEDGMENTS

We thank the many individuals who were kind enough to assist us in this endeavor. The following professors provided insights that guided us in this and prior revisions:

Shahid Ali
Rockhurst University

Stephen Allen
Truman State University

Sema Alptekin
University of Missouri-Rolla

Suad Alwan
Chicago State University

Jean-Pierre Amor
University of San Diego

Moshen Attaran
California State University-Bakersfield

William Barnes
Emporia State University

Leon Bazil
Stevens Institute of Technology

Ali Behnezhad
California State University-Northridge

Victor Berardi
Kent State University

Mark Berenson
Montclair State University

Joe Biggs
California Polytechnic State University

Peter Billington
Colorado State University-Pueblo

John H. Blackstone
University of Georgia

Theodore Boreki
Hofstra University

Lesley Buehler
Ohlone College

Darlene Burk
Western Michigan University

David Cadden
Quinnipiac College

James Campbell
University of Missouri-St. Louis

Rick Carlson
Metropolitan State University

Wen-Chyuan Chiang
University of Tulsa

William Christensen
Dixie State College of Utah

Roy Clinton
University of Louisiana at Monroe

Henry Crouch
Pittsburgh State University

Hugh Daniel
Lipscomb University

Anne Deidrich
Warner Pacific College

John Drabouski
DeVry University

Richard E. Dulski
Daemen College

Charles Englehardt
Salem International University

Wade Ferguson
Western Kentucky University

Warren W. Fisher
Stephen F. Austin State University

Larry A. Flick
Norwalk Community Technical College

Barbara Flynn
Indiana University

Rita Gibson
Embry-Riddle Aeronautical University

Damodar Golhar
Western Michigan University

Jim Goodwin
University of Richmond

James R. Gross
University of Wisconsin-Oshkosh

Eugene Hahn
Salisbury University

Donald Hammond
University of South Florida

John Harpell
West Virginia University

Marilyn K. Hart (retired)
University of Wisconsin-Oshkosh

James S. Hawkes
University of Charleston

George Heinrich
Wichita State University

Sue Helms
Wichita State University

Johnny Ho
Columbus State University

John Hoft
Columbus State University

Zialu Hug
University of Nebraska-Omaha

Garland Hunnicutt
Texas State University

Peter Ittig
University of Massachussetts

Wooseung Jang
University of Missouri-Columbia

Dana Johnson
Michigan Technological University

Paul Jordan
University of Alaska

William Kime
University of New Mexico

Beate Klingenberg
Marist College

Jean Pierre Kuilboer
University of Massachusetts-Boston

Larry LaForge
Clemson University

Gregg Lattier
Lee College

Ronald Lau
Hong Kong University of Science and Technology

Hugh Leach
Washburn University

B.P. Lingeraj
Indiana University

Andy Litteral
University of Richmond

Laurie E. Macdonald
Bryant College

Henry S. Maddux III
Sam Houston State University

Mike Maggard
Northeastern University

Zafar Malik
Governors State University

Mary Marrs
University of Missouri-Columbia

Richard Martin
California State University-Long Beach

Mark McKay
University of Washington

Arthur C. Meiners, Jr.
Marymount University

Gordon Miller
Portland State University

John Miller
Mercer University

Doug Moodie
Michigan Tech University

Donna Mosier
SUNY Potsdam

Philip F. Musa
University of Alabama at Birmingham

Arunachalam Narayanan
Texas A&M University

Joao Neves
Trenton State College

John Nicolay
University of Minnesota

Susan K. Norman
Northern Arizona University

Prafulla Oglekar
LaSalle University

Niranjan Pati
University of Wisconsin-LaCrosse

David Pentico
Duquesne University

Elizabeth Perry
SUNY Binghamton

Michael Pesch
St. Cloud State University

Frank Pianki
Anderson University

Michael Plumb
Tidewater Community College

Leonard Presby
William Paterson University

Zinovy Radovilsky
California State University–Hayward

Ranga V. Ramasesh
Texas Christian University

William Reisel
St. John's University

Spyros Reveliotis
Georgia Institute of Technology

Emma Jane Riddle
Winthrop University

M.J. Riley
Kansas State University

Scott Roberts
Northern Arizona University

Stanford Rosenberg
LaRoche College

Edward Rosenthal
Temple University

Peter Rourke
Wentworth Institute of Technology

Narendrea K. Rustagi
Howard University

X. M. Safford
Milwaukee Area Technical College

Teresita S. Salinas
Washburn University

Chris Sandvig
Western Washington University

Ronald K. Satterfield
University of South Florida

Robert J. Schlesinger
San Diego State University

Shane J. Schvaneveldt
Weber State University

Avanti P. Sethi
Wichita State University

Girish Shambu
Canisius Callege

L.Wayne Shell (retired)
Nicholls State University

Susan Sherer
Lehigh University

Daniel Shimshak
University of Massachusetts-Boston

Theresa A. Shotwell
Florida A&M University

Ernest Silver
Curry College

Samuel Y. Smith Jr.
University of Baltimore

Vicki L. Smith-Daniels
Arizona State University

Victor Sower
San Houston State University

John Stec
Oregon Institute of Technology

Stan Stockton
Indiana University

A. Lawrence Summers
University of Missouri

John Swearingen
Bryant College

Susan Sweeney
Providence College

Kambiz Tabibzadeh
Eastern Kentucky University

Rao J. Taikonda
University of Wisconsin-Oshkosh

Cecelia Temponi
Texas State University

Madeline Thimmes (retired)
Utah State University

Rajendra Tibrewala
New York Institute of Technology

Doug Turner
Auburn University

V. Udayabhanu
San Francisco State University

John Visich-Disc
University of Houston

Ray Walters
Fayetteville Technical Community College

Rick Wing
San Francisco State University

Bruce M. Woodworth
University of Texas-El Paso

Jianghua Wu
Purdue University

Lifang Wu
University of Iowa

Xin Zhai
Purdue University

In addition, we appreciate the wonderful people at Prentice Hall who provided both help and advice: Mark Pfaltzgraff, our decision sciences executive editor; Anne Howard, our marketing manager; Vanessa Bain, our editorial assistant; Ashley Lulling, our media project development manager; Judy Leale, our senior managing editor; Suzanne Grappi, our production project manager; Susie Abraham, our editorial project manager, and Heidi Allgair, our senior production editor at GGS Book Services. Reva Shader developed the exemplary subject indexes for this text. Donna Render and Kay Heizer provided the accurate typing and proofing so critical in a rigorous textbook. We are truly blessed to have such a fantastic team of experts directing, guiding, and assisting us.

We also appreciate the efforts of colleagues who have helped to shape the entire learning package that accompanies this text. Professor Howard Weiss (Temple University) developed the active models, Excel OM, and POM for Windows microcomputer software; Professor Jeff Heyl (Lincoln University) created the PowerPoints. Professor Pedro Reyes (Baylor University) edited the Instructor's Resource Manual; Professor Charles Munson (Washington State University) prepared the Test Bank; Professor Geoff Willis (University of Central Oklahoma) created the online study guide and online virtual tours; Professor Kevin Watson (University of New Orleans) prepared the Study Guide; Angela Sandberg created the Vango Notes; Beverly Amer (Northern Arizona University) produced and directed our videos and DVD video case series; Professors Keith Willoughby (Bucknell University) and Ken Klassen (Brock University) contributed the two Excel-based simulation games; Prof. Gary LaPoint (Syracuse University) developed the MS Project Crashing exercise; and the dice game for SPC. And finally, thanks to our accuracy checkers Annie Puciloski and Vijay Gupta for their attention to detail. We have been fortunate to have been able to work with all these people.

We wish you a pleasant and productive introduction to operations management.

BARRY RENDER
GRADUATE SCHOOL OF BUSINESS
ROLLINS COLLEGE
WINTER PARK, FL 32789
EMAIL: BRENDER@CFL.RR.COM

JAY HEIZER
TEXAS LUTHERAN UNIVERSITY
1000 W. COURT STREET
SEGUIN, TX 78155
EMAIL: JHEIZER@SATX.RR.COM

CHAPTER

1

Operations and Productivity

Chapter Outline

Learning Objectives

When you complete this chapter you should be able to

1. Define operations management
2. Explain the distinction between goods and services
3. Explain the difference between production and productivity
4. Compute single-factor productivity
5. Compute multifactor productivity
6. Identify the critical variables in enhancing productivity

1

Operations Management at Hard Rock Cafe

Operations managers throughout the world are producing products every day to provide for the well-being of society. These products take on a multitude of forms. They may be washing machines at Whirlpool, motion pictures at Dreamworks, rides at Disney World, or food at Hard Rock Cafe. These firms produce thousands of complex products every day—to be delivered as the customer ordered them, when the customers wants them, and where the customer wants them. Hard Rock does this for over 35 million guests worldwide every year. This is a challenging task, and the operations manager's job, whether at Whirlpool, Dreamworks, Disney, or Hard Rock, is demanding.

Orlando-based Hard Rock Cafe opened its first restaurant in London in 1971, making it over 35 years old and the granddaddy of theme restaurants. Although other theme restaurants have come and gone, Hard Rock is still going strong, with 121 restaurants in more than 40 countries—and new restaurants opening each year. Hard Rock made its name with rock music memorabilia, having started when Eric Clapton, a regular customer, marked his favorite bar stool by hanging his guitar on the wall in the London cafe. Now Hard Rock has millions of dollars invested in memorabilia. To keep customers coming back time and again, Hard Rock creates value in the form of good food and entertainment.

The operations managers at Hard Rock Cafe at Universal Studios in Orlando provide more than

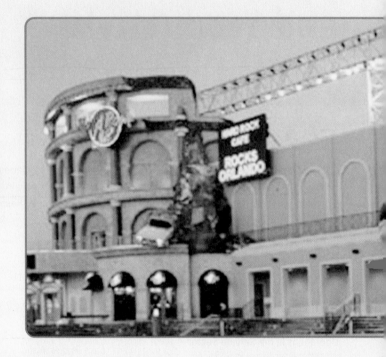

3,500 custom products, in this case meals, every day. These products are designed, tested, and then analyzed for cost of ingredients, labor requirements, and customer satisfaction. On approval, menu items are put into production—and then only if the ingredients are available from qualified suppliers. The production process, from receiving, to cold storage, to grilling or baking or frying, and a dozen other steps, is designed and maintained to yield a quality

▶ *Operations managers are interested in the attractiveness of the layout, but they must be sure that the facility contributes to the efficient movement of people and material with the necessary controls to ensure that proper portions are served.*

▲ Lots of work goes into designing, testing, and costing meals. Then suppliers deliver quality products on time, every time, for well-trained cooks to prepare quality meals. But none of that matters unless an enthusiastic wait staff, such as the one shown here, is doing its job.

◀ Hard Rock Cafe in Orlando, Florida, prepares over 3,500 meals each day. Seating over 1,500 people, it is one of the largest restaurants in the world. But Hard Rock's operations managers serve the hot food hot and the cold food cold.

◀ Efficient kitchen layouts, motivated personnel, tight schedules, and the right ingredients at the right place at the right time are required to delight the customer.

meal. Operations managers, using the best people they can recruit and train, also prepare effective employee schedules and design efficient layouts.

Managers who successfully design and deliver goods and services throughout the world understand operations. In this text, we look not only at how Hard Rock's managers create value but also how operations managers in other services, as well as in manufacturing, do so. Operations management is demanding, challenging, and exciting. It affects our lives every day. Ultimately, operations managers determine how well we live.

3

Video 1.1

Operations Management
at Hard Rock

Operations management (OM) is a discipline that applies to restaurants like Hard Rock Cafe as well as to factories like Sony, Ford, and Whirlpool. The techniques of OM apply throughout the world to virtually all productive enterprises. It doesn't matter if the application is in an office, a hospital, a restaurant, a department store, or a factory—the production of goods and services requires operations management. And the *efficient* production of goods and services requires effective applications of the concepts, tools, and techniques of OM that we introduce in this book.

As we progress through this text, we will discover how to manage operations in a changing global economy. An array of informative examples, charts, text discussions, and pictures illustrates concepts and provides information. We will see how operations managers create the goods and services that enrich our lives.

In this chapter, we first define *operations management*, explaining its heritage and exploring the exciting role operations managers play in a huge variety of businesses. Then we discuss production and productivity in both goods- and service-producing firms. This is followed by a discussion of operations in the service sector and the challenge of managing an effective production system.

WHAT IS OPERATIONS MANAGEMENT?

Learning Objective

1. Define operations management

Production is the creation of goods and services. **Operations management (OM)** is the set of activities that creates value in the form of goods and services by transforming inputs into outputs. Activities creating goods and services take place in all organizations. In manufacturing firms, the production activities that create goods are usually quite obvious. In them, we can see the creation of a tangible product such as a Sony TV or a Harley-Davidson motorcycle.

Production
The creation of goods and services.

In an organization that does not create a tangible good or product, the production function may be less obvious. We often call these activities *services*. The services may be "hidden" from the public and even from the customer. The product may take such forms as the transfer of funds from a savings account to a checking account, the transplant of a liver, the filling of an empty seat on an airplane, or the education of a student. Regardless of whether the end product is a good or service, the production activities that go on in the organization are often referred to as operations, or *operations management*.

Operations management (OM)
Activities that relate to the creation of goods and services through the transformation of inputs to outputs.

ORGANIZING TO PRODUCE GOODS AND SERVICES

To create goods and services, all organizations perform three functions (see Figure 1.1). These functions are the necessary ingredients not only for production but also for an organization's survival. They are:

1. *Marketing*, which generates the demand, or at least takes the order for a product or service (nothing happens until there is a sale).
2. *Production/operations*, which creates the product.
3. *Finance/accounting*, which tracks how well the organization is doing, pays the bills, and collects the money.

Universities, churches or synagogues, and businesses all perform these functions. Even a volunteer group such as the Boy Scouts of America is organized to perform these three basic functions. Figure 1.1 shows how a bank, an airline, and a manufacturing firm organize themselves to perform these functions. The blue-shaded areas of Figure 1.1 show the operations functions in these firms.

WHY STUDY OM?

We study OM for four reasons:

1. OM is one of the three major functions of any organization, and it is integrally related to all the other business functions. All organizations market (sell), finance (account), and produce (operate), and it is important to know how the OM activity functions. Therefore, we study *how people organize themselves for productive enterprise*.
2. We study OM because we want to know *how goods and services are produced*. The production function is the segment of our society that creates the products and services we use.
3. We study OM to *understand what operations managers do*. By understanding what these managers do, you can develop the skills necessary to become such a manager. This will help you explore the numerous and lucrative career opportunities in OM.

4. We study OM *because it is such a costly part of an organization*. A large percentage of the revenue of most firms is spent in the OM function. Indeed, OM provides a major opportunity for an organization to improve its profitability and enhance its service to society. Example 1 considers how a firm might increase its profitability via the production function.

◀ **Figure 1.1**

Organization Charts for Two Service Organizations and One Manufacturing Organization

(A) A bank, (B) an airline, and (C) a manufacturing organization. The blue areas are OM activities.

EXAMPLE 1

Examining the options for increasing contribution

Fisher Technologies is a small firm that must double its dollar contribution to fixed cost and profit in order to be profitable enough to purchase the next generation of production equipment. Management has determined that if the firm fails to increase contribution, its bank will not make the loan and the equipment cannot be purchased. If the firm cannot purchase the equipment, the limitations of the old equipment will force Fisher to go out of business and, in doing so, put its employees out of work and discontinue producing goods and services for its customers.

Approach: Table 1.1 shows a simple profit-and-loss statement and three strategic options (marketing, finance/accounting, and operations) for the firm. The first option is a *marketing option*, where good marketing management may increase sales by 50%. By increasing sales by 50%, contribution will in turn increase 71%. But increasing sales 50% may be difficult; it may even be impossible.

▶ **Table 1.1**

Options for Increasing Contribution

	Current	Marketing Option[a] Increase Sales Revenue 50%	Finance/ Accounting Option[b] Reduce Finance Costs 50%	OM Option[c] Reduce Production Costs 20%
Sales	$100,000	$150,000	$100,000	$100,000
Costs of goods	−80,000	−120,000	−80,000	−64,000
Gross margin	20,000	30,000	20,000	36,000
Finance costs	− 6,000	− 6,000	− 3,000	− 6,000
Subtotal	14,000	24,000	17,000	30,000
Taxes at 25%	− 3,500	− 6,000	− 4,250	− 7,500
Contribution[d]	$ 10,500	$ 18,000	$ 12,750	$ 22,500

[a]Increasing sales 50% increases contribution by $7,500, or 71% (7,500/10,500).
[b]Reducing finance costs 50% increases contribution by $2,250, or 21% (2,250/10,500).
[c]Reducing production costs 20% increases contribution by $12,000, or 114% (12,000/10,500).
[d]Contribution to fixed cost (excluding finance costs) and profit.

The second option is a *finance/accounting option*, where finance costs are cut in half through good financial management. But even a reduction of 50% is still inadequate for generating the necessary increase in contribution. Contribution is increased by only 21%.

The third option is an *OM option*, where management reduces production costs by 20% and increases contribution by 114%.

Solution: Given the conditions of our brief example, Fisher Technologies has increased contribution from $10,500 to $22,500. It may now have a bank willing to lend it additional funds.

Insight: The OM option not only yields the greatest improvement in contribution but also may be the only feasible option. Increasing sales by 50% and decreasing finance cost by 50% may both be virtually impossible. Reducing operations cost by 20% may be difficult but feasible.

Learning exercise: What is the impact of only a 15% decrease in costs in the OM option? [Answer: A $19,500 contribution.]

Example 1 underscores the importance of an effective operations activity of a firm. Development of increasingly effective operations is the approach taken by many companies as they face growing global competition.[1]

[1]See related discussion in Michael Hammer, "Deep Change: How Operational Innovation Can Transform Your Company," *Harvard Business Review* 82, no. 4 (2004): 85–93.

WHAT OPERATIONS MANAGERS DO

All good managers perform the basic functions of the management process. The **management process** consists of *planning*, *organizing*, *staffing*, *leading*, and *controlling*. Operations managers apply this management process to the decisions they make in the OM function. The 10 major decisions of OM are shown in Table 1.2. Successfully addressing each of these decisions requires planning, organizing, staffing, leading, and controlling. Typical issues relevant to these decisions and the chapter where each is discussed are also shown.

How This Book Is Organized

The 10 decisions shown in Table 1.2 are activities required of operations managers. The ability to make good decisions in these areas and allocate resources to ensure their effective execution goes a long way toward an efficient operations function. The text is structured around these 10 decisions. Throughout the book, we discuss the issues and tools that help managers make these 10 decisions. We also consider the impact that these decisions can have on the firm's strategy and productivity.

Where Are the OM Jobs?   How does one get started on a career in operations? The 10 OM decisions identified in Table 1.2 are made by individuals who work in the disciplines shown in the blue areas of Figure 1.1. Competent business students who know their accounting, statistics, finance, and OM have an opportunity to assume entry-level positions in all of these areas. As you read this text, identify disciplines that can assist you in making these decisions. Then take courses in those areas. The more background an OM student has in accounting, statistics, information systems, and mathematics, the more job opportunities will be available. About 40% of *all* jobs are in OM. Figure 1.2 shows some recent job opportunities.

Management process

The application of planning, organizing, staffing, leading, and controlling to the achievement of objectives.

Ten OM Strategy Decisions

Design of Goods and Services
Managing Quality
Process Strategy
Location Strategies
Layout Strategies
Human Resources
Supply Chain Management
Inventory Management
Scheduling
Maintenance

◀ **Table 1.2**

Ten Critical Decisions of Operations Management

Ten Decision Areas	Issues	Chapter(s)
Design of goods and services	What good or service should we offer? How should we design these products?	5
Managing quality	How do we define the quality? Who is responsible for quality?	6, Supplement 6
Process and capacity design	What process and what capacity will these products require? What equipment and technology is necessary for these processes?	7, Supplement 7
Location strategy	Where should we put the facility? On what criteria should we base the location decision?	8
Layout strategy	How should we arrange the facility? How large must the facility be to meet our plan?	9
Human resources and job design	How do we provide a reasonable work environment? How much can we expect our employees to produce?	10, Supplement 10
Supply chain management	Should we make or buy this component? Who are our suppliers and who can integrate into our e-commerce program?	11, Supplement 11
Inventory, material requirements planning, and JIT (just-in-time)	How much inventory of each item should we have? When do we reorder?	12, 14, 16
Intermediate and short-term scheduling	Are we better off keeping people on the payroll during slowdowns? Which job do we perform next?	13, 15
Maintenance	Who is responsible for maintenance? When do we do maintenance?	17

PLANT MANAGER

Division of Fortune 1000 company seeks plant manager for plant located in the upper Hudson Valley area. This plant manufactures loading dock equipment for commercial markets. The candidate must be experienced in plant management including expertise in production planning, purchasing, and inventory management. Good written and oral communication skills are a must along with excellent understanding of and application skills in managing people.

Operations Analyst

Expanding national coffee shop; top 10 "Best Places to Work" wants junior level systems analyst to join our excellent store improvement team. Business or I.E. degree, work methods, labor standards, ergonomics, cost accounting knowledge a plus. This is a hands on job and excellent opportunity for team player with good people skills. West Coast location. Some travel required.

Quality Manager

Several openings exist in our small package processing facilities in the Northeast, Florida, and Southern California for quality managers. These highly visible positions require extensive use of statistical tools to monitor all aspects of service timeliness and workload measurement. The work involves (1) a combination of hands-on applications and detailed analysis using databases and spreadsheets, (2) process audits to identify areas for improvement, and (3) management of implementation of changes. Positions involve night hours and weekends. Send resume.

Supply Chain Manager and Planner

Responsibilities entail negotiating contracts and establishing long-term relationships with suppliers. We will rely on the selected candidate to maintain accuracy in the purchasing system, invoices, and product returns. A bachelor's degree and up to 2 years related experience are required. Working knowledge of MRP, ability to use feedback to master scheduling and suppliers and consolidate orders for best price and delivery are necessary. Proficiency in all PC Windows applications, particularly Excel and Word, is essential. Knowledge of Oracle business system I is a plus. Effective verbal and written communication skills are essential.

Process Improvement Consultants

An expanding consulting firm is seeking consultants to design and implement lean production and cycle time reduction plans in both service and manufacturing processes. Our firm is currently working with an international bank to improve its back office operations, as well as with several manufacturing firms. A business degree required; APICS certification a plus.

▲ **Figure 1.2** Many Opportunities Exist for Operations Managers

THE HERITAGE OF OPERATIONS MANAGEMENT

The field of OM is relatively young, but its history is rich and interesting. Our lives and the OM discipline have been enhanced by the innovations and contributions of numerous individuals. We now introduce a few of these people, and we provide a summary of significant events in operations management in Figure 1.3.

Eli Whitney (1800) is credited for the early popularization of interchangeable parts, which was achieved through standardization and quality control. Through a contract he signed with the U.S. government for 10,000 muskets, he was able to command a premium price because of their interchangeable parts.

Frederick W. Taylor (1881), known as the father of scientific management, contributed to personnel selection, planning and scheduling, motion study, and the now popular field of ergonomics. One of his major contributions was his belief that management should be much more resourceful and aggressive in the improvement of work methods. Taylor and his colleagues, Henry L. Gantt and Frank and Lillian Gilbreth, were among the first to systematically seek the best way to produce.

Another of Taylor's contributions was the belief that management should assume more responsibility for:

> *Taylor revolutionized manufacturing: his scientific approach to the analysis of daily work and the tools of industry frequently increased productivity 400%.*

1. Matching employees to the right job.
2. Providing the proper training.
3. Providing proper work methods and tools.
4. Establishing legitimate incentives for work to be accomplished.

By 1913, Henry Ford and Charles Sorensen combined what they knew about standardized parts with the quasi-assembly lines of the meatpacking and mail-order industries and added the revolutionary concept of the assembly line, where men stood still and material moved.[2]

Quality control is another historically significant contribution to the field of OM. Walter Shewhart (1924) combined his knowledge of statistics with the need for quality control and provided the foundations for statistical sampling in quality control. W. Edwards Deming (1950)

> *Charles Sorensen towed an automobile chassis on a rope over his shoulders through the Ford plant while others added parts.*

---

[2]Jay Heizer, "Determining Responsibility for the Development of the Moving Assembly Line," *Journal of Management History* 4, no. 2 (1998): 94–103.

Customization Focus

**Mass Customization Era
1995–2010**
Globalization
Internet/E-Commerce
Enterprise Resource Planning
Learning Organization
International Quality Standards
Finite Scheduling
Supply Chain Management
Mass Customization
Build-to-Order

Quality Focus

Cost Focus

**Lean Production Era
1980–1995**
Just-in-Time
Computer-Aided Design
Electronic Data Interchange
Total Quality Management
Baldrige Award
Empowerment
Kanbans

**Early Concepts
1776–1880**
Labor Specialization
   (Smith, Babbage)
Standardized Parts (Whitney)

**Scientific Management Era
1880–1910**
Gantt Charts (Gantt)
Motion & Time Studies
   (Gilbreth)
Process Analysis (Taylor)
Queuing Theory (Erlang)

**Mass Production Era
1910–1980**
Moving Assembly Line
   (Ford/Sorensen)
Statistical Sampling
   (Shewhart)
Economic Order
   Quantity (Harris)
Linear Programming
   PERT/CPM (DuPont)
Material Requirements
   Planning

▲ **Figure 1.3**   **Significant Events in Operations Management**

believed, as did Frederick Taylor, that management must do more to improve the work environment and processes so that quality can be improved.

Operations management will continue to progress with contributions from other disciplines, including *industrial engineering* and *management science*. These disciplines, along with statistics, management, and economics, contribute to improved models and decision making.

Innovations from the *physical sciences* (biology, anatomy, chemistry, physics) have also contributed to advances in OM. These innovations include new adhesives, faster integrated circuits, gamma rays to sanitize food products, and higher-quality glass for LCD and plasma TVs. Innovation in products and processes often depends on advances in the physical sciences.

Especially important contributions to OM have come from *information technology*, which we define as the systematic processing of data to yield information. Information technology—with wireless links, Internet, and e-commerce—is reducing costs and accelerating communication.

Decisions in operations management require individuals who are well versed in management science, in information technology, and often in one of the biological or physical sciences. In this textbook, we look at the diverse ways a student can prepare for a career in operations management.

OPERATIONS IN THE SERVICE SECTOR

Manufacturers produce a tangible product, while service products are often intangible. But many products are a combination of a good and a service, which complicates the definition of a service. Even the U.S. government has trouble generating a consistent definition. Because definitions vary, much of the data and statistics generated about the service sector are inconsistent. However, we define **services** as including repair and maintenance, government, food and

Services
Economic activities that typically produce an intangible product (such as education, entertainment, lodging, government, financial, and health services).

lodging, transportation, insurance, trade, financial, real estate, education, legal, medical, entertainment, and other professional occupations.[3]

Differences between Goods and Services

Let's examine some of the differences between goods and services:

- Services are usually *intangible* (for example, your purchase of a ride in an empty airline seat between two cities) as opposed to a tangible good.
- Services are often *produced and consumed simultaneously*; there is no stored inventory. For instance, the beauty salon produces a haircut that is "consumed" simultaneously, or the doctor produces an operation that is "consumed" as it is produced. We have not yet figured out how to inventory haircuts or appendectomies.
- Services are often *unique*. Your mix of financial coverage, such as investments and insurance policies, may not be the same as anyone else's, just as the medical procedure or a haircut produced for you is not exactly like anyone else's.
- Services have *high customer interaction*. Services are often difficult to standardize, automate, and make as efficient as we would like because customer interaction demands uniqueness. In fact, in many cases this uniqueness is what the customer is paying for; therefore, the operations manager must ensure that the product is designed (i.e., customized) so that it can be delivered in the required unique manner.
- Services have *inconsistent product definition*. Product definition may be rigorous, as in the case of an auto insurance policy, but inconsistent because policyholders change cars and mature.
- Services are often *knowledge based*, as in the case of educational, medical, and legal services, and therefore hard to automate.
- Services are frequently *dispersed*. Dispersion occurs because services are frequently brought to the client/customer via a local office, a retail outlet, or even a house call.

Table 1.3 indicates some additional differences between goods and services that affect OM decisions. Although service products are different from goods, the operations function continues to transform resources into products. Indeed, the activities of the operations function are often very similar for both goods and services. For instance, both goods and services must have quality standards established, and both must be designed and processed on a schedule in a facility where human resources are employed.

Having made the distinction between goods and services, we should point out that in many cases, the distinction is not clear-cut. In reality, almost all services and almost all goods are a mixture of a service and a tangible product. Even services such as consulting may require a tangible report. Similarly, the sale of most goods includes a service. For instance, many products have the service components of financing and delivery (e.g., automobile sales). Many also require after-sale training and maintenance (e.g., office copiers and machinery). "Service" activ-

▶ **Table 1.3**

Differences between Goods and Services

Attributes of Goods (tangible product)	Attributes of Services (intangible product)
Product can be resold.	Reselling a service is unusual.
Product can be inventoried.	Many services cannot be inventoried.
Some aspects of quality are measurable.	Many aspects of quality are difficult to measure.
Selling is distinct from production.	Selling is often a part of the service.
Product is transportable.	Provider, not product, is often transportable.
Site of facility is important for cost.	Site of facility is important for customer contact.
Often easy to automate.	Service is often difficult to automate.
Revenue is generated primarily from the tangible product.	Revenue is generated primarily from the intangible services.

[3]This definition is similar to the categories used by the U.S. Bureau of Labor Statistics.

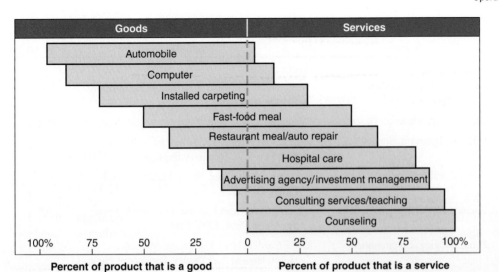

◄ **Figure 1.4**

**Most Goods Contain a
Service, and Most Services
Contain a Good**

ities may also be an integral part of production. Human resource activities, logistics, accounting, training, field service, and repair are all service activities, but they take place within a manufacturing organization.

When a tangible product is *not* included in the service, we may call it a **pure service**. Although there are not very many pure services, in some instances counseling may be an example. Figure 1.4 shows the range of *services* in a product. The range is extensive and shows the pervasiveness of service activities.

Pure service

A service that does not include a tangible product.

Growth of Services

Services now constitute the largest economic sector in postindustrial societies. Until about 1900, most Americans were employed in agriculture. Increased agricultural productivity allowed people to leave the farm and seek employment in the city. Similarly, manufacturing employment has decreased somewhat in the last 25 years. The changes in manufacturing and service employment, in millions, are shown in Figure 1.5(a). Interestingly, as Figure 1.5(b)

▼ **Figure 1.5**   **Development of the Service Economy and Manufacturing Productivity**

Sources: U.S. Bureau of Labor Statistics; Federal Reserve Board, Industrial Production and Capacity Utilization (2003); Statistical Abstract of the United States (2005).

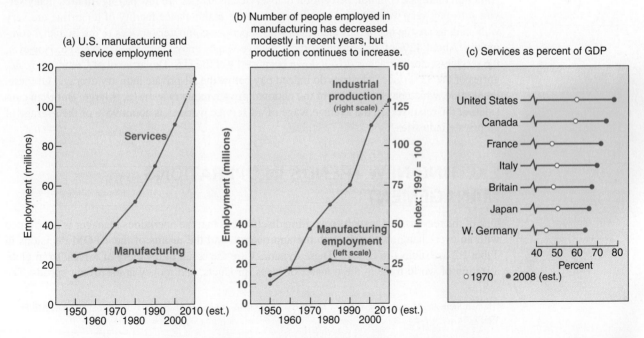

▶ **Table 1.4**

Examples of Organizations in Each Sector

Source: Statistical Abstract of the United States (2007), Table 606 and Bureau of Labor Statistics, 2007.

Sector	Example	Percent of All Jobs
Service Sector		
Education, Legal, Medical, and other services	Notre Dame University, San Diego Zoo, Arnold Palmer Hospital	25.5
Trade (retail, wholesale)	Walgreen's, Wal-Mart, Nordstrom	15.1
Utilities, Transportation	Pacific Gas & Electric, American Airlines, Santa Fe R.R., Roadway Express	5.2
Professional and Business Services	Snelling and Snelling, Waste Management, Inc., Pitney-Bowes	10.1
Finance, Information, Real Estate	Citicorp, American Express, Prudential, Aetna, Trammell Crow, EDS, IBM	9.6
Food, Lodging, Entertainment	Olive Garden, Hard Rock Cafe, Motel 6, Hilton Hotels, Walt Disney, Paramount Pictures	8.5
Public Administration	U.S., State of Alabama, Cook County	4.6
Manufacturing Sector	General Electric, Ford, U.S. Steel, Intel	11.5
Construction Sector	Bechtel, McDermott	7.9
Agriculture	King Ranch	1.6
Mining Sector	Homestake Mining	.4
Grand Total		100.0

(Service Sector subtotal: 78.6)

---

indicates, while the *number* of people employed in manufacturing has held relatively steady since 1950, each person is now producing about 20 times more than in 1950. Services became the dominant employer in the early 1920s, with manufacturing employment peaking at about 32% in 1950. The huge productivity increases in agriculture and manufacturing have allowed more of our economic resources to be devoted to services, as shown in Figure 1.5(c). Consequently, much of the world can now enjoy the pleasures of education, health services, entertainment, and myriad other things that we call services. Examples of firms and percentage of employment in the U.S. **service sector** are shown in Table 1.4. Table 1.4 also provides employment percentages for the nonservice sectors of manufacturing, construction, agriculture, and mining on the bottom four lines.

Service sector

The segment of the economy that includes trade, financial, lodging, education, legal, medical, and other professional occupations.

Service Pay

Although there is a common perception that service industries are low paying, in fact, many service jobs pay very well. Operations managers in the maintenance facility of an airline are very well paid, as are the operations managers who supervise computer services to the financial community. About 42% of all service workers receive wages above the national average. However, the service-sector average is driven down because 14 of the U.S. Department of Commerce categories of the 33 service industries do indeed pay below the all-private industry average. Of these, retail trade, which pays only 61% of the national private industry average, is large. But even considering the retail sector, the average wage of all service workers is about 96% of the average of all private industries.[4]

EXCITING NEW TRENDS IN OPERATIONS MANAGEMENT

One of the reasons OM is such an exciting discipline is that the operations manager is confronted with an ever-changing world. Both the approach to and the results of the 10 OM decisions in Table 1.2 are subject to change. These dynamics are the result of a variety of forces, from globalization of world trade to the transfer of ideas, products, and money at electronic speeds. The

---

[4]Herbert Stein and Murray Foss, *The New Illustrated Guide to the American Economy* (Washington, DC: The AIE Press, 1995): 30.

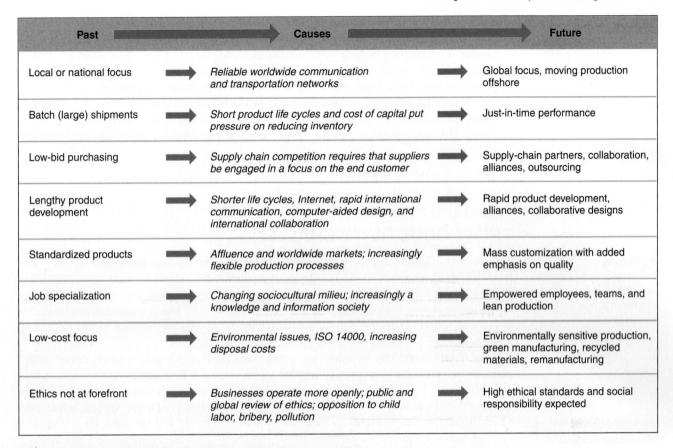

Past		Causes		Future
Local or national focus	→	*Reliable worldwide communication and transportation networks*	→	Global focus, moving production offshore
Batch (large) shipments	→	*Short product life cycles and cost of capital put pressure on reducing inventory*	→	Just-in-time performance
Low-bid purchasing	→	*Supply chain competition requires that suppliers be engaged in a focus on the end customer*	→	Supply-chain partners, collaboration, alliances, outsourcing
Lengthy product development	→	*Shorter life cycles, Internet, rapid international communication, computer-aided design, and international collaboration*	→	Rapid product development, alliances, collaborative designs
Standardized products	→	*Affluence and worldwide markets; increasingly flexible production processes*	→	Mass customization with added emphasis on quality
Job specialization	→	*Changing sociocultural milieu; increasingly a knowledge and information society*	→	Empowered employees, teams, and lean production
Low-cost focus	→	*Environmental issues, ISO 14000, increasing disposal costs*	→	Environmentally sensitive production, green manufacturing, recycled materials, remanufacturing
Ethics not at forefront	→	*Businesses operate more openly; public and global review of ethics; opposition to child labor, bribery, pollution*	→	High ethical standards and social responsibility expected

▲ **Figure 1.6** Changing Challenges for the Operations Manager

direction now being taken by OM—where it has been and where it is going—is shown in Figure 1.6. We now introduce some of the challenges shown in Figure 1.6:

- *Global focus:* The rapid decline in communication and transportation costs has made markets global. At the same time, resources in the form of capital, materials, talent, and labor have also become global. Contributing to this rapid globalization are countries throughout the world that are vying for economic growth and industrialization. Operations managers are responding with innovations that generate and move ideas, production, and finished goods rapidly.

- *Just-in-time performance:* Vast financial resources are committed to inventory, making it costly. Inventory also impedes response to rapid changes in the marketplace. Operations managers are viciously cutting inventories at every level, from raw materials to finished goods.

- *Supply chain partnering:* Shorter product life cycles, driven by demanding customers, as well as rapid changes in material and processes, require suppliers to be more in tune with the needs of the end user. And because suppliers often have unique expertise, operations managers are outsourcing and building long-term partnerships with critical players in the supply chain.

- *Rapid product development:* Rapid international communication of news, entertainment, and lifestyles is dramatically chopping away at the life span of products. Operations managers are responding with management structures and technology that are faster and alliances (partners) that are more effective.

- *Mass customization:* Once managers begin to recognize the world as the marketplace, then the individual differences become quite obvious. Cultural differences, compounded by individual differences, in a world where consumers are increasingly aware of innovation and options, places substantial pressure on firms to respond. Operations managers are responding with production processes that are flexible enough to cater to individual whims of consumers. The goal is to produce customized products, whenever and wherever needed.

- *Empowered employees:* The knowledge explosion and a more technical workplace have combined to require more competence at the workplace. Operations managers are responding by moving more decision making to the individual worker.
- *Environmentally sensitive production:* The operation manager's continuing battle to improve productivity is increasingly concerned with designing products and processes that are environmentally friendly. That means designing products that are biodegradable, or automobile components that can be reused or recycled, or making packaging more efficient.
- *Ethics:* Operations managers are taking their place in the continuing challenge to enhance ethical behavior.

These and many more topics that are part of the exciting challenges to operations managers are discussed in this text.

THE PRODUCTIVITY CHALLENGE

Productivity

The ratio of outputs (goods and services) divided by one or more inputs (such as labor, capital, or management).

The creation of goods and services requires changing resources into goods and services. The more efficiently we make this change, the more productive we are and the more value is added to the good or service provided. **Productivity** is the ratio of outputs (goods and services) divided by the inputs (resources, such as labor and capital) (see Figure 1.7). The operations manager's job is to enhance (improve) this ratio of outputs to inputs. Improving productivity means improving efficiency.[5]

This improvement can be achieved in two ways: reducing inputs while keeping output constant or increasing output while keeping inputs constant. Both represent an improvement in productivity. In an economic sense, inputs are labor, capital, and management, which are integrated into a production system. Management creates this production system, which provides the conversion of inputs to outputs. Outputs are goods and services, including such diverse items as guns, butter, education, improved judicial systems, and ski resorts. *Production* is the making of goods and services. High production may imply only that more people are working and that employment levels are high (low unemployment), but it does not imply high *productivity*.

Measurement of productivity is an excellent way to evaluate a country's ability to provide an improving standard of living for its people. *Only through increases in productivity can the standard of living improve.* Moreover, only through increases in productivity can labor, capital, and management receive additional payments. If returns to labor, capital, or management are increased without increased productivity, prices rise. On the other hand, downward pressure is placed on prices when productivity increases, because more is being produced with the same resources.

The benefits of increased productivity are illustrated in the *OM in Action* box "Improving Productivity at Starbucks."

Learning Objective

3. Explain the difference between production and productivity

▶ **Figure 1.7**

The Economic System Adds Value by Transforming Inputs to Outputs

An effective feedback loop evaluates process performance against a plan or standard. It also evaluates customer satisfaction and sends signals to managers controlling the inputs and process.

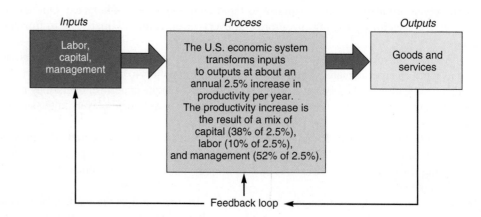

[5]*Efficiency* means doing the job well—with a minimum of resources and waste. Note the distinction between being *efficient*, which implies doing the job well, and *effective*, which means doing the right thing. A job well done—say, by applying the 10 decisions of operations management—helps us be *efficient*; developing and using the correct strategy helps us be *effective*.

OM in Action   Improving Productivity at Starbucks

"This is a game of seconds . . . " says Silva Peterson, whom Starbucks has put in charge of saving seconds. Her team of 10 analysts is constantly asking themselves: "How can we shave time off this?"

Peterson's analysis suggested that there were some obvious opportunities. First, stop requiring signatures on credit-card purchases under $25. This sliced 8 seconds off the transaction time at the cash register.

Then analysts noticed that Starbucks's largest cold beverage, the Venti size, required two bending and digging motions to scoop up enough ice. The scoop was too small. Redesign of the scoop provided the proper amount in one motion and cut 14 seconds off the average time of one minute.

Third were new espresso machines; with the push of a button, the machines grind coffee beans and brew. This

allowed the server, called a "barista" in Starbucks's vocabulary, to do other things. The savings: about 12 seconds per espresso shot.

As a result, operations improvements at Starbucks outlets have increased the average yearly volume by nearly $200,000, to about $940,000 in the past 6 years. This is a 27% improvement in productivity—about 4.5% per year. In the service industry, a 4.5% per year increase is very tasty.

Sources: The Wall Street Journal (April 12, 2005): B2:B7; *Knight Ridder Tribune Business News* (July 25, 2003):1; **www.finfacts.com**, October 6, 2005.

For well over a century (from about 1869), the U.S. has been able to increase productivity at an average rate of almost 2.5% per year. Such growth has doubled U.S. wealth every 30 years. The manufacturing sector, although a decreasing portion of the U.S. economy, has recently seen annual productivity increases exceeding 4%, and the service sector, with increases of almost 1%, has also shown some improvement. The combination has moved U.S. annual productivity growth in this early part of the 21st century slightly above the 2.5% range for the economy as a whole.[6]

In this text, we examine how to improve productivity through the operations function. Productivity is a significant issue for the world and one that the operations manager is uniquely qualified to address.

 Video 1.2

The Transformation Process at Regal Marine

Productivity Measurement

The measurement of productivity can be quite direct. Such is the case when productivity is measured by labor-hours per ton of a specific type of steel. Although labor-hours is a common measure of input, other measures such as capital (dollars invested), materials (tons of ore), or energy (kilowatts of electricity) can be used.[7] An example of this can be summarized in the following equation:

$$\text{Productivity} = \frac{\text{Units produced}}{\text{Input used}} \qquad (1\text{-}1)$$

For example, if units produced = 1,000 and labor-hours used is 250, then:

$$\text{Productivity} = \frac{\text{Units produced}}{\text{Labor-hours used}} = \frac{1{,}000}{250} = 4 \text{ units per labor-hour}$$

The use of just one resource input to measure productivity, as shown in Equation (1-1), is known as **single-factor productivity**. However, a broader view of productivity is **multifactor productivity**, which includes all inputs (e.g., capital, labor, material, energy). Multifactor productivity is also known as *total factor productivity*. Multifactor productivity is calculated by combining the input units as shown here:

$$\text{Productivity} = \frac{\text{Output}}{\text{Labor} + \text{Material} + \text{Energy} + \text{Capital} + \text{Miscellaneous}} \qquad (1\text{-}2)$$

Single-factor productivity
Indicates the ratio of one resource (input) to the goods and services produced (outputs).

Multifactor productivity
Indicates the ratio of many or all resources (inputs) to the goods and services produced (outputs).

---

[6]According to the *Statistical Abstract of the United States*, non-farm business sector productivity increase for 1995 was 0.9%; 1996, 2.5%; 1997, 2.0%; 1998, 2.6%; 1999, 2.4%; 2000, 2.9%; 2001, 1.1%; 2002, 4.8%; (see Table 633). Productivity increase for 2003, 4.5%; 2004, 4.0%; 2005, 2.9%; and 2006, 1.6% (U.S. Dept. of Labor, April 2007). **www.bls.gov/newsreleases/archives**.

[7]The quality and time period are assumed to remain constant.

To aid in the computation of multifactor productivity, the individual inputs (the denominator) can be expressed in dollars and summed as shown in Example 2.

EXAMPLE 2

Computing single- and multifactor gains in productivity

Learning Objective

5. Compute multifactor productivity

Collins Title wants to evaluate its labor and multifactor productivity with a new computerized title-search system. The company has a staff of four, each working 8 hours per day (for a payroll cost of $640/day) and overhead expenses of $400 per day. Collins processes and closes on 8 titles each day. The new computerized title-search system will allow the processing of 14 titles per day. Although the staff, their work hours, and pay are the same, the overhead expenses are now $800 per day.

Approach: Collins uses Equation (1-1) to compute labor productivity and Equation (1-2) to compute multifactor productivity.

Solution:

$$\text{Labor productivity with the old system: } \frac{8 \text{ titles per day}}{32 \text{ labor-hours}} = .25 \text{ titles per labor-hour}$$

$$\text{Labor productivity with the new system: } \frac{14 \text{ titles per day}}{32 \text{ labor-hours}} = .4375 \text{ titles per labor-hour}$$

$$\text{Multifactor productivity with the old system: } \frac{8 \text{ titles per day}}{\$640 + 400} = .0077 \text{ titles per dollar}$$

$$\text{Multifactor productivity with the new system: } \frac{14 \text{ titles per day}}{\$640 + 800} = .0097 \text{ titles per dollar}$$

Labor productivity has increased from .25 to .4375. The change is .4375/.25 = 1.75, or a 75% increase in labor productivity. Multifactor productivity has increased from .0077 to .0097. This change is .0097/.0077 = 1.26, or a 26% increase in multifactor productivity.

Insight: Both the labor (single-factor) and multifactor productivity measures show an increase in productivity. However, the multifactor measure provides a better picture of the increase because it includes all the costs connected with the increase in output.

Learning exercise: If the overhead goes to $960 (rather than $800), what is the multifactor productivity? [Answer: .00875.]

Related problems: 1.1, 1.2, 1.5, 1.6, 1.7, 1.8, 1.9, 1.11, 1.12, 1.14, 1.15

Use of productivity measures aids managers in determining how well they are doing. But results from the two measures can be expected to vary. If labor productivity growth is entirely the result of capital spending, measuring just labor distorts the results. Multifactor productivity is usually better, but more complicated. Labor productivity is the more popular measure. The multifactor-productivity measures provide better information about the trade-offs among factors, but substantial measurement problems remain. Some of these measurement problems are listed here:

1. *Quality* may change while the quantity of inputs and outputs remains constant. Compare an HDTV of this decade with a black-and-white TV of the 1950s. Both are TVs, but few people would deny that the quality has improved. The unit of measure—a TV—is the same, but the quality has changed.
2. *External elements*[8] may cause an increase or a decrease in productivity for which the system under study may not be directly responsible. A more reliable electric power service may greatly improve production, thereby improving the firm's productivity because of this support system rather than because of managerial decisions made within the firm.
3. *Precise units of measure* may be lacking. Not all automobiles require the same inputs: Some cars are subcompacts, others are 911 Turbo Porsches.

Productivity measurement is particularly difficult in the service sector, where the end product can be hard to define. For example, economic statistics ignore the quality of your haircut, the outcome of a court case, or service at a retail store. In some cases, adjustments are made for the quality of the product sold but *not* the quality of the sales presentation or the advantage of a

Video 1.3

Productivity at Whirlpool

[8]These are exogenous variables—that is, variables outside the system under study that influence it.

broader product selection. Productivity measurements require specific inputs and outputs, but a free economy is producing worth—what people want—which includes convenience, speed, and safety. Traditional measures of outputs may be a very poor measure of these other measures of worth. Note the quality-measurement problems in a law office, where each case is different, altering the accuracy of the measure "cases per labor-hour" or "cases per employee."

Productivity Variables

As we saw in Figure 1.7, productivity increases are dependent on three **productivity variables**:

1. *Labor,* which contributes about 10% of the annual increase.
2. *Capital,* which contributes about 38% of the annual increase.
3. *Management,* which contributes about 52% of the annual increase.

These three factors are critical to improved productivity. They represent the broad areas in which managers can take action to improve productivity.[9]

Labor   Improvement in the contribution of labor to productivity is the result of a healthier, better-educated, and better-nourished labor force. Some increase may also be attributed to a shorter workweek. Historically, about 10% of the annual improvement in productivity is attributed to improvement in the quality of labor. Three key variables for improved labor productivity are:

1. Basic education appropriate for an effective labor force.
2. Diet of the labor force.
3. Social overhead that makes labor available, such as transportation and sanitation.

Illiteracy and poor diets are a major impediment to productivity, costing countries up to 20% of their productivity.[10] Infrastructure that yields clean drinking water and sanitation is also an opportunity for improved productivity, as well as an opportunity for better health, in much of the world.

In developed nations, the challenge becomes *maintaining and enhancing the skills of labor* in the midst of rapidly expanding technology and knowledge. Recent data suggest that the average American 17-year-old knows significantly less mathematics than the average Japanese at the same age, and about half cannot answer the questions in Figure 1.8. Moreover, more than 38% of American job applicants tested for basic skills were deficient in reading, writing, or math.[11]

Overcoming shortcomings in the quality of labor while other countries have a better labor force is a major challenge. Perhaps improvements can be found not only through increasing competence of labor but also via *better utilized labor with a stronger commitment.* Training, motivation, team building, and the human resource strategies discussed in Chapter 10, as well as improved education, may be among the many techniques that will contribute to increased labor productivity. Improvements in labor productivity are possible; however, they can be expected to be increasingly difficult and expensive.

Productivity variables
The three factors critical to productivity improvement—labor, capital, and the art and science of management.

Learning Objective

6. Identify the critical variables in enhancing productivity

Many American high schools exceed a 50% dropout rate in spite of offering a wide variety of programs.

Between 20% and 30% of U.S. workers lack the basic skills they need for their current jobs.
(Source: Nan Stone, Harvard Business Review.)

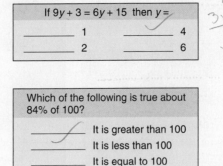

$9y = 6y + 12$
$3y = 12$
$\frac{}{3}$
$y = 4$

◄ **Figure 1.8**

About Half of the 17-Year-Olds in the U.S. Cannot Correctly Answer Questions of This Type

[9]The percentages are from Herbert Stein and Murray Foss, *The New Illustrated Guide to the American Economy* (Washington, DC: AIE Press, 1995): 67.
[10]See report by Christopher Wanjek, "Food at Work: Workplace Solutions for Malnutrition, Obesity, and Chronic Diseases," *International Labor Office*, 2005.
[11]"Can't Read, Can't Count," *Scientific American* (October 2001): 24; and "Economic Time Bomb: U.S. Teens are Among Worst at Math," *The Wall Street Journal* (December 7, 2004):B1.

Capital   Human beings are tool-using animals. Capital investment provides those tools. Capital investment has increased in the U.S. every year except during a few very severe recession periods. Annual capital investment in the U.S. has increased at an annual rate of 1.5% after allowances for depreciation.

Inflation and taxes increase the cost of capital, making capital investment increasingly expensive. When the capital invested per employee drops, we can expect a drop in productivity. Using labor rather than capital may reduce unemployment in the short run, but it also makes economies less productive and therefore lowers wages in the long run. Capital investment is often a necessary, but seldom a sufficient ingredient in the battle for increased productivity.

The trade-off between capital and labor is continually in flux. The higher the interest rate, the more projects requiring capital are "squeezed out": they are not pursued because the potential return on investment for a given risk has been reduced. Managers adjust their investment plans to changes in capital cost.

Management   Management is a factor of production and an economic resource. Management is responsible for ensuring that labor and capital are effectively used to increase productivity. Management accounts for over half of the annual increase in productivity. This increase includes improvements made through the use of knowledge and the application of technology.

Using knowledge and technology is critical in postindustrial societies. Consequently, postindustrial societies are also known as knowledge societies. **Knowledge societies** are those in which much of the labor force has migrated from manual work to technical and information-processing tasks requiring ongoing education. The required education and training are important high-cost items that are the responsibility of operations managers as they build organizations and workforces. The expanding knowledge base of contemporary society requires that managers use *technology and knowledge effectively.*

More effective use of capital also contributes to productivity. It falls to the operations manager, as a productivity catalyst, to select the best new capital investments as well as to improve the productivity of existing investments.

The productivity challenge is difficult. A country cannot be a world-class competitor with second-class inputs. Poorly educated labor, inadequate capital, and dated technology are second-class inputs. High productivity and high-quality outputs require high-quality inputs, including good operations managers.

Knowledge society
A society in which much of the labor force has migrated from manual work to work based on knowledge.

▼ *The effective use of capital often means finding the proper trade-off between investment in capital assets (automation, left) and human assets (a manual process, right). While there are risks connected with any investment, the cost of capital and physical investments is fairly clear-cut, but the cost of employees has many hidden costs including fringe benefits, social insurance, and legal constraints on hiring, employment, and termination.*

◄ *Siemens, the multi-billion-dollar German conglomerate, has long been known for its apprentice programs in its home country. Because education is often the key to efficient operations in a technological society, Siemens has spread its apprentice-training programs to its U.S. plants. These programs are laying the foundation for the highly skilled workforce that is essential for global competitiveness.*

Productivity and the Service Sector

The service sector provides a special challenge to the accurate measurement of productivity and productivity improvement. The traditional analytical framework of economic theory is based primarily on goods-producing activities. Consequently, most published economic data relate to goods production. But the data do indicate that, as our contemporary service economy has increased in size, we have had slower growth in productivity.

Productivity of the service sector has proven difficult to improve because service-sector work is:

1. Typically labor-intensive (for example, counseling, teaching).
2. Frequently focused on unique individual attributes or desires (for example, investment advice).
3. Often an intellectual task performed by professionals (for example, medical diagnosis).
4. Often difficult to mechanize and automate (for example, a haircut).
5. Often difficult to evaluate for quality (for example, performance of a law firm).

The more intellectual and personal the task, the more difficult it is to achieve increases in productivity. Low-productivity improvement in the service sector is also attributable to the growth of low-productivity activities in the service sector. These include activities not previously a part of the measured economy, such as child care, food preparation, house cleaning, and laundry service. These activities have moved out of the home and into the measured economy as more and more women have joined the workforce. Inclusion of these activities has probably resulted in lower measured productivity for the service sector, although, in fact, actual productivity has probably increased because these activities are now more efficiently produced than previously.[12]

However, in spite of the difficulty of improving productivity in the service sector, improvements are being made. And this text presents a multitude of ways to make these improvements. Indeed, what can be done when management pays attention to how work actually gets done is astonishing![13]

Although the evidence indicates that all industrialized countries have the same problem with service productivity, the U.S. remains the world leader in overall productivity *and* service productivity. Retailing is twice as productive in the U.S. as in Japan, where laws protect shopkeepers from discount chains. The U.S. telephone industry is at least twice as productive as Germany's. The U.S. banking system is also 33% more efficient than Germany's banking oligopolies. However, because productivity is central to the operations manager's job and because the service sector is so large, we take special note in this text of how to improve productivity in the service sector. (See, for instance, the *OM in Action* box "Taco Bell Improves Productivity to Lower Costs.")

[12]Allen Sinai and Zaharo Sofianou, "The Service Economy—Productivity Growth Issues" (CSI Washington, DC), *The Service Economy* (January 1992): 11–16.

[13]These conclusions are not unique. See the work of Michael van Biema and Bruce Greenwald, "Managing Our Way to Higher Service-Sector Productivity," *Harvard Business Review* 75, no. 4 (July–August 1997): 89.

OM IN ACTION   Taco Bell Improves Productivity to Lower Costs

Founded in 1962 by Glenn Bell, Taco Bell is seeking competitive advantage via low cost. Like many other services, Taco Bell increasingly relies on its operations function to improve productivity and reduce cost.

First, it revised its menu and designed meals that were easy to prepare. Taco Bell then shifted a substantial portion of food preparation to suppliers who could perform food processing more efficiently than a standalone restaurant. Ground beef is now precooked prior to arrival and then reheated, as are many dishes that arrive in plastic boil bags for easy sanitary reheating. Similarly, tortillas arrive already fried and onions prediced. Efficient layout and automation has cut to 8 seconds the time needed to prepare tacos and burritos and has cut time in the drive-thru lines by one minute.

These advances have been combined with training and empowerment to increase the span of management from one supervisor for 5 restaurants to one supervisor for 30 or more.

Operations managers at Taco Bell believe they have cut in-store labor by 15 hours per day and reduced floor space by more than 50%. The result is a store that can handle twice the volume with half the labor. Effective operations management has resulted in productivity increases that support Taco Bell's low-cost strategy. Taco Bell is now the fast-food low-cost leader and has a 73% share of the Mexican fast-food market.

Sources: Jackie Hueter and William Swart, *Interfaces* (January–February 1998): 75–91; and *Nation's Restaurant News* (August 15, 2005):68–70.

ETHICS AND SOCIAL RESPONSIBILITY

Operations managers are subjected to constant changes and challenges. The systems they build to convert resources into goods and services are complex. The physical and social environment changes, as do laws and values. These changes present a variety of challenges that come from the conflicting perspectives of stakeholders such as customers, distributors, suppliers, owners, lenders, and employees. These stakeholders, as well as government agencies at various levels, require constant monitoring and thoughtful responses.

Identifying ethical and socially responsible responses while building productive systems is not always clear-cut. Among the many ethical challenges facing operations managers are:

- Efficiently developing and producing safe, quality products.
- Maintaining a clean environment.
- Providing a safe workplace.
- Honoring community commitments.

Managers must do all of this in an ethical and socially responsible way while meeting the demands of the marketplace. If operations managers have a *moral awareness and focus on increasing productivity* in a system where all stakeholders have a voice, then many of the ethical challenges will be successfully addressed. The organization will use fewer resources, the employees will be committed, the market will be satisfied, and the ethical climate will be enhanced. Throughout this text, we note a variety of ways in which operations managers can take ethical and socially responsible actions to successfully address these challenges. We also end each chapter with an *Ethical Dilemma* exercise.

Summary

Operations, marketing, and finance/accounting are the three functions basic to all organizations. The operations function creates goods and services. Much of the progress of operations management has been made in the twentieth century, but since the beginning of time, humankind has been attempting to improve its material well-being. Operations managers are key players in the battle for improved productivity.

However, as societies become increasingly affluent, more of their resources are devoted to services. In the U.S., more than three-quarters of the workforce is employed in the service sector. Productivity improvements are difficult to achieve, but operations managers are the primary vehicle for making improvements.

Key Terms

Production *(p. 4)*
Operations management (OM) *(p. 4)*
Management process *(p. 7)*
Services *(p. 9)*

Pure service *(p. 11)*
Service sector *(p. 12)*
Productivity *(p. 14)*
Single-factor productivity *(p. 15)*

Multifactor productivity *(p. 15)*
Productivity variables *(p. 17)*
Knowledge society *(p. 18)*

Solved Problems

Virtual Office Hours help is available on Student DVD.

Solved Problem 1.1

Productivity can be measured in a variety of ways, such as by labor, capital, energy, material usage, and so on. At Modern Lumber, Inc., Art Binley, president and producer of apple crates sold to growers, has been able, with his current equipment, to produce 240 crates per 100 logs. He currently purchases 100 logs per day, and each log requires 3 labor-hours to process. He believes that he can hire a professional buyer who can buy a better-quality log at the same cost. If this is the case, he can increase his production to 260 crates per 100 logs. His labor-hours will increase by 8 hours per day.

What will be the impact on productivity (measured in crates per labor-hour) if the buyer is hired?

Solution

(a)
$$\text{Current labor productivity} = \frac{240 \text{ crates}}{100 \text{ logs} \times 3 \text{ hours/log}}$$
$$= \frac{240}{300}$$
$$= .8 \text{ crates per labor-hour}$$

(b)
$$\begin{array}{c}\text{Labor productivity}\\\text{with buyer}\end{array} = \frac{260 \text{ crates}}{(100 \text{ logs} \times 3 \text{ hours/log}) + 8 \text{ hours}}$$
$$= \frac{260}{308}$$
$$= .844 \text{ crates per labor-hour}$$

Using current productivity (.80 from [a]) as a base, the increase will be 5.5% (.844/.8 = 1.055, or a 5.5% increase).

Solved Problem 1.2

Art Binley has decided to look at his productivity from a multifactor (total factor productivity) perspective (refer to Solved Problem 1.1). To do so, he has determined his labor, capital, energy, and material usage and decided to use dollars as the common denominator. His total labor-hours are now 300 per day and will increase to 308 per day. His capital and energy costs will remain constant at $350 and $150 per day, respectively. Material costs for the 100 logs per day are $1,000 and will remain the same. Because he pays an average of $10 per hour (with fringes), Binley determines his productivity increase as follows:

Solution

	Current System			System with Professional Buyer	
Labor:	300 hrs. @ $10 =	$3,000	308 hrs. @ $10 =		$3,080
Material:	100 logs/day	1,000			1,000
Capital:		350			350
Energy:		150			150
Total Cost:		$4,500			$4,580

Multifactor productivity of current system:
= 240 crates/4,500 = .0533 crates/dollar

Multifactor productivity of proposed system:
= 260 crates/4,580 = .0568 crates/dollar

Using current productivity (.0533) as a base, the increase will be .066. That is, .0568/.0533 = 1.066, or a 6.6% increase.

Self-Test

- **Before taking the self-test**, refer to the learning objectives listed at the beginning of the chapter and the key terms listed at the end of the chapter.
- Use the key at the back of the text to **correct** your answers.
- **Restudy** pages that correspond to any questions you answered incorrectly or material you feel uncertain about.

1. OM jobs constitute what percentage of all jobs?
   a) 20%
   b) 35%
   c) 18%
   d) 40%

2. Productivity increases when:
   a) inputs increase while outputs remain the same.
   b) inputs decrease while outputs remain the same.
   c) outputs decrease while inputs remain the same.
   d) inputs and outputs increase proportionately.
   e) inputs increase at the same rate as outputs.

3. The capital investment each year in the U.S. usually:
   a) decreases.
   b) remains constant.
   c) increases.
   d) decreases unless favorably taxed.
   e) is very cyclical.

4. Productivity increases each year in the U.S. are the result of three factors:
   a) labor, capital, management
   b) engineering, labor, capital
   c) engineering, capital, quality control
   d) engineering, labor, data processing
   e) engineering, capital, data processing

5. Which appears to provide the best opportunity for increases in productivity?
   a) labor
   b) capital
   c) management
   d) engineering

6. When returns to labor, capital, or management are increased without increased productivity, prices:
   a) rise.
   b) fall.
   c) stay the same.
   d) unable to determine.

7. Problems in the measurement of productivity include:
   a) the unknown effect of external elements.
   b) the absence of precise units of measure.
   c) the effects of quality over time.
   d) all of the above.

8. The person who introduced standardized, interchangeable parts was:
   a) Eli Whitney.
   b) Henry Ford.
   c) Adam Smith.
   d) W. Edwards Deming.
   e) Frederick W. Taylor.

Internet and Student CD-ROM/DVD Exercises

Visit our Companion Web site or use your student CD-ROM/DVD to help with material in this chapter.

 On Our Companion Web site,
www.prenhall.com/heizer
- Self-Study Quizzes
- Practice Problems
- Virtual Company Tour
- Power Point Lecture

 On Your Student CD-ROM
- Practice Problems
- POM for Windows

On Your Student DVD
- Video Clips and Video Case
- Virtual Office Hours for Solved Problems

Discussion Questions

1. Why should one study operations management?
2. Identify four people who have contributed to the theory and techniques of operations management.
3. Briefly describe the contributions of the four individuals identified in the preceding question.
4. Figure 1.1 outlines the operations, finance/accounting, and marketing functions of three organizations. Prepare a chart similar to Figure 1.1 outlining the same functions for one of the following:
   (a) a newspaper
   (b) a drugstore
   (c) a college library
   (d) a summer camp
   (e) a small costume-jewelry factory
5. Answer question 4 for some other organization, perhaps an organization where you have worked.
6. What are the three basic functions of a firm?

7. Name the 10 decision areas of operations management.
8. Name four areas that are significant to improving labor productivity.
9. The U.S., and indeed much of the world, has been described as a "knowledge society." How does this affect productivity measurement and the comparison of productivity between the U.S. and other countries?
10. What are the measurement problems that occur when one attempts to measure productivity?
11. Mass customization and rapid product development were identified as current trends in modern manufacturing operations. What is the relationship, if any, between these trends? Can you cite any examples?
12. What are the five reasons productivity is difficult to improve in the service sector?
13. Describe some of the actions taken by Taco Bell to increase productivity that have resulted in Taco Bell's ability to serve "twice the volume with half the labor."

Ethical Dilemma

Major corporations with overseas subcontractors (such as Ikea in Bangladesh, Unilever in India, and Nike in China) have been criticized, often with substantial negative publicity, when children as young as 10 have been found working in the subcontractor's facilities. The standard response is to perform an audit and then enhance controls so it does not happen again. In one such case, a 10-year-old was terminated. Shortly thereafter, the family, without the 10-year-old's contribution to the family income, lost its modest home, and the 10-year-old was left to scrounge in the local dump for scraps of metal. Was the decision to hire the 10-year-old ethical? Was the decision to terminate the 10-year-old ethical?

Problems*

•   **1.1**   John Lucy makes wooden boxes in which to ship motorcycles. John and his three employees invest a total of 40 hours per day making the 120 boxes.
a)   What is their productivity?
b)   John and his employees have discussed redesigning the process to improve efficiency. If they can increase the rate to 125 per day, what will be their new productivity?
c)   What will be their percentage *increase* in productivity and percentage change? **Px**

•   **1.2**   Riverside Metal Works produces cast bronze valves on a 10-person assembly line. On a recent day, 160 valves were produced during an 8-hour shift. Calculate the labor productivity of the line. **Px**

•   **1.3**   This year, Benson, Inc., will produce 57,600 hot water heaters at its plant in Yulee, Florida, in order to meet expected global demand. To accomplish this, each laborer at the Yulee plant will work 160 hours per month. If the labor productivity at the plant is 0.15 hot water heaters per labor hour, how many laborers are employed at the plant?

•   **1.4**   As a library or Internet assignment, find the U.S. productivity rate (increase) last year for the (a) national economy, (b) manufacturing sector, and (c) service sector.

•   **1.5**   Lori produces "Final Exam Care Packages" for resale by her sorority. She is currently working a total of 5 hours per day to produce 100 care packages.
a)   What is Lori's productivity?
b)   Lori thinks that by redesigning the package, she can increase her total productivity to 133 care packages per day. What will be her new productivity?
c)   What will be the percentage increase in productivity if Lori makes the change? **Px**

••   **1.6**   Eric Johnson makes billiard balls in his New England plant. With recent increases in his costs, he has a newfound interest in efficiency. Eric is interested in determining the productivity of his organization. He would like to know if his organization is maintaining the manufacturing average of 3% increase in productivity. He has the following data representing a month from last year and an equivalent month this year:

	Last Year	**Now**
Units produced	1,000	1,000
Labor (hours)	300	275
Resin (pounds)	50	45
Capital invested ($)	10,000	11,000
Energy (BTU)	3,000	2,850

*Note: **Px** means the problem may be solved with POM for Windows and/or Excel OM.

Show the productivity percentage change for each category and then determine the improvement for labor-hours, the typical standard for comparison. **Px**

••   **1.7**   Eric Johnson (using data from Problem 1.6) determines his costs to be as follows:
•   *Labor:* $10 per hour
•   *Resin:* $5 per pound
•   *Capital expense:* 1% per month of investment
•   *Energy:* $.50 per BTU.
Show the percent change in productivity for one month last year versus one month this year, on a multifactor basis with dollars as the common denominator. **Px**

•   **1.8**   Kleen Karpet cleaned 65 rugs in October, consuming the following resources:

Labor:	520 hours at $13 per hour
Solvent:	100 gallons at $5 per gallon
Machine rental:	20 days at $50 per day

a)   What is the labor productivity per dollar?
b)   What is the multifactor productivity? **Px**

••   **1.9**   David Upton is president of Upton Manufacturing, a producer of Go-Kart tires. Upton makes 1,000 tires per day with the following resources:

Labor:	400 hours per day @ $12.50 per hour
Raw material:	20,000 pounds per day @ $1 per pound
Energy:	$5,000 per day
Capital:	$10,000 per day

a)   What is the labor productivity per labor-hour for these tires at Upton Manufacturing?
b)   What is the multifactor productivity for these tires at Upton Manufacturing?
c)   What is the percent change in multifactor productivity if Upton can reduce the energy bill by $1,000 per day without cutting production or changing any other inputs? **Px**

••   **1.10**   Sawyer's, a local bakery, is worried about increased costs—particularly energy. Last year's records can provide a fairly good estimate of the parameters for this year. Judy Sawyer, the owner, does not believe things have changed much, but she did invest an additional $3,000 for modifications to the bakery's ovens to make them more energy-efficient. The modifications were supposed to make the ovens at least 15% more efficient. Sawyer has asked you to check the energy savings of the new ovens and also to look over other measures of the bakery's productivity to see if the modifications were beneficial. You have the following data to work with:

	Last Year	Now
Production (dozen)	1,500	1,500
Labor (hours)	350	325
Capital investment ($)	15,000	18,000
Energy (BTU)	3,000	2,750

•• **1.11** Cunningham Performance Auto, Inc., modifies 375 autos per year. The manager, Peter Cunningham, is interested in obtaining a measure of overall performance. He has asked you to provide him with a multifactor measure of last year's performance as a benchmark for future comparison. You have assembled the following data. Resource inputs were: labor, 10,000 hours; 500 suspension and engine modification kits; and energy, 100,000 kilowatt-hours. Average labor cost last year was $20 per hour, kits cost $1,000 each, and energy costs were $3 per kilowatt-hour. What do you tell Mr. Cunningham? **Px**

•• **1.12** Lake Charles Seafood makes 500 wooden packing boxes for fresh seafood per day, working in two 10-hour shifts. Due to increased demand, plant managers have decided to operate three 8-hour shifts instead. The plant is now able to produce 650 boxes per day. Calculate the company's productivity before the change in work rules and after the change. What is the percent increase in productivity? **Px**

••• **1.13** Charles Lackey operates a bakery in Idaho Falls, Idaho. Because of its excellent product and excellent location, demand has increased by 25% in the last year. On far too many occasions, customers have not been able to purchase the bread of their choice. Because of the size of the store, no new ovens can be added. At a staff meeting, one employee suggested ways to load the ovens differently so that more loaves of bread can be baked at one time. This new process will require that the ovens be loaded by hand, requiring additional manpower. This is the only thing to be changed. If the bakery makes 1,500 loaves per month with a labor productivity of 2.344 loaves per labor-hour, how many workers will Lackey need to add? (*Hint:* Each worker works 160 hours per month.)

•• **1.14** Refer to Problem 1.13. The pay will be $8 per hour for employees. Charles Lackey can also improve the yield by purchasing a new blender. The new blender will mean an increase in his investment. This added investment has a cost of $100 per month, but he will achieve the same output (an increase to 1,875) as the change in labor hours. Which is the better decision?
a) Show the productivity change, in loaves per dollar, with an increase in labor cost (from 640 to 800 hours).
b) Show the new productivity, in loaves per dollar, with only an increase in investment ($100 per month more).
c) Show the percent productivity change for labor and investment.

••• **1.15** Refer to Problems 1.13 and 1.14. If Charles Lackey's utility costs remain constant at $500 per month, labor at $8 per hour, and cost of ingredients at $0.35 per loaf, but Charles does not purchase the blender suggested in Problem 1.14, what will the productivity of the bakery be? What will be the percent increase or decrease?

•• **1.16** In December, General Motors produced 6,600 customized vans at its plant in Detroit. The labor productivity at this plant is known to have been 0.10 vans per labor-hour during that month. If 300 laborers were employed at the plant that month, how many hours did the average laborer work that month?

•• **1.17** Natalie Attired runs a small job shop where garments are made. The job shop employs eight workers. Each worker is paid $10 per hour. During the first week of March, each worker worked 45 hours. Together, they produced a batch of 132 garments. Of these garments, 52 were "seconds" (meaning that they were flawed). The seconds were sold for $90 each at a factory outlet store. The remaining 80 garments were sold to retail outlets at a price of $198 per garment. What was the labor productivity, in dollars per labor-hour, at this job shop during the first week of March?

Case Studies

National Air Express

National Air is a competitive air-express firm with offices around the country. Frank Smith, the Chattanooga, Tennessee, station manager, is preparing his quarterly budget report, which will be presented at the Southeast regional meeting next week. He is very concerned about adding capital expense to the operation when business has not increased appreciably. This has been the worst first quarter he can remember: snowstorms, earthquakes, and bitter cold. He has asked Martha Lewis, field services supervisor, to help him review the available data and offer possible solutions.

Service Methods

National Air offers door-to-door overnight air-express delivery within the U.S. Smith and Lewis manage a fleet of 24 trucks to handle freight in the Chattanooga area. Routes are assigned by area, usually delineated by zip code boundaries, major streets, or key geographical features, such as the Tennessee River. Pickups are generally handled between 3:00 P.M. and 6:00 P.M., Monday through Friday. Driver routes are a combination of regularly scheduled daily stops and pickups that the customer calls in as needed. These call-in pickups are dispatched by radio to the driver. Most call-in customers want as late a pickup as possible, just before closing (usually at 5:00 P.M.).

When the driver arrives at each pickup location, he or she provides supplies as necessary (an envelope or box if requested) and must receive a completed air waybill for each package. Because the industry is extremely competitive, a professional, courteous driver is essential to retaining customers. Therefore, Smith has always been concerned that drivers not rush a customer to complete his or her package and paperwork.

Budget Considerations

Smith and Lewis have found that they have been unable to meet their customers' requests for a scheduled pickup on many occasions in the past quarter. Although, on average, drivers are not handling any more business, they are unable on some days to arrive at each location on time. Smith does not think he can justify increasing costs by $1,200 per week for additional trucks and drivers while productivity (measured in shipments per truck/day) has remained flat. The company has established itself as the low-cost operator in

the industry but has at the same time committed itself to offering quality service and value for its customers.

Discussion Questions

1. Is the productivity measure of shipments per day per truck still useful? Are there alternatives that might be effective?
2. What, if anything, can be done to reduce the daily variability in pickup call-ins? Can the driver be expected to be at several locations at once at 5:00 P.M.?
3. How should package pickup performance be measured? Are standards useful in an environment that is affected by the weather, traffic, and other random variables? Are other companies having similar problems?

Source: Adapted from a case by Phil Pugliese under the supervision of Professor Marilyn M. Helms, University of Tennessee at Chattanooga. Reprinted by permission.

Zychol Chemicals Corporation

Bob Richards, the production manager of Zychol Chemicals, in Houston, Texas, is preparing his quarterly report, which is to include a productivity analysis for his department. One of the inputs is production data prepared by Sharon Walford, his operations analyst. The report, which she gave him this morning, showed the following:

	2006	2007
Production (units)	4,500	6,000
Raw material used (barrels of petroleum by-products)	700	900
Labor hours	22,000	28,000
Capital cost applied to the department ($)	$375,000	$620,000

Bob knew that his labor cost per hour had increased from an average of $13 per hour to an average of $14 per hour, primarily due to a move by management to become more competitive with a new company that had just opened a plant in the area. He also knew that his average cost per barrel of raw material had increased from $320 to $360. He was concerned about the accounting procedures that increased his capital cost from

$375,000 to $620,000, but earlier discussions with his boss suggested that there was nothing that could be done about that allocation.

Bob wondered if his productivity had increased at all. He called Sharon into the office and conveyed the above information to her and asked her to prepare this part of the report.

Discussion Questions

1. Prepare the productivity part of the report for Mr. Richards. He probably expects some analysis of productivity inputs for all factors, as well as a multifactor analysis for both years with the change in productivity (up or down) and the amount noted.
2. The producer price index had increased from 120 to 125, and this fact seemed to indicate to Mr. Richards that his costs were too high. What do you tell him are the implications of this change in the producer price index?
3. Management's expectation for departments such as Mr. Richards's is an annual productivity increase of 5%. Did he reach this goal?

Source: Professor Hank Maddux III, Sam Houston State University.

Hard Rock Cafe: Operations Management in Services **Video Case**

In its 37 years of existence, Hard Rock has grown from a modest London pub to a global power managing 121 cafes, 5 hotels, casinos, live music venues, and a huge annual Rockfest concert. This puts Hard Rock firmly in the service industry—a sector that employs over 75% of the people in the U.S. Hard Rock moved its world headquarters to Orlando, Florida, in 1988 and has expanded to more than 40 locations throughout the U.S., serving over 100,000 meals each day. Hard Rock chefs are modifying the menu from classic American—burgers and chicken wings—to include higher-end items such as stuffed veal chops and lobster tails. Just as taste in music changes over time, so does Hard Rock Cafe, with new menus, layouts, memorabilia, services, and strategies.

At Orlando's Universal Studios, a traditional tourist destination, Hard Rock Cafe serves over 3,500 meals each day. The cafe employs about 400 people. Most are employed in the restaurant, but some work in the retail shop. Retail is now a standard and increasingly prominent feature in Hard Rock Cafes (since close to 48% of revenue comes from this source). Cafe employees include kitchen and wait staff, hostesses, and bartenders. Hard Rock employees are not only competent in their job skills but are also passionate about music and have engaging personalities. Cafe staff is scheduled down to 15-minute intervals to meet seasonal and daily demand changes in the tourist environment of Orlando. Surveys are done on a regular basis to evaluate quality of food and service at the cafe.

Scores are rated on a 1 to 7 scale, and if the score is not a 7, the food or service is a failure.

Hard Rock is adding a new emphasis on live music and is redesigning its restaurants to accommodate the changing tastes. Since Eric Clapton hung his guitar on the wall to mark his favorite bar stool, Hard Rock has become the world's leading collector and exhibitor of rock 'n' roll memorabilia, with changing exhibits at its cafes throughout the world. The collection includes 1,000's of pieces, valued at $40 million. In keeping with the times, Hard Rock also maintains a Web site, **www.hardrock.com**, which receives over 100,000 hits per week, and a weekly cable television program on VH-1. Hard Rock's brand recognition, at 92%, is one of the highest in the world.

Discussion Questions*

1. From your knowledge of restaurants, from the video, from the *Global Company Profile* that opens this chapter, and from the case itself, identify how each of the 10 decisions of operations management is applied at Hard Rock Cafe.

2. How would you determine the productivity of the kitchen staff and wait staff at Hard Rock?

3. How are the 10 decisions of OM different when applied to the operations manager of a service operation such as Hard Rock versus an automobile company such as Ford Motor Company?

*You may wish to play this video case on your DVD before addressing these questions.

Additional Case Study

Harvard has selected this Harvard Business School case to accompany this chapter:

harvardbusinessonline.hbsp.harvard.edu

• **Taco Bell Corp.** (#692-058): Illustrates the power of breakthrough thinking in a service industry.

Bibliography

Deo, Balbinder S., and Doug Strong. "Cost: The Ultimate Measure of Productivity." *Industrial Management* 42, no. 3 (May–June 2000): 20–23.

Dewan, Sanjeev. "Information Technology and Productivity: Evidence from Country-Level Data." *Management Science* 46, no. 4 (April 2000): 548–562.

Hounshell, D. A. *From the American System to Mass Production 1800–1932: The Development of Manufacturing.* Baltimore: Johns Hopkins University Press, 1985.

Lewis, William W., *The Power of Productivity.* Chicago: University of Chicago Press, 2004.

Sahay, B. S. "Multi-factor Productivity Measurement Model for Service Organization." *International Journal of Productivity and Performance Management* 54, no. 1–2 (2005):7–23.

Tangen, S. "Demystifying Productivity and Performance." *International Journal of Productivity and Performance Measurement* 54, no. 1–2 (2005):34–47.

Taylor, F. W. *The Principles of Scientific Management.* New York: Harper & Brothers, 1911.

van Biema, Michael, and Bruce Greenwald. "Managing Our Way to Higher Service-Sector Productivity." *Harvard Business Review* 75, no. 4 (July–August 1997): 87–95.

Wrege, C. D. *Frederick W. Taylor, the Father of Scientific Management: Myth and Reality.* Homewood, IL: Business One Irwin, 1991.

Internet Resources

American Productivity and Quality Center: **www.apqc.org**

American Statistical Association (ASA) offers business and economics DataLinks, a searchable index of statistical data: **www.econ-datalinks.org**

Economics and Statistics Administration: **www.esa.doc.gov**

Federal Statistics: **www.fedstats.gov**

National Bureau of Economic Research: **www.nber.org**

U.S. Bureau of Labor Statistics: **stats.bls.gov**

U.S. Census Bureau: **www.census.gov**

CHAPTER 2

Operations Strategy in a Global Environment

Chapter Outline

Learning Objectives

When you complete this chapter you should be able to

1. Define mission and strategy
2. Identify and explain three strategic approaches to competitive advantage
3. Identify and define the 10 decisions of operations management
4. Identify five OM strategy insights provided by PIMS research
5. Identify and explain four global operations strategy options

Global Company Profile: Boeing

Boeing's Global Strategy Yields Competitive Advantage

Boeing's strategy for its 787 Dreamliner is unique from both an engineering and global perspective.

The Dreamliner incorporates the latest in a wide range of aerospace technologies, from airframe and engine design to superlightweight titanium graphite laminate, carbon fiber and epoxy, and composites. Another innovation is the electronic monitoring system that allows the airplane to report maintenance requirements to ground-based computer systems. Boeing has also worked with General Electric and Rolls-Royce to develop more efficient engines. The advances in engine technology contribute as much as 8% of the increased fuel/payload efficiency of the new airplane, representing a nearly two-generation jump in technology.

▲ With the 787's state-of-the-art design, more spacious interior, and global suppliers, Boeing has garnered record sales worldwide.

Some of the International Suppliers of Boeing 787 Components

Latecoere	France	Passenger doors
Labinel	France	Wiring
Dassault	France	Design and PLM software
Messier-Bugatti	France	Electric brakes
Thales	France	Electrical power conversion system and integrated standby flight display
Messier-Dowty	France	Landing gear structure
Diehl	Germany	Interior lighting
Cobham	UK	Fuel pumps and valves
Rolls-Royce	UK	Engines
Smiths Aerospace	UK	Central computer system
BAE Systems	UK	Electronics
Alenia Aeronautica	Italy	Upper center fuselage and horizontal stabilizer
Toray Industries	Japan	Carbon fiber for wing and tail units
Fuji Heavy Industries	Japan	Center wing box
Kawasaki Heavy Industries	Japan	Forward fuselage, fixed sections of wing, landing gear wheel well
Teijin Seiki	Japan	Hydraulic actuators
Mitsubishi Heavy Industries	Japan	Wing box
Chengdu Aircraft Group	China	Rudder
Hafei Aviation	China	Parts
Korean Airlines	South Korea	Wingtips
Saab	Sweden	Cargo and access doors

This state-of-the-art Boeing 787 is also *global*. Led by Boeing at its Everett, Washington, facility, an international team of aerospace companies developed the airplane. New technologies, new design, new manufacturing processes, and committed international suppliers are helping Boeing and its partners achieve unprecedented levels of performance in design, manufacture, and operation.

The 787 is global with a range of 8,300 miles. And it is global because it is being built across the world. With a huge financial risk of over $5 billion, Boeing needed partners. The global nature of both technology and the aircraft market meant finding exceptional developers and suppliers, wherever they might be. It also meant finding firms willing to step up to the risk associated with a very expensive new product. These partners not only spread the risk but also bring commitment to the table. Countries that have a stake in the 787 are more likely to buy from Boeing than from the European competitor Airbus Industries.

Boeing teamed with more than 20 international systems suppliers to develop technologies and design concepts for the 787. Boeing found its 787 partners in over a dozen countries; a few of them are shown in the table on the left.

The Japanese companies Toray, Teijin Seiki, Fuji, Kawasaki, and Mitsubishi are producing over 35% of the project, providing whole composite fuselage sections. Italy's Alenia Aeronautica is building an additional 10% of the plane.

Many U.S. companies, including Crane Aerospace, Fairchild Controls, Goodrich, General Dynamics, Hamilton Sundstrand, Honeywell, Moog, Parker Hannifin, Rockwell Collins, Vought Aircraft, and Triumph Group are also suppliers. Boeing has 70% to 80% of the Dreamliner built by other companies. And even some of the portion built by Boeing is produced at Boeing facilities outside the U.S., in Australia and Canada.

The global Dreamliner is efficient, has a global range, and is made from components produced around the world. The result: a state-of-the-art airplane reflecting the global nature of business in the 21st century and one of the fastest-selling commercial jets in history.

▲ *Boeing's collaborative technology enables a "virtual workspace" that allows engineers on the 787, including partners in Australia, Japan, Italy, Canada and across the United States, to make concurrent design changes to the airplane in real time. Designing, building, and testing the 787 digitally before production reduced design errors and improved production efficiencies.*

◄ *Components from Boeing's worldwide supply chain come together on an assembly line in Everett, Washington. Although components come from throughout the world, about 35% of the 787 structure comes from Japanese companies.*

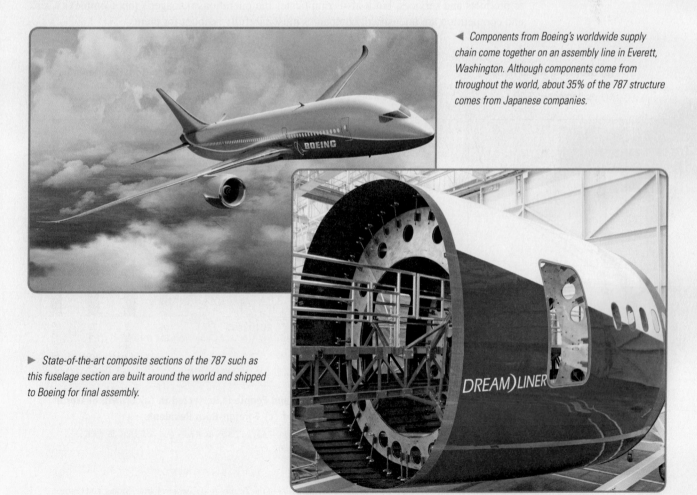

▶ *State-of-the-art composite sections of the 787 such as this fuselage section are built around the world and shipped to Boeing for final assembly.*

Today's operations manager must have a global view of operations strategy. Since the early 1990s, nearly 3 billion people in developing countries have overcome the cultural, religious, ethnic, and political barriers that constrain productivity and are now players on the global economic stage. As these barriers disappear, simultaneous advances are being made in technology, reliable shipping, and cheap communication. The unsurprising result is the growth of world trade, global capital markets, and the international movement of people; see Figure 2.1(a), (b), and (c). This means: increasing economic integration and interdependence of countries—in a word, globalization.[1] In response, organizations are hastily extending their operations globally with innovative strategies. For instance:

"No great civilization has developed in isolation."

Thomas Sewell

- Boeing is competitive because both its sales and production are worldwide.
- Italy's Benetton moves inventory to stores around the world faster than its competition by building flexibility into design, production, and distribution.
- Sony purchases components from suppliers in Thailand, Malaysia, and elsewhere around the world for assembly in its electronic products.
- Volvo, considered a Swedish company, is controlled by a U.S. company, Ford. But the current Volvo S40 is built in Belgium on a platform shared with the Mazda 3 (built in Japan) and the Ford Focus (built and sold in Europe.)
- China's Haier (pronounced "higher") is now producing compact refrigerators (it has one-third of the U.S. market) and refrigerated wine cabinets (it has half of the U.S. market) in South Carolina.

Globalization means that domestic production and exporting may no longer be a viable business model; local production and exporting no longer guarantee success or even survival. There are new standards of global competitiveness that impact quality, variety, customization, convenience, timeliness, and cost. The globalization of strategy contributes efficiency and adds value to products and services, but it also complicates the operations manager's job. Complexity, risk and competition are intensified; companies must carefully account for them.

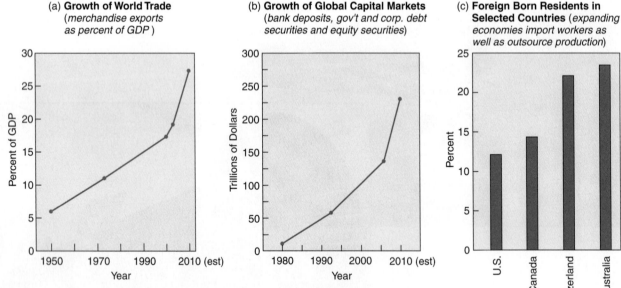

▲ **Figure 2.1**   Movement of Goods, Capital, and People is Reflected in (a) Growth of World Trade, (b) Growth of Global Capital Markets, and (c) Foreign-Born Residents

Sources: Federal Reserve Bank of Dallas (May–June 2006) and (July–August 2005); *McKinsey Quarterly* (July 26, 2006); and Organization for Economic Cooperation and Development (OECD).

---

[1]See Thomas Friedman's *The World Is Flat: A Brief History of the Twenty-first Century*, Farrar, Straus, and Giroux, 2005, for his stimulating discussion of how new players, new playing field, and new processes ensure the rapid expansion of globalization.

A GLOBAL VIEW OF OPERATIONS

We have identified six reasons domestic business operations decide to change to some form of international operation. They are:

1. Reduce costs (labor, taxes, tariffs, etc.).
2. Improve supply chain.
3. Provide better goods and services.
4. Understand markets.
5. Learn to improve operations.
6. Attract and retain global talent.

Let us examine, in turn, each of the six reasons.

Reduce Costs   Many international operations seek to take advantage of the tangible opportunities to reduce their costs. Foreign locations with lower wages can help lower both direct and indirect costs. (See the *OM in Action* box "U.S. Cartoon Production at Home in Manila.") Less stringent government regulations on a wide variety of operation practices (e.g., environmental control, health and safety, etc.) reduce costs. Opportunities to cut the cost of taxes and tariffs also encourage foreign operations. In Mexico, the creation of **maquiladoras** (free trade zones) allows manufacturers to cut their costs of taxation by paying only on the value added by Mexican workers. If a U.S. manufacturer, such as GM, brings a $500 engine to a maquiladora operation for assembly work costing $25, tariff duties will be charged only on the $25 of work performed in Mexico.

Shifting low-skilled jobs to another country has several potential advantages. First, and most obviously, the firm may reduce costs. Second, moving the lower skilled jobs to a lower cost location frees higher cost workers for more valuable tasks. Third, reducing wage costs allows the savings to be invested in improved products and facilities (and the retraining of existing workers, if necessary) at the home location. The impact of this approach is shown in the *OM in Action* box "Going Global to Compete."

Trade agreements have also helped reduce tariffs and thereby reduce the cost of operating facilities in foreign countries. The **World Trade Organization (WTO)** has helped reduce tariffs from 40% in 1940 to less than 3% today. Another important trade agreement is the **North American Free Trade Agreement (NAFTA)**. NAFTA seeks to phase out all trade and tariff barriers among Canada, Mexico, and the U.S. Other trade agreements that are accelerating global trade include APEC (the Pacific Rim countries), SEATO (Australia, New Zealand, Japan, Hong Kong, South Korea, New Guinea, and Chile), and MERCOSUR (Argentina, Brazil, Paraguay, and Uruguay).

Maquiladoras
Mexican factories located along the U.S.–Mexico border that receive preferential tariff treatment.

World Trade Organization (WTO)
An international organization that promotes world trade by lowering barriers to the free flow of goods across borders.

NAFTA
A free trade agreement between Canada, Mexico, and the U.S.

OM in Action   U.S. Cartoon Production at Home in Manila

Fred Flintstone is not from Bedrock. He is actually from Manila, capital of the Philippines. So are Tom and Jerry, Aladdin, and Donald Duck. More than 90% of American television cartoons are produced in Asia and India, with the Philippines leading the way. With their natural advantage of English as an official language and a strong familiarity with U.S. culture, animation companies in Manila now employ more than 1,700 people. Filipinos think Western, and "you need to have a group of artists that can understand the humor that goes with it," says Bill Dennis, a Hanna-Barbera executive.

Major studios like Disney, Marvel, Warner Brothers, and Hanna-Barbera send *storyboards*—cartoon action

outlines—and voice tracks to the Philippines. Artists there draw, paint, and film about 20,000 sketches for a 30-minute episode. The cost of $130,000 to produce an episode in the Philippines compares with $160,000 in Korea and $500,000 in the U.S.

Sources: The New York Times (February 26, 2004): A29; and *The Wall Street Journal* (August 9, 2005): D8.

European Union (EU)
A European trade group that has 27 member states.

Another trading group is the **European Union (EU)**.[2] The European Union has reduced trade barriers among the participating European nations through standardization and a common currency, the euro. However, this major U.S. trading partner, with 490 million people, is also placing some of the world's most restrictive conditions on products sold in the EU. Everything from recycling standards to automobile bumpers to hormone-free farm products must meet EU standards, complicating international trade.

Improve the Supply Chain   The supply chain can often be improved by locating facilities in countries where unique resources are available. These resources may be expertise, labor, or raw material. For example, auto-styling studios from throughout the world are migrating to the auto mecca of southern California to ensure the necessary expertise in contemporary auto design. Similarly, world athletic shoe production has migrated from South Korea to Guangzhou, China: this location takes advantage of the low-cost labor and production competence in a city where 40,000 people work making athletic shoes for the world. And a perfume essence manufacturer wants a presence in Grasse, France, where much of the world's perfume essences are prepared from the flowers of the Mediterranean.

Provide Better Goods and Services   Although the characteristics of goods and services can be objective and measurable (e.g., number of on-time deliveries), they can also be subjective and less measurable (e.g., sensitivity to culture). We need an ever better understanding of differences in culture and of the way business is handled in different countries. Improved understanding as the result of a local presence permits firms to customize products and services to meet unique cultural needs in foreign markets.

Another reason for international operations is to reduce response time to meet customers' changing product and service requirements. Customers who purchase goods and services from U.S. firms are increasingly located in foreign countries. Providing them with quick and adequate service is often improved by locating facilities in their home countries.

Understand Markets   Because international operations require interaction with foreign customers, suppliers, and other competitive businesses, international firms inevitably learn about opportunities for new products and services. Europe led the way with cell phone innovations, and now the Japanese lead with the latest cell phone fads. Knowledge of these markets not only helps firms understand where the market is going but also helps firms diversify their customer base, add production flexibility, and smooth the business cycle.

OM in Action   Going Global to Compete

Banking giant Wachovia Corp. of Charlotte, North Carolina, has inked a $1.1 billion deal with India's Genpact to outsource finance and accounting jobs. Wachovia has also handed over administration of its human resources programs to Illinois-based Hewitt Associates. This is "what we need to do to become a great customer-relationship company," says Wachovia executive P. J. Sidebottom. The expected cost savings of $600 million to $1 billion over the next three years will be invested in the U.S. to boost the core banking business. These investments will be made in new ATMs, branches, and personnel.

Similarly, Dana Corp. of Toledo, Ohio, is also taking a global approach. Dana established a joint venture with Cardanes S.A. to produce truck transmissions in Queretaro, Mexico. Then Dana switched 288 U.S. employees in its Jonesboro, Arkansas, plant from producing truck transmissions at breakeven to axle production at a profit. Productivity is up in Jonesboro, and the Mexican joint venture is making money. Employees in both Jonesboro and Queretaro, as well as stockholders, came out ahead on the move. Dana is also moving operations to China, India, Eastern Europe, and South America.

Resourceful organizations like Wachovia and Dana use a global perspective to become more efficient, which allows them to develop new products, retrain employees, and invest in new plant and equipment.

Sources: Business Week (January 30, 2006): 50–64; *Forbes* (May 8, 2006): 58; and **www.dana.com/news/**.

[2]The 27 members of the European Union (EU) as of 2007 were Austria, Belgium, Bulgaria, Cyprus, Czech Republic, Denmark, Estonia, Finland, France, Germany, Greece, Hungary, Ireland, Italy, Latvia, Lithuania, Luxembourg, Malta, the Netherlands, Poland, Portugal, Romania, Slovakia, Slovenia, Spain, Sweden, United Kingdom: not all have adopted the Euro.

◀ *A worldwide strategy places added burdens on operations management. Because of economic and lifestyle differences, designers must target products to each market. For instance, clothes washers sold in northern countries must spin-dry clothes much better than those in warmer climates, where consumers are likely to line-dry them. Similarly, as shown here, Whirlpool refrigerators sold in Bangkok are manufactured in bright colors because they are often put in living rooms.*

Another reason to go into foreign markets is the opportunity to expand the *life cycle* (i.e., stages a product goes through; see Chapter 5) of an existing product. While some products in the U.S. are in a "mature" stage of their product life cycle, they may represent state-of-the-art products in less developed countries. For example, the U.S. market for personal computers could be characterized as "mature" but as in the "introductory" stage in many developing countries, such as Albania, Vietnam, and Myanmar (Burma).

Learn to Improve Operations   Learning does not take place in isolation. Firms serve themselves and their customers well when they remain open to the free flow of ideas. For example, GM found that it could improve operations by jointly building and running, with the Japanese, an auto assembly plant in San Jose, California. This strategy allows GM to contribute its capital and knowledge of U.S. labor and environmental laws while the Japanese contribute production and inventory ideas. GM also used its employees and experts from Japan to help design its U.S. Saturn plant around production ideas from Japan. Similarly, operations managers have improved equipment and layout by learning from the ergonomic competence of the Scandinavians.

Attract and Retain Global Talent   Global organizations can attract and retain better employees by offering more employment opportunities. They need people in all functional areas and areas of expertise worldwide. Global firms can recruit and retain good employees because they provide both greater growth opportunities and insulation against unemployment during times of economic downturn. During economic downturns in one country or continent, a global firm has the means to relocate unneeded personnel to more prosperous locations. Global organizations also provide incentives for people who like to travel or take vacations in foreign countries.

So, to recap, successfully achieving a competitive advantage in our shrinking world means maximizing all of the possible opportunities, from tangible to intangible, that international operations can offer.

Cultural and Ethical Issues

One of the great challenges as operations go global is reconciling differences in social and cultural behavior. With issues ranging from bribery, to child labor, to the environment, managers sometimes do not know how to respond when operating in a different culture. What one country's culture deems acceptable may be considered unacceptable or illegal in another.

In the last decade, changes in international laws, agreements, and codes of conduct have been applied to define ethical behavior among managers around the world. The World Trade Organization, for example, helps to make uniform the protection of both governments and industries from foreign firms that engage in unethical conduct. Even on issues where significant differences between cultures exist, as in the area of bribery or the protection of intellectual property, global uniformity is slowly being accepted by most nations.

Globalization may take us to the floating factory: A six-person crew will take a factory from port to port to obtain the best market, material, labor, and tax advantages. The service industry, by way of the floating resort (the cruise ship), already provides such an example.

"The ethics of the world market are very clear. Manufacturers will move wherever it is cheapest or most convenient to their interests."

Carlos Arias Macelli, owner of a Guatemala plant that supplies JCPenney

In spite of cultural and ethical differences, we live in a period of extraordinary mobility of capital, information, goods, and even people. We can expect this to continue. The financial sector, the telecommunications sector, and the logistics infrastructure of the world are healthy institutions that foster efficient and effective use of capital, information, and goods. Globalization, with all its opportunities and risks, is here and will continue. It must be embraced as managers develop their missions and strategies.

DEVELOPING MISSIONS AND STRATEGIES

Learning Objective

1. Define mission and strategy

An effective operations management effort must have a *mission* so it knows where it is going and a *strategy* so it knows how to get there. This is the case for a small or domestic organization, as well as a large international organization.

Mission

Mission
The purpose or rationale for an organization's existence.

Economic success, indeed survival, is the result of identifying missions to satisfy a customer's needs and wants. We define the organization's **mission** as its purpose—what it will contribute to society. Mission statements provide boundaries and focus for organizations and the concept around which the firm can rally. The mission states the rationale for the organization's existence. Developing a good strategy is difficult, but it is much easier if the mission has been well defined. Figure 2.2 provides examples of mission statements.

Once an organization's mission has been decided, each functional area within the firm determines its supporting mission. By *functional area* we mean the major disciplines required by the firm, such as marketing, finance/accounting, and production/operations. Missions for each function are developed to support the firm's overall mission. Then within that function lower-level supporting missions are established for the OM functions. Figure 2.3 provides such a hierarchy of sample missions.

▶ **Figure 2.2**

Mission Statements for Four Organizations

Sources: Annual reports: courtesy of FedEx and Merck; Hard Rock Cafe: *Employee Handbook.* Arnold Palmer Hospital.

FedEx
FedEx is committed to our People-Service-Profit philosophy. We will produce outstanding financial returns by providing totally reliable, competitively superior, global air–ground transportation of high-priority goods and documents that require rapid, time-certain delivery. Equally important, positive control of each package will be maintained utilizing real time electronic tracking and tracing systems. A complete record of each shipment and delivery will be presented with our request for payment. We will be helpful, courteous, and professional to each other and the public. We will strive to have a completely satisfied customer at the end of each transaction.
Merck
The mission of Merck is to provide society with superior products and services—innovations and solutions that improve the quality of life and satisfy customer needs—to provide employees with meaningful work and advancement opportunities and investors with a superior rate of return.
Hard Rock Cafe
Our Mission: To spread the spirit of Rock 'n' Roll by delivering an exceptional entertainment and dining experience. We are committed to being an important, contributing member of our community and offering the Hard Rock family a fun, healthy, and nurturing work environment while ensuring our long-term success.
Arnold Palmer Hospital
Arnold Palmer Hospital is a healing environment providing family-centered care with compassion, comfort and respect … when it matters most.

Sample Company Mission
To manufacture and service an innovative, growing, and profitable worldwide microwave communications business that exceeds our customers' expectations.

Sample Operations Management Mission
To produce products consistent with the company's mission as the worldwide low-cost manufacturer.

Sample OM Department Missions	
Product design	To design and produce products and services with outstanding quality and inherent customer value.
Quality management	To attain the exceptional value that is consistent with our company mission and marketing objectives by close attention to design, procurement, production, and field service opportunities.
Process design	To determine and design or produce the production process and equipment that will be compatible with low-cost product, high quality, and a good quality of work life at economical cost.
Location	To locate, design, and build efficient and economical facilities that will yield high value to the company, its employees, and the community.
Layout design	To achieve, through skill, imagination, and resourcefulness in layout and work methods, production effectiveness and efficiency while supporting a high quality of work life.
Human resources	To provide a good quality of work life, with well-designed, safe, rewarding jobs, stable employment, and equitable pay, in exchange for outstanding individual contribution from employees at all levels.
Supply-chain management	To collaborate with suppliers to develop innovative products from stable, effective, and efficient sources of supply.
Inventory	To achieve low investment in inventory consistent with high customer service levels and high facility utilization.
Scheduling	To achieve high levels of throughput and timely customer delivery through effective scheduling.
Maintenance	To achieve high utilization of facilities and equipment by effective preventive maintenance and prompt repair of facilities and equipment.

◀ **Figure 2.3**

Sample Missions for a Company, the Operations Function, and Major OM Departments

Strategy

With the mission established, strategy and its implementation can begin. **Strategy** is an organization's action plan to achieve the mission. Each functional area has a strategy for achieving its mission and for helping the organization reach the overall mission. These strategies exploit opportunities and strengths, neutralize threats, and avoid weaknesses. In the following sections we will describe how strategies are developed and implemented.

Firms achieve missions in three conceptual ways: (1) differentiation, (2) cost leadership, and (3) response.[3] This means operations managers are called on to deliver goods and services that are (1) *better*, or at least different, (2) *cheaper*, and (3) more *responsive*. Operations managers translate these *strategic concepts* into tangible tasks to be accomplished. Any one or combination

Strategy
How an organization expects to achieve its missions and goals.

Learning Objective

2. Identify and explain three strategic approaches to competitive advantage

[3]See related discussion in Michael E. Porter, *Competitive Strategy: Techniques for Analyzing Industries and Competitors* (New York: The Free Press, 1980). Also see Donald C. Hambrick and James W. Fredrickson, "Are You Sure You Have a Strategy?" *Academy of Management Executive* 15, no. 4 (November 2001): 48–59.

Video 2.1

Operations Strategy at Regal Marine

of these three strategic concepts can generate a system that has a unique advantage over competitors. For example, Hunter Fan has differentiated itself as a premier maker of quality ceiling fans that lower heating and cooling costs for its customers. Nucor Steel, on the other hand, satisfies customers by being the lowest-cost steel producer in the world. And Dell achieves rapid response by building personal computers with each customer's requested software in a matter of hours.

Clearly, strategies differ. And each strategy puts different demands on operations management. Hunter Fan's strategy is one of *differentiating* itself via quality from others in the industry. Nucor focuses on value at *low cost*, and Dell's dominant strategy is quick, reliable *response*.

ACHIEVING COMPETITIVE ADVANTAGE THROUGH OPERATIONS

Each of the three strategies provides an opportunity for operations managers to achieve competitive advantage. **Competitive advantage** implies the creation of a system that has a unique advantage over competitors. The idea is to create customer value in an efficient and sustainable way. Pure forms of these strategies may exist, but operations managers will more likely be called on to implement some combination of them. Let us briefly look at how managers achieve competitive advantage via *differentiation*, *low cost*, and *response*.

Competitive advantage
The creation of a unique advantage over competitors.

Competing on Differentiation

Safeskin Corporation is number one in latex exam gloves because it has differentiated itself and its products. It did so by producing gloves that were designed to prevent allergic reactions about which doctors were complaining. When other glove makers caught up, Safeskin developed hypoallergenic gloves. Then it added texture to its gloves. Then it developed a synthetic disposable glove for those allergic to latex—always staying ahead of the competition. Safeskin's strategy is to develop a reputation for designing and producing reliable state-of-the-art gloves, thereby differentiating itself.

Differentiation is concerned with providing *uniqueness*. A firm's opportunities for creating uniqueness are not located within a particular function or activity but can arise in virtually everything the firm does. Moreover, because most products include some service, and most services include some product, the opportunities for creating this uniqueness are limited only by imagination. Indeed, **differentiation** should be thought of as going beyond both physical characteristics and service attributes to encompass everything about the product or service that influences the value that the customers derive from it. Therefore, effective operations managers assist in defining everything about a product or service that will influence the potential value to the customer. This may be the convenience of a broad product line, product features, or a service related to the product. Such services can manifest themselves through convenience (location of distribution centers, stores, or branches), training, product delivery and installation, or repair and maintenance services.

Differentiation
Distinguishing the offerings of an organization in a way that the customer perceives as adding value.

In the service sector, one option for extending product differentiation is through an *experience*. Differentiation by experience in services is a manifestation of the growing "experience economy."[4] The idea of **experience differentiation** is to engage the customer—to use people's five senses so they become immersed, or even an active participant, in the product. Disney does this with the Magic Kingdom. People no longer just go on a ride; they are immersed in the Magic Kingdom—surrounded by a dynamic visual and sound experience that complements the physical ride. Some rides further engage the customer by having them steer the ride or shoot targets or villains.

Experience differentiation
Engaging the customer with a product through imaginative use of the five senses, so the customer "experiences" the product.

Theme restaurants, such as Hard Rock Cafe, likewise differentiate themselves by providing an "experience." Hard Rock engages the customer with classic rock music, big-screen rock videos, memorabilia, and staff who can tell stories. In many instances, a full-time guide is available to explain the displays, and there is always a convenient retail store so the guest can take home a tangible part of the experience. The result is a "dining experience" rather than just a

Video 2.2

Hard Rock's Global Strategy

[4]For an engaging book on the experience economy, see Joseph Pine II and James H. Gilmore, *The Experience Economy*, (Boston: Harvard Business School Press, 1999). Also see Leonard L. Berry, Lewis P. Carbone, and Stephan H. Haeckel, "Managing the Total Customer Experience," *MIT Sloan Management Review* (spring 2002): 85–90.

meal. In a less dramatic way, your local supermarket delivers an experience when it provides music and the aroma of freshly baked bread, and when it has samples for you to taste.

Competing on Cost

Southwest Airlines has been a consistent moneymaker while other U.S. airlines have lost billions. Southwest has done this by fulfilling a need for low-cost and short-hop flights. Its operations strategy has included use of secondary airports and terminals, first-come, first-served seating, few fare options, smaller crews flying more hours, snacks-only or no-meal flights, and no downtown ticket offices.

Additionally, and less obviously, Southwest has very effectively matched capacity to demand and effectively utilized this capacity. It has done this by designing a route structure that matches the capacity of its Boeing 737, the only plane in its fleet. Second, it achieves more air miles than other airlines through faster turnarounds—its planes are on the ground less.

One driver of a low-cost strategy is a facility that is effectively utilized. Southwest and others with low-cost strategies understand this and utilize resources effectively. Identifying the optimum size (and investment) allows firms to spread overhead costs, providing a cost advantage. For instance, Wal-Mart continues to pursue its low-cost strategy with superstores, open 24 hours a day. For 20 years, it has successfully grabbed market share. Wal-Mart has driven down store overhead costs, shrinkage, and distribution costs. Its rapid transportation of goods, reduced warehousing costs, and direct shipment from manufacturers have resulted in high inventory turnover and made it a low-cost leader. Franz Colruyt, as discussed in the *OM in Action* box, is also winning with a low-cost strategy.

Low-cost leadership entails achieving maximum *value* as defined by your customer. It requires examining each of the 10 OM decisions in a relentless effort to drive down costs while meeting customer expectations of value. A low-cost strategy does *not* imply low value or low quality.

Low-cost leadership
Achieving maximum value as perceived by the customer.

Competing on Response

The third strategy option is response. Response is often thought of as *flexible* response, but it also refers to *reliable* and *quick* response. Indeed, we define **response** as including the entire range of values related to timely product development and delivery, as well as reliable scheduling and flexible performance.

Response
A set of values related to rapid, flexible, and reliable performance.

OM in Action   Low-Cost Strategy Wins at Franz Colruyt

Belgian discount food retailer Franz Colruyt NV is so obsessed with cutting costs that there are no shopping bags at its checkout counters, the lighting at its stores is dimmed to save money on electricity, and employees clock out when they go on 5-minute coffee breaks. And to keep costs down at the company's spartan headquarters on the outskirts of Brussels, employees don't have voice mail on their phones. Instead, two receptionists take messages for nearly 1,000 staffers. The messages are bellowed out every few minutes from loudspeakers peppered throughout the building.

This same approach is evident at all 160 of Colruyt's shopping outlets, which are converted factory warehouses, movie theaters, or garages, with black concrete floors, exposed electrical wires, metal shelves, and discarded boxes strewn about. There is no background music (estimated annual cost saving: 2 million euros or $2.5 million), nor are there bags for packing groceries (estimated annual cost saving: 5 million euros). And all the store's freezers have doors, so the company can save about 3 million euros a year on electricity for refrigeration.

The company also employs a team of 30 "work simplifiers"—in Colruyt jargon—whose job is to come up with new ways to improve productivity. One recently discovered that 5 seconds could be shaved from every minute it takes customers to check out if they paid at a separate station from where groceries are scanned, so that when one customer steps away from the scanner, another can step up right away.

Chief Executive Rene De Wit says Colruyt's strategy is simple: cut costs at every turn and undersell your competitors. In an industry where margins of 1% to 2% are typical, Colruyt's cost cutting is so effective that a profit margin of 6.5% dwarfs those of rivals.

A low-cost strategy places significant demands on operations management, but Franz Colruyt, like Wal-Mart, makes it work.

Sources: The Wall Street Journal (September 22, 2003): R3, R7; and *DC Velocity* (September 2004): 38–40.

▶ *Response strategy wins orders at Super Fast Pizza. Using a wireless connection, orders are transmitted to $20,000 kitchens in vans. The driver, who works solo, receives a printed order, goes to the kitchen area, pulls premade pizzas from the cooler, and places them in the oven— it takes about 1 minute. The driver then delivers the pizza—sometimes even arriving before the pizza is ready.*

Flexible response may be thought of as the ability to match changes in a marketplace where design innovations and volumes fluctuate substantially.

Hewlett-Packard is an exceptional example of a firm that has demonstrated flexibility in both design and volume changes in the volatile world of personal computers. HP's products often have a life cycle of months, and volume and cost changes during that brief life cycle are dramatic. However, HP has been successful at institutionalizing the ability to change products and volume to respond to dramatic changes in product design and costs—thus building a *sustainable competitive advantage*.

The second aspect of response is the *reliability* of scheduling. One way the German machine industry has maintained its competitiveness despite having the world's highest labor costs is through reliable response. This response manifests itself in reliable scheduling. German machine firms have meaningful schedules—and they perform to these schedules. Moreover, the results of these schedules are communicated to the customer and the customer can, in turn, rely on them. Consequently, the competitive advantage generated through reliable response has value to the end customer.

The third aspect of response is *quickness*. Johnson Electric, discussed in the *OM in Action* box, competes on speed—speed in design, production, and delivery. Whether it is a production

OM in Action   Response Strategy at Hong Kong's Johnson Electric

Patrick Wang, managing director of Johnson Electric Holdings, Ltd., walks through his Hong Kong headquarters with a micromotor in his hand. This tiny motor, about twice the size of his thumb, powers a Dodge Viper power door lock. Although most people have never heard of Johnson Electric, we all have several of its micromotors nearby. This is because Johnson is the world's leading producer of micromotors for cordless tools, household appliances (such as coffee grinders and food processors), personal care items (such as hair dryers and electric shavers), and cars. A luxury Mercedes, with its headlight wipers, power windows, power seat adjustments, and power side mirrors, may use 50 Johnson micromotors.

Like all truly global businesses, Johnson spends liberally on communications to tie together its global network of factories, R&D facilities, and design centers. For example, Johnson Electric installed a $20 million videoconfer-

encing system that allows engineers in Cleveland, Ohio, and Stuttgart, Germany, to monitor trial production of their micromotors in China.

Johnson's first strength is speed in product development, speed in production, and speed in delivering—13 million motors a month, mostly assembled in China but delivered throughout the world. Its second strength is the ability to stay close to its customers. Johnson has design and technical centers scattered across the U.S., Europe, and Japan. "The physical limitations of the past are gone" when it comes to deciding where to locate a new center, says Patrick Wang. "Customers talk to us where they feel most comfortable, but products are made where they are most competitive."

Sources: Hoover's Company Records (January 1, 2006): 58682; Far Eastern Economic Review (May 16, 2002): 44–45; and The Economist (June 22, 1996): 65.

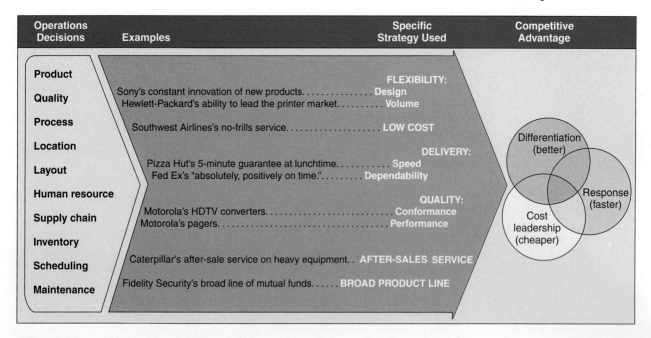

▲ **Figure 2.4**   Operations Management's Contribution to Strategy

system at Johnson Electric, a lunch delivered in 15 minutes at Bennigan's, or customized pagers delivered in three days from Motorola, the operations manager who develops systems that respond quickly can have a competitive advantage.

In practice, these three *concepts* —differentiation, low cost, and response—are often implemented via the six *specific strategies* shown in Figure 2.4: (1) flexibility in design and volume, (2) low cost, (3) delivery, (4) quality, (5) after-sales service, and (6) a broad product line. Through these six specific strategies, OM can increase productivity and generate a sustainable competitive advantage. Proper implementation of the following decisions by operations managers will allow these strategies to be achieved.

"In the future, there will be just two kinds of firms: those who disrupt their markets and those who don't survive the assault."

Professor Richard D'Aveni, author of Hypercompetition

TEN STRATEGIC OM DECISIONS

Differentiation, low cost, and response can be achieved when managers make effective decisions in 10 areas of OM. These are collectively known as **operations decisions**. The 10 decisions of OM that support missions and implement strategies follow:

1. *Goods and service design:* Designing goods and services defines much of the transformation process. Costs, quality, and human resource decisions are often determined by design decisions. Designs usually determine the lower limits of cost and the upper limits of quality.
2. *Quality:* The customer's quality expectations must be determined and policies and procedures established to identify and achieve that quality.
3. *Process and capacity design:* Process options are available for products and services. Process decisions commit management to specific technology, quality, human resource use, and maintenance. These expenses and capital commitments determine much of the firm's basic cost structure.
4. *Location selection:* Facility location decisions for both manufacturing and service organizations may determine the firm's ultimate success. Errors made at this juncture may overwhelm other efficiencies.
5. *Layout design:* Material flows, capacity needs, personnel levels, technology decisions, and inventory requirements influence layout.
6. *Human resources and job design:* People are an integral and expensive part of the total system design. Therefore, the quality of work life provided, the talent and skills required, and their costs must be determined.

Learning Objective

3. Identify and define the 10 decisions of operations management

Operations decisions
The strategic decisions of OM are goods and service design, quality, process design, location selection, layout design, human resources and job design, supply chain management, inventory, scheduling, and maintenance.

> *"Operations is typically thought of as an execution of strategy; for us it is the strategy."*
>
> *Joe R. Lee,*
> *Former chairman of*
> *Darden Restaurants*

7. *Supply chain management:* These decisions determine what is to be made and what is to be purchased. Consideration is also given to quality, delivery, and innovation, all at a satisfactory price. Mutual trust between buyer and supplier is necessary for effective purchasing.

8. *Inventory:* Inventory decisions can be optimized only when customer satisfaction, suppliers, production schedules, and human resource planning are considered.

9. *Scheduling:* Feasible and efficient schedules of production must be developed; the demands on human resources and facilities must be determined and controlled.

10. *Maintenance:* Decisions must be made regarding desired levels of reliability and stability, and systems must be established to maintain that reliability and stability.

Operations managers implement these 10 decisions by identifying key tasks and the staffing needed to achieve them. However, the implementation of decisions is influenced by a variety of issues, including a product's proportion of goods and services (see Table 2.1). Few products are either all goods or all services. Although the 10 decisions remain the same for both goods and services, their relative importance and method of implementation depend on this ratio of goods and services. Throughout this text, we discuss how strategy is selected and implemented for both goods and services through these 10 operations management decisions.

Let's look at an example of strategy development through one of the 10 decisions.

EXAMPLE 1

Strategy development

Pierre Alexander has just completed chef school and is ready to open his own restaurant. After examining both the external environment and his prospective strengths and weaknesses, he makes a decision on the mission for his restaurant, which he defines as "To provide outstanding French fine dining for the people of Chicago."

Approach: Alexander's supporting operations strategy is to ignore the options of *cost leadership* and *quick response* and focus on *differentiation*. Consequently, his operations strategy requires him to evaluate product designs (menus and meals) and selection of process, layout, and location. He must also evaluate the human resources, suppliers, inventory, scheduling, and maintenance that will support his mission and a differentiation strategy.

Solution: Examining just one of these 10 decisions, *process design*, requires that Alexander consider the issues presented in the following figure.

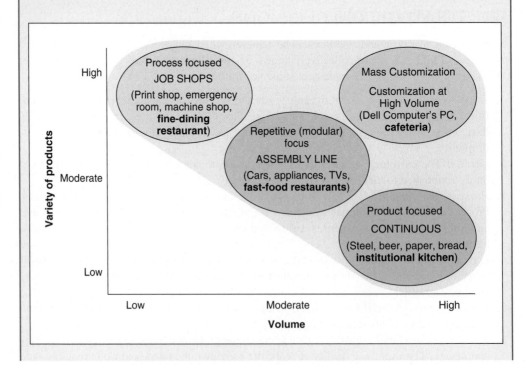

The first option is to operate in the lower right corner of the preceding figure, where he could produce high volumes of food with a limited variety, much as in an institutional kitchen. Such a process could produce large volumes of standard items such as baked goods and mashed potatoes prepared with state-of-the-art automated equipment. Alexander concludes that this is not an acceptable process option.

Alternatively, he can move to the middle of the figure, where he could produce more variety and lower volumes. Here he would have less automation and use prepared modular components for meals, much as a fast-food restaurant does. Again, he deems such process designs inappropriate for his mission.

Another option is to move to the upper right corner and produce a high volume of customized meals, but neither Alexander nor anyone else knows how to do this with gourmet meals.

Finally, Alexander can design a process that operates in the upper left corner of the figure, which requires little automation but lends itself to high variety. This process option suggests that he build an extremely flexible kitchen suitable for a wide variety of custom meals catering to the whims of each customer. With little automation, such a process would be suitable for a huge variety. This process strategy will support his mission and desired product differentiation. Only with a process such as this can he provide the fine French-style gourmet dining that he has in mind.

Insight: By considering the options inherent in each of the 10 OM decisions, managers—Alexander, in this case—can make decisions that support the mission.

Learning exercise: If Alexander's mission were to offer less expensive meals and reduce the variety offered but still do so with a French flair, what might his process strategy be? [Answer: Alexander might try a repetitive (modular) strategy and mimic the La Madeleine cafeteria-style restaurants.]

▼ **Table 2.1**   The Differences Between Goods and Services Influence How the 10 Operations Management Decisions Are Applied

Operations Decisions	Goods	Services
Goods and service design	Product is usually tangible.	Product is not tangible. A new range of product attributes—a smile.
Quality	Many objective quality standards.	Many subjective quality standards—nice color.
Process and capacity design	Customer is not involved in most of the process.	Customer may be directly involved in the process—a haircut.
		Capacity must match demand to avoid lost sales—customers often avoid waiting.
Location selection	May need to be near raw materials or labor force.	May need to be near customer—car rental.
Layout design	Layout can enhance production efficiency.	Can enhance product as well as production—layout of a fine-dining restaurant.
Human resources and job design	Workforce focused on technical skills. Labor standards can be consistent. Output-based wage system possible.	Direct workforce usually needs to be able to interact well with customer—bank teller. Labor standards vary depending on customer requirements—legal cases.
Supply chain management	Supply chain relationships critical to final product.	Supply chain relationships important but may not be critical
Inventory	Raw materials, work-in-process, and finished goods may be inventoried.	Most services cannot be stored; so other ways must be found to accommodate fluctuations in demand—can't store haircuts.
Scheduling	Ability to inventory may allow leveling of production rates.	Often concerned with meeting the customer's immediate schedule with human resources.
Maintenance	Maintenance is often preventive and takes place at the production site.	Maintenance is often "repair" and takes place at the customer's site.

▼ **Table 2.2** **Operations Strategies of Two Drug Companies**

	Brand Name Drugs, Inc.	**Generic Drug Corp.**
Competitive Advantage	**Product Differentiation**	**Low Cost**
Product Selection and Design	Heavy R&D investment; extensive labs; focus on development in a broad range of drug categories	Low R&D investment; focus on development of generic drugs
Quality	Quality is major priority, standards exceed regulatory requirements	Meets regulatory requirements on a country-by-country basis as necessary
Process	Product and modular production process; tries to have long product runs in specialized facilities; builds capacity ahead of demand	Process focused; general production processes; "jobshop" approach, short-run production; focus on high utilization
Location	Still located in city where it was founded	Recently moved to low-tax, low-labor-cost environment
Layout	Layout supports automated product-focused production	Layout supports process-focused "job shop" practices
Human Resources	Hire the best; nationwide searches	Very experienced top executives provide direction; other personnel paid below industry average
Supply Chain	Long-term supplier relationships	Tends to purchase competitively to find bargains
Inventory	Maintains high finished goods inventory primarily to ensure all demands are met	Process focus drives up work-in-process inventory; finished goods inventory tends to be low
Scheduling	Centralized production planning	Many short-run products complicate scheduling
Maintenance	Highly trained staff; extensive parts inventory	Highly trained staff to meet changing demands

The 10 decisions of operations management are implemented in ways that provide competitive advantage, not just for fine-dining restaurants, but for all the goods and services that enrich our lives. How this might be done for two drug companies, one seeking a competitive advantage via differentiation, and the other via low cost, is shown in Table 2.2.

ISSUES IN OPERATIONS STRATEGY

Once a firm has formed a mission, developing and implementing a specific strategy requires that the operations manager consider a number of issues. We will examine these issues in three ways. First, we look at what *research* tells us about effective operations management strategies. Second, we identify some of the *preconditions* to developing effective OM strategy. Third, we look at the *dynamics* of OM strategy development.

Research

PIMS

A program established in cooperation with GE to identify characteristics of high-return-on-investment firms.

Strategic insight has been provided by the findings of the Strategic Planning Institute.[5] Its **PIMS** program (profit impact of market strategy) was established in cooperation with the General Electric Corporation. PIMS has collected nearly 100 data items from about 3,000 cooperating organizations. Using the data collected and high *return on investment* (ROI)[6] as a measure of success, PIMS has been able to identify some characteristics of high-ROI firms. Among those characteristics that affect strategic OM decisions are:

1. High product quality (relative to the competition).
2. High capacity utilization.
3. High operating efficiency (the ratio of expected to actual employee productivity).
4. Low investment intensity (the amount of capital required to produce a dollar of sales).
5. Low direct cost per unit (relative to the competition).

[5]See B. Leavy, "Assessing Your Strategic Alternatives," *Strategy and Leadership* (2003): 29, or R. D. Buzzel and B. T. Gale, *The PIMS Principles* (New York: The Free Press, 1987).
[6]Like other performance measures, *return on investment* (ROI) has limitations, including sensitivity to the business cycle, depreciation policies and schedules, book value (goodwill), and transfer pricing.

These five findings support a high return on investment and should therefore be considered as an organization develops a strategy. In the analysis of a firm's relative strengths and weaknesses, these characteristics can be measured and evaluated. The specific strategic approaches suggested earlier, in Figure 2.4, indicate where an operations manager may want to go, but without achieving the five characteristics of firms with a high return on investment, that journey may not be successful.

Another research study indicates the significant role that OM can play in competitive strategy. When a wide mix of 248 businesses were asked to evaluate the importance of 32 categories in obtaining a sustainable competitive advantage, 28% of the categories selected fell under operations management. When quality/service is added, the total goes to 44%. The study supports the major role OM strategy plays in developing a competitive advantage.[7]

Preconditions

Before establishing and attempting to implement a strategy, the operations manager needs to understand that the firm is operating in an open system in which a multitude of factors exists. These factors influence strategy development and execution. The more thorough the analysis and understanding of both the external and internal factors, the more the likelihood of success. Although the list of factors to be considered is extensive, at a minimum it entails an understanding of:

1. Strengths and weaknesses of competitors, as well as possible new entrants into the market, substitute products, and commitment of suppliers and distributors.
2. Current and prospective environmental, technological, legal, and economic issues.
3. Product life cycle, which may dictate the limitations of operations strategy.
4. Resources available within the firm and within the OM function.
5. Integration of the OM strategy with the company's strategy and other functional areas.

Dynamics

Strategies change for two reasons. First, strategy is dynamic because of *changes within the organization*. All areas of the firm are subject to change. Changes may occur in a variety of areas, including personnel, finance, technology, and product life. All may make a difference in an organization's strengths and weaknesses and therefore its strategy. Figure 2.5 shows possible change in both overall strategy and OM strategy during the product's life. For instance, as a product moves from introduction to growth, product and process design typically move from development to stability. As the product moves to the growth stage, forecasting and capacity planning become issues.

Strategy is also dynamic because of *changes in the environment*.[8] Boeing provides an example, in the opening *Global Company Profile* in this chapter, of how strategy must change as the environment changes. Its strategies, like many OM strategies, are increasingly global. Microsoft also had to adapt quickly to a changing environment. Microsoft's shift in strategy was caused by changing customer demand, security, and the Internet. Microsoft moved from operating systems to office products, to Internet service provider, and now to an integrator of computers and television.

STRATEGY DEVELOPMENT AND IMPLEMENTATION

Once firms understand the issues involved in developing an effective strategy, they evaluate their internal strengths and weaknesses as well as the opportunities and threats of the environment. This is known as **SWOT analysis** (for *S*trengths, *W*eaknesses, *O*pportunities, and *T*hreats). Beginning with SWOT analyses, firms position themselves, through their strategy, to have a competitive advantage. The firm may have excellent design skills or great talent at identifying outstanding locations. However, the firm may recognize limitations of its manufacturing process or in finding good suppliers. The idea is to maximize opportunities and minimize threats in the environment while maximizing the advantages of the organization's strengths and minimizing the weaknesses. Any preconceived ideas about mission are then reevaluated to ensure they are consistent with the SWOT analysis. Subsequently, a strategy for achieving the mission is developed. This strategy is continually evaluated against the value provided customers and competi-

> *"To the Japanese, strategy is so dynamic as to be thought of as 'accommodation' or 'adaptive persistence.'"*
> *Richard Pascale, MIT Sloan Management Review*

SWOT analysis
A method of determining internal strengths and weaknesses and external opportunities and threats.

---

[7]See David A. Aaker, "Creating a Sustainable Competitive Advantage," *California Management Review* (winter 1989): 91–106.
[8]Anita M. McGahan, "How Industries Change," *Harvard Business Review* 82, no. 10 (October 11, 2004): 87–94.

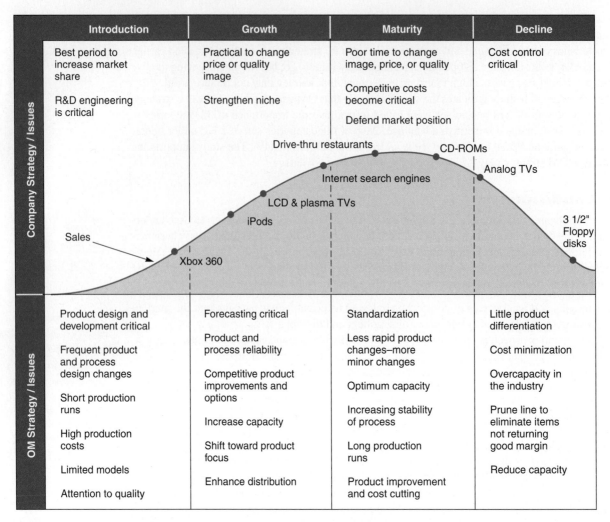

	Introduction	Growth	Maturity	Decline
Company Strategy / Issues	Best period to increase market share R&D engineering is critical	Practical to change price or quality image Strengthen niche	Poor time to change image, price, or quality Competitive costs become critical Defend market position	Cost control critical
OM Strategy / Issues	Product design and development critical Frequent product and process design changes Short production runs High production costs Limited models Attention to quality	Forecasting critical Product and process reliability Competitive product improvements and options Increase capacity Shift toward product focus Enhance distribution	Standardization Less rapid product changes–more minor changes Optimum capacity Increasing stability of process Long production runs Product improvement and cost cutting	Little product differentiation Cost minimization Overcapacity in the industry Prune line to eliminate items not returning good margin Reduce capacity

Within the sales curve: Sales; Xbox 360; iPods; LCD & plasma TVs; Internet search engines; Drive-thru restaurants; CD-ROMs; Analog TVs; 3 1/2" Floppy disks

▲ **Figure 2.5** **Strategy and Issues During a Product's Life**

tive realities. The process is shown in Figure 2.6. From this process critical success factors are identified.

Critical Success Factors and Core Competencies

Critical success factors (CSFs)
Activities or factors that are *key* to achieving competitive advantage.

Because no firm does everything exceptionally well, a successful strategy requires determining the firm's critical success factors and core competencies. **Critical success factors (CSFs)** are those activities that are necessary for a firm to achieve its goals. Critical success factors can be so significant that a firm must get them right to survive in the industry. A CSF for McDonald's, for example,

▶ **Figure 2.6**

Strategy Development Process

Environmental Analysis
Identify the strengths, weaknesses, opportunities, and threats.
Understand the environment, customers, industry, and competitors.

Determine Corporate Mission
State the reason for the firm's existence and identify the value it wishes to create.

Form a Strategy
Build a competitive advantage, such as low price, design or volume flexibility, quality, quick delivery, dependability, after-sale services, or broad product lines.

| Generators | Automobiles | 4-Wheel Scooters | Water Pumps |
| Marine Motors | Formula One Race Cars | Motorcycles | Snow Blowers |

◄ *Honda's core competence is the design and manufacture of gas-powered engines. This competence has allowed Honda to become a leader in the design and manufacture of a wide range of gas-powered products. Tens of millions of these products are produced and shipped around the world.*

is layout. Without a play area, an effective drive-thru, and an efficient kitchen, McDonald's cannot be successful. CSFs are often necessary, but not sufficient for competitive advantage. On the other hand, **core competencies** are the set of unique skills, talents, and capabilities that a firm does at a world-class standard. They allow a firm to set itself apart and develop a competitive advantage. Organizations that prosper identify their core competencies and nurture them. While McDonald's CSFs may include layout, its core competency may be consistency and quality. Honda Motors's core competence is gas-powered engines—engines for automobiles, motorcycles, lawn mowers, generators, snow blowers, and more. The idea is to build CSFs and core competencies that provide a competitive advantage and support a successful strategy and mission. A core competence may be a subset of CSFs or a combination of CSFs. The operations manager begins this inquiry by asking:

Core competencies
A set of skills, talents, and activities that a firm does particularly well.

- "What tasks must be done particularly well for a given strategy to succeed?"
- "Which activities will help the OM function provide a competitive advantage?"
- "Which elements contain the highest likelihood of failure, and which require additional commitment of managerial, monetary, technological, and human resources?"

Only by identifying and strengthening critical success factors and core competencies can an organization achieve sustainable competitive advantage.

In this text we focus on the 10 OM decisions that typically include the CSFs. Potential CSFs for marketing, finance, and operations are shown in Figure 2.7. The 10 operations management

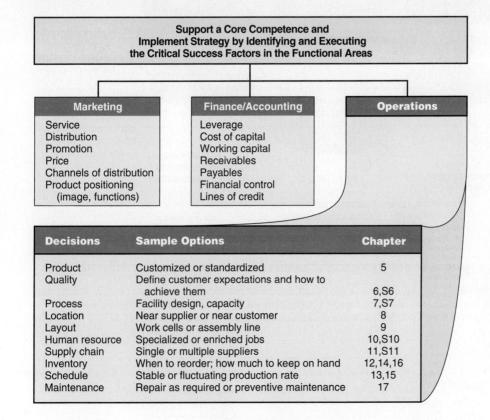

Support a Core Competence and Implement Strategy by Identifying and Executing the Critical Success Factors in the Functional Areas

Marketing	Finance/Accounting	Operations
Service	Leverage	
Distribution	Cost of capital	
Promotion	Working capital	
Price	Receivables	
Channels of distribution	Payables	
Product positioning (image, functions)	Financial control	
	Lines of credit	

Decisions	Sample Options	Chapter
Product	Customized or standardized	5
Quality	Define customer expectations and how to achieve them	6,S6
Process	Facility design, capacity	7,S7
Location	Near supplier or near customer	8
Layout	Work cells or assembly line	9
Human resource	Specialized or enriched jobs	10,S10
Supply chain	Single or multiple suppliers	11,S11
Inventory	When to reorder; how much to keep on hand	12,14,16
Schedule	Stable or fluctuating production rate	13,15
Maintenance	Repair as required or preventive maintenance	17

◄ **Figure 2.7**

Implement Strategy by Identifying and Executing Critical Success Factors and Supporting the Core Competence

decisions we develop in this text provide an excellent initial checklist for determining CSFs and identifying core competencies within the operations function. For instance, the 10 decisions, related CSFs, and core competencies can allow a firm to differentiate its product or service. That differentiation may be via a core competence of innovation and new products, where the CSFs are product design and speed to market, as is the case for 3M and Rubbermaid. Similarly, differentiation may be via quality, where the core competence is institutionalizing quality, as at Toyota. Differentiation may also be via maintenance, where the CSFs are product reliability and after-sale service, as is the case at IBM and Canon.

Whatever the CSFs and core competences, they must be supported by the related activities. One approach to identifying the activities is an **activity map**, which links competitive advantage, CSFs, and supporting activities. For example, Figure 2.8 shows how Southwest Airlines, whose core competence is operations, built a set of integrated activities to support its low-cost competitive advantage. Notice how the CSFs support operations and in turn are supported by other activities.[9] The activities fit together and reinforce each other. And the better they fit and reinforce each other, the more sustainable the competitive advantage. By focusing on enhancing its core competence and CSFs with a supporting set of activities, Southwest Airlines has become one of the great airline success stories.

Activity map

A graphical link of competitive advantage, CSFs, and supporting activities.

Build and Staff the Organization

The operations manager's job is a three-step process. Once a strategy and critical success factors have been identified, the second step is to group the necessary activities into an organizational structure. The third step is to staff it with personnel who will get the job done. The manager

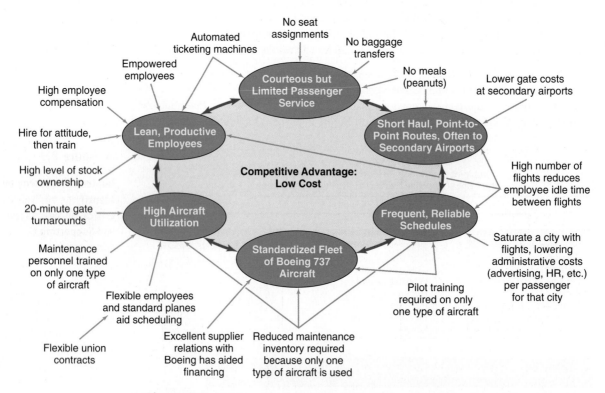

▲ **Figure 2.8** **Activity Mapping of Southwest Airlines's Low-Cost Competitive Advantage**

To achieve a low-cost competitive advantage, Southwest has identified a number of critical success factors (connected by red arrows) and support activities (shown by blue arrows). As this figure indicates, a low-cost advantage is highly dependent on a very well run operations function.

[9]Michael E. Porter and C. Roland Christensen, "What Is Strategy?" *Harvard Business Review* (November–December 1996): 61–75.

works with subordinate managers to build plans, budgets, and programs that will successfully implement strategies that achieve missions. Firms tackle this organization of the operations function in a variety of ways. The organization charts shown in Chapter 1 (Figure 1.1) indicate the way some firms have organized to perform the required activities.

Integrate OM with Other Activities

The organization of the operations function and its relationship to other parts of the organization vary with the OM mission. Moreover, the operations function is most likely to be successful when the operations strategy is integrated with other functional areas of the firm, such as marketing, finance, information technology, and human resources. In this way, all of the areas support the company's objectives. For example, short-term scheduling in the airline industry is dominated by volatile customer travel patterns. Day-of-week preference, holidays, seasonality, college schedules, and so on, all play a role in changing flight schedules. Consequently, airline scheduling, although an OM activity, can be a part of marketing. Effective scheduling in the trucking industry is reflected in the amount of time trucks travel loaded. However, scheduling of trucks requires information from delivery and pickup points, drivers, and other parts of the organization. When the OM function results in effective scheduling in the air passenger and commercial trucking industries, a competitive advantage can exist.

The operations manager provides a means of transforming inputs into outputs. The transformations may be in terms of storage, transportation, manufacturing, dissemination of information, and utility of the product or service. *The operations manager's job is to implement an OM strategy, provide competitive advantage, and increase productivity.*

> "The manufacturing business of tomorrow will not be run by financial executives, marketers, or lawyers inexperienced in manufacturing, as so many U.S. companies are today."
>
> *Peter Drucker*

GLOBAL OPERATIONS STRATEGY OPTIONS

As we suggested early in this chapter, many operations strategies now require an international dimension. We tend to call a firm with an international dimension an international business or a multinational corporation. An **international business** is any firm that engages in international trade or investment. This is a very broad category and is the opposite of a domestic, or local, firm.

A **multinational corporation (MNC)** is a firm with *extensive* international business involvement. MNCs buy resources, create goods or services, and sell goods or services in a variety of countries. The term *multinational corporation* applies to most of the world's large, well-known businesses. Certainly IBM is a good example of an MNC. It imports electronics components to the U.S. from over 50 countries, exports computers to over 130 countries, has facilities in 45 countries, and earns more than half its sales and profits abroad.

Operations managers of international and multinational firms approach global opportunities with one of four operations strategies: *international, multidomestic, global,* and *transnational* (see Figure 2.9). The matrix of Figure 2.9 has a vertical axis of cost reduction and a horizontal axis of local responsiveness. Local responsiveness implies quick response and/or the differentiation necessary for the local market. The operations manager must know how to position the firm in this matrix. Let us briefly examine each of the four strategies.

International business
A firm that engages in cross-border transactions.

Multinational corporation (MNC)
A firm that has extensive involvement in international business, owning or controlling facilities in more than one country.

International Strategy

An **international strategy** uses exports and licenses to penetrate the global arena. As Figure 2.9 suggests, the international strategy is the least advantageous, with little local responsiveness and little cost advantage. There is little responsiveness because we are exporting or licensing a good from the home country. And the cost advantages may be few because we are using the existing production process at some distance from the new market. However, an international strategy is often the easiest, as exports can require little change in existing operations, and licensing agreements often leave much of the risk to the licensee.

International strategy
A strategy in which global markets are penetrated using exports and licenses.

Multidomestic Strategy

The **multidomestic strategy** has decentralized authority with substantial autonomy at each business. Organizationally these are typically subsidiaries, franchises, or joint ventures with substantial independence. The advantage of this strategy is maximizing a competitive response for the

Multidomestic strategy
A strategy in which operating decisions are decentralized to each country to enhance local responsiveness.

▶ **Figure 2.9**

Four International Operations Strategies

Sources: See a similar presentation in M. Hitt, R. D. Ireland, and R. E. Hoskisson, *Strategic Management, Competitiveness and Globalization,* 6th ed. (Cincinnati: Southwestern College Publishing, 2006).

Learning Objective

5. Identify and explain four global operations strategy options

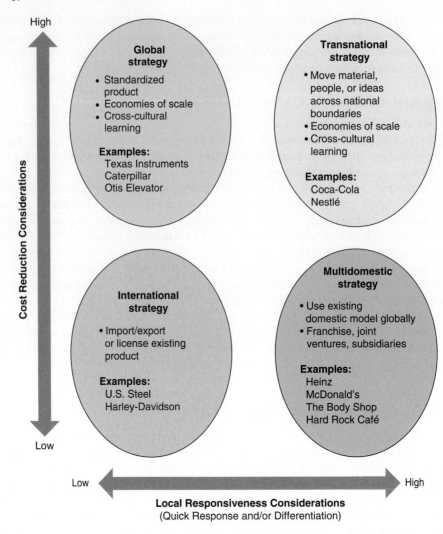

Global strategy

A strategy in which operating decisions are centralized and headquarters coordinates the standardization and learning between facilities.

local market; however, the strategy has little or no cost advantage. Many food producers, such as Heinz, use a multidomestic strategy to accommodate local tastes because global integration of the production process is not critical. The concept is one of "we were successful in the home market, let's export the management talent and processes, not necessarily the product, to accommodate another market." McDonald's is operating primarily as a multidomestic, which gives it the local responsiveness needed to modify its menu country by country. McDonald's can then serve beer in Germany, wine in France, McHuevo (poached egg hamburger) in Uruguay, and hamburgers without beef in India. With over 2,000 restaurants in Japan and a presence of more than a generation, the average Japanese family thinks Japan invented McDonald's. Interestingly, McDonald's prefers to call itself *multilocal*.[10]

Global Strategy

A **global strategy** has a high degree of centralization, with headquarters coordinating the organization to seek out standardization and learning between plants, thus generating economies of scale. This strategy is appropriate when the strategic focus is cost reduction but has little to recommend it when the demand for local responsiveness is high. Caterpillar, the world leader in earth-moving equipment, and Texas Instruments, a world leader in semiconductors, pursue global strategies. Caterpillar and Texas Instruments find this strategy advantageous because the end products are similar throughout the world. Earth-moving equipment is the same in Nigeria as

[10]James L. Watson, ed., *Golden Arches East: McDonald's in East Asia* (Stanford University Press, 1997): 12. *Note:* McDonald's also operates with some of the advantages of a global organization. By using very similar product lines throughout the world, McDonald's obtains some of the standardization advantages of a global strategy. However, it manages to retain the advantages of a multidomestic strategy.

▲ *In a continuing fierce worldwide battle, both Komatsu and Caterpillar seek global advantage in the heavy equipment market. As Komatsu (left) moved west to the UK, Caterpillar (right) moved east, with 13 facilities and joint ventures in China. Both firms are building equipment throughout the world as cost and logistics dictate. Their global strategies allow production to move as markets, risk, and exchange rates dictate.*

in Iowa, which allows Caterpillar to have individual factories focus on a limited line of products to be shipped worldwide. This results in economies of scale and learning within each facility. A global strategy also allows Texas Instruments to build optimum-size plants with similar process and to then maximize learning by aggressive communication between plants. The result is an effective cost reduction advantage for Texas Instruments.

Transnational Strategy

A **transnational strategy** exploits the economies of scale and learning, as well as pressure for responsiveness, by recognizing that core competence does not reside in just the "home" country but can exist anywhere in the organization. *Transnational* describes a condition in which material, people, and ideas cross—or *transgress*—national boundaries. These firms have the potential to pursue all three operations strategies (i.e., differentiation, low cost, and response). Such firms can be thought of as "world companies" whose country identity is not as important as its interdependent network of worldwide operations. Key activities in a transnational company are neither centralized in the parent company nor decentralized so that each subsidiary can carry out its own tasks on a local basis. Instead, the resources and activities are dispersed, but specialized, so as to be both efficient and flexible in an interdependent network. Nestlé is a good example of such a company. Although it is legally Swiss, 95% of its assets are held and 98% of its sales are made outside Switzerland. Fewer than 10% of its workers are Swiss. Similarly, service firms such as Asea Brown Boveri (an engineering firm that is Swedish but headquartered in Switzerland), Reuters (a news agency), Bertelsmann (a publisher), and Citicorp (a banking corporation) can be viewed as transnationals. We can expect the national identities of these transnationals to continue to fade.

Transnational strategy
A strategy that combines the benefits of global-scale efficiencies with the benefits of local responsiveness.

Summary

Global operations provide an increase in both the challenges and opportunities for operations managers. Although the task is challenging, operations managers can and do improve productivity. They can build and manage OM functions that contribute in a significant way to competitiveness. Organizations identify their strengths and weaknesses. They then develop effective missions and strategies that account for these strengths and weaknesses and complement the opportunities and threats in the environment. If this procedure is performed well, the organization can have competitive advantage through some combination of product differentiation, low cost, and response. This competitive advantage is often achieved via a move to international, multidomestic, global, or transnational strategies.

Effective use of resources, whether domestic or international, is the responsibility of the professional manager, and professional managers are among the few in our society who *can* achieve this performance. The challenge is great, and the rewards to the manager and to society substantial.

Key Terms

Maquiladoras *(p. 31)*
World Trade Organization (WTO) *(p. 31)*
North American Free Trade Agreement
  (NAFTA) *(p. 31)*
European Union (EU) *(p. 32)*
Mission *(p. 34)*
Strategy *(p. 35)*
Competitive advantage *(p. 36)*

Differentiation *(p. 36)*
Experience differentiation *(p. 36)*
Low-cost leadership *(p. 37)*
Response *(p. 37)*
Operations decisions *(p. 39)*
PIMS *(p. 42)*
SWOT analysis *(p. 43)*
Critical success factors *(p. 44)*

Core competencies *(p. 45)*
Activity map *(p. 46)*
International business *(p. 47)*
Multinational corporation (MNC) *(p. 47)*
International strategy *(p. 47)*
Multidomestic strategy *(p. 47)*
Global strategy *(p. 48)*
Transnational strategy *(p. 49)*

Solved Problem

 Virtual Office Hours help is available on Student DVD.

Solved Problem 2.1

Strategy at Pirelli SpA The global tire industry continues to consolidate. Michelin buys Goodrich and Uniroyal and builds plants throughout the world. Bridgestone buys Firestone, expands its research budget, and focuses on world markets. Goodyear spends almost 4% of its sales revenue on research. These three aggressive firms have come to dominate the world tire market, with total market share approaching 60%. And the German tire maker Continental AG has strengthened its position as fourth in the world, with a dominant presence in Germany. Against this formidable array, the old-line Italian tire company Pirelli SpA found it difficult to respond effectively. Although Pirelli still had 5% of the market, it was losing millions a year while the competition was getting stronger. Tires are a tough, competitive business that rewards companies having strong market shares and long production runs. Pirelli has some strengths: an outstanding reputation for excellent high-performance tires and an innovative manufacturing function.

Use a SWOT analysis to establish a feasible strategy for Pirelli.

Solution

First, find an opportunity in the world tire market that avoids the threat of the mass-market onslaught by the big three tire makers. Second, utilize the internal marketing strength represented by Pirelli's strong brand name and history of winning World Rally Championships. Third, maximize the internal innovative capabilities of the operations function.

To achieve these goals, Pirelli made a strategic shift out of low-margin standard tires and into higher-margin performance tires. Pirelli established deals with luxury brands Jaguar, BMW, Maserati, Ferrari, Bentley, and Lotus Elise and established itself as a provider of a large share of tires on new Porsches, S-class Mercedes, and Saabs. As a result, more than 70% of the company's tire production is now high-performance tires. People are willing to pay a premium for Pirellis.

The operations function continued to focus its design efforts on performance tires and developing a system of modular tire manufacture that allows much faster switching between models. This modular system, combined with investments in new manufacturing flexibility, has driven batch sizes down to as small as 150 to 200, making small-lot performance tires economically feasible. Manufacturing innovations at Pirelli have streamlined the production process, moving it from a 14-step process to a 3-step process. A threat from the big three going after the performance market remains, but Pirelli has bypassed its weakness of having a small market share. The firm now has a presence in 120 countries and sales exceeding $3.5 billion.

Sources: Just Auto (September 2005): 8–14; *Hoover's Company Records* (October 15, 2005): 41369; and *Frankfurter Allgemeine Zeitung* (February 11, 2002): 5.

Discussion Questions

1. Based on the descriptions and analyses in this chapter, would Boeing be better described as a global firm or a transnational firm? Discuss.
2. List six reasons to internationalize operations.
3. Coca-Cola is called a global product. Does this mean that Coca-Cola is formulated in the same way throughout the world? Discuss.
4. Define *mission*.
5. Define *strategy*.
6. Describe how an organization's *mission* and *strategy* have different purposes.
7. Identify the mission and strategy of your automobile repair garage. What are the manifestations of the 10 OM decisions at the garage? That is, how is each of the 10 decisions accomplished?
8. As a library or Internet assignment, identify the mission of a firm and the strategy that supports that mission.
9. How does an OM strategy change during a product's life cycle?
10. There are three primary ways to achieve competitive advantage. Provide an example, not included in the text, of each. Support your choices.
11. Describe PIMS's five characteristics of high-return-on-investment (ROI) firms.
12. Given the discussion of Southwest Airlines in the text, define an *operations* strategy for that firm.
13. How must an operations strategy integrate with marketing and accounting?

Self-Test

- **Before taking the self-test**, *refer to the learning objectives listed at the beginning of the chapter and the key terms listed at the end of the chapter.*
- *Use the key at the back of the text to* **correct** *your answers.*
- **Restudy** *pages that correspond to any questions you answered incorrectly or material you feel uncertain about.*

1. Among the ways for a firm to effectively use its OM function to yield competitive advantage are:
   a) rapid design changes.
   b) speed of delivery.
   c) maintain a variety of product options.
   d) all of the above.

2. A mission statement is beneficial to an organization because it:
   a) is a statement of the organization's economic purpose.
   b) provides a basis for the organization's culture.
   c) identifies important constituencies.
   d) establishes a basis for strategy formulation.
   e) ensures profitability.

3. A strategy is:
   a) a functional area of the firm.
   b) the purpose for which an organization is established.
   c) the goal that is to be achieved.
   d) an action plan to achieve a mission.
   e) a critical success factor.

4. The PIMS program developed a number of criteria that were based on evaluating firms who did well at:
   a) profitability.
   b) sustained sales growth.
   c) achieving their mission.

   d) high return on investments.
   e) establishing goals.

5. Which of the following are not characteristics of high return-on-investment firms?
   a) high variety of product options
   b) high product quality relative to the competition
   c) high capacity utilization
   d) low investment intensity
   e) all are characteristic of high ROI firms

6. A company that is organized across international boundaries with decentralized authority and substantial autonomy at each business via subsidiaries, franchises, or joint ventures has:
   a) a global strategy.
   b) a transnational strategy.
   c) an international straetgy.
   d) a multidomestic strategy.
   e) a regional strategy.

7. The relatively few activities that make a difference between a firm having and not having a competitive advantage are known as:
   a) activity maps.
   b) SWOT.
   c) critical success factors.
   d) global profile.
   e) response strategy.

8. The three strategic approaches to competitive advantage are _____, _____, and _____.

Internet and Student CD-ROM/DVD Exercises

Visit our Companion Web site or use your student CD-ROM/DVD to help with material in this chapter.

 On Our Companion Web site,
www.prenhall.com/heizer
- Self-Study Quizzes
- Practice Problems
- Virtual Company Tour
- Internet Case
- Power Point Lecture

On Your Student CD-ROM
- Practice Problems

On Your Student DVD
- Video Clips and Video Cases
- Virtual Office Hours for Solved Problem

Ethical Dilemma

As a manufacturer of athletic shoes whose image, indeed performance, is widely regarded as socially responsible, you find your costs increasing. Traditionally, your athletic shoes have been made in Indonesia and South Korea. Although the ease of doing business in those countries has been improving, wage rates have also been increasing. The labor-cost differential between your present suppliers and a contractor who will get the shoes made in China now exceeds $1 per pair. Your sales next year are projected to be 10 million pairs, and

your analysis suggests that this cost differential is not offset by any other tangible costs; you face only the political risk and potential damage to your commitment to social responsibility. Thus, this $1 per pair savings should flow directly to your bottom line. There is no doubt that the Chinese government engages in censorship, remains repressive, and is a long way from a democracy. Moreover, you will have little or no control over working conditions, sexual harassment, and pollution. What do you do and on what basis do you make your decision?

Problems

•   **2.1** The text provides three primary ways—strategic approaches (differentiation, cost, and response)—for achieving competitive advantage. Provide an example of each not given in the text. Support your choices. (*Hint:* Note the examples provided in the text.)

••   **2.2** Within the food service industry (restaurants that serve meals to customers, but not just fast food), find examples of firms that have sustained competitive advantage by competing on the basis of (1) cost leadership, (2) response, and (3) differentiation. Cite one example in each category; provide a sentence or two in

support of each choice. Do not use fast-food chains for all categories. (*Hint:* A "99¢ menu" is very easily copied and is not a good source of sustained advantage.)

••   **2.3** Browse through *The Wall Street Journal*, the financial section of a daily paper, or read business news online. Seek articles that constrain manufacturing innovation and productivity—workers aren't allowed to do this, workers are not or cannot be trained to do that, this technology is not allowed, this material cannot be handled by workers, and so forth. Be prepared to share your articles in class discussion.

••   **2.4** Match the product with the proper parent company and country in the table below:

Product	Parent Company	Country
Arrow Shirts	**a.** Volkswagen	**1.** France
Braun Household Appliances	**b.** Bidermann International	**2.** Great Britain
Lotus Autos	**c.** Bridgestone	**3.** Germany
Firestone Tires	**d.** Campbell Soup	**4.** Japan
Godiva Chocolate	**e.** Credit Lyonnais	**5.** U.S.
Häagen-Daz Ice Cream (USA)	**f.** Ford Motor Company	**6.** Switzerland
Jaguar Autos	**g.** Procter & Gamble	**7.** Malaysia
MGM Movies	**h.** Michelin	
Lamborghini Autos	**i.** Nestlé	
Goodrich Tires	**j.** Proton	
Alpo Pet Foods		

•••   **2.5** Identify how changes within an organization affect the OM strategy for a company. For instance, discuss what impact the following internal factors might have on OM strategy:
a) Maturing of a product.
b) Technology innovation in the manufacturing process.
c) Changes in laptop computer design that move disk drives from CD-ROM drives to DVD drives.

•••   **2.6** Identify how changes in the external environment affect the OM strategy for a company. For instance, discuss what impact the following external factors might have on OM strategy:
a) Major increases in oil prices.
b) Water- and air-quality legislation.
c) Fewer young prospective employees entering the labor market.

d) Inflation versus stable prices.
e) Legislation moving health insurance from a pretax benefit to taxable income.

••   **2.7** Develop a ranking for corruption in the following countries: Mexico, Turkey, Denmark, the U.S., Taiwan, Brazil, and another country of your choice. (*Hint:* See sources such as *Transparency International*, *Asia Pacific Management News*, and *The Economist*.)

••   **2.8** Develop a ranking for competitiveness and/or business environment for Britain, Singapore, the U.S., Hong Kong, and Italy. (*Hint:* See the *Global Competitive Report*, *World Economic Forum*, Geneva, and *The Economist*.)

Case Studies

Minit-Lube

A substantial market exists for automobile tune-ups, oil changes, and lubrication service for more than 200 million cars on U.S. roads. Some of this demand is filled by full-service auto dealerships, some by Sears and Firestone, and some by other tire/service dealers. However, Minit-Lube, Mobil-Lube, Jiffy-Lube and others have also developed strategies to accommodate this opportunity.

Minit-Lube stations perform oil changes, lubrication, and interior cleaning in a spotless environment. The buildings are clean,

painted white, and often surrounded by neatly trimmed landscaping. To facilitate fast service, cars can be driven through three abreast. At Minit-Lube, the customer is greeted by service representatives who are graduates of Minit-Lube U. The Minit-Lube school is not unlike McDonald's Hamburger University near Chicago or Holiday Inn's training school in Memphis. The greeter takes the order, which typically includes fluid checks (oil, water, brake fluid, transmission fluid, differential grease) and the necessary lubrication, as well as filter changes for air and oil. Service personnel in neat uniforms then move into action. The standard three-person team has one person checking fluid levels under the hood, another assigned interior vacuuming and window cleaning, and the third in the garage pit, removing the oil filter, draining the oil, checking the differential and transmission, and lubricating as necessary. Precise task assignments and good training are designed to move the car into and out of the bay in 10 minutes. The idea is to charge no more, and hopefully less, than gas stations, automotive repair chains, and auto dealers, while providing better service.

Discussion Questions

1. What constitutes the mission of Minit-Lube?
2. How does the Minit-Lube operations strategy provide competitive advantage? (*Hint:* Evaluate how Minit-Lube's traditional competitors perform the 10 decisions of operations management vs. how Minit-Lube performs them.)
3. Is it likely that Minit-Lube has increased productivity over its more traditional competitors? Why? How would we measure productivity in this industry?

Strategy at Regal Marine

Video Case

Regal Marine, one of the U.S.'s 10 largest power-boat manufacturers, achieves its mission—providing luxury performance boats to customers worldwide—using the strategy of differentiation. It differentiates its products through constant innovation, unique features, and high quality. Increasing sales at the Orlando, Florida, family-owned firm suggest that the strategy is working.

As a quality boat manufacturer, Regal Marine starts with continuous innovation, as reflected in computer-aided design (CAD), high-quality molds, and close tolerances that are controlled through both defect charts and rigorous visual inspection. In-house quality is not enough, however. Because a product is only as good as the parts put into it, Regal has established close ties with a large number of its suppliers to ensure both flexibility and perfect parts. With the help of these suppliers, Regal can profitably produce a product line of 22 boats, ranging from the $14,000 19-foot boat to the $500,000 44-foot Commodore yacht.

"We build boats," says VP Tim Kuck, "but we're really in the 'fun' business. Our competition includes not only 300 other boat, canoe, and yacht manufacturers in our $17 billion industry, but home theaters, the Internet, and all kinds of alternative family enter-

tainment." Fortunately for Regal, with the strong economy and the repeal of the boat luxury tax on its side, it has been paying down debt and increasing market share.

Regal has also joined with scores of other independent boat makers in the American Boat Builders Association. Through economies of scale in procurement, Regal is able to navigate against billion-dollar competitor Brunswick (makers of the Sea Ray and Bayliner brands). The *Global Company Profile* featuring Regal Marine (which opens Chapter 5) provides further background on Regal and its strategy.

Discussion Questions*

1. State Regal Marine's mission in your own words.
2. Identify the strengths, weaknesses, opportunities, and threats that are relevant to the strategy of Regal Marine.
3. How would you define Regal's strategy?
4. How would each of the 10 operations management decisions apply to operations decision making at Regal Marine?

*You may wish to play this video case on your DVD before addressing these questions.

Hard Rock Cafe's Global Strategy

Video Case

Hard Rock is bringing the concept of the "experience economy" to its cafe operation. The strategy is to incorporate a unique "experience" into its operations. This innovation is somewhat akin to mass customization in manufacturing. At Hard Rock, the experience concept is to provide not only a custom meal from the menu but a dining event that includes a unique visual and sound experience not duplicated anywhere else in the world. This strategy is succeeding. Other theme restaurants have come and gone while Hard Rock continues to grow. As Professor C. Markides of the London Business School says, "The trick is not to play the game better than the competition, but to develop and play an altogether different game."* At Hard Rock, the different game is the experience game.

From the opening of its first cafe in London in 1971, during the British rock music explosion, Hard Rock has been serving food and rock music with equal enthusiasm. Hard Rock Cafe has 40 U.S. locations, about a dozen in Europe, and the remainder scattered throughout the world, from Bangkok and Beijing to Beirut. New construction, leases, and investment in remodeling are long term; so a global strategy means special consideration of political risk, currency risk, and social norms in a context of a brand fit. Although

Hard Rock is one of the most recognized brands in the world, this does not mean its cafe is a natural everywhere. Special consideration must be given to the supply chain for the restaurant and its accompanying retail store. About 48% of a typical cafe's sales are from merchandise.

The Hard Rock Cafe business model is well defined, but because of various risk factors and differences in business practices and employment law, Hard Rock elects to franchise about half of its cafes. Social norms and preferences often suggest some tweaking of menus for local taste. For instance, Europeans, particularly the British, still have some fear of mad cow disease; therefore, Hard Rock is focusing less on hamburgers and beef and more on fish and lobster in its British cafes.

Because 70% of Hard Rock's guests are tourists, recent years have found it expanding to "destination" cities. While this has been a winning strategy for decades, allowing the firm to grow from 1 London cafe to 110 facilities in 41 countries, it has made Hard Rock susceptible to economic fluctuations that hit the tourist business hardest. So Hard Rock is signing a long-term lease for a new location in Nottingham, England, to join recently opened cafes in Manchester and Birmingham—cities that are not standard tourist destinations. At the same time, menus are being upgraded. Hopefully, repeat business from locals in these cities will smooth demand and make Hard Rock less dependent on tourists.

Discussion Questions[†]

1. Identify the strategy changes that have taken place at Hard Rock Cafe since its founding in 1971.

2. As Hard Rock Cafe has changed its strategy, how has its responses to some of the 10 decisions of OM changed?

3. Where does Hard Rock fit in the four international operations strategies outlined in Figure 2.9? Explain your answer.

*Constantinos Markides, "Strategic Innovation," *MIT Sloan Management Review* 38, no. 3 (spring 1997): 9.

†You may wish to play this video case on your DVD before addressing these questions.

Additional Case Studies

Internet Case Study: Visit our Companion Web site at www.prenhall.com/heizer for this free case study:
• **Motorola's Global Strategy:** Focuses on Motorola's international strategy.

Harvard has selected these Harvard Business School cases to accompany this chapter.

harvardbusinessonline.hbsp.harvard.edu

• **Eli Lilly and Co.: Manufacturing Process Technology Strategy—1991** (#692056): Manufacturing pursues comparative advantage in an industry where R&D is the primary competitive advantage.
• **Fresh Connections** (#600-022): Investigates how to structure operations to take advantage of the continued growth in the home meal replacement market.
• **Hitting the Wall: Nike and International Labor Practices** (#7000047): Nike must deal with a spate of alarmingly bad publicity regarding wages in developing countries.
• **Hewlett-Packard Singapore (A)** (#694035): Product development issues when source and recipients of knowledge are separated both geographically and culturally.
• **Komatsu Ltd.** (#398-016): Describes strategic and organizational transformations at Komatsu, a major Japan-based producer of construction equipment.
• **McDonald's Corp.** (#693028): Changing environment and competition forces McDonald's to rethink its operating strategy.
• **Southwest Airlines—1993 (A)** (#694023): Provides insight into Southwest's strategy, operations, marketing, and culture.
• **Toys "Я" Us Japan** (#796-077): Documents Toys "Я" Us difficulties as it enters the Japanese toy market.
• **Lenzing AG: Expanding in Indonesia** (#796-099): Presents the issues surrounding expansion in a foreign country.

Bibliography

Bhagwati, J. *In Defense of Globalization.* Oxford, UK: Oxford University Press, 2004.

Crotts, J. C., D. R. Dickson, and R. C. Ford. "Aligning Organizational Processes with Mission: The Case of Service Excellence." *Academy of Management Executive* 19, no. 3 (August 2005): 54–68.

Drucker, P. F. "The Emerging Theory of Manufacturing." *Harvard Business Review* 68, no. 3 (May–June 1990): 94–103.

Flynn, B. B., R. G. Schroeder, and E. J. Flynn. "World Class Manufacturing: An Investigation of Hayes and Wheelwright's Foundation." *Journal of Operations Management* 17, no. 3 (March 1999): 249–269.

Friedman, Thomas. *The World Is Flat: A Brief History of the Twenty-first Century.* New York: Farrar, Straus, and Giroux, 2005.

Greenwald, Bruce, and Judd Kahn. "All Strategy Is Local." *Harvard Business Review*, 83, no. 9 (September 2005): 94–104.

Kaplan, Robert S., and David P. Norton. *Strategy Maps.* Boston: Harvard Business School Publishing, 2003.

Luke, Royce D., Stephen L. Walston, and Patrick Michael Plummer. *Healthcare Strategy: In Pursuit of Competitive Advantage.* Chicago: Health Administration Press, 2003.

Porter, M. E. *The Competitive Advantage of Nations.* New York: The Free Press, 1990.

Wolf, Martin. *Why Globalization Works.* London: Yale University Press, 2004.

Womack, J. P., D. T. Jones, and D. Roos. *The Machine That Changed the World.* New York: Rawson Associates, 1990.

Internet Resources

Business Policy and Strategy, Division of the Academy of Management: **www.aom.pace.edu/bps**
European Union: **europa.eu.int/index_en.htm**
International Trade Administration: **www.ita.doc.gov**
Manufacturing Strategies, maintained at Cranfield University: **www.cranfield.ac.uk/som**

Transparency International maintains a Bribe Payers Perception Index (BPI) and a Corruption Perceptions Index: **www.transparency.de, www.globalcorruptionreport.org**
World Bank: **www.worldbank.org**
World Economic Forum: **www.weforum.org**
World Trade Organization: **www.wto.org**

CHAPTER 3

Project Management

Chapter Outline

Learning Objectives

When you complete this chapter you should be able to

1. Create a work breakdown structure
2. Draw AOA and AON networks
3. Complete both forward and backward passes for a project
4. Determine a critical path
5. Calculate the variance of activity times
6. Crash a project
7. Use Microsoft Project software to create a project

55

Project Management Provides a Competitive Advantage for Bechtel

Now in its 110th year, the San Francisco–based Bechtel Group (**www.bechtel.com**) is the world's premier manager of massive construction and engineering projects. Known for billion-dollar projects, Bechtel is famous for its construction feats on the Hoover Dam, the Boston Central Artery/Tunnel project, and rebuilding of Kuwait's oil and gas infrastructure after the invasion by Iraq in 1990.

Conditions weren't what Bechtel expected when it won a series of billion-dollar contracts from the U.S. government to help reconstruct Iraq in 2003–2006. Saddam Hussein's defeat by Allied forces hadn't caused much war damage. Instead, what Bechtel found was a country that had been crumbling for years. None of the sewage plants in Baghdad worked. Power flicked on and off. Towns

▲ *Workers wrestle with a 1,500-ton boring machine, measuring 25 feet in diameter, that was used to dig the Eurotunnel between England and France in the early 1990s. With overruns that boosted the cost of the project to $13 billion, a Bechtel Group VP was brought in to head operations.*

◄ *A massive dredge hired by Bechtel removes silt from Iraq's port at Umm Qasr. This paved the way for large-scale deliveries of U.S. food and the return of commercial shipping.*

and cities in the anti-Hussein south had been left to decay as punishment. And to complicate matters even more, scavengers were stealing everything from museum artifacts to electric power lines. Bechtel's job was to oversee electric power, sewage, transportation, and airport repairs.

Bechtel's crews travelled under armed escort and slept in trailers surrounded by razor wire. But the company's efforts have paid off. Iraq's main seaport, Umm Qasr, was reopened when Bechtel dredged the water and repaired the grain elevators. Electrical generation was back to prewar levels in 10 months. Bechtel refurbished more than 1,200 schools.

With a global procurement program, Bechtel easily tapped the company's network of suppliers and

▶ Managing massive construction projects such as this is the strength of Bechtel. With large penalties for late completion and incentives for early completion, a good project manager is worth his or her weight in gold.

▲ Reconstructed terminal at Baghdad International Airport

▶ Bechtel was the construction contractor for the Hoover Dam. This dam, on the Colorado River, is the highest in the Western Hemisphere.

buyers worldwide to help rebuild Iraq's infrastructure. Other interesting recent Bechtel projects include:

- Building 26 massive distribution centers, in just 2 years, for the Internet company Webvan Group ($1 billion).
- Constructing 30 high-security data centers worldwide for Equinix, Inc. ($1.2 billion).
- Building and running a rail line between London and the Channel Tunnel ($4.6 billion).
- Developing an oil pipeline from the Caspian Sea region to Russia ($850 million).
- Expanding the Dubai Airport in the United Arab Emirates ($600 million) and the Miami International Airport ($2 billion).

- Building liquefied natural gas plants in Trinidad, West Indies ($1 billion).
- Building a new subway for Athens, Greece ($2.6 billion).
- Constructing a natural gas pipeline in Thailand ($700 million).
- Building 30 plants for iMotors.com, a company that sells refurbished autos online ($300 million).
- Building a highway to link the north and south of Croatia ($303 million).

When companies or countries seek out firms to manage massive projects, they go to Bechtel, which, again and again, through outstanding project management, has demonstrated its competitive advantage.

THE IMPORTANCE OF PROJECT MANAGEMENT

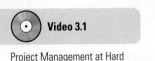

- When the Bechtel project management team entered Iraq after the 2003 war, it quickly had to mobilize an international force of manual workers, construction professionals, cooks, medical personnel, and security forces. It had to access millions of tons of supplies to rebuild ports, roads, schools, and electrical systems.
- When Microsoft Corporation set out to develop Windows Vista—its biggest, most complex, and most important program to date—time was the critical factor for the project manager. With hundreds of programmers working on millions of lines of code in a program costing hundreds of millions of dollars to develop, immense stakes rode on timely delivery of the project.
- When Hard Rock Cafe sponsors Rockfest, hosting 100,000 plus fans at its annual concert, the project manager begins planning some 9 months earlier. Using the software package Microsoft Project, described in this chapter, each of the hundreds of details can be monitored and controlled. When a band can't reach the Rockfest site by bus because of massive traffic jams, Hard Rock's project manager is ready with a helicopter backup.

Bechtel, Microsoft, and Hard Rock are just three examples of firms that face a modern phenomenon: growing project complexity and collapsing product/service life cycles. This change stems from awareness of the strategic value of time-based competition and a quality mandate for continuous improvement. Each new product/service introduction is a unique event—a project. In addition, projects are a common part of our everyday life. We may be planning a wedding or a surprise birthday party, remodeling a house, or preparing a semester-long class project.

Scheduling projects is a difficult challenge for operations managers. The stakes in project management are high. Cost overruns and unnecessary delays occur due to poor scheduling and poor controls.

▲ **Figure 3.1**   Project Planning, Scheduling, and Controlling

Projects that take months or years to complete are usually developed outside the normal production system. Project organizations within the firm may be set up to handle such jobs and are often disbanded when the project is complete. On other occasions, managers find projects just a part of their job. The management of projects involves three phases (see Figure 3.1):

1. *Planning:* This phase includes goal setting, defining the project, and team organization.
2. *Scheduling:* This phase relates people, money, and supplies to specific activities and relates activities to each other.
3. *Controlling:* Here the firm monitors resources, costs, quality, and budgets. It also revises or changes plans and shifts resources to meet time and cost demands.

We begin this chapter with a brief overview of these functions. Three popular techniques to allow managers to plan, schedule, and control—Gantt charts, PERT, and CPM—are also described.

PROJECT PLANNING

Projects can be defined as a series of related tasks directed toward a major output. In some firms a **project organization** is developed to make sure existing programs continue to run smoothly on a day-to-day basis while new projects are successfully completed.

For companies with multiple large projects, such as a construction firm, a project organization is an effective way of assigning the people and physical resources needed. It is a temporary organization structure designed to achieve results by using specialists from throughout the firm. NASA and many other organizations use the project approach. You may recall Project Gemini and Project Apollo. These terms were used to describe teams that NASA organized to reach space exploration objectives.

The project organization works best when:

1. Work can be defined with a specific goal and deadline.
2. The job is unique or somewhat unfamiliar to the existing organization.
3. The work contains complex interrelated tasks requiring specialized skills.
4. The project is temporary but critical to the organization.
5. The project cuts across organizational lines.

Project organization
An organization formed to ensure that programs (projects) receive the proper management and attention.

The Project Manager

An example of a project organization is shown in Figure 3.2. Project team members are temporarily assigned to a project and report to the project manager. The manager heading the project coordinates activities with other departments and reports directly to top management. Project managers receive high visibility in a firm and are responsible for making sure that (1) all necessary activities are finished in proper sequence and on time; (2) the project comes in within budget; (3) the project meets its quality goals; and (4) the people assigned to the project receive the motivation, direction, and information needed to do their jobs. This means that project managers should be good coaches and communicators, and be able to organize activities from a variety of disciplines.

When a project organization is made permanent, it is usually called a "matrix organization."

◀ **Figure 3.2**

A Sample Project Organization

Ethical Issues Faced in Project Management   Project managers not only have high visibility but they also face ethical decisions on a daily basis. How they act establishes the code of conduct for everyone on their project. On the personal level, project managers often deal with (1) offers of gifts from contractors, (2) pressure to alter status reports to mask the reality of delays, (3) false reports for charges of time and expenses, and (4) pressures to compromise quality to meet bonus or penalty schedules.

Other major problems in projects large and small are:

- Bid rigging—divulging confidential information to some bidders to give them an unfair advantage.
- "Low-balling" contractors—who try to "buy" the project by bidding low with the hope of recovering costs later by contract renegotiations or by simply cutting corners.
- Bribery—particularly on international projects.
- Expense account padding, use of substandard materials, compromising health/safety standards, withholding needed information.
- Failure to admit project failure at the close of the project.

Codes of ethics such as those established by the Project Management Institute (**www.pmi.org**) are one means of trying to establish standards. Research has shown that without good leadership and a strong organizational culture most people follow their own set of ethical standards and values.[1]

Work Breakdown Structure

Work breakdown structure (WBS)

Division of a project into more and more detailed components.

The project management team begins its task well in advance of project execution so that a plan can be developed. One of its first steps is to carefully establish the project's objectives, then break the project down into manageable parts. This **work breakdown structure (WBS)** defines the project by dividing it into its major subcomponents (or tasks), which are then subdivided into more detailed components, and finally into a set of activities and their related costs. The division of the project into smaller and smaller tasks can be difficult, but is critical to managing the project and to scheduling success. Gross requirements for people, supplies, and equipment are also estimated in this planning phase.

The work breakdown structure typically decreases in size from top to bottom and is indented like this:

Level
1   Project
2   Major tasks in the project
3   Subtasks in major tasks
4   Activities (or "work packages") to be completed

This hierarchical framework can be illustrated with the development of Microsoft's operating system Windows Vista. As we see in Figure 3.3, the project, creating a new operating system, is labeled 1.0. The first step is to identify the major tasks in the project (level 2). Two examples would be development of graphic user interfaces or GUIs (1.1), and creating compatibility with previous versions of Windows (1.2). The major subtasks for 1.2 are creating a team to handle

▶ **Figure 3.3**

Work Breakdown Structure

Level	Level ID Number	Activity
1	1.0	Develop/launch Windows Vista operating system
2	1.1	Develop GUIs
2	1.2	Ensure compatibility with earlier Windows versions
3	1.21	Compatibility with Windows ME
3	1.22	Compatibility with Windows XP
3	1.23	Compatibility with Windows 2000
4	1.231	Ensure ability to import files

[1]See P. J. Rutland, "Ethical Codes and Personal Values," *Cost Engineering* 44 (December 2002): 22; and K. K. Humphreys, *What Every Engineer Should Know About Ethics* (New York: Marcel Dekker, 2004).

compatibility with Windows ME (1.21), a compatibility team for Windows XP (1.22), and compatibility with Windows 2000 (1.23). Then, each major subtask is broken down into level-4 activities that need to be done, such as "importing files" created in Windows 2000 (1.231). There are usually many level-4 activities.

PROJECT SCHEDULING

Project scheduling involves sequencing and allotting time to all project activities. At this stage, managers decide how long each activity will take and compute how many people and materials will be needed at each stage of production. Managers also chart separate schedules for personnel needs by type of skill (management, engineering, or pouring concrete, for example). Charts also can be developed for scheduling materials.

One popular project scheduling approach is the Gantt chart. **Gantt charts** are low-cost means of helping managers make sure that (1) all activities are planned for, (2) their order of performance is accounted for, (3) the activity time estimates are recorded, and (4) the overall project time is developed. As Figure 3.4 shows, Gantt charts are easy to understand. Horizontal bars are drawn for each project activity along a time line. This illustration of a routine servicing of a Delta jetliner during a 40-minute layover shows that Gantt charts also can be used for scheduling repetitive operations. In this case, the chart helps point out potential delays. The *OM in Action* box on Delta provides additional insights. (A second illustration of a Gantt chart is also provided in Chapter 15, Figure 15.4.)

On simple projects, scheduling charts such as these can be used alone. They permit managers to observe the progress of each activity and to spot and tackle problem areas. Gantt charts, though, do not adequately illustrate the interrelationships between the activities and the resources.

PERT and CPM, the two widely used network techniques that we shall discuss shortly, *do* have the ability to consider precedence relationships and interdependency of activities. On complex projects, the scheduling of which is almost always computerized, PERT and CPM thus have an edge over the simpler Gantt charts. Even on huge projects, though, Gantt charts can be used as summaries of project status and may complement the other network approaches.

To summarize, whatever the approach taken by a project manager, project scheduling serves several purposes:

1. It shows the relationship of each activity to others and to the whole project.
2. It identifies the precedence relationships among activities.
3. It encourages the setting of realistic time and cost estimates for each activity.
4. It helps make better use of people, money, and material resources by identifying critical bottlenecks in the project.

Gantt charts

Planning charts used to schedule resources and allocate time.

Gnatt charts are an example of a widely used, nonmathematical technique that is very popular with managers because it is simple and visual.

◀ **Figure 3.4**

Gantt Chart of Service Activities for a Delta Jet during a 40-Minute Layover

Delta hopes to save $50 million a year with this turnaround time, which is a reduction from its traditional 60-minute routine.

OM in Action   Delta's Ground Crew Orchestrates a Smooth Takeoff

Flight 574's engines screech its arrival as the jet lumbers down Richmond's taxiway with 140 passengers arriving from Atlanta. In 40 minutes, the plane is to be airborne again.

However, before this jet can depart, there is business to attend to: passengers, luggage, and cargo to unload and load; thousands of gallons of jet fuel and countless drinks to restock; cabin and restrooms to clean; toilet holding tanks to drain; and engines, wings, and landing gear to inspect.

The 10-person ground crew knows that a miscue anywhere—a broken cargo loader, lost baggage, misdirected passengers—can mean a late departure and trigger a chain reaction of headaches from Richmond to Atlanta to every destination of a connecting flight.

Carla Sutera, the operations manager for Delta's Richmond International Airport, views the turnaround operation like a pit boss awaiting a race car. Trained crews

are in place for Flight 574 with baggage carts and tractors, hydraulic cargo loaders, a truck to load food and drinks, another to lift the cleanup crew, another to put fuel on, and a fourth to take water off. The "pit crew" usually performs so smoothly that most passengers never suspect the proportions of the effort. Gantt charts, such as the one in Figure 3.4, aid Delta and other airlines with the staffing and scheduling that are needed for this task.

Sources: Knight Ridder Tribune Business News (July 16, 2005): 1 and (November 21, 2002): 1.

PROJECT CONTROLLING

The control of large projects, like the control of any management system, involves close monitoring of resources, costs, quality, and budgets. Control also means using a feedback loop to revise the project plan and having the ability to shift resources to where they are needed most. Computerized PERT/CPM reports and charts are widely available today on personal computers. Some of the more popular of these programs are Primavera (by Primavera Systems, Inc.), MacProject (by Apple Computer Corp.), Pertmaster (by Westminster Software, Inc.), VisiSchedule (by Paladin Software Corp.), Time Line (by Symantec Corp.), and Microsoft Project (by Microsoft Corp.), which we illustrate in this chapter.

These programs produce a broad variety of reports, including (1) detailed cost breakdowns for each task, (2) total program labor curves, (3) cost distribution tables, (4) functional cost and hour summaries, (5) raw material and expenditure forecasts, (6) variance reports, (7) time analysis reports, and (8) work status reports.

 Video 3.2

Project Management at Arnold Palmer Hospital

▲ *Construction of the new 11-story building at Arnold Palmer Hospital in Orlando, Florida, was an enormous project for the hospital administration. The photo on the left shows the first six floors under construction. The photo on the right shows the building as completed in 2006, two years later. Prior to beginning actual construction, regulatory and funding issues added, as they do with most projects, substantial time to the overall project. Cities have zoning and parking issues, the EPA has drainage and waste issues, and regulatory authorities have their own requirements, as do issuers of bonds. The $100 million, four-year project at Arnold Palmer Hospital is discussed in the Video Case Study at the end of this chapter.*

PROJECT MANAGEMENT TECHNIQUES: PERT AND CPM

Program evaluation and review technique (PERT) and the **critical path method (CPM)** were both developed in the 1950s to help managers schedule, monitor, and control large and complex projects. CPM arrived first, in 1957, as a tool developed by J. E. Kelly of Remington Rand and M. R. Walker of duPont to assist in the building and maintenance of chemical plants at duPont. Independently, PERT was developed in 1958 by Booz, Allen, and Hamilton for the U.S. Navy.

The Framework of PERT and CPM

PERT and CPM both follow six basic steps:

1. Define the project and prepare the work breakdown structure.
2. Develop the relationships among the activities. Decide which activities must precede and which must follow others.
3. Draw the network connecting all the activities.
4. Assign time and/or cost estimates to each activity.
5. Compute the *longest* time path through the network. This is called the **critical path**.
6. Use the network to help plan, schedule, monitor, and control the project.

Step 5, finding the critical path, is a major part of controlling a project. The activities on the critical path represent tasks that will delay the entire project if they are not completed on time. Managers can gain the flexibility needed to complete critical tasks by identifying noncritical activities and replanning, rescheduling, and reallocating labor and financial resources.

Although PERT and CPM differ to some extent in terminology and in the construction of the network, their objectives are the same. Furthermore, the analysis used in both techniques is very similar. The major difference is that PERT employs three time estimates for each activity. These time estimates are used to compute expected values and standard deviations for the activity. CPM makes the assumption that activity times are known with certainty and hence requires only one time factor for each activity.

For purposes of illustration, the rest of this section concentrates on a discussion of PERT. Most of the comments and procedures described, however, apply just as well to CPM.

PERT and CPM are important because they can help answer questions such as the following about projects with thousands of activities:

1. When will the entire project be completed?
2. What are the critical activities or tasks in the project—that is, which activities will delay the entire project if they are late?
3. Which are the noncritical activities—the ones that can run late without delaying the whole project's completion?
4. What is the probability that the project will be completed by a specific date?
5. At any particular date, is the project on schedule, behind schedule, or ahead of schedule?
6. On any given date, is the money spent equal to, less than, or greater than the budgeted amount?
7. Are there enough resources available to finish the project on time?
8. If the project is to be finished in a shorter amount of time, what is the best way to accomplish this goal at the least cost?

Network Diagrams and Approaches

The first step in a PERT or CPM network is to divide the entire project into significant activities in accordance with the work breakdown structure. There are two approaches for drawing a project network: **activity on node (AON)** and **activity on arrow (AOA)**. Under the AON convention, *nodes* designate activities. Under AOA, *arrows* represent activities. Activities consume time and resources. The basic difference between AON and AOA is that the nodes in an AON diagram represent activities. In an AOA network, the nodes represent the starting and finishing times of an activity and are also called *events*. So nodes in AOA consume neither time nor resources.

Figure 3.5 illustrates both conventions for a small portion of the airline turnaround Gantt chart (in Figure 3.4). The examples provide some background for understanding six common activity

Program evaluation and review technique (PERT)
A project management technique that employs three time estimates for each activity.

Critical path method (CPM)
A project management technique that uses only one time factor per activity.

Critical path
The computed *longest* time path(s) through a network.

Activity-on-node (AON)
A network diagram in which nodes designate activities.

Activity-on-arrow (AOA)
A network diagram in which arrows designate activities.

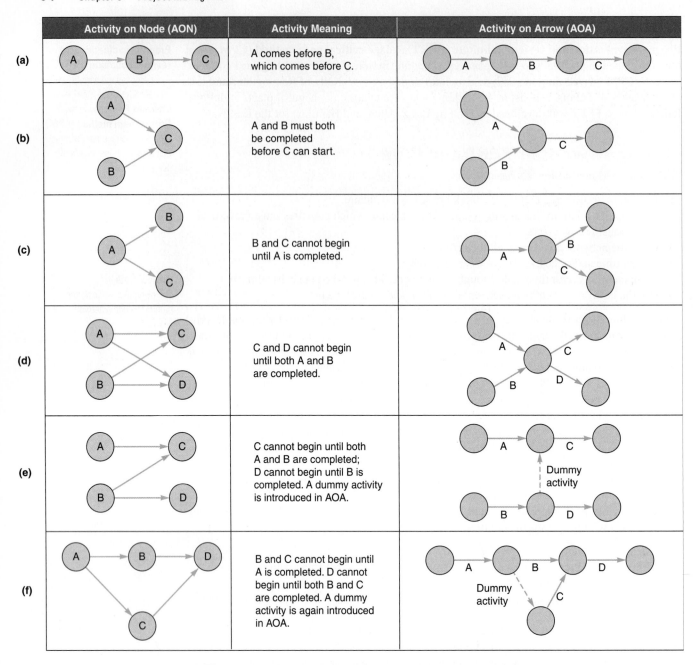

Activity on Node (AON)	Activity Meaning	Activity on Arrow (AOA)
(a) A → B → C	A comes before B, which comes before C.	A → B → C
(b) A, B → C	A and B must both be completed before C can start.	A, B → C
(c) A → B, C	B and C cannot begin until A is completed.	A → B, C
(d) A, B → C, D	C and D cannot begin until both A and B are completed.	A, B → C, D
(e) A → C; B → C, D	C cannot begin until both A and B are completed; D cannot begin until B is completed. A dummy activity is introduced in AOA.	A → C; Dummy activity; B → D
(f) A → B → D; A → C → D	B and C cannot begin until A is completed. D cannot begin until both B and C are completed. A dummy activity is again introduced in AOA.	A → B → D; Dummy activity; C

▲ **Figure 3.5** A Comparison of AON and AOA Network Conventions

relationships in networks. In Figure 3.5(a), activity A must be finished before activity B is started, and B must, in turn, be completed before C begins. Activity A might represent "deplaning passengers," while B is "cabin cleaning," and C is "boarding new passengers."

Figures 3.5(e) and 3.5(f) illustrate that the AOA approach sometimes needs the addition of a **dummy activity** to clarify relationships. A dummy activity consumes no time or resources, but is required when a network has two activities with identical starting and ending events, or when two or more follow some, but not all, "preceding" activities. The use of dummy activities is also important when computer software is employed to determine project completion time. A dummy activity has a completion time of zero.

Although both AON and AOA are popular in practice, many of the project management software packages, including Microsoft Project, use AON networks. For this reason, although we illustrate both types of networks in the next example, we focus on AON networks in subsequent discussions in this chapter.

Dummy activity

An activity having no time that is inserted into a network to maintain the logic of the network.

Activity-on-Node Example

EXAMPLE 1

Activity-on-node for EPA problem at Milwaukee Paper

Milwaukee Paper Manufacturing, Inc., located near downtown Milwaukee, has long been trying to avoid the expense of installing air pollution control equipment in its facility. The Environmental Protection Agency (EPA) has recently given the manufacturer 16 weeks to install a complex air filter system. Milwaukee Paper has been warned that it may be forced to close the facility unless the device is installed in the allotted period. Joni Steinberg, the plant manager, wants to make sure that installation of the filtering system progresses smoothly and on time.

Given the following information, develop a table showing activity precedence relationships.

Approach: Milwaukee Paper has identified the eight activities that need to be performed in order for the project to be completed. When the project begins, two activities can be simultaneously started: building the internal components for the device (activity A) and the modifications necessary for the floor and roof (activity B). The construction of the collection stack (activity C) can begin when the internal components are completed. Pouring the concrete floor and installation of the frame (activity D) can be started as soon as the internal components are completed and the roof and floor have been modified.

After the collection stack has been constructed, two activities can begin: building the high-temperature burner (activity E) and installing the pollution control system (activity F). The air pollution device can be installed (activity G) after the concrete floor has been poured, the frame has been installed, and the high-temperature burner has been built. Finally, after the control system and pollution device have been installed, the system can be inspected and tested (activity H).

Learning Objective

2. Draw AOA and AON networks

Solution: Activities and precedence relationships may seem rather confusing when they are presented in this descriptive form. It is therefore convenient to list all the activity information in a table, as shown in Table 3.1. We see in the table that activity A is listed as an *immediate predecessor* of activity C. Likewise, both activities D and E must be performed prior to starting activity G.

◄ **Table 3.1**

Milwaukee Paper Manufacturing's Activities and Predecessors

Activity	Description	Immediate Predecessors
A	Build internal components	—
B	Modify roof and floor	—
C	Construct collection stack	A
D	Pour concrete and install frame	A, B
E	Build high-temperature burner	C
F	Install pollution control system	C
G	Install air pollution device	D, E
H	Inspect and test	F, G

Insight: To complete a network, all predecessors must be clearly defined.

Learning exercise: What is the impact on the sequence of activities if EPA approval is required after *Inspect and Test?* [Answer: The immediate predecessor for the new activity would be H, *Inspect and Test*, with *EPA approval* as the last activity.]

Related problem: 3.27

Note that in Example 1, it is enough to list just the *immediate predecessors* for each activity. For instance, in Table 3.1, since activity A precedes activity C, and activity C precedes activity E, the fact that activity A precedes activity E is *implicit*. This relationship need not be explicitly shown in the activity precedence relationships.

When there are many activities in a project with fairly complicated precedence relationships, it is difficult for an individual to comprehend the complexity of the project from just the tabular information. In such cases, a visual representation of the project, using a *project network*, is convenient and useful. A project network is a diagram of all the activities and the precedence relationships that exist between these activities in a project. Example 2 illustrates how to construct a project network for Milwaukee Paper Manufacturing.

Networks consist of nodes that are connected by lines (or arcs).

OM in Action | Rebuilding the Pentagon after 9/11

On September 11, 2001, American Airlines Flight 77 slammed into the Pentagon. The world was shocked by this and the other terrorist attacks on the Twin Towers in New York City. One hundred and twenty-five people died when a large portion of the Pentagon was severely damaged. Among the first to react were construction workers renovating another portion of the Pentagon. Their heroism saved lives and eased suffering. Within hours of the disaster, heavy equipment began arriving on the site, accompanied by hundreds of volunteer construction workers driven by patriotism and pride.

Just four days after the attack, Walker Lee Evey, named program manager for "Project Phoenix," promised to rebuild the damaged portions of the Pentagon "faster than anyone has a right to expect . . . and to have people back in the damaged portion of the building, right where the plane hit, by September 11, 2002."

Preliminary construction reports estimated it would take 3 to 4 years and $\$\frac{3}{4}$ billion to rebuild. By directing the project with teamwork, handshake contracts, creativity, and ingenuity—not to mention emotional 20-hour days 6 to 7 days a week—Evey's Project Phoenix met its psychological and physical goal. In less than 11 months,

and for only $501 million, workers demolished and rebuilt the damaged sections—400,000 square feet of structure, 2 million square feet of offices, 50,000 tons of debris—using 1,000 construction workers from 80 companies. By September 9, 2002, over 600 military and civilian personnel were sitting at their desks in rebuilt Pentagon offices.

Outside, the blackened gash is long gone. Instead, some 4,000 pieces of limestone—mined from the same Indiana vein that the Pentagon's original stone came from 65 years ago—have been placed on the building's façade. For this impressive accomplishment, the Pentagon and Walker Evey were nominated for the Project Management Institute's 2003 Project of the Year Award.

Sources: Knight-Ridder Tribune Business News (February 1, 2004): 1; *ENR* (September 2, 2002): 6; *U.S. News & World Report* (September 16, 2002): 35.

EXAMPLE 2

AON graph for Milwaukee Paper

Draw the AON network for Milwaukee Paper, using the data in Example 1.

Approach: In the AON approach, we denote each activity by a node. The lines, or arcs, represent the precedence relationships between the activities.

Solution: In this example, there are two activities (A and B) that do not have any predecessors. We draw separate nodes for each of these activities, as shown in Figure 3.6. Although not required, it is usually convenient to have a unique starting activity for a project. We have therefore included a *dummy activity* called *Start* in Figure 3.6. This dummy activity does not really exist and takes up zero time and resources. Activity *Start* is an immediate predecessor for both activities A and B, and serves as the unique starting activity for the entire project.

▶ **Figure 3.6**

Beginning AON Network for Milwaukee Paper

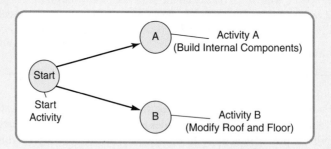

We now show the precedence relationships using lines with arrow symbols. For example, an arrow from activity Start to activity A indicates that Start is a predecessor for activity A. In a similar fashion, we draw an arrow from Start to B.

Next, we add a new node for activity C. Since activity A precedes activity C, we draw an arc from node A to node C (see Figure 3.7). Likewise, we first draw a node to represent activity D. Then, since activities A and B both precede activity D, we draw arrows from A to D and from B to D (see Figure 3.7).

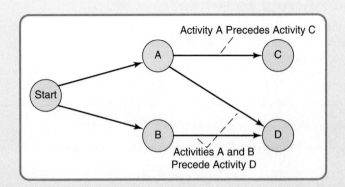

◀ **Figure 3.7**

Intermediate AON Network for Milwaukee Paper

We proceed in this fashion, adding a separate node for each activity and a separate line for each precedence relationship that exists. The complete AON project network for the Milwaukee Paper Manufacturing project is shown in Figure 3.8.

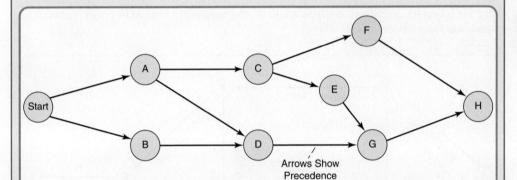

◀ **Figure 3.8**

Complete AON Network for Milwaukee Paper

Insight: Drawing a project network properly takes some time and experience. We would like the lines to be straight and arrows to move to the right when possible.

Learning exercise: If *EPA Approval* occurs after *Inspect and Test*, what is the impact on the graph? [Answer: A straight line is extended to the right beyond H to reflect the additional activity.]

Related problems: 3.3, 3.6, 3.7, 3.9a, 3.10, 3.12, 3.15a

When we first draw a project network, it is not unusual that we place our nodes (activities) in the network in such a fashion that the arrows (precedence relationships) are not straight lines. That is, the lines could be intersecting each other, and even facing in opposite directions. For example, if we had switched the location of the nodes for activities E and F in Figure 3.8, the lines from F to H and E to G would have intersected. Although such a project network is perfectly valid, it is good practice to have a well-drawn network. One rule that we especially recommend is to place the nodes in such a fashion that all arrows point in the same direction. To achieve this, we suggest that you first draw a rough draft of the network, making sure all the relationships are shown. Then you can redraw the network to make appropriate changes in the location of the nodes.

As with the unique starting node, it is convenient to have the project network finish with a unique ending node. In the Milwaukee Paper example, it turns out that a unique activity, H, is the last activity in the project. We therefore automatically have a unique ending node.

In situations in which a project has multiple ending activities, we include a "dummy" ending activity. This dummy activity has all the multiple ending activities in the project as immediate predecessors. We illustrate this type of situation in Solved Problem 3.2 at the end of this chapter.

It is convenient, but not required, to have unique starting and ending activities in a project.

Activity-on-Arrow Example

We saw earlier that in an AOA project network we can represent activities by arrows. A node represents an *event*, which marks the start or completion time of an activity. We usually identify an event (node) by a number.

EXAMPLE 3

Activity-on-arrow for Milwaukee Paper

Draw the complete AOA project network for Milwaukee Paper's problem.

Approach: Using the data from Table 3.1 in Example 1, draw one activity at a time, starting with A.

Solution: We see that activity A starts at event 1 and ends at event 2. Likewise, activity B starts at event 1 and ends at event 3. Activity C, whose only immediate predecessor is activity A, starts at node 2 and ends at node 4. Activity D, however, has two predecessors (i.e., A and B). Hence, we need both activities A and B to end at event 3, so that activity D can start at that event. However, we cannot have multiple activities with common starting and ending nodes in an AOA network. To overcome this difficulty, in such cases, we may need to add a dummy line (activity) to enforce the precedence relationship. The dummy activity, shown in Figure 3.9 as a dashed line, is inserted between events 2 and 3 to make the diagram reflect the precedence between A and D. The remainder of the AOA project network for Milwaukee Paper's example is also shown.

▶ **Figure 3.9**

Complete AOA Network (with Dummy Activity) for Milwaukee Paper

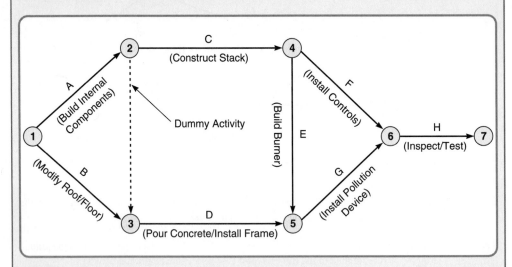

Insight: Dummy activities are common in AOA networks. They do not really exist in the project and take zero time.

Learning exercise: A new activity, *EPA Approval*, follows activity H. Add it to Figure 3.9. [Answer: Insert an arrowed line from node 7, which ends at a new node 8, and is labeled I (EPA Approval).]

Related problems: 3.4, 3.5, 3.9b

DETERMINING THE PROJECT SCHEDULE

Look back to Figure 3.8 (in Example 2) for a moment to see Milwaukee Paper's completed AON project network. Once this project network has been drawn to show all the activities and their precedence relationships, the next step is to determine the project schedule. That is, we need to identify the planned starting and ending time for each activity.

Let us assume Milwaukee Paper estimates the time required for each activity, in weeks, as shown in Table 3.2. The table indicates that the total time for all eight of the company's activities is 25 weeks. However, since several activities can take place simultaneously, it is clear that the total project completion time may be less than 25 weeks. To find out just how long the project will take, we perform the **critical path analysis** for the network.

Critical path analysis

A process that helps determine a project schedule.

Activity	Description	Time (weeks)
A	Build internal components	2
B	Modify roof and floor	3
C	Construct collection stack	2
D	Pour concrete and install frame	4
E	Build high-temperature burner	4
F	Install pollution control system	3
G	Install air pollution device	5
H	Inspect and test	2
	Total time (weeks)	25

◄ **Table 3.2**

Time Estimates for Milwaukee Paper Manufacturing

As mentioned earlier, the critical path is the *longest* time path through the network. To find the critical path, we calculate two distinct starting and ending times for each activity. These are defined as follows:

Earliest start (ES) = earliest time at which an activity can start, assuming all predecessors have been completed

Earliest finish (EF) = earliest time at which an activity can be finished

Latest start (LS) = latest time at which an activity can start so as to not delay the completion time of the entire project

Latest finish (LF) = latest time by which an activity has to finish so as to not delay the completion time of the entire project

We use a two-pass process, consisting of a forward pass and a backward pass, to determine these time schedules for each activity. The early start and finish times (ES and EF) are determined during the **forward pass**. The late start and finish times (LS and LF) are determined during the backward pass.

Forward pass
A process that identifies all the earliest times.

Forward Pass

To clearly show the activity schedules on the project network, we use the notation shown in Figure 3.10. The ES of an activity is shown in the top left corner of the node denoting that activity. The EF is shown in the top right corner. The latest times, LS and LF, are shown in the bottom-left and bottom-right corners, respectively.

Learning Objective

3. Complete both forward and backward passes for a project

Earliest Start Time Rule   Before an activity can start, *all* its immediate predecessors must be finished:

- If an activity has only a single immediate predecessor, its ES equals the EF of the predecessor.
- If an activity has multiple immediate predecessors, its ES is the maximum of all EF values of its predecessors. That is,

$$ES = Max\{EF \text{ of all immediate predecessors}\} \qquad (3\text{-}1)$$

All predecessor activities must be completed before an activity can begin.

Earliest Finish Rule   The earliest finish time (EF) of an activity is the sum of its earliest start time (ES) and its activity time. That is,

$$EF = ES + \text{Activity time} \qquad (3\text{-}2)$$

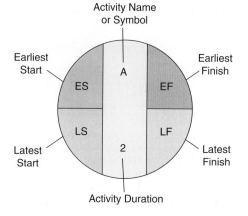

Activity Name or Symbol

Earliest Start — ES

Earliest Finish — EF

A

LS   LF

2

Latest Start — Latest Finish

Activity Duration

◄ **Figure 3.10**

Notation Used in Nodes for Forward and Backward Pass

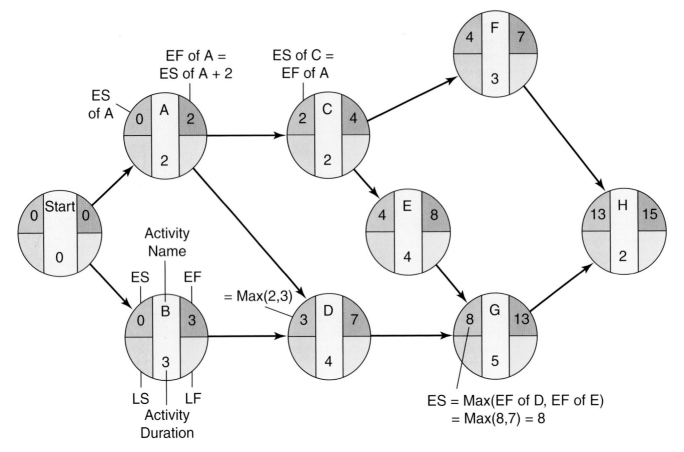

▲ **Figure 3.11**   Earliest Start and Earliest Finish Times for Milwaukee Paper

EXAMPLE 4

Computing earliest start and finish times for Milwaukee paper

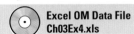
**Excel OM Data File
Ch03Ex4.xls**

Calculate the earliest start and finish times for the activities in the Milwaukee Paper Manufacturing project.

Approach: Use Table 3.2, which contains the activity times. Complete the project network for the company's project, along with the ES and EF values for all activities.

Solution: With the help of Figure 3.11, we describe how these values are calculated.

Since activity Start has no predecessors, we begin by setting its ES to 0. That is, activity Start can begin at the *end* of week 0, which is the same as the beginning of week 1.[2] If activity Start has an ES of 0, its EF is also 0, since its activity time is 0.

Next, we consider activities A and B, both of which have only Start as an immediate predecessor. Using the earliest start time rule, the ES for both activities A and B equals zero, which is the EF of activity Start. Now, using the earliest finish time rule, the EF for A is 2 (= 0 + 2), and the EF for B is 3 (= 0 + 3).

Since activity A precedes activity C, the ES of C equals the EF of A (= 2). The EF of C is therefore 4 (= 2 + 2).

We now come to activity D. Both activities A and B are immediate predecessors for B. Whereas A has an EF of 2, activity B has an EF of 3. Using the earliest start time rule, we compute the ES of activity D as follows:

$$\text{ES of D} = \text{Max(EF of A, EF of B)} = \text{Max}(2, 3) = 3$$

The EF of D equals 7 (= 3 + 4). Next, both activities E and F have activity C as their only immediate predecessor. Therefore, the ES for both E and F equals 4 (= EF of C). The EF of E is 8 (= 4 + 4), and the EF of F is 7 (= 4 + 3).

[2]In writing all earliest and latest times, we need to be consistent. For example, if we specify that the ES value of activity *i* is week 4, do we mean the *beginning* of week 4 or the *end* of week 4? Note that if the value refers to the *beginning* of week 4, it means that week 4 is also available for performing activity *i*. In our discussions, *all* earliest and latest time values correspond to the *end* of a period. That is, if we specify that the ES of activity *i* is week 4, it means that activity *i* starts work only at the beginning of week 5.

Activity G has both activities D and E as predecessors. Using the earliest start time rule, its ES is therefore the maximum of the EF of D and the EF of E. Hence, the ES of activity G equals 8 (= maximum of 7 and 8), and its EF equals 13 (= 8 + 5).

Finally, we come to activity H. Since it also has two predecessors, F and G, the ES of H is the maximum EF of these two activities. That is, the ES of H equals 13 (= maximum of 13 and 7). This implies that the EF of H is 15 (= 13 + 2). Since H is the last activity in the project, this also implies that the earliest time in which the entire project can be completed is 15 weeks.

Insight: The ES of an activity that has only one predecessor is simply the EF of that predecessor. For an activity with more than one predecessor, we must carefully examine the EFs of all immediate predecessors and choose the largest one.

Learning exercise: A new activity I, *EPA Approval*, takes 1 week. Its predecessor is activity H. What are I's ES and EF? [Answer: 15, 16]

Related problems: 3.11, 3.14c

Although the forward pass allows us to determine the earliest project completion time, it does not identify the critical path. To identify this path, we need to now conduct the backward pass to determine the LS and LF values for all activities.

Backward Pass

Just as the forward pass began with the first activity in the project, the **backward pass** begins with the last activity in the project. For each activity, we first determine its LF value, followed by its LS value. The following two rules are used in this process.

Backward pass
An activity that finds all the latest times.

Latest Finish Time Rule   This rule is again based on the fact that before an activity can start, all its immediate predecessors must be finished:

- If an activity is an immediate predecessor for just a single activity, its LF equals the LS of the activity that immediately follows it.
- If an activity is an immediate predecessor to more than one activity, its LF is the minimum of all LS values of all activities that immediately follow it. That is,

$$LF = \text{Min}\{\text{LS of all immediate following activities}\} \qquad (3\text{-}3)$$

LF of an activity = minimum LS of all activities that follow.

Latest Start Time Rule   The latest start time (LS) of an activity is the difference of its latest finish time (LF) and its activity time. That is,

$$LS = LF - \text{Activity time} \qquad (3\text{-}4)$$

EXAMPLE 5

Computing latest start and finish times for Milwaukee Paper

Calculate the latest start and finish times for each activity in Milwaukee Paper's pollution project.

Approach: Use Figure 3.11 as a beginning point. Overlay 1 of Figure 3.11 shows the complete project network for Milwaukee Paper, along with LS and LF values for all activities. In what follows, we see how these values were calculated.

Solution: We begin by assigning an LF value of 15 weeks for activity H. That is, we specify that the latest finish time for the entire project is the same as its earliest finish time. Using the latest start time rule, the LS of activity H is equal to 13 (= 15 − 2).

Since activity H is the lone succeeding activity for both activities F and G, the LF for both F and G equals 13. This implies that the LS of G is 8 (= 13 − 5), and the LS of F is 10 (= 13 − 3).

Proceeding in this fashion, we see that the LF of E is 8 (= LS of G), and its LS is 4 (= 8 − 4). Likewise, the LF of D is 8 (= LS of G), and its LS is 4 (= 8 − 4).

We now consider activity C, which is an immediate predecessor to two activities: E and F. Using the latest finish time rule, we compute the LF of activity C as follows:

$$LF \text{ of } C = \text{Min}(LS \text{ of } E, LS \text{ of } F) = \text{Min}(4, 10) = 4$$

The LS of C is computed as 2 (= 4 − 2). Next, we compute the LF of B as 4 (= LS of D), and its LS as 1 (= 4 − 3).

We now consider activity A. We compute its LF as 2 (= minimum of LS of C and LS of D). Hence, the LS of activity A is 0 (= 2 − 2). Finally, both the LF and LS of activity Start are equal to 0.

> *Insight:* The LF of an activity that is the predecessor of only one activity is just the LS of that following activity. If the activity is the predecessor to more than one activity, its LF is the smallest LS value of all activities that follow immediately.
>
> *Learning exercise:* A new activity I, *EPA Approval*, takes 1 week. Its predecessor is activity H, What are I's LS and LF? [Answer: 15, 16]
>
> *Related problems:* 3.11, 3.14c.

Calculating Slack Time and Identifying the Critical Path(s)

After we have computed the earliest and latest times for all activities, it is a simple matter to find the amount of **slack time**, or free time, that each activity has. Slack is the length of time an activity can be delayed without delaying the entire project. Mathematically,

Slack time
Free time for an activity.

$$\text{Slack} = \text{LS} - \text{ES} \quad \text{or} \quad \text{Slack} = \text{LF} - \text{EF} \tag{3-5}$$

EXAMPLE 6

Calculating slack times for Milwaukee Paper

Calculate the slack for the activities in the Milwaukee Paper project.

Approach: Start with the data in Overlay 1 of Figure 3.11 in Example 5 and develop Table 3.3 one line at a time.

Solution: Table 3.3 summarizes the ES, EF, LS, LF, and slack time for all of the firm's activities. Activity B, for example, has 1 week of slack time since its LS is 1 and its ES is 0 (alternatively, its LF is 4 and its EF is 3). This means that activity B can be delayed by up to 1 week, and the whole project can still be finished in 15 weeks.

▶ **Table 3.3**

Milwaukee Paper's Schedule and Slack Times

Activity	Earliest Start ES	Earliest Finish EF	Latest Start LS	Latest Finish LF	Slack LS − ES	On Critical Path
A	0	2	0	2	0	Yes
B	0	3	1	4	1	No
C	2	4	2	4	0	Yes
D	3	7	4	8	1	No
E	4	8	4	8	0	Yes
F	4	7	10	13	6	No
G	8	13	8	13	0	Yes
H	13	15	13	15	0	Yes

On the other hand, activities A, C, E, G, and H have *no* slack time. This means that none of them can be delayed without delaying the entire project. Conversely, if plant manager Joni Steinberg wants to reduce the total project times, she will have to reduce the length of one of these activities.

Overlay 2 of Figure 3.11 shows the slack computed for each activity.

Insight: Slack may be computed from either early/late starts or early/late finishes. The key is to find which activities have zero slack.

Learning exercise: A new activity I, *EPA Approval*, follows activity H and takes 1 week. Is it on the critical path? [Answer: Yes, it's LS − ES = 0]

Related problems: 3.6, 3.11, 3.27

Active Model 3.1

This example is further illustrated in Active Model 3.1 on the Student CD-ROM and in the exercise located on page 91.

Learning Objective

4. Determine a critical path

The activities with zero slack are called *critical activities* and are said to be on the critical path. The critical path is a continuous path through the project network that:

- Starts at the first activity in the project (Start in our example).
- Terminates at the last activity in the project (H in our example).
- Includes only critical activities (i.e., activities with no slack time).

Show Milwaukee Paper's critical path and find the project completion time.

Approach: We use Table 3.3 and Overlay 3 of Figure 3.11. Overlay 3 of Figure 3.11 indicates that the total project completion time of 15 weeks corresponds to the longest path in the network. That path is start-A-C-E-G-H in network form. It is shown with thick blue arrows.

Insight: The critical path follows the activities with slack = 0. This is considered the longest path through the network.

Learning exercise: Why are activities B, D, and F not on the path with the thick blue line? [Answer: They are not critical and have slack values of 1, 1, and 6 weeks, respectively.]

Related problems: 3.3, 3.4, 3.5, 3.6, 3.7, 3.12, 3.14b, 3.15, 3.17, 3.20a, 3.22a, 3.23, 3.26, 3.27

Total Slack Time versus Free Slack Time   Look again at the project network in Overlay 3 of Figure 3.11. Consider activities B and D, which have slack of 1 week each. Does it mean that we can delay *each* activity by 1 week, and still complete the project in 15 weeks? The answer is no.

Let's assume that activity B is delayed by 1 week. It has used up its slack of 1 week and now has an EF of 4. This implies that activity D now has an ES of 4 and an EF of 8. Note that these are also its LS and LF values, respectively. That is, activity D also has no slack time now. Essentially, the slack of 1 week that activities B and D had is, for that path, *shared* between them. Delaying either activity by 1 week causes not only that activity, but also the other activity, to lose its slack. This type of a slack time is referred to as **total slack**. Typically, when two or more non-critical activities appear successively in a path, they share total slack.

In contrast, consider the slack time of 6 weeks in activity F. Delaying this activity decreases only its slack time and does not affect the slack time of any other activity. This type of a slack time is referred to as **free slack**. Typically, if a noncritical activity has critical activities on either side of it in a path, its slack time is free slack.

Total slack
Time shared among more than one activity.

Free slack
Time associated with a single activity.

VARIABILITY IN ACTIVITY TIMES

In identifying all earliest and latest times so far, and the associated critical path(s), we have adopted the CPM approach of assuming that all activity times are known and fixed constants. That is, there is no variability in activity times. However, in practice, it is likely that activity completion times vary depending on various factors.

◀ *To plan, monitor, and control the huge number of details involved in sponsoring a rock festival attended by more than 100,000 fans, Hard Rock Cafe uses Microsoft Project and the tools discussed in this chapter. The* Video Case Study *"Managing Hard Rock's Rockfest," at the end of the chapter, provides more details of the management task.*

For example, building internal components (activity A) for Milwaukee Paper Manufacturing is estimated to finish in 2 weeks. Clearly, factors such as late arrival of raw materials, absence of key personnel, and so on, could delay this activity. Suppose activity A actually ends up taking 3 weeks. Since A is on the critical path, the entire project will now be delayed by 1 week to 16 weeks. If we had anticipated completion of this project in 15 weeks, we would obviously miss our deadline.

Although some activities may be relatively less prone to delays, others could be extremely susceptible to delays. For example, activity B (modify roof and floor) could be heavily dependent on weather conditions. A spell of bad weather could significantly affect its completion time.

This means that we cannot ignore the impact of variability in activity times when deciding the schedule for a project. PERT addresses this issue.

Three Time Estimates in PERT

In PERT, we employ a probability distribution based on three time estimates for each activity, as follows:

Optimistic time (a) = time an activity will take if everything goes as planned. In estimating this value, there should be only a small probability (say, 1/100) that the activity time will be < a.

Pessimistic time (b) = time an activity will take assuming very unfavorable conditions. In estimating this value, there should also be only a small probability (also, 1/100) that the activity time will be > b.

Most likely time (m) = most realistic estimate of the time required to complete an activity.

When using PERT, we often assume that activity time estimates follow the beta probability distribution (see Figure 3.12). This continuous distribution is often appropriate for determining the expected value and variance for activity completion times.

To find the *expected activity time*, t, the beta distribution weights the three time estimates as follows:

$$t = (a + 4m + b)/6 \tag{3-6}$$

That is, the most likely time (m) is given four times the weight as the optimistic time (a) and pessimistic time (b). The time estimate t computed using Equation 3-6 for each activity is used in the project network to compute all earliest and latest times.

To compute the *dispersion* or *variance of activity completion time*, we use the formula[3]:

$$\text{Variance} = [(b - a)/6]^2 \tag{3-7}$$

Optimistic time

The "best" activity completion time that could be obtained in a PERT network.

Pessimistic time

The "worst" activity time that could be expected in a PERT network.

Most likely time

The most probable time to complete an activity in a PERT network.

▶ **Figure 3.12**

Beta Probability Distribution with Three Time Estimates

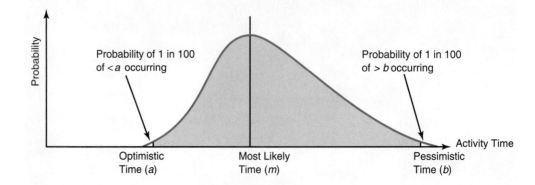

[3]This formula is based on the statistical concept that from one end of the beta distribution to the other is 6 standard deviations (±3 standard deviations from the mean). Since $(b - a)$ is 6 standard deviations, the variance is $[(b - a/6]^2$.

Joni Steinberg and the project management team at Milwaukee Paper want an expected time and variance for Activity F (Installing the Pollution Control System) where:

$$a = 1 \text{ week}, m = 2 \text{ weeks}, b = 9 \text{ weeks}$$

Approach: Use Equations 3-6 and 3-7 to compute the expected time and variance for F.

Solution: The expected time for Activity F is

$$t = \frac{a+4m+b}{6} = \frac{1+4(2)+9}{6} = \frac{18}{6} = 3 \text{ weeks}$$

The variance for Activity F is

$$\text{Variance} = \left[\frac{(b-a)}{6}\right]^2 = \left[\frac{(9-1)}{6}\right]^2 = \left(\frac{8}{6}\right)^2 = \frac{64}{36} = 1.78$$

Insight: Steinberg now has information that allows her to understand and manage Activity F. The expected time is, in fact, the activity time used in our earlier computation and identification of the critical path.

Learning exercise: Review the expected times and variances for all of the other activities in the project. These are shown in Table 3.4.

◄ **Table 3.4**

Time Estimates (in weeks) for Milwaukee Paper's Project

Activity	Optimistic *a*	Most Likely *m*	Pessimistic *b*	Expected Time $t = (a + 4m + b)/6$	Variance $[(b - a)/6]^2$
A	1	2	3	2	$[(3-1)/6]^2 = 4/36 = .11$
B	2	3	4	3	$[(4-2)/6]^2 = 4/36 = .11$
C	1	2	3	2	$[(3-1)/6]^2 = 4/36 = .11$
D	2	4	6	4	$[(6-2)/6]^2 = 16/36 = .44$
E	1	4	7	4	$[(7-1)/6]^2 = 36/36 = 1.00$
F	1	2	9	3	$[(9-1)/6]^2 = 64/36 = 1.78$
G	3	4	11	5	$[(11-3)/6]^2 = 64/36 = 1.78$
H	1	2	3	2	$[(3-1)/6]^2 = 4/36 = .11$

Related problems: 3.13, 3.14a, 3.17a,b, 3.21a

Excel OM Data
FileCh03Ex8.xls

◄ *We see here a ship being built at the Hyundi shipyard, Asia's largest shipbuilder, in Korea. Managing this project uses the same techniques as managing the remodeling of a store or installing a new production line.*

Probability of Project Completion

We compute the project variance by summing variances of only those activities on the critical path.

The critical path analysis helped us determine that Milwaukee Paper's expected project completion time is 15 weeks. Joni Steinberg knows, however, that there is significant variation in the time estimates for several activities. Variation in activities that are on the critical path can affect the overall project completion time—possibly delaying it. This is one occurrence that worries the plant manager considerably.

PERT uses the variance of critical path activities to help determine the variance of the overall project. Project variance is computed by summing variances of *critical* activities:

$$\sigma_p^2 = \text{Project variance} = \Sigma \text{ (variances of activities on critical path)} \tag{3-8}$$

EXAMPLE 9

Computing project variance and standard deviation for Milwaukee Paper

Milwaukee Paper's managers now wish to know the project's variance and standard deviation.

Approach: Because the activities are independent, we can add the variances of the activities on the critical path and then take the square root to determine the project's standard deviation.

Solution: From Example 8 (Table 3.4), we have the variances of all of the activities on the critical path. Specifically, we know that the variance of activity A is 0.11, variance of activity C is 0.11, variance of activity E is 1.00, variance of activity G is 1.78, and variance of activity H is 0.11.

Compute the total project variance and project standard deviation:

$$\text{Project variance } (\sigma_p^2) = 0.11 + 0.11 + 1.00 + 1.78 + 0.11 = 3.11$$

which implies:

$$\text{Project standard deviation } (\sigma_p) = \sqrt{\text{Project variance}} = \sqrt{3.11} = 1.76 \text{ weeks}$$

Insight: Management now has an estimate not only of expected completion time for the project but also of the standard deviation of that estimate.

Learning exercise: If the variance for activity A is actually 0.30 (instead of 0.11), what is the new project standard deviation? [Answer: 1.817.]

Related problem: 3.17e

How can this information be used to help answer questions regarding the probability of finishing the project on time? PERT makes two more assumptions: (1) total project completion times follow a normal probability distribution, and (2) activity times are statistically independent. With these assumptions, the bell-shaped normal curve shown in Figure 3.13 can be used to represent project completion dates. This normal curve implies that there is a 50% chance that the manufacturer's project completion time will be less than 15 weeks and a 50% chance that it will exceed 15 weeks.

▶ **Figure 3.13**

Probability Distribution for Project Completion Times at Milwaukee Paper

Standard Deviation = 1.76 Weeks

15 Weeks

(Expected Completion Time)

Joni Steinberg would like to find the probability that her project will be finished on or before the 16-week deadline.

Approach: To do so, she needs to determine the appropriate area under the normal curve. This is the area to the left of the 16th week.

Solution: The standard normal equation can be applied as follows:

$$Z = (\text{Due date} - \text{expected date of completion})/\sigma_p \qquad (3\text{-}9)$$

$$= (16 \text{ weeks} - 15 \text{ weeks})/1.76 \text{ weeks} = 0.57$$

where Z is the number of standard deviations the due date or target date lies from the mean or expected date.

    Referring to the Normal Table in Appendix I, we find a Z value of 0.57 to the right of the mean indicates a probability of 0.7157. Thus, there is a 71.57% chance that the pollution control equipment can be put in place in 16 weeks or less. This is shown in Figure 3.14.

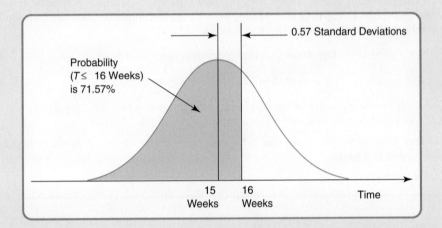

Insight: The shaded area to the left of the 16th week (71.57%) represents the probability that the project will be completed in less than 16 weeks.

Learning exercise: What is the probability that the project will be completed on or before the 17th week? [Answer: About 87.2%.]

Related problems: 3.14d, 3.17f, 3.21d,e, 3.22b, 3.24

Determining Project Completion Time for a Given Confidence Level   Let's say Joni Steinberg is worried that there is only a 71.57% chance that the pollution control equipment can be put in place in 16 weeks or less. She thinks that it may be possible to plead with the environmental group for more time. However, before she approaches the group, she wants to arm herself with sufficient information about the project. Specifically, she wants to find the deadline by which she has a 99% chance of completing the project. She hopes to use her analysis to convince the group to agree to this extended deadline.

    Clearly, this due date would be greater than 16 weeks. However, what is the exact value of this new due date? To answer this question, we again use the assumption that Milwaukee Paper's project completion time follows a normal probability distribution with a mean of 15 weeks and a standard deviation of 1.76 weeks.

Joni Steinberg wants to find the due date that gives her company's project a 99% chance of *on-time* completion.

Approach: She first needs to compute the Z-value corresponding to 99%, as shown in Figure 3.15. Mathematically, this is similar to Example 10, except the unknown is now Z rather than the due date.

EXAMPLE 10

Probability of completing a project on time

◀ **Figure 3.14**

Probability That Milwaukee Paper will Meet the 16-Week Deadline

EXAMPLE 11

Computing probability for any completion date

▶ **Figure 3.15**

Z-Value for 99% Probability of Project Completion at Milwaukee Paper

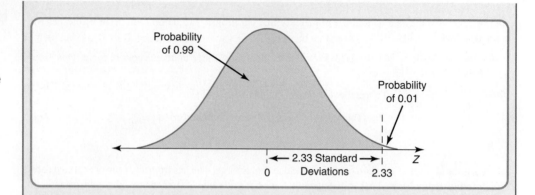

Solution: Referring again to the Normal Table in Appendix I, we identify a Z-value of 2.33 as being closest to the probability of 0.99. That is, Joni Steinberg's due date should be 2.33 standard deviations above the mean project completion time. Starting with the standard normal equation (see Equation 3-9), we can solve for the due date and rewrite the equation as:

$$\text{Due date} = \text{Expected completion time} + (Z \times \sigma_p) \qquad (3\text{-}10)$$

$$= 15 + (2.33 \times 1.76) = 19.1 \text{ weeks}$$

Insight: If Steinberg can get the environmental group to agree to give her a new deadline of 19.1 weeks (or more), she can be 99% sure of finishing the project on time.

Learning exercise: What due date gives the project a 95% chance of on-time completion? [Answer: About 17.9 weeks.]

Related problems: 3.22c, 3.24e

Variability in Completion Time of Noncritical Paths   In our discussion so far, we have focused exclusively on the variability in the completion times of activities on the critical path. This seems logical since these activities are, by definition, the more important activities in a project network. However, when there is variability in activity times, it is important that we also investigate the variability in the completion times of activities on *noncritical* paths.

Consider, for example, activity D in Milwaukee Paper's project. Recall from Overlay 3 in Figure 3.11 (in Example 7) that this is a noncritical activity, with a slack time of 1 week. We have therefore not considered the variability in D's time in computing the probabilities of project completion times. We observe, however, that D has a variance of 0.44 (see Table 3.4 in Example 8). In fact, the pessimistic completion time for D is 6 weeks. This means that if D ends up taking its pessimistic time to finish, the project will not finish in 15 weeks, even though D is not a critical activity.

For this reason, when we find probabilities of project completion times, it may be necessary for us to not focus only on the critical path(s). Indeed, some research has suggested that expending project resources to reduce the variability of activities not on the critical path can be an effective element in project management.[4] We may need also to compute these probabilities for noncritical paths, especially those that have relatively large variances. It is possible for a noncritical path to have a smaller probability of completion within a due date, when compared with the critical path. Determining the variance and probability of completion for a noncritical path is done in the same manner as Examples 9 and 10.

Noncritical paths with large variances should also be closely monitored.

What Project Management Has Provided So Far   Project management techniques have thus far been able to provide Joni Steinberg with several valuable pieces of management information:

1. The project's expected completion date is 15 weeks.
2. There is a 71.57% chance that the equipment will be in place within the 16-week deadline. PERT analysis can easily find the probability of finishing by any date Steinberg is interested in.

---

[4]F. M. Pokladnik, T. F. Anthony, R. R. Hill, G. Ulrich, "A Fresh Look at Estimated Project Duration: Noncritical Path Activity Contribution to Project Variance in PERT/CPM," *Proceedings of the 2003 Southwest Decision Science Conference*, Houston.

3. Five activities (A, C, E, G, and H) are on the critical path. If any one of these is delayed for any reason, the entire project will be delayed.

4. Three activities (B, D, F) are not critical and have some slack time built in. This means that Steinberg can borrow from their resources, and, if necessary, she may be able to speed up the whole project.

5. A detailed schedule of activity starting and ending dates has been made available (see Table 3.3 in Example 6).

COST–TIME TRADE-OFFS AND PROJECT CRASHING

While managing a project, it is not uncommon for a project manager to be faced with either (or both) of the following situations: (1) the project is behind schedule, and (2) the scheduled project completion time has been moved forward. In either situation, some or all of the remaining activities need to be speeded up to finish the project by the desired due date. The process by which we shorten the duration of a project in the cheapest manner possible is called project **crashing**.

CPM is a technique in which each activity has a *normal* or *standard* time that we use in our computations. Associated with this normal time is the *normal* cost of the activity. However, another time in project management is the *crash time*, which is defined as the shortest duration required to complete an activity. Associated with this crash time is the *crash cost* of the activity. Usually, we can shorten an activity by adding extra resources (e.g., equipment, people) to it. Hence, it is logical for the crash cost of an activity to be higher than its normal cost.

The amount by which an activity can be shortened (i.e., the difference between its normal time and crash time) depends on the activity in question. We may not be able to shorten some activities at all. For example, if a casting needs to be heat-treated in the furnace for 48 hours, adding more resources does not help shorten the time. In contrast, we may be able to shorten some activities significantly (e.g., frame a house in 3 days instead of 10 days by using three times as many workers).

Likewise, the cost of crashing (or shortening) an activity depends on the nature of the activity. Managers are usually interested in speeding up a project at the least additional cost. Hence, when choosing which activities to crash, and by how much, we need to ensure the following:

- The amount by which an activity is crashed is, in fact, permissible
- Taken together, the shortened activity durations will enable us to finish the project by the due date
- The total cost of crashing is as small as possible

Crashing a project involves four steps:

Step 1: Compute the crash cost per week (or other time period) for each activity in the network. If crash costs are linear over time, the following formula can be used:

$$\text{Crash cost per period} = \frac{(\text{Crash cost} - \text{Normal cost})}{(\text{Normal time} - \text{Crash time})} \quad \text{(3-11)}$$

Step 2: Using the current activity times, find the critical path(s) in the project network. Identify the critical activities.

Step 3: If there is only one critical path, then select the activity on this critical path that (a) can still be crashed and (b) has the smallest crash cost per period. Crash this activity by one period.

If there is more than one critical path, then select one activity from each critical path such that (a) each selected activity can still be crashed and (b) the total crash cost per period of *all* selected activities is the smallest. Crash each activity by one period. Note that the same activity may be common to more than one critical path.

Step 4: Update all activity times. If the desired due date has been reached, stop. If not, return to Step 2.

We illustrate project crashing in Example 12.

Crashing
Shortening activity time in a network to reduce time on the critical path so total completion time is reduced.

We want to find the cheapest way of crashing a project to the desired due date.

Learning Objective

6. Crash a project

EXAMPLE 12

Project crashing to meet a deadline at Milwaukee Paper

Suppose that Milwaukee Paper Manufacturing has been given only 13 weeks (instead of 16 weeks) to install the new pollution control equipment or face a court-ordered shutdown. As you recall, the length of Joni Steinberg's critical path was 15 weeks, but she must now complete the project in 13.

Approach: Steinberg needs to determine which activities to crash, and by how much, to meet this 13-week due date. Naturally, Steinberg is interested in speeding up the project by 2 weeks, at the least additional cost.

Solution: The company's normal and crash times, and normal and crash costs, are shown in Table 3.5. Note, for example, that activity B's normal time is 3 weeks (the estimate used in computing the critical path), and its crash time is 1 week. This means that activity B can be shortened by up to 2 weeks if extra resources are provided. The cost of these additional resources is $4,000 (= difference between the crash cost of $34,000 and the normal cost of $30,000). If we assume that the crashing cost is linear over time (i.e., the cost is the same each week), activity B's crash cost per week is $2,000 (= $4,000/2).

▶ **Table 3.5**

Normal and Crash Data for Milwaukee Paper Manufacturing

	Time (Weeks)		Cost ($)			
Activity	**Normal**	**Crash**	**Normal**	**Crash**	**Crash Cost Per Week ($)**	**Critical Path?**
A	2	1	22,000	22,750	750	Yes
B	3	1	30,000	34,000	2,000	No
C	2	1	26,000	27,000	1,000	Yes
D	4	3	48,000	49,000	1,000	No
E	4	2	56,000	58,000	1,000	Yes
F	3	2	30,000	30,500	500	No
G	5	2	80,000	84,500	1,500	Yes
H	2	1	16,000	19,000	3,000	Yes

This calculation for Activity B is shown in Figure 3.16. Crash costs for all other activities can be computed in a similar fashion.

▶ **Figure 3.16**

Crash and Normal Times and Costs for Activity B

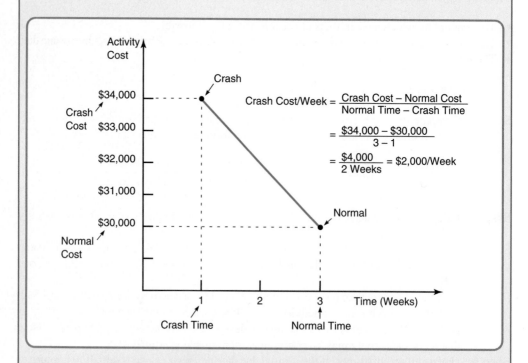

Steps 2, 3, and 4 can now be applied to reduce Milwaukee Paper's project completion time at a minimum cost. We show the project network for Milwaukee Paper again in Figure 3.17.

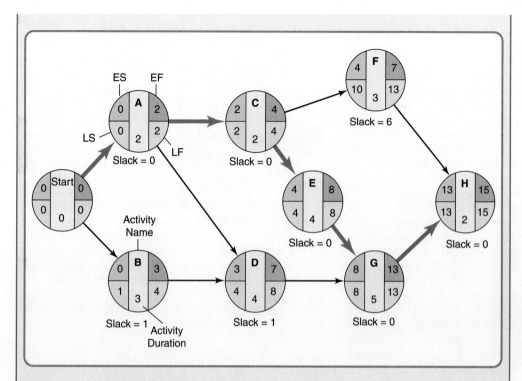

The current critical path (using normal times) is Start-A-C-E-G-H, in which Start is just a dummy starting activity. Of these critical activities, activity A has the lowest crash cost per week of $750. Joni Steinberg should therefore crash activity A by 1 week to reduce the project completion time to 14 weeks. The cost is an additional $750. Note that activity A cannot be crashed any further, since it has reached its crash limit of 1 week.

At this stage, the original path Start-A-C-E-G-H remains critical with a completion time of 14 weeks. However, a new path Start-B-D-G-H is also critical now, with a completion time of 14 weeks. Hence, any further crashing must be done to both critical paths.

On each of these critical paths, we need to identify one activity that can still be crashed. We also want the total cost of crashing an activity on each path to be the smallest. We might be tempted to simply pick the activities with the smallest crash cost per period in each path. If we did this, we would select activity C from the first path and activity D from the second path. The total crash cost would then be $2,000 (= $1,000 + $1,000).

But we spot that activity G is common to both paths. That is, by crashing activity G, we will simultaneously reduce the completion time of both paths. Even though the $1,500 crash cost for activity G is higher than that for activities C and D, we would still prefer crashing G, since the total cost will now be only $1,500 (compared with the $2,000 if we crash C and D).

Insight: To crash the project down to 13 weeks, Steinberg should crash activity A by 1 week, and activity G by 1 week. The total additional cost will be $2,250 (= $750 + $1,500). This is important because many contracts for projects include bonuses or penalties for early or late finishes.

Learning exercise: Say the crash cost for activity B is $31,000 instead of $34,000. How does this change the answer? [Answer: no change.]

Related problems: 3.16, 3.18, 3.19, 3.20, 3.25

A CRITIQUE OF PERT AND CPM

As a critique of our discussions of PERT, here are some of its features about which operations managers need to be aware:

Advantages
1. Especially useful when scheduling and controlling large projects.
2. Straightforward concept and not mathematically complex.
3. Graphical networks help highlight relationships among project activities.

OM in Action   The Mismanagement of Amtrak's Massive Acela Project

With pressure from Congress to break Amtrak into smaller, less-government-dependent pieces, the U.S. passenger rail service embarked in 1996 on a huge project: Acela. Acela's goal was to become the first U.S. train service to compete with airlines in the Washington DC–New York–Boston corridor. One key component was the Acela Express, a sleek 150-mile-per-hour train, with Internet connections at every seat and microbrews on tap. The $32 billion project, when complete, was expected to cut the New York–Boston run by almost 2 hours and add $180 million in annual profits to the besieged Amtrak Corporation.

But according to the U.S. General Accounting Office (GAO) (the nation's auditing arm) both Amtrak and its major suppliers mismanaged the project. "Amtrak's management was not comprehensive, and it was focused primarily on the short term," states a recent GAO report. Amtrak spokesman Cliff Black says "The GAO report is accurate . . . as it relates to project planning and management." Amtrak was faulted for not tackling infrastructure problems like track improvements, bridges, and overhead electrical wires. As a result Acela makes the journey much more slowly than planned.

It didn't help the project that the firms jointly building the $1 billion worth of Acela trains, Bombardier of Quebec and Britain's GEC Alston, produced a locomotive with defective wheels. As in most large projects, the penalties for late delivery were painful. The fines started at $1,000 per train per day and escalated to $13,500 per train per day.

Now, having redefined the scope of the project, clarified the work breakdown structure, addressed many of the infrastructure problems, and invested billions more, Amtrak reports that Acela's speed is finally increasing. The train may one day beat the plane.

Sources: The Wall Street Journal (April 21, 2005): D3; *Knight Ridder Tribune Business News* (March 19, 2004): 1; and *The New York Times* (July 17, 2004): C7.

---

4. Critical path and slack time analyses help pinpoint activities that need to be closely watched.
5. Project documentation and graphs point out who is responsible for various activities.
6. Applicable to a wide variety of projects.
7. Useful in monitoring not only schedules but costs as well.

In large networks there are too many activities to monitor closely, but managers can concentrate on the critical and near critical activities.

Limitations
1. Project activities have to be clearly defined, independent, and stable in their relationships.
2. Precedence relationships must be specified and networked together.
3. Time estimates tend to be subjective and are subject to fudging by managers who fear the dangers of being overly optimistic or not pessimistic enough.
4. There is the inherent danger of placing too much emphasis on the longest, or critical, path. Near-critical paths need to be monitored closely as well.

USING MICROSOFT PROJECT TO MANAGE PROJECTS

Learning Objective

7. Use Microsoft Project software to create a project

The approaches discussed so far are effective for managing small projects. However, for large or complex projects, specialized project management software is much preferred. In this section, we provide a brief introduction to the most popular example of such specialized software, Microsoft Project.

We should note that at this introductory level, our intent here is not to describe the full capabilities of this program. Rather, we illustrate how it can be used to perform some of the basic calculations in managing projects. We leave it to you to explore the advanced capabilities and functions of Microsoft Project (or any other project management software) in greater detail. A time-limited version of Microsoft Project may be requested with this text.

Microsoft Project is useful for project scheduling and control.

Microsoft Project is extremely useful in drawing project networks, identifying the project schedule, and managing project costs and other resources. It does not, however, perform PERT probability calculations.

Creating a Project Schedule Using Microsoft Project

First, we define a new project.

Let us again consider the Milwaukee Paper Manufacturing project. Recall that this project has eight activities (repeated on page 83). The first step is to define the activities and their precedence relationships. To do so, we start Microsoft Project and click File|New to open a blank

◄ **Program 3.1**

Project Summary Information in Microsoft Project

Durations	
Activity	**Time in Weeks**
A	2
B	3
C	2
D	4
E	4
F	3
G	5
H	2

project. We can now enter the project start date in the summary information that is first presented (see Program 3.1). Note that dates are referred to by actual calendar dates rather than as day 0, day 1, and so on. For example, we have used July 1 as our project starting date in Program 3.1. Microsoft Project will automatically update the project finish date once we have entered all the project information. In Program 3.1, we have specified the current date as January 10.

Entering Activity Information   After entering the summary information, we now use the window shown in Program 3.2 to enter all activity information. For each activity (or task, as Microsoft Project calls it), we enter its name and duration. Microsoft Project identifies tasks by numbers (e.g., 1, 2) rather than letters. Hence, for convenience, we have shown both the letter

Next, we enter the activity information.

▼ **Program 3.2**   **Activity Entry in Microsoft Project for Milwaukee Paper Manufacturing**

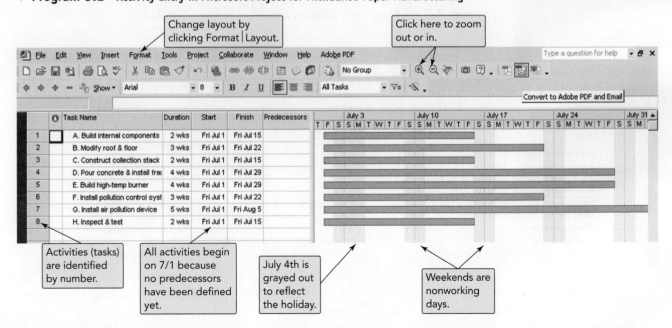

(e.g., A, B) and the description of the activity in the *Task Name* column in Program 3.2. By default, the duration is measured in days. To specify weeks, we include the letter "*w*" after the duration of each activity. For example, we enter the duration of activity A as 2*w*.

As we enter the activities and durations, the software automatically inserts start and finish dates. Note that all activities have the same start date (i.e., July 1), since we have not yet defined the precedence relationships. Also, as shown in Program 3.2, if the Gantt Chart option is selected in the View menu, a horizontal bar corresponding to the duration of each activity appears on the right pane of the window.

> *The schedule automatically takes nonworking days into account.*

Observe that Saturdays and Sundays are automatically grayed out in the Gantt chart to reflect that these are nonworking days. In most project management software, the entire project is linked to a master calendar (or alternatively, each activity is linked to its own specific calendar). Additional nonworking days can be defined using these calendars. For example, we have used Tools|Change Working Time to specify July 4 as a nonworking day in Program 3.2. This automatically extends all activity completion times by one day. Since activity A starts on Friday, July 1, and takes 2 weeks (i.e., 10 working days), its finish time is now Friday, July 15 (rather than Thursday, July 14).

Precedences	
Activity	**Predecessors**
A	—
B	—
C	A
D	A, B
E	C
F	C
G	D, E
H	F, G

Defining Precedence Relationships   The next step is to define precedence relationships (or links) between these activities. There are two ways of specifying these links. The first is to enter the relevant activity numbers (e.g., 1, 2) in the *Predecessor* column, as shown in Program 3.3 for activities C and D. The other approach uses the Link icon. For example, to specify the precedence relationship between activities C and E, we click activity C first, hold the Ctrl key down, and then click activity E. We then click the Link icon, as shown in Program 3.3. As soon as we define a link, the bars in the Gantt chart are automatically repositioned to reflect the new start and finish times for the linked activities. Further, the link itself is shown as an arrow extending from the predecessor activity.

Viewing the Project Schedule   When all links have been defined, the complete project schedule can be viewed as a Gantt chart, as shown in Program 3.4. We can also select View|Network Diagram to view the schedule as a project network (shown in Program 3.5). The critical path is shown in red on the screen (bold in Program 3.5) in the network diagram. We can click on any of the activities in the project network to view details of the activities. Likewise, we can easily add or remove activities and/or links from the project network. Each time we do so, Microsoft Project automatically updates all start dates, finish dates, and the critical path(s). If desired, we can manually change the layout of the network (e.g., reposition activities) by changing the options in Format|Layout.

> *The project can be viewed either as a Gantt chart or as a network.*

▼ **Program 3.3**   **Defining Links Between Activities in Microsoft Project**

▲ **Program 3.4**   Gantt Chart in Microsoft Project for Milwaukee Paper Manufacturing

Programs 3.4 and 3.5 show that if Milwaukee Paper's project starts on July 1, it can be finished on October 14. The start and finish dates for all activities are also clearly identified. This schedule takes into account the nonworking days on all weekends, and on July 4. These programs illustrate how the use of specialized project management software can greatly simplify the scheduling procedures discussed earlier in this chapter.

PERT Analysis   As mentioned, Microsoft Project does not perform the PERT probability calculations discussed in Examples 10 and 11. However, by clicking **View|Toolbars|PERT Analysis**, we can get Microsoft Project to allow us to enter optimistic, most likely, and pessimistic times for each activity. We can then choose to view Gantt charts based on any of these three times for each activity.

▼ **Program 3.5**   Project Network in Microsoft Project for Milwaukee Paper Manufacturing

▶ *Using PERT/CPM, Taco Bell built and opened this fast-food restaurant in Compton, California, in just 2 days! Typically, 2 months are needed to accomplish such a task. Good project management means a faster revenue stream instead of money tied up in construction.*

Tracking Progress and Managing Costs Using Microsoft Project

Pollution Project Percent Completed on Aug. 12	
Activity	**Completed**
A	100
B	100
C	100
D	10
E	20
F	20
G	0
H	0

Perhaps the biggest advantage of using specialized software to manage projects is that they can track the progress of the project. In this regard, Microsoft Project has many features available to track individual activities in terms of time, cost, resource usage, and so on. In this section, we illustrate how we can track the progress of a project in terms of time.

Tracking the Time Status of a Project An easy way to track the time progress of tasks is to enter the percent of work completed for each task. One way to do so is to double-click on any activity in the *Task Name* column in Program 3.4. A window, like the one shown in Program 3.6 is displayed. Let us now enter the percent of work completed for each task.

The table in the margin provides data regarding the percent of each of Milwaukee Paper's activities as of today. (Assume today is Friday, August 12, i.e., the end of the sixth week of the project schedule.)[5] Program 3.6 shows that activity A is 100% complete. We enter the percent completed for all other activities in a similar fashion.

▶ **Program 3.6**

Updating Activity Progress in Microsoft Project

[5]Remember that the nonworking day on July 4 has moved all schedules by one day. Therefore, activities end on Fridays rather than on Thursdays.

▲ **Program 3.7** Tracking Project Progress in Microsoft Project

As shown in Program 3.7, the Gantt chart immediately reflects this updated information by drawing a thick line within each activity's bar. The length of this line is proportional to the percent of that activity's work that has been completed.

How do we know if we are on schedule? Notice that there is a vertical line shown on the Gantt chart corresponding to today's date. Microsoft Project will automatically move this line to correspond with the current date. If the project is on schedule, we should see all bars to the *left* of today's line indicate that they have been completed. For example, Program 3.7 shows that activities A, B, and C are on schedule. In contrast, activities D, E, and F appear to be behind schedule. These activities need to be investigated further to determine the reason for the delay. This type of easy *visual* information is what makes such software so useful in practice for project management.

In addition to reading this section on Microsoft Project, we encourage you to load the software from the CD-ROM that may be ordered with your text and try these procedures.

> *"Poorly managed projects are costly, not only financially, but also in wasted time and demoralized personnel. But failure is almost never the result of poor software."*
>
> *C. Fujinami and A. Marshall, consultants at Kepner Tregoe, Inc.*

Summary

PERT, CPM, and other scheduling techniques have proven to be valuable tools in controlling large and complex projects. With these tools, managers understand the status of each activity and know which activities are critical and which have slack; in addition, they know where crashing makes the most sense. Projects are segmented into discrete activities, and specific resources are identified. This allows project managers to respond aggressively to global competition. Effective project management also allows firms to create products and services

for global markets. As with Microsoft Project illustrated in this chapter, a wide variety of software packages are available to help managers handle network modeling problems.

PERT and CPM do not, however, solve all the project scheduling and management problems. Good management practices, clear responsibilities for tasks, and straightforward and timely reporting systems are also needed. It is important to remember that the models we described in this chapter are only tools to help managers make better decisions.

Key Terms

Project organization (p. 59)
Work breakdown structure (WBS) (p. 60)
Gantt charts (p. 61)
Program evaluation and review technique (PERT) (p. 63)
Critical path method (CPM) (p. 63)
Critical path (p. 63)

Activity-on-node (AON) (p. 63)
Activity-on-arrow (AOA) (p. 63)
Dummy activity (p. 64)
Critical path analysis (p. 68)
Forward pass (p. 69)
Backward pass (p. 71)
Slack time (p. 72)

Total slack (p. 73)
Free slack (p. 73)
Optimistic time (p. 74)
Pessimistic time (p. 74)
Most likely time (p. 74)
Crashing (p. 79)

Using Software to Solve Project Management Problems

In addition to the Microsoft Project software just illustrated, both Excel OM and POM for Windows are available to readers of this text as project management tools.

✖ Using Excel OM

Excel OM has a Project Scheduling module. Program 3.8 uses the data from the Milwaukee Paper Manufacturing example in this chapter (see Examples 4 and 5). The PERT/CPM analysis also handles activities with three time estimates.

🅿 Using POM for Windows

POM for Window's Project Scheduling module can also find the expected project completion time for a CPM and PERT network with either one or three time estimates. POM for Windows also performs project crashing. For further details refer to Appendix IV.

▶ **Program 3.8**

Excel OM's Use of Milwaukee Paper Manufacturing's Data from Examples 4 and 5

Solved Problems

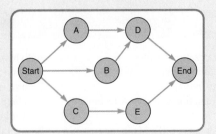

Virtual Office Hours help is available on Student DVD.

Solved Problem 3.1

Construct an AON network based on the following:

Activity	Immediate Predecessor(s)
A	—
B	—
C	—
D	A, B
E	C

Solution

Solved Problem 3.2

Insert a dummy activity and event to correct the following AOA network:

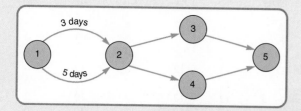

Solution

Since we cannot have two activities starting and ending at the same node, we add the following dummy activity and dummy event to obtain the correct AOA network:

Solved Problem 3.3

Calculate the critical path, project completion time T, and project variance σ_p^2, based on the following AON network information:

Activity	Time	Variance	ES	EF	LS	LF	Slack
A	2	$\frac{2}{6}$	0	2	0	2	0
B	3	$\frac{2}{6}$	0	3	1	4	1
C	2	$\frac{4}{6}$	2	4	2	4	0
D	4	$\frac{4}{6}$	3	7	4	8	1
E	4	$\frac{2}{6}$	4	8	4	8	0
F	3	$\frac{1}{6}$	4	7	10	13	6
G	5	$\frac{1}{6}$	8	13	8	13	0

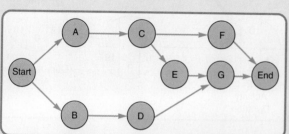

Solution

We conclude that the critical path is Start-A-C-E-G-End:

$$\text{Total project time} = T = 2 + 2 + 4 + 5 = 13$$

and

$$\sigma_p^2 = \Sigma \text{ Variances on the critical path} = \frac{2}{6} + \frac{4}{6} + \frac{2}{6} + \frac{1}{6} = \frac{9}{6} = 1.5$$

Solved Problem 3.4

To complete the wing assembly for an experimental aircraft, Jim Gilbert has laid out the seven major activities involved. These activities have been labeled A through G in the following table, which also shows their estimated completion times (in weeks) and immediate predecessors. Determine the expected time and variance for each activity:

Activity	a	m	b	Immediate Predecessors
A	1	2	3	—
B	2	3	4	—
C	4	5	6	A
D	8	9	10	B
E	2	5	8	C, D
F	4	5	6	D
G	1	2	3	E

Solution

Expected times and variances can be computed using Equations (3-6) and (3-7) presented on page 74 in this chapter. The results are summarized in the following table:

Activity	Expected Time (in weeks)	Variance
A	2	$\frac{1}{9}$
B	3	$\frac{1}{9}$
C	5	$\frac{1}{9}$
D	9	$\frac{1}{9}$
E	5	1
F	5	$\frac{1}{9}$
G	2	$\frac{1}{9}$

Solved Problem 3.5

Referring to Solved Problem 3.4, now Jim Gilbert would like to determine the critical path for the entire wing assembly project as well as the expected completion time for the total project. In addition, he would like to determine the earliest and latest start and finish times for all activities.

Solution

The AON network for Gilbert's project is shown in Figure 3.18. Note that this project has multiple activities (A and B) with no immediate predecessors, and multiple activities (F and G) with no successors. Hence, in addition to a unique starting activity (Start), we have included a unique finishing activity (End) for the project.

Figure 3.18 shows the earliest and latest times for all activities. The results are also summarized in the following table:

| | *Activity Time* | | | | |
Activity	ES	EF	LS	LF	Slack
A	0	2	5	7	5
B	0	3	0	3	0
C	2	7	7	12	5
D	3	12	3	12	0
E	12	17	12	17	0
F	12	17	14	19	2
G	17	19	17	19	0

Expected project length = 19 weeks

Variance of the critical path = 1.333

Standard deviation of the critical path = 1.155 weeks

The activities along the critical path are B, D, E, and G. These activities have zero slack as shown in the table.

▶ **Figure 3.18**

Critical Path for Solved Problem 3.5

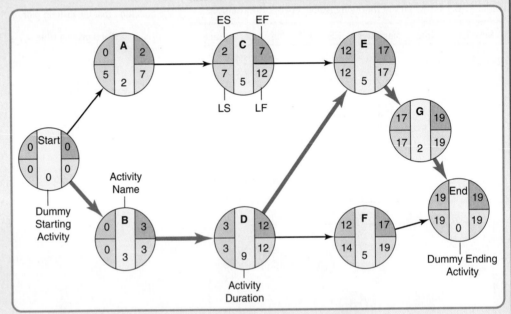

Solved Problem 3.6

The following information has been computed from a project:

$$\text{Expected total project time} = T = 62 \text{ weeks}$$
$$\text{Project variance} \left(\sigma_p^2 \right) = 81$$

What is the probability that the project will be completed 18 weeks *before* its expected completion date?

Solution

The desired completion date is 18 weeks before the expected completion date, 62 weeks. The desired completion date is 44 (or 62 − 18) weeks:

$$\sigma_p = \sqrt{\text{Project variance}}$$

$$Z = \frac{\text{Due date} - \text{Expected completion date}}{\sigma_p}$$

$$= \frac{44 - 62}{9} = \frac{-18}{9} = -2.0$$

The normal curve appears as follows:

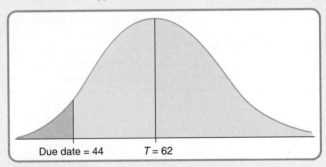

Because the normal curve is symmetrical and table values are calculated for positive values of Z, the area desired is equal to 1 − (table value). For Z = +2.0, the area from the table is .97725. Thus, the area corresponding to a Z value of −2.0 is .02275 (or 1 − .97725). Hence, the probability of completing the project 18 weeks before the expected completion date is approximately .023, or 2.3%.

Solved Problem 3.7

Determine the least cost of reducing the project completion date by 3 months based on the following information:

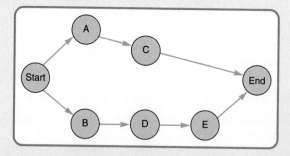

Activity	Normal Time (months)	Crash Time (months)	Normal Cost	Crash Cost
A	6	4	$2,000	$2,400
B	7	5	3,000	3,500
C	7	6	1,000	1,300
D	6	4	2,000	2,600
E	9	8	8,800	9,000

Solution

The first step in this problem is to compute ES, EF, LS, LF, and slack for each activity:

Activity	ES	EF	LS	LF	Slack
A	0	6	9	15	9
B	0	7	0	7	0
C	6	13	15	22	9
D	7	13	7	13	0
E	13	22	13	22	0

The critical path consists of activities B, D, and E.

Next, crash cost/month must be computed for each activity:

Activity	Normal Time – Crash Time	Crash Cost – Normal Cost	Crash Cost/ Month	Critical Path?
A	2	$400	$200/month	No
B	2	500	250/month	Yes
C	1	300	300/month	No
D	2	600	300/month	Yes
E	1	200	200/month	Yes

Finally, we will select that activity on the critical path with the smallest crash cost/month. This is activity E. Thus, we can reduce the total project completion date by 1 month for an additional cost of $200. We still need to reduce the project completion date by 2 more months. This reduction can be achieved at least cost along the critical path by reducing activity B by 2 months for an additional cost of $500. This solution is summarized in the following table:

Activity	Months Reduced	Cost
E	1	$200
B	2	500
		Total: $700

Active Model Exercise

Milwaukee Paper Manufacturing. This Active Model allows you to evaluate changes in important elements on the hospital network we saw in this chapter, using your CD-ROM. See Active Model 3.1.

◄ **Active Model 3.1**

Project Management

This graph contains a Gantt chart for the single time estimate Milwaukee Paper project. The critical activities appear in red in both the data table and the Gantt chart. Noncritical activities appear in green in the Gantt chart, and the right side of these noncritical activities displays the amount of slack they have. You can use the scrollbars to change the times of the individual activities. For critical activities, when you change the times the project times will change. For noncritical activities, if you increase the time, then they will eventually become critical.

Questions

1. Both A and H are critical activities. Describe the difference between what happens on the graph when you increase A vs. increasing H.

2. Activity F is not critical. By how many weeks can you increase activity F until it becomes critical?

3. Activity B is not critical. By how many weeks can you increase activity B until it becomes critical? What happens when B becomes critical?

4. What happens when you increase B by 1 more week after it becomes critical?

5. Suppose that building codes change and as a result activity B would have to be completed before activity C could be started. How would this affect the project?

Self-Test

- **Before taking the self-test**, *refer to the learning objectives listed at the beginning of the chapter and the key terms listed at the end of the chapter.*
- *Use the key at the back of the text to **correct** your answers.*
- ***Restudy** pages that correspond to any questions you answered incorrectly or material you feel uncertain about.*

1. With respect to PERT and CPM, an event:
   a) marks the start or completion of a task.
   b) is a task or subproject that must be completed.
   c) is the amount of time a task may be delayed without affecting any other task in the network.
   d) is the amount of time a task may be delayed without changing the overall project completion time.

2. With respect to PERT and CPM, free slack:
   a) marks the start or completion of a task.
   b) is a task or subproject that must be completed.
   c) is the amount of time a task may be delayed without affecting any other task in the network.
   d) is the amount of time a task may be delayed without changing the overall project completion time.

3. A dummy activity is required when:
   a) the network contains two or more activities that have identical starting and ending events.
   b) two or more activities have the same starting events.
   c) two or more activities have the same ending events.
   d) all of the above are true.

4. Critical path analysis is used to determine:
   a) the earliest activity start time.
   b) the latest activity start time.
   c) activity slack time.
   d) all of the above.

5. The critical path of a network is the:
   a) shortest time path through the network.
   b) path with the fewest activities.
   c) path with the most activities.
   d) longest time path through the network.

6. Slack time equals:
   a) $ES + t$.
   b) $LS - ES$.
   c) zero.
   d) $EF - ES$.

7. If an activity with free slack time of 2 weeks is delayed by 1 week:
   a) the project will be delayed by 1 week.
   b) the slack time of all activities that follow this activity is reduced by 1 week.
   c) no other activity in the project is affected.
   d) the probability of completing the project on time decreases.

8. In PERT, if the pessimistic time was 14 weeks, the optimistic time was 8 weeks, and the most likely time was 11 weeks:
   a) the variance would be 1 week.
   b) the variance would be 11 weeks.
   c) the expected time would be 6 weeks.
   d) the expected time would be $5\frac{1}{2}$ weeks.
   e) there is not enough information.

9. The crash cost per week:
   a) is the difference in costs divided by the difference in times (crash and normal).
   b) is considered to be linear in the range between normal and crash.
   c) needs to be determined so that the smallest cost values on the critical path may be considered for time reduction first.
   d) all of the above.

10. PERT analysis computes the variance of the total project completion time as:
    a) the sum of the variances of all activities in the project.
    b) the sum of the variances of all activities on the critical path.
    c) the sum of the variances of all activities not on the critical path.
    d) the variance of the final activity of the project.

Internet and Student CD-ROM/DVD Exercises

Visit our Companion Web site or use your student CD-ROM/DVD to help with the material in this chapter.

 On Our Companion Web site, www.prenhall.com/heizer
- Self-Study Quizzes
- Practice Problems
- Virtual Company Tour
- Internet Cases
- PowerPoint Lecture
- Microsoft Project (upon request)

On Your Student CD-ROM
- Practice Problems
- ExcelOM
- Excel OM Data Files
- Active Model Exercise
- POM for Windows

On Your Student DVD
- Video Clips and Video Cases
- Virtual Office Hours for Solved Problems

Discussion Questions

1. Give an example of a situation in which project management is needed.
2. Explain the purpose of project organization.
3. What are the three phases involved in the management of a large project?
4. What are some of the questions that can be answered with PERT and CPM?
5. Define *work breakdown structure*. How is it used?
6. What is the use of Gantt charts in project management?
7. What is the difference between an activity-on-arrow (AOA) network and an activity-on-node (AON) network? Which is primarily used in this chapter?
8. What is the significance of the critical path?
9. What would a project manager have to do to crash an activity?
10. Describe how expected activity times and variances can be computed in a PERT network.
11. Define *early start*, *early finish*, *late finish*, and *late start* times.
12. Students are sometimes confused by the concept of critical path, and want to believe that it is the *shortest* path through a network. Convincingly explain why this is not so.
13. What are dummy activities? Why are they used in activity-on-arrow (AOA) project networks?
14. What are the three time estimates used with PERT?
15. Would a project manager ever consider crashing a noncritical activity in a project network? Explain convincingly.
16. How is the variance of the total project computed in PERT?
17. Describe the meaning of slack, and discuss how it can be determined.
18. How can we determine the probability that a project will be completed by a certain date? What assumptions are made in this computation?
19. Name some of the widely used project management software programs.

Ethical Dilemma

Two examples of massively mismanaged projects are TAURUS and the "Big Dig." The first, formally called the London Stock Exchange Automation Project, cost $575 million before it was finally abandoned. Although most IT projects have a reputation for cost overruns, delays, and underperformance, TAURUS set a new standard.

But even TAURUS paled next to the biggest, most expensive public works project in U.S. history—Boston's 15-year-long Central Artery/Tunnel Project. Called the Big Dig, this was perhaps the poorest and most felonious case of project mismanagement in decades. From a starting $2 billion budget to a final price tag of $15 billion, the Big Dig cost more than the Panama Canal, Hoover Dam, or Interstate 95, the 1,919-mile highway between Maine and Florida.

Read about one of these two projects (or another of your choice) and explain why it faced such problems. How and why do project managers allow such massive endeavors to fall into such a state? What do you think are the causes?

Problems*

•   **3.1**   The work breakdown structure for building a house (levels 1 and 2) is shown below:

Note: **Px** means the problem may be solved with POM for Windows and/or Excel OM.

a) Add two level-3 activities to each of the level-2 activities to provide more detail to the WBS.
b) Select one of your level-3 activities and add two level-4 activities below it.

••   **3.2**   Robert Mefford has decided to run for a seat as Congressman from the House of Representative district 34 in California. He views his 8-month campaign for office as a major project and wishes to create a work breakdown structure (WBS) to help control the detailed scheduling. So far, he has developed the following pieces of the WBS:

Level	Level ID No.	Activity
1	1.0	Develop political campaign
2	1.1	Fund-raising plan
3	1.11	_____
3	1.12	_____
3	1.13	_____
2	1.2	Develop a position on major issues
3	1.21	_____
3	1.22	_____
3	1.23	_____
2	1.3	Staffing for campaign
3	1.31	_____
3	1.32	_____
3	1.33	_____
3	1.34	_____
2	1.4	Paperwork compliance for candidacy
3	1.41	_____
3	1.42	_____
2	1.5	Ethical plan/issues
3	1.51	_____

Help Mr. Mefford by providing details where the blank lines appear. Are there any other major (level-2) activities to create? If so, add an ID no. 1.6 and insert them.

• **3.3** Draw the activity-on-node (AON) project network associated with the following activities for Dave Carhart's consulting company project. How long should it take Dave and his team to complete this project? What are the critical path activities?

Activity	Immediate Predecessor(s)	Time (days)
A	—	3
B	A	4
C	A	6
D	B	6
E	B	4
F	C	4
G	D	6
H	E, F	8

Px

• **3.4** Given the activities whose sequence is described by the following table, draw the appropriate activity-on-arrow (AOA) network diagram.
a) Which activities are on the critical path?
b) What is the length of the critical path?

Activity	Immediate Predecessor(s)	Time (days)
A	—	5
B	A	2
C	A	4
D	B	5
E	B	5
F	C	5
G	E, F	2
H	D	3
I	G, H	5

Px

• **3.5** Using AOA, diagram the network described below for Sarah McComb's construction project. Calculate its critical path. How long is the minimum duration of this network?

Activity	Nodes	Time (weeks)	Activity	Nodes	Time (weeks)
J	1–2	10	N	3–4	2
K	1–3	8	O	4–5	7
L	2–4	6	P	3–5	5
M	2–3	3			

Px

•• **3.6** Shirley Hopkins is developing a program in leadership training for middle-level managers. Shirley has listed a number of activities that must be completed before a training program of this nature could be conducted. The activities, immediate predecessors, and times appear in the accompanying table:

Activity	Immediate Predecessor(s)	Time (days)
A	—	2
B	—	5
C	—	1
D	B	10
E	A, D	3
F	C	6
G	E, F	8

a) Develop an AON network for this problem.
b) What is the critical path?
c) What is the total project completion time?
d) What is the slack time for each individual activity? **Px**

•• **3.7** Task time estimates for a production line setup project at Robert Klassen's Ontario factory are as follows:

Activity	Time (in hours)	Immediate Predecessors
A	6.0	—
B	7.2	—
C	5.0	A
D	6.0	B, C
E	4.5	B, C
F	7.7	D
G	4.0	E, F

a) Draw the project network using AON.
b) Identify the critical path.
c) What is the expected project length?
d) Draw a Gantt chart for the project. **Px**

•• **3.8** The City Commission of Nashville has decided to build a botanical garden and picnic area in the heart of the city for the recreation of its citizens. The precedence table for all the activities required to construct this area successfully is given on page 95. Draw the Gantt chart for the whole construction activity.

Table for 3.8

Code	Activity	Description	Time (in hours)	Immediate Predecessor(s)
A	Planning	Find location; determine resource requirements	20	None
B	Purchasing	Requisition of lumber and sand	60	Planning
C	Excavation	Dig and grade	100	Planning
D	Sawing	Saw lumber into appropriate sizes	30	Purchasing
E	Placement	Position lumber in correct locations	20	Sawing, excavation
F	Assembly	Nail lumber together	10	Placement
G	Infill	Put sand in and under the equipment	20	Assembly
H	Outfill	Put dirt around the equipment	10	Assembly
I	Decoration	Put grass all over the garden, landscape, paint	30	Infill, outfill

•• **3.9** Refer to the table in Problem 3.8.
a) Draw the AON network for the construction activity.
b) Draw the AOA network for the construction activity.

• **3.10** The activities needed to build an experimental chemical contaminant tracking machine at Charlie Cook Corp. are listed in the following table. Construct an AON network for these activities.

Activity	Immediate Predecessor(s)	Activity	Immediate Predecessor(s)
A	—	E	B
B	—	F	B
C	A	G	C, E
D	A	H	D, F

• **3.11** Charlie Cook (see Problem 3.10) was able to determine the activity times for constructing his chemical contaminant tracking machine. Cook would like to determine ES, EF, LS, LF, and slack for each activity. The total project completion time and the critical path should also be determined. Here are the activity times:

Activity	Time (weeks)	Activity	Time (weeks)
A	6	E	4
B	7	F	6
C	3	G	10
D	2	H	7

3.12 The activities described by the following table are given for the Duplaga Corporation:

Activity	Immediate Predecessor(s)	Time
A	—	9
B	A	7
C	A	3
D	B	6
E	B	9
F	C	4
G	E, F	6
H	D	5
I	G, H	3

a) Draw the appropriate AON PERT diagram for Ed Duplaga's management team.
b) Find the critical path.
c) What is the project completion time? **P✕**

• **3.13** A small renovation of a Hard Rock Cafe gift shop has six activities (in hours). For the following estimates of a, m, and b, calculate the expected time and the standard deviation for each activity:

Activity	a	m	b
A	11	15	19
B	27	31	41
C	18	18	18
D	8	13	19
E	17	18	20
F	16	19	22	**P✕**

•• **3.14** McGee Carpet and Trim installs carpet in commercial offices. Andrea McGee has been very concerned with the amount of time it took to complete several recent jobs. Some of her workers are very unreliable. A list of activities and their optimistic completion time, the most likely completion time, and the pessimistic completion time (all in days) for a new contract are given in the following table:

Activity	Time (days) a	m	b	Immediate Predecessor(s)
A	3	6	8	—
B	2	4	4	—
C	1	2	3	—
D	6	7	8	C
E	2	4	6	B, D
F	6	10	14	A, E
G	1	2	4	A, E
H	3	6	9	F
I	10	11	12	G
J	14	16	20	C
K	2	8	10	H, I

a) Determine the expected completion time and variance for each activity.
b) Determine the total project completion time and the critical path for the project.
c) Determine ES, EF, LS, LF, and slack for each activity.
d) What is the probability that McGee Carpet and Trim will finish the project in 40 days or less? **P✕**

• •   3.15 The following is a table of activities associated with a project at Bill Figg Enterprises, their durations and what activities each must precede:

Activity	Duration (weeks)	Precedes
A (start)	1	B, C
B	1	E
C	4	F
E	2	F
F (end)	2	—

a) Draw an AON diagram of the project, including activity durations.
b) Define the critical path, listing all critical activities in chronological order.
c) What is the project duration (in weeks)?
d) What is the slack (in weeks) associated with any and all noncritical paths through the project? **Px**

• •   3.16 Assume that the activities in Problem 3.15 have the following costs to shorten: A, $300/week; B, $100/week; C, $200/week; E, $100/week; and F, $400/week. Assume also that you can crash an activity down to 0 weeks in duration and that every week you can shorten the project is worth $250 to you. What activities would you crash? What is the total crashing cost?

• • •   3.17 Bill Fennema, president of Fennema Construction, has developed the tasks, durations, and predecessor relationships in the following table for building new motels. Draw the AON network and answer the questions that follow.

Activity	Immediate Predecessor(s)	Time Estimates (in weeks)		
		Optimistic	Most Likely	Pessimistic
A	—	4	8	10
B	A	2	8	24
C	A	8	12	16
D	A	4	6	10
E	B	1	2	3
F	E, C	6	8	20
G	E, C	2	3	4
H	F	2	2	2
I	F	6	6	6
J	D, G, H	4	6	12
K	I, J	2	2	3

a) What is the expected (estimated) time for activity C?
b) What is the variance for activity C?
c) Based on the calculation of estimated times, what is the critical path?
d) What is the estimated time of the critical path?
e) What is the activity variance along the critical path?
f) What is the probability of completion of the project before week 36? **Px**

• • •   3.18 What is the minimum cost of crashing the following project that James Walters manages at Ball State University by 4 days?

Activity	Normal Time (days)	Crash Time (days)	Normal Cost	Crash Cost	Immediate Predecessor(s)
A	6	5	$ 900	$1,000	—
B	8	6	300	400	—
C	4	3	500	600	—
D	5	3	900	1,200	A
E	8	5	1,000	1,600	C

Px

• •   3.19 Three activities are candidates for crashing on a project network for a large computer installation (all are, of course, critical). Activity details are in the following table:

Activity	Predecessor	Normal Time	Normal Cost	Crash Time	Crash Cost
A	—	7 days	$6,000	6 days	$6,600
B	A	4 days	1,200	2 days	3,000
C	B	11 days	4,000	9 days	6,000

a) What action would you take to reduce the critical path by 1 day?
b) Assuming no other paths become critical, what action would you take to reduce the critical path one additional day?
c) What is the total cost of the 2-day reduction? **Px**

• • •   3.20 Development of a new deluxe version of a particular software product is being considered by Ravi Behara's software house. The activities necessary for the completion of this project are listed in the following table:

Activity	Normal Time (weeks)	Crash Time (weeks)	Normal Cost	Crash Cost	Immediate Predecessor(s)
A	4	3	$2,000	$2,600	—
B	2	1	2,200	2,800	—
C	3	3	500	500	—
D	8	4	2,300	2,600	A
E	6	3	900	1,200	B
F	3	2	3,000	4,200	C
G	4	2	1,400	2,000	D, E

a) What is the project completion date?
b) What is the total cost required for completing this project on normal time?
c) If you wish to reduce the time required to complete this project by 1 week, which activity should be crashed, and how much will this increase the total cost?
d) What is the maximum time that can be crashed? How much would costs increase? **Px**

• • •   3.21 The estimated times and immediate predecessors for the activities in a project at Caesar Douglas's retinal scanning company are given in the following table. Assume that the activity times are independent.

Activity	Immediate Predecessor	Time (weeks)		
		a	m	b
A	—	9	10	11
B	—	4	10	16
C	A	9	10	11
D	B	5	8	11

a) Calculate the expected time and variance for each activity.
b) What is the expected completion time of the critical path? What is the expected completion time of the other path in the network?
c) What is the variance of the critical path? What is the variance of the other path in the network?
d) If the time to complete path A–C is normally distributed, what is the probability that this path will be finished in 22 weeks or less?
e) If the time to complete path B–D is normally distributed, what is the probability that this path will be finished in 22 weeks or less?
f) Explain why the probability that the *critical path* will be finished in 22 weeks or less is not necessarily the probability that the *project* will be finished in 22 weeks or less. **Px**

••• **3.22** Jack Kanet Manufacturing produces custom-built pollution control devices for medium-size steel mills. The most recent project undertaken by Jack requires 14 different activities.

a) Jack's managers would like to determine the total project completion time (in days) and those activities that lie along the critical path. The appropriate data are shown in the following table.
b) What is the probability of being done in 53 days?
c) What date results in a 99% probability of completion?

Activity	Immediate Predecessor(s)	Optimistic Time	Most Likely Time	Pessimistic Time
A	—	4	6	7
B	—	1	2	3
C	A	6	6	6
D	A	5	8	11
E	B, C	1	9	18
F	D	2	3	6
G	D	1	7	8
H	E, F	4	4	6
I	G, H	1	6	8
J	I	2	5	7
K	I	8	9	11
L	J	2	4	6
M	K	1	2	3
N	L, M	6	8	10

Px

••• **3.23** Dream Team Productions, a firm hired to coordinate the release of the movie *Paycheck* (starring Uma Thurman and Ben Affleck), identified 16 activities to be completed before the release of the film.

a) How many weeks in advance of the film release should Dream Team have started its marketing campaign? What is the critical path? The tasks (in time units of weeks) are as follows:

Activity	Immediate Predecessors	Optimistic Time	Most Likely Time	Pessimistic Time
A	—	1	2	4
B	—	3	3.5	4
C	—	10	12	13
D	—	4	5	7
E	—	2	4	5
F	A	6	7	8
G	B	2	4	5.5
H	C	5	7.7	9
I	C	9.9	10	12
J	C	2	4	5
K	D	2	4	6
L	E	2	4	6
M	F, G, H	5	6	6.5
N	J, K, L	1	1.1	2
O	I, M	5	7	8
P	N	5	7	9

b) If activities I and J were not necessary, what impact would this have on the critical path and the number of weeks needed to complete the marketing campaign? **Px**

•• **3.24** Using PERT, Harold Benson was able to determine that the expected project completion time for the construction of a pleasure yacht is 21 months, and the project variance is 4.

a) What is the probability that the project will be completed in 17 months?
b) What is the probability that the project will be completed in 20 months?

c) What is the probability that the project will be completed in 23 months?

d) What is the probability that the project will be completed in 25 months?

e) What is the due date that yields a 95% chance of completion? **Px**

••• **3.25** Bolling Electronics manufactures DVD players for commercial use. W. Blaker Bolling, president of Bolling Electronics, is contemplating producing DVD players for home use. The activities necessary to build an experimental model and related data are given in the following table:

Activity	Normal Time (weeks)	Crash Time (weeks)	Normal Cost ($)	Crash Cost ($)	Immediate Predecessor(s)
A	3	2	1,000	1,600	—
B	2	1	2,000	2,700	—
C	1	1	300	300	—
D	7	3	1,300	1,600	A
E	6	3	850	1,000	B
F	2	1	4,000	5,000	C
G	4	2	1,500	2,000	D, E

a) What is the project completion date?

b) Crash this project to 10 weeks at the least cost.

c) Crash this project to 7 weeks (which is the maximum it can be crashed) at the least cost. **Px**

••• **3.26** The Maser is a new custom-designed sports car. An analysis of the task of building the Maser reveals the following list of relevant activities, their immediate predecessors, and their duration[6]:

Job Letter	Description	Immediate Predecessor(s)	Normal Time (days)
A	Start	—	0
B	Design	A	8
C	Order special accessories	B	0.1
D	Build frame	B	1
E	Build doors	B	1
F	Attach axles, wheels, gas tank	D	1
G	Build body shell	B	2
H	Build transmission and drivetrain	B	3
I	Fit doors to body shell	G, E	1
J	Build engine	B	4
K	Bench-test engine	J	2
L	Assemble chassis	F, H, K	1
M	Road-test chassis	L	0.5
N	Paint body	I	2
O	Install wiring	N	1
P	Install interior	N	1.5
Q	Accept delivery of special accessories	C	5
R	Mount body and accessories on chassis	M, O, P, Q	1
S	Road test car	R	0.5
T	Attach exterior trim	S	1
U	Finish	T	0

a) Draw a network diagram for the project.

b) Mark the critical path and state its length.

c) If the Maser had to be completed 2 days earlier, would it help to:
   i) Buy preassembled transmissions and drivetrains?
   ii) Install robots to halve engine-building time?
   iii) Speed delivery of special accessories by 3 days?

d) How might resources be borrowed from activities on the noncritical path to speed activities on the critical path? **Px**

••• **3.27** You are asked to manage the morning seminars at Miami's South Beach Wine and Food Festival next year. There are three seminars, each requiring several tasks. You must begin by recruiting a committee of six people to help you. You must also recruit one assistant. This is task A and you expect it will take 12 hours. Then, you will concurrently work on developing ideas for each of the seminars. The business college dean, Bill Quain, says two of the seminars will be on "Dining in South Beach." You know this won't take you long. In fact, you plan to divide your committee into two groups to define the topic and then recruit a speaker. You think that these two groups, working concurrently, will take about 4 hours each to complete the task.

The third seminar is more difficult. Dean Quain wants something on "Great Wines I Found in Cheap Restaurants." You are going to work on this yourself, along with your most trusted assistant. This will be done at the same time as the planning for the other two seminars. It will probably take about 12 hours to complete. All three tasks must be completed before moving on to the next phase.

The next phase (task E) will require only you and your assistant. You will write the material for the programs. This will take about 6 hours to complete. For task F, your assistant faxes the program material to four printers, asking them for bids (1 hour). You will use specifications that were developed last year. You receive the bids, make copies, and provide them to the committee members (3 hours). In tasks H and I, the committee again splits up into two groups. Each group reviews all four bids and rates them (4 hours). Then, in task J, the committee members all meet and discuss the bids (2 hours). They then vote on the winning bid. This takes an additional hour.

After you and your assistant receive the vote, you both meet with the winning printer (task L), another hour. After the printer returns the proof, you and your assistant are required to have another 1-hour meeting with the printer to give your final approval. Two members of the committee make final arrangements for the venue (5 hours). The printer takes 10 hours to print the programs. Finally, the three seminars are run, concurrently. Each of them takes 2 hours and requires two committee members to be present at each seminar. After it is all over, your entire committee, including you and your assistant, meet for a 1-hour debriefing.

a) How long does the project take?

b) Which task has the *most* slack time?

c) Which tasks have no slack time?

d) What is the slack time for the critical path?

e) How many different tasks are there in this project?

f) Calculate how many hours you, your assistant, and the committee spend on this project.

g) You value your time, your assistant's time, and the time of your committee members at $25/hour. A consultant has bid $5,000 to take over the whole project (excluding the actual printing) and do all the work. Should you accept the bid? **Px**

Case Studies

Southwestern University: (A)*

Southwestern University (SWU), a large state college in Stephenville, Texas, 30 miles southwest of the Dallas/Fort Worth metroplex, enrolls close to 20,000 students. In a typical town–gown relationship, the school is a dominant force in the small city, with more students during fall and spring than permanent residents.

A longtime football powerhouse, SWU is a member of the Big Eleven conference and is usually in the top 20 in college football rankings. To bolster its chances of reaching the elusive and long-desired number-one ranking, in 2001, SWU hired the legendary Bo Pitterno as its head coach.

One of Pitterno's demands on joining SWU had been a new stadium. With attendance increasing, SWU administrators began to face the issue head-on. After 6 months of study, much political arm wrestling, and some serious financial analysis, Dr. Joel Wisner, president of Southwestern University, had reached a decision to expand the capacity at its on-campus stadium.

Adding thousands of seats, including dozens of luxury skyboxes, would not please everyone. The influential Pitterno had argued the need for a first-class stadium, one with built-in dormitory rooms for his players and a palatial office appropriate for the coach of a future NCAA champion team. But the decision was made, and *everyone*, including the coach, would learn to live with it.

The job now was to get construction going immediately after the 2007 season ended. This would allow exactly 270 days until the 2008 season opening game. The contractor, Hill Construction (Bob Hill being an alumnus, of course), signed his contract. Bob Hill looked at the tasks his engineers had outlined and looked President Wisner in the eye. "I guarantee the team will be able to take the field on schedule next year," he said with a sense of confidence. "I sure hope so," replied Wisner. "The contract penalty of $10,000 per day for running late is nothing compared to what Coach Pitterno will do to you if our opening game with Penn State is delayed or canceled." Hill, sweating slightly, did not need to respond. In football-crazy Texas, Hill Construction would be *mud* if the 270-day target was missed.

Back in his office, Hill again reviewed the data (see Table 3.6) and noted that optimistic time estimates can be used as crash times. He then gathered his foremen. "Folks, if we're not 75% sure we'll finish this stadium in less than 270 days, I want this project crashed! Give me the cost figures for a target date of 250 days—also for 240 days. I want to be *early*, not just on time!"

▼ **Table 3.6**   **Southwestern University Project**

| Activity | Description | Predecessor(s) | Time Estimates (days) | | | Crash Cost/Day |
			Optimistic	Most Likely	Pessimistic	
A	Bonding, insurance, tax structuring	—	20	30	40	$1,500
B	Foundation, concrete footings for boxes	A	20	65	80	3,500
C	Upgrading skybox stadium seating	A	50	60	100	4,000
D	Upgrading walkways, stairwells, elevators	C	30	50	100	1,900
E	Interior wiring, lathes	B	25	30	35	9,500
F	Inspection approvals	E	0.1	0.1	0.1	0
G	Plumbing	D, E	25	30	35	2,500
H	Painting	G	10	20	30	2,000
I	Hardware/AC/metal workings	H	20	25	60	2,000
J	Tile/carpeting/windows	H	8	10	12	6,000
K	Inspection	J	0.1	0.1	0.1	0
L	Final detail work/cleanup	I, K	20	25	60	4,500

Discussion Questions

1. Develop a network drawing for Hill Construction and determine the critical path. How long is the project expected to take?
2. What is the probability of finishing in 270 days?
3. If it is necessary to crash to 250 or 240 days, how would Hill do so, and at what costs? As noted in the case, assume that optimistic time estimates can be used as crash times.

*This integrated study runs throughout the text. Other issues facing Southwestern's football expansion include (B) forecasting game attendance (Chapter 4); (C) quality of facilities (Chapter 6); (D) break-even analysis for food services (Supplement 7 Web site); (E) location of the new stadium (Chapter 8 Web site); (F) inventory planning of football programs (Chapter 12 Web site); and (G) scheduling of campus security officers/staff for game days (Chapter 13).

Project Management at Arnold Palmer Hospital

The equivalent of a new kindergarten class is born every day at Orlando's Arnold Palmer Hospital. With more than 12,300 births in 2005 in a hospital that was designed in 1989 for a capacity of 6,500 births a year, the newborn intensive care unit was stretched to the limit. Moreover, with continuing strong population growth in central Florida, the hospital was often full. It was clear that new facilities were needed. After much analysis, forecasting, and discussion, the management team decided to build a new 273-bed building across the street from the existing hospital. But the facility had to be built in accordance with the hospital's Guiding Principles and its uniqueness as a health center dedicated to the specialized needs of women and infants. Those Guiding Principles are: *Family-centered focus, a healing environment where privacy and dignity are respected, sanctuary of caring that includes warm, serene surroundings with natural lighting, sincere and dedicated staff providing the highest quality care, and patient-centered flow and function.*

The vice president of business development, Karl Hodges, wanted a hospital that was designed from the inside out by the people who understood the Guiding Principles, who knew most about the current system, and who were going to use the new system, namely, the doctors and nurses. Hodges and his staff spent 13 months discussing expansion needs with this group, as well as with patients and the community before developing a proposal for the new facility on December 17, 2001. An administrative team created 35 user groups, which held over 1,000 planning meetings (lasting from 45 minutes to a whole day). They even created a "Supreme Court" to deal with conflicting views on the multifaceted issues facing the new hospital.

Funding and regulatory issues added substantial complexity to this major expansion, and Hodges was very concerned that the project stay on time and within budget. Tom Hyatt, director of facility development, was given the task of onsite manager of the $100 million project, in addition to overseeing ongoing renovations, expansions, and other projects. The activities in the multiyear project for the new building at Arnold Palmer are shown in Table 3.7.

▼ **Table 3.7**   Expansion Planning and Arnold Palmer Hospital Construction Activities and Times[a]

Activity	Scheduled Time	Precedence Activity(ies)
1. Proposal and review	1 month	—
2. Establish master schedule	2 weeks	1
3. Architect selection process	5 weeks	1
4. Survey whole campus and its needs	1 month	1
5. Conceptual architect's plans	6 weeks	3
6. Cost estimating	2 months	2, 4, 5
7. Deliver plans to board for consideration/decision	1 month	6
8. Surveys/regulatory review	6 weeks	6
9. Construction manager selection	9 weeks	6
10. State review of need for more hospital beds ("Certificate of Need")	3.5 months	7, 8
11. Design drawings	4 months	10
12. Construction documents	5 months	9, 11
13. Site preparation/demolish existing building	9 weeks	11
14. Construction start/building pad	2 months	12, 13
15. Relocate utilities	6 weeks	12
16. Deep foundations	2 months	14
17. Building structure in place	9 months	16
18. Exterior skin/roofing	4 months	17
19. Interior buildout	12 months	17
20. Building inspections	5 weeks	15, 19
21. Occupancy	1 month	20

[a]This list of activities is abbreviated for purposes of this case study. For simplification, assume each week = .25 months (i.e., 2 weeks = .5 month, 6 weeks = 1.5 months, etc.).

Discussion Questions*

1. Develop the network for planning and construction of the new hospital at Arnold Palmer.
2. What is the critical path and how long is the project expected to take?
3. Why is the construction of this 11-story building any more complex than construction of an equivalent office building?
4. What percent of the whole project duration was spent in planning that occurred prior to the proposal and reviews? Prior to the actual building construction? Why?

*You may wish to review this video case on your DVD before answering these questions.

Source: Professors Barry Render (Rollins College), Jay Heizer (Texas Lutheran University), and Beverly Amer (Northern Arizona University).

Managing Hard Rock's Rockfest

At the Hard Rock Cafe, like many organizations, project management is a key planning tool. With Hard Rock's constant growth in hotels and cafes, remodeling of existing cafes, scheduling for Hard Rock Live concert and event venues, and planning the annual Rockfest, managers rely on project management techniques and software to maintain schedule and budget performance.

"Without Microsoft Project," says Hard Rock Vice-President Chris Tomasso, "there is no way to keep so many people on the same page." Tomasso is in charge of the Rockfest event, which is attended by well over 100,000 enthusiastic fans. The challenge is pulling it off within a tight 9-month planning horizon. As the event approaches, Tomasso devotes greater energy to its activities. For the first 3 months, Tomasso updates his Microsoft Project charts monthly. Then

at the 6-month mark, he updates his progress weekly. At the 9-month mark, he checks and corrects his schedule twice a week.

Early in the project management process, Tomasso identifies 10 major tasks (called level-2 activities in a work breakdown structure, or WBS)[†]: talent booking, ticketing, marketing/PR, online promotion, television, show production, travel, sponsorships, operations, and merchandising. Using a WBS, each of these is further divided into a series of subtasks. Table 3.8 identifies 26 of the major activities and subactivities, their immediate predecessors, and time estimates. Tomasso enters all these into the Microsoft Project software.[‡] Tomasso alters the Microsoft Project document and the time line as the project progresses. "It's okay to change it as long as you keep on track," he states.

Activity	Description	Predecessor(s)	Time (weeks)
A	Finalize site and building contracts	—	7
B	Select local promoter	A	3
C	Hire production manager	A	3
D	Design promotional Web site	B	5
E	Set TV deal	D	6
F	Hire director	E	4
G	Plan for TV camera placement	F	2
H	Target headline entertainers	B	4
I	Target support entertainers	H	4
J	Travel accommodations for talent	I	10
K	Set venue capacity	C	2
L	Ticketmaster contract	D, K	3
M	On-site ticketing	L	8
N	Sound and staging	C	6
O	Passes and stage credentials	G, R	7
P	Travel accommodations for staff	B	20
Q	Hire sponsor coordinator	B	4
R	Finalize sponsors	Q	4
S	Define/place signage for sponsors	R, X	3
T	Hire operations manager	A	4
U	Develop site plan	T	6
V	Hire security director	T	7
W	Set police/fire security plan	V	4
X	Power, plumbing, AC, toilet services	U	8
Y	Secure merchandise deals	B	6
Z	Online merchandise sales	Y	6

◀ **Table 3.8**

Some of the Major Activities and Subactivities in the Rockfest Plan

The day of the rock concert itself is not the end of the project planning. "It's nothing but surprises. A band not being able to get to the venue because of traffic jams is a surprise, but an 'anticipated' surprise. We had a helicopter on stand-by ready to fly the band in," says Tomasso.

On completion of Rockfest in July, Tomasso and his team have a 3-month reprieve before starting the project planning process again.

Discussion Questions[§]

1. Identify the critical path and its activities for Rockfest. How long does the project take?
2. Which activities have a slack time of 8 weeks or more?

3. Identify five major challenges a project manager faces in events such as this one.
4. Why is a work breakdown structure useful in a project such as this? Take the 26 activities and break them into what you think should be level-2, level-3, and level-4 tasks.

[†]The level-1 activity is the Rockfest concert itself.

[‡]There are actually 127 activities used by Tomasso; the list is abbreviated for this case study.

[§]You may wish to play this video case on your DVD before addressing these questions.

Source: Professors Barry Render (Rollins College), Jay Heizer (Texas Lutheran University), and Beverly Amer (Northern Arizona University).

Additional Case Studies

Internet Case Study: Visit our Companion Web site at **www.prenhall.com/heizer** *for this free case study:*
*   **Shale Oil Company:** This oil refinery must shut down for maintenance of a major piece of equipment.

Harvard has selected these Harvard Business School cases to accompany this chapter:

harvardbusinessonline.hbsp.harvard.edu
*   **Microsoft Office 2000** (#600-097): An analysis of the evolution of the Office 2000 project.
*   **Chrysler and BMW: Tritec Engine Joint Venture** (#600-004): A gifted project leader defines a new product strategy.
*   **BAE Automated Systems (A): Denver International Baggage-Handling System** (#396-311): The project management of the construction of Denver's baggage-handling system.
*   **Turner Construction Co.** (#190-128): Deals with the project management control system at a construction company.

Bibliography

Balakrishnan, R., B. Render, and R. M. Stair. *Managerial Decision Modeling with Spreadsheets*, 2nd ed. Upper Saddle River, NJ: Prentice Hall (2007).

Barkley, B. T. *Integrated Project Management.* New York: McGraw-Hill/Irwin (2006).

Cleland, D. L., and L. R. Ireland. *Project Management*, 5th ed. New York: McGraw-Hill/Irwin (2007).

Dusenberry, W. "CPM for New Product Introductions." *Harvard Business Review* (July–August 1967): 124–139.

Gray, C. L., and E. W. Larson. *Project Management: The Management Process.* New York: McGraw-Hill/Irwin (2006).

Herroslen, W., and R. Leus. "Project Scheduling Under Uncertainty: Survey and Research Potentials." *European Journal of Operations Research* 165, no. 2 (September, 2005): 289.

Kerzner, H. *Using the Project Management Maturity Model*, 2nd ed. New York: Wiley (2005).

Kumar, P. P. "Effective Use of Gantt Chart for Managing Large-Scale Projects." *Cost Engineering* 47, no. 7 (July 2005): 14–21.

Meredith, J. R., and S. Mantel. *Project Management*, 6th ed. New York: Wiley (2006).

Matta, N. F., and R. N. Ashkenas. "Why Good Projects Fail Anyways." *Harvard Business Review* (September 2003): 109–114.

Oates, David. "Understanding and Solving the Causes of Project Failure." *Knowledge Management Review* 9, no. 5 (May–June 2006): 5.

Render, B., R. M. Stair, and M. Hanna. *Quantitative Analysis for Management*, 10th ed. Upper Saddle River, NJ: Prentice Hall (2009).

Shtub, A. F., et al. *Project Management*, 2nd ed. Upper Saddle River, NJ: Prentice Hall (2005).

Vanhoucke, M., and E. Demeulemeester. "The Application of Project Scheduling Techniques in a Real-Life Environment." *Project Management Journal* (March 2003): 30–43.

Wysocki, R. K. *Effective Project Management.* New York: Wiley (2007).

Internet Resources

E-Business Solutions for project management: **www.eprojectcentral.com**

PERT Chart EXPERT is an add-on product for Microsoft Project that adds extensive PERT charting: **www.criticaltools.com**

PERT Chart and WBS Chart add-on products for Microsoft Project: **www.criticaltools.com**

Project Management Forum: **www.pmforum.org**

Project Management Institute, Inc.: **www.pmi.org**

Project Management Software: **www.project-management-software.org**

Project workspace for the construction industry: **www.buzzsaw.com**

Project time collection: **www.journeyx.com**

CHAPTER 4

Forecasting

Chapter Outline

Learning Objectives

When you complete this chapter you should be able to

1. Understand the three time horizons and which models apply for each
2. Explain when to use each of the four qualitative models
3. Apply the naive, moving average, exponential smoothing, and trend methods

4. Compute three measures of forecast accuracy
5. Develop seasonal indexes
6. Conduct a regression and correlation analysis
7. Use a tracking signal

103

Forecasting Provides a Competitive Advantage for Disney

When it comes to the world's most respected global brands, Walt Disney Parks & Resorts is a visible leader. Although the monarch of this magic kingdom is no man but a mouse—Mickey Mouse—it's CEO Robert Iger who daily manages the entertainment giant.

Disney's global portfolio includes Hong Kong Disneyland (opened 2005), Disneyland Paris (1992), and Tokyo Disneyland (1983). But it is Disney World (in Florida) and Disneyland (in California) that drive profits in this $32 billion corporation, which is ranked 54th in the *Fortune* 500 and 79th in the *Financial Times* Global 500.

Revenues at Disney are all about people—how many visit the parks and how they spend money while there. When Iger receives a daily report from his six theme parks in Orlando, the report contains only two numbers: the *forecast* of yesterday's attendance at the parks (Magic Kingdom, Epcot, Animal Kingdom, MGM Studios, Typhoon Lagoon, and Blizzard Beach) and the *actual* attendance. An error close to zero is expected. Iger takes his forecasts very seriously.

The forecasting team at Disney World doesn't just do a daily prediction, however, and Iger is not its only customer. The team also provides daily,

▲ Mickey and Minnie Mouse, and other Disney characters, with Cinderella's Castle in the background, provide the public image of Disney to the world. Forecasts drive the work schedules of 56,000 cast members working at Disney World's Orlando parks.

◄ The giant sphere is the symbol of Epcot, one of Disney's six Orlando parks, for which forecasts of meals, lodging, entertainment, and transportation must be made. This Disney monorail moves guests among parks and the 20 hotels on the massive 47-square-mile property (about the size of San Francisco and twice the size of Manhattan).

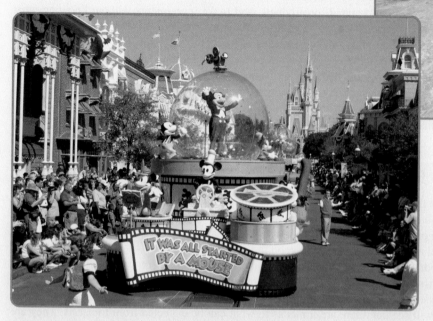

◀ Forecasts are critical to making sure rides are not overcrowded. Disney is good at "managing demand" with techniques such as adding more street activities to reduce long lines for rides.

weekly, monthly, annual, and 5-year forecasts to the labor management, maintenance, operations, finance, and park scheduling departments. Forecasters use judgmental models, econometric models, moving-average models, and regression analysis.

With 20% of Disney World's customers coming from outside the United States, its economic model includes such variables as gross domestic product, cross-exchange rates, and arrivals into the U.S. Disney also uses 35 analysts and 70 field people to survey 1 million people each year. The surveys, administered to guests at the parks and its 20 hotels, to employees, and to travel industry professionals, examine future travel plans and experiences at the parks. This helps forecast not only attendance but behavior at each ride (e.g., how long people will wait, how many times they will ride). Inputs to the monthly forecasting model include airline specials, speeches by the chair of the Federal Reserve, and Wall Street trends. Disney even monitors 3,000 school districts inside and outside the U.S. for holiday/vacation schedules. With this approach, Disney's 5-year attendance forecast yields just a 5% error on average. Its annual forecasts have a 0% to 3% error.

Attendance forecasts for the parks drive a whole slew of management decisions. For example, capacity on any day can be increased by opening at 8 A.M. instead of the usual 9 A.M., by opening more shows or rides, by adding more food/beverage carts (9 million hamburgers and 50 million Cokes are sold per year!), and by bringing in more employees

▲ Disney uses characters such as Minnie Mouse to entertain customers when lines are forecast to be long. On slow days, Disney calls fewer cast members to work.

(called "cast members"). Cast members are scheduled in 15-minute intervals throughout the parks for flexibility. Demand can be managed by limiting the number of guests admitted to the parks, with the "fast pass" reservation system, and by shifting crowds from rides to more street parades.

At Disney, forecasting is a key driver in the company's success and competitive advantage.

Every day, managers like those at Disney make decisions without knowing what will happen in the future. They order inventory without knowing what sales will be, purchase new equipment despite uncertainty about demand for products, and make investments without knowing what profits will be. Managers are always trying to make better estimates of what will happen in the future in the face of uncertainty. Making good estimates is the main purpose of forecasting.

In this chapter, we examine different types of forecasts and present a variety of forecasting models. Our purpose is to show that there are many ways for managers to forecast. We also provide an overview of business sales forecasting and describe how to prepare, monitor, and judge the accuracy of a forecast. Good forecasts are an *essential* part of efficient service and manufacturing operations.

WHAT IS FORECASTING?

Forecasting
The art and science of predicting future events.

Forecasting is the art and science of predicting future events. Forecasting may involve taking historical data and projecting them into the future with some sort of mathematical model. It may be a subjective or intuitive prediction. Or it may involve a combination of these—that is, a mathematical model adjusted by a manager's good judgment.

As we introduce different forecasting techniques in this chapter, you will see that there is seldom one superior method. What works best in one firm under one set of conditions may be a complete disaster in another organization, or even in a different department of the same firm. In addition, you will see that there are limits as to what can be expected from forecasts. They are seldom, if ever, perfect. They are also costly and time-consuming to prepare and monitor.

Few businesses, however, can afford to avoid the process of forecasting by just waiting to see what happens and then taking their chances. Effective planning in both the short run and long run depends on a forecast of demand for the company's products.

Forecasting Time Horizons

A forecast is usually classified by the *future time horizon* that it covers. Time horizons fall into three categories:

1. *Short-range forecast:* This forecast has a time span of up to 1 year but is generally less than 3 months. It is used for planning purchasing, job scheduling, workforce levels, job assignments, and production levels.
2. *Medium-range forecast:* A medium-range, or intermediate, forecast generally spans from 3 months to 3 years. It is useful in sales planning, production planning and budgeting, cash budgeting, and analysis of various operating plans.
3. *Long-range forecast:* Generally 3 years or more in time span, long-range forecasts are used in planning for new products, capital expenditures, facility location or expansion, and research and development.

Medium and long-range forecasts are distinguished from short-range forecasts by three features:

1. First, intermediate and long-run forecasts *deal with more comprehensive issues* and support management decisions regarding planning and products, plants, and processes. Implementing some facility decisions, such as GM's decision to open a new Brazilian manufacturing plant, can take 5 to 8 years from inception to completion.
2. Second, short-term forecasting usually *employs different methodologies* than longer-term forecasting. Mathematical techniques, such as moving averages, exponential smoothing, and trend extrapolation (all of which we shall examine shortly), are common to short-run projections. Broader, *less* quantitative methods are useful in predicting such issues as whether a new product, like the optical disk recorder, should be introduced into a company's product line.
3. Finally, as you would expect, short-range forecasts *tend to be more accurate* than longer-range forecasts. Factors that influence demand change every day. Thus, as the time horizon lengthens, it is likely that forecast accuracy will diminish. It almost goes without saying, then, that sales forecasts must be updated regularly to maintain their value and integrity. After each sales period, forecasts should be reviewed and revised.

Our forecasting ability has improved, but it has been outpaced by an increasingly complex world economy.

The Influence of Product Life Cycle

Another factor to consider when developing sales forecasts, especially longer ones, is product life cycle. Products, and even services, do not sell at a constant level throughout their lives. Most successful products pass through four stages: (1) introduction, (2) growth, (3) maturity, and (4) decline.

Products in the first two stages of the life cycle (such as virtual reality and LCD TVs) need longer forecasts than those in the maturity and decline stages (such as $3\frac{1}{2}$" floppy disks and skateboards). Forecasts that reflect life cycle are useful in projecting different staffing levels, inventory levels, and factory capacity as the product passes from the first to the last stage. The challenge of introducing new products is treated in more detail in Chapter 5.

TYPES OF FORECASTS

Organizations use three major types of forecasts in planning future operations:

1. **Economic forecasts** address the business cycle by predicting inflation rates, money supplies, housing starts, and other planning indicators.
2. **Technological forecasts** are concerned with rates of technological progress, which can result in the birth of exciting new products, requiring new plants and equipment.
3. **Demand forecasts** are projections of demand for a company's products or services. These forecasts, also called *sales forecasts*, drive a company's production, capacity, and scheduling systems and serve as inputs to financial, marketing, and personnel planning.

Economic and technological forecasting are specialized techniques that may fall outside the role of the operations manager. The emphasis in this book will therefore be on demand forecasting.

THE STRATEGIC IMPORTANCE OF FORECASTING

Good forecasts are of critical importance in all aspects of a business: *The forecast is the only estimate of demand until actual demand becomes known.* Forecasts of demand therefore drive decisions in many areas. Let's look at the impact of product forecast on three activities: (1) human resources, (2) capacity, and (3) supply chain management.

Human Resources

Hiring, training, and laying off workers all depend on anticipated demand. If the human resources department must hire additional workers without warning, the amount of training declines and the quality of the workforce suffers. A large Louisiana chemical firm almost lost its biggest customer when a quick expansion to around-the-clock shifts led to a total breakdown in quality control on the second and third shifts.

Capacity

When capacity is inadequate, the resulting shortages can mean undependable delivery, loss of customers, and loss of market share. This is exactly what happened to Nabisco when it underestimated the huge demand for its new low-fat Snackwell Devil's Food Cookies. Even with production lines working overtime, Nabisco could not keep up with demand, and it lost customers. When excess capacity is built, on the other hand, costs can skyrocket.

Supply Chain Management

Good supplier relations and the ensuing price advantages for materials and parts depend on accurate forecasts. For example, auto manufacturers who want TRW Corp. to guarantee sufficient airbag capacity must provide accurate forecasts to justify TRW plant expansions. In the global marketplace, where expensive components for Boeing 787 jets are manufactured in dozens of countries, coordination driven by forecasts is critical. Scheduling transportation to Seattle for final assembly at the lowest possible cost means no last-minute surprises that can harm already-low profit margins.

Economic forecasts
Planning indicators that are valuable in helping organizations prepare medium- to long-range forecasts.

Technological forecasts
Long-term forecasts concerned with the rates of technological progress.

Demand forecasts
Projections of a company's sales for each time period in the planning horizon.

Video 4.1

Forecasting at Hard Rock Cafe

SEVEN STEPS IN THE FORECASTING SYSTEM

Forecasting follows seven basic steps. We use Disney World, the focus of this chapter's *Global Company Profile*, as an example of each step:

1. *Determine the use of the forecast:* Disney uses park attendance forecasts to drive staffing, opening times, ride availability, and food supplies.
2. *Select the items to be forecasted:* For Disney World, there are six main parks. A forecast of daily attendance at each is the main number that determines labor, maintenance, and scheduling.
3. *Determine the time horizon of the forecast:* Is it short, medium, or long term? Disney develops daily, weekly, monthly, annual, and 5-year forecasts.
4. *Select the forecasting model(s):* Disney uses a variety of statistical models that we shall discuss, including moving averages, econometrics, and regression analysis. It also employs judgmental, or nonquantitative, models.
5. *Gather the data needed to make the forecast:* Disney's forecasting team employs 35 analysts and 70 field personnel to survey 1 million people/businesses every year. It also uses a firm called Global Insights for travel industry forecasts and gathers data on exchange rates, arrivals into the U.S., airline specials, Wall Street trends, and school vacation schedules.
6. *Make the forecast.*
7. *Validate and implement the results:* At Disney, forecasts are reviewed daily at the highest levels to make sure that the model, assumptions, and data are valid. Error measures are applied; then the forecasts are used to schedule personnel down to 15-minute intervals.

These seven steps present a systematic way of initiating, designing, and implementing a forecasting system. When the system is to be used to generate forecasts regularly over time, data must be routinely collected. Then actual computations are usually made by computer.

Regardless of the system that firms like Disney use, each company faces several realities:

1. Forecasts are seldom perfect. This means that outside factors that we cannot predict or control often impact the forecast. Companies need to allow for this reality.
2. Most forecasting techniques assume that there is some underlying stability in the system. Consequently, some firms automate their predictions using computerized forecasting software, then closely monitor only the product items whose demand is erratic.
3. Both product family and aggregated forecasts are more accurate than individual product forecasts. Disney, for example, aggregates daily attendance forecasts by park. This approach helps balance the over- and underpredictions of each of the six attractions.

FORECASTING APPROACHES

There are two general approaches to forecasting, just as there are two ways to tackle all decision modeling. One is a quantitative analysis; the other is a qualitative approach. **Quantitative forecasts** use a variety of mathematical models that rely on historical data and/or causal variables to forecast demand. Subjective or **qualitative forecasts** incorporate such factors as the decision maker's intuition, emotions, personal experiences, and value system in reaching a forecast. Some firms use one approach and some use the other. In practice, a combination of the two is usually most effective.

Overview of Qualitative Methods

In this section, we consider four different *qualitative* forecasting techniques:

1. **Jury of executive opinion:** Under this method, the opinions of a group of high-level experts or managers, often in combination with statistical models, are pooled to arrive at a group estimate of demand. Bristol-Meyers Squibb Company, for example, uses 220 well-known research scientists as its jury of executive opinion to get a grasp on future trends in the world of medical research.
2. **Delphi method:** There are three different types of participants in the Delphi method: decision makers, staff personnel, and respondents. Decision makers usually consist of a group of

Quantitative forecasts
Forecasts that employ one or more mathematical models that rely on historical data and/or causal variables to forecast demand.

Qualitative forecasts
Forecasts that incorporate such factors as the decision maker's intuition, emotions, personal experiences, and value system.

Jury of executive opinion
A forecasting technique that takes the opinion of a small group of high-level managers and results in a group estimate of demand.

Delphi method
A forecasting technique using a group process that allows experts to make forecasts.

5 to 10 experts who will be making the actual forecast. Staff personnel assist decision makers by preparing, distributing, collecting, and summarizing a series of questionnaires and survey results. The respondents are a group of people, often located in different places, whose judgments are valued. This group provides inputs to the decision makers before the forecast is made.

Learning Objective

2. Explain when to use each of the four qualitative models

The state of Alaska, for example, has used the Delphi method to develop its long-range economic forecast. An amazing 90% of the state's budget is derived from 1.5 million barrels of oil pumped daily through a pipeline at Prudhoe Bay. The large Delphi panel of experts had to represent all groups and opinions in the state and all geographic areas. Delphi was the perfect forecasting tool because panelist travel could be avoided. It also meant that leading Alaskans could participate because their schedules were not affected by meetings and distances.

3. **Sales force composite:** In this approach, each salesperson estimates what sales will be in his or her region. These forecasts are then reviewed to ensure that they are realistic. Then they are combined at the district and national levels to reach an overall forecast. A variation of this approach occurs at Lexus, where every quarter Lexus dealers have a "make meeting." At this meeting, they talk about what is selling, in what colors, and with what options, so the factory knows what to build.[1]

Sales force composite
A forecasting technique based on salespersons' estimates of expected sales.

4. **Consumer market survey:** This method solicits input from customers or potential customers regarding future purchasing plans. It can help not only in preparing a forecast but also in improving product design and planning for new products. The consumer market survey and sales force composite methods can, however, suffer from overly optimistic forecasts that arise from customer input. The 2001 crash of the telecommunication industry was the result of overexpansion to meet "explosive customer demand." Where did these data come from? Oplink Communications, a Nortel Networks supplier, says its "company forecasts over the last few years were based mainly on informal conversations with customers."[2]

Consumer market survey
A forecasting method that solicits input from customers or potential customers regarding future purchasing plans.

Overview of Quantitative Methods

Five quantitative forecasting methods, all of which use historical data, are described in this chapter. They fall into two categories:

1. Naive approach
2. Moving averages
3. Exponential smoothing } **time-series models**
4. Trend projection
5. Linear regression   } **associative model**

Time-Series Models **Time-series** models predict on the assumption that the future is a function of the past. In other words, they look at what has happened over a period of time and use a series of past data to make a forecast. If we are predicting sales of lawn mowers, we use the past sales for lawn mowers to make the forecasts.

Time series
A forecasting technique that uses a series of past data points to make a forecast.

Associative Models Associative models, such as linear regression, incorporate the variables or factors that might influence the quantity being forecast. For example, an associative model for lawn mower sales might use factors such as new housing starts, advertising budget, and competitors' prices.

TIME-SERIES FORECASTING

A time series is based on a sequence of evenly spaced (weekly, monthly, quarterly, and so on) data points. Examples include weekly sales of Nike Air Jordans, quarterly earnings reports of Microsoft stock, daily shipments of Coors beer, and annual consumer price indices. Forecasting

---

[1]Jonathan Fahey, "The Lexus Nexus," *Forbes* (June 21, 2004): 68–70.
[2]"Lousy Sales Forecasts Helped Fuel the Telecom Mess," *The Wall Street Journal* (July 9, 2001): B1–B4.

time-series data implies that future values are predicted *only* from past values and that other variables, no matter how potentially valuable, may be ignored.

Decomposition of a Time Series

Analyzing time series means breaking down past data into components and then projecting them forward. A time series has four components:

1. *Trend* is the gradual upward or downward movement of the data over time. Changes in income, population, age distribution, or cultural views may account for movement in trend.
2. *Seasonality* is a data pattern that repeats itself after a period of days, weeks, months, or quarters. There are six common seasonality patterns:

Period of Pattern	"Season" Length	Number of "Seasons" in Pattern
Week	Day	7
Month	Week	$4-4\frac{1}{2}$
Month	Day	28–31
Year	Quarter	4
Year	Month	12
Year	Week	52

Restaurants and barber shops, for example, experience weekly seasons, with Saturday being the peak of business. See the *OM in Action* box "Forecasting at Olive Garden and Red Lobster." Beer distributors forecast yearly patterns, with monthly seasons. Three "seasons"—May, July, and September—each contain a big beer-drinking holiday.

3. *Cycles* are patterns in the data that occur every several years. They are usually tied into the business cycle and are of major importance in short-term business analysis and planning. Predicting business cycles is difficult because they may be affected by political events or by international turmoil.
4. *Random variations* are "blips" in the data caused by chance and unusual situations. They follow no discernible pattern, so they cannot be predicted.

Figure 4.1 illustrates a demand over a 4-year period. It shows the average, trend, seasonal components, and random variations around the demand curve. The average demand is the sum of the demand for each period divided by the number of data periods.

Naive Approach

The simplest way to forecast is to assume that demand in the next period will be equal to demand in the most recent period. In other words, if sales of a product—say, Nokia cell phones—were 68 units in January, we can forecast that February's sales will also be 68

▶ **Figure 4.1**

Product Demand Charted over 4 Years with a Growth Trend and Seasonality Indicated

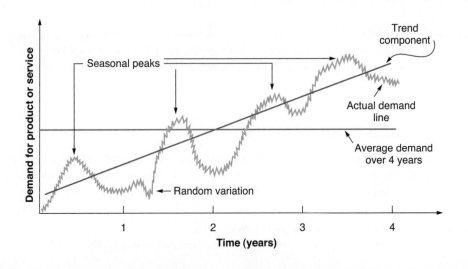

OM in Action   Forecasting at Olive Garden and Red Lobster

It's Friday night in the college town of Gainesville, Florida, and the local Olive Garden restaurant is humming. Customers may wait an average of 30 minutes for a table, but they can sample new wines and cheeses and admire scenic paintings of Italian villages on the restaurant's walls. Then comes dinner with portions so huge that many people take home a doggie bag. The typical bill: under $15 per person.

Crowds flock to the Darden restaurant chain's Olive Garden, Red Lobster, Seasons 52, and Bahama Breeze for value and consistency *and* they get it.

Every night, Darden's computers crank out forecasts that tell store managers what demand to anticipate the next day. The forecasting software generates a total meal forecast and breaks that down into specific menu items. The system tells a manager, for instance, that if 625 meals will be served the next day, "you will serve these items in these quantities. So before you go home, pull 25 pounds of shrimp and 30 pounds of crab out, and tell your operations

people to prepare 42 portion packs of chicken, 75 scampi dishes, 8 stuffed flounders, and so on." Managers often fine tune the quantities based on local conditions, such as weather or a convention, but they know what their customers are going to order.

By relying on demand history, the forecasting system has cut millions of dollars of waste out of the system. The forecast also reduces labor costs by providing the necessary information for improved scheduling. Labor costs decreased almost a full percent in the first year, translating in additional millions in savings for the Darden chain. In the low-margin restaurant business, every dollar counts.

Source: Interviews with Darden executives, 2006, 2007.

---

phones. Does this make any sense? It turns out that for some product lines, this **naive approach** is the most cost-effective and efficient objective forecasting model. At least it provides a starting point against which more sophisticated models that follow can be compared.

> **Naive approach**
> A forecasting technique that assumes demand in the next period is equal to demand in the most recent period.

Moving Averages

A **moving-average** forecast uses a number of historical actual data values to generate a forecast. Moving averages are useful *if we can assume that market demands will stay fairly steady over time*. A 4-month moving average is found by simply summing the demand during the past 4 months and dividing by 4. With each passing month, the most recent month's data are added to the sum of the previous 3 months' data, and the earliest month is dropped. This practice tends to smooth out short-term irregularities in the data series.

Mathematically, the simple moving average (which serves as an estimate of the next period's demand) is expressed as

> **Moving averages**
> A forecasting method that uses an average of the *n* most recent periods of data to forecast the next period.

$$\text{Moving average} = \frac{\Sigma \text{ Demand in previous } n \text{ periods}}{n} \tag{4-1}$$

where *n* is the number of periods in the moving average—for example, 4, 5, or 6 months, respectively, for a 4-, 5-, or 6-period moving average.

Example 1 shows how moving averages are calculated.

> **Learning Objective**
> 3. Apply the naive, moving average, exponential smoothing, and trend methods

Donna's Garden Supply wants a 3-month moving-average forecast, including a forecast for next January, for shed sales.

Approach: Storage shed sales are shown in the middle column of the table on the top of the next page. A 3-month moving average appears on the right.

> **EXAMPLE 1**
>
> Determining the moving average

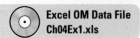

Month	Actual Shed Sales	3-Month Moving Average
January	10	
February	12	
March	13	
April	16	$(10 + 12 + 13)/3 = 11\frac{2}{3}$
May	19	$(12 + 13 + 16)/3 = 13\frac{2}{3}$
June	23	$(13 + 16 + 19)/3 = 16$
July	26	$(16 + 19 + 23)/3 = 19\frac{1}{3}$
August	30	$(19 + 23 + 26)/3 = 22\frac{2}{3}$
September	28	$(23 + 26 + 30)/3 = 26\frac{1}{3}$
October	18	$(26 + 30 + 28)/3 = 28$
November	16	$(30 + 28 + 18)/3 = 25\frac{1}{3}$
December	14	$(28 + 18 + 16)/3 = 20\frac{2}{3}$

Solution: The forecast for December is $20\frac{2}{3}$. To project the demand for sheds in the coming January, we sum the October, November, and December sales and divide by 3: January forecast = $(18 + 16 + 14)/3 = 16$.

Insight: Management now has a forecast that averages sales for the last 3 months. It is easy to use and understand.

Learning exercise: If actual sales in December were 18 (rather than 14), what is the new January forecast? [Answer: $17\frac{1}{3}$.]

Related problems: 4.1a, 4.2b, 4.5a, 4.6, 4.8a,b, 4.10a, 4.13b, 4.15, 4.47

When a detectable trend or pattern is present, *weights* can be used to place more emphasis on recent values. This practice makes forecasting techniques more responsive to changes because more recent periods may be more heavily weighted. Choice of weights is somewhat arbitrary because there is no set formula to determine them. Therefore, deciding which weights to use requires some experience. For example, if the latest month or period is weighted too heavily, the forecast may reflect a large unusual change in the demand or sales pattern too quickly.

A weighted moving average may be expressed mathematically as:

$$\text{Weighted moving average} = \frac{\Sigma \ (\text{Weight for period } n)(\text{Demand in period } n)}{\Sigma \ \text{Weights}} \qquad (4\text{-}2)$$

Example 2 shows how to calculate a weighted moving average.

EXAMPLE 2

Determining the weighted moving average

Donna's Garden Supply (see Example 1) wants to forecast storage shed sales by weighting the past 3 months, with more weight given to recent data to make them more significant.

Approach: Assign more weight to recent data, as follows:

Weights Applied	Period
3	Last month
2	Two months ago
1	Three months ago
6	Sum of weights

Forecast for this month =

$$\frac{3 \times \text{Sales last mo.} + 2 \times \text{Sales 2 mos. ago} + 1 \times \text{Sales 3 mos. ago}}{\text{Sum of the weights}}$$

Solution: The results of this weighted-average forecast are as follows:

Month	Actual Shed Sales	Three-Month Weighted Moving Average
January	10	
February	12	
March	13	
April	16	$[(3 \times 13) + (2 \times 12) + (10)]/6 = 12\frac{1}{6}$
May	19	$[(3 \times 16) + (2 \times 13) + (12)]/6 = 14\frac{1}{3}$
June	23	$[(3 \times 19) + (2 \times 16) + (13)]/6 = 17$
July	26	$[(3 \times 23) + (2 \times 19) + (16)]/6 = 20\frac{1}{2}$
August	30	$[(3 \times 26) + (2 \times 23) + (19)]/6 = 23\frac{5}{6}$
September	28	$[(3 \times 30) + (2 \times 26) + (23)]/6 = 27\frac{1}{2}$
October	18	$[(3 \times 28) + (2 \times 30) + (26)]/6 = 28\frac{1}{3}$
November	16	$[(3 \times 18) + (2 \times 28) + (30)]/6 = 23\frac{1}{3}$
December	14	$[(3 \times 16) + (2 \times 18) + (28)]/6 = 18\frac{2}{3}$

Insight: In this particular forecasting situation, you can see that more heavily weighting the latest month provides a much more accurate projection.

Learning exercise: If the assigned weights were 4, 2, and 1 (instead of 3, 2, and 1) what is the forecast for January's weighted moving average? [Answer: $15\frac{1}{7}$.]

Related problems: 4.1b, 4.2c, 4.5c, 4.6, 4.7, 4.10b

Both simple and weighted moving averages are effective in smoothing out sudden fluctuations in the demand pattern to provide stable estimates. Moving averages do, however, present three problems:

1. Increasing the size of *n* (the number of periods averaged) does smooth out fluctuations better, but it makes the method less sensitive to *real* changes in the data.
2. Moving averages cannot pick up trends very well. Because they are averages, they will always stay within past levels and will not predict changes to either higher or lower levels. That is, they *lag* the actual values.
3. Moving averages require extensive records of past data.

Figure 4.2, a plot of the data in Examples 1 and 2, illustrates the lag effect of the moving-average models. Note that both the moving-average and weighted-moving-average lines lag the actual demand. The weighted moving average, however, usually reacts more quickly to demand changes. Even in periods of downturn (see November and December), it more closely tracks the demand.

Exponential Smoothing

Exponential smoothing is a sophisticated weighted-moving-average forecasting method that is still fairly easy to use. It involves very *little* record keeping of past data. The basic exponential smoothing formula can be shown as follows:

$$\text{New forecast} = \text{Last period's forecast} + \alpha \,(\text{Last period's actual demand} - \text{Last period's forecast}) \quad \text{(4-3)}$$

Data that are 20 years old may not be so useful. It is not always necessary to use all data.

Exponential smoothing
A weighted-moving-average forecasting technique in which data points are weighted by an exponential function.

► **Figure 4.2**

**Actual Demand vs.
Moving-Average and
Weighted-Moving-Average
Methods for Donna's
Garden Supply**

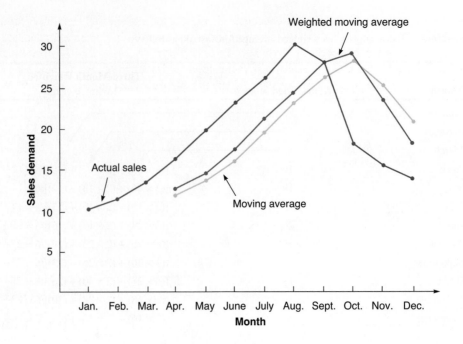

Smoothing constant

The weighting factor used in an exponential smoothing forecast, a number between 0 and 1.

where α is a weight, or **smoothing constant**, chosen by the forecaster, that has a value between 0 and 1. Equation (4-3) can also be written mathematically as:

$$F_t = F_{t-1} + \alpha(A_{t-1} - F_{t-1}) \tag{4-4}$$

where F_t = new forecast
          F_{t-1} = previous period's forecast
          α = smoothing (or weighting) constant $(0 \le \alpha \le 1)$
          A_{t-1} = previous period's actual demand

The concept is not complex. The latest estimate of demand is equal to the old estimate adjusted by a fraction of the difference between the last period's actual demand and the old estimate. Example 3 shows how to use exponential smoothing to derive a forecast.

EXAMPLE 3

Determining a forecast via exponential smoothing

In January, a car dealer predicted February demand for 142 Ford Mustangs. Actual February demand was 153 autos. Using a smoothing constant chosen by management of $\alpha = .20$, the dealer wants to forecast March demand using the exponential smoothing model.

Approach: The exponential smoothing model in Equations 4-3 and 4-4 can be applied.

Solution: Substituting the sample data into the formula, we obtain:

New forecast (for March demand) $= 142 + .2(153 - 142) = 142 + 2.2$

$= 144.2$

Thus, the March demand forecast for Ford Mustangs is rounded to 144.

Insight: Using just two pieces of data, the forecast and the actual demand, plus a smoothing constant, we developed a forecast of 144 Ford Mustangs for March.

Learning exercise: If the smoothing constant is changed to .30, what is the new forecast? [Answer: 145.3]

Related problems: 4.1c, 4.3, 4.4, 4.5d, 4.6, 4.9d, 4.11, 4.12, 4.13a, 4.17, 4.18, 4.37, 4.43, 4.47, 4.49

The *smoothing constant*, α, is generally in the range from .05 to .50 for business applications. It can be changed to give more weight to recent data (when α is high) or more weight to past data (when α is low). When α reaches the extreme of 1.0, then in Equation (4-4), $F_t = 1.0A_{t-1}$. All the older values drop out, and the forecast becomes identical to the naive model mentioned earlier in this chapter. That is, the forecast for the next period is just the same as this period's demand.

The following table helps illustrate this concept. For example, when $\alpha = .5$, we can see that the new forecast is based almost entirely on demand in the last three or four periods. When $\alpha = .1$, the forecast places little weight on recent demand and takes many periods (about 19) of historical values into account.

Exponential smoothing is widely used in business and is an important part of many computerized inventory control systems.

	Weight Assigned to				
Smoothing Constant	Most Recent Period (α)	2nd Most Recent Period $\alpha(1-\alpha)$	3rd Most Recent Period $\alpha(1-\alpha)^2$	4th Most Recent Period $\alpha(1-\alpha)^3$	5th Most Recent Period $\alpha(1-\alpha)^4$
$\alpha = .1$	.1	.09	.081	.073	.066
$\alpha = .5$	.5	.25	.125	.063	.031

Selecting the Smoothing Constant   The exponential smoothing approach is easy to use, and it has been successfully applied in virtually every type of business. However, the appropriate value of the smoothing constant, α, can make the difference between an accurate forecast and an inaccurate forecast. High values of α are chosen when the underlying average is likely to change. Low values of α are used when the underlying average is fairly stable. In picking a value for the smoothing constant, the objective is to obtain the most accurate forecast.

Measuring Forecast Error

The overall accuracy of any forecasting model—moving average, exponential smoothing, or other—can be determined by comparing the forecasted values with the actual or observed values. If F_t denotes the forecast in period t, and A_t denotes the actual demand in period t, the *forecast error* (or deviation) is defined as:

$$\text{Forecast error} = \text{Actual demand} - \text{Forecast value}$$
$$= A_t - F_t$$

The forecast error tells us how well the model performed against itself using past data.

Several measures are used in practice to calculate the overall forecast error. These measures can be used to compare different forecasting models, as well as to monitor forecasts to ensure they are performing well. Three of the most popular measures are mean absolute deviation (MAD), mean squared error (MSE), and mean absolute percent error (MAPE). We now describe and give an example of each.

Learning Objective

4. Compute three measures of forecast accuracy

Mean Absolute Deviation   The first measure of the overall forecast error for a model is the **mean absolute deviation (MAD)**. This value is computed by taking the sum of the absolute values of the individual forecast errors and dividing by the number of periods of data (n):

$$\text{MAD} = \frac{\sum |\text{Actual} - \text{Forecast}|}{n} \tag{4-5}$$

Mean absolute deviation (MAD)

A measure of the overall forecast error for a model.

Example 4 applies MAD, as a measure of overall forecast error, by testing two values of α.

During the past 8 quarters, the Port of Baltimore has unloaded large quantities of grain from ships. The port's operations manager wants to test the use of exponential smoothing to see how well the technique works in predicting tonnage unloaded. He guesses that the forecast of grain unloaded in the first quarter was 175 tons. Two values of α are to be examined: $\alpha = .10$ and $\alpha = .50$.

Approach: Compare the actual data with the data we forecast (using each of the two α values) and then find the absolute deviation and MADs.

EXAMPLE 4

Determining the mean absolute deviation (MAD)

Solution: The following table shows the *detailed* calculations for $\alpha = .10$ only:

Quarter	Actual Tonnage Unloaded	Forecast with $\alpha = .10$	Forecast with $\alpha = .50$
1	180	175	175
2	168	$175.50 = 175.00 + .10(180 - 175)$	177.50
3	159	$174.75 = 175.50 + .10(168 - 175.50)$	172.75
4	175	$173.18 = 174.75 + .10(159 - 174.75)$	165.88
5	190	$173.36 = 173.18 + .10(175 - 173.18)$	170.44
6	205	$175.02 = 173.36 + .10(190 - 173.36)$	180.22
7	180	$178.02 = 175.02 + .10(205 - 175.02)$	192.61
8	182	$178.22 = 178.02 + .10(180 - 178.02)$	186.30
9	?	$178.59 = 178.22 + .10(182 - 178.22)$	184.15

To evaluate the accuracy of each smoothing constant, we can compute forecast errors in terms of absolute deviations and MADs:

Active Model 4.2

Example 4 is further illustrated in Active Model 4.2 on the CD-ROM and in the Exercise located on page 142.

Quarter	Actual Tonnage Unloaded	Forecast with $\alpha = .10$	Absolute Deviation for $\alpha = .10$	Forecast with $\alpha = .50$	Absolute Deviation for $\alpha = .50$
1	180	175	5.00	175	5.00
2	168	175.50	7.50	177.50	9.50
3	159	174.75	15.75	172.75	13.75
4	175	173.18	1.82	165.88	9.12
5	190	173.36	16.64	170.44	19.56
6	205	175.02	29.98	180.22	24.78
7	180	178.02	1.98	192.61	12.61
8	182	178.22	3.78	186.30	4.30
		Sum of absolute deviations:	82.45		98.62
		$\text{MAD} = \dfrac{\Sigma\lvert\text{Deviations}\rvert}{n}$	10.31		12.33

Insight: On the basis of this comparison of the two MADs, a smoothing constant of $\alpha = .10$ is preferred to $\alpha = .50$ because its MAD is smaller.

Learning exercise: If the smoothing constant is changed from $\alpha = .10$ to $\alpha = .20$, what is the new MAD? [Answer: 10.21.]

Related problems: 4.5b, 4.8c, 4.9c, 4.14, 4.23, 4.37a

Most computerized forecasting software includes a feature that automatically finds the smoothing constant with the lowest forecast error. Some software modifies the α value if errors become larger than acceptable.

Mean squared error (MSE)
The average of the squared differences between the forecasted and observed values.

Mean Squared Error   The **mean squared error (MSE)** is a second way of measuring overall forecast error. MSE is the average of the squared differences between the forecasted and observed values. Its formula is:

$$\text{MSE} = \frac{\Sigma(\text{Forecast errors})^2}{n}$$ (4-6)

Example 5 finds the MSE for the Port of Baltimore introduced in Example 4.

EXAMPLE 5

Determining the mean squared error (MSE)

The operations manager for the Port of Baltimore now wants to compute MSE for $\alpha = .10$.

Approach: Use the same forecast data for $\alpha = .10$ from Example 4, then compute the MSE using Equation (4-6).

Solution:

Quarter	Actual Tonnage Unloaded	Forecast for $\alpha = .10$	(Error)^2
1	180	175	$5^2 = 25$
2	168	175.50	$(-7.5)^2 = 56.25$
3	159	174.75	$(-15.75)^2 = 248.06$
4	175	173.18	$(1.82)^2 = 3.33$
5	190	173.36	$(16.64)^2 = 276.89$
6	205	175.02	$(29.98)^2 = 898.70$
7	180	178.02	$(1.98)^2 = 3.92$
8	182	178.22	$(3.78)^2 = 14.31$
			Sum of errors squared = 1,526.46

$$\text{MSE} = \frac{\Sigma(\text{Forecast errors})^2}{n} = 1,526.54/8 = 190.8$$

Insight: Is this MSE = 190.8 good or bad? It all depends on the MSEs for other forecasting approaches. A low MSE is better because we want to minimize MSE. MSE exaggerates errors because it squares them.

Learning exercise: Find the MSE for $\alpha = .50$. [Answer: MSE = 195.24. The result indicates that $\alpha = .10$ is a better choice because we seek a lower MSE. Coincidentally, this is the same conclusion we reached using MAD in Example 4.]

Related problems: 4.8d, 4.14, 4.20

A drawback of using the MSE is that it tends to accentuate large deviations due to the squared term. For example, if the forecast error for period 1 is twice as large as the error for period 2, the squared error in period 1 is four times as large as that for period 2. Hence, using MSE as the measure of forecast error typically indicates that we prefer to have several smaller deviations rather than even one large deviation.

Mean Absolute Percent Error   A problem with both the MAD and MSE is that their values depend on the magnitude of the item being forecast. If the forecast item is measured in thousands, the MAD and MSE values can be very large. To avoid this problem, we can use the **mean absolute percent error (MAPE)**. This is computed as the average of the absolute difference between the forecasted and actual values, expressed as a percentage of the actual values. That is, if we have forecasted and actual values for n periods, the MAPE is calculated as:

Mean absolute percent error (MAPE)
The average of the absolute differences between the forecast and actual values, expressed as a percent of actual values.

$$\text{MAPE} = \frac{\sum_{i=1}^{n} 100 \left| \text{Actual}_i - \text{Forecast}_i \right| / \text{Actual}_i}{n} \qquad \text{(4-7)}$$

Example 6 illustrates the calculations using the data from Examples 4 and 5.

EXAMPLE 6

Determining the mean absolute percent error (MAPE)

The Port of Baltimore wants to now calculate the MAPE when $\alpha = .10$.

Approach: Equation (4-7) is applied to the forecast data computed in Example 4.

Solution:

Quarter	Actual Tonnage Unloaded	Forecast for $\alpha = .10$	Absolute Percent Error 100 (|error|/actual)
1	180	175.00	$100(5/180) = 2.78\%$
2	168	175.50	$100(7.5/168) = 4.46\%$
3	159	174.75	$100(15.75/159) = 9.90\%$
4	175	173.18	$100(1.82/175) = 1.05\%$
5	190	173.36	$100(16.64/190) = 8.76\%$
6	205	175.02	$100(29.98/205) = 14.62\%$
7	180	178.02	$100(1.98/180) = 1.10\%$
8	182	178.22	$100(3.78/182) = 2.08\%$
			Sum of % errors = 44.75%

$$\text{MAPE} = \frac{\Sigma \text{ Absolute percent errors}}{n} = \frac{44.75\%}{8} = 5.59\%$$

Insight: MAPE expresses the error as a percent of the actual values, undistorted by a single large value.

Learning exercise: What is MAPE when α is .50? [Answer: MAPE = 6.75%. As was the case with MAD and MSE, the $\alpha = .1$ was preferable for this series of data.]

Related problems: 4.8e, 4.33c

The MAPE is perhaps the easiest measure to interpret. For example, a result that the MAPE is 6% is a clear statement that is not dependent on issues such as the magnitude of the input data.

Exponential Smoothing with Trend Adjustment

Simple exponential smoothing, the technique we just illustrated in Examples 3 to 6, is like any other moving-average technique: It fails to respond to trends. Other forecasting techniques that can deal with trends are certainly available. However, because exponential smoothing is such a popular modeling approach in business, let us look at it in more detail.

Here is why exponential smoothing must be modified when a trend is present. Assume that demand for our product or service has been increasing by 100 units per month and that we have been forecasting with $\alpha = 0.4$ in our exponential smoothing model. The following table shows a severe lag in the 2nd, 3rd, 4th, and 5th months, even when our initial estimate for month 1 is perfect:

Month	Actual Demand	Forecast for Month $T(F_T)$
1	100	$F_1 = 100$ (given)
2	200	$F_2 = F_1 + \alpha (A_1 - F_1) = 100 + .4(100 - 100) = 100$
3	300	$F_3 = F_2 + \alpha (A_2 - F_2) = 100 + .4(200 - 100) = 140$
4	400	$F_4 = F_3 + \alpha (A_3 - F_3) = 140 + .4(300 - 140) = 204$
5	500	$F_5 = F_4 + \alpha (A_4 - F_4) = 204 + .4(400 - 204) = 282$

To improve our forecast, let us illustrate a more complex exponential smoothing model, one that adjusts for trend. The idea is to compute an exponentially smoothed average of the data and then adjust for positive or negative lag in trend. The new formula is:

$$\text{Forecast including trend}(FIT_t) = \text{Exponentially smoothed forecast}(F_t) + \text{Exponentially smoothed trend}(T_t) \tag{4-8}$$

With trend-adjusted exponential smoothing, estimates for both the average and the trend are smoothed. This procedure requires two smoothing constants: α for the average and β for the trend. We then compute the average and trend each period:

F_t = α(Actual demand last period) + $(1 - \alpha)$(Forecast last period + Trend estimate last period)

or:

$$F_t = \alpha(A_{t-1}) + (1 - \alpha)(F_{t-1} + T_{t-1}) \qquad \text{(4-9)}$$

T_t = β(Forecast this period – Forecast last period)
            + $(1 - \beta)$(Trend estimate last period)

or:

$$T_t = \beta(F_t - F_{t-1}) + (1 - \beta)T_{t-1} \qquad \text{(4-10)}$$

where F_t = exponentially smoothed forecast of the data series in period t
        T_t = exponentially smoothed trend in period t
        A_t = actual demand in period t
        α = smoothing constant for the average $(0 \leq \alpha \leq 1)$
        β = smoothing constant for the trend $(0 \leq \beta \leq 1)$

So the three steps to compute a trend-adjusted forecast are:

Step 1: Compute F_t, the exponentially smoothed forecast for period t, using Equation (4-9).
Step 2: Compute the smoothed trend, T_t, using Equation (4-10).
Step 3: Calculate the forecast including trend, FIT_t, by the formula $FIT_t = F_t + T_t$.

Example 7 shows how to use trend-adjusted exponential smoothing.

EXAMPLE 7

Computing a trend-adjusted exponential smoothing forecast

A large Portland manufacturer wants to forecast demand for a piece of pollution-control equipment. A review of past sales, as shown below, indicates that an increasing trend is present:

Month (t)	Actual Demand (A_t)	Month (t)	Actual Demand (A_t)
1	12	6	21
2	17	7	31
3	20	8	28
4	19	9	36
5	24	10	?

Smoothing constants are assigned the values of α = .2 and β = .4. The firm assumes the initial forecast for month 1 (F_1) was 11 units and the trend over that period (T_1) was 2 units.

Approach: A trend-adjusted exponential smoothing model, using Equations (4-9) and (4-10) and the three steps above, is employed.

Solution:

Step 1:   Forecast for month 2:

$$F_2 = \alpha A_1 + (1 - \alpha)(F_1 + T_1)$$
$$F_2 = (.2)(12) + (1 - .2)(11 + 2)$$
$$= 2.4 + (.8)(13) = 2.4 + 10.4 = 12.8 \text{ units}$$

Step 2:   Compute the trend in period 2:

$$T_2 = \beta(F_2 - F_1) + (1 - \beta)T_1$$
$$= .4(12.8 - 11) + (1 - .4)(2)$$
$$= (.4)(1.8) + (.6)(2) = .72 + 1.2 = 1.92$$

Step 3:   Compute the forecast including trend (FIT_t):

$$FIT_2 = F_2 + T_2$$
$$= 12.8 + 1.92$$
$$= 14.72 \text{ units}$$

   Active Model 4.3

Example 7 is further illustrated in Active Model 4.3 on the CD-ROM.

We will also do the same calculations for the third month:

Step 1. $F_3 = \alpha A_2 + (1 - \alpha)(F_2 + T_2) = (.2)(17) + (1 - .2)(12.8 + 1.92)$
$= 3.4 + (.8)(14.72) = 3.4 + 11.78 = 15.18$

Step 2. $T_3 = \beta(F_3 - F_2) + (1 - \beta)T_2 = (.4)(15.18 - 12.8) + (1 - .4)(1.92)$
$= (.4)(2.38) + (.6)(1.92) = .952 + 1.152 = 2.10$

Step 3. $FIT_3 = F_3 + T_3$
$= 15.18 + 2.10 = 17.28.$

Table 4.1 completes the forecasts for the 10-month period.

▶ **Table 4.1**

Forecast with $\alpha = .2$
and $\beta = .4$

Month	Actual Demand	Smoothed Forecast, F_t	Smoothed Trend, T_t	Forecast Including Trend FIT_t
1	12	11	2	13.00
2	17	12.80	1.92	14.72
3	20	15.18	2.10	17.28
4	19	17.82	2.32	20.14
5	24	19.91	2.23	22.14
6	21	22.51	2.38	24.89
7	31	24.11	2.07	26.18
8	28	27.14	2.45	29.59
9	36	29.28	2.32	31.60
10	—	32.48	2.68	35.16

Insight: Figure 4.3 compares actual demand (A_t) to an exponential smoothing forecast that includes trend (FIT_t). FIT picks up the trend in actual demand. A simple exponential smoothing model (like we saw in Examples 3 and 4) trails far behind.

▶ **Figure 4.3**

Exponential Smoothing with Trend-Adjustment Forecasts Compared to Actual Demand Data

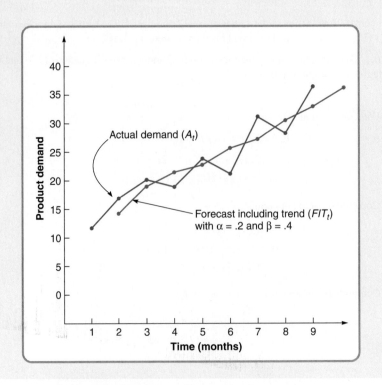

Learning exercise: Using the data for actual demand for the 9 months, compute the exponentially smoothed forecast *without* trend (using Equation (4-4) as we did earlier in Examples 3 and 4). Apply α = .2 and assume an initial forecast for month 1 of 11 units. Then plot the months 2–10 forecast values on Figure 4.3. What do you notice? [Answer: Month 10 forecast = 24.65. All the points are below and lag the trend-adjusted forecast.]

Related problems: 4.19, 4.20, 4.21, 4.22, 4.44

The value of the trend-smoothing constant, β, resembles the α constant because a high β is more responsive to recent changes in trend. A low β gives less weight to the most recent trends and tends to smooth out the present trend. Values of β can be found by the trial-and-error approach or by using sophisticated commercial forecasting software, with the MAD used as a measure of comparison.

Simple exponential smoothing is often referred to as *first-order smoothing*, and trend-adjusted smoothing is called *second-order*, or *double smoothing*. Other advanced exponential-smoothing models are also used, including seasonal-adjusted and triple smoothing, but these are beyond the scope of this book.[3]

Trend Projections

The last time-series forecasting method we will discuss is **trend projection**. This technique fits a trend line to a series of historical data points and then projects the line into the future for medium to long-range forecasts. Several mathematical trend equations can be developed (for example, exponential and quadratic), but in this section, we will look at *linear* (straight-line) trends only.

If we decide to develop a linear trend line by a precise statistical method, we can apply the *least-squares method*. This approach results in a straight line that minimizes the sum of the squares of the vertical differences or deviations from the line to each of the actual observations. Figure 4.4 illustrates the least-squares approach.

A least-squares line is described in terms of its *y*-intercept (the height at which it intercepts the *y*-axis) and its slope (the angle of the line). If we can compute the *y*-intercept and slope, we can express the line with the following equation:

$$\hat{y} = a + bx \qquad (4\text{-}11)$$

Trend projection

A time-series forecasting method that fits a trend line to a series of historical data points and then projects the line into the future for forecasts.

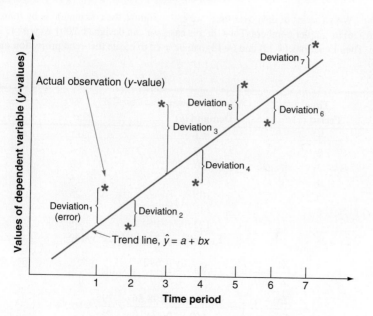

◀ **Figure 4.4**

The Least-Squares Method for Finding the Best-Fitting Straight Line, Where the Asterisks Are the Locations of the Seven Actual Observations or Data Points

[3]For more details, see D. Groebner, P. Shannon, P. Fry, and K. Smith, *Business Statistics*, 7th ed. (Upper Saddle River, NJ: Prentice Hall, 2008).

where $\hat{y}$ (called "y hat") = computed value of the variable to be predicted (called the *dependent variable*)

a = y-axis intercept

b = slope of the regression line (or the rate of change in y for given changes in x)

x = the independent variable (which in this case is *time*)

Statisticians have developed equations that we can use to find the values of a and b for any regression line. The slope b is found by:

$$b = \frac{\Sigma xy - n\bar{x}\bar{y}}{\Sigma x^2 - n\bar{x}^2}$$

(4-12)

where b = slope of the regression line

Σ = summation sign

x = known values of the independent variable

y = known values of the dependent variable

$\bar{x}$ = average of the x-values

$\bar{y}$ = average of the y-values

n = number of data points or observations

We can compute the y-intercept a as follows:

$$a = \bar{y} - b\bar{x}$$

(4-13)

Example 8 shows how to apply these concepts.

EXAMPLE 8

Forecasting with least squares

Excel OM Data File Ch04Ex8.xls

Active Model 4.4

Example 8 is further illustrated in Active Model 4.4 on the CD-ROM.

The demand for electric power at N.Y. Edison over the period 2001 to 2007 is shown in the following table, in megawatts. The firm wants to forecast 2008 demand by fitting a straight-line trend to these data.

Year	Electrical Power Demand	Year	Electrical Power Demand
2001	74	2005	105
2002	79	2006	142
2003	80	2007	122
2004	90		

Approach: With a series of data over time, we can minimize the computations by transforming the values of x (time) to simpler numbers. Thus, in this case, we can designate 2001 as year 1, 2002 as year 2, and so on. Then Equations (4-12) and (4-13) can be used to create the trend projection model.

Solution:

Year	Time Period (x)	Electric Power Demand (y)	x^2	xy
2001	1	74	1	74
2002	2	79	4	158
2003	3	80	9	240
2004	4	90	16	360
2005	5	105	25	525
2006	6	142	36	852
2007	7	122	49	854
	$\Sigma x = 28$	$\Sigma y = 692$	$\Sigma x^2 = 140$	$\Sigma xy = 3,063$

$$\bar{x} = \frac{\Sigma x}{n} = \frac{28}{7} = 4 \qquad \bar{y} = \frac{\Sigma y}{n} = \frac{692}{7} = 98.86$$

$$b = \frac{\Sigma xy - n\bar{x}\bar{y}}{\Sigma x^2 - n\bar{x}^2} = \frac{3,063 - (7)(4)(98.86)}{140 - (7)(4^2)} = \frac{295}{28} = 10.54$$

$$a = \bar{y} - b\bar{x} = 98.86 - 10.54(4) = 56.70$$

Thus, the least squares trend equation is $\hat{y} = 56.70 + 10.54x$. To project demand in 2008, we first denote the year 2008 in our new coding system as $x = 8$:

$$\text{Demand in } 2008 = 56.70 + 10.54(8)$$
$$= 141.02, \text{ or } 141 \text{ megawatts}$$

Insight: To evaluate the model, we plot both the historical demand and the trend line in Figure 4.5. In this case, we may wish to be cautious and try to understand the 2006 to 2007 swing in demand.

◀ **Figure 4.5**

Electrical Power and the Computed Trend Line

Learning exercise: Estimate demand for 2009. [Answer: 151.56 or 152 megawatts.]

Related problems: 4.6, 4.13c, 4.16, 4.25, 4.39, 4.49

Notes on the Use of the Least-Squares Method   Using the least-squares method implies that we have met three requirements:

1. We always plot the data because least-squares data assume a linear relationship. If a curve appears to be present, curvilinear analysis is probably needed.
2. We do not predict time periods far beyond our given database. For example, if we have 20 months' worth of average prices of Microsoft stock, we can forecast only 3 or 4 months into the future. Forecasts beyond that have little statistical validity. Thus, you cannot take 5 years' worth of sales data and project 10 years into the future. The world is too uncertain.
3. Deviations around the least-squares line (see Figure 4.4) are assumed to be random. They are normally distributed, with most observations close to the line and only a smaller number farther out.

Seasonal Variations in Data

Seasonal variations in data are regular up-and-down movements in a time series that relate to recurring events such as weather or holidays. Demand for coal and fuel oil, for example, peaks during cold winter months. Demand for golf clubs or sunscreen may be highest in summer.

   Seasonality may be applied to hourly, daily, weekly, monthly, or other recurring patterns. Fast-food restaurants experience *daily* surges at noon and again at 5 P.M. Movie theaters see higher demand on Friday and Saturday evenings. The post office, Toys "Я" Us, The Christmas Store, and Hallmark Card Shops also exhibit seasonal variation in customer traffic and sales.

Seasonal variations

Regular upward or downward movements in a time series that tie to recurring events.

► *Demand for many products is seasonal. Yamaha, the manufacturer of these jet skis and snowmobiles, produces products with complementary demands to address seasonal fluctuations.*

Because John Deere understands seasonal variations in sales, it has been able to obtain 70% of its orders in advance of seasonal use (through price reductions and incentives such as 0% interest) so it can smooth production.

Similarly, understanding seasonal variations is important for capacity planning in organizations that handle peak loads. These include electric power companies during extreme cold and warm periods, banks on Friday afternoons, and buses and subways during the morning and evening rush hours.

Time-series forecasts like those in Example 8 involve reviewing the trend of data over a series of time periods. The presence of seasonality makes adjustments in trend-line forecasts necessary. Seasonality is expressed in terms of the amount that actual values differ from average values in the time series. Analyzing data in monthly or quarterly terms usually makes it easy for a statistician to spot seasonal patterns. Seasonal indices can then be developed by several common methods.

In what is called a *multiplicative seasonal model*, seasonal factors are multiplied by an estimate of average demand to produce a seasonal forecast. Our assumption in this section is that trend has been removed from the data. Otherwise, the magnitude of the seasonal data will be distorted by the trend.

Here are the steps we will follow for a company that has "seasons" of 1 month:

1. Find the *average historical demand each season* (or month in this case) by summing the demand for that month in each year and dividing by the number of years of data available. For example, if, in January, we have seen sales of 8, 6, and 10 over the past 3 years, average January demand equals $(8 + 6 + 10)/3 = 8$ units.
2. Compute the *average demand over all months* by dividing the total average annual demand by the number of seasons. For example, if the total average demand for a year is 120 units and there are 12 seasons (each month), the average monthly demand is $120/12 = 10$ units.
3. Compute a *seasonal index* for each season by dividing that month's actual historical demand (from step 1) by the average demand over all months (from step 2). For example, if the average historical January demand over the past 3 years is 8 units and the average demand over all months is 10 units, the seasonal index for January is $8/10 = .80$. Likewise, a seasonal index of 1.20 for February would mean that February's demand is 20% larger than the average demand over all months.
4. Estimate next year's total annual demand.
5. Divide this estimate of total annual demand by the number of seasons, then multiply it by the seasonal index for that month. This provides the *seasonal forecast*.

Example 9 illustrates this procedure as it computes seasonal indices from historical data.

EXAMPLE 9

Determining seasonal indices

A Des Moines distributor of Sony laptop computers wants to develop monthly indices for sales. Data from 2005–2007, by month, are available.

Approach: Follow the five steps listed above.

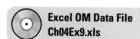

Solution:

Month	Demand 2005	2006	2007	Average 2005–2007 Demand	Average Monthly Demand[a]	Seasonal Index[b]
Jan.	80	85	105	90	94	.957 (= 90/94)
Feb.	70	85	85	80	94	.851 (= 80/94)
Mar.	80	93	82	85	94	.904 (= 85/94)
Apr.	90	95	115	100	94	1.064 (= 100/94)
May	113	125	131	123	94	1.309 (= 123/94)
June	110	115	120	115	94	1.223 (= 115/94)
July	100	102	113	105	94	1.117 (= 105/94)
Aug.	88	102	110	100	94	1.064 (= 100/94)
Sept.	85	90	95	90	94	.957 (= 90/94)
Oct.	77	78	85	80	94	.851 (= 80/94)
Nov.	75	82	83	80	94	.851 (= 80/94)
Dec.	82	78	80	80	94	.851 (= 80/94)

Total average annual demand = 1,128

[a]Average monthly demand = $\frac{1,128}{12 \text{ months}}$ = 94.   [b]Seasonal index = $\frac{\text{Average 2005–2007 monthly demand}}{\text{Average monthly demand}}$.

If we expected the 2008 annual demand for computers to be 1,200 units, we would use these seasonal indices to forecast the monthly demand as follows:

Month	Demand	Month	Demand
Jan.	$\frac{1,200}{12} \times .957 = 96$	July	$\frac{1,200}{12} \times 1.117 = 112$
Feb.	$\frac{1,200}{12} \times .851 = 85$	Aug.	$\frac{1,200}{12} \times 1.064 = 106$
Mar.	$\frac{1,200}{12} \times .904 = 90$	Sept.	$\frac{1,200}{12} \times .957 = 96$
Apr.	$\frac{1,200}{12} \times 1.064 = 106$	Oct.	$\frac{1,200}{12} \times .851 = 85$
May	$\frac{1,200}{12} \times 1.309 = 131$	Nov.	$\frac{1,200}{12} \times .851 = 85$
June	$\frac{1,200}{12} \times 1.223 = 122$	Dec.	$\frac{1,200}{12} \times .851 = 85$

Insight: Think of these indices as percentages of average sales. The average sales (without seasonality) would be 94, but with seasonality, sales fluctuate from 85% to 131% of average.

Learning exercise: If 2008 annual demand is 1,150 laptops (instead of 1,200), what will the January, February, and March forecasts be? [Answer: 92, 82, and 87.]

Related problems: 4.27, 4.28

For simplicity, only 3 periods are used for each monthly index in the preceding example. Example 10 illustrates how indices that have already been prepared can be applied to adjust trend-line forecasts for seasonality.

San Diego Hospital wants to improve its forecasting by applying both trend and seasonal indices to 66 months of data it has collected. It will then forecast "patient-days" over the coming year.

Approach: A trend line is created; then monthly seasonal indices are computed. Finally, a multiplicative seasonal model is used to forecast months 67 to 78.

EXAMPLE 10

Applying both trend and seasonal indices

Solution: Using 66 months of adult inpatient hospital days, the following equation was computed:

$$\hat{y} = 8,090 + 21.5x$$

where

$\hat{y}$ = patient days
x = time, in months

Based on this model, which reflects only trend data, the hospital forecasts patient days for the next month (period 67) to be:

Patient days = 8,090 + (21.5)(67) = 9,530 (trend only)

While this model, as plotted in Figure 4.6, recognized the upward trend line in the demand for inpatient services, it ignored the seasonality that the administration knew to be present.

▶ **Figure 4.6**

Trend Data for San Diego Hospital

Source: From "Modern Methods Improve Hospital Forecasting" by W. E. Sterk and E. G. Shryock from *Healthcare Financial Management*, Vol. 41, no. 3, p. 97. Reprinted by permission of Healthcare Financial Management Association.

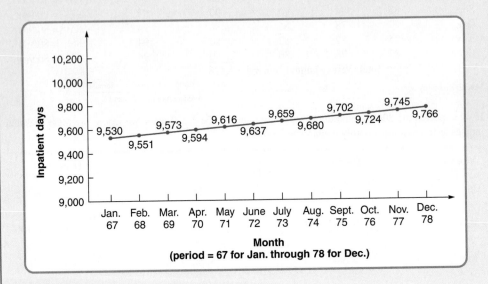

The following table provides seasonal indices based on the same 66 months. Such seasonal data, by the way, were found to be typical of hospitals nationwide.

Seasonality Indices for Adult Inpatient Days at San Diego Hospital

Month	Seasonality Index	Month	Seasonality Index
January	1.04	July	1.03
February	0.97	August	1.04
March	1.02	September	0.97
April	1.01	October	1.00
May	0.99	November	0.96
June	0.99	December	0.98

These seasonal indices are graphed in Figure 4.7. Note that January, March, July, and August seem to exhibit significantly higher patient days on average, while February, September, November, and December experience lower patient days.

However, neither the trend data nor the seasonal data alone provide a reasonable forecast for the hospital. Only when the hospital multiplied the trend-adjusted data times the appropriate seasonal index did it obtain good forecasts. Thus, for period 67 (January):

Patient days = (Trend-adjusted forecast) (Monthly seasonal index) = (9,530)(1.04) = 9,911

The patient days for each month are:

Period	67	68	69	70	71	72	73	74	75	76	77	78
Month	Jan.	Feb.	March	April	May	June	July	Aug.	Sept.	Oct.	Nov.	Dec.
Forecast with Trend & Seasonal	9,911	9,265	9,764	9,691	9,520	9,542	9,949	10,068	9,411	9,724	9,355	9,572

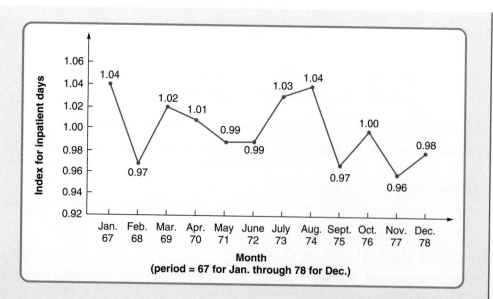

A graph showing the forecast that combines both trend and seasonality appears in Figure 4.8.

Insight: Notice that with trend only, the September forecast is 9,702, but with both trend and seasonal adjustments the forecast is 9,411. By combining trend and seasonal data the hospital was better able to forecast inpatient days and the related staffing and budgeting vital to effective operations.

Learning exercise: If the slope of the trend line for patient-days is 22.0 (rather than 21.5) and the index for December is .99 (instead of .98), what is the new forecast for December inpatient days? [Answer: 9,708.]

Related problems: 4.26, 4.29

Example 11 further illustrates seasonality for quarterly data at a department store.

Management at Davis's Department Store has used time-series regression to forecast retail sales for the next 4 quarters. Sales estimates are $100,000, $120,000, $140,000, and $160,000 for the respective quarters. Seasonal indices for the 4 quarters have been found to be 1.30, .90, .70, and 1.15, respectively.

Approach: To compute a seasonalized or adjusted sales forecast, we just multiply each seasonal index by the appropriate trend forecast:

$$\hat{y}_{\text{seasonal}} = \text{Index} \times \hat{y}_{\text{trend forecast}}$$

EXAMPLE 11

Adjusting trend data with seasonal indices

Solution: Quarter I: $\hat{y}_{I} = (1.30)(\$100,000) = \$130,000$

Quarter II: $\hat{y}_{II} = (.90)(\$120,000) = \$108,000$

Quarter III: $\hat{y}_{III} = (.70)(\$140,000) = \$98,000$

Quarter IV: $\hat{y}_{IV} = (1.15)(\$160,000) = \$184,000$

Insight: The straight-line trend forecast is now adjusted to reflect the seasonal changes.

Learning exercise: If the sales forecast for Quarter IV was 180,000 (rather than 160,000), what would be the seasonally adjusted forecast? [Answer: $207,000.]

Related problems: 4.26, 4.29

Cyclical Variations in Data

Cycles
Patterns in the data that occur every several years.

Cycles are like seasonal variations in data but occur every several *years*, not weeks, months, or quarters. Forecasting cyclical variations in a time series is difficult. This is because cycles include a wide variety of factors that cause the economy to go from recession to expansion to recession over a period of years. These factors include national or industrywide overexpansion in times of euphoria and contraction in times of concern. Demand forecasting cycles for individual products can also be driven by product life cycles—the stages products go through from introduction through decline. Life cycles exist for virtually all products; striking examples include floppy disks, video recorders, and the original Game Boy. We leave cyclical analysis to forecasting texts.

Developing associative techniques of variables that affect one another is our next topic.

ASSOCIATIVE FORECASTING METHODS: REGRESSION AND CORRELATION ANALYSIS

Unlike time-series forecasting, *associative forecasting* models usually consider *several* variables that are related to the quantity being predicted. Once these related variables have been found, a statistical model is built and used to forecast the item of interest. This approach is more powerful than the time-series methods that use only the historical values for the forecasted variable.

Many factors can be considered in an associative analysis. For example, the sales of Dell PCs may be related to Dell's advertising budget, the company's prices, competitors' prices and promotional strategies, and even the nation's economy and unemployment rates. In this case, PC sales would be called the *dependent variable*, and the other variables would be called *independent variables*. The manager's job is to develop *the best statistical relationship between PC sales and the independent variables*. The most common quantitative associative forecasting model is **linear-regression analysis**.

Linear-regression analysis
A straight-line mathematical model to describe the functional relationships between independent and dependent variables.

Using Regression Analysis for Forecasting

Learning Objective

6. Conduct a regression and correlation analysis

We can use the same mathematical model that we employed in the least squares method of trend projection to perform a linear-regression analysis. The dependent variables that we want to forecast will still be $\hat{y}$. But now the independent variable, x, need no longer be time. We use the equation:

$$\hat{y} = a + bx$$

where
$\hat{y}$ = value of the dependent variable (in our example, sales)
a = y-axis intercept
b = slope of the regression line
x = independent variable

Example 12 shows how to use linear regression.

EXAMPLE 12

Nodel Construction Company renovates old homes in West Bloomfield, Michigan. Over time, the company has found that its dollar volume of renovation work is dependent on the West Bloomfield area payroll. Management wants to establish a mathematical relationship to help predict sales.

Computing a linear regression equation

Approach: Nodel's VP of operations has prepared the following table, which lists company revenues and the amount of money earned by wage earners in West Bloomfield during the past 6 years:

 Excel OM Data File
Ch04Ex12.xls

Nodel's Sales (in $ millions), y	Local Payroll (in $ billions), x	Nodel's Sales (in $ millions), y	Local Payroll (in $ billions), x
2.0	1	2.0	2
3.0	3	2.0	1
2.5	4	3.5	7

The VP needs to determine whether there is a straight-line (linear) relationship between area payroll and sales. He plots the known data on a scatter diagram:

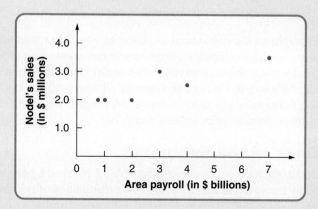

It appears from the six data points that there is a slight positive relationship between the independent variable (payroll) and the dependent variable (sales): As payroll increases, Nodel's sales tend to be higher.

Solution: We can find a mathematical equation by using the least-squares regression approach:

Sales, y	Payroll, x	x^2	xy
2.0	1	1	2.0
3.0	3	9	9.0
2.5	4	16	10.0
2.0	2	4	4.0
2.0	1	1	2.0
3.5	7	49	24.5
$\Sigma y = 15.0$	$\Sigma x = 18$	$\Sigma x^2 = 80$	$\Sigma xy = 51.5$

$$\bar{x} = \frac{\Sigma x}{6} = \frac{18}{6} = 3$$

$$\bar{y} = \frac{\Sigma y}{6} = \frac{15}{6} = 2.5$$

$$b = \frac{\Sigma xy - n\bar{x}\bar{y}}{\Sigma x^2 - n\bar{x}^2} = \frac{51.5 - (6)(3)(2.5)}{80 - (6)(3^2)} = .25$$

$$a = \bar{y} - b\bar{x} = 2.5 - (.25)(3) = 1.75$$

The estimated regression equation, therefore, is:

$$\hat{y} = 1.75 + .25x$$

or:

$$\text{Sales} = 1.75 + .25\ (\text{payroll})$$

If the local chamber of commerce predicts that the West Bloomfield area payroll will be $6 billion next year, we can estimate sales for Nodel with the regression equation:

$$\text{Sales (in \$ millions)} = 1.75 + .25(6)$$
$$= 1.75 + 1.50 = 3.25$$

or:

$$\text{Sales} = \$3,250,000$$

Insight: Given our assumptions of a straight-line relationship between payroll and sales, we now have an indication of the slope of that relationship: Sales increases at the rate of a million dollars for every quarter billion dollars in the local payroll. This is because $b = .25$.

Learning exercise: What are Nodel's sales when the local payroll is $8 billion? [Answer: $3.75 million.]

Related problems: 4.24, 4.30, 4.31, 4.32, 4.33, 4.35, 4.38, 4.40, 4.41, 4.46, 4.48, 4.49

The final part of Example 12 shows a central weakness of associative forecasting methods like regression. Even when we have computed a regression equation, we must provide a forecast of the independent variable x—in this case, payroll—before estimating the dependent variable y for the next time period. Although this is not a problem for all forecasts, you can imagine the difficulty of determining future values of *some* common independent variables (such as unemployment rates, gross national product, price indices, and so on).

Standard Error of the Estimate

The forecast of $3,250,000 for Nodel's sales in Example 12 is called a *point estimate* of y. The point estimate is really the *mean*, or *expected value*, of a distribution of possible values of sales. Figure 4.9 illustrates this concept.

Standard error of the estimate

A measure of variability around the regression line—its standard deviation.

To measure the accuracy of the regression estimates, we must compute the **standard error of the estimate**, $S_{y,x}$. This computation is called the *standard deviation of the regression:* It measures the error from the dependent variable, y, to the regression line, rather than to the mean. Equation (4-14) is a similar expression to that found in most statistics books for computing the standard deviation of an arithmetic mean:

$$S_{y,x} = \sqrt{\frac{\Sigma(y - y_c)^2}{n-2}}$$

(4-14)

where $y = y$-value of each data point
y_c = computed value of the dependent variable, from the regression equation
n = number of data points

▶ **Figure 4.9**

Distribution about the Point Estimate of $3.25 Million Sales

◀ *Glidden Paints' assembly lines fill thousands of cans per hour. To predict demand, the firm uses associative forecasting methods such as linear regression, with independent variables such as disposable personal income and GNP. Although housing starts would be a natural variable, Glidden found that it correlated poorly with past sales. It turns out that most Glidden paint is sold through retailers to customers who already own homes or businesses.*

Equation (4-15) may look more complex, but it is actually an easier-to-use version of Equation (4-14). Both formulas provide the same answer and can be used in setting up prediction intervals around the point estimate.[4]

$$S_{y,x} = \sqrt{\frac{\Sigma y^2 - a\Sigma y - b\Sigma xy}{n-2}}$$ (4-15)

Example 13 shows how we would calculate the standard error of the estimate in Example 12.

EXAMPLE 13

Computing the standard error of the estimate

Nodel's VP of operations now wants to know the error associated with the regression line computed in Example 12.

Approach: Compute the standard error of the estimate, $S_{y,x}$, using Equation (4-15).

Solution: The only number we need that is not available to solve for $S_{y,x}$ is Σy^2. Some quick addition reveals $\Sigma y^2 = 39.5$. Therefore:

$$
\begin{aligned}
S_{y,x} &= \sqrt{\frac{\Sigma y^2 - a\Sigma y - b\Sigma xy}{n-2}} \\
&= \sqrt{\frac{39.5 - 1.75(15.0) - .25(51.5)}{6-2}} \\
&= \sqrt{.09375} = .306 \text{ (in \$ millions)}
\end{aligned}
$$

The standard error of the estimate is then $306,000 in sales.

Insight: The interpretation of the standard error of the estimate is similar to the standard deviation; namely, ±1 standard deviation = .6827. So there is a 68.27% chance of sales being ±$306,000 from the point estimate of $3,250,000.

Learning exercise: What is the probability sales will exceed $3,556,000? [Answer: About 16%.]

Related problems: 4.41e, 4.48b

Correlation Coefficients for Regression Lines

The regression equation is one way of expressing the nature of the relationship between two variables. Regression lines are not "cause-and-effect" relationships. They merely describe the relationships among variables. The regression equation shows how one variable relates to the value and changes in another variable.

Another way to evaluate the relationship between two variables is to compute the **coefficient of correlation**. This measure expresses the degree or strength of the linear relationship. Usually

Coefficient of correlation

A measure of the strength of the relationship between two variables.

---

[4]When the sample size is large ($n > 30$), the prediction interval value of y can be computed using normal tables. When the number of observations is small, the t-distribution is appropriate. See D. Groebner et al., *Business Statistics*, 7th ed. (Upper Saddle River, NJ: Prentice Hall, 2008).

▶ **Figure 4.10**

Four Values of the Correlation Coefficient

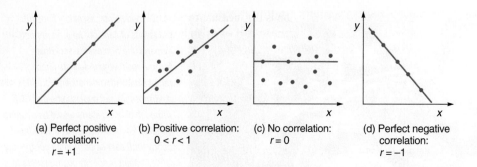

(a) Perfect positive correlation:
$r = +1$

(b) Positive correlation:
$0 < r < 1$

(c) No correlation:
$r = 0$

(d) Perfect negative correlation:
$r = -1$

identified as r, the coefficient of correlation can be any number between +1 and −1. Figure 4.10 illustrates what different values of r might look like.

To compute r, we use much of the same data needed earlier to calculate a and b for the regression line. The rather lengthy equation for r is:

$$r = \frac{n\Sigma xy - \Sigma x\Sigma y}{\sqrt{[n\Sigma x^2 - (\Sigma x)^2][n\Sigma y^2 - (\Sigma y)^2]}}$$

(4-16)

Example 14 shows how to calculate the coefficient of correlation for the data given in Examples 12 and 13.

EXAMPLE 14

Determining the coefficient of correlation

In Example 12, we looked at the relationship between Nodel Construction Company's renovation sales and payroll in its hometown of West Bloomfield. The VP now wants to know the strength of the association between local payroll and sales.

Approach: We compute the r value using Equation 4-16. We need to first add one more column of calculations—for y^2.

Solution: The data, including the column for y^2 and the calculations, are shown here:

y	x	x^2	xy	y^2
2.0	1	1	2.0	4.0
3.0	3	9	9.0	9.0
2.5	4	16	10.0	6.25
2.0	2	4	4.0	4.0
2.0	1	1	2.0	4.0
3.5	7	49	24.5	12.25
$\Sigma y = 15.0$	$\Sigma x = 18$	$\Sigma x^2 = 80$	$\Sigma xy = 51.5$	$\Sigma y^2 = 39.5$

> A high r doesn't always mean one variable will be a good predictor of the other. skirt lengths and stock market prices may be correlated, but a rise in one doesn't mean the other will also go up.

$$r = \frac{(6)(51.5) - (18)(15.0)}{\sqrt{[(6)(80) - (18)^2][(6)(39.5) - (15.0)^2]}}$$

$$= \frac{309 - 270}{\sqrt{(156)(12)}} = \frac{39}{\sqrt{1,872}}$$

$$= \frac{39}{43.3} = .901$$

Insight: This r of .901 appears to be a significant correlation and helps confirm the closeness of the relationship between the two variables.

Learning exercise: If the coefficient of correlation was −.901 rather than +.901, what would this tell you? [Answer: The negative correlation would tell you that as payroll went up, Nodel's sales went down—a rather unlikely occurrence that would suggest you recheck your math.]

Related problems: 4.24d, 4.35d, 4.38c, 4.41f, 4.48b

Although the coefficient of correlation is the measure most commonly used to describe the relationship between two variables, another measure does exist. It is called the **coefficient of determination** and is simply the square of the coefficient of correlation—namely, r^2. The value of r^2 will always be a positive number in the range $0 \leq r^2 \leq 1$. The coefficient of determination is the percent of variation in the dependent variable (y) that is explained by the regression equation. In Nodel's case, the value of r^2 is .81, indicating that 81% of the total variation is explained by the regression equation.

Coefficient of determination
A measure of the amount of variation in the dependent variable about its mean that is explained by the regression equation.

Multiple-Regression Analysis

Multiple regression is a practical extension of the simple regression model we just explored. It allows us to build a model with several independent variables instead of just one variable. For example, if Nodel Construction wanted to include average annual interest rates in its model for forecasting renovation sales, the proper equation would be:

Multiple regression
An associative forecasting method with more than one independent variable.

$$\hat{y} = a + b_1 x_1 + b_2 x_2 \tag{4-17}$$

where
$\hat{y}$ = dependent variable, sales
a = a constant, the y intercept
x_1 and x_2 = values of the two independent variables, area payroll and interest rates, respectively
b_1 and b_2 = coefficients for the two independent variables

The mathematics of multiple regression becomes quite complex (and is usually tackled by computer), so we leave the formulas for a, b_1, and b_2 to statistics textbooks. However, Example 15 shows how to interpret Equation (4-17) in forecasting Nodel's sales.

> **EXAMPLE 15**
>
> **Using a multiple-regression equation**
>
> Nodel Construction wants to see the impact of a second independent variable, interest rates, on its sales.
>
> *Approach:*   The new multiple-regression line for Nodel Construction, calculated by computer software, is:
>
> $$\hat{y} = 1.80 + .30x_1 - 5.0x_2$$
>
> We also find that the new coefficient of correlation is .96, implying the inclusion of the variable x_2, interest rates, adds even more strength to the linear relationship.
>
> *Solution:*   We can now estimate Nodel's sales if we substitute values for next year's payroll and interest rate. If West Bloomfield's payroll will be $6 billion and the interest rate will be .12 (12%), sales will be forecast as:
>
> $$\text{Sales (\$ millions)} = 1.80 + .30(6) - 5.0(.12)$$
> $$= 1.8 + 1.8 - .6$$
> $$= 3.00$$
>
> or:
>
> $$\text{Sales} = \$3,000,000$$
>
> *Insight:*   By using both variables, payroll and interest rates, Nodel now has a sales forecast of $3 million and a higher coefficient of correlation. This suggests a stronger relationship between the two variables and a more accurate estimate of sales.
>
> *Learning exercise:*   If interest rates were only 6%, what would be the sales forecast? [Answer: $3,300,000.]
>
> *Related problems:*   4.34, 4.36

MONITORING AND CONTROLLING FORECASTS

Once a forecast has been completed, it should not be forgotten. No manager wants to be reminded that his or her forecast is horribly inaccurate, but a firm needs to determine why actual demand (or whatever variable is being examined) differed significantly from that projected.

If the forecaster is accurate, that individual usually makes sure that everyone is aware of his or her talents. Very seldom does one read articles in *Fortune*, *Forbes*, or *The Wall Street Journal*, however, about money managers who are consistently off by 25% in their stock market forecasts.

One way to monitor forecasts to ensure that they are performing well is to use a tracking signal. A **tracking signal** is a measurement of how well a forecast is predicting actual values. As forecasts are updated every week, month, or quarter, the newly available demand data are compared to the forecast values.

The tracking signal is computed as the *running sum of the forecast errors (RSFE)* divided by the *mean absolute deviation (MAD)*:

$$
\begin{pmatrix} \text{Tracking} \\ \text{signal} \end{pmatrix} = \frac{\text{RSFE}}{\text{MAD}}
$$

$$
= \frac{\Sigma(\text{Actual demand in period } i - \text{Forecast demand in period } i)}{\text{MAD}}
$$

(4-18)

where

$$
\text{MAD} = \frac{\Sigma \left| \text{Actual} - \text{Forecast} \right|}{n}
$$

as seen earlier in Equation (4-5).

Positive tracking signals indicate that demand is *greater* than forecast. *Negative* signals mean that demand is *less* than forecast. A good tracking signal—that is, one with a low RSFE—has about as much positive error as it has negative error. In other words, small deviations are okay, but positive and negative errors should balance one another so that the tracking signal centers closely around zero. A consistent tendency for forecasts to be greater or less than the actual values (that is, for a high RSFE) is called a **bias** error. Bias can occur if, for example, the wrong variables or trend line are used or if a seasonal index is misapplied.

Once tracking signals are calculated, they are compared with predetermined control limits. When a tracking signal exceeds an upper or lower limit, there is a problem with the forecasting method, and management may want to reevaluate the way it forecasts demand. Figure 4.11 shows the graph of a tracking signal that is exceeding the range of acceptable variation. If the model being used is exponential smoothing, perhaps the smoothing constant needs to be readjusted.

How do firms decide what the upper and lower tracking limits should be? There is no single answer, but they try to find reasonable values—in other words, limits not so low as to be triggered with every small forecast error and not so high as to allow bad forecasts to be regularly overlooked. One MAD is equivalent to approximately .8 standard deviation, ±2 MADs = ±1.6 standard deviations, ±3 MADs = ±2.4 standard deviations, and ±4 MADs = ±3.2 standard deviations. This fact suggests that for a forecast to be "in control," 89% of the errors are expected to fall within ±2 MADs, 98% within ±3 MADs, or 99.9% within ±4 MADs.[5]

Example 16 shows how the tracking signal and RSFE can be computed.

Tracking signal

A measurement of how well the forecast is predicting actual values.

Bias

A forecast that is consistently higher or consistently lower than actual values of a time series.

Learning Objective

7. Use a tracking signal

▶ **Figure 4.11**

A Plot of Tracking Signals

---

[5]To prove these three percentages to yourself, just set up a normal curve for ±1.6 standard deviations (*z*-values). Using the normal table in Appendix I, you find that the area under the curve is .89. This represents ±2 MADs. Likewise, ±3 MADs = ±2.4 standard deviations encompass 98% of the area, and so on for ±4 MADs.

Carlson's Bakery wants to evaluate performance of its croissant forecast.

EXAMPLE 16

Computing the tracking signal at Carlson Bakery

Approach: Develop a tracking signal for the forecast and see if it stays within acceptable limits, which we define as ±4 MADs.

Solution: Using the forecast and demand data for the last 6 quarters for croissant sales, we develop a tracking signal in the table below:

Quarter	Actual Demand	Forecast Demand	Error	RSFE	Absolute Forecast Error	Cumulative Absolute Forecast Error	MAD	Tracking Signal (RSFE/MAD)
1	90	100	−10	−10	10	10	10.0	−10/10 = −1
2	95	100	−5	−15	5	15	7.5	−15/7.5 = −2
3	115	100	+15	0	15	30	10.0	0/10 = 0
4	100	110	−10	−10	10	40	10.0	−10/10 = −1
5	125	110	+15	+5	15	55	11.0	+5/11 = +0.5
6	140	110	+30	+35	30	85	14.2	+35/14.2 = +2.5

$$\text{At the end of quarter 6, MAD} = \frac{\Sigma |\text{Forecast errors}|}{n} = \frac{85}{6} = 14.2$$

$$\text{and Tracking signal} = \frac{\text{RSFE}}{\text{MAD}} = \frac{35}{14.2} = 2.5 \text{ MADs}$$

Insight: Because the tracking signal drifted from −2 MAD to +2.5 MAD (between 1.6 and 2.0 standard deviations), we can conclude that it is within acceptable limits.

Learning exercise: If actual demand in quarter 6 was 130 (rather than 140), what would be the MAD and resulting tracking signal? [Answer: MAD for quarter 6 would be 12.5, and the tracking signal for period 6 would be 2 MADs.]

Related problems: 4.37, 4.45

Adaptive Smoothing

Adaptive forecasting refers to computer monitoring of tracking signals and self-adjustment if a signal passes a preset limit. For example, when applied to exponential smoothing, the α and β coefficients are first selected on the basis of values that minimize error forecasts and then adjusted accordingly whenever the computer notes an errant tracking signal. This process is called **adaptive smoothing**.

Adaptive smoothing
An approach to exponential smoothing forecasting in which the smoothing constant is automatically changed to keep errors to a minimum.

Focus Forecasting

Rather than adapt by choosing a smoothing constant, computers allow us to try a variety of forecasting models. Such an approach is called focus forecasting. **Focus forecasting** is based on two principles:

1. Sophisticated forecasting models are not always better than simple ones.
2. There is no single technique that should be used for all products or services.

Bernard Smith, inventory manager for American Hardware Supply, coined the term *focus forecasting*. Smith's job was to forecast quantities for 100,000 hardware products purchased by American's 21 buyers.[6] He found that buyers neither trusted nor understood the exponential smoothing model then in use. Instead, they used very simple approaches of their own. So Smith developed his new computerized system for selecting forecasting methods.

Focus forecasting
Forecasting that tries a variety of computer models and selects the best one for a particular application.

[6]Bernard T. Smith, *Focus Forecasting: Computer Techniques for Inventory Control* (Boston: CBI Publishing, 1978).

Smith chose seven forecasting methods to test. They ranged from the simple ones that buyers used (such as the naive approach) to statistical models. Every month, Smith applied the forecasts of all seven models to each item in stock. In these simulated trials, the forecast values were subtracted from the most recent actual demands, giving a simulated forecast error. The forecast method yielding the least error is selected by the computer, which then uses it to make next month's forecast. Although buyers still have an override capability, American Hardware finds that focus forecasting provides excellent results.

FORECASTING IN THE SERVICE SECTOR

Forecasting in the service sector presents some unusual challenges. A major technique in the retail sector is tracking demand by maintaining good short-term records. For instance, a barbershop catering to men expects peak flows on Fridays and Saturdays. Indeed, most barbershops are closed on Sunday and Monday, and many call in extra help on Friday and Saturday. A downtown restaurant, on the other hand, may need to track conventions and holidays for effective short-term forecasting. The *OM in Action* box "Forecasting at FedEx's Customer Service Center" provides an example of a major service-sector industry, the call center.

Specialty Retail Shops Specialty retail facilities, such as flower shops, may have other unusual demand patterns, and those patterns will differ depending on the holiday. When Valentine's Day falls on a weekend, for example, flowers can't be delivered to offices, and those romantically inclined are likely to celebrate with outings rather than flowers. If a holiday falls on a Monday, some of the celebration may also take place on the weekend, reducing flower sales. However, when Valentine's Day falls in midweek, busy midweek schedules often make flowers the optimal way to celebrate. Because flowers for Mother's Day are to be delivered on Saturday or Sunday, this holiday forecast varies less. Due to special demand patterns, many service firms maintain records of sales, noting not only the day of the week but also unusual events, including the weather, so that patterns and correlations that influence demand can be developed.

Fast-Food Restaurants Fast-food restaurants are well aware not only of weekly, daily, and hourly but even 15-minute variations in demands that influence sales. Therefore, detailed forecasts of demand are needed. Figure 4.12(a) shows the hourly forecast for a typical fast-food

▲ **Figure 4.12** Forecasts Are Unique: Note the Variations Between (a) Hourly Sales at a Fast-Food Restaurant and (b) Hourly Call Volume at FedEx

*Based on historical data: see *Journal of Business Forecasting* (Winter 1999–2000): 6–11.

OM in Action   Forecasting at FedEx's Customer Service Centers

The world's largest express shipping company, FedEx, generates $30 billion in revenues, using 650 planes, 42,000 trucks, and a workforce of 145,000 in 210 countries. To support this global network, the company has 51 customer service call centers, whose service goal is to answer 90% of all calls within 20 seconds. With a half-million daily calls just in the U.S., FedEx makes extensive use of forecasting models for staffing decisions and to ensure that customer satisfaction levels stay the highest in the industry.

FedEx's Forecasting & Modeling department makes several different forecasts. *One-year* and *five-year* models predict number of calls, average handle time, and staffing needs. They break forecasts into weekday, Saturday, and Sunday and then use the Delphi method and time-series analysis.

FedEx's *tactical forecasts* are monthly and use 8 years of historical daily data. This time-series model addresses

month, day of week, and day of month to predict caller volume. Finally, the *operational forecast* uses a weighted moving average and 6 weeks of data to project the number of calls on a half-hourly basis.

FedEx's forecasts are consistently accurate to within 1% to 2% of actual call volumes. This means coverage needs are met, service levels are maintained, and costs are controlled.

Sources: Baseline (January 2005): 54; and *Journal of Business Forecasting* (Winter 1999–2000): 7–11.

restaurant. Note the lunchtime and dinnertime peaks. This contrasts to the 10:30 A.M. and 4:30 P.M. peaks at FedEx's call center in Figure 14.12(b).

Firms like Taco Bell now use point-of-sale computers that track sales every quarter hour. Taco Bell found that a 6-week moving average was the forecasting technique that minimized its mean squared error (MSE) of these quarter-hour forecasts. Building this forecasting methodology into each of Taco Bell's 6,500 stores' computers, the model makes weekly projections of customer transactions. These in turn are used by store managers to schedule staff, who begin in 15-minute increments, not 1-hour blocks as in other industries. The forecasting model has been so successful that Taco Bell has increased customer service while documenting more than $50 million in labor cost savings in 4 years of use.[7]

Summary

Forecasts are a critical part of the operations manager's function. Demand forecasts drive a firm's production, capacity, and scheduling systems and affect the financial, marketing, and personnel planning functions.

There are a variety of qualitative and quantitative forecasting techniques. Qualitative approaches employ judgment, experience, intuition, and a host of other factors that are difficult to quantify. Quantitative forecasting uses historical data and causal, or associative, relations to project future demands. Table 4.2 summarizes the formulas we introduced in quantitative forecasting. Forecast calculations are seldom performed by hand. Most operations managers turn to software packages such as Forecast PRO, SAP, tsMetrix, AFS, SAS, SPSS, or Excel.

No forecasting method is perfect under all conditions. And even once management has found a satisfactory approach, it must still monitor and control forecasts to make sure errors do not get out of hand. Forecasting can often be a very challenging, but rewarding, part of managing.

---

[7]J. Hueter and W. Swart, "An Integrated Labor Management System for Taco Bell," *Interfaces* 28, no. 1 (January-February 1998): 75–91.

▶ **Table 4.2**

Summary of Forecasting Formulas

Moving averages—forecasts based on an average of recent values

$$\text{Moving average} = \frac{\Sigma \text{ Demand in previous } n \text{ periods}}{n} \tag{4-1}$$

Weighted moving averages—a moving average with weights that vary

$$\text{Weighted moving average} = \frac{\Sigma \text{ (Weight for period } n)(\text{Demand in period } n)}{\Sigma \text{ Weights}} \tag{4-2}$$

Exponential smoothing—a moving average with weights following an exponential distribution

$$\text{New forecast} = \text{Last period's forecast} + \alpha \text{ (Last period's actual} \\ \text{demand} - \text{Last period's forecast)} \tag{4-3}$$

$$F_t = F_{t-1} + \alpha(A_{t-1} - F_{t-1}) \tag{4-4}$$

Mean absolute deviation—a measure of overall forecast error

$$\text{MAD} = \Sigma \,|\, \text{Actual} - \text{Forecast}\,|\,/n = \frac{\Sigma \,|\text{Forecast Errors}|}{n} \tag{4-5}$$

Mean squared error—a second measure of forecast error

$$\text{MSE} = \frac{\Sigma(\text{Forecast errors})^2}{n} \tag{4-6}$$

Mean absolute percent error—a third measure of forecast error

$$\text{MAPE} = \frac{\displaystyle\sum_{i=1}^{n} 100 \,|\text{Actual}_i - \text{Forecast}_i|\,/\,\text{Actual}_i}{n} \tag{4-7}$$

Exponential smoothing with trend adjustment—an exponential smoothing model that can accommodate trend

$$\text{Forecast including trend}(FIT_t) = \text{Exponentially smoothed forecast}(F_t) \\ + \text{Exponentially smoothed trend}(T_t) \tag{4-8}$$

$$F_t = \alpha(A_{t-1}) + (1 - \alpha)(F_{t-1} + T_{t-1}) \tag{4-9}$$

$$T_t = \beta(F_t - F_{t-1}) + (1 - \beta)T_{t-1} \tag{4-10}$$

Trend projection and regression analysis—fitting a trend line to historical data or a regression line to an independent variable

$$\hat{y} = a + bx \tag{4-11}$$

$$b = \frac{\Sigma xy - n\bar{x}\,\bar{y}}{\Sigma x^2 - n\bar{x}^2} \tag{4-12}$$

$$a = \bar{y} - b\bar{x} \tag{4-13}$$

Multiple regression analysis—a regression model with more than one independent (predicting) variable

$$\hat{y} = a + b_1 x_1 + b_2 x_2 + \quad + b_n x_n \tag{4-17}$$

Tracking signal—a measurement of how well the forecast is predicting actual values

$$\text{Tracking signal} = \frac{\text{RSFE}}{\text{MAD}} = \frac{\Sigma(\text{Actual demand in period } i - \text{Forecast demand in period } i)}{\text{MAD}} \tag{4-18}$$

Key Terms

Using Software in Forecasting

This section presents three ways to solve forecasting problems with computer software. First, you can create your own Excel spreadsheets to develop forecasts. Second, you can use the Excel OM software that comes with the text and is found on the student CD. Third, POM for Windows is another program that is located on the student CD.

Creating Your Own Excel Spreadsheets

Excel spreadsheets (and spreadsheets in general) are frequently used in forecasting. Exponential smoothing, trend analysis, and regression analysis (simple and multiple) are supported by built-in Excel functions.

Program 4.1 illustrates how to build an Excel forecast for the data in Example 8. The goal for N.Y. Edison is to create a trend analysis of the 2001–2007 data. Note that in cell D4 you can enter either = $B$16 + $B$17 * C4 *or* = TREND ($B$4: $B$10, $C$4: $C$10, C4).

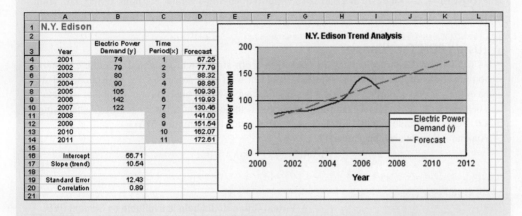

◀ **Program 4.1**

**Using Excel to Develop
Your Own Forecast with
Data from Example 8**

	Computations		
Value	**Cell**	**Excel Formula**	**Action**
Trend line column	D4	=$B$16+$B$17*C4	Copy to D5:D14
		(or =TREND($B$4:$B$10,$C$4:$C$10,C4))	
Intercept	B16	=INTERCEPT(B4:B10, C4:C10)	
Slope (trend)	B17	=SLOPE(B4:B10, C4:C10)	
Standard error	B19	=STEYX(B4:B10, C4:C10)	
Correlation	B20	=CORREL(B4:B10, C4:C10)	

As an alternative, you may want to experiment with Excel's built-in regression analysis. To do so, under the *Tools* menu bar selection choose *Data Analysis*, then *Regression*. Enter your Y and X data into two columns (say B and C). When the regression window appears, enter the Y and X ranges, then select *OK*. Excel offers several plots and tables to those interested in more rigorous analysis of regression problems.

X Using Excel OM

Excel OM's forecasting module has five components: (1) moving averages, (2) weighted moving averages, (3) exponential smoothing, (4) regression (with one variable only), and (5) decomposition. Excel OM's error analysis is much more complete than that available with the Excel add-in.

Program 4.2 illustrates Excel OM's input and output, using Example 2's weighted moving-average data.

Enter the weights to be placed on each of the last three periods at the top of column C: Weights must be entered from oldest to most recent.

Forecast is the weighted sum of past sales (SUMPRODUCT) divided by the sum of the weights (SUM) because weights do not sum to 1.

Error (B11 – E11) is the difference between the demand and the forecast.

= AVERAGE(H11: H19)

= SUMPRODUCT(B17:B19, $C$8:$C$10)/SUM($C$8:$C$10)

The standard error is given by the square root of the total error divided by *n* – 2, where *n* is the number of periods for which forecasts exist, i.e., 9.

▲ **Program 4.2**   Analysis of Excel OM's Weighted Moving-Average Program, Using Data from Example 2 as Input

P Using POM for Windows

POM for Windows can project moving averages (both simple and weighted), handle exponential smoothing (both simple and trend adjusted), forecast with least squares trend projection, and solve linear-regression (associative) models. A summary screen of error analysis and a graph of the data can also be generated. As a special example of exponential smoothing adaptive forecasting, when using an α of 0, POM for Windows will find the α value that yields the minimum MAD.

Appendix IV provides further details.

Solved Problems

Virtual Office Hours help is available on Student DVD.

Solved Problem 4.1

Sales of Volkswagen's popular Beetle have grown steadily at auto dealerships in Nevada during the past 5 years (see table below). The sales manager had predicted in 2002 that 2003 sales would be 410 VWs. Using exponential smoothing with a weight of $\alpha = .30$, develop forecasts for 2004 through 2008.

Year	Sales	Forecast
2003	450	410
2004	495	
2005	518	
2006	563	
2007	584	
2008	?	

Solution

Year	Forecast
2003	410.0
2004	$422.0 = 410 + .3 (450 - 410)$
2005	$443.9 = 422 + .3 (495 - 422)$
2006	$466.1 = 443.9 + .3 (518 - 443.9)$
2007	$495.2 = 466.1 + .3 (563 - 466.1)$
2008	$521.8 = 495.2 + .3 (584 - 495.2)$

Solved Problem 4.2

In Example 7, we applied trend-adjusted exponential smoothing to forecast demand for a piece of pollution-control equipment for months 2 and 3 (out of 9 months of data provided). Let us now continue this process for month 4. We want to confirm the forecast for month 4 shown in Table 4.1 (p. 120) and Figure 4.3 (p. 120).

For month 4, $A_4 = 19$, with $\alpha = .2$, and $\beta = .4$

solution

$$F_4 = \alpha A_3 + (1-\alpha)(F_3 + T_3)$$
$$= (.2)(20) + (1-.2)(15.18 + 2.10)$$
$$= 4.0 + (.8)(17.28)$$
$$= 4.0 + 13.82$$
$$= 17.82$$

$$T_4 = \beta(F_4 - F_3) + (1-\beta)T_3$$
$$= (.4)(17.82 - 15.18) + (1-.4)(2.10)$$
$$= (.4)(2.64) + (.6)(2.10)$$
$$= 1.056 + 1.26$$
$$= 2.32$$

$$FIT_4 = 17.82 + 2.32$$
$$= 20.14$$

Solved Problem 4.3

Room registrations in the Toronto Towers Plaza Hotel have been recorded for the past 9 years. To project future occupancy, management would like to determine the mathematical trend of guest registration. This estimate will help the hotel determine whether future expansion will be needed. Given the following time-series data, develop a regression equation relating registrations to time (e.g., a trend equation). Then forecast 2009 registrations. Room registrations are in the thousands:

1999: 17   2000: 16   2001: 16   2002: 21   2003: 20
2004: 20   2005: 23   2006: 25   2007: 24

solution

Year	Transformed Year, x	Registrants, y (in thousands)	x^2	xy
1999	1	17	1	17
2000	2	16	4	32
2001	3	16	9	48
2002	4	21	16	84
2003	5	20	25	100
2004	6	20	36	120
2005	7	23	49	161
2006	8	25	64	200
2007	9	24	81	216
	$\Sigma x = 45$	$\Sigma y = 182$	$\Sigma x^2 = 285$	$\Sigma xy = 978$

$$b = \frac{\Sigma xy - n\bar{x}\bar{y}}{\Sigma x^2 = n\bar{x}^2} = \frac{978 - (9)(5)(20.22)}{285 - (9)(25)} = \frac{978 - 909.9}{285 - 225} = \frac{68.1}{60} = 1.135$$

$$a = \bar{y} - b\bar{x} = 20.22 - (1.135)(5) = 20.22 - 5.675 = 14.545$$

$$\hat{y}(\text{registrations}) = 14.545 + 1.135x$$

The projection of registrations in the year 2009 (which is $x = 11$ in the coding system used) is:

$$\hat{y} = 14.545 + (1.135)(11) = 27.03$$

or 27,030 guests in 2009

Solved Problem 4.4

Quarterly demand for Ford F150 pickups at a New York auto dealer is forecast with the equation:

$$\hat{y} = 10 + 3x$$

where x = quarters, and:

$$
\begin{aligned}
\text{Quarter I of 2006} &= 0 \\
\text{Quarter II of 2006} &= 1 \\
\text{Quarter III of 2006} &= 2 \\
\text{Quarter IV of 2006} &= 3 \\
\text{Quarter I of 2007} &= 4 \\
&\text{and so on}
\end{aligned}
$$

and:

$$\hat{y} = \text{quarterly demand}$$

The demand for trucks is seasonal, and the indices for Quarters I, II, III, and IV are 0.80, 1.00, 1.30, and 0.90, respectively. Forecast demand for each quarter of 2008. Then, seasonalize each forecast to adjust for quarterly variations.

Solution

Quarter II of 2007 is coded $x = 5$; Quarter III of 2007, $x = 6$; and Quarter IV of 2007, $x = 7$. Hence, Quarter I of 2008 is coded $x = 8$; Quarter II, $x = 9$; and so on.

$$\hat{y}(2008 \text{ Quarter I}) = 10 + 3(8) = 34$$
$$\hat{y}(2008 \text{ Quarter II}) = 10 + 3(9) = 37$$
$$\hat{y}(2008 \text{ Quarter III}) = 10 + 3(10) = 40$$
$$\hat{y}(2008 \text{ Quarter IV}) = 10 + 3(11) = 43$$

$$\text{Adjusted forecast} = (.80)(34) = 27.2$$
$$\text{Adjusted forecast} = (1.00)(37) = 37$$
$$\text{Adjusted forecast} = (1.30)(40) = 52$$
$$\text{Adjusted forecast} = (.90)(43) = 38.7$$

Active Model Exercise

This active model, as well as the three others in this chapter, appears on your CD-ROM. It allows you to evaluate important elements of an exponential smoothing forecast.

▶ **Active Model 4.2**

Exponential Smoothing Using Data from Example 4

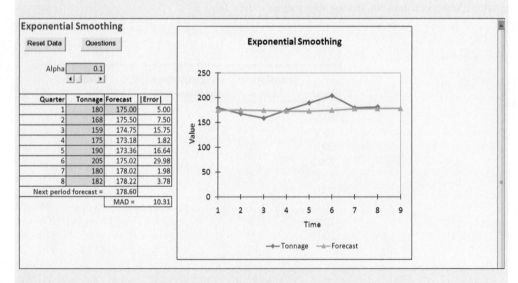

Questions

1. What happens to the graph when $\alpha = 0$?

2. What happens to the graph when $\alpha = 1$?

3. Generalize what happens to a forecast as alpha increases.

4. At what level of alpha is the mean absolute deviation (MAD) minimized?

Self-Test

- *Before taking the self-test*, refer to the learning objectives at the beginning of the chapter, the notes in the margins, and the glossary at the end of the chapter.
- *Use the key at the back of the book to **correct** your answers.*
- ***Restudy*** *pages that correspond to any questions you answered incorrectly or material you feel uncertain about.*

1. Forecasting time horizons include:
   a) long range
   b) medium range
   c) short range
   d) all of the above

2. Quantitative methods of forecasting include:
   a) sales force composite
   b) jury of executive opinion
   c) consumer market survey
   d) exponential smoothing
   e) all are quantitative methods

3. The method that considers the relationship between data and the variable being predicted is:
   a) exponential smoothing
   b) associative forecasting
   c) weighted moving average
   d) all of the above

4. Three popular measures of forecast accuracy are:
   a) total error, average error, and mean error
   b) average error, median error, and maximum error
   c) median error, minimum error, and maximum absolute error
   d) mean absolute error, mean squared error, and mean absolute percent error

5. In exponential smoothing, when the smoothing constant is high:
   a) more weight is placed on the more recent data
   b) less weight is placed on the more recent data
   c) the forecast will be a high number
   d) the forecast is a number between -1 and $+1$

6. With regard to a regression-based forecast, the *standard error of the estimate* gives a measure of:
   a) the overall accuracy of the forecast
   b) the time period for which the forecast is valid
   c) the time required to derive the forecast equation
   d) the maximum error of the forecast
   e) all of the above

7. The main difference between simple and multiple regression is _____.

8. The difference between a *moving average* model and an *exponential smoothing* model is that _____.

9. The purpose of drawing a scatter diagram is to _____.

Internet and Student CD-ROM/DVD Exercises

Visit our Companion Web site or use your student CD-ROM/DVD to help with material in this chapter.

 On Our Companion Web Site,
www.prenhall.com/heizer
- Self-Study Quizzes
- Practice Problems
- Virtual Company Tour
- Internet Case
- PowerPoint Lecture

 On Your Student CD-ROM
- Practice Problems
- Active Model Exercises
- Excel OM
- Excel OM Data Files
- POM for Windows

On Your Student DVD
- Video Clip and Video Case
- Virtual Office Hours for Solved Problems

Discussion Questions

1. What is a qualitative forecasting model, and when is its use appropriate?
2. Identify and briefly describe the two general forecasting approaches.
3. Identify the three forecasting time horizons. State an approximate duration for each.
4. Briefly describe the steps that are used to develop a forecasting system.
5. A skeptical manager asks what medium-range forecasts can be used for. Give the manager three possible uses/purposes.
6. Explain why such forecasting devices as moving averages, weighted moving averages, and exponential smoothing are not well suited for data series that have trends.
7. What is the basic difference between a weighted moving average and exponential smoothing?

8. What three methods are used to determine the accuracy of any given forecasting method? How would you determine whether time-series regression or exponential smoothing is better in a specific application?
9. Research and briefly describe the Delphi technique. How would it be used by an employer you have worked for?
10. What is the primary difference between a time-series model and an associative model?
11. Define time series.
12. What effect does the value of the smoothing constant have on the weight given to the recent values?
13. Explain the value of seasonal indices in forecasting. How are seasonal patterns different from cyclical patterns?
14. Which forecasting technique can place the most emphasis on recent values? How does it do this?

15. In your own words, explain adaptive forecasting.
16. What is the purpose of a tracking signal?
17. Explain, in your own words, the meaning of the correlation coefficient. Discuss the meaning of a negative value of the correlation coefficient.
18. What is the difference between a dependent and an independent variable?

19. Give examples of industries that are affected by seasonality. Why would these businesses want to filter out seasonality?
20. Give examples of industries in which demand forecasting is dependent on the demand for other products.
21. What happens to the ability to forecast for periods farther into the future?

Ethical Dilemma

In 2006, the board of regents responsible for all public higher education funding in a large Midwestern state hired a consultant to develop a series of enrollment forecasting models, one for each college. These models used historical data and exponential smoothing to forecast the following year's enrollments. Based on the model, which included a smoothing constant (α) for each school, each college's budget was set by the board. The head of the board personally selected each smoothing constant, based on what she called her "gut reactions and political acumen."

What do you think the advantages and disadvantages of this system are? Answer from the perspective of (a) the board of regents and (b) the president of each college. How can this model be abused and what can be done to remove any biases? How can a *regression model* be used to produce results that favor one forecast over another?

Problems*

• **4.1** The following gives the number of pints of type A blood used at Woodlawn Hospital in the past 6 weeks:

Week Of	Pints Used
August 31	360
September 7	389
September 14	410
September 21	381
September 28	368
October 5	374

a) Forecast the demand for the week of October 12 using a 3-week moving average.
b) Use a 3-week weighted moving average, with weights of .1, .3, and .6, using .6 for the most recent week. Forecast demand for the week of October 12.
c) Compute the forecast for the week of October 12 using exponential smoothing with a forecast for August 31 of 360 and $\alpha = .2$. **Px**

•• **4.2**

Year	1	2	3	4	5	6	7	8	9	10	11
Demand	7	9	5	9	13	8	12	13	9	11	7

a) Plot the above data on a graph. Do you observe any trend, cycles, or random variations?
b) Starting in year 4 and going to year 12, forecast demand using a 3-year moving average. Plot your forecast on the same graph as the original data.
c) Starting in year 4 and going to year 12, forecast demand using a 3-year moving average with weights of .1, .3, and .6, using .6 for the most recent year. Plot this forecast on the same graph.
d) As you compare forecasts with the original data, which seems to give the better results? **Px**

Note: **Px** means the problem may be solved with POM for Windows and/or Excel OM.

• **4.3** Refer to Problem 4.2. Develop a forecast for years 2 through 12 using exponential smoothing with $\alpha = .4$ and a forecast for year 1 of 6. Plot your new forecast on a graph with the actual data and the naive forecast. Based on a visual inspection, which forecast is better? **Px**

• **4.4** A check-processing center uses exponential smoothing to forecast the number of incoming checks each month. The number of checks received in June was 40 million, while the forecast was 42 million. A smoothing constant of .2 is used.
a) What is the forecast for July?
b) If the center received 45 million checks in July, what would be the forecast for August?
c) Why might this be an inappropriate forecasting method for this situation? **Px**

•• **4.5** The Carbondale Hospital is considering the purchase of a new ambulance. The decision will rest partly on the anticipated mileage to be driven next year. The miles driven during the past 5 years are as follows:

Year	Mileage
1	3,000
2	4,000
3	3,400
4	3,800
5	3,700

a) Forecast the mileage for next year using a 2-year moving average.
b) Find the MAD based on the 2-year moving average forecast in part (a). (Hint: You will have only 3 years of matched data.)
c) Use a weighted 2-year moving average with weights of .4 and .6 to forecast next year's mileage. (The weight of .6 is for the most recent year.) What MAD results from using this approach to forecasting? (Hint: You will have only 3 years of matched data.)
d) Compute the forecast for year 6 using exponential smoothing, an initial forecast for year 1 of 3,000 miles, and $\alpha = .5$. **Px**

•• **4.6** The monthly sales for Telco Batteries, Inc., were as follows:

Month	Sales
January	20
February	21
March	15
April	14
May	13
June	16
July	17
August	18
September	20
October	20
November	21
December	23

a) Plot the monthly sales data.
b) Forecast January sales using each of the following:
  i) Naive method.
  ii) A 3-month moving average.
  iii) A 6-month weighted average using .1, .1, .1, .2, .2, and .3, with the heaviest weights applied to the most recent months.
  iv) Exponential smoothing using an $\alpha = .3$ and a September forecast of 18.
  v) A trend projection.
c) With the data given, which method would allow you to forecast next March's sales? **PX**

• **4.7** The actual demand for the patients at Omaha Emergency Medical Clinic for the first six weeks of this year follows:

Week	Actual No. of Patients
1	65
2	62
3	70
4	48
5	63
6	52

Clinic administrator Marc Schniederjans wants you to forecast patient demand at the clinic for week 7 by using this data. You decide to use a weighted moving average method to find this forecast. Your method uses four actual demand levels, with weights of 0.333 on the present period, 0.25 one period ago, 0.25 two periods ago, and 0.167 three periods ago.
What is the value of your forecast? **PX**

• **4.8** Daily high temperatures in St. Louis for the last week were as follows: 93, 94, 93, 95, 96, 88, 90 (yesterday).
a) Forecast the high temperature today, using a 3-day moving average.
b) Forecast the high temperature today, using a 2-day moving average.
c) Calculate the mean absolute deviation based on a 2-day moving average.
d) Compute the mean squared error for the 2-day moving average.
e) Calculate the mean absolute percent error for the 2-day moving average. **PX**

••• **4.9** Dell uses the CR5 chip in some of its laptop computers. The prices for the chip during the last 12 months were as follows:

Month	Price per Chip	Month	Price per Chip
January	$1.80	July	1.80
February	1.67	August	1.83
March	1.70	September	1.70
April	1.85	October	1.65
May	1.90	November	1.70
June	1.87	December	1.75

a) Use a 2-month moving average on all the data and plot the averages and the prices.
b) Use a 3-month moving average and add the 3-month plot to the graph created in part (a).
c) Which is better (using the mean absolute deviation): the 2-month average or the 3-month average?
d) Compute the forecasts for each month using exponential smoothing, with an initial forecast for January of $1.80. Use $\alpha = .1$, then $\alpha = .3$, and finally $\alpha = .5$. Using MAD, which α is the best? **PX**

•• **4.10** Data collected on the yearly registrations for a Six Sigma seminar at the Quality College are shown in the following table:

Year	1	2	3	4	5	6	7	8	9	10	11
Registrations (000)	4	6	4	5	10	8	7	9	12	14	15

a) Develop a 3-year moving average to forecast registrations from year 4 to year 12.
b) Estimate demand again for years 4 to 12 with a 3-year weighted moving average in which registrations in the most recent year are given a weight of 2, and registrations in the other 2 years are each given a weight of 1.
c) Graph the original data and the two forecasts. Which of the two forecasting methods seems better? **PX**

• **4.11** a) Use exponential smoothing with a smoothing constant of 0.3 to forecast the registrations at the seminar given in Problem 4.10. To begin the procedure, assume that the forecast for year 1 was 5,000 people signing up.
b) What is the MAD? **PX**

•• **4.12** Consider the following actual and forecast demand levels for Big Mac hamburgers at a local McDonald's restaurant:

Day	Actual Demand	Forecast Demand
Monday	88	88
Tuesday	72	88
Wednesday	68	84
Thursday	48	80
Friday		

The forecast for Monday was derived by observing Monday's demand level and setting Monday's forecast level equal to this demand level. Subsequent forecasts were derived by using exponential smoothing with a smoothing constant of 0.25. Using this exponential smoothing method, what is the forecast for Big Mac demand for Friday? **PX**

••• **4.13** As you can see in the following table, demand for heart transplant surgery at Washington General Hospital has increased steadily in the past few years:

Year	1	2	3	4	5	6
Heart Transplants	45	50	52	56	58	?

The director of medical services predicted 6 years ago that demand in year 1 would be 41 surgeries.

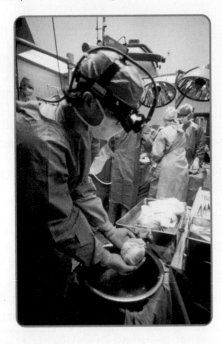

Time Period t	Actual Demand A_t	Forecast Demand F_t
1	50	50
2	42	50
3	56	48
4	46	50
5		

The first forecast, F_1, was derived by observing A_1 and setting F_1 equal to A_1. Subsequent forecasts were derived by exponential smoothing. Using the exponential smoothing method, find the forecast for time period 5. (Hint: You need to first find the smoothing constant, α.)

••• **4.19** Income at the law firm of Smith and Wesson for the period February to July was as follows:

Month	February	March	April	May	June	July
Income **(in \$ thousand)**	70.0	68.5	64.8	71.7	71.3	72.8

Use trend-adjusted exponential smoothing to forecast the law firm's August income. Assume that the initial forecast for February is \$65,000 and the initial trend adjustment is 0. The smoothing constants selected are $\alpha = .1$ and $\beta = .2$. **Px**

••• **4.20** Resolve Problem 4.19 with $\alpha = .1$ and $\beta = .8$. Using MSE, determine which smoothing constants provide a better forecast. **Px**

• **4.21** Refer to the trend-adjusted exponential smoothing illustration in Example 7 on pages 119–121. Using $\alpha = .2$ and $\beta = .4$, we forecast sales for 9 months, showing the detailed calculations for months 2 and 3. In Solved Problem 4.2, we continued the process for month 4.

In this problem, show your calculations for months 5 and 6 for F_t, T_t, and FIT_t. **Px**

• **4.22** Refer to Problem 4.21. Complete the trend-adjusted exponential-smoothing forecast computations for periods 7, 8, and 9. Confirm that your numbers for F_t, T_t, and FIT_t match those in Table 4.1 (p. 120). **Px**

•• **4.23** Sales of vegetable dehydrators at Bud Banis's discount department store in St. Louis over the past year are shown below. Management prepared a forecast using a combination of exponential smoothing and its collective judgment for the 4 months (March, April, May, and June of 2007):

Month	2006–2007 Unit Sales	Management's Forecast
July	100	
August	93	
September	96	
October	110	
November	124	
December	119	
January	92	
February	83	
March	101	120
April	96	114
May	89	110
June	108	108

a) Use exponential smoothing, first with a smoothing constant of .6 and then with one of .9, to develop forecasts for years 2 through 6.
b) Use a 3-year moving average to forecast demand in years 4, 5, and 6.
c) Use the trend-projection method to forecast demand in years 1 through 6.
d) With MAD as the criterion, which of the four forecasting methods is best? **Px**

•• **4.14** Following are two weekly forecasts made by two different methods for the number of gallons of gasoline, in thousands, demanded at a local gasoline station. Also shown are actual demand levels, in thousands of gallons:

	Forecasts		
Week	**Method 1**	**Method 2**	**Actual Demand**
1	0.90	0.80	0.70
2	1.05	1.20	1.00
3	0.95	0.90	1.00
4	1.20	1.11	1.00

What are the MAD and MSE for each method?

• **4.15** Refer to Solved Problem 4.1 on page 139. Use a 3-year moving average to forecast the sales of Volkswagen Beetles in Nevada through 2008. What is the MAD? **Px**

• **4.16** Refer to Solved Problem 4.1. Using the trend projection method, develop a forecast for the sales of Volkswagen Beetles in Nevada through 2008. What is the MAD? **Px**

• **4.17** Refer to Solved Problem 4.1. Using smoothing constants of .6 and .9, develop forecasts for the sales of VW Beetles. What effect did the smoothing constant have on the forecast? Use MAD to determine which of the three smoothing constants (.3, .6, or .9) gives the most accurate forecast. **Px**

•••• **4.18** Consider the following actual (A_t) and forecast (F_t) demand levels for a product:

a) Compute MAD and MAPE for management's technique.
b) Do management's results outperform (i.e., have smaller MAD and MAPE than) a naive forecast?
c) Which forecast do you recommend, based on lower forecast error?

•• **4.24** Howard Weiss, owner of a musical instrument distributorship, thinks that demand for bass drums may be related to the number of television appearances by the popular group Stone Temple Pilots during the previous month. Weiss has collected the data shown in the following table:

Demand for Bass Drums	3	6	7	5	10	7
Stone Temple Pilots' TV Appearances	3	4	7	6	8	5

a) Graph these data to see whether a linear equation might describe the relationship between the group's television shows and bass drum sales.
b) Use the least-squares regression method to derive a forecasting equation.
c) What is your estimate for bass drum sales if the Stone Temple Pilots performed on TV nine times last month?
d) What are the correlation coefficient (r) and the coefficient of determination (r^2) for this model, and what do they mean? **Px**

• **4.25** The following gives the number of accidents that occurred on Florida State Highway 101 during the last 4 months:

Month	Number of Accidents
January	30
February	40
March	60
April	90

Forecast the number of accidents that will occur in May, using least-squares regression to derive a trend equation. **Px**

• **4.26** In the past, Arup Mukherjee's tire dealership in Pensacola sold an average of 1,000 radials each year. In the past 2 years, 200 and 250, respectively, were sold in fall, 350 and 300 in winter, 150 and 165 in spring, and 300 and 285 in summer. With a major expansion planned, Mukherjee projects sales next year to increase to 1,200 radials. What will be the demand during each season?

•• **4.27** Mark Cotteleer owns a company that manufactures sailboats. Actual demand for Mark's sailboats during each season in 2004 through 2007 was as follows:

Season	Year			
	2004	2005	2006	2007
Winter	1,400	1,200	1,000	900
Spring	1,500	1,400	1,600	1,500
Summer	1,000	2,100	2,000	1,900
Fall	600	750	650	500

Mark has forecasted that annual demand for his sailboats in 2009 will equal 5,600 sailboats. Based on this data and the multiplicative seasonal model, what will the demand level be for Mark's sailboats in the spring of 2009?

•• **4.28** Attendance at Los Angeles's newest Disneylike attraction, Vacation World, has been as follows:

Quarter	Guests (in thousands)	Quarter	Guests (in thousands)
Winter '05	73	Summer '06	124
Spring '05	104	Fall '06	52
Summer '05	168	Winter '07	89
Fall '05	74	Spring '07	146
Winter '06	65	Summer '07	205
Spring '06	82	Fall '07	98

Compute seasonal indices using all of the data. **Px**

• **4.29** Central States Electric Company estimates its demand trend line (in millions of kilowatt hours) to be:

$$D = 77 + 0.43Q$$

where Q refers to the sequential quarter number and $Q = 1$ for winter 1984. In addition, the multiplicative seasonal factors are as follows:

Quarter	Factor (Index)
Winter	.8
Spring	1.1
Summer	1.4
Fall	.7

Forecast energy use for the four quarters of 2009, beginning with winter.

• **4.30** Brian Buckley has developed the following forecasting model:

$$\hat{y} = 36 + 4.3x$$

where $\hat{y}$ = demand for Aztec air conditioners and
 x = the outside temperature (°F)

a) Forecast demand for the Aztec when the temperature is 70°F.
b) What is demand when the temperature is 80°F?
c) What is demand when the temperature is 90°F? **Px**

•• **4.31** Coffee Palace's manager, Joe Felan, suspects that demand for mocha latte coffees depends on the price being charged. Based on historical observations, Joe has gathered the following data, which show the numbers of these coffees sold over six different price values:

Price	Number Sold
$2.70	760
$3.50	510
$2.00	980
$4.20	250
$3.10	320
$4.05	480

Using these data, how many mocha latte coffees would be forecast to be sold according to simple linear regression if the price per cup were $1.80? **Px**

• **4.32** The following data relate the sales figures of the bar in Marty and Polly Starr's small bed-and-breakfast inn in Marathon, Florida, to the number of guests registered that week:

Week	Guests	Bar Sales
1	16	$330
2	12	270
3	18	380
4	14	300

a) Perform a linear regression that relates bar sales to guests (not to time).
b) If the forecast is for 20 guests next week, what are the sales expected to be? **Px**

• **4.33** The number of transistors (in millions) made at a plant in Japan during the past 5 years follows:

Year	Transistors
1	140
2	160
3	190
4	200
5	210

a) Forecast the number of transistors to be made next year, using linear regression.
b) Compute the mean squared error (MSE) when using linear regression.
c) Compute the mean absolute percent error (MAPE). **Px**

• **4.34** The number of auto accidents in a certain region is related to the regional number of registered automobiles in thousands (X_1), alcoholic beverage sales in $10,000s (X_2), and rainfall in inches (X_3). Furthermore, the regression formula has been calculated as:

$$Y = a + b_1 X_1 + b_2 X_2 + b_3 X_3$$

where
Y = number of automobile accidents
$a = 7.5$
$b_1 = 3.5$
$b_2 = 4.5$
$b_3 = 2.5$

Calculate the expected number of automobile accidents under conditions a, b, and c:

	X_1	X_2	X_3
(a)	2	3	0
(b)	3	5	1
(c)	4	7	2

Px

•• **4.35** John Howard, a Mobile, Alabama, real estate developer, has devised a regression model to help determine residential housing prices in South Alabama. The model was developed using recent sales in a particular neighborhood. The price (Y) of the house is based on the size (square footage = X) of the house. The model is:

$$Y = 13,473 + 37.65X$$

The coefficient of correlation for the model is 0.63.
a) Use the model to predict the selling price of a house that is 1,860 square feet.

b) An 1,860-square-foot house recently sold for $95,000. Explain why this is not what the model predicted.
c) If you were going to use multiple regression to develop such a model, what other quantitative variables might you include?
d) What is the value of the coefficient of determination in this problem? **Px**

• **4.36** Accountants at the firm Michael Vest, CPAs, believed that several traveling executives were submitting unusually high travel vouchers when they returned from business trips. First, they took a sample of 200 vouchers submitted from the past year. Then they developed the following multiple-regression equation relating expected travel cost to number of days on the road (x_1) and distance traveled (x_2) in miles:

$$\hat{y} = \$90.00 + \$48.50x_1 + \$.40x_2$$

The coefficient of correlation computed was .68.
a) If Wanda Fennell returns from a 300-mile trip that took her out of town for 5 days, what is the expected amount she should claim as expenses?
b) Fennell submitted a reimbursement request for $685. What should the accountant do?
c) Should any other variables be included? Which ones? Why? **P**

•• **4.37** Sales of music stands at Johnny Ho's music store in Columbus, Ohio, over the past 10 weeks are shown in the table below. Forecast demand for each week, including week 10, using exponential smoothing with $\alpha = .5$ (initial forecast = 20):

Week	Demand	Week	Demand
1	20	6	29
2	21	7	36
3	28	8	22
4	37	9	25
5	25	10	28

a) Compute the MAD.
b) Compute the tracking signal. **Px**

•• **4.38** City government has collected the following data on annual sales tax collections and new car registrations:

Annual Sales Tax Collections (in millions)	1.0	1.4	1.9	2.0	1.8	2.1	2.3
New Car Registrations (in thousands)	10	12	15	16	14	17	20

Determine the following:
a) The least-squares regression equation.
b) Using the results of part (a), find the estimated sales tax collections if new car registrations total 22,000.
c) The coefficients of correlation and determination. **Px**

•• **4.39** Dr. Susan Sweeney, a Providence psychologist, specializes in treating patients who are agoraphobic (i.e., afraid to leave their homes). The following table indicates how many patients Dr. Sweeney has seen each year for the past 10 years. It also indicates what the robbery rate was in Providence during the same year:

Year	1	2	3	4	5	6	7	8	9	10
Number of Patients	36	33	40	41	40	55	60	54	58	61
Robbery Rate per 1,000 Population	58.3	61.1	73.4	75.7	81.1	89.0	101.1	94.8	103.3	116.2

Using trend analysis, predict the number of patients Dr. Sweeney will see in years 11 and 12. How well does the model fit the data? **Px**

•• **4.40** Using the data in Problem 4.39, apply linear regression to study the relationship between the robbery rate and Dr. Sweeney's patient load. If the robbery rate increases to 131.2 in year 11, how many phobic patients will Dr. Sweeney treat? If the robbery rate drops to 90.6, what is the patient projection? **Px**

••• **4.41** Bus and subway ridership for the summer months in London, England, is believed to be tied heavily to the number of tourists visiting the city. During the past 12 years, the following data have been obtained:

Year (summer months)	Number of Tourists (in millions)	Ridership (in millions)
1	7	1.5
2	2	1.0
3	6	1.3
4	4	1.5
5	14	2.5
6	15	2.7
7	16	2.4
8	12	2.0
9	14	2.7
10	20	4.4
11	15	3.4
12	7	1.7

a) Plot these data and decide if a linear model is reasonable.
b) Develop a regression relationship.
c) What is expected ridership if 10 million tourists visit London in a year?
d) Explain the predicted ridership if there are no tourists at all.
e) What is the standard error of the estimate?
f) What is the model's correlation coefficient and coefficient of determination? **Px**

••• **4.42** Des Moines Power and Light has been collecting data on demand for electric power in its western subregion for only the past 2 years. Those data are shown in the following table:

Demand in Megawatts		
Month	Last Year	This Year
January	5	17
February	6	14
March	10	20
April	13	23
May	18	30
June	15	38
July	23	44
August	26	41
September	21	33
October	15	23
November	12	26
December	14	17

To plan for expansion and to arrange to borrow power from neighboring utilities during peak periods, the utility needs to be able to forecast demand for each month next year. However, the standard forecasting models discussed in this chapter will not fit the data observed for the 2 years.
a) What are the weaknesses of the standard forecasting techniques as applied to this set of data?
b) Because known models are not appropriate here, propose your own approach to forecasting. Although there is no perfect solution to tackling data such as these (in other words, there are no 100% right or wrong answers), justify your model.
c) Forecast demand for each month next year using the model you propose.

••• **4.43** Emergency calls to the 911 system of Gainesville, Florida, for the past 24 weeks are shown in the following table:

Week	1	2	3	4	5	6	7	8	9	10	11	12
Calls	50	35	25	40	45	35	20	30	35	20	15	40
Week	13	14	15	16	17	18	19	20	21	22	23	24
Calls	55	35	25	55	55	40	35	60	75	50	40	65

a) Compute the exponentially smoothed forecast of calls for each week. Assume an initial forecast of 50 calls in the first week, and use $\alpha = .2$. What is the forecast for week 25?
b) Reforecast each period using $\alpha = .6$.
c) Actual calls during week 25 were 85. Which smoothing constant provides a superior forecast? Explain and justify the measure of error you used. **Px**

••• **4.44** Using the 911 call data in Problem 4.43, forecast calls for weeks 2 through 25 with a trend-adjusted exponential smoothing model. Assume an initial forecast for 50 calls for week 1 and an initial trend of zero. Use smoothing constants of $\alpha = .3$ and $\beta = .2$. Is this model better than that of Problem 4.43? What adjustment might be useful for further improvement? (Again, assume that actual calls in week 25 were 85.) **Px**

••• **4.45** The following are monthly actual and forecast demand levels for May through December for units of a product manufactured by the N. Tamimi Pharmaceutical Company:

Month	Actual Demand	Forecast Demand
May	100	100
June	80	104
July	110	99
August	115	101
September	105	104
October	110	104
November	125	105
December	120	109

What is the value of the tracking signal as of the end of December?

•• **4.46** Thirteen students entered the business program at Hillcrest College 2 years ago. The following table indicates what each student scored on the high school SAT math exam and their grade-point averages (GPAs) after students were in the Hillcrest program for 2 years.

a) Is there a meaningful relationship between SAT math scores and grades?
b) If a student scores a 350, what do you think his or her GPA will be?
c) What about a student who scores 800?

Student	A	B	C	D	E	F	G
SAT Score	421	377	585	690	608	390	415
GPA	2.90	2.93	3.00	3.45	3.66	2.88	2.15
Student	H	I	J	K	L	M	
SAT Score	481	729	501	613	709	366	
GPA	2.53	3.22	1.99	2.75	3.90	1.60	**Px**

••• **4.47** City Cycles has just started selling the new Z-10 mountain bike, with monthly sales as shown in the table. First, co-owner Amit wants to forecast by exponential smoothing by initially setting February's forecast equal to January's sales with $\alpha = .1$. Co-owner, Barbara wants to use a three-period moving average.

	Sales	Amit	Barbara	Amit's Error	Barbara's Error
January	400	—			
February	380	400			
March	410				
April	375				
May					

a) Is there a strong linear trend in sales over time?
b) Fill in the table with what Amit and Barbara each forecast for May and the earlier months, as relevant.
c) Assume that May's actual sales figure turns out to be 405. Complete the table's columns and then calculate the mean absolute deviation for both Amit's and Barbara's methods.
d) Based on these calculations, which method seems more accurate? **Px**

•• **4.48** Sundar Balakrishnan, the general manager of Precision Engineering Corporation (PEC), thinks that his firm's engineering services contracted to highway construction firms are directly related to the volume of highway construction business contracted with companies in his geographic area. He wonders if this is really so, and if it is, can this information help him plan his operations better by forecasting the quantity of his engineering services required by construction firms in each quarter of the year? The following table presents the sales of his services and total amounts of contracts for highway construction over the last 8 quarters:

Quarter	1	2	3	4	5	6	7	8
Sales of PEC Services (in $ thousands)	8	10	15	9	12	13	12	16
Contracts Released (in $ thousands)	153	172	197	178	185	199	205	226

a) Using this data, develop a regression equation for predicting the level of demand of Precision's services.
b) Determine the coefficient of correlation and the standard error of the estimate. **Px**

•••• **4.49** Salinas Savings and Loan is proud of its long tradition in Topeka, Kansas. Begun by Teresita Salinas 18 years after World War II, the S&L has bucked the trend of financial and liquidity problems that has plagued the industry since 1985. Deposits have increased slowly but surely over the years, despite recessions in 1983, 1988, 1991, and 2001. Ms. Salinas believes it is necessary to have a long-range strategic plan for her firm, including a 1-year forecast and preferably even a 5-year forecast of deposits. She examines the past deposit data and also peruses Kansas's gross state product (GSP), over the same 44 years. (GSP is analogous to gross national product [GNP] but on the state level.) The resulting data are in the following table:

Year	Deposits[a]	GSP[b]	Year	Deposits[a]	GSP[b]
1964	.25	.4	1986	6.2	2.5
1965	.24	.4	1987	4.1	2.8
1966	.24	.5	1988	4.5	2.9
1967	.26	.7	1989	6.1	3.4
1968	.25	.9	1990	7.7	3.8
1969	.30	1.0	1991	10.1	4.1
1970	.31	1.4	1992	15.2	4.0
1971	.32	1.7	1993	18.1	4.0
1972	.24	1.3	1994	24.1	3.9
1973	.26	1.2	1995	25.6	3.8
1974	.25	1.1	1996	30.3	3.8
1975	.33	.9	1997	36.0	3.7
1976	.50	1.2	1998	31.1	4.1
1977	.95	1.2	1999	31.7	4.1
1978	1.70	1.2	2000	38.5	4.0
1979	2.3	1.6	2001	47.9	4.5
1980	2.8	1.5	2002	49.1	4.6
1981	2.8	1.6	2003	55.8	4.5
1982	2.7	1.7	2004	70.1	4.6
1983	3.9	1.9	2005	70.9	4.6
1984	4.9	1.9	2006	79.1	4.7
1985	5.3	2.3	2007	94.0	5.0

[a]In $ millions.
[b]In $ billions.

a) Using exponential smoothing, with $\alpha = .6$, then trend analysis, and finally linear regression, discuss which forecasting model fits best for Salinas's strategic plan. Justify the selection of one model over another.
b) Carefully examine the data. Can you make a case for excluding a portion of the information? Why? Would that change your choice of model? **Px**

Case Studies

Southwestern University: (B)*

Southwestern University (SWU), a large state college in Stephenville, Texas, enrolls close to 20,000 students. The school is a dominant force in the small city, with more students during fall and spring than permanent residents.

Always a football powerhouse, SWU is usually in the top 20 in college football rankings. Since the legendary Bo Pitterno was hired as its head coach in 2001 (in hopes of reaching the elusive number 1 ranking), attendance at the five Saturday home games each year increased. Prior to Pitterno's arrival, attendance generally averaged 25,000 to 29,000 per game. Season ticket sales bumped up by 10,000 just with the announcement of the new coach's arrival. Stephenville and SWU were ready to move to the big time!

The immediate issue facing SWU, however, was not NCAA ranking. It was capacity. The existing SWU stadium, built in 1953, has seating for 54,000 fans. The following table indicates attendance at each game for the past 6 years.

One of Pitterno's demands upon joining SWU had been a stadium expansion, or possibly even a new stadium. With attendance increasing, SWU administrators began to face the issue head-on. Pitterno had wanted dormitories solely for his athletes in the stadium as an additional feature of any expansion.

SWU's president, Dr. Joel Wisner, decided it was time for his vice president of development to forecast when the existing stadium would "max out." The expansion was, in his mind, a given. But Wisner needed to know how long he could wait. He also sought a revenue projection, assuming an average ticket price of $20 in 2008 and a 5% increase each year in future prices.

Discussion Questions

1. Develop a forecasting model, justifying its selection over other techniques, and project attendance through 2009.
2. What revenues are to be expected in 2008 and 2009?
3. Discuss the school's options.

*This integrated case study runs throughout the text. Other issues facing Southwestern's football stadium include (A) managing the stadium project (Chapter 3); (C) quality of facilities (Chapter 6); (D) break-even analysis of food services (Supplement 7 web site); (E) locating the new stadium (Chapter 8 web site); (F) inventory planning of football programs (Chapter 12 web site); and (G) scheduling of campus security officers/staff for game days (Chapter 13).

Southwestern University Football Game Attendance, 2002–2007

Game	2002 Attendees	Opponent	2003 Attendees	Opponent	2004 Attendees	Opponent
1	34,200	Baylor	36,100	Oklahoma	35,900	TCU
2[a]	39,800	Texas	40,200	Nebraska	46,500	Texas Tech
3	38,200	LSU	39,100	UCLA	43,100	Alaska
4[b]	26,900	Arkansas	25,300	Nevada	27,900	Arizona
5	35,100	USC	36,200	Ohio State	39,200	Rice

Game	2005 Attendees	Opponent	2006 Attendees	Opponent	2007 Attendees	Opponent
1	41,900	Arkansas	42,500	Indiana	46,900	LSU
2[a]	46,100	Missouri	48,200	North Texas	50,100	Texas
3	43,900	Florida	44,200	Texas A&M	45,900	Prairie View A&M
4[b]	30,100	Miami	33,900	Southern	36,300	Montana
5	40,500	Duke	47,800	Oklahoma	49,900	Arizona State

[a]Homecoming games.

[b]During the 4th week of each season, Stephenville hosted a hugely popular southwestern crafts festival. This event brought tens of thousands of tourists to the town, especially on weekends, and had an obvious negative impact on game attendance.

Digital Cell Phone, Inc.

Paul Jordan has just been hired as a management analyst at Digital Cell Phone, Inc. Digital Cell manufactures a broad line of phones for the consumer market. Paul's boss, John Smithers, chief operations officer, has asked Paul to stop by his office this morning. After a brief exchange of pleasantries over a cup of coffee, he says he has a special assignment for Paul: "We've always just made an educated guess about how many phones we need to make each month. Usually we just look at how many we sold last month and plan to produce about the same number. This sometimes works fine. But most months we either have too many phones in inventory or we are out of stock. Neither situation is good."

Handing Paul the table shown here, Smithers continues, "Here are our actual orders entered for the past 36 months. There are 144 phones per case. I was hoping that since you graduated recently from the University of Alaska, you might have studied some techniques that would help us plan better. It's been awhile since I was in college—I think I forgot most of the details I learned then. I'd like you to analyze these data and give me an idea of what our business will look like over the next 6 to 12 months. Do you think you can handle this?"

"Of course," Paul replies, sounding more confident than he really is. "How much time do I have?"

"I need your report on the Monday before Thanksgiving—that would be November 20th. I plan to take it home with me and read it during the holiday. Since I'm sure you will not be around during the holiday, be sure that you explain things carefully so that I can understand your recommendation without having to ask you any more questions. Since you are new to the company, you should know that I like to see all the details and complete justification for recommendations from my staff."

With that, Paul was dismissed. Arriving back at his office, he began his analysis.

Orders Received by Month

Month	Cases 2005	Cases 2006	Cases 2007
January	480	575	608
February	436	527	597
March	482	540	612
April	448	502	603
May	458	508	628
June	489	573	605
July	498	508	627
August	430	498	578
September	444	485	585
October	496	526	581
November	487	552	632
December	525	587	656

Discussion Question

1. Prepare Paul Jordan's report to John Smithers using regression analysis. Provide a summary of the cell phone industry outlook as part of Paul's response.
2. Adding seasonality into your model, how does the analysis change?

Source: Professor Victor E. Sower, Sam Houston State University.

Forecasting at Hard Rock Cafe

Video Case

With the growth of Hard Rock Cafe—from one pub in London in 1971 to more than 110 restaurants in more than 40 countries today—came a corporatewide demand for better forecasting. Hard Rock uses long-range forecasting in setting a capacity plan and intermediate-term forecasting for locking in contracts for leather goods (used in jackets) and for such food items as beef, chicken, and pork. Its short-term sales forecasts are conducted each month, by cafe, and then aggregated for a headquarters view.

The heart of the sales forecasting system is the point-of-sale system (POS), which, in effect, captures transaction data on nearly every person who walks through a cafe's door. The sale of each entrée represents one customer; the entrée sales data are transmitted daily to the Orlando corporate headquarters' database. There, the financial team, headed by Todd Lindsey, begins the forecast process. Lindsey forecasts monthly guest counts, retail sales, banquet sales, and concert sales (if applicable) at each cafe. The general managers of individual cafes tap into the same database to prepare a daily forecast for their sites. A cafe manager pulls up prior years' sales for that day, adding information from the local Chamber of Commerce or Tourist Board on upcoming events such as a major convention, sporting event, or concert in the city where the cafe is located. The daily forecast is further broken into hourly sales, which drives employee scheduling. An hourly forecast of $5,500 in sales translates into 19 workstations, which are further broken down into a specific number of wait staff, hosts, bartenders, and kitchen staff. Computerized scheduling software plugs in people based on their availability. Variances between forecast and actual sales are then examined to see why errors occurred.

Hard Rock doesn't limit its use of forecasting tools to sales. To evaluate managers and set bonuses, a 3-year weighted moving average is applied to cafe sales. If cafe general managers exceed their

targets, a bonus is computed. Todd Lindsey, at corporate headquarters, applies weights of 40% to the most recent year's sales, 40% to the year before, and 20% to sales 2 years ago in reaching his moving average.

An even more sophisticated application of statistics is found in Hard Rock's menu planning. Using multiple regression, managers can compute the impact on demand of other menu items if the price of one item is changed. For example, if the price of a cheeseburger increases from $7.99 to $8.99, Hard Rock can predict the effect this will have on sales of chicken sandwiches, pork sandwiches, and salads. Managers do the same analysis on menu placement, with the center section driving higher sales volumes. When an item such as a hamburger is moved off the center to one of the side flaps, the corresponding effect on related items, say french fries, is determined.

Hard Rock's Moscow Cafe[a]

Month	1	2	3	4	5	6	7	8	9	10
Guest count (in thousands)	21	24	27	32	29	37	43	43	54	66
Advertising (in $ thousand)	14	17	25	25	35	35	45	50	60	60

[a]These figures are used for purposes of this case study.

Discussion Questions*

1. Describe three different forecasting applications at Hard Rock. Name three other areas in which you think Hard Rock could use forecasting models.
2. What is the role of the POS system in forecasting at Hard Rock?

3. Justify the use of the weighting system used for evaluating managers for annual bonuses.
4. Name several variables besides those mentioned in the case that could be used as good predictors of daily sales in each cafe.
5. At Hard Rock's Moscow restaurant, the manager is trying to evaluate how a new advertising campaign affects guest counts.

Using data for the past 10 months (see the table) develop a least squares regression relationship and then forecast the expected guest count when advertising is $65,000.

*You may wish to review this video case on your DVD before answering these questions.

Additional Case Studies

Internet Case Study: Visit our Companion Web site at www.prenhall.com/heizer *for this free case study:*

• **North–South Airline:** Reflects the merger of two airlines and addresses their maintenance costs.

Harvard has selected these Harvard Business School case studies to accompany this chapter:

harvardbusinessonline.hbsp.harvard.edu

• **Merchandising at Nine West Retail Stores** (# 698-098): This large retail shoe store chain faces a merchandising decision.
• **New Technologies, New Markets: The Launch of Hong Kong Telecom's Video-on-Demand** (# HKU-011): Asks students to examine the forecasting behind a new technology.
• **Sport Obermeyer Ltd.** (# 695-022): This skiwear company has short-life-cycle products with uncertain demand and a globally dispersed supply chain.
• **L.L. Bean, Inc.** (# 893-003): L.L. Bean must forecast and manage thousands of inventory items sold through its catalogs.

Bibliography

Balakrishnan, R., B. Render, and R. M. Stair. *Managerial Decision Modeling with Spreadsheets*, 2nd ed. Upper Saddle River, NJ: Prentice Hall, 2007.

Berenson, Mark, Tim Krehbiel, and David Levine. *Basic Business Statistics*, 10th ed. Upper Saddle River, NJ: Prentice Hall, 2006.

Diebold, F. X. *Elements of Forecasting*, 4th ed. Cincinnati: Southwestern College Publishing, 2007.

Georgoff, D. M., and R. G. Murdick. "Manager's Guide to Forecasting." *Harvard Business Review* 64 (January–February 1986): 110–120.

Gilliland, M. "Is Forecasting a Waste of Time?" *Supply Chain Management Review* 1 (July 2002).

Gilliland, M., and M. Leonard. "Forecasting Software—The Past and the Future." *The Journal of Business Forecasting* 25, no. 1 (Spring 2006): 33–36.

Hanke, J. E., A. G. Reitsch, and D. W. Wichern. *Business Forecasting*, 9th ed. Upper Saddle River, NJ: Prentice Hall, 2007.

Heizer, Jay. "Forecasting with Stagger Charts." *IIE Solutions* 34 (June 2002): 46–49.

Jain, C. L. "Benchmarking Forecasting Models." *The Journal of Business Forecasting* 24, no. 4 (Winter 2005/2006): 9–11.

Lapide, Larry. "Evolution of the Forecasting Function." *The Journal of Business Forecasting* 25, no. 1 (Spring 2006): 22–24.

Meade, Nigel. "Evidence for the Selection of Forecasting Models." *Journal of Forecasting* 19, no. 6 (November 2000): 515–535.

Portougal, V. "Demand Forecast for a Catalog Retailing Company." *Production and Inventory Management Journal* (first–second quarter 2002): 29–34.

Render, B., R. M. Stair, and M. Hanna. *Quantitative Analysis for Management*, 9th ed. Upper Saddle River, NJ: Prentice Hall, 2006.

Sanders, N. R., and K. B. Manrodt. "Forecasting Software in Practice." *Interfaces* 33 (September–October 2003): 90–93.

Snyder, Ralph D., and Roland G. Shami. "Exponential Smoothing of Seasonal Data." *Journal of Forecasting* 20, no. 3 (April 2001): 197–202.

Wilson, J. H., B. Keating, and J. Galt. *Business Forecasting with Forecast X Software*. New York: McGraw-Hill, 2007.

Internet Resources

American Statistical Association: **www.amstat.org**
Institute of Business Forecasting: **www.ibf.org**
International Institute of Forecasters: **www.forecasters.org**

Journal of Time Series Analysis: **www.blackwellpublishers.co.uk**
Royal Statistical Society: **www.rss.org.uk**

CHAPTER 5

Design of Goods and Services

Chapter Outline

Ten OM Strategy Decisions

Design of Goods and Services

Managing Quality

Process Strategy

Location Strategies

Layout Strategies

Human Resources

Supply Chain Management

Inventory Management

Scheduling

Maintenance

Learning Objectives

When you complete this chapter you should be able to

1. Define product life cycle
2. Describe a product development system
3. Build a house of quality
4. Describe how time-based competition is implemented
5. Describe how products and services are defined
6. Prepare the documents needed for production
7. Describe customer participation in the design and production of services
8. Apply decision trees to product issues

Product Strategy Provides Competitive Advantage at Regal Marine

Thirty years after its founding by potato farmer Paul Kuck, Regal Marine has become a powerful force on the waters of the world. The world's third-largest boat manufacturer (by global sales), Regal exports to 30 countries, including Russia and China. Almost one-third of its sales are overseas.

Product design is critical in the highly competitive pleasure boat business: "We keep in touch with our customers and we respond to the marketplace," says Kuck. "We're introducing six new models this year alone. I'd say we're definitely on the aggressive end of the spectrum."

With changing consumer tastes, compounded by material changes and ever-improving marine engineering, the design function is under constant pressure. Added to these pressures is the constant issue of cost competitiveness combined with the need to provide good value for customers.

Consequently, Regal Marine is a frequent user of computer-aided design (CAD). New designs come to life via Regal's three-dimensional CAD system, borrowed from automotive technology. Regal's naval architects' goal is to continue to reduce the time

▲ CAD/CAM is used to design the hull of a new product. This process results in faster and more efficient design and production.

◄ Once a hull has been pulled from the mold, it travels down a monorail assembly path. JIT inventory delivers engines, wiring, seats, flooring, and interiors when needed.

from concept to prototype to production. The sophisticated CAD system not only has reduced product development time but also has reduced problems with tooling and production, resulting in a superior product.

All of Regal's products, from its $14,000 19-foot boat to the $500,000 44-foot Commodore yacht, follow a similar production process. Hulls and decks are separately hand-produced by spraying preformed molds with three to five layers of a fiberglass laminate. The hulls and decks harden and are removed to become the lower and upper structure

► Here the deck, suspended from ceiling cranes, is being finished prior to being moved to join the hull.

◄ Larger boats, such as this luxurious Commodore 4260 Express, are water tested on a lake or ocean. Regal is one of the few boat builders in the world to earn the ISO 9001:2000 quality certification.

► At the final stage, smaller boats, such as this one, are placed in this test tank, where a rain machine ensures watertight fits.

of the boat. As they move to the assembly line, they are joined and components added at each workstation.

Wooden components, precut in-house by computer-driven routers, are delivered on a just-in-time basis for installation at one station. Engines—one of the few purchased components—are installed at another. Racks of electrical wiring harnesses, engineered and rigged in-house, are then installed. An in-house upholstery department delivers customized seats, beds, dashboards, or other cushioned components. Finally, chrome fixtures are put in place, and the boat is sent to Regal's test tank for watertight, gauge, and system inspection.

Global firms like Regal Marine know that the basis for an organization's existence is the good or service it provides society. Great products are the keys to success. Anything less than an excellent product strategy can be devastating to a firm. To maximize the potential for success, top companies focus on only a few products and then concentrate on those products. For instance, Honda's focus is engines. Virtually all of Honda's sales (autos, motorcycles, generators, lawn mowers) are based on its outstanding engine technology. Likewise, Intel's focus is on microprocessors and chips, and Microsoft's is PC software. However, because most products have a limited and even predictable life cycle, companies must constantly be looking for new products to design, develop, and take to market. Good operations managers insist on strong communication among customer, product, processes, and suppliers that results in a high success rate for their new products. 3M's goal is to produce 30% of its profit from products introduced in the last 4 years. Benchmarks, of course, vary by industry, but Regal introduces six new boats a year, and Rubbermaid introduces a new product each day!

One product strategy is to build particular competence in customizing an established family of goods or services. This approach allows the customer to choose product variations while reinforcing the organization's strength. Dell Computers, for example, has built a huge market by delivering computers with the exact hardware and software desired by end users. And Dell does it fast—it understands that speed to market is imperative to gain a competitive edge.

Note that many service firms also refer to their offerings as products. For instance, when Allstate Insurance offers a new homeowner's policy, it is referred to as a new "product." Similarly, when Citicorp opens a mortgage department, it offers a number of new mortgage "products." Although the term *products* may often refer to tangible goods, it also refers to offerings by service organizations.

An effective product strategy links product decisions with investment, market share, and product life cycle, and defines the breadth of the product line. The *objective of the* **product decision** *is to develop and implement a product strategy that meets the demands of the marketplace with a competitive advantage.* As one of the 10 decisions of OM, product strategy may focus on developing a competitive advantage via differentiation, low cost, rapid response, or a combination of these.

GOODS AND SERVICES SELECTION

Product Strategy Options Support Competitive Advantage

A world of options exists in the selection, definition, and design of products. Product selection is choosing the good or service to provide customers or clients. For instance, hospitals specialize in various types of patients and various types of medical procedures. A hospital's management may decide to operate a general-purpose hospital or a maternity hospital or, as in the case of the Canadian hospital Shouldice, to specialize in hernias. Hospitals select their products when they decide what kind of hospital to be. Numerous other options exist for hospitals, just as they exist for McDonald's or General Motors.

Service organizations like Shouldice Hospital *differentiate* themselves through their product. Shouldice differentiates itself by offering a distinctly unique and high-quality product. Its world-renowned specialization in hernia-repair service is so effective it allows patients to return to normal living in 8 days as opposed to the average 2 weeks—and with very few complications. The entire production system is designed for this one product. Local anesthetics are used; patients enter and leave the operating room on their own; rooms are spartan, and meals are served in a common dining room, encouraging patients to get out of bed for meals and join fellow patients in the lounge. As Shouldice has demonstrated, product selection affects the entire production system.

Taco Bell has developed and executed a *low-cost* strategy through product design. By designing a product (its menu) that can be produced with a minimum of labor in small kitchens, Taco Bell has developed a product line that is both low cost and high value. Successful product design has allowed Taco Bell to increase the food content of its products from 27¢ to 45¢ of each sales dollar.

Toyota's strategy is *rapid response* to changing consumer demand. By executing the fastest automobile design in the industry, Toyota has driven the speed of product development down to well under 2 years in an industry whose standard is still over 2 years. The shorter design time allows Toyota to get a car to market before consumer tastes change and to do so with the latest technology and innovations.

Product decisions are fundamental to an organization's strategy and have major implications throughout the operations function. For instance, GM's steering columns are a good example of the strong role product design plays in both quality and efficiency. The redesigned steering column has a simpler design, with about 30% fewer parts than its predecessor. The result: Assembly

Video 5.1

Product Strategy at
Regal Marine

Product decision

The selection, definition, and
design of products.

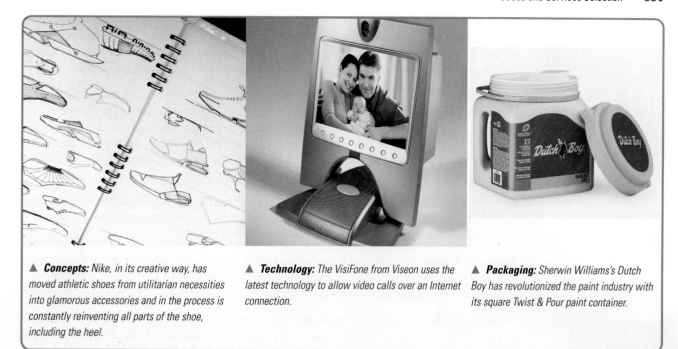

▲ **Concepts:** Nike, in its creative way, has moved athletic shoes from utilitarian necessities into glamorous accessories and in the process is constantly reinventing all parts of the shoe, including the heel.

▲ **Technology:** The VisiFone from Viseon uses the latest technology to allow video calls over an Internet connection.

▲ **Packaging:** Sherwin Williams's Dutch Boy has revolutionized the paint industry with its square Twist & Pour paint container.

▲ **Product Design Can Manifest Itself in Concepts, Technology, and Packaging.** Whether it is a design focused on style at Nike, the application of technology at Viseon, or a new container at Sherwin-Williams, operations managers need to remind themselves that the creative process is ongoing with major implications for production.

time is one-third that of the older column, and the new column's quality is about seven times higher. As an added bonus, machinery on the new line costs a third less than that in the old line.

Product Life Cycles

Products are born. They live and they die. They are cast aside by a changing society. It may be helpful to think of a product's life as divided into four phases. Those phases are introduction, growth, maturity, and decline.

Product life cycles may be a matter of a few hours (a newspaper), months (seasonal fashions and personal computers), years (video cassette tapes), or decades (Volkswagen Beetle). Regardless of the length of the cycle, the task for the operations manager is the same: to design a system that helps introduce new products successfully. If the operations function cannot perform effectively at this stage, the firm may be saddled with losers—products that cannot be produced efficiently and perhaps not at all.

Figure 5.1 shows the four life cycle stages and the relationship of product sales, cash flow, and profit over the life cycle of a product. Note that typically a firm has a negative cash flow while it develops a product. When the product is successful, those losses may be recovered. Eventually, the successful product may yield a profit prior to its decline. However, the profit is fleeting—hence, the constant demand for new products.

Learning Objective

1. Define product life cycle

Life Cycle and Strategy

Just as operations managers must be prepared to develop new products, they must also be prepared to develop *strategies* for new and existing products. Periodic examination of products is

◄ **Figure 5.1**

Product Life Cycle, Sales, Cost, and Profit

appropriate because *strategies change as products move through their life cycle*. Successful product strategies require determining the best strategy for each product based on its position in its life cycle. A firm, therefore, identifies products or families of products and their position in the life cycle. Let us review some strategy options as products move through their life cycles.

Introductory Phase   Because products in the introductory phase are still being "fine-tuned" for the market, as are their production techniques, they may warrant unusual expenditures for (1) research, (2) product development, (3) process modification and enhancement, and (4) supplier development. For example, when cellular phones were first introduced, the features desired by the public were still being determined. At the same time, operations managers were still groping for the best manufacturing techniques.

Growth Phase   In the growth phase, product design has begun to stabilize, and effective forecasting of capacity requirements is necessary. Adding capacity or enhancing existing capacity to accommodate the increase in product demand may be necessary.

Maturity Phase   By the time a product is mature, competitors are established. So high-volume, innovative production may be appropriate. Improved cost control, reduction in options, and a paring down of the product line may be effective or necessary for profitability and market share.

Decline Phase   Management may need to be ruthless with those products whose life cycle is at an end. Dying products are typically poor products in which to invest resources and managerial talent. Unless dying products make some unique contribution to the firm's reputation or its product line or can be sold with an unusually high contribution, their production should be terminated.[1]

Product-by-Value Analysis

Product-by-value analysis

A listing of products in descending order of their individual dollar contribution to the firm, as well as the *total annual dollar contribution* of the product.

The effective operations manager selects items that show the greatest promise. This is the Pareto principle (i.e., focus on the critical few, not the trivial many) applied to product mix: Resources are to be invested in the critical few and not the trivial many. **Product-by-value analysis** lists products in descending order of their *individual dollar contribution* to the firm. It also lists the *total annual dollar contribution* of the product. Low contribution on a per-unit basis by a particular product may look substantially different if it represents a large portion of the company's sales.

A product-by-value report allows management to evaluate possible strategies for each product. These may include increasing cash flow (e.g., increasing contribution by raising selling price or lowering cost), increasing market penetration (improving quality and/or reducing cost or price), or reducing costs (improving the production process). The report may also tell management which product offerings should be eliminated and which fail to justify further investment in research and development or capital equipment. The report focuses management's attention on the strategic direction for each product.

GENERATING NEW PRODUCTS

Because products die; because products must be weeded out and replaced; because firms generate most of their revenue and profit from new products— product selection, definition, and design take place on a continuing basis. Consider recent product changes: TV to HDTV, radio to satellite radio, coffee shops to Starbucks lifestyle coffee, traveling circuses to Cirque du Soleil, land lines to cell phones, cell phone to Blackberry, Walkman to iPod, mops to Swiffers—and the list goes on. Knowing how to successfully find and develop new products is a requirement.

New Product Opportunities

"Companies that are successful today . . . are those that can get closest to their customers' needs."

Federal Reserve Board

Aggressive new product development requires that organizations build structures internally that have open communication with customers, innovative organizational cultures, aggressive R&D, strong leadership, formal incentives, and training. Only then can a firm profitably and energetically focus on specific opportunities such as the following:

1. *Understanding the customer* is the premier issue in new-product development. Many commercially important products are initially thought of and even prototyped by users rather

---

[1]*Contribution* is defined as the difference between direct cost and selling price. Direct costs are labor and material that go into the product.

than producers. Such products tend to be developed by "lead users"—companies, organizations, or individuals that are well ahead of market trends and have needs that go far beyond those of average users.[2] The operations manager must be "tuned in" to the market and particularly these lead users.

2. *Economic change* brings increasing levels of affluence in the long run but economic cycles and price changes in the short run. In the long run, for instance, more and more people can afford automobiles, but in the short run, a recession may weaken the demand for automobiles.

3. *Sociological and demographic change* may appear in such factors as decreasing family size. This trend alters the size preference for homes, apartments, and automobiles.

4. *Technological change* makes possible everything from cell phones to iPods to artificial hearts.

5. *Political/legal change* brings about new trade agreements, tariffs, and government requirements.

6. Other changes may be brought about through *market practice*, *professional standards*, *suppliers*, and *distributors*.

Operations managers must be aware of these dynamics and be able to anticipate changes in product opportunities, the products themselves, product volume, and product mix.

Importance of New Products

The importance of new products cannot be overestimated. As Figure 5.2(a) shows, leading companies generate a substantial portion of their sales from products less than 5 years old.[3] Even Disney (Figure 5.2(b)) needs new theme parks to boost attendance. The need for new products is why Gillette developed its multi-blade razors, in spite of continuing high sales of its phenomenally successful Sensor razor and why Disney innovates in spite of being the leading family entertainment company in the world.

Despite constant efforts to introduce viable new products, many new products do not succeed. Indeed, for General Mills to come up with a winner in the breakfast cereal market—defined as a cereal that gets a scant half of 1% of the market—isn't easy. Among the top 10 brands of cereal, the youngest, Honey Nut Cheerios, was created in 1979. DuPont estimates that it takes 250 ideas to yield one *marketable* product.[4]

▼ **Figure 5.2** Innovation and New Products Yield Results for Both Goods and Services

(a) The higher the percentage of sales from the last 5 years, the more likely the firm is to be a leader.
(b) Disney World innovates with new parks, rides, and attractions to boost attendance.

Source: *Orlando Sentinel* (May 2, 2005): A8.

[2]Eric von Hipple, Stefan Thomke, and Mary Sonnack, "Creating Breakthroughs at 3M," *Harvard Business Review* 71, no. 5 (September–October 1999): 47–57.
[3]Barry L. Bayus, Gary Erickson, and Robert Jacobson, "The Financial Rewards of New Product Introductions in the Personal Computer Industry," *Management Science* 49, no. 2 (February 2003): 197–210.
[4]Rosabeth Kanter, John Kao, and Fred Wiersema, *Innovation Breakthrough Thinking at 3M, DuPont, GE, Pfizer, and Rubbermaid* (New York: Harper-Business, 1997).

▶ *The 3M Corporation has a strong internal culture of creativity, formal incentives, and a customer focus that has resulted in its being one of the most innovative companies in the world. Scotch-Brite Never Rust Soap Pads (shown here) captured 22% of the U.S. market within 18 months of introduction.*

Motorola went through 3,000 working models to develop its first pocket-size cell phone.

As one can see, product selection, definition, and design occur frequently—perhaps hundreds of times for each financially successful product. Operations managers and their organizations must be able to accept risk and tolerate failure. They must accommodate a high volume of new product ideas while maintaining the activities to which they are already committed.

PRODUCT DEVELOPMENT

Product Development System

Learning Objective

2. Describe a product development system

An effective product strategy links product decisions with cash flow, market dynamics, product life cycle, and the organization's capabilities. A firm must have the cash for product development, understand the changes constantly taking place in the marketplace, and have the necessary talents and resources available. The product development system may well determine not only product success but also the firm's future. Figure 5.3 shows the stages of product development. In this system, product options go through a series of steps, each having its own screening and evaluation criteria and providing feedback to prior steps.

The screening process extends to the operations function. Optimum product development depends not only on support from other parts of the firm but also on the successful integration of all 10 of the OM decisions, from product design to maintenance. Identifying products that appear likely to capture market share, be cost effective, and profitable, but are in fact very difficult to produce, may lead to failure rather than success.[5]

Quality function deployment (QFD)

A process for determining customer requirements (customer "wants") and translating them into the attributes (the "hows") that each functional area can understand and act on.

Quality Function Deployment (QFD)

Quality function deployment (QFD) refers to both (1) determining what will satisfy the customer and (2) translating those customer desires into the target design.[6] The idea is to capture a rich understanding of customer wants and to identify alternative process solutions. This information is then integrated into the evolving product design. QFD is used early in the design process to help determine *what will satisfy the customer* and *where to deploy quality efforts*.

---

[5]Rohit Verma, Gary M. Thompson, William L. Moore, and Jordan J. Louviere, "Effective Design of Products/Services: An Approach Based on Integration of Marketing and Operations Management Decisions," *Decision Sciences* 32, no. 1 (winter 2001): 165–193.

[6]See work by the developer of QFD, Yoji Akao, in Yoji Akao and Glenn H. Mazur, "The Leading Edge in QFD: Past, Present, and Future," *The International Journal of Quality and Reliability Management* 20, no. 1 (2003): 20–35.

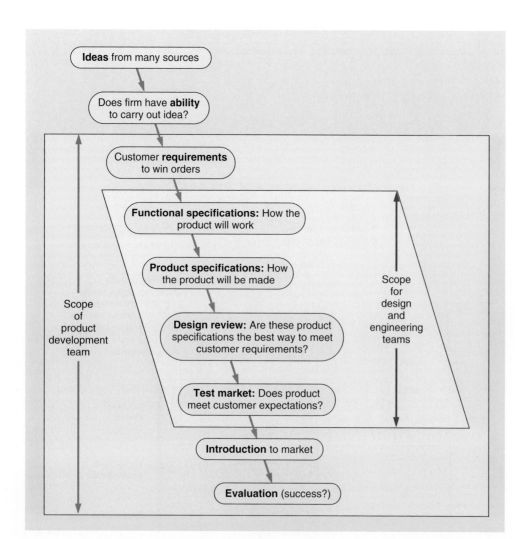

Product Development Stages

Product concepts are developed from a variety of sources, both external and internal to the firm. Concepts that survive the product idea stage progress through various stages, with nearly constant review, feedback, and evaluation in a highly participative environment to minimize failure.

One of the tools of QFD is the house of quality. The **house of quality** is a graphic technique for defining the relationship between customer desires and product (or service). Only by defining this relationship in a rigorous way can operations managers design products and processes with features desired by customers. Defining this relationship is the first step in building a world-class production system. To build the house of quality, we perform seven basic steps:

1. Identify customer *wants*. (What do prospective customers want in this product?)
2. Identify *how* the good/service will satisfy customer wants. (Identify specific product characteristics, features, or attributes and show how they will satisfy customer *wants*.)
3. Relate customer *wants* to product *hows*. (Build a matrix, as in Example 1, that shows this relationship.)
4. Identify relationships between the firm's *hows*. (How do our *hows* tie together? For instance, in the following example, there is a high relationship between low electricity requirements and auto focus, auto exposure, and a paint pallet because they all require electricity. This relationship is shown in the "roof" of the house in Example 1.)
5. Develop importance ratings. (Using the *customer's* importance ratings and weights for the relationships shown in the matrix, compute *our* importance ratings, as in Example 1.)
6. Evaluate competing products. (How well do competing products meet customer wants? Such an evaluation, as shown in the two columns on the right of the figure in Example 1, would be based on market research.)
7. Determine the desirable technical attributes, your performance, and the competitor's performance against these attributes. (This is done at the bottom of the figure in Example 1).

The following series of overlays for Example 1 show how to construct a house of quality.

House of quality

A part of the quality function deployment process that utilizes a planning matrix to relate customer "wants" to "how" the firm is going to meet those "wants."

Learning Objective

3. Build a house of quality

EXAMPLE 1

Constructing a house of quality

Great Cameras, Inc., wants a methodology that strengthens its ability to meet customer desires with its new digital camera.

Approach: Use QFD's house of quality.

Solution: Build the house of quality for Great Cameras, Inc. We do so here using Overlays 1, 2, 3, and 4.

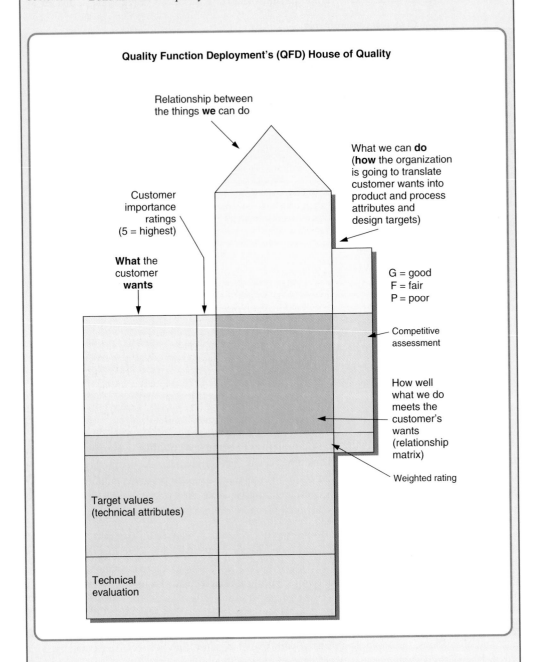

Quality Function Deployment's (QFD) House of Quality

Insight: QFD provides an analytical tool that structures design features and technical issues, as well as providing importance rankings and competitor comparison.

Learning exercise: If the market research for another country indicates that "lightweight" has the most important customer ranking (5), and reliability a 3, what is the new total importance ranking for low electricity requirements, aluminum components, and ergonomic design? [Answer: 18, 15, 27, respectively.]

Related problems: 5.1, 5.2, 5.3, 5.4

Another use of quality function deployment (QFD) is to show how the quality effort will be *deployed*. As Figure 5.4 shows, *design characteristics* of House 1 become the inputs to House 2, which are satisfied by *specific components* of the product. Similarly, the concept is carried to House 3, where the specific components are to be satisfied through particular *production processes*. Once those production processes are defined, they become requirements of House 4 to be satisfied by a *quality plan* that will ensure conformance of those processes. The quality plan is a set of specific tolerances, procedures, methods, and sampling techniques that will ensure that the production process meets the customer requirements.

Much of the QFD effort is devoted to meeting customer requirements with design characteristics (House 1 in Figure 5.4), and its importance is not to be underestimated. However, the *sequence* of houses is a very effective way of identifying, communicating, and allocating resources throughout the system. The series of houses helps operations managers determine where to *deploy* quality resources. In this way we meet customer requirements, produce quality products, and win orders.

Organizing for Product Development

Let's look at four approaches to organizing for product development. *First*, the traditional U.S. approach to product development is an organization with distinct departments: a research and development department to do the necessary research; an engineering department to design the product; a manufacturing engineering department to design a product that can be produced; and a production department that produces the product. The distinct advantage of this approach is that fixed duties and responsibilities exist. The distinct disadvantage is lack of forward thinking: How will downstream departments in the process deal with the concepts, ideas, and designs presented to them, and ultimately what will the customer think of the product?

A *second* and popular approach is to assign a product manager to "champion" the product through the product development system and related organizations. However, a *third*, and perhaps the best, product development approach used in the U.S. seems to be the use of teams. Such teams are known variously as *product development teams, design for manufacturability teams*, and *value engineering teams*.

The Japanese use a *fourth* approach. They bypass the team issue by not subdividing organizations into research and development, engineering, production, and so forth. Consistent with the Japanese style of group effort and teamwork, these activities are all in one organization. Japanese culture and management style are more collegial and the organization less structured than in most Western countries. Therefore, the Japanese find it unnecessary to have "teams" provide the necessary communication and coordination. However, the typical Western style, and the conventional wisdom, is to use teams.

Product development teams are charged with the responsibility of moving from market requirements for a product to achieving a product success (refer to Figure 5.3 on page 163). Such teams often include representatives from marketing, manufacturing, purchasing, quality assurance, and field service personnel. Many teams also include representatives from vendors. Regardless of the formal nature of the product development effort, research suggests that success is more likely in an open, highly participative environment where those with potential contributions are allowed to make them. The objective of a product development team is to make the good or service a success. This includes marketability, manufacturability, and serviceability.

Product excellence means determining what the customer wants and providing it.

Product development teams
Teams charged with moving from market requirements for a product to achieving product success.

▼ **Figure 5.4** **House of Quality Sequence Indicates How to Deploy Resources to Achieve Customer Requirements**

OM in Action   Designing Trident Splash

Cadbury Schweppes PLC sells a lot of gum—Dentyne, Bubbaloo, and Trident—some $4.2 billion of a $15.4 billion market that is growing about 6% per year. However, Cadbury perceived a niche for a new gum that would be a low calorie substitute for unhealthy snacks. Cadbury wanted the new product to compete with the creamy or crunchy mouth experience one gets from snacks other than gum.

The R & D team eventually designed a unique three-layer pellet with a candy shell over a sugarless gum with a liquid center. For the liquid center Cadbury scientists searched for and evaluated scores of long lasting flavors before settling on two unusual blends: strawberry-lime and peppermint-vanilla.

Development wasn't easy; neither was designing a product that could be produced. Although Cadbury acquired the liquid center technology from Pfizer, some of the flavors were too water-soluble—making the gum

soft. Early formulations leaked during production. Others survived production only to fail when subjected to the punishment of transportation.

Adding to production problems was the lack of sugar in the gum. Sugar traditionally adds strength and bulk to aid the production process, but with artificial sweeteners, the centers were not strong enough for the application of the candy coating. The machinery crushed the weakened pellets and the liquid flavors oozed out. This in turn contributed to some messy production equipment.

It took two years and millions of dollars, but Cadbury's biggest ever new-product development effort, Trident Splash, is now on the market.

Sources: The Wall Street Journal (January 12, 2006): A1, A8; *Fortune* (April 3, 2006): 33

Concurrent engineering
Use of participating teams in design and engineering activities.

Use of such teams is also called **concurrent engineering** and implies a team representing all affected areas (known as a *cross-functional* team). Concurrent engineering also implies speedier product development through simultaneous performance of various aspects of product development.[7] The team approach is the dominant structure for product development by leading organizations in the U.S.

Manufacturability and Value Engineering

Manufacturability and value engineering
Activities that help improve a product's design, production, maintainability, and use.

Manufacturability and value engineering activities are concerned with improvement of design and specifications at the research, development, design, and production stages of product development. (See the *OM in Action* box "Designing Trident Splash".) In addition to immediate, obvious cost reduction, design for manufacturability and value engineering may produce other benefits. These include:

1. Reduced complexity of the product.
2. Additional standardization of components.
3. Improvement of functional aspects of the product.
4. Improved job design and job safety.
5. Improved maintainability (serviceability) of the product.
6. Robust design.

Manufacturability and value engineering activities may be the best cost-avoidance technique available to operations management. They yield value improvement by focusing on achieving the functional specifications necessary to meet customer requirements in an optimal way. Value engineering programs, when effectively managed, typically reduce costs between 15% and 70% without reducing quality. Some studies have indicated that for every dollar spent on value engineering, $10 to $25 in savings can be realized.

QFD CAPTURE software is a management aid for prioritizing choices for better products and services. A free evaluation version is available at www.qfdcapture.com.

Product design affects virtually all aspects of operating expense. Consequently, the development process needs to ensure a thorough evaluation of design prior to a commitment to produce. The cost reduction achieved for a specific bracket via value engineering is shown in Figure 5.5.

▶ **Figure 5.5**

Cost Reduction of a Bracket via Value Engineering

Each time the bracket is redesigned and simplified, we are able to produce it for less.

[7]Firms that have high technological or product change in their competitive environment tend to use more concurrent engineering practices. See Xenophon Koufteros, Mark Vonderembse, and William Doll, "Concurrent Engineering and Its Consequences," *Journal of Operations Management* 19, no. 1 (January 2001): 97–115.

ISSUES FOR PRODUCT DESIGN

In addition to developing an effective system and organization structure for product development, several *techniques* are important to the design of a product. We will now review seven of these: (1) robust design, (2) modular design, (3) computer-aided design (CAD), (4) computer-aided manufacturing (CAM), (5) virtual reality technology, (6) value analysis, and (7) environmentally friendly designs.

Robust Design

Robust design means that the product is designed so that small variations in production or assembly do not adversely affect the product. For instance, Lucent developed an integrated circuit that could be used in many products to amplify voice signals. As originally designed, the circuit had to be manufactured very precisely to avoid variations in the strength of the signal. Such a circuit would have been costly to make because of stringent quality controls needed during the manufacturing process. However, after testing and analyzing the design, Lucent engineers realized that if the resistance of the circuit was reduced—a minor change with no associated costs—the circuit would be far less sensitive to manufacturing variations. The result was a 40% improvement in quality.

Robust design
A design that can be produced to requirements even with unfavorable conditions in the production process.

Modular Design

Products designed in easily segmented components are known as **modular designs**. Modular designs offer flexibility to both production and marketing. The production department typically finds modularity helpful because it makes product development, production, and subsequent changes easier. Moreover, marketing may like modularity because it adds flexibility to the ways customers can be satisfied. For instance, virtually all premium high-fidelity sound systems are produced and sold this way. The customization provided by modularity allows customers to mix and match to their own taste. This is also the approach taken by Harley-Davidson, where relatively few different engines, chassis, gas tanks, and suspension systems are mixed to produce a huge variety of motorcycles. It has been estimated that many automobile manufacturers can, by mixing the available modules, never make two cars alike. This same concept of modularity is carried over to many industries, from airframe manufacturers to fast-food restaurants. Airbus uses the same wing modules on several planes, just as McDonald's and Burger King use relatively few modules (cheese, lettuce, buns, sauces, pickles, meat patties, french fries, etc.) to make a variety of meals.

Modular design
A design in which parts or components of a product are subdivided into modules that are easily interchanged or replaced.

 Video 5.2

Modular Assembly at Harley-Davidson

Computer-Aided Design (CAD)

Computer-aided design (CAD) is the use of computers to interactively design products and prepare engineering documentation. Use and variety of CAD software is extensive and is rapidly expanding. CAD software allows designers to use three-dimensional drawings to save time and money by shortening development cycles for virtually all products (see the 3-D design photos on page 168). The speed and ease with which sophisticated designs can be manipulated, analyzed, and modified with CAD makes review of numerous options possible before final commitments are made. Faster development, better products, accurate flow of information to other departments—all contribute to a tremendous payoff for CAD. The payoff is particularly significant because most product costs are determined at the design stage.

Computer-aided design (CAD)
Interactive use of a computer to develop and document a product.

One extension of CAD is **design for manufacture and assembly (DFMA)** software, which focuses on the effect of design on assembly. It allows designers to examine the integration of product designs before the product is manufactured. For instance, DFMA allows automobile designers to examine how a transmission will be placed in a car on the production line, even while both the transmission and the car are still in the design stage.

Design for manufacture and assembly (DFMA)
Software that allows designers to look at the effect of design on manufacturing of the product.

A second CAD extension is **3-D object modeling**. The technology is particularly useful for small prototype development (as shown in the photo on page 169). 3-D object modeling rapidly builds up a model in very thin layers of synthetic materials for evaluation. This technology speeds development by avoiding a more lengthy and formal manufacturing process. 3-D printers, costing from $20,000 to $50,000, are also now available. Shoemaker Timberland, Inc., uses

3-D object modeling
An extension of CAD that builds small prototypes.

theirs to allow footwear designers to see their constructions overnight rather than waiting a week for model-makers to carve them.[8]

Some CAD systems have moved to the Internet through e-commerce, where they link computerized design with purchasing, outsourcing, manufacturing, and long-term maintenance. This move supports rapid product change and the growing trend toward "mass customization." With CAD on the Internet, customers can enter a supplier's design libraries and make design changes. The supplier's software can then automatically generate the drawings, update the bill of material, and prepare instructions for the supplier's production process. The result is customized products produced faster and at less expense.

Standard for the exchange of product data (STEP)
A standard that provides a format allowing the electronic transmittal of three-dimensional data.

As product life cycles shorten and design becomes more complex, collaboration among departments, facilities and suppliers throughout the world becomes critical. The potential of such collaboration has proven so important that a standard for its exchange has been developed, known as the **standard for the exchange of product data (STEP)**. STEP permits manufacturers to express 3-D product information in a standard format so it can be exchanged internationally, allowing geographically dispersed manufacturers to integrate design, manufacture, and support processes.[9]

Computer-Aided Manufacturing (CAM)

Computer-aided manufacturing (CAM)
The use of information technology to control machinery.

Computer-aided manufacturing (CAM) refers to the use of specialized computer programs to direct and control manufacturing equipment. When computer-aided design (CAD) information is translated into instructions for computer-aided manufacturing (CAM), the result of these two technologies is CAD/CAM.

The benefits of CAD and CAM include:

1. *Product quality:* CAD permits the designer to investigate more alternatives, potential problems, and dangers.
2. *Shorter design time:* A shorter design phase lowers cost and allows a more rapid response to the market.
3. *Production cost reductions:* Reduced inventory, more efficient use of personnel through improved scheduling, and faster implementation of design changes lower costs.

▲ *The increasing sophistication of CAD software provides (a) 3D solid design, (b) integrated assembly, and (c) analysis of stress, pressure, and thermal issues, which improves design, speeds the design process, and provides code for CAM equipment while reducing costs.*

[8]See Jose A. Ceroni and Alvaro A. Velasquez, "Conflict Detection and Resolution in Distributed Design," *Production Planning and Control*, 14, no. 8 (December 2003): 734–742 and "New Copiers Create 3D Plastic Models on Demand," *The Wall Street Journal* (August 2, 2006): B1, B4.
[9]The STEP format is documented in the European Community's standard ISO 10303.

◀ *This prototype wheel for a tire (at the left of the photo) is being built using 3-D System's Stereolithography technology, a 3-D object modeling system. This technology uses data from CAD and builds structures layer by layer in .001-inch increments. The technique reduces the time it takes to create a sample from weeks to hours while also reducing costs. The technique is also known as* rapid prototyping.

4. *Database availability:* Provides information for other manufacturing software and accurate product data so everyone is operating from the same information, resulting in dramatic cost reductions.

5. *New range of capabilities:* For instance, the abilities to rotate and depict objects in three-dimensional form, to check clearances, to relate parts and attachments, and to improve the use of numerically controlled machine tools—all provide new capability for manufacturing. CAD/CAM removes substantial detail work, allowing designers to concentrate on the conceptual and imaginative aspects of their task.

Procter & Gamble used CAD when designing its Crest toothpaste pump dispenser.

Virtual Reality Technology

Virtual reality is a visual form of communication in which images substitute for the real thing but still allow the user to respond interactively. The roots of virtual reality technology in operations are in computer-aided design. Once design information is in a CAD system, it is also in electronic digital form for other uses. For instance, General Motors creates its version of an Opel "virtual car" using ceiling-mounted video projectors to project stereoscopic images in a small, stark room (see the photo on page 170). After donning a special pair of glasses, both designers and customers see a three-dimensional model of what the inside of a new design looks like. Virtual reality is also being used to develop 3-D layouts of everything from restaurants to amusement parks. Changes to the car, restaurant, or ride are made much less expensively at this design stage than later.

Virtual reality
A visual form of communication in which images substitute for reality and typically allow the user to respond interactively.

Value Analysis

Although value engineering (discussed on page 166) focuses on *preproduction* design improvement, value analysis, a related technique, takes place *during* the production process, when it is clear that a new product is a success. **Value analysis** seeks improvements that lead to either a better product or a product made more economically. The techniques and advantages for value analysis are the same as for value engineering, although minor changes in implementation may be necessary because value analysis is taking place while the product is being produced.

Value analysis
A review of successful products that takes place during the production process.

Ethics and Environmentally Friendly Designs

An operations manager's most ethical, and an environmentally sound, activity is to enhance productivity while delivering desired goods and services. Operations managers can drive down costs while preserving resources. The entire product life cycle—from design, to production, to final destruction—provides an opportunity to preserve resources. Planet Earth is finite; managers who squeeze more out of its resources are its heroes. Here are examples of how three firms are ethically and environmentally responsible:

• *At the design stage*, DuPont developed a polyester film stronger and thinner so it uses less material and costs less to make. Also, because the film performs better, customers are willing to pay more for it.

▶ *Computer-aided design programs developed during the past three decades have made drafting tables and modeling clay a thing of the past. Three-dimensional images are now displayed on four sides of a transparent room, creating a realistic environment, which is perfect for evaluating GM's Opel car interior shown here.*

- *At the production stage*, Bristol-Meyers Squibb established an environmental and pollution prevention program designed to address environmental, health, and safety issues at all stages of the product life cycle. Ban Roll-On was one of the first products studied and an early success. Repackaging Ban in smaller cartons resulted in a reduction of 600 tons of recycled paperboard. The product then required 55% less shelf space for display. As a result, not only is pollution prevented but store operating costs are also reduced.
- *At the destruction stage*, the automobile industry has been very successful: The industry now recycles more than 75% of the material by weight of 10 million cars scrapped each year. Some of this success is because of care at the design stage. For instance, BMW, with environmentally friendly designs, recycles much of a car, including many plastic components (see the photo on the next page).

These efforts are consistent with the environmental issues raised by the ISO 14000 standard, a topic we address in Chapter 6.

The Ethical Approach   One way to accomplish programs like those at DuPont, Bristol-Meyers Squibb, and BMW is to add an ethical and environmental charge to the job of operations managers and their value engineering/analysis teams. Team members from different functional areas working together can present a wide range of environmental perspectives and approaches. Managers and teams should consider two issues:

- First, they need to view products from a "systems" perspective—that is, view the product in terms of its impact on the entire economy. This means a comprehensive look at the inputs to the firm, the processes, and the outputs, recognizing that some of the resources, long considered free, are in fact not free. Particulates and sulfur in the air are pollution for someone else; similarly, bacteria and phosphates in the water going downstream become someone else's problem. In the case of the battle between styrofoam and paper containers, which one is really "better," and by what criteria? We may know which is more economical for the firm, but is that one also most economical for society?
- Second, operations managers must consider the life cycle of the product, that is, from design, through production, to final disposition. The goal is to reduce the environmental impact of a product throughout its life—a challenging task.[10]

The likelihood that ethical decisions will be made is enhanced when managers maintain these two perspectives and maintain an open dialogue among all stakeholders.

---

[10]For an article on management's perception of "environmentally responsible manufacturing," see Steven A. Melnyk, Robert Sroufe, and Frank Montabon, "How Does Management View Environmentally Responsible Manufacturing?" *Production and Inventory Management Journal* 42, nos. 3 and 4 (third and fourth quarters 2001): 55–63.

Goals   Goals for ethical and environmentally friendly designs are:

1. Developing safe and more environmentally sound products.
2. Minimizing waste of raw materials and energy.
3. Reducing environmental liabilities.
4. Increasing cost-effectiveness of complying with environmental regulations.
5. Being recognized as a good corporate citizen.

Guidelines   The following six guidelines may help operations managers achieve ethical and environmentally friendly designs:

1. *Make products recyclable:* Many firms are doing this on their own, but the U.S. and the EU now have take-back laws that affect a variety of products, from automobiles and tires to computers. Not only is most of a car recycled but so are over half the aluminum cans and a large portion of paper, plastic, and glass. In some cases, as with tires, the manufacturer is responsible for 100% disposal.
2. *Use recycled materials:* Scotch-Brite soap pads at 3M are designed to use recycled plastics, as are the park benches and other products at Plastic Recycling Corporation.
3. *Use less harmful ingredients:* Standard Register, like most of the printing industry, has replaced environmentally dangerous inks with soy-based inks that reduce air and water pollution.
4. *Use lighter components:* The auto and truck industries continue to expand the use of aluminum and plastic components to reduce weight. Mercedes is even building car exteriors from a banana plant fiber that is both biodegradable and lightweight.[11] Similarly, Boeing is using carbon fiber, epoxy composites, and titanium graphite laminate to reduce weight in its new 787 Dreamliner. These changes can be expensive, but they make autos, trucks, and aircraft more environmentally friendly by improving payload and mileage.
5. *Use less energy:* While the auto, truck, and airframe industries are redesigning to improve mileage, General Electric is designing a new generation of refrigerators that requires substantially less electricity during their lifetime. DuPont is so good at energy efficiency that it has turned its expertise into a consulting business.
6. *Use less material:* Many organizations waste material—in the plant and in the packaging. An employee team at a Sony semiconductor plant achieved a 50% reduction in the amount of chemicals used in the silicon wafer etching process. This and similar successes reduce both production costs and environmental concerns. To conserve packaging, Boston's Park Plaza Hotel eliminated bars of soap and bottles of shampoo by installing pump dispensers in its bathrooms, saving the need for a million plastic containers a year.

◀ *BMW uses parts made of recycled plastics (blue) and parts that can be recycled (green). "Green manufacturing" means companies can reuse, refurbish, or dispose of a product's components safely and reduce total life cycle product costs.*

[11]"Take It Back," *The Wall Street Journal* (April 17, 2006): R6.

▶ *With increasing restrictions on disposal of TVs, cell phones, computers, and other electronic waste, much of such waste (left) ends its life in Guangdong province on China's southern coast (right). Here, under less-than-ideal conditions, Chinese women strip old circuit boards to salvage the chips.*

Legal and Industry Standards Laws and industry standards can help operations managers make ethical and socially responsible decisions. In the last 100 years we have seen development of law and industry standards to guide managers in product design, manufacture/assembly, and disassembly/disposal.

Design: On the legal side, U.S. laws and regulations such as those promulgated by the Federal Drug Administration, Consumer Product Safety Commission, National Highway Safety Administration, and Children's Product Safety Act provide guidance, if not explicit law, to aid decision making. Guidance is also provided by phrases in case law like "design for foreseeable misuse" and in regard to children's toys, "The concept of a prudent child . . . is a grotesque combination."

Manufacture/assembly: The manufacture and assembly of products has standards and guidelines from the Occupational Safety and Health Administration (OSHA), Environmental Protection Agency (EPA), professional ergonomic standards, and a wide range of state and federal laws that deal with employment standards, disabilities, discrimination, and the like.

Disassembly/disposal: Product disassembly and disposal in the U.S., Canada, and the EU are governed by increasingly rigid laws. In the U.S., the Vehicle Recycling Partnership, supported by the auto industry, provides *Design for Disassembly Standards* for auto disassembly and disposal. However, in the fragmented electronics industry, safe disposal of TVs, computers, and cell phones is much more difficult and dangerous (see the photo).

Ethical, socially responsible decisions can be difficult and complex—often with no easy answers—but such decisions are appreciated by the public, and they can save money, material, and the environment. These are the types of win-win situations that operations managers seek.

TIME-BASED COMPETITION

As product life cycles shorten, the need for faster product development increases. Additionally, as technological sophistication of new products increases, so do the expense and risk. For instance, drug firms invest an average of 12 to 15 years and $400 million before receiving regulatory approval of each new drug. And even then, only 1 of 5 will actually be a success. Those operations managers who master this art of product development continually gain on slower product developers. To the swift goes the competitive advantage (see Table 5.1). This concept is called **time-based competition**.

Often, the first company into production may have its product adopted for use in a variety of applications that will generate sales for years. It may become the "standard." Consequently, there is often more concern with getting the product to market than with optimum product design or process efficiency. Even so, rapid introduction to the market may be good management because until competition begins to introduce copies or improved versions, the product can sometimes be priced high enough to justify somewhat inefficient production design and methods. For example, when Kodak first introduced its Ektar film, it sold for 10% to 15% more than conventional film. Motorola's innovative pocket-size cellular telephone was 50% smaller than any competitor's and sold for twice the price.

Because time-based competition is so important, instead of developing new products from scratch (which has been the focus thus far in this chapter) a number of other strategies can be

---

▼ **Table 5.1**

Ever Faster Product Development

DELL NOTEBOOK
10 yrs ago: **18 mos**
last yr: **9 mos**
CELL PHONE
5 yrs ago: **12–18 mos**
now: **3–6 mos**
IPOD
first 6 versions: **2 yrs**
latest 8: **8 mos**
PLAYAWAY
From idea to production:
13 mos

Source: Forbes (December 26, 2005).

Time-based competition
Competition based on time; rapidly developing products and moving them to market.

Learning Objective

4. Describe how time-based competition is implemented

Product Development Continuum

◀ **Figure 5.6**

Product Development Continuum

External development strategies

Alliances

Joint ventures

Purchase technology or expertise
by acquiring the developer

Internal development strategies

Migrations of existing products

Enhancements to existing products

New internally developed products

Internal ◀———	*Cost of product development*	———▶ Shared
Lengthy ◀———	*Speed of product development*	———▶ Rapid and/or Existing
High ◀———	*Risk of product development*	———▶ Shared

used. Figure 5.6 shows a continuum that goes from new, internally developed products (on the lower left) to "alliances." *Enhancements* and *migrations* use the organization's existing product strengths for innovation and therefore are typically faster while at the same time being less risky than developing entirely new products. Enhancements may be changes in color, size, weight, or features, such as are taking place in cellular phones (see *OM in Action* box "Chasing Fads in the Cell Phone Industry"), or even changes in commercial aircraft. Boeing's enhancements of the 737 since its introduction in 1967 has made the 737 the largest-selling commercial aircraft in history. Boeing also uses its engineering prowess in air frames to *migrate* from one model to the next. This allows Boeing to speed development while reducing both cost and risk for new designs. This approach is also referred to as building on *product platforms*. Black & Decker has used its "platform" expertise in hand-powered tools to build a leading position in that market. Similarly, Hewlett-Packard has done the same in the printer business. Enhancements and migrations are a way of building on existing expertise and extending a product's life cycle.[12]

> *Much of the current competitive battlefield is focused around the speed of product to market. The president of one huge U.S. firm says: "If I miss one product cycle, I'm dead."*

OM in Action — Chasing Fads in the Cell Phone Industry

In the shrinking world marketplace, innovations that appeal to customers in one region rapidly become global trends. The process shakes up the structure of one industry after another, from computers to automobiles to consumer electronics.

Nowhere has this impact been greater in recent years than in the $73 billion cell phone industry. The product life cycle is short. Competition is intense because higher margins go to the innovator—and manufacturers that jump on an emerging trend early can reap substantial rewards. The swiftest Chinese manufacturers, such as Ningbo Bird and TCL, now replace some phone models after just 6 months. In the past, Motorola, Nokia, and other industry veterans enjoyed what are now considered long life cycles—2 years. New styles and technological advances in cell phones constantly appear somewhere in the world. Wired, well-traveled consumers seek the latest innovation; local retailers rush to offer it; and telecommunication providers order it.

Contemporary cell phones may be a curvy, boxy, or clamshell fashion item; have a tiny keyboard for quick and easy typing or a more limited number pad for a phone; have a built-in radio or a digital music player; have a camera, Internet access, or TV clips; function on cellular or wireless (Wi-Fi) networks; or have games or personal organizers. Mattel and Nokia even have Barbie phones for preteen girls, complete with prepaid minutes, customized ringtones, and faceplates. The rapid changes in features and demand are forcing manufacturers into a frenzied race to keep up or simply to pull out.

"We got out of the handset business because we couldn't keep up with the cycle times," says Jeffrey Belk, Marketing V.P. for Qualcomm Inc., the San Diego company that now focuses on making handset chips.

Developing new products is always a challenge, but in the dynamic global market place of cell phones, product development takes on new technology and new markets at breakneck speed.

Sources: DSN Retailing Today (April 25, 2005): 42–43; and *The Wall Street Journal* (October 30, 2003): A1 and (Sept. 8, 2004): D5.

---

[12]Y. Moon, "Break Free from the Product Life Cycle," *Harvard Business Review* 83, no. 5 (May 2005): 86–94.

The product development strategies on the lower left of Figure 5.6 are *internal* development strategies, while the three approaches we now introduce can be thought of as *external* development strategies. Firms use both. The external strategies are (1) purchase the technology, (2) establish joint ventures, and (3) develop alliances.

Purchasing Technology by Acquiring a Firm

Microsoft and Cisco Systems are examples of companies on the cutting edge of technology that often speed development by *acquiring entrepreneurial firms* that have already developed the technology that fits their mission. The issue then becomes fitting the purchased organization, its technology, its product lines, and its culture into the buying firm, rather than a product development issue.

Joint Ventures

Joint ventures

Firms establishing joint ownership to pursue new products or markets.

Joint ventures are combined ownership, usually between just two firms, to form a new entity. Ownership can be 50–50, or one owner can assume a larger portion to ensure tighter control. Joint ventures are often appropriate for exploiting specific product opportunities that may not be central to the firm's mission. Such ventures are more likely to work when the risks are known and can be equitably shared. For instance, GM and Toyota formed a joint venture with their NUMMI plant in northern California to produce the GM Prism and the Toyota Corolla. Both companies saw a learning opportunity as well as a product they both needed in the North American market. Toyota wanted to learn about building and managing a plant in North America, and GM wanted to learn about manufacturing a small car with Toyota's manufacturing techniques. The risks were well understood, as were the respective commitments. Similarly, Fuji-Xerox, a manufacturer and marketer of photocopiers, is a joint venture of Xerox, the U.S. maker of photocopiers, and Fuji, Japan's largest manufacturer of film.

Alliances

Alliances

Cooperative agreements that allow firms to remain independent, but that pursue strategies consistent with their individual missions.

Alliances are cooperative agreements that allow firms to remain independent but use complementing strengths to pursue strategies consistent with their individual missions. When new products are central to the mission, but substantial resources are required and sizable risk is present, then alliances may be a good strategy for product development. Alliances are particularly beneficial when the products to be developed also have technologies that are in ferment. Additionally, if the boundaries between firms will be difficult to specify, alliances may be the best strategy. For example, Microsoft is pursuing a number of alliances with a variety of companies to deal with the convergence of computing, the Internet, and television broadcasting. Alliances in this case are appropriate because the technological unknowns, capital demands, and risks are significant. Similarly, three firms, Mercedes Benz, Ford Motor, and Ballard Power Systems, have formed an alliance to develop "green" cars powered by fuel cells. However, alliances are much more difficult to achieve and maintain than joint ventures because of the ambiguities associated with them.[13] It may be helpful to think of an alliance as an incomplete contract between the firms. The firms remain separate.

Enhancements, migration, acquisitions, joint ventures, and alliances are all strategies for speeding product development. Moreover, they typically reduce the risk associated with product development while enhancing the human and capital resources available.

DEFINING A PRODUCT

Learning Objective

5. Describe how products and services are defined

Once new goods or services are selected for introduction, they must be defined. First, a good or service is defined in terms of its *functions*—that is, what it is to *do*. The product is then designed, and the firm determines how the functions are to be achieved. Management typically has a variety of options as to how a product should achieve its functional purpose. For instance, when an

---

[13]Jeffrey H. Dyer, Prashant Kale, and Harbir Singh, "When to Ally & When to Acquire," *Harvard Business Review*, 82, 7/8 (July–August 2004): 108–115; and Donald Gerwin, "Coordinating New Product Development in Strategic Alliances," *The Academy of Management Review*, 29, 2 (April 2004): 241–257.

◀ **Figure 5.7**

Monterey Jack

A portion of the general requirements for the U.S. grades of Monterey cheese is shown here.

---

§ 58.2469 Specifications for U.S. grades of Monterey (Monterey Jack) cheese

(a) *U.S. grade AA.* Monterey Cheese shall conform to the following requirements:

(1) *Flavor.* Is fine and highly pleasing, free from undesirable flavors and odors. May possess a very slight acid or feed flavor.

(2) *Body and texture.* A plug drawn from the cheese shall be reasonably firm. It shall have numerous small mechanical openings evenly distributed throughout the plug. It shall not possess sweet holes, yeast holes, or other gas holes.

(3) *Color.* Shall have a natural, uniform, bright, attractive appearance.

(4) *Finish and appearance—bandaged and paraffin-dipped.* The rind shall be sound, firm, and smooth, providing a good protection to the cheese.

Code of Federal Regulation, Parts 53 to 109, General Service Administration.

---

alarm clock is produced, aspects of design such as the color, size, or location of buttons may make substantial differences in ease of manufacture, quality, and market acceptance.

Rigorous specifications of a product are necessary to assure efficient production. Equipment, layout, and human resources cannot be determined until the product is defined, designed, and documented. Therefore, every organization needs documents to define its products. This is true of everything from meat patties, to cheese, to computers, to a medical procedure. In the case of cheese, a written specification is typical. Indeed, written specifications or standard grades exist and provide the definition for many products. For instance, Monterey Jack cheese has a written description that specifies the characteristics necessary for each Department of Agriculture grade. A portion of the Department of Agriculture grade for Monterey Jack Grade AA is shown in Figure 5.7. Similarly, McDonald's Corp. has 60 specifications for potatoes that are to be made into french fries.

Most manufactured items as well as their components are defined by a drawing, usually referred to as an engineering drawing. An **engineering drawing** shows the dimensions, tolerances, materials, and finishes of a component. The engineering drawing will be an item on a bill of material. An engineering drawing is shown in Figure 5.8. The **bill of material (BOM)** lists the components, their description, and the quantity of each required to make one unit of a product. A bill of material for a manufactured item is shown in Figure 5.9(a). Note that subassemblies and components (lower-level items) are indented at each level to indicate their subordinate position. An engineering drawing shows how to make one item on the bill of material.

In the food-service industry, bills of material manifest themselves in *portion-control standards.* The portion-control standard for Hard Rock Cafe's hickory BBQ bacon cheeseburger is shown in Figure 5.9(b). In a more complex product, a bill of material is referenced on other bills of material of which they are a part. In this manner, subunits (subassemblies) are part of the next higher unit (their parent bill of material) that ultimately makes a final product. In addition to being defined by written specifications, portion-control documents, or bills of material, products can be defined in other ways. For example, products such as chemicals, paints, and petroleums may be defined by formulas or proportions that describe how they are to be made. Movies are defined by scripts, and insurance coverage by legal documents known as policies.

Engineering drawing
A drawing that shows the dimensions, tolerances, materials, and finishes of a component.

Bill of material (BOM)
A listing of the components, their description, and the quantity of each required to make one unit of a product.

◀ **Figure 5.8**

Engineering Drawings Such as This One Show Dimensions, Tolerances, Materials, and Finishes

► **Figure 5.9**

Bills of Material Take Different Forms in a (a) Manufacturing Plant and a (b) Restaurant, but in Both Cases, the Product Must Be Defined

(a)   Bill of Material for a Panel Weldment

NUMBER	DESCRIPTION	QTY
A 60-71	PANEL WELDM'T	1
A 60-7	LOWER ROLLER ASSM.	1
R 60-17	ROLLER	1
R 60-428	PIN	1
P 60-2	LOCKNUT	1
A 60-72	GUIDE ASSM. REAR	1
R 60-57-1	SUPPORT ANGLE	1
A 60-4	ROLLER ASSEM.	1
02-50-1150	BOLT	1
A 60-73	GUIDE ASSM. FRONT	1
A 60-74	SUPPORT WELDM'T	1
R 60-99	WEAR PLATE	1
02-50-1150	BOLT	1

(b)   Hard Rock Cafe's Hickory BBQ Bacon Cheeseburger

DESCRIPTION	QTY
Bun	1
Hamburger patty	8 oz.
Cheddar cheese	2 slices
Bacon	2 strips
BBQ onions	1/2 cup
Hickory BBQ sauce	1 oz.
Burger set	
Lettuce	1 leaf
Tomato	1 slice
Red onion	4 rings
Pickle	1 slice
French fries	5 oz.
Seasoned salt	1 tsp.
11-inch plate	1
HRC flag	1

Make-or-Buy Decisions

Make-or-buy decision

The choice between producing a component or a service and purchasing it from an outside source.

For many components of products, firms have the option of producing the components themselves or purchasing them from outside sources. Choosing between these options is known as the make-or-buy decision. The **make-or-buy decision** distinguishes between what the firm wants to *produce* and what it wants to *purchase*. Because of variations in quality, cost, and delivery schedules, the make-or-buy decision is critical to product definition. Many items can be purchased as a "standard item" produced by someone else. Such a standard item does not require its own bill of material or engineering drawing because its specification as a standard item is adequate. Examples are the standard bolts listed on the bill of material shown in Figure 5.9(a), for which there will be SAE (Society of Automotive Engineers) specifications. Therefore, there typically is no need for the firm to duplicate this specification in another document. We discuss the make-or-buy decision in more detail in Chapter 11.

Group Technology

Group technology

A product and component coding system that specifies the type of processing and the parameters of the processing; it allows similar products to be grouped.

Engineering drawings may also include codes to facilitate group technology. **Group technology** requires that components be identified by a coding scheme that specifies the type of processing (such as drilling) and the parameters of the processing (such as size). This facilitates standardization of materials, components, and processes as well as the identification of families of parts. As families of parts are identified, activities and machines can be grouped to minimize setups, routings, and material handling. An example of how families of parts may be grouped is shown in Figure 5.10. Group technology provides a systematic way to review a family of components to see if an existing component might suffice on a new project. Using existing or standard components eliminates all the costs connected with the design and development of the new part, which is a major cost reduction. For these reasons, successful implementation of group technology leads to the following advantages:

1. Improved design (because more design time can be devoted to fewer components).
2. Reduced raw material and purchases.
3. Simplified production planning and control.
4. Improved layout, routing, and machine loading.
5. Reduced tooling setup time, and work-in-process and production time.

The application of group technology helps the entire organization, as many costs are reduced.

DOCUMENTS FOR PRODUCTION

Once a product is selected, designed, and ready for production, production is assisted by a variety of documents. We will briefly review some of these.

◀ **Figure 5.10**

A Variety of Group Technology Coding Schemes Move Manufactured Components from (a) Ungrouped to (b) Grouped (families of parts)

(a) Ungrouped Parts	(b) Grouped Cylindrical Parts (families of parts)				
	Grooved	Slotted	Threaded	Drilled	Machined

An **assembly drawing** simply shows an exploded view of the product. An assembly drawing is usually a three-dimensional drawing, known as an *isometric drawing*; the relative locations of components are drawn in relation to each other to show how to assemble the unit (see Figure 5.11[a]).

The **assembly chart** shows in schematic form how a product is assembled. Manufactured components, purchased components, or a combination of both may be shown on an assembly chart. The assembly chart identifies the point of production at which components flow into subassemblies and ultimately into a final product. An example of an assembly chart is shown in Figure 5.11(b).

The **route sheet** lists the operations (including assembly and inspection) necessary to produce the component with the material specified in the bill of material. The route sheet for an item will have one entry for each operation to be performed on the item. When route sheets include specific methods of operation and labor standards, they are often known as *process sheets*.

The **work order** is an instruction to make a given quantity of a particular item, usually to a given schedule. The ticket that a waiter writes in your favorite restaurant is a work order. In a hospital or factory, the work order is a more formal document that provides authorization to draw various pharmaceuticals or items from inventory, to perform various functions, and to assign personnel to perform those functions.

Assembly drawing
An exploded view of the product, usually via a three-dimensional or isometric drawing.

Assembly chart
A graphic means of identifying how components flow into subassemblies and ultimately into a final product.

Route sheet
A listing of the operations necessary to produce a component with the material specified in the bill of material.

Work order
An instruction to make a given quantity of a particular item, usually to a given schedule.

◀ **Figure 5.11**

Assembly Drawing and Assembly Chart

(a) Assembly Drawing

(b) Assembly Chart

▶ *Each year the JR Simplot potato-processing facility in Caldwell, Idaho, produces billions of french fries for McDonald's (left photo). Sixty specifications (including a special blend of frying oil, a unique steaming process, and exact time and temperature for prefrying and drying) define how these potatoes become french fries. Further, 40% of all french fries must be 2 to 3 inches long, 40% must be over 3 inches long, and a few stubby ones constitute the final 20%. Quality control personnel use a micrometer to measure the fries (right photo).*

Engineering change notice (ECN)

A correction or modification of an engineering drawing or bill of material.

Configuration management

A system by which a product's planned and changing components are accurately identified and the accountability of change is maintained.

Engineering change notices (ECNs) change some aspect of the product's definition or documentation, such as an engineering drawing or a bill of material. For a complex product that has a long manufacturing cycle, such as a Boeing 777, the changes may be so numerous that no two 777s are built exactly alike—which is indeed the case. Such dynamic design change has fostered the development of a discipline known as configuration management, which is concerned with product identification, control, and documentation. **Configuration management** is the system by which a product's planned and changing configurations are accurately identified and for which control and accountability of change are maintained.

Product Life-Cycle Management (PLM)

Product life-cycle management (PLM) is an umbrella of software programs that attempts to bring together phases of product design and manufacture—including tying together many of the techniques discussed in the prior two sections, *Defining a Product* and *Documents for Production*. The idea behind PLM software is that product design and manufacture decisions can be performed more creatively, faster, and more economically when the data are integrated and consistent.

Product life-cycle management (PLM)

Software programs that tie together many phases of product design and manufacture.

Although there is not one standard, PLM products often start with product design (CAD/CAM); move on to design for manufacture and assembly (DFMA); and then into product routing, materials, layout, assembly, maintenance and even environmental issues.[14] Integration of these tasks makes sense because many of these decisions areas require overlapping pieces of data. PLM software, a $9 billion market, is now a tool of many large organizations, including Lockheed Martin, GE, Procter & Gamble, Toyota, and Boeing. Boeing estimates that PLM is cutting final assembly of its 787 jet from 2 weeks to 3 days. PLM is now finding its way into medium and small manufacture as well.[15]

Shorter life cycles, more technologically challenging products, more regulations about materials and manufacturing processes, and more environmental issues all make PLM an appealing tool for operations managers.

SERVICE DESIGN

Much of our discussion so far has focused on what we can call tangible products, that is, goods. On the other side of the product coin are, of course, services. Service industries include banking, finance, insurance, transportation, and communications. The products offered by service firms

---

[14]Some PLM vendors include supply chain elements such as sourcing, material management, and vendor evaluation in their packages, but in most instances, these are considered part of the ERP systems discussed along with MRP in Chapter 14. See, for instance, SAP PLM (**www.mySAP.com**), Parametric Technology Corp. (**www.ptc.com**), UGS Corp. (**www.ugs.com**), and Proplanner (**www.proplanner.com**).

[15]*Business Week* (May 31, 2004): 19; and *Industry Week* (August 2004): 54.

range from a medical procedure that leaves only the tiniest scar after an appendectomy, to a shampoo and cut at a hair salon, to a great movie.

Learning Objective

7. Describe customer participation in the design and production of services

Designing services is challenging because they often have unique characteristics. One reason productivity improvements in services are so low is because both the design and delivery of service products include customer interaction. When the customer participates in the design process, the service supplier may have a menu of services from which the customer selects options (see Figure 5.12[a]). At this point, the customer may even participate in the *design* of the service. Design specifications may take the form of a contract or a narrative description with photos (such as for cosmetic surgery or a hairstyle). Similarly, the customer may be involved in the *delivery* of a service (see Figure 5.12[b]) or in both design and delivery, a situation that maximizes the product design challenge (see Figure 5.12[c]).

However, as with goods, a large part of cost and quality of a service is defined at the design stage. Also as with goods, a number of techniques can both reduce costs and enhance the product. One technique is to design the product so that *customization is delayed* as late in the process as possible. This is the way a hair salon operates: Although shampoo and rinse are done in a standard way with lower-cost labor, the tint and styling (customizing) are done last. It is also the way most restaurants operate: How would you like that cooked? Which dressing would you prefer with your salad?

The second approach is to *modularize* the product so that customization takes the form of changing modules. This strategy allows modules to be designed as "fixed," standard entities. The modular approach to product design has applications in both manufacturing and service. Just as modular design allows you to buy a Harley-Davidson motorcycle or a high-fidelity sound system with just the features you want, modular flexibility also lets you buy meals, clothes, and insurance on a mix-and-match (modular) basis. Similarly, investment portfolios are put together on a modular basis, as are college curricula. Both are examples of how the modular approach can be used to customize a service.

A third approach to the design of services is to divide the service into small parts and identify those parts that lend themselves to *automation* or *reduced customer interaction*. For instance, by isolating check-cashing activity via ATM machines, banks have been very effective at designing

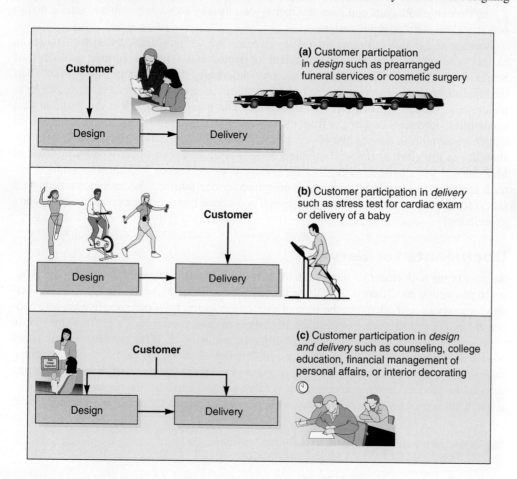

◀ **Figure 5.12**

Customer Participation in the Design of Services

(a) Customer participation in *design* such as prearranged funeral services or cosmetic surgery

Customer

Design → Delivery

(b) Customer participation in *delivery* such as stress test for cardiac exam or delivery of a baby

Customer

Design → Delivery

(c) Customer participation in *design and delivery* such as counseling, college education, financial management of personal affairs, or interior decorating

Customer

Design → Delivery

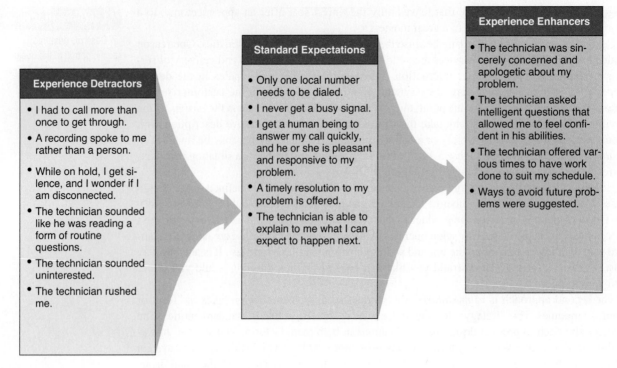

Experience Detractors

- I had to call more than once to get through.
- A recording spoke to me rather than a person.
- While on hold, I get silence, and I wonder if I am disconnected.
- The technician sounded like he was reading a form of routine questions.
- The technician sounded uninterested.
- The technician rushed me.

Standard Expectations

- Only one local number needs to be dialed.
- I never get a busy signal.
- I get a human being to answer my call quickly, and he or she is pleasant and responsive to my problem.
- A timely resolution to my problem is offered.
- The technician is able to explain to me what I can expect to happen next.

Experience Enhancers

- The technician was sincerely concerned and apologetic about my problem.
- The technician asked intelligent questions that allowed me to feel confident in his abilities.
- The technician offered various times to have work done to suit my schedule.
- Ways to avoid future problems were suggested.

▲ **Figure 5.13**   **Moment of Truth: The Customer Contacts the Service Hotline at a Computer Company**

a product that both increases customer service and reduces costs. Similarly, airlines are moving to ticketless service. Because airlines spend $15 to $30 to produce a single ticket (including labor, printing, and travel agent's commission), ticketless systems save the industry a billion dollars a year. Reducing both costs and lines at airports—and thereby increasing customer satisfaction—provides a win–win "product" design.

Because of the high customer interaction in many service industries, a fourth technique is to focus design on the so-called moment of truth. Jan Carlzon, former president of Scandinavian Airways, believes that in the service industry there is a moment of truth when the relationship between the provider and the customer is crucial.[16] At that moment, the customer's satisfaction with the service is defined. The *moment of truth* is the moment that exemplifies, enhances, or detracts from the customer's expectations. That moment may be as simple as a smile or having the checkout clerk focus on you rather than talking over his shoulder to the clerk at the next counter. Moments of truth can occur when you order at McDonald's, get a haircut, or register for college courses. Figure 5.13 shows a moment-of-truth analysis for a computer company's customer service hotline. The operations manager's task is to identify moments of truth and design operations that meet or exceed the customer's expectations.

Documents for Services

Because of the high customer interaction of most services, the documents for moving the product to production are different from those used in goods-producing operations. The documentation for a service will often take the form of explicit *job instructions* that specify what is to happen at the moment of truth. For instance, regardless of how good a bank's products may be in terms of checking, savings, trusts, loans, mortgages, and so forth, if the moment of truth is not done well, the product may be poorly received. Example 2 shows the kind of documentation a bank may use to move a product (drive-up window banking) to "production." In a telemarketing service, the product design is communicated to production personnel in the form of *telephone script*, while a *storyboard* (see the photo on the next page) is used for movie and TV production.

---

[16]Jan Carlzon, *Moments of Truth* (Cambridge, MA: Ballinger Publishing, 1987).

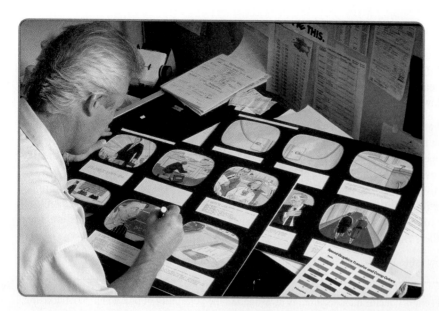

◄ *This storyboard lays out the product clearly so that each activity is identified and its contribution to the process known.*

EXAMPLE 2

Service
documentation
for production

First Bank Corp. wants to ensure effective delivery of service to its drive-up customers.

Approach: Develop a "production" document for the tellers at the drive-up window that provides the information necessary to do an effective job.

Solution:

Documentation for Tellers at Drive-up Windows

Customers who use the drive-up teller windows rather than walk-in lobbies require a different customer relations technique. The distance and machinery between the teller and the customer raises communication barriers. Guidelines to ensure good customer relations at the drive-up window are:

- Be especially discreet when talking to the customer through the microphone.
- Provide written instructions for customers who must fill out forms you provide.
- Mark lines to be completed or attach a note with instructions.
- Always say "please" and "thank you" when speaking through the microphone.
- Establish eye contact with the customer if the distance allows it.
- If a transaction requires that the customer park the car and come into the lobby, apologize for the inconvenience.

Source: Adapted with permission from *Teller Operations* (Chicago, IL: The Institute of Financial Education, 1999): 32.

Insight: By providing documentation in the form of a script/guideline for tellers, the likelihood of effective communication and a good product/service is improved.

Learning exercise: Modify the guidelines above to show how they would be different for a drive-through restaurant. [Answer: Written instructions, marking lines to be completed, or coming into the store are seldom necessary, but techniques for making change, and proper transfer of the order should be included.]

Related problem: 5.7

APPLICATION OF DECISION TREES TO PRODUCT DESIGN

Decision trees can be used for new-product decisions as well as for a wide variety of other management problems. They are particularly helpful when there are a series of decisions and various outcomes that lead to *subsequent* decisions followed by other outcomes. To form a decision tree, we use the following procedure:

1. Be sure that all possible alternatives and states of nature are included in the tree. This includes an alternative of "doing nothing."
2. Payoffs are entered at the end of the appropriate branch. This is the place to develop the payoff of achieving this branch.
3. The objective is to determine the expected value of each course of action. We accomplish this by starting at the end of the tree (the right-hand side) and working toward the beginning of the tree (the left), calculating values at each step and "pruning" alternatives that are not as good as others from the same node.

Example 3 shows the use of a decision tree applied to product design.

EXAMPLE 3

Decision tree applied to product design

Silicon, Inc., a semiconductor manufacturer, is investigating the possibility of producing and marketing a microprocessor. Undertaking this project will require either purchasing a sophisticated CAD system or hiring and training several additional engineers. The market for the product could be either favorable or unfavorable. Silicon, Inc., of course, has the option of not developing the new product at all.

With favorable acceptance by the market, sales would be 25,000 processors selling for $100 each. With unfavorable acceptance, sales would be only 8,000 processors selling for $100 each. The cost of CAD equipment is $500,000, but that of hiring and training three new engineers is only $375,000. However, manufacturing costs should drop from $50 each when manufacturing without CAD, to $40 each when manufacturing with CAD.

The probability of favorable acceptance of the new microprocessor is .40; the probability of unfavorable acceptance is .60.

► **Figure 5.14**

Decision Tree for Development of a New Product

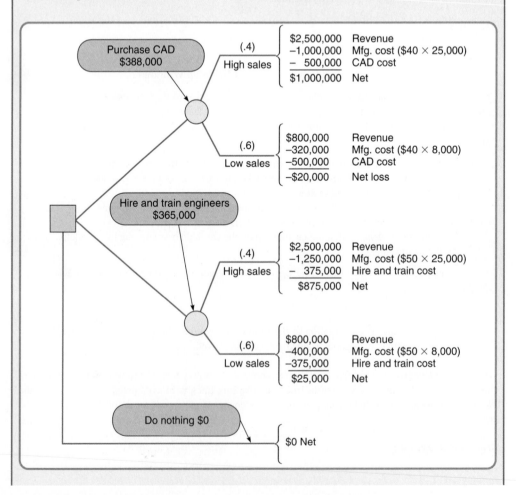

Approach: Use of a decision tree seems appropriate as Silicon, Inc., has the basic ingredients: a choice of decisions, probabilities, and payoffs.

Solution: In Figure 5.14 we draw a decision tree with a branch for each of the three decisions, assign the respective probabilities payoff for each branch, and then compute the respective EMVs. The expected monetary values (EMVs) have been circled at each step of the decision tree. For the top branch:

$$\text{EMV (Purchase CAD system)} = (.4)(\$1{,}000{,}000) + (.6)(-\$20{,}000)$$
$$= \$388{,}000$$

This figure represents the results that will occur if Silicon, Inc., purchases CAD.

The expected value of hiring and training engineers is the second series of branches:

$$\text{EMV (Hire/train engineers)} = (.4)(\$875{,}000) + (.6)(\$25{,}000)$$
$$= \$365{,}000$$

The EMV of doing nothing is $0.

Because the top branch has the highest expected monetary value (an EMV of $388,000 vs. $365,000 vs. $0), it represents the best decision. Management should purchase the CAD system.

Insight: Use of the decision tree provides both objectivity and structure to our analysis of the Silicon, Inc., decision.

Learning exercise: If Silicon, Inc., thinks the probabilities of high sales and low sales may be equal, at .5 each, what is the best decision? [Answer: Purchase CAD remains the best decision, but with an EMV of $490,000.]

Related problems: 5.10, 5.11, 5.12, 5.13, 5.14, 5.15, 5.16, 5.18

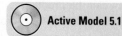

Active Model 5.1

Example 3 is further illustrated in Active Model 5.1 on the CD-ROM and in the Exercise located on page 186.

TRANSITION TO PRODUCTION

Eventually, a product, whether a good or service, has been selected, designed, and defined. It has progressed from an idea to a functional definition, and then perhaps to a design. Now, management must make a decision as to further development and production or termination of the product idea. One of the arts of modern management is knowing when to move a product from development to production; this move is known as *transition to production.* The product development staff is always interested in making improvements in a product. Because this staff tends to see product development as evolutionary, they may never have a completed product, but as we noted earlier, the cost of late product introduction is high. Although these conflicting pressures exist, management must make a decision—more development or production.

Once this decision is made, there is usually a period of trial production to ensure that the design is indeed producible. This is the manufacturability test. This trial also gives the operations staff the opportunity to develop proper tooling, quality control procedures, and training of personnel to ensure that production can be initiated successfully. Finally, when the product is deemed both marketable and producible, line management will assume responsibility.

Some companies appoint a *project manager*; others use *product development teams* to ensure that the transition from development to production is successful. Both approaches allow a wide range of resources and talents to be brought to bear to ensure satisfactory production of a product that is still in flux. A third approach is *integration of the product development and manufacturing organizations.* This approach allows for easy shifting of resources between the two organizations as needs change. The operations manager's job is to make the transition from R&D to production seamless or as smooth as possible.

Summary

Effective product strategy requires selecting, designing, and defining a product and then transitioning that product to production. Only when this strategy is carried out effectively can the production function contribute its maximum to the organization. The operations manager must build a product development system that has the ability to conceive, design, and produce products that will yield a competitive advantage for the firm. As products move through their life cycle (introduction, growth, maturity, and decline), the options that the operations manager should pursue change. Both manufactured and service products

have a variety of techniques available to aid in performing this activity efficiently.

Written specifications, bills of material, and engineering drawings aid in defining products. Similarly, assembly drawings, assembly charts, route sheets, and work orders are often used to assist in the actual production of the product. Once a product is in production, value analysis is appropriate to ensure maximum product value. Engineering change notices and configuration management provide product documentation.

Key Terms

Product decision *(p. 158)*
Product-by-value analysis *(p. 160)*
Quality function deployment (QFD) *(p. 162)*
House of quality *(p. 163)*
Product development teams *(p. 165)*
Concurrent engineering *(p. 166)*
Manufacturability and value engineering
    (p. 166)
Robust design *(p. 167)*
Modular design *(p. 167)*
Computer-aided design (CAD) *(p. 167)*
Design for manufacture and assembly
    (DFMA) *(p. 167)*

3-D object modeling *(p. 167)*
Standard for the Exchange of Product Data
    (STEP) *(p. 168)*
Computer-aided manufacturing (CAM)
    (p. 168)
Virtual reality *(p. 169)*
Value analysis *(p. 169)*
Time-based competition *(p. 172)*
Joint ventures *(p. 174)*
Alliances *(p. 174)*
Engineering drawing *(p. 175)*

Bill of material (BOM) *(p. 175)*
Make-or-buy decision *(p. 176)*
Group technology *(p. 176)*
Assembly drawing *(p. 177)*
Assembly chart *(p. 177)*
Route sheet *(p. 177)*
Work order *(p. 177)*
Engineering change notice (ECN) *(p. 178)*
Configuration management *(p. 178)*
Product life-cycle management (PLM)
    (p. 178)

Solved Problem

⊙ **Virtual Office Hours help is available on Student DVD.**

Solved Problem 5.1

Sarah King, president of King Electronics, Inc., has two design options for her new line of high-resolution cathode-ray tubes (CRTs) for CAD workstations. The life cycle sales forecast for the CRT is 100,000 units.

Design option A has a .90 probability of yielding 59 good CRTs per 100 and a .10 probability of yielding 64 good CRTs per 100. This design will cost $1,000,000.

Design option B has a .80 probability of yielding 64 good units per 100 and a .20 probability of yielding 59 good units per 100. This design will cost $1,350,000.

Good or bad, each CRT will cost $75. Each good CRT will sell for $150. Bad CRTs are destroyed and have no salvage value. We ignore any disposal costs in this problem.

Solution

We draw the decision tree to reflect the two decisions and the probabilities associated with each decision. We then determine the payoff associated with each branch. The resulting tree is shown in Figure 5.15.

For design A:

$$\text{EMV (design A)} = (.9)(\$350,000) + (.1)(\$1,100,000)$$
$$= \$425,000$$

For design B:

$$\text{EMV (design B)} = (.8)(\$750,000) + (.2)(\$0)$$
$$= \$600,000$$

The highest payoff is design option B, at $600,000.

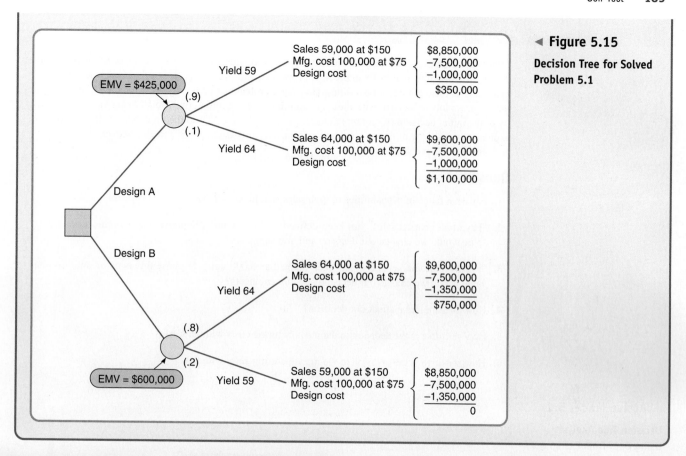

◄ Figure 5.15

Decision Tree for Solved Problem 5.1

Self-Test

- **Before taking the self-test**, refer to the learning objectives listed at the beginning of the chapter and the key terms listed at the end of the chapter.
- Use the key at the back of the text to **correct** your answers.
- **Restudy** pages that correspond to any questions you answered incorrectly or material you feel uncertain about.

1. A product's life cycle is divided into four stages, which include:
   a) introduction
   b) growth
   c) maturity
   d) all of the above

2. Listing products in descending order of their individual dollar contribution to the firm is called:
   a) product-by-value analysis
   b) value analysis
   c) value engineering
   d) design database
   e) all of the above

3. The benefits of CAD/CAM include:
   a) shorter design time
   b) production cost reductions
   c) product quality improvement
   d) design database availability
   e) all of the above

4. A route sheet:
   a) lists the operations necessary to produce the component

   b) is an instruction to make a given quantity of a particular item
   c) is a schematic showing how a product is assembled
   d) is a document showing the flow of product components
   e) all of the above

5. An assembly chart is:
   a) an exploded view of the product
   b) a schematic showing how the product is put together
   c) a list of the operations necessary to produce the component
   d) an instruction to make a given quantity of a particular item
   e) a set of detailed instructions about how to perform a task

6. Four techniques that are available when a service is designed are:
   a) recognize political or legal change, technological change, sociological demographic change, and economic change
   b) understand product introduction, growth, maturity, and decline
   c) recognize functional specifications, product specifications, design review, and test markets
   d) ensure customization is done as late in the process as possible, modularize the product, reduce customer interaction, focus on the moment of truth

7. A product-by-value analysis report is _____
   _____.

8. Products must be continually developed because _____
   _____.

9. Products are documented by _____
   _____.

Active Model Exercise

This Active Model appears on your student CD-ROM. It allows you to evaluate important elements in a decision tree such as that in Example 3. A sequential decision tree is one of the models in operations management that contains probabilities. Generally, probabilities are estimates (forecasts), and there is much uncertainty associated with these probabilities. We use this Active Model to explore the sensitivity of the initial decision (hiring more engineers or purchase CAD) to the probabilities. In addition, we explore the sensitivity of the decision to the estimated (forecasted) payoffs in each sequence of decisions and probabilistic events.

Questions

1. For what range of probabilities of high sales should we purchase the CAD system?

2. "Favorable market sales" has been defined as 25,000 units. Suppose this is optimistic. At what value would we change our decision and hire engineers?

3. "Unfavorable market sales" has been defined as 8,000 units. Suppose this is optimistic. At what value would we change our decision and hire engineers?

4. How does the price affect our decision?

5. How sensitive is the decision to the manufacturing costs without CAD?

6. How sensitive is the decision to the manufacturing costs with CAD?

► **Active Model 5.1**

Decision Tree Analysis Using Data from Example 3

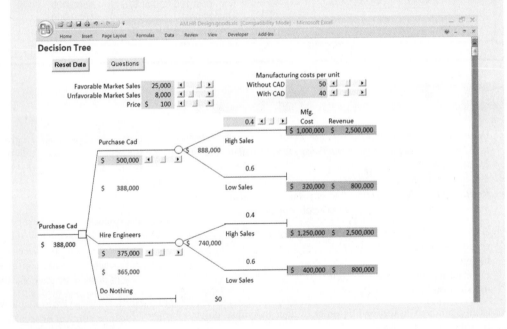

Internet and Student CD-ROM/DVD Exercises

Visit our Companion Web site or use your student CD-ROM/DVD to help with material in this chapter.

 On Our Companion Web Site, www.prenhall.com/heizer
- Self-Study Quizzes
- Practice Problems
- Virtual Company Tour
- PowerPoint Lecture

On Your Student CD-ROM
- Practice Problems
- Active Model Exercise
- Link to QFD Capture Software
- POM for Windows

On Your Student DVD
- Video Clips and Video Case
- Virtual Office Hours for Solved Problem

Discussion Questions

1. Why is it necessary to document a product explicitly?
2. What techniques do we use to define a product?
3. In what ways is product strategy linked to product decisions?
4. Once a product is defined, what documents are used to assist production personnel in its manufacture?
5. What is time-based competition?
6. Describe the differences between joint ventures and alliances.
7. Describe four organizational approaches to product development. Which of these is generally thought to be best?
8. Explain what is meant by robust design.
9. What are three specific ways in which computer-aided design (CAD) benefits the design engineer?
10. What information is contained in a bill of material?
11. What information is contained in an engineering drawing?
12. What information is contained in an assembly chart? In a process sheet?
13. Explain what is meant in service design by the "moment of truth."
14. Explain how the house of quality translates customer desires into product/service attributes.
15. What are the advantages of computer-aided design?
16. What strategic advantages does computer-aided design provide?

Ethical Dilemma

John Edwards, president of Edwards Toy Company, Inc., in South Carolina, has just reviewed the design of a new pull-toy locomotive for 1- to 3-year-olds. John's design and marketing staff are very enthusiastic about the market for the product and the potential of follow-on circus train cars. The sales manager is looking forward to a very good reception at the annual toy show in Dallas next month. John, too, is delighted, as he is faced with a layoff if orders do not improve.

John's production people have worked out the manufacturing issues and produced a successful pilot run. However, the quality testing staff suggests that under certain conditions, a hook to attach cars to the locomotive and the crank for the bell can be broken off. This is an issue because children can choke on small parts such as these. In the quality test, 1- to 3-year-olds were unable to break off these parts; there were *no* failures. But when the test simulated the force of an adult tossing the locomotive into a toy box or a 5-year-old throwing it on the floor, there were failures. The estimate is that one of the two parts can be broken off 4 times out of 100,000 throws. Neither the design nor the material people know how to make the toy safer and still perform as designed. The failure rate is low and certainly normal for this type of toy, but not at the Six Sigma level that John's firm strives for. And, of course, someone, someday may sue. A child choking on the broken part is a serious matter. Also, John was recently reminded in a discussion with legal counsel that U.S. case law suggests that new products may not be produced if there is "actual or foreseeable knowledge of a problem" with the product.

The design of successful, ethically produced, new products, as suggested in this chapter, is a complex task. What should John do?

Problems*

•• **5.1** Construct a house of quality matrix for a wristwatch. Be sure to indicate specific customer wants that you think the general public desires. Then complete the matrix to show how an operations manager might identify specific attributes that can be measured and controlled to meet those customer desires.

•• **5.2** Using the house of quality, pick a real product (a good or service) and analyze how an existing organization satisfies customer requirements.

•• **5.3** Prepare a house of quality for a mousetrap.

•• **5.4** Conduct an interview with a prospective purchaser of a new bicycle and translate the customer's *wants* into the specific *hows* of the firm.

•• **5.5** Prepare a bill of material for (a) a pair of eyeglasses and its case or (b) a fast-food sandwich (visit a local sandwich shop like

Subway, McDonald's, Blimpie, Quizno's; perhaps a clerk or the manager will provide you with details on the quantity or weight of various ingredients—otherwise, estimate the quantities).

•• **5.6** Draw an assembly chart for a pair of eyeglasses and its case.

•• **5.7** Prepare a script for telephone callers at the university's annual "phone-a-thon" fund raiser.

•• **5.8** Prepare an assembly chart for a table lamp.

••• **5.9** Prepare a product-by-value analysis for the following products, and given the position in its life cycle, identify the issues likely to confront the operations manager, and his or her possible actions. Product Alpha has annual sales of 1,000 units and a contribution of $2,500; it is in the introductory stage. Product Bravo has annual sales of 1,500 units and a contribution of $3,000; it is in the growth stage. Product Charlie has annual sales of 3,500 units and a contribution of $1,750; it is in the decline stage.

*Note: **PX** means the problem may be solved with POM for Windows and/or Excel OM.

•• **5.10** Given the contribution made on each of the three products in the following table and their position in the life cycle, identify a reasonable operations strategy for each:

Product	Product Contribution (% of selling price)	Company Contribution (%: total annual contribution divided by total annual sales)	Position in Life Cycle
Notebook computer	30	40	Growth
Palmheld computer	30	50	Introduction
Hand calculator	50	10	Decline

•• **5.11** The product design group of Flores Electric Supplies, Inc., has determined that it needs to design a new series of switches. It must decide on one of three design strategies. The market forecast is for 200,000 units. The better and more sophisticated the design strategy and the more time spent on value engineering, the less will be the variable cost. The chief of engineering design, Dr. W. L. Berry, has decided that the following costs are a good estimate of the initial and variable costs connected with each of the three strategies:

a) *Low-tech:* a low-technology, low-cost process consisting of hiring several new junior engineers. This option has a fixed cost of $45,000 and variable-cost probabilities of .3 for $.55 each, .4 for $.50, and .3 for $.45.

b) *Subcontract:* a medium-cost approach using a good outside design staff. This approach would have a fixed cost of $65,000 and variable-cost probabilities of .7 of $.45, .2 of $.40, and .1 of $.35.

c) *High-tech:* a high-technology approach using the very best of the inside staff and the latest computer-aided design technology. This approach has a fixed cost of $75,000 and variable-cost probabilities of .9 of $.40 and .1 of $.35. What is the best decision based on an expected monetary value (EMV) criterion? (*Note:* We want the lowest EMV, as we are dealing with costs in this problem.) **Px**

•• **5.12** Clarkson Products, Inc., of Clarkson, New York, has the option of (a) proceeding immediately with production of a new top-of-the-line stereo TV that has just completed prototype testing or (b) having the value analysis team complete a study. If Ed Lusk, VP for operations, proceeds with the existing prototype (option a), the firm can expect sales to be 100,000 units at $550 each, with a probability of .6 and a .4 probability of 75,000 at $550. If, however, he uses the value analysis team (option b), the firm expects sales of 75,000 units at $750, with a probability of .7 and a .3 probability of 70,000 units at $750. Value analysis, at a cost of $100,000, is only used in option b. Which option has the highest expected monetary value (EMV)? **Px**

•• **5.13** Residents of Mill River have fond memories of ice skating at a local park. An artist has captured the experience in a drawing and is hoping to reproduce it and sell framed copies to current and former residents. He thinks that if the market is good he can sell 400 copies of the elegant version at $125 each. If the market is not good, he will sell only 300 at $90 each. He can make a deluxe version of the same drawing instead. He feels that if the market is good he can sell 500 copies of the deluxe version at $100 each. If the market is not good, he will sell only 400 copies at $70 each. In either case, production costs will be approximately $35,000. He can also choose to do nothing at this time. If he believes there is a 50% probability of a good market, what should he do? Why? **Px**

•• **5.14** Ritz Products's materials manager, Bruce Elwell, must determine whether to make or buy a new semiconductor for the wrist TV that the firm is about to produce. One million units are expected to be produced over the life cycle. If the product is made, start-up and production costs of the *make* decision total $1 million, with a probability of .4 that the product will be satisfactory and a .6 probability that it will not. If the product is not satisfactory, the firm will have to reevaluate the decision. If the decision is reevaluated, the choice will be whether to spend another $1 million to redesign the semiconductor or to purchase. Likelihood of success the second time that the make decision is made is .9. If the second *make* decision also fails, the firm must purchase. Regardless of when the purchase takes place, Elwell's best judgment of cost is that Ritz will pay $.50 for each purchased semiconductor plus $1 million in vendor development cost.

a) Assuming that Ritz must have the semiconductor (stopping or doing without is not a viable option), what is the best decision?

b) What criteria did you use to make this decision?

c) What is the worst that can happen to Ritz as a result of this particular decision? What is the best that can happen? **Px**

•• **5.15** Page Engineering designs and constructs air conditioning and heating (HVAC) systems for hospitals and clinics. Currently the company's staff is overloaded with design work. There is a major design project due in 8 weeks. The penalty for completing the design late is $14,000 per week, since any delay will cause the facility to open later than anticipated, and cost the client significant revenue. If the company uses its inside engineers to complete the design, it will have to pay them overtime for all work. Page has estimated that it will cost $12,000 per week (wages and overhead), including late weeks, to have company engineers complete the design. Page is also considering having an outside engineering firm do the design. A bid of $92,000 has been received for the completed design. Yet another option for completing the design is to conduct a joint design by having a third engineering company complete all electromechanical components of the design at a cost of $56,000. Page would then complete the rest of the design and control systems at an estimated cost of $30,000.

Page has estimated the following probabilities of completing the project within various time frames when using each of the three options. Those estimates are shown in the following table:

		Probability of Completing the Design		
Option	**On Time**	**One Week Late**	**Two Weeks Late**	**Three Weeks Late**
Internal Engineers	.4	.5	.1	—
External Engineers	.2	.4	.3	.1
Joint Design	.1	.3	.4	.2

What is the best decision based on an expected monetary value criterion? (*Note:* You want the lowest EMV because we are dealing with costs in this problem.) **Px**

••• **5.16** Use the data in Solved Problem 5.1 to examine what happens to the decision if Sarah King can increase yields from 59,000 to 64,000 by applying an expensive phosphorus to the screen at an added cost of $250,000. Prepare the modified decision tree. What are the payoffs, and which branch has the greatest EMV?

•••• **5.17** Using the house of quality sequence, as described in Figure 5.4 on page 165, determine how you might deploy resources to achieve the desired quality for a product or service whose production process you understand.

•••• **5.18** McBurger, Inc., wants to redesign its kitchens to improve productivity and quality. Three designs, called designs K1, K2, and K3, are under consideration. No matter which design is used, daily demand for sandwiches at a typical McBurger restaurant is for 500 sandwiches. A sandwich costs $1.30 to produce. Non-defective sandwiches sell, on the average, for $2.50 per sandwich. Defective sandwiches cannot be sold and are scrapped. The goal is to choose a design that maximizes the expected profit at a typical restaurant over a 300-day period. Designs K1, K2, and K3 cost $100,000, $130,000, and $180,000, respectively. Under design K1, there is a .80 chance that 90 out of each 100 sandwiches are non-defective and a .20 chance that 70 out of each 100 sandwiches are non-defective. Under design K2, there is a .85 chance that 90 out of each 100 sandwiches are non-defective and a .15 chance that 75 out of each 100 sandwiches are non-defective. Under design K3, there is a .90 chance that 95 out of each 100 sandwiches are non-defective and a .10 chance that 80 out of each 100 sandwiches are non-defective. What is the expected profit level of the design that achieves the maximum expected 300-day profit level?

Case Studies

De Mar's Product Strategy

De Mar, a plumbing, heating, and air-conditioning company located in Fresno, California, has a simple but powerful product strategy: *Solve the customer's problem no matter what, solve the problem when the customer needs it solved, and make sure the customer feels good when you leave.* De Mar offers guaranteed, same-day service for customers requiring it. The company provides 24-hour-a-day, 7-day-a-week service at no extra charge for customers whose air conditioning dies on a hot summer Sunday or whose toilet overflows at 2:30 A.M.. As assistant service coordinator Janie Walter puts it: "We will be there to fix your A/C on the fourth of July, and it's not a penny extra. When our competitors won't get out of bed, we'll be there!"

De Mar guarantees the price of a job to the penny before the work begins. Whereas most competitors guarantee their work for 30 days, De Mar guarantees all parts and labor for one year. The company assesses no travel charge because "it's not fair to charge customers for driving out." Owner Larry Harmon says: "We are in an industry that doesn't have the best reputation. If we start making money our main goal, we are in trouble. So I stress customer satisfaction; money is the by-product."

De Mar uses selective hiring, ongoing training and education, performance measures and compensation that incorporate customer satisfaction, strong teamwork, peer pressure, empowerment, and aggressive promotion to implement its strategy. Says credit manager Anne Semrick: "The person who wants a nine-to-five job needs to go somewhere else."

De Mar is a premium pricer. Yet customers respond because De Mar delivers value—that is, benefits for costs. In 8 years, annual sales increased from about $200,000 to more than $3.3 million.

Discussion Questions

1. What is De Mar's product? Identify the tangible parts of this product and its service components.
2. How should other areas of De Mar (marketing, finance, personnel) support its product strategy?
3. Even though De Mar's product is primarily a service product, how should each of the 10 OM decisions in the text be managed to ensure that the product is successful?

Source: Reprinted with the permission of The Free Press, from *On Great Service: A Framework for Action* by Leonard L. Berry. Copyright © 1995 by Leonard L. Berry.

Product Design at Regal Marine

Video Case

With hundreds of competitors in the boat business, Regal Marine must work to differentiate itself from the flock. As we saw in the *Global Company Profile* that opened this chapter, Regal continuously introduces innovative, high-quality new boats. Its differentiation strategy is reflected in a product line consisting of 22 models.

To maintain this stream of innovation, and with so many boats at varying stages of their life cycles, Regal constantly seeks design input from customers, dealers, and consultants. Design ideas rapidly find themselves in the styling studio, where they are placed onto CAD machines in order to speed the development process. Existing boat designs are always evolving as the company tries to stay stylish and competitive. Moreover, with life cycles as short as 3 years, a steady stream of new products is required. A few years ago, the new product was the three-passenger $11,000 Rush, a small but powerful boat capable of pulling a water-skier. This was followed with a 20-foot inboard–outboard performance boat with so many innovations that it won prize after prize in the industry. Another new boat is a redesigned 44-foot Commodore that sleeps six in luxury staterooms. With all these models and innovations, Regal designers and production personnel are under pressure to respond quickly.

By getting key suppliers on board early and urging them to participate at the design stage, Regal improves both innovations and quality while speeding product development. Regal finds that the sooner it brings suppliers on board, the faster it can bring new boats to the market. After a development stage that constitutes concept and styling, CAD designs yield product specifications. The first stage in actual production is the creation of the "plug," a foam-based carving used to make the molds for fiberglass hulls and decks. Specifications from the CAD system drive the carving process. Once the plug is carved, the permanent molds for each new hull and deck design are formed. Molds take about 4 to 8 weeks to make and are all handmade. Similar molds are made for many of the other features in Regal boats—from galley and stateroom components to lavatories and steps. Finished molds can be joined and used to make thousands of boats.

Discussion Questions*

1. How does the concept of product life cycle apply to Regal Marine products?
2. What strategy does Regal use to stay competitive?
3. What kind of engineering savings is Regal achieving by using CAD technology rather than traditional drafting techniques?
4. What are the likely benefits of the CAD design technology?

*You may wish to view this video case on your DVD before addressing these questions.

Additional Case Studies

Harvard has selected these Harvard Business School cases to accompany this chapter:

harvardbusinessonline.hbsp.harvard.edu

- **The Ritz-Carlton (#601-163):** Allows students to examine innovation and service improvement in the hospitality industry.
- **Product Development at Dell Computer Corp. (#699-010):** Focuses on how Dell redesigned its new-product development process.
- **Innovation at 3M Corp. (A) (#699-012):** Describes how 3M Corp.'s new-product development process obtains customer input.
- **CIBA Vision: The Daily Disposable Lens Project (A) (#696-100):** Examines CIBA Vision's evaluation of a new low-cost disposable contact lens.
- **Apple Powerbook (A) (#994-023):** Examines tension between perfection and time to market.
- **BMW: The 7 Series Project (A) (#692-083):** Explores decision about how to manufacture prototype vehicles.

Bibliography

Baldwin, C. Y., and K. B. Clark. *Design Rules. Volume 1: The Power of Modularity.* Cambridge, MA: MIT Press, 2000.

Brockman, Beverly K., and Robert M. Morgan. "The Role of Existing Knowledge in New Product Innovativeness and Performance." *Decision Sciences* 34, no. 2 (Spring 2003): 385–419.

Ceroni, J. A., and A. A. Velasquez. "Conflict Detection and Resolution in Distributed Design." *Production Planning & Control* 14, no. 8 (December 2003): 734–742.

Cohen, Lou. *Quality Function Deployment.* Upper Saddle River, NJ: Prentice Hall, 1995.

Ernst, David, and James Bamford. "Your Alliances Are Too Stable." *Harvard Business Review* 83, no. 5 (June 2005): 133–141.

Gerwin, Donald. "Coordinating New Product Development in Strategic Alliances." *The Academy of Management Review* 29, no. 2 (April 2004): 241–257.

Krishnan, V., and Karl T. Ulrich. "Product Development Decisions: A Review of the Literature." *Management Science* 47, no. 1 (January 2001): 1–21.

Loch, C. H., and C. Terwiesch. "Rush and Be Wrong or Wait and Be Late? A Model of Information in Collaborative Processes." *Production and Operations Management* 14, no. 3 (Fall 2005): 331–343.

Otto, K., and K. Wood. *Product Design.* Upper Saddle River, NJ: Prentice Hall, 2001.

Revelle, J. B., J. W. Moran, and C. A. Cox. *The Quality Function Deployment Handbook.* New York: Wiley, 1999.

Saaksvuori, A., and A. Immonen. *Product Lifecycle Management.* Berlin: Springer-Verlag (2004).

Thomke, Stefan. "Enlightened Experimentation: The New Imperative for Innovation." *Harvard Business Review* 79, no. 2 (February 2001): 67–72.

Ulrich, K., and S. Eppinger. *Product Design and Development*, 3rd ed. New York: McGraw-Hill, 2004.

Internet Resources

Agile Manufacturing Project at MIT: **web.mit.edu/ctpid/www/agile/atlanta.html**

Centre for Design at the Royal Melbourne Institute of Technology: **www.cfd.rmit.edu.au/**

Concurrent Engineering Virtual Environment Demo: University of Hertfordshire: **www.ider.herts.ac.uk/ider/design.html**

Consortium on Green Design and Manufacturing: **cgdm.berkeley.edu**

EH&S Management Systems Center: **ems-hsms.com**

Examples of bad design: **www.baddesigns.com**

Green Design Initiative at Carnegie Mellon University: **www.ce.cmu.edu/GreenDesign/**

Design Safety Engineering Risk Assessment Software, Training, and Consulting: **www.designsafe.com**

CHAPTER 6

Managing Quality

Chapter Outline

Ten OM Strategy Decisions

Design of Goods and Services

Managing Quality

Process Strategy

Location Strategies

Layout Strategies

Human Resources

Supply Chain Management

Inventory Management

Scheduling

Maintenance

Learning Objectives

When you complete this chapter you should be able to

1. Define quality and TQM
2. Describe the ISO international quality standards
3. Explain Six Sigma
4. Explain how benchmarking is used
5. Explain quality robust products and Taguchi concepts
6. Use the seven tools of TQM

Managing Quality Provides a Competitive Advantage at Arnold Palmer Hospital

Since 1989, the Arnold Palmer Hospital, named after its famous golfing benefactor, has touched the lives of over 7 million children and women and their families. Its patients come not only from its Orlando location but from all 50 states and around the world. More than 13,000 babies are delivered every year at Arnold Palmer, and its huge neonatal intensive care unit boasts one of the highest survival rates in the U.S.

Every hospital professes quality health care, but at Arnold Palmer quality is the mantra—practiced in a fashion like the Ritz-Carlton practices it in the hotel industry. The hospital typically scores in the top 10% of national benchmark studies in terms of patient satisfaction. And its managers follow patient questionnaire results daily. If anything is amiss, corrective action takes place immediately.

Virtually every quality management technique we present in this chapter is employed at Arnold Palmer Hospital:

- *Continuous improvement:* The hospital constantly seeks new ways to lower infection rates, readmission rates, deaths, costs, and hospital stay times.
- *Employee empowerment:* When employees see a problem, they are trained to take care of it. Just like at the Ritz, staff are empowered to give gifts to patients displeased with some aspect of service.
- *Benchmarking:* The hospital belongs to a 2,000-member organization that monitors standards in many areas and provides monthly feedback to the hospital.
- *Just-in-time:* Supplies are delivered to Arnold Palmer on a JIT basis. This keeps inventory costs low and keeps quality problems from hiding.

▼ *The lobby of Arnold Palmer Hospital, with its 20-foot-high Genie, is clearly intended as a warm and friendly place for children.*

▼ *The Storkboard is a visible chart of the status of each baby about to be delivered, so all nurses and doctors are kept up-to-date at a glance.*

This PYXIS inventory station gives nurses quick access to medicines and supplies needed in their departments. When the nurse removes an item for patient use, the item is automatically billed to that account, and usage is noted at the main supply area.

► The Mark Twain quote on the board reads "Always Do Right. This will gratify some people and astonish most." The hospital has redesigned its neonatal rooms. In the old system, there were 16 neonatal beds in an often noisy and large room. The new rooms are semiprivate, with a quiet simulated-night atmosphere. These rooms have proven to help babies develop and improve more quickly.

◄ When Arnold Palmer Hospital began planning for a new 11-story hospital across the street from its existing building, it decided on a circular pod design, creating a patient-centered environment. Rooms use warm colors, have pull-down Murphy beds for family members, 14-foot ceilings, and natural lighting with oversized windows. The pod concept also means there is a nursing station within a few feet of each 10-bed pod, saving much wasted walking time by nurses to reach the patient. The Video Case Study in Chapter 9 examines this layout in detail.

- *Tools such as Pareto charts and flowcharts:* These tools monitor processes and help the staff graphically spot problem areas and suggest ways they can be improved.

From their first day of orientation, employees from janitors to nurses learn that the patient comes first.

Staff standing in hallways will never be heard discussing their personal lives or commenting on confidential issues of health care. This culture of quality at Arnold Palmer Hospital makes a hospital visit, often traumatic to children and their parents, a warmer and more comforting experience.

QUALITY AND STRATEGY

As Arnold Palmer Hospital and many other organizations have found, quality is a wonderful tonic for improving operations. Managing quality helps build successful strategies of *differentiation*, *low cost*, and *response*. For instance, defining customer quality expectations has helped Bose Corp. successfully *differentiate* its stereo speakers as among the best in the world. Nucor has learned to produce quality steel at *low cost* by developing efficient processes that produce consistent quality. And Dell Computers rapidly *responds* to customer orders because quality systems, with little rework, have allowed it to achieve rapid throughput in its plants. Indeed, quality may be the critical success factor for these firms just as it is at Arnold Palmer Hospital.

As Figure 6.1 suggests, improvements in quality help firms increase sales and reduce costs, both of which can increase profitability. Increases in sales often occur as firms speed response, lower selling prices as a result of economies of scale, and improve their reputation for quality products. Similarly, improved quality allows costs to drop as firms increase productivity and lower rework, scrap, and warranty costs. One study found that companies with the highest quality were five times as productive (as measured by units produced per labor-hour) as companies with the poorest quality. Indeed, when the implications of an organization's long-term costs and the potential for increased sales are considered, total costs may well be at a minimum when 100% of the goods or services are perfect and defect free.

Quality, or the lack of quality, affects the entire organization from supplier to customer and from product design to maintenance. Perhaps more importantly, *building* an organization that can achieve quality also affects the entire organization—and it is a demanding task. Figure 6.2 lays out the flow of activities for an organization to use to achieve total quality management (TQM). A successful quality strategy begins with an organizational environment that fosters quality, followed by an understanding of the principles of quality, and then an effort to engage employees in the necessary activities to implement quality. When these things are done well, the organization typically satisfies its customers and obtains a competitive advantage. The ultimate goal is to win customers. Because quality causes so many other good things to happen, it is a great place to start.

DEFINING QUALITY

Quality
The ability of a product or service to meet customer needs.

The operations manager's objective is to build a total quality management system that identifies and satisfies customer needs. Total quality management takes care of the customer. Consequently, we accept the definition of **quality** as adopted by the American Society for Quality: "The totality of features and characteristics of a product or service that bears on its ability to satisfy stated or implied needs."[1]

Others, however, believe that definitions of quality fall into several categories. Some definitions are *user based*. They propose that quality "lies in the eyes of the beholder." Marketing people like this approach and so do customers. To them, higher quality means better performance, nicer features, and other (sometimes costly) improvements. To production managers, quality is *manufacturing based*. They believe that quality means conforming to standards and "making it right the first time." Yet a third approach is *product based*, which views quality as a precise and measurable variable. In this view, for example, really good ice cream has high butterfat levels.

▶ **Figure 6.1**

**Ways Quality Improves
Profitability**

[1]See the American Society for Quality Web site, at **www.asq.org**.

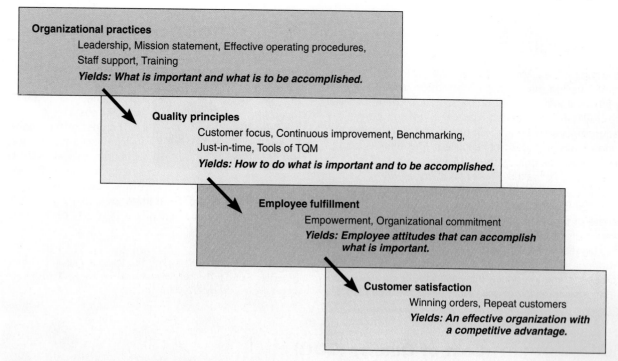

Organizational practices
Leadership, Mission statement, Effective operating procedures,
Staff support, Training
Yields: What is important and what is to be accomplished.

Quality principles
Customer focus, Continuous improvement, Benchmarking,
Just-in-time, Tools of TQM
Yields: How to do what is important and to be accomplished.

Employee fulfillment
Empowerment, Organizational commitment
*Yields: Employee attitudes that can accomplish
what is important.*

Customer satisfaction
Winning orders, Repeat customers
*Yields: An effective organization with
a competitive advantage.*

▲ **Figure 6.2**   **The Flow of Activities that Are Necessary to Achieve Total Quality Management**

This text develops approaches and techniques to address all three categories of quality. The characteristics that connote quality must first be identified through research (a user-based approach to quality). These characteristics are then translated into specific product attributes (a product-based approach to quality). Then, the manufacturing process is organized to ensure that products are made precisely to specifications (a manufacturing-based approach to quality). A process that ignores any one of these steps will not result in a quality product.

> *Quality may be in the eyes of the beholder, but to create a good or a service, operations managers must define what the beholder (the consumer) expects.*

Implications of Quality

In addition to being a critical element in operations, quality has other implications. Here are three other reasons why quality is important:

1. *Company reputation:* An organization can expect its reputation for quality—be it good or bad—to follow it. Quality will show up in perceptions about the firm's new products, employment practices, and supplier relations. Self-promotion is not a substitute for quality products.
2. *Product liability:* The courts increasingly hold organizations that design, produce, or distribute faulty products or services liable for damages or injuries resulting from their use. Legislation such as the Consumer Product Safety Act sets and enforces product standards by banning products that do not reach those standards. Impure foods that cause illness, nightgowns that burn, tires that fall apart, or auto fuel tanks that explode on impact can all lead to huge legal expenses, large settlements or losses, and terrible publicity.
3. *Global implications:* In this technological age, quality is an international, as well as OM, concern. For both a company and a country to compete effectively in the global economy, products must meet global quality, design, and price expectations. Inferior products harm a firm's profitability and a nation's balance of payments.

Malcolm Baldrige National Quality Award

The global implications of quality are so important that the U.S. has established the *Malcolm Baldrige National Quality Award* for quality achievement. The award is named for former Secretary of Commerce Malcolm Baldrige. Winners include such firms as Motorola, Milliken, Xerox, FedEx, Ritz-Carlton Hotels, AT&T, Cadillac, and Texas Instruments.

The Japanese have a similar award, the Deming Prize, named after an American, Dr. W. Edwards Deming.

> *For further information regarding the Baldrige Award and its 1,000-point scoring system, visit* ***www.quality.nist.gov.***

Perhaps it was Mercedes's merger with Chrysler that first diverted management's attention from quality. Or perhaps it was the $4.7 billion operating loss at Chrysler in 2001. But Mercedes made the difficult decision—squeeze costs to pump out better corporate profits and demand lower prices from suppliers. The result: suppliers cut corners on quality. By 2003, Mercedes had fallen to the bottom of the J.D. Power reliability survey.

Mercedes is still reeling from a series of recalls from its $50,000 E-Class sedan. In 2004, the company suffered a spate of problems with brake control systems; 680,000 cars were recalled. Then in 2005, Mercedes announced the biggest recall in its history—1.3 million cars with faulty fuel pumps made by supplier Robert Bosch. Software problems and interfaces that failed to let complex electronics systems talk to each other were to blame for many

Mercedes E-Class on fire in Tokyo.

other defects. All totaled, Mercedes spent $600 million in one year to cover warranty costs.

The cost of the quality fiasco takes a toll in sales, of course, as well. Market shares in the U.S. and Europe are down. And rival BMW has just overtaken Mercedes as the world's number-one luxury carmaker. BMW's strategy: build only premium quality cars . . . and don't get diverted.

Sources: Business Week (August 15, 2005): 31–38; *Motor Trend* (November 2005): 4; *The Wall Street Journal* (January 30, 2006): B4; and *Automotive News* (May 2, 2005); 3.

Cost of Quality (COQ)

Cost of quality (COQ)
The cost of doing things wrong—that is, the price of nonconformance.

Four major categories of costs are associated with quality. Called the **cost of quality (COQ)**, they are:

- *Prevention costs:* costs associated with reducing the potential for defective parts or services (e.g., training, quality improvement programs).
- *Appraisal costs:* costs related to evaluating products, processes, parts, and services (e.g., testing, labs, inspectors).
- *Internal failure:* costs that result from production of defective parts or services before delivery to customers (e.g., rework, scrap, downtime).
- *External costs:* costs that occur after delivery of defective parts or services (e.g., rework, returned goods, liabilities, lost goodwill, costs to society).

The first three costs can be reasonably estimated, but external costs are very hard to quantify. When GE had to recall 3.1 million dishwashers recently (because of a defective switch alleged to have started seven fires), the cost of repairs exceeded the value of all the machines. This leads to the belief by many experts that the cost of poor quality is consistently underestimated. The *OM in Action* box "The Very High Cost of Quality at Mercedes" certainly reinforces that point.

Observers of quality management believe that, on balance, the cost of quality products is only a fraction of the benefits. They think the real losers are organizations that fail to work aggressively at quality. For instance, Philip Crosby stated that quality is free. "What costs money are the unquality things—all the actions that involve not doing it right the first time."[2]

TAKUMI

Takumi is a Japanese character that symbolizes a broader dimension than quality, a deeper process than education, and a more perfect method than persistence.

Leaders in Quality Besides Crosby there are several other giants in the field of quality management, including Deming, Feigenbaum, and Juran. Table 6.1 summarizes their philosophies and contributions.

Ethics and Quality Management

For operations managers, one of the most important jobs is to deliver healthy, safe, and quality products and services to customers. The development of poor-quality products, because of inadequate design and production processes, results not only in higher production costs but also leads to injuries, lawsuits, and increased government regulation.

---

[2]Philip B. Crosby, *Quality Is Free* (New York: McGraw-Hill, 1979). Further, J. M. Juran states, in his book *Juran on Quality by Design* (The Free Press 1992, p. 119), that costs of poor quality "are huge, but the amounts are not known with precision. In most companies the accounting system provides only a minority of the information needed to quantify this cost of poor quality. It takes a great deal of time and effort to extend the accounting system so as to provide full coverage."

▼ **Table 6.1**   Leaders in the Field of Quality Management

Leader	Philosophy/Contribution
W. Edwards Deming	Deming insisted management accept responsibility for building good systems. The employee cannot produce products that on average exceed the quality of what the process is capable of producing. His 14 points for implementing quality improvement are presented in this chapter.
Joseph M. Juran	A pioneer in teaching the Japanese how to improve quality, Juran believes strongly in top-management commitment, support, and involvement in the quality effort. He is also a believer in teams that continually seek to raise quality standards. Juran varies from Deming somewhat in focusing on the customer and defining quality as fitness for use, not necessarily the written specifications.
Armand Feigenbaum	His 1961 book, *Total Quality Control*, laid out 40 steps to quality improvement processes. He viewed quality not as a set of tools but as a total field that integrated the processes of a company. His work in how people learn from each other's successes led to the field of cross-functional teamwork.
Philip B. Crosby	*Quality is Free* was Crosby's attention-getting book published in 1979. Crosby believed that in the traditional trade-off between the cost of improving quality and the cost of poor quality, the cost of poor quality is understated. The cost of poor quality should include all of the things that are involved in not doing the job right the first time. Crosby coined the term *zero defects* and stated, "There is absolutely no reason for having errors or defects in any product or service."

If a firm believes that it has introduced a questionable product, ethical conduct must dictate the responsible action. This may be a worldwide recall, as conducted by both Johnson & Johnson (for Tylenol) and Perrier (for sparkling water), when each of these products was found to be contaminated. A manufacturer must accept responsibility for any poor-quality product released to the public. Neither Ford (the Explorer SUV maker) nor Firestone (the radial tire maker) did this. In recent years, both firms have been accused of failing to issue product recalls, of withholding damaging information, and of handling complaints on an individual basis.[3]

> *High-quality products and services are the most profitable.*

There are many stakeholders involved in the production and marketing of poor-quality products, including stockholders, employees, customers, suppliers, distributors, and creditors. As a matter of ethics, management must ask if any of these stakeholders are being wronged. Every company needs to develop core values that become day-to-day guidelines for everyone from the CEO to production-line employees.

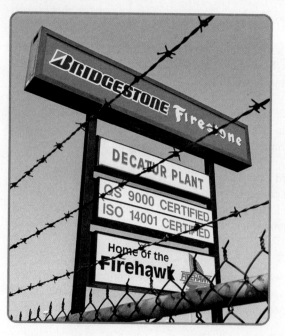

◄ *The ISO 9000 Certified sign is up, but this Bridgestone/Firestone plant in Decatur, Illinois, produced millions of defective tires that resulted in thousands of accidents and 271 deaths. After lying before Congress, the firm was forced to admit that the Firestone 500 radial had 17.5% return rates (vs. 2.9% for competitor Goodyear). Before the investigation became public knowledge, Firestone held a half-price clearance sale of defective tires in the Southeast U.S. Congress later discovered that Firestone continued to manufacture the 500 radial tire after claiming it had stopped production. This case of unethical conduct eventually resulted in the recall of 14.4 million tires and cost Bridgestone/Firestone hundreds of millions of dollars.*

[3]For further reading, see M. R. Nayebpour and D. Koehn, "The Ethics of Quality: Problems and Preconditions" *Journal of Business Ethics* 44 (April, 2003): 37–48.

INTERNATIONAL QUALITY STANDARDS

ISO 9000

Quality is so important globally that the world is uniting around a single quality standard, **ISO 9000**. ISO 9000 is the only quality standard with international recognition. In 1987, 91 member nations (including the U.S.) published a series of quality assurance standards, known collectively as ISO 9000. The U.S., through the American National Standards Institute, has adopted the ISO 9000 series as the ANSI/ASQ Q9000 series.[4] The focus of the standards is to establish quality management procedures, through leadership, detailed documentation, work instructions, and recordkeeping. These procedures, we should note, say nothing about the actual quality of the product—they deal entirely with standards to be followed.

"ISO" is Greek for equal or uniform, as in uniform throughout the world.

To become ISO 9000 certified, organizations go through a 9- to 18-month process that involves documenting quality procedures, an on-site assessment, and an ongoing series of audits of their products or services. To do business globally—and especially in Europe—being listed in the ISO directory is critical. As of 2007, there were well over 600,000 certifications awarded to firms in 158 countries. About 50,000 U.S. firms are ISO 9000 certified.

*Visit the Web sites **www.iso.ch** and **www.asq.org** to learn more about ISO standards.*

ISO revised its standards in 2000 into more of a quality management system, which is detailed in its **ISO 9001: 2000** component. Leadership by top management and customer requirements and satisfaction play a much larger role, while documented procedures receive less emphasis under **ISO 9001: 2000**.

Learning Objective

2. Describe the ISO international quality standards

ISO 14000

ISO 14000

An environmental management standard established by the International Organization for Standardization (ISO).

The continuing internationalization of quality is evident with the development of **ISO 14000**. ISO 14000 is an environmental management standard that contains five core elements: (1) environmental management, (2) auditing, (3) performance evaluation, (4) labeling, and (5) life cycle assessment. The new standard could have several advantages:

- Positive public image and reduced exposure to liability.
- Good systematic approach to pollution prevention through the minimization of ecological impact of products and activities.
- Compliance with regulatory requirements and opportunities for competitive advantage.
- Reduction in need for multiple audits.

This standard is being accepted worldwide.

TOTAL QUALITY MANAGEMENT

Total quality management (TQM)

Management of an entire organization so that it excels in all aspects of products and services that are important to the customer.

Total quality management (TQM) refers to a quality emphasis that encompasses the entire organization, from supplier to customer. TQM stresses a commitment by management to have a continuing companywide drive toward excellence in all aspects of products and services that are important to the customer.

TQM is important because quality decisions influence each of the 10 decisions made by operations managers. Each of those 10 decisions deals with some aspect of identifying and meeting customer expectations. Meeting those expectations requires an emphasis on TQM if a firm is to compete as a leader in world markets.

Quality expert W. Edwards Deming used 14 points (see Table 6.2) to indicate how he implemented TQM. We develop these into seven concepts for an effective TQM program: (1) continuous improvement, (2) Six Sigma, (3) employee empowerment, (4) benchmarking, (5) just-in-time (JIT), (6) Taguchi concepts, and (7) knowledge of TQM tools.

Continuous Improvement

Respect for people is a cornerstone of continuous improvement.

Total quality management requires a never-ending process of continuous improvement that covers people, equipment, suppliers, materials, and procedures. The basis of the philosophy is that every aspect of an operation can be improved. The end goal is perfection, which is never achieved but always sought.

[4]ASQ is the American Society for Quality.

1. Create consistency of purpose.
2. Lead to promote change.
3. Build quality into the product; stop depending on inspections to catch problems.
4. Build long-term relationships based on performance instead of awarding business on the basis of price.
5. Continuously improve product, quality, and service.
6. Start training.
7. Emphasize leadership.
8. Drive out fear.
9. Break down barriers between departments.
10. Stop haranguing workers.
11. Support, help, and improve.
12. Remove barriers to pride in work.
13. Institute a vigorous program of education and self-improvement.
14. Put everybody in the company to work on the transformation.

◄ **Table 6.2**

Deming's 14 Points for Implementing Quality Improvement

Source: Deming revised his 14 points a number of times over the years. See J. Spigener and P. J. Angelo, "What Would Deming Say?" *Quality Progress* (March 2001): 61–65.

Plan-Do-Check-Act Walter Shewhart, another pioneer in quality management, developed a circular model known as **PDCA** (plan, do, check, act) as his version of continuous improvement. Deming later took this concept to Japan during his work there after World War II. The PDCA cycle is shown in Figure 6.3 as a circle to stress the continuous nature of the improvement process.

The Japanese use the word *kaizen* to describe this ongoing process of unending improvement—the setting and achieving of ever-higher goals. In the U.S., *TQM* and *zero defects* are also used to describe continuous improvement efforts. But whether it's PDCA, *kaizen*, TQM, or zero defects, the operations manager is a key player in building a work culture that endorses continuous improvement.

▲ **Figure 6.3** PDCA Cycle

PDCA
A continuous improvement model of plan, do, check. act.

Six Sigma

The term **Six Sigma**, popularized by Motorola, Honeywell, and General Electric, has two meanings in TQM. In a *statistical* sense, it describes a process, product, or service with an extremely high capability (99.9997% accuracy). For example, if 1 million passengers pass through the St. Louis Airport with checked baggage each month, a Six Sigma program for baggage handling will result in only 3.4 passengers with misplaced luggage. The more common three-sigma program (which we address in the supplement to this chapter) would result in 2,700 passengers with misplaced bags every month. See Figure 6.4.

The second TQM definition of Six Sigma is a program designed to reduce defects to help lower costs, save time, and improve customer satisfaction. Six Sigma is a comprehensive system—a strategy, a discipline, and a set of tools—for achieving and sustaining business success:

- It is a *strategy* because it focuses on total customer satisfaction.
- It is a *discipline* because it follows the formal Six Sigma Improvement Model known as **DMAIC**. This five-step process improvement model (1) **Defines** the project's purpose, scope, and outputs and then identifies the required process information, keeping in mind the customer's definition of quality; (2) **Measures** the process and collects data; (3) **Analyzes** the

Six Sigma
A program to save time, improve quality, and lower costs.

Learning Objective

3. Explain what Six Sigma is

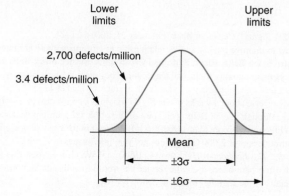

◄ **Figure 6.4**

Defects per Million for ±3σ vs. ± 6σ

data, ensuring repeatability (the results can be duplicated), and reproducibility (others get the same result); (4) *Improves*, by modifying or redesigning, existing processes and procedures; and (5) *Controls* the new process to make sure performance levels are maintained.

- It is a *set of seven tools* that we introduce shortly in this chapter: check sheets, scatter diagrams, cause-and-effect diagrams, Pareto charts, flowcharts, histograms, and statistical process control.

Motorola developed Six Sigma in the 1980s in response to customer complaints about its products, and to stiff competition. The company first set a goal of reducing defects by 90%. Within 1 year it had achieved such impressive results—through benchmarking competitors, soliciting new ideas from employees, changing reward plans, adding training, revamping critical processes—that it documented the procedures into what it called Six Sigma. Although the concept was rooted in manufacturing, GE later expanded Six Sigma into services, including human resources, sales, customer services, and financial/credit services. The concept of wiping out defects turns out to be the same in both manufacturing and services.

Implementing Six Sigma Implementing Six Sigma "is a big commitment," says the head of that program at Praxair, a major industrial gas company. "We're asking our executives to spend upward of 15% of their time on Six Sigma. If you don't spend the time you don't get the results."[5] Indeed, successful Six Sigma programs in every firm, from GE to Motorola to DuPont to Texas Instruments require a major time commitment, especially from top management. These leaders have to formulate the plan, communicate their buy-in and the firm's objectives, and take a visible role in setting the example for others.

Successful Six Sigma projects are clearly related to the strategic direction of a company. It is a management-directed, team-based, and expert-led approach.[6]

Employee Empowerment

Employee empowerment

Enlarging employee jobs so that the added responsibility and authority is moved to the lowest level possible in the organization.

Employee empowerment means involving employees in every step of the production process. Consistently, business literature suggests that some 85% of quality problems have to do with materials and processes, not with employee performance. Therefore, the task is to design equipment and processes that produce the desired quality. This is best done with a high degree of involvement by those who understand the shortcomings of the system. Those dealing with the system on a daily basis understand it better than anyone else. One study indicated that TQM programs that delegate responsibility for quality to shop-floor employees tend to be twice as likely to succeed as those implemented with "top-down" directives.[7]

When nonconformance occurs, the worker is seldom wrong. Either the product was designed wrong, the system that makes the product was designed wrong, or the employee was improperly trained. Although the employee may be able to help solve the problem, the employee rarely causes it.

Techniques for building employee empowerment include (1) building communication networks that include employees; (2) developing open, supportive supervisors; (3) moving responsibility from both managers and staff to production employees; (4) building high-morale organizations; (5) and creating such formal organization structures as teams and quality circles.

Quality circle

A group of employees meeting regularly with a facilitator to solve work-related problems in their work area.

Teams can be built to address a variety of issues. One popular focus of teams is quality. Such teams are often known as quality circles. A **quality circle** is a group of employees who meet regularly to solve work-related problems. The members receive training in group planning, problem solving, and statistical quality control. They generally meet once a week (usually after work but

[5]B. Schmitt, "Expanding Six Sigma," *Chemical Week* (February 21, 2001): 21–24.

[6]To train employees in how to improve quality and its relationship to customers, there are three other key players in the Six Sigma program: Master Black Belts, Black Belts, and Green Belts. Master Black Belts are full-time teachers who have extensive training in statistics, quality tools, and leadership. They mentor Black Belts, who in turn are project team leaders, directing perhaps a half-dozen projects per year (with average savings of $175,000 per project, according to the Six Sigma Academy). They receive about 4 weeks of Six Sigma training but must also have solid "people skills," so as to be able to see their changes through. Green Belts spend part of their time on team projects and the rest on their normal jobs. Dow Chemical and DuPont have more than 1,000 Black Belts each in their global operations. DuPont also has 160 Master Black Belts and introduces over 2,000 Green Belts per year into its ranks.

[7]"The Straining of Quality," *The Economist* (January 14, 1995): 55. We also see that this is one of the strengths of Southwest Airlines, which offers bare-bones domestic service but whose friendly and humorous employees help it obtain number one ranking for quality. (See *Fortune* [March 6, 2006]: 65–69.)

◀ *Workers at this TRW airbag manufacturing plant in Marshall, Illinois, are their own inspectors. Empowerment is an essential part of TQM. This man is checking the quality of a crash sensor he built.*

sometimes on company time). Although the members are not rewarded financially, they do receive recognition from the firm. A specially trained team member, called the *facilitator*, usually helps train the members and keeps the meetings running smoothly. Teams with a quality focus have proven to be a cost-effective way to increase productivity as well as quality.

Benchmarking

Benchmarking is another ingredient in an organization's TQM program. **Benchmarking** involves selecting a demonstrated standard of products, services, costs, or practices that represent the very best performance for processes or activities very similar to your own. The idea is to develop a target at which to shoot and then to develop a standard or benchmark against which to compare your performance. The steps for developing benchmarks are:

1. Determine what to benchmark.
2. Form a benchmark team.
3. Identify benchmarking partners.
4. Collect and analyze benchmarking information.
5. Take action to match or exceed the benchmark.

Typical performance measures used in benchmarking include percentage of defects, cost per unit or per order, processing time per unit, service response time, return on investment, customer satisfaction rates, and customer retention rates. When considering company Web sites, this benchmark list is quite different, as we see in Table 6.3.

In the ideal situation, you find one or more similar organizations that are leaders in the particular areas you want to study. Then you compare yourself (benchmark yourself) against them. The

Benchmarking

Selecting a demonstrated standard of performance that represents the very best performance for a process or an activity.

Learning Objective

4. Explain how benchmarking is used in TQM

1. Use of meta tags (keywords)	Yes: 70%, No: 30%
2. A meaningful homepage title	Yes: 97%, No: 3%
3. Unique domain name	Yes: 91%, No: 9%
4. Search engine site registration	Above 96%
5. Average speed of homepage loading (in seconds)	28K: 19.31; 56K: 10.88; T1: 2.59
6. Average number of spelling errors	0.16
7. Visibility of contact information	Yes: 74%, No: 26%
8. Presence of a search engine	Yes: 59%, No: 41%
9. Translation to multiple languages	Yes: 11%; No: 89%

◀ **Table 6.3**

Benchmarking Factors Deemed Critical to Quality at *Fortune* 500 Company Web Sites (and survey results)

Sources: Adopted from M. Jenamani, P. K. J. Mohapatra, and S. Ghose, *Internet Research* 16, no. 3 (2006): 248; and N. Tamini, M. Rajan, and R. Sebastianelli, *Quality Progress* 33, no. 7 (July 2000): 47–51.

▶ **Table 6.4**

Best Practices for Resolving Customer Complaints

- *Make it easy for clients to complain:* It is free market research.
- *Respond quickly to complaints:* It adds customers and loyalty.
- *Resolve complaints on the first contact:* It reduces cost.
- *Use computers to manage complaints:* Discover trends, share them, and align your services.
- *Recruit the best for customer service jobs:* It should be part of formal training and career advancement.

Source: Canadian Government Guide on Complaint Mechanism.

company need not be in your industry. Indeed, to establish world-class standards, it may be best to look outside your industry. If one industry has learned how to compete via rapid product development while yours has not, it does no good to study your industry.

This is exactly what Xerox and Mercedes Benz did when they went to L.L. Bean for order-filling and warehousing benchmarks. Xerox noticed that L.L. Bean was able to "pick" orders three times as fast as it could. After benchmarking, it was immediately able to pare warehouse costs by 10%. Mercedes Benz observed that L.L. Bean warehouse employees used flowcharts to spot wasted motions. The auto giant followed suit and now relies more on problem solving at the worker level.

Benchmarks often take the form of "best practices" found in other firms or in other divisions. Table 6.4 illustrates best practices for resolving customer complaints.

Likewise, British computer manufacturer ICL benchmarked Marks and Spencer (the food and clothing retailer) to improve its distribution system.

Internal Benchmarking   When an organization is large enough to have many divisions or business units, a natural approach is the internal benchmark. Data are usually much more accessible than from outside firms. Typically, one internal unit has superior performance worth learning from.

Xerox's almost religious belief in benchmarking has paid off not only by looking outward to L.L. Bean but by examining the operations of its various country divisions. For example, Xerox Europe, a $6 billion subsidiary of Xerox Corp., formed teams to see how better sales could result through internal benchmarking. Somehow, France sold five times as many color copiers as did other divisions in Europe. By copying France's approach, namely, better sales training and use of dealer channels to supplement direct sales, Norway increased sales by 152%, Holland by 300%, and Switzerland by 328%!

Benchmarks can and should be established in a variety of areas. Total quality management requires no less.[8]

Video 6.2

Xerox's Benchmarking Strategy

Just-in-Time (JIT)

The philosophy behind just-in-time (JIT) is one of continuing improvement and enforced problem solving. JIT systems are designed to produce or deliver goods just as they are needed. JIT is related to quality in three ways:

- *JIT cuts the cost of quality:* This occurs because scrap, rework, inventory investment, and damage costs are directly related to inventory on hand. Because there is less inventory on hand with JIT, costs are lower. Additionally, inventory hides bad quality, whereas JIT immediately *exposes* bad quality.
- *JIT improves quality:* As JIT shrinks lead time it keeps evidence of errors fresh and limits the number of potential sources of error. JIT creates, in effect, an early warning system for quality problems, both within the firm and with vendors.
- *Better quality means less inventory and a better, easier-to-employ JIT system:* Often the purpose of keeping inventory is to protect against poor production performance resulting from unreliable quality. If consistent quality exists, JIT allows firms to reduce all the costs associated with inventory.

---

[8]Note that benchmarking is good for evaluating how well you are doing the thing you are doing compared with the industry, but the more imaginative approach to process improvement is to ask, Should we be doing this at all? Comparing your warehousing operations to the marvelous job that L.L. Bean does is fine, but maybe you should be outsourcing the warehousing function (see Supplement 11).

Taguchi Concepts

Most quality problems are the result of poor product and process design. Genichi Taguchi has provided us with three concepts aimed at improving both product and process quality: *quality robustness*, *quality loss function*, and *target-oriented quality*.[9]

Quality robust products are products that can be produced uniformly and consistently in adverse manufacturing and environmental conditions. Taguchi's idea is to remove the *effects* of adverse conditions instead of removing the causes. Taguchi suggests that removing the effects is often cheaper than removing the causes and more effective in producing a robust product. In this way, small variations in materials and process do not destroy product quality.

A **quality loss function (QLF)** identifies all costs connected with poor quality and shows how these costs increase as the product moves away from being exactly what the customer wants. These costs include not only customer dissatisfaction but also warranty and service costs; internal inspection, repair, and scrap costs; and costs that can best be described as costs to society. Notice that Figure 6.5(a) shows the quality loss function as a curve that increases at an increasing rate. It takes the general form of a simple quadratic formula:

$$L = D^2 C$$

where L = loss to society
D^2 = square of the distance from the target value
C = cost of the deviation at the specification limit

All the losses to society due to poor performance are included in the loss function. The smaller the loss, the more desirable the product. The farther the product is from the target value, the more severe the loss.

Taguchi observed that traditional conformance-oriented specifications (i.e., the product is good as long as it falls within the tolerance limits) are too simplistic. As shown in Figure 6.5(b), conformance-oriented quality accepts all products that fall within the tolerance limits, producing more units farther from the target. Therefore, the loss (cost) is higher in terms of customer satisfaction and benefits to society. Target-oriented quality, on the other hand, strives to keep the product at the desired specification, producing more (and better) units near the target. **Target-oriented quality** is a philosophy of continuous improvement to bring the product exactly on target.

Quality robust
Products that are consistently built to meet customer needs in spite of adverse conditions in the production process.

Quality loss function (QLF)
A mathematical function that identifies all costs connected with poor quality and shows how these costs increase as product quality moves from what the customer wants.

Target-oriented quality
A philosophy of continuous improvement to bring the product exactly on target.

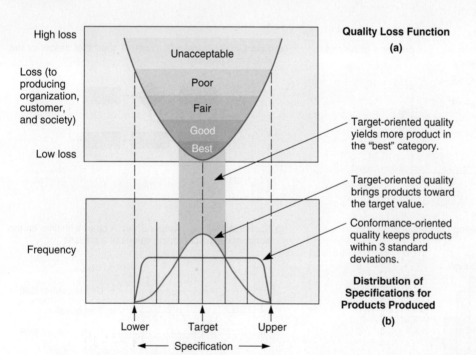

◄ **Figure 6.5**

(a) Quality Loss Function and (b) Distribution of Products Produced

Taguchi aims for the target because products produced near the upper and lower acceptable specifications result in higher quality loss function.

Quality Loss Function
(a)

Target-oriented quality yields more product in the "best" category.

Target-oriented quality brings products toward the target value.

Conformance-oriented quality keeps products within 3 standard deviations.

Distribution of Specifications for Products Produced
(b)

[9]G. Taguchi, S. Chowdhury, and Y. Wu, *Taguchi's Quality Engineering Handbook* (New York: Wiley, 2004).

Knowledge of TQM Tools

"Quality is never an accident; it is always the result of intelligent effort."

John Ruskin

To empower employees and implement TQM as a continuing effort, everyone in the organization must be trained in the techniques of TQM. In the following section, we focus on some of the diverse and expanding tools that are used in the TQM crusade.

TOOLS OF TQM

Seven tools that are particularly helpful in the TQM effort are shown in Figure 6.6. We will now introduce these tools.

Learning Objective

6. Use the seven tools of TQM

Check Sheets

A check sheet is any kind of a form that is designed for recording data. In many cases, the recording is done so the patterns are easily seen while the data are being taken (see Figure 6.6[a]). Check sheets help analysts find the facts or patterns that may aid subsequent analysis. An example might be a drawing that shows a tally of the areas where defects are occurring or a check sheet showing the type of customer complaints.

Tools for Generating Ideas

(a) *Check Sheet:* An organized method of recording data

Defect	Hour							
	1	2	3	4	5	6	7	8
A	///	/		/	/	/	///	/
B	//	/	/	/			//	///
C	/	//					//	////

(b) *Scatter Diagram:* A graph of the value of one variable vs. another variable

(c) *Cause-and-Effect Diagram:* A tool that identifies process elements (causes) that may effect an outcome

Tools for Organizing the Data

(d) *Pareto Chart:* A graph to identify and plot problems or defects in descending order of frequency

(e) *Flow Chart (Process Diagram):* A chart that describes the steps in a process

Tools for Identifying Problems

(f) *Histogram:* A distribution showing the frequency of occurrences of a variable

(g) *Statistical Process Control Chart:* A chart with time on the horizontal axis for plotting values of a statistic

▲ **Figure 6.6**   Seven Tools of TQM

Scatter Diagrams

Scatter diagrams show the relationship between two measurements. An example is the positive relationship between length of a service call and the number of trips the repairperson makes back to the truck for parts (as discussed in the *OM in Action* box "TQM Improves Copier Service"). Another example might be a plot of productivity and absenteeism, as shown in Figure 6.6(b). If the two items are closely related, the data points will form a tight band. If a random pattern results, the items are unrelated.

Cause-and-Effect Diagrams

Another tool for identifying quality issues and inspection points is the **cause-and-effect diagram**, also known as an **Ishikawa diagram** or a **fish-bone chart**. Figure 6.7 illustrates a chart (note the shape resembling the bones of a fish) for a basketball quality control problem—missed free throws. Each "bone" represents a possible source of error.

Cause-and-effect diagram
A schematic technique used to discover possible locations of quality problems.

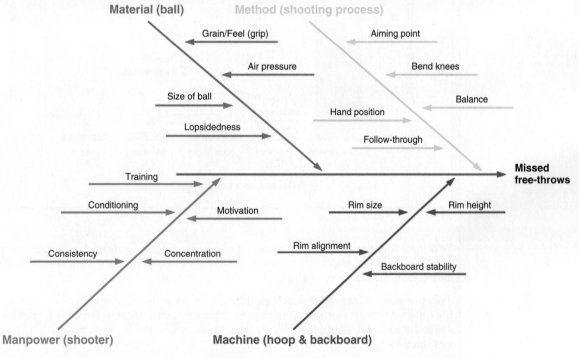

▲ **Figure 6.7**   **Fish-Bone Chart (or Cause-and-Effect Diagram) for Problems with Missed Free Throws**

Source: Adapted from MoreSteam.com, 2007.

The operations manager starts with four categories: material, machinery/equipment, manpower, and methods. These four *M*s are the "causes." They provide a good checklist for initial analysis. Individual causes associated with each category are tied in as separate bones along that branch, often through a brainstorming process. For example, the method branch in Figure 6.7 has problems caused by hand position, follow-through, aiming point, bent knees, and balance. When a fish-bone chart is systematically developed, possible quality problems and inspection points are highlighted.

Pareto Charts

Pareto charts are a method of organizing errors, problems, or defects to help focus on problem-solving efforts. They are based on the work of Vilfredo Pareto, a nineteenth-century economist. Joseph M. Juran popularized Pareto's work when he suggested that 80% of a firm's problems are a result of only 20% of the causes.

Example 1 indicates that of the five types of complaints identified, the vast majority were of one type, poor room service.

Pareto charts
Graphics that identify the few critical items as opposed to many less important ones.

EXAMPLE 1

A Pareto chart at the Hard Rock Hotel

The Hard Rock Hotel in Bali has just collected the data from 75 complaint calls to the general manager during the month of October. The manager wants to prepare an analysis of the complaints. The data provided are room service, 54; check-in delays, 12; hours the pool is open, 4; minibar prices, 3; and miscellaneous, 2.

Approach: A Pareto chart is an excellent choice for this analysis.

Solution: The Pareto chart shown below indicates that 72% of the calls were the result of one cause: room service. The majority of complaints will be eliminated when this one cause is corrected.

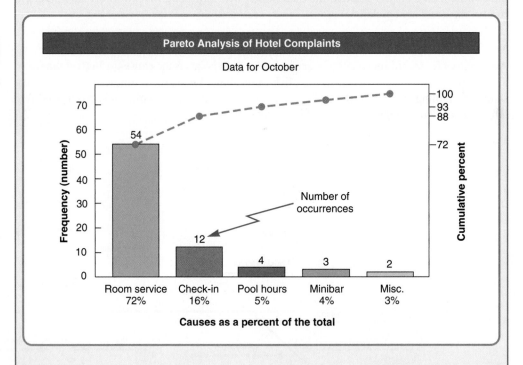

Pareto Analysis of Hotel Complaints

Data for October

Insight: This visual means of summarizing data is very helpful—particularly with large amounts of data, as in the Southwestern University case study at the end of this chapter. We can immediately spot the top problems and prepare a plan to address them.

Learning exercise: Hard Rock's bar manager decides to do a similar analysis on complaints she has collected over the past year: too expensive, 22; weak drinks, 15; slow service, 65; short hours, 8; unfriendly bartender, 12. Prepare a Pareto chart. [Answer: slow service, 53%; expensive, 18%; drinks, 12%; bartender, 10%; hours, 7%.]

Related problems: 6.1, 6.3, 6.7b, 6.12, 6.13, 6.16c

Active Model 6.1

Example 1 is further illustrated in Active Model 6.1 in the CD-ROM and in the Exercise located on page 213.

Pareto analysis indicates which problems may yield the greatest payoff. Pacific Bell discovered this when it tried to find a way to reduce damage to buried phone cable, the number-one cause of phone outages. Pareto analysis showed that 41% of cable damage was caused by construction work. Armed with this information, Pacific Bell was able to devise a plan to reduce cable cuts by 24% in one year, saving $6 million.

Flowcharts

Flowcharts graphically present a process or system using annotated boxes and interconnected lines (see Figure 6.6[e]). They are a simple, but great tool for trying to make sense of a process or explain a process. Example 2 uses a flowchart to show the process of completing an MRI at a hospital.

Flowcharts

Block diagrams that graphically describe a process or system.

EXAMPLE 2

A flowchart for hospital MRI service

Arnold Palmer Hospital has undertaken a series of process improvement initiatives. One of these is to make the MRI service efficient for patient, doctor, and hospital. The first step, the administrator believes, is to develop a flowchart for this process.

Approach: A process improvement staffer observed a number of patients and followed them (and information flow) from start to end. Here are the 11 steps:

1. Physician schedules MRI after examining patient (START).
2. Patient taken to the MRI lab with test order and copy of medical records.
3. Patient signs in, completes required paperwork.
4. Patient is prepped by technician for scan.
5. Technician carries out the MRI scan.
6. Technician inspects film for clarity.
7. If MRI not satisfactory (20% of time), steps 5 and 6 are repeated.
8. Patient taken back to hospital room.
9. MRI is read by radiologist and report is prepared.
10. MRI and report are transferred electronically to physician.
11. Patient and physician discuss report (END).

Solution: Here is the flowchart:

Insight: With the flowchart in hand, the hospital can analyze each step and identify value-added activities and activities that can be improved or eliminated.

Learning exercise: If the patient's blood pressure is over 200/120 when being prepped for the MRI, she is taken back to her room for 2 hours and the process returns to step 2. How does the flowchart change? Answer:

Related problems: 6.6, 6.15

▶ **Figure 6.8**

Control Chart for Percentage of Free Throws Missed by the Chicago Bulls in Their First Nine Games of the New Season

Histograms

Histograms show the range of values of a measurement and the frequency with which each value occurs (see Figure 6.6[f]). They show the most frequently occurring readings as well as the variations in the measurements. Descriptive statistics, such as the average and standard deviation, may be calculated to describe the distribution. However, the data should always be plotted so the shape of the distribution can be "seen." A visual presentation of the distribution may also provide insight into the cause of the variation.

Statistical Process Control (SPC)

Statistical process control (SPC)

A process used to monitor standards, make measurements and take corrective action as a product or service is being produced.

Control charts

Graphic presentations of process data over time, with predetermined control limits.

Statistical process control monitors standards, makes measurements, and takes corrective action as a product or service is being produced. Samples of process outputs are examined; if they are within acceptable limits, the process is permitted to continue. If they fall outside certain specific ranges, the process is stopped and, typically, the assignable cause located and removed.

Control charts are graphic presentations of data over time that show upper and lower limits for the process we want to control (see Figure 6.6[g]). Control charts are constructed in such a way that new data can be quickly compared with past performance data. We take samples of the process output and plot the average of these samples on a chart that has the limits on it. The upper and lower limits in a control chart can be in units of temperature, pressure, weight, length, and so on.

Figure 6.8 shows the plot of percentages of a sample in a control chart. When the average of the samples falls within the upper and lower control limits and no discernible pattern is present, the process is said to be in control with only natural variation present. Otherwise, the process is out of control or out of adjustment.

The supplement to this chapter details how control charts of different types are developed. It also deals with the statistical foundation underlying the use of this important tool.

THE ROLE OF INSPECTION

Inspection

A means of ensuring that an operation is producing at the quality level expected.

To make sure a system is producing at the expected quality level, control of the process is needed. The best processes have little variation from the standard expected. The operations manager's task is to build such systems and to verify, often by inspection, that they are performing to standard. This **inspection** can involve measurement, tasting, touching, weighing, or testing of the product (sometimes even destroying it when doing so). Its goal is to detect a bad process immediately. Inspection does not correct deficiencies in the system or defects in the products; nor does it change a product or increase its value. Inspection only finds deficiencies and defects, and it is expensive.

Inspection should be thought of as an audit. Audits do not add value to the product. However, operations managers, like financial managers, need audits, and they need to know when and where to audit. Thus there are two basic issues relating to inspection: (1) *when to inspect* and (2) *where to inspect*.

When and Where to Inspect

Deciding when and where to inspect depends on the type of process and the value added at each stage. Inspections (audits) can take place at any of the following points:

1. At your supplier's plant while the supplier is producing.
2. At your facility upon receipt of goods from your supplier.

3. Before costly or irreversible processes.
4. During the step-by-step production process.
5. When production or service is complete.
6. Before delivery to your customer.
7. At the point of customer contact.

The seven tools of TQM discussed in the previous section aid in this "when and where to inspect" decision. However, inspection is not a substitute for a robust product produced by well-trained employees in a good process. In one well-known experiment conducted by an independent research firm, 100 defective pieces were added to a "perfect" lot of items and then subjected to 100% inspection.[10] The inspectors found only 68 of the defective pieces in their first inspection. It took another three passes by the inspectors to find the next 30 defects. The last two defects were never found. So the bottom line is that there is variability in the inspection process. Additionally, inspectors are only human: They become bored, they become tired, and the inspection equipment itself has variability. Even with 100% inspection, inspectors cannot guarantee perfection. Therefore, good processes, employee empowerment, and source control are a better solution than trying to find defects by inspection.

For example, at Velcro Industries, as in many organizations, quality was viewed by machine operators as the job of "those quality people." Inspections were based on random sampling, and if a part showed up bad, it was thrown out. The company decided to pay more attention to operators, machine repair and design, measurement methods, communications, and responsibilities, and to invest more money in training. Over time as defects declined, Velcro was able to pull half its quality control people out of the process.

One of the themes of our treatment of quality is that "quality cannot be inspected into a product."

Source Inspection

The best inspection can be thought of as no inspection at all; this "inspection" is always done at the source—it is just doing the job properly with the operator ensuring that this is so. This may be called **source inspection** (or source control) and is consistent with the concept of employee empowerment, where individual employees self-check their own work. The idea is that each supplier, process, and employee *treats the next step in the process as the customer*, ensuring perfect product to the next "customer." This inspection may be assisted by the use of checklists and controls such as a fail-safe device called a *poka-yoke*, a name borrowed from the Japanese.

A **poka-yoke** is a foolproof device or technique that ensures production of good units every time.[11] These special devices avoid errors and provide quick feedback of problems. A simple example of a poka-yoke device is the diesel or leaded gas pump nozzle that will not fit into the "unleaded" gas tank opening on your car. In McDonald's, the french fry scoop and standard-size

Source inspection
Controlling or monitoring at the point of production or purchase—at the source.

Poka-yoke
Literally translated, "foolproof"; it has come to mean a device or technique that ensures the production of a good unit every time.

◀ Good methods analysis and the proper tools can result in poka-yokes that improve both quality and speed. Here, two poka-yokes are demonstrated. First, the aluminum scoop automatically positions the French fries vertically, and second, the properly sized container ensures that the portion served is correct. This combination also speeds delivery, ensuring that french fries are delivered just as the customer requests them.

[10] *Statistical Quality Control* (Springfield, MA: Monsanto Chemical Company, n.d.): 19.
[11] For further discussion, see D. M. Stewart and S. A. Melnyk, "Effective Process Improvement Developing Poka-Yoke Procedures," *Production & Inventory Management Journal* 41, no. 4 (4th quarter, 2000): 11–17.

▶ **Table 6.5**

Examples of Inspection in Services

Organization	What Is Inspected	Standard
Jones Law Offices	Receptionist performance	Phone answered by the second ring
	Billing	Accurate, timely, and correct format
	Attorney	Promptness in returning calls
Hard Rock Hotel	Reception desk	Use customer's name
	Doorman	Greet guest in less than 30 seconds
	Room	All lights working, spotless bathroom
	Minibar	Restocked and charges accurately posted to bill
Arnold Palmer Hospital	Billing	Accurate, timely, and correct format
	Pharmacy	Prescription accuracy, inventory accuracy
	Lab	Audit for lab-test accuracy
	Nurses	Charts immediately updated
	Admissions	Data entered correctly and completely
Olive Garden Restaurant	Busboy	Serves water and bread within 1 minute
	Busboy	Clears all entrée items and crumbs prior to dessert
	Waiter	Knows and suggests specials, desserts
Nordstrom Department Store	Display areas	Attractive, well organized, stocked, good lighting
	Stockrooms	Rotation of goods, organized, clean
	Salesclerks	Neat, courteous, very knowledgeable

bag used to measure the correct quantity are poka-yokes. Similarly, in a hospital, the prepackaged surgical coverings that contain exactly the items needed for a medical procedure are poka-yokes. Checklists are another type of poka-yoke. The idea of source inspection and poka-yokes is to ensure that 100% good product or service is provided at each step in the process.

Service Industry Inspection

In *service*-oriented organizations, inspection points can be assigned at a wide range of locations, as illustrated in Table 6.5. Again, the operations manager must decide where inspections are justified and may find the seven tools of TQM useful when making these judgments.

Inspection of Attributes versus Variables

Attribute inspection

An inspection that classifies items as being either good or defective.

When inspections take place, quality characteristics may be measured as either *attributes* or *variables*. **Attribute inspection** classifies items as being either good or defective. It does not address the *degree* of failure. For example, the lightbulb burns or it does not. **Variable inspection** measures such dimensions as weight, speed, height, or strength to see if an item falls within an acceptable range. If a piece of electrical wire is supposed to be 0.01 inch in diameter, a micrometer can be used to see if the product is close enough to pass inspection.

Variable inspection

Classifications of inspected items as falling on a continuum scale, such as dimension, size, or strength.

Knowing whether attributes or variables are being inspected helps us decide which statistical quality control approach to take, as we will see in the supplement to this chapter.

TQM IN SERVICES

The personal component of services is more difficult to measure than the quality of the tangible component. Generally, the user of a service, like the user of a good, has features in mind that form a basis for comparison among alternatives. Lack of any one feature may eliminate the service from further consideration. Quality also may be perceived as a bundle of attributes in which many lesser characteristics are superior to those of competitors. This approach to product comparison differs little between goods and services. However, what is very different about the selection of services is the poor definition of the (1) *intangible differences between products* and (2) *the intangible expectations customers have of those products*.[12] Indeed, the intangible attributes may not

---

[12] V. Zeithaml, L. Berry, and A. Parasuraman, "The Behavioral Consequence of Service Quality," *Journal of Marketing* (April 1996): 31–47.

Turn in **sales leads**

Hair can't grow below shirt collar

Sideburns can't grow below the bottom of the ear

No smoking in front of customers

Undershirts must be either white or brown

Use **DIAD** to log everything from driver's miles per gallon to tracking data on parcels

Key ring held on the pinky finger

"All Good Kids Love Milk": the five seeing habits of drivers: Aim high in steering, Get the big picture, Keep your eyes moving, Leave yourself an out, Make sure they see you

No beards

Shirts can't be unbuttoned below the first button

Toot horn when arriving at business or residence

Present parcels for five stops ahead

Load boxes neatly and evenly like a stack of bricks

Walk briskly. No running allowed

Sport **clean uniform** every day

Black or brown **polishable shoes,** nonslip soles

◄ *UPS drivers are taught 340 precise methods of how to correctly deliver a package. Regimented? Absolutely. But UPS credits its uniformity and efficiency with laying the foundation for its high-quality service.*

Source: Forbes (January 10, 2000): 80.

be defined at all. They are often unspoken images in the purchaser's mind. This is why all of those marketing issues such as advertising, image, and promotion can make a difference (see the photo of the UPS driver).

The operations manager plays a significant role in addressing several major aspects of service quality. First, the *tangible component of many services is important.* How well the service is designed and produced does make a difference. This might be how accurate, clear, and complete your checkout bill at the hotel is, how warm the food is at Taco Bell, or how well your car runs after you pick it up at the repair shop.

Second, another aspect of service and service quality is the process. Notice in Table 6.6 that 9 out of 10 of the determinants of service quality are related to *the service process.* Such things as reliability and courtesy are part of the process. An operations manager can *design processes (service products) that have these attributes* and can ensure their quality through the TQM techniques discussed in this chapter.

Third, the operations manager should realize that the customer's expectations are the standard against which the service is judged. Customers' perceptions of service quality result from a comparison of their before-service expectations with their actual-service experience. In other words, service quality is judged on the basis of whether it meets expectations. The *manager may be able to influence both the quality of the service and the expectation.* Don't promise more than you can deliver.

Fourth, the manager must expect exceptions. There is a standard quality level at which the regular service is delivered, such as the bank teller's handling of a transaction. However, there are "exceptions" or "problems" initiated by the customer or by less-than-optimal operating conditions (e.g., the computer "crashed"). This implies that the quality control system must recognize and *have a set of alternative plans for less-than-optimal operating conditions.*

Video 6.3

TQM at Ritz-Carlton Hotels

▶ **Table 6.6**

Determinants of Service Quality

Reliability involves consistency of performance and dependability. It means that the firm performs the service right the first time and that the firm honors its promises.

Responsiveness concerns the willingness or readiness of employees to provide service. It involves timeliness of service.

Competence means possession of the required skills and knowledge to perform the service.

Access involves approachability and ease of contact.

Courtesy involves politeness, respect, consideration, and friendliness of contact personnel (including receptionists, telephone operators, etc.).

Communication means keeping customers informed in language they can understand and listening to them. It may mean that the company has to adjust its language for different consumers—increasing the level of sophistication with a well-educated customer and speaking simply and plainly with a novice.

Credibility involves trustworthiness, believability, and honesty. It involves having the customer's best interests at heart.

Security is the freedom from danger, risk, or doubt.

Understanding/knowing the customer involves making the effort to understand the customer's needs.

Tangibles include the physical evidence of the service.

Source: Adapted from A. Parasuranam, Valarie A. Zeithaml, and Leonard L. Berry, *Delivering Quality Service and Balancing Customer Expectations* (New York: The Free Press, 1990).

Service recovery

Training and empowering frontline workers to solve a problem immediately.

Well-run companies have **service recovery** strategies. This means they train and empower frontline employees to immediately solve a problem. Staff at Marriott Hotels are drilled in the LEARN routine—*L*isten, *E*mpathize, *A*pologize, *R*eact, *N*otify—with the final step ensuring that the complaint is fed back into the system. The Ritz-Carlton trains its staff not to say merely "sorry" but "please accept my apology" and gives them a budget for reimbursing upset guests.

Designing the product, managing the service process, matching customer expectations to the product, and preparing for the exceptions are keys to quality services. The *OM in Action* box "Richey International's Spies" provides another glimpse of how OM managers improve quality in services.

OM in Action   Richey International's Spies

How do luxury hotels maintain quality? They inspect. But when the product is one-on-one service, largely dependent on personal behavior, how do you inspect? You hire spies!

Richey International is the spy. Preferred Hotels and Resorts Worldwide and Intercontinental Hotels have both hired Richey to do quality evaluations via spying. Richey employees posing as customers perform the inspections. However, even then management must have established what the customer expects and specific services that yield customer satisfaction. Only then do managers know where and how to inspect. Aggressive training and objective inspections reinforce behavior that will meet those customer expectations.

The hotels use Richey's undercover inspectors to ensure performance to exacting standards. The hotels do not know when the evaluators will arrive or what aliases they will use. More than 50 different standards are evaluated before the inspectors even check in at a luxury hotel. Over the next 24 hours, using checklists, tape recordings, and photos, written reports are prepared and include evaluation of standards such as the following:

- Does the doorman greet each guest in less than 30 seconds?
- Does the front-desk clerk use the guest's name during check-in?
- Is the bathroom tub and shower spotlessly clean?
- How many minutes does it take to get coffee after the guest sits down for breakfast?
- Did the waiter make eye contact?
- Were minibar charges posted correctly on the bill?

Established standards, aggressive training, and inspections are part of the TQM effort at these hotels. Quality does not happen by accident.

Sources: Hotel and Motel Management (August 2002): 128; *The Wall Street Journal* (May 12, 1999): B1, B12; and *Forbes* (October 5, 1998): 88–89.

Summary

Quality is a term that means different things to different people. It is defined in this chapter as "the totality of features and characteristics of a product or service that bears on its ability to satisfy stated or implied needs." Defining quality expectations is critical to effective and efficient operations.

Quality requires building a total quality management (TQM) environment because quality cannot be inspected into a product. The chapter also addresses seven TQM *concepts* : continuous improvement, Six Sigma, employee empowerment, benchmarking, just-in-time, Taguchi concepts, and knowledge of TQM tools. The seven TQM *tools* introduced in this chapter are check sheets, scatter diagrams, cause-and-effect diagrams, Pareto charts, flowcharts, histograms, and statistical process control (SPC).

Key Terms

Quality *(p. 194)*
Cost of quality (COQ) *(p. 196)*
ISO 9000 *(p. 198)*
ISO 14000 *(p. 198)*
Total quality management (TQM) *(p. 198)*
PDCA *(p. 199)*
Six Sigma *(p. 199)*
Employee empowerment *(p. 200)*
Quality circle *(p. 200)*

Benchmarking *(p. 201)*
Quality robust *(p. 203)*
Quality loss function (QLF) *(p. 203)*
Target-oriented quality *(p. 203)*
Cause-and-effect diagram, Ishikawa diagram, or fish-bone chart *(p. 205)*
Pareto charts *(p. 206)*
Flowcharts *(p. 207)*
Statistical process control (SPC) *(p. 208)*

Control charts *(p. 208)*
Inspection *(p. 208)*
Source inspection *(p. 209)*
Poka-yoke *(p. 209)*
Attribute inspection *(p. 210)*
Variable inspection *(p. 210)*
Service recovery *(p. 212)*

Active Model Exercise

This Active Model appears on your CD-ROM. It allows you to evaluate important elements in the Pareto chart.

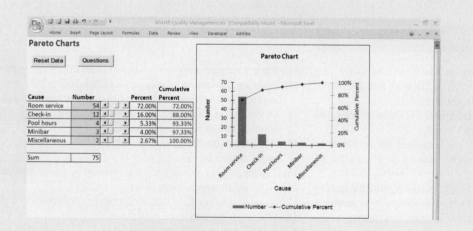

◀ **Active Model 6.1**

Pareto Analysis of Hotel Data from Example 1

Questions

1. What percentage of overall defects do the room service complaints account for?

2. If we could reduce the room service complaints in half how would this affect the chart?

Self-Test

- *Before taking the self-test*, refer to the learning objectives listed at the beginning of the chapter and the key terms listed at the end of the chapter.
- Use the key at the back of the text to **correct** your answers.
- *Restudy* pages that correspond to any questions you answered incorrectly or material you feel uncertain about.

1. In this chapter, *quality* is defined as:
   a) the degree of excellence at an acceptable price and the control of variability at an acceptable cost
   b) how well a product fits patterns of consumer preferences
   c) the totality or features and characteristics of a product or service that bears on its ability to satisfy stated or implied needs
   d) even though it cannot be defined, you know what it is

2. 100% inspection:
   a) will always catch all of the defective parts
   b) means that only good parts will be shipped to a customer
   c) is practical and generally a good idea
   d) means that every part is checked to see whether or not it is defective

3. The seven basic concepts of TQM are _____, _____, _____, _____, _____, _____, and _____.

4. ISO 14000 is an EC standard to address _____.

5. The seven tools of total quality management are _____, _____, _____, _____, _____, _____, and _____.

6. Cause-and-effect diagrams are also known as:
   a) quality loss charts
   b) target specification graphs
   c) fish-bone charts
   d) Ishikawa diagrams
   e) a and b
   f) c and d

7. The Taguchi method includes all except which of the following major concepts:
   a) employee involvement
   b) remove the effects of adverse conditions
   c) quality loss function
   d) target specifications

8. Quality cannot be _____ into a product.

Internet and Student CD-ROM/DVD Exercises

Visit our Companion Web site or your student CD-ROM/DVD to help with material in this chapter.

 On Our Companion Web Site,
www.prenhall.com/heizer
- Self-Study Quizzes
- Practice Problems
- Virtual Company Tour
- Internet Case
- PowerPoint Lecture

On Your Student CD-ROM
- Practice Problems
- Active Model Exercise

 On Your Student DVD
- Video Clips and Video Cases

Discussion Questions

1. Explain how improving quality can lead to reduced costs.
2. As an Internet exercise, determine the Baldrige Award Criteria. See the Web site **www.quality.nist.gov**.
3. Which 3 of Deming's 14 points do you feel are most critical to the success of a TQM program? Why?
4. List the seven concepts that are necessary for an effective TQM program. How are these related to Deming's 14 points?
5. Name three of the important people associated with the quality concepts of this chapter. In each case, write a short sentence about each one summarizing their primary contribution to the field of quality management.
6. What are seven tools of TQM?
7. How does fear in the workplace (and in the classroom) inhibit learning?
8. How can a university control the quality of its output (that is, its graduates)?
9. Philip Crosby said that quality is free. Why?
10. List the three concepts central to Taguchi's approach.
11. What is the purpose of using a Pareto chart for a given problem?
12. What are the four broad categories of "causes" to help initially structure an Ishikawa diagram or cause-and-effect diagram?
13. Of the several points where inspection may be necessary, which apply especially well to manufacturing?
14. What roles do operations managers play in addressing the major aspects of service quality?
15. Explain, in your own words, what is meant by *source inspection*.
16. What are 10 determinants of service quality?
17. Name several products that do not require high quality.
18. What does the formula $L = D^2C$ mean?
19. In this chapter, we have suggested that building quality into a process and its people is difficult. Inspections are also difficult. To indicate just how difficult inspections are, count the number of *E*s (both capital *E* and lowercase *e*) in the *OM in Action* box "Richey International's Spies" on page 212 (include the title but not the footnote). How many did you find? If each student does this individually, you are very likely to find a distribution rather than a single number!

Ethical Dilemma

A lawsuit a few years ago made headlines worldwide when a McDonald's drive-through customer spilled a cup of scalding hot coffee on herself. Claiming the coffee was too hot to be safely consumed in a car, the badly burned 80-year-old woman won $2.9 million in court. (The judge later reduced the award to $640,000.) McDonald's claimed the product was served to the correct specifications and was of proper quality. Further, the cup read "Caution—Contents May Be Hot." McDonald's coffee, at 180°, is substantially hotter (by corporate rule) than typical restaurant coffee,

despite hundreds of coffee-scalding complaints in the past 10 years. Similar court cases, incidentally, resulted in smaller verdicts, but again in favor of the plaintiffs. For example, Motor City Bagel Shop was sued for a spilled cup of coffee by a drive-through patron, and Starbucks by a customer who spilled coffee on her own ankle.

Are McDonald's, Motor City, and Starbucks at fault in situations such as these? How do quality and ethics enter into these cases?

Problems

• **6.1** An avant-garde clothing manufacturer runs a series of high-profile, risqué ads on a billboard on Highway 101 and regularly collects protest calls from people who are offended by them. The company has no idea how many people in total see the ad, but it has been collecting statistics on the number of phone calls from irate viewers:

Type	Description	Number of Complaints
R	Offensive racially/ethnically	10
M	Demeaning to men	4
W	Demeaning to women	14
I	Ad is Incomprehensible	6
O	Other	2

a) Depict this data with a Pareto chart. Also depict the cumulative complaint line.
b) What percent of the total complaints can be attributed to the most prevalent complaint?

• **6.2** Develop a scatter diagram for two variables of interest (say pages in the newspaper by day of the week; see example in Figure 6.6b).

• **6.3** Develop a Pareto chart of the following causes of poor grades on an exam:

Reason for Poor Grade	Frequency
Insufficient time to complete	15
Late arrival to exam	7
Difficulty understanding material	25
Insufficient preparation time	2
Studied wrong material	2
Distractions in exam room	9
Calculator batteries died during exam	1
Forgot exam was scheduled	3
Felt ill during exam	4

• **6.4** Develop a histogram of the time it took for you or your friends to receive six recent orders at a fast-food restaurant.

•• **6.5** Theresa Shotwell's restaurant in Tallahassee, Florida, has recorded the following data for eight recent customers:

Customer Number, i	Minutes from Time Food Ordered Until Food Arrived (y_i)	No. of Trips to Kitchen by Waitress (x_i)
1	10.50	4
2	12.75	5
3	9.25	3
4	8.00	2
5	9.75	3
6	11.00	4
7	14.00	6
8	10.75	5

a) Theresa wants you to graph the eight points (x_i, y_i), i = 1, 2, . . . 8. She has been concerned because customers have been waiting too long for their food, and this graph is intended to help her find possible causes of the problem.
b) This is an example of what type of graph?

•• **6.6** Develop a flowchart (as in Figure 6.6[e] and Example 2) showing all the steps involved in planning a party.

•• **6.7** Consider the types of poor driving habits that might occur at a traffic light. Make a list of the 10 you consider most likely to happen. Add the category of "other" to that list.
a) Compose a check sheet (like that in Figure 6.6[a]) to collect the frequency of occurrence of these habits. Using your check sheet, visit a busy traffic light intersection at four different times of the day, with two of these times being during high-traffic periods (rush hour, lunch hour). For 15 to 20 minutes each visit, observe the frequency with which the habits you listed occurred.
b) Construct a Pareto chart showing the relative frequency of occurrence of each habit.

•• **6.8** Draw a fish-bone chart detailing reasons why an airline customer might be dissatisfied.

•• **6.9** Consider the everyday task of getting to work on time or arriving at your first class on time in the morning. Draw a fish-bone chart showing reasons why you might arrive late in the morning.

•• **6.10** Construct a cause-and-effect diagram to reflect "student dissatisfied with university registration process." Use the "four Ms" or create your own organizing scheme. Include at least 12 causes.

•• **6.11** Draw a fish-bone chart depicting the reasons that might give rise to an incorrect fee statement at the time you go to pay for your registration at school.

• • • **6.12** Mary Beth Marrs, the manager of an apartment complex, feels overwhelmed by the number of complaints she is receiving. Below is the check sheet she has kept for the last 12 weeks. Develop a Pareto chart using this information. What recommendations would you make?

Week	Grounds	Parking/ Drives	Pool	Tenant Issues	Electrical/ Plumbing
1	✓✓✓	✓✓	✓	✓✓✓	
2	✓	✓✓✓	✓✓	✓✓	✓
3	✓✓✓	✓✓✓	✓✓	✓	
4	✓	✓✓✓✓	✓	✓	✓✓
5	✓✓	✓✓✓	✓✓✓✓	✓✓	
6	✓	✓✓✓✓	✓✓		
7		✓✓✓	✓✓	✓✓	
8	✓	✓✓✓✓	✓✓	✓✓✓	✓
9	✓	✓✓	✓		
10	✓	✓✓✓✓	✓✓	✓✓	
11		✓✓✓	✓✓	✓	
12	✓✓	✓✓✓	✓✓✓	✓	

• **6.13** Use Pareto analysis to investigate the following data collected on a printed-circuit-board assembly line:

Defect	Number of Defect Occurrences
Components not adhering	143
Excess adhesive	71
Misplaced transistors	601
Defective board dimension	146
Mounting holes improperly positioned	12
Circuitry problems on final test	90
Wrong component	212

a) Prepare a graph of the data.
b) What conclusions do you reach?

• • **6.14** A list of 16 issues that led to incorrect formulations in Richard Dulski's jam manufacturing unit is provided below:

List of Issues

1. Incorrect measurement	9. Variability
2. Antiquated scales	10. Equipment in disrepair
3. Lack of clear instructions	11. Technician calculation off
4. Damaged raw material	12. Jars mislabeled
5. Operator misreads display	13. Temperature controls off
6. Inadequate cleanup	14. Incorrect weights
7. Incorrect maintenance	15. Priority miscommunication
8. Inadequate flow controls	16. Inadequate instructions

Create a fish-bone diagram and categorize each of these issues correctly, using the "four *M*s" method.

• • **6.15** Develop a flowchart for one of the following:
a) Filling up with gasoline at a self-serve station.
b) Determining your account balance and making a withdrawal at an ATM.
c) Getting a cone of yogurt or ice cream from an ice cream store.

• • • • **6.16** Boston Electric Generators has been getting many complaints from its major customer, Home Station, about the quality of its shipments of home generators. Daniel Shimshak, the plant manager, is alarmed that a customer is providing him with the only information the company has on shipment quality. He decides to collect information on defective shipments through a form he has asked his drivers to complete on arrival at customers' stores. The forms for the first 279 shipments have been turned in. They show the following over the last 8 weeks:

			Reason for Defective Shipment			
Week	No. of Ship- ments	No. of Ship- ments with Defects	Incorrect Bill of Lading	Incorrect Truck- load	Damaged Product	Trucks Late
1	23	5	2	2	1	
2	31	8	1	4	1	2
3	28	6	2	3	1	
4	37	11	4	4	1	2
5	35	10	3	4	2	1
6	40	14	5	6	3	
7	41	12	3	5	3	1
8	44	15	4	7	2	2

Even though Daniel increased his capacity by adding more workers to his normal contingent of 30, he knew that for many weeks he exceeded his regular output of 30 shipments per week. A review of his turnover over the last 8 weeks shows the following:

Week	No. of New Hires	No. of Terminations	Total No. of Workers
1	1	0	30
2	2	1	31
3	3	2	32
4	2	0	34
5	2	2	34
6	2	4	32
7	4	1	35
8	3	2	36

a) Develop a scatter diagram using total number of shipments and number of defective shipments. Does there appear to be any relationship?
b) Develop a scatter diagram using the variable "turnover" (number of new hires plus number of terminations) and the number of defective shipments. Does the diagram depict a relationship between the two variables?
c) Develop a Pareto chart for the type of defects that have occurred.
d) Draw a fish-bone chart showing the possible causes of the defective shipments.

Case Study

Southwestern University: (C)*

The popularity of Southwestern University's football program under its new coach, Bo Pitterno, surged in each of the 5 years since his arrival at the Stephenville, Texas, college. (See Southwestern University: (A) in Chapter 3 and (B) in Chapter 4.) With a football stadium close to maxing out at 54,000 seats and a vocal coach pushing for a new stadium, SWU president Joel Wisner faced some difficult decisions. After a phenomenal upset victory over its archrival, the University of Texas, at the homecoming game in the fall, Dr. Wisner was not as happy as one would think. Instead of ecstatic alumni, students, and faculty, all Wisner heard were complaints. "The lines at the concession stands were too long"; "Parking was harder to find and farther away than in the old days" (that is, before the team won regularly); "Seats weren't comfortable"; "Traffic was backed up halfway to Dallas"; and on and on. "A college president just can't win," muttered Wisner to himself.

At his staff meeting the following Monday, Wisner turned to his VP of administration, Leslie Gardner. "I wish you would take care of these football complaints, Leslie," he said. "See what the *real* problems are and let me know how you've resolved them." Gardner wasn't surprised at the request. "I've already got a handle on it, Joel," she replied. "We've been randomly surveying 50 fans per game for the past year to see what's on their minds. It's all part of my campuswide TQM effort. Let me tally things up and I'll get back to you in a week."

When she returned to her office, Gardner pulled out the file her assistant had compiled (see Table 6.7). "There's a lot of information here," she thought.

		Overall Grade				
		A	**B**	**C**	**D**	**E**
Game Day	A. Parking	90	105	45	5	5
	B. Traffic	50	85	48	52	15
	C. Seating	45	30	115	35	25
	D. Entertainment	160	35	26	10	19
	E. Printed Program	66	34	98	22	30
Tickets	A. Pricing	105	104	16	15	10
	B. Season Ticket Plans	75	80	54	41	0
Concessions	A. Prices	16	116	58	58	2
	B. Selection of Foods	155	60	24	11	0
	C. Speed of Service	35	45	46	48	76

Respondents

Alumnus	113
Student	83
Faculty/Staff	16
None of the above	38

Open-Ended Comments on Survey Cards:

Parking a mess	More hot dog stands	Put in bigger seats	My company will buy a
Add a skybox	Seats are all metal	Friendly ushers	skybox—build it!
Get better cheerleaders	Need skyboxes	Need better seats	Programs overpriced
Double the parking attendants	Seats stink	Expand parking lots	Want softer seats
Everything is okay	Go SWU!	Hate the bleacher seats	Beat those Longhorns!
Too crowded	Lines are awful	Hot dogs cold	I'll pay for a skybox
Seats too narrow	Seats are uncomfortable	$3 for a coffee? No way!	Seats too small
Great food	I will pay more for better view	Get some skyboxes	Band was terrific
Joe P. for President!	Get a new stadium	Love the new uniforms	Love Pitterno
I smelled drugs being smoked	Student dress code needed	Took an hour to park	Everything is great
Stadium is ancient	I want cushioned seats	Coach is terrific	Build new stadium
Seats are like rocks	Not enough police	More water fountains	Move games to Dallas
Not enough cops for traffic	Students too rowdy	Better seats	No complaints
Game starts too late	Parking terrible	Seats not comfy	Dirty bathroom
Hire more traffic cops	Toilets weren't clean	Bigger parking lot	
Need new band	Not enough handicap spots in lot	I'm too old for bench seats	
Great!	Well done, SWU	Cold coffee served at game	

▲ **Table 6.7** Fan Satisfaction Survey Results (*N* = 250)

Discussion Questions

1. Using at least two different quality tools, analyze the data and present your conclusions.
2. How could the survey have been more useful?
3. What is the next step?

*This integrated case study runs throughout the text. Other issues facing Southwestern's football stadium include: (A) Managing the renovation project (Chapter 3); (B) Forecasting game attendance (Chapter 4); (D) Break-even analysis of food services (Supplement 7 Web site); (E) Locating the new stadium (Chapter 8 Web site); (F) Inventory planning of football programs (Chapter 12 Web site); and (G) Scheduling of campus security officers/staff for game days (Chapter 13).

The Culture of Quality at Arnold Palmer Hospital

Video Case

Founded in 1989, Arnold Palmer Hospital is one of the largest hospitals for women and children in the U.S., with 431 beds in two facilities totaling 676,000 square feet. Located in downtown Orlando, Florida, and named after its famed golf benefactor, the hospital, with more than 2,000 employees serves an 18-county area in central Florida and is the only Level 1 trauma center for children in that region. Arnold Palmer Hospital provides a broad range of medical services including neonatal and pediatric intensive care, pediatric oncology and cardiology, care for high-risk pregnancies, and maternal intensive care.

The Issue of Assessing Quality Health Care

Quality health care is a goal all hospitals profess, but Arnold Palmer Hospital has actually developed comprehensive and scientific means of asking customers to judge the quality of care they receive. Participating in a national benchmark comparison against other hospitals, Arnold Palmer Hospital consistently scores in the top 10% in overall patient satisfaction. Executive Director Kathy Swanson states, "Hospitals in this area will be distinguished largely on the basis of their customer satisfaction. We must have accurate information about how our patients and their families judge the quality of our care, so I follow the questionnaire results daily. The in-depth survey helps me and others on my team to gain quick knowledge from patient feedback." Arnold Palmer Hospital employees are empowered to provide gifts in value up to $200 to patients who find reason to complain about any hospital service such as food, courtesy, responsiveness, or cleanliness.

Swanson doesn't focus just on the customer surveys, which are mailed to patients one week after discharge, but also on a variety of internal measures. These measures usually start at the grassroots level, where the staff sees a problem and develops ways to track performance. The hospital's longstanding philosophy supports the concept that each patient is important and respected as a person. That patient has the right to comprehensive, compassionate family-centered health care provided by a knowledgeable physician-directed team.

Some of the measures Swanson carefully monitors for continuous improvement are morbidity, infection rates, readmission rates, costs per case, and length of stays. The tools she uses daily include Pareto charts, flowcharts and process charts, in addition to benchmarking against hospitals both nationally and in the southeast region.

The result of all of these efforts has been a quality culture as manifested in Arnold Palmer's high ranking in patient satisfaction and one of the highest survival rates of critically ill babies.

Discussion Questions*

1. Why is it important for Arnold Palmer Hospital to get a patient's assessment of health care quality? Does the patient have the expertise to judge the health care she receives?
2. How would you build a culture of quality in an organization, such as Arnold Palmer Hospital?
3. What techniques does Arnold Palmer Hospital practice in its drive for quality and continuous improvement?
4. Develop a fish-bone diagram illustrating the quality variables for a patient who just gave birth at Arnold Palmer Hospital (or any other hospital).

*You may wish to review this video case on your DVD before answering these questions.

Quality at the Ritz-Carlton Hotel Company

Video Case

Ritz-Carlton. The name alone evokes images of luxury and quality. As the first hotel company to win the Malcolm Baldrige National Quality Award, the Ritz treats quality as if it is the heartbeat of the company. This means a daily commitment to meeting customer expectations and making sure that each hotel is free of any deficiency.

In the hotel industry, quality can be hard to quantify. Guests do not purchase a product when they stay at the Ritz: They buy an experience. Thus, creating the right combination of elements to make the experience stand out is the challenge and goal of every employee, from maintenance to management.

Before applying for the Baldrige Award, company management undertook a rigorous self-examination of its operations in an attempt to measure and quantify quality. Nineteen processes were studied, including room service delivery, guest reservation and registration, message delivery, and breakfast service. This period of self-study included statistical measurement of process work flows and cycle times for areas ranging from room service delivery times and reservations to valet parking and housekeeping efficiency. The results were used to develop performance benchmarks against which future activity could be measured.

With specific, quantifiable targets in place, Ritz-Carlton managers and employees now focus on continuous improvement. The goal is 100% customer satisfaction: If a guest's experience does not meet expectations, the Ritz-Carlton risks losing that guest to competition.

One way the company has put more meaning behind its quality efforts is to organize its employees into "self-directed" work teams. Employee teams determine work scheduling, what work needs to be done, and what to do about quality problems in their own areas. In order that they can see the relationship of their specific area to the overall goals, employees are also given the opportunity to take additional training in hotel operations. Ritz-Carlton believes that a more educated and informed employee is in a better position to make decisions in the best interest of the organization.

Discussion Questions*

1. In what ways could the Ritz-Carlton monitor its success in achieving quality?
2. Many companies say that their goal is to provide quality products or services. What actions might you expect from a company that intends quality to be more than a slogan or buzzword?
3. Why might it cost the Ritz-Carlton less to "do things right" the first time?
4. How could control charts, Pareto diagrams, and cause-and-effect diagrams be used to identify quality problems at a hotel?
5. What are some nonfinancial measures of customer satisfaction that might be used by the Ritz-Carlton?

*You may wish to view this video case on your DVD before addressing these questions.

Source: Adapted from C. T. Horngren, S. M. Datar, and G. Foster, *Cost Accounting*, 12th ed. (Upper Saddle River, NJ: Prentice Hall, 2006).

Additional Case Studies

Internet Case Study: Visit our Companion Web site at www.prenhall.com/heizer for this free case study:

- **Westover Electrical, Inc.:** This electric motor manufacturer has a large log of defects in its wiring process.

Harvard has selected these Harvard Business School cases to accompany this chapter:

harvardbusinessonline.hbsp.harvard.edu

- **GE: We Bring Good Things to Life (A)** (#899-162): Illustrates the complexity of managing change and the momentum that initiatives can provide.
- **Wainwright Industries (A): Beyond the Baldrige** (#396-219): Traces the growth of an auto supply company and its culture of quality.
- **Romeo Engine Plant** (#197-100): The employees at this auto engine plant must solve problems and ensure quality, not watch parts being made.
- **Motorola-Penang** (#494-135): The female manager of this Malaysia factory is skeptical of empowerment efforts at other Motorola sites.
- **Measure of Delight: The Pursuit of Quality at AT&T Universal Card Service (A)** (#694-047): Links performance measurement and compensation policies to precepts of quality management.

Bibliography

Aikens, C. *Quality*. Upper Saddle River, NJ: Prentice Hall, 2006.

Beer, M. "Why Total Quality Management Programs Do Not Persist." *Decision Sciences* 34, no. 4 (Fall 2003): 623–642.

Brown, Mark G. *Baldrige Award Winning Quality*, 13th ed. University Park, IL: Productivity Press, 2004.

Crosby, P. B. *Quality Is Still Free*. New York: McGraw-Hill, 1996.

Evans, J. R., and W. M. Lindsay. *An Introduction to Six Sigma and Process Improvement*. Mason, OH: Thompson-Southwestern, 2005.

Foster, S. Thomas. *Managing Quality*, 3rd ed. Upper Saddle River, NJ: Prentice Hall, 2007.

Gitlow, H. S., et al. *Quality Management*, 3rd ed. New York: McGraw-Hill, 2005.

Goetsch, David L., and Stanley B. Davis. *Quality Management*, 5th ed. Upper Saddle River, NJ: Prentice Hall, 2006.

Gryna, F. M., R. C. H. Chua, and J. A. DeFeo. *Juran's Quality Planning and Analysis for Enterprise Quality*, 5th ed. New York: McGraw-Hill, 2007.

Henderson, G. R. *Six Sigma Quality Improvement with Minitab*. New York: Wiley, 2006.

King, J., and R. Cichy. *Managing for Quality in the Hospitality Industry*. Upper Saddle River, NJ: Prentice Hall, 2006.

Pande, P. S., R. P. Neuman, R. R. Cavanagh. *What Is Design for Six Sigma?* New York: McGraw-Hill, 2005.

Pil, F. K., and S. Rothenberg. "Environmental Performance as a Driver of Superior Quality." *Production and Operations Management* 12, no. 3 (Fall 2003): 404–415.

Prahalad, C. K., and M. S. Krishnan. "The New Meaning of Quality in the Information Age." *Harvard Business Review* (September–October, 1999): 109–118.

Stewart, D. M. "Piecing Together Service Quality: A Framework for Robust Service." *Production and Operations Management* (Summer 2003): 246–265.

Summers, Donna. *Quality*. 4th ed. Upper Saddle River, NJ: Prentice Hall, 2006.

Tonkin, L. P. "Supercharging Business Improvements: Motorola's Six Sigma Leadership Tools." *Target: Innovation at Work* 20, no. 1 (first issue 2004): 50–53.

Vastag, Gyula. "Revisiting ISO 14000 Diffusion: A New 'Look' at the Drivers of Certification." *Production and Operations Management* 13, no. 3 (Fall 2004): 260–267.

Internet Resources

American Society for Quality: **www.asq.org/**
ISO Central Secretariat: **www.iso.ch/**
Juran Institute: **www.juran.com/**
Links to benchmarking sites: **www.ebenchmarking.com**

National Institute of Standards and Technology: **www.quality.nist.gov/**
Quality Assurance Institute: **www.qai.worldwide.org**
Quality Digest: **www. qualitydigest.com**
Quality Progress: **www.qualityprogress.asq.org**

SUPPLEMENT 6

Statistical Process Control

Supplement Outline

Learning Objectives

When you complete this supplement you should be able to

1. Explain the purpose of a control chart
2. Explain the role of the central limit theorem in SPC
3. Build $\bar{x}$-charts and R-charts
4. List the five steps involved in building control charts
5. Build p-charts and c-charts
6. Explain process capability and compute C_p and C_{pk}
7. Explain acceptance sampling
8. Compute the AOQ

► *BetzDearborn, A Division of Hercules Incorporated, is headquartered in Trevose, Pennsylvania. It is a global supplier of specialty chemicals for the treatment of industrial water, wastewater, and process systems. The company uses statistical process control to monitor the performance of treatment programs in a wide variety of industries throughout the world. BetzDearborn's quality assurance laboratory (shown here) also uses statistical sampling techniques to monitor manufacturing processes at all of the company's production plants.*

Statistical process control (SPC)
A process used to monitor standards by taking measurements and corrective action as a product or service is being produced.

In this supplement, we address statistical process control—the same techniques used at BetzDearborn, at IBM, at GE, and at Motorola to achieve quality standards. We also introduce acceptance sampling. **Statistical process control** is the application of statistical techniques to the control of processes. *Acceptance sampling* is used to determine acceptance or rejection of material evaluated by a sample.

STATISTICAL PROCESS CONTROL (SPC)

Statistical process control (SPC) is a statistical technique that is widely used to ensure that processes meet standards. All processes are subject to a certain degree of variability. While studying process data in the 1920s, Walter Shewhart of Bell Laboratories made the distinction between the common and special causes of variation. Many people now refer to these variations as *natural* and *assignable* causes. He developed a simple but powerful tool to separate the two— the **control chart**.

Control chart
A graphical presentation of process data over time.

We use statistical process control to measure performance of a process. A process is said to be operating *in statistical control* when the only source of variation is common (natural) causes. The process must first be brought into statistical control by detecting and eliminating special (assignable) causes of variation.[1] Then its performance is predictable, and its ability to meet customer expectations can be assessed. The *objective* of a process control system is to *provide a statistical signal when assignable causes of variation are present*. Such a signal can quicken appropriate action to eliminate assignable causes.

Natural variations
Variability that affects every production process to some degree and is to be expected; also known as common cause.

Natural Variations Natural variations affect almost every production process and are to be expected. **Natural variations** are the many sources of variation that occur within a process that is in statistical control. Natural variations behave like a constant system of chance causes. Although individual values are all different, as a group they form a pattern that can be described as a *distribution*. When these distributions are *normal*, they are characterized by two parameters:

- Mean, μ (the measure of central tendency—in this case, the average value)
- Standard deviation, σ (the measure of dispersion)

As long as the distribution (output measurements) remains within specified limits, the process is said to be "in control," and natural variations are tolerated.

---

[1]Removing assignable causes is work. Quality expert W. Edwards Deming observed that a state of statistical control is not a natural state for a manufacturing process. Deming instead viewed it as an achievement, arrived at by elimination, one by one, by determined effort, of special causes of excessive variation. See J. R. Thompson and J. Koronacki, *Statistical Process Control, The Deming Paradigm and Beyond.* Boca Raton, FL: Chapman and Hall, 2002.

Assignable Variations   **Assignable variation** in a process can be traced to a specific reason. Factors such as machine wear, misadjusted equipment, fatigued or untrained workers, or new batches of raw material are all potential sources of assignable variations.

Natural and assignable variations distinguish two tasks for the operations manager. The first is to *ensure that the process is capable* of operating under control with only natural variation. The second is, of course, to *identify and eliminate assignable variations* so that the processes will remain under control.

Samples   Because of natural and assignable variation, statistical process control uses averages of small samples (often of four to eight items) as opposed to data on individual parts. Individual pieces tend to be too erratic to make trends quickly visible.

Figure S6.1 provides a detailed look at the important steps in determining process variation. The horizontal scale can be weight (as in the number of ounces in boxes of cereal) or length (as in fence posts) or any physical measure. The vertical scale is frequency. The samples of five boxes of cereal in Figure S6.1 (**a**) are weighed; (**b**) form a distribution, and (**c**) can vary. The distributions formed in (**b**) and (**c**) will fall in a predictable pattern (**d**) if only natural variation is present. If assignable causes of variation are present, then we can expect either the mean to vary or the dispersion to vary, as is the case in (**e**).

Control Charts   The process of building control charts is based on the concepts presented in Figure S6.2. This figure shows three distributions that are the result of outputs from three types of processes. We plot small samples and then examine characteristics of the resulting data to see if the process is within "control limits." The purpose of control charts is to help distinguish between natural variations and variations due to assignable causes. As seen in Figure S6.2, a process is (**a**) in control *and the process is capable of producing within established control limits*, (**b**) in control *but the process is not capable of producing within established limits*, or (**c**) out of control. We now look at ways to build control charts that help the operations manager keep a process under control.

Assignable variation
Variation in a production process that can be traced to specific causes.

    Video S6.1

SPC at Harley-Davidson

Learning Objective

1. Explain the purpose of a control chart

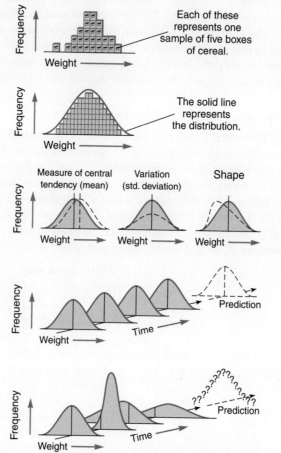

(a) Samples of the product, say five boxes of cereal taken off the filling machine line, vary from one another in weight.

Each of these represents one sample of five boxes of cereal.

(b) After enough samples are taken from a stable process, they form a pattern called a *distribution*.

The solid line represents the distribution.

(c) There are many types of distributions, including the normal (bell-shaped) distribution, but distributions do differ in terms of central tendency (mean), standard deviation or variance, and shape.

(d) If only natural causes of variation are present, the output of a process forms a distribution that is stable over time and is predictable.

(e) If assignable causes of variation are present, the process output is not stable over time and is not predictable. That is, when causes that are not an expected part of the process occur, the samples will yield unexpected distributions that vary by central tendency, standard deviation, and shape.

◀ **Figure S6.1**

Natural and Assignable Variation

▶ **Figure S6.2**

Process Control: Three Types of Process Outputs

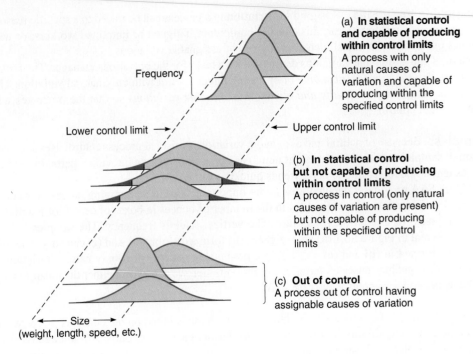

Frequency

Lower control limit →

← Upper control limit

(a) **In statistical control and capable of producing within control limits**
A process with only natural causes of variation and capable of producing within the specified control limits

(b) **In statistical control but not capable of producing within control limits**
A process in control (only natural causes of variation are present) but not capable of producing within the specified control limits

(c) **Out of control**
A process out of control having assignable causes of variation

← Size →
(weight, length, speed, etc.)

Control Charts for Variables

$\bar{x}$-chart

A quality control chart for variables that indicates when changes occur in the central tendency of a production process.

R-chart

A control chart that tracks the "range" within a sample; it indicates that a gain or loss in uniformity has occurred in dispersion of a production process.

Central limit theorem

The theoretical foundation for $\bar{x}$-charts, which states that regardless of the distribution of the population of all parts or services, the distribution of $\bar{x}$s will tend to follow a normal curve as the number of samples increases.

The variables of interest here are those that have continuous dimensions. They have an infinite number of possibilities. Examples are weight, speed, length, or strength. Control charts for the mean, $\bar{x}$ or x-bar, and the range, R, are used to monitor processes that have continuous dimensions. The **$\bar{x}$-chart** tells us whether changes have occurred in the central tendency (the mean, in this case) of a process. These changes might be due to such factors as tool wear, a gradual increase in temperature, a different method used on the second shift, or new and stronger materials. The **R-chart** values indicate that a gain or loss in dispersion has occurred. Such a change may be due to worn bearings, a loose tool, an erratic flow of lubricants to a machine, or to sloppiness on the part of a machine operator. The two types of charts go hand in hand when monitoring variables because they measure the two critical parameters: central tendency and dispersion.

The Central Limit Theorem

The theoretical foundation for $\bar{x}$-charts is the **central limit theorem**. This theorem states that regardless of the distribution of the population, the distribution of $\bar{x}$s (each of which is a mean of a sample drawn from the population) will tend to follow a normal curve as the number of samples increases. Fortunately, even if the sample (n) is fairly small (say, 4 or 5), the distributions of the averages will still roughly follow a normal curve. The theorem also states that: (1) the mean of the distribution of the $\bar{x}$s (called $\bar{\bar{x}}$) will equal the mean of the overall population (called μ); and (2) the standard deviation of the *sampling distribution*, $\sigma_{\bar{x}}$, will be the *population standard deviation*, σ, divided by the square root of the sample size, n. In other words:[2]

$$\bar{\bar{x}} = \mu \tag{S6-1}$$

and:

$$\sigma_{\bar{x}} = \frac{\sigma}{\sqrt{n}} \tag{S6-2}$$

Figure S6.3 shows three possible population distributions, each with its own mean, μ, and standard deviation, σ. If a series of random samples ($\bar{x}_1, \bar{x}_2, \bar{x}_3, \bar{x}_4$, and so on), each of size n, is

---

[2]*Note:* The standard deviation is easily calculated as $\sigma = \sqrt{\dfrac{\displaystyle\sum_{i=1}^{n}(x_i - \bar{x})^2}{n-1}}$.

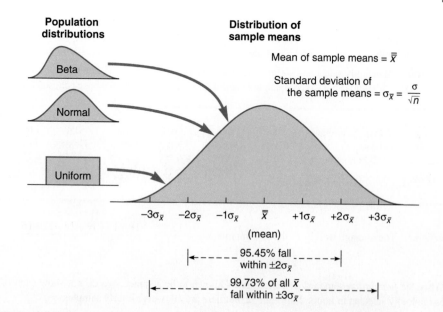

The Relationship between Population and Sampling Distributions

Regardless of the population distribution (e.g., normal, beta, uniform), each with its own mean (μ) and standard deviation (σ), the distribution of sample means is normal.

drawn from any population distribution (which could be normal, beta, uniform, and so on), the resulting distribution of $\bar{x}_i$s will appear as they do in Figure S6.3.

Moreover, the sampling distribution, as is shown in Figure S6.4, will have less variability than the process distribution. Because the sampling distribution is normal, we can state that:

- 95.45% of the time, the sample averages will fall within $\pm 2\sigma_{\bar{x}}$ if the process has only natural variations.
- 99.73% of the time, the sample averages will fall within $\pm 3\sigma_{\bar{x}}$ if the process has only natural variations.

If a point on the control chart falls outside of the $\pm 3\sigma_{\bar{x}}$ control limits, then we are 99.73% sure the process has changed. This is the theory behind control charts.

Learning Objective

2. Explain the role of the central limit theorem in SPC

Setting Mean Chart Limits ($\bar{x}$-Charts)

If we know, through past data, the standard deviation of the process population, σ, we can set upper and lower control limits by using these formulas:

$$\text{Upper control limit (UCL)} = \bar{\bar{x}} + z\sigma_{\bar{x}} \tag{S6-3}$$

$$\text{Lower control limit (LCL)} = \bar{\bar{x}} - z\sigma_{\bar{x}} \tag{S6-4}$$

where $\bar{\bar{x}}$ = mean of the sample means or a target value set for the process
   z = number of normal standard deviations (2 for 95.45% confidence, 3 for 99.73%)
   $\sigma_{\bar{x}}$ = standard deviation of the sample means = $\sigma / \sqrt{n}$
   σ = population (process) standard deviation
   n = sample size

Example S1 shows how to set control limits for sample means using standard deviations.

Learning Objective

3. Build $\bar{x}$-charts and R-charts

The Sampling Distribution of Means Is Normal and Has Less Variability Than the Process Distribution

In this figure, the process distribution from which the sample was drawn was also normal, but it could have been any distribution.

EXAMPLE S1

Setting control limits using samples

The weights of boxes of Oat Flakes within a large production lot are sampled each hour. Managers want to set control limits that include 99.73% of the sample means.

Approach: Randomly select and weigh nine ($n = 9$) boxes each hour. Then find the overall mean and use Equations (S6-3) and (S6-4) to compute the control limits. Here are the nine boxes chosen for Hour 1:

Oat Flakes	Oat Flakes	Oat Flakes	Oat Flakes	Oat Flakes	Oat Flakes	Oat Flakes	Oat Flakes	Oat Flakes
17 oz.	13 oz.	16 oz.	18 oz.	17 oz.	16 oz.	15 oz.	17 oz.	16 oz.

Solution: The average weight in the first sample $= \dfrac{17+13+16+18+17+16+15+17+16}{9}$

$$= 16.1 \text{ oz.}$$

Also, the *population* standard deviation (σ) is known to be 1 ounce. We do not show each of the boxes randomly selected in hours 2 through 12, but here are all twelve hourly samples:

Weight of Sample		Weight of Sample		Weight of Sample	
Hour	**(Avg. of 9 Boxes)**	**Hour**	**(Avg. of 9 Boxes)**	**Hour**	**(Avg. of 9 Boxes)**
1	16.1	5	16.5	9	16.3
2	16.8	6	16.4	10	14.8
3	15.5	7	15.2	11	14.2
4	16.5	8	16.4	12	17.3

The average mean of the 12 samples is calculated to be exactly 16 ounces. We therefore have $\bar{\bar{x}} = 16$ ounces, $\sigma = 1$ ounce, $n = 9$, and $z = 3$. The control limits are:

$$\text{UCL}_{\bar{x}} = \bar{\bar{x}} + z\sigma_{\bar{x}} = 16 + 3\left(\frac{1}{\sqrt{9}}\right) = 16 + 3\left(\frac{1}{3}\right) = 17 \text{ ounces}$$

$$\text{LCL}_{\bar{x}} = \bar{\bar{x}} - z\sigma_{\bar{x}} = 16 - 3\left(\frac{1}{\sqrt{9}}\right) = 16 - 3\left(\frac{1}{3}\right) = 15 \text{ ounces}$$

The 12 samples are then plotted on the following control chart:

Insight: Because the means of recent sample averages fall outside the upper and lower control limits of 17 and 15, we can conclude that the process is becoming erratic and is *not* in control.

Learning exercise: If Oat Flakes's population standard deviation (σ) is 2 (instead of 1), what is your conclusion? [Answer: LCL = 14, UCL = 18; the process would be in control.]

Related problems: S6.1, S6.2, S6.4, S6.8, S6.10a,b

Sample Size, n	Mean Factor, A_2	Upper Range, D_4	Lower Range, D_3
2	1.880	3.268	0
3	1.023	2.574	0
4	.729	2.282	0
5	.577	2.115	0
6	.483	2.004	0
7	.419	1.924	0.076
8	.373	1.864	0.136
9	.337	1.816	0.184
10	.308	1.777	0.223
12	.266	1.716	0.284

◄ **Table S6.1**

Factors for Computing Control Chart Limits (3 sigma)

Source: Reprinted by permission of American Society for Testing Materials. Copyright 1951. Taken from Special Technical Publication 15-C, "Quality Control of Materials," pp. 63 and 72.

Because process standard deviations are either not available or difficult to compute, we usually calculate control limits based on the average *range* values rather than on standard deviations. Table S6.1 provides the necessary conversion for us to do so. The *range* is defined as the difference between the largest and smallest items in one sample. For example, the heaviest box of Oat Flakes in Hour 1 of Example S1 was 18 ounces and the lightest was 13 ounces, so the range for that hour is 5 ounces. We use Table S6.1 and the equations:

The range is the difference between the largest and the smallest items in a sample.

$$UCL_{\bar{x}} = \bar{\bar{x}} + A_2\bar{R}$$ (S6-5)

and:

$$LCL_{\bar{x}} = \bar{\bar{x}} - A_2\bar{R}$$ (S6-6)

where $\bar{R}$ = average range of the samples

A_2 = value found in Table S6.1

$\bar{\bar{x}}$ = mean of the sample means

Example S2 shows how to set control limits for sample means by using Table S6.1 and the average range.

EXAMPLE S2

Setting mean limits using table values

 Excel OM Data File Ch06SExS2.xls

Super Cola bottles soft drinks labeled "net weight 12 ounces." Indeed, an overall process average of 12 ounces has been found by taking many samples, in which each sample contained 5 bottles. The average range of the process is .25 ounce. The OM team wants to determine the upper and lower control limits for averages in this process.

Approach: Super Cola applies Equations (S6-5) and (S6-6) and uses the A_2 column of Table S6.1.

Solution: Looking in Table S6.1 for a sample size of 5 in the mean factor A_2 column, we find the value .577. Thus, the upper and lower control chart limits are:

$$UCL_{\bar{x}} = \bar{\bar{x}} + A_2\bar{R}$$
$$= 12 + (.577)(.25)$$
$$= 12 + .144$$
$$= 12.144 \text{ ounces}$$
$$LCL_{\bar{x}} = \bar{\bar{x}} - A_2\bar{R}$$
$$= 12 - .144$$
$$= 11.856 \text{ ounces}$$

Insight: The advantage of using this range approach, instead of the standard deviation, is that it is easy to apply and may be less confusing.

Learning exercise: If the sample size was $n = 4$ and the average range = .20 ounces, what are the revised $UCL_{\bar{x}}$ and $LCL_{\bar{x}}$? [Answer: 12.146, 11.854.]

Related problems: S6.3a, S6.5, S6.6, S6.7, S6.9, S6.10b,c,d S6.11, S6.34

▶ *Salmon filets are monitored by Darden Restaurant's SPC software, which includes C_p, C_{pk}, $\bar{x}$-, and R-charts and a process capability histogram. The video case study "Farm to Fork," at the end of this supplement, asks you to interpret these figures.*

Video S6.2

Farm to Fork: Quality of Darden Restaurants

Setting Range Chart Limits (*R*-Charts)

In Examples S1 and S2, we determined the upper and lower control limits for the process *average*. In addition to being concerned with the process average, operations managers are interested in the process *dispersion*, or *range*. Even though the process average is under control, the dispersion of the process may not be. For example, something may have worked itself loose in a piece of equipment that fills boxes of Oat Flakes. As a result, the average of the samples may remain the same, but the variation within the samples could be entirely too large. For this reason, operations managers use control charts for ranges to monitor the process variability, as well as control charts for averages, which monitor the process central tendency. The theory behind the control charts for ranges is the same as that for process average control charts. Limits are established that contain ±3 standard deviations of the distribution for the average range $\bar{R}$. We can use the following equations to set the upper and lower control limits for ranges:

When determining the UCL_R and LCL_R, use the average range, $\bar{R}$. But when plotting points once the R-chart is developed, use the individual range values for each sample.

$$UCL_R = D_4\bar{R} \tag{S6-7}$$

$$LCL_R = D_3\bar{R} \tag{S6-8}$$

where UCL_R = upper control chart limit for the range
LCL_R = lower control chart limit for the range
D_4 and D_3 = values from Table S6.1

Example S3 shows how to set control limits for sample ranges using Table S6.1 and the average range.

EXAMPLE S3

Setting range limits using table values

The average *range* of a product at Clinton Manufacturing is 5.3 pounds. With a sample size of 5, owner Roy Clinton wants to determine the upper and lower control chart limits.

Approach: Looking in Table S6.1 for a sample size of 5, he finds that $D_4 = 2.115$ and $D_3 = 0$.

Solution: The range control limits are:

$$UCL_R = D_4\bar{R} = (2.115)(5.3 \text{ pounds}) = 11.2 \text{ pounds}$$

$$LCL_R = D_3\bar{R} = (0)(5.3 \text{ pounds}) = 0$$

Insight: Computing ranges with Table S6.1 is straightforward and an easy way to evaluate dispersion.

Learning exercise: Clinton decides to increase the sample size to $n = 7$. What are the new UCL_R and LCL_R values? [Answer: 10.197, 0.40.]

Related problems: S6.3b, S6.5, S6.6, S6.7, S6.9, S6.10c, S6.11, S6.12, S6.34

Using Mean and Range Charts

The normal distribution is defined by two parameters, the *mean* and *standard deviation*. The $\bar{x}$ (mean)-chart and the R-chart mimic these two parameters. The $\bar{x}$-chart is sensitive to shifts in the process mean, whereas the R-chart is sensitive to shifts in the process standard deviation. Consequently, by using both charts we can track changes in the process distribution.

For instance, the samples and the resulting $\bar{x}$-chart in Figure S6.5(a) show the shift in the process mean, but because the dispersion is constant, no change is detected by the R-chart. Conversely, the samples and the $\bar{x}$-chart in Figure S6.5(b) detect no shift (because none is present), but the R-chart does detect the shift in the dispersion. Both charts are required to track the process accurately.

Steps to Follow When Using Control Charts   There are five steps that are generally followed in using $\bar{x}$- and R-charts:

1. Collect 20 to 25 samples, often of $n = 4$ or $n = 5$ observations each, from a stable process and compute the mean and range of each.
2. Compute the overall means ($\bar{\bar{x}}$ and $\bar{R}$), set appropriate control limits, usually at the 99.73% level, and calculate the preliminary upper and lower control limits. Refer to Table S6.2 for other control limits. *If the process is not currently stable*, use the desired mean, μ, instead of $\bar{\bar{x}}$ to calculate limits.

▼ Table S6.2
Common z Values

Desired Control Limit (%)	z-Value (standard deviation required for desired level of confidence)
90.0	1.65
95.0	1.96
95.45	2.00
99.0	2.58
99.73	3.00

Learning Objective

4. List the five steps involved in building control charts

The two parameters are:
Mean → measure of central tendency.
Range → measure of dispersion.

◀ **Figure S6.5**

Mean and Range Charts Complement Each Other by Showing the Mean and Dispersion of the Normal Distribution

OM in Action   Frito-Lay Uses SPC to Keep Its Ruffles Tasty

No one wants to bite into a potato chip that is too salty—nor one that has no taste at all. Frito-Lay's Ruffles brand potato chips have to have just the right salt content, crispiness, and thickness.

Frito-Lay uses $\bar{x}$ charts and SPC to control its production at critical points in the process—instead of its old system of inspecting chips at the end of the process. Every 15 minutes, three batches of chips are taken from the conveyor, ground up, weighed, dissolved in distilled water, and filtered into a beaker. The salt content of the batches is analyzed electronically and averaged to get a mean for that sample. The sample mean is then plotted on an $\bar{x}$ chart whose target value is 1.6%. The lower and upper control limits are 1.12% and 2.08%, respectively;

so if a batch is out of control, the process can be corrected before a huge number of defective Ruffles are produced. With SPC, variability among bags of chips has decreased by 50%.

Sources: Knight Ridder Tribune Business News (October 24, 2004): 1; COMAP, Annenberg/CPB Project (Needham Heights, MA: Allyn & Bacon); and Strategic Direction (February 2002): 8–11.

3. Graph the sample means and ranges on their respective control charts and determine whether they fall outside the acceptable limits.
4. Investigate points or patterns that indicate the process is out of control. Try to assign causes for the variation, address the causes, and then resume the process.
5. Collect additional samples and, if necessary, revalidate the control limits using the new data.

Applications of control charts appear in examples in this supplement, as well as in the *OM in Action* box "Frito-Lay Uses SPC to Keep Its Ruffles Tasty."

Learning Objective

5. Build *p*-charts and *c*-charts

Control Charts for Attributes

Control charts for $\bar{x}$ and R do not apply when we are sampling *attributes*, which are typically classified as *defective* or *nondefective*. Measuring defectives involves counting them (for example, number of bad lightbulbs in a given lot, or number of letters or data entry records typed with errors), whereas *variables* are usually measured for length or weight. There are two kinds of attribute control charts: (1) those that measure the *percent* defective in a sample—called *p*-charts—and (2) those that count the *number* of defects—called *c*-charts.

p-chart

A quality control chart that is used to control attributes.

*p***-Charts**   Using **p-charts** is the chief way to control attributes. Although attributes that are either good or bad follow the binomial distribution, the normal distribution can be used to calculate *p*-chart limits when sample sizes are large. The procedure resembles the $\bar{x}$-chart approach, which is also based on the central limit theorem.

▶ *Although SPC charts can be generated by computer, this one is being prepared by hand. This chart is updated each hour and reflects a week of workshifts.*

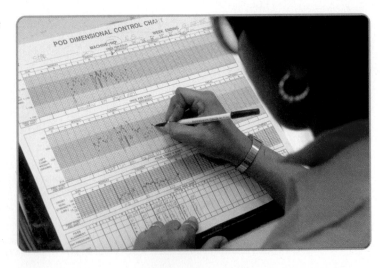

The formulas for *p*-chart upper and lower control limits follow:

$$\text{UCL}_p = \bar{p} + z\sigma_{\hat{p}} \tag{S6-9}$$

$$\text{LCL}_p = \bar{p} - z\sigma_{\hat{p}} \tag{S6-10}$$

where $\bar{p}$ = mean fraction defective in the sample
         z = number of standard deviations ($z = 2$ for 95.45% limits; $z = 3$ for 99.73% limits)
         $\sigma_{\hat{p}}$ = standard deviation of the sampling distribution

$\sigma_{\hat{p}}$ is estimated by the formula

$$\sigma_{\hat{p}} = \sqrt{\frac{\bar{p}(1 - \bar{p})}{n}} \tag{S6-11}$$

where n = number of observations in *each* sample

Example S4 shows how to set control limits for *p*-charts for these standard deviations.

Clerks at Mosier Data Systems key in thousands of insurance records each day for a variety of client firms. CEO Donna Mosier wants to set control limits to include 99.73% of the random variation in the data entry process when it is in control.

Approach: Samples of the work of 20 clerks are gathered (and shown in the table). Mosier carefully examines 100 records entered by each clerk and counts the number of errors. She also computes the fraction defective in each sample. Equations (S6-9), (S6-10), and (S6-11) are then used to set the control limits.

Sample Number	Number of Errors	Fraction Defective	Sample Number	Number of Errors	Fraction Defective
1	6	.06	11	6	.06
2	5	.05	12	1	.01
3	0	.00	13	8	.08
4	1	.01	14	7	.07
5	4	.04	15	5	.05
6	2	.02	16	4	.04
7	5	.05	17	11	.11
8	3	.03	18	3	.03
9	3	.03	19	0	.00
10	2	.02	20	$\underline{4}$	.04
				80	

Solution: $\bar{p} = \dfrac{\text{Total number of errors}}{\text{Total number of records examined}} = \dfrac{80}{(100)(20)} = .04$

$\sigma_{\hat{p}} = \sqrt{\dfrac{(.04)(1 - .04)}{100}} = .02$ (rounded up from .0196)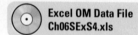

(*Note:* 100 is the size of *each* sample = *n*.)

$$\text{UCL}_p = \bar{p} + z\sigma_{\hat{p}} = .04 + 3(.02) = .10$$

$$\text{LCL}_p = \bar{p} - z\sigma_{\hat{p}} = .04 - 3(.02) = 0$$

(because we cannot have a negative percent defective)

Insight: When we plot the control limits and the sample fraction defectives, we find that only one data-entry clerk (number 17) is out of control. The firm may wish to examine that individual's work a bit more closely to see if a serious problem exists (see Figure S6.6).

EXAMPLE S4

Setting control limits for percent defective

Excel OM Data File
Ch06SExS4.xls

 Active Model S6.1

Example S4 is further illustrated in Active Model S6.1 on the CD-ROM and in the Exercise on page 242.

▶ **Figure S6.6**

p-Chart for Data Entry
for Example S4

Learning exercise: Mosier decides to set control limits at 95.45% instead. What are the new UCL_p and LCL_p? [Answer: 0.08, 0.]

Related problems: S6.13, S6.14, S6.15, S6.16, S6.17, S6.18, S6.19, S6.20, S6.25

The *OM in Action* box "Unisys Corp.'s Costly Experiment in Health Care Services" provides a real-world follow-up to Example S4.

c-chart

A quality control chart used to control the number of defects per unit of output.

c-**Charts**   In Example S4, we counted the number of defective records entered. A defective record was one that was not exactly correct because it contained at least one defect. However, a bad record may contain more than one defect. We use *c*-**charts** to control the *number* of defects per unit of output (or per insurance record, in the preceding case).

Control charts for defects are helpful for monitoring processes in which a large number of potential errors can occur, but the actual number that do occur is relatively small. Defects may be errors in newspaper words, bad circuits in a microchip, blemishes on a table, or missing pickles on a fast-food hamburger.

OM in Action   **Unisys Corp.'s Costly Experiment in Health Care Services**

When Unisys Corp. expanded into the computerized health care service business things looked rosy. It had just beat out Blue Cross/Blue Shield of Florida for an $86 million contract to serve Florida's state employee health-insurance services. Its job was to handle the 215,000 Florida employees' claims processing—a seemingly simple and lucrative growth area for an old-line computer company like Unisys.

But 1 year later the contract was not only torn up, Unisys was fined more than $500,000 for not meeting quality standards. Here are two of the measures of quality, both attributes (that is, either "defective" or "not defective") on which the firm was out of control:

1. *Percent of claims processed with errors:* An audit over a 3-month period, by Coopers & Lybrand, found that Unisys made errors in 8.5% of claims processed. The industry standard is 3.5% "defectives."

2. *Percent of claims processed within 30 days:* For this attribute measure, a "defect" is a processing time longer than the contract's time allowance. In one month's sample, 13% of the claims exceeded the 30-day limit, far above the 5% allowed by the State of Florida.

The Florida contract was a migraine for Unisys, which underestimated the labor-intensiveness of health claims. CEO James Unruh pulled the plug on future ambitions in health care. Meanwhile, the State of Florida's Ron Poppel says, "We really need somebody that's in the insurance business."

Sources: Knight Ridder Tribune Business News (October 20, 2004): 1 and (February 7, 2002): 1; and *Business Week* (June 16, 1997): 6.

◀ *Sampling wine from these wooden barrels, to make sure it is aging properly, uses both SPC (for alcohol content and acidity) and subjective measures (for taste).*

The Poisson probability distribution,[3] which has a variance equal to its mean, is the basis for *c*-charts. Because $\bar{c}$ is the mean number of defects per unit, the standard deviation is equal to $\sqrt{\bar{c}}$. To compute 99.73% control limits for $\bar{c}$, we use the formula:

$$\text{Control limits} = \bar{c} \pm 3\sqrt{\bar{c}} \qquad \text{(S6-12)}$$

Example S5 shows how to set control limits for a $\bar{c}$-chart.

EXAMPLE S5

Setting control limits for number defective

Red Top Cab Company receives several complaints per day about the behavior of its drivers. Over a 9-day period (where days are the units of measure), the owner, Gordon Hoft, received the following numbers of calls from irate passengers: 3, 0, 8, 9, 6, 7, 4, 9, 8, for a total of 54 complaints. Hoft wants to compute 99.73% control limits.

Approach: He applies Equation (S6-12).

Solution: $\bar{c} = \dfrac{54}{9} = 6$ complaints per day

Thus:

$$\text{UCL}_c = \bar{c} + 3\sqrt{\bar{c}} = 6 + 3\sqrt{6} = 6 + 3(2.45) = 13.35, \text{ or } 13$$

$$\text{LCL}_c = \bar{c} - 3\sqrt{\bar{c}} = 6 - 3\sqrt{6} = 6 - 3(2.45) = 0 \leftarrow \text{(since it cannot be negative)}$$

Insight: After Hoft plotted a control chart summarizing these data and posted it prominently in the drivers' locker room, the number of calls received dropped to an average of three per day. Can you explain why this occurred?

Learning exercise: Hoft collects 3 more days' worth of complaints (10, 12, and 8 complaints) and wants to combine them with the original 9 days to compute updated control limits. What are the revised UCL_c and LCL_c? [Answer: 14.94, 0.]

Related problems: S6.21, S6.22, S6.23, S6.24

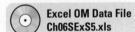

Excel OM Data File Ch06SExS5.xls

Managerial Issues and Control Charts

In an ideal world, there is no need for control charts. Quality is uniform and so high that employees need not waste time and money sampling and monitoring variables and attributes. But because most processes have not reached perfection, managers must make three major decisions regarding control charts.

---

[3]A Poisson probability distribution is a discrete distribution commonly used when the items of interest (in this case, defects) are infrequent and/or occur in time and space.

▶ **Table S6.3**

Helping You Decide Which Control Chart to Use

Variable Data

Using an $\bar{x}$-Chart and an R-Chart

1. Observations are *variables*, which are usually products measured for size or weight. Examples are the width or length of a wire being cut and the weight of a can of Campbell's soup.
2. Collect 20 to 25 samples, usually of $n = 4$, $n = 5$, or more, each from a stable process, and compute the mean for an $\bar{x}$-chart and the range for an R-chart.
3. We track samples of n observations each, as in Example S1.

Attribute Data

Using a p-Chart

1. Observations are *attributes* that can be categorized as good or bad (or pass–fail, or functional–broken), that is, in two states.
2. We deal with fraction, proportion, or percent defectives.
3. There are several samples, with many observations in each. For example, 20 samples of $n = 100$ observations in each, as in Example S4.

Using a c-Chart

1. Observations are *attributes* whose defects per unit of output can be counted.
2. We deal with the number counted, which is a small part of the possible occurrences.
3. Defects may be: number of blemishes on a desk; complaints in a day; crimes in a year; broken seats in a stadium; typos in a chapter of this text; or flaws in a bolt of cloth, as is shown in Example S5.

First, managers must select the points in their process that need SPC. They may ask "Which parts of the job are critical to success?" or "Which parts of the job have a tendency to become out of control?"

Second, managers need to decide if variable charts (i.e., $\bar{x}$ and R) or attribute charts (i.e., p and c) are appropriate. Variable charts monitor weights or dimensions. Attribute charts are more of a "yes–no" or "go–no go" gauge and tend to be less costly to implement. Table S6.3 can help you understand when to use each of these types of control charts.

Third, the company must set clear and specific SPC policies for employees to follow. For example, should the data-entry process be halted if a trend is appearing in percent defective records being keyed? Should an assembly line be stopped if the average length of five successive samples is above the centerline? Figure S6.7 illustrates some of the patterns to look for over time in a process.

Run test

A test used to examine the points in a control chart to see if nonrandom variation is present.

A tool called a **run test** is available to help identify the kind of abnormalities in a process that we see in Figure S6.7. In general, a run of 5 points above or below the target or centerline may suggest that an assignable, or nonrandom, variation is present. When this occurs, even though all the points

▶ **Figure S6.7**

Patterns to Look for on Control Charts

Source: Adapted from Bertrand L. Hansen, *Quality Control: Theory and Applications* (1991): 65. Reprinted by permission of Prentice Hall, Upper Saddle River, New Jersey.

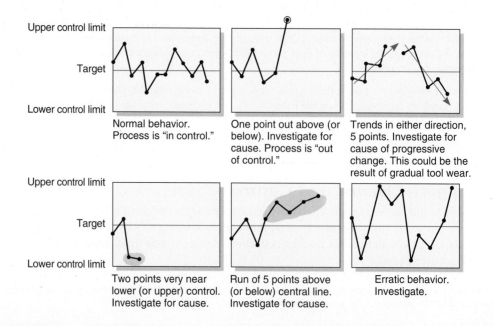

may fall inside the control limits, a flag has been raised. This means the process may not be statistically in control. A variety of run tests are described in books on the subject of quality methods.[4]

PROCESS CAPABILITY

Statistical process control means keeping a process in control. This means that the natural variation of the process must be stable. But a process that is in statistical control may not yield goods or services that meet their *design specifications* (tolerances). The ability of a process to meet design specifications, which are set by engineering design or customer requirements, is called **process capability**. Even though that process may be statistically in control (stable), the output of that process may not conform to specifications.

For example, let's say the time a customer expects to wait for the completion of a lube job at Quik Lube is 12 minutes, with an acceptable tolerance of ±2 minutes. This tolerance gives an upper specification of 14 minutes and a lower specification of 10 minutes. The lube process has to be capable of operating within these design specifications—if not, some customers will not have their requirements met. As a manufacturing example, the tolerances for Harley-Davidson cam gears are extremely low, only 0.0005 inch—and a process must be designed that is capable of achieving this tolerance.

There are two popular measures for quantitatively determining if a process is capable: process capability ratio (C_p) and process capability index (C_{pk}).

Process Capability Ratio (C_p)

For a process to be capable, its values must fall within upper and lower specifications. This typically means the process capability is within ±3 standard deviations from the process mean. Since this range of values is 6 standard deviations, a capable process tolerance, which is the difference between the upper and lower specifications, must be greater than or equal to 6.

The process capability ratio, C_p, is computed as:

$$C_p = \frac{\text{Upper specification} - \text{Lower specification}}{6\sigma} \qquad \text{(S6-13)}$$

Example S6 shows the computation of C_p.

> In a GE insurance claims process, $\bar{x} = 210.0$ minutes, and $\sigma = .516$ minutes.
>
> The design specification to meet customer expectations is 210 ± 3 minutes. So the Upper Specification is 213 minutes and the lower specification is 207 minutes. The OM manager wants to compute the process capability ratio.
>
> *Approach:* GE applies Equation (S6-13).
>
> *Solution:* $C_p = \dfrac{\text{Upper specification} - \text{Lower specification}}{6\sigma} = \dfrac{213 - 207}{6(.516)} = 1.938$
>
> *Insight:* Since a ratio of 1.00 means that 99.73% of a process's outputs are within specifications, this ratio suggests a very capable process, with nonconformance of less than 4 claims per million.
>
> *Learning exercise:* If $\sigma = .60$ (instead of .516), what is the new C_p? [Answer: 1.667, a very capable process still.]
>
> *Related problems:* S6.26, S6.27

A capable process has a C_p of at least 1.0. If the C_p is less than 1.0, the process yields products or services that are outside their allowable tolerance. With a C_p of 1.0, 2.7 parts in 1,000 can be expected to be "out of spec."[5] The higher the process capability ratio, the greater the likelihood

Sidebar

Process capability
The ability to meet design specifications.

Learning Objective
6. Explain process capability and compute C_p and C_{pk}

C_p
A ratio for determining whether a process meets design specifications; a ratio of the specification to the process variation.

EXAMPLE S6

Process capability ratio (C_p)

 Active Model S6.2

Example S6 is further illustrated in Active Model S6.2 on the CD-ROM.

---

[4]See Gerald Smith, *Statistical Process Control and Process Improvement*, 6th ed. (Upper Saddle River, NJ: Prentice Hall, 2007).

[5]This is because a C_p of 1.0 has 99.73% of outputs within specifications. So $1.00 - .9973 = .0027$; with 1,000 parts, there are $.0027 \times 1,000 = 2.7$ defects.

For a C_p of 2.0, 99.99966% of outputs are "within spec." So $1.00 - .9999966 = .0000034$; with 1 million parts, there are 3.4 defects.

the process will be within design specifications. Many firms have chosen a C_p of 1.33 (a 4-sigma standard) as a target for reducing process variability. This means that only 64 parts per million can be expected to be out of specification.

Recall that in Chapter 6 we mentioned the concept of *Six Sigma* quality, championed by GE and Motorola. This standard equates to a C_p of 2.0, with only 3.4 defective parts per million (very close to zero defects) instead of the 2.7 parts per 1,000 with 3-sigma limits.

Although C_p relates to the spread (dispersion) of the process output relative to its tolerance, it does not look at how well the process average is centered on the target value.

Process Capability Index (C_{pk})

C_{pk}
A proportion of variation (3σ) between the center of the process and the nearest specification limit.

The process capability index, **C_{pk}**, measures the difference between the desired and actual dimensions of goods or services produced.

The formula for C_{pk} is:

$$C_{pk} = \text{Minimum of}\left[\frac{\text{Upper specification limit} - \bar{X}}{3\sigma}, \frac{\bar{X} - \text{Lower specification limit}}{3\sigma}\right] \quad \text{(S6-14)}$$

where $\bar{X}$ = process mean
σ = standard deviation of the process population

When the C_{pk} index for both the upper and lower specification limits equals 1.0, the process variation is centered and the process is capable of producing within ±3 standard deviations (fewer than 2,700 defects per million). A C_{pk} of 2.0 means the process is capable of producing fewer than 3.4 defects per million. For C_{pk} to exceed 1, σ must be less than $\frac{1}{3}$ of the difference between the specification and the process mean ($\bar{X}$). Figure S6.8 shows the meaning of various measures of C_{pk}, and Example S7 shows an application of C_{pk}.

EXAMPLE S7

Process capability index (C_{pk})

You are the process improvement manager and have developed a new machine to cut insoles for the company's top-of-the-line running shoes. You are excited because the company's goal is no more than 3.4 defects per million and this machine may be the innovation you need. The insoles cannot be more than ±.001 of an inch from the required thickness of .250″. You want to know if you should replace the existing machine, which has a C_{pk} of 1.0.

Approach: You decide to determine the C_{pk}, using Equation (S6-14), for the new machine and make a decision on that basis.

Solution: Upper specification limit = .251 inch

Lower specification limit = .249 inch

Mean of the new process $\bar{X}$ = .250 inch.
Estimated standard deviation of the new process = σ = .0005 inch.

$$C_{pk} = \text{Minimum of}\left[\frac{\text{Upper specification limit} - \bar{X}}{3\sigma}, \frac{\bar{X} - \text{Lower specification limit}}{3\sigma}\right]$$

$$C_{pk} = \text{Minimum of}\left[\frac{(.251) - .250}{(3).0005}, \frac{.250 - (.249)}{(3).0005}\right]$$

Both calculations result in: $\frac{.001}{.0015} = .67$.

Insight: Because the new machine has a C_{pk} of only 0.67, the new machine should *not* replace the existing machine.

Learning exercise: If the insoles can be ±.002″ (instead of .001″) from the required .250″, what is the new C_{pk}? [Answer: 1.33 and the new machine *should* replace the existing one.]

Related problems: S6.27, S6.28, S6.29, S6.30, S6.31

Note that C_p and C_{pk} will be the same when the process is centered. However, if the mean of the process is not centered on the desired (specified) mean, then the smaller numerator in Equation (S6-14) is used (the minimum of the difference between the upper specification limit and the mean or the lower specification limit and the mean). This application of C_{pk} is shown in Solved Problem S6.4. C_{pk} is the standard criterion used to express process performance.

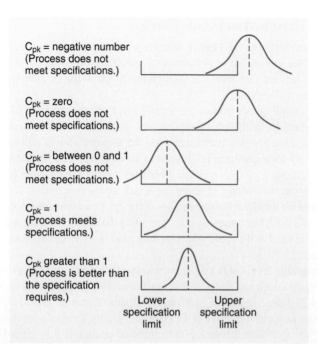

◀ **Figure S6.8**

Meanings of C$_{pk}$ Measures

A C$_{pk}$ index of 1.0 for both the upper and lower control limits indicates that the process variation is within the upper and lower control limits. As the C$_{pk}$ index goes above 1.0, the process becomes increasingly target-oriented with fewer defects. If the C$_{pk}$ is less than 1.0, the process will not produce within the specified tolerance. Because a process may not be centered, or may "drift," a C$_{pk}$ above 1 is desired.

Within the figure:

C_{pk} = negative number (Process does not meet specifications.)

C_{pk} = zero (Process does not meet specifications.)

C_{pk} = between 0 and 1 (Process does not meet specifications.)

C_{pk} = 1 (Process meets specifications.)

C_{pk} greater than 1 (Process is better than the specification requires.)

Lower specification limit   Upper specification limit

ACCEPTANCE SAMPLING[6]

Acceptance sampling is a form of testing that involves taking random samples of "lots," or batches, of finished products and measuring them against predetermined standards. Sampling is more economical than 100% inspection. The quality of the sample is used to judge the quality of all items in the lot. Although both attributes and variables can be inspected by acceptance sampling, attribute inspection is more commonly used, as illustrated in this section.

Acceptance sampling can be applied either when materials arrive at a plant or at final inspection, but it is usually used to control incoming lots of purchased products. A lot of items rejected, based on an unacceptable level of defects found in the sample, can (1) be returned to the supplier or (2) be 100% inspected to cull out all defects, with the cost of this screening usually billed to the supplier. However, acceptance sampling is not a substitute for adequate process controls. In fact, the current approach is to build statistical quality controls at suppliers so that acceptance sampling can be eliminated.

Acceptance sampling
A method of measuring random samples of lots or batches of products against predetermined standards.

Learning Objective

7. Explain acceptance sampling

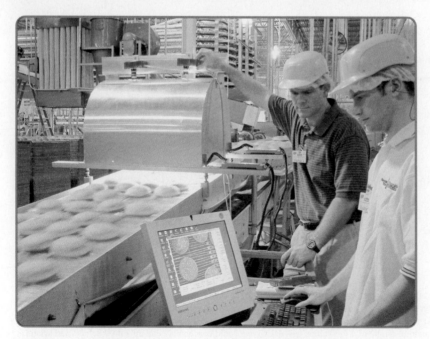

◀ *Flowers Bakery in Villa Rica, Georgia, uses a digital camera to inspect just-baked sandwich buns as they move along the production line. Items that don't measure up in terms of color, shape, seed distribution, or size are identified and removed automatically from the conveyor.*

[6]Refer to Tutorial 2 on your CD-ROM for an extended discussion of Acceptance Sampling.

Operating Characteristic Curve

Operating characteristic (OC) curve

A graph that describes how well an acceptance plan discriminates between good and bad lots.

Producer's risk

The mistake of having a producer's good lot rejected through sampling.

Consumer's risk

The mistake of a customer's acceptance of a bad lot overlooked through sampling.

Acceptable quality level (AQL)

The quality level of a lot considered good.

Lot tolerance percent defective (LTPD)

The quality level of a lot considered bad.

The **operating characteristic (OC) curve** describes how well an acceptance plan discriminates between good and bad lots. A curve pertains to a specific plan—that is, to a combination of *n* (sample size) and *c* (acceptance level). It is intended to show the probability that the plan will accept lots of various quality levels.

With acceptance sampling, two parties are usually involved: the producer of the product and the consumer of the product. In specifying a sampling plan, each party wants to avoid costly mistakes in accepting or rejecting a lot. The producer usually has the responsibility of replacing all defects in the rejected lot or of paying for a new lot to be shipped to the customer. The producer, therefore, wants to avoid the mistake of having a good lot rejected (**producer's risk**). On the other hand, the customer or consumer wants to avoid the mistake of accepting a bad lot because defects found in a lot that has already been accepted are usually the responsibility of the customer (**consumer's risk**). The OC curve shows the features of a particular sampling plan, including the risks of making a wrong decision.[7]

Figure S6.9 can be used to illustrate one sampling plan in more detail. Four concepts are illustrated in this figure.

The **acceptable quality level (AQL)** is the poorest level of quality that we are willing to accept. In other words, we wish to accept lots that have this or a better level of quality, but no lower. If an acceptable quality level is 20 defects in a lot of 1,000 items or parts, then AQL is 20/1,000 = 2% defectives.

The **lot tolerance percent defective (LTPD)** is the quality level of a lot that we consider bad. We wish to reject lots that have this or a poorer level of quality. If it is agreed that an unacceptable quality level is 70 defects in a lot of 1,000, then the LTPD is 70/1,000 = 7% defective.

To derive a sampling plan, producer and consumer must define not only "good lots" and "bad lots" through the AQL and LTPD, but they must also specify risk levels.

Producer's risk (α) is the probability that a "good" lot will be rejected. This is the risk that a random sample might result in a much higher proportion of defects than the population of all items. A lot with an acceptable quality level of AQL still has an α chance of being rejected. Sampling plans are often designed to have the producer's risk set at $\alpha = .05$, or 5%.

▶ **Figure S6.9**

An Operating Characteristic (OC) Curve Showing Producer's and Consumer's Risks

A good lot for this particular acceptance plan has less than or equal to 2% defectives. A bad lot has 7% or more defectives.

Active Model S6.3

Figure S6.9 is further illustrated in Active Model S6.3 on the CD.

[7]Note that sampling always runs the danger of leading to an erroneous conclusion. Let us say in one company that the total population under scrutiny is a load of 1,000 computer chips, of which in reality only 30 (or 3%) are defective. This means that we would want to accept the shipment of chips, because for this particular firm 4% is the allowable defect rate. However, if a random sample of $n = 50$ chips was drawn, we could conceivably end up with 0 defects and accept that shipment (that is, it is okay), or we could find all 30 defects in the sample. If the latter happened, we could wrongly conclude that the whole population was 60% defective and reject them all.

◄ *This laser tracking device, by Faro Technologies, enables quality control personnel to measure and inspect parts and tools during production. The tracker can measure objects from 100 feet away and takes up to 1,000 readings per second.*

Consumer's risk (β) is the probability that a "bad" lot will be accepted. This is the risk that a random sample may result in a lower proportion of defects than the overall population of items. A common value for consumer's risk in sampling plans is $\beta = .10$, or 10%.

The probability of rejecting a good lot is called a **type I error**. The probability of accepting a bad lot is a **type II error**.

Sampling plans and OC curves may be developed by computer (as seen in the software available with this text), by published tables, or by calculation, using binomial or Poisson distributions.

Type I error

Statistically, the probability of rejecting a good lot.

Type II error

Statistically, the probability of accepting a bad lot.

Average Outgoing Quality

In most sampling plans, when a lot is rejected, the entire lot is inspected and all defective items replaced. Use of this replacement technique improves the average outgoing quality in terms of percent defective. In fact, given (1) any sampling plan that replaces all defective items encountered and (2) the true incoming percent defective for the lot, it is possible to determine the **average outgoing quality (AOQ)** in percent defective. The equation for AOQ is:

$$AOQ = \frac{(P_d)(P_a)(N - n)}{N} \tag{S6-15}$$

where P_d = true percent defective of the lot
P_a = probability of accepting the lot for a given sample size and quantity defective
N = number of items in the lot
n = number of items in the sample

The maximum value of AOQ corresponds to the highest average percent defective or the lowest average quality for the sampling plan. It is called the *average outgoing quality limit (AOQL)*.

Acceptance sampling is useful for screening incoming lots. When the defective parts are replaced with good parts, acceptance sampling helps to increase the quality of the lots by reducing the outgoing percent defective.

Figure S6.10 compares acceptance sampling, SPC, and C_{pk}. As Figure S6.10 shows, (a) acceptance sampling by definition accepts some bad units, (b) control charts try to keep the process in control, but (c) the C_{pk} index places the focus on improving the process. As operations managers, that is what we want to do—improve the process.

Average outgoing quality (AOQ)

The percent defective in an average lot of goods inspected through acceptance sampling.

Learning Objective

8. Compute the AOQ

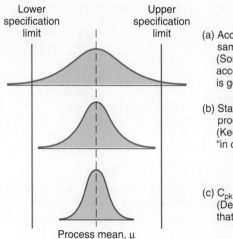

Lower specification limit

Upper specification limit

(a) Acceptance sampling
(Some bad units accepted; the "lot" is good or bad.)

(b) Statistical process control
(Keep the process "in control.")

(c) $C_{pk} > 1$
(Design a process that is in control.)

Process mean, μ

◄ **Figure S6.10**

The Application of Statistical Process Techniques Contributes to the Identification and Systematic Reduction of Process Variability

Summary

Statistical process control is a major statistical tool of quality control. Control charts for SPC help operations managers distinguish between natural and assignable variations. The $\bar{x}$-chart and the R-chart are used for variable sampling, and the p-chart and the c-chart for attribute sampling. The C_{pk} index is a way to express process capability. Operating characteristic (OC) curves facilitate acceptance sampling and provide the manager with tools to evaluate the quality of a production run or shipment.

Key Terms

Statistical process control (SPC) *(p. 222)*
Control chart *(p. 222)*
Natural variations *(p. 222)*
Assignable variation *(p. 223)*
$\bar{x}$-chart *(p. 224)*
R-chart *(p. 224)*
Central limit theorem *(p. 224)*
p-chart *(p. 230)*

c-chart *(p. 232)*
Run test *(p. 234)*
Process capability *(p. 235)*
C_p *(p. 235)*
C_{pk} *(p. 236)*
Acceptance sampling *(p. 237)*
Operating characteristic (OC) curve *(p. 238)*
Producer's risk *(p. 238)*

Consumer's risk *(p. 238)*
Acceptable quality level (AQL) *(p. 238)*
Lot tolerance percent defective (LTPD) *(p. 238)*
Type I error *(p. 239)*
Type II error *(p. 239)*
Average outgoing quality (AOQ) *(p. 239)*

Using Software for SPC

Excel, Excel OM, and POM for Windows may be used to develop control charts for most of the problems in this chapter.

✗ Creating Excel Spreadsheets to Determine Control Limits for a c-Chart

Excel and other spreadsheets are extensively used in industry to maintain control charts. Program S6.1 is an example of how to use Excel to determine the control limits for a c-chart. C-charts are used when the number of defects per unit of output is known. The data from Example S5 are used. In this example, 54 complaints occurred over 9 days. Excel also contains a built-in graphing ability with Chart Wizard.

▶ **Program S6.1**

An Excel Spreadsheet for Creating a c-Chart for Example S5

	A	B	C	D	E	F	G	H
1	Red Top Cab Company							
2								
3	Number of samples	9						
4								
5		Complaints		Results				
6	Day 1	3		Total Defects	54			
7	Day 2	0		Defect rate, λ	6			
8	Day 3	8		Standard deviation	2.45			
9	Day 4	9		z value	3			99.73%
10	Day 5	6						
11	Day 6	7		Upper Control Limit	13.348469			
12	Day 7	4		Center Line	6			
13	Day 8	9		Lower Control Limit	0			
14	Day 9	8						

Value	Cell	Excel Formula
Total Defects	E6	=SUM(B6:B14)
Defect rate, λ	E7	=E6/B3
Standard deviation	E8	=SQRT(E7)
Upper Control Limit	E11	=E7+E9*E8
Center Line	E12	=E7
Lower Control Limit	E13	=IF(E7-E9*E8>0,E7-E9*E8,0)

✗ Using Excel OM

Excel OM's Quality Control module has the ability to develop $\bar{x}$-charts, p-charts, and c-charts. It also handles OC curves, acceptance sampling, and process capability. Program S6.2 illustrates Excel OM's spreadsheet approach to computing the $\bar{x}$ control limits for the Oat Flakes company in Example S1.

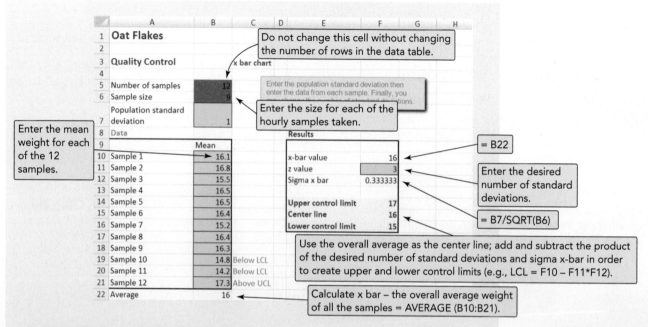

▲ **Program S6.2** **Excel OM Input and Selected Formulas for the Oat Flakes Example S1**

P Using POM for Windows

The POM for Windows Quality Control module has the ability to compute all the SPC control charts we introduced in this supplement, as well as OC curves, acceptance sampling, and process capability. See Appendix IV for further details.

Solved Problems

  Virtual Office Hours help is available on Student DVD.

Solved Problem S6.1

A manufacturer of precision machine parts produces round shafts for use in the construction of drill presses. The average diameter of a shaft is .56 inch. Inspection samples contain 6 shafts each. The average range of these samples is .006 inch. Determine the upper and lower $\bar{x}$ control chart limits.

solution

The mean factor A_2 from Table S6.1 where the sample size is 6, is seen to be .483. With this factor, you can obtain the upper and lower control limits:

$$\text{UCL}_{\bar{x}} = .56 + (.483)(.006)$$
$$= .56 + .0029$$
$$= .5629 \text{ inch}$$
$$\text{LCL}_{\bar{x}} = .56 - .0029$$
$$= .5571 \text{ inch}$$

Solved Problem S6.2

Nocaf Drinks, Inc., a producer of decaffeinated coffee, bottles Nocaf. Each bottle should have a net weight of 4 ounces. The machine that fills the bottles with coffee is new, and the operations manager wants to make sure that it is properly adjusted. Bonnie Crutcher, the operations manager, randomly selects and weighs $n = 8$ bottles and records the average and range in ounces for each sample. The data for several samples is given in the following table. Note that every sample consists of 8 bottles.

Sample	Sample Range	Sample Average	Sample	Sample Range	Sample Average
A	.41	4.00	E	.56	4.17
B	.55	4.16	F	.62	3.93
C	.44	3.99	G	.54	3.98
D	.48	4.00	H	.44	4.01

Is the machine properly adjusted and in control?

solution

We first find that $\bar{\bar{x}} = 4.03$ and $\bar{R} = .505$. Then, using Table S6.1, we find:

$$\text{UCL}_{\bar{x}} = \bar{\bar{x}} + A_2\bar{R} = 4.03 + (.373)(.505) = 4.22$$

$$\text{LCL}_{\bar{x}} = \bar{\bar{x}} - A_2\bar{R} = 4.03 - (.373)(.505) = 3.84$$

$$\text{UCL}_R = D_4\bar{R} = (1.864)(.505) = .94$$

$$\text{LCL}_R = D_3\bar{R} = (.136)(.505) = .07$$

It appears that the process average and range are both in statistical control.

The operations manager needs to determine if a process with a mean (4.03) slightly above the desired mean of 4.00 is satisfactory; if it is not, the process will need to be changed.

Solved Problem S6.3

Altman Distributors, Inc., fills catalog orders. Samples of size $n = 100$ orders have been taken each day over the past six weeks. The average defect rate was .05. Determine the upper and lower limits for this process for 99.73% confidence.

solution

$z = 3$, $\bar{p} = .05$. Using Equations S6-9, S6-10, and S6-11,

$$\text{UCL}_p = \bar{p} + 3\sqrt{\frac{\bar{p}(1-\bar{p})}{n}} = .05 + 3\sqrt{\frac{(.05)(1-.05)}{100}}$$

$$= .05 + 3(0.0218) = .1154$$

$$\text{LCL}_p = \bar{p} - 3\sqrt{\frac{\bar{p}(1-\bar{p})}{n}} = .05 - 3(.0218)$$

$$= .05 - .0654 = 0 \text{ (because percent defective cannot be negative)}$$

Solved Problem S6.4

Ettlie Engineering has a new catalyst injection system for your countertop production line. Your process engineering department has conducted experiments and determined that the mean is 8.01 grams with a standard deviation of .03. Your specifications are:

$\mu = 8.0$ and $\sigma = .04$, which means an upper specification limit of 8.12 [$= 8.0 + 3(.04)$] and a lower specification limit of 7.88 [$= 8.0 - 3(.04)$].

What is the C_{pk} performance of the injection system?

solution

Using Equation (S6-14):

$$C_{pk} = \text{Minimum of} \left[\frac{\text{Upper specification limit} - \bar{X}}{3\sigma}, \frac{\bar{X} - \text{Lower specification limit}}{3\sigma} \right]$$

where
$\bar{X}$ = process mean
σ = standard deviation of the process population

$$C_{pk} = \text{minimum of} \left[\frac{8.12 - 8.01}{(3)(.03)}, \frac{8.01 - 7.88}{(3)(.03)} \right]$$

$$\left[\frac{.11}{.09} = 1.22, \frac{.13}{.09} = 1.44 \right]$$

The minimum is 1.22, so the C_{pk} of 1.22 is within specifications and has an implied error rate of less than 2,700 defects per million.

Active Model Exercise

This Active Model, as well as Active Models S6.2 and S6.3, appears on your CD. Active Model S6.1 allows you to evaluate important elements in the *p*-charts.

Questions

1. Has the process been in control?

2. Suppose we use a 95 percent *p*-chart. What are the upper and lower control limits? Has the process gotten more out of control?

p-Chart

Reset Data	Questions

Number of samples	20
Sample size	100
z value	3.0000
Confidence	99.73%

	# Defects	Fraction Defective
Sample 1	6	0.06
Sample 2	5	0.05
Sample 3	0	0.00
Sample 4	1	0.01
Sample 5	4	0.04
Sample 6	2	0.02
Sample 7	5	0.05
Sample 8	3	0.03
Sample 9	3	0.03
Sample 10	2	0.02
Sample 11	6	0.06
Sample 12	1	0.01
Sample 13	8	0.08
Sample 14	7	0.07
Sample 15	5	0.05
Sample 16	4	0.04
Sample 17	11	0.11 Above UCL
Sample 18	3	0.03
Sample 19	0	0.00
Sample 20	4	0.04

Total Sample Size	2000	Upper Control Limit	0.10
Total Defects	80	Center Line	0.04
Percentage defects	0.04	Lower Control Limit	0.00
Std dev of p-bar	0.019596		

◄ **Active Model S6.1**

p-Chart for the Mosier Data Systems in Example S4.

3. Suppose that the sample size used was actually 120 instead of the 100 that it was supposed to be. How would this affect the chart?

4. What happens to the chart as we reduce the *z*-value?

5. What happens to the chart as we reduce the percentage defects?

Self-Test

- *Before taking the self-test*, refer to the learning objectives listed at the beginning of the supplement and the key terms listed at the end of the supplement.
- Use the key at the back of the text to **correct** your answers.
- *Restudy* pages that correspond to any questions you answered incorrectly or material you feel uncertain about.

1. The type of chart used to control the central tendency of variables with continuous dimensions is:
   a) $\bar{x}$-bar chart
   b) *R*-chart
   c) *p*-chart
   d) *c*-chart
   e) none of the above

2. Control charts for attributes are:
   a) *p*-charts
   b) *c*-charts
   c) *R*-charts
   d) $\bar{x}$-charts
   e) all of the above

3. If parts in a sample are measured and the mean of the sample measurement is outside the tolerance limits:
   a) the process is out of control, and the cause should be established
   b) the process is in control, but not capable of producing within the established control limits
   c) the process is within the established control limits with only natural causes of variation
   d) all of the above are true

4. If *parts* in a sample are measured and the mean of the sample measurement is in the middle of the tolerance limits but some parts measure outside the control limits:
   a) the process is in control, with only assignable causes of variation
   b) the process is not producing within the established control limits
   c) the process is within the established control limits with only natural causes of variation
   d) the process has both natural and assignable causes of variation

5. If a 95.45% level of confidence is desired, the $\bar{x}$-chart limits will be set plus or minus _____.

6. The two techniques discussed to find and resolve assignable variations in process control are the _____ and the _____.

7. The _____ risk is the probability that a lot will be rejected despite the quality level exceeding or meeting the _____.

8. The ability of a process to meet design specifications is called:
   a) Taguchi
   b) process capability
   c) capability index
   d) acceptance sampling
   e) average outgoing quality

Internet and Student CD-ROM/DVD Exercises

Visit our Companion Web site or use your student CD-ROM/DVD to help with material in this supplement.

 On Our Companion Web Site,
www.prenhall.com/heizer
- Self-Study Quizzes
- Practice Problems
- Virtual Company Tour
- Internet Case Study
- PowerPoint Lecture

On Your Student CD-ROM
- Practice Problems
- Active Model Exercises
- Excel OM Software
- Excel OM Data Files
- POM for Windows

On Your Student DVD
- Video Clips and Video Case Study
- Virtual Office Hours for Solved Problems

Discussion Questions

1. List Shewhart's two types of variation. What are they also called?
2. Define "in statistical control."
3. Explain briefly what an $\bar{x}$-chart and an R-chart do.
4. What might cause a process to be out of control?
5. List five steps in developing and using $\bar{x}$-charts and R-charts.
6. List some possible causes of assignable variation.
7. Explain how a person using 2-sigma control charts will more easily find samples "out of bounds" than 3-sigma control charts. What are some possible consequences of this fact?
8. When is the desired mean, μ, used in establishing the centerline of a control chart instead of $\bar{\bar{x}}$?
9. Can a production process be labeled as "out of control" because it is too good? Explain.
10. In a control chart, what would be the effect on the control limits if the sample size varied from one sample to the next?
11. Define C_{pk} and explain what a C_{pk} of 1.0 means. What is C_p?
12. What does a run of 5 points above or below the centerline in a control chart imply?
13. What are the acceptable quality level (AQL) and the lot tolerance percent defective (LTPD)? How are they used?
14. What is a run test and when is it used?
15. Discuss the managerial issues regarding the use of control charts.
16. What is an OC curve?
17. What is the purpose of acceptance sampling?
18. What two risks are present when acceptance sampling is used?
19. Is a *capable* process a *perfect* process? That is, does a capable process generate only output that meets specifications? Explain.

Problems*

• **S6.1** Boxes of Organic Flakes are produced to contain 14 ounces, with a standard deviation of .1 ounce. Set up the 3-sigma $\bar{x}$-chart for a sample size of 36 boxes. **Px**

• **S6.2** The overall average on a process you are attempting to monitor is 50 units. The process standard deviation is 1.72. Determine the upper and lower control limits for a mean chart, if you choose to use a sample size of 5. Set $z = 3$. **Px**

• **S6.3** Thirty-five samples of size 7 each were taken from a fertilizer-bag-filling machine. The results were: Overall mean = 57.75 lb; Average range = 1.78 lb.
a) Determine the upper and lower control limits of the $\bar{x}$-chart, where $\sigma = 3$.
b) Determine the upper and lower control limits of the R-chart, where $\sigma = 3$. **Px**

• **S6.4** Pioneer Chicken advertises "lite" chicken with 30% fewer calories than standard chicken. When the process for "lite" chicken breast production is in control, the average chicken breast contains 420 calories, and the standard deviation in caloric content of the chicken breast population is 25 calories.

Pioneer wants to design an $\bar{x}$-chart to monitor the caloric content of chicken breasts, where 25 chicken breasts would be chosen at random to form each sample. What are the lower and upper control limits for this chart if these limits are chosen to be *four* standard deviations from the target? **Px**

• **S6.5** Cordelia Barrera is attempting to monitor a filling process that has an overall average of 705 cc. The average range is 6 cc. If you use a sample size of 10, what are the upper and lower control limits for the mean and range? **Px**

•• **S6.6** Sampling 4 pieces of precision-cut wire (to be used in computer assembly) every hour for the past 24 hours has produced the following results:

Hour	$\bar{x}$	R	Hour	$\bar{x}$	R
1	3.25"	.71"	13	3.11"	.85"
2	3.10	1.18	14	2.83	1.31
3	3.22	1.43	15	3.12	1.06
4	3.39	1.26	16	2.84	.50
5	3.07	1.17	17	2.86	1.43
6	2.86	.32	18	2.74	1.29
7	3.05	.53	19	3.41	1.61
8	2.65	1.13	20	2.89	1.09
9	3.02	.71	21	2.65	1.08
10	2.85	1.33	22	3.28	.46
11	2.83	1.17	23	2.94	1.58
12	2.97	.40	24	2.64	.97

Develop appropriate control charts and determine whether there is any cause for concern in the cutting process. Plot the information and look for patterns. **Px**

Note: **Px** means the problem may be solved with POM for Windows and/or Excel OM/Excel.

•• S6.7 Auto pistons at Yongpin Zhou's plant in Shanghai are produced in a forging process, and the diameter is a critical factor that must be controlled. From sample sizes of 10 pistons produced each day, the mean and the range of this diameter have been as follows: ●

Day	Mean (mm)	Range (mm)
1	156.9	4.2
2	153.2	4.6
3	153.6	4.1
4	155.5	5.0
5	156.6	4.5

Construct the 3-sigma $\bar{x}$-chart and the 3-sigma R-chart for this dimension, using the data observed in the table above. **Px**

•• S6.8 Bill Kime's bowling ball factory makes bowling balls of adult size and weight only. The standard deviation in the weight of a bowling ball produced at the factory is known to be 0.12 pounds. Each day for 24 days, the average weight, in pounds, of nine of the bowling balls produced that day has been assessed as follows:

Day	Average (lb)	Day	Average (lb)
1	16.3	13	16.3
2	15.9	14	15.9
3	15.8	15	16.3
4	15.5	16	16.2
5	16.3	17	16.1
6	16.2	18	15.9
7	16.0	19	16.2
8	16.1	20	15.9
9	15.9	21	15.9
10	16.2	22	16.0
11	15.9	23	15.5
12	15.9	24	15.8

Establish a control chart for monitoring the average weights of the bowling balls in which the upper and lower control limits are each two standard deviations from the mean. What are the values of the control limits? **Px**

•• S6.9 Whole Grains LLC uses statistical process control to ensure that its health-conscious, low-fat, multigrain sandwich loaves have the proper weight. Based on a previously stable and in-control process, the control limits of the $\bar{x}$- and R-charts are: $UCL_{\bar{x}} = 6.56$, $LCL_{\bar{x}} = 5.84$, $UCL_R = 1.141$, $LCL_R = 0$. Over the past few days, they have taken five random samples of four loaves each and have found the following:

	Net Weight			
Sample	Loaf #1	Loaf #2	Loaf #3	Loaf #4
1	6.3	6.0	5.9	5.9
2	6.0	6.0	6.3	5.9
3	6.3	4.8	5.6	5.2
4	6.2	6.0	6.2	5.9
5	6.5	6.6	6.5	6.9

Is the process still in control? **Px**

••• S6.10 A process that is considered to be in control measures an ingredient in ounces. Below are the last 10 samples (each of size $n = 5$) taken. The population standard deviation is 1.36.

	Samples									
1	**2**	**3**	**4**	**5**	**6**	**7**	**8**	**9**	**10**
10	9	13	10	12	10	10	13	8	10
9	9	9	10	10	10	11	10	8	12
10	11	10	11	9	8	10	8	12	9
9	11	10	10	11	12	8	10	12	8
12	10	9	10	10	9	9	8	9	12

a) What is the process standard deviation σ? What is $\sigma_{\bar{x}}$?
b) If $z = 3$, what are the control limits for the mean chart?
c) What are the control limits for the range chart?
d) Is the process in control? **Px**

••• S6.11 Twelve samples, each containing five parts, were taken from a process that produces steel rods. The length of each rod in the samples was determined. The results were tabulated and sample means and ranges were computed. The results were:

Sample	Sample Mean (in.)	Range (in.)
1	10.002	0.011
2	10.002	0.014
3	9.991	0.007
4	10.006	0.022
5	9.997	0.013
6	9.999	0.012
7	10.001	0.008
8	10.005	0.013
9	9.995	0.004
10	10.001	0.011
11	10.001	0.014
12	10.006	0.009

Determine the upper and lower control limits and the overall means for $\bar{x}$-charts and R-charts. Draw the chart and plot the values of the sample means and ranges. Do the data indicate a process that is in control? Why or why not? **Px**

•• S6.12 Eagletrons are all-electric automobiles produced by Mogul Motors, Inc. One of the concerns of Mogul Motors is that the Eagletrons be capable of achieving appropriate maximum speeds. To monitor this, Mogul executives take samples of eight Eagletrons at a time. For each sample, they determine the average maximum speed and the range of the maximum speeds within the sample. They repeat this with 35 samples to obtain 35 sample means and 35 ranges. They find that the average sample mean is 88.50 miles per hour, and the average range is 3.25 miles per hour. Using these results, the executives decide to establish an R chart. They would like this chart to be established so that when it shows that the range of a sample is not within the control limits, there is only approximately a 0.0027 probability that this is due to natural variation. What will be the upper control limit (UCL) and the lower control limit (LCL) in this chart? **Px**

• S6.13 The defect rate for data entry of insurance claims has historically been about 1.5%. What are the upper and lower control chart limits if you wish to use a sample size of 100 and 3-sigma limits? **Px**

•• S6.14 You are attempting to develop a quality monitoring system for some parts purchased from Charles Sox Manufacturing Co. These parts are either good or defective. You have decided to take a sample of 100 units. Develop a table of the appropriate upper and lower control chart limits for various values of the average fraction defective in the samples taken. The values for $\bar{p}$ in this table should range from 0.02 to 0.10 in increments of 0.02. Develop the upper and lower control limits for a 99.73% confidence level.

	n = 100	
$\bar{p}$	UCL	LCL
0.02		
0.04		
0.06		
0.08		
0.10		

•• **S6.15** The results of inspection of DNA samples taken over the past 10 days are given below. Sample size is 100.

Day	1	2	3	4	5	6	7	8	9	10
Defectives	7	6	6	9	5	6	0	8	9	1

a) Construct a 3-sigma p-chart using this information.
b) If the number of defectives on the next three days are 12, 5, and 13, is the process in control? **Px**

• **S6.16** In the past, the defect rate for your product has been 1.5%. What are the upper and lower control chart limits if you wish to use a sample size of 500 and $z = 3$? **Px**

• **S6.17** Refer to Problem S6.16. If the defect rate was 3.5% instead of 1.5%, what would be the control limits ($z = 3$)? **Px**

•• **S6.18** Five data entry operators work at the data processing department of the Georgia Bank. Each day for 30 days, the number of defective records in a sample of 250 records typed by these operators has been noted, as follows:

Sample No.	No. Defective	Sample No.	No. Defective	Sample No.	No. Defective
1	7	11	18	21	17
2	5	12	5	22	12
3	19	13	16	23	6
4	10	14	4	24	7
5	11	15	11	25	13
6	8	16	8	26	10
7	12	17	12	27	14
8	9	18	4	28	6
9	6	19	6	29	12
10	13	20	16	30	3

Establish 3σ upper and lower control limits. **Px**

•• **S6.19** Detroit Central Hospital is trying to improve its image by providing a positive experience for its patients and their relatives. Part of the "image" program involves providing tasty, inviting patient meals that are also healthful. A questionnaire accompanies each meal served, asking the patient, among other things, whether he or she is satisfied or unsatisfied with the meal. A 100-patient sample of the survey results over the past 7 days yielded the following data:

Day	No. of Unsatisfied Patients	Sample Size
1	24	100
2	22	100
3	8	100
4	15	100
5	10	100
6	26	100
7	17	100

Construct a p-chart that plots the percentage of patients unsatisfied with their meals. Set the control limits to include 99.73% of the random variation in meal satisfaction. Comment on your results. **Px**

•• **S6.20** Chicago Supply Company manufactures paper clips and other office products. Although inexpensive, paper clips have provided the firm with a high margin of profitability. Samples of 200 are taken. Results are given for the last 10 samples. Establish upper and lower control limits for the control chart and graph the data. Is the process in control?

Sample	1	2	3	4	5	6	7	8	9	10
Defectives	5	7	4	4	6	3	5	6	2	8

Px

• **S6.21** Peter Ittig's department store, Ittig Brothers, is Amherst's largest independent clothier. The store receives an average of six returns per day. Using $z = 3$, would nine returns in a day warrant action? **Px**

•• **S6.22** An ad agency tracks the complaints, by week received, about the billboards in its city:

Week	No. of Complaints
1	4
2	5
3	4
4	11
5	3
6	9

a) What type of control chart would you use to monitor this process and why?
b) What are the 3-sigma control limits for this process? Assume that the historical complaint rate is unknown.
c) Is the process mean in control, according to the control limits? Why or why not?
d) Assume now that the historical complaint rate has been 4 calls a week. What would the 3-sigma control limits for this process be now? Is the process in control according to the control limits? **Px**

•• **S6.23** The school board is trying to evaluate a new math program introduced to second-graders in five elementary schools across the county this year. A sample of the student scores on standardized math tests in each elementary school yielded the following data:

School	No. of Test Errors
A	52
B	27
C	35
D	44
E	55

Construct a *c*-chart for test errors, and set the control limits to contain 99.73% of the random variation in test scores. What does the chart tell you? Has the new math program been effective? **Px**

•• **S6.24** Telephone inquiries of 100 IRS "customers" are monitored daily at random. Incidents of incorrect information or other nonconformities (such as impoliteness to customers) are recorded. The data for last week follow:

Day	No. of Nonconformities
1	5
2	10
3	23
4	20
5	15

Construct a 3-standard deviation *c*-chart of nonconformities. What does the control chart tell you about the IRS telephone operators? **Px**

••• **S6.25** The accounts receivable department at Rick Wing Manufacturing has been having difficulty getting customers to pay the full amount of their bills. Many customers complain that the bills are not correct and do not reflect the materials that arrived at their receiving docks. The department has decided to implement SPC in its billing process. To set up control charts, 10 samples of 50 bills each were taken over a month's time and the items on the bills checked against the bill of lading sent by the company's shipping department to determine the number of bills that were not correct. The results were:

Sample No.	No. of Incorrect Bills	Sample No.	No. of Incorrect Bills
1	6	6	5
2	5	7	3
3	11	8	4
4	4	9	7
5	0	10	2

a) Determine the value of *p*-bar, the mean fraction defective. Then determine the control limits for the *p*-chart using a 99.73% confidence level (3 standard deviations). Is this process in control? If not, which sample(s) were out of control?

b) How might you use the quality tools discussed in Chapter 6 to determine the source of the billing defects and where you might start your improvement efforts to eliminate the causes? **Px**

• **S6.26** The difference between the upper specification and the lower specification for a process is 0.6″. The standard deviation is 0.1″. What is the process capability ratio, C_p? Interpret this number. **Px**

•• **S6.27** Meena Chavan Corp.'s computer chip production process yields DRAM chips with an average life of 1,800 hours and $\sigma = 100$ hours. The tolerance upper and lower specification limits are 2,400 hours and 1,600 hours, respectively. Is this process capable of producing DRAM chips to specification? **Px**

•• **S6.28** Blackburn, Inc., an equipment manufacturer in Nashville, has submitted a sample cutoff valve to improve your manufacturing process. Your process engineering department has conducted experiments and found that the valve has a mean (μ) of 8.00 and a standard deviation (σ) of .04. Your desired performance is $\mu = 8.0$ and $\sigma = .045$. What is the C_{pk} of the Blackburn valve? **Px**

•• **S6.29** The specifications for a plastic liner for concrete highway projects calls for a thickness of 3.0 mm ±.1 mm. The standard deviation of the process is estimated to be .02 mm. What are the upper and lower specification limits for this product? The process is known to operate at a mean thickness of 3.0 mm. What is the C_{pk} for this process? About what percentage of all units of this liner will meet specifications? **Px**

•• **S6.30** The manager of a food processing plant desires a quality specification with a mean of 16 ounces, an upper specification limit of 16.5, and a lower specification limit of 15.5. The process has a mean of 16 ounces and a standard deviation of 1 ounce. Determine the C_{pk} of the process. **Px**

•• **S6.31** A process filling small bottles with baby formula has a target of 3 ounces ±0.150 ounce. Two hundred bottles from the process were sampled. The results showed the average amount of formula placed in the bottles to be 3.042 ounces. The standard deviation of the amounts was 0.034 ounce. Determine the value of C_{pk}. Roughly what proportion of bottles meet the specifications? **Px**

••• **S6.32** As the supervisor in charge of shipping and receiving, you need to determine *the average outgoing quality* in a plant where the known incoming lots from your assembly line have an average defective rate of 3%. Your plan is to sample 80 units of every 1,000 in a lot. The number of defects in the sample is not to exceed 3. Such a plan provides you with a probability of acceptance of each lot of .79 (79%). What is your average outgoing quality? **Px**

••• **S6.33** An acceptance sampling plan has lots of 500 pieces and a sample size of 60. The number of defects in the sample may not exceed 2. This plan, based on an OC curve, has a probability of .57 of accepting lots when the incoming lots have a defective rate of 4%, which is the historical average for this process. What do you tell your customer the average outgoing quality is? **Px**

•••• **S6.34** West Battery Corp. has recently been receiving complaints from retailers that its 9-volt batteries are not lasting as long as other name brands. James West, head of the TQM program at West's Austin plant, believes there is no problem because his batteries have had an average life of 50 hours, about 10% longer than competitors' models. To raise the lifetime above this level would require a new level of technology not available to West. Nevertheless, he is concerned enough to set up hourly assembly line checks. Previously, after ensuring that the process was running properly, West took size-5 samples of 9-volt batteries for each of 25 hours to establish the standards for control chart limits. Those 25 samples are shown in the following table:

West Battery Data—Battery Lifetimes (in hours)

Hour	Sample 1	2	3	4	5	$\bar{x}$	R
1	51	50	49	50	50	50.0	2
2	45	47	70	46	36	48.8	34
3	50	35	48	39	47	43.8	15
4	55	70	50	30	51	51.2	40
5	49	38	64	36	47	46.8	28
6	59	62	40	54	64	55.8	24
7	36	33	49	48	56	44.4	23
8	50	67	53	43	40	50.6	27
9	44	52	46	47	44	46.6	8
10	70	45	50	47	41	50.6	29
11	57	54	62	45	36	50.8	26
12	56	54	47	42	62	52.2	20
13	40	70	58	45	44	51.4	30
14	52	58	40	52	46	49.6	18
15	57	42	52	58	59	53.6	17
16	62	49	42	33	55	48.2	29
17	40	39	49	59	48	47.0	20
18	64	50	42	57	50	52.6	22
19	58	53	52	48	50	52.2	10

Hour	Sample 1	2	3	4	5	$\bar{x}$	R
20	60	50	41	41	50	48.4	19
21	52	47	48	58	40	49.0	18
22	55	40	56	49	45	49.0	16
23	47	48	50	50	48	48.6	3
24	50	50	49	51	51	50.2	2
25	51	50	51	51	62	53.0	12

With these limits established, West now takes 5 more hours of data, which are shown in the following table:

Hour	Sample 1	2	3	4	5
26	48	52	39	57	61
27	45	53	48	46	66
28	63	49	50	45	53
29	57	70	45	52	61
30	45	38	46	54	52

a) Determine means and the upper and lower control limits for $\bar{x}$ and R (using the first 25 hours only).
b) Is the manufacturing process in control?
c) Comment on the lifetimes observed. **Px**

Case Studies

Bayfield Mud Company

In November 2007, John Wells, a customer service representative of Bayfield Mud Company, was summoned to the Houston warehouse of Wet-Land Drilling, Inc., to inspect three boxcars of mud-treating agents that Bayfield had shipped to the Houston firm. (Bayfield's corporate offices and its largest plant are located in Orange, Texas, which is just west of the Louisiana–Texas border.) Wet-Land had filed a complaint that the 50-pound bags of treating agents just received from Bayfield were short-weight by approximately 5%.

The short-weight bags were initially detected by one of Wet-Land's receiving clerks, who noticed that the railroad scale tickets indicated that net weights were significantly less on all three boxcars than those of identical shipments received on October 25, 2007. Bayfield's traffic department was called to determine if lighter-weight pallets were used on the shipments. (This might explain the lighter net weights.) Bayfield indicated, however, that no changes had been made in loading or palletizing procedures. Thus, Wet-Land engineers randomly checked 50 bags and discovered that the average net weight was 47.51 pounds. They noted from past shipments that the process yielded bag net weights averaging exactly 50.0 pounds, with an acceptable standard deviation σ of 1.2 pounds. Consequently, they concluded that the sample indicated a significant short-weight. (The reader may wish to verify this conclusion.) Bayfield was then contacted, and Wells was sent to investigate the complaint. Upon arrival, Wells verified the complaint and issued a 5% credit to Wet-Land.

Wet-Land management, however, was not completely satisfied with the issuance of credit. The charts followed by their mud engineers on the drilling platforms were based on 50-pound bags of treating agents. Lighter-weight bags might result in poor chemical control during the drilling operation and thus adversely affect drilling efficiency. (Mud-treating agents are used to control the pH and other chemical properties of the core during drilling operation.) This defect could cause severe economic consequences because of the extremely high cost of oil and natural gas well-drilling operations. Consequently, special-use instructions had to accompany the delivery of these shipments to the drilling platforms. Moreover, the short-weight shipments had to be isolated in Wet-Land's warehouse, causing extra handling and poor space utilization. Thus, Wells was informed that Wet-Land might seek a new supplier of mud-treating agents if, in the future, it received bags that deviated significantly from 50 pounds.

The quality control department at Bayfield suspected that the lightweight bags might have resulted from "growing pains" at the Orange plant. Because of the earlier energy crisis, oil and natural gas exploration activity had greatly increased. In turn, this increased activity created increased demand for products produced by related industries, including drilling muds. Consequently, Bayfield had to expand from a one-shift (6:00 A.M. to 2:00 P.M.) to a two-shift (2:00 P.M. to 10:00 P.M.) operation in mid-2005, and finally to a three-shift operation (24 hours per day) in the fall of 2007.

The additional night-shift bagging crew was staffed entirely by new employees. The most experienced foremen were temporarily assigned to supervise the night-shift employees. Most emphasis was placed on increasing the output of bags to meet ever-increasing demand. It was suspected that only occasional reminders were made to double-check the bag weight-feeder. (A double-check is per-

Time	Average Weight (pounds)	Range		Time	Average Weight (pounds)	Range	
		Smallest	Largest			Smallest	Largest
6:00 A.M.	49.6	48.7	50.7	6:00	46.8	41.0	51.2
7:00	50.2	49.1	51.2	7:00	50.0	46.2	51.7
8:00	50.6	49.6	51.4	8:00	47.4	44.0	48.7
9:00	50.8	50.2	51.8	9:00	47.0	44.2	48.9
10:00	49.9	49.2	52.3	10:00	47.2	46.6	50.2
11:00	50.3	48.6	51.7	11:00	48.6	47.0	50.0
12 Noon	48.6	46.2	50.4	12 Midnight	49.8	48.2	50.4
1:00 P.M.	49.0	46.4	50.0	1:00 A.M.	49.6	48.4	51.7
2:00	49.0	46.0	50.6	2:00	50.0	49.0	52.2
3:00	49.8	48.2	50.8	3:00	50.0	49.2	50.0
4:00	50.3	49.2	52.7	4:00	47.2	46.3	50.5
5:00	51.4	50.0	55.3	5:00	47.0	44.1	49.7
6:00	51.6	49.2	54.7	6:00	48.4	45.0	49.0
7:00	51.8	50.0	55.6	7:00	48.8	44.8	49.7
8:00	51.0	48.6	53.2	8:00	49.6	48.0	51.8
9:00	50.5	49.4	52.4	9:00	50.0	48.1	52.7
10:00	49.2	46.1	50.7	10:00	51.0	48.1	55.2
11:00	49.0	46.3	50.8	11:00	50.4	49.5	54.1
12 Midnight	48.4	45.4	50.2	12 Noon	50.0	48.7	50.9
1:00 A.M.	47.6	44.3	49.7	1:00 P.M.	48.9	47.6	51.2
2:00	47.4	44.1	49.6	2:00	49.8	48.4	51.0
3:00	48.2	45.2	49.0	3:00	49.8	48.8	50.8
4:00	48.0	45.5	49.1	4:00	50.0	49.1	50.6
5:00	48.4	47.1	49.6	5:00	47.8	45.2	51.2
6:00	48.6	47.4	52.0	6:00	46.4	44.0	49.7
7:00	50.0	49.2	52.2	7:00	46.4	44.4	50.0
8:00	49.8	49.0	52.4	8:00	47.2	46.6	48.9
9:00	50.3	49.4	51.7	9:00	48.4	47.2	49.5
10:00	50.2	49.6	51.8	10:00	49.2	48.1	50.7
11:00	50.0	49.0	52.3	11:00	48.4	47.0	50.8
12 Noon	50.0	48.8	52.4	12 Midnight	47.2	46.4	49.2
1:00 P.M.	50.1	49.4	53.6	1:00 A.M.	47.4	46.8	49.0
2:00	49.7	48.6	51.0	2:00	48.8	47.2	51.4
3:00	48.4	47.2	51.7	3:00	49.6	49.0	50.6
4:00	47.2	45.3	50.9	4:00	51.0	50.5	51.5
5:00	46.8	44.1	49.0	5:00	50.5	50.0	51.9

formed by systematically weighing a bag on a scale to determine if the proper weight is being loaded by the weight-feeder. If there is significant deviation from 50 pounds, corrective adjustments are made to the weight-release mechanism.)

To verify this expectation, the quality control staff randomly sampled the bag output and prepared the chart above. Six bags were sampled and weighed each hour.

Discussion Questions

1. What is your analysis of the bag-weight problem?
2. What procedures would you recommend to maintain proper quality control?

Source: Professor Jerry Kinard, Western Carolina University.

Alabama Airlines's On-Time Schedule

Alabama Airlines opened its doors in December 2001 as a commuter service with its headquarters and only hub located in Birmingham. A product of airline deregulation, Alabama Air joined the growing number of short-haul, point-to-point airlines, including Lone Star, Comair, Atlantic Southeast, and Skywest.

Alabama Air was started and managed by two former pilots, David Douglas (who had been with now-defunct Midway Airlines) and Michael Hanna (formerly with Continental). It acquired a fleet of 12 used prop-jet planes and the airport gates vacated by Delta Airlines in 2001 when it curtailed flights due to the terrorist attacks of 9/11.

One of Alabama Air's top competitive priorities is on-time arrivals. The airline defines "on-time" to mean any arrival that is within 20 minutes of the scheduled time.

Mike Hanna decided to personally monitor Alabama Air's performance. Each week for the past 30 weeks, Hanna checked a random sample of 100 flight arrivals for on-time performance. The table that follows contains the number of flights that did not meet Alabama Air's definition of on time:

Sample (week)	Late Flights	Sample (week)	Late Flights
1	2	16	2
2	4	17	3
3	10	18	7
4	4	19	3
5	1	20	2
6	1	21	3
7	13	22	7
8	9	23	4
9	11	24	3
10	0	25	2
11	3	26	2
12	4	27	0
13	2	28	1
14	2	29	3
15	8	30	4

Discussion Questions

1. Using a 95% confidence level, plot the overall percentage of late flights (p) and the upper and lower control limits on a control chart.
2. Assume that the airline industry's upper and lower control limits for flights that are not on time are .1000 and .0400, respectively. Draw them on your control chart.
3. Plot the percentage of late flights in each sample. Do all samples fall within Alabama Airlines's control limits? When one falls outside the control limits, what should be done?
4. What can Mike Hanna report about the quality of service?

Farm to Fork: Quality at Darden Restaurants

Video Case

Darden Restaurants, the $5.2 billion owner of such popular brands as Olive Garden, Red Lobster, Seasons 52, and Bahama Breeze, serves more than 300 million meals annually in its 1,450 restaurants across the U.S. and Canada. Before any one of these meals is placed before a guest, the ingredients for each recipe must pass quality control inspections from the source, ranging from measurement and weighing, to tasting, touching, or lab testing. Darden has differentiated itself from its restaurant peers by developing the gold standard in continuous improvement.

To assure both customers and the company that quality expectations are met, Darden uses a rigorous inspection process, employing statistical process control (SPC) as part of its "Farm to Fork" program. More than 50 food scientists, microbiologists, and public health professionals report to Ana Hooper, director of quality assurance.

As part of Darden's Point Source program, Hooper's team, based in Southeast Asia (in China, Thailand, and Singapore) and Latin America (in Equador, Honduras, and Chile), approves and inspects—and works with Darden buyers to purchase—more than 50 million pounds of seafood each year for restaurant use. Darden used to build quality in at the end by inspecting shipments as they reached U.S. distribution centers. Now, thanks to coaching and partnering with vendors abroad, Darden needs but a few domestic inspection labs to verify compliance to its exacting standards. Food vendors in source countries know that when supplying Darden, they are subject to regular audits that are stricter than U.S. Food & Drug Administration (FDA) standards.

Two Quality Success Stories

Quality specialists' jobs include raising the bar and improving quality and safety at all plants in their geographic area. The Thai quality representative, for example, worked closely with several of Darden's largest shrimp vendors to convert them to a production-line-integrated quality assurance program. The vendors were able to improve the quality of shrimp supplied and reduce the percentage of defects by 19%.

Likewise, when the Darden quality teams visited fields of growers/shippers in Mexico recently, it identified challenges such as low employee hygiene standards, field food safety problems, lack of portable toilets, child labor, and poor working conditions. Darden addressed these concerns and hired third party independent food safety verification firms to ensure continued compliance to standards.

SPC Charts

SPC charts, such as the one shown on page 228 in this supplement, are particularly important. These charts document precooked food weights; meat, seafood and poultry temperatures; blemishes on produce; and bacteria counts on shrimp—just to name a few. Quality assurance is part of a much bigger process that is key to Darden's success—its supply chain (see Chapter 11 and Supplement 11 for discussion and case studies on this topic). That's because quality comes from the source and flows through distribution to the restaurant and guests.

Discussion Questions*

1. How does Darden build quality into the supply chain?
2. Select two potential problems—one in the Darden supply chain and one in a restaurant—that can be analyzed with a fish-bone chart. Draw a complete chart to deal with each problem.
3. Darden applies SPC in many product attributes. Identify where these are probably used.
4. The SPC chart on page 228 illustrates Darden's use of control charts to monitor the weight of salmon filets. Given these data, what conclusion do you, as a Darden quality control inspector, draw? What report do you issue to your supervisor? How do you respond to the salmon vendor?

*You might want to watch this video case on your DVD before answering these questions.

Additional Case Studies

Internet Case Study: Visit our Companion Web site at www.prenhall.com/heizer for this free case study:

- **Green River Chemical Company:** Involves a company that needs to set up a control chart to monitor sulfate content because of customer complaints.

Harvard has selected these Harvard Business School cases to accompany this supplement:

harvardbusinessonline.hbsp.harvard.edu

- **Deutsche Allgemeinversicherung** (#696-084): A German insurance company tries to adopt *p*-charts to a variety of services it performs.
- **Process Control at Polaroid (A)** (#696-047): This film-production plant moves from traditional QC inspection to worker-based SPC charts.

Bibliography

Bakir, S. T. "A Quality Control Chart for Work Performance Appraisal." *Quality Engineering* 17, no. 3 (2005): 429.

Burr, J. T. *Elementary Statistical Quality Control.* Boca Raton, FL: CRC Press, 2005.

Goetsch, David L., and Stanley B. Davis. *Quality Management,* 5th ed. Upper Saddle River, NJ: Prentice Hall, 2006.

Gryna, F. M., R. C. H. Chua, and J. A. DeFeo. *Juran's Quality Planning and Analysis*, 5th ed. New York: McGraw-Hill, 2007.

Johnson, K. "Six Sigma Delivers On-Time Service." *Quality Progress* 38, no. 12 (December 2005): 57–60.

Lin, H., and G. Sheen. "Practical Implementation of the Capability Index C_{pk} Based on Control Chart Data." *Quality Engineering* 17, no. 3 (2005): 371.

Montgomery, D. C. *Introduction to Statistical Quality Control,* 5th ed. New York: Wiley, 2004.

Roth, H. P. "How SPC Can Help Cut Costs." *Journal of Corporate Accounting and Finance* 16, no. 3 (March–April 2005): 21–30.

Smith, Gerald. *Statistical Process Control and Process Improvement.* 6th ed. Upper Saddle River, NJ: Prentice Hall, 2007.

Summers, Donna. *Quality*, 4th ed. Upper Saddle River, NJ: Prentice Hall, 2006.

Spigener, J. B., and P. J. Angelo. "What Would Deming Say?" *Quality Progress* 34, no. 3 (March 2001): 61–65.

Sumukadas, N., J. W. Fairfield-Sonn, and S. Morgan. "Ready-to-Use Simulation: Demystifying Statistical Process Control." *Simulation & Gaming* 36, no. 1 (March 2005): 134.

Internet Resources

American Society for Quality: **www.asq.org**
American Statistical Association: **www.amstat.org**
Associated Quality Consultants: **www.quality.org**
Business Process Improvement: **spcforexcel.com**
Institute of Statistics and Decision Science at Duke University: **www.isds.duke.edu**

Statistical Engineering Division of the Department of Commerce: **www.itl.nist.gov/div898/**
Total Quality Engineering: **www.tqe.com**

CHAPTER 7

Process Strategy

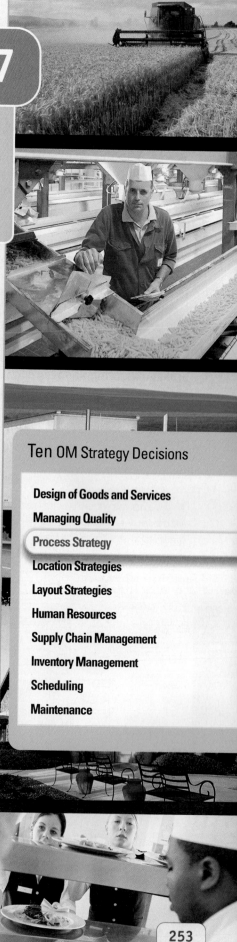

Chapter Outline

Ten OM Strategy Decisions

Design of Goods and Services

Managing Quality

Process Strategy

Location Strategies

Layout Strategies

Human Resources

Supply Chain Management

Inventory Management

Scheduling

Maintenance

Learning Objectives

When you complete this chapter you should be able to

1. Describe four production processes
2. Compute crossover points for different processes
3. Use the tools of process analysis
4. Describe customer interaction in process design
5. Identify recent advances in production technology

Global Company Profile: Dell Computer Corp.

Mass Customization Provides Dell Computer's Competitive Advantage

Dell Computer started with a single premise: selling a custom PC directly to end customers, thus eliminating markups in the distribution chain that accounted for a high percentage of a PC's price. Dell's concept and manufacturing process made the company an innovative business model, allowing Dell to grab first place in sales worldwide.

Dell's plants in Austin, Texas, and Nashville, Tennessee, are showcases of efficient custom manufacturing. Dell's direct-sales model and lean production practices provide instantaneous customer feedback. Because of this, Dell is the first to know of changes in the market. Dell has been so successful at manufacturing and knowing its customers that huge productivity increases are the norm, with manufacturing space constantly reduced. Robots shave seconds from the time required to load computers into cartons. Additional seconds are saved by com-

▼ *Dell computers are sold over the Internet and then efficiently produced and shipped directly to individual customers. No inventories are kept. Mass customization allows models to change continually as new technologies become available.*

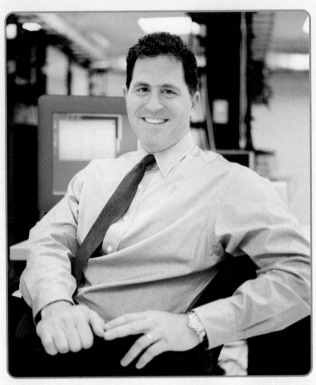

▲ *Michael Dell founded Dell Computer, at age 19, from his college dorm at the University of Texas. He dreamed of competing with IBM and in 1999 bypassed IBM in PC sales. Dell is now number one in the world.*

bining the downloading of software and computer testing into one step. Dell keeps product design under constant review, simplifying components, speeding assembly, and saving even more seconds. Time saved improves throughput, adds capacity, and contributes to flexibility. The added throughput, capacity, and flexibility allow Dell to respond to the sudden and frequent shifts in demand that characterize the PC market.

Both Dell's suppliers and in-house purchasing personnel evaluate inventories on an hour-by-hour basis to hold work-in-process (WIP) to a minimum. Despite a long and diverse global supply chain, Dell operates with just 4 days of inventory, a fraction of its competitors'. Six-person teams assemble 18 computers each hour, with parts that arrive via an overhead conveyor system. When a work cell has a prob-

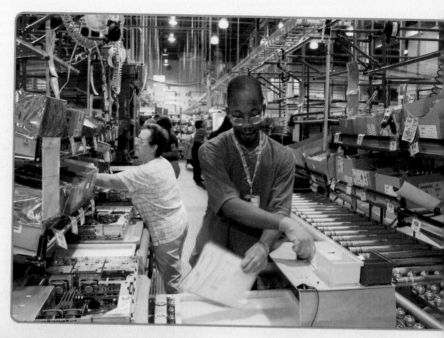

▶ Although more than 90% of Dell's personal computer business is build to order, the throughput time for each machine is less than 8 hours, and manufacturing cycle time is about 3 hours.

◀ Kits of components are prepared for each customer. Parts are then delivered as needed to work cells, and the final product is assembled by highly trained generalists who put together the entire computer.

lem, parts are instantly shifted to another cell, avoiding delays that are common in traditional assembly lines.

Dell's direct sales model embraces the Internet. Few companies have been as successful in turning the Internet into an everyday tool to enhance productivity. Dell has integrated the Web into every aspect of its business—design, production, sales, and service. Dell has set the standard for quick delivery and mass customization. This process has prevented the major problem of outdated inventory and obsolete PCs. Dell trims inventory by taking

delivery of components just *minutes* before they are needed.

One reason mass customization works at Dell is because instead of investing resources in developing computer components (as many competitors do), it focuses much of its research and development on software designed to make the installation and configuration of its PCs fast and simple. Dell's performance impresses many large organizations that now use Dell as their de facto supplier. The firm's reputation is such that CEO Michael Dell now counsels other firms on mass customization.

In Chapter 5, we examined the need for the selection, definition, and design of goods and services. We now turn to their production. A major decision for an operations manager is finding the best way to produce. Let's look at ways to help managers design a process for achieving this goal.

A **process** (or transformation) **strategy** is an organization's approach to transforming resources into goods and services. *The objective of a process strategy is to build a production process that meets customer requirements and product specifications within cost and other managerial constraints.* The process selected will have a long-term effect on efficiency and flexibility of production, as well as on cost and quality of the goods produced. Therefore, much of a firm's operations strategy is determined at the time of this process decision.

Process strategy
An organization's approach to transforming resources into goods and services.

FOUR PROCESS STRATEGIES

Virtually every good or service is made by using some variation of one of four process strategies: (1) process focus, (2) repetitive focus, (3) product focus, and (4) mass customization. The relationship of these four strategies to volume and variety is shown in Figure 7.1. Although the figure shows only four strategies, an innovative operations manager can build processes anywhere in the matrix to meet the necessary volume and variety requirements.

Let's look at each of these strategies with an example and a flow diagram. We examine *Standard Register* as a process-focused firm, *Harley-Davidson* as a repetitive producer, *Nucor Steel* as a product-focused operation, and *Dell* as a mass customizer.

Learning Objective

1. Describe four production processes

Process Focus

The vast majority of global production is devoted to making *low-volume, high-variety* products in places called "job shops." Such facilities are organized around specific activities or processes. In a factory, these processes might be departments devoted to welding, grinding, and painting. In an office, the processes might be accounts payable, sales, and payroll. In a restaurant, they might be bar, grill, and bakery. Such facilities are **process focused** in terms of equipment, layout, and supervision. They provide a high degree of product flexibility as products move intermittently between processes. Each process is designed to perform a wide variety of activities and handle frequent changes. Consequently, they are also called *intermittent processes*.

These facilities have high variable costs with extremely low utilization of facilities, as low as 5%. This is the case for many restaurants, hospitals, and machine shops. However, some facilities now do somewhat better through the use of innovative equipment, often with electronic controls. With the development of machines controlled by computer software, it is possible to program machine tools, piece movement, and tool changing, and even to automate placement of the parts on the machine and the movement of materials between machines.

Process focus
A production facility organized around processes to facilitate low-volume, high-variety production.

▶ **Figure 7.1**

Process Selected Must Fit with Volume and Variety

Example 1 shows how Standard Register, a billion-dollar printer and document processor headquartered in Dayton, Ohio, produces paper business forms.

EXAMPLE 1

Job Shop Process Focus at Standard Register

If you've had a pizza delivered to your home recently, there is a good chance that Standard Register printed the order and delivery tag on the box. You probably came in contact with one of Standard's forms this week without knowing it. Thousands of different products are made by the firm, a typical one being a multisheet (three- or four-layer) business form. Forms used for college student applications, hospital patient admissions, bank drafts, store orders, and job applications are examples. The company has 11 U.S. plants in its Forms Division.

Figure 7.2 is a flow diagram of the entire production process, from order submission to shipment, at Standard's Kirksville, Missouri, plant. This job shop groups people and machines that perform specific activities, such as printing, cutting, or binding, into departments. Entire orders are processed in batches, moving from department to department.

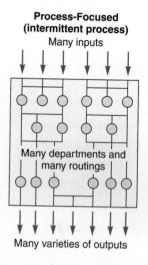

Process-Focused (intermittent process)
Many inputs

Many departments and many routings

Many varieties of outputs

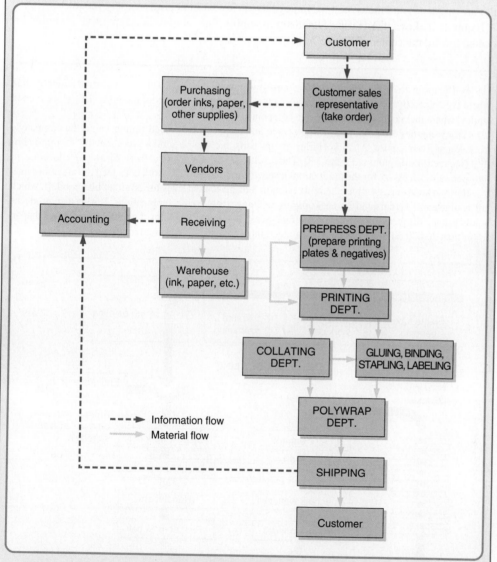

Information flow
Material flow

◄ **Figure 7.2**

Flow Diagram of the Production Process at Standard Register's Plant in Kirksville, Missouri

Source: Adapted with permission from J. S. Martinich, *Production and Operations Management* (New York: Wiley, 1997): 79–87.

The process begins with a sales representative helping the customer design the business form. Once the form is established, the order is transmitted electronically to the Sales Support Department at the manufacturing plant. An order coordinator determines what materials will be needed in production (ink, paper, labels, etc.), computes the production *time* needed, and schedules the job on a particular machine.

The Prepress Department uses computer-aided design (CAD) to convert the product design into printing plates for the presses and then "burns" the image of the form onto an aluminum printing plate. Machine operators in the Printing Department install the plates and inks on their presses and print the forms. After leaving the presses, most products are collated on a machine that places up to 14 copies together. Some products undergo additional processing (for example, gluing, binding, stapling, or labeling). When the forms are completed, most are wrapped in polyethylene before being placed in cartons for shipping. The order is shipped, a "job ticket" is sent to Accounting, and an invoice goes to the customer.

Repetitive Focus

A repetitive process falls between the product and process focuses seen in Figure 7.1. Repetitive processes use modules. Modules are parts or components previously prepared, often in a continuous process.

The **repetitive process** line is the classic assembly line. Widely used in the assembly of virtually all automobiles and household appliances, it has more structure and consequently less flexibility than a process-focused facility.

Fast-food firms are an example of a repetitive process using **modules**. This type of production allows more customizing than a continuous process; modules (for example, meat, cheese, sauce, tomatoes, onions) are assembled to get a quasi-custom product, a cheeseburger. In this manner, the firm obtains both the economic advantages of the continuous model (where many of the modules are prepared) and the custom advantage of the low-volume, high-variety model.

Example 2 shows the Harley-Davidson assembly line. Harley is a repetitive manufacturer located toward the center of Figure 7.1.

Repetitive process

A product-oriented production process that uses modules.

Modules

Parts or components of a product previously prepared, often in a continuous process.

EXAMPLE 2

Repetitive Manufacturing at Harley-Davidson

Harley-Davidson assembles modules. Most repetitive manufacturers produce on a form of assembly line where the end product can take a variety of shapes depending on the mix of modules. This is the case at Harley, where the modules are motorcycle components and options.

Harley engines are produced in Milwaukee and shipped on a just-in-time basis to the company's York, Pennsylvania, plant. At York, Harley groups parts that require similar processes together into families (see the flow diagram in Figure 7.3). The result is *work cells*. Work cells perform in one location all the operations necessary for the production of specific modules. These work cells feed the assembly line.

Harley-Davidson assembles 2 engine types in 3 displacement sizes for 20 street bike models, which are available in 13 colors and 2 wheel options, adding up to 95 total combinations. Harley also produces 4 police and 2 Shriner motorcycles, and offers many custom paint options. This strategy requires that no fewer than 20,000 different pieces be assembled into modules and then into motorcycles.

Repetitive Focus
Raw material and module inputs

Few modules

Modules combined for many output options

 Video 7.1

Saturn Auto's Mass Production

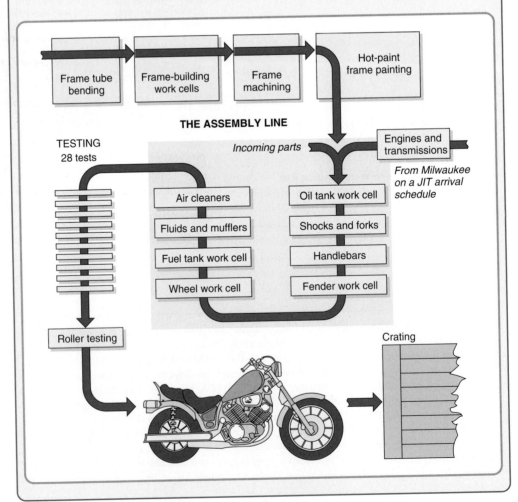

▶ **Figure 7.3**

Flow Diagram Showing the Production Process at Harley-Davidson's York, Pennsylvania, Assembly Plant

Product Focus

High-volume, low-variety processes are **product focused**. The facilities are organized around *products*. They are also called *continuous processes*, because they have very long, continuous production runs. Products such as glass, paper, tin sheets, lightbulbs, beer, and bolts are made via a continuous process. Some products, such as lightbulbs, are discrete; others, such as rolls of paper, are nondiscrete. Still others, such as repaired hernias at Shouldice Hospital, are services. It is only with standardization and effective quality control that firms have established product-focused facilities. An organization producing the same lightbulb or hot dog bun day after day can organize around a product. Such an organization has an inherent ability to set standards and maintain a given quality, as opposed to an organization that is producing unique products every day, such as a print shop or general-purpose hospital.

A product-focused facility produces high volume and low variety. The specialized nature of the facility requires high fixed cost, but low variable costs reward high facility utilization. The Nucor example follows.

Product focus

A facility organized around products; a product-oriented, high-volume, low-variety process.

 Video 7.2

Wassau Paper's Continuous Work Flow

EXAMPLE 3

Product-Focused Production at Nucor Steel

Steel is manufactured in a product-oriented facility. Figure 7.4 illustrates Nucor's product-focused flow.

Product-Focused (continuous process)
Few inputs

Output variations in size, shape, and packaging

◄ **Figure 7.4**

A Flow Diagram Showing the Steelmaking Process at Nucor's Crawfordsville, Indiana, Plant

In this process flow diagram, cold scrap steel is first lowered into a furnace that uses an electric arc to melt the steel in 20 seconds (A). Then molten steel pours from the furnace into a preheated ladle (B). The ladle moves on an overhead-track crane to the continuous caster (C). The ladle then opens and steel exits into the caster (D). Shaped steel exits the caster mold as a 2″ × 52″ slab (E). The slab exits the tunnel furnace (F) at a specific temperature needed for rolling. A higher-quality sheet can be produced if the slab temperature is uniform. The steel then enters the rolling mill (G). Water cools the hot-rolled steel before it is coiled (H). The rolled sheet of steel is coiled into rolls of about 25 tons each (I). Finally, a variety of finishing operations can modify the characteristics of the sheet steel to meet customer needs.

Nucor operates 24 hours a day, 6 days a week, with the seventh day reserved for scheduled maintenance.

Mass Customization Focus

Our increasingly wealthy and sophisticated world demands individualized goods and services. A peek at the rich variety of goods and services that operations managers are called on to supply is shown in Table 7.1. The explosion of variety has taken place in automobiles, movies, breakfast cereals, and thousands of other areas. In spite of this proliferation of products, operations managers have improved product quality while reducing costs. Consequently, the variety of products continues to grow. Operations managers use *mass customization* to produce this vast array of goods and services. **Mass customization** is the rapid, low-cost production of goods and services that fulfill increasingly unique customer desires. But mass customization (see the upper-right section of Figure 7.1) is not just about variety; it is about making precisely *what* the customer wants *when* the customer wants it economically.

Mass customization

Rapid, low-cost production that caters to constantly changing unique customer desires.

Mass customization brings us the variety of products traditionally provided by low-volume manufacture (a process focus) at the cost of standardized high-volume (product-focused) production. However, achieving mass customization is a challenge that requires sophisticated operational capabilities. Building agile processes that rapidly and inexpensively produce custom products requires imaginative and aggressive use of organizational resources. And the link between sales, design, production, supply chain, and logistics must be tight.[1]

Dell Computer has demonstrated that the payoff for mass customization can be substantial. More traditional manufacturers include General Motors, which builds six different styles on its Fairfax, Kansas, assembly line. GM adjusts robot welders and other equipment electronically as different models come down the assembly line. Moreover, GM's Cadillac division is now custom manufacturing cars with a 10-day lead time. Not to be outdone, Toyota recently announced delivery of custom-ordered cars in 5 days. Similarly, electronic controls allow designers in the textile industry to rapidly revamp their lines and respond to changes.

The service industry is also moving toward mass customization. For instance, not very many years ago, most people had the same telephone service. Now, not only is the phone service full of options, from caller ID to voice mail, but contemporary phones are hardly phones. They may also be part camera, computer, game player, and Web browser. Insurance companies are adding and

▶ **Table 7.1**

Mass Customization Provides More Choices Than Ever[a]

Source: Various; however, many of the data are from the Federal Reserve Bank of Dallas.

| Item | Number of Choices | |
	1970s	21st Century
Vehicle models	140	286
Vehicle styles	18	1,212
Bicycle types	8	211,000[c]
Software titles	0	400,000
Web sites	0	98,116,993[d]
Movie releases	267	458
New book titles	40,530	77,446
Houston TV channels	5	185
Breakfast cereals	160	340
Items (SKUs) in supermarkets	14,000[b]	150,000[e]
LCD TVs	0	102

[a]Variety available in America; worldwide the variety increases even more.
[b]1989.
[c]Possible combinations for one manufacturer.
[d]2007, **www.ipwalk.com** (July 2, 2007).
[e]SKUs managed by H. E. Butts grocery chain.

[1]Paul Zipkin, "The Limits of Mass Customization," *MIT Sloan Management Review* (spring 2001): p. 81.

So you want a hard-to-get, high-quality paperback book in 15 minutes? Borders can take care of you—even if you want a book that the store does not carry or have in stock. First, a Borders employee checks the digital database of titles that have been licensed from publishers. If the title is available, a digital file of the book is downloaded to two printers from a central server in Atlanta. One printer makes the book cover and the other the pages. Then the employee puts the two pieces together in a bookbinding machine. A separate machine cuts the book to size. And your book is ready. You get the book you want now, and Borders gets a sale. Books sold this way also avoid both inventory and incoming shipping cost, as well as the cost of returning books that do not sell.

Smooth FM provides a "customized" radio broadcast for Houston, Boston, Milwaukee, Albany, and Jacksonville from its midtown Manhattan station. Here is how it works. During Smooth FM's 40-minute music blocks, an announcer in Manhattan busily records 30-second blocks of local weather and traffic, commercials, promotions, and 5-second station IDs. Then the recorded material is transmitted to the affiliate stations. When the music block is over, the Manhattan announcer hits a button that signals computers at all the affiliates to simultaneously air the prerecorded "local" segments. Any "national" news or "national" ads can also be added from Manhattan. The result is the economy of mass production *and* a customized product for the local market. Radio people call it "local customization."

Sources: Hoover's Company Records (January 15, 2006): 51511; *The New York Times* (February 16, 2004): C3; *The Wall Street Journal* (June 1, 1999): B1, B4.

tailoring new products with shortened development times to meet the unique needs of their customers. And emusic of California maintains a music sound bite inventory on the Internet that allows customers to select a dozen songs of their choosing and have them made into a custom CD.[2] Similarly, the number of new books and movies increases each year. Mass customization places new demands on operations managers who must build the processes that provide this expanding variety of goods and services.

One of the essential ingredients in mass customization is a reliance on modular design. In all the examples cited, as well as those in the *OM in Action* box "Mass Customization at Borders Books and at Smooth FM Radio," modular design is the key. However, as Figure 7.5 shows, very effective scheduling, personnel and facility flexibility, supportive supply chains, and rapid throughput are also required. These items influence all 10 of the OM decisions and therefore require excellent operations management.

Making Mass Customization Work   Mass customization suggests a system in which products are built-to-order.[3] **Build-to-order** means producing to customer orders, not forecasts.

Build-to-order (BTO)
Produce to customer order rather than to a forecast.

◀ **Figure 7.5**

Requirements to Achieve Mass Customization

---

[2]**www.emusic.com**.
[3]Build-to-order (BTO) may be referred to and refined as engineer-to-order (ETO) and design-to-order (DTO), depending on the extent of the customization.

As Dell Computers has shown, build-to-order can be a successful order-winning strategy when executed successfully. But build-to-order is difficult. Some major challenges are:

- *Product design* must be imaginative and fast. Successful build-to-order designs often use modules. Ping Inc. uses different combinations of club heads, grips, shafts, and angles to make 20,000 variations of its golf clubs. Another design technique is to do the customization as late in the production process as possible. For instance, to accommodate different orders, Dell installs both requested hardware and software modules at final assembly. At organizations such as Ping and Dell, the individual modules are made to a forecast but assembled on a "mix and match" basis to meet mass customization demands.

- *Process design* must be rapid, flexible, and able to accommodate changes in design and technology. Flexibility allows a BMW customer to change an order up to 6 days before the car's final assembly. In addition to process flexibility that facilitates change, a process technique that has proven effective is to postpone customization until late in the production process. The auto industry installs or outsources unique interior modules until very late in the production, as they do with customized vans.

- *Inventory management* requires tight control. To be successful, a firm must avoid being stuck with unpopular or obsolete components. With virtually no raw material, work in process, or finished goods, Dell puts custom computers together in less than a day.

Postponement

The delay of any modifications or customization to a product as long as possible in the production process.

- *Tight schedules* that track orders and material from design through delivery can be effectively implemented only with dedicated personnel. National Bicycle (see the photo) accomplishes this with virtually no inventory and a 3-hour build schedule. Product and process design that allow customization to be scheduled late in the production process also contribute to efficient mass customization. This type of scheduling is often referred to as **postponement** and is discussed further in Chapter 11.

- *Responsive partners* in the supply chain yield effective collaboration. Cooperation with fast, open information exchange is critical as operations moves to an era in which competition is not between individual companies but between supply chains. Vans Inc. can custom tailor a pair of shoes, have them manufactured thousands of miles away in a Chinese factory, and have them delivered in a matter of weeks. Forecasting, inventory management, and ordering for JCPenney men's dress shirts are all handled by a supplier in Hong Kong.

Mass customization/build-to-order is difficult, but is the new imperative for operations. There are advantages to mass customization and building to order: first, by meeting the demands of the market place, firms win orders and stay in business; in addition, they reduce the enormous expenses present in organizations (from personnel to inventory to facilities) that exist because of inaccurate sales forecasting. Mass customization and build-to-order can be done—and operations managers in leading organizations are accepting the challenge.

▲ *Mass customization improves customer service and provides competitive advantage. National Bicycle's customized bicycle production process begins by defining individual customer needs. The customer mounts the special frame in a bicycle store from which measurements are taken. These custom measurements are then sent to the factory, where CAD software produces a blueprint in about 3 minutes. At the same time, a bar-code label is prepared that will identify bicycle components as they move through production. Time—from beginning to end—is only 3 hours.*

Comparison of Process Choices

The characteristics of the four processes are shown in Table 7.2 and Figure 7.5 (on page 261). Advantages exist across the continuum of processes, and firms may find strategic advantage in any process. Each of the processes, when properly matched to volume and variety, can produce a low-cost advantage. For instance, unit costs will be less in the continuous-process case if high volume (and high utilization) exists. However, we do not always use the continuous-process (that is, specialized equipment and facilities) because it is too expensive when volumes are low or flexibility is required. A low-volume, unique, highly differentiated good or service is more economical when produced under process focus; this is the way fine-dining restaurants and general-purpose hospitals are organized. Just as all four processes, when appropriately selected and well managed, can yield low cost, so too can all four be responsive and produce differentiated products.

Figure 7.5 indicated that equipment utilization in a process-focused facility is often in the range of 5% to 25%. When utilization goes above 15%, moving toward a repetitive or product

Manufactured housing is now used for 32% of all new homes sold in the U.S. This industry has increased sales, reduced costs, and moved production from a process focus to a repetitive focus.

▼ **Table 7.2** Comparison of the Characteristics of Four Types of Processes

Process Focus (low volume, high variety) (e.g., Standard Register)	Repetitive Focus (modular) (e.g., Harley-Davidson)	Product Focus (high volume, low variety) (e.g., Nucor Steel)	Mass Customization (high volume, high variety) (e.g., Dell Computer)
1. Small quantity and large variety of products are produced.	1. Long runs, usually a standardized product with options, are produced from modules.	1. Large quantity and small variety of products are produced.	1. Large quantity and large variety of products are produced.
2. Equipment used is general purpose.	2. Special equipment aids in use of an assembly line.	2. Equipment used is special purpose.	2. Rapid changeover on flexible equipment.
3. Operators are broadly skilled.	3. Employees are modestly trained.	3. Operators are less broadly skilled.	3. Flexible operators are trained for the necessary customization.
4. There are many job instructions because each job changes.	4. Repetitive operations reduce training and changes in job instructions.	4. Work orders and job instructions are few because they are standardized.	4. Custom orders require many job instructions.
5. Raw-material inventories are high relative to the value of the product.	5. Just-in-time procurement techniques are used.	5. Raw material inventories are low relative to the value of the product.	5. Raw material inventories are low relative to the value of the product.
6. Work-in-process is high compared to output.	6. Just-in-time inventory techniques are used.	6. Work-in-process inventory is low compared to output.	6. Work-in-process inventory is driven down by JIT, kanban, lean production.
7. Units move slowly through the plant.	7. Movement is measured in hours and days.	7. Swift movement of units through the facility is typical.	7. Goods move swiftly through the facility.
8. Finished goods are usually made to order and not stored.	8. Finished goods are made to frequent forecasts.	8. Finished goods are usually made to a forecast and stored.	8. Finished goods are often build-to-order (BTO).
9. Scheduling orders is complex and concerned with the trade-off between inventory availability, capacity, and customer service.	9. Scheduling is based on building various models from a variety of modules to forecasts.	9. Scheduling is relatively simple and concerned with establishing a rate of output sufficient to meet sales forecasts.	9. Sophisticated scheduling is required to accommodate custom orders.
10. Fixed costs tend to be low and variable costs high.	10. Fixed costs are dependent on flexibility of the facility.	10. Fixed costs tend to be high and variable costs low.	10. Fixed costs tend to be high, but variable costs must be low.
11. Costing, often done by the job, is estimated prior to doing the job, but known only after the job.	11. Costs are usually known because of extensive prior experience.	11. Because fixed costs are high, costs are highly dependent on utilization of capacity.	11. High fixed costs and dynamic variable costs make costing a challenge.

► **Figure 7.6**

Crossover Charts

Three different processes can be expected to have three different costs. However, at any given volume, only one will have the lowest cost.

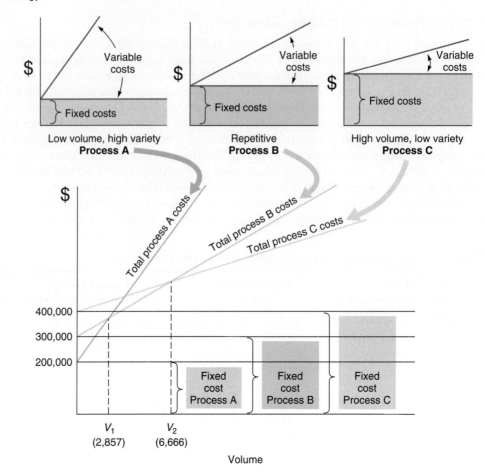

Learning Objective

2. Compute crossover points for different processes

focus, or even mass customization, may be advantageous. A cost advantage usually exists by improving utilization, provided the necessary flexibility is maintained. McDonald's started an entirely new industry by moving its limited menu from process focus to repetitive focus. McDonald's is now trying to add more variety by moving toward mass customization.

Much of what is produced in the world is still produced in very small lots—often as small as one. This is true for legal services, medical services, dental services, and restaurants. An X-ray machine in a dentist's office and much of the equipment in a fine-dining restaurant have low utilization. Hospitals, too, have low utilization, which suggests why their costs are considered high. Why such low utilization? In part because excess capacity for peak loads is desirable. Hospital administrators, as well as managers of other service facilities and their patients and customers, expect equipment to be available as needed. Another reason is poor scheduling (although substantial efforts have been made to forecast demand in the service industry) and the resulting imbalance in the use of facilities.

Crossover Charts

A chart of costs at the possible volumes for more than one process.

Crossover Charts   The comparison of processes can be further enhanced by looking at the point where the total cost of the processes changes. For instance, Figure 7.6 shows three alternative processes compared on a single chart. Such a chart is sometimes called a **crossover chart**. Process A has the lowest cost for volumes below V_1, process B has the lowest cost between V_1 and V_2, and process C has the lowest cost at volumes above V_2.

Example 4 illustrates how to determine the exact volume where one process becomes more expensive than another.

EXAMPLE 4

Crossover chart

Kleber Enterprises would like to evaluate three accounting software products (A, B, and C) to support changes in its internal accounting processes. The resulting processes will have cost structures similar to those shown in Figure 7.6. The costs of the software for these processes are:

	Total Fixed Cost	Dollars Required per Accounting Report
Software A	$200,000	$60
Software B	$300,000	$25
Software C	$400,000	$10

Approach: Solve for the crossover point for software A and B and then the crossover point for software B and C.

Solution: Software A yields a process that is most economical up to V_1, but to exactly what number of reports (volume)? To determine the volume at V_1, we set the cost of software A equal to the cost of software B. V_1 is the unknown volume:

$$200,000 + (60)V_1 = 300,000 + (25)V_1$$

$$35V_1 = 100,000$$

$$V_1 = 2,857$$

This means that software A is most economical from 0 reports to 2,857 reports (V_1).

Similarly, to determine the crossover point for V_2, we set the cost of software B equal to the cost of software C:

$$300,000 + (25)V_2 = 400,000 + (10)V_2$$

$$15V_2 = 100,000$$

$$V_2 = 6,666$$

This means that software B is most economical if the number of reports is between 2,857 (V_1) and 6,666 (V_2) and that software C is most economical if reports exceed 6,666 (V_2).

Insight: As you can see, the software and related process chosen is highly dependent on the forecasted volume.

Learning exercise: If the vendor of software A reduces the fixed cost to $150,000, what is the new crossover point between A and B? [Answer: 4,286.]

Related problems: 7.5, 7.6, 7.7, 7.8, 7.9, 7.10, 7.11, 7.12, 7.14

Active Model 7.1

Example 4 is further illustrated in Active Model 7.1 on the CD-ROM and in the Exercise located on page 280.

Focused Processes   In an ongoing quest for efficiency, industrialized societies continue to move toward specialization. The focus that comes with specialization contributes to efficiency. Managers who focus on a limited number of activities, products, and technologies do better. As the variety of products in a facility increase, overhead costs increase even faster. Similarly, as the variety of products, customers, and technology increases, so does complexity. The resources necessary to cope with the complexity expand disproportionately. A focus on depth of product line as opposed to breadth is typical of outstanding firms, of which Intel, Motorola, L.M. Ericsson, Nokia, and Bosch are world-class examples. Specialization, simplification, concentration, and *focus* yield efficiency. They also contribute to building a core competence that yields market and financial success. The focus can be:

Video 7.3

Process Strategy at Wheeled Coach Ambulance

- *Customers* (such as Winterhalter Gastronom, a German company that focuses on dishwashers for hotels and restaurants, for whom spotless glasses and dishes are critical)
- *Products* with similar attributes (such as Nucor Steel's Crawford, Ohio, plant, which processes only high-quality sheet steels, and Gallagher, a New Zealand company, which has 45% of the world market in electric fences)
- *Service* (such as Orlando's Arnold Palmer Hospital, with a focus on children and women; or Shouldice Hospital, in Canada, with a focus on hernia repair).
- *Technology* (such as Texas Instruments, with a focus on only certain specialized kinds of semiconductors; and SAP, which in spite of a world of opportunities, remains focused on software).

The key for the operations manager is to move continuously toward specialization, focusing on the products, technology, customers, processes, and talents necessary to excel in that specialty.

Changing Processes   Changing the production system from one process model to another is difficult and expensive. In some cases, the change may mean starting over. Consider what would be required of a rather simple change—McDonald's adding the flexibility necessary to serve you a charbroiled hamburger. What appears to be rather straightforward would require changes in

Agile organizations are quick and flexible in their response to changing customer requirements.

many of our 10 OM decisions. For instance, changes may be necessary in (1) purchasing (a different quality of meat, perhaps with more fat content, and supplies such as charcoal); (2) quality standards (how long and at what temperature the patty will cook); (3) equipment (the charbroiler); (4) layout (space for the new process and for new exhaust vents); and (5) training. So choosing where to operate on the process strategy continuum may determine the transformation strategy for an extended period. This critical decision must be done right the first time.

PROCESS ANALYSIS AND DESIGN

When analyzing and designing processes to transform resources into goods and services, we ask questions such as the following:

- Is the process designed to achieve competitive advantage in terms of differentiation, response, or low cost?
- Does the process eliminate steps that do not add value?
- Does the process maximize customer value as perceived by the customer?
- Will the process win orders?

A number of tools help us understand the complexities of process design and redesign. They are simply ways of making sense of what happens or must happen in a process. Let's look at five of them: flow diagrams, time-function mapping, value-stream mapping, process charts, and service blueprinting.

Flow Diagrams

Flow diagram

A drawing used to analyze movement of people or material.

The first tool is the **flow diagram**, which is a schematic or drawing of the movement of material, product, or people. For instance, Figures 7.2, 7.3, and 7.4 showed the processes for Standard Register, Harley-Davidson, and Nucor Steel, respectively. Such diagrams can help understanding, analysis, and communication of a process.

Time-Function Mapping

Time-function mapping (or process mapping)

A flow diagram with time added on the horizontal axis.

A second tool for process analysis and design is a flow diagram, but with time added on the horizontal axis. Such charts are sometimes called **time-function mapping**, or **process mapping**. With time-function mapping, nodes indicate the activities and the arrows indicate the flow direction, with time on the horizontal axis. This type of analysis allows users to identify and eliminate waste such as extra steps, duplication, and delay. Figure 7.7 shows the use of process mapping before and after

▼ **Figure 7.7** **Time-Function Mapping (Process Mapping) for a Product Requiring Printing and Extruding Operations at American National Can Company**

This technique clearly shows that waiting and order processing contributed substantially to the 46 days that can be eliminated in this operation.

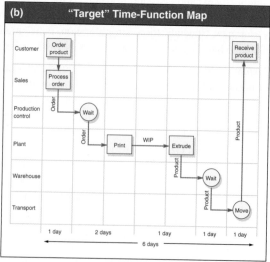

Source: Excerpted from Elaine J. Labach, "Faster, Better, and Cheaper," *Target* no. 5: 43 with permission of the Association for Manufacturing Excellence, 380 West Palatine Road, Wheeling, IL 60090-5863, 847/520-3282. **www.ame.org**.

process improvement at American National Can Company. In this example, substantial reduction in waiting time and process improvement in order processing contributed to a savings of 46 days.

Value-Stream Mapping

A variation of time-function mapping is **value-stream mapping (VSM)**; however, value-stream mapping takes an expanded look at where value is added (and not added) in the entire production process, including the supply chain. As with time-function mapping, the idea is to start with the customer and understand the production process, but value-stream mapping extends the analysis back to suppliers.[4]

Value-stream mapping (VSM)

A process that helps managers understand how to add value in the flow of material and information through the entire production process.

EXAMPLE 5

Value-stream mapping

Motorola has received an order for 11,000 cell phones per month and wants to understand how the order will be processed through manufacturing.

Approach: To fully understand the process from customer to supplier, Motorola wants to prepare a value-stream map.

Solution: Although value-stream maps appear complex, their construction is easy. Here are the steps needed to complete the value-stream map shown in Figure 7.8

◄ **Figure 7.8**

Value-Stream Mapping (VSM)

1. Begin with symbols for customer, supplier, and production to ensure the big picture.
2. Enter customer order requirements.
3. Calculate the daily production requirements.
4. Enter the outbound shipping requirements and delivery frequency.
5. Determine inbound shipping method and delivery frequency.
6. Add the process steps (i.e., machine, assemble) in sequence, left to right.

[4]See Mike Rother and John Shook, *Learning to See*. Brookline, MA: Lean Enterprise Institute, Inc., 1999.

7. Add communication methods, add their frequency, and show the direction with arrows.
8. Add inventory quantities (shown with ▲I) between every step of the entire flow.
9. Determine total working time (value-added time) and delay (non-value-added time).

Insight: From Figure 7.8 we note that large inventories exist in incoming raw material and between processing steps, and that the value-added time is low as a proportion of the entire process.

Learning exercise: How might raw material inventory be reduced? [Answer: Have deliveries twice per week rather than once per week.]

Related problem: 7.13

Value-stream mapping takes into account not only the process but, as shown in Example 5, also the management decisions and information systems that support the process.

Process Charts

Process charts

Charts that use symbols to analyze the movement of people or material.

The fourth tool is the *process chart*. **Process charts** use symbols, time, and distance to provide an objective and structured way to analyze and record the activities that make up a process.[5] They allow us to focus on value-added activities. For instance, the process chart shown in Figure 7.9, which includes the present method of hamburger assembly at a fast-food restaurant, includes a value-added line to help us distinguish between value-added activities and waste. Identifying all value-added operations (as opposed to inspection, storage, delay, and transportation, which add no value) allows us to determine the percent of value added to total activities.[6] We can see from the computation at the bottom of Figure 7.9 that the value added in this case is 85.7%. The operations manager's job is to reduce waste and increase the percent of value added. The non-value-added items are a waste; they are resources lost to the firm and to society forever.

▶ **Figure 7.9**

Process Chart Showing a Hamburger Assembly Process at a Fast-Food Restaurant

Present Method [X]		PROCESS CHART	Proposed Method [ ]
SUBJECT CHARTED	*Hamburger Assembly Process*		DATE *8 / 1 / 07*
DEPARTMENT		CHART BY *KH*	SHEET NO. *1* OF *1*

DIST. IN FEET	TIME IN MINS.	CHART SYMBOLS	PROCESS DESCRIPTION
	—	○ ⇨ □ D ▽	*Meat Patty in Storage*
1.5	.05	○ ⇨ □ D ▽	*Transfer to Broiler*
	2.50	○ ⇨ □ D ▽	*Broiler*
	.05	○ ⇨ □ D ▽	*Visual Inspection*
1.0	.05	○ ⇨ □ D ▽	*Transfer to Rack*
	.15	○ ⇨ □ D ▽	*Temporary Storage*
.5	.10	○ ⇨ □ D ▽	*Obtain Buns, Lettuce, etc.*
	.20	○ ⇨ □ D ▽	*Assemble Order*
.5	.05	○ ⇨ □ D ▽	*Place in Finish Rack*
		○ ⇨ □ D ▽	
3.5	3.15	2 4 1 – 2	TOTALS

Value-added time = Operation time/Total time = (2.50+.20)/3.15 = 85.7%

○ = operation; ⇨ = transportation; □ = inspection; D = delay; ▽ = storage.

[5]An additional example of a process chart is shown in Chapter 10.
[6]Waste includes *inspection* (if the task is done properly, then inspection is unnecessary); *transportation* (movement of material within a process may be a necessary evil, but it adds no value); *delay* (an asset sitting idle and taking up space is waste); *storage* (unless part of a "curing" process, storage is waste).

Service Blueprinting

Products with a high service content may warrant use of yet a fifth process technique. **Service blueprinting** is a process analysis technique that focuses on the customer and the provider's interaction with the customer.[7] For instance, the activities at level one of Figure 7.10 are under the control of the customer. In the second level are activities of the service provider interacting with the customer. The third level includes those activities that are performed away from, and not immediately visible to, the customer. Each level suggests different management issues. For instance, the top level may suggest educating the customer or modifying expectations, whereas the second level may require a focus on personnel selection and training. Finally, the third level lends itself to more typical process innovations. The service blueprint shown in Figure 7.10 also notes potential failure points and shows how poka-yoke techniques can be added to improve quality. The consequences of these failure points can be greatly reduced if identified at the design stage when modifications or appropriate poka-yokes can be included. A time dimension is included in Figure 7.10 to aid understanding, extend insight, and provide a focus on customer service.[8]

Service blueprinting
A process analysis technique that lends itself to a focus on the customer and the provider's interaction with the customer.

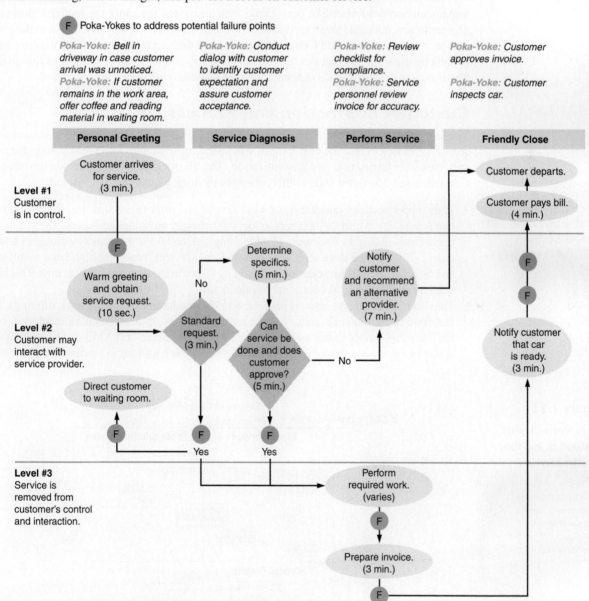

▲ **Figure 7.10**   **Service Blueprint for Service at Speedy Lube, Inc.**

[7]G. L. Shostack is given credit for the term *service blueprint*. See G. L. Shostack, "Designing Services That Deliver," *Harvard Business Review* 62, no. 1 (January–February, 1984): 133–139.

[8]See related work by James P. Womack and Daniel T. Jones, "Lean Consumption," *Harvard Business Review* 84, no. 4 (March 2005): 58–68.

Each of these five process analysis tools has its strengths and variations. Flowcharts are a quick way to view the big picture and try to make sense of the entire system. Time-function mapping adds some rigor and a time element to the macro analysis. Value-stream mapping extends beyond the immediate organization to customers and suppliers. Process charts are designed to provide a much more detailed view of the process, adding items such as value-added time, delay, distance, storage, and so forth. Service blueprinting, on the other hand, is designed to help us focus on the customer interaction part of the process. Because customer interaction is often an important variable in process design, we now examine some additional aspects of service process design.

SERVICE PROCESS DESIGN

Interaction with the customer often affects process performance adversely. But a service, by its very nature, implies that some interaction and customization is needed. Recognizing that the customer's unique desires tend to play havoc with a process, the more the manager designs the process to accommodate these special requirements, the more effective and efficient the process will be. Notice how well Dell Computer has managed the interface between the customer and the process by using the Internet (see the *Global Company Profile* at the beginning of this chapter). The trick is to find the right combination of cost and customer interaction.

Customer Interaction and Process Design

The four quadrants of Figure 7.11 provide additional insight on how operations managers design service processes to find the best level of specialization and focus while maintaining the necessary customer interaction and customization. The 10 operations decisions we introduced in Chapters 1 and 2 are used with a different emphasis in each quadrant. For instance:

- In the upper sections (quadrants) of *mass service* and *professional service*, where *labor content is high*, we expect the manager to focus extensively on human resources. These quadrants require that managers find ways of addressing unique issues that satisfy customers and win orders. This is often done with very personalized services, requiring high labor involvement and therefore significant selection and training issues in the human resources area. This is particularly true in the professional service quadrant.
- The quadrants with *low customization* tend to (1) standardize or restrict some offerings, as do fast-food restaurants, (2) automate, as have airlines with ticket-vending machines, or (3) remove some services, such as seat assignments, as has Southwest Airlines. Off-loading some aspect of the service through automation may require innovations in process design as well as

▶ **Figure 7.11**

Services Moving toward Specialization and Focus within the Service Process Matrix

Source: Adapted from work by Roger Schmenner, "Service Business and Productivity," *Decision Sciences* 35, no. 3 (summer 2004): 333–347.

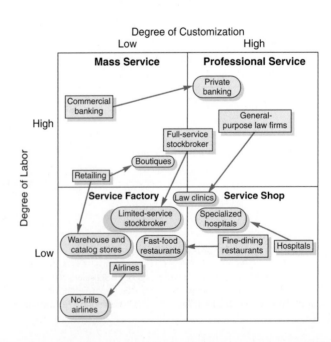

Strategy	Technique	Example
Separation	*Structuring service* so customers must go where the service is offered	Bank customers go to a manager to open a new account, to loan officers for loans, and to tellers for deposits
Self-service	*Self-service* so customers examine, compare, and evaluate at their own pace	Supermarkets and department stores Internet ordering
Postponement	*Customizing at delivery*	Customizing vans at delivery rather than at production
Focus	*Restricting* the offerings	Limited-menu restaurant
Modules	*Modular* selection of service *Modular* production	Investment and insurance selection Prepackaged food modules in restaurants
Automation	*Separating services* that may lend themselves to some type of automation	Automatic teller machines
Scheduling	Precise personnel *scheduling*	Scheduling ticket counter personnel at 15-minute intervals at airlines
Training	*Clarifying the service* options *Explaining how to avoid problems*	Investment counselor, funeral directors After-sale maintenance personnel

capital investment. Such is the case with airline ticket vending and bank ATMs. This move to standardization and automation may require added capital expenditure, as well as putting operations managers under pressure to develop new skills for the purchase and maintenance of such equipment. A reduction in a customization capability will require added strength in other areas.

- Because customer feedback is lower in the quadrants with *low customization*, tight control may be required to maintain quality standards.
- Operations with *low labor intensity* may lend themselves particularly well to innovations in process technology and scheduling.

Table 7.3 shows some additional techniques for innovative process design in services. Managers focus on designing innovative processes that enhance the service. For instance, super-market *self-service* reduces cost while it allows customers to check for the specific features they want, such as freshness or color. Dell Computer provides another version of self-service by allowing customers to design their own product on the Web. Customers seem to like this, and it is cheaper and faster for Dell.

More Opportunities to Improve Service Processes

Layout   Layout design is an integral part of many service processes, particularly in retailing, dining, and banking. In retailing, layout can provide not only product exposure but also customer education and product enhancement. In restaurants, layout can enhance the dining experience as well as provide an effective flow between bar, kitchen, and dining area. In banks, layout provides security as well as work flow and personal comfort. Because layout is such an integral part of many services, it provides continuing opportunity for winning orders.

Video 7.4

Process Analysis at Arnold Palmer Hospital

Human Resources   Because so many services involve direct interaction with the customer (as the upper quadrants of Figure 7.11 suggest), the human resource issues of recruiting and training can be particularly important ingredients in service processes. Additionally, a committed workforce that exhibits flexibility when schedules are made and is cross-trained to fill in when the process requires less than a full-time person, can have a tremendous impact on overall process performance.

SELECTION OF EQUIPMENT AND TECHNOLOGY

Ultimately, the decisions about a particular process require decisions about equipment and technology. Those decisions can be complex because alternative methods of production are present in virtually all operations functions, be they hospitals, restaurants, or manufacturing facilities.

Picking the best equipment means understanding the specific industry and available processes and technology. That choice of equipment, be it an X-ray machine for a hospital, a computer-controlled lathe for a factory, or a new computer for an office, requires considering cost, quality, capacity, and flexibility. To make this decision, operations personnel develop documentation that indicates the capacity, size, and tolerances of each option, as well as its maintenance requirements. Any one of these attributes may be the deciding factor regarding selection.

The selection of equipment for a particular type of process can also provide competitive advantage. Many firms, for instance, develop unique machines or techniques within established processes that provide an advantage. This advantage may result in added flexibility in meeting customer requirements, lower cost, or higher quality. Innovations and equipment modification might also allow for a more stable production process that takes less adjustment, maintenance, and operator training. In any case, specialized equipment often provides a way to win orders.

Modern technology also allows operations managers to enlarge the scope of their processes. As a result, an important attribute to look for in new equipment and process selection is flexible equipment. **Flexibility** is the ability to respond with little penalty in time, cost, or customer value. This may mean modular, movable, even cheap equipment. Flexibility may also mean the development of sophisticated electronic equipment, which increasingly provides the rapid changes that mass customization demands. The technological advances that influence OM process strategy are substantial and are discussed next.

Flexibility

The ability to respond with little penalty in time, cost, or customer value.

PRODUCTION TECHNOLOGY

Advances in technology that enhance production and productivity have a wide range of applications in both manufacturing and services. In this section, we introduce nine areas of technology: (1) machine technology, (2) automatic identification systems (AIS), (3) process control, (4) vision systems, (5) robots, (6) automated storage and retrieval systems (ASRSs), (7) automated guided vehicles (AGVs), (8) flexible manufacturing systems (FMSs), and (9) computer-integrated manufacturing (CIM).

Learning Objective

5. Identify recent advances in production technology

Machine Technology

Most of the world's machinery that performs operations such as cutting, drilling, boring, and milling is undergoing tremendous progress in both precision and control. New machinery turns out metal components that vary less than a micron—1/76 the width of a human hair. They can accelerate water to three times the speed of sound to cut titanium for surgical tools. Machinery of the 21st century is often five times more productive than that of previous generations while being smaller and using less power. The space and power savings are both significant. And continuing advances in lubricants now allow the use of water-based lubricants rather than oil based. Using water-based lubricants eliminates hazardous waste and allows shavings to be easily recovered and recycled.

▶ *Three critical success factors in the trucking industry are (1) getting shipments to customers promptly (rapid response); (2) keeping trucks busy (capacity utilization); and (3) buying inexpensive fuel (driving down costs). Many firms have now developed devices like the one shown here (on the right) to track location of trucks and facilitate communication between drivers and dispatchers. Some systems use global positioning satellites (shown on the left),*

to speed shipment response, maximize utilization of the truck, and ensure purchase of fuel at the most economical location. Sensors are also being added inside trailers. These sensors communicate whether the trailer is empty or full and detect if the trailer is connected to a truck or riding on a railroad car.

The intelligence now available for the control of new machinery via computer chips allows more complex and precise items to be made faster. Electronic controls increase speed by reducing changeover time, reducing waste (because of fewer mistakes), and enhancing flexibility. Machinery with its own computer and memory is called **computer numerical control (CNC)** machinery.

Computer numerical control (CNC)
Machinery with its own computer and memory.

Advanced versions of such technology are used on Pratt and Whitney's turbine blade plant in Connecticut. The machinery has improved the loading and alignment task so much that Pratt has cut the total time for the grinding process of a turbine blade from 10 days to 2 hours. The new machinery has also contributed to process improvements that mean the blades now travel just 1,800 feet in the plant, down from 8,100 feet. The total throughput time for a turbine blade has been cut from 22 days to 7 days.

Automatic Identification Systems (AISs) and RFID

New equipment, from numerically controlled manufacturing machinery to ATM machines, is controlled by digital electronic signals. Electrons are a great vehicle for transmitting information, but they have a major limitation—most OM data does not start out in bits and bytes. Therefore, operations managers must get the data into an electronic form. Making data digital is done via computer keyboards, bar codes, radio frequencies, optical characters on bank checks, and so forth. These **automatic identification systems (AISs)** help us move data into electronic form, where it is easily manipulated.

Automatic identification system (AIS)
A system for transforming data into electronic form, for example, bar codes.

Because of its decreasing cost and increasing pervasiveness, **radio frequency identification (RFID)** warrants special note. RFID is integrated circuitry with its own tiny antennas that use radio waves to send signals a limited range—usually a matter of yards. These RFID tags (sometimes called RFID circuits) provide unique identification that enables the tracking and monitoring of parts, pallets, people, and pets—virtually everything that moves. RFID requires no line of sight between tag and reader.

Radio frequency identification (RFID)
A wireless system in which integrated circuits with antennas send radio waves.

Innovative OM examples of AISs and RFID include:[9]

- Nurses reduce errors in hospitals by matching bar codes on medication to ID bracelets on patients.
- RFID tags in agriculture monitor the temperature at which fruit is kept. They can also track what chemicals and fertilizers have been used on the fruit.
- Transponders attached to cars allow McDonald's to identify and bill customers who can now zip through the drive-through line without having to stop and pay. The transponders use the same technology that permits motorists to skip stops on some toll roads. McDonald's estimates that the change speeds up throughput time by 15 seconds.
- Stanford University School of Medicine doctors are using sponges embedded with RFID tags. Waving a detector over an incision can tell if a surgeon accidentally left a sponge in the patient.
- FedEx tags major airplane parts, which allows them to be scanned so maintenance data (e.g., part number, installation date, country of origin) can be tracked.

With RFID, a cashier could scan the entire contents of a shopping cart in seconds.

Process Control

Process control is the use of information technology to monitor and control a physical process. For instance, process control is used to measure the moisture content and thickness of paper as it travels over a paper machine at thousands of feet per minute. Process control is also used to determine and control temperatures, pressures, and quantities in petroleum refineries, petrochemical processes, cement plants, steel mills, nuclear reactors, and other product-focused facilities.

Process control
The use of information technology to control a physical process.

Process control systems operate in a number of ways, but the following is typical:

- Sensors collect data.
- Devices read data on some periodic basis, perhaps once a minute or once every second.
- Measurements are translated into digital signals, which are transmitted to a digital computer.
- Computer programs read the file (the digital data) and analyze the data.
- The resulting output may take numerous forms. These include messages on computer consoles or printers, signals to motors to change valve settings, warning lights or horns, statistical process control charts, or schematics as shown in the photo on page 274.

[9]See *Industrial Engineer* 38, no. 8 (August 2006): 10; and *The Wall Street Journal* (July 18, 2006): D3.

▶ *Process control software, such as Factory Link IV, shown here, controls the flow of sugars and fruits into a juice mixer. The production report in the lower left corner provides a current status report.*

Vision Systems

Vision systems

Systems that use video cameras and computer technology in inspection roles.

Vision systems combine video cameras and computer technology and are often used in inspection roles. Visual inspection is an important task in most food-processing and manufacturing organizations. Moreover, in many applications, visual inspection performed by humans is tedious, mind-numbing, and error prone. Thus vision systems are widely used when the items being inspected are very similar. For instance, vision systems are used to inspect french fries so that imperfections can be identified as the fries proceed down the production line. Vision systems are used to ensure that sealant is present and in the proper amount on Whirlpool's washing-machine transmissions, and to inspect switch assemblies at the Foster Plant in Des Plaines, Illinois. Vision systems are consistently accurate, do not become bored, and are of modest cost. These systems are vastly superior to individuals trying to perform these tasks.

Robots

Robot

A flexible machine with the ability to hold, move, or grab items. It functions through electronic impulses that activate motors and switches.

When a machine is flexible and has the ability to hold, move, and perhaps "grab" items, we tend to use the word *robot*. **Robots** are mechanical devices that may have a few electronic impulses stored on semiconductor chips that will activate motors and switches. Robots may be used effectively to perform tasks that are especially monotonous or dangerous or those that can be improved by the substitution of mechanical for human effort. Such is the case when consistency, accuracy, speed, strength, or power can be enhanced by the substitution of machines for people. Ford, for example, uses robots to do 98% of the welding on some automobiles.

Automated Storage and Retrieval Systems (ASRSs)

Automated storage and retrieval system (ASRS)

Computer-controlled warehouses that provide for the automatic placement of parts into and from designated places within a warehouse.

Because of the tremendous labor involved in error-prone warehousing, computer-controlled warehouses have been developed. These systems, known as **automated storage and retrieval systems (ASRSs)**, provide for the automatic placement and withdrawal of parts and products into and from designated places in a warehouse. Such systems are commonly used in distribution facilities of retailers such as Wal-Mart, Tupperware, and Benetton. These systems are also found in inventory and test areas of manufacturing firms.

Automated Guided Vehicles (AGVs)

Automated material handling can take the form of monorails, conveyors, robots, or automated guided vehicles. **Automated guided vehicles (AGVs)** are electronically guided and controlled carts used in manufacturing to move parts and equipment. They are also used in offices to move mail and in hospitals and in jails to deliver meals.

Automated guided vehicle (AGV)

Electronically guided and controlled cart used to move materials.

Flexible Manufacturing Systems (FMSs)

When a central computer provides instructions to each workstation *and* to the material-handling equipment (which moves material to that station), the system is known as an automated work cell or, more commonly, a **flexible manufacturing system (FMS)**. An FMS is flexible because both the material-handling devices and the machines themselves are controlled by easily changed electronic signals (computer programs). Operators simply load new programs, as necessary, to produce different products. The result is a system that can economically produce low volume but high variety. For example, the Lockheed Martin facility, near Dallas, efficiently builds one-of-a-kind spare parts for military aircraft. The costs associated with changeover and low utilization have been reduced substantially. FMSs bridge the gap between product-focused and process-focused facilities.

FMSs are not a panacea, however, because the individual components (machines and material-handling devices) have their own physical constraints. The Lockheed Martin plant, for example, handles only light machining. Other FMSs are capable of handling electronic assembly of products of only limited size. Moreover, an FMS also has stringent communications requirements between the unique components within it. And, of course, sophisticated equipment means substantial capital investment. However, reduced changeover time and more accurate scheduling result in faster throughput and improved utilization. Because there are fewer mistakes, reduced waste also contributes to lowering costs. These features are what operations managers are looking for: flexibility to provide customized products, improved utilization to reduce costs, and improved throughput to improve response.

Flexible manufacturing system (FMS)

A system that uses an automated work cell controlled by electronic signals from a common centralized computer facility.

Computer-Integrated Manufacturing (CIM)

Flexible manufacturing systems can be extended backward electronically into the engineering and inventory control departments and forward to the warehousing and shipping departments. In this way, computer-aided design (CAD) generates the necessary electronic instructions to run a numerically controlled machine. In a computer-integrated manufacturing environment, a design change initiated at a CAD terminal can result in that change being made in the part produced on the shop floor in a matter of minutes. When this capability is integrated with inventory control, warehousing, and shipping as a part of a flexible manufacturing system, the entire system is called **computer-integrated manufacturing (CIM)** (Figure 7.12).

Flexible manufacturing systems and computer-integrated manufacturing are reducing the distinction between low-volume/high-variety and high-volume/low-variety production. Information technology is allowing FMS and CIM to handle increasing variety while expanding to include a growing range of volumes.

Video 7.5

Computer-Integrated Manufacturing at Harley-Davidson

Computer-integrated manufacturing (CIM)

A manufacturing system in which CAD, FMS, inventory control, warehousing, and shipping are integrated.

TECHNOLOGY IN SERVICES

Just as we have seen rapid advances in technology in the manufacturing sector, so we also find dramatic changes in the service sector. These range from electronic diagnostic equipment at auto repair shops, to blood- and urine-testing equipment in hospitals, to retinal security scanners at airports and high-security facilities. The hospitality industry provides other examples, as discussed

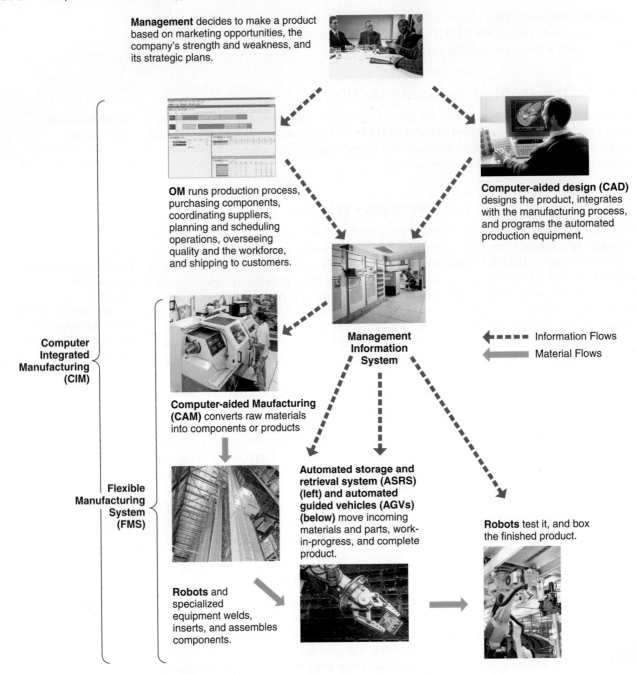

Management decides to make a product based on marketing opportunities, the company's strength and weakness, and its strategic plans.

OM runs production process, purchasing components, coordinating suppliers, planning and scheduling operations, overseeing quality and the workforce, and shipping to customers.

Computer-aided design (CAD) designs the product, integrates with the manufacturing process, and programs the automated production equipment.

Management Information System

Information Flows

Material Flows

Computer-aided Maufacturing (CAM) converts raw materials into components or products

Computer Integrated Manufacturing (CIM)

Flexible Manufacturing System (FMS)

Automated storage and retrieval system (ASRS) (left) and automated guided vehicles (AGVs) (below) move incoming materials and parts, work-in-progress, and complete product.

Robots test it, and box the finished product.

Robots and specialized equipment welds, inserts, and assembles components.

▲ **Figure 7.12   Computer-Integrated Manufacturing (CIM)**

CIM includes computer-aided design (CAD), computer-aided manufacturing (CAM), flexible manufacturing systems (FMSs), automated storage and retrieval systems (ASRSs), automated guided vehicles (AGVs), and robots to provide an integrated and flexible manufacturing process.

in the *OM in Action* box "Technology Changes the Hotel Industry." The McDonald's approach is to use self-serve kiosks. The labor savings when ordering and speedier checkout service provide valuable productivity increases for both the restaurant and the customer.

Similarly, Andersen Windows, of Minnesota, has developed user-friendly computer software that enables customers to design their own window specifications. The customer calls up a product information guide, promotion material, a gallery of designs, and a sketch pad to create the designs desired. The software also allows the customer to determine likely energy savings and see a graphic view of their home fitted with the new window.

In retail stores, POS terminals now download prices quickly to reflect changing costs or market conditions, and sales are tracked in 15-minute segments to aid production and scheduling.

OM in Action   Technology Changes the Hotel Industry

Technology is introducing "intelligent rooms" to the hotel industry. Hotel management can now precisely track a maid's time through the use of a security system. When a maid enters a room, a card is inserted that notifies the front-desk computer of the maid's location. "We can show her a printout of how long she takes to do a room," says one manager.

Security systems also enable guests to use their own credit cards as keys to unlock their doors. There are also other uses for the system. The computer can bar a guest's access to the room after checkout time and automatically control the air conditioning or heat, turning it on at check-in and off at checkout.

Minibars are now equipped with sensors that alert the central computer system at the hotel when an item is removed. Such items are immediately billed to the room. And now, with a handheld infrared unit, housekeeping staff can check, from the hallway, to see if a room is physically occupied. This both eliminates the embarrassment of having a hotel staffer walk in on a guest *and* improves security for housekeepers.

At Loew's Portofino Bay Hotel at Universal Studios, Orlando, guest smart cards act as credit cards in both the theme park and the hotel, and staff smart cards (programmed for different levels of security access) create an audit trail of employee movement. Starwood Hotels, which runs such properties as Sheraton and Westins, use Casio Pocket PCs to communicate with a hotel wireless network. Now guests can check in and out from any place on the property, such as at their restaurant table after breakfast or lunch.

Sources: Hotel and Motel Management (August 2004): 128–133; *Hotels* (April, 2004): 51–54; and *Newsweek* (international ed.) (September 27, 2004): 73.

Drug companies, such as Purdue Pharma LP, have begun tracking critical medications with radio frequency identification (RFID) tags to reduce counterfeiting and theft.

Table 7.4 provides a glimpse of the impact of technology on services. Operations managers in services, as in manufacturing, must be able to evaluate the impact of technology on their firm. This ability requires particular skill when evaluating reliability, investment analysis, human resource requirements, and maintenance/service.

PROCESS REDESIGN

Often a firm finds that the initial assumptions of its process are no longer valid. The world is a dynamic place, and customer desires, product technology, and product mix change. Consequently, processes are redesigned. **Process redesign** is the fundamental rethinking of business processes to

Process redesign
The fundamental rethinking of business processes to bring about dramatic improvements in performance.

▲ *At Orlando's Wet 'n Wild water park, instead of using credit cards or cash, visitors use RFID technology. The technology is embedded in wristbands that can transmit a serial number to scanners alongside the park's cash registers. At the end of the day, visitors get a receipt that lists all their charges. The bands are disabled once they are cut off.*

▲ *Pharmaceutical companies are counting on RFID to aid the tracking and tracing of drugs in the distribution system to reduce losses that total over $30 billion a year.*

▶ **Table 7.4**

Examples of Technology's Impact on Services

Service Industry	Example
Financial Services	Debit cards, electronic funds transfer, automatic teller machines, Internet stock trading
Education	Online newspapers, online journals, interactive assignments via Web CT and Blackboard
Utilities and government	Automated one-man garbage trucks, optical mail and bomb scanners, flood-warning systems.
Restaurants and foods	Wireless orders from waiters to the kitchen, robot butchering, transponders on cars that track sales at drive-throughs.
Communications	Electronic publishing, interactive TV
Hotels	Electronic check-in/checkout, electronic key/lock systems
Wholesale/retail trade	Use of ATM-like kiosks, point-of-sale (POS) terminals, e-commerce, electronic communication between store and supplier, bar-coded data
Transportation	Automatic toll booths, satellite-directed navigation systems
Health care	Online patient-monitoring systems, online medical information systems, robotic surgery
Airlines	Ticketless travel, scheduling, Internet purchases

bring about dramatic improvements in performance.[10] Effective process redesign relies on reevaluating the purpose of the process and questioning both purpose and underlying assumptions. It works only if the basic process and its objectives are reexamined (see the *OM in Action* box "Operations Management at the Barber Shop?").

Process redesign also focuses on those activities that cross functional lines. Because managers are often in charge of specific "functions" or specialized areas of responsibility, those activities (processes) that cross from one function or specialty to another may be neglected.

OM in Action   **Operations Management at the Barber Shop?**

While Kuniyoshi Konishi was getting his hair cut one day, he found himself growing irritated with the drawn-out ritual of hot towels and shoulder rubs that is standard practice in Japanese barber shops. For the haircut and other amenities, Tokyo barbers charge 3,000 to 6,000 yen ($25 to $50).

Mr. Konishi recognized the need for a new system of delivering fast, inexpensive haircuts, so he formed QB House, a fast, no-frills men's barber shop: no reservations, no phones, and no shampoo (just an "air wash" system, to vacuum heads clean).

To free barbers from any task that took them away from snipping, each QB House is equipped with a ticket vending machine. Customers buy a ticket from the machine and then give the ticket to the barber before getting their cut.

High-tech touches were added along the way. Sensors under each seat in the waiting area convey signals to a signpost in front of each shop. A green light on the sign-

post means there is no waiting, a yellow light indicates a wait of about 5 minutes, and a red light indicates the waiting time may be as long as 15 minutes. The barber chair sensor and the ticket vending machine sensor transmit data over the Internet to the head office in Tokyo, where traffic volume and sales can be monitored in real time. When sales volume for a particular store is much higher than average, QB House looks into opening another outlet nearby.

Seven years after opening his first barber shop, Konishi has 200 outlets nationwide providing the formerly impossible: 10-minute haircuts for 1,000 yen. With OM techniques, the company has creatively improved productivity in a very traditional service and is now going global. Next stop Singapore.

Sources: The Wall Street Journal (September 22, 2003): R4, R7; and *American Way* (December 15, 2003): 54–60.

---

[10]Michael Hammer and Steven Stanton call process redesign *process reengineering* in *The Reengineering Revolution* (New York: HarperCollins, 1995): 3.

Redesign casts aside all notions of how the process is currently being done and focuses on dramatic improvements in cost, time, and customer value. Any process is a candidate for radical redesign. The process can be a factory layout, a purchasing procedure, a new way of processing credit applications, or a new order-fulfillment process.

Shell Lubricants, for example, reinvented its order-fulfillment process by replacing a group of people who handled different parts of an order with one individual who does it all. As a result, Shell has cut the cycle time of turning an order into cash by 75%, reduced operating expenses by 45%, and boosted customer satisfaction 105%—all by introducing a new way of handling orders. Time, cost, and customer satisfaction—the dimension of performance shaped by operations—get major boosts from operational innovation.[11]

ETHICS AND ENVIRONMENTALLY FRIENDLY PROCESSES

In Chapter 5 we discussed ethics and environment-friendly design techniques; now we introduce some process approaches that address ethics, social responsibility, and environmental concerns. Many firms have found opportunities in their production processes to reduce the negative impact on the environment. The opportunities range from activities that society perceives as ethical and socially responsible to actions that are legally required, such as pollution prevention. These activities include a focus on such issues as efficient use of resources, reduction of waste by-products, emission controls, and recycling.

Operations managers can be environmentally sensitive and still achieve a differentiation strategy—and even a low-cost strategy. Here are four examples:

- British cosmetic firm The Body Shop has successfully differentiated its products by stressing environmental sensitivity. It pursues a product design, development, and testing strategy that it believes to be ethical and socially responsible. This includes environment-friendly ingredients and elimination of animal testing.
- Ben & Jerry's pursues its socially responsible image (and saves $250,000 annually) just by using energy-efficient lighting.
- Standard Register, described in Example 1, produces considerable paper scrap—almost 20 tons of punch holes alone per month—which creates a significant waste issue. But the company developed ways to recycle the paper scrap, as well as aluminum and silver from the plate-making process shown in the flow diagram in Figure 7.2.
- Anheuser-Busch saves $30 million per year in energy and waste-treatment costs by using treated plant wastewater to generate the gas that powers its St. Louis brewery.

Processes can be ethical, environmentally friendly, and socially responsible while still contributing to profitable strategies.

Summary

Effective operations managers understand how to use process strategy as a competitive weapon. They select a production process with the necessary quality, flexibility, and cost structure to meet product and volume requirements. They also seek creative ways to combine the low unit cost of high-volume, low-variety manufacturing with the customization available through low-volume, high-variety facilities. Managers use the techniques of lean production and employee participation to encourage the development of efficient equipment and processes. They design their equipment and processes to have capabilities beyond the tolerance required by their customers, while ensuring the flexibility needed for adjustments in technology, features, and volumes.

[11]Michael Hammer, "Deep Change: How Operational Innovation Can Transform Your Company," *Harvard Business Review* 82, no. 4 (April 2004): 85–93.

Key Terms

Solved Problem

Virtual Office Hours help is available on Student DVD.

Solved Problem 7.1

Bagot Copy Shop has a volume of 125,000 black-and-white copies per month. Two salesmen have made presentations to Gordon Bagot for machines of equal quality and reliability. The Print Shop 5 has a cost of $2,000 per month and a variable cost of $.03. The other machine (a Speed Copy 100) will cost only $1,500 per month but the toner is more expensive, driving the cost per copy up to $.035. If cost and volume are the only considerations, which machine should Bagot purchase?

Solution

$$2,000 + .03\,X = 1,500 + .035\,X$$
$$2,000 - 1,500 = .035\,X - .03\,X$$
$$500 = .005\,X$$
$$100,000 = X$$

Because Bagot expects his volume to exceed 100,000 units, he should choose the Print Shop 5.

Active Model Exercise

This active model appears on your CD-ROM. It allows you to evaluate important elements in the crossover chart in Example 4.

▶ **Active Model 7.1**

Crossover Chart Illustration of Example 4's Three Software Products

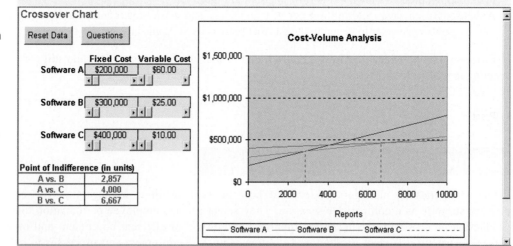

Questions

1. Suppose that Kleber Enterprises wants to lower the point of indifference between software A and software B to 2,000 units. What would the fixed costs need to be for software B?

2. Examine the graph. If the expected volume is 1,500 reports, which process should be used?

3. Examine the graph. If the expected volume is 15,000 reports, which process should be used?

4. As the fixed costs for developing software B drop, what happens to the graph?

Self-Test

- *Before taking the self-test*, refer to the learning objectives listed at the beginning of the chapter and the key terms listed at the end of the chapter.
- Use the key at the back of the text to **correct** your answers.
- *Restudy* pages that correspond to any questions you answered incorrectly or material you feel uncertain about.

1. Low-volume, high-variety processes are also known as:
   a) continuous processes
   b) intermittent processes
   c) repetitive processes
   d) product focused

2. Advantages of a flexible manufacturing system (FMS) include:
   a) lower direct labor cost
   b) consistent and perhaps better quality
   c) reduced inventory
   d) all of the above

3. Repetitive process lines:
   a) use modules
   b) are the classic assembly lines
   c) have more structure and less flexibility than a job shop layout
   d) include the assembly of basically all automobiles
   e) all of the above

4. Computer-integrated manufacturing (CIM) includes manufacturing systems that have:
   a) computer-aided design, direct numerical control machines, material handling equipment controlled by automation
   b) transaction processing, management information system, and decision support systems

   c) automated guided vehicles, robots, and process control
   d) robots, automated guided vehicles, and transfer equipment

5. As the quantity produced increases and you move toward product-focused production:
   a) the variable cost per unit increases
   b) the total fixed cost for the production operation increases
   c) the equipment utilization rate decreases
   d) more general-purpose equipment is used
   e) all of the above

6. Characteristics of a modular production process (repetitive focus) include:
   a) the use of just-in-time procurement techniques
   b) the use of just-in-time inventory control techniques
   c) costs are usually known
   d) standardized product options
   e) all of the above

7. Advantages of flexible manufacturing systems include all of the following except:
   a) lower setup costs
   b) ability to adapt to wide range of sizes and configuration
   c) high utilization of facilities
   d) lower direct labor costs
   e) all of the above are advantages

8. Process control is used to control physical processes in:
   a) discrete manufacturing facilities
   b) repetitive manufacturing facilities
   c) intermittent facilities
   d) job shops
   e) product-oriented facilities

Internet and Student CD-ROM/DVD Exercises

Visit our Companion Web Site or use your student CD-ROM/DVD to help with material in this chapter.

 On Our Companion Web Site,
   www.prenhall.com/heizer
- Self-Study Quizzes
- Practice Problems
- Virtual Company Tour
- Internet Case
- PowerPoint Lecture

On Your Student CD-ROM
- Practice Problems
- Active Model Exercise
- POM for Windows

On Your Student DVD
- Video Clips and Video Cases
- Virtual Office Hours for Solved Problem

Discussion Questions

1. What is process strategy?
2. What type of process is used for making each of the following products?
   (a) beer
   (b) wedding invitations
   (c) automobiles
   (d) paper
   (e) Big Macs
   (f) custom homes
   (g) motorcycles

3. What is service blueprinting?
4. What is process redesign?
5. What are the techniques for improving service productivity?
6. Name the four quadrants of the service process matrix. Discuss how the matrix is used to classify services into categories.
7. What is CIM?
8. What do we mean by a process-control system and what are the typical elements in such systems?
9. Identify *manufacturing* firms that compete on each of the four processes shown in Figure 7.1.

10. Identify the competitive advantage of each of the four firms identified in discussion question 9.
11. Identify *service* firms that compete on each of the four processes shown in Figure 7.1.
12. Identify the competitive advantage of each of the four firms identified in discussion question 11.
13. What are numerically controlled machines?
14. Describe briefly what an automatic identification system (AIS) is and how service organizations could use AIS to increase productivity and at the same time increase the variety of services offered.
15. Name some of the advances being made in technology that enhance production and productivity.
16. Explain what a flexible manufacturing system (FMS) is.
17. In what ways do CAD and FMS connect?

Ethical Dilemma

For the sake of efficiency and lower costs, Premium Standard Farms of Princeton, Missouri, has turned pig production into a standardized product-focused process. Slaughterhouses have done this for a hundred years—but after the animal was dead. Doing it while the animal is alive is a relatively recent innovation. Here is how it works.

Impregnated female sows wait for 40 days in metal stalls so small that they cannot turn around. After an ultrasound test, they wait 67 days in a similar stall until they give birth. Two weeks after delivering 10 or 11 piglets, the sows are moved back to breeding rooms for another cycle. After 3 years, the sow is slaughtered. Animal-welfare advocates say such confinement drives pigs crazy. Premium Standard replies that its hogs are in fact comfortable, arguing that only 1% die before Premium Standard wants them to.

Discuss the productivity and ethical implications of this industry and these two divergent opinions.

Problems*

• **7.1** Prepare a flow diagram for one of the following:
a) The registration process at a school.
b) The process at the local car wash.
c) A shoe shine.
d) Some other process with the approval of the instructor.

• **7.2** Prepare a process chart for one of the activities in Problem 7.1.

•• **7.3** Prepare a time-function map for one of the activities in Problem 7.1.

•• **7.4** Prepare a service blueprint for one of the activities in Problem 7.1.

• **7.5** Meile Machine Shop, Inc., has a 1-year contract for the production of 200,000 gear housings for a new off-road vehicle. Owner Larry Meile hopes the contract will be extended and the volume increased next year. Meile has developed costs for three alternatives. They are general-purpose equipment (GPE), flexible manufacturing system (FMS), and expensive, but efficient, dedicated machine (DM). The cost data follow:

	General-Purpose Equipment (GPE)	Flexible Manufacturing System (FMS)	Dedicated Machine (DM)
Annual contracted units	200,000	200,000	200,000
Annual fixed cost	$100,000	$200,000	$500,000
Per unit variable cost	$ 15.00	$ 14.00	$ 13.00

Which process is best for this contract? **Px**

• **7.6** Using the data in Problem 7.5, determine the economical volume for each process. **Px**

• **7.7** Using the data in Problem 7.5, determine the best process for each of the following volumes: (1) 75,000, (2) 275,000, and (3) 375,000.

• **7.8** Refer to Problem 7.5. If a contract for the second and third years is pending, what are the implications for process selection?

•• **7.9** Stan Fawcett's company is considering producing a gear assembly that it now purchases from Salt Lake Supply, Inc. Salt Lake Supply charges $4 per unit with a minimum order of 3,000 units. Stan estimates that it will cost $15,000 to set up the process and then $1.82 per unit for labor and materials.
a) Draw a graph illustrating the crossover (or indifference) point.
b) Determine the number of units where either choice has the same cost. **Px**

•• **7.10** Ski Boards, Inc., wants to enter the market quickly with a new finish on its ski boards. It has three choices: (a) refurbish the old equipment at a cost of $800, (b) make major modifications at the

Note: **Px** means the problem may be solved with POM for Windows and/or Excel OM.

cost of $1,100, or (c) purchase new equipment at a net cost of $1,800. If the firm chooses to refurbish the equipment, materials and labor will be $1.10 per board. If it chooses to make modifications, materials and labor will be $0.70 per board. If it buys new equipment, variable costs are estimated to be $.40 per board.

a) Graph the three total cost lines on the same chart.

b) Which alternative should Ski Boards, Inc., choose if it thinks it can sell more than 3,000 boards?

c) Which alternative should the firm use if it thinks the market for boards will be between 1,000 and 2,000? **Px**

•• **7.11** Susan Meyer, owner/manager of Meyer's Motor Court in Key West, is considering outsourcing the daily room cleanup for her motel to Duffy's Maid Service. Susan rents an average of 50 rooms for each of 365 nights (365 × 50 equals the total rooms rented for the year). Susan's cost to clean a room is $12.50. The Duffy's Maid Service quote is $18.50 per room plus a fixed cost of $25,000 for sundry items such as uniforms with the motel's name. Susan's annual fixed cost for space, equipment, and supplies is $61,000. Which is the preferred process for Susan, and why? **Px**

•• **7.12** Keith Whittingham, as manager of Designs by Whittingham, is upgrading his CAD software. The high-performance (HP) software rents for $3,000 per month per workstation. The standard-performance (SP) software rents for $2,000 per month per workstation. The productivity figures that he has available suggest that the HP software is faster for his kind of design. Therefore, with the HP software he will need five engineers and with the SP soft-

ware he will need six. This translates into a variable cost of $200 per drawing for the HP system and $240 per drawing for the SP system. At his projected volume of 80 drawings per month, which system should he rent? **Px**

•• **7.13** Using Figure 7.8 in the discussion of value-stream mapping as a starting point, analyze an opportunity for improvement in a process with which you are familiar and develop an improved process.

••• **7.14** Creative Cabinets, Inc., needs to choose a production method for its new office shelf, the Maxistand. To help accomplish this, the firm has gathered the following production cost data:

Process Type	Annualized Fixed Cost of Plant & Equip.	Variable Costs (per unit) ($)		
		Labor	Material	Energy
Mass Customization	$1,260,000	30	18	12
Intermittent	$1,000,000	24	26	20
Repetitive	$1,625,000	28	15	12
Continuous	$1,960,000	25	15	10

Creative Cabinets projects an annual demand of 24,000 units for the Maxistand. The Maxistand will sell for $120 per unit.

a) Which process type will maximize the annual profit from producing the Maxistand?

b) What is the value of this annual profit? **Px**

Case Studies

Rochester Manufacturing Corporation

Rochester Manufacturing Corporation (RMC) is considering moving some of its production from traditional numerically controlled machines to a flexible manufacturing system (FMS). Its computer numerical control machines have been operating in a high-variety, low-volume, intermittent manner. Machine utilization, as near as it can determine, is hovering around 10%. The machine tool salespeople and a consulting firm want to put the machines together in an FMS. They believe that a $3 million expenditure on machinery and the transfer machines will handle about 30% of RMC's work. There will, of course, be transition and startup costs in addition to this.

The firm has not yet entered all its parts into a comprehensive group technology system, but believes that the 30% is a good estimate of products suitable for the FMS. This 30% should fit very nicely into a "family." A reduction, because of higher utilization, should take place in the number of pieces of machinery. The firm should be able to go from 15 to about 4 machines and personnel should go from 15 to perhaps as low as 3. Similarly, floor space reduction will go from 20,000 square feet to about 6,000. Throughput of orders should also

improve with processing of this family of parts in 1 to 2 days rather than 7 to 10. Inventory reduction is estimated to yield a one-time $750,000 savings, and annual labor savings should be in the neighborhood of $300,000.

Although the projections all look very positive, an analysis of the project's return on investment showed it to be between 10% and 15% per year. The company has traditionally had an expectation that projects should yield well over 15% and have payback periods of substantially less than 5 years.

Discussion Questions

1. As a production manager for RMC, what do you recommend? Why?

2. Prepare a case by a conservative plant manager for maintaining the status quo until the returns are more obvious.

3. Prepare the case for an optimistic sales manager that you should move ahead with the FMS now.

Process Analysis at Arnold Palmer Hospital

Video Case

The Arnold Palmer Hospital (APH) in Orlando, Florida, is one of the busiest and most respected hospitals for the medical treatment of children and women in the U.S. Since its opening on golfing legend

Arnold Palmer's birthday September 10, 1989, more than 1.6 million children and women have passed through its doors. It is the fourth busiest labor and delivery hospital in the U.S. and one of the largest neonatal intensive care units in the Southeast. APH ranks in the top 10% of hospitals nationwide in patient satisfaction.

"Part of the reason for APH's success," says Executive Director Kathy Swanson, "is our continuous improvement process. Our goal is 100% patient satisfaction. But getting there means constantly examining and reexamining everything we do, from patient flow, to cleanliness, to layout space, to a work-friendly environment, to speed of medication delivery from the pharmacy to a patient. Continuous improvement is a huge and never-ending task."

One of the tools the hospital uses consistently is the process flowchart (like those in Figures 7.1 to 7.3 in this chapter and Figure 6.6e in Chapter 6). Staffer Diane Bowles, who carries the title "clinical practice improvement consultant," charts scores of processes. Bowles's flowcharts help study ways to improve the turnaround of a vacated room (especially important in a hospital that has pushed capacity for years), speed up the admission process, and deliver warm meals warm.

Lately, APH has been examining the flow of maternity patients (and their paperwork) from the moment they enter the hospital until they are discharged, hopefully with their healthy baby a day or two later. The flow of maternity patients follows these steps:

1. Enter APH's Labor & Delivery check-in desk entrance.
2. If the baby is born en route or if birth is imminent, the mother and baby are taken directly to Labor & Delivery on the second floor and registered and admitted directly at the bedside. If there are no complications, the mother and baby go to step 6.
3. If the baby is *not* yet born, the front desk asks if the mother is pre-registered. (Most do pre-register at the 28- to 30-week pregnancy mark). If she is not, she goes to the registration office on the first floor.
4. The pregnant woman is then taken to Labor & Delivery Triage on the 8th floor for assessment. If she is in active labor, she is taken to a Labor & Delivery (L&D) room on the 2nd floor until the baby is born. If she is not ready, she goes to step 5.

5. Pregnant women not ready to deliver (i.e., no contractions or false alarm) are either sent home to return on a later date and reenter the system at that time, or if contractions are not yet close enough, they are sent to walk around the hospital grounds (to encourage progress) and then return to Labor & Delivery Triage at a prescribed time.
6. When the baby is born, if there are no complications, after 2 hours the mother and baby are transferred to a "mother–baby care unit" room on floors 3, 4, or 5 for an average of 40–44 hours.
7. If there *are* complications with the mother, she goes to an operating room and/or intensive care unit. From there, she goes back to a mother–baby care room upon stabilization—or is discharged at another time if not stabilized. Complications for the baby may result in a stay in the neonatal intensive care unit (NICU) before transfer to the baby nursery near the mother's room. If the baby is not stable enough for discharge with the mother, the baby is discharged later.
8. Mother and/or baby, when ready, are discharged and taken by wheelchair to the discharge exit for pickup to travel home.

Discussion Questions*

1. As Diane's new assistant, you need to flowchart this process. Explain how the process might be improved once you have completed the chart.
2. If a mother is scheduled for a Caesarean-section birth (i.e., the baby is removed from the womb surgically), how would this flowchart change?
3. If *all* mothers were electronically (or manually) preregistered, how would the flowchart change? Redraw the chart to show your changes.
4. Describe in detail a process that the hospital could analyze, besides the ones mentioned in this case.

*You may wish to view this video case on your DVD before addressing these questions.

Process Strategy at Wheeled Coach

Video Case

Wheeled Coach, based in Winter Park, Florida, is the world's largest manufacturer of ambulances. Working four 10-hour days each week, 350 employees make only custom-made ambulances: Virtually every vehicle is unique. Wheeled Coach accommodates the marketplace by providing a wide variety of options and an engineering staff accustomed to innovation and custom design. Continuing growth, which now requires that more than 20 ambulances roll off the assembly line each week, makes process design a continuing challenge. Wheeled Coach's response has been to build a focused factory: Wheeled Coach builds nothing but ambulances. Within the focused factory, Wheeled Coach established work cells for every major module feeding an assembly line, including aluminum bodies, electrical wiring harnesses, interior cabinets, windows, painting, and upholstery.

Labor standards drive the schedule so that every work cell feeds the assembly line on schedule, just-in-time for installations. The chassis, usually that of a Ford truck, moves to a station at which the aluminum body is mounted. Then the vehicle is moved to painting. Following a custom paint job, it moves to the assembly line, where it will spend 7 days. During each of these 7 workdays, each work cell delivers its respective module to the appropriate position

on the assembly line. During the first day, electrical wiring is installed; on the second day, the unit moves forward to the station at which cabinetry is delivered and installed, then to a window and lighting station, on to upholstery, to fit and finish, to further customizing, and finally to inspection and road testing. The *Global Company Profile* featuring Wheeled Coach, which opens Chapter 14, provides further details about this process.

Discussion Questions*

1. Why do you think major auto manufacturers do not build ambulances?
2. What is an alternative process strategy to the assembly line that Wheeled Coach currently uses?
3. Why is it more efficient for the work cells to prepare "modules" and deliver them to the assembly line than it would be to produce the component (e.g., interior upholstery) on the line?
4. How does Wheeled Coach manage the tasks to be performed at each work station?

*You may wish to view this video case on your DVD before addressing these questions.

Additional Case Studies

Internet case study: Visit our Companion Web site at **www.prenhall.com/heizer** *for this free case study:*

- **Matthew Yachts, Inc.:** Examines a possible process change as the market for yachts changes.

Harvard has selected these Harvard Business School cases to accompany this chapter:

harvardbusinessonline.hbsp.harvard.edu

- **Massachusetts General Hospital** (#696-015): Describes efforts at Massachusetts General Hospital to reengineer the service delivery process for heart bypass surgery.
- **John Crane UK Ltd.: The CAD/CAM Link** (#691-021): Describes the improvement of manufacturing performance in a job shop.
- **Product Development at Dell** (#699-010): Discusses the new product and process and the management of development risk.

Bibliography

Carrillo, Janice E., and Cheryl Gaimon. "Improving Manufacturing Performance through Process Change and Knowledge Creation." *Management Science* 46, no. 2 (February 2000): 265–288.

Davenport, T. H. "The Coming Commoditization of Processes." *Harvard Business Review* 83, no. 6 (June 2005): 101–108.

Debo, L. G., L. B. Toktay, and L. N. Van Wassenhove. "Market Segmentation and Product Technology Selection for Remanufacturable Products." *Management Science* 51, no. 8 (August 2005): 1193–1205.

Duray, R., P. T. Ward, G. W. Milligan, and W. L. Berry. "Approaches to Mass Customization: Configurations and Empirical Validation." *Journal of Operations Management* 18, no. 6 (November 2000): 605–625.

Gilmore, James H., and Joseph Pine II (eds.). *Markets of One: Creating Customer-Unique Value through Mass Customization.* Harvard Business Review Book, 2000.

Hegde, V. G. et al. "Customization: Impact on Product and Process Performance." *Production and Operations Management* 14, no. 4 (Winter 2005): 388–399.

Hounshell, D. A. *From the American System to Mass Production, 1800–1932.* Baltimore: Johns Hopkins University Press, 1984.

Inderfurth, Karl, I. M. Langella. "An Approach for Solving Disassembly-to-order Problems under Stochastic Yields." In *Logistik Management.* Heidelberg: Physica, 2004: 309–331.

Moeeni, F. "From Light Frequency Identification to Radio Frequency Identification in the Supply Chain," *Decision Line* 37, no. 3 (May 2006): 8–13.

Su, J. C. P., Y. Chang, and M. Ferguson. "Evaluation of Postponement Structures to Accommodate Mass Customization." *Journal of Operations Management* 23, nos. 3–4 (April 2005): 305–318.

Swamidass, Paul M. *Innovations in Competitive Manufacturing.* Dordrecht, NL: Kluwer, 2000.

Tu, Qiang, et al. "Measuring Modularity-Based Manufacturing Practices and Their Impact on Mass Customization Capability: A Customer-Driven Perspective." *Decision Sciences* 35, no. 2 (Spring 2004): 147–168.

Zipkin, Paul. "The Limits of Mass Customization." *MIT Sloan Management Review* 40, no. 1 (spring 2001): 81–88.

Internet Resources

American Council of Engineering Companies: **www.acec.org**

Association of Automatic Identification and Mobility: **www.aimglobal.org**

Association for Manufacturing Excellence: **www.ame.org**

Business Process Reengineering online learning center tutorial: **www.prosci.com/index.html**

DARPA: U.S. Defense Dept., Innovative Prototype Systems: **www.ARPA.mil**

Dassault Systems: **www.dsweb.com**

Graham Process Improvement Methodology: **www.worksimp.com**

iGraphic's approach to Value Stream Mapping: **www.iGrafx.com**

Strategos Inc.'s approach to value-stream mapping: **www.strategosinc.com**

Traleon GMBH's approach to value-stream mapping: **www.valuestreamdesigner.com**

WARIA, the Workflow and Reengineering International Association: **www.waria.com**

SUPPLEMENT 7

Capacity Planning

Supplement Outline

Learning Objectives

When you complete this supplement you should be able to

1. Define capacity
2. Determine design capacity, effective capacity, and utilization
3. Compute break-even
4. Apply decision trees to capacity decisions
5. Compute net present value

▶ *When designing a concert hall, management hopes that the forecasted capacity (the product mix—opera, symphony, and special events—and the technology needed for these events) is accurate and adequate for operation above the break-even point. However, in many concert halls, even when operating at full capacity, break-even is not achieved, and supplemental funding must be obtained.*

CAPACITY

How many concertgoers should a facility seat? How many customers per day should an Olive Garden or a Hard Rock Cafe be able to service? How many computers should Dell's Nashville plant be able to produce in an 8-hour shift? And how should we build facilities to meet these uncertain demands?

Capacity

The "throughput" or number of units a facility can hold, receive, store, or produce in a period of time.

After selection of a production process (Chapter 7), we need to determine capacity. **Capacity** is the "throughput," or the number of units a facility can hold, receive, store, or produce in a period of time. The capacity often determines capital requirements and therefore a large portion of fixed cost. Capacity also determines if demand will be satisfied or if facilities will be idle. If the facility is too large, portions of it will sit idle and add cost to existing production. If the facility is too small, customers and perhaps entire markets are lost. So determining facility size, with an objective of achieving high levels of utilization and a high return on investment, is critical.

Capacity planning can be viewed in three time horizons. In Figure S7.1 we note that long-range capacity (greater than 1 year) is a function of adding facilities and equipment that have a long lead time. In the intermediate range (3 to 18 months), we can add equipment, personnel, and shifts; we can subcontract; and we can build or use inventory. This is the aggregate planning task. In the short run (usually up to 3 months), we are primarily concerned with scheduling jobs and people, and allocating machinery. It is difficult to modify capacity in the short run; we are using capacity that already exists.

Learning Objective

1. Define capacity

▶ **Figure S7.1**

Types of Planning over a Time Horizon

	Modify capacity	Use capacity
Long-range planning	Add facilities. Add long lead time equipment.	★
Intermediate-range planning (aggregate planning)	Subcontract. Add equipment. Add shifts.	Add personnel. Build or use inventory.
Short-range planning (scheduling)	★	Schedule jobs. Schedule personnel. Allocate machinery.

* Limited options exist

Design and Effective Capacity

Design capacity is the maximum theoretical output of a system in a given period under ideal conditions. It is normally expressed as a rate, such as the number of tons of steel that can be produced per week, per month, or per year. For many companies, measuring capacity can be straightforward: It is the maximum number of units produced in a specific time. However, for some organizations, determining capacity can be more difficult. Capacity can be measured in terms of beds (a hospital), active members (a church), or classroom size (a school). Other organizations use total work time available as a measure of overall capacity.

Most organizations operate their facilities at a rate less than the design capacity. They do so because they have found that they can operate more efficiently when their resources are not stretched to the limit. Instead, they expect to operate at perhaps 82% of design capacity. This concept is called effective capacity.

Effective capacity is the capacity a firm *expects* to achieve given the current operating constraints. Effective capacity is often lower than design capacity because the facility may have been designed for an earlier version of the product or a different product mix than is currently being produced.

Two measures of system performance are particularly useful: utilization and efficiency. **Utilization** is simply the percent of *design capacity* actually achieved. **Efficiency** is the percent of *effective capacity* actually achieved. Depending on how facilities are used and managed, it may be difficult or impossible to reach 100% efficiency. Operations managers tend to be evaluated on efficiency. The key to improving efficiency is often found in correcting quality problems and in effective scheduling, training, and maintenance. Utilization and efficiency are computed below:

$$\text{Utilization} = \text{Actual output/Design capacity} \tag{S7-1}$$

$$\text{Efficiency} = \text{Actual output/Effective capacity} \tag{S7-2}$$

In Example S1 we determine these values.

> **Design capacity**
> The theoretical maximum output of a system in a given period under ideal conditions.

> **Effective capacity**
> The capacity a firm can expect to achieve, given its product mix, methods of scheduling, maintenance, and standards of quality.

> **Utilization**
> Actual output as a percent of design capacity.

> **Efficiency**
> Actual output as a percent of effective capacity.

EXAMPLE S1

Determing capacity utilization and efficiency

Sara James Bakery has a plant for processing *Deluxe* breakfast rolls and wants to better understand its capability. Determine the design capacity, utilization, and efficiency for this plant when producing this *Deluxe* roll.

Approach: Last week the facility produced 148,000 rolls. The effective capacity is 175,000 rolls. The production line operates 7 days per week, with three 8-hour shifts per day. The line was designed to process the nut-filled, cinnamon-flavored *Deluxe* roll at a rate of 1,200 per hour. The firm first computes the design capacity and then uses Equation (S7-1) to determine utilization and Equation (S7-2) to determine efficiency.

Solution: Design capacity = (7 days × 3 shifts × 8 hours) × (1,200 rolls per hour) = 201,600 rolls

Utilization = Actual output/Design capacity = 148,000/201,600 = 73.4%

Efficiency = Actual output/Effective capacity = 148,000/175,000 = 84.6%

Insight: The bakery now has the information necessary to evaluate efficiency.

Learning exercise: If the actual output is 150,000, what is the efficiency? [Answer: 85.7%.]

Related problems: S7.1, S7.2, S7.4, S7.5, S7.11

 Active Model S7.1

Example S1 is further illustrated in Active Model S7.1 on your CD-ROM.

Design capacity, utilization, and efficiency are all important measures for an operations manager. But managers often need to know the expected output of a facility or process. To do this, we solve for actual (or in this case, future or expected) output as shown in Equation (S7-3):

$$\text{Actual (or Expected) output} = (\text{Effective capacity})(\text{Efficiency}) \tag{S7-3}$$

Expected output is sometimes referred to as *rated capacity*. With a knowledge of effective capacity and efficiency, a manager can find the expected output of a facility. We do so in Example S2.

> **Learning Objective**
> 2. Determine design capacity, effective capacity, and utilization

EXAMPLE S2

Determining expected output

The manager of Sara James Bakery (see Example S1) now needs to increase production of the increasingly popular *Deluxe* roll. To meet this demand, she will be adding a second production line.

Approach: The manager must determine the expected output of this second line for the sales department. Effective capacity on the second line is the same as on the first line, which is 175,000 *Deluxe* rolls. The first line is operating at an efficiency of 84.6%, as computed in Example S1. But output on the second line will be less than the first line because the crew will be primarily new hires; so the efficiency can be expected to be no more than 75%. What is the expected output?

Solution: Use Equation (S7-3) to determine the expected output:

Expected output = (Effective capacity)(Efficiency) = (175,000)(.75) = 131,250 rolls

Insight: The sales department can now be told the expected output is 131,250 *Deluxe* rolls.

Learning exercise: After 1 month of training, the crew on the second production line is expected to perform at 80% efficiency. What is the revised expected output of *Deluxe* rolls? [Answer: 140,000.]

Related problems: S7.3, S7.6, S7.7, S7.8, S7.10

If the expected output is inadequate, additional capacity may be needed. Much of the remainder of this supplement addresses how to effectively and efficiently add that capacity.

Capacity and Strategy

Sustained profits come from building competitive advantage, not just from a good financial return on a specific process. Capacity decisions must be integrated into the organization's mission and strategy. Investments are not to be made as isolated expenditures, but as part of a coordinated plan that will place the firm in an advantageous position.[1] The questions to be asked are, Will these investments eventually win customers? and What competitive advantage (such as process flexibility, speed of delivery, improved quality, and so on) do we obtain?

All 10 decisions of operations management we discuss in this text, as well as other organizational elements such as marketing and finance, are affected by changes in capacity. Change in capacity will have sales and cash flow implications, just as capacity changes have quality, supply chain, human resource, and maintenance implications. All must be considered.

Capacity Considerations

In addition to tight integration of strategy and investments, there are four special considerations for a good capacity decision:

1. *Forecast demand accurately:* An accurate forecast is paramount to the capacity decision. The new product may be Olive Garden's veal scampi, a dish that places added demands on the restaurant's food service, or the product may be a new maternity capability at Arnold Palmer Hospital, or the new hybrid Lexus. Whatever the new product, its prospects and the life cycle of existing products, must be determined. Management must know which products are being added and which are being dropped, as well as their expected volumes.

2. *Understand the technology and capacity increments:* The number of initial alternatives may be large, but once the volume is determined, technology decisions may be aided by analysis of cost, human resources required, quality, and reliability. Such a review often reduces the number of alternatives to a few. The technology may dictate the capacity increment. Meeting added demand with a few extra tables in an Olive Garden may not be difficult, but meeting increased demand for a new automobile by adding a new assembly line at BMW may be very difficult—and expensive. The operations manager is held responsible for the technology and the correct capacity increment.

3. *Find the optimum operating level (volume):* Technology and capacity increments often dictate an optimal size for a facility. A roadside motel may require 50 rooms to be viable. If

[1]For an excellent discussion on investments that support competitive advantage, see Terry Hill, *Operations Management*, 2nd ed. (New York: Palgrave Macmillan, 2005).

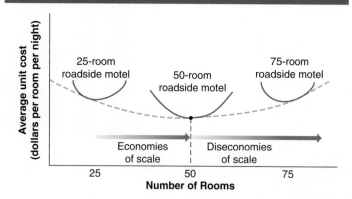

smaller, the fixed cost is too burdensome; if larger, the facility becomes more than one manager can supervise. A hypothetical optimum for the motel is shown in Figure S7.2. This issue is known as *economies and diseconomies of scale*. GM at one time believed that the optimum auto plant was one with 600 employees. As the Krispy Kreme photo suggests, most businesses have an optimal size—at least until someone comes along with a new business model. For decades, very large integrated steel mills were considered optimal. Then along came Nucor, CMC, and other minimills with a new process and a new business model that changed the optimum size of a steel mill.

4. *Build for change:* In our fast-paced world, change is inevitable. So operations managers build flexibility into the facility and equipment (see Figure S7.3. They evaluate the sensitivity of the decision by testing several revenue projections on both the upside and downside for potential risks. Buildings can often be built in phases; and buildings and equipment can be designed with modifications in mind to accommodate future changes in product, product mix, and processes.

Rather than strategically manage capacity, managers may tactically manage demand.

Managing Demand

Even with good forecasting and facilities built to that forecast, there may be a poor match between the actual demand that occurs and available capacity. A poor match may mean demand exceeds capacity or capacity exceeds demand. However, in both cases, firms have options.

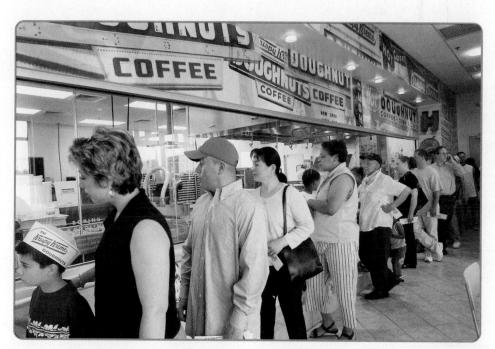

◀ *Krispy Kreme originally had 8,000-square-foot stores but found them too large and too expensive for many markets. Then they tried tiny 1,300-square-foot stores, which required less investment, but such stores were too small to provide the mystique of seeing and smelling Krispy Kreme donuts being made. Krispy Kreme finally got it right with a 2,600-foot-store. This one includes a huge glass window to view doughnut production.*

▶ **Figure S7.3**   **Percent of North American Vehicles Made on Flexible Assembly Lines***

A large and growing percent of cars are made on flexible assembly lines. Chrysler, for example, discovered several years ago that its underutilized Belvidere, Illinois, plant was not flexible enough to paint a PT Cruiser (which was 1″ too tall). The company learned its lesson and is now a leader in investing in design flexibility.

*2007 estimate, *The Wall Street Journal* (April 11, 2006): A1 and (January 14–15, 2006): B14.

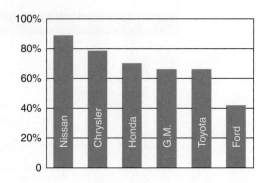

Demand Exceeds Capacity   When *demand exceeds capacity*, the firm may be able to curtail demand simply by raising prices, scheduling long lead times (which may be inevitable), and discouraging marginally profitable business. However, because inadequate facilities reduce revenue below what is possible, the long-term solution is usually to increase capacity (as we see in the *OM in Action* box "Too Little Capacity at Dalrymple Bay").

Capacity Exceeds Demand   When *capacity exceeds demand*, the firm may want to stimulate demand through price reductions or aggressive marketing, or it may accommodate the market through product changes. When decreasing customer demand is combined with old and inflexible processes, layoffs and plant closings may be necessary to bring capacity in line with demand. The *OM in Action* box "Too Much Capacity at G.M. and Ford" indicates how difficult adjusting capacity to declining demand can be.

Adjusting to Seasonal Demands   A seasonal or cyclical pattern of demand is another capacity challenge. In such cases, management may find it helpful to offer products with complementary demand patterns—that is, products for which the demand is high for one when low for the other. For example, in Figure S7.4 the firm is adding a line of snowmobile motors to its line of jet skis to smooth demand. With appropriate complementing of products, perhaps the utilization of facility, equipment, and personnel can be smoothed.

OM in Action   Too Little Capacity at Dalrymple Bay

Nearly 20 ships were anchored in the Coral Sea on a recent morning. They were waiting to be loaded with coal to fuel Asia's voracious steel mills. Australia has some of the most prolific coal mines in the world, but its key port of Dalrymple Bay, just outside Queensland, isn't big enough to meet demand. So the ships sit idle for days. Capacity at the port is far below what is needed for the current worldwide demand. This makes Dalrymple Bay one of the key choke points.

The process is rather simple but expensive. Trains are loaded with coal at the mines, travel several hours to the port, and dump their coal into piles that are sprayed with water to prevent black coal dust from blowing onto homes and beaches. Eventually, the coal is loaded onto a conveyor belt that moves 2.5 miles out into the Coral Sea, to be loaded onto ships.

The current plan is to invest $610 million to expand port capacity to 85 million metric tons of coal in the next 3 years. But this is still less than the estimated demand requirement of 107 million metric tons needed. As a result, coal companies, even after the expansion is completed, may still find access to shipping rationed.

The demand must exist, the port must expand, and the mines must enlarge. Without that assurance, the risk remains high and the necessary ROI (return on investment) is not there. Managers are not going to put significant money into expanding port capacity until they are comfortable that both the demand and coal supply support a larger port. To justify investment in capacity, each phase of the chain must support that investment.

Source: Australasian Business Intelligence (June 22, 2006); and *The Wall Street Journal* (July 7, 2005): C1, C4.

OM in Action   Too Much Capacity at G.M. and Ford

For decades G.M. and Ford added capacity. The auto and truck market expanded, and they expanded along with it. They were the world's greatest automobile companies. They built specialized product-focused plants with little flexibility. And they grew capacity to millions of cars per year. G.M. alone produced over half of the cars sold in the U.S. But the world changed. Cars now arrive in the U.S. from every corner of the world. Germany, Italy, Japan, Korea, and now even Mexico and Brazil are making inroads into the U.S. market—with China on the horizon. And G.M. now makes fewer than one-fourth of the cars sold in the U.S.

Toyota, VW, Honda, BMW, Mercedes, and others are stealing sales. They are stealing sales with imports, and they are stealing sales with domestic production. Recently Toyota's U.S. plants were operating at 111% of expected output compared with 87% for G.M. and 79% for Ford.

G.M. and Ford are not sitting still. In an effort to drive down costs, both companies are increasing productivity and flexibility. For instance, in the past 6 years, the total labor-hours per vehicle necessary for stamping, assembly, and engine production have dropped by 26%, from 46.5 hours to 34.3 hours. The number of stamping machines necessary to make the fenders, hoods, doors, and so on have dropped from 330 to 241. This potent combination of lower sales and increased productivity means G.M. and Ford must cut capacity. By 2010, employment at the two automakers will drop by 50,000 people. Capacity adjustments, particularly on the down side, can be painful.

Source: The Wall Street Journal (January 21–22, 2006): A2; *The Economist* (January 7, 2006): 61; and *Knight Ridder Tribune Business News* (January 4, 2006): 1.

Tactics for Matching Capacity to Demand   Various tactics for matching capacity to demand exist. Options for adjusting capacity include:

1. Making staffing changes (increasing or decreasing the number of employees or shifts)
2. Adjusting equipment (purchasing additional machinery or selling or leasing out existing equipment)
3. Improving processes to increase throughput
4. Redesigning products to facilitate more throughput
5. Adding process flexibility to better meet changing product preferences
6. Closing facilities

The foregoing tactics can be used to adjust demand to existing facilities. The strategic issue is, of course, how to have a facility of the correct size.

Demand and Capacity Management in the Service Sector

In the service sector, scheduling customers is *demand management*, and scheduling the workforce is *capacity management*.

Demand Management   When demand and capacity are fairly well matched, demand management can often be handled with appointments, reservations, or a first-come, first-served rule. In some businesses, such as doctors' and lawyers' offices, an *appointment system* is the schedule and is adequate. *Reservations systems* work well in rental car agencies, hotels, and some restaurants as

Time (months)

◀ **Figure S7.4**

By Combining Products That Have Complementary Seasonal Patterns, Capacity Can Be Better Utilized

A smoother sales demand contributes to improved scheduling and better human resource strategies.

▶ *Many U.S. hospitals use services abroad to manage capacity for radiologists during night shifts. Night Hawk, an Idaho-based service with 50 radiologists in Zurich and Sydney, contracts with 900 facilities (20% of all U.S. hospitals). These trained experts, wide awake and alert in their daylight hours, usually return a diagnosis in 10 to 20 minutes, with a guarantee of 30 minutes.*

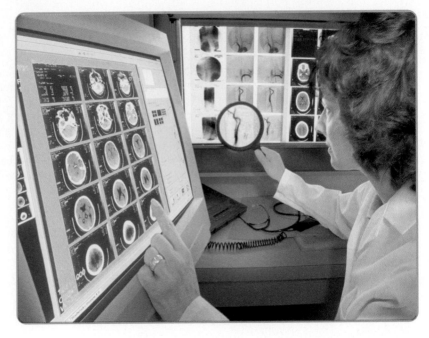

a means of minimizing customer waiting time and avoiding disappointment over unfilled service. In retail shops, a post office, or a fast-food restaurant, a *first-come, first-served* rule for serving customers may suffice. Each industry develops its own approaches to matching demand and capacity. Other more aggressive approaches to demand management include many variations of discounts: "early bird" specials in restaurants, discounts for matinee performances or for seats at odd hours on an airline, and cheap weekend phone calls.

Capacity Management   When managing demand is not feasible, then managing capacity through changes in full-time, temporary, or part-time staff may be an option. This is the approach in many services. For instance, hospitals may find capacity limited by a shortage of board-certified radiologists willing to cover the graveyard shifts. Getting fast and reliable radiology readings can be the difference between life and death for an emergency room patient. As the photo above illustrates, when an overnight reading is required (and 40% of CT scans are done between 8 P.M. and 8 A.M.), the image can be sent by e-mail to a doctor in Europe or Australia for immediate analysis.

▶ *FedEx's huge aircraft fleet is used to near capacity for nighttime delivery of packages but is 100% idle during the daytime. In an attempt to better utilize capacity (and leverage assets), FedEx considered two services with opposite or countercyclical demand patterns to its nighttime service—commuter passenger service and passenger charter service. However, after a thorough analysis, the 12% to 13% return on investment was judged insufficient for the risks involved. Facing the same issues, though, UPS decided to begin a charter airline that operates on weekends.*

CAPACITY PLANNING

Video S7.1

Capacity Planning at
Arnold Palmer Hospital

Setting future capacity requirements can be a complicated procedure, one based in large part on future demand. When demand for goods and services can be forecast with a reasonable degree of precision, determining capacity requirements can be straightforward. Determining capacity normally requires two phases. During the first phase, future demand is forecast with traditional models, as we saw in Chapter 4. During the second phase, this forecast is used to determine capacity requirements and the incremental size of each addition to capacity.[2] Interestingly, demand growth is typically gradual in small units, while capacity additions are typically instantaneous in large units. This contradiction often makes capacity expansion difficult.

Figure S7.5 reveals four approaches to new capacity. As we see in Figure S7.5(a), new capacity is acquired at the beginning of year 1. This capacity will handle increased demand until the beginning of year 2. At the beginning of year 2, new capacity is again acquired, which will allow the organization to stay ahead of demand until the beginning of year 3. This process can be continued indefinitely into the future.

The capacity plan shown in Figure S7.5(a) is only one of an almost limitless number of plans to satisfy future demand. In this figure, new capacity was acquired *incrementally*—at the beginning of year 1 *and* at the beginning of year 2. In Figure S7.5(b), a large increase in capacity is acquired at the beginning of year 1 to satisfy expected demand until the beginning of year 3.

The excess capacity provided by plans Figure S7.5(a) and Figure S7.5(b) gives operations managers flexibility. For instance, in the hotel industry, added capacity in the form of rooms can

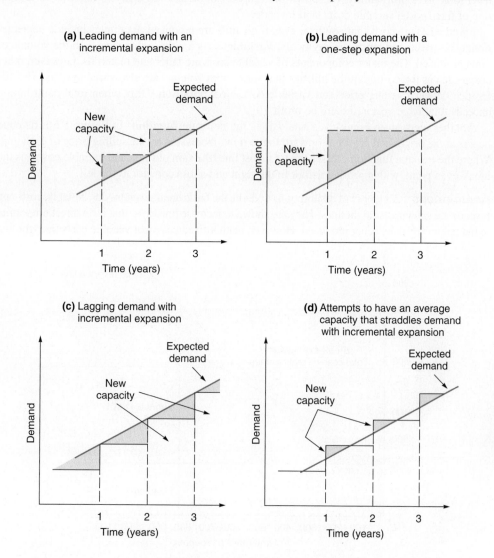

(a) Leading demand with an incremental expansion

(b) Leading demand with a one-step expansion

(c) Lagging demand with incremental expansion

(d) Attempts to have an average capacity that straddles demand with incremental expansion

◀ **Figure S7.5**

Approaches to Capacity Expansion

---

[2]At this point, we make the assumption that management knows the technology and the *type* of facilities to be employed to satisfy future demand requirements—not a minor issue, but beyond the scope of this text.

allow a wider variety of room options and perhaps flexibility in room cleanup schedules. In manufacturing, the excess capacity can be used to do more setups to shorten production runs, driving down inventory. The added capacity may also allow management to build excess inventory and thus delay the capital expenditure and disruption that come with adding additional new capacity.[3]

Alternatives Figure S7.5(a) and Figure S7.5(b) *lead* capacity—that is, acquire capacity to stay ahead of demand—but Figure S7.5(c) shows an option that *lags* capacity, perhaps using overtime or subcontracting to accommodate excess demand. Figure S7.5(d) straddles demand by building capacity that is "average," sometimes lagging demand and sometimes leading it.

In some cases, deciding between alternatives can be relatively easy. The total cost of each alternative can be computed, and the alternative with the least total cost can be selected. In other cases, determining the capacity and how to achieve it can be much more complicated. In most cases, numerous subjective factors are difficult to quantify and measure. These factors include technological options; competitor strategies; building restrictions; cost of capital; human resource options; and local, state, and federal laws and regulations.

Learning Objective

3. Compute break-even

Break-even analysis
A means of finding the point, in dollars and units, at which costs equal revenues.

Fixed costs
Costs that continue even if no units are produced.

Variable costs
Costs that vary with the volume of units produced.

Contribution
The difference between selling price and variable costs.

Revenue function
The function that increases by the selling price of each unit.

BREAK-EVEN ANALYSIS

Break-even analysis is a critical tool for determining the capacity a facility must have to achieve profitability. The objective of **break-even analysis** is to find the point, in dollars and units, at which costs equal revenue. This point is the break-even point. Firms must operate above this level to achieve profitability. As shown in Figure S7.6, break-even analysis requires an estimation of fixed costs, variable costs, and revenue.

Fixed costs are costs that continue even if no units are produced. Examples include depreciation, taxes, debt, and mortgage payments. **Variable costs** are those that vary with the volume of units produced. The major components of variable costs are labor and materials. However, other costs, such as the portion of the utilities that varies with volume, are also variable costs. The difference between selling price and variable cost is **contribution**. Only when total contribution exceeds total fixed cost will there be profit.

Another element in break-even analysis is the **revenue function**. In Figure S7.6, revenue begins at the origin and proceeds upward to the right, increasing by the selling price of each unit. Where the revenue function crosses the total cost line (the sum of fixed and variable costs), is the break-even point, with a profit corridor to the right and a loss corridor to the left.

Assumptions A number of assumptions underlie the basic break-even model. Notably, costs and revenue are shown as straight lines. They are shown to increase linearly—that is, in direct proportion to the volume of units being produced. However, neither fixed costs nor variable costs (nor, for that

▶ **Figure S7.6**

Basic Break-Even Point

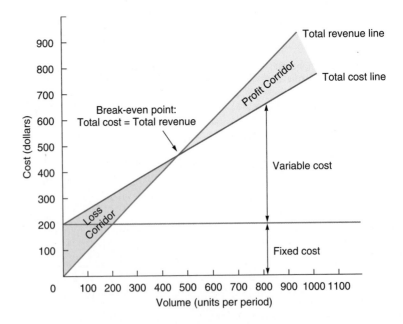

[3]See related discussion in S. Rajagopalan and J. M. Swaminathan, "Coordinated Production Planning Model with Capacity Expansion and Inventory Management," *Management Science* 47, no. 11, (November 2001): 1562–1580.

matter, the revenue function) need be a straight line. For example, fixed costs change as more capital equipment or warehouse space is used; labor costs change with overtime or as marginally skilled workers are employed; the revenue function may change with such factors as volume discounts.

Graphic Approach   The first step in the graphic approach to break-even analysis is to define those costs that are fixed and sum them. The fixed costs are drawn as a horizontal line beginning at that dollar amount on the vertical axis. The variable costs are then estimated by an analysis of labor, materials, and other costs connected with the production of each unit. The variable costs are shown as an incrementally increasing cost, originating at the intersection of the fixed cost on the vertical axis and increasing with each change in volume as we move to the right on the volume (or horizontal) axis. Both fixed- and variable-cost information is usually available from a firm's cost accounting department, although an industrial engineering department may also maintain cost information.

Fixed costs do not remain constant over all volume; new warehouses and new overhead charges result in step functions in fixed cost.

Algebraic Approach   The respective formulas for the break-even point in units and dollars are shown below. Let:

BEP_x = break-even point in units
$BEP_\$$ = break-even point in dollars
P = price per unit (after all discounts)
x = number of units produced

TR = total revenue = Px
F = fixed costs
V = variable costs per unit
TC = total costs = $F + Vx$

The break-even point occurs where total revenue equals total costs. Therefore:

$$TR = TC \quad \text{or} \quad Px = F + Vx$$

Solving for x, we get

$$BEP_x = \frac{F}{P - V}$$

and:

$$BEP_\$ = BEP_x P = \frac{F}{P - V} P = \frac{F}{(P - V)/P}$$

$$= \frac{F}{1 - V/P}$$

$$\text{Profit} = TR - TC$$
$$= Px - (F + Vx) = Px - F - Vx$$
$$= (P - V)x - F$$

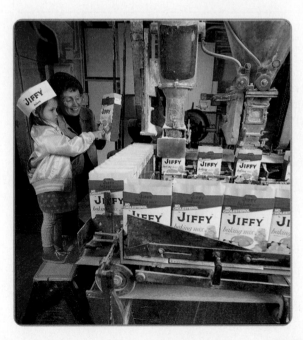

◀ Some companies adjust for a capacity change by modifying machinery or using older equipment—even though it may not be the most efficient. For instance, managers at the family-owned maker of Jiffy brand mixes decided that their OM strategy did not support additional capital investment in new equipment. Consequently, when making repairs, modifying equipment, or adjusting for peak loads, they draw on spare, often old, equipment.

Using these equations, we can solve directly for break-even point and profitability. The two break-even formulas of particular interest are:

$$\text{Break-even in units} = \frac{\text{Total fixed cost}}{\text{Price} - \text{Variable cost}} \tag{S7-4}$$

$$\text{Break-even in dollars} = \frac{\text{Total fixed cost}}{1 - \dfrac{\text{Variable cost}}{\text{Selling price}}} \tag{S7-5}$$

Single-Product Case

In Example S3, we determine the break-even point in dollars and units for one product.

EXAMPLE S3

Single product break-even analysis

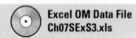
Excel OM Data File
Ch07SExS3.xls

Active Model S7.2

Example S3 is further illustrated in Active Model S7.2 on the CD-ROM.

Stephens, Inc., wants to determine the minimum dollar volume and unit volume needed at its new facility to break even.

Approach: The firm first determines that it has fixed costs of $10,000 this period. Direct labor is $1.50 per unit, and material is $.75 per unit. The selling price is $4.00 per unit.

Solution: The break-even point in dollars is computed as follows:

$$BEP_\$ = \frac{F}{1 - (V/P)} = \frac{\$10,000}{1 - [(1.50 + .75)/(4.00)]} = \frac{\$10,000}{.4375} = \$22,857.14$$

The break-even point in units is:

$$BEP_x = \frac{F}{P - V} = \frac{\$10,000}{4.00 - (1.50 + .75)} = 5,714$$

Note that we use total variable costs (that is, both labor and material).

Insight: The management of Stevens, Inc., now has an estimate in both units and dollars of the volume necessary for the new facility.

Learning exercise: If Stevens finds that fixed cost will increase to $12,000, what happens to the break-even in units and dollars? [Answer: The break-even in units increases to 6,857, and break-even in dollars increases to $27,428.57.]

Related problems: S7.9, S7.12, S7.13, S7.14, S7.15, S7.16, S7.17, S7.18, S7.19, S7.20, S7.21, S7.22, S7.23

Multiproduct Case

Most firms, from manufacturers to restaurants (even fast-food restaurants), have a variety of offerings. Each offering may have a different selling price and variable cost. Utilizing break-even analysis, we modify Equation (S7-5) to reflect the proportion of sales for each product. We do this by "weighting" each product's contribution by its proportion of sales. The formula is then:

$$BEP_\$ = \frac{F}{\sum \left[\left(1 - \dfrac{V_i}{P_i} \right) \times (W_i) \right]} \tag{S7-6}$$

where V = variable cost per unit
           P = price per unit
           F = fixed cost
           W = percent each product is of total dollar sales
           i = each product

Example S4 shows how to determine the break-even point for the multiproduct case at the Le Bistro restaurant.

◀ *Paper machines such as the one shown here, at International Paper, require a high capital investment. This investment results in a high fixed cost but allows production of paper at a very low variable cost. The production manager's job is to maintain utilization above the break-even point to achieve profitability.*

EXAMPLE S4

Multiproduct break-even analysis

Le Bistro makes more than one product and would like to know its break-even point in dollars.

Approach: Information for Le Bistro follows. Fixed costs are $3,500 per month.

Item	Price	Cost	Annual Forecasted Sales Units
Sandwich	$2.95	$1.25	7,000
Soft drink	.80	.30	7,000
Baked potato	1.55	.47	5,000
Tea	.75	.25	5,000
Salad bar	2.85	1.00	3,000

With a variety of offerings, we proceed with break-even analysis just as in a single-product case, except that we weight each of the products by its proportion of total sales using Equation (S7.6).

Solution: Multiproduct Break-Even: Determining Contribution

1	2	3	4	5	6	7	8
Item (i)	Selling Price (P)	Variable Cost (V)	(V/P)	$1 - (V/P)$	Annual Forecasted Sales $	% of Sales	Weighted Contribution (col. 5 × col. 7)
Sandwich	$2.95	$1.25	.42	.58	$20,650	.446	.259
Soft drink	.80	.30	.38	.62	5,600	.121	.075
Baked potato	1.55	.47	.30	.70	7,750	.167	.117
Tea	.75	.25	.33	.67	3,750	.081	.054
Salad bar	2.85	1.00	.35	.65	8,550	.185	.120
					$46,300	1.000	.625

Note: Revenue for sandwiches is $20,650 (2.95 × 7,000), which is 44.6% of the total revenue of $46,300. Therefore, the contribution for sandwiches is "weighted" by .446. The weighted contribution is .446 × .58 = .259. In this manner, its *relative* contribution is properly reflected.

Using this approach for each product, we find that the total weighted contribution is .625 for each dollar of sales, and the break-even point in dollars is $67,200:

$$BEP_\$ = \frac{F}{\sum \left[\left(1 - \frac{V_i}{P_i}\right) \times (W_i) \right]} = \frac{\$3,500 \times 12}{.625} = \frac{\$42,000}{.625} = \$67,200$$

The information given in this example implies total daily sales (52 weeks at 6 days each) of:

$$\frac{\$67{,}200}{312 \text{ days}} = \$215.38$$

Insight: The management of Le Bistro now knows that it must generate average sales of $215.38 each day to break even. Management also knows that if the forecasted sales of $46,300 are correct, Le Bistro will lose money, as break-even is $67,200.

Learning exercise: If the manager of Le Bistro wants to make an additional $2,000 per month and considers this a fixed cost, what is the new break-even point in average sales per day? [Answer: $338.46.]

Related problems: S7.24a, S7.25, S7.26a

Break-even figures by product provide the manager with added insight as to the realism of his or her sales forecast. They indicate exactly what must be sold each day, as we illustrate in Example S5.

EXAMPLE S5

Unit sales at break-even

Le Bistro also wants to know the break-even for the number of sandwiches that must be sold every day.

Approach: Using the data in Example S4, we take the forecast sandwich sales of 44.6% times the daily break-even of $215.38 divided by the selling price of each sandwich ($2.95).

Solution: At break-even, sandwich sales must then be:

$$\frac{.446 \times \$215.38}{\$2.95} = \text{Number of sandwiches} = 32.6 \approx 33 \text{ sandwiches each day}$$

Insight: With knowledge of individual product sales, the manager has a basis for determining material and labor requirements.

Learning exercise: At a dollar break-even of $338.46 per day, how many sandwiches must Le Bistro sell each day? [Answer: 51.]

Related problems: S7.24b, S7.26b, S7.35

Once break-even analysis has been prepared, analyzed, and judged to be reasonable, decisions can be made about the type and capacity of equipment needed. Indeed, a better judgment of the likelihood of success of the enterprise can now be made.

When capacity requirements are subject to significant unknowns, "probabilistic" models may be appropriate. One technique for making successful capacity planning decisions with an uncertain demand is decision theory, including the use of decision trees.

Learning Objective

4. Apply decision trees to capacity decisions

APPLYING DECISION TREES TO CAPACITY DECISIONS

Decision trees require specifying alternatives and various states of nature. For capacity planning situations, the state of nature usually is future demand or market favorability. By assigning probability values to the various states of nature, we can make decisions that maximize the expected value of the alternatives. Example S6 shows how to apply decision trees to a capacity decision.

EXAMPLE S6

Decision tree applied to capacity decision

Southern Hospital Supplies, a company that makes hospital gowns, is considering capacity expansion.

Approach: Southern's major alternatives are to do nothing, build a small plant, build a medium plant, or build a large plant. The new facility would produce a new type of gown, and currently the potential or marketability for this product is unknown. If a large plant is built and a favorable market exists, a profit of $100,000 could be realized. An unfavorable market would yield a $90,000 loss.

However, a medium plant would earn a $60,000 profit with a favorable market. A $10,000 loss would result from an unfavorable market. A small plant, on the other hand, would return $40,000 with favorable market conditions and lose only $5,000 in an unfavorable market. Of course, there is always the option of doing nothing.

Recent market research indicates that there is a .4 probability of a favorable market, which means that there is also a .6 probability of an unfavorable market. With this information, the alternative that will result in the highest expected monetary value (EMV) can be selected.

Solution: Prepare a decision tree and compute the EMV for each branch:

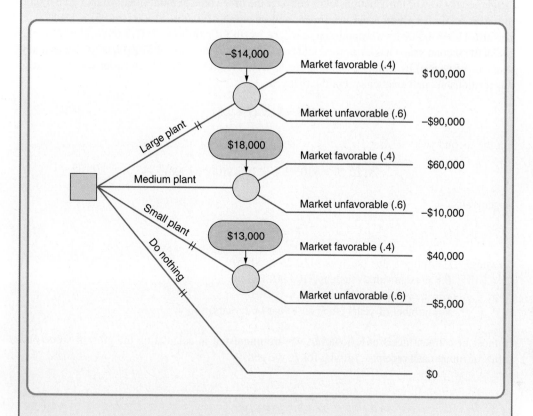

$$\text{EMV (large plant)} = (.4)(\$100,000) + (.6)(-\$90,000) = -\$14,000$$
$$\text{EMV (medium plant)} = (.4)(\$60,000) + (.6)(-\$10,000) = +\$18,000$$
$$\text{EMV (small plant)} = (.4)(\$40,000) + (.6)(-\$5,000) = +\$13,000$$
$$\text{EMV (do nothing)} = \$0$$

Based on EMV criteria, Southern should build a medium plant.

Insight: If Southern makes many decisions like this, then determining the EMV for each branch and selecting the highest EMV is a good decision criterion.

Learning exercise: If a new estimate of the loss from a medium plant in an unfavorable market increases to −$20,000 what is the new EMV for this branch? [Answer: $12,000, which changes the decision because the small plant EMV is now higher.]

Related problems: S7.27, S7.28.

APPLYING INVESTMENT ANALYSIS TO STRATEGY-DRIVEN INVESTMENTS

Once the strategy implications of potential investments have been considered, traditional investment analysis is appropriate. We introduce the investment aspects of capacity next.

An operations manager may be the one held responsible for return on investment (ROI).

Investment, Variable Cost, and Cash Flow

Capital investment requires cash flow as well as an evaluation of return on investments.

Because capacity and process alternatives exist, so do options regarding capital investment and variable cost. Managers must choose from among different financial options as well as capacity and process alternatives. Analysis should show the capital investment, variable cost, and cash flows as well as net present value for each alternative.

Net Present Value

Net present value
A means of determining the discounted value of a series of future cash receipts.

Determining the discount value of a series of future cash receipts is known as the **net present value** technique. By way of introduction, let us consider the time value of money. Say you invest $100.00 in a bank at 5% for 1 year. Your investment will be worth $100.00 + ($100.00)(.05) = $105.00. If you invest the $105.00 for a second year, it will be worth $105.00 + ($105.00)(.05) = $110.25 at the end of the second year. Of course, we could calculate the future value of $100.00 at 5% for as many years as we wanted by simply extending this analysis. However, there is an easier way to express this relationship mathematically. For the first year:

$$\$105 = \$100(1 + .05)$$

For the second year:

$$\$110.25 = \$105(1 + .05) = \$100(1 + .05)^2$$

In general:

$$F = P(1 + i)^N \tag{S7-7}$$

where F = future value (such as $110.25 or $105)
P = present value (such as $100.00)
i = interest rate (such as .05)
N = number of years (such as 1 year or 2 years)

Learning Objective

5. Compute net present value

In most investment decisions, however, we are interested in calculating the present value of a series of future cash receipts. Solving for P, we get:

$$P = \frac{F}{(1 + i)^N} \tag{S7-8}$$

When the number of years is not too large, the preceding equation is effective. However, when the number of years, N, is large, the formula is cumbersome. For 20 years, you would have to compute $(1 + i)^{20}$. Without a sophisticated calculator, this computation would be difficult.

▲ *Matching capacity and demand can be a challenge. When market share is declining and facilities are old and inflexible, as is the case at this General Motors plant, the mismatch between demand and capacity means empty plants and laying off employees (left photo). On the other hand, when demand exceeds capacity, as at this opening of the Apple store on the outskirts of Rome, Italy, the mismatch may mean frustrated customers and lost revenue (right photo).*

Year	5%	6%	7%	8%	9%	10%	12%	14%
1	.952	.943	.935	.926	.917	.909	.893	.877
2	.907	.890	.873	.857	.842	.826	.797	.769
3	.864	.840	.816	.794	.772	.751	.712	.675
4	.823	.792	.763	.735	.708	.683	.636	.592
5	.784	.747	.713	.681	.650	.621	.567	.519
6	.746	.705	.666	.630	.596	.564	.507	.456
7	.711	.665	.623	.583	.547	.513	.452	.400
8	.677	.627	.582	.540	.502	.467	.404	.351
9	.645	.592	.544	.500	.460	.424	.361	.308
10	.614	.558	.508	.463	.422	.386	.322	.270
15	.481	.417	.362	.315	.275	.239	.183	.140
20	.377	.312	.258	.215	.178	.149	.104	.073

Interest-rate tables, such as Table S7.1, alleviate this situation. First, let us restate the present value equation:

$$P = \frac{F}{(1+i)^N} = FX \qquad \text{(S7-9)}$$

where X = a factor from Table S7.1 defined as = $1/(1+i)^N$ and F = future value

Thus, all we have to do is find the factor X and multiply it by F to calculate the present value, P. The factors, of course, are a function of the interest rate, i, and the number of years, N. Table S7.1 lists some of these factors.

Equations (S7-8) and (S7-9) are used to determine the present value of one future cash amount, but there are situations in which an investment generates a series of uniform and equal cash amounts. This type of investment is called an *annuity*. For example, an investment might yield $300 per year for 3 years. Of course, you could use Equation (S7-8) three times, for 1, 2, and 3 years, but there is a shorter method. Although there is a formula that can be used to solve for the present value of an annual series of uniform and equal cash flows (an annuity), an easy-to-use table has been developed for this purpose. Like the customary present value computations, this calculation involves a factor. The factors for annuities are in Table S7.2. The basic relationship is

$$S = RX$$

where X = factor from Table S7.2
S = present value of a series of uniform annual receipts
R = receipts that are received every year for the life of the investment (the annuity)

The present value of a uniform annual series of amounts is an extension of the present value of a single amount, and thus Table S7.2 can be directly developed from Table S7.1. The factors for any given interest rate in Table S7.2 are nothing more than the cumulative sum of the values in

Year	5%	6%	7%	8%	9%	10%	12%	14%
1	.952	.943	.935	.926	.917	.909	.893	.877
2	1.859	1.833	1.808	1.783	1.759	1.736	1.690	1.647
3	2.723	2.673	2.624	2.577	2.531	2.487	2.402	2.322
4	3.546	3.465	3.387	3.312	3.240	3.170	3.037	2.914
5	4.329	4.212	4.100	3.993	3.890	3.791	3.605	3.433
6	5.076	4.917	4.766	4.623	4.486	4.355	4.111	3.889
7	5.786	5.582	5.389	5.206	5.033	4.868	4.564	4.288
8	6.463	6.210	5.971	5.747	5.535	5.335	4.968	4.639
9	7.108	6.802	6.515	6.247	5.985	5.759	5.328	4.946
10	7.722	7.360	7.024	6.710	6.418	6.145	5.650	5.216
15	10.380	9.712	9.108	8.559	8.060	7.606	6.811	6.142
20	12.462	11.470	10.594	9.818	9.128	8.514	7.469	6.623

Table S7.1. In Table S7.1, for example, .952, .907, and .864 are the factors for years 1, 2, and 3 when the interest rate is 5%. The cumulative sum of these factors is 2.723 = .952 + .907 + .864. Now look at the point in Table S7.2 where the interest rate is 5% and the number of years is 3. The factor for the present value of an annuity is 2.723, as you would expect. Table S7.2 can be very helpful in reducing the computations necessary to make financial decisions. (Note, however, that there may be minor rounding differences between the tables.)

Example S7 shows how to determine the present value of an annuity.

EXAMPLE S7

Determining net present value of future receipts of equal value

River Road Medical Clinic is thinking of investing in a sophisticated new piece of medical equipment. It will generate $7,000 per year in receipts for 5 years.

Approach: Determine the present value of this cash flow; assume an interest rate of 6%.

Solution: The factor from Table S7.2 (4.212) is obtained by finding that value when the interest rate is 6% and the number of years is 5:

$$S = RX = \$7,000(4.212) = \$29,484$$

Insight: There is another way of looking at this example. If you went to a bank and took a loan for $29,484 today, your payments would be $7,000 per year for 5 years if the bank used an interest rate of 6% compounded yearly. Thus, $29,484 is the present value.

Learning exercise: If the interest rate is 8%, what is the present value? [Answer: $27,951.]

Related problems: S7.29, S7.30, S7.31

The net present value method is one of the best methods of ranking investment alternatives. The procedure is straightforward: You simply compute the present value of all cash flows for each investment alternative. When deciding among investment alternatives, you pick the investment with the highest net present value. Similarly, when making several investments, those with higher net present values are preferable to investments with lower net present values.

Example S8 shows how to use the net present value to choose between investment alternatives.

EXAMPLE S8

Determining net present value of future receipts of different value

Quality Plastics, Inc., is considering two different investment alternatives.

Approach: To find the net present value of each investment, Quality first needs to determine the initial investment, cash flows, and interest rate. Investment A has an initial cost of $25,000, and investment B has an initial cost of $26,000. Both investments have a useful life of 4 years. The cash flows for these investments follow. The cost of capital or the interest rate (*i*) is 8%. (Factors come from Table S7.1).

Investment A's Cash Flow	Investment B's Cash Flow	Year	Present Value Factor at 8%
$10,000	$9,000	1	.926
9,000	9,000	2	.857
8,000	9,000	3	.794
7,000	9,000	4	.735

Solution: To find the present value of the cash flows for each investment, we multiply the present value factor by the cash flow for each investment for each year. The sum of these present value calculations minus the initial investment is the net present value of each investment. The computations appear in the following table:

Year	Investment A's Present Values	Investment B's Present Values
1	$ 9,260 = (.926)($10,000)	$ 8,334 = (.926)($9,000)
2	7,713 = (.857)($9,000)	7,713 = (.857)($9,000)
3	6,352 = (.794)($8,000)	7,146 = (.794)($9,000)
4	5,145 = (.735)($7,000)	6,615 = (.735)($9,000)
Totals	$28,470	$29,808
Minus initial investment	−25,000	−26,000
Net present value	$ 3,470	$ 3,808

> *Insight:* The net present value criterion shows investment B to be more attractive than investment A because it has a higher present value.
>
> *Learning exercise:* If the interest rate is 10%, does this change the decision? [Answer: no, but the difference between the two investments does narrow. NPV of investment A = $2,243; B = $2,500.]
>
> *Related problems:* S7.32, S7.33, S7.34, S7.36

In Example S8, it was not necessary to make all those present value computations for investment B. Because the cash flows are uniform, Table S7.2, the annuity table, gives the present value factor. Of course, we would expect to get the same answer. As you recall, Table S7.2 gives factors for the present value of an annuity. In this example, for payments of $9,000, cost of capital is 8% and the number of years is 4. Looking at Table S7.2 under 8% and 4 years, we find a factor of 3.312. Thus, the present value of this annuity is (3.312)($9,000) = $29,808, the same value as in Example S8.

Although net present value is one of the best approaches to evaluating investment alternatives, it does have its faults. Limitations of the net present value approach include the following:

1. Investments with the same net present value may have significantly different projected lives and different salvage values.
2. Investments with the same net present value may have different cash flows. Different cash flows may make substantial differences in the company's ability to pay its bills.
3. The assumption is that we know future interest rates, which we do not.
4. Payments are always made at the end of the period (week, month, or year), which is not always the case.

Summary

Managers tie equipment selection and capacity decisions to the organization's missions and strategy. They design their equipment and processes to have capabilities beyond the tolerance required by their customers while ensuring the flexibility needed for adjustments in technology, features, and volumes.

Good forecasting, break-even analysis, decision trees, cash flow, and net present value (NPV) techniques are particularly useful to operations managers when making capacity decisions.

Capacity investments are made effective by ensuring that the investments support a long-term strategy. The criteria for investment decisions are contributions to the overall strategic plan and winning profitable orders, not just return on investment. Efficient firms select the correct process and the correct capacity that contributes to their long-term strategy.

Key Terms

Capacity *(p. 288)*
Design capacity *(p. 289)*
Effective capacity *(p. 289)*
Utilization *(p. 289)*

Efficiency *(p. 289)*
Break-even analysis *(p. 296)*
Fixed costs *(p. 296)*
Variable costs *(p. 296)*

Contribution *(p. 296)*
Revenue function *(p. 296)*
Net present value *(p. 302)*

Using Software for Break-Even Analysis

Excel, Excel OM, and POM for Windows all handle break-even and cost–volume analysis problems.

Using Excel

It is a straightforward task to develop the formulas to do a break-even analysis in Excel. Although we do not demonstrate the basics here, you can see most of the spreadsheet analysis in the Excel OM preprogrammed software that accompanies this text.

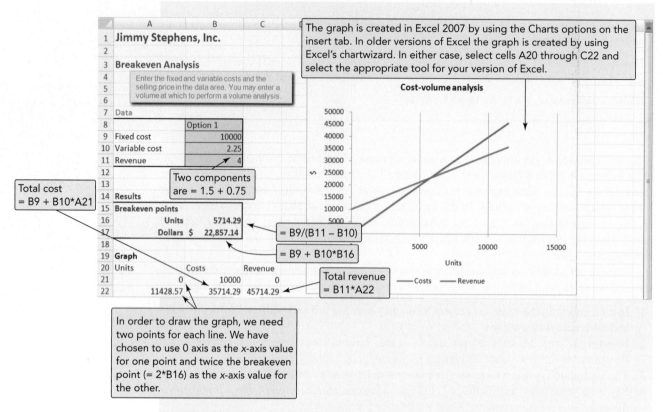

Total cost
= B9 + B10*A21

Two components
are = 1.5 + 0.75

= B9/(B11 – B10)

= B9 + B10*B16

Total revenue
= B11*A22

In order to draw the graph, we need two points for each line. We have chosen to use 0 axis as the x-axis value for one point and twice the breakeven point (= 2*B16) as the x-axis value for the other.

The graph is created in Excel 2007 by using the Charts options on the insert tab. In older versions of Excel the graph is created by using Excel's chartwizard. In either case, select cells A20 through C22 and select the appropriate tool for your version of Excel.

▲ **Program S7.1**   Excel OM's Break-Even Analysis, Using Example S3 Data

✕ Using Excel OM

Excel OM's Break-Even Analysis module is illustrated in Program S7.1. Using the Stephens, Inc., information in Example S3, Program S7.1 shows input data, the Excel formulas used to compute the break-even points, and the solution and graphical output.

P Using POM for Windows

Similar to Excel OM, POM for Windows also contains a break-even/cost–volume analysis module.

Solved Problems

 Virtual Office Hours help is available on Student DVD.

Solved Problem S7.1

Sara James Bakery, described earlier in Examples S1 and S2, has decided to increase its facilities by adding one additional process line. The firm will have two process lines, each working 7 days a week, 3 shifts per day, 8 hours per shift. Effective capacity is now 300,000 rolls. This addition, however, will reduce overall system efficiency to 85%. Compute the expected production with this new effective capacity.

Solution

Expected production = (Effective capacity)(Efficiency)

= 300,000(.85)

= 255,000 rolls per week

Solved Problem S7.2

Marty McDonald has a business packaging software in Wisconsin. His annual fixed cost is $10,000, direct labor is $3.50 per package, and material is $4.50 per package. The selling price will be $12.50 per package. What is the break-even point in dollars? What is break-even in units?

Solution

$$BEP_\$ = \frac{F}{1-(V/P)} = \frac{\$10,000}{1-(\$8.00/\$12.50)} = \frac{\$10,000}{.36} = \$27,777$$

$$BEP_x = \frac{F}{P-V} = \frac{\$10,000}{\$12.50-\$8.00} = \frac{\$10,000}{\$4.50} = 2,222 \text{ units}$$

Solved Problem S7.3

John has been asked to determine whether the $22.50 cost of tickets for the community dinner theater will allow the group to achieve break-even and whether the 175 seating capacity is adequate. The cost for each performance of a 10-performance run is $2,500. The facility rental cost for the entire 10 performances is $10,000. Drinks and parking are extra charges and have their own price and variable costs, as shown below:

1	2	3	4	5	6	7	8	9
	Selling Price (P)	Variable Cost (V)	Percent Variable Cost (V/P)	Contribution 1 − (V/P)	Estimated Quantity of Sales Units (sales)	Dollar Sales (Sales × P)	Percent of Sales	Contribution Weighted by Percent Sales (col. 5 × col. 8)
Tickets with Dinner	$22.50	$10.50	0.467	0.533	175	$3,938	0.741	0.395
Drinks	$ 5.00	$ 1.75	0.350	0.650	175	$ 875	0.165	0.107
Parking	$ 5.00	$ 2.00	0.400	0.600	100	$ 500	0.094	0.056
					450	$5,313	1.000	0.558

Solution

$$BEP_\$ = \frac{F}{\sum\left[\left(1 - \frac{V_i}{P_i}\right) \times (W_i)\right]} = \frac{\$(10 \times 2,500) + \$10,000}{0.558} = \frac{\$35,000}{0.558} = \$62,724$$

Revenue for each day (from column 7) = $5,313
Total forecasted revenue for the 10 performances = $(10 \times \$5,313) = \$53,130$
Forecasted revenue with this mix of sales shows a breakeven of $62,724

Thus, given this mix of costs, sales, and capacity John determines that the theatre will not break even.

Solved Problem S7.4

Your boss has told you to evaluate the cost of two machines. After some questioning, you are assured that they have the costs shown at the right. Assume:
a)   The life of each machine is 3 years, and
b)   The company thinks it knows how to make 14% on investments no riskier than this one.
Determine via the present value method which machine to purchase.

	Machine A	Machine B
Original cost	$13,000	$20,000
Labor cost per year	2,000	3,000
Floor space per year	500	600
Energy (electricity) per year	1,000	900
Maintenance per year	2,500	500
Total annual cost	$ 6,000	$ 5,000
Salvage value	$ 2,000	$ 7,000

Solution

			Machine A			Machine B	
		Column 1	Column 2	Column 3	Column 4	Column 5	Column 6
Now	Expense	1.000	$13,000	$13,000	1.000	$20,000	$20,000
1 yr.	Expense	.877	6,000	5,262	.877	5,000	4,385
2 yr.	Expense	.769	6,000	4,614	.769	5,000	3,845
3 yr.	Expense	.675	6,000	4,050	.675	5,000	3,375
				$26,926			$31,605
3 yr.	Salvage Revenue	.675	$ 2,000	−1,350	.675	$ 7,000	−4,725
				$25,576			$26,880

We use 1.0 for payments with no discount applied against them (that is, when payments are made now, there is no need for a discount). The other values in columns 1 and 4 are from the 14% column and the respective year in Table S7.1 (for example, the intersection of 14% and 1 year is .877, etc.). Columns 3 and 6 are the products of the present value figures times the combined costs. This computation is made for each year and for the salvage value.

The calculation for machine A for the first year is:

$$.877 \times (\$2,000 + \$500 + \$1,000 + \$2,500) = \$5,262$$

The salvage value of the product is *subtracted* from the summed costs, because it is a receipt of cash. Since the sum of the net costs for machine B is larger than the sum of the net costs for machine A, machine A is the low-cost purchase, and your boss should be so informed.

Self-Test

- *Before taking the self-test*, refer to the learning objectives listed at the beginning of the supplement and the key terms listed at the end of the supplement.
- *Use the key at the back of the text to **correct** your answers.*
- *Restudy* pages that correspond to any questions you answered incorrectly or material you feel uncertain about.

1. Capacity decisions should be made on the basis of:
   a) building sustained competitive advantage
   b) good financial returns
   c) a coordinated plan
   d) integration into the company's strategy
   e) all of the above

2. Assumptions of the standard break-even model are:
   a) fixed and variable costs are linear and revenue is exponential
   b) fixed cost is linear and variable and revenue are exponential
   c) fixed cost, variable cost and revenue are linear
   d) break-even is computed in dollars only
   e) break-even is computed in units only

3. Effective capacity is:
   a) the capacity a firm expects to achieve given the current operating constraints
   b) percent of design capacity actually achieved
   c) the percent of capacity actually achieved
   d) actual output
   e) efficiency

4. Utilization is:
   a) the capacity a firm expects to achieve given the current operating constraints
   b) percent of design capacity actually achieved

   c) the percent of capacity actually achieved
   d) actual output
   e) efficiency

5. Efficiency is:
   a) the capacity a firm expects to achieve given the current operating constraints
   b) percent of design capacity actually achieved
   c) the percent of effective capacity actually achieved
   d) actual output
   e) design capacity

6. Capacity adjustments are accomplished through:
   a) making staffing changes
   b) adjusting equipment
   c) improving processes
   d) product redesign
   e) all of the above

7. The break-even point is:
   a) adding processes to meet the point of changing product demands
   b) improving processes to increase throughput point
   c) the point in dollars or units at which cost equals revenue
   d) adding or removing capacity to meet demand
   e) the total cost of a process alternative

8. Contribution is
   a) cost that continues even if no units are produced
   b) the difference between selling price and the variable costs
   c) the revenue that is directly in proportion to the units sold
   d) those cost that vary with the units sold
   e) all of the above

Internet and Student CD-ROM/DVD Exercises

Visit our Companion Web site or use your student CD-ROM/DVD to help with material in this supplement.

 On Our Companion Web Site,
     www.prenhall.com/heizer
- Self-Study Quizzes
- Practice Problems
- Virtual Company Tour
- Internet Cases
- PowerPoint Lecture

 On Your Student CD-ROM
- Practice Problems
- Active Model Exercises
- Excel OM
- Excel OM Data Files
- POM for Windows

 On Your Student DVD
- Video Clips and Video Case
- Virtual Office Hours for Solved Problems

Discussion Questions

1. Distinguish between design capacity and effective capacity.
2. What are the assumptions of break-even analysis?
3. Where does the manager obtain data for break-even analysis?
4. What keeps plotted revenue data from falling on a straight line in a break-even analysis?
5. Under what conditions would a firm want its capacity to lag demand? to lead demand?

6. Explain how net present value is an appropriate tool for comparing investments.
7. What is effective capacity?
8. What is efficiency?
9. How is actual, or expected, output computed?

Problems*

• **S7.1** If a plant was designed to produce 7,000 hammers per day but is limited to making 6,000 hammers per day because of the time needed to change equipment between styles of hammers, what is the utilization?

• **S7.2** For the past month, the plant in Problem S7.1, which has an effective capacity of 6,500, has made only 4,500 hammers per day because of material delay, employee absences, and other problems. What is its efficiency?

• **S7.3** If a plant has an effective capacity of 6,500 and an efficiency of 88%, what is the actual (planned) output?

• **S7.4** A plant has an effective capacity of 900 units per day and produces 800 units per day with its product mix; what is its efficiency?

• **S7.5** Material delays have routinely limited production of household sinks to 400 units per day. If the plant efficiency is 80%, what is the effective capacity?

•• **S7.6** What is the expected output for a plant with a design capacity of 108 chairs per day, if its effective capacity is 90 chairs and its efficiency is 90%?

• **S7.7** A work center containing 4 machines of equal capability operates 2 shifts per day 5 days per week (8 hours per shift). This is the effective capacity. If the work center has a system efficiency of 95%, what is the expected output in hours per week?

• **S7.8** The effective capacity and efficiency for the next quarter at MMU Mfg. in Waco, Texas, for each of three departments are shown:

Department	Effective Capacity	Recent Efficiency
Design	93,600	.95
Fabrication	156,000	1.03
Finishing	62,400	1.05

Compute the expected production for next quarter for each department.

• **S7.9** Smithson Cutting is opening a new line of scissors for supermarket distribution. It estimates its fixed cost to be $500.00 and its variable cost to be $0.50 per unit. Selling price is expected to average $0.75 per unit.
a) What is Smithson's break-even point in units?
b) What is the break-even point in dollars? **PX**

•• **S7.10** Under ideal conditions, a service bay at a Fast Lube can serve 6 cars per hour. The effective capacity and efficiency of a Fast Lube service bay are known to be 5.5 and 0.880, respectively. What is the minimum number of service bays Fast Lube needs to achieve an anticipated production of 200 cars per 8-hour day?

•• **S7.11** Southeastern Oklahoma State University's business program has the facilities and faculty to handle an enrollment of 2,000 new students per semester. However, in an effort to limit class sizes to a "reasonable" level (under 200, generally), Southeastern's dean, Tom Choi, placed a ceiling on enrollment of 1,500 new students. Although there was ample demand for business courses last semester, conflicting schedules allowed only 1,450 new students to take business courses. What are the utilization and efficiency of this system?

Note: **PX** means the problem may be solved with POM for Windows and/or Excel OM.

• **S7.12** Markland Manufacturing intends to increase capacity by overcoming a bottleneck operation by adding new equipment. Two vendors have presented proposals. The fixed costs for proposal A are $50,000, and for proposal B, $70,000. The variable cost for A is $12.00, and for B, $10.00. The revenue generated by each unit is $20.00.
a) What is the break-even point in units for proposal A?
b) What is the break-even point in units for proposal B? **PX**

• **S7.13** Using the data in Problem S7.12:
a) What is the break-even point in dollars for proposal A if you add $10,000 installation to the fixed cost?
b) What is the break-even point in dollars for proposal B if you add $10,000 installation to the fixed cost? **PX**

• **S7.14** Given the data in Problem S7.12, at what volume (units) of output would the two alternatives yield the same profit? **PX**

•• **S7.15** Janelle Heinke, the owner of Ha'Peppas!, is considering a new oven in which to bake the firm's signature dish, vegetarian pizza. Oven type A can handle 20 pizzas an hour. The fixed costs associated with oven A are $20,000 and the variable costs are $2.00 per pizza. Oven B is larger and can handle 40 pizzas an hour. The fixed costs associated with oven B are $30,000 and the variable costs are $1.25 per pizza. The pizzas sell for $14 each.
a) What is the break-even point for each oven?
b) If the owner expects to sell 9,000 pizzas, which oven should she purchase?
c) If the owner expects to sell 12,000 pizzas, which oven should she purchase?
d) At what volume should Janelle switch ovens? **PX**

• **S7.16** Given the following data, calculate: a) *BEP(x)*; b) *BEP($)*; and c) the profit at 100,000 units:

$$P = \$8/\text{unit} \quad V = \$4/\text{unit} \quad F = \$50,000 \text{ PX}$$

•• **S7.17** You are considering opening a copy service in the student union. You estimate your fixed cost at $15,000 and the variable cost of each copy sold at $.01. You expect the selling price to average $.05.
a) What is the break-even point in dollars?
b) What is the break-even point in units? **PX**

•• **S7.18** Dr. Aleda Roth, a prolific author, is considering starting her own publishing company. She will call it DSI Publishing, Inc. DSI's estimated costs are:

Fixed	$250,000.00
Variable cost per book	$20.00
Selling price per book	$30.00

How many books must DSI sell to break even? What is its break-even point in dollars? **Px**

•• **S7.19** In addition to the costs in Problem S7.18, Dr. Roth wants to pay herself a salary of $75,000 per year.
a) Now what is her break-even point in units?
b) What is her break-even point in dollars? **Px**

•• **S7.20** An electronics firm is currently manufacturing an item that has a variable cost of $.50 per unit and a selling price of $1.00 per unit. Fixed costs are $14,000. Current volume is 30,000 units. The firm can substantially improve the product quality by adding a new piece of equipment at an additional fixed cost of $6,000. Variable cost would increase to $.60, but volume should jump to 50,000 units due to a higher-quality product. Should the company buy the new equipment? **Px**

•• **S7.21** The electronics firm in Problem S7.20 is now considering the new equipment and increasing the selling price to $1.10 per unit. With the higher-quality product, the new volume is expected to be 45,000 units. Under these circumstances, should the company purchase the new equipment and increase the selling price? **Px**

•••• **S7.22** Zan Azlett and Angela Zesiger have joined forces to start A&Z Lettuce Products, a processor of packaged shredded lettuce for institutional use. Zan has years of food processing experience, and Angela has extensive commercial food preparation experience. The process will consist of opening crates of lettuce and then sorting, washing, slicing, preserving, and finally packaging the prepared lettuce. Together, with help from vendors, they feel they can adequately estimate demand, fixed costs, revenues, and variable cost per 5-pound bag of lettuce. They think a largely manual process will have monthly fixed costs of $37,500 and variable costs of $1.75 per bag. A more mechanized process will have fixed costs of $75,000 per month with variable costs of $1.25 per 5-pound bag. They expect to sell the shredded lettuce for $2.50 per 5-pound bag.
a) What is the break-even quantity for the manual process?
b) What is the revenue at the break-even quantity for the manual process?
c) What is the break-even quantity for the mechanized process?
d) What is the revenue at the break-even quantity for the mechanized process?
e) What is the monthly profit or loss of the *manual* process if they expect to sell 60,000 bags of lettuce per month?
f) What is the monthly profit or loss of the *mechanized* process if they expect to sell 60,000 bags of lettuce per month?
g) At what quantity would Zan and Angela be indifferent to the process selected?
h) Over what range of demand would the *manual* process be preferred over the mechanized process? Over what range of demand would the *mechanized* process be preferred over the manual process? **Px**

•• **S7.23** Carter Manufacturing is currently producing a tape holder that has a variable cost of $0.75 per unit and a selling price of $2.00 per unit. Fixed costs are $20,000. Current volume is 40,000

units. The firm can produce a better product by adding a new piece of equipment to the process line. This equipment represents an increase of $5,000 in fixed cost. The variable cost would decrease $0.25 per unit. Volume for the new and improved product should rise to 50,000 units.
a) Should the company invest in the new equipment?
b) At what volume does the equipment choice change?
c) At a volume of 15,000 units, which process should be used?

••• **S7.24** As a prospective owner of a club known as the Red Rose, you are interested in determining the volume of sales dollars necessary for the coming year to reach the break-even point. You have decided to break down the sales for the club into four categories, the first category being beer. Your estimate of the beer sales is that 30,000 drinks will be served. The selling price for each unit will average $1.50; the cost is $.75. The second major category is meals, which you expect to be 10,000 units with an average price of $10.00 and a cost of $5.00. The third major category is desserts and wine, of which you also expect to sell 10,000 units, but with an average price of $2.50 per unit sold and a cost of $1.00 per unit. The final category is lunches and inexpensive sandwiches, which you expect to total 20,000 units at an average price of $6.25 with a food cost of $3.25. Your fixed cost (that is, rent, utilities, and so on) is $1,800 per month plus $2,000 per month for entertainment.
a) What is your break-even point in dollars per month?
b) What is the expected number of meals each day if you are open 30 days a month?

••• **S7.25** Using the data in Problem S7.24, make the problem more realistic by adding labor cost (as a variable cost) at one-third the total cost of meals and sandwiches. Also add variable expenses (kitchen supplies, tablecloths, napkins, etc.) at 10% of the food cost for each category.
a) What is your break-even point?
b) If you expect to make an annual profit of $35,000 (before taxes) for your 12-hour days, what must your total sales be?

••• **S7.26** As manager of the St. Cloud Theatre Company, you have decided that concession sales will support themselves. The following table provides the information you have been able to put together thus far:

Item	Selling Price	Variable Cost	% of Revenue
Soft drink	$1.00	$ .65	25
Wine	1.75	.95	25
Coffee	1.00	.30	30
Candy	1.00	.30	20

Last year's manager, Jim Freeland, has advised you to be sure to add 10% of variable cost as a waste allowance for all categories.

You estimate labor cost to be $250.00 (5 booths with 3 people each). Even if nothing is sold, your labor cost will be $250.00, so you decide to consider this a fixed cost. Booth rental, which is a contractual cost at $50.00 for *each* booth per night, is also a fixed cost.
a) What is break-even volume per evening performance?
b) How much wine would you expect to sell at the break-even point?

•• **S7.27** James Lawson's Bed and Breakfast, in a small historic Mississippi town, must decide how to subdivide (remodel) the large old home that will become its inn. There are three alternatives: Option A would modernize all baths and combine rooms, leaving the inn with four suites, each suitable for two to four adults.

Option B would modernize only the second floor; the results would be six suites, four for two to four adults, two for two adults only. Option C (the status quo option) leaves all walls intact. In this case, there are eight rooms available, but only two are suitable for four adults, and four rooms will not have private baths. Below are the details of profit and demand patterns that will accompany each option:

	Annual Profit under Various Demand Patterns			
Alternatives	**High**	**p**	**Average**	**p**
A (modernize all)	$90,000	.5	$25,000	.5
B (modernize 2nd)	$80,000	.4	$70,000	.6
C (status quo)	$60,000	.3	$55,000	.7

a) Draw the decision tree for Lawson.
b) Which option has the highest expected value? **Px**

••• **S7.28** As operations manager of Holz Furniture, you must make a decision about adding a line of rustic furniture. In discussing the possibilities with your sales manager, Steve Gilbert, you decide that there will definitely be a market and that your firm should enter that market. However, because rustic furniture has a different finish than your standard offering, you decide you need another process line. There is no doubt in your mind about the decision, and you are sure that you should have a second process. But you do question how large to make it. A large process line is going to cost $400,000; a small process line will cost $300,000. The question, therefore, is the demand for rustic furniture. After extensive discussion with Mr. Gilbert and Tim Ireland of Ireland Market Research, Inc., you determine that the best estimate you can make is that there is a two-out-of-three chance of profit from sales as large as $600,000 and a one-out-of-three chance as low as $300,000.

With a large process line, you could handle the high figure of $600,000. However, with a small process line you could not and would be forced to expand (at a cost of $150,000), after which time your profit from sales would be $500,000 rather than the $600,000 because of the lost time in expanding the process. If you do not expand the small process, your profit from sales would be held to $400,000. If you build a small process and the demand is low, you can handle all of the demand.

Should you open a large or small process line?

•• **S7.29** What is the net present value of an investment that costs $75,000 and has a salvage value of $45,000? The annual profit from the investment is $15,000 each year for 5 years. The cost of capital at this risk level is 12%. **Px**

• **S7.30** The initial cost of an investment is $65,000 and the cost of capital is 10%. The return is $16,000 per year for 8 years. What is the net present value? **Px**

• **S7.31** An investment will produce $2,000 three years from now. What is the amount worth today? That is, what is the present value if the interest rate is 9%? **Px**

• **S7.32** What is the present value of $5,600 when the interest rate is 8% and the return of $5,600 will not be received for 15 years? **Px**

•• **S7.33** Tim Smunt has been asked to evaluate two machines. After some investigation, he determines that they have the costs shown in the following table. He is told to assume that:
a) the life of each machine is 3 years, and
b) the company thinks it knows how to make 12% on investments no more risky than this one.

	Machine A	Machine B
Original cost	$10,000	$20,000
Labor per year	2,000	4,000
Maintenance per year	4,000	1,000
Salvage value	2,000	7,000

Determine, via the present value method, which machine Tim should recommend.

•• **S7.34** Your boss has told you to evaluate two ovens for Tink-the-Tinkers, a gourmet sandwich shop. After some questioning of vendors and receipt of specifications, you are assured that the ovens have the attributes and costs shown in the following table. The following two assumptions are appropriate:
1) The life of each machine is 5 years.
2) The company thinks it knows how to make 14% on investments no more risky than this one.

	Three Small Ovens at $1,250 Each	Two Large Ovens at $2,500 Each
Original cost	$3,750	$5,000
Labor per year in excess of larger models	$ 750 (total)	
Cleaning/ maintenance	$ 750 ($250 each)	$ 400 ($200 each)
Salvage value	$ 750 ($250 each)	$1,000 ($500 each)

a) Determine via the present value method which machine to tell your boss to purchase.
b) What assumption are you making about the ovens?
c) What assumptions are you making in your methodology?

•••• **S7.35** Andre is investigating setting up a crepe stand on campus. He could rent space in the student union (which costs $300/month in rent and overhead). His materials and labor costs are $1 per crepe, and the sale price is $4 per crepe.
a) What is the break-even quantity for this option (i.e., how many crepes per month will Andre have to sell before making a profit)?
b) Andre could use a portable crepe maker from a friend and set up a booth outside the student union. He'd have no rent or other general overhead costs (i.e., no fixed costs), but his friend would demand $1.50 per crepe sold. What is the break-even quantity for this option?
c) Assume that an informal survey shows that Andre could expect 350 crepes to be sold per month. Which capacity option should he elect: student union stand or portable crepe maker?
d) What would his total monthly profit be on the better option?
e) By how much (and in what direction) would the demand have to be different before he would consider switching to the other capacity option?

•••• **S7.36** Bold's Gym, a health club chain, is considering expanding into a new location: the initial investment would be $1 million in equipment, renovation, and a 6-year lease, and its annual upkeep and expenses would be $75,000. Its planning horizon is 6 years out, and at the end, it can sell the equipment for $50,000. Club capacity is 500 members who would pay an annual fee of $600. Bold's expects to have no problems filling membership slots. Assume that the interest rate is 10%. (See Table S7.1)
a) What is the present value profit/loss of the deal?
b) The club is considering offering a special deal to the members in the first year. For $3,000 upfront they get a full 6-year membership (i.e., 1 year free). Would it make financial sense to offer this deal?

Case Study

Capacity Planning at Arnold Palmer Hospital

Since opening day in 1989, the Arnold Palmer Hospital has experienced an explosive growth in demand for its services. One of only six hospitals in the U.S. to specialize in health care for women and children, Arnold Palmer Hospital has cared for over 1,500,000 patients who came to the Orlando facility from all 50 states and more than 100 countries. With patient satisfaction scores in the top 10% of U.S. hospitals surveyed (over 95% of patients would recommend the hospital to others), one of Arnold Palmer Hospital's main focuses is delivery of babies. Originally built with 281 beds and a capacity for 6,500 births per year, the hospital steadily approached and then passed 10,000 births. Looking at Table S7.3, Executive Director Kathy Swanson knew an expansion was necessary.

▼ **Table S7.3** Births at Arnold Palmer Hospital

Year	Births
1995	6,144
1996	6,230
1997	6,432
1998	6,950
1999	7,377
2000	8,655
2001	9,536
2002	9,825
2003	10,253
2004	10,555
2005	12,316
2006	13,070
2007 (est.)	13,600

With continuing population growth in its market area serving 18 central Florida counties, Arnold Palmer Hospital was delivering the equivalent of a kindergarten class of babies every day and still not meeting demand. Supported with substantial additional demographic analysis, the hospital was ready to move ahead with a capacity expansion plan and a new 11-story hospital building across the street from the existing facility.

Thirty-five planning teams were established to study such issues as (1) their specific forecasts, (2) services that would transfer to the new facility, (3) services that would remain in the existing facility, (4) staffing needs, (5) capital equipment, (6) pro forma accounting data, and (7) regulatory requirements. Ultimately, Arnold Palmer Hospital was ready to move ahead with a budget of $100 million and a commitment to an additional 150 beds. But given the growth of the central Florida region, Swanson decided to expand the hospital in stages: the top two floors would be empty interiors ("shell") to be completed at a later date, and the fourth-floor operating room could be doubled in size when needed. "With the new facility in place, we are now able to handle up to 16,000 births per year," says Swanson.

Discussion Questions*

1. Given the capacity planning discussion in the text (see Figure S7.5) what approach is being taken by Arnold Palmer Hospital toward matching capacity to demand?
2. What kind of major changes could take place in Arnold Palmer Hospital's demand forecast that would leave the hospital with an underutilized facility (namely, what are the risks connected with this capacity decision)?
3. Use regression analysis to forecast the point at which Swanson needs to "build out" the top two floors of the new building, namely, when demand will exceed 16,000 births.

*You may wish to view this video case on your DVD before addressing these questions.

Additional Case Studies

Internet case study: Visit our Companion Web site at www.prenhall.com/heizer for this free case study:

- **Southwestern University D:** Requires the development of a multiproduct break-even solution.

Harvard has selected these Harvard Business School cases to accompany this supplement:

harvardbusinessonline.hbsp.harvard.edu

- **National Cranberry Cooperative** (#688-122): Requires the student to analyze process, bottlenecks, and capacity.
- **Lenzing AG: Expanding in Indonesia** (#796-099): Considers how expansion affects the company's competitive position.
- **Chaparral Steel** (#687-045): Examines a major capacity expansion proposal of Chaparral Steel, a steel minimill.
- **Align Technology, Inc., Matching Manufacturing Capacity to Sales Demand** (#603-058): Analyzing and planning production capacity.
- **Samsung Heavy Industries: The Koje Shipyard** (#695-032): Explores manufacturing improvement but falling performance after major capital expansion.

Bibliography

Atamturk, A., and D. S. Hochbaum. "Capacity Acquisition, Subcontracting, and Lot-Sizing." *Management Science* 47, no. 8 (August 2001): 1081–1100.

Bowers, John, et al. "Modelling Outpatient Capacity for a Diagnosis and Treatment Center." *Health Care Management Science* 8, no. 3 (August 2005): 205.

Cheng, H. K., K. Dogan, R. A. Einicki. "Pricing and Capacity Decisions for Non-Profit Internet Service Providers." *Information Technology and Management* 7, no. 2 (April, 2006): 91.

Goodale, John C., Rohit Verma, and Madeleine E. Pullman. "A Market Utility-Based Model for Capacity Scheduling in Mass Services." *Production and Operations Management* 12, no. 2 (summer 2003): 165–185.

Hanfield, Robert B., and Kevin McCormack. "What You Need to Know About Sourcing from China." *Supply Chain Management Review* 9, no. 6 (September 2005): 28–37.

Jack, Eric P., and Amitabh S. Raturi. "Measuring and Comparing Volume Flexibility in the Capital Goods Industry." *Production and Operations Management* 12, no. 4 (winter 2003): 480–501.

Jonsson, Patrik, and Stig-Arne Mattsson. "Use and Applicability of Capacity Planning Methods." *Production and Inventory Management Journal* (3rd/4th quarter 2002): 89–95.

Kekre, Sunder, et al. "Reconfiguring a Remanufacturing Line at Visteon, Mexico." *Interfaces* 33, no. 6 (November–December 2003): 30–43.

Koste, L. L., M. K. Malhotra, and S. Sharma. "Measuring Dimensions of Manufacturing Flexibility." *Journal of Operations Management* 22, no. 2 (April 2004): 171–196.

Lovejoy, William S., and Ying Li. "Hospital Operating Room Expansion." *Management Science* 48, no. 11 (November 2002): 1369–1387.

Wacker, J. G., and C. Sheu. "Effectiveness of Manufacturing Planning and Central Systems on Manufacturing Competitiveness." *International Journal of Production Research* 44, no. 5 (March 2006): 1015.

Internet Resources

American Council of Engineering Companies: **www.acec.org**
Association for Manufacturing Excellence: **www.ame.org**

DARPA: U.S. Defense Dept., Innovative Prototype Systems: **www.DARPA.mil**

CHAPTER 8

Location Strategies

Chapter Outline

Ten OM Strategy Decisions

Design of Goods and Services
Managing Quality
Process Strategy
Location Strategies
Layout Strategies
Human Resources
Supply Chain Management
Inventory Management
Scheduling
Maintenance

Learning Objectives

When you complete this chapter you should be able to

1. Identify and explain seven major factors that affect location decisions
2. Compute labor productivity
3. Apply the factor-rating method
4. Complete a locational break-even analysis graphically and mathematically
5. Use the center-of-gravity method

Location Provides Competitive Advantage for FedEx

Overnight-delivery powerhouse FedEx has believed in the hub concept for its 43-year existence. Even though Fred Smith, founder and CEO, got a C on his college paper proposing a hub for small-package delivery, the idea has proven extremely successful. Starting with a hub in Memphis, Tennessee (now called its *superhub*), the $30 billion firm has added a European hub in Paris, an Asian hub in Guangzhou, China, a Latin American hub in Miami, and a Canadian hub in Toronto. FedEx's fleet of 650 planes flies into 378 airports worldwide, then delivers to the door with more than 42,000 vans.

Why was Memphis picked as FedEx's central location? (1) It is located in the middle of the U.S. (2) It has very few hours of bad weather closures, perhaps contributing to the firm's excellent flight-safety record.

Each night, except Sunday, FedEx brings to Memphis packages from throughout the world that are going to cities for which FedEx does not have

▶ At the FedEx hub in Memphis, Tennessee, approximately 100 FedEx aircraft converge each night around midnight with more than 1 million documents and packages.

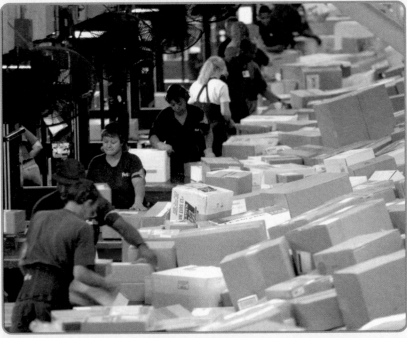

▶ At the preliminary sorting area, packages and documents are sorted and sent to a secondary sorting area. The Memphis facility covers 1.5 million square feet; it is big enough to hold 33 football fields. Packages are sorted and exchanged until 4 A.M.

▶ Packages and documents that have already gone through the primary and secondary sorts are checked by city, state, and zip code. They are then placed in containers that are loaded onto aircraft for delivery to their final destinations in 215 countries.

◀ FedEx's fleet of 650 planes makes it the second-largest airline in the world. Over 42,000 trucks complete the delivery process.

▶ The brand-new $150 million hub in Guangzhou lies in the heart of one of China's fastest-growing manufacturing districts. FedEx controls 39% of the China-to-U.S. air express market.

direct flights. The central hub permits service to a far greater number of points with fewer aircraft than the traditional City A–to–City B system. It also allows FedEx to match aircraft flights with package loads each night and to reroute flights when load volume requires it, a major cost savings. Moreover, FedEx also believes that the central hub system helps reduce mishandling and delay in transit because there is total control over the packages from pickup point through delivery.

THE STRATEGIC IMPORTANCE OF LOCATION

When FedEx opened its Asian super-hub in Guangzhou, China in 2008, it set the stage for "round-the-world" flights linking its Paris and Memphis package hubs to Asia. When Mercedes announced its plans to build its first major overseas plant in Vance, Alabama, it completed a year of competition among 170 sites in 30 states and two countries. When Hard Rock Cafe opened in Moscow, it ended 3 years of advance preparation of a Russian food supply chain.

One of the most important strategic decisions made by companies like FedEx, Mercedes, and Hard Rock is where to locate their operations. The international aspect of these decisions is an indication of the global nature of location decisions. With the opening of the Soviet and Chinese blocs, a great transformation is taking place. World markets have doubled, and the global nature of business is accelerating.

Firms throughout the world are using the concepts and techniques of this chapter to address the location decision because location greatly affects both fixed and variable costs. Location has a major impact on the overall risk and profit of the company. For instance, depending on the product and type of production or service taking place, transportation costs alone can total as much as 25% of the product's selling price. That is, one-fourth of a firm's total revenue may be needed just to cover freight expenses of the raw materials coming in and finished products going out. Other costs that may be influenced by location include taxes, wages, raw material costs, and rents.

Companies make location decisions relatively infrequently, usually because demand has outgrown the current plant's capacity or because of changes in labor productivity, exchange rates, costs, or local attitudes. Companies may also relocate their manufacturing or service facilities because of shifts in demographics and customer demand.

Location options include (1) expanding an existing facility instead of moving, (2) maintaining current sites while adding another facility elsewhere, or (3) closing the existing facility and moving to another location.

The location decision often depends on the type of business. For industrial location decisions, the strategy is usually minimizing costs, although innovation and creativity may also be critical. For retail and professional service organizations, the strategy focuses on maximizing revenue. Warehouse location strategy, however, may be driven by a combination of cost and speed of delivery. *The objective of location strategy is to maximize the benefit of location to the firm.*

Video 8.1

Hard Rock's Location Selection

> *The objective of location strategy is to maximize the benefit of location to a firm.*

Location and Costs Because location is such a significant cost and revenue driver, location often has the power to make (or break) a company's business strategy. Key multinationals in every major industry, from automobiles to cellular phones, now have or are planning a presence in each of their major markets. Location decisions to support a low-cost strategy require particularly careful consideration.

Once management is committed to a specific location, many costs are firmly in place and difficult to reduce. For instance, if a new factory location is in a region with high energy costs, even good management with an outstanding energy strategy is starting at a disadvantage. Management is in a similar bind with its human resource strategy if labor in the selected location is expensive, ill-trained, or has a poor work ethic. Consequently, hard work to determine an optimal facility location is a good investment.

Location and Innovation When creativity, innovation, and research and development investments are critical to the operations strategy, the location criteria may change from a focus on costs. When innovation is the focus, four attributes seem to affect overall competitiveness as well as innovation[1]:

- The presence of high-quality and specialized inputs such as scientific and technical talent
- An environment that encourages investment and intense local rivalry
- Pressure and insight gained from a sophisticated local market
- Local presence of related and supporting industries

---

[1]See Michael E. Porter and Scott Stern, "Innovation: Location Matters," *MIT Sloan Management Review* 42, no. 4 (summer 2001): 28–36.

Motorola and Intel are among those firms that have rejected low-cost locations when those locations could not support other important aspects of the strategy. In the case of Motorola, when analysis indicated that the infrastructure and education levels could not support specific production technologies, the locations were removed from consideration, even if they were low cost. And Intel opened its newest plant not in Asia but in the U.S. The $3 billion semiconductor facility, with 1,000 workers, ended up in Arizona in 2007 for four reasons: (1) the skilled labor requirements (for employees who understand statistics and scientific principles), (2) protection of intellectual property in the U.S., (3) tax breaks to help cover the cost of equipment, and (4) easy oversight from Intel's California headquarters.

FACTORS THAT AFFECT LOCATION DECISIONS

Selecting a facility location is becoming much more complex with the globalization of the workplace. As we saw in Chapter 2, globalization has taken place because of the development of (1) market economics; (2) better international communications; (3) more rapid, reliable travel and shipping; (4) ease of capital flow between countries; and (5) high differences in labor costs. Many firms now consider opening new offices, factories, retail stores, or banks outside their home country. Location decisions transcend national borders. In fact, as Figure 8.1 shows, the sequence of location decisions often begins with choosing a country in which to operate.

One approach to selecting a country is to identify what the parent organization believes are critical success factors (CSFs) needed to achieve competitive advantage. Six possible country CSFs are listed at the top of Figure 8.1. Using such factors (including some negative ones, such as crime) the World Economic Forum biannually ranks the global competitiveness of 125 countries (see Table 8.1). Switzerland landed first in 2006–2007 because of its high rates of saving and investment, openness to trade, quality education, and efficient government.

Once a firm decides which country is best for its location, it focuses on a region of the chosen country and a community. The final step in the location decision process is choosing a specific site within a community. The company must pick the one location that is best suited for shipping and receiving, zoning, utilities, size, and cost. Again, Figure 8.1 summarizes this series of decisions and the factors that affect them.

▼ **Table 8.1**

Competitiveness of 125 Selected Countries, Based on Annual Surveys of 11,000 Business Executives

Country	2006–2007 Ranking
Switzerland	1
⋮	
U.S.	6
Japan	7
Germany	8
⋮	
UK	10
⋮	
Israel	15
Canada	16
⋮	
Italy	42
⋮	
China	54
⋮	
Mexico	58
⋮	
Russia	62
⋮	
Vietnam	77
⋮	
Angola	125

Source: **www.weforum.org**, 2007.

Country Decision

Critical Success Factors

1. Political risks, government rules, attitudes, incentives
2. Cultural and economic issues
3. Location of markets
4. Labor talent, attitudes, productivity, costs
5. Availability of supplies, communications, energy
6. Exchange rates and currency risk

Region/Community Decision

1. Corporate desires
2. Attractiveness of region (culture, taxes, climate, etc.)
3. Labor availability, costs, attitudes toward unions
4. Cost and availability of utilities
5. Environmental regulations of state and town
6. Government incentives and fiscal policies
7. Proximity to raw materials and customers
8. Land/construction costs

Site Decision

1. Site size and cost
2. Air, rail, highway, waterway systems
3. Zoning restrictions
4. Proximity of services/supplies needed
5. Environmental impact issues

◀ **Figure 8.1**

Some Considerations and Factors That Affect Location Decisions

OM in Action   Quality Coils Pulls the Plug on Mexico

Keith Gibson, president of Quality Coils, Inc., saw the savings of low Mexican wages and headed south. He shut down a factory in Connecticut and opened one in Juarez, where he could pay Mexicans one-third the wage rates he was paying Americans. "All the figures pointed out we should make a killing," says Gibson.

Instead, his company was nearly destroyed. The electromagnetic coil maker regularly lost money during 4 years in Mexico. High absenteeism, low productivity, and problems of long-distance management wore down Gibson until he finally pulled the plug on Juarez.

Moving back to the U.S. and rehiring some of his original workers, Gibson learned, "I can hire one person in Connecticut for what three were doing in Juarez."

When U.S. unions complain that they cannot compete against the low wages in other countries and when the teamster rallies chant "$4 a day/No way!" they overlook several factors. First, productivity in low-wage countries often erases a wage advantage that is not nearly as great as people believe. Second, a host of problems, from poor roads to corrupt governments, run up operating costs. Third, although labor costs in many underdeveloped countries are only one-third of those in the U.S., they may represent less than 10% of total manufacturing costs. Thus, the difference may not overcome other disadvantages. And most importantly, the cost of labor for most U.S. manufacturers is less important than such factors as the skill of the workforce, the quality of transportation, and access to technology.

Sources: Global Information Network (January 8, 2004): 1; and *The Wall Street Journal* (January 13, 2004): A12 and (September 15, 1993): A1.

Learning Objective

1. Identify and explain seven major factors that affect location decisions

Besides globalization, a number of other factors affect the location decision. Among these are labor productivity, foreign exchange, culture, changing attitudes toward the industry, and proximity to markets, suppliers, and competitors.

Labor Productivity

When deciding on a location, management may be tempted by an area's low wage rates. However, wage rates cannot be considered by themselves, as Quality Coils, Inc., discovered when it opened its plant in Mexico (see the *OM in Action* box "Quality Coils Pulls the Plug on Mexico"). Management must also consider productivity.

As discussed in Chapter 1, differences exist in productivity in various countries. What management is really interested in is the combination of productivity and the wage rate. For example, if Quality Coils pays $70 per day with 60 units produced per day in Connecticut, it will spend less on labor than at a Mexican plant that pays $25 per day with a productivity of 20 units per day:

It is generally cheaper to make clothes in developing countries and ship them to the U.S. than it is to produce them in the U.S. However, final cost is the critical factor, and low productivity can negate low cost.

$$\frac{\text{Labor cost per day}}{\text{Productivity (that is, units per day)}} = \text{Cost per unit}$$

Case 1: Connecticut plant:

$$\frac{\$70 \text{ Wages per day}}{60 \text{ Units produced per day}} = \frac{\$70}{60} = \$1.17 \text{ per unit}$$

Case 2: Juarez, Mexico, plant:

$$\frac{\$25 \text{ Wages per day}}{20 \text{ Units produced per day}} = \frac{\$25}{20} = \$1.25 \text{ per unit}$$

Learning Objective

2. Compute labor productivity

Employees with poor training, poor education, or poor work habits may not be a good buy even at low wages. By the same token, employees who cannot or will not always reach their places of work are not much good to the organization, even at low wages. (Labor cost per unit is sometimes called the *labor content* of the product.)

Exchange Rates and Currency Risk

Although wage rates and productivity may make a country seem economical, unfavorable exchange rates may negate any savings. Sometimes, though, firms can take advantage of a particularly favorable exchange rate by relocating or exporting to a foreign country. However, the values of foreign currencies continually rise and fall in most countries. Such changes could well make what was a good location in 2007 a disastrous one in 2011.

◀ *Assembly plants operating along the Mexican side of the border, from Texas to California, are called maquiladoras. Some 3,200 firms and industrial giants such as GM, Zenith, Hitachi, and GE operate these plants, which employ over 1.5 million workers. Mexican wages are low, but at current exchange rates, companies also look to Asia.*

Costs

We can divide location costs into two categories, tangible and intangible. **Tangible costs** are those costs that are readily identifiable and precisely measured. They include utilities, labor, material, taxes, depreciation, and other costs that the accounting department and management can identify. In addition, such costs as transportation of raw materials, transportation of finished goods, and site construction are all factored into the overall cost of a location. Government incentives, as we see in the *OM in Action* box "How Big Incentives Won Alabama the Auto Industry," certainly affect a location's cost.

Intangible costs are less easily quantified. They include quality of education, public transportation facilities, community attitudes toward the industry and the company, and quality and attitude of prospective employees. They also include quality-of-life variables, such as climate and sports teams, that may influence personnel recruiting.

Ethical Issues   Location decisions based on costs alone may create ethical situations such as the United Airlines case in Indianapolis (see the "Ethical Dilemma" at the end of this chapter). United accepted $320 million in incentives to open a facility in that location, only to renege a decade later, leaving residents and government holding the bag.[2]

Tangible costs
Readily identifiable costs that can be measured with some precision.

Intangible costs
A category of location costs that cannot be easily quantified, such as quality of life and government.

In 1993, Alabama persuaded Mercedes-Benz to build its first U.S. auto plant in the town of Vance by offering the luxury carmaker $253 million worth of incentives—$169,000 for every job Mercedes promised the state.

Taxpayers considered the deal such a boondoggle that they voted Governor Jim Folsom out of office long before the first Mercedes SUV rolled off the new assembly line in 1997. Today, with 84,000 car-related jobs in Alabama, the deal looks a little more like a bargain—suggesting that the practice of paying millions of taxpayer dollars to lure big employers can *sometimes* have a big payoff.

Mercedes surpassed its pledge to create 1,500 jobs at the Vance plant and in 2007 has a workforce of 4,000.

In 2001, Honda opened a factory 70 miles east of the Mercedes plant, to build its Odyssey minivan. Toyota Motor Corp.'s plant near Huntsville started producing engines in 2002. Those two automakers also received incentives.

To cement Alabama's reputation as the South's busiest auto-making center, Hyundai Motor Co. of South Korea picked a site near Montgomery for its first U.S. assembly plant. The factory began production in 2005, employing 2,000 workers to make 300,000 sedans and SUVs a year.

Is the state giving away more than it gets in return? That's what many economists argue. Other former foes of incentives now argue that manufacturers' arrivals herald "Alabama's new day."

Sources: Knight Ridder Tribune Business News (August 25, 2005): 1 and (October 17, 2004): 1; and *The Wall Street Journal* (April 5, 2002): 1.

[2]So what's a city, county, or state to do? According to *Forbes* (June 19, 2006) page 42, "Keep taxes low. Don't grant favors. Pursue non-discriminatory reforms like reining in debt and public spending. Remove barriers rather than trying to steer economic growth to this favored corporation or that one." While many inner cities have languished, Chicago has prospered by focusing on infrastructure and quality-of-life issues. Also see "Is There a Better Way to Court a Company?" *Business Week* (July 23, 2007): 55.

To what extent do companies owe long-term allegiance to a particular country or state or town if they are losing money—or if the firm can make greater profits elsewhere? Is it ethical for developed countries to locate plants in undeveloped countries where sweatshops and child labor are commonly used? Where low wages and poor working conditions are the norm? It has been said that the factory of the future will be a large ship, capable of moving from port to port as costs in one port become noncompetitive.

Political Risk, Values, and Culture

The political risk associated with national, state, and local governments' attitudes toward private and intellectual property, zoning, pollution, and employment stability may be in flux. Governmental positions at the time a location decision is made may not be lasting ones. However, management may find that these attitudes can be influenced by their own leadership.

Worker values may also differ from country to country, region to region, and small town to city. Worker views regarding turnover, unions, and absenteeism are all relevant factors. In turn, these values can affect a company's decision whether to make offers to current workers if the firm relocates to a new location. The case study at the end of this chapter, "Southern Recreational Vehicle Company," describes a St. Louis firm that actively chose *not to relocate* any of its workers when it moved to Mississippi.

One of the greatest challenges in a global operations decision is dealing with another country's culture. Cultural variations in punctuality by employees and suppliers make a marked difference in production and delivery schedules. Bribery likewise creates substantial economic inefficiency, as well as ethical and legal problems in the global arena. As a result, operations managers face significant challenges when building effective supply chains that include foreign firms. Table 8.2 provides one ranking of corruption in countries around the world.

Proximity to Markets

For many firms it is extremely important to locate near customers. Particularly, service organizations, like drugstores, restaurants, post offices, or barbers, find that proximity to market is *the* primary location factor. Manufacturing firms find it useful to be close to customers when transporting finished goods is expensive or difficult (perhaps because they are bulky, heavy, or fragile). Foreign-owned auto giants are joining their customers' desires for European and Asian cars and trucks by building in the U.S. Over 4 million cars per year are now made in the U.S. by such firms as Mercedes, Honda, Toyota, and Hyundai.

In addition, with just-in-time production, suppliers want to locate near users. For a firm like Coca-Cola, whose product's primary ingredient is water, it makes sense to have bottling plants in many cities rather than shipping heavy (and sometimes fragile glass) containers cross country.

Proximity to Suppliers

Firms locate near their raw materials and suppliers because of (1) perishability, (2) transportation costs, or (3) bulk. Bakeries, dairy plants, and frozen seafood processors deal with *perishable* raw materials, so they often locate close to suppliers. Companies dependent on inputs of heavy or bulky raw materials (such as steel producers using coal and iron ore) face expensive inbound *transportation costs*, so transportation costs become a major factor. And goods for which there is a *reduction in bulk* during production (such as lumber mills locating in the Northwest near timber resources) typically need to be near the raw material.

Proximity to Competitors (Clustering)

Companies also like to locate, somewhat surprisingly, near competitors. This tendency, called **clustering**, often occurs when a major resource is found in that region. Such resources include natural resources, information resources, venture capital resources, and talent resources. Table 8.3 presents nine examples of industries that exhibit clustering, and the reasons why.

Italy may be the true leader when it comes to clustering, however, with northern zones of that country holding world leadership in such specialties as ceramic tile (Modena), gold jewelry (Vicenza), machine tools (Busto Arsizio), cashmere and wool (Biella), designer eyeglasses (Belluma), and pasta machines (Parma).

▼ **Table 8.2**

Ranking Corruption in Selected Countries (score of 10 represents a corruption-free country)

Rank		Score
1	Finland, Iceland, New Zealand	9.6 (tie)
11	UK	8.6
14	Canada	8.5
17	Japan	7.6
20	U.S., Belgium	7.3 (tie)
34	Israel, Taiwan	5.9 (tie)
70	Brazil, China, India, Saudi Arabia	3.3 (tie)
105	Iran, Uganda	2.7 (tie)
121	Russia, Rwanda	2.5 (tie)
163	Haiti	1.8

Source: Transparency International's 2006 survey, at **www.transparency.org**.

Clustering

The location of competing companies near each other, often because of a critical mass of information, talent, venture capital, or natural resources.

▼ **Table 8.3**   **Clustering of Companies**

Industry	Locations	Reason for Clustering
Wine making	Napa Valley (U.S.), Bordeaux region (France)	Natural resources of land and climate
Software firms	Silicon Valley, Boston, Bangalore (India)	Talent resources of bright graduates in scientific/technical areas, venture capitalists nearby
Race car building	Huntington/North Hampton region (England)	Critical mass of talent and information
Theme parks (including Disney World, Universal Studios, and Sea World)	Orlando, Florida	A hot spot for entertainment, warm weather, tourists, and inexpensive labor
Electronics firms (such as Sony, IBM, HP, Motorola, and Panasonic)	Northern Mexico	NAFTA, duty-free export to U.S. (24% of all TVs are built here)
Computer hardware manufacturing	Singapore, Taiwan	High technological penetration rates and per capita GDP, skilled/educated workforce with large pool of engineers
Fast-food chains (such as Wendy's, McDonald's, Burger King, and Pizza Hut)	Sites within 1 mile of one another	Stimulate food sales, high traffic flows
General aviation aircraft (including Cessna, Learjet, Boeing, and Raytheon)	Wichita, Kansas	Mass of aviation skills (60–70% of world's small planes/jets built here)
Orthopedic devices	Warsaw, Indiana	Ready supply of skilled workers, strong U.S. market

METHODS OF EVALUATING LOCATION ALTERNATIVES

Four major methods are used for solving location problems: the factor-rating method, locational break-even analysis, the center-of-gravity method, and the transportation model. This section describes these approaches.

The Factor-Rating Method

There are many factors, both qualitative and quantitative, to consider in choosing a location. Some of these factors are more important than others, so managers can use weightings to make the decision process more objective. The **factor-rating method** is popular because a wide variety of factors, from education to recreation to labor skills, can be objectively included. Figure 8.1 listed a few of the many factors that affect location decisions.

The factor-rating method has six steps:

Factor-rating method
A location method that instills objectivity into the process of identifying hard-to-evaluate costs.

1. Develop a list of relevant factors called *critical success factors* (such as those in Figure 8.1).
2. Assign a weight to each factor to reflect its relative importance in the company's objectives.
3. Develop a scale for each factor (for example, 1 to 10 or 1 to 100 points).
4. Have management score each location for each factor, using the scale in step 3.
5. Multiply the score by the weights for each factor and total the score for each location.
6. Make a recommendation based on the maximum point score, considering the results of other quantitative approaches as well.

Five Flags over Florida, a U.S. chain of 10 family-oriented theme parks, has decided to expand overseas by opening its first park in Europe. It wishes to select between France and Denmark.

Approach: The ratings sheet in Table 8.4 lists critical success factors that management has decided are important; their weightings and their rating for two possible sites—Dijon, France, and Copenhagen, Denmark—are shown.

EXAMPLE 1

Factor-rating method for an expanding theme park

▼ **Table 8.4** Weights, Scores, and Solution

Critical Success Factor	Weight	Scores (out of 100)		Weighted Scores	
		France	Denmark	France	Denmark
Labor availability and attitude	.25	70	60	(.25)(70) = 17.5	(.25)(60) = 15.0
People-to-car ratio	.05	50	60	(.05)(50) = 2.5	(.05)(60) = 3.0
Per capita income	.10	85	80	(.10)(85) = 8.5	(.10)(80) = 8.0
Tax structure	.39	75	70	(.39)(75) = 29.3	(.39)(70) = 27.3
Education and health	.21	60	70	(.21)(60) = 12.6	(.21)(70) = 14.7
Totals	1.00			70.4	68.0

Learning Objective

3. Apply the factor-rating method

Solution: Table 8.4 uses weights and scores to evaluate alternative site locations. Given the option of 100 points assigned to each factor, the French location is preferable.

Insight: By changing the points or weights slightly for those factors about which there is some doubt, we can analyze the sensitivity of the decision. For instance, we can see that changing the scores for "labor availability and attitude" by 10 points can change the decision. The numbers used in factor weighting can be subjective and the model's results are not "exact" even though this is a quantitative approach.

Learning exercise: If the weight for "tax structure" drops to .20 and the weight for "education and health" increases to .40, what is the new result? [Answer: Denmark is now chosen, with a 68.0 vs. a 67.5 score for France.]

Related problems: 8.5, 8.6, 8.7, 8.8, 8.9, 8.10, 8.11, 8.12, 8.13, 8.14, 8.15, 8.24, 8.25

When a decision is sensitive to minor changes, further analysis of the weighting and the points assigned may be appropriate. Alternatively, management may conclude that these intangible factors are not the proper criteria on which to base a location decision. Managers therefore place primary weight on the more quantitative aspects of the decision.

Locational Break-Even Analysis

Locational break-even analysis

A cost–volume analysis to make an economic comparison of location alternatives.

Locational break-even analysis is the use of cost–volume analysis to make an economic comparison of location alternatives. By identifying fixed and variable costs and graphing them for each location, we can determine which one provides the lowest cost. Locational break-even analysis can be done mathematically or graphically. The graphic approach has the advantage of providing the range of volume over which each location is preferable.

The three steps to locational break-even analysis are as follows:

1. Determine the fixed and variable cost for each location.
2. Plot the costs for each location, with costs on the vertical axis of the graph and annual volume on the horizontal axis.
3. Select the location that has the lowest total cost for the expected production volume.

EXAMPLE 2

Locational break-even for a parts manufacturer

John Kros, owner of Carolina Ignitions Manufacturing, needs to expand his capacity. He is considering three locations—Akron, Bowling Green, and Chicago—for a new plant. The company wishes to find the most economical location for an expected volume of 2,000 units per year.

Approach: Kros conducts locational break-even analysis. To do so, he determines that fixed costs per year at the sites are $30,000, $60,000, and $110,000, respectively; and variable costs are $75 per unit, $45 per unit, and $25 per unit, respectively. The expected selling price of each ignition system produced is $120.

Solution: For each of the three locations, Kros can plot the fixed costs (those at a volume of zero units) and the total cost (fixed costs + variable costs) at the expected volume of output. These lines have been plotted in Figure 8.2.

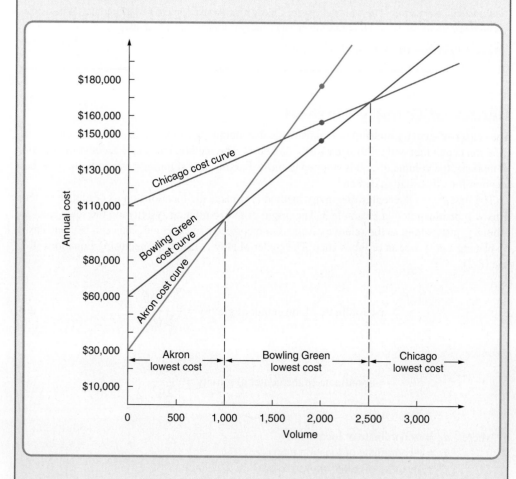

◄ **Figure 8.2**

Crossover Chart for Locational Break-Even Analysis

Excel OM Data File Ch08Ex2.xls

For Akron:

$$\text{Total cost} = \$30,000 + \$75(2,000) = \$180,000$$

For Bowling Green:

$$\text{Total cost} = \$60,000 + \$45(2,000) = \$150,000$$

For Chicago:

$$\text{Total cost} = \$110,000 + \$25(2,000) = \$160,000$$

With an expected volume of 2,000 units per year, Bowling Green provides the lowest cost location. The expected profit is:

$$\text{Total revenue} - \text{Total cost} = \$120(2,000) - \$150,000 = \$90,000 \text{ per year}$$

The crossover point for Akron and Bowing Green is:

$$30,000 + 75(x) = 60,000 + 45(x)$$
$$30(x) = 30,000$$
$$x = 1,000$$

and the crossover point for Bowling Green and Chicago is:

$$60,000 + 45(x) = 110,000 + 25(x)$$
$$20(x) = 50,000$$
$$x = 2,500$$

Learning Objective

4. Complete a locational break-even analysis graphically and mathematically

Insight: As with every other OM model, locational break-even results can be sensitive to input data. For example, for a volume of less than 1,000, Akron would be preferred. For a volume greater than 2,500, Chicago would yield the greatest profit.

Learning exercise: The variable cost for Chicago is now expected to be $22 per unit. What is the new crossover point between Bowling Green and Chicago? [Answer: 2,174 units.]

Related problems: 8.16, 8.17, 8.18, 8.19

Center-of-Gravity Method

Center-of-gravity method

A mathematical technique used for finding the best location for a single distribution point that services several stores or areas.

The **center-of-gravity method** is a mathematical technique used for finding the location of a distribution center that will minimize distribution costs. The method takes into account the location of markets, the volume of goods shipped to those markets, and shipping costs in finding the best location for a distribution center.[3]

The first step in the center-of-gravity method is to place the locations on a coordinate system. This will be illustrated in Example 3. The origin of the coordinate system and the scale used are arbitrary, just as long as the relative distances are correctly represented. This can be done easily by placing a grid over an ordinary map. The center of gravity is determined using Equations (8-1) and (8-2):

$$x\text{-coordinate of the center of gravity} = \frac{\sum_i d_{ix} Q_i}{\sum_i Q_i} \tag{8-1}$$

$$y\text{-coordinate of the center of gravity} = \frac{\sum_i d_{iy} Q_i}{\sum_i Q_i} \tag{8-2}$$

Learning Objective

5. Use the center-of-gravity method

where d_{ix} = x-coordinate of location i
d_{iy} = y-coordinate of location i
Q_i = Quantity of goods moved to or from location i

Note that Equations (8-1) and (8-2) include the term Q_i, the quantity of supplies transferred to or from location i.

Since the number of containers shipped each month affects cost, distance alone should not be the principal criterion. The center-of-gravity method assumes that cost is directly proportional to both distance and volume shipped. The ideal location is that which minimizes the weighted distance between the warehouse and its retail outlets, where the distance is weighted by the number of containers shipped.[4]

EXAMPLE 3

Center of gravity

Quain's Discount Department Stores, a chain of four large Target-type outlets, has store locations in Chicago, Pittsburgh, New York, and Atlanta; they are currently being supplied out of an old and inadequate warehouse in Pittsburgh, the site of the chain's first store. The firm wants to find some "central" location in which to build a new warehouse.

---

[3]For a discussion of the use of the center-of-gravity method in a warehouse location and consolidation problem, see Charles A. Watts, "Using a Personal Computer to Solve a Warehouse Location/Consolidation Problem," *Production and Inventory Management Journal* (4th quarter 2000): 23–28.

[4]Equations (8-1) and (8-2) compute a center of gravity (COG) under "squared Euclidean" distances and may actually result in transportation costs slightly (less than 2%) higher than an *optimal* COG computed using "Euclidean" (straight-line) distances. The latter, however, is a more complex and involved procedure mathematically, so the formulas we present are generally used as an attractive substitute. See C. Kuo and R. E. White, "A Note on the Treatment of the Center-of-Gravity Method in Operations Management Textbooks," *Decision Sciences Journal of Innovative Education* 2 (fall 2004): 219–227.

Approach: Quain will apply the center-of-gravity method. It gathers data on demand rates at each outlet (see Table 8.5).

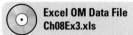
Excel OM Data File
Ch08Ex3.xls

▼ **Table 8.5** **Demand for Quain's Discount Department Stores**

Store Location	Number of Containers Shipped per Month
Chicago	2,000
Pittsburgh	1,000
New York	1,000
Atlanta	2,000

Its current store locations are shown in Figure 8.3. For example, location 1 is Chicago, and from Table 8.5 and Figure 8.3, we have:

$$d_{1x} = 30$$
$$d_{1y} = 120$$
$$Q_1 = 2,000$$

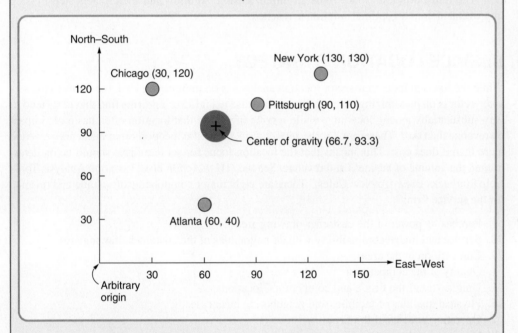

◄ **Figure 8.3**

Coordinate Locations of Four Quain's Department Stores and Center of Gravity

solution: Using the data in Table 8.5 and Figure 8.3 for each of the other cities, in Equations (8-1) and (8-2) we find:

x-coordinate of the center of gravity:

$$= \frac{(30)(2000)+(90)(1000)+(130)(1000)+(60)(2000)}{2000+1000+1000+2000} = \frac{400,000}{6,000}$$

$$= 66.7$$

y-coordinate of the center of gravity:

$$= \frac{(120)(2000)+(110)(1000)+(130)(1000)+(40)(2000)}{2000+1000+1000+2000} = \frac{560,000}{6,000}$$

$$= 93.3$$

This location (66.7, 93.3) is shown by the crosshairs in Figure 8.3.

Active Model 8.1

Example 3 is further illustrated in Active Model 8.1 on the CD-ROM and in the Exercise on page 335.

Insight: By overlaying a U.S. map on this exhibit, we find this location is near central Ohio. The firm may well wish to consider Columbus, Ohio, or a nearby city as an appropriate location. But it is important to have both North–South and East–West interstate highways near the city selected to make delivery times quicker.

Transportation Model

Transportation model

A technique for solving a class of linear programming problems.

The objective of the **transportation model** is to determine the best pattern of shipments from several points of supply (sources) to several points of demand (destinations) so as to minimize total production and transportation costs. Every firm with a network of supply-and-demand points faces such a problem. The complex Volkswagen supply network (shown in Figure 8.4) provides one such illustration. We note in Figure 8.4, for example, that VW de Mexico ships vehicles for assembly and parts to VW of Nigeria, sends assemblies to VW do Brasil, and receives parts and assemblies from headquarters in Germany.

Although the linear programming (LP) technique can be used to solve this type of problem, more efficient, special-purpose algorithms have been developed for the transportation application. The transportation model finds an initial feasible solution and then makes step-by-step improvement until an optimal solution is reached.

SERVICE LOCATION STRATEGY

While the focus in industrial-sector location analysis is on minimizing cost, the focus in the service sector is on maximizing revenue. This is because manufacturing firms find that costs tend to vary substantially among locations, while service firms find that location often has more impact on revenue than cost. Therefore, for the service firm, a specific location often influences revenue more than it does cost. This means that the location focus for service firms should be on determining the volume of business and revenue. See the *OM in Action* box "Location Analysis Tools Help Starbucks Brew Up New Cafes." There are eight major components of volume and revenue for the service firm:

It is often desirable to locate near competition; large department stores often attract more shoppers when competitors are close by. The same applies to shoe stores, fast-food restaurants, and others.

1. Purchasing power of the customer-drawing area
2. Service and image compatibility with demographics of the customer-drawing area
3. Competition in the area
4. Quality of the competition
5. Uniqueness of the firm's and competitors' locations
6. Physical qualities of facilities and neighboring businesses
7. Operating policies of the firm
8. Quality of management

▶ **Figure 8.4**

Worldwide Distribution of Volkswagens and Parts

Source: The Economist, Ltd.
Distributed by *The New York Times*/Special Features.

OM in Action   Location Analysis Tools Help Starbucks Brew Up New Cafes

The secret to Starbucks Coffee's plan to open three new cafes around the world every day isn't in the coffee beans—it is in the location. The company's phenomenal growth has been fueled by site-selection software that strengthens the strategic decision-making process. The analysis is as follows: If a site's potential is not within a certain ROI parameter, the company doesn't waste its time.

Every site-acquisition decision evaluates geocoded demographic and consumer data. In the U.S., this is simple. Data from geographic information systems provides population, age, purchasing power, traffic counts, and competition on virtually every block in the country. Planners instantly see all the surrounding shops, proposed locations, and competing sites. When Starbucks entered Japan and China, the unavailability of these data was the biggest challenge.

"In the U.S., if you see a mall, it will probably still be there in two years," says Ernest Luk, VP for Starbucks Asia–Pacific. "A year passes by in a Chinese location, and you almost won't know your way around there anymore." So a team of "hot-spot" seekers traces the paths of where potential customers live, work, and play. Although Starbucks is a barely affordable luxury (at $2.65 for a medium latte where the average income is $143 per month in Shanghai), people don't go for just the coffee. "They go there to present themselves as modern Chinese in a public setting. Chinese are proudly conspicuous," says the North Asia director of the ad firm J. Walter Thompson.

With more than 500 stores in Japan and reaching saturation in key cities like Tokyo, Starbucks and its competition are finding more innovative locations. New cafes in a Nissan auto showroom, in office building lobbies, and in supermarkets remind us that it all boils down to location, location, location . . . determined by the latest site-selection technology.

Sources: The Wall Street Journal (April 3, 2007): B1 and (February 14, 2001): B1, B4; and SinoCast China Business Daily News (September 21, 2005): 1.

Realistic analysis of these factors can provide a reasonable picture of the revenue expected. The techniques used in the service sector include correlation analysis, traffic counts, demographic analysis, purchasing power analysis, the factor-rating method, the center-of-gravity method, and geographic information systems. Table 8.6 provides a summary of location strategies for both service and goods-producing organizations.

How Hotel Chains Select Sites

One of the most important decisions in the hospitality industry is location. Hotel chains that pick good sites more accurately and quickly than competitors have a distinct strategic advantage. La Quinta Corporation is a moderately priced chain of 590 motels oriented toward frequent business travelers. To model motel-selection behavior and predict success of a site, La Quinta turned to statistical regression analysis.[5]

▲ *Picking good sites for service operations such as fast-food restaurants and hotels is increasingly harder because of saturated markets. But opportunities still exist. Subway (on the left), with over 20,000 U.S. outlets (vs. 13,700 for McDonald's) has found success with "nontraditional" locations. True Bethel Baptist Church in Buffalo, New York, now houses a Subway. Similarly, a kosher Subway just opened in the Jewish Community Center of Cleveland. Good sites for hotels include those near hospitals and medical centers (right photo). Outpatient care, shorter hospital stays, and more diagnostic tests increase this need to house patients and their families.*

[5]Sheryl Kimes and James Fitzsimmons, "Selecting Profitable Hotel Sites at La Quinta Motor Inns," *Interfaces* (March–April 1990): 12–20. Also see *The Wall Street Journal* (July 19, 1995): B1, B5, for a discussion of how Amerihost Inns makes its location decisions.

▶ **Table 8.6**

**Location Strategies—
Service vs. Goods-
Producing Organizations**

Service/Retail/Professional Location	Goods-Producing Location
Revenue Focus	**Cost Focus**

Volume/revenue
   Drawing area; purchasing power
   Competition; advertising/pricing
 	
 Physical quality
   Parking/access; security/lighting;
     appearance/image
 	
 Cost determinants
   Rent
   Management caliber
   Operation policies (hours, wage rates)
	Tangible costs
	   Transportation cost of raw material
	   Shipment cost of finished goods
	   Energy and utility cost; labor; raw material;
	     taxes, and so on
	
	 Intangible and future costs
	   Attitude toward union
	   Quality of life
	   Education expenditures by state
	   Quality of state and local government

Techniques	**Techniques**
Regression models to determine importance of various factors Factor-rating method Traffic counts Demographic analysis of drawing area Purchasing power analysis of area Center-of-gravity method Geographic information systems	Transportation method Factor-rating method Locational break-even analysis Crossover charts
Assumptions	**Assumptions**

Location is a major determinant of revenue
 High customer-contact issues are critical
 Costs are relatively constant for a given area;
   therefore, the revenue function is critical
	Location is a major determinant of cost
	 Most major costs can be identified explicitly
	   for each site
	 Low customer contact allows focus on the
	   identifiable costs
	 Intangible costs can be evaluated

The hotel started by testing 35 independent variables, trying to find which of them would have the highest correlation with predicted profitability, the dependent variable. "Competitive" independent variables included the number of hotel rooms in the vicinity and average room rates. "Demand generator" variables were such local attractions as office buildings and hospitals that drew potential customers to a 4-mile-radius trade area. "Demographic" variables, such as local population and unemployment rate, can also affect the success of a hotel. "Market awareness" factors, such as the number of inns in a region, were a fourth category. Finally, "physical characteristics" of the site, such as ease of access or sign visibility, provided the last group of the 35 independent variables.

In the end, the regression model chosen, with a coefficient of determination (r^2) of 51%, included just four predictive variables. They are the *price of the inn*, *median income levels*, the *state population per inn*, and the *location of nearby colleges* (which serves as a proxy for other demand generators). La Quinta then used the regression model to predict profitability and developed a cutoff that gave the best results for predicting success or failure of a site. A spreadsheet is now used to implement the model, which applies the decision rule and suggests "build" or "don't build."

The Call Center Industry

Industries and office activities that require neither face-to-face contact with the customer nor movement of material broaden location options substantially. A case in point is the call center industry, in which the traditional variables (as noted earlier) are no longer relevant. Where inexpensive fiber-optic phone lines are available, the cost and availability of labor may drive the location decision.

A decade or so ago, big U.S. companies starting hiring call center staff in low-wage countries like India to deal with customer contact jobs, such as product support, hotel reservations, and bill collection. India's highly educated, English-speaking workforce still attracts a large call center business. But the Philippines, Mexico, Canada, Ireland, and small-town U.S. are increasingly destinations of choice for matching employees and in-depth knowledge of American popular culture. The VP of Client–Logic, Inc., a firm that sets up call centers for companies such as DIRECTV, Sony, and TiVo, says "I'm looking for people who already know that Barbie's boyfriend is Ken." He increasingly likes Monterrey, Mexico, because the town's mall has an American-style 13-screen Cineplex, which shows almost all Hollywood films—meaning locals pick up U.S. slang, fashion trends, brands, and geography.[6]

How to use quantitative techniques to locate call centers is discussed in detail in Supplement 11.

Geographic Information Systems

Geographic information systems are an important tool to help firms make successful, analytical decisions with regard to location. A **geographic information system (GIS)** stores and displays information that can be linked to a geographical location. For instance, retailers, banks, food chains, gas stations, and print shop franchises can all use geographically coded files from a GIS to conduct demographic analyses. By combining population, age, income, traffic flow, and density figures with geography, a retailer can pinpoint the best location for a new store or restaurant.

Here are some of the geographic databases available in many GISs:

- Census data by block, tract, city, county, congressional district, metropolitan area, state, zip code
- Maps of every street, highway, bridge, and tunnel in the U.S.
- Utilities such as electrical, water, and gas lines
- All rivers, mountains, lakes, forests
- All major airports, colleges, hospitals

For example, airlines use GISs to identify airports where ground services are the most effective. This information is then used to help schedule and to decide where to purchase fuel, meals, and other services.

Commercial office building developers use GISs in the selection of cities for future construction. Building new office space takes several years so developers value the database approach that a GIS can offer. GIS is used to analyze factors that influence the location decisions by addressing five elements for each city: (1) residential areas, (2) retail shops, (3) cultural and entertainment centers, (4) crime incidence, and (5) transportation options. For example, one study of Tampa, Florida, showed that the city's central business district lacks the characteristics to sustain a viable high-demand office market, suggesting that builders should look elsewhere.

Geographic information system (GIS)

A system that stores and displays information that can be linked to a geographic location.

◄ *Geographic information systems (GISs) are used by a variety of firms, including Darden Restaurants, to identify target markets by income, ethnicity, product use, age, etc. Here, data from MapInfo helps with competitive analysis. Three concentric blue rings, each representing various mile radii, were drawn around the competitor's store. The heavy red line indicates the "drive" time to the firm's own central store (the red dot).*

---

[6]"Siting a Call Center? Check Out the Mall First." *The Wall Street Journal* (July 3, 2006): B1, B3.

Here are four more examples of how location-scouting GIS software is turning commercial real estate into a science[7]:

- *Carvel Ice Cream:* This 73-year-old chain of ice cream shops uses GIS to create a demographic profile of what a typically successful neighborhood for a Carvel looks like—mostly in terms of income and ages.
- *Arby's:* As this fast-food chain learned, specific products can affect behavior. Using MapInfo, Arby's discovered that diners drove up to 20% farther for their roast beef sandwich (which they consider a "destination" product) than for its chicken sandwich.
- *Home Depot:* Wanting a store in New York City, even though Home Depot demographics are usually for customers who own big homes, the company opened in Queens when GIS software predicted it would do well. Although most people there live in apartments and very small homes, the store has become one of the chain's highest-volume outlets. Similarly, Home Depot thought it had saturated Atlanta two decades ago, but GIS analysis suggested expansion. There are now over 40 Home Depots in that area.
- *Jo-Ann Stores:* This fabric and craft retailer's 70 superstores were doing well a few years ago, but managers were afraid more big-box stores could not justify building expenses. So Jo-Ann used its GIS to create an ideal customer profile—female homeowners with families—and mapped it against demographics. The firm found it could build 700 superstores, which in turn increased the sales from $105 to $150 per square foot.

Other packages similar to MapInfo are Hemisphere Solutions (by Unisys Corp.), Atlas GIS (from Strategic Mapping, Inc.), Arc/Info (by ESRI), SAS/GIS (by SAS Institute, Inc.), Market Base (by National Decision Systems, Inc.), and MapPoint 2006 (by Microsoft).

To illustrate how extensive some of these GISs can be, consider Microsoft's MapPoint 2006, which includes a comprehensive set of map and demographic data. Its North American maps have more than 5.9 million miles of streets and 1.8 million points of interest to allow users to locate restaurants, airports, hotels, gas stations, ATMs, museums, campgrounds, and freeway exits. Demographic data includes statistics for population, age, income, education, and housing for 1980, 1990, 2000, and 2005. These data can be mapped by state, county, city, zip code, or census tract. MapPoint 2006 produces maps that identify business trends; pinpoint market graphics; locate clients, customers, and competitors; and visualize sales performance and product distribution. The European version of MapPoint includes 4.2 million kilometers of roads as well as 400,000 points of interest.[8]

 Video 8.2

Locating the Next Red Lobster Restaurant

The Video Case Study "Locating the Next Red Lobster Restaurant" that appears at the end of this chapter describes how that chain uses its GIS to define trade areas based on market size and population density.

Summary

Location may determine up to 10% of the total cost of an industrial firm. Location is also a critical element in determining revenue for the service, retail, or professional firm. Industrial firms need to consider both tangible and intangible costs. Industrial location problems are typically addressed via a factor-rating method, locational break-even analysis, the center-of-gravity method, and the transportation method of linear programming.

For service, retail, and professional organizations, analysis is typically made of a variety of variables including purchasing power of a drawing area, competition, advertising and promotion, physical qualities of the location, and operating policies of the organization.

Key Terms

Tangible costs *(p. 321)*
Intangible costs *(p. 321)*
Clustering *(p. 322)*

Factor-rating method *(p. 323)*
Locational break-even analysis *(p. 324)*
Center-of-gravity method *(p. 326)*

Transportation model *(p. 328)*
Graphical information system (GIS) *(p. 331)*

---

[7]"Location, Location, Technology," *The Wall Street Journal* (July 18, 2005): R-7; and "Is Your Business in the Right Spot?" *Business 2.0* (May 2004): 76–77.
[8]*Source:* **www.mapapps.net**.

Using Software to Solve Location Problems

This section presents three ways to solve location problems with computer software. First, you can create your own spreadsheets to compute factor ratings, the center of gravity, and break-even analysis. Second, Excel OM (free with your text and found in the student CD) is programmed to solve all three models. Third, POM for Windows is also found on your CD and can solve all problems labelled with a **P**.

Creating Your Own Excel Spreadsheets

Excel (and other spreadsheets) are easily developed to solve most of the problems in this chapter. We do not provide an example here, but you can see from Program 8.1 how the formulas are created.

✕ Using Excel OM

Excel OM may be used to solve Example 1 (with the Factor Rating module), Example 2 (with the Break-Even Analysis module), and Example 3 (with the Center of Gravity module), as well as other location problems. To illustrate the factor-rating method, consider the case of Five Flags over Florida (Example 1), which wishes to expand its corporate presence to Europe. Program 8.1 provides the data inputs for five important factors, including their weights, and ratings on a 1–100 scale (where 100 is the highest rating) for each country. As we see, France is more highly rated, with a 70.4 score versus 68.0 for Denmark.

P Using POM for Windows

POM for Windows also includes three different facility location models: the factor-rating method, the center-of-gravity model, and locational break-even analysis. For details, refer to Appendix IV.

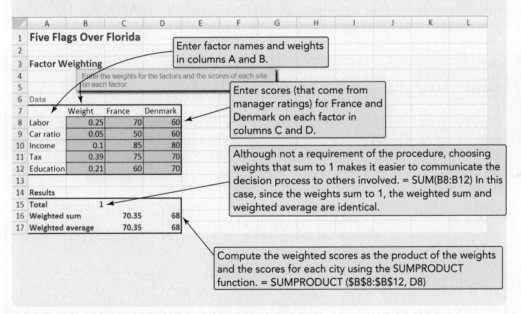

◀ **Program 8.1**

Excel OM's Factor Rating Module, Including Inputs, Selected Formulas, and Outputs Using Five Flags over Florida Data in Example 1

Solved Problems

 Virtual Office Hours help is available on Student DVD.

Solved Problem 8.1

Just as cities and communities can be compared for location selection by the weighted approach model, as we saw earlier in this chapter, so can actual site decisions within those cities. Table 8.7 (on the next page) illustrates four factors of importance to Washington, DC, and the health officials charged with opening that city's first public drug treatment clinic. Of primary concern (and given a weight of 5) was location of the clinic so it would be as accessible as possible to the largest number of patients. Due to a tight budget, the annual lease cost was also of some concern. A suite in the new city hall, at 14th and U Streets, was highly rated because its rent would be free. An old office building near the downtown bus station received a much lower rating because of its cost. Equally important as lease

cost was the need for confidentiality of patients and, therefore, for a relatively inconspicuous clinic. Finally, because so many of the staff at the clinic would be donating their time, the safety, parking, and accessibility of each site were of concern as well.

Using the factor-rating method, which site is preferred?

Solution

From the three rightmost columns in Table 8.7, the weighted scores are summed. The bus terminal area has a low score and can be excluded from further consideration. The other two sites are virtually identical in total score. The city may now want to consider other factors, including political ones, in selecting between the two remaining sites.

▼ **Table 8.7** Potential Clinic Sites in Washington, DC

		Potential Locations[a]			Weighted Scores		
Factor	Importance Weight	Homeless Shelter (2nd and D, SE)	City Hall (14th and U, NW)	Bus Terminal Area (7th and H, NW)	Homeless Shelter	City Hall	Bus Terminal Area
Accessibility for addicts	5	9	7	7	45	35	35
Annual lease cost	3	6	10	3	18	30	9
Inconspicuous	3	5	2	7	15	6	21
Accessibility for health staff	2	3	6	2	6	12	4
				Total scores:	84	83	69

[a]All sites are rated on a 1 to 10 basis, with 10 as the highest score and 1 as the lowest.

Source: From *Service Management and Operations*, 2/e, by Haksever/Render/Russell/Murdick, p. 266. Copyright © 2000. Reprinted by permission of Prentice Hall, Inc., Upper Saddle River, NJ.

Solved Problem 8.2

Ching-Chang Kau is considering opening a new foundry in Denton, Texas; Edwardsville, Illinois; or Fayetteville, Arkansas, to produce high-quality rifle sights. He has assembled the following fixed-cost and variable-cost data:

		Per-Unit Costs		
Location	Fixed Cost per Year	Material	Variable Labor	Overhead
Denton	$200,000	$ .20	$ .40	$ .40
Edwardsville	$180,000	$ .25	$ .75	$ .75
Fayetteville	$170,000	$1.00	$1.00	$1.00

a) Graph the total cost lines.
b) Over what range of annual volume is each facility going to have a competitive advantage?
c) What is the volume at the intersection of the Edwardsville and Fayetteville cost lines?

solution

(a) A graph of the total cost lines is shown in Figure 8.5.

(b) Below 8,000 units, the Fayetteville facility will have a competitive advantage (lowest cost); between 8,000 units and 26,666 units, Edwardsville has an advantage; and above 26,666, Denton has the advantage. (We have made the assumption in this problem that other costs—that is, delivery and intangible factors—are constant regardless of the decision.)

(c) From Figure 8.5, we see that the cost line for Fayetteville and the cost line for Edwardsville cross at about 8,000. We can also determine this point with a little algebra:

$$\$180,000 + 1.75Q = \$170,000 + 3.00Q$$
$$\$10,000 = 1.25Q$$
$$8,000 = Q$$

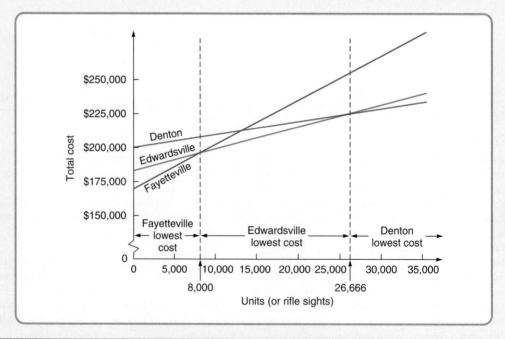

► **Figure 8.5**

Graph of Total Cost Lines for Ching-Chang Kau

Self-Test

- ***Before taking the self-test***, *refer to the learning objectives listed at the beginning of the chapter and the key terms listed at the end of the chapter.*
- *Use the key at the back of the text to **correct** your answers.*
- ***Restudy*** *pages that correspond to any questions you answered incorrectly or material you feel uncertain about.*

1. Which of the following methods best considers intangible costs related to a location decision?
  a) weighted methods like factor rating
  b) locational break-even analysis
  c) transportation method
  d) assignment method

2. What is the major difference in focus between location decisions in the service sector and in the manufacturing sector?
  a) there is no difference in focus
  b) the focus in manufacturing is revenue maximization, while the focus in service is cost minimization
  c) the focus in service is revenue maximization, while the focus in manufacturing is cost minimization
  d) the focus in manufacturing is on raw materials, while the focus in service is on labor

3. Service/retail/professional locational analysis typically has:
  a) a cost focus
  b) a revenue focus
  c) a labor focus
  d) an environmental focus

4. The factors involved in location decisions include:
  a) foreign exchange
  b) attitudes
  c) labor productivity
  d) all of the above

5. Industrial locational analysis typically has:
  a) a cost focus
  b) a revenue focus
  c) a labor focus
  d) an environmental focus

6. The major types of methods used to solve location problems are:
  a) _____
  b) _____
  c) _____
  d) _____

7. The call center industry seeks locations that have:
  a) good electronic movement of data
  b) low cost labor
  c) adequate availability of labor
  d) all of the above

8. Factors affecting location decisions include:
  a) proximity to markets and suppliers
  b) labor productivity
  c) average age of labor force, labor costs
  d) political risk, values, and culture
  e) all of the above

Active Model Exercise

This active model appears on your CD-ROM. It allows you to evaluate important elements in a center-of-gravity model.

Center of Gravity

City	Number of containers shipped per month	X coord	Y coord	Total weighted distance to this city	Total weighted distance to trial location
Chicago	2000	30	120	332,206	90,676
Pittsburgh	1000	90	110	318,692	28,674
New York	1000	130	130	473,754	73,182
Atlanta	2000	60	40	361,055	107,497
Sum of Total Wtd Distances to Trial Location					300,029

	X coord	Y coord
Trial Location	67	93

	X coord	Y coord
Center of Gravity	67	93
Total Weighted Distance to Center of Gravity	300,029	

◄ **Active Model 8.1**

Center-of-Gravity Model Using Quain's Department Store Data in Example 3.

Questions

1. What is the total weighted distance from their current old and inadequate warehouse in Pittsburgh?

2. If they relocate their warehouse to the center of gravity, by how much will this reduce the total weighted shipping distance?

3. Observe the graph. If the number of shipments from New York doubles, how does this affect the center of gravity?

4. The center of gravity does not necessarily find the site with the minimum total weighted distance. Use the scrollbars to move the trial location and see if you can improve (lower) the distance.

5. If you have Solver set up in Excel, from Excel's main menu use Tools, Solver, Solve to see the best answer to the previous question.

Internet and Student CD-ROM/DVD Exercises

Visit our Companion Web site or use your student CD-ROM/DVD to help with material in this chapter.

 On Our Companion Web Site,
www.prenhall.com/heizer
- Self-Study Quizzes
- Practice Problems
- Virtual Company Tour
- Internet Cases
- PowerPoint Lecture

 On Your Student CD-ROM
- Practice Problems
- Excel OM
- Excel OM Data Files
- Active Model Exercise
- POM for Windows

 On Your Student DVD
- Video Cases and Video Clips
- Virtual Office Hours for Solved Problems

Discussion Questions

1. How is FedEx's location a competitive advantage? Discuss.
2. Why do so many U.S. firms build facilities in other countries?
3. Why do so many foreign companies build facilities in the U.S.?
4. What is clustering?
5. How does factor weighting incorporate personal preference in location choices?
6. What are the advantages and disadvantages of a qualitative (as opposed to a quantitative) approach to location decision making?
7. Provide two examples of clustering in the service sector.
8. What are the major factors that firms consider when choosing a country in which to locate?
9. What factors affect region/community location decisions?
10. Although most organizations may make the location decision infrequently, there are some organizations that make the decision quite regularly and often. Provide one or two examples. How might their approach to the location decision differ from the norm?
11. List those factors, other than globalization, that affect the location decision.

12. Explain the assumptions behind the center-of-gravity method. How can the model be used in a service facility location?
13. What are the three steps to locational break-even analysis?
14. "Manufacturers locate near their resources, retailers locate near their customers." Discuss this statement, with reference to the proximity-to-markets arguments covered in the text. Can you think of a counterexample in each case? Support your choices.
15. Why shouldn't low wage rates alone be sufficient to select a location?
16. List the techniques used by service organizations to select locations.
17. Contrast the location of a food distributor and a supermarket. (The distributor sends truckloads of food, meat, produce, etc., to the supermarket.) Show the relevant considerations (factors) they share; show those where they differ.
18. Elmer's Fudge Factory is planning to open 10 retail outlets in Oregon over the next 2 years. Identify (and weight) those factors relevant to the decision. Provide this list of factors and weights.

Ethical Dilemma

In this chapter, we have discussed a number of location decisions. Consider another: United Airlines announced its competition to select a town for a new billion-dollar aircraft-repair base. The bidding for the prize of 7,500 jobs paying at least $25 per hour was fast and furious, with Orlando offering $154 million in incentives and Denver more than twice that amount. Kentucky's

governor angrily rescinded Louisville's offer of $300 million, likening the bidding to "squeezing every drop of blood out of a turnip."

When United finally selected from among the 93 cities bidding on the base, the winner was Indianapolis and its $320 million offer of taxpayers' money.

But in 2003, with United near bankruptcy, and having fulfilled its legal obligation, the company walked away from the massive center. This left the city and state governments out all that money, with no new tenant in sight. The city now even owns the tools, neatly arranged in each of the 12 elaborately equipped hangar bays. United outsourced its maintenance to mechanics at a Southern firm (which pays one-third of what United gave out in salary and benefits in Indianapolis).

What are the ethical, legal, and economic implications of such location bidding wars? Who pays for such giveaways? Are local citizens allowed to vote on offers made by their cities, counties, or states? Should there be limits on these incentives?

Problems*

• **8.1** In Cambodia, six laborers, each making the equivalent of $3 per day, can produce 40 units per day. In China, 10 laborers, each making the equivalent of $2 per day, can produce 45 units. In Billings, Montana, two laborers, each making $60 per day, can make 100 units. Based on labor costs only, which location would be most economical to produce the item?

• **8.2** Refer to Problem 8.1. Shipping cost from Cambodia to Denver, Colorado, the final destination, is $1.50 per unit. Shipping cost from China to Denver is $1 per unit, while the shipping cost from Billings to Denver is $.25 per unit. Considering both labor and transportation costs, which is the most favorable production location?

•• **8.3** You have been asked to analyze the bids for 200 polished disks used in solar panels. These bids have been submitted by three suppliers: Thailand Polishing, India Shine, and Sacramento Glow. Thailand Polishing has submitted a bid of 2,000 baht. India Shine has submitted a bid of 2,000 rupee. Sacramento Glow has submitted a bid of $200. You check with your local bank and find that $1 = 10 baht and $1 = 8 rupee. Which company should you choose?

• **8.4** Refer to Problem 8.3. If the final destination is New Delhi, India, and there is a 30% import tax, which firm should you choose?

•• **8.5** Subway, with more than 20,000 outlets in the U.S., is planning for a new restaurant in Buffalo, New York. Three locations are being considered. The following table gives the factors for each site. At which site should Subway open the new restaurant?

Factor	Weight	Maitland	Baptist Church	Northside Mall
Space	.30	60	70	80
Costs	.25	40	80	30
Traffic density	.20	50	80	60
Neighborhood income	.15	50	70	40
Zoning laws	.10	80	20	90 PX

• **8.6** Gayla Delong owns the Oklahoma Warriors, a minor league baseball team in northwest Oklahoma. She wishes to move the Warriors east, to either Atlanta or Charlotte. The table below

Factor	Weight	Atlanta	Charlotte
Incentive	.4	80	60
Player satisfaction	.3	20	50
Sports interest	.2	40	90
Size of city	.1	70	30 PX

*Note: PX means the problem may be solved with POM for Windows and/or Excel OM.

gives the factors that Gayla thinks are important, their weights, and the scores for Atlanta and Charlotte. Which site should she select?

•• **8.7** Insurance Company of Latin America (ILA) is considering opening an office in the U.S. The two cities under consideration are Philadelphia and New York. The factor ratings (higher scores are better) for the two cities are given in the following table. In which city should ILA locate?

Factor	Weight	Philadelphia	New York
Customer convenience	.25	70	80
Bank accessibility	.20	40	90
Computer support	.20	85	75
Rental costs	.15	90	55
Labor costs	.10	80	50
Taxes	.10	90	50 PX

•• **8.8** Marilyn Helm Retailers is attempting to decide on a location for a new retail outlet. At the moment, the firm has three alternatives—stay where it is but enlarge the facility; locate along the main street in nearby Newbury; or locate in a new shopping mall in Hyde Park. The company has selected the four factors listed in the following table as the basis for evaluation and has assigned weights as shown:

Factor	Factor Description	Weight
1	Average community income	.30
2	Community growth potential	.15
3	Availability of public transportation	.20
4	Labor availability, attitude, and cost	.35

Helm has rated each location for each factor, on a 100-point basis. These ratings are given below:

	Location		
Factor	Present Location	Newbury	Hyde Park
1	40	60	50
2	20	20	80
3	30	60	50
4	80	50	50 Px

•• **8.9** A location analysis for Temponi Controls, a small manufacturer of parts for high-technology cable systems, has been narrowed down to four locations. Temponi will need to train assemblers, testers, and robotics maintainers in local training centers. Cecilia Temponi, the president, has asked each potential site to offer training programs, tax breaks, and other industrial incentives. The critical factors, their weights, and the ratings for each location are shown in the following table. High scores represent favorable values.

		Location			
Factor	Weight	Akron, OH	Biloxi, MS	Carthage, TX	Denver, CO
Labor availability	.15	90	80	90	80
Technical school quality	.10	95	75	65	85
Operating cost	.30	80	85	95	85
Land and construction cost	.15	60	80	90	70
Industrial incentives	.20	90	75	85	60
Labor cost	.10	75	80	85	75

a) Compute the composite (weighted average) rating for each location.
b) Which site would you choose?
c) Would you reach the same conclusion if the weights for operating cost and labor cost were reversed? Recompute as necessary and explain. Px

• **8.10** Consolidated Refineries, headquartered in Houston, must decide among three sites for the construction of a new oil-processing center. The firm has selected the six factors listed below as a basis for evaluation and has assigned rating weights from 1 to 5 on each factor:

Factor	Factor Name	Rating Weight
1	Proximity to port facilities	5
2	Power-source availability and cost	3
3	Workforce attitude and cost	4
4	Distance from Houston	2
5	Community desirability	2
6	Equipment suppliers in area	3

Management has rated each location for each factor on a 1 to 100 point basis.

Factor	Location A	Location B	Location C
1	100	80	80
2	80	70	100
3	30	60	70
4	10	80	60
5	90	60	80
6	50	60	90

Which site will be recommended? Px

•• **8.11** A company is planning on expanding and building a new plant in one of three Southeast Asian countries. David Pentico, the manager charged with making the decision, has determined that five critical success factors (CSFs) can be used to evaluate the prospective countries. Pentico used a rating system of 1 (least desirable country) to 5 (most desirable) to evaluate each CSF. Which country should be selected for the new plant?

Critical Success Factors		Candidate Country Ratings		
	Weight	Taiwan	Thailand	Singapore
Technology	0.2	4	5	1
Level of education	0.1	4	1	5
Political and legal aspects	0.4	1	3	3
Social and cultural aspects	0.1	4	2	3
Economic factors	0.2	3	3	2 Px

• **8.12** Thomas Green College is contemplating opening a European campus where students from the main campus could go to take courses for 1 of the 4 college years. At the moment, it is considering five countries: Holland, Great Britain, Italy, Belgium, and Greece. The college wishes to consider eight factors in its decision. All the factors have equal weight. The following table illustrates its assessment of each factor for each country (5 is best).

Factor	Factor Description	Holland	Great Britain	Italy	Belgium	Greece
1	Stability of government	5	5	3	5	4
2	Degree to which the population can converse in English	4	5	3	4	3
3	Stability of the monetary system	5	4	3	4	3
4	Communications infrastructure	4	5	3	4	3
5	Transportation infrastructure	5	5	3	5	3
6	Availability of historic/cultural sites	3	4	5	3	5
7	Import restrictions	4	4	3	4	4
8	Availability of suitable quarters	4	4	3	4	3

a) In which country should Thomas Green College choose to set up its European campus?
b) How would the decision change if the "degree to which the population can converse in English" were not an issue? **Px**

• **8.13** Daniel Tracy, owner of Martin Manufacturing, must expand by building a new factory. The search for a location for this factory has been narrowed to four sites: A, B, C, or D. The following table shows the results thus far obtained by Tracy by using the factor-rating method to analyze the problem. The scale used for each factor scoring is 1 through 5.

Factor	Weight	Site Scores			
		A	B	C	D
Quality of Labor	10	5	4	4	5
Construction Cost	8	2	3	4	1
Transportation Costs	8	3	4	3	2
Proximity to Markets	7	5	3	4	4
Taxes	6	2	3	3	4
Weather	6	2	5	5	4
Energy Costs	5	5	4	3	3

Which site should Tracy choose? **Px**

•• **8.14** An American consulting firm is planning to expand globally by opening a new office in one of four countries: Germany, Italy, Spain, or Greece. The chief partner entrusted with the decision, L. Wayne Shell, has identified eight critical success factors (CSFs) that he views as essential for the success of any consultancy. He used a rating system of 1 (least desirable country) to 5 (most desirable) to evaluate each CSF. Which country should be selected for the new office?

Critical Success Factors	Candidate Country Ratings			
	Weight	Germany	Italy	Spain	Greece
Level of education					
Number of consultants	.05	5	5	5	2
National literacy rate	.05	4	2	1	1
Political aspects					
Stability of government	0.2	5	5	5	2
Product liability laws	0.2	5	2	3	5
Environmental regulations	0.2	1	4	1	3
Social and cultural aspects					
Similarity in language	0.1	4	2	1	1
Acceptability of consultants	0.1	1	4	4	3
Economic factors					
Incentives	0.1	2	3	1	5 **Px**

•• **8.15** A British hospital chain wishes to make its first entry into the U.S. market by building a medical facility in the Midwest, a region with which its director, Doug Moodie, is comfortable because he got his medical degree at Northwestern University. After a preliminary analysis, four cities are chosen for further consideration. They are rated and weighted according to the factors shown at top of next column:

Factor		City			
	Weight	Chicago	Milwaukee	Madison	Detroit
Costs	2.0	8	5	6	7
Need for a facility	1.5	4	9	8	4
Staff availability	1.0	7	6	4	7
Local incentives	0.5	8	6	5	9

a) Which city should Moodie select?
b) Assume a minimum unweighted score of 5 is now required for all factors. Which city should be chosen? **Px**

•• **8.16** The fixed and variable costs for three potential manufacturing plant sites for a rattan chair weaver are shown:

Site	Fixed Cost per Year	Variable Cost per Unit
1	$ 500	$11
2	1,000	7
3	1,700	4

a) Over what range of production is each location optimal?
b) For a production of 200 units, which site is best? **Px**

• **8.17** Peter Billington Stereo, Inc., supplies car radios to auto manufacturers and is going to open a new plant. The company is undecided between Detroit and Dallas as the site. The fixed costs in Dallas are lower due to cheaper land costs, but the variable costs in Dallas are higher because shipping distances would increase. Given the following costs, perform an analysis of the volume over which each location is preferable:

	Dallas	Detroit
Fixed costs	$600,000	$800,000
Variable costs	$28/radio	$22/radio **Px**

••• **8.18** Audi Motors is considering three sites—A, B, and C—at which to locate a factory to build its new-model automobile, the Audi SUV XL500. The goal is to locate at a minimum-cost site, where cost is measured by the annual fixed plus variable costs of production. Audi Motors has gathered the following data:

Site	Annualized Fixed Cost	Variable Cost per Auto Produced
A	$10,000,000	$2,500
B	$20,000,000	$2,000
C	$25,000,000	$1,000

The firm knows it will produce between 0 and 60,000 SUV XL500s at the new plant each year, but, thus far, that is the extent of its knowledge about production plans. For what values of volume, V, of production, if any, is site C a recommended site? **Px**

•• **8.19** Hugh Leach Corp., a producer of machine tools, wants to move to a larger site. Two alternative locations have been identified: Bonham and McKinney. Bonham would have fixed costs of $800,000 per year and variable costs of $14,000 per standard unit produced. McKinney would have annual fixed costs of $920,000 and variable costs of $13,000 per standard unit. The finished items sell for $29,000 each.

a) At what volume of output would the two locations have the same profit?
b) For what range of output would Bonham be superior (have higher profits)?
c) For what range would McKinney be superior?
d) What is the relevance of break-even points for these cities? **Px**

•• **8.20** The following table gives the map coordinates and the shipping loads for a set of cities that we wish to connect through a central hub. Near which map coordinates should the hub be located?

City	Map Coordinate (x, y)	Shipping Load
A	(5, 10)	5
B	(6, 8)	10
C	(4, 9)	15
D	(9, 5)	5
E	(7, 9)	15
F	(3, 2)	10
G	(2, 6)	5 **Px**

•• **8.21** A chain of home health care firms in Louisiana needs to locate a central office from which to conduct internal audits and other periodic reviews of its facilities. These facilities are scattered throughout the state, as detailed in the following table. Each site, except for Houma, will be visited three times each year by a team of workers, who will drive from the central office to the site. Houma will be visited five times a year. Which coordinates represent a good central location for this office? What other factors might influence the office location decision? Where would you place this office? Explain.

City	Map Coordinates X	Map Coordinates Y
Covington	9.2	3.5
Donaldsonville	7.3	2.5
Houma	7.8	1.4
Monroe	5.0	8.4
Natchitoches	2.8	6.5
New Iberia	5.5	2.4
Opelousas	5.0	3.6
Ruston	3.8	8.5 **Px**

•• **8.22** A small rural county has experienced unprecedented growth over the past 6 years, and as a result, the local school district built the new 500-student North Park Elementary School. The district has three older and smaller elementary schools: Washington, Jefferson, and Lincoln. Now the growth pressure is being felt at the secondary level. The school district would like to build a centrally located middle school to accommodate students and reduce busing costs. The older middle school is adjacent to the high school and will become part of the high school campus.

a) What are the coordinates of the central location?

b) What other factors should be considered before building a school? **Px**

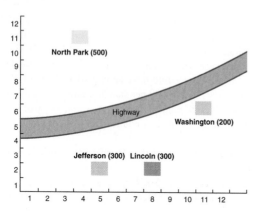

•• **8.23** Todd's Video, a major video rental and TV sales chain headquartered in New Orleans, is about to open its first outlet in Mobile, Alabama, and wants to select a site that will place the new outlet in the center of Mobile's population base. Todd examines the seven census tracts in Mobile, plots the coordinates of the center of each from a map, and looks up the population base in each to use as a weighting. The information gathered appears in the following table. At what center-of-gravity coordinates should the new store be located?

Census Tract	Population in Census Tract	X, Y Map Coordinates
101	2,000	(25, 45)
102	5,000	(25, 25)
103	10,000	(55, 45)
104	7,000	(50, 20)
105	10,000	(80, 50)
106	20,000	(70, 20)
107	14,000	(90, 25) **Px**

•••• **8.24** Eagle Electronics must expand by building a second facility. The search has been narrowed down to locating the new facility in one of four cities: Atlanta (A), Baltimore (B), Chicago (C), or Dallas (D). The factors, scores, and weights follow:

i	Factor	Weight (W_i)	Scores by Site A	B	C	D
1	Labor quality	20	5	4	4	5
2	Quality of life	16	2	3	4	1
3	Transportation	16	3	4	3	2
4	Proximity to markets	14	5	3	4	4
5	Proximity to suppliers	12	2	3	3	4
6	Taxes	12	2	5	5	4
7	Energy supplies	10	5	4	3	3

a) Using the factor-rating method, what is the recommended site for Eagle Electronics's new facility?

b) For what range of values for the weight (currently $w_7 = 10$) does the site given as the answer to part (a) remain a recommended site?

•••• **8.25** The unification of Europe has brought about changes in airline regulation that dramatically affect major European carriers such as British International Air, KLM, Air France, Alitalia, and Swiss. With ambitious expansion plans, British International Air (BIA) has decided it needs a second service hub on the continent, to

| | | | | Location | | | | | |
| | | Italy | | | France | | | Germany | |
Factor	Importance Weight	Milan	Rome	Genoa	Paris	Lyon	Nice	Munich	Bonn	Berlin
Financial incentives	85	8	8	8	7	7	7	7	7	7
Skilled labor pool	80	4	6	5	9	9	7	10	8	9
Existing facility	70	5	3	2	9	6	5	9	9	2
Wage rates	70	9	8	9	4	6	6	4	5	5
Competition for jobs	70	7	3	8	2	8	7	4	8	9
Ease of air traffic access	65	5	4	6	2	8	8	4	8	9
Real estate cost	40	6	4	7	4	6	6	3	4	5
Communication links	25	6	7	6	9	9	9	10	9	8
Attractiveness to relocating executives	15	4	8	3	9	6	6	2	3	3
Political considerations	10	6	6	6	8	8	8	8	8	8
Expansion possibilities	10	10	2	8	1	5	4	4	5	6
Union strength	10	1	1	1	5	5	5	6	6	6

complement its large Heathrow (London) repair facility. The location selection is critical, and with the potential for 4,000 new skilled blue-collar jobs on the line, virtually every city in Western Europe is actively bidding for BIA's business.

After initial investigations by Holmes Miller, head of the Operations Department, BIA has narrowed the list to 9 cities. Each is then rated on 12 factors, as shown in the table above.

a) Help Miller rank the top three cities that BIA should consider as its new site for servicing aircraft.

b) After further investigation, Miller decides that an existing set of hangar facilities for repairs is not nearly as important as earlier thought. If he lowers the weight of that factor to 30, does the ranking change?

c) After Miller makes the change in part (b), Germany announces it has reconsidered its offer of financial incentives, with an additional 200-million-euro package to entice BIA. Accordingly, BIA has raised Germany's rating to 10 on that factor. Is there any change in top rankings in part (b)? **Px**

Case Studies

Southern Recreational Vehicle Company

In October 2007, top management of Southern Recreational Vehicle Company of St. Louis, Missouri, announced its plans to relocate its manufacturing and assembly operations to a new plant in Ridgecrest, Mississippi. The firm, a major producer of pickup campers and camper trailers, had experienced 5 consecutive years of declining profits as a result of spiraling production costs. The costs of labor and raw materials had increased alarmingly, utility costs had gone up sharply, and taxes and transportation expenses had steadily climbed upward. In spite of increased sales, the company suffered its first net loss since operations were begun in 1982.

When management initially considered relocation, it closely scrutinized several geographic areas. Of primary importance to the relocation decision were the availability of adequate transportation facilities, state and municipal tax structures, an adequate labor supply, positive community attitudes, reasonable site costs, and financial inducements. Although several communities offered essentially the same incentives, the management of Southern Recreational Vehicle Company was favorably impressed by the efforts of the Mississippi Power and Light Company to attract "clean, labor-intensive" industry and the enthusiasm exhibited by state and local officials, who actively sought to bolster the state's economy by enticing manufacturing firms to locate within its boundaries.

Two weeks prior to the announcement, management of Southern Recreational Vehicle Company finalized its relocation plans. An existing building in Ridgecrest's industrial park was selected (the physical facility had previously housed a mobile home manufacturer that had gone bankrupt due to inadequate financing and poor management); initial recruiting was begun through the state employment office; and efforts to lease or sell the St. Louis property were initiated. Among the inducements offered Southern Recreational Vehicle Company to locate in Ridgecrest were:

1. Exemption from county and municipal taxes for 5 years
2. Free water and sewage services
3. Construction of a second loading dock—free of cost—at the industrial site
4. An agreement to issue $500,000 in industrial bonds for future expansion
5. Public-financed training of workers in a local industrial trade school

In addition to these inducements, other factors weighed heavily in the decision to locate in the small Mississippi town. Labor costs would be significantly less than those incurred in St. Louis; organized labor was not expected to be as powerful (Mississippi is a right-to-work state); and utility costs and taxes would be moderate. All in all, management of Southern Recreational Vehicle Company felt that its decision was sound.

On October 15, the following announcement was attached to each employee's paycheck:

To: Employees of Southern Recreational Vehicle Company

From: Gerald O'Brian, President

The Management of Southern Recreational Vehicle Company regretfully announces its plans to cease all manufacturing operations in St. Louis on December 31. Because of increased operating costs and the unreasonable demands forced upon the company by the union, it has become impossible to operate profitably. I sincerely appreciate the fine service that each of you has rendered to the company during the past years. If I can be of assistance in helping you find suitable employment with another firm, please let me know. Thank you again for your cooperation and past service.

Discussion Questions

1. Evaluate the inducements offered Southern Recreational Vehicle Company by community leaders in Ridgecrest, Mississippi.
2. What problems would a company experience in relocating its executives from a heavily populated industrialized area to a small rural town?
3. Evaluate the reasons cited by O'Brian for relocation. Are they justifiable?
4. What legal and ethical responsibilities does a firm have to its employees when a decision to cease operations is made?

Source: Reprinted by permission of Professor Jerry Kinard (Western Carolina University).

Locating the Next Red Lobster Restaurant

Video Case

From its first Red Lobster in 1968, Darden Restaurants has grown the chain to 648 locations, with over $2 billion in U.S. sales annually. The casual dining market may be crowded, with competitors such as Chili's, Ruby Tuesday, Applebee's, TGI Friday's, and Outback, but Darden's continuing success means the chain thinks there is still plenty of room to grow. Robert Reiner, director of market development, is charged with identifying the sites that will maximize new store sales without cannibalizing sales at the existing Red Lobster locations.

Characteristics for identifying a good site have not changed in 40 years; they still include real estate prices, customer age, competition, ethnicity, income, family size, population density, nearby hotels, and buying behavior, to name just a few. What *has* changed is the powerful software that allows Reiner to analyze a new site in 5 minutes, as opposed to the 8 hours he spent just a few years ago.

Darden has partnered with MapInfo Corp., whose geographic information system (GIS) contains a powerful module for analyzing a trade area (see the discussion of GIS in the chapter). With the U.S. geo-coded down to the individual block, MapInfo allows Reiner to create a psychographic profile of existing and potential Red Lobster trade areas. "We can now target areas with greatest sales potential," says Reiner.

The U.S. is segmented into 72 "clusters" of customer profiles by MapInfo. If, for example, cluster #7, Equestrian Heights (see MapInfo description in the next column), represents 1.7% of a household base within a Red Lobster trade area, but this segment also accounts for 2.4% of sales, Reiner computes that this segment is effectively spending 1.39 times more than average (Index = 2.4/1.7) and adjusts his analysis of a new site to reflect this added weight.

When Reiner maps the U.S., a state, or a region for a new site, he wants one that is at least 3 miles from the nearest Red Lobster and won't negatively impact its sales by more than 8%; MapInfo pinpoints the best spot. The software also recognizes the nearness of non-Darden competition and assigns a probability of success (as measured by reaching sales potential).

The specific spot selected depends on Darden's seven real estate brokers, whose list of considerations include proximity to a vibrant retail area, proximity to a freeway, road visibility, nearby hotels, and a corner location at a primary intersection.

"Picking a new Red Lobster location is one of the most critical functions we can do at Darden," says Reiner. "And the software we use serves as an independent voice in assessing the quality of an existing or proposed location."

Cluster	PSYTE 2003	Snap Shot Description
7	Equestrian Heights	They may not have a stallion in the barn, but they likely pass a corral on the way home. These families with teens live in older, larger homes adjacent to, or between, suburbs but not usually tract housing. Most are married with teenagers, but 40% are empty nesters. They use their graduate and professional school education—56% are dual earners. Over 90% are white, non-Hispanic. Their mean family income is $99,000, and they live within commuting distance of central cities. They have white-collar jobs during the week but require a riding lawn mower to keep the place up on weekends.

Discussion Questions*

1. Visit the Web site for MapInfo (**www.mapinfo.com**). Describe the psychological profiling (PSYTE) clustering system. Select an industry, other than restaurants, and explain how the software can be used for that industry.
2. What are the major differences in site location for a restaurant vs. a retail store vs. a manufacturing plant?
3. Red Lobster also defines its trade areas based on market size and population density. Here are its seven density classes:

Density Class	Description	Households per Sq. Mile
1	Super Urban	8,000+
2	Urban	4,000–7,999
3	Light Urban	2,000–3,999
4	First Tier Suburban	1,000–1,999
5	Second Tier Suburban	600–999
6	Exurban/Small	100–599
7	Rural	0–99

Note: Density classes are based on the households and land area within 3 miles of the geography (e.g., census tract) using population-weighted centroids.

Ninety-two percent of the Red Lobster restaurants fall into three of these classes. Which three classes do you think the chain has the most restaurants in? Why?

*You may wish to view this video case on your DVD before answering the questions.

Source: Professors Barry Render (Rollins College), Jay Heizer (Texas Lutheran University), and Beverly Amer (Northern Arizona University).

Where to Place the Hard Rock Cafe

Some people would say that Oliver Munday, Hard Rock's vice president for cafe development, has the best job in the world. Travel the world to pick a country for Hard Rock's next cafe, select a city, and find the ideal site. It's true that selecting a site involves lots of incognito walking around, visiting nice restaurants, and drinking in bars. But that is not where Mr. Munday's work begins, nor where it ends. At the front end, selecting the country and city first involves a great deal of research. At the back end, Munday not only picks the final site and negotiates the deal but then works with architects and planners and stays with the project through the opening and first year's sales.

Munday is currently looking heavily into global expansion in Europe, Latin America, and Asia. "We've got to look at political risk, currency, and social norms—how does our brand fit into the country," he says. Once the country is selected, Munday focuses on the region and city. His research checklist is extensive:

Hard Rock's Standard Market Report (for offshore sites)

A. Demographics (local, city, region, SMSA), with trend analysis
  1. Population of area
  2. Economic indicators
B. Visitor market, with trend analysis
  1. Tourists/business visitors
  2. Hotels
  3. Convention center
  4. Entertainment
  5. Sports
  6. Retail
C. Transportation
  1. Airport ←   subcategories include:
  2. Rail   (a) age of airport,
  3. Road   (b) no. of passengers,
  4. Sea/river   (c) airlines,
                   (d) direct flights,
                   (e) hubs
D. Restaurants and nightclubs (a selection in key target market areas)
E. Political risk
F. Real estate market
G. Hard Rock Cafe comparable market analysis

Site location now tends to focus on the tremendous resurgence of "city centers," where nightlife tends to concentrate. That's what Munday selected in Moscow and Bogota, although in both locations he chose to find a local partner and franchise the operation. In these two political environments, "Hard Rock wouldn't dream of operating by ourselves," says Munday. The location decision also is at least a 10- to 15-year commitment by Hard Rock, which employs tools such as break-even analysis to help decide whether to purchase land and build, or to remodel an existing facility.

Currently, Munday is considering four European cities for Hard Rock's next expansion. Although he could not provide the names, for competitive reasons, the following is known:

	European City under Consideration				Importance of This Factor at This Time
Factor	**A**	**B**	**C**	**D**	
A. Demographics	70	70	60	90	20
B. Visitor market	80	60	90	75	20
C. Transportation	100	50	75	90	20
D. Restaurants/ nightclubs	80	90	65	65	10
E. Low political risk	90	60	50	70	10
F. Real estate market	65	75	85	70	10
G. Comparable market analysis	70	60	65	80	10

Discussion Questions*

1. From Munday's Standard Market Report checklist, select any other four categories, such as population (A1), hotels (B2), or restaurants/nightclubs (D), and provide three subcategories that should be evaluated. (See item C1 (airport) for a guide.)
2. Which is the highest rated of the four European cities under consideration, using the table above?
3. Why does Hard Rock put such serious effort into its location analysis?
4. Under what conditions do you think Hard Rock prefers to franchise a cafe?

*You may wish to view this video case on your DVD before answering the questions.

Additional Case Studies

Internet case study: Visit our Companion Web site at **www.prenhall.com/heizer** *for this free case study:*

- **Southwestern University (E):** The university faces three choices in where to locate its football stadium.

Harvard has selected these Harvard Business School case studies to accompany this chapter of our text:

harvardbusinessonline.hbsp.harvard.edu

- **Filene's Basement** (#594-018): This retailer is trying to decide where to add two new stores in its Chicago operation.
- **To Move or Not to Move: Cathay Pacific Airlines** (#HKU-003): Should this airline relocate its data center from Hong Kong to a new country?
- **Wriston Manufacturing** (#698-049): An auto parts producer is trying to decide whether to close one of its Detroit plants.
- **Ellis Manufacturing** (#682-103): This kitchen appliance manufacturer has duplication of resources in its plants.

Bibliography

Ballou, Ronald H. *Business Logistics Management*, 5th ed. Upper Saddle River, NJ: Prentice Hall, 2004.

Bartness, A. D. "The Plant Location Puzzle." *Harvard Business Review* 72, no. 2 (March–April 1994).

Denton, B. "Decision Analysis, Location Models, and Scheduling Problems." *Interfaces* 30, no. 3 (May–June 2005): 262–263.

Drezner, Z. *Facility Location: Applications and Theory*, Berlin: Springer-Verlag, 2002.

Florida, R. *The Flight of the Creative Class: The New Global Competition for Talent*. New York: HarperCollins, 2005.

Francica, J. "Location, Location, Location." *Intelligent Enterprise* 9, no. 4 (April 2006): 37–40.

Klamroth, K. *Single Facility Location Problems*. Berlin: Springer-Verlag, 2002.

Kennedy, M. *Introducing Geographic Information Systems with ArcGIS*. New York: Wiley, 2006.

Partovi, F. Y. "An Analytic Model for Locating Facilities Strategically." *Omega* 34, no. 1 (January 2006): 41.

Porter, Michael E., and Scott Stern. "Innovation: Location Matters." *MIT Sloan Management Review* (summer 2001): 28–36.

Render, B., R. M. Stair, and M. Hanna. *Quantitative Analysis for Management*, 9th ed. Upper Saddle River, NJ: Prentice Hall, 2006.

Snyder, L. V. "Facility Location Under Uncertainty." *IIE Transactions* 38, no. 7 (July 2006): 547.

Tallman, Stephen, et al. "Knowledge, Clusters, and Competitive Advantage." *The Academy of Management Review* 29, no. 2 (April 2004): 258–271.

Wan, William P., and Robert E. Hoskisson. "Home Country Environments, Corporate Diversification Strategies, and Firm Performance." *Academy of Management Journal* 46, no. 1 (2003): 27–45.

Internet Resources

Economic Development Service (consulting service): **www.sitelocationassistance.com**

Location Strategies: **locationstrategies.com**

National Association of Manufacturers: **www.nam.org**

Site Selection magazine: **www.conway.com**

Transparency International, which maintains a bribe payers perception index (BPI) and a corruption perceptions index: **www.transparency.org**

Layout Strategies

Chapter Outline

Ten OM Strategy Decisions

Design of Goods and Services

Managing Quality

Process Strategy

Location Strategies

Layout Strategies

Human Resources

Supply Chain Management

Inventory Management

Scheduling

Maintenance

Learning Objectives

When you complete this chapter you should be able to

1. Discuss important issues in office layout
2. Define the objectives of retail layout
3. Discuss modern warehouse management and terms such as ASRS, cross-docking, and random stocking
4. Identify when fixed-position layouts are appropriate
5. Explain how to achieve a good process-oriented facility layout
6. Define work cell and the requirements of a work cell
7. Define product-oriented layout
8. Explain how to balance production flow in a repetitive or product-oriented facility

McDonald's Looks for Competitive Advantage through Layout

In its half century of existence, McDonald's revolutionized the restaurant industry by inventing the limited-menu fast-food restaurant. It has also made seven major innovations. The first, the introduction of *indoor seating* (1950s), was a layout issue, as was the second, *drive-through windows* (1970s). The third, adding *breakfasts* to the menu (1980s), was a product strategy. The fourth, *adding play areas* (late 1980s), was again a layout decision.

In the 1990s, McDonald's completed its fifth innovation, a radically new *redesign of the kitchens* in its 13,500 North America outlets to facilitate a mass customization process. Dubbed the "Made by You" kitchen system, sandwiches were assembled to order with the revamped layout.

In 2004, the chain began the rollout of its sixth innovation, a new food ordering layout: the *self-service kiosk*. Self-service kiosks have been infiltrating the service sector since the introduction of ATMs in 1985 (there are over ½ million ATMs in banking). Alaska Airlines was the first airline to provide self-service airport check-in, in 1996. Most passengers of the major airlines now check themselves in for flights. Kiosks take up less space than an employee and reduce waiting line time.

Now, McDonald's is working on its seventh innovation, and not surprisingly, it also deals with restaurant layout. The company, on an unprecedented scale, is redesigning all 30,000 eateries around the globe to take on a *21st century look*. The dining area will be separated into three sections with distinct personalities: (1) the "linger" zone focuses on young adults and offers comfortable furniture and Wi-Fi connections; (2) the "grab and go" zone features tall counters, bar stools, and plasma TVs; and (3) the "flexible" zone has colorful family booths, flexible seating, and kid-oriented music. The cost per outlet: a whopping $300,000–$400,000 renovation fee.

As McDonald's has discovered, facility layout is indeed a source of competitive advantage.

▼ *McDonald's finds that kiosks reduce both space requirements and waiting; order taking is faster. An added benefit is that customers like them. Also, kiosks are reliable—they don't call in sick. And, most importantly, sales are up 10%–15% (an average of $1) when a customer orders from a kiosk, which consistently recommends the larger size and other extras.*

► *The redesigned kitchen of a McDonald's in Manhattan. The more efficient layout requires less labor, reduces waste, and provides faster service. A graphic of this "assembly line" is shown in Figure 9.12.*

▼ Linger Zone
Cozy armchairs and sofas, plus Wi-Fi connections, make these areas attractive to those who want to hang out and socialize.

▼ Grab & Go Zone
This section has tall counters with bar stools for customers who eat alone. Plasma TVs keep them company.

▲ Flexible Zone
Booths with colorful fabric cushions make up the area geared to family and larger groups. Tables and chairs are movable.

THE STRATEGIC IMPORTANCE OF LAYOUT DECISIONS

Layout is one of the key decisions that determines the long-run efficiency of operations. Layout has numerous strategic implications because it establishes an organization's competitive priorities in regard to capacity, processes, flexibility, and cost, as well as quality of work life, customer contact, and image. An effective layout can help an organization achieve a strategy that supports differentiation, low cost, or response. Benetton, for example, supports a *differentiation* strategy by heavy investment in warehouse layouts that contribute to fast, accurate sorting and shipping to its 5,000 outlets. Wal-Mart store layouts support a strategy of *low cost*, as do its warehouse and store layouts. Hallmark's office layouts, where many professionals operate with open communication in work cells, support *rapid development* of greeting cards. *The objective of layout strategy is to develop an effective and efficient layout that will meet the firm's competitive requirements.* These firms have done so.

In all cases, layout design must consider how to achieve the following:

1. Higher utilization of space, equipment, and people
2. Improved flow of information, materials, or people
3. Improved employee morale and safer working conditions
4. Improved customer/client interaction
5. Flexibility (whatever the layout is now, it will need to change).

> *The objective of layout strategy is to develop a cost-effective layout that meets a firm's competitive needs.*

In our increasingly short-life-cycle, mass-customized world, layout designs need to be viewed as dynamic. This means considering small, movable, and flexible equipment. Store displays need to be movable, office desks and partitions modular, and warehouse racks prefabricated. To make quick and easy changes in product models and in production rates, operations managers must design flexibility into layouts. To obtain flexibility in layout, managers cross train their workers, maintain equipment, keep investments low, place workstations close together, and use small, movable equipment. In some cases, equipment on wheels is appropriate, in anticipation of the next change in product, process, or volume.

TYPES OF LAYOUT

Layout decisions include the best placement of machines (in production settings), offices and desks (in office settings), or service centers (in settings such as hospitals or department stores). An effective layout facilitates the flow of materials, people, and information within and between areas. To achieve these objectives, a variety of approaches has been developed. We will discuss seven of them in this chapter:

Video 9.1

Layout at Service Organizations

1. *Office layout:* Positions workers, their equipment, and spaces/offices to provide for movement of information.
2. *Retail layout:* Allocates shelf space and responds to customer behavior.
3. *Warehouse layout:* Addresses trade-offs between space and material handling.
4. *Fixed-position layout:* Addresses the layout requirements of large, bulky projects such as ships and buildings.
5. *Process-oriented layout:* Deals with low-volume, high-variety production (also called "job shop," or intermittent production).
6. *Work-cell layout:* Arranges machinery and equipment to focus on production of a single product or group of related products.
7. *Product-oriented layout:* Seeks the best personnel and machine utilization in repetitive or continuous production.

Examples for each of these classes of layout problems are noted in Table 9.1.

Because only a few of these seven classes can be modeled mathematically, layout and design of physical facilities are still something of an art. However, we do know that a good layout requires determining the following:

1. *Material handling equipment:* Managers must decide about equipment to be used, including conveyors, cranes, automated storage and retrieval systems, and automatic carts to deliver and store material.
2. *Capacity and space requirements:* Only when personnel, machines, and equipment requirements are known can managers proceed with layout and provide space for each component.

▼ **Table 9.1** Layout Strategies

Office	Retail	Warehouse (storage)	Project (fixed position)	Job Shop (process oriented)	Work Cell (product families)	Repetitive/ Continuous (product oriented)
Examples						
Allstate Insurance	Kroger's Supermarket	Federal-Mogul's warehouse	Ingall Ship Building Corp.	Arnold Palmer Hospital	Hallmark Cards	Sony's TV assembly line
Microsoft Corp.	Walgreen's	The Gap's distribution center	Trump Plaza	Hard Rock Cafe	Wheeled Coach	Toyota Scion
	Bloomingdale's		Pittsburgh Airport	Olive Garden	Standard Aero	
Problems/Issues						
Locate workers requiring frequent contact close to one another	Expose customer to high-margin items	Balance low-cost storage with low-cost material handling	Move material to the limited storage areas around the site	Manage varied material flow for each product	Identify a product family, build teams, cross train team members	Equalize the task time at each workstation

In the case of office work, operations managers must make judgments about the space requirements for each employee. It may be a 6 × 6-foot cubicle plus allowance for hallways, aisles, rest rooms, cafeterias, stairwells, elevators, and so forth, or it may be spacious executive offices and conference rooms. Management must also consider allowances for requirements that address safety, noise, dust, fumes, temperature, and space around equipment and machines.

3. *Environment and aesthetics:* Layout concerns often require decisions about windows, planters, and height of partitions to facilitate air flow, reduce noise, provide privacy, and so forth.

4. *Flows of information:* Communication is important to any organization and must be facilitated by the layout. This issue may require decisions about proximity as well as decisions about open spaces versus half-height dividers versus private offices.

5. *Cost of moving between various work areas:* There may be unique considerations related to moving materials or to the importance of having certain areas next to each other. For example, moving molten steel is more difficult than moving cold steel.

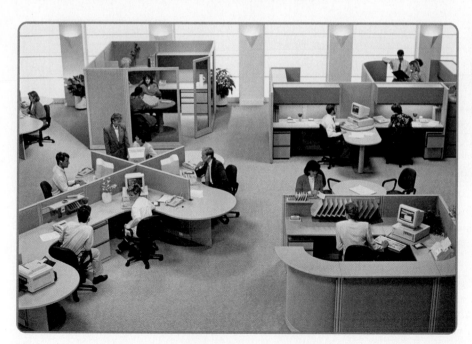

◄ *This open office offers a large shared space that encourages employees to interact. Before Steelcase, the office furniture maker, went to an open office system, 80% of its office space was private; now it is just 20% private. The CEO even went from a private 700-square-foot office to a 48-square-foot enclosure in an open area. This dramatically increases unplanned and spontaneous communication between employees.*

OFFICE LAYOUT

Learning Objective

1. Discuss important issues in office layout

Concepts of office space are not universal. In the Tokyo office of Toyota about 110 people work in one large room. When important visitors arrive for meetings, they are ushered into special rooms and do not see these cramped offices.

Office layouts require the grouping of workers, their equipment, and spaces to provide for comfort, safety, and movement of information. The main distinction of office layouts is the importance placed on the flow of information. Office layouts are in constant flux as the technological change sweeping society alters the way offices function.

Even though the movement of information is increasingly electronic, analysis of office layouts still requires a task-based approach. Paper correspondence, contracts, legal documents, confidential patient records, and hard-copy scripts, artwork, and designs still play a major role in many offices. Managers therefore examine both electronic and conventional communication patterns, separation needs, and other conditions affecting employee effectiveness. A useful tool for such an analysis is the *relationship chart* shown in Figure 9.1. This chart, prepared for an office of product designers, indicates that the chief marketing officer must be (1) near the designers' area, (2) less near the secretary and central files, and (3) not at all near the copy center or accounting department.

General office-area guidelines allot an average of about 100 square feet per person (including corridors). A major executive is allotted about 400 square feet, and a conference room area is based on 25 square feet per person.

On the other hand, some layout considerations are universal (many of which apply to factories as well as to offices). They have to do with working conditions, teamwork, authority, and status. Should offices be private or open cubicles, have low file cabinets to foster informal communication or high cabinets to reduce noise and contribute to privacy? (See the Steelcase photo on the previous page). Should all employees use the same entrance, rest rooms, lockers, and cafeteria? As mentioned earlier, layout decisions are part art and part science.

As a final comment on office layout, we note two major trends. First, technology, such as cell phones, iPods, faxes, the Internet, laptop computers, and PDAs, allows increasing layout flexibility by moving information electronically and allowing employees to work offsite. Second, modern firms create dynamic needs for space and services.

Here are two examples[1]:

1. When Deloitte & Touche found that 30% to 40% of desks were empty at any given time, the firm developed its "hoteling programs." Consultants lost their permanent offices; anyone who plans to be in the building (rather than out with clients) books an office through a "concierge," who hangs that consultant's name on the door for the day and stocks the space with requested supplies.
2. Cisco Systems cut rent and workplace service costs by 37% and saw productivity benefits of $2.4 billion per year by reducing square footage, reconfiguring space, creating movable, everything-on-wheels offices, and designing "get away from it all" innovation areas.

▶ **Figure 9.1**

Office Relationship Chart

Source: Adapted from Richard Muther, *Simplified Systematic Layout Planning*, 3rd ed. (Kansas City, Mgt. & Ind'l Research Publications). Used by permission of the publisher.

Value	CLOSENESS
A	Absolutely necessary
E	Especially important
I	Important
O	Ordinary OK
U	Unimportant
X	Not desirable

[1]"Square Feet. Oh, How Square!" *Business Week* (July 3, 2006): 100–101.

RETAIL LAYOUT

Retail layouts are based on the idea that sales and profitability vary directly with customer exposure to products. Thus, most retail operations managers try to expose customers to as many products as possible. Studies do show that the greater the rate of exposure, the greater the sales and the higher the return on investment. The operations manager can alter *both* with the overall arrangement of the store and the allocation of space to various products within that arrangement.

Five ideas are helpful for determining the overall arrangement of many stores:

1. Locate the high-draw items around the periphery of the store. Thus, we tend to find dairy products on one side of a supermarket and bread and bakery products on another. An example of this tactic is shown in Figure 9.2.
2. Use prominent locations for high-impulse and high-margin items. Best Buy puts fast-growing, high-margin digital goods—such as cameras and DVDs—in the front and center of its stores.
3. Distribute what are known in the trade as "power items"—items that may dominate a purchasing trip—to both sides of an aisle, and disperse them to increase the viewing of other items.
4. Use end-aisle locations because they have a very high exposure rate.
5. Convey the mission of the store by carefully selecting the position of the lead-off department. For instance, if prepared foods are part of a supermarket's mission, position the bakery and deli up front to appeal to convenience-oriented customers. Wal-Mart's push to increase sales of clothes means those departments are in broad view upon entering a store.

Once the overall layout of a retail store has been decided, products need to be arranged for sale. Many considerations go into this arrangement. However, the main *objective of retail layout is to maximize profitability per square foot of floor space* (or, in some stores, on linear foot of shelf space). Big-ticket, or expensive, items may yield greater dollar sales, but the profit per square foot may be lower. Computerized programs are available to assist managers in evaluating the profitability of various merchandising plans for hundreds of categories: this technique is know as category management.

An additional, and somewhat controversial, issue in retail layout is called slotting. **Slotting fees** are fees manufacturers pay to get their goods on the shelf in a retail store or supermarket chain. The result of massive new-product introductions, retailers can now demand up to $25,000 to place an item in their chain. During the last decade, marketplace economics, consolidations, and technology have provided retailers with this leverage. The competition for shelf space is advanced by POS systems and scanner technology, which improve supply chain management and inventory control. Many small firms question the legality and ethics of slotting fees, claiming the fees stifle new products, limit their ability to expand, and cost consumers money.[2] (See the Ethical Dilemma at the end of this chapter).

Retail layout
An approach that addresses flow, allocates space, and responds to customer behavior.

Slotting fees
Fees manufacturers pay to get shelf space for their products.

Wal-Mart is one of the few major retailers that does not demand slotting fees. This removes the barrier to entry that small companies usually face.

► **Figure 9.2**

Store Layout with Dairy and Bakery, High-Draw Items, in Different Areas of the Store

[2]For an interesting discussion of slotting fees, see J. G. Kaikati and A. M. Kaikati, "Slotting and Promotional Allowances," *Supply Chain Management* 11, no. 2 (2006): 140–147; or J. L. Stanton and K. C. Herbst, "Slotting Allowances," *International Journal of Retail & Distribution Management* 34, no. 2/3 (2006): 187–197.

▶ *Trying to penetrate urban areas that have lofty land prices and strong antidevelopment movements, Wal-Mart is changing its layout to up, not out. A new generation of multilevel stores take only one-third the space of the traditional 25-acre swaths. Here, in the El Cajon, California, store, Wal-Mart trained workers to help shoppers confused by the device next to the escalator that carries shopping carts from one floor to another.*

Servicescapes

Although the main objective of retail layout is to maximize profit through product exposure, there are other aspects of the service that managers consider. The term **servicescape** describes the physical surroundings in which the service is delivered and how the surroundings have a humanistic effect on customers and employees.[3] To provide a good service layout, a firm considers three elements:

1. *Ambient conditions*, which are background characteristics such as lighting, sound, smell, and temperature. All these affect workers *and* customers and can affect how much is spent and how long a person stays in the building.
2. *Spatial layout and functionality*, which involve customer circulation path planning, aisle characteristics (such as width, direction, angle, and shelf spacing), and product grouping.
3. *Signs, symbols, and artifacts*, which are characteristics of building design that carry social significance (such as carpeted areas of a department store that encourage shoppers to slow down and browse).

▶ *A critical element contributing to the bottom line at Hard Rock Cafe is the layout of each cafe's retail shop space. The retail space, from 600 to 1,300 square feet in size, is laid out in conjunction with the restaurant area to create the maximum traffic flow before and after eating. The payoffs for cafes like this one in London are huge. Almost half of a cafe's annual sales are generated from these small shops, which have very high retail sales per square foot.*

---

[3]See either A. Tombs and J. R. McColl-Kennedy, "Social Servicescapes Conceptual Model," *Marketing Theory* (December 2003): 447; or Mary Jo Bitner, "Servicescapes: The Impact of Physical Surroundings on Customers and Employees," *Journal of Marketing* 56 (April 1992): 57–71.

Examples of each of these three elements of servicescape are:

- *Ambient conditions:* Fine-dining restaurant with linen tablecloths and candlelit atmosphere; Mrs. Field's Cookie bakery smells permeating the shopping mall; leather chairs at Starbucks
- *Layout/functionality:* Kroger's long aisles and high shelves; Best Buys' wide center aisle
- *Signs, symbols, and artifacts:* Wal-Mart's greeter at the door; Hard Rock Cafe's wall of guitars

WAREHOUSING AND STORAGE LAYOUTS

The objective of **warehouse layout** is to find the optimum trade-off between handling cost and costs associated with warehouse space. Consequently, management's task is to maximize the utilization of the total "cube" of the warehouse—that is, utilize its full volume while maintaining low material handling costs. We define *material handling costs* as all the costs related to the transaction. This consists of incoming transport, storage, and outgoing transport of the materials to be warehoused. These costs include equipment, people, material, supervision, insurance, and depreciation. Effective warehouse layouts do, of course, also minimize the damage and spoilage of material within the warehouse.

Warehouse layout
A design that attempts to minimize total cost by addressing trade-offs between space and material handling.

Management minimizes the sum of the resources spent on finding and moving material plus the deterioration and damage to the material itself. The variety of items stored and the number of items "picked" has direct bearing on the optimum layout. A warehouse storing a few unique items lends itself to higher density than a warehouse storing a variety of items. Modern warehouse management is, in many instances, an automated procedure using *automated storage and retrieval systems* (ASRSs).

The Stop & Shop grocery chain, with 350 supermarkets in New England, has recently completed the largest ASRS in the world. The 1.3 million-square-foot distribution center in Freetown, Massachusetts, employs 77 rotating-fork automated storage and retrieval machines. These 77 cranes each access 11,500 pick slots on 90 aisles—a total of 64,000 pallets of food. The Wolfsburg, Germany parking garage photo (below) indicates that an ASRS can take many forms.

An important component of warehouse layout is the relationship between the receiving/unloading area and the shipping/loading area. Facility design depends on the type of supplies unloaded, what they are unloaded from (trucks, rail cars, barges, and so on), and where they are unloaded. In some companies, the receiving and shipping facilities, or *docks*, as they are called, are even the same area; sometimes they are receiving docks in the morning and shipping docks in the afternoon.

Learning Objective

3. Discuss modern warehouse management and terms such as ASRS, cross-docking, and random stocking

◄ Automated storage and retrieval systems are not found only in traditional warehouses. This parking garage in Wolfsburg, Germany, occupies only 20% of the space of a traditionally designed garage. The ASRS "retrieves" autos in less time, without the potential of the cars being damaged by an attendant.

Automated storage and retrieval systems are reported to improve productivity by an estimated 500% over manual methods.

Cross-docking

Avoiding the placement of materials or supplies in storage by processing them as they are received for shipment.

INBOUND

No delay

No storage

System in place for information exchange and product movement

OUTBOUND

Random stocking

Used in warehousing to locate stock wherever there is an open location.

Customizing

Using warehousing to add value to a product through component modification, repair, labeling, and packaging.

Cross-Docking

Cross-docking means to avoid placing materials or supplies in storage by processing them as they are received. In a manufacturing facility, product is received directly to the assembly line. In a distribution center, labeled and presorted loads arrive at the shipping dock for immediate rerouting, thereby avoiding formal receiving, stocking/storing, and order-selection activities. Because these activities add no value to the product, their elimination is 100% cost savings. Wal-Mart, an early advocate of cross-docking, uses the technique as a major component of its continuing low-cost strategy. With cross-docking, Wal-Mart reduces distribution costs and speeds restocking of stores, thereby improving customer service. Although cross-docking reduces product handling, inventory, and facility costs, it requires both (1) tight scheduling and (2) accurate inbound product identification.

Random Stocking

Automatic identification systems (AISs), usually in the form of bar codes, allow accurate and rapid item identification. When automatic identification systems are combined with effective management information systems, operations managers know the quantity and location of every unit. This information can be used with human operators or with automatic storage and retrieval systems to load units anywhere in the warehouse—randomly. Accurate inventory quantities and locations mean the potential utilization of the whole facility because space does not need to be reserved for certain stock-keeping units (SKUs) or part families. Computerized **random stocking** systems often include the following tasks:

1. Maintaining a list of "open" locations
2. Maintaining accurate records of existing inventory and its locations
3. Sequencing items to minimize the travel time required to "pick" orders
4. Combining orders to reduce picking time
5. Assigning certain items or classes of items, such as high-usage items, to particular warehouse areas so that the total distance traveled within the warehouse is minimized

Random stocking systems can increase facility utilization and decrease labor cost, but they require accurate records.

Customizing

Although we expect warehouses to store as little product as possible and hold it for as short a time as possible, we are now asking warehouses to customize products. Warehouses can be places where value is added through **customizing**. Warehouse customization is a particularly useful way to generate competitive advantage in markets with rapidly changing products. For instance, a warehouse can be a place where computer components are put together, software

▶ *The Gap strives for both high quality and low costs. It does so by (1) designing its own clothes, (2) ensuring quality control among its vendors, and (3) maintaining downward pressure on distribution costs. A new automatic distribution center near Baltimore allows The Gap to stock East Coast stores daily rather than only three times a week.*

loaded, and repairs made. Warehouses may also provide customized labeling and packaging for retailers so items arrive ready for display.

Increasingly, this type of work goes on adjacent to major airports, in facilities such as the FedEx terminal in Memphis. Adding value at warehouses adjacent to major airports also facilitates overnight delivery. For example, if your computer terminal has failed, the replacement may be sent to you from such a warehouse for delivery the next morning. When your old terminal arrives back at the warehouse, it is repaired and sent to someone else. These value-added activities at "quasi-warehouses" contribute to strategies of differentiation, low cost, and rapid response.

FIXED-POSITION LAYOUT

In a **fixed-position layout**, the project remains in one place and workers and equipment come to that one work area. Examples of this type of project are a ship, a highway, a bridge, a house, and an operating table in a hospital operating room.

The techniques for addressing the fixed-position layout are not well developed and are complicated by three factors. First, there is limited space at virtually all sites. Second, at different stages of a project, different materials are needed; therefore, different items become critical as the project develops. Third, the volume of materials needed is dynamic. For example, the rate of use of steel panels for the hull of a ship changes as the project progresses.

Fixed-position layout
A system that addresses the layout requirements of stationary projects.

Here are three versions of the fixed-position layout.

◄ *A house built via traditional fixed-position layout would be constructed onsite, with equipment, materials, and workers brought to the site for a "meeting of the trades" to assign space for various time periods. However, the home pictured here can be built at a much lower cost. The house is built in two movable modules in a factory. Scaffolding and hoists make the job easier, quicker, and cheaper, and the indoor work environment aids labor productivity.*

▲ *A service example of a fixed-position layout is an operating room; the patient remains stationary on the table, and medical personnel and equipment are brought to the site.*

▲ *In shipbuilding, there is limited space next to the fixed-position layout. Shipyards call these loading areas platens, and they are assigned for various time periods to each contractor.*

Because problems with fixed-position layouts are so difficult to solve well onsite, an alternative strategy is to complete as much of the project as possible offsite. This approach is used in the shipbuilding industry when standard units—say, pipe-holding brackets—are assembled on a nearby assembly line (a product-oriented facility). In an attempt to add efficiency to shipbuilding, Ingall Ship Building Corporation has moved toward product-oriented production when sections of a ship (modules) are similar or when it has a contract to build the same section of several similar ships. Also, as the top photo on the previous page shows, many home builders are moving from a fixed-position layout strategy to one that is more product oriented. About one-third of all new homes in the U.S. are built this way. In addition, many houses that are built onsite (fixed position) have the majority of components such as doors, windows, fixtures, trusses, stairs, and wallboard built as modules with more efficient offsite processes.

PROCESS-ORIENTED LAYOUT

Process-oriented layout

A layout that deals with low-volume, high-variety production in which like machines and equipment are grouped together.

A **process-oriented layout** can simultaneously handle a wide variety of products or services. This is the traditional way to support a product differentiation strategy. It is most efficient when making products with different requirements or when handling customers, patients, or clients with different needs. A process-oriented layout is typically the low-volume, high-variety strategy discussed in Chapter 7. In this job-shop environment, each product or each small group of products undergoes a different sequence of operations. A product or small order is produced by moving it from one department to another in the sequence required for that product. A good example of the process-oriented layout is a hospital or clinic. Figure 9.3 illustrates the process for two patients, A and B, at an emergency clinic in Chicago. An inflow of patients, each with his or her own needs, requires routing through admissions, laboratories, operating rooms, radiology, pharmacies, nursing beds, and so on. Equipment, skills, and supervision are organized around these processes.

A big advantage of process-oriented layout is its flexibility in equipment and labor assignments. The breakdown of one machine, for example, need not halt an entire process; work can be transferred to other machines in the department. Process-oriented layout is also especially good for handling the manufacture of parts in small batches, or **job lots**, and for the production of a wide variety of parts in different sizes or forms.

Job lots

Groups or batches of parts processed together.

The disadvantages of process-oriented layout come from the general-purpose use of the equipment. Orders take more time to move through the system because of difficult scheduling, changing setups, and unique material handling. In addition, general-purpose equipment requires high labor skills, and work-in-process inventories are higher because of imbalances in the production process. High labor-skill needs also increase the required level of training and experience, and high work-in-process levels increase capital investment.

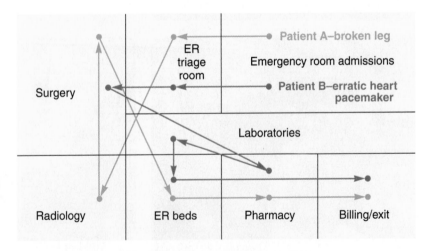

▲ **Figure 9.3**   **An Emergency Room Process Layout Showing the Routing of Two Patients**

Patient A (broken leg) proceeds (blue arrow) to ER triage, to radiology, to surgery, to a bed, to pharmacy, to billing. Patient B (pacemaker problem) moves (purple arrow) to ER triage, to surgery, to pharmacy, to lab, to a bed, to billing.

When designing a process layout, the most common tactic is to arrange departments or work centers so as to minimize the costs of material handling. In other words, departments with large flows of parts or people between them should be placed next to one another. Material handling costs in this approach depend on (1) the number of loads (or people) to be moved between two departments during some period of time and (2) the distance-related costs of moving loads (or people) between departments. Cost is assumed to be a function of distance between departments. The objective can be expressed as follows:

$$\text{Minimize cost} = \sum_{i=1}^{n}\sum_{j=1}^{n} X_{ij}C_{ij} \qquad (9\text{-}1)$$

where
- n = total number of work centers or departments
- i, j = individual departments
- X_{ij} = number of loads moved from department i to department j
- C_{ij} = cost to move a load between department i and department j

Process-oriented facilities (and fixed-position layouts as well) try to minimize loads or trips, times distance-related costs. The term C_{ij} combines distance and other costs into one factor. We thereby assume not only that the difficulty of movement is equal but also that the pickup and set-down costs are constant. Although they are not always constant, for simplicity's sake we summarize these data (that is, distance, difficulty, and pickup and setdown costs) in this one variable, cost. The best way to understand the steps involved in designing a process layout is to look at an example.

Walters Company management wants to arrange the six departments of its factory in a way that will minimize interdepartmental material handling costs. They make an initial assumption (to simplify the problem) that each department is 20 × 20 feet and that the building is 60 feet long and 40 feet wide.

EXAMPLE 1

Designing a process layout

Approach and Solution: The process layout procedure that they follow involves six steps:

Step 1: *Construct a "from–to matrix"* showing the flow of parts or materials from department to department (see Figure 9.4).

Number of loads per week

Department	Assembly (1)	Painting (2)	Machine Shop (3)	Receiving (4)	Shipping (5)	Testing (6)
Assembly (1)		50	100	0	0	20
Painting (2)			30	50	10	0
Machine Shop (3)				20	0	100
Receiving (4)					50	0
Shipping (5)						0
Testing (6)						

◄ **Figure 9.4**

Interdepartmental Flow of Parts

The high flows between 1 and 3 and between 3 and 6 are immediately apparent. Departments 1, 3, and 6, therefore, should be close together.

Step 2: *Determine the space requirements* for each department. (Figure 9.5 shows available plant space.)

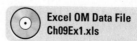

▶ **Figure 9.5**

Building Dimensions and One Possible Department Layout

Step 3: *Develop an initial schematic diagram* showing the sequence of departments through which parts must move. Try to place departments with a heavy flow of materials or parts next to one another. (See Figure 9.6.)

▶ **Figure 9.6**

Interdepartmental Flow Graph Showing Number of Weekly Loads

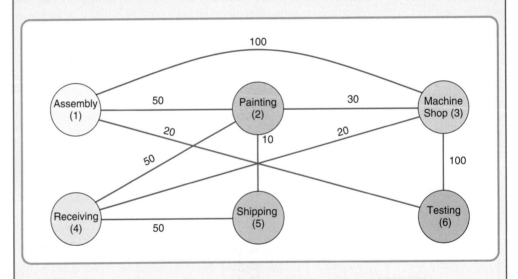

Step 4: *Determine the cost of this layout* by using the material-handling cost equation:

$$\text{Cost} = \sum_{i=1}^{n} \sum_{j=1}^{n} X_{ij} C_{ij}$$

For this problem, Walters Company assumes that a forklift carries all interdepartmental loads. The cost of moving one load between adjacent departments is estimated to be $1. Moving a load between nonadjacent departments costs $2. Looking at Figures 9.4 and 9.5, we thus see that the handling cost between departments 1 and 2 is $50 ($1 × 50 loads), $200 between departments 1 and 3 ($2 × 100 loads), $40 between departments 1 and 6 ($2 × 20 loads), and so on. Work areas that are diagonal to one another, such as 2 and 4, are treated as adjacent. The total cost for the layout shown in Figure 9.6 is:

$$
\begin{aligned}
\text{Cost} = \ &\$50 \ + \ \$200 \ + \ \$40 \ + \ \$30 \ + \ \$50 \\
&\text{(1 and 2)} \ \text{(1 and 3)} \ \text{(1 and 6)} \ \text{(2 and 3)} \ \text{(2 and 4)} \\
&+ \ \$10 \ + \ \$40 \ + \ \$100 \ + \ \$50 \\
&\text{(2 and 5)} \ \text{(3 and 4)} \ \text{(3 and 6)} \ \text{(4 and 5)} \\
= \ &\$570
\end{aligned}
$$

Active Model 9.1

Example 1 is further illustrated in Active Model 9.1 on the CD-ROM in the Exercise located on pages 375–376.

Step 5: By trial and error (or by a more sophisticated computer program approach that we discuss shortly), *try to improve the layout* pictured in Figure 9.5 to establish a better arrangement of departments.

By looking at both the flow graph (Figure 9.6) and the cost calculations, we see that placing departments 1 and 3 closer together appears desirable. They currently are nonadjacent, and the high volume of flow between them causes a large handling expense. Looking the situation over, we need to check the effect of shifting departments and possibly raising, instead of lowering, overall costs.

One possibility is to switch departments 1 and 2. This exchange produces a second departmental flow graph (Figure 9.7), which shows a reduction in cost to $480, a savings in material handling of $90:

$$
\begin{aligned}
\text{Cost} = \ &\$50 \ + \ \$100 \ + \ \$20 \ + \ \$60 \ + \ \$50 \\
&\text{(1 and 2)} \ \text{(1 and 3)} \ \text{(1 and 6)} \ \text{(2 and 3)} \ \text{(2 and 4)} \\[4pt]
&+ \ \$10 \ + \ \$40 \ + \ \$100 \ + \ \$50 \\
&\quad\text{(2 and 5)} \ \text{(3 and 4)} \ \text{(3 and 6)} \ \text{(4 and 5)} \\[4pt]
&= \$480
\end{aligned}
$$

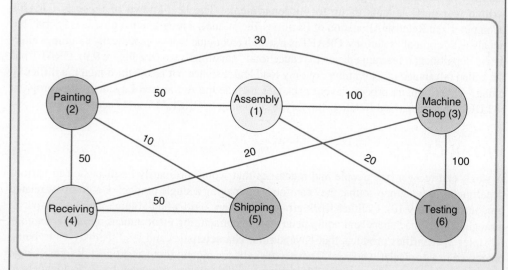

Suppose Walters Company is satisfied with the cost figure of $480 and the flow graph of Figure 9.7. The problem may not be solved yet. Often, a sixth step is necessary:

Step 6: *Prepare a detailed plan* arranging the departments to fit the shape of the building and its non-movable areas (such as the loading dock, washrooms, and stairways). Often this step involves ensuring that the final plan can be accommodated by the electrical system, floor loads, aesthetics, and other factors.

In the case of Walters Company, space requirements are a simple matter (see Figure 9.8).

Area A	Area B	Area C
Painting Department (2)	Assembly Department (1)	Machine Shop Department (3)
Receiving Department (4)	Shipping Department (5)	Testing Department (6)
Area D	Area E	Area F

Insight: This switch of departments is only one of a large number of possible changes. For a six-department problem, there are actually 720 (or 6! = 6 × 5 × 4 × 3 × 2 × 1) potential arrangements! In layout problems, we may not find the optimal solution and may have to be satisfied with a "reasonable" one.

Learning exercise: Can you improve on the layout in Figures 9.7 and 9.8? [Answer: Yes, it can be lowered to $430 by placing Shipping in area A, Painting in area B, Assembly in area C, Receiving in area D (no change), Machine Shop in area E, and Testing in area F (no change).]

Related problems: 9.1, 9.2, 9.3, 9.4, 9.5, 9.6, 9.7, 9.8, 9.9

Computer Software for Process-Oriented Layouts

CRAFT

A computer program that systematically examines alternative departmental rearrangements to reduce total material handling cost.

The graphic approach in Example 1 is fine for small problems. It does not, however, suffice for larger problems. When 20 departments are involved in a layout problem, more than 600 *trillion* different department configurations are possible. Fortunately, computer programs have been written to handle layouts of up to 40 departments. The best-known of these is **CRAFT** (Computerized Relative Allocation of Facilities Technique), a program that produces "good" but not always "optimal" solutions. CRAFT is a search technique that systematically examines alternative departmental rearrangements to reduce total "handling" cost (see Figure 9.9). CRAFT has the added advantage of examining not only load and distance but also a third factor, a difficulty rating.[4] Other popular process layout packages include the Automated Layout Design program (ALDEP), Computerized Relationship Layout Planning (CORELAP), and Factory Flow.

WORK CELLS

Work cell

An arrangement of machines and personnel that focuses on making a single product or family of related products.

A **work cell** reorganizes people and machines that would ordinarily be dispersed in various departments into a group so that they can focus on making a single product or a group of related products (Figure 9.10). Cellular work arrangements are used when volume warrants a special arrangement of machinery and equipment. In a manufacturing environment, *group technology* (Chapter 5) identifies products that have similar characteristics and lend themselves to being processed in a particular work cell. These work cells are reconfigured as product designs change or volume fluctuates. Although the idea of work cells was first presented by R. E. Flanders in 1925, only with the increasing use of group technology has the technique reasserted itself. The advantages of work cells are:

1. *Reduced work-in-process inventory* because the work cell is set up to provide one-piece flow from machine to machine.
2. *Less floor space* required because less space is needed between machines to accommodate work-in-process inventory.

▶ **Figure 9.9**

In This Six-Department Outpatient Hospital Example, (a) CRAFT Has Rearranged the Initial Layout, with a Cost of $20,100, into (b) the New Layout with a Lower Cost of $14,390.

CRAFT does this by systematically testing pairs of departments to see if moving them closer to each other lowers total cost.

Legend:

☐ A = X-ray/MRI rooms

☐ B = laboratories

☐ C = admissions

☐ D = exam rooms

☐ E = operating rooms

☐ F = recovery rooms

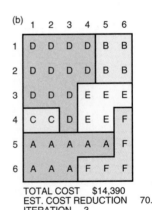

[4]Y. A. Bozer, R. R. Meller, and S. J. Erlebacher, "An Improvement-Type Layout Algorithm for Single and Multiple Floor Facilities," *Management Science* 40, no. 7 (1994): 918–933.

◀ *Contemporary software such as this from e-factory (UGS Corp.) allows operations managers to quickly place and connect symbols for factory equipment for a full three-dimensional view of the layout. Such presentations provide added insight into the issues of facility layout in terms of process, material handling, efficiency, and safety.*

3. *Reduced raw material and finished goods inventories* because less work-in-process allows more rapid movement of materials through the work cell.
4. *Reduced direct labor cost* because of improved communication among employees, better material flow, and improved scheduling.
5. *Heightened sense of employee participation* in the organization and the product: employees accept the added responsibility of product quality because it is directly associated with them and their work cell.
6. *Increased equipment and machinery utilization* because of better scheduling and faster material flow.
7. *Reduced investment in machinery and equipment* because good utilization reduces the number of machines and the amount of equipment and tooling.

Learning Objective

6. Define work cell and the requirements of a work cell

Requirements of Work Cells

The requirements of cellular production include:

1. Identification of families of products, often through the use of group technology codes or equivalents
2. A high level of training, flexibility, and empowerment of employees
3. Being self-contained, with its own equipment and resources.
4. Test (poka-yoke) at each station in the cell

Work cells have at least five advantages over assembly lines and process facilities: (1) because tasks are grouped, inspection is often immediate; (2) fewer workers are needed; (3) workers can reach more of the work area; (4) the work area can be more efficiently balanced; and (5) communication is enhanced. Work cells are sometimes organized in a U shape, as shown on the right side of Figure 9.10.

About half of U.S. plants with fewer than 100 employees use some sort of cellular system, whereas 75% of larger plants have adopted cellular production methods. Bayside Controls in Queens, New York, for example, has in the past decade increased sales from $300,000 per year to $11 million. Much of the gain was attributed to its move to cellular manufacturing. As noted in the *OM in Action* box, Rowe Furniture has had similar success with work cells.

 Video 9.3

Work Cells at Kurt Manufacturing

Staffing and Balancing Work Cells

Once the work cell has the appropriate equipment located in the proper sequence, the next task is to staff and balance the cell. Efficient production in a work cell requires appropriate staffing.

▶ **Figure 9.10**

Improving Layouts by Moving to the Work Cell Concept

Note in both (a) and (b) that U-shaped work cells can reduce material and employee movement. The U shape may also reduce space requirements, enhance communication, cut the number of workers, and make inspection easier.

(a)

Current layout–workers in small closed areas. Cannot increase output without a third worker.

Improved layout–cross-trained workers can assist each other. May be able to add a third worker as added output is needed.

(b)

Current layout–straight lines make it hard to balance tasks because work may not be divided evenly.

Improved layout–in U shape, workers have better access. Four cross-trained workers were reduced to three.

Takt time

Pace of production to meet customer demands.

This involves two steps. First, determine the **takt time**,[5] which is the pace (frequency) of production units necessary to meet customer orders:

$$\text{Takt time} = \text{Total work time available} / \text{Units required} \qquad (9\text{-}2)$$

Second, determine the number of operators required. This requires dividing the total operation time in the work cell by the takt time:

$$\text{Workers required} = \text{Total operation time required} / \text{Takt time} \qquad (9\text{-}3)$$

Example 2 considers these two steps when staffing work cells.

OM in Action   Work Cells at Rowe Furniture

Furniture customers usually want a much wider selection of options than showrooms display. What they really want is customization—unique styles, fabrics, and colors. And they are unhappy waiting months to get them. With imports claiming over 50% of the U.S. dining room/bedroom market, custom furniture is an opportunity for American manufacturers. Rowe Furniture Corp. of Salem, Virginia, took advantage of this opportunity by creating a computer network on which customers could order customized combinations of styles, fabrics, and colors. This strategy provided the orders for customization, but the real trick was how operations people could build ordered furniture quickly (in 10 days from order to delivery), with no increase in cost.

First, Rowe got rid of its old assembly line. Then it formed unique work cells, called "focused factories," each containing teams of workers with the necessary skills—gluers, sewers, staplers, and stuffers. Instead of being scattered along an assembly line, about three dozen team members found themselves in work cells. The work cells enhanced communication among team members and with management. Cross-training followed; gluers began to understand what staplers needed, and stuffers began to understand sewing requirements. Soon, team members realized that they could successfully deal with daily problems and began to develop improved methods. Moreover, both team members and management began to work together to solve problems.

The work cells yielded record productivity. The plant now produces 5% more with 10% fewer workers, and absenteeism has been cut in half. In addition, immediate feedback in the work cell has driven the error rate down to 1/10 of 1%.

Sources: Upholstery Design and Management (February 2001): 16–22; Fast Company (July 2004): 80–82; The Wall Street Journal (September 13, 1996): B1; and www.rowefurniture.com.

---

[5]*Takt* is German for "time," "measure," "beat" and is used in this context as the rate at which completed units must be produced to satisfy customer demand.

EXAMPLE 2

Staffing work cells

Stephen Hall's company in Dayton makes auto mirrors. The major customer is the Honda plant nearby. Honda expects 600 mirrors delivered daily, and the work cell producing the mirrors is scheduled for 8 hours. Hall wants to determine the takt time and the number of workers required.

Approach: Hall uses Equations (9-2) and (9-3) and develops a work balance chart to help determine the time for each operation in the work cell, as well as total time.

Solution: Takt time = (8 hours × 60 minutes) / 600 units = 480/600 =.8 minute = 48 seconds

Therefore, the customer requirement is one mirror every 48 seconds.

The *work balance chart* in Figure 9.11 shows that 5 operations are necessary, for a total operation time of 140 seconds:

$$\text{Workers required} = \text{Total operation time required} / \text{Takt time}$$
$$= (50 + 45 + 10 + 20 + 15) / 48$$
$$= 140 / 48 = 2.91$$

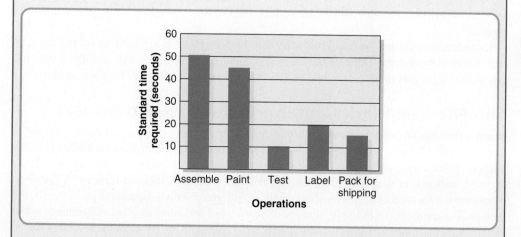

◄ **Figure 9.11**

Work Balance Chart for Mirror Production

Insight: To produce one unit every 48 seconds will require 2.91 people. With three operators this work cell will be producing one unit each 46.67 seconds (140 seconds / 3 employees = 46.67) and 617 units per day (480 minutes available × 60 seconds) / 46.67 seconds for each unit = 617).

Learning exercise: If testing time is expanded to 20 seconds, what is the staffing requirement? [Answer: 3.125 employees.]

Related problem: 9.10

A *work balance chart* (like the one in Example 2) is also valuable for evaluating the operation times in work cells. Some consideration must be given to determining the bottleneck operation. Bottleneck operations can constrain the flow through the cell. Imbalance in a work cell is seldom an issue if the operation is manual, as cell members by definition are part of a cross-trained team. Consequently, the many advantages of work cells typically overcome modest imbalance issues within a cell. However, if the imbalance is a machine constraint, then an adjustment in machinery, process, or operations may be necessary. In such situations the use of traditional assembly-line-balancing analysis, the topic of our next section, may be helpful.

In many arrangements, without cells and without cross training, if one operation is halted for whatever reason (reading a drawing, getting a tool, machine maintenance, etc.), the entire flow stops. Multiple-operator cells are therefore preferred.

The success of work cells is not limited to manufacturing. Kansas City's Hallmark, which has over half the U.S. greeting card market and produces some 40,000 different cards, has modified the offices into a cellular design. In the past, its 700 creative professionals would take up to 2 years to develop a new card. Hallmark's decision to create work cells consisting of artists, writers, lithographers, merchandisers, and accountants, all located in the same area, has resulted in card preparation in a fraction of the time that the old layout required. Work cells have also

Work Cell	Focused Work Center	Focused Factory
A work cell is a temporary product-oriented arrangement of machines and personnel in what is ordinarily a process-oriented facility	A focused work center is a permanent product-oriented arrangement of machines and personnel in what is ordinarily a process-oriented facility	A focused factory is a permanent facility to produce a product or component in a product-oriented facility. Many of the focused factories currently being built were originally part of a process-oriented facility
Example: A job shop with machinery and personnel rearranged to produce 300 unique control panels	*Example:* Pipe bracket manufacturing at a shipyard	*Example:* A plant to produce window mechanisms for automobiles

yielded higher performance and better service for the American Red Cross blood donation process.[6]

Commercial software, such as ProPlanner and Factory Flow, is available to aid managers in their move to work cells. These programs typically require information that includes AutoCAD layout drawings; part routing data; and cost, times, and speeds of material handling systems.

The Focused Work Center and the Focused Factory

When a firm has *identified a family of similar products that have a large and stable demand*, it may organize a focused work center. A **focused work center** moves production from a general-purpose, process-oriented facility to a large work cell that remains part of the present plant. If the focused work center is in a separate facility, it is often called a **focused factory**. A fast-food restaurant is a focused factory—most are easily reconfigured for adjustments to product mix and volume. Burger King, for example, changes the number of personnel and task assignments rather than moving machines and equipment. In this manner, Burger King balances the assembly line to meet changing production demands. In effect, the "layout" changes numerous times each day.

The term *focused factories* may also refer to facilities that are focused in ways other than by product line or layout. For instance, facilities may be focused in regard to meeting quality, new product introduction, or flexibility requirements.

Focused facilities in manufacturing and in services appear to be better able to stay in tune with their customers, to produce quality products, and to operate at higher margins. This is true whether they are steel mills like CMC, Nucor, or Chaparral; restaurants like McDonald's and Burger King; or a hospital like Arnold Palmer.

Table 9.2 summarizes our discussion of work cells, focused work centers, and focused factories.

Focused work center

A permanent or semi-permanent product-oriented arrangement of machines and personnel.

Focused factory

A facility designed to produce similar products or components.

REPETITIVE AND PRODUCT-ORIENTED LAYOUT

Product-oriented layouts are organized around products or families of similar high-volume, low-variety products. Repetitive production and continuous production, which are discussed in Chapter 7, use product layouts. The assumptions are that:

1. Volume is adequate for high equipment utilization
2. Product demand is stable enough to justify high investment in specialized equipment
3. Product is standardized or approaching a phase of its life cycle that justifies investment in specialized equipment
4. Supplies of raw materials and components are adequate and of uniform quality (adequately standardized) to ensure that they will work with the specialized equipment

Two types of a product-oriented layout are fabrication and assembly lines. The **fabrication line** builds components, such as automobile tires or metal parts for a refrigerator, on a series of

Learning Objective

7. Define product-oriented layout

Fabrication line

A machine-paced, product-oriented facility for building components.

[6]Mark Pagell and Steven A. Melnyk, "Assessing the Impact of Alternative Manufacturing Layouts in a Service Setting," *Journal of Operations Management* 22 (2004): 413–429.

machines. An **assembly line** puts the fabricated parts together at a series of workstations. Both are repetitive processes, and in both cases, the line must be "balanced": That is, the time spent to perform work on one machine must equal or "balance" the time spent to perform work on the next machine in the fabrication line, just as the time spent at one workstation by one assembly-line employee must "balance" the time spent at the next workstation by the next employee. The same issues arise when designing the "disassembly lines" of slaughterhouses and automobile makers (see the *OM in Action* box "From Assembly Lines to Disassembly Lines").

Fabrication lines tend to be machine-paced and require mechanical and engineering changes to facilitate balancing. Assembly lines, on the other hand, tend to be paced by work tasks assigned to individuals or to workstations. Assembly lines, therefore, can be balanced by moving tasks from one individual to another. The central problem, then, in product-oriented layout planning is to balance the tasks at each workstation on the production line so that it is nearly the same while obtaining the desired amount of output.

Management's goal is to create a smooth, continuous flow along the assembly line with a minimum of idle time at each workstation. A well-balanced assembly line has the advantage of high personnel and facility utilization and equity among employees' work loads. Some union contracts require that work loads be nearly equal among those on the same assembly line. The term most often used to describe this process is **assembly-line balancing**. Indeed, the *objective of the product-oriented layout is to minimize imbalance in the fabrication or assembly line.*

The main advantages of product-oriented layout are:

1. The low variable cost per unit usually associated with high-volume, standardized products
2. Low material handling costs
3. Reduced work-in-process inventories
4. Easier training and supervision
5. Rapid throughput

The disadvantages of product layout are:

1. The high volume required because of the large investment needed to establish the process
2. That work stoppage at any one point ties up the whole operation
3. A lack of flexibility when handling a variety of products or production rates

Assembly line
An approach that puts fabricated parts together at a series of workstations; used in repetitive processes.

Assembly-line balancing
Obtaining output at each workstation on a production line so delay is minimized.

Product layout can handle only a few products and process designs.

OM in Action   From Assembly Lines to Disassembly Lines

Almost 100 years have passed since assembly lines were developed to *make* automobiles—and now we're developing disassembly lines to take them apart. Sprawling graveyards of rusting cars and trucks bear testimony to the need for automotive disassembly lines. But those graveyards are slowly beginning to shrink as we learn the art of automobile disassembly. New *disassembly* lines now take apart so many automobiles that recycling is the 16th-largest industry in the U.S. The motivation for this disassembly comes from many sources, including mandated industry recycling standards and a growing consumer interest in purchasing cars based on how "green" they are.

New car designs have traditionally been unfriendly to recyclers, with little thought given to disassembly. However, manufacturers now design in such a way that materials can be easily reused in the next generation of cars. The 2007 Mercedes S-class is 95% recyclable and already meets the 2015 EU standard. BMW has disassembly plants in Europe and Japan as well as U.S. salvage centers in New York, Los Angeles, and Orlando. A giant 200,000-square-foot facility in Baltimore (called CARS) can disassemble up to 30,000 vehicles per year. At CARS's ini-

tial "greening station," special tools puncture tanks and drain fluids, and the battery and gas tank are removed. Then on a semi-automated track, which includes a giant steel vise that can flip a 7,500-pound car upside-down, wheels, doors, hood, and trunk are removed; next comes the interior items; then plastic parts are removed and sorted for recycling; then glass and interior and trunk materials. Eventually the chassis is in a bale and sold as a commodity to minimills that use scrap steel.

Disassembly lines are not easy. Some components, like air bags, are hard to handle and dangerous. Reusable parts are bar coded and entered into a database. Various color-coded plastics must be recycled differently to support being remelted and turned into new parts, such as intake manifolds. After the engines, transmissions, radios, and exhausts have been removed, the remaining metal parts of the disassembly line are easier: with shredders and magnets, baseball-sized chunks of metal are sorted. Assembly lines put cars together, and disassembly lines take them apart.

Sources: The New York Times (September 19, 2005): D5; *Forbes* (April 16, 2001): 314–315; and *Automotive Industry Trends* (March 2004).

► *The Boeing 737, the world's most popular commercial airplane, is produced on a moving production line, traveling at 2 inches a minute through the final assembly process. The moving line, one of several lean manufacturing innovations at the Renton, Washington, facility, has enhanced quality, reduced flow time, slashed inventory levels, and cut space requirements. Final assembly is only 11 days—a time savings of 50%—and inventory is down more than 55%. Boeing has expanded the moving line concept to its 747 jumbo jet.*

 Video 9.4

Facility Layout at Wheeled Coach Ambulances

Because the problems of fabrication lines and assembly lines are similar, we focus our discussion on assembly lines. On an assembly line, the product typically moves via automated means, such as a conveyor, through a series of workstations until completed. This is the way automobiles and some planes (see the photo of the Boeing 737) are assembled, television sets and ovens are produced, and fast-food hamburgers are made (see Figure 9.12). Product-oriented layouts use more automated and specially designed equipment than do process layouts.

Assembly-Line Balancing

Line balancing is usually undertaken to minimize imbalance between machines or personnel while meeting a required output from the line. To produce at a specified rate, management must know the tools, equipment, and work methods used. Then the time requirements for each assembly task (e.g., drilling a hole, tightening a nut, or spray-painting a part) must be determined. Management also needs to know the *precedence relationship* among the activities—that is, the sequence in which various tasks must be performed. Example 3 shows how to turn these task data into a precedence diagram.

► **Figure 9.12**

McDonald's Hamburger Assembly Line

EXAMPLE 3

Developing a
precedence diagram
for an assembly line

Boeing wants to develop a precedence diagram for an electrostatic wing component that requires a total assembly time of 66 minutes.

Approach: Staff gather tasks, assembly times, and sequence requirements for the component in Table 9.3.

Task	Performance Time (minutes)	Task Must Follow Task Listed Below	
A	10	—	
B	11	A	This means that
C	5	B	tasks B and E
D	4	B	cannot be done
E	12	A	until task A has
F	3	C, D	been completed.
G	7	F	
H	11	E	
I	3	G, H	
	Total time 66		

◀ **Table 9.3**

Precedence Data for Wing Component

Solution: Figure 9.13 shows the precedence diagram.

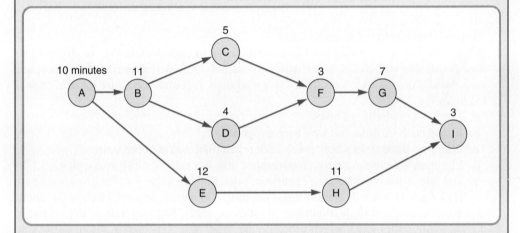

◀ **Figure 9.13**

Precedence Diagram

Insight: The diagram helps structure an assembly line and workstations, and it makes it easier to visualize the sequence of tasks.

Learning exercise: If task D had a second preceding task (C), how would Figure 9.13 change? [Answer: There would also be an arrow pointing from C to D.]

Related problems: 9.12a, 9.14a, 9.15a, 9.16a, 9.19a

Once we have constructed a precedence chart summarizing the sequences and performance times, we turn to the job of grouping tasks into job stations so that we can meet the specified production rate. This process involves three steps:

1. Take the units required (demand or production rate) per day and divide it into the productive time available per day (in minutes or seconds). This operation gives us what is called the **cycle time**[7]—namely, the maximum time allowed at each workstation if the production rate is to be achieved:

$$\text{Cycle time} = \frac{\text{Production time available per day}}{\text{Units required per day}} \qquad (9\text{-}4)$$

Cycle time
The maximum time that a product is allowed at each workstation.

[7]*Cycle time* is the actual time to accomplish a task or process step. Several process steps may be necessary to complete the product. *Takt time*, discussed earlier, is determined by the customer and is the speed at which completed units must be produced to satisfy customer demand.

▶ **Table 9.4**

Layout Heuristics That May Be Used to Assign Tasks to Work Stations in Assembly-Line Balancing

1. *Longest task (operation) time*	From the available tasks, choose the task with the largest (longest) time.
2. *Most following tasks*	From the available tasks, choose the task with the largest number of following tasks.
3. *Ranked positional weight*	From the available tasks, choose the task for which the sum of the times for each following task is longest. (In Example 4 we will see that the ranked positional weight of task C = 5(C) + 3(F) + 7(G) + 3(I) = 18, whereas the ranked positional weight of task D = 4(D) + 3(F) + 7(G) + 3(I) = 17; therefore, C would be chosen first.)
4. *Shortest task (operations) time*	From the available tasks, choose the task with the shortest task time.
5. *Least number of following tasks*	From the available tasks, choose the task with the least number of subsequent tasks.

2. Calculate the theoretical minimum number of workstations. This is the total task-duration time (the time it takes to make the product) divided by the cycle time. Fractions are rounded to the next higher whole number:

$$\text{Minimum number of workstations} = \frac{\sum_{i=1}^{n} \text{Time for task } i}{\text{Cycle time}} \qquad (9\text{-}5)$$

where n is the number of assembly tasks.

3. Balance the line by assigning specific assembly tasks to each workstation. An efficient balance is one that will complete the required assembly, follow the specified sequence, and keep the idle time at each workstation to a minimum. A formal procedure for doing this is the following:

   a. Identify a master list of tasks.
   b. Eliminate those tasks that have been assigned.
   c. Eliminate those tasks whose precedence relationship has not been satisfied.
   d. Eliminate those tasks for which inadequate time is available at the workstation.
   e. Use one of the line-balancing "heuristics" described in Table 9.4. The five choices are (1) longest task time, (2) most following tasks, (3) ranked positional weight, (4) shortest task time, and (5) least number of following tasks. You may wish to test several of these **heuristics** to see which generates the "best" solution—that is, the smallest number of workstations and highest efficiency. Remember, however, that although heuristics provide solutions, they do not guarantee an optimal solution.

Heuristic
Problem solving using procedures and rules rather than mathematical optimization.

Example 4 illustrates a simple line-balancing procedure.

EXAMPLE 4

Balancing the assembly line

On the basis of the precedence diagram and activity times given in Example 3, Boeing determines that there are 480 productive minutes of work available per day. Furthermore, the production schedule requires that 40 units of the wing component be completed as output from the assembly line each day. It now wants to group the tasks into workstations.

Approach: Following the three steps above, we compute the cycle time using Equation (9-4) and minimum number of workstations using Equation (9-5), and we assign tasks to workstations—in this case using the *most following tasks* heuristic.

Solution:

$$\text{Cycle time (in minutes)} = \frac{480 \text{ minutes}}{40 \text{ units}}$$
$$= 12 \text{ minutes/unit}$$

$$\text{Minimum number of workstations} = \frac{\text{Total task time}}{\text{Cycle time}} = \frac{66}{12}$$
$$= 5.5 \text{ or 6 stations}$$

Figure 9.14 shows one solution that does not violate the sequence requirements and that groups tasks into six stations. To obtain this solution, activities with the most following tasks were moved into workstations to use as much of the available cycle time of 12 minutes as possible. The first workstation consumes 10 minutes and has an idle time of 2 minutes.

◄ **Figure 9.14**

A Six-Station Solution to the Line-Balancing Problem

Insight: This is a reasonably well-balanced assembly line. The second workstation uses 11 minutes, and the third consumes the full 12 minutes. The fourth workstation groups three small tasks and balances perfectly at 12 minutes. The fifth has 1 minute of idle time, and the sixth (consisting of tasks G and I) has 2 minutes of idle time per cycle. Total idle time for this solution is 6 minutes per cycle.

Learning exercise: If task I required 6 minutes (instead of 3 minutes), how would this change the solution? [Answer: The cycle time would not change, and the *theoretical* minimum number of workstations would still be 6 (rounded up from 5.75), but it would take 7 stations to balance the line.]

Related problems: 9.11, 9.12, 9.13, 9.14, 9.15, 9.16, 9.17, 9.18, 9.19, 9.20, 9.21, 9.22, 9.23

We can compute the efficiency of a line balance by dividing the total task time by the product of the number of workstations required times the assigned (actual) cycle time of the longest workstation:

$$\text{Efficiency} = \frac{\Sigma \text{ Task times}}{(\text{Actual number of workstations}) \times (\text{Largest assigned cycle time})} \quad (9\text{-}6)$$

Operations managers compare different levels of efficiency for various numbers of workstations. In this way, a firm can determine the sensitivity of the line to changes in the production rate and workstation assignments.

Two issues in line balancing are the production rate and the efficiency.

EXAMPLE 5

Determining line efficiency

Boeing needs to calculate the balance efficiency for Example 4.

Approach: Equation (9-6) is applied.

Solution: $\text{Efficiency} = \dfrac{66 \text{ minutes}}{(6 \text{ stations}) \times (12 \text{ minutes})} = \dfrac{66}{72} = 91.7\%$

Note that opening a seventh workstation, for whatever reason, would decrease the efficiency of the balance to 78.6% (assuming that at least one of the workstations still required 12 minutes):

$$\text{Efficiency} = \frac{66 \text{ minutes}}{(7 \text{ stations}) \times (12 \text{ minutes})} = 78.6\%$$

Some tasks simply cannot be grouped together in one workstation. There may be a variety of physical reasons for this.

Insight: Increasing efficiency may require that some tasks be divided into smaller elements and reassigned to other tasks. This facilitates a better balance between workstations and means higher efficiency.

Learning exercise: What is the efficiency if an eighth workstation is opened? [Answer: Efficiency = 68.75%.]

Related problems: 9.12f, 9.13c, 9.14f, 9.16c, 9.17b, 9.18b, 9.19e,g

Large-scale line-balancing problems, like large process-layout problems, are often solved by computers. Several computer programs are available to handle the assignment of workstations on assembly lines with 100 (or more) individual work activities. Two computer routines, COMSOAL (Computer Method for Sequencing Operations for Assembly Lines)[8] and ASYBL (General Electric's Assembly Line Configuration program), are widely used in larger problems to evaluate the thousands, or even millions, of possible workstation combinations much more efficiently than could ever be done by hand.

▶ *In the case of slaughtering operations, the assembly line is actually a disassembly line. The line-balancing procedures described in this chapter are the same as for an assembly line. The chicken-processing plant shown here must balance the work of several hundred employees. The total labor content in each of the chickens processed is a few minutes.*

Summary

Layouts make a substantial difference in operating efficiency. The seven layout situations discussed in this chapter are (1) office, (2) retail, (3) warehouse, (4) fixed position, (5) process oriented, (6) work cells, and (7) product oriented. A variety of techniques have been developed to solve these layout problems. Office layouts often seek to maximize information flows, retail firms focus on product exposure, and warehouses attempt to optimize the trade-off between storage space and material handling cost.

The fixed-position layout problem attempts to minimize material handling costs within the constraint of limited space

at the site. Process layouts minimize travel distances times the number of trips. Product layouts focus on reducing waste and the imbalance in an assembly line. Work cells are the result of identifying a family of products that justify a special configuration of machinery and equipment that reduces material travel and adjusts imbalances with cross-trained personnel.

Often, the issues in a layout problem are so wide-ranging that finding an optimal solution is not possible. For this reason, layout decisions, although the subject of substantial research effort, remain something of an art.

[8]G. W. De Puy, "Applying the COMSOAL Computer Heuristic," *Computers & Industrial Engineering* 38, no. 3 (October 2000): 413–422.

Key Terms

Office layout *(p. 350)*
Retail layout *(p. 351)*
Slotting fees *(p. 351)*
Servicescape *(p. 352)*
Warehouse layout *(p. 353)*
Cross-docking *(p. 354)*
Random stocking *(p. 354)*

Customizing *(p. 354)*
Fixed-position layout *(p. 355)*
Process-oriented layout *(p. 356)*
Job lots *(p. 356)*
CRAFT *(p. 360)*
Work cell *(p. 360)*
Takt time *(p. 362)*

Focused work center *(p. 364)*
Focused factory *(p. 364)*
Fabrication line *(p. 364)*
Assembly line *(p. 365)*
Assembly-line balancing *(p. 365)*
Cycle time *(p. 367)*
Heuristic *(p. 368)*

Using Software to Solve Layout Problems

In addition to the many commercial software packages available for addressing layout problems, Excel OM and POM for Windows, both of which accompany this text, contain modules for the process problem and the assembly-line-balancing problem.

✕ Using Excel OM

Excel OM can assist in evaluating a series of department to work area assignments like the one we saw for the Walters Company in Example 1. The layout module can generate an optimal solution by enumeration or by computing the "total movement" cost for each layout you wish to examine. As such, it provides a speedy calculator for each flow–distance pairing.

Program 9.1 illustrates our inputs in the top two tables. We first enter department flows, then provide distances between work areas. Entering area assignments on a trial-and-error basis in the upper left of the top table generates movement computations at the bottom of the screen. Total movement is recalculated each time we try a new area assignment. It turns out that the assignment shown is optimal at 430 feet of movement.

P Using POM for Windows

The POM for Windows facility layout module can be used to place up to 10 departments in 10 rooms to minimize the total distance traveled as a function of the distances between the rooms and the flow between departments. The program exchanges departments until no exchange will reduce the total amount of movement, meaning an optimal solution has been reached.

▲ **Program 9.1** Using Excel OM's Process Layout Module to Solve the Walters Company Problem in Example 1

The POM for Windows and Excel OM modules for line balancing can handle a line with up to 99 tasks, each with up to 6 immediate predecessors. In this program, cycle time can be entered either (1) *given*, if known, or (2) the *demand* rate can be entered with time available as shown. All five "heuristic rules" are used: (1) longest operation (task) time, (2) most following tasks, (3) ranked positional weight, (4) shortest operation (task) time, and (5) least number of following tasks. No one rule can guarantee an optimal solution, but POM for Windows displays the number of stations needed for each rule.

Appendix IV discusses further details regarding POM for Windows.

Solved Problems

 Virtual Office Hours help is available on Student DVD.

Solved Problem 9.1

Aero Maintenance is a small aircraft engine maintenance facility located in Wichita, Kansas. Its new administrator, Ann Daniel, decides to improve material flow in the facility, using the process-layout method she studied at Wichita State University. The current layout of Aero Maintenance's eight departments is shown in Figure 9.15.

Current Aero Maintenance Layout

Area A	Area B	Area C	Area D
Entrance (1)	Receiving (2)	Parts (3)	Metallurgy (4)
Breakdown (5)	Assembly (6)	Inspection (7)	Test (8)
Area E	Area F	Area G	Area H

10' / 10' / 40'

▲ **Figure 9.15**   **Aero Maintenance Layout**

The only physical restriction perceived by Daniel is the need to keep the entrance in its current location. All other departments can be moved to a different work area (each 10 feet square) if layout analysis indicates a move would be beneficial.

First, Daniel analyzes records to determine the number of material movements among departments in an average month. These data are shown in Figure 9.16. Her objective, Daniel decides, is to lay out the departments so as to minimize the total movement (distance traveled) of material in the facility. She writes her objective as:

$$\text{Minimize material movement} = \sum_{i=1}^{8}\sum_{j=1}^{8} X_{ij} C_{ij}$$

where X_{ij} = number of material movements per month (loads or trips) moving from department i to department j

C_{ij} = distance in feet between departments i and j (which, in this case, is the equivalent of cost per load to move between departments)

Note that this is only a slight modification of the cost-objective equation shown earlier in the chapter.

▶ **Figure 9.16**

Number of Material Movements (Loads) between Departments in One Month

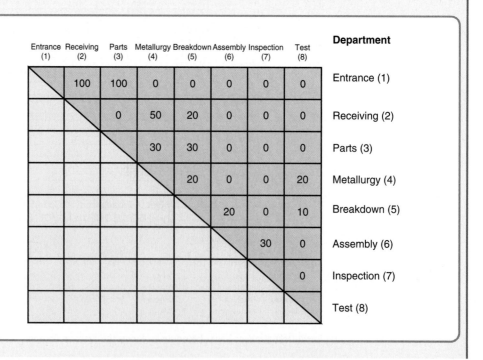

	Entrance (1)	Receiving (2)	Parts (3)	Metallurgy (4)	Breakdown (5)	Assembly (6)	Inspection (7)	Test (8)	Department
		100	100	0	0	0	0	0	Entrance (1)
			0	50	20	0	0	0	Receiving (2)
				30	30	0	0	0	Parts (3)
					20	0	0	20	Metallurgy (4)
						20	0	10	Breakdown (5)
							30	0	Assembly (6)
								0	Inspection (7)
									Test (8)

Daniel assumes that adjacent departments, such as entrance (now in work area A) and receiving (now in work area B), have a walking distance of 10 feet. Diagonal departments are also considered adjacent and assigned a distance of 10 feet. Nonadjacent departments, such as the entrance and parts (now in area C) or the entrance and inspection (area G) are 20 feet apart, and nonadjacent rooms, such as entrance and metallurgy (area D), are 30 feet apart. (Hence, 10 feet is considered 10 units of cost, 20 feet is 20 units of cost, and 30 feet is 30 units of cost.)

Given the above information, redesign Aero Maintenance's layout to improve its material flow efficiency.

solution

First, establish Aero Maintenance's current layout, as shown in Figure 9.17. Then, by analyzing the current layout, compute material movement:

$$
\begin{aligned}
\text{Total movement} = \quad & \underset{\text{1 to 2}}{(100 \times 10')} + \underset{\text{1 to 3}}{(100 \times 20')} + \underset{\text{2 to 4}}{(50 \times 20')} + \underset{\text{2 to 5}}{(20 \times 10')} \\
+ \quad & \underset{\text{3 to 4}}{(30 \times 10')} + \underset{\text{3 to 5}}{(30 \times 20')} + \underset{\text{4 to 5}}{(20 \times 30')} + \underset{\text{4 to 8}}{(20 \times 10')} \\
+ \quad & \underset{\text{5 to 6}}{(20 \times 10')} + \underset{\text{5 to 8}}{(10 \times 30')} + \underset{\text{6 to 7}}{(30 \times 10')} \\
= \quad & 1,000 + 2,000 + 1,000 + 200 + 300 + 600 + 600 \\
& + 200 + 200 + 300 + 300 \\
= \quad & 6,700 \text{ feet}
\end{aligned}
$$

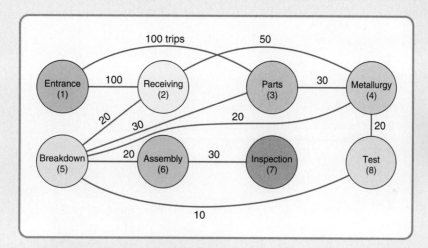

▲ **Figure 9.17** **Current Material Flow**

Propose a new layout that will reduce the current figure of 6,700 feet. Two useful changes, for example, are to switch departments 3 and 5 and to interchange departments 4 and 6. This change would result in the schematic shown in Figure 9.18:

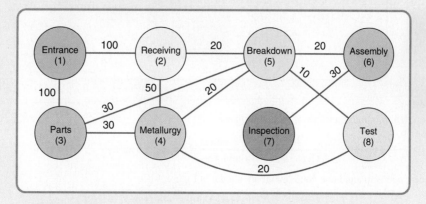

▲ **Figure 9.18** **Improved Layout**

$$\text{Total movement} = \begin{array}{cccc} (100 \times 10') & + & (100 \times 10') & + & (50 \times 10') & + & (20 \times 10') \\ \text{1 to 2} & & \text{1 to 3} & & \text{2 to 4} & & \text{2 to 5} \end{array}$$

$$+ \begin{array}{cccc} (30 \times 10') & + & (30 \times 20') & + & (20 \times 10') & + & (20 \times 20') \\ \text{3 to 4} & & \text{3 to 5} & & \text{4 to 5} & & \text{4 to 8} \end{array}$$

$$+ \begin{array}{ccc} (20 \times 10') & + & (10 \times 10') & + & (30 \times 10') \\ \text{5 to 6} & & \text{5 to 8} & & \text{6 to 7} \end{array}$$

$$= 1,000 + 1,000 + 500 + 200 + 300 + 600 + 200$$
$$+ 400 + 200 + 100 + 300$$

$$= 4,800 \text{ feet}$$

Do you see any room for further improvement?

Solved Problem 9.2

The assembly line whose activities are shown in Figure 9.19 has an 8-minute cycle time. Draw the precedence graph and find the minimum possible number of workstations. Then arrange the work activities into workstations so as to balance the line. What is the efficiency of your line balance?

Task	Performance Time (minutes)	Task Must Follow This Task
A	5	—
B	3	A
C	4	B
D	3	B
E	6	C
F	1	C
G	4	D, E, F
H	2	G
	28	

▶ **Figure 9.19**

Four-Station Solution to the Line-Balancing Problem

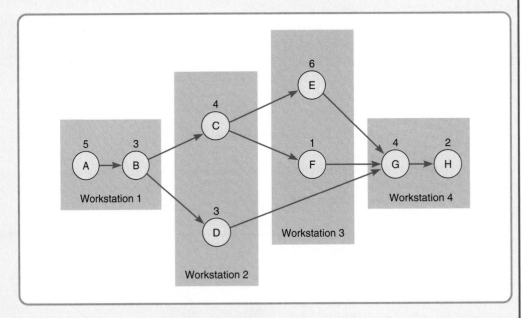

solution

The theoretical minimum number of workstations is:

$$\frac{\Sigma t_i}{\text{Cycle time}} = \frac{28 \text{ minutes}}{8 \text{ minutes}} = 3.5, \text{ or 4 stations}$$

The precedence graph and one good layout are shown in Figure 9.19.

$$\text{Efficiency} = \frac{\text{Total task time}}{(\text{Number of workstations}) \times (\text{Largest cycle time})} = \frac{28}{(4)(8)} = 87.5\%$$

Self-Test

- *Before taking the self-test*, refer to the learning objectives listed at the beginning of the chapter and the key terms listed at the end of the chapter.
- *Use the key at the back of the text to **correct** your answers.*
- *Restudy pages that correspond to any questions you answered incorrectly or material you feel uncertain about.*

1. In process-oriented and fixed-position layouts, it is important to minimize the costs of:
   a) raw materials
   b) material handling
   c) special purpose machinery
   d) skilled labor

2. A major assumption of stability of demand is important for justifying which of the following layout types?
   a) product layout
   b) process layout
   c) fixed-position layout
   d) all of the above

3. A fixed-position layout:
   a) groups workers to provide for movement of information
   b) addresses the layout requirements of large, bulky projects such as ships and buildings
   c) seeks the best machine utilization in continuous production
   d) allocates shelf space based on customer behavior
   e) deals with low-volume, high-variety production

4. A process-oriented layout:
   a) groups workers to provide for movement of information
   b) addresses the layout requirements of large, bulky projects such as ships and buildings
   c) seeks the best machine utilization in continuous production
   d) allocates shelf space based on customer behavior
   e) deals with low-volume, high-variety production

5. A big advantage of a process-oriented layout is:
   a) its low cost
   b) its flexibility in equipment and labor assignment
   c) the simplified scheduling problem presented by this layout strategy
   d) the ability to employ low-skilled labor

6. The fundamental layout strategies include:
   a) _____
   b) _____
   c) _____
   d) _____
   e) _____
   f) _____

7. For a focused work center or focused factory to be appropriate requires:
   a) _____
   b) _____
   c) _____

8. Before considering a product-oriented layout, we would wish to be certain that:
   a) _____
   b) _____
   c) _____
   d) _____

Active Model Exercise

This active model appears on your CD-ROM. It allows you to evaluate parameters in a process layout analysis. Active Model 9.1 contains a device for pairwise exchange of processes in work areas. There is a drop-down box that tells the software which two processes to swap. There is a Swap button that will make the switch. If the switch does not help, pressing the Swap button a second time will return the two processes to the work areas they were in before the swap.

Questions

1. What is the current total cost?

2. Assembly and Machine Shop have the highest degree of interaction. Would it be better to swap Assembly and Painting or Machine Shop and Painting to get Assembly and Machine Shop next to each other?

3. Use the Swap button one swap at a time. If the swap helps, move to the next pair. If not, press Swap to put the departments back. What is the minimum total cost after all swaps have been tried?

4. Look at the two data tables and use the yellow-shaded column to put processes in areas. What assignments lead to the minimum cost? What is this cost?

▼ **Active Model 9.1**   **Process Layout Model Using Walters Co. Data in Example 1**

Process - Oriented Layout

Area A	Area B	Area C
Assembly	Painting	Machine Shop
Receiving	Shipping	Testing
Area D	Area E	Area F

Reset Data   Questions

Assigned Work Area	Load Table	Assembly	Painting	Machine Shop	Receiving	Shipping	Testing
Area A	Assembly		50	100	0	0	20
Area B	Painting			30	50	10	0
Area C	Machine Shop				20	0	100
Area D	Receiving					50	0
Area E	Shipping						0
Area F	Testing						

Assembly & Painting   Swap

Total cost $ 570

Assigned Department	Cost table	Area A	Area B	Area C	Area D	Area E	Area F
Assembly	Area A		1	2	1	2	2
Painting	Area B			1	1	1	2
Machine Shop	Area C				2	2	1
Receiving	Area D					1	2
Shipping	Area E						1
Testing	Area F						

Cost/Movement computations

First Department	Second Department	Loads	First Area	Second Area	Cost	Loads x Cost
Assembly	Assembly	0	Area A	Area A	0	0
Assembly	Painting	50	Area A	Area B	1	50
Assembly	Machine Shop	100	Area A	Area C	2	200
Assembly	Receiving	0	Area A	Area D	1	0
Assembly	Shipping	0	Area A	Area E	2	0
Assembly	Testing	20	Area A	Area F	2	40
Painting	Assembly	0	Area B	Area A	1	0
Painting	Painting	0	Area B	Area B	0	0

Internet and Student CD-ROM/DVD Exercises

Visit our Companion Web site or use your student CD-ROM/DVD to help with material in this chapter.

 On Our Companion Web Site, www.prenhall.com/heizer
- Self-Study Quizzes
- Internet Case
- Practice Problems
- Virtual Company Tour
- PowerPoint Lecture

 On Your Student CD-ROM
- Practice Problems
- Active Model Exercise
- Excel OM
- Excel OM Data Files
- POM for Windows

 On Your Student DVD
- Video Clips and Video Cases
- Virtual Office Hours for Solved Problems

Discussion Questions

1. What are the seven layout strategies presented in this chapter?
2. What are the three factors that complicate a fixed-position layout?
3. What are the advantages and disadvantages of process layout?
4. How would an analyst obtain data and determine the number of trips in:
   (a) a hospital?
   (b) a machine shop?
   (c) an auto-repair shop?
5. What are the advantages and disadvantages of product layout?
6. What are the four assumptions (or preconditions) of establishing layout for high-volume, low-variety products?
7. What are the three forms of work cells discussed in the textbook?
8. What are the advantages and disadvantages of work cells?
9. What are the requirements for a focused work center or focused factory to be appropriate?
10. What are the two major trends influencing office layout?
11. What layout variables would you consider particularly important in an office layout where computer programs are written?
12. What layout innovations have you noticed recently in retail establishments?
13. What are the variables that a manager can manipulate in a retail layout?
14. Visit a local supermarket and sketch its layout. What are your observations regarding departments and their locations?
15. What is random stocking?
16. What information is necessary for random stocking to work?
17. Explain the concept of cross-docking.
18. What is a heuristic? Name several that can be used in assembly-line balancing.

Ethical Dilemma

Although buried by mass customization and a proliferation of new products of numerous sizes and variations, grocery chains continue to seek to maximize payoff from their layout. Their layout includes a marketable commodity—shelf space—and they charge for it. This charge is known as a *slotting fee*. Recent estimates are that food manufacturers now spend some 13% of sales on trade promotions, which is paid to grocers to get them to promote and discount the manufacturer's products. A portion of these fees is for slotting; but slotting fees drive up the manufacturer's cost. They also put the small company with a new product at a disadvantage, because small companies with limited resources are squeezed out of the market place. Slotting fees may also mean that customers may no longer be able to find the special local brand. How ethical are slotting fees?

Problems*

•• **9.1** Michael Plumb's job shop has four work areas, A, B, C, and D. Distances in feet between centers of the work areas are:

	A	B	C	D
A	—	4	9	7
B	—	—	6	8
C	—	—	—	10
D	—	—	—	—

Workpieces moved, in 100s of workpieces per week, between pairs of work areas, are:

	A	B	C	D
A	—	8	7	4
B	—	—	3	2
C	—	—	—	6
D	—	—	—	—

It costs Michael $1 to move 1 work piece 1 foot. What is the weekly total material handling cost of the layout? **PX**

•• **9.2** A Missouri job shop has four departments—machining (M), dipping in a chemical bath (D), finishing (F), and plating (P)—assigned to four work areas. The operations manager, Mary Marrs, has gathered the following data for this job shop as it is currently laid out (Plan A).

100s of Workpieces Moved Between Work Areas Each Year
Plan A

	M	D	F	P
M	—	6	18	2
D	—	—	4	2
F	—	—	—	18
P	—	—	—	—

Distances Between Work Areas (Departments) in Feet

	M	D	F	P
M	—	20	12	8
D	—	—	6	10
F	—	—	—	4
P	—	—	—	—

It costs $0.50 to move 1 workpiece 1 foot in the job shop. Marrs' goal is to find a layout that has the lowest material handling cost.
a) Determine cost of the current layout, Plan A, from the data above.

b) One alternative is to switch those departments with the high loads, namely, finishing (F) and plating (P), which alters the distance between them and machining (M) and dipping (D), as follows:

Distances Between Work Areas (Departments) in Feet
Plan B

	M	D	F	P
M	—	20	8	12
D	—	—	10	6
F	—	—	—	4
P	—	—	—	—

What is the cost of *this* layout?
c) Marrs now wants you to evaluate Plan C, which also switches milling (M) and drilling (D), below.

Distance Between Work Areas (Departments) in Feet
Plan C

	M	D	F	P
M	—	20	10	6
D	—	—	8	12
F	—	—	—	4
P	—	—	—	—

What is the cost of *this* layout?
d) Which layout is best from a cost perspective? **PX**

• **9.3** Three departments—milling (M), drilling (D), and sawing (S)—are assigned to three work areas in Samuel Smith's machine shop in Baltimore. The number of work pieces moved per day and the distances between the centers of the work areas, in feet, are shown below.

Pieces Moved Between Work Areas Each Day

	M	D	S
M	—	23	32
D	—	—	20
S	—	—	—

Distances Between Centers of Work Areas (Departments) in Feet

	M	D	S
M	—	10	5
D	—	—	8
S	—	—	—

It costs $2 to move 1 workpiece 1 foot.
What is the cost? **PX**

Note: **PX** means the problem may be solved with POM for Windows and/or Excel OM.

•• **9.4**   Roy Creasey Enterprises, a machine shop, is planning to move to a new, larger location. The new building will be 60 feet long by 40 feet wide. Creasey envisions the building as having six distinct production areas, roughly equal in size. He feels strongly about safety and intends to have marked pathways throughout the building to facilitate the movement of people and materials. See the following building schematic.

Building Schematic (with work areas 1–6)

His foreman has completed a month-long study of the number of loads of material that have moved from one process to another in the current building. This information is contained in the following flow matrix.

Flow Matrix between Production Processes

To From	Materials	Welding	Drills	Lathes	Grinders	Benders
Materials	0	100	50	0	0	50
Welding	25	0	0	50	0	0
Drills	25	0	0	0	50	0
Lathes	0	25	0	0	20	0
Grinders	50	0	100	0	0	0
Benders	10	0	20	0	0	0

Finally, Creasey has developed the following matrix to indicate distances between the work areas shown in the building schematic.

Distance between Work Areas

	1	2	3	4	5	6
1		20	40	20	40	60
2			20	40	20	40
3				60	40	20
4					20	40
5						20
6						

What is the appropriate layout of the new building?

•• **9.5**   Registration at Southern University has always been a time of emotion, commotion, and lines. Students must move among four stations to complete the trying semiannual process. Last semes-

Interstation Activity Mix

	Pick up paperwork and forms (A)	Advising station (B)	Pick up class cards (C)	Verification of status and payment (D)
Paperwork/forms (A)	---	450	550	50
Advising (B)	350	---	200	0
Class cards (C)	0	0	---	750
Verification/payment (D)	0	0	0	---

Existing Layout

▲ **Figure 9.20**   Registration Flow of Students

ter's registration, held in the fieldhouse, is described in Figure 9.20. You can see, for example, that 450 students moved from the paperwork station (A) to advising (B), and 550 went directly from A to picking up their class cards (C). Graduate students, who for the most part had preregistered, proceeded directly from A to the station where registration is verified and payment collected (D). The layout used last semester is also shown in Figure 9.20. The registrar is preparing to set up this semester's stations and is anticipating similar numbers.

a) What is the "load × distance," or "movement cost," of the layout shown?

b) Provide an improved layout and compute its movement cost. **Px**

••• **9.6**   You have just been hired as the director of operations for Reid Chocolates, a purveyor of exceptionally fine candies. Reid Chocolates has two kitchen layouts under consideration for its recipe making and testing department. The strategy is to provide the best kitchen layout possible so that food scientists can devote their time and energy to product improvement, not wasted effort in the kitchen. You have been asked to evaluate these two kitchen layouts and to prepare a recommendation for your boss, Mr. Reid, so that he can proceed to place the contract for building the kitchens. (See Figure 9.21(a), and Figure 9.21(b) on the next page.) **Px**

▼ **Figure 9.21(a)**   Layout Options

Number of trips between work centers:

From: \ To:	Refrigerator 1	Counter 2	Sink 3	Storage 4	Stove 5
Refrig. 1	0	8	13	0	0
Counter 2	5	0	3	3	8
Sink 3	3	12	0	4	0
Storage 4	3	0	0	0	5
Stove 5	0	8	4	10	0

(continued)

Kitchen layout #1

Walking distance in feet

Kitchen layout #2

Walking distance in feet

▲ **Figure 9.21(b)** *(continued)*

Kitchen layout #5

Walking distance in feet

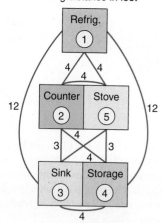

•• **9.7** Reid Chocolates (see Problem 9.6) is considering a third layout, as shown below. Evaluate its effectiveness in trip-distance feet. **Px**

Kitchen layout #3

Walking distance in feet

•• **9.8** Reid Chocolates (see Problems 9.6 and 9.7) has yet two more layouts to consider.
a) Layout 4 is shown below. What is the total trip distance?
b) Layout 5, which also follows, has what total trip distance? **Px**

Kitchen layout #4

Walking distance in feet

•• **9.9** Six processes are to be laid out in six areas along a long corridor at Linda Babat Accounting Services. The distance between adjacent work centers is 40 feet. The number of trips between work centers is given in the following table:

	Trips between Processes					
			To			
From	**A**	**B**	**C**	**D**	**E**	**F**
A		18	25	73	12	54
B			96	23	31	45
C				41	22	20
D					19	57
E						48
F						

a) Assign the processes to the work areas in a way that minimizes the total flow, using a method that places processes with highest flow adjacent to each other.
b) What assignment minimizes the total traffic flow? **Px**

•• **9.10** After an extensive product analysis using group technology, Bob Buerlein has identified a product he believes should be pulled out of his process facility and handled in a work cell. Bob has identified the following operations as necessary for the work cell. The customer expects delivery of 250 units per day, and the work day is 420 minutes.
a) What is the takt time?
b) How many employees should be cross-trained for the cell?
c) Which operations may warrant special consideration?

Operation	**Standard Time (min)**
Shear	1.1
Bend	1.1
Weld	1.7
Clean	3.1
Paint	1.0

•• **9.11** Stanford Rosenberg Electronics wants to establish an assembly line for producing a new product, the Personal Little

Assistant (PLA). The tasks, task times, and immediate predecessors for the tasks are as follows:

Task	Time (sec)	Immediate Predecessors
A	12	—
B	15	A
C	8	A
D	5	B, C
E	20	D

Rosenberg's goal is to produce 180 PLAs per hour.
a) What is the cycle time?
b) What is the theoretical minimum for the number of workstations that Rosenberg can achieve in this assembly line?
c) Can the theoretical minimum actually be reached when workstations are assigned? **Px**

•• **9.12** South Carolina Furniture, Inc., produces all types of office furniture. The "Executive Secretary" is a chair that has been designed using ergonomics to provide comfort during long work hours. The chair sells for $130. There are 480 minutes available during the day, and the average daily demand has been 50 chairs. There are eight tasks:

Task	Performance Time (min)	Task Must Follow Task Listed Below
A	4	—
B	7	—
C	6	A, B
D	5	C
E	6	D
F	7	E
G	8	E
H	6	F, G

a) Draw a precedence diagram of this operation.
b) What is the cycle time for this operation?
c) What is the *theoretical* minimum number of workstations?
d) Assign tasks to workstations.
e) How much total idle time is present each day?
f) What is the overall efficiency of the assembly line? **Px**

•• **9.13** Rita Gibson Appliances wants to establish an assembly line to manufacture its new product, the Mini-Me Microwave Oven. The goal is to produce five Mini-Me Microwave Ovens per hour. The tasks, task times, and immediate predecessors for producing one Mini-Me Microwave Oven are as follows:

Task	Time (min)	Immediate Predecessors
A	10	—
B	12	A
C	8	A, B
D	6	B, C
E	6	C
F	6	D, E

a) What is the *theoretical* minimum for the smallest number of workstations that Gibson can achieve in this assembly line?
b) Graph the assembly line and assign workers to workstations. Can you assign them with the theoretical minimum?
c) What is the efficiency of *your* assignment? **Px**

•• **9.14** The Temple Toy Company has decided to manufacture a new toy tractor, the production of which is broken into six steps. The demand for the tractor is 4,800 units per 40-hour workweek:

Task	Performance Time (sec)	Predecessors
A	20	None
B	30	A
C	15	A
D	15	A
E	10	B, C
F	30	D, E

a) Draw a precedence diagram of this operation.
b) Given the demand, what is the cycle time for this operation?
c) What is the *theoretical* minimum number of workstations?
d) Assign tasks to workstations.
e) How much total idle time is present each cycle?
f) What is the overall efficiency of the assembly line with five stations; and with six stations? **Px**

•• **9.15** The following table details the tasks required for Dallas-based T. Liscio Industries to manufacture a fully portable industrial vacuum cleaner. The times in the table are in minutes. Demand forecasts indicate a need to operate with a cycle time of 10 minutes.

Activity	Activity Description	Immediate Predecessors	Time
A	Attach wheels to tub	—	5
B	Attach motor to lid	—	1.5
C	Attach battery pack	B	3
D	Attach safety cutoff	C	4
E	Attach filters	B	3
F	Attach lid to tub	A, E	2
G	Assemble attachments	—	3
H	Function test	D, F, G	3.5
I	Final inspection	H	2
J	Packing	I	2

a) Draw the appropriate precedence diagram for this production line.
b) Assign tasks to workstations and determine how much idle time is present each cycle?
c) Discuss how this balance could be improved to 100%
d) What is the *theoretical* minimum number of workstations? **Px**

•• **9.16** Tailwind, Inc., produces high-quality but expensive training shoes for runners. The Tailwind shoe, which sells for $210, contains both gas- and liquid-filled compartments to provide more stability and better protection against knee, foot, and back injuries. Manufacturing the shoes requires 10 separate tasks. There are 400 minutes available for manufacturing the shoes in the plant each day. Daily demand is 60. The information for the tasks is as follows:

Task	Performance Time (min)	Task Must Follow Task Listed Below
A	1	—
B	3	A
C	2	B
D	4	B
E	1	C, D
F	3	A
G	2	F
H	5	G
I	1	E, H
J	3	I

a) Draw the precedence diagram.

b) Assign tasks to the minimum feasible number of workstations according to the "ranked positioned weight" decision rule.

c) What is the efficiency of the process?

d) What is the idle time per cycle? **Px**

•• **9.17** Mach 10 is a one-person sailboat designed to be used in the ocean. Manufactured by Creative Leisure, Mach 10 can handle 40-mph winds and seas over 10 feet. The final assembly plant is in Cupertino, California. At this time, 200 minutes are available each day to manufacture Mach 10. The daily demand is 60 boats. Given the following information,

a) Draw the precedence diagram and assign tasks to the fewest workstations possible.

b) What is the efficiency of the assembly line?

c) What is the *theoretical* minimum number of workstations?

d) What is the idle time?

Task	Performance Time (min)	Task Must Follow Task Listed Below
A	1	—
B	1	A
C	2	A
D	1	C
E	3	C
F	1	C
G	1	D, E, F
H	2	B
I	1	G, H **Px**

•• **9.18** Because of the expected high demand for Mach 10, Creative Leisure has decided to increase manufacturing time available to produce the Mach 10 (see Problem 9.17).

a) If demand remained the same and 300 minutes were available each day, how many workstations would be needed?

b) What would be the efficiency of the new system?

c) What would be the impact on the system if 400 minutes were available? **Px**

••• **9.19** Dr. Lori Baker, operations manager at Nesa Electronics, prides herself on excellent assembly-line balancing. She has been told that the firm needs to complete 96 instruments per 24-hour day. The assembly-line activities are:

Task	Time (min)	Predecessors
A	3	—
B	6	—
C	7	A
D	5	A, B
E	2	B
F	4	C
G	5	F
H	7	D, E
I	1	H
J	6	E
K	4	G, I, J
	50	

a) Draw the precedence diagram.

b) If the daily (24-hour) production rate is 96 units, what is the highest allowable cycle time?

c) If the cycle time after allowances is given as 10 minutes, what is the daily (24-hour) production rate?

d) With a 10-minute cycle time, what is the theoretical minimum number of stations with which the line can be balanced?

e) With a 10-minute cycle time and six workstations, what is the efficiency?

f) What is the total idle time per cycle with a 10-minute cycle time and six workstations?

g) What is the best work station assignment you can make without exceeding a 10-minute cycle time and what is its efficiency? **Px**

•• **9.20** Suppose production requirements in Solved Problem 9.2 (see page 374) increase and require a reduction in cycle time from 8 minutes to 7 minutes. Balance the line once again, using the new cycle time. Note that it is not possible to combine task times so as to group tasks into the minimum number of workstations. This condition occurs in actual balancing problems fairly often. **Px**

•• **9.21** The preinduction physical examination given by the U.S. Army involves the following seven activities:

Activity	Average Time (min)
Medical history	10
Blood tests	8
Eye examination	5
Measurements (i.e., weight, height, blood pressure)	7
Medical examination	16
Psychological interview	12
Exit medical evaluation	10

These activities can be performed in any order, with two exceptions: Medical history must be taken first, and exit medical evaluation is last. At present, there are three paramedics and two physicians on duty during each shift. Only physicians can perform exit evaluations and conduct psychological interviews. Other activities can be carried out by either physicians or paramedics.

a) Develop a layout and balance the line.

b) How many people can be processed per hour?

c) Which activity accounts for the current bottleneck?

d) What is the total idle time per cycle?

e) If one more physician and one more paramedic can be placed on duty, how would you redraw the layout? What is the new throughput?

••• **9.22** Frank Pianki's company wants to establish an assembly line to manufacture its new product, the iScan phone. Frank's goal is to produce 60 iScans per hour. Tasks, task times, and immediate predecessors are as follows:

Task	Time (sec)	Immediate Predecessors	Task	Time (sec)	Immediate Predecessors
A	40	—	F	25	C
B	30	A	G	15	C
C	50	A	H	20	D, E
D	40	B	I	18	F, G
E	6	B	J	30	H, I

a) What is the theoretical minimum for the number of workstations that Frank can achieve in this assembly line?

b) Use the *most following tasks* heuristic to balance an assembly line for the iScan phone.

c) How many workstations are in your answer to (b)?

d) What is the efficiency of your answer to (b)? **Px**

•••• **9.23** As the Cottrell Bicycle Co. of St. Louis completes plans for its new assembly line, it identifies 25 different tasks in the production process. VP of Operations Jonathan Cottrell now faces the job of balancing the line. He lists precedences and provides time estimates for each step based on work-sampling tech-

niques. His goal is to produce 1,000 bicycles per standard 40-hour workweek.

Task	Time (sec)	Precedence Tasks	Task	Time (sec)	Precedence Tasks
K3	60	—	E3	109	F3
K4	24	K3	D6	53	F4
K9	27	K3	D7	72	F9, E2, E3
J1	66	K3	D8	78	E3, D6
J2	22	K3	D9	37	D6
J3	3	—	C1	78	F7
G4	79	K4, K9	B3	72	D7, D8, D9, C1
G5	29	K9, J1	B5	108	C1
F3	32	J2	B7	18	B3
F4	92	J2	A1	52	B5
F7	21	J3	A2	72	B5
F9	126	G4	A3	114	B7, A1, A2
E2	18	G5, F3			

a) Balance this operation, using various heuristics. Which is best and why?

b) What happens if the firm can change to a 41-hour workweek? **Px**

Case Studies

State Automobile License Renewals

Henry Coupe, the manager of a metropolitan branch office of the state department of motor vehicles, attempted to analyze the driver's license–renewal operations. He had to perform several steps. After examining the license-renewal process, he identified those steps and associated times required to perform each step, as shown in the following table:

State Automobile License-Renewal Process Times

Step	Average Time to Perform (sec)
1. Review renewal application for correctness	15
2. Process and record payment	30
3. Check file for violations and restrictions	60
4. Conduct eye test	40
5. Photograph applicant	20
6. Issue temporary license	30

Coupe found that each step was assigned to a different person. Each application was a separate process in the sequence shown. He determined that his office should be prepared to accommodate a maximum demand of processing 120 renewal applicants per hour.

He observed that work was unevenly divided among clerks and that the clerk responsible for checking violations tended to shortcut her task to keep up with the others. Long lines built up during the maximum-demand periods.

Coupe also found that steps 1 to 4 were handled by general clerks who were each paid $12 per hour. Step 5 was performed by a photographer paid $16 per hour. (Branch offices were charged $10 per hour for each camera to perform photography.) Step 6, issuing temporary licenses, was required by state policy to be handled by uniformed motor vehicle officers. Officers were paid $18 per hour but could be assigned to any job except photography.

A review of the jobs indicated that step 1, reviewing applications for correctness, had to be performed before any other step could be taken. Similarly, step 6, issuing temporary licenses, could not be performed until all the other steps were completed.

Henry Coupe was under severe pressure to increase productivity and reduce costs, but he was also told by the regional director that he must accommodate the demand for renewals. Otherwise, "heads would roll."

Discussion Questions

1. What is the maximum number of applications per hour that can be handled by the present configuration of the process?

2. How many applications can be processed per hour if a second clerk is added to check for violations?

3. Assuming the addition of a second clerk, what is the maximum number of applications the process can handle?

4. How would you suggest modifying the process to accommodate 120 applications per hour?

Source: Updated from a case by W. Earl Sasser, Paul R. Olson, and D. Daryl Wyckoff, *Management of Services Operations: Text, Cases, and Readings* (Boston: Allyn & Bacon).

Laying Out Arnold Palmer Hospital's New Facility

When Orlando's Arnold Palmer Hospital began plans to create a new 273-bed, 11-story hospital across the street from its existing facility, which was bursting at the seams in terms of capacity, a massive planning process began. The $100 million building, opened in 2006, was long overdue, according to Executive Director Kathy Swanson. "We started Arnold Palmer Hospital in 1989, with a mission to provide quality services for children and women in a comforting, family-friendly environment. Since then we have served well over 1.5 million women and children and now deliver more than 12,000 babies a year. By 2001, we simply ran out of room, and it was time for us to grow."

The new hospital's unique, circular pod design provides a maximally efficient layout in all areas of the hospital, creating a patient-centered environment. *Servicescape* design features include a serene environment created through the use of warm colors, private rooms with pull-down Murphy beds for family members, 14-foot ceilings, and natural lighting with oversized windows in patient

rooms. But these radical new features did not come easily. "This pod concept with a central nursing area and pie-shaped rooms resulted from over 1,000 planning meetings of 35 user groups, extensive motion and time studies, and computer simulations of the daily movements of nurses," says Swanson.

In a traditional linear hospital layout, called the *racetrack* design, patient rooms line long hallways, and a nurse might walk 2.7 miles per day serving patient needs at Arnold Palmer. "Some nurses spent 30% of their time simply walking. With the nursing shortage and the high cost of health care professionals, efficiency is a major concern," added Swanson. With the nursing station in the center of 10- or 12-bed circular pods, no patient room is more than 14 feet from a station. The time savings are in the 20% range. Swanson pointed to Figures 9.22 and 9.23 as examples of the old and new walking and trip distances.*

*Layout and walking distances, including some of the numbers in Figures 9.22 and 9.23, have been simplified for purposes of this case.

▶ **Figure 9.22**

Traditional Hospital Layout

Patient rooms are on two linear hallways with exterior windows. Supply rooms are on interior corridors. This layout is called a "racetrack" design.

▶ **Figure 9.23**

New Pod Design for Hospital Layout

Note that each room is 14 feet from the pod's *local* nursing station. The *break rooms* and the *central medical station* are each about 60 feet from the local nursing pod. Pod *linen supply* rooms are also 14 feet from the local nursing station.

"We have also totally redesigned our neonatal rooms," says Swanson. "In the old system, there were 16 neonatal beds in a large and often noisy rectangular room. The new building features semiprivate rooms for these tiny babies. The rooms are much improved, with added privacy and a quiet, simulated night atmosphere, in addition to pull-down beds for parents to use. Our research shows that babies improve and develop much more quickly with this layout design. Layout and environment indeed impact patient care!"

Discussion Questions**

1. Identify the many variables that a hospital needs to consider in layout design.
2. What are the advantages of the circular pod design over the traditional linear hallway layout found in most hospitals?
3. Figure 9.22 illustrates a sample linear hallway layout. During a period of random observation, nurse Thomas Smith's day includes 6 trips from the nursing station to each of the 12 patient rooms (back and forth), 20 trips to the medical supply room, 5 trips to the break room, and 12 trips to the linen supply room. What is his total distance traveled in miles?
4. Figure 9.23 illustrates an architect's drawing of Arnold Palmer Hospital's new circular pod system. If nurse Susan Jones's day includes 7 trips from the nursing pod to each of the 12 rooms (back and forth), 20 trips to central medical supply, 6 trips to the break room, and 12 trips to the pod linen supply, how many miles does she walk during her shift? What are the differences in the travel times between the two nurses for this random day?
5. The concept of *servicescapes* is discussed in this chapter. Describe why this is so important at Arnold Palmer Hospital and give examples of its use in layout design.

**You may wish to view this video case on your DVD before addressing these questions.

Facility Layout at Wheeled Coach

When President Bob Collins began his career at Wheeled Coach, the world's largest manufacturer of ambulances, there were only a handful of employees. Now the firm's Florida plant has a workforce of 350. The physical plant has also expanded, with offices, R&D, final assembly, and wiring, cabinetry, and upholstery work cells in one large building. Growth has forced the painting work cell into a separate building, aluminum fabrication and body installation into another, inspection and shipping into a fourth, and warehousing into yet another.

Like many other growing companies, Wheeled Coach was not able to design its facility from scratch. And although management realizes that material handling costs are a little higher than an ideal layout would provide, Collins is pleased with the way the facility has evolved and employees have adapted. The aluminum cutting work cell lies adjacent to body fabrication, which, in turn, is located next to the body-installation work cell. And while the vehicle must be driven across a street to one building for painting and then to another for final assembly, at least the ambulance is on wheels. Collins is also satisfied with the flexibility shown in design of the work cells. Cell construction is flexible and can accommodate changes in product mix and volume. Additionally, work cells are typically small and movable, with many work benches and staging racks borne on wheels so that they can be easily rearranged and products transported to the assembly line.

Assembly-line balancing is one key problem facing Wheeled Coach and every other repetitive manufacturer. Produced on a schedule calling for four 10-hour work days per week, once an ambulance is on one of the six final assembly lines, it *must* move forward each day to the next workstation. Balancing just enough workers and tasks at each of the seven workstations is a never-ending challenge. Too many workers end up running into each other; too few can't finish an ambulance in 7 days. Constant shifting of design and mix and improved analysis has led to frequent changes.

Discussion Questions*

1. What analytical techniques are available to help a company like Wheeled Coach deal with layout problems?
2. What suggestions would you make to Bob Collins about his layout?
3. How would you measure the "efficiency" of this layout?

*You may wish to view this video case on your DVD before addressing these questions.

Additional Case Studies

Internet case study: Visit our Companion Web site at www.prenhall.com/heizer for this free case study:

- **Microfix, Inc.:** This company needs to balance its PC manufacturing assembly line and deal with sensitivity analysis of time estimates.

Harvard has selected these Harvard Business School cases to accompany this chapter:

harvardbusinessonline.hbsp.harvard.edu

- **Toshiba; Ome Works** (#696-059): Deals with the design of an efficient notebook computer assembly line in the Ome, Japan, factory.
- **Mouawad Bangkok Rare Jewels Manufacturers Co. Ltd. (A)** (#696-056): This small Thai factory faces a challenging production control process.
- **Copeland Corp. (B)** (#686-089): A plant layout must be selected from two alternatives available to this Sydney, Australia, manufacturer.

Bibliography

Dekker, R., et al. "Improving Order-Picking Response Time at Ankor's Warehouse." *Interfaces* 34, no. 4 (July–August 2004): 303–313.

Francis, R. L., L. F. McGinnis, and J. A. White. *Facility Layout and Location*, 3rd ed. Upper Saddle River, NJ: Prentice Hall, 1998.

Heyer, N., and U. Wemmerlöv. *Reorganizing the Factory: Competing through Cellular Manufacturing.* Portland, OR: Productivity Press, 2002.

Kee, Micah R. "The Well-Ordered Warehouse." *APICS: The Performance Advantage* (March 2003): 20–24.

Kulwiec, Ray. "Crossdocking as a Supply Chain Strategy." *Target* 20, no. 3 (third issue 2004): 28–35.

Larson, S. "Extreme Makover—OR Edition." *Nursing Management* (November 2005): 26.

Owen, Robin. "Modeling Future Factories." *IIE Solutions* (August 2001): 24–35.

Panchalavarapu, P. R., and V. Chankong. "Design of Cellular Manufacturing System with Assembly Considerations."

Computers & Industrial Engineering 48, no. 3 (May 2005): 448.

Roodbergen, K. J., and I. F. A. Vis. "A Model for Warehouse Layout." *IIE Transactions* 38, no. 10 (October 2006): 799–811.

Seppala, P. "How to Carry Out Sustainable Change? An Analysis of Introducing Manufacturing Cells in a Finnish Engineering Company." *Human Factors and Ergonomics in Manufacturing* 16, no. 1 (Winter 2006): 17.

Stanowy, A. "Evolutionary Strategy for Manufacturing Cell Design." *Omega* 34, no. 1 (January 2006): 1.

Upton, David. "What Really Makes Factories Flexible?" *Harvard Business Review* 73, no. 4 (July–August 1995): 74–84.

Zeng, A. Z., M. Mahan, and N. Fleut. "Designing an Efficient Warehouse Layout to Facilitate the Order-Filling Process." *Production and Inventory Management Journal* 43, no. 3–4 (3rd/4th quarter 2002): 83–88.

Internet Resources

Commercial layout software from Cimtechnologies: **www.cimtech.com**
Factory flow for layout analysis: **www.ugs.com**
Layout iQ: **www.rapidmodeling.com**

Proplanner's Flow Planner calculator:
  www.proplanner.com/product/details/flowpath.aspx
Various facility designs plans: **www.manufacturing.net**

CHAPTER 10

Human Resources and Job Design

Chapter Outline

Ten OM Strategy Decisions

Design of Goods and Services

Managing Quality

Process Strategy

Location Strategies

Layout Strategies

Human Resources

Supply Chain Management

Inventory Management

Scheduling

Maintenance

Learning Objectives

When you complete this chapter you should be able to

1. Describe labor planning policies
2. Identify the major issues in job design
3. Identify major ergonomic and work environment issues
4. Use the tools of methods analysis
5. Understand the contribution of the visual workplace

High-Performance Teamwork from the Pit Crew Makes the Difference between Winning and Losing

In the 1990s, the popularity of NASCAR (National Association for Stock Car Auto Racing) exploded, bringing $100s of millions of TV and sponsorship dollars into the sport. With more money, competition increased, as did the rewards for winning on Sunday. The teams, headed by such names as Rusty Wallace, Jeff Gordon, Dale Earnhardt, Jr., and Tony Stewart, are as famous as the New York Yankees, Atlanta Hawks, or Chicago Bears.

The race car drivers may be famous, but it's the pit crews who often determine the outcome of a race. Twenty years ago, crews were auto mechanics during the week that simply did double duty on Sundays in the pits. They did pretty well to change four tires in less than 30 seconds. Today, because NASCAR teams find competitive advantage wherever they can, taking more than 16 seconds can be disastrous. A botched pit stop is the equivalent of ramming your car against the wall—crushing all hopes for the day.

On Rusty Wallace's team, as on all the top NASCAR squads, the crewmen who go "over the wall" are now athletes, usually ex-college football or basketball players with proven agility and strength. The Evernham team, for example, includes a former defensive back from Fairleigh Dickinson (who is now a professional tire carrier) and a 300-pound lineman from East Carolina University (who handles the jack). The Chip Ganassi racing team includes baseball players from Wake Forest, football players from University of Kentucky and North Carolina, and a hockey player from Dartmouth.

Tire changers—the guys who wrench lug nuts off and on—are a scarce human resource and average $100,000 a year in salary. Jeff Gordon was reminded of the importance of coordinated teamwork when five of his "over-the-wall" guys jumped to Dale

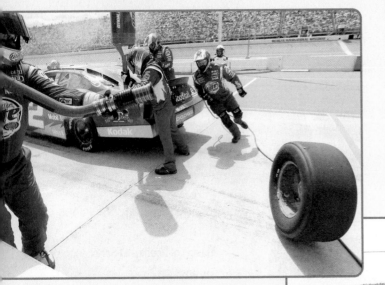

▲ This Goodyear tire comes off Rusty Wallace's car and is no longer needed after going around the track for more than 40 laps in a June 19 Michigan International Speedway race.

▼ Lap 91—Tire is removed from Rusty Wallace's car.

◄ Jamie Rolewicz takes tires from pile of used tires and puts them onto a cart.

388

1 Wallace's car pulls into the pit; the crew rushes to the right side of the car to begin service.

CFT JM
FTC CRT
RTC
GM#1 GM#2

Wall

2 Right side is jacked up, tire starts to come off; gas man is emptying his first can.

3.1

CFT FTC JM CRT RTC
GM#2
GM#1

Wall

3 Action shifts to driver's side of the car; gas man carries second can of gas in.

8.9

GM#2
GM#1
FTC CFT RTC JM CRT

Wall

4 The second can of gas is being emptied; driver's side tires are being changed.

.7

GM#2
GM#1
FTC CFT RTC JM CRT

Wall

5 Service is complete. The jackman drops the car, which is the signal to the Wallace driver to exit the pit.

15.4

A good pit stop will take about 16 seconds.

FTC CFT JM RTC CRT GM#2
GM#1

Wall

Movement of the pit crew members who go over the wall...

FTC = Front tire carrier
CFT = Changer front tire
GM#1 = Gas man #1
GM#2 = Gas man #2
RTC = Rear tire carrier
CRT = Changer rear tire
JM = Jackman

▲ **JM (Jackman)** *The jackman carries the hydraulic jack from the pit wall to raise the car's right side. After new tires are bolted on, he drops the car to the ground and repeats the process on the left side. His timing is crucial during this left side change, because when he drops the car again, it's the signal for the driver to go. The jackman has the most dangerous job of all the crew members; during the right-side change, he is exposed to oncoming traffic down pit row.* **FTC (Front tire carrier)** *Each tire carrier hauls a new 75-pound tire to the car's right side, places it on the wheel studs and removes the old tire after the tire change. They repeat this process on the left side of the car with a new tire rolled to them by crew members behind the pit wall.* **CFT (Changer front tire)** *Tire changers run to the car's right side and using an air impact wrench, they remove five lug nuts off the old tire and bolt on a new tire. They repeat the process on the left side.* **RTC (Rear tire carrier)** *Same as front tire carrier, except RTC may also adjust the rear jack bolt to alter the car's handling.* **CRT (Changer rear tire)** *Same as FT but on two rear tires.* **Gas man #1** *This gas man is usually the biggest and strongest person on the team. He goes over the wall carrying a 75-pound, 11-gallon "dump can" whose nozzle he jams into the car's fuel cell receptacle. He is then handed (or tossed) another can, and the process is repeated.* **Gas man #2** *Gets second gas can to Gas man #1 and catches excess fuel that spills out.*

Jarrett's organization a few years ago; it was believed to be a $500,000 per year deal.

A pit crew consists of seven men: a front-tire changer; a rear-tire changer; front- and rear-tire carriers; a man who jacks the car up; and two gas men with an 11-gallon can.

Every sport has its core competencies and key metrics—for example, the speed of a pitcher's fastball, a running back's time on the 40-yard dash. In NASCAR, a tire changer should get 5 lug nuts off in 1.2 seconds. The jackman should haul his 25-pound aluminum jack from the car's right side to left in 3.8 seconds. For tire carriers, it should take .7 seconds to get a tire from the ground to mounted on the car.

The seven men who go over the wall are coached and orchestrated. Coaches use the tools of OM and watch "game tape" of pit stops and make intricate adjustments to the choreography.

"There's a lot of pressure," says D. J. Richardson, a Rusty Wallace team tire changer—and one of the best in the business. Richardson trains daily with the rest of the crew in the shop of the team owner. They focus on cardiovascular work and two muscle groups daily.

Twice a week, they simulate pit stops—there can be from 12 to 14 variations—to work on their timing.

In a recent race in Michigan, Richardson and the rest of the Rusty Wallace team, with ergonomically designed gas cans, tools, and special safety gear, were ready. On lap 43, the split-second frenzy began, with Richardson—air gun in hand—jumping over a 2-foot white wall and sprinting to the right side of the team's Dodge. A teammate grabbed the tire and set it in place while Richardson secured it to the car. The process was repeated on the left side while the front crew followed the same procedure. Coupled with refueling, the pit stop took 12.734 seconds.

After catching their breath for a minute, Richardson and the other pit crew guys reviewed a videotape, looking for split-second flaws.

The same process was repeated on lap 91. The Wallace driver made a late charge on Jeff Burton and Kurt Busch on the last lap and went from 14th place to a 10th place finish.

Sources: The Wall Street Journal (June 15, 2005): A1; and Orlando Sentinel (June 26, 2005): C10–C12 and (February 11, 2001): M10–M11.

Various work cultures, of which NASCAR racing teams is just one example, exist all over the world. How are these cultures built and what are the human resource issues for the operations manager? In this chapter, we will examine a variety of human resource issues because organizations do not function without people. Moreover, they do not function well without competent, motivated people. The operations manager's human resource strategy determines the talents and skills available to operations.

As many organizations from Hard Rock Cafe to Southwest Airlines have demonstrated, competitive advantage can be built through human resource strategy. Good human resource strategies are expensive, difficult to achieve, and hard to sustain. However, the payoff potential is substantial because they are hard to copy! So a competitive advantage in this area is particularly beneficial. For these reasons, we now look at the operations manager's human resource options.

Video 10.1

Human Resources at
Hard Rock Cafe

HUMAN RESOURCE STRATEGY FOR COMPETITIVE ADVANTAGE

The objective of a human resource strategy is to manage labor and design jobs so people are effectively and efficiently utilized. As we focus on a human resource strategy, we want to ensure that people:

1. Are efficiently utilized within the constraints of other operations management decisions.
2. Have a reasonable quality of work life in an atmosphere of mutual commitment and trust.

By reasonable *quality of work life* we mean a job that is not only reasonably safe and for which the pay is equitable but that also achieves an appropriate level of both physical and psychological requirements. *Mutual commitment* means that both management and employee strive to meet common objectives. *Mutual trust* is reflected in reasonable, documented employment policies that are honestly and equitably implemented to the satisfaction of both management and employee.[1] When management has a genuine respect for its employees and their contributions to the firm, establishing a reasonable quality of work life and mutual trust is not particularly difficult.

This chapter is devoted to showing how operations managers can achieve an effective human resource strategy, which, as we have suggested in our opening profile of NASCAR racing teams, may provide a competitive advantage.

Constraints on Human Resource Strategy

As Figure 10.1 suggests, many decisions made about people are constrained by other decisions. First, the product mix may determine seasonality and stability of employment. Second, technology, equipment, and processes may have implications for safety and job content. Third, the location decision may have an impact on the ambient environment in which the employees work. Finally, layout decisions, such as assembly line versus work cell, influence job content.

Technology decisions impose substantial constraints. For instance, some of the jobs in steel mills are dirty, noisy, and dangerous; slaughterhouse jobs may be stressful and subject workers to stomach-crunching stench; assembly-line jobs are often boring and mind numbing; and high capital investments such as those required for manufacturing semiconductor chips may require 24-hour, 7-day-a-week operation in restrictive clothing.

We are not going to change these jobs without making changes in our other strategic decisions. So, the trade-offs necessary to reach a tolerable quality of work life are difficult. Effective managers consider such decisions simultaneously. The result: an effective, efficient system in which both individual and team performance are enhanced through optimum job design.

Acknowledging the constraints imposed on human resource strategy, we now look at three distinct decision areas of human resource strategy: *labor planning*, *job design*, and *labor standards*. The supplement to this chapter expands on the discussion of labor standards and introduces work measurement.

"It's possible to achieve sustainable competitive advantage by how you manage people."

Stanford University Prof. Jeffrey Pfeffer

---

[1] With increasing frequency, we find companies calling their employees *associates*, *individual contributors*, or members of a particular team.

◀ **Figure 10.1**

Constraints on Human Resource Strategy

An effective operations manager understands how decisions blend together to constrain the human resource strategy.

LABOR PLANNING

Labor planning is determining staffing policies that deal with (1) employment stability, (2) work schedules, and (3) work rules.

Employment-Stability Policies

Employment stability deals with the number of employees maintained by an organization at any given time. There are two very basic policies for dealing with stability:

1. *Follow demand exactly:* Following demand exactly keeps direct labor costs tied to production but incurs other costs. These other costs include (a) hiring and termination costs, (b) unemployment insurance, and (c) premium wages to entice personnel to accept unstable employment. This policy tends to treat labor as a variable cost.

2. *Hold employment constant:* Holding employment levels constant maintains a trained workforce and keeps hiring, termination, and unemployment costs to a minimum. However, with employment held constant, employees may not be utilized fully when demand is low, and the firm may not have the human resources it needs when demand is high. This policy tends to treat labor as a fixed cost.

Maintaining a stable workforce may allow a firm to pay lower wages than a firm that follows demand. This savings may provide a competitive advantage. However, firms with highly seasonal work and little control over demand may be best served by a fluctuating workforce. For example, a salmon canner on the Columbia River processes salmon only when the salmon are running. However, the firm may find complementary labor demands in other products or operations, such as making cans and labels or repairing and maintaining facilities.

The above policies are only two of many that can be efficient *and* provide a reasonable quality of work life. Firms must determine policies about employment stability. Employment policies are partly determined by management's view of labor costs—as a variable cost or a fixed cost.

Work Schedules

Although the standard work schedule in the U.S. is still five 8-hour days, many variations exist. A currently popular variation is a work schedule called flextime. *Flextime* allows employees, within limits, to determine their own schedules. A flextime policy might allow an employee (with proper notification) to be at work at 8 A.M. plus or minus 2 hours. This policy allows more autonomy and independence on the part of the employee. Some firms have found flextime a

Labor planning
A means of determining staffing policies dealing with employment stability, work schedules, and work rules.

Learning Objective

1. Describe labor planning policies

low-cost fringe benefit that enhances job satisfaction. The problem from the OM perspective is that much production work requires full staffing for efficient operations. A machine that requires three people cannot run at all if only two show up. Having a waiter show up to serve lunch at 1:30 P.M. rather than 11:30 A.M. is not much help either.

Similarly, some industries find that their process strategies severely constrain their human resource scheduling options. For instance, paper manufacturing, petroleum refining, and power stations require around-the-clock staffing except for maintenance and repair shutdown.

Another option is the *flexible workweek*. This plan often calls for fewer but longer days, such as four 10-hour days or, as in the case of light-assembly plants, 12-hour shifts. Working 12-hour shifts usually means working 3 days one week and 4 the next. Such shifts are sometimes called *compressed workweeks*. These schedules are viable for many operations functions—as long as suppliers and customers can be accommodated. Firms that have high process startup times (say, to get a boiler up to operating temperature) find longer workday options particularly appealing. Compressed workweeks have long been common in fire and utility departments, where physical exertion is modest but 24-hour coverage desirable. A recent Gallup survey showed that two-thirds of working adults would prefer toiling four 10-hour days to the standard 5-day schedule. Duke Power Co., Los Angeles County, AT&T, and General Motors are just a few organizations to offer the 4-day week.

Another option is shorter days rather than longer days. This plan often moves employees to *part-time status*. Such an option is particularly attractive in service industries, where staffing for peak loads is necessary. Banks and restaurants often hire part-time workers. Also, many firms reduce labor costs by reducing fringe benefits for part-time employees.

Job Classifications and Work Rules

"We've got product flexibility. Now we need manpower flexibility."

Former Chrysler CEO Tom LaSorda (The Wall Street Journal, August 15, 2005)

Many organizations have strict job classifications and work rules that specify who can do what, when they can do it, and under what conditions they can do it, often as a result of union pressure. These job classifications and work rules restrict employee flexibility on the job, which in turn reduces the flexibility of the operations function. Yet part of an operations manager's task is to manage the unexpected. Therefore, the more flexibility a firm has when staffing and establishing work schedules, the more efficient and responsive it *can* be. This is particularly true in service organizations, where extra capacity often resides in extra or flexible staff. Building morale and meeting staffing requirements that result in an efficient, responsive operation are easier if managers have fewer job classifications and work-rule constraints. If the strategy is to achieve a competitive advantage by responding rapidly to the customer, a flexible workforce may be a prerequisite.

JOB DESIGN

Job design

An approach that specifies the tasks that constitute a job for an individual or a group.

Job design specifies the tasks that constitute a job for an individual or a group. We examine five components of job design: (1) job specialization, (2) job expansion, (3) psychological components, (4) self-directed teams, and (5) motivation and incentive systems.

Labor Specialization

Labor specialization (or job specialization)

The division of labor into unique ("special") tasks.

The importance of job design as a management variable is credited to the 18th-century economist Adam Smith.[2] Smith suggested that a division of labor, also known as **labor specialization** (or **job specialization**), would assist in reducing labor costs of multiskilled artisans. This is accomplished in several ways:

1. *Development of dexterity* and faster learning by the employee because of repetition
2. *Less loss of time* because the employee would not be changing jobs or tools
3. *Development of specialized tools* and the reduction of investment because each employee has only a few tools needed for a particular task

---

[2]Adam Smith, *The Wealth of Nations* (London, 1776).

The 19th-century British mathematician Charles Babbage determined that a fourth consideration was also important for labor efficiency.[3] Because pay tends to follow skill with a rather high correlation, Babbage suggested *paying exactly the wage needed for the particular skill required*. If the entire job consists of only one skill, then we would pay for only that skill. Otherwise, we would tend to pay for the highest skill contributed by the employee. These four advantages of labor specialization are still valid today.

A classic example of labor specialization is the assembly line. Such a system is often very efficient, although it may require employees to do repetitive, mind-numbing jobs. The wage rate for many of these jobs, however, is very good. Given the relatively high wage rate for the modest skills required in many of these jobs, there is often a large pool of employees from which to choose. This is not an incidental consideration for the manager with responsibility for staffing the operations function. It is estimated that 2% to 3% of the workforce in industrialized nations perform highly specialized, repetitive assembly-line jobs. The traditional way of developing and maintaining worker commitment under labor specialization has been good selection (matching people to the job), good wages, and incentive systems.

From the manager's point of view, a major limitation of specialized jobs is their failure to bring the whole person to the job. Job specialization tends to bring only the employee's manual skills to work. In an increasingly sophisticated knowledge-based society, managers may want employees to bring their mind to work as well.

Learning Objective

2. Identify the major issues in job design

Job Expansion

In recent years, there has been an effort to improve the quality of work life by moving from labor specialization toward more varied job design. Driving this effort is the theory that variety makes the job "better" and that the employee therefore enjoys a higher quality of work life. This flexibility thus benefits the employee and the organization.

We modify jobs in a variety of ways. The first approach is **job enlargement**, which occurs when we add tasks requiring similar skill to an existing job. **Job rotation** is a version of job enlargement that occurs when the employee is allowed to move from one specialized job to another. Variety has been added to the employee's perspective of the job. Another approach is **job enrichment**, which adds planning and control to the job. An example is to have department store salespeople responsible for ordering, as well as selling, their goods. Job enrichment can be thought of as *vertical expansion*, as opposed to job enlargement, which is *horizontal*. These ideas are shown in Figure 10.2.

Job enlargement
The grouping of a variety of tasks about the same skill level; horizontal enlargement.

Job rotation
A system in which an employee is moved from one specialized job to another.

Job enrichment
A method of giving an employee more responsibility that includes some of the planning and control necessary for job accomplishment; vertical expansion.

▼ **Figure 10.2**   An Example of Job Enlargement (*horizontal* job expansion) and Job Enrichment (*vertical* job expansion)

The job can be enlarged horizontally by job rotation to tasks 2 and 3, or these tasks can be made a part of the present job. Job enrichment, expanding the job vertically, can occur by adding other types of tasks, such as participation in a quality team (planning) and testing tasks (control).

[3]Charles Babbage, *On the Economy of Machinery and Manufacturers* (London: C. Knight, 1832), Chapter 18.

Employee empowerment

Enlarging employee jobs so that the added responsibility and authority is moved to the lowest level possible in the organization; including perhaps even planning, quality, purchasing, hiring.

A popular extension of job enrichment, **employee empowerment** is the practice of enriching jobs so employees accept responsibility for a variety of decisions normally associated with staff specialists. Empowering employees helps them take "ownership" of their jobs so they have a personal interest in improving performance.

Psychological Components of Job Design

An effective human resources strategy also requires consideration of the psychological components of job design. These components focus on how to design jobs that meet some minimum psychological requirements.

Hawthorne Studies   The Hawthorne studies introduced psychology to the workplace. They were conducted in the late 1920s at Western Electric's Hawthorne plant near Chicago. Publication of the findings in 1939[4] showed conclusively that there is a dynamic social system in the workplace. Ironically, these studies were initiated to determine the impact of lighting on productivity. Instead, they found the social system and distinct roles played by employees to be more important than the intensity of the lighting. They also found that individual differences may be dominant in what an employee expects from the job and what the employee thinks her or his contribution to the job should be.

Core Job Characteristics   In the eight decades since the Hawthorne studies, substantial research regarding the psychological components of job design has taken place.[5] Hackman and Oldham have incorporated much of that work into five desirable characteristics of job design.[6] Their summary suggests that jobs should include the following characteristics:

> *"We hired workers and human beings came instead."*
>
> Max Frisch

1. *Skill variety*, requiring the worker to use a variety of skills and talents
2. *Job identity*, allowing the worker to perceive the job as a whole and recognize a start and a finish
3. *Job significance*, providing a sense that the job has an impact on the organization and society
4. *Autonomy*, offering freedom, independence, and discretion
5. *Feedback*, providing clear, timely information about performance

Including these five ingredients in job design is consistent with job enlargement, job enrichment, and employee empowerment. We now want to look at some of the ways in which teams can be used to expand jobs and achieve these five job characteristics.

Self-Directed Teams

Self-directed team

A group of empowered individuals working together to reach a common goal.

Many world-class organizations have adopted teams to foster mutual trust and commitment, and provide the core job characteristics. One team concept of particular note is the **self-directed team**: a group of empowered individuals working together to reach a common goal. These teams may be organized for long- or short-term objectives. Teams are effective primarily because they can easily provide employee empowerment, ensure core job characteristics, and satisfy many of the psychological needs of individual team members. A job design continuum is shown in Figure 10.3.

Of course, many good job designs *can* provide these psychological needs. Therefore, to maximize team effectiveness, managers do more than just form "teams." For instance, they (1) ensure that those who have a legitimate contribution are on the team, (2) provide management support, (3) ensure the necessary training, and (4) endorse clear objectives and goals. Successful teams should also receive financial or nonfinancial rewards. Finally, supervisors must release some control and learn to accept different job responsibilities. Self-directed teams may mean having no supervisors on the factory floor. Removing supervisors from the

---

[4]F. J. Roethlisberger and William J. Dickinson, *Management and the Workers* (New York: Wiley, 1964, copyright 1939, by the President & Fellows of Harvard College).

[5]See, for instance, the work of Gary P. Latham and Craig C. Pinder, "Work Motivation Theory and Research at the Dawn of the Twenty-First Century," *Annual Review of Psychology* 56 (2005): 485–517; Abraham H. Maslow, "A Theory of Human Motivation," *Psychological Review* 50 (1943): 370–396; and Frederick Herzberg, B. Mausner, and B. B. Snyderman, *The Motivation to Work* (New York: Wiley, 1965).

[6]See "Motivation Through the Design of Work," in Jay Richard Hackman and Greg R. Oldham, eds., *Work Redesign* (Reading, MA: Addison-Wesley, 1980) and A. Thomas, W. C. Buboltz, and C. Winkelspecht, "Job Characteristics and Personality as Predictors of Job Satisfaction," *Organizational Analysis*, 12, no. 2 (2004): 205–219.

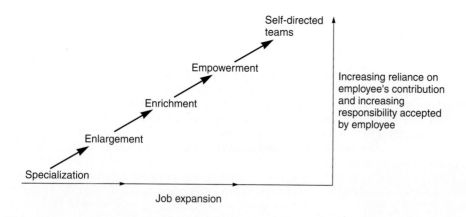

◀ **Figure 10.3**

Job Design Continuum

factory floor at M2 Global Inc. was a major culture change but one that led to new performance standards.

Limitations of Job Expansion   If job designs that enlarge, enrich, empower, and use teams are so good, why are they not universally used? Mostly it is because of costs. Here are a few limitations of expanded job designs:

- *Higher capital cost:* Job expansion may require facilities that cost more than those with a conventional layout.
- *Individual differences:* Some studies indicate that many employees opt for the less complex jobs.
- *Higher wage rates:* Expanded jobs may well require a higher average wage than jobs that are not expanded.
- *Smaller labor pool:* Because expanded jobs require more skill and acceptance of more responsibility, job requirements have increased.
- *Higher training costs:* Job expansion requires training and cross-training. Therefore, training budgets (especially in the U.S.) need to increase. (See Table 10.1.)

Despite these limitations, firms are finding a substantial payoff in job expansion.

▼ **Table 10.1**

Average Annual Training Hours per Employee

U.S.	7
Sweden	170
Japan	200

Source: APICS Newsletter.

Motivation and Incentive Systems

Our discussion of the psychological components of job design provides insight into the factors that contribute to job satisfaction and motivation. In addition to these psychological factors, there are monetary factors. Money often serves as a psychological as well as financial motivator. Monetary rewards take the form of bonuses, profit and gain sharing, and incentive systems.

Bonuses, typically in cash or stock options, are often used at executive levels to reward management. Profit-sharing systems provide some part of the profit for distribution to employees. A variation of profit sharing is gain sharing, which rewards employees for improvements made in an organization's performance. The most popular of these is the Scanlon plan, in which any reduction in the cost of labor is shared between management and labor.

The gain-sharing approach used by Panhandle Eastern Corp. of Houston, Texas, allows for employees to receive a bonus of 2% of their salary at year's end if the company earns at least $2.00 per share. When Panhandle earns $2.10 per share, the bonus climbs to 3%. Employees have become much more sensitive about costs since the plan began. Similarly, a bonus tied to the production of defect-free steel at Nucor, by an employee's shift, can triple a steelworker's take-home pay. Last year the average Nucor steelworker took home $100,000 based on profit and gain sharing.[7]

Incentive systems based on individual or group productivity are used throughout the world in a wide variety of applications, including nearly half of the manufacturing firms in America. Production incentives often require employees or crews to produce at or above a predetermined standard. The standard can be based on a "standard time" per task or number of pieces made. Both systems typically guarantee the employee at least a base rate. Incentives, of course, need not be monetary. Awards, recognition, and other kinds of preferences such as a preferred work schedule can be effective. (See the *OM in Action* box "Using Incentives to Unsnarl Traffic Jams in the

The only thing worse than training an employee and having them go to work somewhere else—is not training them and having them stay!

[7]N. Byrnes. "The Art of Motivation." *Business Week* (May 1, 2006): 57–62.

OM in Action — Using Incentives to Unsnarl Traffic Jams in the OR

Hospitals have long offered surgeons a precious perk: scheduling the bulk of their elective surgeries in the middle of the week so they can attend conferences, teach, or relax during long weekends. But at Boston Medical Center, St. John's Health Center (in Missouri), and Elliot Health System (in New Hampshire), this practice, one of the biggest impediments to a smooth-running hospital, is changing. "Block scheduling" jams up operating rooms, overloads nurses at peak times, and bumps scheduled patients for hours and even days.

Boston Medical Center's delays and cancellations of elective surgeries were nearly eliminated after surgeons agreed to stop block scheduling and to dedicate one OR for emergency cases. Cancellations dropped to 3, from 334, in just one 6-month period. In general, hospitals changing to the new system of spreading out elective surgeries during the week increase their surgery capacity by 10%, move patients through the operating room faster, and reduce nursing overtime.

To get doctors on board at St. John's, the hospital offered a carrot and two sticks: Doctors who were more than 10 minutes late 10% of the time lost their coveted 7:30 A.M. start times *and* were fined a portion of their fee—with proceeds going to a kitty that rewarded the best on-time performers. Surgeons' late start times quickly dropped from 16% to 5% and then to less than 1% within a year.

Sources: International Journal of Production Economics (January–February, 2006): 52; The Wall Street Journal (August 10, 2005): D1, D3; and Hospitals & Health Networks (September, 2005): 24–25.

OR.") Hard Rock Cafe has successfully reduced its turnover by giving every employee—from the CEO to the busboys—a $10,000 gold Rolex watch on their 10th anniversary with the firm.

With the increasing use of teams, various forms of team-based pay are also being developed. Many are based on traditional pay systems supplemented with some form of bonus or incentive system. However, because many team environments require cross training of enlarged jobs, *knowledge-based* pay systems have also been developed. Under knowledge-based (or skill-based) pay systems, a portion of the employee's pay depends on demonstrated knowledge or skills possessed. Knowledge-based pay systems are designed to reward employees for the enlarged scope of their jobs. Some of these pay systems have three dimensions: *horizontal skills* that reflect the variety of tasks the employee can perform; *vertical skills* that reflect the planning and control aspects of the job; and *depth of skills* that reflect quality and productivity. At Wisconsin's Johnsonville Sausage Co., employees receive pay raises *only* by mastering new skills such as scheduling, budgeting, and quality control.

 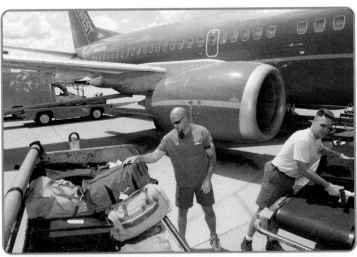

▲ *Southwest Airlines—consistently at the top of the airline pack in travel surveys, fewest lost bags and complaints, and highest profits—hires people with enthusiasm and empowers them to excel. A barefoot chairman of the board, Herb Kelleher, clings to the tail of a jet (left photo). Says Kelleher, "I've tried to create a culture of caring for people in the totality of their lives, not just at work. Someone can go out and buy airplanes and ticket counters, but they can't buy our culture, our esprit de corps."*

ERGONOMICS AND THE WORK ENVIRONMENT

With the foundation provided by Frederick W. Taylor, the father of the era of scientific management, we have developed a body of knowledge about people's capabilities and limitations. This knowledge is necessary because humans are hand/eye animals possessing exceptional capabilities and some limitations. Because managers must design jobs that can be done, we now introduce a few of the issues related to people's capabilities and limitations.

Ergonomics   The operations manager is interested in building a good interface between human and machine. Studies of this interface are known as **ergonomics**. Ergonomics means "the study of work." (*Ergon* is the Greek word for *work*.) In the U.S., the term *human factors* is often substituted for the word *ergonomics*. Understanding ergonomics issues helps to improve human performance.

Male and female adults come in limited configurations. Therefore, design of tools and the workplace depends on the study of people to determine what they can and cannot do. Substantial data have been collected that provide basic strength and measurement data needed to design tools and the workplace. The design of the workplace can make the job easier or impossible. Additionally, we now have the ability, through the use of computer modeling, to analyze human motions and efforts.

Let's look briefly at one instance of human measurements: determining the proper height for a writing desk. The desk has an optimum height depending on the size of the individual and the task to be performed. The common height for a writing desk is 29 inches. For typing or data entry at a computer, the surface should be lower. The preferred chair and desk height should result in a very slight angle between the body and arm when the individual is viewed from the front and when the back is straight. This is the critical measurement; it can be achieved via adjustment in either table or chair height.

Operator Input to Machines   Operator response to machines, be they hand tools, pedals, levers, or buttons, needs to be evaluated. Operations managers need to be sure that operators have the strength, reflexes, perception, and mental capacity to provide necessary control. Such problems as *carpal tunnel syndrome* may result when a tool as simple as a keyboard is poorly designed.[8] The photos in Figure 10.4 indicate recent innovations designed to improve this common tool.

> **Learning Objective**
>
> 3. Identify major ergonomic and work environment issues

Ergonomics

The study of work; often called *human factors*.

> *Many bicycle riders have seats set too low. The correct height is 103% of crotch-to-foot distance.*

◄ *Ergonomics issues occur in the office as well as in the factory. Here an ergonomics consultant is measuring the angle of a terminal operator's neck. Posture, which is related to desk height, chair height and position, keyboard placement, and computer screen, is an important factor in reducing back and neck pain that can be caused by extended hours at a computer.*

---

[8]Although carpal tunnel syndrome is routinely referred to as a work-related condition, there is some evidence that an underlying disease, such as diabetes or arthritis, may be the chief cause. See "Diseases, Not Work, May Be Carpal Tunnel Culprit," *IIE Solutions* (February 1999): 13.

The Infogrip 'keyboard' has only seven keys, one for each finger and three for the thumb, but replicates all the functions of a traditional QWERTY keyboard. Since finger placement is constant, strain on the hand is reduced. (Infogrip, Ventura, CA)

The TouchStream LP incorporates technology that allows computer users to enter information not only by keyboard and mouse but also with simple gesture commands. The system includes a specialized keyboard, a standard mouse, and an extensive two-handed gesture set. Typing, pointing, and gesturing are all done in the same area, eliminating the need to reach for a mouse. (Finger Works)

The "Data-Hand" keyboard allows each hand to rest on its own ergonomically shaped and padded palm support. Five keys surround each fingertip and thumb. (Industrial Innovations, Inc., Scottsdale, AZ)

▲ **Figure 10.4**   **Job Design and the Keyboard**

Feedback to Operators   Feedback to operators is provided by sight, sound, and feel; it should not be left to chance. The mishap at the Three Mile Island nuclear facility, America's worst nuclear experience, was in large part the result of poor feedback to the operators about reactor performance. Nonfunctional groups of large, unclear instruments and inaccessible controls, combined with hundreds of confusing warning lights, contributed to that nuclear failure. Such relatively simple issues make a difference in operator response and, therefore, performance.

The Work Environment   The physical environment in which employees work affects their performance, safety, and quality of work life. Illumination, noise and vibration, temperature, humidity, and air quality are work-environment factors under the control of the organization and the operations manager. The manager must approach them as controllable.

Illumination is necessary, but the proper level depends on the work being performed. Table 10.2 provides some guidelines. However, other lighting factors are important. These include reflective ability, contrast of the work surface with surroundings, glare, and shadows. (See the contrast in the cockpit photos).

Noise of some form is usually present in the work area, and most employees seem to adjust well. However, high levels of sound will damage hearing. Table 10.3 provides indications of the sound generated by various activities. Extended periods of exposure to decibel levels above 85

▶ **Table 10.2**

Levels of Illumination Recommended for Various Task Conditions

Task Condition	Type of Task or Area	Illumination Level (ft-c)[a]	Type of Illumination
Small detail, extreme accuracy	Sewing, inspecting dark materials	100	Overhead ceiling lights and desk lamp
Normal detail, prolonged periods	Reading, parts assembly, general office work	20–50	Overhead ceiling lights
Good contrast, fairly large objects	Recreational facilities	5–10	Overhead ceiling lights
Large objects	Restaurants, stairways, warehouses	2–5	Overhead ceiling lights

[a]ft-c (the foot-candle) is a measure of illumination.

Source: C. T. Morgan, J. S. Cook III, A. Chapanis, and M. W. Lund, eds., *Human Engineering Guide to Equipment Design* (New York: McGraw-Hill, 1963).

▲ *An important human factor/ergonomic issue in the aircraft industry is cockpit design. Newer "glass cockpits" (on the right) display information in more concise form than the traditional rows of round analog dials and gauges (on the left). New displays reduce the chance of human error, which is a factor in about two-thirds of commercial air accidents. Fractions of a second in the cockpit can literally mean the difference between life and death.*

dB are permanently damaging. The Occupational Safety and Health Administration (OSHA) requires ear protection above this level if exposure equals or exceeds 8 hours. Even at low levels, noise and vibration can be distracting and can raise a person's blood pressure, so managers make substantial effort to reduce noise and vibration through good machine design, enclosures, or insulation.

Temperature and humidity parameters have been well established. Managers with activities operating outside the established comfort zone should expect adverse effect on performance.

> *Recent research shows that noise in the work environment can increase the risk of heart attack by 50% or more.*

METHODS ANALYSIS

Methods analysis focuses on *how* a task is accomplished. Whether controlling a machine or making or assembling components, how a task is done makes a difference in performance, safety, and quality. Using knowledge from ergonomics and methods analysis, methods engineers are charged with ensuring that quality and quantity standards are achieved efficiently and safely.

Methods analysis
A system that involves developing work procedures that are safe and produce quality products efficiently.

Environment Noises	Common Noise Sources	Decibels	
	Jet takeoff (200 ft)	120	
		|	
Electric furnace area	Pneumatic hammer	100	Very annoying
		|	
Printing press plant	Subway train (20 ft)	90	
		|	
	Pneumatic drill (50 ft)	80	Ear protection required
Inside sports car (50 mph)		|	if exposed for 8 or
	Vacuum cleaner (10 ft)	70	more hours
Near freeway (auto traffic)	Speech (1 ft)	|	Intrusive
		60	
Private business office		|	
Light traffic (100 ft)	Large transformer (200 ft)	50	Quiet
		|	
Minimum levels, residential areas in Chicago at night		40	
		|	
Studio (speech)	Soft whisper (5 ft)	30	Very quiet

Source: Adapted from A. P. G. Peterson and E. E. Gross, Jr., *Handbook of Noise Measurement*, 7th ed. (New Concord, MA: General Radio Co.).

◀ **Table 10.3**

Decibel (dB) Levels for Various Sounds

Decibel levels are A-weighted sound levels measured with a sound-level meter.

= operation; ➡ = transportation; ☐ = inspection; ◗ = delay; ▽ = storage

▲ **Figure 10.5**   **Flow Diagram of Axle-Stand Production Line at Paddy Hopkirk Factory**

(a) Old method; (b) new method; (c) process chart of axle-stand production using Paddy Hopkirk's new method (shown in b).

Methods analysis and related techniques are useful in office environments as well as in the factory. Methods techniques are used to analyze:

1. **Movement of individuals or material.** The analysis is performed using *flow diagrams* and *process charts* with varying amounts of detail.
2. **Activity of human and machine and crew activity.** This analysis is performed using *activity charts* (also known as man–machine charts and crew charts).
3. **Body movement (primarily arms and hands).** This analysis is performed using *micro-motion charts*.

Flow diagram

A drawing used to analyze movement of people or material.

Process chart

Graphic representations that depict a sequence of steps for a process.

Activity chart

A way of improving utilization of an operator and a machine or some combination of operators (a crew) and machines.

Flow diagrams are schematics (drawings) used to investigate movement of people or material. As shown for Britain's Paddy Hopkirk Factory in Figure 10.5 and the *OM in Action* box "Saving Steps on the B-2 Bomber," the flow diagram provides a systematic procedure for looking at long-cycle repetitive tasks. The old method is shown in Figure 10.5(a), and a new method, with improved work flow and requiring less storage and space, is shown in Figure 10.5(b). **Process charts** use symbols, as in Figure 10.5(c), to help us understand the movement of people or material. In this way, movement and delays can be reduced and operations made more efficient. Figure 10.5(c) is a process chart used to supplement the flow diagram shown in Figure 10.5(b).

Activity charts are used to study and improve the utilization of an operator and a machine or some combination of operators (a "crew") and machines. The typical approach is for the analyst to record the present method through direct observation and then propose the improvement on a

OM in Action   Saving Steps on the B-2 Bomber

The aerospace industry is noted for making exotic products, but it is also known for doing so in a very expensive way. The historical batch-based processes used in the industry have left a lot of room for improvement. In leading the way, Northrop Grumman analyzed the work flow of a mechanic whose job in the Palmsdale, California, plant was to apply about 70 feet of tape to the B-2 stealth bomber. The mechanic (see the graphic below) walked away from the plane 26 times and took 3 hours just to

The mechanic's work path is reduced to the small area of purple lines shown here.

gather chemicals, hose, gauges, and other material needed just to get ready for the job. By making prepackaged kits for the job, Northrop Grumman cut preparation time to zero and the time to complete the job dropped from 8.4 hours to 1.6 hours (as seen above).

Sources: Business Week (May 28, 2001): 14; *Aviation Week & Space Technology* (January 17, 2000): 44; and *New York Times* (March 9, 1999): C1, C9.

The 26 trips to various workstations to gather the tools and equipment to apply tape to the B2 bomber are shown as purple lines above.

second chart. Figure 10.6 is an activity chart to show a proposed improvement for a two-person crew at Quick Car Lube.

Body movement is analyzed by an **operations chart**. It is designed to show economy of motion by pointing out wasted motion and idle time (delay). The operations chart (also known as a *right-hand/left-hand chart*) is shown in Figure 10.7.

Operations chart
A chart depicting right- and left-hand motions.

ACTIVITY CHART

	OPERATOR #1		OPERATOR #2	
	TIME	%	TIME	%
WORK	12	100	12	100
IDLE	0	0	0	0

OPERATION: Oil change & fluid check
EQUIPMENT: One bay/pit
OPERATOR: Two-person crew
STUDY NO.: _____ ANALYST: NG

SUBJECT *Quick Car Lube*   DATE *8-1-08*
PRESENT (PROPOSED) DEPT.   SHEET *1* OF *1*   CHART BY *LSA*

TIME	Operator #1	TIME	Operator #2	TIME
2	Take order		Move car to pit	
4	Vacuum car		Drain oil	
6	Clean windows		Check transmission	
8	Check under hood		Change oil filter	
10	Fill with oil		Replace oil plug	
12	Complete bill		Move car to front for customer	
14	Greet next customer		Move next car to pit	
16	Vacuum car		Drain oil	
18	Clean windows		Check transmission	

Repeat cycle

▲ **Figure 10.6** Activity Chart for Two-Person Crew Doing an Oil Change in 12 Minutes at Quick Car Lube

OPERATION CHART

SYMBOLS	PRESENT		PROPOSED	
	LH	RH	LH	RH
◯ OPERATION	2	3		
⇨ TRANSPORT.	1	1		
☐ INSPECTION				
D DELAY	4	3		
▽ STORAGE				

PROCESS: Bolt–washer assembly
EQUIPMENT:
OPERATOR: KJH
STUDY NO: _____ ANALYST:
DATE: 8 /1 /08   SHEET NO. 1 of 1
METHOD (PRESENT / PROPOSED)
REMARKS:

LEFT-HAND ACTIVITY Present METHOD	DIST.	SYMBOLS	SYMBOLS	DIST.	RIGHT-HAND ACTIVITY Present METHOD
1 Reach for bolt		●⇨☐D▽	◯⇨☐D▽		Idle
2 Grasp bolt		●⇨☐D▽	◯⇨☐D▽		Idle
3 Move bolt	6"	◯➡☐D▽	◯⇨☐D▽		Idle
4 Hold bolt		◯⇨☐●▽	◯⇨☐D▽		Reach for washer
5 Hold bolt		◯⇨☐●▽	◯⇨☐D▽		Grasp washer
6 Hold bolt		◯⇨☐●▽	◯➡☐D▽	8"	Move washer to bolt
7 Hold bolt		◯⇨☐●▽	◯⇨☐D▽		Place washer on bolt

▲ **Figure 10.7** Operations Chart (right-hand/left-hand chart) for Bolt-Washer Assembly

THE VISUAL WORKPLACE

Visual workplace
Uses a variety of visual communication techniques to rapidly communicate information to stakeholders.

A **visual workplace** uses low-cost visual devices to share information quickly and accurately. Well-designed displays and graphs root out confusion and replace difficult-to-understand print-outs and paperwork. Because workplace data change quickly and often, operations managers need to share accurate and up-to-date information. Workplace dynamics, with changing customer requirements, specifications, schedules, and other details on which an enterprise depends, must be rapidly communicated.

All visual systems should focus on improvement, because progress almost always has motivational benefits. An assortment of visual signals and charts is an excellent tool for communication not only among people doing the work but also among support staff, management, visitors, and suppliers. All these stakeholders deserve feedback on the organization. Management reports, if held only in the hands of management, are often useless and perhaps counterproductive. Visual management is a way of communicating to those who can make things happen.

Visual signals in the workplace can take many forms, as shown in Figure 10.8 and as noted below and on page 403.

Learning Objective

5. Understand the contribution of the visual workplace

Present the big picture

- Visual systems can communicate the larger picture, helping employees understand the link between their day-to-day activities and the organization's overall performance. At Baldor Electric Co. in Fort Smith, Arkansas, the prior day's closing price of Baldor's stock is posted for all to see. The stock price is to remind employees that a portion of their pay is based on profit sharing and stock options and to encourage them to keep looking for ways to increase productivity.
- Missouri's Springfield Re Manufacturing Corp. has developed a concept called "open book management," where every employee is trained to understand the importance of financial measures (such as return on equity) and is provided with these measures regularly.

Performance

- Details of quality, accidents, service levels, delivery performance, costs, and such traditional variables as attendance and tardiness can all be presented, often in the form of statistical process control (SPC) charts.
- Kanbans are a type of visual signal indicating the need for more production.
- Some organizations have found it helpful to show performance standards against cycle time or hourly quotas; for instance, the 3-minute clocks found in Burger Kings are a type of visual standard indicating the acceptable wait for service.

▼ **Figure 10.8** The Visual Workplace

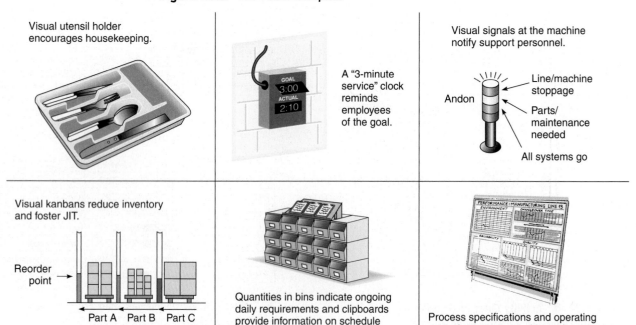

Visual utensil holder encourages housekeeping.

A "3-minute service" clock reminds employees of the goal.

Visual signals at the machine notify support personnel.

Andon — Line/machine stoppage — Parts/maintenance needed — All systems go

Visual kanbans reduce inventory and foster JIT.

Reorder point

Part A   Part B   Part C

Quantities in bins indicate ongoing daily requirements and clipboards provide information on schedule changes.

Process specifications and operating procedures are posted in each work area.

Housekeeping

- *Shadow boards and footprinting:* Painted symbols indicating the place for tools and the position of machinery and equipment are visual ways to aid housekeeping.
- *Labeling:* Proper identification of parts, bins, and tools is a basic, but substantial, aid to reducing waste.
- *Color-coded signs and lights:* Andon lights are another visual signal. An **andon** is a signal that there is a problem. Andons can be manually initiated by employees when they notice a problem or defect. They can also be triggered automatically when machine performance drops below a certain pace or when the number of cycles indicate that it is time for maintenance.

Andon
A call light that signals problems.

The purpose of the visual workplace is to eliminate non-value-added activities by making problems, abnormalities, and standards visual. This concept enhances communication and feedback by providing immediate information. The visual workplace needs less supervision because employees understand the standard, see the results, and know what to do.

ETHICS AND THE WORK ENVIRONMENT

Ethics in the workplace presents some interesting challenges. As we have suggested in this chapter, many constraints influence job design. The issues of fairness, equity, and ethics are pervasive. Whether the issue is equal opportunity, equal pay for equal work, or safe working conditions, the operations manager is often the one responsible.

Managers do have some guidelines. By knowing the law, working with OSHA,[9] MSDS,[10] state agencies, unions, trade associations, insurers, and employees, managers can often determine the parameters of their decisions. Human resource and legal departments are also available for help and guidance through the labyrinth of laws and regulations.

Jobs can be hot, difficult, and dangerous. Indeed, many jobs have been found to be very dangerous even years after they were successfully accomplished by thousands of people. For instance, asbestos, once known as the "magic mineral" for its insulation and ability to withstand flames, is now a notorious and feared killer. The issue may be what is known about jobs and their inherent dangers. In some cases, management and society were ignorant of the dangers, whether they were keyboards, a noisy environment, or materials in the workplace such as asbestos. In other cases, the risks are well known, and appropriate action must be taken promptly. (Many firms failed to take prompt action in the case of asbestos, and all the stakeholders paid the price when bankruptcy was declared.)

Insurance companies can provide good estimates of how many people will die in certain occupations each year. Nevertheless, society doesn't stop building skyscrapers or stop making cast-iron pipe even though we can document that ironworkers and foundry workers have dangerous jobs. Management's job is to mitigate the danger and take timely action once the dangers are known.

Management's role is to educate the employee, even when employees think it is "macho" not to wear safety equipment. Management's role is to define the necessary equipment, work rules, and work environment and to enforce those requirements. We began this chapter with a discussion of mutual trust and commitment, and that is the environment that managers should foster. Ethical management requires no less.

LABOR STANDARDS

So far in this chapter, we have discussed labor planning and job design. The third requirement of an effective human resource strategy is the establishment of labor standards. Effective manpower planning is dependent on a knowledge of the labor required.

Labor standards are the amount of time required to perform a job or part of a job. Every firm has labor standards, although they may vary from those established via informal methods to those established by professionals. Only when accurate labor standards exist can management know what its labor requirements are, what its costs should be, and what constitutes a fair day's work. Techniques for setting labor standards are presented in the supplement to this chapter.

Labor standards
The amount of time required to perform a job or part of a job.

[9]Occupational Safety and Health Administration (OSHA), a federal government agency whose task it is to assure the safety and health of U.S. workers.
[10]Material Safety Data Sheets (MSDS) contain details of hazards associated with chemicals and give information on their safe use.

Summary

Outstanding firms know the importance of an effective and efficient human resource strategy. Often a large percentage of employees and a large part of labor costs are under the direction of OM. Consequently, the operations manager usually has a large role to play in achieving human resource objectives. A prerequisite is to build an environment with mutual respect and commitment and a reasonable quality of work life. Outstanding organizations have designed jobs that use both the mental and physical capabilities of their employees. Regardless of the strategy chosen, the skill with which a firm manages its human resources ultimately determines its success.

Key Terms

Labor planning *(p. 391)*
Job design *(p. 392)*
Labor specialization (or job specialization) *(p. 392)*
Job enlargement *(p. 393)*
Job rotation *(p. 393)*

Job enrichment *(p. 393)*
Employee empowerment *(p. 394)*
Self-directed team *(p. 394)*
Ergonomics *(p. 397)*
Methods analysis *(p. 399)*
Flow diagram *(p. 400)*

Process chart *(p. 400)*
Activity chart *(p. 400)*
Operations chart *(p. 401)*
Visual workplace *(p. 402)*
Andon *(p. 403)*
Labor standards *(p. 404)*

Solved Problem

 Virtual Office Hours help is available on Student DVD.

Solved Problem 10.1

As pit crew manager for Rusty Wallace's NASCAR team (see the *Global Company Profile* that opens this chapter), you would like to evaluate how your "Jackman" and "Gas Man #1" are utilized. Recent stopwatch studies have verified the following times:

Activity	Time (seconds)
Move to right side of car and raise car	4.0
Move to rear gas filler	2.5
Move to left side of car and raise car	3.8
Load fuel (per gallon)	0.5
Move back over wall from left side	2.5
Move back over the wall from gas filler	2.5

Use an activity chart similar to the one in Figure 10.6 as an aid.

solution

	Jackman (Seconds)	Gas Man #1 (Seconds)	
Move to right side of car and raise car	4.0	2.5	Move to rear gas filler
Wait for tire exchange to finish	1.0	5.5	Load 11 gallons of fuel (one can of fuel)
Move to left side of car and raise car	3.8		
Wait for tire exchange to finish	1.2	2.5	Move back over the wall from gas filler
Move back over wall from left side	2.5		

Self-Test

- *Before taking the self-test*, refer to the learning objectives listed at the beginning of the chapter and the key terms listed at the end of the chapter.
- Use the key at the back of the text to **correct** your answers.
- *Restudy* pages that correspond to any questions you answered incorrectly or material you feel uncertain about.

1. Methods analysis techniques are used to analyze:
   a) movement of individuals or materials
   b) activity of man and machine and crew activity
   c) body movement
   d) all of the above

2. When product demand fluctuates and yet you maintain a constant level of employment, some of your cost savings might include:
   a) reduction in hiring costs
   b) reduction in firing costs and unemployment insurance costs
   c) lack of need to pay a premium wage to get workers to accept unstable employment
   d) having a trained workforce rather than having to retrain new employees each time you hire for an upswing in demand
   e) all of the above

3. Job enrichment:
   a) is the same as job enlargement
   b) includes a modest increase in pay
   c) is a concept promoted by Adam Smith and Charles Babbage in books they wrote
   d) includes some of the planning and control necessary for job accomplishment
   e) includes all of the above

4. The difference between *job enrichment* and *job enlargement* is that:
   a) enlarged jobs contain a larger number of similar tasks, while enriched jobs include some of the planning and control necessary for job accomplishment
   b) enriched jobs contain a larger number of similar tasks, while enlarged jobs include some of the planning and control necessary for job accomplishment
   c) enriched jobs enable an employee to do a number of boring jobs instead of just one
   d) all of the above

5. Ergonomics is the study of:
   a) ergos
   b) the management of technology
   c) the man–machine interface
   d) the use of automation in a manufacturing organization

6. *Methods analysis* focuses on:
   a) the design of the machines used to perform a task
   b) *how* a task is accomplished
   c) the raw materials that are consumed in performing a task
   d) reducing the number of steps required to perform a task

7. Gain sharing rewards employees for:
   a) executives' leadership
   b) working longer hours
   c) improvements in the company's performance
   d) stock price increases that exceed 10%

8. Southwest Airlines's success is heavily based on its:
   a) cheap tickets
   b) long flight routes
   c) culture of hiring people who are team oriented
   d) first-class seating and service

9. The work environment includes these factors:
   a) lighting, noise, temperature, and air quality
   b) illumination, carpeting, and high ceilings
   c) enough space for meetings and videoconferencing
   d) noise, humidity, and number of coworkers
   e) job enlargement and space analysis

Internet and Student CD-ROM/DVD Exercises

Visit our Companion Web site or use your student CD-ROM/DVD to help with material in this chapter.

 On Our Companion Web Site, www.prenhall.com./heizer
- Self-Study Quizzes
- Practice Problems
- Virtual Company Tour
- Internet Case
- PowerPoint Lecture

 On Your Student CD-ROM
- Practice Problems

 On Your Student DVD
- Video Clip and Video Case
- Virtual Office Hours for Solved Problem

Discussion Questions

1. How would you define a good quality of work life?
2. What are some of the worst jobs you know about? Why are they bad jobs? Why do people want these jobs?
3. If you were redesigning the jobs described in Question 2, what changes would you make? Are your changes realistic? Would they improve productivity (not just *production*, but *productivity*)?
4. Can you think of any jobs that push the man–machine interface to the limits of human capabilities?
5. What are the five core characteristics of a good job design?
6. What are the differences among job enrichment, job enlargement, job rotation, job specialization, and employee empowerment?
7. Define vertical job expansion and horizontal job expansion. Explain clearly how they differ.
8. Explain how job expansion can lead to higher accident rates.
9. Define ergonomics. Discuss the role of ergonomics in job design.
10. List the techniques available for carrying out methods analysis.
11. What are the constraints on human resource strategy as presented in the text?

Ethical Dilemma

Birmingham's McWane Inc., with 10 major foundries, is one of the world's largest makers of cast-iron water and sewer pipes. In one of the nation's most dangerous industries, McWane is perhaps the most unsafe, with four times the injury rate of its six competitors combined. Its worker death rate is six times that of its industry's. McWane plants were also found in violation of pollution and emission limits 450 times in a recent 7-year period.

Workers who protest dangerous work conditions claim they are "bull's-eyed"—marked for termination. Supervisors have bullied injured workers and intimidated union leaders. Line workers who fail to make daily quotas get disciplinary actions. Managers have put up safety signs *after* a worker was injured to make it appear the worker ignored posted policies. They alter safety records and doctor machines to cover up hazards. When the government investigated one worker's death in 2000, inspectors found the McWane policy "was not to correct anything until OSHA found it."

McWane plants have also been repeatedly fined for failing to stop production to repair broken pollution controls. Five plants have been designated "high priority" violators by the EPA. Inside the plants, workers have repeatedly complained of blurred vision, severe headaches, and respiratory problems after being exposed, without training or protection, to chemicals used to make pipes. Near one plant in Phillipsburg, New Jersey, school crossing guards have had to wear gas masks—that location alone received 150 violations between 1995 and 2002. McWane's "standard procedure" (according to a former plant manager) is to illegally dump industrial contaminants into local rivers and creeks. Workers wait for night or heavy rainstorms before flushing thousands of gallons from their sump pumps.

Given the following fictional scenarios: What is your position, and what action should you take?

a. On your spouse's recent move to Birmingham, you accepted a job, perhaps somewhat naively, as a company nurse in one of the McWane plants. After 2 weeks on the job you became aware of the work environment noted above.

b. You are a contractor who has traditionally used McWane's products, which meet specifications. McWane is consistently the low bidder. Your customers are happy with the product.

c. You are McWane's banker.

d. You are a supplier to McWane.

Sources: The New York Times (May 26, 2004): A19 and (August 30, 2005): A16; and *The Wall Street Journal* (May 27, 2004): A8.

Problems

• **10.1** Make a process chart for changing the right rear tire on an automobile.

• **10.2** Draw an activity chart for a machine operator with the following operation. The relevant times are as follows:

Prepare mill for loading (cleaning, oiling, and so on)	.50 min.
Load mill	1.75 min.
Mill operating (cutting material)	2.25 min.
Unload mill	.75 min.

••• **10.3** Draw an activity chart (a crew chart similar to Figure 10.6) for a concert (for example, Nickelback, Linkin Park, Fall Out Boy, or Bruce Springsteen) and determine how to put the concert together so the star has reasonable breaks. For instance, at what point is there an instrumental number, a visual effect, a duet, a dance moment, that allows the star to pause and rest physically or at least rest his or her voice? Do other members of the show have moments of pause or rest?

•• **10.4** Make an operations chart of one of the following:
a) Putting a new eraser in (or on) a pencil
b) Putting a paper clip on two pieces of paper
c) Putting paper in a printer

• **10.5** Develop a process chart for installing a new memory board in your personal computer.

• **10.6** Rate a job you have had using Hackman and Oldham's core job characteristics (see page 394) on a scale from 1 to 10. What is your total score? What about the job could have been changed to make you give it a higher score?

•• **10.7** Using the data in Solved Problem 10.1, prepare an activity chart like the one in the solved problem, but a second Gas Man also delivers 11 gallons.

•• **10.8** Prepare a process chart for the jack man in Solved Problem 10.1.

•• **10.9** Draw an activity chart for changing the right rear tire on an automobile with:
a) Only one person working
b) Two people working

••• **10.10** Draw an activity chart for washing the dishes in a double-sided sink. Two people participate, one washing, the other rinsing and drying. The rinser dries a batch of dishes from the drip rack as the washer fills the right sink with clean but unrinsed dishes. Then the rinser rinses the clean batch and places them on the drip rack. All dishes are stacked before being placed in the cabinets.

• • • **10.11** Your campus club is hosting a car wash. Due to demand, three people are going to be scheduled per wash line. (Three people have to wash each vehicle.) Design an activity chart for washing and drying a typical sedan. You must wash the wheels but ignore the cleaning of the interior, because this part of the operation will be done at a separate vacuum station.

• • • • **10.12** Design a process chart for printing a short document on a laser printer at an office. Unknown to you, the printer in the hallway is out of paper. The paper is located in a supply room at the

other end of the hall. You wish to make five stapled copies of the document once it is printed. The copier, located next to the printer, has a sorter but no stapler. How could you make the task more efficient with the existing equipment?

• • • • **10.13** Make an operations chart for taping two 5-inch-by-4-inch pictures onto a piece of paper (letter size) in a portrait layout. (Each picture is part of a presentation that you will copy and hand out to participants.) The tape comes from a dispenser, and you have unlimited space on the top of your desk.

Case Studies

The Fleet That Wanders

In March 2007, Bill Southard, owner of Southard Truck Lines, in Canyon, Texas, purchased a dozen new tractors from ARC Trucks.* His relations with his drivers have been excellent, but the new tractors are creating a problem. His drivers do not like them. They complain that the new tractors are hard to control on the highway; they "wander." By wandering, the drivers seem to mean the tractors take more work to control at highway speeds. Moreover, when the drivers have a choice, they choose the older tractors. Two drivers have even left the company and Southard believes that, instead of helping him keep good drivers, the new trucks have actually contributed to losing them. After many talks with the drivers, Southard concludes that the new tractors do indeed have a problem. He further believes that this situation has serious negative implications for the future of the firm. The new tractors are fully outfitted with the newest navigation features, as well as numerous expensive creature comforts. They get better gas mileage, should have lower maintenance costs, and have the latest antilocking brakes.

Because each tractor costs over $100,000, Southard's investment exceeds $1 million. He is desperately trying to improve his fleet performance by reducing maintenance and fuel costs; however, these improvements have not happened. Additionally, he wants to keep his drivers happy. This has not happened either. Consequently, Southard has had a series of talks with the manufacturer of the trucks.

The manufacturer, ARC Trucks of Denton, Texas, redesigned the front suspension for the trucks that Southard purchased. However,

ARC insists that the new front end is great and operates without a problem. Southard finds out, however, that since he purchased his trucks, there have been further (though minor) changes in some front-suspension parts. ARC claims these changes are the normal product improvement that it makes as part of its policy of continuous product improvement.

Despite several strongly worded requests by Southard, ARC Trucks has refused to make any changes in the tractors Southard purchased. The new trucks do not seem to have a higher accident rate, but they do not have many miles on them either. No one has suggested there is a significant safety problem, but Bill's drivers are adamant that they have to work harder to keep the new tractors on the road. The result is Southard has new tractors spending much of their time sitting in the yard while drivers use the old tractors. Southard's costs, therefore, are higher than they should be. He is considering court action, but legal counsel suggests that he document his case.

Discussion Questions

1. What suggestions do you have for Mr. Southard?
2. Having been exposed to introductory material about ergonomics, can you imagine an analytical approach to documenting the problems reported by the drivers?

*Large highway trucks are made up of two components; a tractor that pulls a trailer.

Hard Rock's Human Resource Strategy

Video Case

Everyone—managers and hourly employees alike—who goes to work for Hard Rock Cafe takes Rock 101, an initial 2-day training class. There they receive their wallet-sized "Hard Rock Values" card which they carry at all times. The Hard Rock value system is to bring a fun, healthy, nurturing environment into the Hard Rock Cafe culture.* This initial course and many other courses help employees develop both personally and professionally. The human resource department plays a critical role in any service organization, but at Hard Rock, with its "experience strategy," the human resource department takes on added importance.

Long before Jim Knight, manager of corporate training, begins the class, the human resource strategy of Hard Rock has had an impact. Hard Rock's strategic plan includes building a culture that allows for acceptance of substantial diversity and individuality. From

a human resource perspective, this has the benefit of enlarging the pool of applicants as well as contributing to the Hard Rock culture.

Creating a work environment above and beyond a paycheck is a unique challenge. Outstanding pay and benefits are a start, but the key is to provide an environment that works for the employees. This includes benefits that start for part-timers who work at least 19 hours per week (while others in the industry start at 35 hours per week); a unique respect for individuality; continuing training; and a high level of internal promotions—some 60% of the managers are promoted from hourly employee ranks. The company's training is very specific, with job-oriented interactive CDs covering kitchen, retail, and front-of-the-house service. Outside volunteer work is especially encouraged to foster a bond between the workers, their community, and issues of importance to them.

Applicants also are screened on their interest in music and their ability to tell a story. Hard Rock builds on a hiring criterion of bright, positive-attitude, self-motivated individuals with an employee bill of rights and substantial employee empowerment. The result is a unique culture and work environment which, no doubt, contributes to the low turnover of hourly people—one-half the industry average.

The layout, memorabilia, music, and videos are important elements in the Hard Rock "experience," but it falls on the waiters and waitresses to make the experience come alive. They are particularly focused on providing an authentic and memorable dining experience. Like Southwest Airlines, Hard Rock is looking for people with a cause—people who like to serve. By succeeding with its human resource strategy, Hard Rock obtains a competitive advantage.

Discussion Questions†

1. What has Hard Rock done to lower employee turnover to half the industry average?
2. How does Hard Rock's human resource department support the company's overall strategy?
3. How would Hard Rock's value system work for automobile assembly line workers? (Hint: Consider Hackman and Oldham's core job characteristics.)
4. How might you adjust a traditional assembly line to address more "core job characteristics"?

*Hard Rock Cafe's mission statement appears in Chapter 2 in Figure 2.2.

†Before answering these questions, you may wish to view this video case on your DVD.

Additional Case Studies

Internet case study: Visit our Companion Web site at www.prenhall.com/heizer for this free case study:

- **Karstadt versus JCPenney:** Compares the work culture in retailing in the U.S. to Germany.

Harvard has selected these Harvard Business School cases to accompany this chapter:

harvardbusinessonline.hbsp.harvard.edu

- **Southwest Airlines: Using Human Resources for Competitive Advantage** (#HR1A): Considers how Southwest Airlines developed a sustainable competitive advantage via human resources.
- **Eli Lilly: The Evista Project** (#699-016): Explores operational realities of two product development teams.
- **PPG: Developing a Self-Directed Workforce** (#693-020): Considers the process of creating a self-directed workforce, including the theory and difficulties.

Bibliography

Barnes, R. M. *Motion and Time Study, Design and Measurement of Work.* 7th ed. New York: Wiley, 1980.

De Jong, A., K. De Ruyter, and J. Lemmink. "Service Climate in Self-Managing Teams." *The Journal of Management Studies* 42, no. 8 (December 2005): 1593.

Goldstein, Susan M. "Employee Development: An Examination of Service Strategy in a High-Contact Service Environment." *Production and Operations Management* 12, no. 2 (summer 2003): 186–203.

Guthrie, James P. "High-Involvement Work Practices, Turnover, and Productivity: Evidence from New Zealand." *Academy of Management Journal* 44, no. 1 (2001): 180–190.

Hays, J. M., and A. V. Hill. "A Preliminary Investigation of the Relationships between Employee Motivation/Vision, Service Learning, and Perceived Service Quality." *Journal of Operations Management* 19, no. 3 (May 2001): 335–349.

Housel, Debra J. *Team Dynamics: Professional Development Series.* Cincinnati: South-Western Publishing, 2002.

Huselid, Mark A., Richard W. Beatty, and Brian E. Becker, " 'A Players' or 'A Positions'? The Strategic Logic of Workforce Management." *Harvard Business Review* (December 2005): 110–117.

Muthasamy, S. K., J. V. Wheeler, and B. L. Simmons. "Self-Managing Work Teams." *Organization Development Journal* 23, no. 3 (Fall 2005): 53–66.

Niebel, B., and A. Freivalds. *Methods, Standards, and Work Design*, 11th ed. New York: McGraw-Hill, 2003.

Pfeffer, Jeffrey. "Producing Sustainable Competitive Advantage Through the Effective Management of People." *Academy of Management Executive* 19, no. 4 (2005): 95.

Salvendy, G., ed. *Handbook of Human Factors and Ergonomics*, 3rd ed. New York: Wiley, 2006.

Schultz, George. "More than Measuring." *APICS: The Performance Advantage* (January 2004): 23–26.

Stratman, J. K., A. V. Roth, and W. G. Gilland. "The Deployment of Temporary Production Workers in Assembly Operations." *Journal of Operations Management* 21, no. 6 (January 2004): 689–707.

Internet Resources

Bibliography on interpersonal relationships and team success:
www.hq.nasa.gov/office/hqlibrary/ppm/ppm29.htm
Bibliography on teams and teamwork:
www.hq.nasa.gov/office/hqlibrary/ppm/ppm5.htm
Ergonomics at University of Toronto: **vered.rose.toronto.edu**
Human Measurements by Open Ergonomics Ltd: **www.openerg.com**

Human modeling by UGS: **www.ugs.com/products/efactory**
Occupational Safety and Health Administration: **www.osha.gov**
Visual training systems by Quality Methods International:
www.visual-workplace.com
World at Work: **www.worldatwork.org**

SUPPLEMENT 10

Work Measurement

Supplement Outline

Learning Objectives

When you complete this supplement you should be able to

1. Identify four ways of establishing labor standards
2. Compute the normal and standard times in a time study
3. Find the proper sample size for a time study
4. Explain how predetermined time standards and TMUs are used in work measurement
5. Apply the five steps of work sampling

► *Each day—in fact, 130 times each day—Tim Nelson leans back into a La-Z-Boy recliner, sofa section, or love seat. He is one of 25 inspectors at La-Z-Boy Inc.'s Dayton factory. As Tim leans back into the oversized La-Z-Boy he inspects for overall comfort; he must sink slightly into the chair, but not too far. Like Goldilocks, the chair must not be too firm or too soft; it must be just right—or it is sent back for restuffing. If it passes the "firm" test, he then rocks back and forth, making certain the chair is properly balanced and moves smoothly. Then Tim checks the footrest, arches his back, and holds the position as if he were taking that Sunday afternoon nap. Hopping to his feet, he does a walk-around visual check; then it is on to the next chair. One down, and 129 to go.*

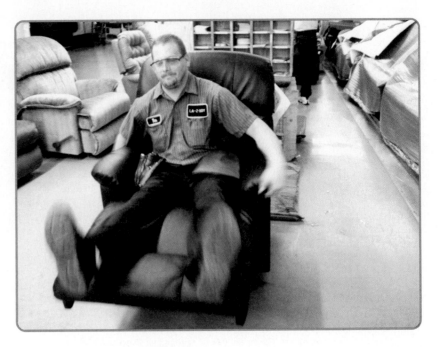

LABOR STANDARDS AND WORK MEASUREMENT

Modern labor standards originated with the works of Frederick Taylor and Frank and Lillian Gilbreth at the beginning of the 20th century. At that time, a large proportion of work was manual, and the resulting labor content of products was high. Little was known about what constituted a fair day's work, so managers initiated studies to improve work methods and understand human effort. These efforts continue to this day. Although we are now at the beginning of the 21st century, and labor costs are often less than 10% of sales, labor standards remain important and continue to play a major role in both service and manufacturing organizations. They are often a beginning point for determining staffing requirements. With over half of the manufacturing plants in America using some form of labor incentive system, good labor standards are a requirement.

Labor standards exist for telephone operators, auto mechanics, and UPS drivers, as well as for many factory workers, such as Tim Nelson at La-Z-Boy, in the photo above.

Effective operations management requires meaningful standards that can help a firm determine the following:

1. Labor content of items produced (the labor cost)
2. Staffing needs (how many people it will take to meet required production)
3. Cost and time estimates prior to production (to assist in a variety of decisions, from cost estimates to make-or-buy decisions)
4. Crew size and work balance (who does what in a group activity or on an assembly line)
5. Expected production (so that both manager and worker know what constitutes a fair day's work)
6. Basis of wage-incentive plans (what provides a reasonable incentive)
7. Efficiency of employees and supervision (a standard is necessary against which to determine efficiency)

Properly set labor standards represent the amount of time that it should take an average employee to perform specific job activities under normal working conditions. Labor standards are set in four ways:

Learning Objective

1. Identify four ways of establishing labor standards

1. Historical experience
2. Time studies
3. Predetermined time standards
4. Work sampling

This supplement covers each of these techniques.

HISTORICAL EXPERIENCE

Labor standards can be estimated based on *historical experience*—that is, how many labor-hours were required to do a task the last time it was performed. Historical standards have the advantage of being relatively easy and inexpensive to obtain. They are usually available from employee time cards or production records. However, they are not objective, and we do not know their accuracy, whether they represent a reasonable or a poor work pace, and whether unusual occurrences are included. Because these variables are unknown, their use is not recommended. Instead, time studies, predetermined time standards, and work sampling are preferred.

TIME STUDIES

The classical stopwatch study, or time study, originally proposed by Frederick W. Taylor in 1881, is still the most widely used time-study method.[1] A **time-study** procedure involves timing a sample of a worker's performance and using it to set a standard. A trained and experienced person can establish a standard by following these eight steps:

1. Define the task to be studied (after methods analysis has been conducted).
2. Divide the task into precise elements (parts of a task that often take no more than a few seconds).
3. Decide how many times to measure the task (the number of job cycles or samples needed).
4. Time and record elemental times and ratings of performance.
5. Compute the average observed (actual) time. The **average observed time** is the arithmetic mean of the times for *each* element measured, adjusted for unusual influence for each element:

$$\text{Average observed time} = \frac{\begin{pmatrix} \text{Sum of the times recorded} \\ \text{to perform each element} \end{pmatrix}}{\text{Number of observations}} \quad \text{(S10-1)}$$

6. Determine performance rating (work pace) and then compute the **normal time** for each element.

$$\text{Normal time} = (\text{Average observed time}) \times (\text{Performance rating factor}) \quad \text{(S10-2)}$$

Time study
Timing a sample of a worker's performance and using it as a basis for setting a standard time.

Average observed time
The arithmetic mean of the times for each element measured, adjusted for unusual influence for each element.

Normal time
The average observed time, adjusted for pace.

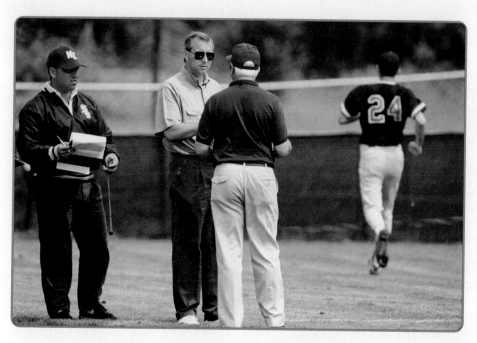

◀ *One of the challenges when conducting time studies is the need to create realistic conditions for the study. For example, in baseball, players often run quicker when they know they are being timed. Similarly, in a job setting, employees may perform faster or slower than a normal pace.*

[1]For an illuminating look at the life and influence of Taylor, see S. Parayitum, M. A. White, and J. R. Hough, *Management Decision* 40, no. 10 (2002): 1003–1012 or Daniel Nelson, "The One Best Way: Frederick Winslow Taylor and the Enigma of Efficiency" *Journal of Economic History* (September 1998): 903–905.

1. Constant allowances:	(ii) Quite inadequate 5
(A) Personal allowance 5	(E) Atmospheric conditions (heat and humidity):
(B) Basic fatigue allowance 4	Variable 0–10
2. Variable allowances:	(F) Close attention:
(A) Standing allowance 2	(i) Fine or exacting 2
(B) Abnormal position allowance:	(ii) Very fine or very exacting 5
(i) Awkward (bending) .2	(G) Noise level:
(ii) Very awkward (lying, stretching) 7	(i) Intermittent—loud 2
(C) Use of force or muscular energy in	(ii) Intermittent—very loud or high pitched 5
lifting, pulling, pushing	(H) Mental strain:
Weight lifted (pounds):	(i) Complex or wide span of attention 4
20 3	(ii) Very complex 8
40 9	(I) Tediousness:
60 17	(i) Tedious 2
(D) Bad light:	(ii) Very tedious 5
(i) Well below recommended 2	

▲ **Figure S10.1** **Allowances (in percentage) for Various Classes of Work**

Source: Niebel, B. W., and A. Freivalds. *Methods, Standards, and Work Design*, 11th ed. (New York: Irwin/McGraw-Hill, 2003).

The performance rating adjusts the average observed time to what a normal worker could expect to accomplish. For example, a normal worker should be able to walk 3 miles per hour. He or she should also be able to deal a deck of 52 cards into 4 equal piles in 30 seconds. A performance rating of 1.05 would indicate that the observed worker performs the task slightly *faster* than average. Numerous videos specify work pace on which professionals agree, and benchmarks have been established by the Society for the Advancement of Management. Performance rating, however, is still something of an art.

Standard time

An adjustment to the total normal time; the adjustment provides allowances for personal needs, unavoidable work delays, and fatigue.

7. Add the normal times for each element to develop a total normal time for the task.

8. Compute the **standard time**. This adjustment to the total normal time provides for allowances such as *personal* needs, unavoidable work *delays*, and worker *fatigue*:

$$\text{Standard time} = \frac{\text{Total normal time}}{1 - \text{Allowance factor}} \qquad \text{(S10-3)}$$

Personal time allowances are often established in the range of 4% to 7% of total time, depending on nearness to rest rooms, water fountains, and other facilities. *Delay allowances* are often set as a result of the actual studies of the delay that occurs. *Fatigue allowances* are based on our growing knowledge of human energy expenditure under various physical and environmental conditions. A sample set of personal and fatigue allowances is shown in Figure S10.1. Example S1 illustrates the computation of standard time.

EXAMPLE S1

Determining normal and standard time

The time study of a work operation at a Red Lobster restaurant yielded an average observed time of 4.0 minutes. The analyst rated the observed worker at 85%. This means the worker performed at 85% of normal when the study was made. The firm uses a 13% allowance factor. Red Lobster wants to compute the normal time and the standard time for this operation.

Approach: The firm needs to apply Equations (S10-2) and (S10-3).

Solution: Average observed time = 4.0 min.

Normal time = (Average observed time) × (Performance rating factor)

= (4.0)(.85)

= 3.4 min.

$$\text{Standard time} = \frac{\text{Normal time}}{1 - \text{Allowance factor}} = \frac{3.4}{1 - .13} = \frac{3.4}{.87}$$

= 3.9 min

Insight: Because the observed worker was rated at 85% (slower than average), the normal time is less than the worker's 4.0-minute average time.

Learning exercise: If the observed worker is rated at 115% (faster than average), what are the new normal and standard times? [Answer: 4.6 min, 5.287 min.]

Related problems: S10.2, S10.3, S10.4, S10.5, S10.6, S10.7, S10.8, S10.9, S10.10, S10.11, S10.25

Example S2 uses a series of actual stopwatch times for each element.

Management Science Associates promotes its management development seminars by mailing thousands of individually composed and typed letters to various firms. A time study has been conducted on the task of preparing letters for mailing. On the basis of the following observations, Management Science Associates wants to develop a time standard for this task. The firm's personal, delay, and fatigue allowance factor is 15%.

Job Element	Observations (minutes)					Performance Rating
	1	2	3	4	5	
(A) Compose and type letter	8	10	9	21*	11	120%
(B) Type envelope address	2	3	2	1	3	105%
(C) Stuff, stamp, seal, and sort envelopes	2	1	5*	2	1	110%

Approach: Once the data have been collected, the procedure is to:

1. Delete unusual or nonrecurring observations.
2. Compute the *average time* for each element, using Equation (S10-1).
3. Compute the *normal time* for each element, using Equation (S10-2).
4. Find the total normal time.
5. Compute the *standard time*, using Equation (S10-3).

Solution:

1. Delete observations such as those marked with an asterisk (*). (These may be due to business interruptions, conferences with the boss, or mistakes of an unusual nature; they are not part of the job element, but may be personal or delay time.)
2. Average time for each job element:

$$\text{Average time for A} = \frac{8+10+9+11}{4}$$
$$= 9.5 \text{ min}$$
$$\text{Average time for B} = \frac{2+3+2+1+3}{5}$$
$$= 2.2 \text{ min}$$
$$\text{Average time for C} = \frac{2+1+2+1}{4}$$
$$= 1.5 \text{ min}$$

3. Normal time for each job element:

$$\text{Normal time for A} = (\text{Average observed time}) \times (\text{Performance rating})$$
$$= (9.5)(1.2)$$
$$= 11.4 \text{ min}$$
$$\text{Normal time for B} = (2.2)(1.05)$$
$$= 2.31 \text{ min}$$
$$\text{Normal time for C} = (1.5)(1.10)$$
$$= 1.65 \text{ min}$$

Note: Normal times are computed for each element because the performance rating factor (work pace) may vary for each element, as it did in this case.

In many service jobs, such as cleaning a Sheraton hotel bathtub, renting a Hertz car, or wrapping a Taco Bell burrito, motion and time studies are effective management tools.

4. Add the normal times for each element to find the total normal time (the normal time for the whole job):

$$\text{Total normal time} = 11.40 + 2.31 + 1.65$$
$$= 15.36 \text{ min}$$

5. Standard time for the job:

$$\text{Standard time} = \frac{\text{Total normal time}}{1 - \text{Allowance factor}} = \frac{15.36}{1 - .15}$$
$$= 18.07 \text{ min}$$

Thus, 18.07 minutes is the time standard for this job.

Insight: When observed times are not consistent they need to be reviewed. Abnormally short times may be the result of an observational error and are usually discarded. Abnormally long times need to be analyzed to determine if they, too, are an error. However, they may *include* a seldom occurring but legitimate activity for the element (such as a machine adjustment) or may be personal, delay, or fatigue time.

Learning exercise: If the two observations marked with an asterisk were *not* deleted, what would be the total normal time and the standard time? [Answer: 18.89 min, 22.22 min.]

Related problems: S10.12, S10.13, S10.14, S10.15, S10.16, S10.20a,b, S10.21a, S10.22a

---

Always let a worker who is going to be observed know about the study in advance to prevent misunderstanding or suspicion.

Time study requires a sampling process; so the question of sampling error in the average observed time naturally arises. In statistics, error varies inversely with sample size. Thus, to determine just how many cycles we should time, we must consider the variability of each element in the study.

To determine an adequate sample size, three items must be considered:

1. How accurate we want to be (e.g., is ±5% of observed time close enough?).
2. The desired level of confidence (e.g., the *z*-value; is 95% adequate or is 99% required?).
3. How much variation exists within the job elements (e.g., if the variation is large, a larger sample will be required).

The formula for finding the appropriate sample size, given these three variables, is:

$$\text{Required sample size} = n = \left(\frac{zs}{h\overline{x}}\right)^2 \tag{S10-4}$$

where h = accuracy level desired in percent of the job element, expressed as a decimal (5% = .05)

z = number of standard deviations required for desired level of confidence (90% confidence = 1.65; see Table S10.1 or Appendix I for more *z*-values)

s = standard deviation of the initial sample

$\overline{x}$ = mean of the initial sample

n = required sample size

We demonstrate with Example S3.

▼ Table S10.1

Common *z*-Values

Desired Confidence (%)	*z*-Value (standard deviation required for desired level of confidence)
90.0	1.65
95.0	1.96
95.45	2.00
99.0	2.58
99.73	3.00

▶ *Sleep Inn® hotels are showing the world that big gains in productivity can be made not only by manufacturers but in the service industry as well. Designed with labor efficiency in mind, Sleep Inn hotels are staffed with 13% fewer employees than similar budget hotels. Its features include a laundry room that is almost completely automated, round shower stalls that eliminate dirty corners, and closets that have no doors for maids to open and shut.*

◀ *Since the days of F. W. Taylor, time studies have been performed by using a stopwatch. However, with the development of PDA software, such as the program shown here, study elements, time, performance rate, and statistical confidence intervals can be created, edited, managed, and logged with a PDA. Handheld technology eliminates the need for data entry and sends the data directly to a program to be analyzed. The software shown here is available from Laubrass Inc.* (**www.laubrass.com**).

Thomas W. Jones Manufacturing Co. has asked you to check a labor standard prepared by a recently terminated analyst. Your first task is to determine the correct sample size. Your accuracy is to be within 5% and your confidence level at 95%. The standard deviation of the sample is 1.0 and the mean 3.00.

Approach: You apply Equation (S10-4).

Solution:
$$h = .05 \qquad \bar{x} = 3.00 \qquad s = 1.0$$
$$z = 1.96 \text{ (from Table S10.1 or Appendix I)}$$
$$n = \left(\frac{zs}{h\bar{x}}\right)^2$$
$$n = \left(\frac{1.96 \times 1.0}{.05 \times 3}\right)^2 = 170.74 \approx 171$$

Therefore, you recommend a sample size of 171.

Insight: Notice that as the confidence level required increases, the sample size also increases. Similarly, as the desired accuracy level increases (say, from 5% to 1%), the sample size increases.

Learning exercise: The confidence level for Jones Manufacturing Co. can be set lower, at 90%, while retaining the same ±5% accuracy levels. What sample size is needed now? [Answer: n = 121.]

Related problems: S10.17, S10.18, S10.19, S10.20c, S10.21b, S10.22b

EXAMPLE S3

Computing sample size

Now let's look at two variations of Example S3.

First, if *h*, the desired accuracy, is expressed as an absolute amount of error (say, 1 minute of error is acceptable), then substitute *e* for $h\bar{x}$, and the appropriate formula is:

$$n = \left(\frac{zs}{e}\right)^2 \qquad \text{(S10-5)}$$

where *e* is the absolute time amount of acceptable error.

Second, for those cases when *s*, the standard deviation of the sample, is not provided (which is typically the case outside the classroom), it must be computed. The formula for doing so is given in Equation (S10-6):

$$s = \sqrt{\frac{\sum (x_i - \bar{x})^2}{n-1}} = \sqrt{\frac{\sum (\text{Each sample observation} - \bar{x})^2}{\text{Number in sample} - 1}} \qquad \text{(S10-6)}$$

where x_i = value of each observation
$\bar{x}$ = mean of the observations
n = number of observations in the sample

An example of this computation is provided in Solved Problem S10.3 on page 424.

Learning Objective

3. Find the proper sample size for a time study

OM in Action
UPS: The Tightest Ship in the Shipping Business

United Parcel Service (UPS) employs 400,000 people and delivers an average of 16 million packages a day to locations throughout the U.S. and 200 other countries. To achieve its claim of "running the tightest ship in the shipping business," UPS methodically trains its delivery drivers in how to do their jobs as efficiently as possible.

Industrial engineers at UPS have time-studied each driver's route and set standards for each delivery, stop, and pickup. These engineers have recorded every second taken up by stoplights, traffic volume, detours, doorbells, walkways, stairways, and coffee breaks. Even bathroom stops are factored into the standards. All this information is then fed into company computers to provide detailed time standards for every driver, every day.

To meet their objective of 200 deliveries and pickups each day (versus only 80 at Federal Express), UPS drivers must follow procedures exactly. As they approach a deliv-

ery stop, drivers unbuckle their seat belts, honk their horns, and cut their engines. In one seamless motion, they are required to yank up their emergency brakes and push their gearshifts into first. Then they slide to the ground with their electronic clipboards under their right arm and their packages in their left hand. Ignition keys, teeth up, are in their right hand. They walk to the customer's door at the prescribed 3 feet per second and knock first to avoid lost seconds searching for the doorbell. After making the delivery, they do the paperwork on the way back to the truck.

Productivity experts describe UPS as one of the most efficient companies anywhere in applying effective labor standards.

Sources: Knight Ridder Tribune Business News (December 21, 2005): 1; *IIE Solutions* (March 2002): 16; and *Industrial Engineer* (November, 2003): 22.

Although time studies provide accuracy in setting labor standards (see the *OM in Action* box "UPS: The Tightest Ship in the Shipping Business"), they have two disadvantages. First, they require a trained staff of analysts. Second, labor standards cannot be set before tasks are actually performed. This leads us to two alternative work-measurement techniques that we discuss next.

PREDETERMINED TIME STANDARDS

Predetermined time standards

A division of manual work into small basic elements that have established and widely accepted times.

In addition to historical experience and time studies, we can set production standards by using predetermined time standards. **Predetermined time standards** divide manual work into small basic elements that already have established times (based on very large samples of workers). To estimate the time for a particular task, the time factors for each basic element of that task are added together. Developing a comprehensive system of predetermined time standards would be prohibitively expensive for any given firm. Consequently, a number of systems are commercially

▶ *Before an assembly line, like this one in China, is set up, the company establishes labor standards to assist in layout and manpower planning.*

GET and PLACE			DISTANCE RANGE IN IN.	<8	>8 <20	>20 <32
WEIGHT	CONDITIONS OF GET	PLACE ACCURACY	CODE	1	2	3
<2 LB	EASY	APPROXIMATE	AA	20	35	50
		LOOSE	AB	30	45	60
		TIGHT	AC	40	55	70
	DIFFICULT	APPROXIMATE	AD	20	45	60
		LOOSE	AE	30	55	70
		TIGHT	AF	40	65	80
	HANDFUL	APPROXIMATE	AG	40	65	80
>2 LB <18 LB		APPROXIMATE	AH	25	45	55
		LOOSE	AJ	40	65	75
		TIGHT	AK	50	75	85
>18 LB <45 LB		APPROXIMATE	AL	90	106	115
		LOOSE	AM	95	120	130
		TIGHT	AN	120	145	160

◀ **Figure S10.2**

Sample MTM Table for GET and PLACE Motion

Time values are in TMUs.

Source: Copyrighted by the MTM Association for Standards and Research. No reprint permission without consent from the MTM Association, 16-01 Broadway, Fair Lawn, NJ 07410.

available. The most common predetermined time standard is *methods time measurement* (MTM), which is a product of the MTM Association.[2]

Predetermined time standards are an outgrowth of basic motions called therbligs. The term *therblig* was coined by Frank Gilbreth (*Gilbreth* spelled backwards with the *t* and *h* reversed). **Therbligs** include such activities as select, grasp, position, assemble, reach, hold, rest, and inspect. These activities are stated in terms of **time measurement units (TMUs)**, which are equal to only .00001 hour, or .0006 minute each. MTM values for various therbligs are specified in very detailed tables. Figure S10.2, for example, provides the set of time standards for the motion GET and PLACE. To use GET and PLACE, one must know what is "gotten," its approximate weight, and where and how far it is supposed to be placed.

Example S4 shows a use of predetermined time standards in setting service labor standards.

Therbligs
Basic physical elements of motion.

Time measurement units (TMUs)
Units for very basic micromotions in which 1 TMU = .0006 min or 100,000 TMUs = 1 hr.

General Hospital wants to set the standard time for lab technicians to pour a tube specimen using MTM.[3]

Approach: This is a repetitive task for which the MTM data in Table S10.2 may be used to develop standard times. The sample tube is in a rack and the centrifuge tubes in a nearby box. A technician removes the sample tube from the rack, uncaps it, gets the centrifuge tube, pours, and places both tubes in the rack.

Element Description	Element	Time
Get tube from rack	AA2	35
Get stopper, place on counter	AA2	35
Get centrifuge tube, place at sample tube	AD2	45
Pour (3 sec)	PT	83
Place tubes in rack (simo)	PC2	40
	Total TMU	238

.0006 × 238 = Total standard minutes = .14

EXAMPLE S4

Using predetermined time (MTM analysis) to determine standard time

◀ **Table S10.2**

MTM-HC Analysis: Pouring Tube Specimen

[2]MTM is really a family of products available from the Methods Time Measurement Association. For example, MTM-HC deals with the health care industry, MTM-C handles clerical activities, MTM-M involves microscope activities, MTM-V deals with machine shop tasks, and so on.
[3]A. S. Helms, B. W. Shaw, and C. A. Lindner, "The Development of Laboratory Workload Standards through Computer-Based Work Measurement Technique, Part I," *Journal of Methods-Time Measurement* 12: 43. Used with permission of MTM Association for Standards and Research.

4. Explain how predetermined time standards and TMUs are used in work measurement

Solution: The first work element involves getting the tube from the rack. The conditions for GETTING the tube and PLACING it in front of the technician are:

- *Weight:* (less than 2 pounds)
- *Conditions of GET:* (easy)
- *Place accuracy:* (approximate)
- *Distance range:* (8 to 20 inches)

Then the MTM element for this activity is AA2 (as seen in Figure S10.2). The rest of Table S10.2 is developed from similar MTM tables.

Insight: Most MTM calculations are computerized, so the user need only key in the appropriate MTM codes, such as AA2 in this example.

Learning exercise: General Hospital decides that the first step in this process really involves a distance range of 4 inches (getting the tube from the rack). The other work elements are unchanged. What is the new standard time? [Answer: .134 min.]

Related problem: S10.28

Some firms use a combination of stopwatch studies and predetermined time standards.

Predetermined time standards have several advantages over direct time studies. First, they may be established in a laboratory environment, where the procedure will not upset actual production activities (which time studies tend to do). Second, because the standard can be set *before* a task is actually performed, it can be used for planning. Third, no performance ratings are necessary. Fourth, unions tend to accept this method as a fair means of setting standards. Finally, predetermined time standards are particularly effective in firms that do substantial numbers of studies of similar tasks. To ensure accurate labor standards, some firms use both time studies and predetermined time standards.

WORK SAMPLING

Work sampling

An estimate, via sampling, of the percent of the time that a worker spends on various tasks.

The fourth method of developing labor or production standards, work sampling, was developed in England by L. Tippet in the 1930s. **Work sampling** estimates the percent of the time that a worker spends on various tasks. Random observations are used to record the activity that a worker is performing. The results are primarily used to determine how employees allocate their time among various activities. Knowledge of this allocation may lead to staffing changes, reassignment of duties, estimates of activity cost, and the setting of delay allowances for labor standards. When work sampling is done to establish delay allowances, it is sometimes called a *ratio delay study*.

▶ *Using the techniques of this supplement to develop labor standards, operations managers at Orlando's Arnold Palmer Hospital determined that nurses walked an average of 2.7 miles per day. This constitutes up to 30% of the nurse's time, a terrible waste of critical talent. Analysis resulted in a new layout design that has reduced walking distances by 20%.*

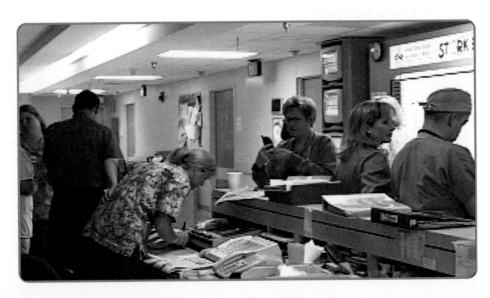

The work-sampling procedure can be summarized in five steps:

1. Take a preliminary sample to obtain an estimate of the parameter value (e.g., percent of time a worker is busy).
2. Compute the sample size required.
3. Prepare a schedule for observing the worker at appropriate times. The concept of random numbers is used to provide for random observation. For example, let's say we draw the following five random numbers from a table: 07, 12, 22, 25, and 49. These can then be used to create an observation schedule of 9:07 A.M., 9:12, 9:22, 9:25, 9:49.
4. Observe and record worker activities.
5. Determine how workers spend their time (usually as a percent).

Learning Objective

5. Apply the five steps of work sampling

To determine the number of observations required, management must decide on the desired confidence level and accuracy. First, however, the analyst must select a preliminary value for the parameter under study (step 1 above). The choice is usually based on a small sample of perhaps 50 observations. The following formula then gives the sample size for a desired confidence and accuracy:

$$n = \frac{z^2 p(1-p)}{h^2}$$

(S10-7)

where n = required sample size

z = number of standard normal deviations for the desired confidence level ($z = 1$ for 68% confidence, $z = 2$ for 95.45% confidence, and $z = 3$ for 99.73% confidence—these values are obtained from Table S10.1 or the normal table in Appendix I)

p = estimated value of sample proportion (of time worker is observed busy or idle)

h = acceptable error level, in percent

Example S5 shows how to apply this formula.

EXAMPLE S5

Determining the number of work sample observations needed

The manager of Michigan County's welfare office, Dana Johnson, estimates that her employees are idle 25% of the time. She would like to take a work sample that is accurate within 3% and wants to have 95.45% confidence in the results.

Approach: Dana applies Equation (S10-7) to determine how many observations should be taken.

Solution: Dana computes n:

$$n = \frac{z^2 p(1-p)}{h^2}$$

where n = required sample size
z = 2 for 95.45% confidence level
p = estimate of idle proportion = 25% = .25
h = acceptable error of 3% = .03

She finds that

$$n = \frac{(2)^2(.25)(.75)}{(.03)^2} = 833 \text{ observations}$$

Insight: Thus, 833 observations should be taken. If the percent of idle time observed is not close to 25% as the study progresses, then the number of observations may have to be recalculated and increased or decreased as appropriate.

Learning exercise: If the confidence level increases to 99.73%, how does the sample size change? [Answer: $n = 1,875$.]

Related problems: S10.23, S10.24, S10.27, S10.29

 Active Model S10.1

Example S5 is further illustrated in Active Model S10.1 on the CD-ROM and in the Exercise located on page 425.

The focus of work sampling is to determine how workers allocate their time among various activities. This is accomplished by establishing the percent of time individuals spend on these activities rather than the exact amount of time spent on specific tasks. The analyst simply records in a random, nonbiased way the occurrence of each activity. Example S6 shows the procedure for evaluating employees at the state welfare office introduced in Example S5.

EXAMPLE S6

Determining employee time allocation with work sampling

Dana Johnson, the manager of Michigan County's welfare office, wants to be sure her employees have adequate time to provide prompt, helpful service. She believes that service to welfare clients who phone or walk in without an appointment deteriorates rapidly when employees are busy more than 75% of the time. Consequently, she does not want her employees to be occupied with client service activities more than 75% of the time.

Approach: The study requires several things: First, based on the calculations in Example S5, 833 observations are needed. Second, observations are to be made in a random, nonbiased way over a period of 2 weeks to ensure a true sample. Third, the analyst must define the activities that are "work." In this case, work is defined as all the activities necessary to take care of the client (filing, meetings, data entry, discussions with the supervisor, etc.). Fourth, personal time is to be included in the 25% of nonwork time. Fifth, the observations are made in a nonintrusive way so as not to distort the normal work patterns. At the end of the 2 weeks, the 833 observations yield the following results:

No. of Observations	Activity
485	On the phone or meeting with a welfare client
126	Idle
62	Personal time
23	Discussions with supervisor
137	Filing, meeting, and computer data entry
833	

Solution: The analyst concludes that all but 188 observations (126 idle and 62 personal) are work related. Since 22.6% (= 188/833) is less idle time than Dana believes necessary to ensure a high client service level, she needs to find a way to reduce current workloads. This could be done through a reassignment of duties or the hiring of additional personnel.

Insight: Work sampling is particularly helpful when determining staffing needs or the reallocation of duties (see Figure S10.3).

Learning exercise: The analyst working for Dana recategorizes several observations. There are now 450 "on the phone/meeting with client" observations, 156 "idle," and 67 "personal time" observations. The last two categories saw no changes. Do the conclusions change? [Answer: Yes; now about 27% of employee time is not work related—over the 25% Dana desires.]

Related problem: S10.26

The cataloger Lands' End expects its sales reps to be busy 85% of the time and idle 15%. When the busy ratio hits 90%, the firm believes it is not reaching its goal of high-quality service.

The results of a similar study of salespeople and assembly-line employees are shown in Figure S10.3.

▶ **Figure S10.3**

Work-Sampling Time Studies

These two work-sampling time studies were done to determine what salespeople do at a wholesale electronics distributor (left) and a composite of several auto assembly-line employees (right).

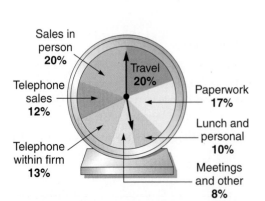

Salespeople

Sales in person 20%
Travel 20%
Telephone sales 12%
Paperwork 17%
Telephone within firm 13%
Lunch and personal 10%
Meetings and other 8%

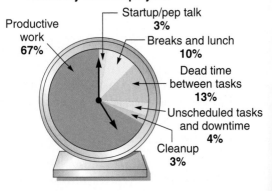

Assembly-Line Employees

Productive work 67%
Startup/pep talk 3%
Breaks and lunch 10%
Dead time between tasks 13%
Unscheduled tasks and downtime 4%
Cleanup 3%

Work sampling offers several advantages over time-study methods. First, because a single observer can observe several workers simultaneously, it is less expensive. Second, observers usually do not require much training, and no timing devices are needed. Third, the study can be temporarily delayed at any time with little impact on the results. Fourth, because work sampling uses instantaneous observations over a long period, the worker has little chance of affecting the study's outcome. Fifth, the procedure is less intrusive and therefore less likely to generate objections.

The disadvantages of work sampling are (1) it does not divide work elements as completely as time studies, (2) it can yield biased or incorrect results if the observer does not follow random routes of travel and observation, and (3) because it is less intrusive, it tends to be less accurate; this is particularly true when job content times are short.

Summary

Labor standards are required for an efficient operations system. They are needed for production planning, labor planning, costing, and evaluating performance. They can also be used as a basis for incentive systems. They are used in both the factory and the office. Standards may be established via historical data, time studies, predetermined time standards, and work sampling.

Key Terms

Time study *(p. 413)*
Average observed time *(p. 413)*
Normal time *(p. 413)*

Standard time *(p. 414)*
Predetermined time standards *(p. 418)*
Therbligs *(p. 419)*

Time measurement units (TMUs) *(p. 419)*
Work sampling *(p. 420)*

Solved Problems

Virtual Office Hours help is available on Student DVD.

Solved Problem S10.1

A work operation consisting of three elements has been subjected to a stopwatch time study. The recorded observations are shown in the following table. By union contract, the allowance time for the operation is personal time 5%, delay 5%, and fatigue 10%. Determine the standard time for the work operation.

Job Element	Observations (minutes)						Performance Rating (%)
	1	2	3	4	5	6	
A	.1	.3	.2	.9	.2	.1	90
B	.8	.6	.8	.5	3.2	.7	110
C	.5	.5	.4	.5	.6	.5	80

Solution

First, delete the two observations that appear to be very unusual (.9 minute for job element A and 3.2 minutes for job element B). Then:

$$\text{A's average observed time} = \frac{.1+.3+.2+.2+.1}{5} = .18 \text{ min}$$

$$\text{B's average observed time} = \frac{.8+.6+.8+.5+.7}{5} = .68 \text{ min}$$

$$\text{C's average observed time} = \frac{.5+.5+.4+.5+.6+.5}{6} = .50 \text{ min}$$

$$\text{A's normal time} = (.18)(.90) = .16 \text{ min}$$
$$\text{B's normal time} = (.68)(1.10) = .75 \text{ min}$$
$$\text{C's normal time} = (.50)(.80) = .40 \text{ min}$$
$$\text{Normal time for job} = .16 + .75 + .40 = 1.31 \text{ min}$$

Note, the total allowance factor = $.05 + .05 + .10 = .20$

$$\text{Then: Standard time} = \frac{1.31}{1 - .20} = 1.64 \text{ min}$$

Solved Problem S10.2

The preliminary work sample of an operation indicates the following:

Number of times operator working	60
Number of times operator idle	40
Total number of preliminary observations	100

What is the required sample size for a 99.73% confidence level with ±4% precision?

Solution

$z = 3$ for 99.73% confidence; $p = {}^{60}\!/_{100} = .6$; $h = .04$
So:

$$n = \frac{z^2 p(1-p)}{h^2} = \frac{(3)^2(.6)(.4)}{(.04)^2} = 1{,}350 \text{ sample size}$$

Solved Problem S10.3

Amor Manufacturing Co. of Geneva, Switzerland, has just observed a job in its laboratory in anticipation of releasing the job to the factory for production. The firm wants rather good accuracy for costing and labor forecasting. Specifically, it wants to provide a 99% confidence level and a cycle time that is within 3% of the true value. How many observations should it make? The data collected so far are as follows:

Observation	Time
1	1.7
2	1.6
3	1.4
4	1.4
5	1.4

solution

First, solve for the mean, $\bar{x}$, and the sample standard deviation, s:

$$s = \sqrt{\frac{\sum (\text{Each sample observation} - \bar{x})^2}{\text{Number in sample} - 1}}$$

Observation	x_i	$\bar{x}$	$x_i - \bar{x}$	$(x_i - \bar{x})^2$
1	1.7	1.5	.2	0.04
2	1.6	1.5	.1	0.01
3	1.4	1.5	−.1	0.01
4	1.4	1.5	−.1	0.01
5	1.4	1.5	−.1	0.01
	$\bar{x} = 1.5$			$0.08 = \Sigma(x_i - \bar{x})^2$

$$s = \sqrt{\frac{.08}{n-1}} = \sqrt{\frac{.08}{4}} = .141$$

Then, solve for $n = \left(\frac{zs}{h\bar{x}}\right)^2 = \left[\frac{(2.58)(.141)}{(.03)(1.5)}\right]^2 = 65.3$

where $\bar{x} = 1.5$
$s = .141$
$z = 2.58$ (from Table S10.1)
$h = .03$

Therefore, you recommend 65 observations.

Solved Problem S10.4

At Maggard Micro Manufacturing, Inc., workers press semiconductors into predrilled slots on printed circuit boards. The elemental motions for normal time used by the company are as follows:

Reach 6 inches for semiconductors	40 TMU
Grasp the semiconductor	10 TMU
Move semiconductor to printed circuit board	30 TMU
Position semiconductor	35 TMU
Press semiconductor into slots	65 TMU
Move board aside	20 TMU

(Each time measurement unit is equal to .0006 min.) Determine the normal time for this operation in minutes and in seconds.

solution

Add the time measurement units:

$$40 + 10 + 30 + 35 + 65 + 20 = 200$$
Time in minutes $= (200)(.0006 \text{ min.}) = .12 \text{ min}$
Time in seconds $= (.12)(60 \text{ sec.}) = 7.2 \text{ sec}$

Solved Problem S10.5

To obtain the estimate of time a worker is busy for a work sampling study, a manager divides a typical workday into 480 minutes. Using a random-number table to decide what time to go to an area to sample work occurrences, the manager records observations on a tally sheet like the following:

Status	Tally
Productively working	⫽⫽⫽ ⫽⫽⫽ ⫽⫽⫽ ⎮
Idle	⎮⎮⎮⎮

solution

In this case, the supervisor made 20 observations and found that employees were working 80% of the time. So, out of 480 minutes in an office workday, 20%, or 96 minutes, was idle time, and 384 minutes was productive. Note that this procedure describes that a worker is busy, not necessarily what he or she *should* be doing.

Active Model Exercise

This work sampling active model, using Example S5, displays the sample size required as a function of the proportion of time spent on a work activity. The scrollbars enable you to change the confidence or number of standard deviations. Alternatively, you may change the degree of allowable error, h, in order to determine the effects of this variable on sample size.

Degree of confidence	0.9545	◄ ┘ ►
Number of standard deviations, z	2.00	◄ ┘ ►
Acceptable error, h	0.03	◄┘ ►
Estimate of idle proportion, p	25%	◄ ┘ ►
Required sample size, n	833	

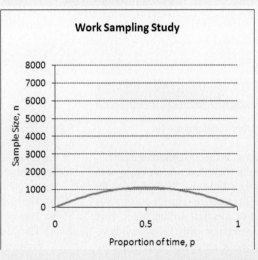

◄ **Active Model S10.1**

Work Sampling Analysis Using Example S5 Data

Questions

1. Scroll the mouse over the graph to determine what the sample size should be if $p = 30\%$.

2. Based on the graph, what value of p requires the largest sample size?

3. Use the scrollbar to determine what happens to the sample size as the number of standard deviations, z, increases.

4. Use the scrollbar to determine what happens to the sample size as the acceptable error, h, increases.

Self-Test

- *Before taking the self-test*, refer to the learning objectives listed at the beginning of the supplement and the key terms listed at the end of the supplement.
- Use the key at the back of the text to **correct** your answers.
- *Restudy pages that correspond to any questions you answered incorrectly or material you feel uncertain about.*

1. Labor standards are necessary to determine which of the following?
   a) the steps necessary to perform a task
   b) cost and time estimates prior to production
   c) the amount of raw materials to be consumed in the process
   d) the machines required by the process

2. The least preferred method of establishing labor standards is:
   a) time studies
   b) work sampling
   c) historical experience
   d) predetermined time standards

3. Classical stopwatch studies:
   a) divide a task into precise elements
   b) compute average observed times
   c) compute the normal time
   d) compute the standard time
   e) all of the above

4. The allowance factor in a time study:
   a) adjusts normal time for errors and rework
   b) adjusts standard time for lunch breaks
   c) adjusts normal time for personal needs, unavoidable delays, and fatigue
   d) allows workers to rest every 20 minutes

5. To set the required sample size in a time study, you must know:
   a) the number of employees
   b) the number of parts produced per day
   c) the desired accuracy and confidence levels
   d) management's philosophy toward sampling

6. Micro hand motions devised by Frank and Lillian Gilbreth are:
   a) flow diagrams
   b) activity charts
   c) therbligs
   d) SAE standards
   e) all of the above

7. Time measurement units (TMUs) are:
   a) equal to .00001 hours
   b) equal to .0006 minutes
   c) part of MTM
   d) tied to therbligs
   e) all of the above

Internet and Student CD-ROM/DVD Exercises

Visit our Companion Web site or use your student CD-ROM/DVD to help with material in this supplement.

 On Our Companion Web Site,
    www.prenhall.com/heizer
- Self-Study Quizzes
- Practice Problems
- Internet Case
- PowerPoint Lecture

On Your Student CD-ROM
- Practice Problems
- Active Model Exercise
- POM for Windows

On Your Student DVD
- Virtual Office Hours for Solved
  Problems

Discussion Questions

1. Identify four ways in which labor standards are set.
2. Define normal time.
3. What are some of the uses to which labor standards are put?
4. As a new time-study engineer in your plant, you are engaged in studying an employee operating a drill press. Somewhat to your surprise, one of the first things you notice is that the operator is performing many operations besides just drilling holes. Your problem is what to include in your time study. From the following examples, indicate how, as the individual responsible for labor standards in your plant, you would handle them.
   (a) Every so often, perhaps every 50 units or so, the drill press operator takes an extra-long look at the piece, which apparently is misshaped, and then typically throws it in the scrap barrel.
   (b) Approximately 1 out of 100 units has a rough edge and will not fit in the jig properly; therefore, the drill press operator picks up the piece, hits the lower right-hand edge with a file a few times, puts the file down, and returns to normal operation.
   (c) About every hour or so, the drill press operator stops to change the drill in the machine, even if he is in the middle of a job. (We can assume that the drill has become dull.)

5. What is the difference between "normal" and "standard" times?
6. What kind of work-pace change might you expect from an employee during a time study? Why?
7. How would you classify the following job elements? Are they personal, fatigue, or delay?
   (a) The operator stops to talk to you.
   (b) The operator lights up a cigarette.
   (c) The operator opens his lunch pail (it is not lunch time), removes an apple, and takes an occasional bite.
8. How do you classify the time for a drill press operator who is idle for a few minutes at the beginning of every job waiting for the setup person to complete the setup? Some of the setup time is used in going for stock, but the operator typically returns with stock before the setup person is finished with the setup.
9. How do you classify the time for a machine operator who, between every job and sometimes in the middle of jobs, turns off the machine and goes for stock?
10. The operator drops a part, which you pick up and hand to him. Does this make any difference in a time study? If so, how?
11. Describe the Gilbreths' approach to setting work standards.

Problems**

• **S10.1** An assembly-line employee had the following times, in seconds, for gluing three separate pieces together: 35, 33, 37, 34, 37, 56. What would you do next in attempting to determine the standard time for this operation?

• **S10.2** If Charlene Brewster has times of 8.4, 8.6, 8.3, 8.5, 8.7, 8.5 and a performance rating of 110%, what is the normal time for this operation? Is she faster or slower than normal?

• **S10.3** If Charlene, the worker in Problem S10.2, has a performance rating of 90%, what is the normal time for the operation? Is she faster or slower than normal?

•• **S10.4** Refer to Problem S10.2.
a) If the allowance factor is 15%, what is the standard time for this operation?
b) If the allowance factor is 18% and the performance rating is now 90%, what is the standard time for this operation?

•• **S10.5** Maurice Browne recorded the following times assembling a watch. Determine (a) the average time, (b) the normal time,

and (c) the standard time taken by him, using a performance rating of 95% and a personal allowance of 8%.

Assembly Times Recorded

Observation No.	Time (minutes)
1	0.11
2	0.10
3	0.11
4	0.10
5	0.14
6	0.10
7	0.10
8	0.09
9	0.12
10	0.09
11	0.12
12	0.11
13	0.10
14	0.12
15	0.14
16	0.09

****Note:** ▯ means the problem may be solved with POM for Windows and/or Excel.

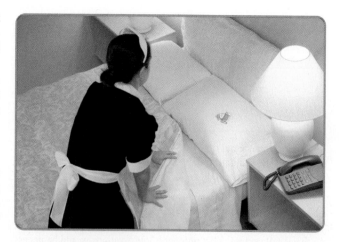

- **S10.6**   A Northeast Airline gate agent, Chip Gilliken, gives out seat assignments to ticketed passengers. He takes an average of 50 seconds per passenger and is rated 110% in performance. How long should a *typical* agent be expected to take to make seat assignments? **Px**

- **S10.7**   After being observed many times, Marilyn Jones, a hospital lab analyst, had an average observed time for blood tests of 12 minutes. Marilyn's performance rating is 105%. The hospital has a personal, fatigue, and delay allowance of 16%.
a) Find the normal time for this process.
b) Find the standard time for this blood test. **Px**

- **S10.8**   Jell Lee Beans is famous for its boxed candies, which are sold primarily to businesses. One operator had the following observed times for gift wrapping in minutes: 2.2, 2.6, 2.3, 2.5, 2.4. The operator has a performance rating of 105% and an allowance factor of 10%. What is the standard time for gift wrapping? **Px**

- **S10.9**   After training, Mary Fernandez, a computer technician, had an average observed time for memory-chip tests of 12 seconds. Shirley's performance rating is 100%. The firm has a personal fatigue and delay allowance of 15%.
a) Find the normal time for this process.
b) Find the standard time for this process. **Px**

- - **S10.10**   Susan Cottenden clocked the observed time for welding a part onto truck doors at 5.3 minutes. The performance rating of the worker timed was estimated at 105%. Find the normal time for this operation.
Note: According to the local union contract, each welder is allowed 3 minutes of personal time per hour and 2 minutes of fatigue time per hour. Further, there should be an average delay allowance of 1 minute per hour. Compute the allowance factor and then find the standard time for the welding activity. **Px**

- **S10.11**   The normal time for a particular task has been clocked at 25 minutes. Assume that the allowances are personal time: 5 minutes per hour; fatigue: 10 minutes per hour; and delay: 2 minutes per hour for setup approval:
a) What is the allowance factor?
b) What is the standard time? **Px**

- - **S10.12**   The data in the following table represent time-study observations for a lab test at Arnold Palmer Hospital. On the basis of these observations, find the standard time for the test. Assume a personal time of 6%, a fatigue allowance of 6%, and a delay allowance of 6%.

		Observation (minutes per cycle)				
Element	**Performance Rating**	**1**	**2**	**3**	**4**	**5**
1	100%	1.5	1.6	1.4	1.5	1.5
2	90%	2.3	2.5	2.1	2.2	2.4
3	120%	1.7	1.9	1.9	1.4	1.6
4	100%	3.5	3.6	3.6	3.6	3.2 **Px**

- - **S10.13**   A hotel housekeeper, Alison Harvey, was observed five times on each of four task elements, as shown in the following table. On the basis of these observations, find the standard time for the process. Assume a 10% allowance factor.

		Observations (minutes per cycle)				
Element	**Performance Rating (%)**	**1**	**2**	**3**	**4**	**5**
Check minibar	100	1.5	1.6	1.4	1.5	1.5
Make one bed	90	2.3	2.5	2.1	2.2	2.4
Vacuum floor	120	1.7	1.9	1.9	1.4	1.6
Clean bath	100	3.5	3.6	3.6	3.6	3.2 **Px**

- - **S10.14**   Virginia College promotes a wide variety of executive-training courses for firms in the Arlington, Virginia, region. Director Marilyn Helms believes that individually typed letters add a personal touch to marketing. To prepare letters for mailing, she conducts a time study of her secretaries. On the basis of the observations shown in the following table, she wishes to develop a time standard for the whole job.

The college uses a total allowance factor of 12%. Helms decides to delete all unusual observations from the time study. What is the standard time?

	Observations (minutes)						
Element	**1**	**2**	**3**	**4**	**5**	**6**	**Performance Rating (%)**
Typing letter	2.5	3.5	2.8	2.1	2.6	3.3	85
Typing envelope	.8	.8	.6	.8	3.1[a]	.7	100
Stuffing envelope	.4	.5	1.9[a]	.3	.6	.5	95
Sealing, sorting	1.0	2.9[b]	.9	1.0	4.4[b]	.9	125

[a]Disregard—secretary stopped to answer the phone.
[b]Disregard—interruption by supervisor. **Px**

- **S10.15**   The results of a time study to perform a quality control test are shown in the following table. On the basis of these observations, determine the normal and standard time for the test, assuming a 23% allowance factor.

		Observations (minutes)				
Task Element	**Performance Rating (%)**	**1**	**2**	**3**	**4**	**5**
1	97	1.5	1.8	2.0	1.7	1.5
2	105	.6	.4	.7	3.7[a]	.5
3	86	.5	.4	.6	.4	.4
4	90	.6	.8	.7	.6	.7

[a]Disregard—employee is smoking a cigarette (included in personal time).

a) What is the normal time?
b) What is the standard time? **Px**

- - **S10.16**   Peter Rourke, a loan processor at Wentworth Bank, has been timed performing four work elements, with the results shown in the following table. The allowances for tasks such as this are personal, 7%; fatigue, 10%; and delay, 3%.

Task Element	Performance Rating (%)	Observations (minutes)				
		1	**2**	**3**	**4**	**5**
1	110	.5	.4	.6	.4	.4
2	95	.6	.8	.7	.6	.7
3	90	.6	.4	.7	.5	.5
4	85	1.5	1.8	2.0	1.7	1.5

a) What is the normal time?
b) What is the standard time? **Px**

•• **S10.17** Each year, Lord & Taylor, Ltd., sets up a gift-wrapping station to assist its customers with holiday shopping. Preliminary observations of one worker at the station produced the following sample time (in minutes per package): 3.5, 3.2, 4.1, 3.6, 3.9. Based on this small sample, what number of observations would be necessary to determine the true cycle time with a 95% confidence level and an accuracy of 5%? **Px**

•• **S10.18** A time study of a factory worker has revealed an average observed time of 3.20 minutes, with a standard deviation of 1.28 minutes. These figures were based on a sample of 45 observations. Is this sample adequate in size for the firm to be 99% confident that the standard time is within 5% of the true value? If not, what should be the proper number of observations? **Px**

••• **S10.19** A time study was done on a data entry operation done by clerical workers at Martin Industries. The mean time and standard deviation for the operation were .4 seconds and .15 seconds, respectively. Only 12 measurements were taken in this initial study, and the accuracy level had to remain at 10%. The measurements found are shown in the table below. A performance rating of 90% is assigned, along with an allowance factor of 6%.
a) What confidence is obtained using $n = 12$?
b) Determine the average cycle (observed) time, the normal time, and the standard time.

Observation	Time (minutes)
1	.331
2	.243
3	.422
4	.521
5	.511
6	.342
7	.468
8	.766
9	.489
10	.391
11	.413
12	.484 **Px**

•• **S10.20** Based on a careful work study in the Richard Dulski Corp., the results shown in the following table have been observed:

Element	Observations (minutes)					Performance Rating (%)
	1	**2**	**3**	**4**	**5**	
Prepare daily reports	35	40	33	42	39	120
Photocopy results	12	10	36[a]	15	13	110
Label and package reports	3	3	5	5	4	90
Distribute reports	15	18	21	17	45[b]	85

[a]Photocopying machine broken; included as delay in the allowance factor.
[b]Power outage; included as delay in the allowance factor.

a) Compute the normal time for each work element.
b) If the allowance for this type of work is 15%, what is the standard time?
c) How many observations are needed for a 95% confidence level within 5% accuracy? (*Hint:* Calculate the sample size of each element.) **Px**

•• **S10.21** The Dubuque Cement Company packs 80-pound bags of concrete mix. Time-study data for the filling activity are shown in the following table. Because of the high physical demands of the job, the company's policy is a 23% allowance for workers.
a) Compute the standard time for the bag-packing task.
b) How many observations are necessary for 99% confidence, within 5% accuracy?

Element	Observations (seconds)					Performance Rating (%)
	1	**2**	**3**	**4**	**5**	
Grasp and place bag	8	9	8	11	7	110
Fill bag	36	41	39	35	112[a]	85
Seal bag	15	17	13	20	18	105
Place bag on conveyor	8	6	9	30[b]	35[b]	90

[a]Bag breaks open; included as delay in the allowance factor.
[b]Conveyor jams; included as delay in the allowance factor. **Px**

•• **S10.22** Installing mufflers at the Stanley Garage in Golden, Colorado, involves five work elements. Linda Stanley has timed workers performing these tasks seven times, with the results shown in the following table.

Job Element	Observations (minutes)							Performance Rating (%)
	1	**2**	**3**	**4**	**5**	**6**	**7**	
1. Select correct mufflers	4	5	4	6	4	15[a]	4	110
2. Remove old muffler	6	8	7	6	7	6	7	90
3. Weld/install new muffler	15	14	14	12	15	16	13	105
4. Check/inspect work	3	4	24[a]	5	4	3	18[a]	100
5. Complete paperwork	5	6	8	—	7	6	7	130

[a]Employee has lengthy conversations with boss (not job related).

By agreement with her workers, Stanley allows a 10% fatigue factor and a 10% personal-time factor. To compute standard time for the work operation, Stanley excludes all observations that appear to be unusual or nonrecurring. She does not want an error of more than 5%.
a) What is the standard time for the task?
b) How many observations are needed to assure a 95% confidence level? **Px**

• **S10.23** Bank manager Art Hill wants to determine the percent of time that tellers are working and idle. He decides to use work sampling, and his initial estimate is that the tellers are idle 15% of the time. How many observations should Hill take to be 95.45% confident that the results will not be more than 4% from the true result? **Px**

•• **S10.24** Supervisor Robert Hall wants to determine the percent of time a machine in his area is idle. He decides to use work sampling, and his initial estimate is that the machine is idle 20% of the time. How many observations should Hall take to be 98% confident that the results will be less than 5% from the true results?

•••**S10.25** In the photo caption that begins this supplement, Tim Nelson's job as an inspector for La-Z-Boy is discussed. Tim is expected to inspect 130 chairs per day.
a) If he works an 8-hour day, how many minutes is he allowed for each inspection (i.e., what is his "standard time")?
b) If he is allowed a 6% fatigue allowance, a 6% delay allowance, and 6% for personal time, what is the normal time that he is assumed to take to perform each inspection?

• **S10.26** A random work sample of operators taken over a 160-hour work month at Tele-Marketing, Inc., has produced the following results. What is the percent of time spent working?

On phone with customer	858
Idle time	220
Personal time	85

•• **S10.27** A total of 300 observations of Bob Ramos, an assembly-line worker, were made over a 40-hour work week. The sample also showed that Bob was busy working (assembling the parts) during 250 observations.
a) Find the percent of time Bob was working.
b) If you want a confidence level of 95% and if 3% is an acceptable error, what size should the sample be?
c) Was the sample size adequate? **Px**

• **S10.28** Sharpening your pencil is an operation that may be divided into eight small elemental motions. In MTM terms, each element may be assigned a certain number of TMUs:

Reach 4 inches for the pencil	6 TMU
Grasp the pencil	2 TMU
Move the pencil 6 inches	10 TMU
Position the pencil	20 TMU
Insert the pencil into the sharpener	4 TMU
Sharpen the pencil	120 TMU
Disengage the pencil	10 TMU
Move the pencil 6 inches	10 TMU

What is the total normal time for sharpening one pencil? Convert your answer into minutes and seconds.

•• **S10.29** Supervisor Vic Sower at Huntsville Equipment Company is concerned that material is not arriving as promptly as needed at work cells. A new kanban system has been installed, but there seems to be some delay in getting the material moved to the work cells so that the job can begin promptly. Sower is interested in determining how much delay there is on the part of his highly paid machinists. Ideally, the delay would be close to zero. He has asked his assistant to determine the delay factor among his 10 work cells. The assistant collects the data on a random basis over the next 2 weeks and determines that of the 1,200 observations, 105 were made while the operators were waiting for materials. Use a 95% confidence level and a 3% acceptable error. What report does he give to Sower? **Px**

••••**S10.30** The Winter Garden Hotel has 400 rooms. Every day, the housekeepers clean any room that was occupied the night before. If a guest is checking out of the hotel, the housekeepers give the room a thorough cleaning to get it ready for the next guest. This takes about 30 minutes. If a guest is staying another night, the housekeeper only "refreshes" the room, which takes 15 minutes.

Each day, each housekeeper reports for her 6-hour shift, then prepares her cart. She pushes the cart to her floor and begins work. She usually has to restock the cart once per day; then she pushes it back to the storeroom at the end of the day and puts the things away. Here is a timetable:
1) Arrive at work and stock cart (10 minutes).
2) Push cart to floor (10 minutes).
3) Take morning break (15 minutes).
4) Stop for lunch (30 minutes).
5) Restock cart (20 minutes).
6) Take afternoon break (15 minutes).
7) Push cart back to laundry and store items (20 minutes).

Last night, the hotel was full (all 400 rooms were occupied). People are checking out of 200 rooms. Their rooms will need to be thoroughly cleaned. The other 200 rooms will need to be refreshed.
a) How many minutes per day of actual room cleaning can each housekeeper do?
b) How many minutes of room cleaning will the Winter Garden Hotel need today?
c) How many housekeepers will be needed to clean the hotel today?
d) If *all* the guests checked out this morning, how many housekeepers would be needed to clean the 400 rooms?

Case Study

Jackson Manufacturing Company

Kathleen McFadden, vice president of operations at Jackson Manufacturing Company, has just received a request for quote (RFQ) from DeKalb Electric Supply for 400 units per week of a motor armature. The components are standard and either easy to work into the existing production schedule or readily available from established suppliers on a JIT basis. But there is some difference in assembly. Ms. McFadden has identified eight tasks that Jackson must perform to assemble the armature. Seven of these tasks are very similar to the

ones performed by Jackson in the past; therefore, the average time and resulting labor standard of those tasks is known.

The eighth task, an *overload* test, requires performing a task that is very different from any performed previously, however. Kathleen has asked you to conduct a time study on the task to determine the standard time. Then an estimate can be made of the cost to assemble the armature. This information, combined with other cost data, will allow the firm to put together the information needed for the RFQ.

To determine a standard time for the task, an employee from an existing assembly station was trained in the new assembly process. Once proficient, the employee was then asked to perform the task 17 times so a standard could be determined. The actual times observed (in minutes) were as follows:

1	2	3	4	5	6	7	8	9	10	11	12	13	14	15	16	17
2.05	1.92	2.01	1.89	1.77	1.80	1.86	1.83	1.93	1.96	1.95	2.05	1.79	1.82	1.85	1.85	1.99

The worker had a 115% performance rating. The task can be performed in a sitting position at a well-designed ergonomic workstation in an air-conditioned facility. Although the armature itself weighs 10.5 pounds, there is a carrier that holds it so that the operator need only rotate the armature. But the detail work remains high; therefore, the fatigue allowance will be 8%. The company has an established personal allowance of 6%. Delay should be very low. Previous studies of delay in this department average 2%. This standard is to use the same figure.

The workday is 7.5 hours, but operators are paid for 8 hours at an average of $12.50 per hour.

Discussion Questions

In your report to Ms. McFadden, you realize you will want to address several factors:

1. How big should the sample be for a statistically accurate standard (at, say, the 99.73% confidence level and accuracy of 5%)?
2. Is the sample size adequate?
3. How many units should be produced at this workstation per day?
4. What is the cost per unit for this task in direct labor cost?

Source: Professor Hank Maddux, Sam Houston State University.

Additional Case Studies

Internet case study: Visit our Companion Web site at www.prenhall.com/heizer for this free case study:

• **Chicago Southern Hospital:** Examines the requirements for a work-sampling plan for nurses.

Harvard has selected this Harvard Business School case to accompany this supplement:

harvardbusinessonline.hbsp.harvard.edu

• **Lincoln Electric** (#376-028): Discusses the compensation system and company culture at this welding equipment manufacturer.

Bibliography

Aft, Larry, and Neil Schmeidler. "Work Measurement Practices." *Industrial Engineer* 35, no. 11 (November 2003): 44.

Elnekave, M., and I. Gilad. "Rapid Video-Based Analysis System for Advanced Work Measurement." *International Journal of Production Research* 44, no. 2 (January 2006): 271.

Konz, S., and Steven Johnson. *Work Design: Industrial Ergonomics*, 6th ed. Scottsdale, AZ: Holcomb Hathaway, 2004.

Myers, Fred E. *Time and Motion Study for Lean Manufacturing*, 3rd ed. Upper Saddle River, NJ: Prentice Hall, 2002.

Niebel, B. W., and Andris Freivalds. *Methods, Standards, and Work Design*, 11th ed. New York: Irwin/McGraw-Hill, 2003.

Ousnamer, Mark. "Time Standards That Make Sense." *IIE Solutions* (December 2000): 28–32.

Sadikoglu, E. "Integration of Work Measurement and Total Quality Management." *Total Quality Management and Business Excellence* 16, no. 5 (July 2005): 597.

Tolo, B. "21st-Century Stopwatch." *Industrial Engineer* 37, no. 7 (July 2005): 34–37.

Walsh, Ellen. "Get Results with Workload Management." *Nursing Management* (October 2003): 16.

Internet Resources

Applied Computer Services, Inc. (measurement software): **www.acsco.com**
Institute of Industrial Engineers: **www.iienet.org**
H. B. Maynard and Company, Inc. (workforce performance): **hbmaynard.com**

Methods Time Measurement Association: **www.mtm.org**
Quetech Ltd. (time studies and work sampling): **www.quetech.com**
Tectime Data Systems Ltd. (work measurement systems): **www.tectime.com**

Part Three   Managing Operations

CHAPTER 11

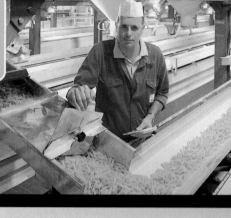

Supply Chain Management

Chapter Outline

Ten OM Strategy Decisions

Design of Goods and Services
Managing Quality
Process Strategy
Location Strategies
Layout Strategies
Human Resources
Supply Chain Management
Inventory Management
Scheduling
Maintenance

Learning Objectives

When you complete this chapter you should be able to

1. Explain the strategic importance
   of the supply chain
2. Identify five supply chain strategies
3. Explain issues and opportunities in the
   supply chain
4. Describe approaches to supply chain
   negotiations

5. Evaluate supply chain performance
6. Compute percent of assets committed
   to inventory
7. Compute inventory turnover

Global Company Profile: Darden Restaurants

Darden's Supply Chain Yields a Competitive Edge

Darden Restaurants, Inc., is the largest publicly traded casual dining restaurant company in the world. It serves over 300 million meals annually from more than 1,400 restaurants in the U.S. and Canada. Each of its well-known flagship brands—Olive Garden and Red Lobster—generates sales of $2.4 billion annually. Darden's other brands include Bahama Breeze and Seasons 52; with the $1.4 billion addition in late 2007 of the Capital Grille and Long Horn Steakhouse chains. The firm employs more than 150,000 people.

"Operations is typically thought of as an execution of strategy. For us it is the strategy," Darden's former chairman, Joe R. Lee, recently stated.

In the restaurant business, a winning strategy requires a winning supply chain. Nothing is more important than sourcing and delivering healthy, high-quality food; and there are very few other industries where supplier performance is so closely tied to the customer.

Darden sources its food from five continents and thousands of suppliers. To meet Darden's needs for fresh ingredients, the company has developed four distinct supply chains: one for seafood; one for dairy/produce/other refrigerated foods; a third for other food items, like baked goods; and a fourth for restaurant supplies (everything from dishes to ovens to uniforms). Over $1.5 billion is spent in these supply chains annually. (See the *Video Case Study* at the end of this chapter for details.)

▲ *Product tracking:* Darden's seafood inspection team developed an integral system that uses a lot ID to track seafood from its origin through shipping and receipt. Darden uses a modified atmosphere packaging (MAP) process to extend the shelf life and preserve the quality of its fresh fish. The tracking includes time temperature monitoring.

 Video 11.1

Darden's Global Supply Chain

▶ *Qualifying the supplier:* Long before a supplier is qualified to sell to Darden, a total quality team is appointed. The team, consisting of personnel from the quality assurance, culinary, purchasing, and distribution departments spends time at the supplier's facility to understand the processes and to evaluate the effectiveness of its food safety/quality management. The team provides guidance, assistance, support, and training to the supplier to ensure that overall objectives and desired results are accomplished.

▶ **Worldwide sources:** *Parts of the supply chain begin in the frigid waters off the coast of Alaska, where crabs are harvested. For many products, temperature monitoring begins immediately and is tracked through the entire supply chain, to the kitchen, and ultimately to the guest.*

◀ **Independent audits of suppliers:** *To provide fair and accurate assessment, Darden's Total Quality Supplier Program includes an independent verification program. Each supplier is evaluated regularly by independent auditors on a risk-based schedule to determine the supplier's effectiveness.*

▶ **JIT delivery:** *JIT delivery and quality service at each of Darden's 1,450 restaurants is the final step in the supply chain.*

Darden's four supply channels have some common characteristics. They all require *supplier qualification*, have *product tracking*, are subject to *independent audits*, and employ *just-in-time delivery*. With best-in-class techniques and processes, Darden creates world-wide supply chain partnerships and alliances that are rapid, transparent, and efficient. Darden achieves competitive advantage through its superior supply chain.

433

Most firms, like Darden, spend a huge portion of their sales dollars on purchases. Because such a high percentage of an organization's costs are determined by purchasing, relationships with suppliers are increasingly integrated and long term. Joint efforts that improve innovation, speed design, and reduce costs are common. Such efforts, when part of a corporate-wide strategy, can dramatically improve both partners' competitiveness. This integrated focus places added emphasis on procurement and supplier relationships which must be managed. The discipline that manages these relationships is known as *supply chain management*.

THE SUPPLY CHAIN'S STRATEGIC IMPORTANCE

Supply chain management

Management of activities that procure materials and services, transforming them into intermediate goods and final products, and delivering the products through a distribution system.

Supply chain management is the integration of the activities that procure materials and services, transform them into intermediate goods and final products, and deliver them to customers. These activities include purchasing and outsourcing activities, plus many other functions that are important to the relationship with suppliers and distributors. As Figure 11.1 suggests, supply-chain management includes determining (1) transportation vendors, (2) credit and cash transfers, (3) suppliers, (4) distributors, (5) accounts payable and receivable, (6) warehousing and inventory, (7) order fulfillment, and (8) sharing customer, forecasting, and production information. The *objective is to build a chain of suppliers that focuses on maximizing value to the ultimate customer*. Competition is no longer between companies; it is between supply chains. And those supply chains are often global.

As firms strive to increase their competitiveness via product customization, high quality, cost reductions, and speed to market, added emphasis is placed on the supply chain. Effective supply chain management makes suppliers "partners" in the firm's strategy to satisfy an ever-changing marketplace. A competitive advantage may depend on a close long-term strategic relationship with a few suppliers.

▼ **Figure 11.1** **A Supply Chain for Beer**

The supply chain includes all the interactions among suppliers, manufacturers, distributors, and customers. The chain includes transportation, scheduling information, cash and credit transfers, as well as ideas, designs, and material transfers. Even can and bottle manufacturers have their own tiers of suppliers providing components such as glass, lids, labels, packing containers, etc. (Costs are approximate and include substantial taxes.)

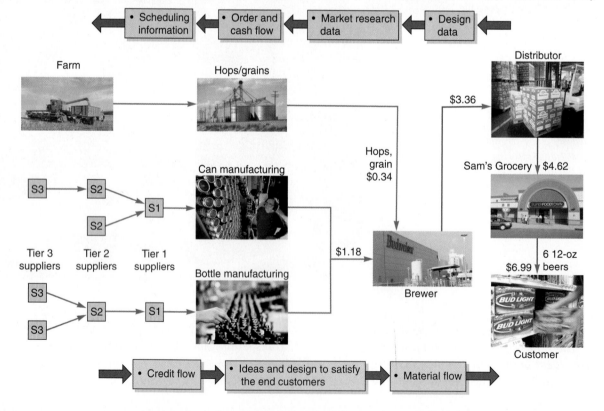

▼ **Table 11.1**   **How Supply Chain Decisions Affect Strategy***

	Low-Cost Strategy	**Response Strategy**	**Differentiation Strategy**
Supplier's goal	Supply demand at lowest possible cost (e.g., Emerson Electric, Taco Bell)	Respond quickly to changing requirements and demand to minimize stockouts (e.g., Dell Computers)	Share market research; jointly develop products and options (e.g., Benetton)
Primary selection criteria	Select primarily for cost	Select primarily for capacity, speed, and flexibility	Select primarily for product development skills
Process characteristics	Maintain high average utilization	Invest in excess capacity and flexible processes	Use modular processes that lend themselves to mass customization
Inventory characteristics	Minimize inventory throughout the chain to hold down costs	Develop responsive system, with buffer stocks positioned to ensure supply	Minimize inventory in the chain to avoid obsolescence
Lead-time characteristics	Shorten lead time as long as it does not increase costs	Invest aggressively to reduce production lead time	Invest aggressively to reduce development lead time
Product-design characteristics	Maximize performance and minimize cost	Use product designs that lead to low setup time and rapid production ramp-up	Use modular design to postpone product differentiation for as long as possible

*See related table and discussion in Marshall L. Fisher, "What Is the Right Supply Chain for Your Product?" *Harvard Business Review* (March–April 1997): 105.

To ensure that the supply chain supports the firm's strategy, managers need to consider the supply chain issues shown in Table 11.1. Activities of supply chain managers cut across accounting, finance, marketing, and the operations discipline. Just as the OM function supports the firm's overall strategy, the supply chain must support the OM strategy. Strategies of low cost or rapid response demand different things from a supply chain than a strategy of differentiation. For instance, a low-cost strategy, as Table 11.1 indicates, requires suppliers be selected based primarily on cost. Such suppliers should have the ability to design low-cost products that meet the functional requirements, minimize inventory, and drive down lead times. The firm must achieve integration of its selected strategy up and down the supply chain, and must expect that strategy to be different for different products and change as products move through their life cycle.

> **Learning Objective**
>
> 1. Explain the strategic importance of the supply chain

Global Supply Chain Issues

When companies enter growing global markets such as eastern Europe, China, South America, or even Mexico, expanding their supply chains becomes a strategic challenge. Quality production in those areas may be a challenge, just as distribution systems may be less reliable, suggesting higher inventory levels than would be needed in one's home country. Also, tariffs and quotas may block nonlocal companies from doing business. Moreover, both political and currency risk remain high in much of the world.[1]

Thus, the development of a successful strategic plan for supply chain management requires innovative planning and careful research. Supply chains in a global environment must be able to:

1. React to sudden changes in parts availability, distribution or shipping channels, import duties, and currency rates
2. Use the latest computer and transmission technologies to schedule and manage the shipment of parts in and finished products out
3. Staff with local specialists who handle duties, freight, customs, and political issues

McDonald's planned for a global supply chain challenge 6 years in advance of its opening in Russia. Creating a $60 million "food town," it developed independently owned supply plants in

---

[1]Note the devaluation of the Mexican peso in 1992, the Thai bhat and the Malaysian ringgit in 1997, and the Argentine peso in 2002, as well as armed conflicts in about two dozen countries at any given time. Even the stable U.S. dollar reached record lows compared with the euro in 2007.

OM in Action   A Rose Is a Rose, But Only if It Is Fresh

Supply chains for food and flowers must be fast, and they must be good. When the food supply chain has a problem, the best that can happen is the customer does not get fed on time; the worst that happens is the customer gets food poisoning and dies. In the floral industry, the timing and temperature are also critical. Indeed, flowers are the most perishable agricultural item—even more so than fish. Flowers not only need to move fast, but they must also be kept cool, at a constant temperature of 33 to 37 degrees. And they must be provided preservative-treated water while in transit. Roses are especially delicate, fragile, and perishable.

Seventy percent of the roses sold in the U.S. market arrive by air from rural Columbia and Ecuador. Roses move through this supply chain via an intricate but fast transportation network. This network stretches from growers who cut, grade, bundle, pack and ship, to importers who make the deal, to the U.S. Department of Agriculture personnel who quarantine and inspect for insects, diseases, and parasites, to U.S. Customs agents

who inspect and approve, to facilitators who provide clearance and labeling, to wholesalers who distribute, to retailers who arrange and sell, and finally to the customer. Each and every minute the product is deteriorating. The time and temperature sensitivity of perishables like roses requires sophistication and refined standards in the supply chain. Success yields quality and low losses. After all, when it's Valentine's Day, what good is a shipment of roses that arrives wilted or late? This is a difficult supply chain; only an excellent one will get the job done.

Sources: IIE Solutions (February 2002): 26–32; and *World Trade* (June 2004): 22–25.

Moscow to keep its transportation costs and handling times low and its quality and customer-service levels high. Every component in this food chain—meat plant, chicken plant, bakery, fish plant, and lettuce plant—is closely monitored to make sure that all the system's links are strong.

Firms like Ford and Boeing also face global procurement decisions. Ford's Mercury has only 227 suppliers worldwide, a small number compared with the 700 involved in previous models. Ford has set a trend to develop a global network of *fewer* suppliers who provide the lowest cost and highest quality regardless of home country. So global is the production of the Boeing 787 that 75% to 80% of the plane is built by non-Boeing companies, with most of that figure outside the U.S. The *OM in Action* box "A Rose Is a Rose, But Only if It Is Fresh" details a global supply chain that ends with your local florist.

SUPPLY CHAIN ECONOMICS

The supply chain receives such attention because it is an integral part of a firm's strategy and the most costly activity in most firms. For both goods and services, supply chain costs as a percent of sales are often substantial (see Table 11.2). Because such a huge portion of revenue is devoted to the supply chain, an effective strategy is vital. The supply chain provides a major opportunity to reduce costs and increase contribution margins.

Table 11.3 and Example 1 illustrate the amount of leverage available to the operations manager through the supply chain.

▼ **Table 11.2**

Supply Chain Costs as a Percent of Sales

Industry	% Purchased
All industry	52
Automobile	67
Food	60
Lumber	61
Paper	55
Petroleum	79
Transportation	62

EXAMPLE 1

Profit potential in the supply chain

Hau Lee Furniture Inc. spends 50% of its sales dollar in the supply chain and has a net profit of 4%. Hau wants to know how many dollars of sales is equivalent to supply chain savings of $1.

Approach: Table 11.3 (given Hau's assumptions) can be used to make the analysis.

Solution: Table 11.3 indicates that every $1 Hau can save in the supply chain results in the same profit that would be generated by $3.70 in sales.

Percent Net Profit of Firm	Percent of Sales Spent in the Supply Chain						
	30%	**40%**	**50%**	**60%**	**70%**	**80%**	**90%**
2	$2.78	$3.23	$3.85	$4.76	$6.25	$9.09	$16.67
4	$2.70	$3.13	$3.70	$4.55	$5.88	$8.33	$14.29
6	$2.63	$3.03	$3.57	$4.35	$5.56	$7.69	$12.50
8	$2.56	$2.94	$3.45	$4.17	$5.26	$7.14	$11.11
10	$2.50	$2.86	$3.33	$4.00	$5.00	$6.67	$10.00

[a]The required increase in sales assumes that 50% of the costs other than purchases are variable and that half the remaining costs (less profit) are fixed. Therefore, at sales of $100 (50% purchases and 2% margin), $50 are purchases, $24 are other variable costs, $24 are fixed costs, and $2 profit. Increasing sales by $3.85 yields the following:

Purchases at 50%	$ 51.93
Other Variable Costs	24.92
Fixed Cost	24.00
Profit	3.00
	$103.85

Through $3.85 of additional sales, we have increased profit by $1, from $2 to $3. The same increase in margin could have been obtained by reducing supply chain costs by $1.

Insight: Effective management of the supply chain can generate substantial benefits.

Learning exercise: If Hau increases his profit to 6%, how much of an increase in sales is necessary to equal $1 savings? [Answer: $3.57.]

Related problems: 11.6, 11.7

These numbers indicate the strong role that procurement can play in profitability.

Make-or-Buy Decisions

A wholesaler or retailer buys everything that it sells; a manufacturing operation hardly ever does. Manufacturers, restaurants, and assemblers of products buy components and subassemblies that go into final products. As we saw in Chapter 5, choosing products and services that can be advantageously obtained *externally* as opposed to produced *internally* is known as the **make-or-buy decision**. Supply chain personnel evaluate alternative suppliers and provide current, accurate, complete data relevant to the buy alternative. Table 11.4 lists a variety of considerations in the make-or-buy decision. Regardless of the decision, supply chain performance should be reviewed periodically. Vendor competence and costs change, as do a firm's own strategy, production capabilities, and costs.

Make-or-buy decision
A choice between producing a component or service in-house or purchasing it from an outside source.

◄ **Table 11.4**

Considerations for the Make-or-Buy Decision

Reasons for Making	Reasons for Buying
1. Maintain core competence	1. Frees management to deal with its core competence
2. Lower production cost	
3. Unsuitable suppliers	2. Lower acquisition cost
4. Assure adequate supply (quantity or delivery)	3. Preserve supplier commitment
5. Utilize surplus labor or facilities and make a marginal contribution	4. Obtain technical or management ability
	5. Inadequate capacity
6. Obtain desired quality	6. Reduce inventory costs
7. Remove supplier collusion	7. Ensure alternative sources
8. Obtain unique item that would entail a prohibitive commitment for a supplier	8. Inadequate managerial or technical resources
9. Protect personnel from a layoff	9. Reciprocity
10. Protect proprietary design or quality	10. Item is protected by a patent or trade secret
11. Increase or maintain size of the company (management preference)	

Outsourcing
Transferring a firm's activities that have traditionally been internal to external suppliers.

Outsourcing

Outsourcing transfers some of what are traditional internal activities and resources of a firm to outside vendors, making it slightly different from the traditional make-or-buy decision. Outsourcing is part of the continuing trend toward utilizing the efficiency that comes with specialization. The vendor performing the outsourced service is an expert in that particular specialty. This leaves the outsourcing firm to focus on its critical success factors, that is, its core competencies that yield a competitive advantage. Outsourcing is the focus of the supplement to this chapter.

ETHICS IN THE SUPPLY CHAIN

As we have stressed throughout this text, ethical decisions are critical to the long-term success of any organization. However, the supply chain is particularly susceptible to ethical lapses, as the opportunities for unethical behavior are enormous. With sales personnel anxious to sell, and purchasing agents spending huge sums, the temptation for unethical behavior is substantial. Many salespeople become friends with customers, do favors for them, take them to lunch, or present small (or large) gifts. Determining when tokens of friendship become a bribe can be a challenge. Many companies have strict rules and codes of conduct that limit what is acceptable. Recognizing these issues, the Institute for Supply Management has developed principles and standards to be used as guidelines for ethical behavior. An abbreviated version is shown in Table 11.5.

As the supply chain becomes international, operations managers need to expect an additional set of ethical issues to manifest themselves as they deal with labor laws, culture, and whole new sets of values. For instance, Gap Inc. recently reported that of its 3,000 plus factories worldwide, about 90% failed their initial evaluation.[2] The report indicated that between 10% and 25% of its Chinese factories engaged in psychological or verbal abuse, and more than 50% of the factories visited in sub-Saharan Africa operate without proper safety devices. The challenge of ethics in the supply chain is significant, but responsible firms such as Gap are finding ways to deal with a difficult issue.

SUPPLY CHAIN STRATEGIES

Learning Objective

2. Identify five supply chain strategies

For goods and services to be obtained from outside sources, the firm must decide on a supply chain strategy. One such strategy is the approach of *negotiating with many suppliers* and playing one supplier against another. A second strategy is to develop *long-term "partnering"* relation-

▶ **Table 11.5**

Principles and Standards of Ethical Supply Management Conduct

LOYALTY TO YOUR ORGANIZATION; JUSTICE TO THOSE WITH WHOM YOU DEAL; FAITH IN YOUR PROFESSION

1. Avoid the intent and appearance of unethical or compromising practice.
2. Demonstrate loyalty to the employer by diligently following the lawful instructions of the employer.
3. Avoid any activity that would create a conflict between personal and employer interest.
4. Avoid any activity that might influence, or appear to influence, supply management decisions.
5. Handle confidential or proprietary information with due care and proper consideration.
6. Promote positive supplier relationships.
7. Avoid improper reciprocal agreements.
8. Know and obey the letter and spirit of laws.
9. Encourage support for small, disadvantaged, and minority-owned businesses.
10. Acquire and maintain professional competence.
11. Conduct activities in accordance with national and international laws, customs, practices, and ethics.
12. Enhance the stature of the supply management profession.

Source: Adapted from the Institute for Supply Management™, **www.ism.ws/about/content/cfm**.

---

[2]Amy Merrick, "Gap Offers Unusual Look at Factory Conditions," *The Wall Street Journal* (May 12, 2004): A1, A12.

ships with a few suppliers to satisfy the end customer. A third strategy is *vertical integration*, in which a firm decides to use vertical backward integration by actually buying the supplier. A fourth variation is a combination of few suppliers and vertical integration, known as a *keiretsu*. In a *keiretsu, suppliers become part of a company coalition.* Finally, a fifth strategy is to develop *virtual companies that use suppliers on an as-needed basis.* We will now discuss each of these strategies.

Video 11.2

Supply Chain Management at Regal Marine

Many Suppliers

With the many-suppliers strategy, a supplier responds to the demands and specifications of a "request for quotation," with the order usually going to the low bidder. This is a common strategy when products are commodities. This strategy plays one supplier against another and places the burden of meeting the buyer's demands on the supplier. Suppliers aggressively compete with one another. Although many approaches to negotiations can be used with this strategy, long-term "partnering" relationships are not the goal. This approach holds the supplier responsible for maintaining the necessary technology, expertise, and forecasting abilities, as well as cost, quality, and delivery competencies.

Few Suppliers

A strategy of few suppliers implies that rather than looking for short-term attributes, such as low cost, a buyer is better off forming a long-term relationship with a few dedicated suppliers. Long-term suppliers are more likely to understand the broad objectives of the procuring firm and the end customer. Using few suppliers can create value by allowing suppliers to have economies of scale and a learning curve that yields both lower transaction costs and lower production costs.

Few suppliers, each with a large commitment to the buyer, may also be more willing to participate in JIT systems as well as provide design innovations and technological expertise. Many firms have moved aggressively to incorporate suppliers into their supply systems. Chrysler, for one, now seeks to choose suppliers even before parts are designed. Motorola also evaluates suppliers on rigorous criteria, but in many instances has eliminated traditional supplier bidding, placing added emphasis on quality and reliability. On occasion these relationships yield contracts that extend through the product's life cycle. The expectation is that both the purchaser and supplier collaborate, becoming more efficient and reducing prices over time. The natural outcome of such relationships is fewer suppliers, but those that remain have long-term relationships.

Service companies like Marks & Spencer, a British retailer, have also demonstrated that cooperation with suppliers can yield cost savings for customers and suppliers alike. This strategy has resulted in suppliers that develop new products, winning customers for Marks & Spencer and the supplier. The move toward tight integration of the suppliers and purchasers is occurring in both manufacturing and services.

Like all strategies, a downside exists. With few suppliers, the cost of changing partners is huge, so both buyer and supplier run the risk of becoming captives of the other. Poor supplier performance is only one risk the purchaser faces. The purchaser must also be concerned about trade secrets and suppliers that make other alliances or venture out on their own. This happened when the U.S. Schwinn Bicycle Co., needing additional capacity, taught Taiwan's Giant Manufacturing Company to make and sell bicycles. Giant Manufacturing is now the largest bicycle manufacturer in the world, and Schwinn was acquired out of bankruptcy by Pacific Cycle LLC.

About 100 years ago, Henry Ford surrounded himself with reliable suppliers, many on his own property, making his assembly operation close to self-sufficient.

Vertical Integration

Purchasing can be extended to take the form of vertical integration. By **vertical integration**, we mean developing the ability to produce goods or services previously purchased or actually buying a supplier or a distributor. As shown in Figure 11.2, vertical integration can take the form of *forward* or *backward integration.*

Backward integration suggests a firm purchase its suppliers, as in the case of Ford Motor Company deciding to manufacture its own car radios. Forward integration, on the other hand, suggests that a manufacturer of components make the finished product. An example is Texas Instruments, a manufacturer of integrated circuits that also makes calculators and flat-screens containing integrated circuits for TVs.

Vertical integration

Developing the ability to produce goods or services previously purchased or actually buying a supplier or a distributor.

▶ **Figure 11.2**

Vertical Integration Can Be Forward or Backward

Vertical integration can offer a strategic opportunity for the operations manager. For firms with the capital, managerial talent, and required demand, vertical integration may provide substantial opportunities for cost reduction, quality adherence, and timely delivery. Other advantages, such as inventory reduction and scheduling can accrue to the company that effectively manages vertical integration or close, mutually beneficial relationships with suppliers.

Because purchased items represent such a large part of the costs of sales, it is obvious why so many organizations find interest in vertical integration. Vertical integration appears to work best when the organization has large market share and the management talent to operate an acquired vendor successfully.

The relentless march of specialization continues, meaning that a model of "doing everything" or "vertical integration" is increasingly difficult. Backward integration may be particularly dangerous for firms in industries undergoing technological change if management cannot keep abreast of those changes or invest the financial resources necessary for the next wave of technology. The alternative, particularly in high-tech industries, is to establish close-relationship suppliers. This allows partners to focus on their specific contribution. Research and development costs are too high and technology changes too rapid for one company to sustain leadership in every component. Most organizations are better served concentrating on their specialty and leveraging the partners' contributions. Exceptions do exist. Where capital, management talent, and technology are available and the components are also highly integrated, vertical integration may make sense. On the other hand, it made no sense for Jaguar to make commodity components for its autos as it did until it was purchased by Ford.

Keiretsu Networks

Many large Japanese manufacturers have found a middle ground between purchasing from few suppliers and vertical integration. These manufacturers are often financial supporters of suppliers through ownership or loans. The supplier becomes part of a company coalition known as a *keiretsu*. Members of the *keiretsu* are assured long-term relationships and are therefore expected to function as partners, providing technical expertise and stable quality production to the manufacturer. Members of the *keiretsu* can also have suppliers farther down the chain, making second- and even third-tier suppliers part of the coalition.

Keiretsu

A Japanese term that describes suppliers who become part of a company coalition.

Virtual Companies

The limitations to vertical integration are severe. Our technological society continually demands more specialization, which complicates vertical integration. Moreover, a firm that has a department or division of its own for everything may be too bureaucratic to be world class. So rather than letting vertical integration lock an organization into businesses that it may not understand or be able to manage, another approach is to find good flexible suppliers. **Virtual companies** rely on a variety of supplier relationships to provide services on demand. Virtual companies have fluid, moving organizational boundaries that allow them to create a unique enterprise to meet changing market demands. Suppliers may provide a variety of services that include doing the payroll, hiring personnel, designing products, providing consulting services, manufacturing

Virtual companies

Companies that rely on a variety of supplier relationships to provide services on demand. Also known as hollow corporations or network companies.

components, conducting tests, or distributing products. The relationships may be short- or long-term and may include true partners, collaborators, or simply able suppliers and subcontractors. Whatever the formal relationship, the result can be exceptionally lean performance. The advantages of virtual companies include specialized management expertise, low capital investment, flexibility, and speed. The result is efficiency.

The apparel business provides a *traditional* example of virtual organizations. The designers of clothes seldom manufacture their designs; rather, they license the manufacture. The manufacturer may then rent space, lease sewing machines, and contract for labor. The result is an organization that has low overhead, remains flexible, and can respond rapidly to the market.

A *contemporary* example is the semiconductor industry, exemplified by Visioneer in Palo Alto. This California firm subcontracts almost everything: Software is written by several partners, hardware is manufactured by a subcontractor in Silicon Valley, printed circuit boards are made in Singapore, and plastic cases are made in Boston, where units are also tested and packed for shipment. In the virtual company, managing the supply chain is demanding and dynamic.

MANAGING THE SUPPLY CHAIN

As managers move toward integration of the supply chain, substantial efficiencies are possible. The cycle of materials—as they flow from suppliers, to production, to warehousing, to distribution, to the customer—takes place among separate and often very independent organizations. Therefore, there are significant management issues that may result in serious inefficiencies. Success begins with mutual agreement on goals, followed by mutual trust, and continues with compatible organizational cultures.

Mutual Agreement on Goals   An integrated supply chain requires more than just agreement on the contractual terms of a buy/sell relationship. Partners in the chain must appreciate that the only entity that puts money into a supply chain is the end customer. Therefore, establishing a mutual understanding of the mission, strategy, and goals of participating organizations is essential. The integrated supply chain is about adding economic value and maximizing the total content of the product.

Trust   Trust is critical to an effective and efficient supply chain. Members of the chain must enter into a relationship that shares information. Visibility throughout the supply chain—what Darden Restaurants calls a transparent supply chain—is a requirement. Supplier relationships are more likely to be successful if risk and cost savings are shared—and activities such as end-customer research, sales analysis, forecasting, and production planning are joint activities. Such relationships are built on mutual trust.

Compatible Organizational Cultures   A positive relationship between the purchasing and supplying organizations that comes with compatible organizational cultures can be a real advantage when making a supply chain hum. A champion within one of the two firms promotes both formal and informal contacts, and those contacts contribute to the alignment of the organizational cultures, further strengthening the relationship.

The operations manager is dealing with a supply chain that is made up of independent specialists, each trying to satisfy its own customers at a profit. This leads to actions that may not optimize the entire chain. On the other hand, the supply chain is replete with opportunities to reduce waste and enhance value. We now look at some of the significant issues and opportunities.

Issues in an Integrated Supply Chain

Three issues complicate development of an efficient, integrated supply chain: local optimization, incentives, and large lots.

Local Optimization   Members of the chain are inclined to focus on maximizing local profit or minimizing immediate cost based on their limited knowledge. Slight upturns in demand are overcompensated for because no one wants to be caught short. Similarly, slight downturns are overcompensated for because no one wants to be caught holding excess inventory. So fluctuations are magnified. For instance, a pasta distributor does not want to run out of pasta for its retail customers;

Video 11.3

Arnold Palmer Hospital's
Supply Chain

The supplier must be treated as an extension of the company.

Learning Objective

3. Explain issues and opportunities in the supply chain

the natural response to an extra large order from the retailer is to compensate with an even larger order to the manufacturer on the assumption that retail sales are picking up. Neither the distributor nor the manufacturer knows that the retailer had a major one-time promotion that moved a lot of pasta. This is exactly the issue that complicated the implementation of efficient distribution at the Italian pasta maker Barilla.

Incentives (Sales Incentives, Quantity Discounts, Quotas, and Promotions)
Incentives push merchandise into the chain for sales that have not occurred. This generates fluctuations that are ultimately expensive to all members of the chain.

Large Lots
There is often a bias toward large lots because large lots tend to reduce unit costs. A logistics manager wants to ship large lots, preferably in full trucks, and a production manager wants long production runs. Both actions drive down unit shipping and production costs, but fail to reflect actual sales and increased holding costs.

These three common occurrences—local optimization, incentives, and large lots—contribute to distortions of information about what is really occurring in the supply chain. A well-running supply system needs to be based on accurate information about how many products are truly being pulled through the chain. The inaccurate information is unintentional, but it results in distortions and fluctuations in the supply chain and causes what is known as the bullwhip effect.

Bullwhip effect
The increasing fluctuation in orders that often occurs as orders move through the supply chain.

The **bullwhip effect** occurs as orders are relayed from retailers, to wholesalers, to manufacturers, with fluctuations increasing at each step in the sequence. The "bullwhip" fluctuations in the supply chain increase the costs associated with inventory, transportation, shipping, and receiving while decreasing customer service and profitability. Procter & Gamble found that although the use of Pampers diapers was steady and the retail-store orders had little fluctuation, as orders moved through the supply chain, fluctuations increased. By the time orders were initiated for raw material, the variability was substantial. Similar behavior has been observed and documented at many companies, including Campbell Soup, Hewlett-Packard, and Applied Materials.[3] A number of opportunities exist for reducing the bullwhip effect and improving opportunities in the supply chain. These are discussed in the following section.

Opportunities in an Integrated Supply Chain
Opportunities for effective management in the supply chain include the following 10 items.

Pull data
Accurate sales data that initiate transactions to "pull" product through the supply chain.

Accurate "Pull" Data
Accurate **pull data** are generated by sharing (1) point-of-sales (POS) information so that each member of the chain can schedule effectively and (2) computer-assisted ordering (CAO). This implies using POS systems that collect sales data and then adjusting that data for market factors, inventory on hand, and outstanding orders. Then a net order is sent directly to the supplier who is responsible for maintaining the finished-goods inventory.

Lot Size Reduction
Lot sizes are reduced through aggressive management. This may include (1) developing economical shipments of less than truckload lots; (2) providing discounts based on total annual volume rather than size of individual shipments; and (3) reducing the cost of ordering through techniques such as standing orders and various forms of electronic purchasing.

Single stage control of replenishment
Fixing responsibility for monitoring and managing inventory for the retailer.

Single Stage Control of Replenishment
Single stage control of replenishment means designating a member in the chain as responsible for monitoring and managing inventory in the supply chain based on the "pull" from the end user. This approach removes distorted information and multiple forecasts that create the bullwhip effect. Control may be in the hands of:

- A sophisticated retailer who understands demand patterns. How Wal-Mart does this for some of its inventory with radio frequency (RFID) tags is shown in the *OM in Action* box "Radio Frequency Tags: Keeping the Shelves Stocked."
- A distributor who manages the inventory for a particular distribution area. Distributors who handle grocery items, beer, and soft drinks may do this. Anheuser-Busch manages beer inventory and delivery for many of its customers.

[3]See R. Croson and K. Donahue, "Behavioral Causes of the Bullwhip Effect," *Management Science* 52, no. 3 (March 2006): 323–336; R. D. H. Warburton, "An Analytical Investigation of the Bullwhip Effect," *Production and Operations Management* 13, no. 2 (summer 2004): 150–160; and Robert Ristelhueber, "Supply Chain Strategies—Applied Materials Seek to Snap Bullwhip Effect," *EBN* (January 22, 2001): 61.

OM in Action   Radio Frequency Tags: Keeping the Shelves Stocked

Supply chains work smoothly when sales are steady, but often break down when confronted by a sudden surge in demand. Radio frequency ID (or RFID) tags can change that by providing real-time information about what's happening on store shelves. Here's how the system works for Procter & Gamble's (P&G's) Pampers.

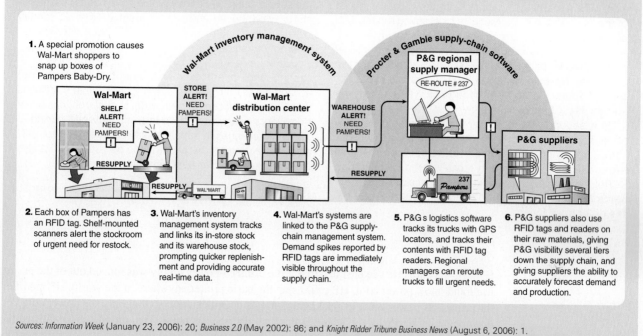

1. A special promotion causes Wal-Mart shoppers to snap up boxes of Pampers Baby-Dry.

2. Each box of Pampers has an RFID tag. Shelf-mounted scanners alert the stockroom of urgent need for restock.

3. Wal-Mart's inventory management system tracks and links its in-store stock and its warehouse stock, prompting quicker replenishment and providing accurate real-time data.

4. Wal-Mart's systems are linked to the P&G supply-chain management system. Demand spikes reported by RFID tags are immediately visible throughout the supply chain.

5. P&G's logistics software tracks its trucks with GPS locators, and tracks their contents with RFID tag readers. Regional managers can reroute trucks to fill urgent needs.

6. P&G suppliers also use RFID tags and readers on their raw materials, giving P&G visibility several tiers down the supply chain, and giving suppliers the ability to accurately forecast demand and production.

Sources: Information Week (January 23, 2006): 20; *Business 2.0* (May 2002): 86; and *Knight Ridder Tribune Business News* (August 6, 2006): 1.

- A manufacturer who has a well-managed forecasting, manufacturing, and distribution system. TAL Apparel Ltd., discussed in the *OM in Action* box on page 444, "The JCPenney Supply Chain for Dress Shirts," does this for JCPenney.

Vendor-Managed Inventory   **Vendor-managed inventory (VMI)** means the use of a local supplier (usually a distributor) to maintain inventory for the manufacturer or retailer. The supplier delivers directly to the purchaser's using department rather than to a receiving dock or stockroom. If the supplier can maintain the stock of inventory for a variety of customers who use the same product or whose differences are very minor (say, at the packaging stage), then there should be a net savings. These systems work without the immediate direction of the purchaser.

Blanket Orders   Blanket orders are unfilled orders with a vendor.[4] A **blanket order** is a contract to purchase certain items from a vendor. It is not an authorization to ship anything. Shipment is made only on receipt of an agreed-on document, perhaps a shipping requisition or shipment release.

Standardization   The purchasing department should make special efforts to increase levels of standardization. That is, rather than obtaining a variety of similar components with labeling, coloring, packaging, or perhaps even slightly different engineering specifications, the purchasing agent should try to have those components standardized. Consider GM's automobile seat frame. GM makes 26 different versions; Toyota makes 2. The cost advantage to Toyota is about $500 million.[5]

Postponement   **Postponement** withholds any modification or customization to the product (keeping it generic) as long as possible. The concept is to minimize internal variety while maximizing external variety. For instance, after analyzing the supply chain for its printers,

Vendor-managed inventory (VMI)
A system in which a supplier maintains material for the buyer, often delivering directly to the buyer's using department.

Blanket order
A long-term purchase commitment to a supplier for items that are to be delivered against short-term releases to ship.

Postponement
Delaying any modifications or customization to a product as long as possible in the production process.

---

[4]Unfilled orders are also referred to as "open" orders, or "incomplete" orders.
[5]David Welch, "Renault—Nissan: Say Hello to Bo," *Business Week* (July 31, 2006): 56–58.

Purchase a white Stafford wrinkle-free dress shirt, size 17 neck, 34/35 sleeve at JCPenney at Atlanta's Northlake Mall on a Tuesday, and the supply chain responds. Within a day, TAL Apparel Ltd. in Hong Kong downloads a record of the sale. After a run through its forecasting model, TAL decides how many shirts to make and in what styles, colors, and sizes. By Wednesday afternoon, the replacement shirt is packed to be shipped directly to the JCPenney Northlake Mall store. The system bypasses the JCPenney warehouse—indeed all warehouses—as well as the JCPenney corporate decision makers.

In a second instance, two shirts are sold, leaving none in stock. TAL, after downloading the data, runs its forecasting model but comes to the decision that this store needs to have two in stock. Without consulting JCPenney, a TAL factory in Taiwan makes two new shirts. It sends one by ship, but because of the outage, the other goes by air.

As retailers deal with mass customization, fads, and seasonal swings they also strive to cut costs—making a responsive supply chain critical. Before globalization of the supply chain, JCPenney would have had thousands of shirts warehoused across the country. Now JCPenney stores, like those of many retailers, hold a very limited inventory of shirts.

JCPenney's supplier, TAL, is providing both sales forecasting and inventory management, a situation not acceptable to many retailers. But what is most startling is that TAL also places its own orders! A supply chain like this works only when there is trust between partners. The rapid changes in supply chain management not only place increasing technical demands on suppliers but also increase demands for trust between the parties.

Sources: Apparel (April 2006): 14–18; *The Wall Street Journal* (September 11, 2003): A1, A9; and *International Trade Forum* (Issue 3, 2005): 12–13.

Hewlett-Packard (HP) determined that if the printer's power supply was moved out of the printer itself and into a power cord, HP could ship the basic printer anywhere in the world. HP modified the printer, its power cord, its packaging, and its documentation so that only the power cord and documentation needed to be added at the final distribution point. This modification allowed the firm to manufacture and hold centralized inventories of the generic printer for shipment as demand changed. Only the unique power system and documentation had to be held in each country. This understanding of the entire supply chain reduced both risk and investment in inventory.

Drop shipping

Shipping directly from the supplier to the end consumer rather than from the seller, saving both time and reshipping costs.

Drop Shipping and Special Packaging **Drop shipping** means the supplier will ship directly to the end consumer, rather than to the seller, saving both time and reshipping costs. Other cost-saving measures include the use of special packaging, labels, and optimal placement of labels and bar codes on containers. The final location down to the department and number of units in each shipping container can also be indicated. Substantial savings can be obtained through management techniques such as these. Some of these techniques can be of particular benefit to wholesalers and retailers by reducing shrinkage (lost, damaged, or stolen merchandise) and handling cost.

For instance, Dell Computer has decided that its core competence is not in stocking peripherals, but in assembling PCs. So if you order a PC from Dell, with a printer and perhaps other components, the computer comes from Dell, but the printer and many of the other components will be drop shipped from the manufacturer.

Pass-through facility

Expedites shipment by holding merchandise and delivering from shipping hubs.

Pass-through Facility A **pass-through facility** is a distribution center where merchandise is held, but it functions less as a holding area and more as a shipping hub. These facilities, often run by logistics vendors, use the latest technology and automated systems to expedite orders. For instance, UPS works with Nike at such a facility in Louisville, Kentucky, to immediately handle orders. Similarly, FedEx's warehouse next to the airport in Memphis can receive an order after a store closes for the evening and can locate, package, and ship the merchandise that night. Delivery is guaranteed by 10 A.M. the next day.

Channel assembly

Postpones final assembly of a product so the distribution channel can assemble it.

Channel Assembly Channel assembly is an extension of the pass-through facility. **Channel assembly** sends individual components and modules, rather than finished products, to the distributor. The distributor then assembles, tests, and ships. Channel assembly treats distributors more as manufacturing partners than as distributors. This technique has proven successful in industries where products are undergoing rapid change, such as personal computers. With this strategy, finished-goods inventory is reduced because units are built to a shorter, more accurate forecast. Consequently, market response is better, with lower investment—a nice combination.

E-PROCUREMENT

E-procurement uses the Internet to facilitate purchasing. E-procurement speeds purchasing, reduces costs, and integrates the supply chain, enhancing an organization's competitive advantage. The traditional supply chain is full of paper transactions, such as requisitions, requests for bids, bid evaluations, purchase orders, order releases, receiving documents, invoices, and the issuance of checks. E-procurement reduces this barrage of paperwork.

In this section, we discuss traditional techniques of electronic ordering and funds transfer and then move on to online catalogs, auctions, RFQs, and real-time inventory tracking.

Electronic Ordering and Funds Transfer   Electronic ordering and bank transfers are traditional approaches to speeding transactions and reducing paperwork. Transactions between firms often use **electronic data interchange (EDI)**, which is a standardized data-transmittal format for computerized communications between organizations. EDI provides data transfer for virtually any business application, including purchasing. Under EDI, data for a purchase order, such as order date, due date, quantity, part number, purchase order number, address, and so forth, are fitted into the standard EDI format. EDI also provides for the use of **advanced shipping notice (ASN)**, which notifies the purchaser that the vendor is ready to ship. Although some firms are still moving to EDI and ASN, the Internet's ease of use and lower cost is proving more popular.

Online Catalogs

Purchase of standard items is often accomplished via online catalogs. Such catalogs provide current information about products in electronic form. Online catalogs support cost comparisons and are efficient for both buyers and sellers. These electronic catalogs can enrich traditional catalogs by incorporating voice and video clips, much as do the CD-ROM and DVD that accompany this text. Online catalogs are available in three versions:

1. Typical of *catalogs provided by vendors* are those of W. W. Grainger and Office Depot. W. W. Grainger is probably the world's largest seller of MRO items (items for maintenance, repair, and operations), while Office Depot provides the same service for office supplies. Systems such as Grainger's and Office Depot's take care of frequent, relatively low-dollar purchases. Customized catalogs can take orders 24 hours a day and reflect discounts applicable to each customer. Online catalogs are often available on every employee's desktop computer. Once approved and established, each employee can do his or her own purchasing. Many of these purchases are individually small dollar value and as such have historically failed to receive the attention of other "normal" purchases. The result has been a huge inefficiency. E-procurement provides an opportunity for substantial savings; and the paper trails related to ordering become less-expensive electronic trails.

2. *Catalogs provided by intermediaries* are Internet sites where business buyers and sellers can meet. These intermediaries typically create industry specific catalogs with content from many suppliers. Qualified buyers can place orders with selling companies. The cost is significantly less than with traditional faxes, telephone calls, and purchase orders.

3. One of the first online *exchanges provided by buyers* was Covisint, created by auto giants GM, Ford, and Chrysler. Although focusing on the auto industry, Covisint buys virtually everything, from paper clips to stamping presses to contract manufacturing. As Figure 11.3 suggests, virtually every other industry quickly followed. For instance, Global Health Care Exchange, the first exchange listed in Figure 11.3, provides similar service for the hospital

Health care products—set up by Johnson & Johnson, GE Medical Systems, Baxter International, Abbott Laboratories, and Medtronic Inc; called the Global Health Care Exchange (**ghx.com**).
Retail Goods—set up by Sears and France's Carrefour; called GlobalNetXchange for retailers (**gnx.com**).
Defense and aerospace products— created by Boeing, Raytheon, Lockheed-Martin, Rolls-Royce, and Britain's BAE Systems; called the Aerospace and Defense Industry Trading Exchange (**exostar.com**).
Food, beverage, consumer products—set up by 49 leading food and beverage firms; called Transora (**transora.com**).
Steel and metal products—such as Metal-Site (**metalsite.com**).
Hotels—created by Marriott and Hyatt, and later joined by Fairmont, Six Continents, and Club Corp; called Avendra (**avendra.com**) buys for 2,800 hotels.

◀ **Figure 11.3**
Internet Trading Exchanges

E-procurement
Purchasing facilitated through the Internet.

Electronic data interchange (EDI)
A standardized data-transmittal format for computerized communications between organizations.

Advanced shipping notice (ASN)
A shipping notice delivered directly from vendor to purchaser.

"...e-procurement... integrates supply chains between different buyers and sellers, and makes a company's supply chain a key competitive advantage."

Robert Derocher
Deloitte Consulting

sector. These exchanges, by moving from a multitude of individual phone calls, faxes, and e-mails to a centralized online exchange, are driving billions of dollars of waste out of the supply chain. Online exchanges can be expected to continue to put downward pressure on price while improving transaction efficiency.

Auctions

Online auction sites can be maintained by sellers, buyers, or intermediaries. GM's approach to selling excess steel is to post it on the Web and expect that its own suppliers who need steel will buy it. Operations managers find online auctions a fertile area for disposing of excess raw material and discontinued or excess inventory. Online auctions lower entry barriers, which encourages sellers to join and simultaneously increase the potential number of buyers.

The key for auction firms, such as Ariba of Sunnyvale, California, is to find and build a huge base of potential bidders (see photo). Indeed, most of Ariba's employees spend their time not running electronic auctions but improving client buying procedures and qualifying new suppliers.

Sun Microsystems claims savings of over $1 billion a year using its in-house reverse auction system (called Dynamic Bidding). The firm now spends 1 hour pricing out items that used to take weeks or months to negotiate. For an operations manager, online auctions are a significant opportunity to improve supply chain performance.

RFQs

When purchasing requirements are nonstandard, time spent preparing requests for quotes (RFQs) and the related bid package can be substantial. Consequently, e-procurement has now moved these often expensive parts of the purchasing process online. At General Electric, for example, e-procurement now provides purchasing personnel with an extensive database of vendor, delivery, and quality data. With this extensive history, supplier selection has improved. Electronic files containing engineering drawings are also available. These resources allow purchasing agents to attach electronic copies of the necessary drawings to RFQs and inexpensively send the entire electronic-encrypted package to vendors in a matter of hours.

Real-Time Inventory Tracking

FedEx's pioneering efforts at tracking packages from pickup to delivery has shown the way for operations managers to do the same for their shipments and inventory. Because tracking cars and trucks has been a chronic and embarrassingly inexact science, Ford has recently hired UPS to track more than 4 million vehicles as they move from factory to dealers. Using bar codes and the Internet, Ford dealers are now able to log onto a Web site and find out exactly where the ordered vehicles are in the distribution system. As operations managers move to an era of mass customization, with customers ordering exactly the cars they want, customers will expect to know

▶ Here an Ariba team monitors an online market from the firm's Global Market Operations Center. Ariba provides support for the entire global sourcing process, including software, supplier development, competitive negotiations, and savings implementation. Online bidding leads to greater cost savings than more traditional procurement.

where their cars are and exactly when they can be picked up. E-procurement, supported by bar codes and RFID, can provide economical inventory tracking on the shop floor, in warehouses, and in logistics.

VENDOR SELECTION

For those goods and services a firm buys, vendors must be selected. Vendor selection considers numerous factors, such as strategic fit, vendor competence, delivery, and quality performance. Because a firm may have some competence in all areas and may have exceptional competence in only a few, selection can be challenging. Procurement policies also need to be established. Those might address issues such as percent of business done with any one supplier or with minority businesses. We now examine vendor selection as a three-stage process: (1) vendor evaluation, (2) vendor development, and (3) negotiations.

Vendor Evaluation

The first stage of vendor selection, *vendor evaluation*, involves finding potential vendors and determining the likelihood of their becoming good suppliers. This phase requires the development of evaluation criteria such as criteria shown in Example 2.[6] However, both the criteria and the weights selected vary depending on the supply chain strategy being implemented. (Refer to Table 11.1 shown earlier in the chapter.)

EXAMPLE 2

Weighted approach to vendor evaluation

Erin Davis, president of Creative Toys in Palo Alto, is interested in evaluating suppliers who will work with him to make nontoxic, environmentally friendly paints and dyes for his line of children's toys. This is a critical strategic element of his supply chain, and he desires a firm that will contribute to his product.

Approach: Erin begins his analysis of one potential supplier, Faber Paint and Dye, by using the weighted approach to vendor evaluation.

Solution: Erin first reviews the supplier differentiation attributes in Table 11.1 and develops the following list of selection criteria. He then assigns the weights shown to help him perform an objective review of potential vendors. His staff assigns the scores shown and computes the total weighted score.

Criteria	Weights	Scores (1–5) (5 highest)	Weight × Score
Engineering/research/innovation skills	.20	5	1.0
Production process capability (flexibility/technical assistance)	.15	4	.6
Distribution/delivery capability	.05	4	.2
Quality systems and performance	.10	2	.2
Facilities/location	.05	2	.1
Financial and managerial strength (stability and cost structure)	.15	4	.6
Information systems capability (e-procurement, ERP)	.10	2	.2
Integrity (environmental compliance/ethics)	.20	5	1.0
	1.00		3.9 Total

Faber Paint and Dye receives an overall score of 3.9.

Insight: Erin now has a basis for comparison with other potential vendors, selecting the one with the highest overall rating.

Learning exercise: If Erin believes that the weight for "engineering/research/innovation skills" should be increased to .25 and the weight for "financial and managerial strength" reduced to .10, what is the new score? [Answer: Faber Paint and Dye now goes to 3.95.]

Related problems: 11.2, 11.3, 11.4

---

[6]A discussion of vendor selection criteria can be found in Chapter 8 of Robert Monczka, Robert Trent, and Robert Handfield, *Purchasing and Supply Chain Management*, 3rd ed. (Mason, Ohio: South-Western, 2005); and Chapters 2 and 3 of Joel D. Wisner, G. Keong Leong, and K. C. Tan, *Principles of Supply Chain Management* (Mason, Ohio: South-Western, 2005).

The selection of competent suppliers is critical. If good suppliers are not selected, then all other supply-chain efforts are wasted. As firms move toward using fewer longer-term suppliers, the issues of financial strength, quality, management, research, technical ability, and potential for a close long-term relationship play an increasingly important role. These attributes should be noted in the evaluation process.

Vendor Development

The second stage of vendor selection is *vendor development*. Assuming that a firm wants to proceed with a particular vendor, how does it integrate this supplier into its system? The buyer makes sure the vendor has an appreciation of quality requirements, product specifications, schedules and delivery, the purchaser's payment system, and procurement policies. *Vendor development* may include everything from training, to engineering and production help, to procedures for information transfer.

Negotiations

Negotiation strategies
Approaches taken by supply chain personnel to develop contractual relationships with suppliers.

Regardless of the supply chain strategy adopted, negotiations regarding the critical elements of the contractual relationship must take place. These negotiations often focus on quality, delivery, payment, and cost. We will look at three classic types of **negotiation strategies**: the cost-based model, the market-based price model, and competitive bidding.

Cost-Based Price Model   The *cost-based price model* requires that the supplier open its books to the purchaser. The contract price is then based on time and materials or on a fixed cost with an escalation clause to accommodate changes in the vendor's labor and materials cost.

Learning Objective

4. Describe approaches to supply chain negotiations

Market-Based Price Model   In the market-based price model, price is based on a published, auction, or index price. Many commodities (agriculture products, paper, metal, etc.) are priced this way. Paperboard prices, for instance, are available via the *Official Board Markets* weekly publication (**www.advanstar.com**). Nonferrous metal prices are quoted in *Platt's Metals Week* (**www.platts.com/plattsmetals/**), and prices of other metals are quoted at **www.metalworld.com**.

Competitive Bidding   When suppliers are not willing to discuss costs or where near-perfect markets do not exist, competitive bidding is often appropriate. Infrequent work (such as construction, tooling, and dies) is usually purchased based on a bid. Bidding may take place via mail, fax, or an Internet auction. Competitive bidding is the typical policy in many firms for the majority of their purchases. Bidding policies usually require that the purchasing agent have several potential suppliers of the product (or its equivalent) and quotations from each. The major disadvantage of this method, as mentioned earlier, is that the development of long-term relations between buyer and seller is hindered. Competitive bidding may effectively determine initial cost. However, it may also make difficult the communication and performance that are vital for engineering changes, quality, and delivery.

Negotiations should not be viewed as a win–lose game; they can be a win–win game.

Yet a fourth approach is *to combine one or more* of the preceding negotiation techniques. The supplier and purchaser may agree on review of certain cost data, accept some form of market data for raw material costs, or agree that the supplier will "remain competitive." In any case, a good supplier relationship is one in which both partners have established a degree of mutual trust and a belief in each other's competence, honesty, and fair dealing.

LOGISTICS MANAGEMENT

Logistics management
An approach that seeks efficiency of operations through the integration of all material acquisition, movement, and storage activities.

Procurement activities may be combined with various shipping, warehousing, and inventory activities to form a logistics system. The purpose of **logistics management** is to obtain efficiency of operations through the integration of all material acquisition, movement, and storage activities. When transportation and inventory costs are substantial on both the input and output sides of the production process, an emphasis on logistics may be appropriate. When logistics issues are significant or expensive, many firms opt for outsourcing the logistics function. Logistics specialists can often bring expertise not available in-house. For instance, logistics companies often have tracking technology that reduces transportation losses and supports delivery schedules that adhere to precise delivery windows. The potential for competitive advantage is found via both reduced costs and improved customer service.

Firms recognize that the distribution of goods to and from their facilities can represent as much as 25% of the cost of products. In addition, the total distribution cost in the U.S. is over 10% of the gross national product (GNP). Because of this high cost, firms constantly evaluate their means of distribution. Five major means of distribution are trucking, railroads, airfreight, waterways, and pipelines.

Distribution Systems

Trucking   The vast majority of manufactured goods moves by truck. The flexibility of shipping by truck is only one of its many advantages. Companies that have adopted JIT programs in recent years have put increased pressure on truckers to pick up and deliver on time, with no damage, with paperwork in order, and at low cost. Trucking firms are using computers to monitor weather, find the most effective route, reduce fuel cost, and analyze the most efficient way to unload. In spite of these advances, the motor carrier industry averages a capacity utilization of only 50%. That under-utilized space costs the U.S. economy over $31 billion per year. To improve logistics efficiency, the industry is establishing Web sites such as Schneider National's connection (**www.schneider.com**), which lets shippers and truckers find each other to use some of this idle capacity. Shippers may pick from thousands of approved North American carriers that have registered with Schneider logistics.

Railroads   Railroads in the U.S. employ 200,000 people and ship 90% of all coal, 67% of autos, 68% of paper products, and about half of all food, lumber, and chemicals. Containerization has made intermodal shipping of truck trailers on railroad flat cars, often piggybacked as double-deckers, a popular means of distribution. More than 13 million trailer loads are moved in the U.S. each year by rail. With the growth of JIT, however, rail transport has been the biggest loser because small-batch manufacture requires frequent, smaller shipments that are likely to move via truck or air.

Airfreight   Airfreight represents only about 1% of tonnage shipped in the U.S. However, the recent proliferation of airfreight carriers such as FedEx, UPS, and DHL makes it the fastest-growing mode of shipping. Clearly, for national and international movement of lightweight items, such as medical and emergency supplies, flowers, fruits, and electronic components, airfreight offers speed and reliability.

Waterways   Waterways are one of the nation's oldest means of freight transportation, dating back to construction of the Erie Canal in 1817. Included in U.S. waterways are the nation's rivers, canals, the Great Lakes, coastlines, and oceans connecting to other countries. The usual cargo on waterways is bulky, low-value cargo such as iron ore, grains, cement, coal, chemicals, limestone, and petroleum products. Internationally, millions of containers are shipped at very

◄ As this photo of the port of Charleston suggests, with 16 million containers entering the U.S. annually, tracking location, content, and condition of trucks and containers is a challenge. But new technology may improve both security and JIT shipments.

▶ *Seven farms within a 2-hour drive of Kenya's Nairobi Airport supply 300 tons of fresh beans, bok choy, okra, and other produce that is packaged at the airport and shipped overnight to Europe. The time between harvest and arrival in Europe is 2 days. When a good supply chain and good logistics work together, the results can be startling—and fresh food.*

low cost via huge oceangoing ships each year. Water transportation is important when shipping cost is more important than speed.

Pipelines Pipelines are an important form of transporting crude oil, natural gas, and other petroleum and chemical products. An amazing 90% of the state of Alaska's budget is derived from the 1.5 million barrels of oil pumped daily through the pipeline at Prudhoe Bay.

Third-Party Logistics

Supply chain managers may find that outsourcing logistics is advantageous in driving down inventory investment and costs while improving delivery reliability and speed. Specialized logistics firms support this goal by coordinating the supplier's inventory system with the service capabilities of the delivery firm. FedEx, for example, has a successful history of using the Internet for online tracking. At **FedEx.com**, a customer can compute shipping costs, print labels, adjust invoices, and track package status all on the same Web site. FedEx, UPS, and DHL play a core role in other firms' logistics processes. In some cases, they even run the server for retailer Web sites. In other cases, such as for Dell Computer, FedEx operates warehouses that pick, pack, test, and assemble products, then it handles delivery and customs clearance when necessary. The *OM in Action* box "DHL's Role in the Supply Chain" provides another example of how outsourcing logistics can reduce costs while shrinking inventory and delivery times.

OM in Action   **DHL's Role in the Supply Chain**

It's the dead of night at DHL International's air express hub in Brussels, yet the massive building is alive with busy forklifts and sorting workers. The boxes going on and off the DHL plane range from Dell computers and Cisco routers to Caterpillar mufflers and Komatsu hydraulic pumps. Sun Microsystems computers from California are earmarked for Finland; CD-ROMs from Teac's plant in Malaysia are destined for Bulgaria.

The door-to-door movement of time-sensitive packages is key to the global supply chain. JIT, short product life cycles, mass customization, and reduced inventories depend on logistics firms such as DHL, FedEx, and UPS. These powerhouses are in continuous motion.

With a decentralized network covering 227 countries and territories (more than are in the UN), DHL is a true multinational. The Brussels headquarters has only 450

of the company's 60,000 employees but includes 26 nationalities.

DHL has assembled an extensive global network of express logistics centers for strategic goods. In its Brussels logistics center, for instance, DHL upgrades, repairs, and configures Fijitsu computers, InFocus projectors, and Johnson & Johnson medical equipment. It stores and provides parts for EMC and Hewlett-Packard and replaces Nokia and Philips phones. "If something breaks down on a Thursday at 4 o'clock, the relevant warehouse knows at 4:05, and the part is on a DHL plane at 7 or 8 that evening," says Robert Kuijpers, DHL International's CEO.

Sources: Journal of Commerce (August 15, 2005): 1; EBN (February 25, 2002): 27; and Forbes (October 18, 1999): 120–124.

Cost of Shipping Alternatives

The longer a product is in transit, the longer the firm has its money invested. But faster shipping is usually more expensive than slow shipping. A simple way to obtain some insight into this trade-off is to evaluate carrying cost against shipping options. We do this in Example 3.

A shipment of new connectors for semiconductors needs to go from San Jose to Singapore for assembly. The value of the connectors is $1,750 and holding cost is 40% per year. One airfreight carrier can ship the connectors 1 day faster than its competitor, at an extra cost of $20.00. Which carrier should be selected?

EXAMPLE 3

Determining daily cost of holding

Approach: First we determine the daily holding cost and then compare the daily holding cost with the cost of faster shipment.

Solution: Daily cost of holding the product = (Annual holding cost × Product value)/365

$$= (.40 \times \$1,750)/365$$
$$= \$1.92$$

Since the cost of saving one day is $20.00, which is much more than the daily holding cost of $1.92, we decide on the less costly of the carriers and take the extra day to make the shipment. This saves $18.08 ($20.00 − $1.92).

Insight: The solution becomes radically different if the 1-day delay in getting the connectors to Singapore delays delivery (making a customer angry) or delays payment of a $150,000 final product. (Even 1 day's interest on $150,000 or an angry customer makes a savings of $18.08 insignificant.)

Learning exercise: If the holding cost is 100% per year, what is the decision? [Answer: Even with a holding cost of $4.79 per day, the less costly carrier is selected.]

Related problems: 11.8, 11.9, 11.10

Example 3 looks only at holding costs versus shipping cost. For the operations or logistics manager there are many other considerations, including coordinating shipments to maintain a schedule, getting a new product to market, and keeping a customer happy.[7] Estimates of these other costs can be added to the estimate of daily holding cost. Determining the impact and cost of these many other considerations makes the evaluation of shipping alternatives interesting.

▲ *Speed and accuracy in the supply chain are supported by bar-code tracking of shipments. At each step of a journey, from initial pickup to final destination, bar codes (left) are read and stored. Within seconds, this tracking information is available online to customers worldwide (right).*

---

[7]The cost of an unhappy customer can be equated to the stockout cost discussed in Chapter 12.

▶ *The global supply chain puts new demands on logistics: In Boeing's case, sections of the 787 Dreamliner need to be moved around the world in a timely fashion. Boeing's in-house solution was to build three of these new Large Cargo Freight liners. "Some people say this plane is ugly, but I call it an elegant logistics solution," says a Boeing supply chain executive. (The Wall Street Journal, January 8, 2007: A1, A14).*

Logistics, Security, and JIT

There is probably no society more open than the U.S. This includes its borders and ports. With removal of the last constraints on the North American Free Trade Agreement (NAFTA), expanding globalization, and increased use of JIT deliveries, U.S. borders and ports are swamped. About 16 million containers enter U.S. ports each year, along with thousands of planes, cars, and trucks each day. Even under the best of conditions, some 5% of the container movements are misrouted, stolen, damaged, or excessively delayed.

Since the September 11, 2001, terrorist attacks, supply chains have become more complex, and they can be expected to become even more so. However, technological innovations in the supply chain are improving logistics, security, and JIT. Technology is now capable of knowing truck and container location, content, and condition. New devices can detect whether someone has broken into a sealed container and can communicate that information to the shipper or receiver via satellite or radio. Motion detectors can also be installed inside containers. Other sensors can record interior data including temperature, shock, radioactivity, and whether a container is moving. Tracking lost containers, identifying delays, or just reminding individuals in the supply chain that a shipment is on its way will help expedite shipments. Improvements in security may aid JIT, and improvements in JIT may aid security—both of which can improve supply chain logistics.

MEASURING SUPPLY CHAIN PERFORMANCE

Learning Objective

5. Evaluate supply chain performance

Like all other managers, supply chain managers require standards (or *metrics*, as they are often called) to evaluate performance. Evaluation of the supply chain is particularly critical for these managers because they spend most of the organization's money. In addition, they make scheduling and quantity decisions that determine the assets committed to inventory. Only with effective metrics can managers determine how well the *supply chain is performing* and *how well assets are utilized*. We will now discuss these two metrics.

Supply Chain Performance   The benchmark metrics shown in Table 11.6 focus on procurement and vendor performance issues. World-class benchmarks are the result of well-managed supply chains that drive down costs, lead times, late deliveries, and shortages while improving quality.

▶ **Table 11.6**

Supply Chain Performance

	Typical Firms	Benchmark Firms
Lead time (weeks)	15	8
Time spent placing an order	42 minutes	15 minutes
Percent of late deliveries	33%	2%
Percent of rejected material	1.5%	.0001%
Number of shortages per year	400	4

Source: Adapted from a McKinsey & Company report.

Assets Committed to Inventory   Three specific measures can be helpful here. The first is the amount of money invested in inventory, usually expressed as a percent of assets, as shown in Equation (11-1):

$$\text{Percent invested in inventory} = (\text{Total inventory investment/Total assets}) \times 100 \quad \text{(11-1)}$$

Learning Objective

6. Compute percent of assets committed to inventory

Home Depot's management wishes to track its investment in inventory as one of its performance measures. Home Depot had $11.4 billion invested in inventory and total assets of $44.4 billion in 2006.

Approach: Determine the investment in inventory and total assets and then use Equation (11-1).

Solution: Percent invested in inventory = $(11.4/44.4) \times 100 = 25.7\%$

Insight: Over one-fourth of Home Depot assets are committed to inventory.

Learning exercise: If Home Depot can drive its investment down to 20% of assets, how much money will it free up for other uses? [Answer: $11.4 - (44.5 \times .2) = \$2.5$ billion.]

Related problems: 11.11b, 11.12b

EXAMPLE 4

Tracking Home Depot's inventory investment

Specific comparisons with competitors may assist evaluation. Total assets committed to inventory in manufacturing approach 20%, in wholesale 34%, and retail 27%—with wide variations, depending on the specific business model and management (see Table 11.7).

The second common measure of supply chain performance is *inventory turnover* (see Table 11.8) and its reciprocal, *weeks of supply*. **Inventory turnover** is computed on an annual basis, using Equation (11-2):

$$\text{Inventory turnover} = \text{Cost of goods sold/Inventory investment} \quad \text{(11-2)}$$

Inventory turnover
Cost of goods sold divided by average inventory.

Cost of goods sold is the cost to produce the goods or services sold for a given period. Average inventory investment is the average inventory value for the same period. This may be the average of several periods of inventory or beginning and ending inventory added together and divided by 2. Often, average inventory investment is based on nothing more than the inventory investment at the end of the period—typically at year-end.[8]

In Example 5, we look at inventory turnover applied to PepsiCo.

Learning Objective

7. Compute inventory turnover

▼ **Table 11.7** **Inventory as Percent of Total Assets (with examples of exceptional performance)**

Manufacturer (Toyota 5%)	20%
Wholesale (Coca-Cola 2.9%)	34%
Restaurants (McDonald's .05%)	2.9%
Retail (Home Depot 25.7%)	27%

▼ **Table 11.8** **Examples of Annual Inventory Turnover**

Food, Beverage, Retail	
Anheuser Busch	15
Coca-Cola	14
Home Depot	5
McDonald's	112
Manufacturing	
Dell Computer	90
Johnson Controls	22
Toyota (overall)	13
Nissan (assembly)	150

[8]Inventory quantities often fluctuate wildly, and various types of inventory exist (e.g., raw material, work-in-process, finished goods, and maintenance, repair, and operating supplies [MRO]). Therefore, care must be taken when using inventory values; they may reflect more than just supply chain performance.

EXAMPLE 5

Inventory turnover at PepsiCo, Inc.

PepsiCo, Inc., manufacturer and distributor of drinks, snacks, and Quaker Foods, provides the following in its 2005 annual report (shown here in $ billions). Determine PepsiCo's turnover and weeks of inventory.

Net revenue		$32.5
Cost of goods sold		$14.2
Inventory:		
Raw material inventory	$.74	
Work-in-process inventory	$.11	
Finished goods inventory	$.84	
Total inventory investment		$1.69

Approach: Use the inventory turnover computation in Equation (11-2) to measure inventory performance. Cost of goods sold is $14.2 billion. Total inventory is the sum of raw material at $.74 billion, work-in-process at $.11 billion, and finished goods at $.84 billion, for total inventory investment of $1.69 billion.

Solution: Inventory Turnover = Cost of goods sold / Inventory investment

$$= 14.2/1.69$$

$$= 8.4$$

Insight: We now have a standard, popular measure by which to evaluate performance.

Learning exercise: If Coca-Cola's cost of goods sold is $10.8 billion and inventory investment is $.76 billion, what is its inventory turnover? [Answer: 14.2.]

Related problems: 11.11a, 11.12c, 11.13

Weeks of supply may have more meaning in the wholesale and retail portions of the service sector than in manufacturing. It is computed below as the reciprocal of inventory turnover:

Weeks of supply = Inventory investment/(Annual cost of goods sold/52 weeks)   (11-3)

EXAMPLE 6

Determining weeks of supply at PepsiCo

Using the PepsiCo data in Example 5, management wants to know the weeks of supply.

Approach: We know that inventory investment is $1.69 billion and that weekly sales equal annual cost of goods sold ($14.2 billion) divided by 52 = $14.2/52 = $.273 billion.

Solution: Using Equation (11-3), we compute weeks of supply as:

Weeks of supply = (Inventory investment/Average weekly cost of goods sold)

$$1.69/.273 = 6.19 \text{ weeks}$$

Insight: We now have a standard measurement by which to evaluate a company's continuing performance or by which to compare companies.

Learning exercise: If Coca-Cola's average inventory investment is $.76 billion and its average weekly cost of goods sold is $.207 billion, what is the firm's weeks of supply? [Answer: 3.67 weeks.]

Related problems: 11.12a, 11.14

For most companies, the percent of revenue spent on labor is going down but the percent spent in the supply chain is going up.

Supply chain management is critical in driving down inventory investment. The rapid movement of goods is key. Wal-Mart, for example, has set the pace in the retailing sector with its world-renowned supply chain management. By doing so, it has established a competitive advantage. With its own truck fleet, distribution centers, and a state-of-the-art communication system, Wal-Mart (with the help of its suppliers) replenishes store shelves an average of twice per week. Competitors resupply every other week. Economical and speedy resupply means both rapid response to product changes and customer preferences, as well as lower inventory investment. Similarly, while many manufacturers struggle to move inventory turnover up to 10 times per year, Dell Computer has inventory turns exceeding 90 and supply measured in *days*—not weeks. Supply chain management provides a competitive advantage when firms effectively respond to the demands of global markets and global sources.

Summary

Competition is not just between companies but between supply chains. For many firms, the supply chain determines a substantial portion of product cost and quality, as well as opportunities for responsiveness and differentiation. Five supply chain strategies have been identified: (1) many suppliers, (2) few suppliers, (3) vertical integration, (4) *keiretsu* networks, and (5) virtual companies. Skillful supply chain management provides a great strategic opportunity for competitive advantage.

Key Terms

Supply chain management *(p. 434)*
Make-or-buy decision *(p. 437)*
Outsourcing *(p. 438)*
Vertical integration *(p. 439)*
Keiretsu (p. 440)
Virtual companies *(p. 440)*
Bullwhip effect *(p. 442)*
Pull data *(p. 442)*

Single stage control of replenishment
   (p. 442)
Vendor-managed inventory (VMI)
   (p. 443)
Blanket order *(p. 443)*
Postponement *(p. 443)*
Drop shipping *(p. 444)*
Pass-through facility *(p. 444)*

Channel assembly *(p. 444)*
E-procurement *(p. 445)*
Electronic data interchange (EDI) *(p. 445)*
Advanced shipping notice (ASN) *(p. 445)*
Negotiation strategies *(p. 448)*
Logistics management *(p. 448)*
Inventory turnover *(p. 453)*

Solved Problem

 Virtual Office Hours help is available on Student DVD.

Solved Problem 11.1

Jack's Pottery Outlet has total end-of-year assets of $5 million. The first-of-the-year inventory was $375,000, with a year-end inventory of $325,000. The annual cost of goods sold was $7 million. The owner, Eric Jack, wants to evaluate his supply chain performance by measuring his percent of assets in inventory, his inventory turnover, and his weeks of supply. We use Equations (11-1), (11-2), and (11-3) to provide these measures.

Solution
First, determine *average inventory*:

$$(\$375{,}000 + \$325{,}000)/2 = \$350{,}000$$

Then, use Equation (11-1) to determine percent invested in inventory:

$$\text{Percent invested in inventory} = (\text{Total inventory investment}/\text{Total assets}) \times 100$$
$$= (350{,}000/5{,}000{,}000) \times 100$$
$$= 7\%$$

Third, determine inventory turnover, using Equation (11-2):

$$\text{Inventory turnover} = \text{Cost of goods sold}/\text{Inventory investment}$$
$$= 7{,}000{,}000/350{,}000$$
$$= 20$$

Finally, to determine weeks of inventory, use Equation (11-3), adjusted to weeks:

$$\text{Weeks of inventory} = \text{Inventory investment}/\text{Weekly cost of goods sold}$$
$$= 350{,}000/(7{,}000{,}000/52)$$
$$= 350{,}000/134{,}615$$
$$= 2.6$$

We conclude that Jack's Pottery Outlet has 7% of its assets invested in inventory, that the inventory turnover is 20, and that weeks of supply is 2.6.

Self-Test

- *Before taking the self-test*, *refer to the learning objectives listed at the beginning of the chapter and the key terms listed at the end of the chapter.*
- *Use the key at the back of the text to **correct** your answers.*
- *Restudy* *pages that correspond to any questions you answered incorrectly or material you feel uncertain about.*

1. A *keiretsu* is:
   a) a purchasing agent
   b) an expediter
   c) a virtual company
   d) part of a company coalition
   e) a variation of the bullwhip effect

2. A pull system is aimed toward _____.

3. Two measures of supply chain performance are:
   a) inventory turnover and amount of vertical integration
   b) assets committed to inventory and amount of vertical integration
   c) weeks of supply and number of blanket orders
   d) inventory turnover and assets committed to inventory
   e) level of bullwhip and inventory turnover

4. The term *vertical integration* means to:
   a) develop the ability to produce products that complement or supplement the original product
   b) produce goods or services previously purchased
   c) develop the ability to produce the specified good more efficiently
   d) all of the above

5. Postponement:
   a) is shipping directly from the supplier to the end customer
   b) requires the use of EDI or the Internet

   c) uses e-procurement to facilitate purchasing
   d) delays modifications as long as possible in the production process
   e) uses single stage replenishment

6. Vendor-managed inventories and blanket orders:
   a) mean the same thing
   b) both lead to vastly reduced overall purchasing costs for a particular item
   c) both tend to reduce the amount of paperwork involved in the transaction
   d) both require multiplicity of suppliers

7. Single-stage replenishment means:
   a) vendor-managed inventory
   b) a single member of the supply chain is responsible for managing resupply
   c) sharing POS information
   d) drop shipping directly to the end customer
   e) delaying modifications to the product as long as possible

8. The objective of supply chain management is: _____.

9. A market-based model for negotiations is based on:
   a) the supplier opening its books to the purchaser
   b) supplier and vendor agreeing on price
   c) competitive bidding
   d) a published, auction, or index price

10. The bullwhip effect can be aggravated by:
   a) local optimization
   b) sales incentives
   c) quantity discounts
   d) promotions
   e) all of the above

Internet and Student CD-ROM/DVD Exercises

Visit our Companion Web site or use your student CD-ROM/DVD to help with material in this chapter.

 On Our Companion Web Site,
   www.prenhall.com/heizer
- Self-Study Quizzes
- Practice Problems
- Virtual Company Tour
- Internet Case
- PowerPoint Lecture

 On Your Student CD-ROM
- Practice Problems

 On Your Student DVD
- Video Clips and Video Cases
- Virtual Office Hours for Solved Problem

Discussion Questions

1. Define supply chain management.
2. What are the objectives of supply chain management?
3. What is the objective of logistics management?
4. How do we distinguish between supply chain management, purchasing, and logistics management?
5. What is vertical integration? Give examples of backward and forward integration.
6. What are three basic approaches to negotiations?

7. How does a traditional adversarial relationship with suppliers change when a firm makes a decision to move to a few suppliers?
8. What is the difference between postponement and channel assembly?
9. Explain each of the three versions of online catalogs.
10. What is the value of online auctions in e-commerce?
11. Explain how FedEx uses the Internet to meet requirements for quick and accurate delivery.

12. How does Wal-Mart use drop shipping?
13. What are blanket orders? How do they differ from invoiceless purchasing?
14. What can purchasing do to implement just-in-time deliveries?
15. What is e-procurement?
16. How does Darden Restaurants, described in the *Global Company Profile*, find competitive advantage in its supply chain?
17. What are the cultural impediments to establishing *keiretsu* networks in countries other than Japan?

Ethical Dilemma

For generations, the policy of Sears Roebuck and Company, the granddaddy of retailers, was not to purchase more than 50% of any of its suppliers' output. The rationale of this policy was that it allowed Sears to move to other suppliers, as the market dictated, without destroying the supplier's ability to stay in business. In contrast, Wal-Mart purchases more and more of a supplier's output. Eventually, Wal-Mart can be expected to sit down with that supplier and explain why the supplier no longer needs a sales force and that the supplier should eliminate the sales force, passing the cost savings on to Wal-Mart.

Sears is losing market share, has been acquired by K-Mart, and is eliminating jobs; Wal-Mart is gaining market share and hiring. What are the ethical issues involved, and which firm has a more ethical position?

Problems

•• **11.1** Choose a local establishment that is a member of a relatively large chain. From interviews with workers and information from the Internet, identify the elements of the supply chain. Determine whether the supply chain represents a low-cost, rapid response, or differentiation strategy (refer to Chapter 2). Are the supply chain characteristics significantly different from one product to another?

•• **11.2** As purchasing agent for Woolsey Enterprises in Golden, Colorado, you ask your buyer to provide you with a ranking of "excellent," "good," "fair," or "poor" for a variety of characteristics for two potential vendors. You suggest that "Products" total be weighted 40% and the other three categories' totals be weighted 20% each. The buyer has returned the following ranking:

VENDOR RATING

Company	Excellent (4)	Good (3)	Fair (2)	Poor (1)
Financial Strength			K	D
Manufacturing Range			KD	
Research Facilities	K		D	
Geographical Locations		K	D	
Management		K	D	
Labor Relations			K	D
Trade Relations			KD	

Service	Excellent (4)	Good (3)	Fair (2)	Poor (1)
Deliveries on Time		KD		
Handling of Problems		KD		
Technical Assistance		K	D	

Products	Excellent (4)	Good (3)	Fair (2)	Poor (1)
Quality	KD			
Price			KD	
Packaging			KD	

Sales	Excellent (4)	Good (3)	Fair (2)	Poor (1)
Product Knowledge			D	K
Sales Calls			K	D
Sales Service		K	D	

DONNA INC. = D
KAY CORP. = K

Which of the two vendors would you select?

•• **11.3** Using the data in Problem 11.2, assume that both Donna, Inc., and Kay Corp. are able to move all their "poor" ratings to "fair." How would you then rank the two firms?

•• **11.4** Develop a vendor-rating form that represents your comparison of the education offered by universities in which you considered (or are considering) enrolling. Fill in the necessary data, and identify the "best" choice. Are you attending that "best" choice? If not, why not?

•• **11.5** Using sources from the Internet, identify some of the problems faced by a company of your choosing as it moves toward, or operates as, a virtual organization. Does its operating as a virtual organization simply exacerbate old problems, or does it create new ones?

• **11.6** Using Table 11.3, determine the sales necessary to equal a dollar of savings on purchases for a company that has:
a) A net profit of 4% and spends 40% of its revenue on purchases.
b) A net profit of 6% and spends 80% of its revenue on purchases.

• **11.7** Using Table 11.3, determine the sales necessary to equal a dollar of savings on purchases for a company that has:
a) A net profit of 6% and spends 60% of its revenue on purchases.
b) A net profit of 8% and spends 80% of its revenue on purchases.

•• **11.8** Your options for shipping $100,000 of machine parts from Baltimore to Kuala Lumpur, Malaysia, are (1) use a ship that will take 30 days at a cost of $3,800, or (2) truck the parts to Los Angeles and then ship at a total cost of $4,800. The second option will take only 20 days. You are paid via a letter of credit the day the parts arrive. Your holding cost is estimated at 30% of the value per year.
a) Which option is more economical?
b) What customer issues are not included in the data presented?

•• **11.9** If you have a third option for the data in Problem 11.8, and it costs only $4,000 and also takes 20 days, what is your most economical plan?

•• **11.10** Monczka-Trent Shipping is the logistics vendor for Handfield Manufacturing Co. in Ohio. Handfield has daily shipments of a power-steering pump from its Ohio plant to an auto assembly line in Alabama. The value of the standard shipment is $250,000. Monczka-Trent has two options: (1) its standard 2-day shipment or (2) a subcontractor who will team drive overnight with an effective delivery of 1 day. The extra driver costs $175. Handfield's holding cost is 35% annually for this kind of inventory.
a) Which option is more economical?
b) What production issues are not included in the data presented?

▼ **Table 11.9** For Problems 11.11 and 11.12

Arrow Distributing Corp.

Net revenue	$16,500
Cost of sales	$13,500
Inventory	$ 1,000
Total assets	$ 8,600

Baker Mfg. Inc.

Net revenue	$27,500
Cost of sales	$21,500
Inventory	$ 1,250
Total assets	$16,600

•• **11.11** Baker Mfg Inc. (see Table 11.9) wishes to compare its inventory turnover to those of industry leaders, who have turnover of about 13 times per year and 8% of their assets invested in inventory.
a) What is Baker's inventory turnover?
b) What is Baker's percent of assets committed to inventory?
c) How does Baker's performance compare to the industry leaders?

•• **11.12** Arrow Distributing Corp. (see Table 11.9) likes to track inventory by using weeks of supply as well as by inventory turnover.
a) What is its weeks of supply?
b) What percent of Arrow's assets are committed to inventory?
c) What is Arrow's inventory turnover?
d) Is Arrow's supply chain performance, as measured by these inventory metrics, better than that of Baker, in Problem 11.11?

• **11.13** The grocery industry has an annual inventory turnover of about 14 times. Organic Grocers, Inc., had a cost of goods sold last year of $10.5 million; its average inventory was $1.0 million. What was Organic Grocers's inventory turnover, and how does that performance compare with that of the industry?

•• **11.14** Mattress Wholesalers, Inc. is constantly trying to reduce inventory in its supply chain. Last year, cost of goods sold was $7.5 million and inventory was $1.5 million. This year, costs of goods sold is $8.6 million and inventory investment is $1.6 million.
a) What were the weeks of supply last year?
b) What are the weeks of supply this year?
c) Is Mattress Wholesalers making progress in its inventory-reduction effort?

Case Studies

Dell's Value Chain

Dell, the computer manufacturer highlighted in Chapter 7's *Global Company Profile*, develops close relationships with suppliers. It encourages suppliers to focus on their individual technological capabilities to sustain leadership in their components. Research and development costs are too high and technological changes are too rapid for any one company to sustain leadership in every component. Suppliers are also pressed to drive down lead times, lot sizes, and inventories. Dell, in turn, keeps its research customer focused

and leverages that research to help itself and suppliers. Dell also constructs special Web pages for suppliers, allowing them to view orders for components they produce as well as current levels of inventory at Dell. This allows suppliers to plan based on actual end customer demand; as a result, it reduces the bullwhip effect. The intent is to work with suppliers to keep the supply chain moving rapidly, products current, and the customer order queue short. Then, with supplier collaboration, Dell can offer the latest options, can build to order, and can achieve rapid throughput. The payoff is a competitive advantage, growing market share, and low capital investment.

On the distribution side, Dell uses direct sales, primarily via the Internet, to increase revenues by offering a virtually unlimited variety of desktops, notebooks, and enterprise products. Options displayed over the Internet allow Dell to attract customers that value choice. Customers select recommended product configurations or customize them. Dell's customers place orders at any time of the day from anywhere in the world. And Dell's price is cheaper; retail stores have additional costs because of their brick-and-mortar model. Dell has also customized Web pages that enable large business customers to track past purchases and place orders consistent with their purchase history and current needs. Assembly begins immediately after receipt of a customer order. Competing firms have previously assembled products filling the distribution channels (including shelves at retailers) before a product reaches the customer. Dell, in contrast, introduces a new product to customers over the Internet as soon as the first of that model is ready. In an industry where products have life cycles measured in months, Dell enjoys a huge early-to-market advantage.

Dell's model also has cash flow advantages. Direct sales allow Dell to eliminate distributor and retailer margins and increase its own margin. Dell collects payment in a matter of days after products are sold. But Dell pays its suppliers according to the more traditional billing schedules. Given its low levels of inventory, Dell is able to operate its business with negative working capital because it manages to receive payment before it pays its suppliers for components. These more traditional supply chains often require 60 or more days for the cash to flow from customer to supplier—a huge demand on working capital.

Dell has designed its order processing, products, and assembly lines so that customized products can be assembled in a matter of hours. This allows Dell to postpone assembly until after a customer order has been placed. In addition, any inventory is often in the form of components that are common across a wide variety of finished products. Postponement, component modularity, and tight scheduling allow low inventory and support mass customization. Dell maximizes the benefit of postponement by focusing on new products for which demand is difficult to forecast. Manufacturers who sell via distributors and retailers find postponement virtually impossible. Therefore, traditional manufacturers are often stuck with product configurations that are not selling while simultaneously being out of the configurations that *are* selling. Dell is better able to match supply and demand.

One of the few negatives for Dell's model is that it results in higher outbound shipping costs than selling through distributors and retailers. Dell sends individual products directly to customers from its factories. But many of these shipments are small (often one or a few products), while manufacturers selling through distributors and retailers ship with some economy of scale, using large shipments via truck to warehouses and retailers, with the end user providing the final portion of delivery. As a result, Dell's outbound transportation costs are higher, but the relative cost is low (typically 2% to 3%), and thus the impact on the overall cost is low.

What Dell has done is build a collaborative supply chain and an innovative ordering and production system. The result is what Dell likes to refer to as its *value chain*—a chain that brings value from supplier to the customer and provides Dell with a competitive advantage.

Discussion Questions

1. How has Dell used its direct sales and build-to-order model to develop an exceptional supply chain?
2. How has Dell exploited the direct sales model to improve operations performance?
3. What are the main disadvantages of Dell's direct sales model?
4. How does Dell compete with a retailer who already has a stock?
5. How does Dell's supply chain deal with the bullwhip effect?

Sources: Adapted from S. Chopra and P. Meindl, *Supply Chain Management*, 3rd ed. (Upper Saddle River, NJ: Prentice Hall, 2007); R. Kapuscinski, et al., "Inventory Decisions in Dell's Supply Chain," *Interfaces* 34, no. 3 (May–June 2004): 191–205; and A. A. Thompson, A. J. Strickland, and J. E. Gamble, "Dell, Inc. in 2006: Can Rivals Beat Its Strategy?" *Crafting and Executing Strategy*, 15th ed. (New York: McGraw-Hill, 2007).

Darden's Global Supply Chains

Video Case

Darden Restaurants (subject of the *Global Company Profile* at the beginning of this chapter), owner of popular brands such as Olive Garden and Red Lobster, requires unique supply chains to serve more than 300 million meals annually. Darden's strategy is operations excellence, and Senior VP Jim Lawrence's task is to ensure competitive advantage via Darden's supply chains. For a firm with purchases exceeding $1.5 billion, managing the supply chains is a complex and challenging task.

Darden, like other casual dining restaurants, has unique supply chains that reflect its menu options. Darden's supply chains are rather shallow, often having just one tier of suppliers. But it has four distinct supply chains.

First, "smallware" is a restaurant industry term for items such as linens, dishes, tableware and kitchenware, and silverware. These are purchased, with Darden taking title as they are received at the Darden Direct Distribution (DDD) warehouse in Orlando, Florida. From this single warehouse, smallware items are shipped via common carrier (trucking companies) to Olive Garden, Red Lobster, Bahama Breeze, and Seasons 52 restaurants.

Second, frozen, dry, and canned food products are handled economically by Darden's 11 distribution centers in North America, which are managed by major U.S. food distributors, such as MBM, Maines, and Sygma. This is Darden's second supply line.

Third, the fresh food supply chain (not frozen and not canned), where life is measured in days, includes dairy products, produce, and meat. This supply chain is B2B, where restaurant managers directly place orders with a preselected group of independent suppliers.

Fourth, Darden's worldwide seafood supply chain is the final link. Here Darden has developed independent suppliers of salmon, shrimp, tilapia, scallops, and other fresh fish that are source inspected by Darden's overseas representatives to ensure quality. These fresh products are flown to the U.S. and shipped to 16 distributors, with 22 locations, for quick delivery to the restaurants. With suppliers in 35 countries, Darden must be on the cutting edge when it comes to collaboration, partnering, communication, and food safety. It does this with heavy travel schedules for purchasing and quality control personnel, native-speaking employees onsite, and aggressive communication.

Communication is a critical element; Darden tries to develop as much forecasting transparency as possible. "Point of sale (POS) terminals," says Lawrence, "feed actual sales every night to suppliers."

Discussion Questions*

1. What are the advantages of each of Darden's four supply chains?
2. What are the complications of having four supply chains?
3. Where would you expect ownership/title to change in each of Darden's four supply chains?

4. How do Darden's four supply chains compare with those of other firms, such as Dell or an automobile manufacturer? Why do the differences exist, and how are they addressed?

*You may wish to view this video on your DVD before answering these questions.

Source: Written by Professors Barry Render (Rollins College), Jay Heizer (Texas Lutheran University), and Beverly Amer (Northern Arizona University).

Arnold Palmer Hospital's Supply Chain

Video Case

Arnold Palmer Hospital, one of the nation's top hospitals dedicated to serving women and children, is a large business with over 2,000 employees working in a 431-bed facility totaling 676,000 square feet in Orlando, Florida. Like many other hospitals, and other companies, Arnold Palmer Hospital had been a long-time member of a large buying group, one servicing 900 members. But the group did have a few limitations. For example, it might change suppliers for a particular product every year (based on a new lower-cost bidder) or stock only a product that was not familiar to the physicians at Arnold Palmer Hospital. The buying group was also not able to negotiate contracts with local manufacturers to secure the best pricing.

So in 2003, Arnold Palmer Hospital, together with seven other partner hospitals in central Florida, formed its own much smaller, but still powerful (with $200 million in annual purchases) Healthcare Purchasing Alliance (HPA) corporation. The new alliance saved the HPA members $7 million in its first year from two main changes. First, it was structured and staffed to assure that the bulk of the savings associated with its contracting efforts went to its eight members. Second, it struck even better deals with vendors by guaranteeing a *committed* volume and signing not 1-year deals but 3–5 year contracts. "Even with a new internal cost of $400,000 to run HPA, the savings and ability to contract for what our member hospitals really want makes the deal a winner," says George DeLong, head of HPA.

Effective supply chain management in manufacturing often focuses on development of new product innovations and efficiency through buyer–vendor collaboration. However, the approach in a service industry has a slightly different emphasis. At Arnold Palmer Hospital, supply chain opportunities often manifest themselves through the Medical Economic Outcomes Committee. This committee (and its subcommittees) consists of users (including the medical and nursing staff) who evaluate purchase options with a goal of

better medicine while achieving economic targets. For instance, the heart pacemaker negotiation by the cardiology subcommittee allowed for the standardization to two manufacturers, with annual savings of $2 million for just this one product.

Arnold Palmer Hospital is also able to develop custom products that require collaboration down to the third tier of the supply chain. This is the case with custom packs that are used in the operating room. The custom packs are delivered by a distributor, McKesson General Medical, but assembled by a pack company that uses materials the hospital wanted purchased from specific manufacturers. The HPA allows Arnold Palmer Hospital to be creative in this way. With major cost savings, standardization, blanket purchase orders, long-term contracts, and more control of product development, the benefits to the hospital are substantial.

Discussion Questions*

1. How does this supply chain differ from that in a manufacturing firm?
2. What are the constraints on making decisions based on economics alone at Arnold Palmer Hospital?
3. What role do doctors and nurses play in supply chain decisions in a hospital? How is this participation handled at Arnold Palmer Hospital?
4. Doctor Smith just returned from the Annual Physician's Orthopedic Conference, where she saw a new hip joint replacement demonstrated. She decides she wants to start using the replacement joint at Arnold Palmer Hospital. What process will Dr. Smith have to go through at the hospital to introduce this new product into the supply chain for future surgical use?

*You may wish to view this video on your DVD before answering the questions.

Supply Chain Management at Regal Marine

Video Case

Like most other manufacturers, Regal Marine finds that it must spend a huge portion of its revenue on purchases. Regal has also found that the better its suppliers understand its end users, the better are both the supplier's product and Regal's final product. As one of the 10 largest U.S. power boat manufacturers, Regal is trying to differentiate its products from the vast number of boats supplied by 300 other companies. Thus, the firm works closely with suppliers to ensure innovation, quality, and timely delivery.

Regal has done a number of things to drive down costs while driving up quality, responsiveness, and innovation. First, working on partnering relationships with suppliers ranging from providers of wind-

shields to providers of instrument panel controls, Regal has brought timely innovation at reasonable cost to its product. Key vendors are so tightly linked with the company that they meet with designers to discuss material changes to be incorporated into new product designs.

Second, the company has joined about 15 other boat manufacturers in a purchasing group, known as American Boat Builders Association, to work with suppliers on reducing the costs of large purchases. Third, Regal is working with a number of local vendors to supply hardware and fasteners directly to the assembly line on a just-in-time basis. In some of these cases, Regal has worked out an arrangement with the vendor so that title does not transfer until parts are used by Regal. In other cases, title transfers when items are delivered to the property. This practice drives down total inventory and the costs associated with large-lot delivery.

Finally, Regal works with a personnel agency to outsource part of the recruiting and screening process for employees. In all these cases, Regal is demonstrating innovative approaches to supply chain management that help the firm and, ultimately, the end user. The *Global Company Profile* featuring Regal Marine (which opens Chapter 5) provides further background on Regal's operations.

Discussion Questions*

1. What other techniques might Regal use to improve supply chain management?
2. What kind of response might members of the supply chain expect from Regal in response to their "partnering" in the supply chain?
3. Why is supply chain management important to Regal?

*You may wish to view this case on your DVD before answering the questions.

Additional Case Studies

Internet case study: Visit our Companion Web site at www.prenhall.com/heizer for this free case study:

- **Amazon.com:** Discusses opportunities and issues in an innovative business model for the Internet.

Harvard has selected these Harvard Business School cases to accompany this chapter:

harvardbusinessonline.hbsp.harvard.edu

- **Supply Chain Management at World Co. Ltd.** (#601-072): Illustrates the value of response times and how response times can be reduced.
- **Ford Motor Co.: Supply Chain Strategy** (#699-198): Evaluation of whether Ford should "virtually integrate" on the Dell Computer model.
- **Sport Obermeyer Ltd.** (#695-022): Examines how to match supply with demand for products with high demand uncertainty.
- **Barilla SpA (A)** (#694-046): Allows students to analyze how a company can implement a continuous replenishment system.
- **Tale of Two Electronic Components Distributors** (#697-064): Examines distributor consolidation and growth of the Internet.

Bibliography

Ballou, Ronald H. *Business Logistics Management*, 5th ed. Upper Saddle River, NJ: Prentice Hall (2004).

Benton, W. C., and Michael Maloni. "The Influence of Power Driven Buyer/Seller Relationships on Supply Chain Satisfaction." *Journal of Operations Management* 23, vol. 1 (January 2005): 1–22.

Boswell, Tim, et al. "How Supplier Development Helps Harley-Davidson Go Lean." *Target: Innovation at Work* 20, no. 1 (first issue 2004): 18–30.

Boyer, Kenneth K., and G. Tomas M. Hult. "Extending the Supply Chain: Integrating Operations and Marketing in the Online Grocery Industry." *Journal of Operations Management* 23, no. 6 (September 2005): 642–661.

Chen, I. J., and A. Paulraj. "Towards a Theory of Supply Chain Management: The Constructs and Measurements." *Journal of Operations Management* 22, no. 2 (April 2004): 119–150.

Chopra, Sunil, and Peter Meindl. *Supply Chain Management*, 3rd ed. Upper Saddle River, NJ: Prentice Hall (2007).

Davenport, Thomas H. "The Coming Commoditization of Processes." *Harvard Business Review* (June 2005): 100–108.

Gardner, Dan. "The Impact of Globalization on Supply Chain Management." *APICS—The Performance Advantage* (April 2004): 30–35.

Gaur, Vishal, Marshall L. Fisher, and Ananth Raman. "An Econometric Analysis of Inventory Turnover Performance in Retail Services." *Management Science* 51, no. 2 (February 2005): 181–194.

Kapuscinski, Roman, et al. "Inventory Decisions in Dell's Supply Chain." *Interfaces* 34, no. 3 (May–June 2004): 191–205.

Kleindorfer, Paul R., and Germaine H. Saad. "Managing Disruption Risks in Supply Chains." *Production and Operations Management* 14, no. 1 (spring 2005): 53–68.

Kreipl, Stephan, and Michael Pinedo. "Planning and Scheduling in Supply Chains: An Overview of Issues in Practice." *Production and Operations Management* 13, no. 1 (spring 2004): 77–92.

Mentzer, John T., Soonhong Min, and L. Michelle Bobbitt. "Toward a Unified Theory of Logistics." *International Journal of Physical Distribution and Logistics Management* 34, no. 8 (2004): 606–627.

Shirodkar, S., and K. Kempf. "Supply Chain Collaboration Through Shared Capacity Models." *Interfaces* 36, no. 5 (September–October 2006): 420–432.

Stanley, L. L., and V. R. Singhal. "Service Quality Along the Supply Chain: Implications for Purchasing." *Journal of Operations Management* 19, no. 3 (May 2001): 287–306.

de Treville, Suzanne, Roy D. Shapiro, and Ari-Pekka Hameri. "From Supply Chain to Demand Chain: The Role of Lead-Time Reduction in Improving Demand Chain Performance." *Journal of Operations Management* 21, no. 6 (January 2004): 613–627.

Wisner, Joel and Linda Stanley. *Process Management: Creating Value Along the Supply Chain*. Mason OH: Thomson (2008).

Internet Resources

American Supplier Institute (ASI): **www.amsup.com**
Commerce One: **www.commerceone.com**
Council of Supply Chain Management: **www.escmp.org**
Erasmus Center for Maritime Economics and Logistics: **www.maritimeeeconomics.com**
Institute for Logistics Management: **www.logistics-edu.com/**

Institute for Supply Management: **www.ism.ws**
Distribution Solutions International: **www2.dsii.com**
Purchasing Magazine's Business Intelligence Center: **www.purchasingdata.com**
Purchasing Magazine Web Site: **www.purchasing.com**

SUPPLEMENT 11

Outsourcing as a Supply Chain Strategy

Supplement Outline

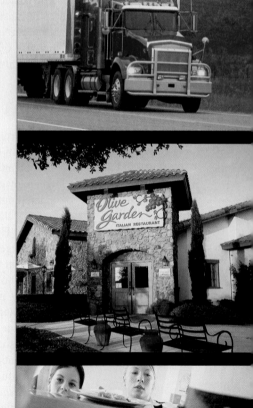

Learning Objectives

When you complete this supplement you should be able to

1. Explain how core competencies relate to outsourcing
2. Describe the risks of outsourcing
3. Use factor rating to evaluate both country and provider outsourcers
4. Use break-even analysis to determine if outsourcing is cost-effective
5. List the advantages and disadvantages of outsourcing

463

► *Sara Lee contracts with external bakeries to prepare many of its food products. By outsourcing most of its supply chain, Sara Lee can focus on managing its most important competitive advantage—its brand name. But there are risks involved in outsourcing. Outsourcing decisions, as part of the supply chain strategy, are explored in this supplement.*

Outsourcing is a creative management strategy. Indeed, some organizations use outsourcing to replace entire purchasing, information systems, marketing, finance, and operations departments. Outsourcing is applicable to firms throughout the world. And because outsourcing decisions are risky and many are not successful, making the right decision may mean the difference between a firm's success and failure.[1]

Because outsourcing grows by double digits every year, students and managers need to understand the issues, concepts, models, philosophies, procedures, and practices of outsourcing. The purpose of this supplement is to provide current concepts and methodologies that can help you understand and use outsourcing strategies.

WHAT IS OUTSOURCING?

Outsourcing
Procuring from external sources services or products that are normally part of an organization.

Offshoring
Moving a business process to a foreign country but retaining control of it.

Client firm
An organization that outsources.

Outsource provider
A firm that provides outsourcing activity.

Outsourcing means procuring from external suppliers services or products that are normally a part of an organization. In other words, a firm takes functions it was performing in-house (such as accounting, janitorial, or call center functions) and has another company do the same job. If a company owns two plants and reallocates production from the first to the second, this is not considered outsourcing. In addition, if a company moves some of its business processes to a foreign country but retains control, we define this move as **offshoring**, not outsourcing. For example, China's Haier Group recently offshored a $40 million refrigerator factory to South Carolina (with huge savings in transportation costs).

A firm that outsources its internal business activities is called the **client firm**. A company that provides outsourcing is called the **outsource provider**.

Early in their life cycle, many businesses handle their activities internally. As businesses mature and grow, however, they often find competitive advantage in the specialization provided by outside firms. They may also find limitations on locally available labor, services, materials, or other resources. So organizations balance the potential benefits of outsourcing with its potential risks. Outsourcing the wrong activities can cause major problems.

Outsourcing is not a new concept; it is simply an extension of the long-standing practice of *subcontracting* production activities. Indeed, the classic make-or-buy decisions concerning products (which we discussed in Chapter 11) are examples of outsourcing.

---

[1]The authors wish to thank Professor Marc J. Schniederjans, of the University of Nebraska–Lincoln, for help with the development of this supplement. His book *Outsourcing and Insourcing in an International Context*, with Ashlyn Schniederjans and Dara Schniederjans (Armonk, NY: M.E. Sharpe, 2005), provided insight, content, and references that shaped our approach to the topic.

So why has outsourcing expanded to become a major strategy in business the world over? From an economic perspective, it is due to the continuing move toward specialization in an increasingly technological society. More specifically, outsourcing's continuing growth is due to (1) increasing expertise, (2) reduced costs of more reliable transportation, and (3) the rapid development and deployment of advancements in telecommunications and computers. Low-cost communication, including the Internet, permits firms anywhere in the world to provide information services that were previously limited geographically. This communication ability also supplies the connectivity needed to support the global outsourcing growth engine.

Examples of outsourcing include:

- Call centers for the French in Angola (a former French colony in Africa) and for the U.S. and England in India
- DuPont's legal services and Procter & Gamble's (P&G's) finance services routed to the Philippines
- Electronic Data Systems (EDS) providing information technology for Delphi Automotive and Nextel
- IBM handling travel services and payroll, and Hewlett-Packard providing IT services to P&G
- ADP providing payroll services for thousands of firms
- Solectron (a specialist in electronic assembly) producing many of IBM's computers
- Production of the Chrysler Crossfire, Audi A4 convertible, and Mercedes CLK convertible by Wilheim Karmann in Osnabruck, Germany

Outsourced manufacturing, also known as contract manufacturing, is becoming standard practice in many industries, from computers (as shown in the photo) to automobiles.

Paralleling the growth of outsourcing is the growth of international trade. With the passage of landmark trade agreements like the North American Free Trade Agreement (NAFTA), the work of the World Trade Organization and the European Union, and other international trade zones established throughout the world, we are witnessing the greatest expansion of international commerce in history.

Types of Outsourcing

Nearly any business activity can be outsourced. A general contractor in the building industry, who subcontracts various construction activities needed to build a home, is a perfect example of an outsourcer. Every component of the building process, including the architect's design, a consultant's site location analysis, a lawyer's work to obtain the building permits, plumbing, electrical work, dry walling, painting, furnace installation, landscaping, and sales, is usually outsourced. Outsourcing implies an agreement (typically a legally binding contract) with an external organization.

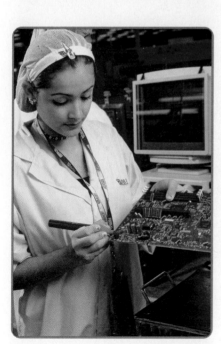

◄ *Contract manufacturers such as Solectron provide outsourcing service not only to IBM but also to Cisco Systems, HP, Microsoft, Motorola, Sony, Nortel, Ericsson, and Sun. Solectron is a high-quality producer that has won over 450 awards, including the Malcolm Baldrige Award. One of the side benefits of outsourcing is that client firms such as IBM can actually improve their performance by using the competencies of an outstanding firm like Solectron.*

"Offshoring is when a company takes one of its factories that it is operating in Canton, Ohio and moves the whole factory to Canton, China."

Thomas Friedman,
The World Is Flat

When outsourcing does work, it can deliver tremendous value.

Among the business processes outsourced are (1) purchasing, (2) logistics, (3) R&D, (4) operation of facilities, (5) management of services, (6) human resources, (7) finance/accounting, (8) customer relations, (9) sales/marketing, (10) training, and (11) legal processes. Note that the first six of these are OM functions that we discuss in this text.

STRATEGIC PLANNING AND CORE COMPETENCIES

As we saw in Chapter 2, organizations develop missions, long-term goals, and strategies as general guides for operating their businesses. The strategic planning process begins with a basic mission statement and establishing goals. Given the mission and goals, strategic planners next undertake an internal analysis of the organization to identify how much or little each business activity contributes to the achievement of the mission.

During such an analysis, firms identify their strengths—what they do well or better than their competitors. These unique skills, talents, and capabilities are called **core competencies**. Core competencies may include specialized knowledge, proprietary technology or information, and unique production methods. The trick is to identify what the organization does better than anyone else. Common sense dictates that core competencies are the activities that a firm should perform. By contrast, *non-core activities*, which can be a sizable portion of an organization's total business, are good candidates for outsourcing.

Sony's core competency, for example, is electromechanical design of chips. This is its core, and Sony is one of the best in the world when it comes to rapid response and specialized production of these chips. But, as Figure S11.1 suggests, outsourcing could offer Sony continuous innovation and flexibility. Leading specialized outsource providers are likely to come up with major innovations in such areas as software, human resources, and distribution. That is their business, not Sony's.

Managers evaluate their strategies and core competencies and ask themselves how to use the assets entrusted to them. Do they want to be the offshore company that does low-margin work at 3%–4% or the innovative firm that makes a 30%–40% margin? PC or iPod assemblers in China and Taiwan earn 3%–4%, but Apple, which innovates, designs, and sells, has a margin 10 times as large.

Core competencies
An organization's unique skills, talents, and capabilities.

Learning Objective

1. Explain how core competencies relate to outsourcing

▶ **Figure S11.1**

Sony, an Outsourcing Company*

*Adapted from J. B. Quinn. "Outsourcing Innovation." *Sloan Management Review* (Summer 2000): 20.

Outsourcers *could* provide Sony with:

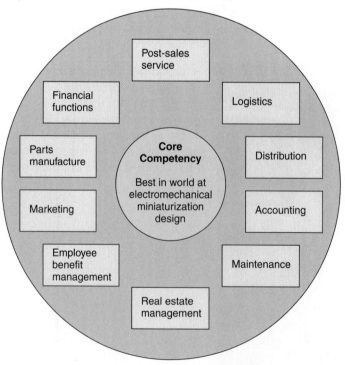

The Theory of Comparative Advantage

The motivation for international outsourcing comes from the **theory of comparative advantage**. This theory focuses on the basic economics of outsourcing internationally. According to the theory, if an external outsourcing provider, regardless of its geographic location, can perform activities more productively than the client firm, the client firm should allow the external outsourcing provider firm to do the work. This allows the client firm to focus on what it does best (namely, on its core competencies).

Countries such as India, China, and Russia have made it a government priority and set up agencies to support the easy transition of foreign-based client firms into their outsourcing markets. Work and jobs go to countries that reduce risk through necessary legal structures, build an infrastructure, and have an educated workforce.

Ford's president calls the theory of comparative advantage "Economics 101, Adam Smith."[2] Ford has told its suppliers to match the world's "optimal" prices on auto parts, which usually means parts companies are forced to move work to Mexico or China. But Mexico is in a precarious position. Foster Electric, Ford's speaker supplier, recently shifted its entire production from Mexico to China to shave an additional 20% off its cost. With wages 1/20 of those in the U.S., the term "China price" has become the global benchmark— interchangeable with "lowest price possible." General Motors, which buys more than $80 billion of parts a year, expects its suppliers to meet the best price the firm can find worldwide—or else face termination.[3]

> **Theory of comparative advantage**
> A theory which states that countries benefit from specializing in (and exporting) products and services in which they have relative advantage, and importing goods in which they have a relative disadvantage.

> "Although you may be good at something tactically, someone else may do it better and at lower cost."
>
> *James Champy*

OUTSOURCING TRENDS AND POLITICAL REPERCUSSIONS

In a survey of 52 major corporations (83% of them U.S. based), executives were asked what they felt were the most important reasons for outsourcing. The top reasons included cost savings (77%), gaining outside expertise (70%), improving services (61%), focusing on core competencies (59%), and gaining access to technology (56%).[4] The study also revealed that in addition to outsourcing business activities (e.g., computer help desk services), whole business departmental functions (e.g., accounting, marketing, finance, operations management, information systems) were being outsourced. When asked about future plans, 35% said they would continue or expand outsourcing, 40% said they would continue outsourcing but revise their outsourcing arrangements, and a significant percent said they would reduce outsourcing or choose to bring their work inside. Apparently, those with experience in outsourcing are not always completely satisfied, suggesting that executives still have a lot to learn about using outsourcing to boost productivity.

One of the risks is the political backlash that results from outsourcing in foreign countries. The loss of U.S. jobs (as well as the loss of jobs in European countries) has fueled anti-outsourcing rhetoric and action from government officials. (See the *OM in Action* box "Outsourcing to Small-Town U.S.A."). In 2004, the governor of Tennessee signed an anti-outsourcing bill that made the state the first to give businesses an incentive for not outsourcing information systems work to cheaper offshore locations. The law requires state procurement officials to give preference in bids for information systems services to contractors employing workers only in the U.S. Almost 100 other bills aimed at keeping jobs in the U.S. have been introduced in 30 states. On the federal level, the *Thomas-Voinovich Amendment*, which also passed in 2004, prohibits some federal contracts from being outsourced overseas if U.S. government employees had previously done the work. One federal bill requires call centers to disclose their locations to consumers.

---

[2]N. Shirouzu, "Big Three's Outsourcing Plan: Make Part Suppliers Do It." *The Wall Street Journal* (June 10, 2004): A1, A6 and (September 26, 2005): A1.

[3]T. C. Fishman, "How China Will Change Your Business." *Inc. Magazine* (March 2005): 70–84.

[4]N. M. Goldsmith, *Outsourcing Trends* (New York: The Conference Board, 2003).

OM in Action   Outsourcing to Small-Town U.S.A.

U.S. companies continue their global search for efficiency by outsourcing call centers and back-office operations, but many find they need to look no farther than a place like Nacogdoches, Texas.

To U.S. firms facing quality problems with their outsourcing operations overseas and bad publicity at home, small-town America is emerging as a pleasant alternative. Nacogdoches (population 29,914) or Twin Falls, Idaho (population 34,469), may be the perfect call center location. Even though the pay is only $7 an hour, the jobs are some of the best available to small-town residents.

By moving out of big cities to the cheaper labor and real estate of small towns, companies can save millions and still increase productivity. A call center in a town that just lost its major manufacturing plant finds the jobs easy to fill. U.S. Bank recently picked Coeur d'Alene, Idaho, for its credit card call center. The city "has pretty serious unemployment," says VP Schott Hansen. "We can go in with 500 jobs and really make a difference in the community."

But taking advantage of cheap wages in countries like India will not stop soon. A few years ago, IBM bought Daksh eServices Ltd., a 9,000-employee Indian call center firm, for $170 million. So is India the unstoppable overseas call center capital? Not necessarily. Despite its population of 1.2 billion, only a small percent of its workers have the language skills and education to be employable in Western-style industries. Already, India has been warned that if call centers can't recruit at reasonable wages, its jobs will move to the Philippines, South Africa, and Ghana. And, indeed, in 2006, Apple Computer and Britain's Powergen pulled the plug on Indian call centers, claiming their costs had become too high.

Sources: Information Week (May 9, 2005): 47–53; *Business Week* (August 7, 2006): 40–41; *Business World* (October 11, 2005): 1; *Knight Ridder Tribune Business News* (October 2, 2005): 1.

Other developed countries have similar restrictions. A 2005 survey by the *Financial Times* found that 59% of French, 56% of Belgian, and 51% of German residents feared their jobs moving to other countries. (Ironically, developing countries are also concerned with developed nations exploiting labor and markets and dominating their countries' economic landscapes.)

Despite the negative impression created by government actions, the press, and current public opinion, the latest U.S. government data suggest that foreigners outsource far more services to the U.S. than American companies send abroad. And while U.S. jobs are outsourced, a minuscule few are outsourced offshore. One estimate is that 2/10 of 1% of jobs are outsourced each year, while the dynamic U.S. economy, in the natural course of capitalism, destroys millions of jobs but creates even more.[5] People flock to the U.S. for jobs, and unemployment remains low. The value of U.S. exports of services (e.g., legal work, computer programming, telecommunications, banking) was recently at $54 billion more than the value of U.S. imports of the same services. But outsourcing is a two-way street. India's cartoon producer Jadoo Works has even outsourced projects to U.S. animators!

In summary, the trend toward outsourcing continues to grow. This does not mean all existing outsourcing practices are perfect. The term **backsourcing** has been created to describe the return of business activity to the original firm. We will now discuss the risks associated with outsourcing.

Backsourcing
The return of business activity to the client firm.

RISKS IN OUTSOURCING

Outsourcing can look very risky. And indeed it is. Perhaps half of all outsourcing agreements fail because of inappropriate planning and analysis.[6] For one thing, few promoters of international outsourcing mention the erratic power grids in some foreign countries or the difficulties with local government officials, inexperienced managers, and unmotivated employees. On the other hand, when managers set an outsourcing goal of 75% cost reduction and receive only a 30%–40% cost reduction, they view the outsourcing as a failure, when, in fact, it may be a success.

Table S11.1 lists some of the risks inherent in outsourcing.

"The biggest challenge executives have is that they see outsourcing as a panacea, without investing sufficient time into making sure they do it right."

Dr. James Tompkins

[5]D. W. Drezner, "The Outsourcing Bogeyman," *Foreign Affairs* 83, no. 3 (May–June 2004): 22.
[6]See S. E. Fawcett, L. M. Ellram, and J. A. Ogden, *Supply Chain Management* [Upper Saddle River, N.J.: Prentice Hall, 2007]: 282–300; P. Puranum and K. Srikanth "Seven Myths of Outsourcing" *The Wall Street Journal* (June 16–17, 2007): R6; and J. A. Tompkins, "Don't Outsource the Relationship," *Industrial Engineer* 87, no. 11 (2005): 28–33.

Outsourcing Process	Examples of Possible Risks
Identify non-core competencies	Can be incorrectly identified as a non-core competency.
Identify non-core activities that should be outsourced	Just because the activity is not a core competency for your firm does not mean an outsource provider is more competent and efficient.
Identify impact on existing facilities, capacity, and logistics	May fail to understand the change in resources and talents needed internally.
Establish goals and draft outsourcing agreement specifications	Goals can be set so high that failure is certain.
Identify and select outsource provider	Can select the wrong outsource provider.
Negotiate goals and measures of outsourcing performance	Can misinterpret measures and goals, how they are measured, and what they mean.
Monitor and control current outsourcing program	May be unable to control product development, schedules, and quality.
Evaluate and give feedback to outsource provider	May have a non-responsive provider (i.e., one that ignores feedback).
Evaluate international political and currency risks	Country's currency may be unstable, a country may be politically unstable, or cultural and language differences may inhibit successful operations.
Evaluate coordination needed for shipping and distribution	May not understand the timing necessary to manage flows to different facilities and markets.

◀ **Table S11.1**

The Outsourcing Process and Related Risks

The *OM in Action* box "Dell Brings Home Its Help Desks" is a case study in the *cultural* risks related to language. Understanding culture and all its implications is fundamental to any international business activity, and it is critically important in outsourcing.

In addition to the external risks, operations managers must deal with other issues that outsourcing brings. These include (1) changes in employment levels, (2) changes in facilities and processes needed to receive components in a different state of assembly, and (3) vastly expanded logistics issues, such as insurance, customs, and timing.

Learning Objective

2. Describe the risks of outsourcing

OM in Action   Dell Brings Home Its Help Desks

Dell Computer is considered one of the best PC manufacturers in the world. Its business model, marketing strategies, and management have succeeded even in the most difficult economic times. When it saw other competitors (Gateway and Hewlett-Packard) moving some operations offshore, Dell quickly decided to adopt an international outsourcing strategy as well.

Dell believed it could cut labor costs by moving some of its technical support ("help desk" services) for corporate customers to Bangalore, India. Customers who had problems with their Dell computers could call a help desk service number, and a Dell service technician in India could provide basic technical information to help the customer to resolve the problems. Unfortunately, customer complaints quickly surfaced concerning the difficulty of understanding Indian service technicians.

Despite the best efforts of the provider firm in India, the accent of the Indian technicians was frequently too difficult

▲ *A call centre in Bangalore, India*

for customers to understand, a problem reported in the media. When Dell's customers started to complain, Dell management responded by backsourcing, shifting some help desk service phone calls previously routed to Bangalore to locations in Idaho, Tennessee, and Texas. Four of Dell's 30 call centers remain in India, partly to handle calls for help from its growing base of PC owners there.

Sources: CIO (June 1, 2006): 1; *Knight Ridder Tribune Business News* (May 29, 2005): 1 and (May 23, 2006): 1; and MSNBC *Nightly News* (February 19, 2004).

What can be done to mitigate the risks of outsourcing? Research indicates that of all the reasons given for outsourcing failure, the most common is that the decision was made without sufficient understanding of the options through quantitative analysis. The next section provides an analytical framework and some methodologies that help analyze the outsourcing decision process.

METHODOLOGIES FOR OUTSOURCING

In this section we introduce two analytical approaches that can be applied to an outsourcing decision: factor rating and break-even analysis.

Evaluating Multiple Criteria with Factor Rating

The factor-rating method, first introduced in Chapter 8, is an excellent tool for dealing with both country risk assessment and source provider selection problems.

Rating International Risk Factors   Suppose a company has identified for outsourcing a functional area of production that is a non-core competency. Example S1 shows how to subjectively rate several international risk factors using an *unweighted* factor rating approach.

EXAMPLE S1
Establishing risk factors for four countries

Toronto Airbags produces auto and truck airbags for Nissan, Chrysler, Mercedes, and BMW. It wants to conduct a risk assessment of outsourcing manufacturing. Four countries—England, Mexico, Spain, and Canada (the current home nation)—are being considered. Only English- or Spanish-speaking countries are included because they "fit" with organizational capabilities.

Approach: Toronto's management identifies nine factors, listed in Table S11.2, and subjectively rates each country on a 0–3 scale, where 0 is no risk and 3 is high risk. Risk ratings are added to find the lowest-risk location.

▶ **Table S11.2**

Toronto Airbag's International Risk Factors, by Country (an unweighted approach)

Risk Factor	England	Mexico	Spain	Canada (home country)
Economic: Labor cost/laws	1	0	2	1
Economic: Capital availability	0	2	1	0
Economic: Infrastructure	0	2	2	0
Culture: Language	0	0	0	0
Culture: Social norms	2	0	1	2
Migration: Uncontrolled	0	2	0	0
Politics: Ideology	2	0	1	2
Politics: Instability	0	1	2	2
Politics: Legalities	3	0	2	3
Total risk rating scores	8	7	11	10

Risk rating scale: 0 = no risk, 1 = minor risk, 2 = average risk, 3 = high risk

Solution: Based on these ratings, Mexico is the least risky of the four locations being considered.

Insight: As with many other quantitative methods, assessing risk factors is not easy and may require considerable research, but the technique adds objectivity to a decision.

Learning exercise: Social norms in England have just been rescored by an economist, and the new rating is "no risk." How does this affect Toronto's decision? [Answer: England now has the lowest rating for risk.]

Related problems: S11.1, S11.3

Learning Objective

3. Use factor rating to evaluate both country and provider outsourcers

In Example S1, Toronto Airbags considered only English- and Spanish-speaking countries. But it is worth mentioning that countries like China, India, and Russia have millions of English-speaking personnel. This may have an impact on the final decision.

Example S1 considered the home country of the client firm. This inclusion helps document the risks that a domestic outsourcing provider poses compared to the risks posed by international

▲ Outsourcing office jobs and technical jobs is often feasible because the distance issue is overcome with electronic communication. However, on occasion, outsourcing can take unusual forms. Here, outsourcing the casting of more than 2,000 individual panels (left) to Pretecsa of Mexico and then shipping them 2,350 miles north for Salt Lake City's public library (right) is unusual, but indicates the growing magnitude of outsourcing.

providers. Including the home country in the analysis also helps justify final strategy selection to stakeholders who might question it.

Indeed, **nearshoring** (i.e., choosing an outsource provider located in the home country or in a nearby country) can be a good strategy for businesses and governments seeking both control and cost advantages. U.S. firms are interested in nearshoring to Canada because of Canada's cultural similarity and geographic nearness to the U.S. This allows the company wanting to outsource to exert more control than would be possible when outsourcing to most other countries. Nearshoring represents a compromise in which some cost savings are sacrificed for greater control because Canada's smaller wage differential limits the labor cost reduction advantage.

Nearshoring
Choosing an outsource provider in the home country or in a nearby country.

Rating Outsource Providers   In Chapter 8 (see Example 1) we illustrated the factor-rating method's computations when each factor has its own importance weight. We now apply that concept in Example S2 to compare outsourcing providers being considered by a firm.

National Architects, Inc., a San Francisco–based designer of high-rise buildings, has decided to outsource its information technology (IT) function. Three outsourcing providers are being actively considered: one in the U.S., one in India, and one in Israel.

Approach: National's VP–Operations, Susan Cholette, has made a list of seven criteria she considers critical. After putting together a committee of four other VPs, she has rated each firm (on a 1–5 scale with 5 being highest) and has also placed an importance weight on each of the factors, as shown in Table S11.3.

EXAMPLE S2

Rating tactical provider selection criteria

◄ **Table S11.3**

Factor Ratings Applied to National Architects's Potential IT Outsourcing Providers

Factor (criterion)*	Importance Weight	Outsource Providers		
		BIM (U.S.)	S.P.C. (India)	Telco (Israel)
1. Can reduce operating costs	.2	3	3	5
2. Can reduce capital investment	.2	4	3	3
3. Skilled personnel	.2	5	4	3
4. Can improve quality	.1	4	5	2
5. Can gain access to technology not in company	.1	5	3	5
6. Can create additional capacity	.1	4	2	4
7. Aligns with policy/ philosophy/culture	.1	2	3	5
Totals	1.0	3.9	3.3	3.8

*These seven major criteria are based on a survey of 165 procurement executives, as reported in J. Schildhouse, "Outsourcing Ins and Outs," *Inside Supply Management* (December 2005): 22–29.

Solution: Susan multiplies each rating by the weight and sums the products in each column to generate a total score for each outsourcing provider. She selects BIM, which has the highest overall rating.

Insight: When the total scores are as close (3.9 vs. 3.8) as they are in this case, it is important to examine the sensitivity of the results to inputs. For example, if one of the importance weights or factor scores changes even marginally, the final selection may change. Management preference may also play a role here.

Learning exercise: Susan decides that "Skilled personnel" should instead get a weight of 0.1 and "Aligns with policy/philosophy/culture" should increase to 0.2. How do the total scores change? [Answer: BIM = 3.6, S.P.C. = 3.2, and Telco = 4.0, so Telco is selected.]

Related problems: S11.2, S11.4, S11.5, S11.6, S11.7

Break-even Analysis

In situations in which a firm's production is identified as a possible candidate for outsourcing, a break-even analysis may be applied. We first define total cost in-house as:

$$TC_{in} = F_{in} + (V_{in} \times X_{in}) \tag{S11-1}$$

where TC_{in} is the total cost of an item produced in-house
           F_{in} is the total in-house fixed cost
           V_{in} is the variable cost/unit produced in-house
           X_{in} is the total number of units produced in-house

Learning Objective

4. Use break-even analysis to determine if outsourcing is cost-effective

Using the same approach, total cost under outsourcing is:

$$TC_{out} = F_{out} + (V_{out} \times X_{out}) \tag{S11-2}$$

At an ideal break-even point, $X_{in} = X_{out}$ and $TC_{in} = TC_{out}$. If we let $X = X_{in} = X_{out}$, the two equations can be restated as:

$$F_{in} + (V_{in} \times X) = F_{out} + (V_{out} \times X) \tag{S11-3}$$

By solving for X in Equation (S11-3), we compute how many units must be outsourced in order to reach a break-even point in total costs from both possible sources:

$$X = \frac{F_{in} - F_{out}}{V_{out} - V_{in}} \tag{S11-4}$$

If X is less than the expected demand, we would select the source with the lower *variable* cost and higher *fixed* cost. If X is greater than the expected demand, the source with lower *fixed* cost and higher *variable* cost is chosen. Example S3 applies Equation (S11-4) to a specific company.[7]

▶ *Most U.S. toy companies now outsource their production to Chinese manufacturers. Cost savings are significant, but there are several downsides, including loss of control over such issues as quality. In 2007 alone, Mattel had to recall 10.5 million Elmos, Big Birds, and SpongeBobs. Thomas & Friends recalled 1.5 million wooden trains, and Target recalled 20,000 kid's flashlights. All these made-in-China toys contained excessive levels of lead in their paint or other life-threatening ingredients.*

[7]The simple unit break-even model in Equation (S11-4) can also be mathematically adjusted to reflect risk factors inherent in financial parameters when using international outsourcing as a strategy. See M. J. Schniederjans and K. Zuckweiler, "A Quantitative Approach to the Outsourcing–Insourcing Decision in an International Context," *Management Decision* 42, no. 8 (2004): 974–986.

Toledo's Baker Toys produces a popular toy, the Astro Transformer, invented by its 30-year-old founder Ron Baker. The present annual fixed cost at the Ohio plant is $2 million, and the variable cost per toy is $3. A Chinese manufacturer, Jumbo Products, has approached Ron. Jumbo can produce an Astro Transformer of equal quality for a yearly fixed-cost payment of $1 million and a variable cost per unit of $4. Baker Toys now faces a yearly demand of 1.1 million Astro Transformers. Should Baker outsource to Jumbo?

Approach: Baker applies the outsource break-even model of Equation (S11-4).

Solution: The unit break-even point is:

$$X = \frac{F_{in} - F_{out}}{V_{out} - V_{in}} = \frac{2,000,000 - 1,000,000}{4 - 3}$$
$$= 1,000,000 \text{ units}$$

Since the computed X of 1,000,000 is less than the expected demand of 1,100,000 units, the decision is to produce in-house since Baker has the lower variable cost.

Insight: For firms looking to outsource the manufacture of a single product or a group of products to an outsource provider, where cost is a major factor, this model may apply.

Learning exercise: Jumbo believes it can lower its variable cost per toy from $4 to $3.80 through better training and quality control. Should Baker now outsource to Jumbo? [Answer: Yes, $X = 1,250,000$ units now. So $X > 1,100,000$ units of expected demand.]

Related problems: S11.8, S11.9

EXAMPLE S3

Outsource break-even analysis for Baker Toys

If cost minimization is a driving force in an outsourcing decision, this break-even approach may be an excellent initial decision methodology. Note that this approach is similar to the crossover chart model introduced in Figure 7.6 in Chapter 7.

ADVANTAGES AND DISADVANTAGES OF OUTSOURCING[8]

Advantages of Outsourcing

As mentioned earlier, companies outsource for five main reasons. They are, in order of importance: (1) cost savings, (2) gaining outside expertise, (3) improving operations and service, (4) focusing on core competencies, and (5) gaining outside technology.

Learning Objective

5. List the advantages and disadvantages of outsourcing

Cost Savings   The number-one reason driving outsourcing for many firms is the possibility of significant cost savings, particularly for labor. (See the *OM in Action* box "Wal-Mart's Competitive Advantage Is Its Supply Chain").

Gaining Outside Expertise   In addition to gaining access to a broad base of skills that are unavailable in-house, an outsourcing provider may be a source of innovation for improving products, processes, and services.

Improving Operations and Service   An outsourcing provider may have production flexibility. This may allow the client firm to win orders by more quickly introducing new products and services.

Focusing on Core Competencies   An outsourcing provider brings *its* core competencies to the supply chain. This frees up the client firm's human, physical, and financial resources to reallocate to core competencies.

[8]See M. Weidenbaum, "Outsourcing: Pros and Cons," *Business Horizons* 48, no. 4 (July/August, 2005): 311; and P. Engardio, "The Future of Outsourcing," *Business Week* (January 30, 2006): 50–64.

OM in Action *Wal-Mart's Competitive Advantage Is Its Supply Chain*

Competition is no longer between companies—it is now between supply chains, and Wal-Mart knows the way. No other company has a more efficient supply chain, and no other company has embraced outsourcing to China more vigorously than Wal-Mart. Perhaps as much as 85% of Wal-Mart's merchandise is made abroad, and Chinese factories are by far the most important and fastest growing of these sources.

A whopping 10%–13% of everything China sends to the U.S. ends up on Wal-Mart's shelves—well over $15 billion worth of goods a year. *The Washington Post* reported in 2004 that "more than 80% of the 6,000 factories in Wal-Mart's worldwide database of suppliers are in China." Wal-Mart has almost 600 people on the ground in China just to negotiate and make purchases.

As much as Wal-Mart has been demonized for its part in offshoring jobs and pushing the "China price" on all producers, it has expertly managed and accelerated that trend. Wal-Mart's critical mass allows Chinese firms to build assembly lines that are so huge that they drive prices down through economies of scale.

Wal-Mart's Chinese suppliers achieve startling, market-shaking price cuts. For example, the price of portable DVDs with 7" LCD screens dropped in half when Wal-Mart found a Chinese factory to build in giant quantities. Likewise, Wal-Mart's Apex brand TVs from Changhong Electric undercut the competition by more than $100. Wal-Mart's success in going abroad and pressing suppliers for price breaks has forced both retailers and manufacturers to seriously reevaluate their supply chains and their operational processes.

Sources: The Booklist (February 1, 2006): 12; *Barron's* (November 20, 2006): 44; *Inc. Magazine* (March 2005): 80; and *Money Marketing* (April 8, 2004): 46.

Gaining Outside Technology The client firm can outsource to state-of-the-art providers instead of retaining "legacy" systems. The client firm does not have to invest in new technology, thereby cutting risks.

Other Advantages There are additional advantages in outsourcing. For example, the client firm may improve its performance and image by associating with an outstanding provider. Outsourcing can also be used as a strategy for downsizing, or "reengineering," a client firm.

Disadvantages of Outsourcing

There are a number of potential disadvantages in outsourcing. Here are just a few:

Increased Transportation Costs Delivery costs may rise substantially if distance increases from an outsourcing provider to a client firm.

Loss of Control This disadvantage can permeate and link to all other problems with outsourcing. When managers lose control of some operations, costs may increase because it's harder to assess and control them. For example, production of most of the world's laptops is now outsourced. This means that companies like Dell and HP find themselves using the same contractor (Quanta) to make their machines in China. This can leave them struggling to maintain control over the supplier.

Creating Future Competition Intel, for example, outsourced a core competency, chip production, to AMD when it could not keep up with early demands. Within a few years, AMD became a leading competitor, manufacturing its own chips.

Negative Impact on Employees Employee morale may drop when functions are outsourced, particularly when friends lose their jobs. Employees believe they may be next, and indeed they may be. Productivity, loyalty, and trust—all of which are needed for a healthy, growing business—may suffer.

Longer-Term Impact Some disadvantages of outsourcing tend to be longer term than the advantages of outsourcing. In other words, many of the risks firms run by outsourcing may not show up on the bottom line until some time in the future. This permits CEOs who prefer short-term planning and are interested only in bottom-line improvements to use the outsourcing strategy to make quick gains at the expense of longer-term objectives.

The advantages and disadvantages of outsourcing may or may not occur but should be thought of as possibilities to be managed effectively.

AUDITS AND METRICS TO EVALUATE OUTSOURCING PERFORMANCE

Regardless of the techniques and success in selection of outsourcing providers, agreements must specify results and outcomes. Whatever the outsourced component or service, management needs an evaluation process to ensure satisfactory continuing performance. At a minimum, the product or service must be defined in terms of quality, customer satisfaction, delivery, cost, and improvement. The mix and detail of the performance measures will depend on the nature of the product.

In situations where the outsourced product or service plays a major role in strategy and winning orders, the relationship needs to be more than after-the-fact audits and reports. It needs to be based on continuing communication, understanding, trust, and performance. The relationship should manifest itself in the mutual belief that "we are in this together" and go well beyond the written agreement.

However, when outsourcing is for less critical components, agreements that include the traditional mix of audits and metrics (such as cost, logistics, quality, and delivery) may be reported weekly or monthly. When a *service* has been outsourced, more imaginative metrics may be necessary. For instance, in an outsourced call center, these metrics may deal with personnel evaluation and training, call volume, call type, and response time, as well as tracking complaints. In this dynamic environment, reporting of such metrics may be required daily.[9]

> *As the client's needs change, the outsourcing agreements need to evolve also.*

ETHICAL ISSUES IN OUTSOURCING

Laws, trade agreements, and business practices are contributing to a growing set of international, ethical practices for the outsourcing industry. Table S11.4 presents several tenets of conduct that have fairly universal acceptance.

In the electronics industry, HP, Dell, IBM, Intel and twelve other companies have created the Electronics Industry Code of Conduct (EICC). The EICC sets environmental standards, bans child labor and excessive overtime, and audits outsourcing producers to ensure compliance.[10]

Ethics Principle	Outsourcing Linkage
Seek to do no harm to indigenous cultures	Don't use outsourcing in a way that violates religious holidays (e.g., making employees work during religious holidays).
Seek to do no harm to the ecological systems of the world	Don't use outsourcing to move pollution from one country to another.
Seek to uphold universal labor standards	Don't use outsourcing to take advantage of cheap child labor that leads to child abuse.
Seek to uphold basic human rights	Don't accept outsourcing that violates basic human rights.
Seek to pursue long-term involvement in foreign countries	Don't use outsourcing as a short-term arrangement to reduce costs; view it as a long-term partnership.
Seek to share knowledge and technology with foreign countries	Don't think an outsourcing agreement will prevent sharing of technology, but use the inevitable sharing to build a good relationship with foreign outsourcing firms.

◀ **Table S11.4**

Ethical Principles and Related Outsourcing Linkages

[9]S. H. Huang and H. Keskar, "Comprehensive and Configurable Metrics for Supplier Selection," *International Journal of Production Economics* 105, no. 2 (February, 2007): 510–523.
[10]P. Burrows, "Stalking High-Tech Sweatshops," *Business Week* (June 19, 2006): 62–63.

Summary

Companies can give many different reasons why they outsource, but the reality is that outsourcing's most attractive feature is that it helps firms cut costs. Workers in low-cost countries simply work much more cheaply, with fewer fringe benefits, work rules, and legal restrictions, than their U.S. and European counterparts. For example, a comparable hourly wage of $20 in the U.S. and $30 in Europe is well above the $1 per hour in China. Yet China often achieves quality levels equivalent to (or even higher than) plants in the West.

There is a growing economic pressure to outsource. But there is also a need for planning outsourcing to make it acceptable to all participants. When outsourcing is done in the right way, it creates a win–win situation.

Key Terms

Outsourcing *(p. 464)*
Offshoring *(p. 464)*
Client firm *(p. 464)*

Outsource provider *(p. 464)*
Core competencies *(p. 466)*
Theory of comparative advantage *(p. 467)*

Backsourcing *(p. 468)*
Nearshoring *(p. 471)*

Using Software to Solve Outsourcing Problems

Excel, Excel OM, and POM for Windows may be used to solve most of the problems in this supplement.

Excel OM and POM for Windows both contain Factor Rating modules that can address issues such as the ones we saw in Examples S1 and S2. They also both contain Cost-volume/Break-even Analysis modules that handle problems like we saw in Example S3. The Factor Rating module was illustrated earlier in Program 8.1 in Chapter 8.

Solved Problem

 Virtual Office Hours help is available on Student DVD.

Solved Problem S11.1

Mark Berenson is CEO of Montclair Electronics. He is currently producing 70,000 video telephones a year in his New Jersey plant, where fixed costs are $900,000 and the variable cost per unit is $6. By outsourcing to a Mexican firm, annual fixed cost (F) payments will rise to $1 million, but the variable cost (V) will drop to $5 per unit. Should Berenson outsource?

Solution

Use Equation (S11-4) to compute how many units must be outsourced to reach a break-even point in total costs:

$$X = \frac{F_{in} - F_{out}}{V_{out} - V_{in}} = \frac{900{,}000 - 1{,}000{,}000}{5 - 6}$$

$$= \frac{-100{,}000}{-1} = 100{,}000 \text{ units}$$

Since a production level of 70,000 units is less than $X = 100{,}000$, Berenson should keep producing in New Jersey, where there are lower fixed costs and higher variable costs.

Self-Test

- *Before taking the self-test*, refer to the learning objectives listed at the beginning of the supplement and the key terms listed at the end of the supplement.
- Use the key at the back of the text to *correct* your answers.
- *Restudy* pages that correspond to any question you answered incorrectly or material you feel uncertain about.

1. Outsourcing is procuring services or products from:
   a) other countries where the company owns facilities
   b) Canada or Mexico
   c) sources external to the organization
   d) offshore firms
   e) all of the above

2. Outsourcing has become a major force in business:
   a) because the Internet allows firms anywhere in the world to provide information services
   b) because of advancement in telecommunications
   c) because of rapid development of technology
   d) because there is more expertise in our knowledge society
   e) all of the above

3. Companies like IBM, HP, and Cisco outsource to Solectron because
   a) they can't build quality products themselves
   b) Solectron is an award-winning company with a good reputation
   c) it is not possible to manufacture computer parts in the U.S. anymore
   d) Solectron only manufactures in India, where costs are lower
   e) IBM, HP, and Cisco do not outsource

4. Core competencies are those strengths in a firm that include:
   a) specialized skills
   b) unique production methods
   c) proprietary information/knowledge
   d) things a company does better than others
   e) all of the above

5. The theory of comparative advantage means:
   a) Russia and China will almost always be selected for outsourcing
   b) a firm should typically outsource if a provider can do the work more productively than the outsourcing firm
   c) international outsourcing is better than outsourcing to other U.S. firms
   d) core competencies are never as strong as a good outsource provider
   e) the same as the theory of constraints

6. Outsourcing can be a risky proposition because:
   a) about half of all outsourcing agreements fail
   b) it only saves about 30% in labor costs
   c) labor costs are increasing throughout the world
   d) a non-core competency is outsourced
   e) shipping costs are increasing

7. Nearshoring is a good strategy for U.S. firms because:
   a) Mexico's culture is identical to that of the U.S.
   b) Canada is a low-cost producer
   c) geographic nearness allows more control than outsourcing to India or China
   d) Latin America is a lower-cost producer than Europe
   e) international trade is declining

8. Advantages of outsourcing include:
   a) focusing on core competencies and cost savings
   b) gaining outside technology and creating new markets in India for U.S. products
   c) improving operations by closing plants in Malaysia
   d) employees will want to leave the firm
   e) reduced problems with logistics

Internet and Student CD-ROM/DVD Exercises

Visit our Companion Web site or use your student CD-ROM/DVD to help with material in this supplement.

 On Our Companion Web Site,
www.prenhall.com/heizer
- Self-Study Quizzes
- Practice Problems
- PowerPoint Lecture

 On Your Student CD-ROM
- Practice Problems
- Excel OM Software
- Excel OM Data Files
- POM for Windows

 On Your Student DVD
- Video Clip and Video Case
- Virtual Office Hours for Solved Problem

Discussion Questions

1. How would you summarize outsourcing trends?
2. What potential cost saving advantages might firms experience by using outsourcing?
3. What internal issues must managers address when outsourcing?
4. How should a company select an outsourcing provider?

5. What are we trying to find the break-even point for in outsourcing break-even analysis?
6. What are international risk factors in the outsourcing decision?
7. How can ethics be beneficial in an outsourcing organization?
8. What are some of the possible consequences of poor outsourcing?

Problems*

• **S11.1** Claudia Pragram Technologies, Inc., has narrowed its choice of outsourcing provider to two firms located in different countries. Pragram wants to decide which one of the two countries is the better choice, based on risk-avoidance criteria. She has polled her executives and established four criteria. The resulting ratings for the two countries are presented in the table below, where 1 is a lower risk and 3 is a higher risk. Using the unweighted factor-rating method, which country would you select?

Selection Criterion	England	Canada
Price of service from outsourcer	2	3
Nearness of facilities to client	3	1
Level of technology	1	3
History of successful outsourcing	1	2 **Px**

• **S11.2** Using the same ratings given in Problem S11.1, assume that the executives have determined four criteria weightings: Price, with a weight of 0.1; Nearness, with 0.6; Technology, with 0.2; and History, with 0.1. Using the weighted factor-rating method, which country would you select? Why? **Px**

• **S11.3** Ranga Ramasesh is the operations manager for a firm that is trying to decide which one of four countries it should research for possible outsourcing providers. The first step is to select a country based on cultural risk factors, which are critical to eventual business success with the provider. Ranga has reviewed outsourcing provider directories and found that the four countries in the table below have an ample number of providers from which they can choose. To aid in the country selection step, he has enlisted the aid of a cultural expert, John Wang, who has provided ratings of the various criteria in the table below. The resulting ratings are on a 1 to 10 scale, where 1 is a low risk and 10 is a high risk. Using the unweighted factor-rating method, which country should Ranga select based on risk avoidance?

Culture Selection Criterion	Mexico	Panama	Costa Rica	Peru
Trust	1	2	2	1
Society value of quality work	7	10	9	10
Religious attitudes	3	3	3	5
Individualism attitudes	5	2	4	8
Time orientation attitudes	4	6	7	3
Uncertainty avoidance attitudes	3	2	4	2 **Px**

•• **S11.4** Using the same ratings given in Problem S11.3, assume that John Wang has determined six criteria weightings: Trust, with a weight of 0.4; Quality, with 0.2; Religious, with 0.1; Individualism, with 0.1; Time, with 0.1; and Uncertainty, with 0.1. Using the weighted factor-rating method, which country should Ranga select? **Px**

Note: **Px** means the problem may be solved with POM for Windows and/or Excel OM.

• **S11.5** Charles Teplitz's firm wishes to use factor rating to help select an outsourcing provider of logistics services. With weights from 1–5 (5 highest) and ratings from 1–100 (100 highest), use the following table to help Teplitz make his decision:

		Rating of Logistics Providers		
Criterion	Weight	Atlanta Shipping	Seattle Delivery	Utah Freight
Quality	5	90	80	75
Delivery	3	70	85	70
Cost	2	70	80	95 **Px**

• **S11.6** Walker Accounting Software is marketed to small accounting firms throughout the U.S. and Canada. Owner George Walker has decided to outsource the company's help desk and is considering three providers: Manila Call Center (Philippines), Delhi Services (India), and Moscow Bell (Russia). The following table summarizes the data Walker has assembled. Which outsourcing firm has the best rating? (Higher weights imply higher importance and higher ratings imply more desirable providers.)

		Provider Ratings		
Criterion	Importance Weight	Manila	Delhi	Moscow
Flexibility	0.5	5	1	9
Trustworthiness	0.1	5	5	2
Price	0.2	4	3	6
Delivery	0.2	5	6	6 **Px**

•••• **S11.7** Price Technologies, a California-based high-tech manufacturer, is considering outsourcing some of its electronics production. Four firms have responded to its request for bids, and CEO Willard Price has started to perform an analysis on the scores his OM team has entered in the table below.

		Ratings of Outsource Providers			
Factor	Weight	A	B	C	D
Labor	w	5	4	3	5
Quality procedures	30	2	3	5	1
Logistics system	5	3	4	3	5
Price	25	5	3	4	4
Trustworthiness	5	3	2	3	5
Technology in place	15	2	5	4	4
Management team	15	5	4	2	1

Weights are on a scale from 1 through 30, and the outsourcing provider scores are on a scale of 1 through 5. The weight for the labor factor is shown as a w because Price's OM team cannot agree on a value for this weight. For what range of values of w, if any, is company C a recommended outsourcing provider, according to the factor-rating method?

•• **S11.8** Kamal-Gursoy Electronics is currently insourcing all its single-product production, with a yearly fixed cost (F_{in}) of $5 million and a variable cost per unit (V_{in}) of $2. The firm is approached by a Vietnamese outsourcing provider that can manufacture the product with equal quality for a yearly fixed cost payment (F_{out}) of $2 million and a variable cost per unit (V_{out}) of $6. Kamal-Gursoy is now facing a yearly demand of 2 million units.

a) Using the unit break-even model, should the firm outsource or continue to insource the manufacture of this product?

b) What is the break-even point in units? **Px**

•• **S11.9**   Nye Products is currently insourcing all its telephone answering machines (its only product), with a yearly fixed cost of $7 million and a variable cost per unit of $3. CEO Harvey Nye has published a request for information and found an outsourcing provider that can manufacture the product with equal quality for a yearly fixed-cost payment of $3 million and a variable cost per unit of $8. Nye Products is now facing a yearly demand of 1.5 million telephones.

a) Using the unit break-even model, should Nye outsource or continue to insource the manufacture of this product?

b) What is the break-even point in units? **Px**

Case Studies

Outsourcing to Tata

While some states, such as Tennessee, have been quick to ban or limit international outsourcing of government activities, other state governments have sought to take advantage of low-cost opportunities that international outsourcing can offer.

The state of New Mexico's Labor Department hired Tata Consultancy Services, an Indian outsourcing firm, to redo New Mexico's unemployment compensation computer system. While Tata had completed work for other states, including Pennsylvania and New York, it had never worked on an unemployment compensation system. Also, New Mexico agreed to allow Tata to do all computer software work in India, apparently with insufficient monitoring of progress by New Mexico officials responsible for the outsourcing project.

The new system should have been completed in 6 months, which put the due date in December 2001. Unfortunately, things did not work out well. The initial system was delivered 1 year later. But in late 2004 it was still not working. Also, the outsourcing project went way over the budget of $3.6 million, up to $13 million. The warranty for the system ended in 2003, leaving New Mexico with a situation of either suing Tata to complete the project (it was estimated at 80% complete) or hiring someone to fix it. Tata's position was that it had complied with the outsourcing agreement and was willing to continue fixing the system if it could receive additional compensation to justify additional work.

Discussion Questions

1. Use the process in Table S11.1 to analyze what New Mexico could have done to achieve a more successful outcome.
2. Is this a case of cultural misunderstanding, or could the same result have occurred if a U.S. firm, such as IBM, had been selected?
3. Conduct your own research to assess the risks of outsourcing any information technology project. (*Computerworld* is one good source.)

Outsourcing Offshore at Darden

Video Case

Darden Restaurants, owner of popular brands such as Olive Garden and Red Lobster, serves more than 300 million meals annually in over 1,400 restaurants across the U.S. and Canada. To achieve competitive advantage via its supply chain, Darden must achieve excellence at each step. With purchases from 35 countries, and seafood products with a shelf life as short as 4 days, this is a complex and challenging task.

Those 300 million meals annually mean 40 million pounds of shrimp and huge quantities of tilapia, swordfish, and other fresh purchases. Fresh seafood is typically flown to the U.S. and monitored each step of the way to ensure that 34°F is maintained.

Darden's purchasing agents travel the world to find competitive advantage in the supply chain. Darden personnel from supply chain and development, quality assurance, and environmental relations contribute to developing, evaluating, and checking suppliers. Darden also has seven native-speaking representatives living on other continents to provide continuing support and evaluation of suppliers. All suppliers must abide by Darden's food standards, which typically exceed FDA and other industry standards. Darden expects continuous improvement in durable relationships that increase quality and reduce cost.

Darden's aggressiveness and development of a sophisticated supply chain provides an opportunity for outsourcing. Much food preparation is labor intensive and is often more efficient when handled in bulk. This is particularly true where large volumes may justify capital investment. For instance, Tyson and Iowa Beef prepare meats to Darden's specifications much more economically than can individual restaurants. Similarly, Darden has found that it can outsource both the cutting of salmon to the proper portion size and the cracking/peeling of shrimp more cost-effectively offshore than in U.S. distribution centers or individual restaurants.

Discussion Questions*

1. What are some outsourcing opportunities in a restaurant?
2. What supply chain issues are unique to a firm sourcing from 35 countries?
3. Examine how other firms or industries develop international supply chains as compared to Darden.
4. Why does Darden outsource harvesting and preparation of much of its seafood?

*You may wish to view this video case study on your DVD before answering the questions.

Source: Professors Barry Render (Rollins College), Jay Heizer (Texas Lutheran University), and Beverly Amer (Northern Arizona University).

Bibliography

Aron, R., and J. V. Singh. "Getting Offshoring Right." *Harvard Business Review* (December 2005): 135–143.

Bravard, J., and R. Morgan. *Smarter Outsourcing.* Upper Saddle River, NJ: Pearson (2006).

Champy, James. *Avoiding the Seven Deadly Sins of Outsourcing Relationships.* Plano, TX: Perot Systems (2005).

Friedman, Thomas. *The World Is Flat: A Brief History of the 21st Century.* New York: Farrar, Straus, and Giroux (2005).

Gray, J. V., A. Roth, and B. Tomlin. "An Empirical Study of Manufacturing Outsourcing." *Annual Decision Sciences Institute Proceedings.* San Francisco (2005).

Halvey, J. K., and B. M. Melby. *Business Process Outsourcing,* 2nd ed. New York: Wiley (2007).

Kotabe, M., and Murray, J. Y. "Global Sourcing Strategy and Sustainable Competitive Advantage." *Industrial Marketing Management* 33, no. 1 (2004): 7–15.

Lee, Hau L., and Chung-Yee Lee. *Building Supply Chain Excellence in Emerging Economies.* Secaucus, NJ: Springer (2007).

Rasheed, A. A., and K. M. Gilley. "Outsourcing: National- and Firm-Level Implications." *Thunderbird International Business Review* 47, no. 5 (September/October 2005): 513.

Schildhouse, Jill. "Outsourcing Ins and Outs." *Inside Supply Management* (December 2005): 22–29.

Schniederjans, Marc J., A. M. Schniederjans, and D. G. Schniederjans. *Outsourcing and Insourcing in an International Context.* Armonk, NY: M.E. Sharpe (2005).

Steak, M., and R. Downing. "Another Look at Offshoring." *Business Horizons* 48, no. 6 (November–December 2005): 513.

Thomas, A. R., and T. J. Wilkinson. "The Outsourcing Compulsion." *MIT Sloan Management Review* 48, no. 1 (Fall 2006): 10.

Tompkins, J. A., et al. *Logistics and Manufacturing Outsourcing: Harness Your Core Competencies.* Raleigh, NC: Tompkins Press (2005).

Webb, L., and J. Laborde. "Crafting a Successful Outsourcing Vendor/Client Relationship." *Business Process Management Journal* 11, no. 5 (2005): 437–443.

Whitten, Dwayne, and Dorothy Leidner. "Bringing IT Back: An Analysis of the Decision to Backsource or Switch Vendors." *Decision Sciences* 37, no. 4 (November 2006): 605–621.

Yourdon, Edward. *Outsource: Competing in the Global Productivity Race.* Upper Saddle River, NJ: Prentice Hall (2005).

Internet Resources

Center for Global Outsourcing **www.outsourceglobal.org**
Council on Foreign Affairs **www.foreignaffairs.org**
Global Aquaculture Alliance **www.gaalliance.org**
Institute for Supply Management **www.ism.ws**

Outsourcing directory **www.offshorexperts.com**
Outsourcing global services directory **www.outsourcing.org**
The Outsourcing Institute **www.outsourcing.com**
World Trade Organization **www.wto.org**

CHAPTER 12

Inventory Management

Chapter Outline

Ten OM Strategy Decisions

Design of Goods and Services

Managing Quality

Process Strategy

Location Strategies

Layout Strategies

Human Resources

Supply Chain Management

Inventory Management
   Independent Demand
   Dependent Demand
   JIT & Lean Operations

Scheduling

Maintenance

Learning Objectives

When you complete this chapter you should be able to

1. Conduct an ABC analysis
2. Explain and use cycle counting
3. Explain and use the EOQ model for independent inventory demand
4. Compute a reorder point and explain safety stock
5. Apply the production order quantity model
6. Explain and use the quantity discount model
7. Understand service levels and probabilistic inventory models

Inventory Management Provides Competitive Advantage at Amazon.com

When Jeff Bezos opened his revolutionary business in 1995, Amazon.com was intended to be a "virtual" retailer—no inventory, no warehouses, no overhead—just a bunch of computers taking orders and authorizing others to fill them. Things clearly didn't work out that way. Now, Amazon stocks millions of items of inventory, amid hundreds of thousands of bins on metal shelves, in warehouses (seven around the U.S. and three in Europe) that have twice the floor space of the Empire State Building.

Precisely managing this massive inventory has forced Amazon into becoming a world-class leader in warehouse management and automation, with annual sales of over $8 billion. This profile shows what goes on behind the scenes.

When you place an order at Amazon.com, not only are you doing business with an Internet company, you are doing business with a company that obtains competitive advantage through inventory management.

▶ 1. **You order three items, and a computer in Seattle takes charge.** *A computer assigns your order—a book, a game, and a digital camera—to one of Amazon's massive U.S. distribution centers, such as the 750,000-square-foot facility in Coffeyville, Kansas.*

2. **The "flow meister" in Coffeyville receives your order.** *She determines which workers go where to fill your order.*

◀ 3. **Rows of red lights show which products are ordered.** *Workers move from bulb to bulb, retrieving an item from the shelf above and pressing a button that resets the light. This is known as a "pick-to-light" system. This system doubles the picking speed of manual operators and drops the error rate to nearly zero.*

▼ 4. **Your items are put into crates on moving belts.** *Each item goes into a large green crate that contains many customers' orders. When full, the crates ride a series of conveyor belts that wind more than 10 miles through the plant at a constant speed of 2.9 feet per second. The bar code on each item is scanned 15 times, by machines and by many of the 600 workers. The goal is to reduce errors to zero—returns are very expensive.*

▶ 5. **All three items converge in a chute and then inside a box.** *All the crates arrive at a central point where bar codes are matched with order numbers to determine who gets what. Your three items end up in a 3-foot-wide chute—one of several thousand—and are placed into a cardboard box with a new bar code that identifies your order. Picking is sequenced to reduce operator travel.*

6. **Any gifts you've chosen are wrapped by hand**. *Amazon trains an elite group of gift wrappers, each of whom processes 30 packages an hour.*

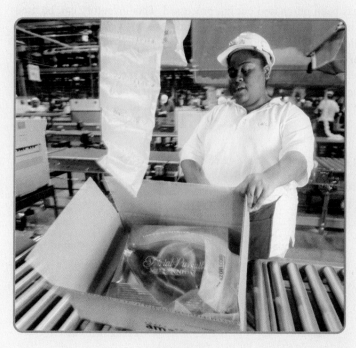

◀ 7. **The box is packed, taped, weighed, and labeled before leaving the warehouse in a truck**. *The Coffeyville plant was designed to ship as many as 200,000 pieces a day. About 60% of orders are shipped via the U.S. Postal Service; nearly everything else goes through United Parcel Service.*

8. **Your order arrives at your doorstep.** *Within a week, your order is delivered.*

As Amazon.com well knows, inventory is one of the most expensive assets of many companies, representing as much as 50% of total invested capital. Operations managers around the globe have long recognized that good inventory management is crucial. On the one hand, a firm can reduce costs by reducing inventory. On the other hand, production may stop and customers become dissatisfied when an item is out of stock. *The objective of inventory management is to strike a balance between inventory investment and customer service.* You can never achieve a low-cost strategy without good inventory management.

All organizations have some type of inventory planning and control system. A bank has methods to control its inventory of cash. A hospital has methods to control blood supplies and pharmaceuticals. Government agencies, schools, and, of course, virtually every manufacturing and production organization are concerned with inventory planning and control.

In cases of physical products, the organization must determine whether to produce goods or to purchase them. Once this decision has been made, the next step is to forecast demand, as discussed in Chapter 4. Then operations managers determine the inventory necessary to service that demand. In this chapter, we discuss the functions, types, and management of inventory. We then address two basic inventory issues: how much to order and when to order.

> *Inventory investment: your company's largest asset.*

FUNCTIONS OF INVENTORY

Inventory can serve several functions that add flexibility to a firm's operations. The four functions of inventory are:

1. To "*decouple*" *or separate various parts of the production process*. For example, if a firm's supplies fluctuate, extra inventory may be necessary to decouple the production process from suppliers.
2. To *decouple the firm from fluctuations in demand* and *provide a stock of goods that will provide a selection for customers*. Such inventories are typical in retail establishments.
3. To *take advantage of quantity discounts*, because purchases in larger quantities may reduce the cost of goods or their delivery.
4. To *hedge against inflation* and upward price changes.

Types of Inventory

To accommodate the functions of inventory, firms maintain four types of inventories: (1) raw material inventory, (2) work-in-process inventory, (3) maintenance/repair/operating supply (MRO) inventory, and (4) finished-goods inventory.

Raw material inventory has been purchased but not processed. This inventory can be used to decouple (i.e., separate) suppliers from the production process. However, the preferred approach is to eliminate supplier variability in quality, quantity, or delivery time so that separation is not needed. **Work-in-process (WIP) inventory** is components or raw material that have undergone some change but are not completed. WIP exists because of the time it takes for a product to be made (called *cycle time*). Reducing cycle time reduces inventory. Often this task is not difficult: During most of the time a product is "being made," it is in fact sitting idle. As Figure 12.1

Raw material inventory
Materials that are usually purchased but have yet to enter the manufacturing process.

Work-in-process (WIP) inventory
Products or components that are no longer raw materials but have yet to become finished products.

▼ **Figure 12.1** The Material Flow Cycle

Most of the time that work is in-process (95% of the cycle time) is not productive time.

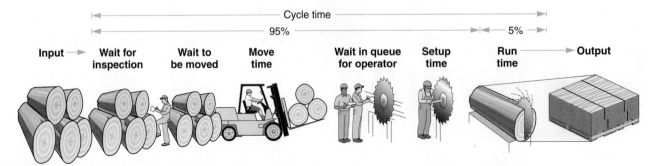

shows, actual work time, or "run" time, is a small portion of the material flow time, perhaps as low as 5%.

MROs are inventories devoted to **maintenance/repair/operating** supplies necessary to keep machinery and processes productive. They exist because the need and timing for maintenance and repair of some equipment are unknown. Although the demand for MRO inventory is often a function of maintenance schedules, other unscheduled MRO demands must be anticipated. **Finished-goods inventory** is completed product awaiting shipment. Finished goods may be inventoried because future customer demands are unknown.

MRO
Maintenance, repair, and operating materials.

Finished-goods inventory
An end item ready to be sold, but still an asset on the company's books.

INVENTORY MANAGEMENT

Operations managers establish systems for managing inventory. In this section, we briefly examine two ingredients of such systems: (1) how inventory items can be classified (called *ABC analysis*) and (2) how accurate inventory records can be maintained. We will then look at inventory control in the service sector.

ABC Analysis

ABC analysis divides on-hand inventory into three classifications on the basis of annual dollar volume. ABC analysis is an inventory application of what is known as the *Pareto principle*. The Pareto principle states that there are a "critical few and trivial many."[1] The idea is to establish inventory policies that focus resources on the *few critical* inventory parts and not the many trivial ones. It is not realistic to monitor inexpensive items with the same intensity as very expensive items.

To determine annual dollar volume for ABC analysis, we measure the *annual demand* of each inventory item times the *cost per unit. Class A* items are those on which the annual dollar volume is high. Although such items may represent only about 15% of the total inventory items, they represent 70% to 80% of the total dollar usage. *Class B* items are those inventory items of medium annual dollar volume. These items may represent about 30% of inventory items and 15% to 25% of the total value. Those with low annual dollar volume are *Class C*, which may represent only 5% of the annual dollar volume but about 55% of the total inventory items.

Graphically, the inventory of many organizations would appear as presented in Figure 12.2. An example of the use of ABC analysis is shown in Example 1.

ABC analysis
A method for dividing on-hand inventory into three classifications based on annual dollar volume.

Learning Objective
1. Conduct an ABC analysis

◄ **Figure 12.2**

Graphic Representation of ABC Analysis

Silicon Chips, Inc., maker of superfast DRAM chips, wants to categorize its 10 major inventory items using ABC analysis.

Approach: ABC analysis organizes the items on an annual dollar-volume basis. Shown on the following page (in columns 1–4) are the 10 items (identified by stock numbers), their annual demands, and unit costs.

Solution: Annual dollar volume is computed in column 5, along with the percent of the total represented by each item in column 6. Column 7 groups the 10 items into A, B, and C categories.

EXAMPLE 1

ABC analysis for a chip manufacturer

[1]After Vilfredo Pareto, 19th-century Italian economist.

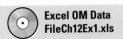

Excel OM Data
FileCh12Ex1.xls

ABC Calculation

(1) Item Stock Number	(2) Percent of Number of Items Stocked	(3) Annual Volume (units)	×	(4) Unit Cost	=	(5) Annual Dollar Volume	(6) Percent of Annual Dollar Volume		(7) Class
#10286	20%	1,000	×	$ 90.00	=	$ 90,000	38.8%	72%	A
#11526		500		154.00		77,000	33.2%		A
#12760	30%	1,550		17.00		26,350	11.3%	23%	B
#10867		350		42.86		15,001	6.4%		B
#10500		1,000		12.50		12,500	5.4%		B
#12572	50%	600		14.17		8,502	3.7%	5%	C
#14075		2,000		.60		1,200	.5%		C
#01036		100		8.50		850	.4%		C
#01307		1,200		.42		504	.2%		C
#10572		250		.60		150	.1%		C
		8,550				$232,057	100.0%		

Insight: The breakdown into A, B, and C categories is not hard and fast. The objective is to try to separate the "important" from the "unimportant."

Learning exercise: The unit cost for Item #10286 has increased from $90.00 to $120.00. How does this impact the ABC analysis? [Answer: The total annual dollar volume increases by $30,000, to $262,057, and the two A items now comprise 75% of that amount.]

Related problems: 12.1, 12.2, 12.3

Most automated inventory management systems include ABC analysis.

Criteria other than annual dollar volume can determine item classification. For instance, anticipated engineering changes, delivery problems, quality problems, or high unit cost may dictate upgrading items to a higher classification. The advantage of dividing inventory items into classes allows policies and controls to be established for each class.

Policies that may be based on ABC analysis include the following:

1. Purchasing resources expended on supplier development should be much higher for individual A items than for C items.
2. A items, as opposed to B and C items, should have tighter physical inventory control; perhaps they belong in a more secure area, and perhaps the accuracy of inventory records for A items should be verified more frequently.
3. Forecasting A items may warrant more care than forecasting other items.

Better forecasting, physical control, supplier reliability, and an ultimate reduction in safety stock can all result from appropriate inventory management policies. ABC analysis guides the development of those policies.

Record Accuracy

Video 12.1

Inventory Control at
Wheeled Coach Ambulance

Good inventory policies are meaningless if management does not know what inventory is on hand. Accuracy of records is a critical ingredient in production and inventory systems. Record accuracy allows organizations to focus on those items that are needed, rather than settling for being sure that "some of everything" is in inventory. Only when an organization can determine accurately what it has on hand can it make precise decisions about ordering, scheduling, and shipping.

To ensure accuracy, incoming and outgoing record keeping must be good, as must be stockroom security. A well-organized stockroom will have limited access, good housekeeping, and storage areas that hold fixed amounts of inventory. Bins, shelf space, and parts will be labeled accurately. The U.S. Marines' approach to improved inventory record accuracy is discussed in the *OM in Action* box "What the Marines Learned about Inventory from Wal-Mart."

The U.S. Marine Corps knew it had inventory problems. A few years ago, when a soldier at Camp Pendleton, near San Diego, put in an order for a spare part, it took him a week to get it—from the other side of the base. Worse, the Corps had 207 computer systems worldwide. Called the "Rats' Nest" by Marine techies, most systems didn't even talk to each other.

To execute a victory over uncontrolled supplies, the Corps studied Wal-Mart, Caterpillar, Inc., and UPS. "We're in the middle of a revolution," says General Gary McKissock. McKissock aims to reduce inventory for the Corps by half, saving $200 million, and to shift 2,000 Marines from inventory detail to the battlefield.

By replacing inventory with information, the Corps won't have to stockpile tons of supplies near the battle-

field, like it did during the Gulf War, only to find it couldn't keep track of what was in containers. Then there was the Marine policy requiring a 60-day supply of everything. McKissock figured out there was no need to overstock commodity items, like office supplies, that can be obtained anywhere. And with advice from the private sector, the Marines have been upgrading warehouses, adding wireless scanners for real-time inventory placement and tracking. Now, if containers need to be sent into a war zone, they will have radio frequency transponders that, when scanned, will link to a database detailing what's inside.

Sources: Modern Materials Handling (August 2005): 24–25; and *Business Week* (December 24, 2001): 24.

Cycle Counting

Even though an organization may have made substantial efforts to record inventory accurately, these records must be verified through a continuing audit. Such audits are known as **cycle counting**. Historically, many firms performed annual physical inventories. This practice often meant shutting down the facility and having inexperienced people count parts and material. Inventory records should instead be verified via cycle counting. Cycle counting uses inventory classifications developed through ABC analysis. With cycle counting procedures, items are counted, records are verified, and inaccuracies are periodically documented. The cause of inaccuracies is then traced and appropriate remedial action taken to ensure integrity of the inventory system. A items will be counted frequently, perhaps once a month; B items will be counted less frequently, perhaps once a quarter; and C items will be counted perhaps once every 6 months. Example 2 illustrates how to compute the number of items of each classification to be counted each day.

Cycle counting
A continuing reconciliation of inventory with inventory records.

Learning Objective

2. Explain and use cycle counting

◀ *At John Deere, two workers fill orders for 3,000 parts from a six-stand carousel system, using a sophisticated computer system. The computer saves time searching for parts and speeds orders in the miles of warehouse shelving. While a worker pulls a part from one carousel, the computer sends the next request to the adjacent carousel.*

Cole's Trucks, Inc., a builder of high-quality refuse trucks, has about 5,000 items in its inventory. It wants to determine how many items to cycle count each day.

Approach: After hiring Matt Clark, a bright young OM student, for the summer, the firm determined that it has 500 A items, 1,750 B items, and 2,750 C items. Company policy is to count all A items every month (every 20 working days), all B items every quarter (every 60 working days), and all C items every 6 months (every 120 working days). The firm then allocates some items to be counted each day.

EXAMPLE 2

Cycle counting at a truck manufacturer

solution:

Item Class	Quantity	Cycle Counting Policy	Number of Items Counted per Day
A	500	Each month (20 working days)	500/20 = 25/day
B	1,750	Each quarter (60 working days)	1,750/60 ≅ 29/day
C	2,750	Every 6 months (120 working days)	2,750/120 = 23/day
			77/day

Seventy-seven items are counted each day.

Insight: This daily audit of 77 items is much more efficient and accurate than conducting a massive inventory count once a year.

Learning exercise: Cole's reclassifies some B and C items so there are now 1,500 B items and 3,000 C items. How does this change the cycle count? [Answer: B and C both change to 25 items each per day, for a total of 75 items per day.]

Related problem: 12.4

In Example 2, the particular items to be cycle counted can be sequentially or randomly selected each day. Another option is to cycle count items when they are reordered.

Cycle counting also has the following advantages:

1. Eliminates the shutdown and interruption of production necessary for annual physical inventories.
2. Eliminates annual inventory adjustments.
3. Trained personnel audit the accuracy of inventory.
4. Allows the cause of the errors to be identified and remedial action to be taken.
5. Maintains accurate inventory records.

Control of Service Inventories

Shrinkage
Retail inventory that is unaccounted for between receipt and sale.

Pilferage
A small amount of theft.

Management of service inventories deserves special consideration. Although we may think of the service sector of our economy as not having inventory, that is not always the case. For instance, extensive inventory is held in wholesale and retail businesses, making inventory management crucial and often a factor in a manager's advancement. In the food-service business, for example, control of inventory can make the difference between success and failure. Moreover, inventory that is in transit or idle in a warehouse is lost value. Similarly, inventory damaged or stolen prior to sale is a loss. In retailing, inventory that is unaccounted for between receipt and time of sale is known as **shrinkage**. Shrinkage occurs from damage and theft as well as from sloppy paperwork. Inventory theft is also known as **pilferage**. Retail inventory loss of 1% of sales is consid-

▶ *Pharmaceutical distributor McKesson Corp., which is one of Arnold Palmer Hospital's main suppliers of surgical materials, makes heavy use of bar-code readers to automate inventory control. The device on the warehouse worker's arm combines a scanner, a computer, and a two-way radio to check orders. With rapid and accurate data, items are easily verified, improving inventory and shipment accuracy.*

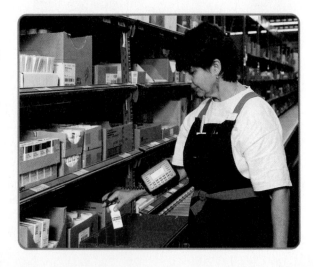

ered good, with losses in many stores exceeding 3%. Because the impact on profitability is substantial, inventory accuracy and control are critical. Applicable techniques include the following:

1. *Good personnel selection, training, and discipline:* These are never easy but very necessary in food-service, wholesale, and retail operations, where employees have access to directly consumable merchandise.
2. *Tight control of incoming shipments:* This task is being addressed by many firms through the use of bar-code and radio frequency ID (RFID) systems that read every incoming shipment and automatically check tallies against purchase orders. When properly designed, these systems are very hard to defeat. Each item has its own unique stock keeping unit (SKU; pronounced "skew").
3. *Effective control of all goods leaving the facility:* This job is accomplished with bar codes on items being shipped, magnetic strips on merchandise, or via direct observation. Direct observation can be personnel stationed at exits (as at Costco and Sam's Club wholesale stores) and in potentially high-loss areas or can take the form of one-way mirrors and video surveillance.

Handheld reader can scan RFID tags, aiding control of both incoming and outgoing shipments.

Successful retail operations require very good store-level control with accurate inventory in its proper location. One recent study found that consumers and clerks could not find 16% of the items at one of the U.S.'s largest retailers—not because the items were out of stock but because they were misplaced (in a backroom, a storage area, or on the wrong aisle). By the researcher's estimates, major retailers lose 10% to 25% of overall profits due to poor or inaccurate inventory records.[2]

INVENTORY MODELS

We now examine a variety of inventory models and the costs associated with them.

Independent vs. Dependent Demand

Inventory control models assume that demand for an item is either independent of or dependent on the demand for other items. For example, the demand for refrigerators is *independent* of the demand for toaster ovens. However, the demand for toaster oven components is *dependent* on the requirements of toaster ovens.

This chapter focuses on managing inventory where demand is *independent*. Chapter 14 presents *dependent* demand management.

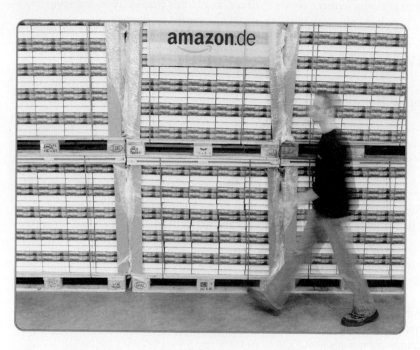

◀ *Even for a firm that manages its inventory better than most, Amazon was overwhelmed with the warehousing costs of the latest Harry Potter book. With popular products and seasonality causing surges in demand, retailers and suppliers often rely on large inventories. Full warehouses in November, in preparation for the holiday season, can mean huge holding costs.*

[2]See E. Malykhina, "Retailers Take Stock," *Information Week* (February 7, 2005): 20–22 and A. Raman, N. DeHoratius, and Z. Ton, "Execution: The Missing Link in Retail Operations," *California Management Review* 43, no. 3 (spring 2001): 136–141.

► **Table 12.1**

Determining Inventory Holding Costs

Category	Cost (and range) as a Percent of Inventory Value
Housing costs (building rent or depreciation, operating cost, taxes, insurance)	6% (3–10%)
Material handling costs (equipment lease or depreciation, power, operating cost)	3% (1–3.5%)
Labor cost (receiving, warehousing, security)	3% (3–5%)
Investment costs (borrowing costs, taxes, and insurance on inventory)	11% (6–24%)
Pilferage, scrap, and obsolescence (much higher in rapid-change industries like PCs and cell phones)	3% (2–5%)
Overall carrying cost	**26%**

Note: All numbers are approximate, as they vary substantially depending on the nature of the business, location, and current interest rates. Any inventory holding cost of less than 15% is suspect, but annual inventory holding costs often approach 40% of the value of inventory and even more in high tech and fashion industries.

Holding, Ordering, and Setup Costs

Holding cost

The cost to keep or carry inventory in stock.

Holding costs are the costs associated with holding or "carrying" inventory over time. Therefore, holding costs also include obsolescence and costs related to storage, such as insurance, extra staffing, and interest payments. Table 12.1 shows the kinds of costs that need to be evaluated to determine holding costs. Many firms fail to include all the inventory holding costs. Consequently, inventory holding costs are often understated.

Ordering cost

The cost of the ordering process.

Ordering cost includes costs of supplies, forms, order processing, purchasing, clerical support, and so forth. When orders are being manufactured, ordering costs also exist, but they are a part of what is called setup costs. **Setup cost** is the cost to prepare a machine or process for manufacturing an order. This includes time and labor to clean and change tools or holders. Operations managers can lower ordering costs by reducing setup costs and by using such efficient procedures as electronic ordering and payment.

Setup cost

The cost to prepare a machine or process for production.

Setup time

The time required to prepare a machine or process for production.

In many environments, setup cost is highly correlated with **setup time**. Setups usually require a substantial amount of work before a setup is actually performed at the work center. With proper planning much of the preparation required by a setup can be done prior to shutting down the machine or process. Setup times can thus be reduced substantially. Machines and processes that traditionally have taken hours to set up are now being set up in less than a minute by the more imaginative world-class manufacturers. As we shall see later in this chapter, reducing setup times is an excellent way to reduce inventory investment and to improve productivity.

INVENTORY MODELS FOR INDEPENDENT DEMAND

In this section, we introduce three inventory models that address two important questions: *when to order* and *how much to order*. These *independent* demand models are:

1. Basic economic order quantity (EOQ) model
2. Production order quantity model
3. Quantity discount model

The Basic Economic Order Quantity (EOQ) Model

Economic order quantity (EOQ) model

An inventory-control technique that minimizes the total of ordering and holding costs.

The **economic order quantity (EOQ) model** is one of the oldest and most commonly known inventory-control techniques.[3] This technique is relatively easy to use but is based on several assumptions:

1. Demand is known, constant, and independent.
2. Lead time—that is, the time between placement and receipt of the order—is known and constant.
3. Receipt of inventory is instantaneous and complete. In other words, the inventory from an order arrives in one batch at one time.
4. Quantity discounts are not possible.

[3]The research on EOQ dates to 1915; see Ford W. Harris, *Operations and Cost* (Chicago: A. W. Shaw, 1915).

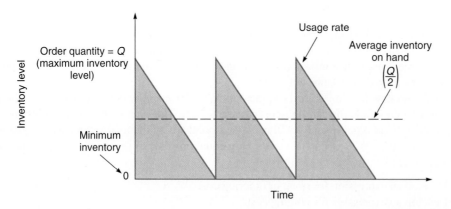

5. The only variable costs are the cost of setting up or placing an order (setup cost) and the cost of holding or storing inventory over time (holding or carrying cost). These costs were discussed in the previous section.
6. Stockouts (shortages) can be completely avoided if orders are placed at the right time.

With these assumptions, the graph of inventory usage over time has a sawtooth shape, as in Figure 12.3. In Figure 12.3, Q represents the amount that is ordered. If this amount is 500 dresses, all 500 dresses arrive at one time (when an order is received). Thus, the inventory level jumps from 0 to 500 dresses. In general, an inventory level increases from 0 to Q units when an order arrives.

Because demand is constant over time, inventory drops at a uniform rate over time. (Refer to the sloped lines in Figure 12.3.) Each time the inventory level reaches 0, the new order is placed and received, and the inventory level again jumps to Q units (represented by the vertical lines). This process continues indefinitely over time.

Minimizing Costs

The objective of most inventory models is to minimize total costs. With the assumptions just given, significant costs are setup (or ordering) cost and holding (or carrying) cost. All other costs, such as the cost of the inventory itself, are constant. Thus, if we minimize the sum of setup and holding costs, we will also be minimizing total costs. To help you visualize this, in Figure 12.4 we graph total costs as a function of the order quantity, Q. The optimal order size, Q^*, will be the quantity that minimizes the total costs. As the quantity ordered increases, the total number of orders placed per year will decrease. Thus, as the quantity ordered increases, the annual setup or ordering cost will decrease. But as the order quantity increases, the holding cost will increase due to the larger average inventories that are maintained.

As we can see in Figure 12.4, a reduction in either holding or setup cost will reduce the total cost curve. A reduction in setup cost curve also reduces the optimal order quantity (lot size). In

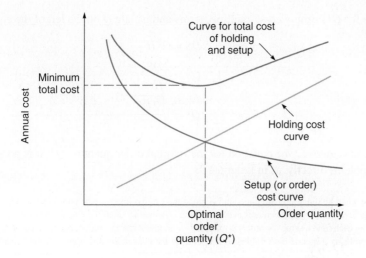

addition, smaller lot sizes have a positive impact on quality and production flexibility. At Toshiba, the $40 billion Japanese conglomerate, workers can make as few as 10 laptop computers before changing models. This lot-size flexibility has allowed Toshiba to move toward a "build-to-order" mass customization system, an important ability in an industry that has product life cycles measured in months, not years.

You should note that in Figure 12.4, the optimal order quantity occurs at the point where the ordering-cost curve and the carrying-cost curve intersect. This was not by chance. With the EOQ model, the optimal order quantity will occur at a point where the total setup cost is equal to the total holding cost.[4] We use this fact to develop equations that solve directly for Q^*. The necessary steps are:

1. Develop an expression for setup or ordering cost.
2. Develop an expression for holding cost.
3. Set setup cost equal to holding cost.
4. Solve the equation for the optimal order quantity.

Using the following variables, we can determine setup and holding costs and solve for Q^*:

$$Q = \text{Number of units per order}$$
$$Q^* = \text{Optimum number of units per order (EOQ)}$$
$$D = \text{Annual demand in units for the inventory item}$$
$$S = \text{Setup or ordering cost for each order}$$
$$H = \text{Holding or carrying cost per unit per year}$$

1. Annual set up cost = (Number of orders placed per year) × (Setup or order cost per order)

$$= \left(\frac{\text{Annual demand}}{\text{Number of units in each order}} \right) (\text{Setup or order cost per order})$$

$$= \left(\frac{D}{Q} \right) (S) = \frac{D}{Q} S$$

2. Annual holding cost = (Average inventory level) × (Holding cost per unit per year)

$$= \left(\frac{\text{Order quantity}}{2} \right) (\text{Holding cost per unit per year})$$

$$= \left(\frac{Q}{2} \right) (H) = \frac{Q}{2} H$$

3. Optimal order quantity is found when annual setup cost equals annual holding cost, namely:

$$\frac{D}{Q} S = \frac{Q}{2} H$$

4. To solve for Q^*, simply cross-multiply terms and isolate Q on the left of the equal sign:

$$2DS = Q^2 H$$

$$Q^2 = \frac{2DS}{H}$$

$$Q^* = \sqrt{\frac{2DS}{H}} \tag{12-1}$$

Now that we have derived the equation for the optimal order quantity, Q^*, it is possible to solve inventory problems directly, as in Example 3.

---

[4]This is the case when holding costs are linear and begin at the origin—that is, when inventory costs do not decline (or they increase) as inventory volume increases and all holding costs are in small increments. Additionally, there is probably some learning each time a setup (or order) is executed—a fact that lowers subsequent setup costs. Consequently, the EOQ model is probably a special case. However, we abide by the conventional wisdom that this model is a reasonable approximation.

Sharp, Inc., a company that markets painless hypodermic needles to hospitals, would like to reduce its inventory cost by determining the optimal number of hypodermic needles to obtain per order.

Approach: The annual demand is 1,000 units; setup or ordering cost is $10 per order; and the holding cost per unit per year is $.50.

Solution: Using these figures, we can calculate the optimal number of units per order:

$$Q^* = \sqrt{\frac{2DS}{H}}$$

$$Q^* = \sqrt{\frac{2(1,000)(10)}{0.50}} = \sqrt{40,000} = 200 \text{ units}$$

Insight: Sharp, Inc., now knows how many needles to order per order. The firm also has a basis for determining ordering and holding costs for this item, as well as the number of orders to be processed by the receiving and inventory departments.

Learning exercise: If D increases to 1,200 units, what is the new Q^*? [Answer: $Q^* = 219$ units.]

Related problems: 12.5, 12.6, 12.7, 12.8, 12.9, 12.12, 12.13, 12.15, 12.36, 12.38

EXAMPLE 3

Finding the optimal order size at Sharp, Inc.

Excel OM Data File Ch12Ex3.xls

We can also determine the expected number of orders placed during the year (N) and the expected time between orders (T), as follows:

$$\text{Expected number of orders} = N = \frac{\text{Demand}}{\text{Order quantity}} = \frac{D}{Q^*} \tag{12-2}$$

$$\text{Expected time between orders} = T = \frac{\text{Number of working days per year}}{N} \tag{12-3}$$

Example 4 illustrates this concept.

Sharp, Inc. (in Example 3), has a 250-day working year and wants to find the number of orders (N) and the expected time between orders (T).

Approach: Using Equations (12-2) and (12-3), Sharp enters the data given in Example 3.

Solution:

$$N = \frac{\text{Demand}}{\text{Order quantity}}$$

$$= \frac{1,000}{200} = 5 \text{ orders per year}$$

$$T = \frac{\text{Number of working days per year}}{\text{Expected number of orders}}$$

$$= \frac{250 \text{ working days per year}}{5 \text{ orders}} = 50 \text{ days between orders}$$

Insight: The company now knows not only how many needles to order per order but that the time between orders is 50 days and that there are five orders per year.

Learning exercise: If $D = 1,200$ units instead of 1,000, find N and T. [Answer: $N \cong 5.48$, $T = 45.62$.]

Related problems: 12.12, 12.13, 12.15

EXAMPLE 4

Computing number of orders and time between orders at Sharp, Inc.

As mentioned earlier in this section, the total annual variable inventory cost is the sum of setup and holding costs:

$$\text{Total annual cost} = \text{Setup (order) cost} + \text{Holding cost} \tag{12-4}$$

In terms of the variables in the model, we can express the total cost TC as:

$$TC = \frac{D}{Q}S + \frac{Q}{2}H \tag{12-5}$$

Example 5 shows how to use this formula.

Active Model 12.1

Examples 3, 4, and 5 are further illustrated in Active Model 12.1 on your CD-ROM and in the Exercise located on page 515.

▶ *This store takes 4 weeks to get an order for Levis 501 jeans filled by the manufacturer. If the store sells 10 pairs of size 30–32 Levis a week, the store manager could set up two containers, keep 40 pairs of jeans in the second container, and place an order whenever the first container is empty. This would be a fixed-quantity reordering system. It is also called a "two-bin" system and is an example of a very elementary, but effective, approach to inventory management*

EXAMPLE 5

Computing combined cost of ordering and holding

Sharp, Inc. (from Examples 3 and 4), wants to determine the combined annual ordering and holding costs.

Approach: Apply Equation (12-5), using the data in Example 3.

Solution:

$$TC = \frac{D}{Q}S + \frac{Q}{2}H$$

$$= \frac{1{,}000}{200}(\$10) + \frac{200}{2}(\$.50)$$

$$= (5)(\$10) + (100)(\$.50)$$

$$= \$50 + \$50 = \$100$$

Insight: These are the annual setup and holding costs. The $100 total does not include the actual cost of goods. Notice that in the EOQ model, holding costs always equal setup (order) costs.

Learning exercise: Find the total annual cost if $D = 1{,}200$ units in Example 3. [Answer: $109.54.]

Related problems: 12.9, 12.12, 12.13, 12.14, 12.38b,c

Inventory costs may also be expressed to include the actual cost of the material purchased. If we assume that the annual demand and the price per hypodermic needle are known values (e.g., 1,000 hypodermics per year at $P = \$10$) and total annual cost should include purchase cost, then Equation (12-5) becomes:

$$TC = \frac{D}{Q}S + \frac{Q}{2}H + PD$$

Because material cost does not depend on the particular order policy, we still incur an annual material cost of $D \times P = (1{,}000)\ (\$10) = \$10{,}000$. (Later in this chapter we will discuss the case in which this may not be true—namely, when a quantity discount is available.)[5]

---

[5]The formula for the economic order quantity (Q^*) can also be determined by finding where the total cost curve is at a minimum (i.e., where the slope of the total cost curve is zero). Using calculus, we set the derivative of the total cost with respect to Q^* equal to 0.

The calculations for finding the minimum of $TC = \frac{D}{Q}S + \frac{Q}{2}H + PD$

are $\dfrac{d(TC)}{dQ} = \left(\dfrac{-DS}{Q^2}\right) + \dfrac{H}{2} + 0 = 0$

Thus, $Q^* = \sqrt{\dfrac{2DS}{H}}$.

Robust Model   A benefit of the EOQ model is that it is robust. By **robust** we mean that it gives satisfactory answers even with substantial variation in its parameters. As we have observed, determining accurate ordering costs and holding costs for inventory is often difficult. Consequently, a robust model is advantageous. Total cost of the EOQ changes little in the neighborhood of the minimum. The curve is very shallow. This means that variations in setup costs, holding costs, demand, or even EOQ make relatively modest differences in total cost. Example 6 shows the robustness of EOQ.

Robust

Giving satisfactory answers even with substantial variation in the parameters.

EXAMPLE 6

EOQ is a robust model

Management in the Sharp, Inc., examples underestimates total annual demand by 50% (say demand is actually 1,500 needles rather than 1,000 needles) while using the same Q. How will the annual inventory cost be impacted?

Approach: We will solve for annual costs twice. First, we will apply the wrong EOQ; then we will recompute costs with the correct EOQ.

Solution: The annual inventory cost increases only $25 ($100 vs. $125), or 25%. Here is why: If demand in Example 5 is actually 1,500 needles rather than 1,000, but management uses an order quantity of $Q = 200$ (when it should be $Q = 244.9$ based on $D = 1,500$), the sum of holding and ordering cost increases 25%:

$$\text{Annual cost} = \frac{D}{Q}S + \frac{Q}{2}H$$
$$= \frac{1,500}{200}(\$10) + \frac{200}{2}(\$.50)$$
$$= \$75 + \$50 = \$125$$

However, had we known that the demand was for 1,500 with an EOQ of 244.9 units, we would have spent $122.47, as shown:

$$\text{Annual cost} = \frac{1,500}{244.9}(\$10) + \frac{244.9}{2}(\$.50)$$
$$= 6.125(\$10) + 122.45(\$.50)$$
$$= \$61.25 + \$61.22 = \$122.47$$

Insight: Note that the expenditure of $125.00, made with an estimate of demand that was substantially wrong, is only 2% ($2.52/$122.47) higher than we would have paid had we known the actual demand and ordered accordingly. Note also, that were if not due to rounding, the annual holding costs and ordering costs would be exactly equal.

Learning exercise: Demand at Sharp remains at 1,000, H is still $.50, and we order 200 needles at a time (as in Example 5). But if the true order cost = $S = \$15$ (rather than $10), what is the annual cost? [Answer: Annual order cost increases to $75, and annual holding cost stays at $50. So the total cost = $125.]

Related problems: 12.8b, 12.14

We may conclude that the EOQ is indeed robust and that significant errors do not cost us very much. This attribute of the EOQ model is most convenient because our ability to accurately forecast demand, holding cost, and ordering cost is limited.

Reorder Points

Now that we have decided *how much* to order, we will look at the second inventory question, *when* to order. Simple inventory models assume that receipt of an order is instantaneous. In other words, they assume (1) that a firm will place an order when the inventory level for that particular item reaches zero and (2) that it will receive the ordered items immediately. However, the time between placement and receipt of an order, called **lead time**, or delivery time, can be as short as a few

Lead time

In purchasing systems, the time between placing an order and receiving it; in production systems, the wait, move, queue, setup, and run times for each component produced.

► **Figure 12.5**

The Reorder Point (ROP)

Q^* is the optimum order quantity, and lead time represents the time between placing and receiving an order.

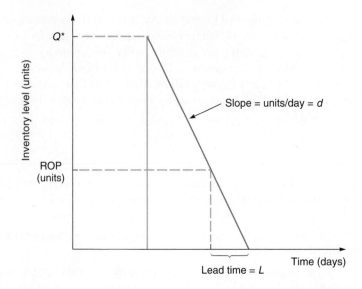

hours or as long as months. Thus, the when-to-order decision is usually expressed in terms of a **reorder point (ROP)**—the inventory level at which an order should be placed (see Figure 12.5).

The reorder point (ROP) is given as:

$$\text{ROP} = (\text{Demand per day}) \times (\text{Lead time for a new order in days})$$
$$= d \times L \tag{12-6}$$

This equation for ROP *assumes that demand during lead time and lead time itself are constant.* When this is not the case, extra stock, often called **safety stock**, should be added.

The demand per day, d, is found by dividing the annual demand, D, by the number of working days in a year:

$$d = \frac{D}{\text{Number of working days in a year}}$$

Computing the reorder point is demonstrated in Example 7.

Reorder point (ROP)
The inventory level (point) at which action is taken to replenish the stocked item.

Safety stock
Extra stock to allow for uneven demand; a buffer.

EXAMPLE 7

Computing reorder points (ROP) for iPods

An Apple distributor has a demand for 8,000 iPods per year. The firm operates a 250-day working year. On average, delivery of an order takes 3 working days. It wants to calculate the reorder point.

Approach: Compute the daily demand and then apply Equation (12-6).

Solution:
$$d = \frac{D}{\text{Number of working days in a year}} = \frac{8,000}{250}$$
$$= 32 \text{ units}$$
$$\text{ROP} = \text{Reorder point} = d \times L = 32 \text{ units per day} \times 3 \text{ days}$$
$$= 96 \text{ units}$$

Insight: Thus, when iPod inventory stock drops to 96 units, an order should be placed. The order will arrive 3 days later, just as the distributor's stock is depleted.

Learning exercise: If there are only 200 working days per year, what is the correct ROP? [Answer: 120 iPods.]

Related problems: 12.9d, 12.10, 12.11, 12.13f

Learning Objective

4. Compute a reorder point and explain safety stock

Safety stock is especially important in firms whose raw material deliveries may be uniquely unreliable. For example, San Miguel Corp. in the Philippines uses cheese curd imported from Europe. Because the normal mode of delivery is lengthy and variable, safety stock may be substantial.

Production Order Quantity Model

In the previous inventory model, we assumed that the entire inventory order was received at one time. There are times, however, when the firm may receive its inventory over a period of time. Such cases require a different model, one that does not require the instantaneous-receipt assumption. This model is applicable under two situations: (1) when inventory continuously flows or builds up over a period of time after an order has been placed or (2) when units are produced and sold simultaneously. Under these circumstances, we take into account daily production (or inventory-flow) rate and daily demand rate. Figure 12.6 shows inventory levels as a function of time.

Because this model is especially suitable for the production environment, it is commonly called the **production order quantity model**. It is useful when inventory continuously builds up over time, and traditional economic order quantity assumptions are valid. We derive this model by setting ordering or setup costs equal to holding costs and solving for optimal order size, Q^*. Using the following symbols, we can determine the expression for annual inventory holding cost for the production order quantity model:

Learning Objective

5. Apply the production order quantity model

Production order quantity model
An economic order quantity technique applied to production orders.

$$Q = \text{Number of units per order}$$
$$H = \text{Holding cost per unit per year}$$
$$p = \text{Daily production rate}$$
$$d = \text{Daily demand rate, or usage rate}$$
$$t = \text{Length of the production run in days}$$

1. $\left(\begin{array}{c}\text{Annual inventory}\\\text{holding cost}\end{array}\right) = (\text{Average inventory level}) \times \left(\begin{array}{c}\text{Holding cost}\\\text{per unit per year}\end{array}\right)$

2. $\left(\begin{array}{c}\text{Average inventory}\\\text{level}\end{array}\right) = (\text{Maximum inventory level})/2$

3. $\left(\begin{array}{c}\text{Maximum}\\\text{inventory level}\end{array}\right) = \left(\begin{array}{c}\text{Total production during}\\\text{the production run}\end{array}\right) - \left(\begin{array}{c}\text{Total used during}\\\text{the production run}\end{array}\right)$
$$= pt - dt$$

However, $Q = \text{total produced} = pt$, and thus $t = Q/p$. Therefore:

$$\text{Maximum inventory level} = p\left(\frac{Q}{p}\right) - d\left(\frac{Q}{p}\right) = Q - \frac{d}{p}Q$$

$$= Q\left(1 - \frac{d}{p}\right)$$

4. Annual inventory holding cost (or simply holding cost) =

$$\frac{\text{Maximum inventory level}}{2}(H) = \frac{Q}{2}\left[1 - \left(\frac{d}{p}\right)\right]H$$

◀ **Figure 12.6**

Change in Inventory Levels over Time for the Production Model

▶ *Each order may require a change in the way a machine or process is set up. Reducing setup time usually means a reduction in setup cost; and reductions in setup costs make smaller batches (lots) economical to produce. Increasingly, set up (and operation) is performed by computer-controlled machines, such as this one, operating from previously written programs.*

Using this expression for holding cost and the expression for setup cost developed in the basic EOQ model, we solve for the optimal number of pieces per order by equating setup cost and holding cost:

$$\text{Setup cost} = (D/Q)S$$

$$\text{Holding cost} = \tfrac{1}{2} HQ[1 - (d/p)]$$

Set ordering cost equal to holding cost to obtain Q_p^*:

$$\frac{D}{Q}S = \tfrac{1}{2} HQ[1 - (d/p)]$$

$$Q^2 = \frac{2DS}{H[1 - (d/p)]}$$

$$Q_p^* = \sqrt{\frac{2DS}{H[1 - (d/p)]}} \tag{12-7}$$

In Example 8, we use the above equation, Q_p^*, to solve for the optimum order or production quantity when inventory is consumed as it is produced.

EXAMPLE 8

A production order quantity model

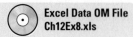

Excel Data OM File Ch12Ex8.xls

Nathan Manufacturing, Inc., makes and sells specialty hubcaps for the retail automobile aftermarket. Nathan's forecast for its wire-wheel hubcap is 1,000 units next year, with an average daily demand of 4 units. However, the production process is most efficient at 8 units per day. So the company produces 8 per day but uses only 4 per day. The company wants to solve for the optimum number of units per order. (*Note:* This plant schedules production of this hubcap only as needed, during the 250 days per year the shop operates.)

Approach: Gather the cost data and apply Equation (12-7):

$$\text{Annual demand} = D = 1,000 \text{ units}$$
$$\text{Setup costs} = S = \$10$$
$$\text{Holding cost} = H = \$0.50 \text{ per unit per year}$$
$$\text{Daily production rate} = p = 8 \text{ units daily}$$
$$\text{Daily demand rate} = d = 4 \text{ units daily}$$

solution:

$$Q_p^* = \sqrt{\frac{2DS}{H[1-(d/p)]}}$$

$$Q_p^* = \sqrt{\frac{2(1,000)(10)}{0.50[1-(4/8)]}}$$

$$= \sqrt{\frac{20,000}{0.50(1/2)}} = \sqrt{80,000}$$

$$= 282.8 \text{ hubcaps, or } 283 \text{ hubcaps}$$

Insight: The difference between the production order quantity model and the basic EOQ model is the annual holding cost, which is reduced in the production order quantity model.

Learning exercise: If Nathan can increase its daily production rate from 8 to 10, how does Q_p^* change? [Answer: $Q_p^* = 258$.]

Related problems: 12.16, 12.17, 12.18, 12.37

Active Model 12.2

Example 8 is further illustrated in Active Model 12.2 on the CD-ROM.

You may want to compare this solution with the answer in Example 3, which had identical *D*, *S*, and *H* values. Eliminating the instantaneous-receipt assumption, where $p = 8$ and $d = 4$, resulted in an increase in *Q** from 200 in Example 3 to 283 in Example 8. This increase in *Q** occurred because holding cost dropped from \$.50 to (\$.50 × $\frac{1}{2}$), making a larger order quantity optimal. Also note that:

$$d = 4 = \frac{D}{\text{Number of days the plant is in operation}} = \frac{1,000}{250}$$

We can also calculate Q_p^* when *annual* data are available. When annual data are used, we can express Q_p^* as:

$$Q_p^* = \sqrt{\frac{2DS}{H\left(1 - \dfrac{\text{Annual demand rate}}{\text{Annual production rate}}\right)}} \tag{12-8}$$

OM in Action   Inventory Accuracy at Milton Bradley

Milton Bradley, a division of Hasbro, Inc., has been manufacturing toys for more than 100 years. Founded by Milton Bradley in 1860, the company started by making a lithograph of Abraham Lincoln. Using his printing skills, Bradley developed games, including the Game of Life, Chutes and Ladders, Candy Land, Scrabble, and Lite Brite. Today, the company produces hundreds of games, requiring billions of plastic parts.

Once Milton Bradley has determined the optimal quantities for each production run, it must make them and assemble them as a part of the proper game. Some games require literally hundreds of plastic parts, including spinners, hotels, people, animals, cars, and so on. According to Gary Brennan, director of manufacturing, getting the right number of pieces to the right toys and production lines is the most important issue for the credibility of the company. Some orders can require 20,000 or more perfectly assembled games delivered to their warehouses in a matter of days.

Games with the incorrect number of parts and pieces can result in some very unhappy customers. It is also

time-consuming and expensive for Milton Bradley to supply the extra parts or to have toys or games returned. When shortages are found during the assembly stage, the entire production run is stopped until the problem is corrected. Counting parts by hand or machine is not always accurate. As a result, Milton Bradley now weighs pieces and completed games to determine if the correct number of parts have been included. If the weight is not exact, there is a problem that is resolved before shipment. Using highly accurate digital scales, Milton Bradley is now able to get the right parts in the right game at the right time. Without this simple innovation, the most sophisticated production schedule is meaningless.

Sources: The Wall Street Journal (April 15, 1999): B1; *Plastics World* (March 1997): 22–26; and *Modern Materials Handling* (September 1997): 55–57.

Quantity Discount Models

To increase sales, many companies offer quantity discounts to their customers. A **quantity discount** is simply a reduced price (P) for an item when it is purchased in larger quantities. Discount schedules with several discounts for large orders are common. A typical quantity discount schedule appears in Table 12.2. As can be seen in the table, the normal price of the item is $5. When 1,000 to 1,999 units are ordered at one time, the price per unit drops to $4.80; when the quantity ordered at one time is 2,000 units or more, the price is $4.75 per unit. As always, management must decide when and how much to order. However, with an opportunity to save money on quantity discounts, how does the operations manager make these decisions?

As with other inventory models discussed so far, the overall objective is to minimize total cost. Because the unit cost for the third discount in Table 12.2 is the lowest, you may be tempted to order 2,000 units or more merely to take advantage of the lower product cost. Placing an order for that quantity, however, even with the greatest discount price, may not minimize total inventory cost. Granted, as discount quantity goes up, the product cost goes down. However, holding cost increases because orders are larger. Thus the major trade-off when considering quantity discounts is between *reduced product cost* and *increased holding cost*. When we include the cost of the product, the equation for the total annual inventory cost can be calculated as follows:

$$\text{Total cost} = \text{Setup cost} + \text{Holding cost} + \text{Product cost}$$

or

$$TC = \frac{D}{Q}S + \frac{Q}{2}H + PD \tag{12-9}$$

where Q = Quantity ordered
   D = Annual demand in units
   S = Ordering or setup cost per order or per setup
   P = Price per unit
   H = Holding cost per unit per year

Now, we have to determine the quantity that will minimize the total annual inventory cost. Because there are several discounts, this process involves four steps:

Step 1: For each discount, calculate a value for optimal order size Q^*, using the following equation:

$$Q^* = \sqrt{\frac{2DS}{IP}} \tag{12-10}$$

Note that the holding cost is IP instead of H. Because the price of the item is a factor in annual holding cost, we cannot assume that the holding cost is a constant when the price per unit changes for each quantity discount. Thus, it is common to express the holding cost as a percent (I) of unit price (P) instead of as a constant cost per unit per year, H.

Step 2: For any discount, if the order quantity is too low to qualify for the discount, adjust the order quantity upward to the *lowest* quantity that will qualify for the discount. For example, if Q^* for discount 2 in Table 12.2 were 500 units, you would adjust this value up to 1,000 units. Look at the second discount in Table 12.2. Order quantities between 1,000 and 1,999 will qualify for the 4% discount. Thus, if Q^* is below 1,000 units, we will adjust the order quantity up to 1,000 units.

▶ **Table 12.2**

A Quantity Discount Schedule

Discount Number	Discount Quantity	Discount (%)	Discount Price (P)
1	0 to 999	no discount	$5.00
2	1,000 to 1,999	4	$4.80
3	2,000 and over	5	$4.75

◀ **Figure 12.7**

**Total Cost Curve for the
Quantity Discount Model**

The reasoning for step 2 may not be obvious. If the order quantity, Q^*, is below the range that will qualify for a discount, a quantity within this range may still result in the lowest total cost.

As shown in Figure 12.7, the total cost curve is broken into three different total cost curves. There is a total cost curve for the first ($0 \leq Q \leq 999$), second ($1,000 \leq Q \leq 1,999$), and third ($Q \geq 2,000$) discount. Look at the total cost (TC) curve for discount 2. Q^* for discount 2 is less than the allowable discount range, which is from 1,000 to 1,999 units. As the figure shows, the lowest allowable quantity in this range, which is 1,000 units, is the quantity that minimizes total cost. Thus, the second step is needed to ensure that we do not discard an order quantity that may indeed produce the minimum cost. Note that an order quantity computed in step 1 that is *greater* than the range that would qualify it for a discount may be discarded.

Step 3: Using the preceding total cost equation, compute a total cost for every Q^* determined in steps 1 and 2. If you had to adjust Q^* upward because it was below the allowable quantity range, be sure to use the adjusted value for Q^*.

Step 4: Select the Q^* that has the lowest total cost, as computed in step 3. It will be the quantity that will minimize the total inventory cost.

Let us see how this procedure can be applied with an example.

Wohl's Discount Store stocks toy race cars. Recently, the store has been given a quantity discount schedule for these cars. This quantity schedule was shown in Table 12.2. Thus, the normal cost for the toy race cars is $5.00. For orders between 1,000 and 1,999 units, the unit cost drops to $4.80; for orders of 2,000 or more units, the unit cost is only $4.75. Furthermore, ordering cost is $49.00 per order, annual demand is 5,000 race cars, and inventory carrying charge, as a percent of cost, I, is 20%, or .2. What order quantity will minimize the total inventory cost?

Approach: We will follow the four steps just outlined for a quantity discount model.

Solution: The first step is to compute Q^* for every discount in Table 12.2. This is done as follows:

$$Q_1^* = \sqrt{\frac{2(5,000)(49)}{(.2)(5.00)}} = 700 \text{ cars per order}$$

$$Q_2^* = \sqrt{\frac{2(5,000)(49)}{(.2)(4.80)}} = 714 \text{ cars per order}$$

$$Q_3^* = \sqrt{\frac{2(5,000)(49)}{(.2)(4.75)}} = 718 \text{ cars per order}$$

EXAMPLE 9

**Quantity discount
model**

**Excel OM Data File
Ch12Ex9.xls**

The second step is to adjust upward those values of Q^* that are below the allowable discount range. Since Q_1^* is between 0 and 999, it need not be adjusted. Because Q_2^* is below the allowable range of 1,000 to 1,999, it must be adjusted to 1,000 units. The same is true for Q_3^*: It must be adjusted to 2,000 units. After this step, the following order quantities must be tested in the total cost equation:

$$Q_1^* = 700$$

$$Q_2^* = 1,000\text{—adjusted}$$

$$Q_3^* = 2,000\text{—adjusted}$$

The third step is to use the total cost equation (12-9) and compute a total cost for each order quantity. This step is taken with the aid of Table 12.3, which presents the computations for each level of discount introduced in Table 12.2.

▶ **Table 12.3**

Total Cost Computations for Wohl's Discount Store

Discount Number	Unit Price	Order Quantity	Annual Product Cost	Annual Ordering Cost	Annual Holding Cost	Total
1	$5.00	700	$25,000	$350	$350	$25,700
2	$4.80	1,000	$24,000	$245	$480	$24,725
3	$4.75	2,000	$23,750	$122.50	$950	$24,822.50

The fourth step is to select that order quantity with the lowest total cost. Looking at Table 12.3, you can see that an order quantity of 1,000 toy race cars will minimize the total cost. You should see, however, that the total cost for ordering 2,000 cars is only slightly greater than the total cost for ordering 1,000 cars. Thus, if the third discount cost is lowered to $4.65, for example, then this quantity might be the one that minimizes total inventory cost.

Insight: The quantity discount model's third cost factor, annual product cost, is now a major variable with impact on the final cost and decision. It takes substantial increases in order and holding costs to compensate for a large quantity price break.

Learning exercise: Wohl's has just been offered a third price break. If it orders 2,500 or more cars at a time, the unit cost drops to $4.60. What is the optimal order quantity now? [Answer: $Q_4^* = 2,500$, for a total cost of $24,248.]

Related problems: 12.19, 12.20, 12.21, 12.22, 12.23, 12.24, 12.25

PROBABILISTIC MODELS AND SAFETY STOCK

All the inventory models we have discussed so far make the assumption that demand for a product is constant and certain. We now relax this assumption. The following inventory models apply when product demand is not known but can be specified by means of a probability distribution. These types of models are called **probabilistic models**.

Probabilistic model

A statistical model applicable when product demand or any other variable is not known but can be specified by means of a probability distribution.

Service level

The complement of the probability of a stockout.

An important concern of management is maintaining an adequate service level in the face of uncertain demand. The **service level** is the *complement* of the probability of a stockout. For instance, if the probability of a stockout is 0.05, then the service level is .95. Uncertain demand raises the possibility of a stockout. One method of reducing stockouts is to hold extra units in inventory. As we noted, such inventory is usually referred to as safety stock. It involves adding a number of units as a buffer to the reorder point. As you recall from our previous discussion:

$$\text{Reorder point} = \text{ROP} = d \times L$$

where d = Daily demand
  L = Order lead time, or number of working days it takes to deliver an order

The inclusion of safety stock (*ss*) changes the expression to:

$$\text{ROP} = d \times L + ss \tag{12-11}$$

The amount of safety stock maintained depends on the cost of incurring a stockout and the cost of holding the extra inventory. Annual stockout cost is computed as follows:

$$\text{Annual stockout costs} = \text{The sum of the units short for each demand level}$$
$$\times \text{The probability of that demand level} \times \text{The stockout cost/unit}$$
$$\times \text{The number of orders per year} \qquad \text{(12-12)}$$

Example 10 illustrates this concept.

David Rivera Optical has determined that its reorder point for eyeglass frames is 50 $(d \times L)$ units. Its carrying cost per frame per year is $5, and stockout (or lost sale) cost is $40 per frame. The store has experienced the following probability distribution for inventory demand during the reorder period. The optimum number of orders per year is six.

Number of Units	Probability
30	.2
40	.2
ROP → 50	.3
60	.2
70	.1
	1.0

How much safety stock should David Rivera keep on hand?

Approach: The objective is to find the amount of safety stock that minimizes the sum of the additional inventory holding costs and stockout costs. The annual holding cost is simply the holding cost per unit multiplied by the units added to the ROP. For example, a safety stock of 20 frames, which implies that the new ROP, with safety stock, is 70 (= 50 + 20), raises the annual carrying cost by $5(20) = $100.

However, computing annual stockout cost is more interesting. For any level of safety stock, stockout cost is the expected cost of stocking out. We can compute it, as in Equation (12-12), by multiplying the number of frames short (Demand – ROP) by the probability of demand at that level, by the stockout cost, by the number of times per year the stockout can occur (which in our case is the number of orders per year). Then we add stockout costs for each possible stockout level for a given ROP.

Solution: We begin by looking at zero safety stock. For this safety stock, a shortage of 10 frames will occur if demand is 60, and a shortage of 20 frames will occur if the demand is 70. Thus the stockout costs for zero safety stock are:

$$\text{(10 frames short) (.2) ($40 per stockout) (6 possible stockouts per year)}$$
$$+ \text{(20 frames short) (.1) ($40) (6)} = $960$$

The following table summarizes the total costs for each of the three alternatives:

Safety Stock	Additional Holding Cost	Stockout Cost		Total Cost
20	(20) ($5) = $100		$ 0	$100
10	(10) ($5) = $ 50	(10) (.1) ($40) (6)	= $240	$290
0	$ 0	(10) (.2) ($40) (6) + (20) (.1) ($40) (6) = $960		$960

The safety stock with the lowest total cost is 20 frames. Therefore, this safety stock changes the reorder point to 50 + 20 = 70 frames.

Insight: The optical company now knows that a safety stock of 20 frames will be the most economical decision.

Learning exercise: David Rivera's holding cost per frame is now estimated to be $20, while the stockout cost is $30 per frame. Does the reorder point change? [Answer: Safety stock = 10 now, with a total cost of $380, which is the lowest of the three. ROP = 60 frames.]

Related problems: 12.29, 12.30, 12.31

EXAMPLE 10

Determining safety stock with probabilistic demand and constant lead time

► **Figure 12.8**

Probabilistic Demand for a Hospital Item

Expected number of kits needed during lead time is 350, but for a 95% service level, the reorder point should be raised to 366.5.

When it is difficult or impossible to determine the cost of being out of stock, a manager may decide to follow a policy of keeping enough safety stock on hand to meet a prescribed customer service level. For instance, Figure 12.8 shows the use of safety stock when demand (for hospital resuscitation kits) is probabilistic. We see that the safety stock in Figure 12.8 is 16.5 units, and the reorder point is also increased by 16.5.

The manager may want to define the service level as meeting 95% of the demand (or, conversely, having stockouts only 5% of the time). Assuming that demand during lead time (the reorder period) follows a normal curve, only the mean and standard deviation are needed to define the inventory requirements for any given service level. Sales data are usually adequate for computing the mean and standard deviation. In the following example we use a normal curve with a known mean (μ) and standard deviation (σ) to determine the reorder point and safety stock necessary for a 95% service level. We use the following formula:

$$\text{ROP} = \text{Expected demand during lead time} + Z\sigma_{dLT} \tag{12-13}$$

where $Z =$ Number of standard deviations
    $\sigma_{dLT} =$ Standard deviation of demand during lead time

EXAMPLE 11

Safety stock with probabilistic demand

Memphis Regional Hospital stocks a "code blue" resuscitation kit that has a normally distributed demand during the reorder period. The mean (average) demand during the reorder period is 350 kits, and the standard deviation is 10 kits. The hospital administrator wants to follow a policy that results in stockouts only 5% of the time.

(a) What is the appropriate value of Z? (b) How much safety stock should the hospital maintain? (c) What reorder point should be used?

Approach: The hospital determines how much inventory is needed to meet the demand 95% of the time. The figure in this example may help you visualize the approach. The data are as follows:

$\mu =$ Mean demand $= 350$ kits

$\sigma_{dLT} =$ Standard deviation of demand during lead time $= 10$ kits

$Z =$ Number of standard normal deviations

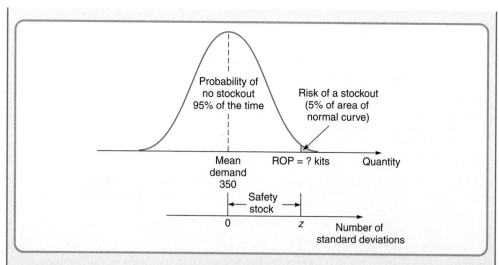

Solution:

a. We use the properties of a standardized normal curve to get a Z-value for an area under the normal curve of .95 (or 1 − .05). Using a normal table (see Appendix I), we find a Z-value of 1.65 standard deviations from the mean.

b. Because: Safety stock $= x - \mu$

And: $Z = \dfrac{x - \mu}{\sigma_{dLT}}$

Then: Safety stock $= Z\sigma_{dLT}$ (12-14)

Solving for safety stock, as in Equation (12-14), gives:

Safety stock $= 1.65(10) = 16.5$ kits

This is the situation illustrated in Figure 12.8.

c. The reorder point is:

ROP = Expected demand during lead time + Safety stock

$= 350$ kits $+ 16.5$ kits of safety stock $= 366.5$, or 367 kits

Insight: The cost of the inventory policy increases dramatically (exponentially) with an increase in service levels.

Learning exercise: What policy results in stockouts 10% of the time? [Answer: Z = 1.28; safety stock = 12.8; ROP = 363 kits.]

Related problems: 12.27, 12.28, 12.38

Other Probabilistic Models

Equations (12-13) and (12-14) assume that both an estimate of expected demand during lead times and its standard deviation are available. When data on lead time demand are *not* at hand, these formulas cannot be applied. However, three other models are available. We need to determine which model to use for three situations:

1. Demand is variable and lead time is constant
2. Lead time is variable, and demand is constant
3. Both demand and lead time are variable

All three models assume that demand and lead time are independent variables. Note that our examples use days, but weeks can also be used. Let us examine these three situations separately, because a different formula for the ROP is needed for each.

Demand Is Variable and Lead Time Is Constant   When *only the demand is variable*, then:

ROP = (*Average* daily demand × Lead time in days) + $Z\sigma_{dLT}$ (12-15)

where σ_{dLT} = Standard deviation of demand during lead time = $\sigma_d \sqrt{\text{Lead time}}$

and σ_d = Standard deviation of demand per day

Learning Objective

7. Understand service levels and probabilistic inventory models

EXAMPLE 12

ROP for variable demand and constant lead time

The *average* daily demand for Apple iPods at a Circuit Town store is 15, with a standard deviation of 5 units. The lead time is constant at 2 days. Find the reorder point if management wants a 90% service level (i.e., risk stockouts only 10% of the time). How much of this is safety stock?

Approach: Apply Equation (12-15) to the following data:

Average daily demand (normally distributed) = 15
Lead time in days (constant) = 2
Standard deviation of daily demand = $\sigma_d = 5$
Service level = 90%

Solution: From the normal table (Appendix I), we derive a Z-value for 90% of 1.28. Then:

$$\text{ROP} = (15 \text{ units} \times 2 \text{ days}) + Z\sigma_d \sqrt{\text{Lead time}}$$
$$= 30 + 1.28(5)(\sqrt{2})$$
$$= 30 + 1.28(5)(1.41) = 30 + 9.02 = 39.02 \cong 39$$

Thus, safety stock is about 9 iPods.

Insight: The value of Z depends on the manager's stockout risk level. The smaller the risk, the higher the Z.

Learning exercise: If the Circuit Town manager wants a 95% service level, what is the new ROP? [Answer: ROP = 41.63, or 42.]

Related problem: 12.32

Lead Time Is Variable and Demand is Constant   When the demand is constant and *only the lead time is variable*, then:

$$\text{ROP} = (\text{Daily demand} \times Average \text{ lead time in days}) + Z(\text{Daily demand}) \times \sigma_{LT} \quad \text{(12-16)}$$

where σ_{LT} = Standard deviation of lead time in days

EXAMPLE 13

ROP for constant demand and variable lead time

The Circuit Town store in Example 12 sells about 10 digital cameras a day (almost a constant quantity). Lead time for camera delivery is normally distributed with a mean time of 6 days and a standard deviation of 3 days. A 98% service level is set. Find the ROP.

Aproach: Apply Equation (12-16) to the following data:

Daily demand = 10
Average lead time = 6 days
Standard deviation of lead time = $\sigma_{LT} = 3$ days
Service level = 98%, so Z (from Appendix I) = 2.055

Solution: From the equation we get:

$$\text{ROP} = (10 \text{ units} \times 6 \text{ days}) + 2.055(10 \text{ units})(3)$$
$$= 60 + 61.65 = 121.65$$

The reorder point is about 122 cameras.

Insight: Note how the very high service level of 98% drives the ROP up.

Learning exercise: If a 90% service level is applied, what does the ROP drop to? [Answer: ROP = 60 + (1.28)(10)(3) = 60 + 38.4 = 98.4, since the Z-value is only 1.28.]

Related problem: 12.33

Both Demand and Lead Time Are Variable   When both the demand and lead time are variable, the formula for reorder point becomes more complex[6]:

$$\text{ROP} = (\text{Average daily demand} \times \text{Average lead time}) + Z\sigma_{dLT} \quad \text{(12-17)}$$

where σ_d = Standard deviation of demand per day

σ_{LT} = Standard deviation of lead time in days

and $\sigma_{dLT} = \sqrt{(\text{Average lead time} \times \sigma_d^2) + (\text{Average daily demand})^2 \sigma_{LT}^2}$

---

[6]Refer to S. Narasimhan, D. W. McLeavey, and P. Billington, *Production Planning and Inventory Control*, 2nd ed. (Upper Saddle River, NJ: Prentice Hall, 1995), Chap. 6, for details. Note that Equation (12-17) can also be expressed as ROP = Average daily demand × Average lead time + $Z\sqrt{(\text{Average lead time} \times \sigma_d^2) + \bar{d}^2\sigma_{LT}^2}$

EXAMPLE 14

ROP for variable
demand and variable
lead time

The Circuit Town store's most popular item is six-packs of 9-volt batteries. About 150 packs are sold per day, following a normal distribution with a standard deviation of 16 packs. Batteries are ordered from an out-of-state distributor; lead time is normally distributed with an average of 5 days and a standard deviation of 1 day. To maintain a 95% service level, what ROP is appropriate?

Approach: Determine a quantity at which to reorder by applying Equation (12-17) to the following data:

Average daily demand = 150 packs
Standard deviation of demand = σ_d = 16 packs
Average lead time = 5 days
Standard deviation of lead time = σ_{LT} = 1 day
Service level = 95%, so Z = 1.65 (from Appendix I)

Solution: From the equation we compute:

$$ROP = (150 \text{ packs} \times 5 \text{ days}) + 1.65 \, \sigma_{dLT}$$

where

$$\sigma_{dLT} = \sqrt{(5 \text{ days} \times 16^2) + (150^2 \times 1^2)}$$
$$= \sqrt{(5 \times 256) + (22{,}500 \times 1)}$$
$$= \sqrt{1{,}280 + 22{,}500} = \sqrt{23{,}780} \cong 154$$

So ROP = $(150 \times 5) + 1.65(154) \cong 750 + 254 = 1{,}004$ packs

Insight: When both demand and lead time are variable, the formula looks quite complex. But it is just the result of squaring the standard deviations in Equations (12-15) and (12-16) to get their variances, then summing them, and finally taking the square root.

Learning exercise: For an 80% service level, what is the ROP? [Answer: Z = .84 and ROP = 879 packs.]

Related problem: 12.34

FIXED-PERIOD (P) SYSTEMS

The inventory models that we have considered so far are **fixed-quantity**, or **Q**, **systems**. That is, the same fixed amount is added to inventory every time an order for an item is placed. We saw that orders are event triggered. When inventory decreases to the reorder point (ROP), a new order for Q units is placed.

To use the fixed-quantity model, inventory must be continuously monitored. This is called a **perpetual inventory system**. Every time an item is added to or withdrawn from inventory, records must be updated to make sure the ROP has not been reached.

In a **fixed-period**, or **P**, **system**, on the other hand, inventory is ordered at the end of a given period. Then, and only then, is on-hand inventory counted. Only the amount necessary to bring total inventory up to a prespecified target level is ordered. Figure 12.9 illustrates this concept.

Fixed-quantity (Q) system
An EOQ ordering system with the same order amount each time.

Perpetual inventory system
A system that keeps track of each withdrawal or addition to inventory continuously, so records are always current.

Fixed-period (P) system
A system in which inventory orders are made at regular time intervals.

◄ **Figure 12.9**

Inventory Level in a Fixed-Period (P) System

Various amounts (Q_1, Q_2, Q_3, etc.) are ordered at regular time intervals (P) based on the quantity necessary to bring inventory up to the target quantity (T).

Fixed-period systems have several of the same assumptions as the basic EOQ fixed-quantity system:

- The only relevant costs are the ordering and holding costs.
- Lead times are known and constant.
- Items are independent of one another.

The downward-sloped line in Figure 12.9 again represents on-hand inventory. But now, when the time between orders (P) passes, we place an order to raise inventory up to the target quantity (T). The amount ordered during the first period may be Q_1, the second period Q_2, and so on. The Q_i value is the difference between current on-hand inventory and the target inventory level. Example 15 illustrates how much to reorder in a simple P system.

EXAMPLE 15

P-system ordering

Hard Rock London has a back order for three leather bomber jackets in its retail shop. There are no jackets in stock, none are expected from earlier orders, and it is time to place an order. The target value is 50 jackets. How many bomber jackets should be ordered?

Approach: Consider the four variables: the target quantity, on-hand inventory, earlier orders en route, and back orders.

Solution: Order amount (Q) = Target quantity (T) – On-hand inventory – Earlier orders not yet received + Back orders = 50 – 0 – 0 + 3 = 53 jackets

Insight: Because demand in a P system is variable, some orders will be larger than the EOQ and some will be smaller.

Learning exercise: Hard Rock has a back order of 5 London T-shirts, no on-hand inventory, a target quantity of 400, and no orders not yet received. What is Q? [Answer: 405 T-shirts.]

Related problem: 12.35

The advantage of the fixed-period system is that there is no physical count of inventory items after an item is withdrawn—this occurs only when the time for the next review comes up. This procedure is also convenient administratively, especially if inventory control is only one of several duties of an employee.

A fixed-period system is appropriate when vendors make routine (i.e., at fixed-time interval) visits to customers to take fresh orders or when purchasers want to combine orders to save ordering and transportation costs (therefore, they will have the same review period for similar inventory items). For example, a vending machine company may come to refill its machines every Tuesday. This is also the case at Anheuser-Busch, whose sales reps may visit a store every 5 days (see the *OM in Action* box "66,207,896 Bottles of Beer on the Wall").

OM in Action   66,207,896 Bottles of Beer on the Wall

When Dereck Gurden pulls up at one of his customers' stores—7-Eleven, Buy N Save, or one of dozens of liquor marts and restaurants in the 800-square-mile territory he covers in California's Central Valley—managers usually stop what they're doing and grab a note pad. This is because, as Gurden claims, "I know more about these guys' businesses than they do . . . at least in the beer section."

What makes Gurden and other sales reps for Anheuser-Busch distributors so smart? It's BudNet, the King of Beer's top-secret crown jewel—a nationwide data network through which drivers and reps report, in excruciating detail, on sales, shelf space, inventory, and displays at thousands of stores. How does it work? As Gurden walks a store, he inputs what he sees to his handheld PC, then plugs into a cell phone and fires off new orders, along with

the data he has gathered. Anheuser has made a deadly accurate science of finding out what beer lovers are buying, as well as when, where, and why.

Matching these data with U.S. census figures of neighborhoods, Anheuser mines data down to the sales at individual stores. The company can pinpoint age, ethnicity, education, political, and sexual orientation of customers at your local 7-Eleven. BudNet is the primary reason Anheuser's share of the $75 billion U.S. beer market continues to increase, and the company has posted double-digit profit gains for 20 straight quarters while its competitors have flat-lined.

Sources: Business 2.0 (January/February 2001): 47–49; *Beverage Industry* (May 2004): 20–23; and *The Wall Street Journal* (March 23, 2004): C3.

The disadvantage of the *P* system is that because there is no tally of inventory during the review period, there is the possibility of a stockout during this time. This scenario is possible if a large order draws the inventory level down to zero right after an order is placed. Therefore, a higher level of safety stock (as compared to a fixed-quantity system) needs to be maintained to provide protection against stockout during both the time between reviews and the lead time.

Summary

Inventory represents a major investment for many firms. This investment is often larger than it should be because firms find it easier to have "just-in-case" inventory rather than "just-in-time" inventory. Inventories are of four types:

1. Raw material and purchased components
2. Work-in-process
3. Maintenance, repair, and operating (MRO)
4. Finished goods

In this chapter, we discussed independent inventory, ABC analysis, record accuracy, cycle counting, and inventory models used to control independent demands. The EOQ model, production order quantity model, and quantity discount model can all be solved using Excel, Excel OM, or POM for Windows software. A summary of the inventory models presented in this chapter is shown in Table 12.4.

◄ **Table 12.4**

Models for Independent Demand Summarized

Q = Number of units per order
EOQ = Optimum order quantity ($Q*$)
D = Annual demand in units
S = Setup or ordering cost for each order
H = Holding or carrying cost per unit per year in dollars
p = Daily production rate
d = Daily demand rate

P = Price
I = Annual inventory carrying cost as a percent
μ = Mean demand
σ_{dLT} = Standard deviation of demand during lead-time
σ_{LT} = Standard deviation of lead time
Z = Standardized value under the normal curve

EOQ:

$$Q* = \sqrt{\frac{2DS}{H}} \tag{12-1}$$

EOQ production order quantity model:

$$Q_p^* = \sqrt{\frac{2DS}{H[1-(d/p)]}} \tag{12-7}$$

Total cost for the EOQ and quantity discount EOQ models:

$$TC = \text{Total cost}$$
$$= \text{Setup cost} + \text{Holding cost} + \text{Product cost}$$
$$= \frac{D}{Q}S + \frac{Q}{2}H + PD \tag{12-9}$$

Quantity discount EOQ model:

$$Q* = \sqrt{\frac{2DS}{IP}} \tag{12-10}$$

Probability model with expected lead time demand known:

$$ROP = \text{Expected demand during lead time} + Z\sigma_{dLT} \tag{12-13}$$

$$\text{Safety stock} = Z\sigma_{dLT} \tag{12-14}$$

Probability model with variable demand and constant lead time:

$$ROP = (\text{Average daily demand} \times \text{Lead time in days}) + Z\sigma_{dLT} \tag{12-15}$$

Probability model with constant demand and variable lead time:

$$ROP = (\text{Daily demand} \times \text{Average lead time in days}) + Z(\text{Daily demand}) \sigma_{LT} \tag{12-16}$$

Probability model with both demand and lead time variable:

$$ROP = (\text{Average daily demand} \times \text{Average lead time in days}) + Z\sigma_{dLT} \tag{12-17}$$

Key Terms

Raw material inventory *(p. 484)*
Work-in-process (WIP) inventory *(p. 484)*
MRO *(p. 485)*
Finished-goods inventory *(p. 485)*
ABC analysis *(p. 485)*
Cycle counting *(p. 487)*
Shrinkage *(p. 488)*
Pilferage *(p. 488)*
Holding cost *(p. 490)*

Ordering cost *(p. 490)*
Setup cost *(p. 490)*
Setup time *(p. 490)*
Economic order quantity (EOQ) model *(p. 490)*
Robust *(p. 495)*
Lead time *(p. 495)*
Reorder point (ROP) *(p. 495)*
Safety stock *(p. 496)*

Production order quantity model *(p. 497)*
Quantity discount *(p. 500)*
Probabilistic model *(p. 502)*
Service level *(p. 502)*
Fixed-quantity (Q) system *(p. 507)*
Perpetual inventory system *(p. 507)*
Fixed-period (P) system *(p. 507)*

Using Software to Solve Inventory Problems

This section presents three ways to solve inventory problems with computer software. First, you can create your own Excel spreadsheets. Second, you can use the Excel OM software that comes with this text and is found on the student CD. Third, POM for Windows, also on your CD, can solve all problems marked with a **P**.

Creating Your Own Excel Spreadsheets

Program 12.1 illustrates how you can make an Excel model to solve Example 8 (p. 498). This is a production order quantity model. Below Program 12.1 is a listing of the formulas needed to create the spreadsheet.

▶ **Program 12.1**

Using Excel for a Production Model, with Data from Example 8

	A	B
1	**Nathan Manufacturing, Inc.**	
2		
3	Demand rate, D	1000
4	Setup cost, S	$ 10.00
5	Holding cost, H	$ 0.50
6	Daily production rate, p	8
7	Daily demand rate, d	4
8	Days per year	250
9	Unit price, P	$ 200.00
10		
11		
12	Optimal production quantity, Q*	282.84
13	Maximum Inventory	141.42
14	Average Inventory	70.71
15	Number of Setups	3.54
16	Time (days) between production runs	70.71
17		
18	Holding cost	$ 35.36
19	Setup cost	$ 35.36
20		
21	Unit costs	$ 200,000
22		
23	Total cost, Tc	$ 200,071
24		

Computations

Value	Cell	Excel Formula
Optimal production quantity, Q*	B12	=SQRT(2*B3*B4/B5)*SQRT(B6/(B6-B7))
Maximum Inventory	B13	=B12*(B6-B7)/B6
Average Inventory	B14	=B13/2
Number of Setups	B15	=B3/B12
Time (days) between production runs	B16	=B8/B15
Holding cost	B18	=B14*B5
Setup cost	B19	=B15*B4
Unit costs	B21	=B9*B3
Total cost, Tc	B22	=B18+B19+B21

X Using Excel OM

Excel OM allows us to easily model inventory problems ranging from ABC analysis, to the basic EOQ model, to the production model, to quantity discount situations.

Program 12.2 shows the input data, selected formulas, and results for an ABC analysis, using data from Example 1 (on p. 485). After the data are entered, we use the *Data* and *Sort* Excel commands to rank the items from largest to smallest dollar volumes.

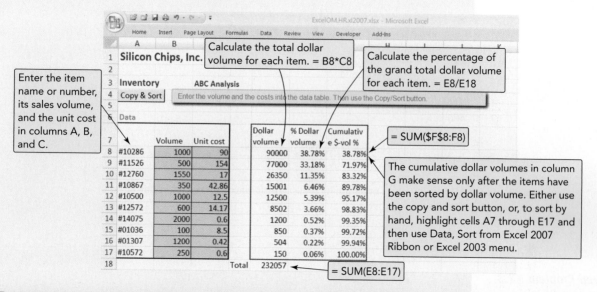

▲ **Program 12.2**   **Using Excel OM for an ABC Analysis, with Data from Example 1**

P Using POM for Windows

The POM for Windows Inventory module can also solve the entire EOQ family of problems. Please refer to Appendix IV for further details.

Solved Problems

 Virtual Office help is available on Student DVD.

Solved Problem 12.1

David Alexander has compiled the following table of six items in inventory at Angelo Products, along with the unit cost and the annual demand in units:

Identification Code	Unit Cost ($)	Annual Demand (units)
XX1	5.84	1,200
B66	5.40	1,110
3CPO	1.12	896
33CP	74.54	1,104
R2D2	2.00	1,110
RMS	2.08	961

Use ABC analysis to determine which item(s) should be carefully controlled using a quantitative inventory technique and which item(s) should not be closely controlled.

solution

The item that needs strict control is 33CP, so it is an A item. Items that do not need to be strictly controlled are 3CPO, R2D2, and RMS; these are C items. The B items will be XX1 and B66.

Code	Annual dollar volume = Unit Cost × Demand
XX1	$ 7,008.00
B66	$ 5,994.00
3CPO	$ 1,003.52
33CP	$82,292.16
R2D2	$ 2,220.00
RMS	$ 1,998.88

Total cost = $100,516.56
70% of total cost = $70,347.92

Solved Problem 12.2

The Warren W. Fisher Computer Corporation purchases 8,000 transistors each year as components in minicomputers. The unit cost of each transistor is $10, and the cost of carrying one transistor in inventory for a year is $3. Ordering cost is $30 per order.

What are (a) the optimal order quantity, (b) the expected number of orders placed each year, and (c) the expected time between orders? Assume that Fisher operates on a 200-day working year.

Solution

(a) $Q^* = \sqrt{\dfrac{2DS}{H}} = \sqrt{\dfrac{2(8,000)(30)}{3}} = 400$ units

(b) $N = \dfrac{D}{Q^*} = \dfrac{8,000}{400} = 20$ orders

(c)   Time between orders $= T = \dfrac{\text{Number of working days}}{N} = \dfrac{200}{20} = 10$ working days

With 20 orders placed each year, an order for 400 transistors is placed every 10 working days.

Solved Problem 12.3

Annual demand for notebook binders at Meyer's Stationery Shop is 10,000 units. Brad Meyer operates his business 300 days per year and finds that deliveries from his supplier generally take 5 working days. Calculate the reorder point for the notebook binders.

Solution

$$L = 5 \text{ days}$$

$$d = \frac{10,000}{300} = 33.3 \text{ units per day}$$

$$\text{ROP} = d \times L = (33.3 \text{ units per day})(5 \text{ days})$$
$$= 166.7 \text{ units}$$

Thus, Brad should reorder when his stock reaches 167 units.

Solved Problem 12.4

Leonard Presby, Inc., has an annual demand rate of 1,000 units but can produce at an average production rate of 2,000 units. Setup cost is $10; carrying cost is $1. What is the optimal number of units to be produced each time?

Solution

$$Q_p^* = \sqrt{\dfrac{2DS}{H\left(1 - \dfrac{\text{Annual demand rate}}{\text{Annual production rate}}\right)}} = \sqrt{\dfrac{2(1,000)(10)}{1[1 - (1,000/2,000)]}}$$

$$= \sqrt{\dfrac{20,000}{1/2}} = \sqrt{40,000} = 200 \text{ units}$$

Solved Problem 12.5

Whole Nature Foods sells a gluten-free product for which the annual demand is 5,000 boxes. At the moment it is paying $6.40 for each box; carrying cost is 25% of the unit cost; ordering costs are $25. A new supplier has offered to sell the same item for $6.00 if Whole Nature Foods buys at least 3,000 boxes per order. Should the firm stick with the old supplier, or take advantage of the new quantity discount?

Solution

Under present price of $6.40 per box:

Economic order quantity, using Equation (12-10):

$$Q^* = \sqrt{\frac{2DS}{IP}}$$

$$Q^* = \sqrt{\frac{2(5,000)(25)}{(0.25)(6.40)}}$$

$$= 395.3, \text{ or } 395 \text{ boxes}$$

where D = period demand
   S = order cost
   P = price per box
   I = holding cost as percent
   H = holding cost = IP

Total cost = Order cost + Holding cost + Purchase cost

$$= \frac{DS}{Q} + \frac{Q}{2}H + PD$$

$$= \frac{(5,000)(25)}{395} + \frac{(395)(0.25)(6.40)}{2} + (6.40)(6,000)$$

$$= 316 + 316 + 32,000$$

$$= \$32,632$$

Note: Order and carrying costs are rounded.

Under the quantity discount price of $6.00 per box:

Total cost = Order cost + Holding cost + Purchase cost

$$= \frac{DS}{Q} + \frac{Q}{2}H + PD$$

$$= \frac{(5,000)(25)}{3000} + \frac{(5,000)(0.25)(6.00)}{2} + (6.00)(5,000)$$

$$= 42 + 3,750 + 30,000$$

$$= \$33,792$$

Therefore, the old supplier with whom Whole Nature Foods would incur a total cost of $32,632 is preferable.

Solved Problem 12.6

Children's art sets are ordered once each year by Ashok Kumar, Inc., and the reorder point, without safety stock (dL) is 100 art sets. Inventory carrying cost is $10 per set per year, and the cost of a stockout is $50 per set per year. Given the following demand probabilities during the reorder period, how much safety stock should be carried?

Demand during Reorder Period	Probability
0	.1
50	.2
ROP → 100	.4
150	.2
200	.1
	1.0

Solution

		Incremental Costs	
Safety Stock	Carrying Cost	Stockout Cost	Total Cost
0	0	50 × (50 × 0.2 + 100 × 0.1) = 1,000	$1,000
50	50 × 10 = 500	50 × (0.1 × 50) = 250	750
100	100 × 10 = 1,000	0	1,000

The safety stock that minimizes total incremental cost is 50 sets. The reorder point then becomes 100 sets + 50 sets, or 150 sets.

Solved Problem 12.7

What safety stock should Ron Satterfield Corporation maintain if mean sales are 80 during the reorder period, the standard deviation is 7, and Ron can tolerate stockouts 10% of the time?

Solution

From Appendix I, Z at an area of .9 (or $1 - .10$) = 1.28, and Equation (12-14):

$$\text{Safety stock} = Z\sigma_{dLT}$$
$$= 1.28(7) = 8.96 \text{ units, or 9 units}$$

Solved Problem 12.8

The daily demand for 52″ plasma TVs at Sarah's Discount Emporium is normally distributed, with an average of 5 and a standard deviation of 2 units. The lead time for receiving a shipment of new TVs is 10 days and is fairly constant. Determine the reorder point and safety stock for a 95% service level.

Solution

The ROP for this variable demand and constant lead time model uses Equation (12-15):

$$\text{ROP} = (\text{Average daily demand} \times \text{Lead time in days}) + Z\sigma_{dLT}$$

where
$$\sigma_{dLT} = \sigma_d \sqrt{\text{Lead time}}$$

So, with $Z = 1.65$,

$$\text{ROP} = (5 \times 10) + 1.65(2)\sqrt{10}$$
$$= 50 + 10.4 = 60.4 \cong 60 \text{ TVs}$$

The safety stock is 10.4, or about 10 TVs.

Solved Problem 12.9

The demand at Arnold Palmer Hospital for a specialized surgery pack is 60 per week, virtually every week. The lead time from McKesson, its main supplier, is normally distributed, with a mean of 6 weeks for this product and a standard deviation of 2 weeks. A 90% weekly service level is desired. Find the ROP.

Solution

Here the demand is constant and lead time is variable, with data given in weeks, not days. We apply Equation (12-16):

$$\text{ROP} = (\text{Weekly demand} \times \text{Average lead time in weeks}) + Z (\text{Weekly demand}) \sigma_{LT}$$

where
$$\sigma_{LT} = \text{standard deviation of lead time in weeks} = 2$$

So, with $Z = 1.28$, for a 90% service level:

$$\text{ROP} = (60 \times 6) + 1.28(60)(2)$$
$$= 360 + 153.6 = 513.6 \cong 514 \text{ surgery packs}$$

Self-Test

- *Before taking the self-test*, refer to the learning objectives listed at the beginning of the chapter and the key terms listed at the end of the chapter.
- Use the key at the back of the text to **correct** your answers.
- **Restudy** pages that correspond to any questions you answered incorrectly or material you feel uncertain about.

1. ABC analysis divides on-hand inventory into three classes based upon:
   a) unit price
   b) the number of units on hand
   c) annual demand
   d) annual dollar values

2. Cycle counting:
   a) provides a measure of inventory turnover
   b) assumes that all inventory records must be verified with the same frequency
   c) is a process by which inventory records are periodically verified
   d) all of the above

3. The service industry is improving inventory management through a number of methods. These include:
   a) shrinkage and pilferage
   b) good personnel selection
   c) bar coding of incoming and outgoing merchandise
   d) a and b above
   e) b and c above

4. Annual holding costs are usually:
   a) under 6% of inventory value
   b) 6% to 9% of inventory value
   c) 9% to 12% of inventory value
   d) 12% to 15% of inventory value
   e) over 15% of inventory value

5. The difference(s) between the basic EOQ model and the production order quantity model is(are) that:
   a) the production order quantity model does not require the assumption of known, constant demand
   b) the EOQ model does not require the assumption of negligible lead time
   c) the production order quantity model does not require the assumption of instantaneous delivery
   d) all of the above

6. Extra units held in inventory to reduce stockouts are called:
   a) reorder point
   b) safety stock
   c) just-in-time inventory
   d) all of the above

7. The two most important inventory-based questions answered by the typical inventory model are:
   a) when to place an order and the cost of the order
   b) when to place an order and how much of an item to order
   c) how much of an item to order and the cost of the order
   d) how much of an item to order and with whom the order should be placed

8. The appropriate level of safety stock is typically determined by:
   a) minimizing an expected stockout cost
   b) choosing the level of safety stock that assures a given service level
   c) carrying sufficient safety stock so as to eliminate all stockouts

9. Inventory record accuracy can be improved through:
   a) cycle counting
   b) reorder points
   c) ABC analysis
   d) all of the above

Active Model Exercise

This active model explores the basics of a typical inventory decision and the sensitivity of the model to changes in demand and costs. It uses the data from Examples 3, 4, and 5.

◄ **Active Model 12.1**

An EOQ Analysis of the Data in Examples 3, 4, and 5 for Sharp, Inc.

Questions

1. What is the EOQ and what is the lowest total cost?

2. What is the annual cost of *carrying* inventory at the EOQ and the annual cost of *ordering* inventory at the EOQ of 200 units?

3. From the graph, what can you conclude about the relationship between the lowest total cost and the costs of ordering and carrying inventory?

4. How much does the total cost increase if the store manager orders 50 more hypodermics than the EOQ? 50 fewer hypodermics?

5. What happens to the EOQ and total cost when demand is doubled? When carrying cost is doubled?

6. Scroll through lower setup cost values and describe the changes to the graph. What happens to the EOQ?

7. Comment on the sensitivity of the EOQ model to errors in demand or cost estimates.

Internet and Student CD-ROM Exercises

Visit our Companion Web site or use your student CD-ROM/DVD to help with material in this chapter.

 On Our Companion Web Site, www.prenhall.com/heizer
- Self-Study Quizzes
- Practice Problems
- Virtual Company Tour
- Internet Cases
- PowerPoint Lecture

 On Your Student CD-ROM
- Practice Problems
- Active Model Exercises
- Excel OM
- Excel OM Example Data Files
- POM for Windows

 On Your Student DVD
- Video Clip and Video Case
- Virtual Office Hours for Solved Problems

Discussion Questions

1. Describe the four types of inventory.
2. With the advent of low-cost computing, do you see alternatives to the popular ABC classifications?
3. What is the purpose of the ABC classification system?
4. Identify and explain the types of costs that are involved in an inventory system.
5. Explain the major assumptions of the basic EOQ model.
6. What is the relationship of the economic order quantity to demand? To the holding cost? To the setup cost?
7. Explain why it is not necessary to include product cost (price or price times quantity) in the EOQ model, but the quantity discount model requires this information.
8. What are the advantages of cycle counting?
9. What impact does a decrease in setup time have on EOQ?
10. When quantity discounts are offered, why is it not necessary to check discount points that are below the EOQ or points above the EOQ that are not discount points?

11. What is meant by *service level*?
12. Explain the following: All things being equal, the production inventory quantity will be larger than the economic order quantity.
13. Describe the difference between a fixed-quantity (Q) and a fixed-period (P) inventory system.
14. Explain what is meant by the expression "robust model." Specifically, what would you tell a manager who exclaimed, "Uh-oh, we're in trouble! The calculated EOQ is wrong, Actual demand is 10% greater than estimated."
15. What is "safety stock"? What does safety stock provide safety against?
16. When demand is not constant, the reorder point is a function of what four parameters?
17. How are inventory levels monitored in retail stores?
18. State a major advantage, and a major disadvantage, of a fixed-period (P) system.

Ethical Dilemma

Wayne Hills Hospital in tiny Wayne, Nebraska, faces a problem common to large, urban hospitals as well as to small, remote ones like itself. That problem is deciding how much of each type of whole blood to keep in stock. Because blood is expensive and has a limited shelf life (up to 5 weeks under 1–6°C refrigeration), Wayne Hills naturally wants to keep its stock as low as possible. Unfortunately, past disasters such as a major tornado and a train wreck demonstrated that lives would be lost when not enough blood was available to handle massive needs. The hospital administrator wants to set an 85% service level based on demand over the past decade. Discuss the implications of this decision. What is the hospital's responsibility with regard to stocking lifesaving medicines with short shelf lives? How would you set the inventory level for a commodity such as blood?

Problems*

•• **12.1** L. Houts Plastics is a large manufacturer of injection-molded plastics in North Carolina. An investigation of the company's manufacturing facility in Charlotte yields the information presented in the table below. How would the plant classify these items according to an ABC classification system?

L. Houts Plastics Charlotte Inventory Levels

Item Code #	Average Inventory (units)	Value ($/unit)
1289	400	3.75
2347	300	4.00
2349	120	2.50
2363	75	1.50
2394	60	1.75
2395	30	2.00
6782	20	1.15
7844	12	2.05
8210	8	1.80
8310	7	2.00
9111	6	3.00 **PX**

• **12.2** Boreki Enterprise has the following 10 items in inventory. Theodore Boreki asks you, a recent OM graduate, to divide these items into ABC classifications. What do you report back?

Item	Annual Demand	Cost/Unit
A2	3,000	$ 50
B8	4,000	12
C7	1,500	45
D1	6,000	10
E9	1,000	20
F3	500	500
G2	300	1,500
H2	600	20
I5	1,750	10
J8	2,500	5 **PX**

•• **12.3** Jean-Marie Bourjolly's restaurant has the following inventory items that it orders on a weekly basis:

Inventory Item	$ Value/Case	# Ordered/Week
Rib eye steak	135	3
Lobster tail	245	3
Pasta	23	12
Salt	3	2
Napkins	12	2
Tomato sauce	23	11
French fries	43	32
Pepper	3	3
Garlic powder	11	3
Trash can liners	12	3
Table cloths	32	5
Fish filets	143	10
Prime rib roasts	166	6
Oil	28	2

Inventory Item	$ Value/Case	# Ordered/Week
Lettuce (case)	35	24
Chickens	75	14
Order pads	12	2
Eggs (case)	22	7
Bacon	56	5
Sugar	4	2

a) Which is the most expensive item, using annual dollar volume?
b) Which are C items?
c) What is the annual dollar volume for all 20 items? **PX**

• **12.4** Howard Electronics, a small manufacturer of electronic research equipment, has approximately 7,000 items in its inventory and has hired Joan Blasco-Paul to manage its inventory. Joan has determined that 10% of the items in inventory are A items, 35% are B items, and 55% are C items. She would like to set up a system in which all A items are counted monthly (every 20 working days), all B items are counted quarterly (every 60 working days), and all C items are counted semiannually (every 120 working days). How many items need to be counted each day?

• **12.5** William Beville's computer training school, in Richmond, stocks workbooks with the following characteristics:

$$\text{Demand } D = 19{,}500 \text{ units/year}$$
$$\text{Ordering cost } S = \$25/\text{order}$$
$$\text{Holding cost } H = \$4/\text{unit/year}$$

a) Calculate the EOQ for the workbooks.
b) What are the annual holding costs for the workbooks?
c) What are the annual ordering costs? **PX**

• **12.6** If D = 8,000 per month, S = $45 per order, and H = $2 per unit per month, what is the economic order quantity? **PX**

•• **12.7** Henry Crouch's law office has traditionally ordered ink refills 60 units at a time. The firm estimates that carrying cost is 40% of the $10 unit cost and that annual demand is about 240 units per year. The assumptions of the basic EOQ model are thought to apply. For what value of ordering cost would its action be optimal?

• **12.8** Madeline Thimmes's Dream Store sells water beds and assorted supplies. Her best-selling bed has an annual demand of 400 units. Ordering cost is $40; holding cost is $5 per unit per year.
a) To minimize the total cost, how many units should be ordered each time an order is placed?
b) If the holding cost per unit was $6 instead of $5, what would the optimal order quantity be? **PX**

• **12.9** Southeastern Bell stocks a certain switch connector at its central warehouse for supplying field service offices. The yearly demand for these connectors is 15,000 units. Southeastern estimates its annual holding cost for this item to be $25 per unit. The cost to place and process an order from the supplier is $75. The company operates 300 days per year, and the lead time to receive an order from the supplier is 2 working days.
a) Find the economic order quantity.
b) Find the annual holding costs.
c) Find the annual ordering costs.
d) What is the reorder point? **PX**

*Note: **PX** means the problem may be solved with POM for Windows and/or Excel OM.

· 12.10 Lead time for one of your fastest-moving products is 21 days. Demand during this period averages 100 units per day. What would be an appropriate reorder point?

· 12.11 Annual demand for the notebook binders at Duncan's Stationery Shop is 10,000 units. Dana Duncan operates her business 300 days per year and finds that deliveries from her supplier generally take 5 working days. Calculate the reorder point for the notebook binders that she stocks.

·· 12.12 Thomas Kratzer is the purchasing manager for the headquarters of a large insurance company chain with a central inventory operation. Thomas's fastest-moving inventory item has a demand of 6,000 units per year. The cost of each unit is $100, and the inventory carrying cost is $10 per unit per year. The average ordering cost is $30 per order. It takes about 5 days for an order to arrive, and the demand for 1 week is 120 units. (This is a corporate operation, and there are 250 working days per year.)
a) What is the EOQ?
b) What is the average inventory if the EOQ is used?
c) What is the optimal number of orders per year?
d) What is the optimal number of days in between any two orders?
e) What is the annual cost of ordering and holding inventory?
f) What is the total annual inventory cost, including cost of the 6,000 units? **Px**

·· 12.13 Joe Henry's machine shop uses 2,500 brackets during the course of a year. These brackets are purchased from a supplier 90 miles away. The following information is known about the brackets:

Annual demand:	2,500
Holding cost per bracket per year:	$1.50
Order cost per order:	$18.75
Lead time:	2 days
Working days per year:	250

a) Given the above information, what would be the economic order quantity (EOQ)?
b) Given the EOQ, what would be the average inventory? What would be the annual inventory holding cost?
c) Given the EOQ, how many orders would be made each year? What would be the annual order cost?
d) Given the EOQ, what is the total annual cost of managing the inventory?
e) What is the time between orders?
f) What is the reorder point (ROP)? **Px**

·· 12.14 Myriah Fitzgibbon, of L.A. Plumbing, uses 1,200 of a certain spare part that costs $25 for each order, with an annual holding cost of $24.
a) Calculate the total cost for order sizes of 25, 40, 50, 60, and 100.
b) Identify the economic order quantity and consider the implications for making an error in calculating economic order quantity. **Px**

··· 12.15 M. Cotteleer Electronics supplies microcomputer circuitry to a company that incorporates microprocessors into refrigerators and other home appliances. One of the components has an annual demand of 250 units, and this is constant throughout the year. Carrying cost is estimated to be $1 per unit per year, and the ordering cost is $20 per order.
a) To minimize cost, how many units should be ordered each time an order is placed?
b) How many orders per year are needed with the optimal policy?

c) What is the average inventory if costs are minimized?
d) Suppose that the ordering cost is not $20, and Cotteleer has been ordering 150 units each time an order is placed. For this order policy (of $Q = 150$) to be optimal, determine what the ordering cost would have to be. **Px**

·· 12.16 Race One Motors is an Indonesian car manufacturer. At its largest manufacturing facility, in Jakarta, the company produces subcomponents at a rate of 300 per day, and it uses these subcomponents at a rate of 12,500 per year (of 250 working days). Holding costs are $2 per item per year, and ordering costs are $30 per order.
a) What is the economic production quantity?
b) How many production runs per year will be made?
c) What will be the maximum inventory level?
d) What percentage of time will the facility be producing components?
e) What is the annual cost of ordering and holding inventory? **Px**

·· 12.17 Radovilsky Manufacturing Company, in Hayward, California, makes flashing lights for toys. The company operates its production facility 300 days per year. It has orders for about 12,000 flashing lights per year and has the capability of producing 100 per day. Setting up the light production costs $50. The cost of each light is $1. The holding cost is $0.10 per light per year.
a) What is the optimal size of the production run?
b) What is the average holding cost per year?
c) What is the average setup cost per year?
d) What is the total cost per year, including the cost of the lights? **Px**

·· 12.18 Arthur Meiners is the production manager of Wheel-Rite, a small producer of metal parts. Wheel-Rite supplies Cal-Tex, a larger assembly company, with 10,000 wheel bearings each year. This order has been stable for some time. Setup cost for Wheel-Rite is $40, and holding cost is $.60 per wheel bearing per year. Wheel-Rite can produce 500 wheel bearings per day. Cal-Tex is a just-in-time manufacturer and requires that 50 bearings be shipped to it each business day.
a) What is the optimum production quantity?
b) What is the maximum number of wheel bearings that will be in inventory at Wheel-Rite?
c) How many production runs of wheel bearings will Wheel-Rite have in a year?
d) What is the total setup + holding cost for Wheel-Rite? **Px**

·· 12.19 Cesar Rogo Computers, a Mississippi chain of computer hardware and software retail outlets, supplies both educational and commercial customers with memory and storage devices. It currently faces the following ordering decision relating to purchases of CD-ROMs:

$$D = 36,000 \text{ disks}$$
$$S = \$25$$
$$H = \$0.45$$
$$\text{Purchase price} = \$0.85$$
$$\text{Discount price} = \$0.82$$
$$\text{Quantity needed to qualify for the discount} = 6,000 \text{ disks}$$

Should the discount be taken? **Px**

·· 12.20 Bell Computers purchases integrated chips at $350 per chip. The holding cost is $35 per unit per year, the ordering cost is $120 per order, and sales are steady, at 400 per month. The company's supplier, Rich Blue Chip Manufacturing, Inc., decides to offer price concessions in order to attract larger orders. The price structure is shown below.

a) What is the optimal order quantity and the minimum cost for Bell Computers to order, purchase, and hold these integrated chips?

Rich Blue Chip's Price Structure

Quantity Purchased	Price/Unit
1–99 units	$350
100–199 units	$325
200 or more units	$300

b) Bell Computers wishes to use a 10% holding cost rather than the fixed $35 holding cost in part a. What is the optimal order quantity, and what is the optimal cost? **Px**

•• **12.21** Wang Distributors has an annual demand for an airport metal detector of 1,400 units. The cost of a typical detector to Wang is $400. Carrying cost is estimated to be 20% of the unit cost, and the ordering cost is $25 per order. If Ping Wang, the owner, orders in quantities of 300 or more, he can get a 5% discount on the cost of the detectors. Should Wang take the quantity discount? **Px**

•• **12.22** The catering manager of LaVista Hotel, Lisa Ferguson, is disturbed by the amount of silverware she is losing every week. Last Friday night, when her crew tried to set up for a banquet for 500 people, they did not have enough knives. She decides she needs to order some more silverware, but wants to take advantage of any quantity discounts her vendor will offer.

For a small order (2,000 pieces or less) her vendor quotes a price of $1.80/piece.

If she orders 2,001–5,000 pieces, the price drops to $1.60/piece. 5,001–10,000 pieces brings the price to $1.40/piece, and 10,001 and above reduces the price to $1.25.

Lisa's order costs are $200 per order, her annual holding costs are 5%, and the annual demand is 45,000 pieces. For the best option:
a) What is the optimal order quantity?
b) What is the annual holding cost?
c) What is the annual ordering (setup) cost?
d) What are the annual costs of the silverware itself with an optimal order quantity?
e) What is the total annual cost, including ordering, holding, and purchasing the silverware? **Px**

•• **12.23** Rocky Mountain Tire Center sells 20,000 go-cart tires per year. The ordering cost for each order is $40, and the holding cost is 20% of the purchase price of the tires per year. The purchase price is $20 per tire if fewer than 500 tires are ordered, $18 per tire if 500 or more—but fewer than 1,000—tires are ordered, and $17 per tire if 1,000 or more tires are ordered. How many tires should Rocky Mountain order each time it places an order? **Px**

•• **12.24** M. P. VanOyen Manufacturing has gone out on bid for a regulator component. Expected demand is 700 units per month. The item can be purchased from either Allen Manufacturing or Baker Manufacturing. Their price lists are shown in the table. Ordering cost is $50, and annual holding cost per unit is $5.

Allen Mfg.		Baker Mfg.	
Quantity	Unit Price	Quantity	Unit Price
1–499	$16.00	1–399	$16.10
500–999	15.50	400–799	15.60
1,000+	15.00	800+	15.10

a) What is the economic order quantity?
b) Which supplier should be used? Why?
c) What is the optimal order quantity and total annual cost of ordering, purchasing, and holding the component? **Px**

••• **12.25** Chris Sandvig Irrigation, Inc., has summarized the price list from four potential suppliers of an underground control valve. See the table below. Annual usage is 2,400 valves; order cost is $10 per order; and annual inventory holding costs are $3.33 per unit.

Which vendor should be selected and what order quantity is best if Sandvig Irrigation wants to minimize total cost?

Vendor A		Vendor B	
Quantity	Price	Quantity	Price
1–49	$35.00	1–74	$34.75
50–74	34.75	75–149	34.00
75–149	33.55	150–299	32.80
150–299	32.35	300–499	31.60
300–499	31.15	500+	30.50
500+	30.75		

Vendor C		Vendor D	
Quantity	Price	Quantity	Price
1–99	$34.50	1–199	$34.25
100–199	33.75	200–399	33.00
200–399	32.50	400+	31.00
400+	31.10		**Px**

••• **12.26** Emery Pharmaceutical uses an unstable chemical compound that must be kept in an environment where both temperature and humidity can be controlled. Emery uses 800 pounds per month of the chemical, estimates the holding cost to be 50% of the purchase price (because of spoilage), and estimates order costs to be $50 per order. The cost schedules of two suppliers are as follows:

Vendor 1		Vendor 2	
Quantity	Price/lb	Quantity	Price/lb
1–499	$17.00	1–399	$17.10
500–999	16.75	400–799	16.85
1,000+	16.50	800–1,199	16.60
		1,200+	16.25

a) What is the economic order quantity for both suppliers?
b) What quantity should be ordered and which supplier should be used?
c) What is the total cost for the most economic order size?
d) What factor(s) should be considered besides total cost? **Px**

•• **12.27** Barbara Flynn is in charge of maintaining hospital supplies at General Hospital. During the past year, the mean lead time demand for bandage BX-5 was 60 (and was normally distributed). Furthermore, the standard deviation for BX-5 was 7. Ms. Flynn would like to maintain a 90% service level.
a) What safety stock level do you recommend for BX-5?
b) What is the appropriate reorder point? **Px**

•• **12.28** Based on available information, lead time demand for PC jump drives averages 50 units (normally distributed), with a standard deviation of 5 drives. Management wants a 97% service level.
a) What value of Z should be applied?
b) How many drives should be carried as safety stock?
c) What is the appropriate reorder point? **Px**

••• **12.29** Authentic Thai rattan chairs (shown in the photo) are delivered to Gary Schwartz's chain of retail stores, called The Kathmandu Shop, once a year. The reorder point, without safety stock, is 200 chairs. Carrying cost is $30 per unit per year, and the cost of a stockout is $70 per chair per year. Given the following demand probabilities during the reorder period, how much safety stock should be carried?

Demand during Reorder Period	Probability
0	0.2
100	0.2
200	0.2
300	0.2
400	0.2 **Px**

•• **12.30** Tobacco is shipped from North Carolina to a cigarette manufacturer in Cambodia once a year. The reorder point, without safety stock, is 200 kilos. The carrying cost is $15 per kilo per year, and the cost of a stockout is $70 per kilo per year. Given the following demand probabilities during the reorder period, how much safety stock should be carried?

Demand During Reorder Period (kilos)	Probability
0	0.1
100	0.1
200	0.2
300	0.4
400	0.2 **Px**

••• **12.31** Mr. Beautiful, an organization that sells weight training sets, has an ordering cost of $40 for the BB-1 set. (BB-1 stands for Body Beautiful Number 1.) The carrying cost for BB-1 is $5 per set per year. To meet demand, Mr. Beautiful orders large quantities of BB-1 seven times a year. The stockout cost for BB-1 is estimated to be $50 per set. Over the past several years, Mr. Beautiful has observed the following demand during the lead time for BB-1:

Demand during Lead Time	Probability
40	.1
50	.2
60	.2
70	.2
80	.2
90	.1
	1.0

The reorder point for BB-1 is 60 sets. What level of safety stock should be maintained for BB-1? **Px**

•• **12.32** Chicago's Hard Rock Hotel distributes a mean of 1,000 bath towels per day to guests at the pool and in their rooms. This demand is normally distributed with a standard deviation of 100 towels per day, based on occupancy. The laundry firm that has the linen contract requires a 2-day lead time. The hotel expects a 98% service level to satisfy high guest expectations.
a) What is the ROP?
b) What is the safety stock? **Px**

•• **12.33** First Printing has contracts with legal firms in San Francisco to copy their court documents. Daily demand is almost constant at 12,500 pages of documents. The lead time for paper delivery is normally distributed with a mean of 4 days and a standard deviation of 1 day. A 97% service level is expected. Compute First's ROP. **Px**

••• **12.34** Gainesville Cigar stocks Cuban cigars that have variable lead times because of the difficulty in importing the product: Lead time is normally distributed with an average of 6 weeks and a standard deviation of 2 weeks. Demand is also a variable and normally distributed with a mean of 200 cigars per week and a standard deviation of 25 cigars. For a 90% service level, what is the ROP? **Px**

• **12.35** Louisiana Power and Light orders utility poles on the first business day of each month from its supplier in Oregon. The target value is 40 poles in this fixed-period system (P-system). It is time to order and there are 5 poles on hand. Because of a delayed shipment last month, 18 poles ordered earlier should arrive shortly. How many poles should be ordered now?

••• **12.36** Kim Clark has asked you to help him determine the best ordering policy for a new product. The demand for the new product has been forecasted to be about 1,000 units annually. To help you get a handle on the carrying and ordering costs, Kim has given you the list of last year's costs. He thought that these costs might be appropriate for the new product.

Cost Factor	Cost ($)	Cost Factor	Cost ($)
Taxes for the warehouse	2,000	Warehouse supplies	280
Receiving and incoming inspection	1,500	Research and development	2,750
New product development	2,500	Purchasing salaries & wages	30,000
Acct. Dept. costs to pay invoices	500	Warehouse salaries & wages	12,800
Inventory insurance	600	Pilferage of inventory	800
Product advertising	800	Purchase order supplies	500
Spoilage	750	Inventory obsolescence	300
Sending purchasing orders	800	Purchasing Dept. overhead	1,000

He also told you that these data were compiled for 10,000 inventory items that were carried or held during the year. You have also determined that 200 orders were placed last year. Your job as a new operations management graduate is to help Kim determine the economic order quantity for the new product.

•••• **12.37** Emarpy Appliance is a company that produces all kinds of major appliances. Bud Banis, the president of Emarpy, is concerned about the production policy for the company's best-selling refrigerator. The annual demand for this has been about 8,000 units each year, and this demand has been constant throughout the year. The production capacity is 200 units per day. Each time production starts, it costs the company $120 to move materials into place, reset the assembly line, and clean the equipment. The holding cost of a refrigerator is $50 per year. The current production plan calls for 400 refrigerators to be produced in each production run. Assume there are 250 working days per year.
a) What is the daily demand of this product?
b) If the company were to continue to produce 400 units each time production starts, how many days would production continue?
c) Under the current policy, how many production runs per year would be required? What would the annual setup cost be?
d) If the current policy continues, how many refrigerators would be in inventory when production stops? What would the average inventory level be?
e) If the company produces 400 refrigerators at a time, what would the total annual setup cost and holding cost be?

f) If Bud Banis wants to minimize the total annual inventory cost, how many refrigerators should be produced in each production run? How much would this save the company in inventory costs compared to the current policy of producing 400 in each production run? **Px**

•••• **12.38** A gourmet coffee shop in downtown San Francisco is open 200 days a year and sells an average of 75 pounds of Kona coffee beans a day. (Demand can be assumed to be distributed normally with a standard deviation of 15 pounds per day). After ordering (fixed cost = $16 per order), beans are always shipped from Hawaii within exactly 4 days. Per-pound annual holding costs for the beans are $3.
a) What is the economic order quantity (EOQ) for Kona coffee beans?
b) What are the total annual holding costs of stock for Kona coffee beans?
c) What are the total annual ordering costs for Kona coffee beans?
d) Assume that management has specified that no more than a 1% risk during stockout is acceptable. What should the reorder point (ROP) be?
e) What is the safety stock needed to attain a 1% risk of stockout during lead time?
f) What is the annual holding cost of maintaining the level of safety stock needed to support a 1% risk?
g) If management specified that a 2% risk of stockout during lead time would be acceptable, would the safety stock holding costs decrease or increase?

Case Studies

Zhou Bicycle Company

Zhou Bicycle Company (ZBC), located in Seattle, is a wholesale distributor of bicycles and bicycle parts. Formed in 1981, by University of Washington Professor Yong-Pin Zhou, the firm's primary retail outlets are located within a 400-mile radius of the distribution center. These retail outlets receive the order from ZBC within 2 days after notifying the distribution center, provided that the stock is available. However, if an order is not fulfilled by the company, no backorder is placed; the retailers arrange to get their shipment from other distributors, and ZBC loses that amount of business.

The company distributes a wide variety of bicycles. The most popular model, and the major source of revenue to the company, is the AirWing. ZBC receives all the models from a single manufacturer in China, and shipment takes as long as 4 weeks from the time an order is placed. With the cost of communication, paperwork, and customs clearance included, ZBC estimates that each time an order is placed, it incurs a cost of $65. The purchase price paid by ZBC, per bicycle, is roughly 60% of the suggested retail price for all the styles available, and the inventory carrying cost is 1% per month (12% per year) of the purchase price paid by ZBC. The retail price (paid by the customers) for the AirWing is $170 per bicycle.

ZBC is interested in making an inventory plan for 2008. The firm wants to maintain a 95% service level with its customers to minimize the losses on the lost orders. The data collected for the past 2 years are summarized in the following table. A forecast for AirWing model sales in 2008 has been developed and will be used to make an inventory plan for ZBC.

Demands for AirWing Model

Month	2006	2007	Forecast for 2008
January	6	7	8
February	12	14	15
March	24	27	31
April	46	53	59
May	75	86	97
June	47	54	60
July	30	34	39
August	18	21	24
September	13	15	16
October	12	13	15
November	22	25	28
December	38	42	47
Total	343	391	439

Discussion Questions

1. Develop an inventory plan to help ZBC.
2. Discuss ROPs and total costs.
3. How can you address demand that is not at the level of the planning horizon?

Source: Professor Kala Chand Seal, Loyola Marymount University.

Sturdivant Sound Systems

Sturdivant Sound Systems manufactures and sells sound systems for both home and auto. All parts of the sound systems, with the exception of DVD players, are produced in the Rochester, New York, plant. DVD players used in the assembly of Sturdivant systems are purchased from Morris Electronics of Concord, New Hampshire.

Sturdivant purchasing agent Mary Kim submits a purchase requisition for DVD players once every 4 weeks. The company's annual requirements total 5,000 units (20 per working day), and the cost per unit is $60. (Sturdivant does not purchase in greater quantities because Morris Electronics does not offer quantity discounts.) Because Morris promises delivery within 1 week following receipt of a purchase requisition, rarely is there a shortage of DVD players. (Total time between date of order and date of receipt is 5 days.)

Associated with the purchase of each shipment are procurement costs. These costs, which amount to $20 per order, include the costs of preparing the requisition, inspecting and storing the delivered goods, updating inventory records, and issuing a voucher and a check for payment. In addition to procurement costs, Sturdivant incurs inventory carrying costs that include insurance, storage, handling, taxes, and so forth. These costs equal $6 per unit per year.

Beginning in August of this year, Sturdivant management will embark on a companywide cost-control program in an attempt to improve its profits. One area to be closely scrutinized for possible cost savings is inventory procurement.

Discussion Questions

1. Compute the optimal order quantity of DVD players.
2. Determine the appropriate reorder point (in units).
3. Compute the cost savings that the company will realize if it implements the optimal inventory procurement decision.
4. Should procurement costs be considered a linear function of the number of orders?

Source: Reprinted by permission of Professor Jerry Kinard, Western Carolina University.

Inventory Control at Wheeled Coach

Video Case

Controlling inventory is one of Wheeled Coach's toughest problems. Operating according to a strategy of mass customization and responsiveness, management knows that success is dependent on tight inventory control. Anything else results in an inability to deliver promptly, chaos on the assembly line, and a huge inventory investment. Wheeled Coach finds that almost 50% of the $40,000 to $100,000 cost of every ambulance it manufactures is purchased materials. A large proportion of that 50% is in chassis (purchased from Ford), aluminum (from Reynolds Metal), and plywood used for flooring and cabinetry construction (from local suppliers). Wheeled Coach tracks these A inventory items quite carefully, maintaining tight security/control and ordering carefully so as to maximize quantity discounts while minimizing on-hand stock. Because of long lead times and scheduling needs at Reynolds, aluminum must actually be ordered as much as 8 months in advance.

In a crowded ambulance industry in which it is the only giant, its 45 competitors don't have the purchasing power to draw the same discounts as Wheeled Coach. But this competitive cost advantage cannot be taken lightly, according to President Bob Collins.

"Cycle counting in our stockrooms is critical. No part can leave the locked stockrooms without appearing on a bill of materials."

Accurate bills of material (BOM) are a requirement if products are going to be built on time. Additionally, because of the custom nature of each vehicle, most orders are won only after a bidding process. Accurate BOMs are critical to cost estimation and the resulting bid. For these reasons, Collins was emphatic that Wheeled Coach maintain outstanding inventory control. The *Global Company Profile* featuring Wheeled Coach (which opens Chapter 14) provides further details about the ambulance inventory control and production process.

Discussion Questions*

1. Explain how Wheeled Coach implements ABC analysis.
2. If you were to take over as inventory control manager at Wheeled Coach, what additional policies and techniques would you initiate to ensure accurate inventory records?
3. How would you go about implementing these suggestions?

*You may wish to view this case on your DVD before answering these questions.

Additional Case Studies

Internet case studies: Visit our Companion Web site at www.prenhall.com/heizer for these free case studies:

- **Southwestern University F:** The university must decide how many football day programs to order, and from whom.
- **LaPlace Power and Light:** This utility company is evaluating its current inventory policies.

Harvard has selected these Harvard Business School cases to accompany this chapter:

harvardbusinessonline.hbsp.harvard.edu

- **Pioneer Hi-Bred International, Inc.** (#898-238): Deals with the challenges in managing inventory in a large, complex agribusiness firm.
- **L.L. Bean, Inc.: Item Forecasting and Inventory** (#893-003): The firm must balance costs of understocking and overstocking when demand for catalog items is uncertain.
- **Blanchard Importing and Distribution Co., Inc.** (#673-033): Illustrates two main types of errors resulting from the use of EOQ models.

Bibliography

Abernathy, Frederick H., et al. "Control Your Inventory in a World of Lean Retailing." *Harvard Business Review* 78, no. 6 (November–December 2000): 169–176.

Arnold, David. "Seven Rules of International Distribution." *Harvard Business Review* 78, no. 6 (November–December 2000): 131–137.

Arnold, J. R., and S. Chapman. *Introduction to Materials Management*, 5th ed. Upper Saddle River, NJ: Prentice Hall (2004).

Balakrishnan, R., B. Render, and R. M. Stair. *Managerial Decision Modeling with Spreadsheets*, 2nd ed. Upper Saddle River, NJ: Prentice Hall (2007).

Bradley, James R., and Richard W. Conway. "Managing Cyclic Inventories." *Production and Operations Management* 12, no. 4 (winter 2003): 464–479.

Cannon, Alan R., and Richard E. Crandall, "The Way Things Never Were." *APICS—The Performance Advantage* (January 2004): 32–35.

Chapmas, Stephen. *Fundamentals of Production Planning and Control*. Upper Saddle River, NJ: Prentice Hall (2006).

Chopra, Sunil, Gilles Reinhardt, and Maqbool Dada. "The Effect of Lead Time Uncertainty on Safety Stocks." *Decision Sciences* 35, no. 1 (winter 2004): 1–24.

Coleman, B. Jay. "Determining the Correct Service Level Target." *Production and Inventory Management Journal* 41, no. 1 (1st quarter 2000): 19–23.

Corsten, Daniel, and Nirmalya Kumar. "Profits in the Pie of the Beholder." *Harvard Business Review* (May 2003): 22–23.

Landvater, D. V. *World Class Production and Inventory Management*. Newburg, NH: Oliver Wight Publications (1997).

Noblitt, James M. "The Economic Order Quantity Model: Panacea or Plague?" *APICS—The Performance Advantage* (February 2001): 53–57.

Robison, James A. "Inventory Profile Analysis." *Production and Inventory Management Journal* 42, no. 2 (2nd quarter 2001): 8–13.

Rubin, Paul A., and W. C. Benton. "A Generalized Framework for Quantity Discount Pricing Schedules." *Decision Sciences* 34, no. 1 (winter 2003): 173–188.

Sell, William H. "Recovering Value from I.O.$." *APICS—The Performance Advantage* (November/December 2003): 50–53.

Vollmann, T. E., W. L. Berry, D. C. Whybark, and F. R. Jacobs. *Manufacturing Planning and Control for Supply Chain Management*, 5th ed. Burr Ridge, IL: Irwin/McGraw (2005).

Witt, Clyde E. "Mobile Warehouse Supplies U.S. Marines in Iraq." *Material Handling Management* 60, no. 8 (August 2005): 24–25.

Zipkin, Paul. *Foundations of Inventory Management*. New York: Irwin/McGraw-Hill (2000).

Internet Resources

APICS: The Educational Society for Resource Management: **www.apics.org**

Center for Inventory Management: **www.inventorymanagement.com**

Institute of Industrial Engineers: **www.iienet.org**

Inventory Control Forum: **www.cris.com/~kthill/sites.htm**

CHAPTER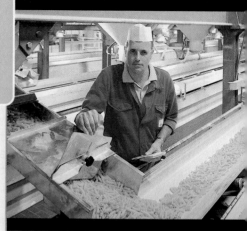

13

Aggregate Planning

Chapter Outline

Ten OM Strategy Decisions

Design of Goods and Services

Managing Quality

Process Strategy

Location Strategies

Layout Strategies

Human Resources

Supply Chain Management

Inventory Management

Scheduling

  Aggregate

  Short-Term

Maintenance

Learning Objectives

When you complete this chapter you should be able to

1. Define aggregate planning
2. Identify optional strategies for developing an aggregate plan
3. Prepare a graphical aggregate plan
4. Solve an aggregate plan via the transportation method of linear programming
5. Understand and solve a yield management problem

Global Company Profile: Anheuser-Busch

Aggregate Planning Provides a Competitive Advantage at Anheuser-Busch

Anheuser-Busch produces close to 40% of the beer consumed in the U.S. The company achieves efficiency at such volume by doing an excellent job of matching capacity to demand.

Matching capacity and demand in the intermediate term (3 to 18 months) is the heart of aggregate planning. Anheuser-Busch matches fluctuating demand by brand to specific plant, labor, and inventory capacity. Meticulous cleaning between batches, effective maintenance, and efficient employee and facility scheduling contribute to high facility utilization, a major factor in all high capital investment facilities.

Beer is made in a product-focused facility—one that produces high volume and low variety. Product-focused production processes usually require high fixed cost but typically have the benefit of low variable costs. Maintaining high use of such facilities is critical because high capital costs require high use to be competitive. Performance above the break-even point requires high use, and downtime is disastrous.

Beer production can be divided into four stages. The first stage is the selection and assurance of raw material delivery and quality. The second stage is the actual brewing process from milling to aging. The third stage is packaging into the wide variety of containers desired by the market.

The fourth and final stage is distribution, which includes temperature-controlled delivery and storage. Each stage has its resource limitations. Developing the aggregate plan to make it all work is demanding. Effective aggregate planning is a major ingredient in competitive advantage at Anheuser-Busch.

▲ Shown are brew kettles in which wort, later to become beer, is boiled and hops are added for the flavor and bitter character they impart.

◀ In the brewhouse control room, process control uses computers to monitor the starting-cellar process, where wort is in its final stage of preparation before being fermented into beer.

▶ The canning line imprints on each can a code that identifies the day, year, and 15-minute period of production; the plant at which the product was brewed and packaged; and the production line used. This system allows any quality-control problems to be tracked and corrected.

◀ A critical ingredient, hops, is being added to give the beer "character."

Manufacturers like Anheuser-Busch, GE, and Yamaha face tough decisions when trying to schedule products like beer, air conditioners, and jet skis, the demand for which is heavily dependent on seasonal variation. If the firms increase output and a summer is warmer than usual, they stand to increase sales and market share. However, if the summer is cool, they may be stuck with expensive unsold product. Developing plans that minimize costs connected with such forecasts is one of the main functions of an operations manager.

Aggregate planning (also known as **aggregate scheduling**) is concerned with determining the quantity and timing of production for the intermediate future, often from 3 to 18 months ahead. Operations managers try to determine the best way to meet forecasted demand by adjusting production rates, labor levels, inventory levels, overtime work, subcontracting rates, and other controllable variables. Usually, *the objective of aggregate planning is to meet forecasted demand while minimizing cost over the planning period*. However, other strategic issues may be more important than low cost. These strategies may be to smooth employment levels, to drive down inventory levels, or to meet a high level of service.

For manufacturers, the aggregate schedule ties the firm's strategic goals to production plans, but for service organizations, the aggregate schedule ties strategic goals to workforce schedules.

Four things are needed for aggregate planning:

- A logical overall unit for measuring sales and output, such as air-conditioning units at GE or cases of beer at Anheuser-Busch
- A forecast of demand for a reasonable intermediate planning period in these aggregate terms
- A method for determining the costs that we discuss in this chapter
- A model that combines forecasts and costs so that scheduling decisions can be made for the planning period

In this chapter we describe the aggregate planning decision, show how the aggregate plan fits into the overall planning process, and describe several techniques that managers use when developing an aggregate plan. We stress both manufacturing and service-sector firms.

THE PLANNING PROCESS

In Chapter 4, we saw that demand forecasting can address short-, medium-, and long-range problems. Long-range forecasts help managers deal with capacity and strategic issues and are the responsibility of top management (see Figure 13.1). Top management formulates policy-related questions, such as facility location and expansion, new product development, research funding, and investment over a period of several years.

Medium-range planning begins once long-term capacity decisions are made. This is the job of the operations manager. **Scheduling decisions** address the problem of matching productivity to fluctuating demands. These plans need to be consistent with top management's long-range strategy and work within the resources allocated by earlier strategic decisions. Medium- (or "intermediate-") range planning is accomplished by building an aggregate production plan.

Short-range planning may extend up to a year but is usually less than 3 months. This plan is also the responsibility of operations personnel, who work with supervisors and foremen to "disaggregate" the intermediate plan into weekly, daily, and hourly schedules. Tactics for dealing with short-term planning involve loading, sequencing, expediting, and dispatching, which are discussed in Chapter 15.

Figure 13.1 illustrates the time horizons and features for short-, intermediate-, and long-range planning.

THE NATURE OF AGGREGATE PLANNING

As the term *aggregate* implies, an aggregate plan means combining appropriate resources into general, or overall, terms. Given demand forecast, facility capacity, inventory levels, workforce size, and related inputs, the planner has to select the rate of output for a facility over the next 3 to 18 months. The plan can be for manufacturing firms such as Anheuser-Busch and Whirlpool, hospitals, colleges, or Prentice Hall, the company that published this textbook.

Take, for a manufacturing example, Snapper, which produces many different models of lawn mowers. It makes walk-behind mowers, rear-engine riding mowers, garden tractors, and many

---

Aggregate planning (or aggregate scheduling)
An approach to determine the quantity and timing of production for the intermediate future (usually 3 to 18 months ahead).

Learning Objective

1. Define aggregate planning

Scheduling decisions
Plans that match production to changes in demand.

◀ **Figure 13.1**

Planning Tasks and Responsibilities

Long-range plans (over one year)
Capacity decisions (Supplement 7) are critical to long-range plans.

Research and Development
New product plans
Capital investments
Facility location/expansion

Top executives

Intermediate-range plans (3 to 18 months)
The aggregate planning techniques of this chapter aid managers in building intermediate-range plans.

Sales planning
Production planning and budgeting
Setting employment, inventory, subcontracting levels
Analyzing operating plans

Operations managers

Short-range plans (up to 3 months)
The scheduling techniques (Chapter 15) help managers prepare short-range plans.
Job assignments
Ordering
Job scheduling
Dispatching
Overtime
Part-time help

Operations managers, supervisors, foremen

Responsibility   **Planning tasks and time horizons**

If top management does a poor or inconsistent job of long-term planning, problems will develop that make the aggregate planner's job very tough.

more, for a total of 145 models. For each month in the upcoming 3 quarters, the aggregate plan for Snapper might have the following output (in units of production) for Snapper's "family" of mowers:

	Quarter 1			Quarter 2			Quarter 3	
Jan.	Feb.	March	April	May	June	July	Aug.	Sept.
150,000	120,000	110,000	100,000	130,000	150,000	180,000	150,000	140,000

Note that the plan looks at production *in the aggregate* (the family of mowers), not as a product-by-product breakdown. Likewise, an aggregate plan for BMW tells the auto manufacturer how many cars to make, but not how many should be two-door versus four-door or red versus green.[1] It tells Nucor Steel how many tons of steel to produce but does not differentiate grades of steel. (We extend the discussion of planning at Snapper in the *OM in Action* box "Building the Plan at Snapper.")

▲ *Operations personnel build an aggregate plan using the total expected demand for all of the family products, such as 145 models at Snapper (a few of which are shown above). Only when the forecasts are assembled in the aggregate plan does the company decide how to meet the total requirement with the available resources. These resource constraints include facility capacity, workforce size, supply chain limitations, inventory issues, and financial resources.*

[1]For detailed discussion on BMW's planning, see B. Fleishman, S. Ferber, and P. Henrich, "Strategic Planning of BMW's Global Production Network," *Interfaces* 36, no. 3 (May–June 2006): 194–208.

Every bright red Snapper lawn mower sold anywhere in the world comes from a factory in McDonough, Georgia. Ten years ago, the Snapper line had about 40 models of mowers, leaf blowers, and snow blowers. Today, reflecting the demands of mass customization, the product line is much more complex. Snapper designs, manufactures, and sells 145 models. This means that aggregate planning and the related short-term scheduling have become more complex, too.

In the past, Snapper met demand by carrying a huge inventory for 52 regional distributors and thousands of independent dealerships. It manufactured and shipped tens of thousands of lawn mowers, worth tens of millions of dollars, without quite knowing when they would be sold—a very expensive approach to meeting demand. Some changes were necessary. The new plan's goal is for each distribution center to receive only the minimum inventory necessary to meet demand. Today, operations managers at Snapper evaluate production capacity and use frequent data from the field as inputs to sophisticated software to forecast sales. The new system tracks customer demand and aggregates forecasts for every model in every region of the country. It even adjusts for holidays and weather. And the number of distribution centers has been cut from 52 to 4.

Once evaluation of the aggregate plan against capacity determines the plan to be feasible, Snapper's planners break down the plan into production needs for each model. Production by model is accomplished by building rolling monthly and weekly plans. These plans track the pace at which various units are selling. Then, the final step requires juggling work assignments to various work centers for each shift, such as 265 lawn mowers in an 8-hour shift. That's a new Snapper every 109 seconds.

Sources: The Wall Street Journal (July 14, 2006): B1, B6; *Fast Company* (January/February 2006): 67–71; and **www.snapper.com**.

In the service sector, consider Computrain, a company that provides microcomputer training for managers. The firm offers courses on spreadsheets, graphics, databases, word processing, and writing Web pages, and employs several instructors to meet the demand for its services from business and government. Demand for training tends to be very low near holiday seasons and during summer, when many people take their vacations. To meet the fluctuating needs for courses, the company can hire and lay off instructors, advertise to increase demand in slow seasons, or subcontract its work to other training agencies during peak periods. Again, aggregate planning makes decisions about intermediate-range capacity, not specific courses or instructors.

Aggregate planning is part of a larger production planning system. Therefore, understanding the interfaces between the plan and several internal and external factors is useful. Figure 13.2 shows that the operations manager not only receives input from the marketing department's demand forecast, but must also deal with financial data, personnel, capacity, and availability of raw materials. In a manufacturing environment, the process of breaking the aggregate plan down into greater detail is called **disaggregation**. Disaggregation results in a **master production schedule**, which provides input to material requirements planning (MRP) systems. The master production schedule addresses the purchasing or production of parts or components needed to make final products (see Chapter 14). Detailed work schedules for people and priority scheduling for products result as the final step of the production planning system (and are discussed in Chapter 15).

Disaggregation
The process of breaking an aggregate plan into greater detail.

Master production schedule
A timetable that specifies what is to be made and when.

AGGREGATE PLANNING STRATEGIES

When generating an aggregate plan, the operations manager must answer several questions:

1. Should inventories be used to absorb changes in demand during the planning period?
2. Should changes be accommodated by varying the size of the workforce?
3. Should part-timers be used, or should overtime and idle time absorb fluctuations?
4. Should subcontractors be used on fluctuating orders so a stable workforce can be maintained?
5. Should prices or other factors be changed to influence demand?

All of these are legitimate planning strategies. They involve the manipulation of inventory, production rates, labor levels, capacity, and other controllable variables. We will now examine eight options in more detail. The first five are called *capacity options* because they do not try to change demand but attempt to absorb the fluctuations in it. The last three are *demand options* through which firms try to smooth out changes in the demand pattern over the planning period.

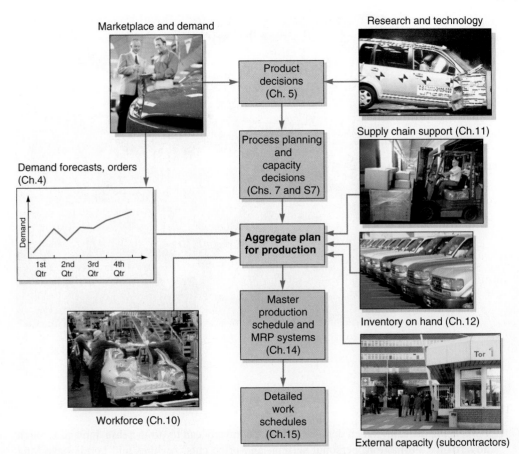

Capacity Options

A firm can choose from the following basic capacity (production) options:

1. *Changing inventory levels:* Managers can increase inventory during periods of low demand to meet high demand in future periods. If this strategy is selected, costs associated with storage, insurance, handling, obsolescence, pilferage, and capital invested will increase. (These costs typically range from 15% to 40% of the value of an item annually.) On the other hand, when the firm enters a period of increasing demand, shortages can result in lost sales due to potentially longer lead times and poorer customer service.
2. *Varying workforce size by hiring or layoffs:* One way to meet demand is to hire or lay off production workers to match production rates. However, often new employees need to be trained, and the average productivity drops temporarily as they are absorbed into the firm. Layoffs or firings, of course, lower the morale of all workers and can lead to lower productivity.
3. *Varying production rates through overtime or idle time:* It is sometimes possible to keep a constant workforce while varying working hours, cutting back the number of hours worked when demand is low and increasing them when it rises. Yet when demand is on a large upswing, there is a limit on how much overtime is realistic. Overtime pay requires more money, and too much overtime can wear workers down to the point that overall productivity drops off. Overtime also implies the increased overhead needed to keep a facility open. On the other hand, when there is a period of decreased demand, the company must somehow absorb workers' idle time—usually a difficult process.
4. *Subcontracting:* A firm can acquire temporary capacity by subcontracting work during peak demand periods. Subcontracting, however, has several pitfalls. First, it may be costly; second, it risks opening the client's door to a competitor. Third, it is often hard to find the perfect subcontract supplier, one who always delivers the quality product on time.
5. *Using part-time workers:* Especially in the service sector, part-time workers can fill unskilled labor needs. This practice is common in restaurants, retail stores, and supermarkets.

Aggregate planning in the real world involves a lot of trial and error.

▶ *John Deere and Company, the "granddaddy" of farm equipment manufacturers, uses sales incentives to smooth demand. During the fall and winter off-seasons, sales are boosted with price cuts and other incentives. About 70% of Deere's big machines are ordered in advance of seasonal use—about double the industry rate. Incentives hurt margins, but Deere keeps its market share and controls costs by producing more steadily all year long. Similarly, in service businesses like L.L. Bean, some customers are offered free shipping on orders placed before the Christmas rush.*

Demand Options

The basic demand options are:

1. *Influencing demand:* When demand is low, a company can try to increase demand through advertising, promotion, personal selling, and price cuts. Airlines and hotels have long offered weekend discounts and off-season rates; telephone companies charge less at night; some colleges give discounts to senior citizens; and air conditioners are least expensive in winter. However, even special advertising, promotions, selling, and pricing are not always able to balance demand with production capacity.

2. *Back ordering during high-demand periods:* Back orders are orders for goods or services that a firm accepts but is unable (either on purpose or by chance) to fill at the moment. If customers are willing to wait without loss of their goodwill or order, back ordering is a possible strategy. Many firms back order, but the approach often results in lost sales.

3. *Counterseasonal product and service mixing:* A widely used active smoothing technique among manufacturers is to develop a product mix of counterseasonal items. Examples include companies that make both furnaces and air conditioners or lawn mowers and snowblowers. However, companies that follow this approach may find themselves involved in products or services beyond their area of expertise or beyond their target market.

> *Negative inventory means a company owes units to customers. It either loses sales or back orders to make it up.*

These eight options, along with their advantages and disadvantages, are summarized in Table 13.1.

Mixing Options to Develop a Plan

Although each of the five capacity options and three demand options may produce an effective aggregate schedule, some combination of capacity options and demand options may be better.

Many manufacturers assume that the use of the demand options has been fully explored by the marketing department and those reasonable options incorporated into the demand forecast. The operations manager then builds the aggregate plan based on that forecast. However, using the five capacity options at his command, the operations manager still has a multitude of possible plans. These plans can embody, at one extreme, a *chase strategy* and, at the other, a *level-scheduling strategy*. They may, of course, fall somewhere in between.

Chase strategy
A planning strategy that sets production equal to forecasted demand.

Chase Strategy   A **chase strategy** attempts to achieve output rates for each period that match the demand forecast for that period. This strategy can be accomplished in a variety of ways. For example, the operations manager can vary workforce levels by hiring or laying off or

▼ **Table 13.1** Aggregate Planning Options: Advantages and Disadvantages

Option	Advantages	Disadvantages	Some Comments
Changing inventory levels	Changes in human resources are gradual or none; no abrupt production changes.	Inventory holding costs may increase. Shortages may result in lost sales.	Applies mainly to production, not service, operations.
Varying workforce size by hiring or layoffs	Avoids the costs of other alternatives.	Hiring, layoff, and training costs may be significant.	Used where size of labor pool is large.
Varying production rates through overtime or idle time	Matches seasonal fluctuations without hiring/training costs.	Overtime premiums; tired workers; may not meet demand.	Allows flexibility within the aggregate plan.
Subcontracting	Permits flexibility and smoothing of the firm's output.	Loss of quality control; reduced profits; loss of future business.	Applies mainly in production settings.
Using part-time workers	Is less costly and more flexible than full-time workers.	High turnover/training costs; quality suffers; scheduling difficult.	Good for unskilled jobs in areas with large temporary labor pools.
Influencing demand	Tries to use excess capacity. Discounts draw new customers.	Uncertainty in demand. Hard to match demand to supply exactly.	Creates marketing ideas. Overbooking used in some businesses.
Back ordering during high-demand periods	May avoid overtime. Keeps capacity constant.	Customer must be willing to wait, but goodwill is lost.	Many companies back order.
Counterseasonal product and service mixing	Fully utilizes resources; allows stable workforce.	May require skills or equipment outside firm's areas of expertise.	Risky finding products or services with opposite demand patterns.

can vary production by means of overtime, idle time, part-time employees, or subcontracting. Many service organizations favor the chase strategy because the inventory option is difficult or impossible to adopt. Industries that have moved toward a chase strategy include education, hospitality, and construction.

Level Strategy   A level strategy (or **level scheduling**) is an aggregate plan in which production is uniform from period to period. Firms like Toyota and Nissan keep production at uniform levels and may (1) let the finished-goods inventory go up or down to buffer the difference between demand and production or (2) find alternative work for employees. Their philosophy is that a stable workforce leads to a better-quality product, less turnover and absenteeism, and more employee commitment to corporate goals. Other hidden savings include employees who are more experienced, easier scheduling and supervision, and fewer dramatic startups and shutdowns. Level scheduling works well when demand is reasonably stable.

Level scheduling
Maintaining a constant output rate, production rate, or workforce level over the planning horizon.

METHODS FOR AGGREGATE PLANNING

For most firms, neither a chase strategy nor a level strategy is likely to prove ideal, so a combination of the eight options (called a **mixed strategy**) must be investigated to achieve minimum cost. However, because there are a huge number of possible mixed strategies, managers find that aggregate planning can be a challenging task. Finding the one "optimal" plan is not always possible. Indeed, some companies have no formal aggregate planning process: They use the same plan from year to year, making adjustments up or down just enough to fit the new annual demand. This method certainly does not provide much flexibility, and if the original plan was suboptimal, the entire production process will be locked into suboptimal performance.

In this section, we introduce several techniques that operations managers use to develop more useful and appropriate aggregate plans. They range from the widely used graphical method to a series of more formal mathematical approaches, including the transportation method of linear programming.

Mixed strategy
A planning strategy that uses two or more controllable variables to set a feasible production plan.

Mixed plans are more complex than single, or "pure," ones but typically yield a better strategy.

Graphical Methods

Graphical techniques

Aggregate planning techniques that work with a few variables at a time to allow planners to compare projected demand with existing capacity.

Graphical techniques are popular because they are easy to understand and use. Basically, these plans work with a few variables at a time to allow planners to compare projected demand with existing capacity. They are trial-and-error approaches that do not guarantee an optimal production plan, but they require only limited computations and can be performed by clerical staff. Following are the five steps in the graphical method:

1. Determine the demand in each period.
2. Determine capacity for regular time, overtime, and subcontracting each period.
3. Find labor costs, hiring and layoff costs, and inventory holding costs.
4. Consider company policy that may apply to the workers or to stock levels.
5. Develop alternative plans and examine their total costs.

These steps are illustrated in Examples 1 to 4.

Learning Objective

3. Prepare a graphical aggregate plan

EXAMPLE 1

Graphical approach to aggregate planning for a roofing supplier

A Juarez, Mexico, manufacturer of roofing supplies has developed monthly forecasts for a family of products. Data for the 6-month period January to June are presented in Table 13.2. The firm would like to begin development of an aggregate plan.

Month	Expected Demand	Production Days	Demand per Day (computed)
Jan.	900	22	41
Feb.	700	18	39
Mar.	800	21	38
Apr.	1,200	21	57
May	1,500	22	68
June	1,100	20	55
	6,200	124	

▶ **Table 13.2**

Monthly Forecasts

Approach: Plot daily and average demand to illustrate the nature of the aggregate planning problem.

Solution: First, compute demand per day by dividing the expected monthly demand by the number of production days (working days) each month and drawing a graph of those forecasted demands (Figure 13.3). Second, draw a dotted line across the chart that represents the production rate required to meet average demand over the 6-month period. The chart is computed as follows:

$$\text{Average requirement} = \frac{\text{Total expected demand}}{\text{Number of production days}} = \frac{6,200}{124} = 50 \text{ units per day}$$

▶ **Figure 13.3**

Graph of Forecast and Average Forecast Demand

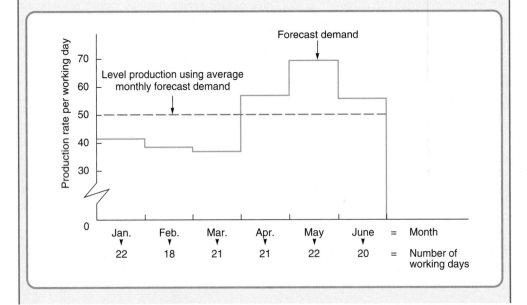

Insight: Changes in the production rate become obvious when the data are graphed. Note that in the first 3 months, expected demand is lower than average, while expected demand in April, May, and June is above average.

Learning exercise: If demand for June increases to 1,200 (from 1,100), what is the impact on Figure 13.3? [Answer: The daily rate for June will go up to 60, and average production will increase to 50.8 (6,300/124).]

Related problem: 13.1

The graph in Figure 13.3 illustrates how the forecast differs from the average demand. Some strategies for meeting the forecast were listed earlier. The firm, for example, might staff in order to yield a production rate that meets *average* demand (as indicated by the dashed line). Or it might produce a steady rate of, say, 30 units and then subcontract excess demand to other roofing suppliers. Other plans might combine overtime work with subcontracting to absorb demand. Examples 2 to 4 illustrate three possible strategies.

One possible strategy (call it plan 1) for the manufacturer described in Example 1 is to maintain a constant workforce throughout the 6-month period. A second (plan 2) is to maintain a constant workforce at a level necessary to meet the lowest demand month (March) and to meet all demand above this level by subcontracting. Both plan 1 and plan 2 have level production and are, therefore, called *level strategies.* Plan 3 is to hire and lay off workers as needed to produce exact monthly requirements—*a chase strategy.* Table 13.3 provides cost information necessary for analyzing these three alternatives:	**EXAMPLE 2** **Plan 1 for the roofing supplier—a constant workforce**

Inventory carrying cost	$ 5 per unit per month
Subcontracting cost per unit	$ 10 per unit
Average pay rate	$ 5 per hour ($40 per day)
Overtime pay rate	$ 7 per hour (above 8 hours per day)
Labor-hours to produce a unit	1.6 hours per unit
Cost of increasing daily production rate (hiring and training)	$300 per unit
Cost of decreasing daily production rate (layoffs)	$600 per unit

 Excel OM Data File Ch13Ex2.xls

◀ **Table 13.3**

Cost Information

Analysis of Plan 1. Approach: Here we assume that 50 units are produced per day and that we have a constant workforce, no overtime or idle time, no safety stock, and no subcontractors. The firm accumulates inventory during the slack period of demand, January through March, and depletes it during the higher-demand warm season, April through June. We assume beginning inventory = 0 and planned ending inventory = 0:

Solution: We construct the table below and accumulate the costs:

Month	Production at 50 Units per Day	Demand Forecast	Monthly Inventory Change	Ending Inventory
Jan.	1,100	900	+200	200
Feb.	900	700	+200	400
Mar.	1,050	800	+250	650
Apr.	1,050	1,200	−150	500
May	1,100	1,500	−400	100
June	1,000	1,100	−100	0
				1,850

Total units of inventory carried over from one month to the next month = 1,850 units

Workforce required to produce 50 units per day = 10 workers

 Active Model 13.1

Example 2 is further illustrated in Active Model 13.1 on the CD-ROM and in the Exercise located on page 550.

Because each unit requires 1.6 labor-hours to produce, each worker can make 5 units in an 8-hour day. Thus to produce 50 units, 10 workers are needed.

Finally, the costs of plan 1 are computed as follows:

Costs		Calculations
Inventory carrying	$ 9,250	(= 1,850 units carried × $5 per unit)
Regular-time labor	49,600	(= 10 workers × $40 per day × 124 days)
Other costs (overtime, hiring, layoffs, subcontracting)	0	
Total cost	$58,850	

Insight: Note the significant cost of carrying the inventory.

Learning exercise: If demand for June decreases to 1,000 (from 1,100), what is the change in cost? [Answer: Total inventory carried will increase to 1,950 at $5, for an inventory cost of $9,750 and total cost of $59,350.]

Related problems: 13.2, 13.3, 13.4, 13.5, 13.6, 13.7, 13.8, 13.9, 13.10, 13.11, 13.12, 13.19

The graph for Example 2 was shown in Figure 13.3. Some planners prefer a *cumulative* graph to display visually how the forecast deviates from the average requirements. Note that both the level production line and the forecast line produce the same total production. Such a graph is provided in Figure 13.4.

▶ **Figure 13.4**

Cumulative Graph for Plan 1

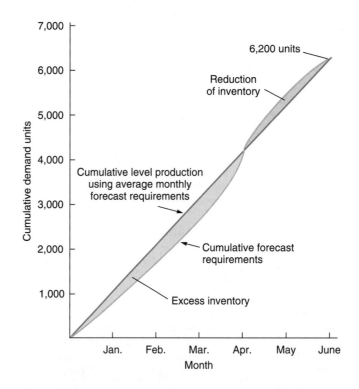

EXAMPLE 3

Plan 2 for the roofing supplier—use of subcontractors within a constant workforce

Analysis of Plan 2. Approach: Although a constant workforce is also maintained in plan 2, it is set low enough to meet demand only in March, the lowest demand-per-day month. To produce 38 units per day in-house, 7.6 workers are needed. (You can think of this as 7 full-time workers and 1 part-timer.) *All* other demand is met by subcontracting. Subcontracting is thus required in every other month. No inventory holding costs are incurred in plan 2.

Solution: Because 6,200 units are required during the aggregate plan period, we must compute how many can be made by the firm and how many must be subcontracted:

$$\text{In-house production} = 38 \text{ units per day} \times 124 \text{ production days}$$

$$= 4,712 \text{ units}$$

$$\text{Subcontract units} = 6,200 - 4,712 = 1,488 \text{ units}$$

The costs of plan 2 are computed as follows:

Costs		Calculations
Regular-time labor	$37,696	(= 7.6 workers × $40 per day × 124 days)
Subcontracting	14,880	(= 1,488 units × $10 per unit)
Total cost	$52,576	

Insight: Note the lower cost of regular labor but the added subcontracting cost.

Learning exercise: If demand for June increases to 1,200 (from 1,100), what is the change in cost? [Answer: Subcontracting requirements increase to 1,588 at $10 per unit, for a subcontracting cost of $15,880 and a total cost of $53,576.]

Related problems: 13.2, 13.3, 13.4, 13.5, 13.6, 13.7, 13.8, 13.9, 13.10, 13.11, 13.12, 13.19

EXAMPLE 4

Plan 3 for the roofing supplier—hiring and firing

Analysis of Plan 3. Approach: The final strategy, plan 3, involves varying the workforce size by hiring and firing as necessary. The production rate will equal the demand, and there is no change in production from the previous month, December.

Solution: Table 13.4 shows the calculations and the total cost of plan 3. Recall that it costs $600 per unit produced to reduce production from the previous month's daily level and $300 per unit change to increase the daily rate of production through hirings.

◀ **Table 13.4**

Cost Computations for Plan 3

Month	Forecast (units)	Daily Production Rate	Basic Production Cost (demand × 1.6 hr per unit × $5 per hr)	Extra Cost of Increasing Production (hiring cost)	Extra Cost of Decreasing Production (layoff cost)	Total Cost
Jan.	900	41	$ 7,200	—	—	$ 7,200
Feb.	700	39	5,600	—	$1,200 (= 2 × $600)	6,800
Mar.	800	38	6,400	—	$ 600 (= 1 × $600)	7,000
Apr.	1,200	57	9,600	$5,700 (= 19 × $300)	—	15,300
May	1,500	68	12,000	$3,300 (= 11 × $300)	—	15,300
June	1,100	55	8,800	—	$7,800 (= 13 × $600)	$16,600
			$49,600	$9,000	$9,600	$68,200

Thus, the total cost, including production, hiring, and layoff, for plan 3 is $68,200.

Insight: Note the substantial cost associated with changing (both increasing and decreasing) the production levels.

Learning exercise: If demand for June increases to 1,200 (from 1,100), what is the change in cost? [Answer: Daily production for June is 60 units, which is a decrease of 8 units in the daily production rate from May's 68 units, so the new layoff cost is $4,800 (= 8 × $600), with a total cost of $65,200.]

Related problems: 13.2, 13.3, 13.4, 13.5, 13.6, 13.7, 13.8, 13.9, 13.10, 13.11, 13.12, 13.19

The final step in the graphical method is to compare the costs of each proposed plan and to select the approach with the least total cost. A summary analysis is provided in Table 13.5. We see that because plan 2 has the lowest cost, it is the best of the three options.

Of course, many other feasible strategies can be considered in a problem like this, including combinations that use some overtime. Although graphing is a popular management tool, its help is in evaluating strategies, not generating them. To generate strategies, a systematic approach that considers all costs and produces an effective solution is needed.

► **Table 13.5**

**Comparison of the
Three Plans**

Cost	Plan 1 (constant workforce of 10 workers)	Plan 2 (workforce of 7.6 workers plus subcontract)	Plan 3 (hiring and layoffs to meet demand)
Inventory carrying	$ 9,250	$ 0	$ 0
Regular labor	49,600	37,696	49,600
Overtime labor	0	0	0
Hiring	0	0	9,000
Layoffs	0	0	9,600
Subcontracting	0	14,880	0
Total cost	$58,850	$52,576	$68,200

Mathematical Approaches

This section briefly describes some of the mathematical approaches to aggregate planning that have been developed over the past 50 years.

The Transportation Method of Linear Programming   When an aggregate planning problem is viewed as one of allocating operating capacity to meet forecasted demand, it can be formulated in a linear programming format. The **transportation method of linear programming** is not a trial-and-error approach like graphing but rather produces an optimal plan for minimizing costs. It is also flexible in that it can specify regular and overtime production in each time period, the number of units to be subcontracted, extra shifts, and the inventory carryover from period to period.

Transportation method of linear programming

A way of solving for the optimal solution to an aggregate planning problem.

In Example 5, the supply consists of on-hand inventory and units produced by regular time, overtime, and subcontracting. Costs per unit, in the upper-right corner of each cell of the matrix in Table 13.7, relate to units produced in a given period or units carried in inventory from an earlier period.

EXAMPLE 5

Aggregate planning with the transportation method

Farnsworth Tire Company would like to develop an aggregate plan via the transportation method. Data that relate to production, demand, capacity, and cost at its West Virginia plant are shown in Table 13.6.

▼ **Table 13.6**   Farnsworth's Production, Demand, Capacity, and Cost Data

	Sales Period		
	Mar.	**Apr.**	**May**
Demand	800	1,000	750
Capacity:			
Regular	700	700	700
Overtime	50	50	50
Subcontracting	150	150	130
Beginning inventory	100 tires		

Costs	
Regular time	$40 per tire
Overtime	$50 per tire
Subcontract	$70 per tire
Carrying cost	$ 2 per tire per month

**Excel OM Data File
Ch13Ex5.xls**

Approach: Solve the aggregate planning problem by minimizing the costs of matching production in various periods to future demands.

solution: Table 13.7 illustrates the structure of the transportation table and an initial feasible solution.

◀ **Table 13.7**

Farnsworth's Transportation Table[a]

SUPPLY FROM		Period 1 (Mar.)	Period 2 (Apr.)	Period 3 (May)	Unused Capacity (dummy)	TOTAL CAPACITY AVAILABLE (supply)
		DEMAND FOR				
Beginning inventory		0 — 100	2	4	0	100
Period 1 Regular time		40 — 700	42	44	0	700
Overtime		50	52 — 50	54	0	50
Subcontract		70	72 — 150	74	0	150
Period 2 Regular time		×	40 — 700	42	0	700
Overtime		×	50 — 50	52	0	50
Subcontract		×	70 — 50	72	0 — 100	150
Period 3 Regular time		×	×	40 — 700	0	700
Overtime		×	×	50 — 50	0	50
Subcontract		×	×	70	0 — 130	130
TOTAL DEMAND		800	1,000	750	230	2,780

[a]Cells with an x indicate that back orders are not used at Farnsworth. When using Excel OM or POM for Windows to solve, you must insert a *very* high cost (e.g., 9999) in each cell that is not used for production.

Learning Objective

4. Solve an aggregate plan via the transportation method of linear programming

When setting up and analyzing this table, you should note the following:

1. Carrying costs are $2/tire per month. Tires produced in 1 period and held for 1 month will have a $2 higher cost. Because holding cost is linear, 2 months' holdover costs $4. So when you move across a row from left to right, regular time, overtime, and subcontracting costs are lowest when output is used the same period it is produced. If goods are made in one period and carried over to the next, holding costs are incurred. Beginning inventory, however, is generally given a unit cost of 0 if it is used to satisfy demand in period 1.

2. Transportation problems require that supply equals demand; so, a dummy column called "unused capacity" has been added. Costs of not using capacity are zero.

3. Because back ordering is not a viable alternative for this particular company, no production is possible in those cells that represent production in a period to satisfy demand in a past period (i.e., those periods with an "X"). If back ordering *is* allowed, costs of expediting, loss of goodwill, and loss of sales revenues are summed to estimate backorder cost.

4. Quantities in red in each column of Table 13.7 designate the levels of inventory needed to meet demand requirements (shown in the bottom row of the table). Demand of 800 tires in March is met by using 100 tires from beginning inventory and 700 tires from regular time.

5. In general, to complete the table, allocate as much production as you can to a cell with the smallest cost without exceeding the unused capacity in that row or demand in that column. If there is still some demand left in that row, allocate as much as you can to the next-lowest-cost cell. You then repeat this process for periods 2 and 3 (and beyond, if necessary). When you are finished, the sum of

all your entries in a row must equal the total row capacity, and the sum of all entries in a column must equal the demand for that period. (This step can be accomplished by the transportation method or by using POM for Windows or Excel OM software.)

Try to confirm that the cost of this initial solution is $105,900. The initial solution is not optimal, however. See if you can find the production schedule that yields the least cost (which turns out to be $105,700) using software or by hand.

Insight: The transportation method is flexible when costs are linear but does not work when costs are nonlinear.

Learning example: What is the impact on this problem if there is no beginning inventory? [Answer: Total capacity (units) available is reduced by 100 units and the need to subcontract increases by 100 units.]

Related problems: 13.13, 13.14, 13.15, 13.16, 13.17, 13.18

The transportation method of linear programming described in the above example was originally formulated by E. H. Bowman in 1956. Although it works well in analyzing the effects of holding inventories, using overtime, and subcontracting, it does not work when nonlinear or negative factors are introduced. Thus, when other factors such as hiring and layoffs are introduced, the more general method of linear programming must be used.

Management coefficients model

A formal planning model built around a manager's experience and performance.

Management Coefficients Model   Bowman's **management coefficients model**[2] builds a formal decision model around a manager's experience and performance. The assumption is that the manager's past performance is pretty good, so it can be used as a basis for future decisions. The technique uses a regression analysis of past production decisions made by managers. The regression line provides the relationship between variables (such as demand and labor) for future decisions. According to Bowman, managers' deficiencies are mostly inconsistencies in decision making.

Other Models   Two additional aggregate planning models are the linear decision rule and simulation. The *linear decision rule (LDR)* attempts to specify an optimum production rate and workforce level over a specific period. It minimizes the total costs of payroll, hiring, layoffs, overtime, and inventory through a series of quadratic cost curves.[3]

A computer model called *scheduling by simulation* uses a search procedure to look for the minimum-cost combination of values for workforce size and production rate.

Comparison of Aggregate Planning Methods

Although these mathematical models have been found by researchers to work well under certain conditions, and linear programming has found some acceptance in industry, the fact is that most sophisticated planning models are not widely used. Why? Perhaps it reflects the average manager's attitude about what he or she views as overly complex models. Like all of us, planners like to understand how and why the models on which they are basing important decisions work. Additionally, operations managers need to make decisions quickly based on the changing dynamics of the workplace—and building good models is time-consuming. This may explain why the simpler graphical approach is more generally accepted.

Table 13.8 highlights some of the main features of graphing, transportation, management coefficients, and simulation planning models.

[2]E. H. Bowman, "Consistency and Optimality in Managerial Decision Making," *Management Science* 9, no. 2 (January 1963): 310–321.
[3]Because LDR was developed by Charles C. Holt, Franco Modigliani, John F. Muth, and Herbert Simon, it is popularly known as the HMMS rule. For details, see Martin K. Starr, *Production and Operations Management* (Cincinnati, OH: Atomic Dog Publishing, 2004): 490–493.

Technique	Solution Approaches	Important Aspects
Graphical methods	Trial and error	Simple to understand and easy to use. Many solutions; one chosen may not be optimal.
Transportation method of linear programming	Optimization	LP software available; permits sensitivity analysis and new constraints; linear functions may not be realistic.
Management coefficients model	Heuristic	Simple, easy to implement; tries to mimic manager's decision process; uses regression.
Simulation	Change parameters	Complex; model may be difficult to build and for managers to understand.

◀ **Table 13.8**

Summary of Four Major Aggregate Planning Methods

AGGREGATE PLANNING IN SERVICES

Some service organizations conduct aggregate planning in exactly the same way as we did in Examples 1 through 5 in this chapter, but with demand management taking a more active role. Because most services pursue *combinations* of the eight capacity and demand options discussed earlier, they usually formulate mixed aggregate planning strategies. In industries such as banking, trucking, and fast foods, aggregate planning may be easier than in manufacturing.

Controlling the cost of labor in service firms is critical. Successful techniques include:

1. Accurate scheduling of labor-hours to assure quick response to customer demand
2. An on-call labor resource that can be added or deleted to meet unexpected demand
3. Flexibility of individual worker skills that permits reallocation of available labor
4. Flexibility in rate of output or hours of work to meet changing demand

These options may seem demanding, but they are not unusual in service industries, in which labor is the primary aggregate planning vehicle. For instance:

- Excess capacity is used to provide study and planning time by real estate and auto salespersons.
- Police and fire departments have provisions for calling in off-duty personnel for major emergencies. Where the emergency is extended, police or fire personnel may work longer hours and extra shifts.
- When business is unexpectedly light, restaurants and retail stores send personnel home early.
- Supermarket stock clerks work cash registers when checkout lines become too lengthy.
- Experienced waitresses increase their pace and efficiency of service as crowds of customers arrive.

Approaches to aggregate planning differ by the type of service provided. Here we discuss five service scenarios.

◀ *The heavy demands of the December holiday season place a special burden on aggregate planning at UPS. UPS maximizes truck and plane resource availability for the season, as well as overtime and temporary workers to match capacity to demand.*

Restaurants

In a business with a highly variable demand, such as a restaurant, aggregate scheduling is directed toward (1) smoothing the production rate and (2) finding the optimal size of the workforce. The general approach usually requires building very modest levels of inventory during slack periods and depleting inventory during peak periods, but using labor to accommodate most of the changes in demand. Because this situation is very similar to those found in manufacturing, traditional aggregate planning methods may be applied to services as well. One difference that should be noted is that even modest amounts of inventory may be perishable. In addition, the relevant units of time may be much smaller than in manufacturing. For example, in fast-food restaurants, peak and slack periods may be measured in fractions of an hour and the "product" may be inventoried for as little as 10 minutes.

Hospitals

Hospitals face aggregate planning problems in allocating money, staff, and supplies to meet the demands of patients. Michigan's Henry Ford Hospital, for example, plans for bed capacity and personnel needs in light of a patient-load forecast developed by moving averages. The necessary labor focus of its aggregate plan has led to the creation of a new floating staff pool serving each nursing pod.

National Chains of Small Service Firms

With the advent of national chains of small service businesses such as funeral homes, oil change outlets, and photocopy/printing centers, the question of aggregate planning versus independent planning at each business establishment becomes an issue. Both purchases and production capacity may be centrally planned when demand can be influenced through special promotions. This approach to aggregate scheduling is often advantageous because it reduces costs and helps manage cash flow at independent sites.

Miscellaneous Services

Most "miscellaneous" services—financial, transportation, and many communication and recreation services—provide intangible output. Aggregate planning for these services deals mainly with planning for human resource requirements and managing demand. The twofold goal is to level demand peaks and to design methods for fully utilizing labor resources during low-demand periods. Example 6 illustrates such a plan for a legal firm.

EXAMPLE 6

Aggregate planning in a law firm

▶ **Table 13.9**

Labor Allocation at Klasson and Avalon, Forecasts for Coming Quarter (1 lawyer = 500 hours of labor)

Klasson and Avalon, a medium-size Tampa law firm of 32 legal professionals, wants to develop an aggregate plan for the next quarter. The firm has developed 3 forecasts of billable hours for the next quarter for each of 5 categories of legal business it performs (column 1, Table 13.9). The 3 forecasts (best, likely, and worst) are shown in columns 2, 3, and 4 of Table 13.9.

	Labor-Hours Required			Capacity Constraints	
	(2)	(3)	(4)	(5)	(6)
	Forecasts			Maximum	Number of
(1) Category of Legal Business	Best (hours)	Likely (hours)	Worst (hours)	Demand in People	Qualified Personnel
Trial work	1,800	1,500	1,200	3.6	4
Legal research	4,500	4,000	3,500	9.0	32
Corporate law	8,000	7,000	6,500	16.0	15
Real estate law	1,700	1,500	1,300	3.4	6
Criminal law	3,500	3,000	2,500	7.0	12
Total hours	19,500	17,000	15,000		
Lawyers needed	39	34	30		

Approach: If we make some assumptions about the workweek and skills, we can provide an aggregate plan for the firm. Assuming a 40-hour workweek and that 100% of each lawyer's hours are billed, about 500 billable hours are available from each lawyer this fiscal quarter.

Solution: We divide hours of billable time (which is the demand) by 500 to provide a count of lawyers needed (lawyers represent the capacity) to cover the estimated demand. Capacity then is shown to be 39, 34, and 30 for the three forecasts, best, likely, and worst, respectively. For example, the best-case scenario of 19,500 total hours, divided by 500 hours per lawyer, equals 39 lawyers needed. Because all 32 lawyers at Klasson and Avalon are qualified to perform basic legal research, this skill has maximum scheduling flexibility (column 6). The most highly skilled (and capacity-constrained) categories are trial work and corporate law. The firm's best-case forecast just barely covers trial work, with 3.6 lawyers needed (see column 5) and 4 qualified (column 6). And corporate law is short 1 full person.

Overtime may be used to cover the excess this quarter, but as business expands, it may be necessary to hire or develop talent in both of these areas. Available staff adequately covers real estate and criminal practice, as long as other needs do not use their excess capacity. With its current legal staff of 32, Klasson and Avalon's best-case forecast will increase the workload by [(39 − 32)/32 =] 22% (assuming no new hires). This represents 1 extra day of work per lawyer per week. The worst-case scenario will result in about a 6% underutilization of talent. For both of these scenarios, the firm has determined that available staff will provide adequate service.

Insight: While our definitions of demand and capacity are different than for a manufacturing firm, aggregate planning is as appropriate, useful, and necessary in a service environment as in manufacturing.

Learning exercise: If the criminal law best-case forecast increases to 4,500 hours, what happens to the number of lawyers needed? [Answer: The demand for lawyers increases to 41.]

Related problems: 13.20, 13.21

Source: Adapted from Glenn Bassett, *Operations Management for Service Industries* (Westport, CT: Quorum Books, 1992): 110.

Airline Industry

Airlines and auto-rental firms also have unique aggregate scheduling problems. Consider an airline that has its headquarters in New York, two hub sites in cities such as Atlanta and Dallas, and 150 offices in airports throughout the country. This planning is considerably more complex than aggregate planning for a single site or even for a number of independent sites.

Aggregate planning consists of tables or schedules for (1) number of flights in and out of each hub; (2) number of flights on all routes; (3) number of passengers to be serviced on all flights; (4) number of air personnel and ground personnel required at each hub and airport; and (5) determining the seats to be allocated to various fare classes. Techniques for determining seat allocation are called yield, or revenue, management, our next topic.

YIELD MANAGEMENT

Most operations models, like most business models, assume that firms charge all customers the same price for a product. In fact, many firms work hard at charging different prices. The idea is to match the demand curve by charging based on differences in the customer's willingness to pay. The management challenge is to identify those differences and price accordingly. The technique for multiple price points is called yield management.

Yield (or **revenue**) **management** is the aggregate planning process of allocating the company's scarce resources to customers at prices that will maximize yield or revenue. Popular use of the technique dates to the 1980s, when American Airlines's reservation system (called SABRE) allowed the airline to alter ticket prices, in real time and on any route, based on demand information. If it looked like demand for expensive seats was low, more discounted seats were offered. If demand for full-fare seats was high, the number of discounted seats was reduced.

Yield (or **revenue**) **management**
Capacity decisions that determine the allocation of resources to maximize profit or yield.

Yield Management at Hertz

For over 90 years, Hertz has been renting standard cars for a fixed amount per day. During the past two decades, however, a significant increase in demand has derived from airline travelers flying for business purposes. As the auto-rental market has changed and matured, Hertz has offered more options, including allowing customers to pick up and drop off in different locations. This option has resulted in excess capacity in some cities and shortages in others.

These shortages and overages alerted Hertz to the need for a yield management system similar to those used in the airline industry. The system is used to set prices, regulate the movement, and ultimately determine the availability of cars at each location. Through research, Hertz found that different city locations peak on different days of the week. So cars are moved to peak-demand locations from locations where the demand is low. By altering both the price and quantity of cars at various locations, Hertz has been able to increase "yield" and boost revenue.

The yield management system is primarily used by regional and local managers to better deal with changes in demand in the U.S. market. Hertz's plan to go global with the system, however, faces major challenges in foreign countries, where restrictions against moving empty cars across national borders are common.

Sources: The Wall Street Journal (December 30, 2003): D1 and (March 3, 2000): W-4; and *Cornell Hotel and Restaurant Quarterly* (December 2001): 33–46.

Learning Objective

5. Understand and solve a yield management problem

American Airlines's success in yield management spawned many other companies and industries to adopt the concept. Yield management in the hotel industry began in the late 1980s at Marriott International, which now claims an additional $400 million a year in profit from its management of revenue. The competing Omni hotel chain uses software that performs more than 100,000 calculations every night at each facility. The Dallas Omni, for example, charges its highest rates (about $279) on weekdays but heavily discounts (to as low as $99) on weekends. Its sister hotel in San Antonio, which is in a more tourist-oriented destination, reverses this rating scheme, with better deals for its consumers on weekdays. Similarly, Walt Disney World has multiple prices: an annual admission pass for an adult was recently quoted at $421; but for a Florida resident, $318; for a member of the AAA, $307; and for active-duty military, $385. The *OM in Action* box "Yield Management at Hertz," describes this practice in the rental car industry.

Organizations that have *perishable inventory*, such as airlines, hotels, car rental agencies, cruise lines, and even electrical utilities, have the following shared characteristics that make yield management of interest[4]:

1. Service or product can be sold in advance of consumption.
2. Demand fluctuates.
3. The resource (capacity) is relatively fixed.
4. Demand can be segmented.
5. Variable costs are low and fixed costs are high.

Example 7 illustrates how yield management works in a hotel.

EXAMPLE 7

Yield management

The Cleveland Downtown Inn is a 100-room hotel that has historically charged one set price for its rooms, $150 per night. The variable cost of a room being occupied is low. Management believes the cleaning, air-conditioning, and incidental costs of soap, shampoo, and so forth, are $15 per room per night. Sales average 50 rooms per night. Figure 13.5 illustrates the current pricing scheme. Net sales are $6,750 per night with a single price point.

Approach: Analyze pricing from the perspective of yield management. We note in Figure 13.5 that some guests would have been willing to spend more than $150 per room—"money left on the table." Others would be willing to pay more than the variable cost of $15 but less than $150—"passed-up contribution."

---

[4]R. Oberwetter, "Revenue Management," *OR/MS Today* (June 2001): 41–44.

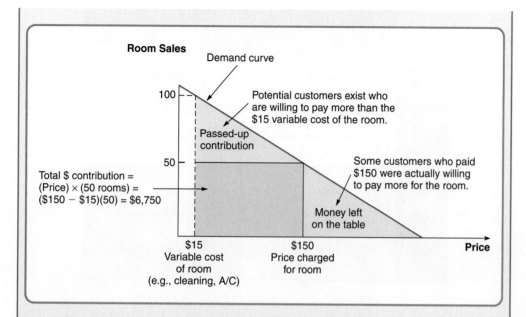

Solution: In Figure 13.6, the inn decides to set *two* price levels. It estimates that 30 rooms per night can be sold at $100 and another 30 rooms at $200, using yield management software that is widely available.

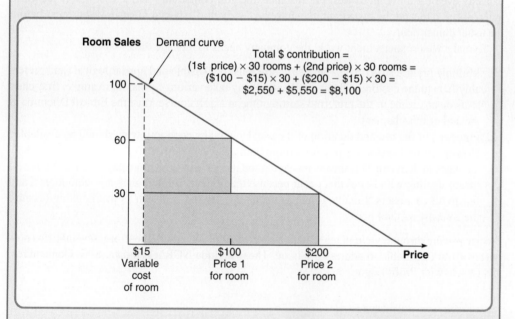

Insight: Yield management has increased total contribution to $8,100 ($2,550 from $100 rooms and $5,550 from $200 rooms). It may be that even more price levels are called for at Cleveland Downtown Inn.

Learning exercise: If the hotel develops a third price of $150 and can sell half of the $100 rooms at the increased rate, what is the contribution? [Answer: $8,850 = (15 × $85) + (15 × $135) + (30 × $185).]

Related problem: 13.22

Industries traditionally associated with revenue management operate in quadrant 2 of Figure 13.7. They are able to apply variable pricing for their product and control product use or availability (number of airline seats or hotel rooms sold at economy rate). On the other hand, movie theaters, arenas, or performing arts centers (quadrant 1) have less pricing flexibility but still use time (evening or matinee) and location (orchestra, side, or balcony) to manage revenue. In both

▶ **Figure 13.7**

Yield Management Matrix

Industries in quadrant 2 are traditionally associated with revenue management.

Source: Adapted from S. Kimes and K. McGuire, "Function Space Revenue Management," *Cornell Hotel and Restaurant Administration Quarterly* 42, no. 6 (December 2001): 33–46.

		Price	
		Tend to be fixed	Tend to be variable
Duration of use	Predictable use	Quadrant 1: Movies Stadiums/arenas Convention centers Hotel meeting space	Quadrant 2: Hotels Airlines Rental cars Cruise lines
	Unpredictable use	Quadrant 3: Restaurants Golf courses Internet service providers	Quadrant 4: Continuing care hospitals

cases, management has control over the amount of the resource used—the duration of the resource—such as a seat for 2 hours.

In the lower half of Figure 13.7, the manager's job is more difficult because the duration of the use of the resource is less controllable. However, with imagination, managers are using excess capacity even for these industries. For instance, the golf course may sell less desirable tee times at a reduced rate, and the restaurant may have an "early bird" special to generate business before the usual dinner hour.

To make yield management work, the company needs to manage three issues:

1. Multiple pricing structures: These structure must be feasible and appear logical (and preferably fair) to the customer. Such justification may take various forms, for example, first-class seats on an airline or the preferred starting time at a golf course. (See the Ethical Dilemma at the end of this chapter).

2. Forecasts of the use and duration of the use: How many economy seats should be available? How much will customers pay for a room with an ocean view?

3. Changes in demand: This means managing the increased use as more capacity is sold. It also means dealing with issues that occur because the pricing structure may not seem logical and fair to all customers. Finally, it means managing new issues, such as overbooking because the forecast was not perfect.

Precise pricing through yield management has substantial potential. Therefore, several firms now have software available to address the issue. These include NCR's Teradata, SPS, DemandTec, and Oracle with Profit Logic.

Summary

Aggregate planning provides companies with a necessary weapon to help capture market shares in the global economy. The aggregate plan provides both manufacturing and service firms the ability to respond to changing customer demands while still producing at low-cost and high-quality levels.

The aggregate schedule sets levels of inventory, production, subcontracting, and employment over an intermediate time range, usually 3 to 18 months. This chapter describes several aggregate planning techniques, ranging from the popular graphical approach to a variety of mathematical models such as linear programming.

The aggregate plan is an important responsibility of an operations manager and a key to efficient production. Output from the aggregate schedule leads to a more detailed master production schedule, which is the basis for disaggregation, job scheduling, and MRP systems.

Aggregate plans for manufacturing firms and service systems are similar. Restaurants, airlines, and hotels are all service systems that employ aggregate plans, and have an opportunity to implement yield management. But regardless of the industry or planning method, the most important issue is the implementation of the plan. In this respect, managers appear to be more comfortable with faster, less complex, and less mathematical approaches to planning.

Key Terms

Aggregate planning (or aggregate scheduling) *(p. 528)*
Scheduling decisions *(p. 528)*
Disaggregation *(p. 530)*
Master production schedule *(p. 530)*

Chase strategy *(p. 532)*
Level scheduling *(p. 533)*
Mixed strategy *(p. 533)*
Graphical techniques *(p. 534)*

Transportation method of linear programming *(p. 538)*
Management coefficients model *(p. 540)*
Yield (or revenue) management *(p. 543)*

Using Software for Aggregate Planning

This section illustrates the use of Excel OM and POM for Windows in aggregate planning.

✗ Using Excel OM

Excel OM's Aggregate Planning module is demonstrated in Program 13.1. Again using data from Example 2, Program 13.1 provides input and some of the formulas used to compute the costs of regular time, overtime, subcontracting, holding, shortage, and increase or decrease in production. The user must provide the production plan for Excel OM to analyze.

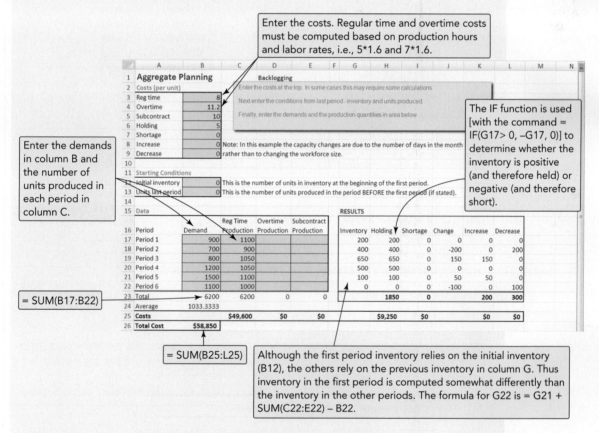

▲ **Program 13.1** **Using Excel OM for Aggregate Planning, with Example 2 Data**

ℙ Using POM for Windows

The POM for Windows Aggregate Planning module performs aggregate or production planning for up to 90 time periods. Given a set of demands for future periods, you can try various plans to determine the lowest-cost plan based on holding, shortage, production, and changeover costs. Four methods are available for planning. More help is available on each after you choose the method. See Appendix IV for further details.

Solved Problem 13.1

The roofing manufacturer described in Examples 1 to 4 of this chapter wishes to consider yet a fourth planning strategy (plan 4). This one maintains a constant workforce of eight people and uses overtime whenever necessary to meet demand. Use the information found in Table 13.3 on page 535. Again, assume beginning and ending inventories are equal to zero.

Solution

Employ eight workers and use overtime when necessary. Note that carrying costs will be encountered in this plan.

Month	Production Days	Production at 40 Units per Day	Beginning-of-Month Inventory	Forecast Demand This Month	Overtime Production Needed	Ending Inventory
Jan.	22	880	—	900	20 units	0 units
Feb.	18	720	0	700	0 units	20 units
Mar.	21	840	20	800	0 units	60 units
Apr.	21	840	60	1,200	300 units	0 units
May	22	880	0	1,500	620 units	0 units
June	20	800	0	1,100	300 units	0 units
					1,240 units	80 units

Carrying cost totals = 80 units × $5/unit/month = $400

Regular pay:

$$8 \text{ workers} \times \$40/\text{day} \times 124 \text{ days} = \$39,680$$

To produce 1,240 units at overtime rate (of $7/hour) requires (1,240 × 1.6 =) 1,984 hours.

$$\text{Overtime pay} = \$7/\text{hour} \times 1,984 \text{ hours} = \$13,888$$

Plan 4

Costs (workforce of 8 plus overtime)

Carrying cost	$ 400	(80 units carried × $5/unit)
Regular labor	39,680	(8 workers × $40/day × 124 days)
Overtime	13,888	(1,984 hours × $7/hour)
Hiring or firing	0	
Subcontracting	0	
Total costs	$53,968	

Plan 2 is still preferable at $52,576.

Solved Problem 13.2

A Dover, Delaware, plant has developed the accompanying supply, demand, cost, and inventory data. The firm has a constant workforce and meets all its demand. Allocate production capacity to satisfy demand at a minimum cost. What is the cost of this plan?

Demand Forecast

Period	Demand (units)
1	450
2	550
3	750

Supply Capacity Available (units)

Period	Regular Time	Overtime	Subcontract
1	300	50	200
2	400	50	200
3	450	50	200

Other Data

Initial inventory	50 units
Regular-time cost per unit	$50
Overtime cost per unit	$65
Subcontract cost per unit	$80
Carrying cost per unit per period	$ 1
Back order cost per unit per period	$ 4

solution

SUPPLY FROM		Period 1	Period 2	Period 3	Unused Capacity (dummy)	TOTAL CAPACITY AVAILABLE (supply)
Beginning inventory		0 / 50	1	2	0	50
Period 1	Regular time	50 / 300	51	52	0	300
	Overtime	65 / 50	66	67	0	50
	Subcontract	80 / 50	81	82	0 / 150	200
Period 2	Regular time	54	50 / 400	51	0	400
	Overtime	69	65 / 50	66	0	50
	Subcontract	84	80 / 100	81 / 50	0 / 50	200
Period 3	Regular time	58	54	50 / 450	0	450
	Overtime	73	69	65 / 50	0	50
	Subcontract	88	84	80 / 200	0	200
TOTAL DEMAND		450	550	750	200	1,950

Cost of plan:

Period 1: $50(\$0) + 300(\$50) + 50(\$65) + 50(\$80) = \$22{,}250$

Period 2: $400(\$50) + 50(\$65) + 100(\$80) = \$31{,}250$

Period 3: $50(\$81) + 450(\$50) + 50(\$65) + 200(\$80) = \underline{\$45{,}800}$ *

Total cost $\$99{,}300$

*Includes 50 units of subcontract and carrying cost.

Self-Test

- *Before taking the self-test*, refer to the learning objectives listed at the beginning of the chapter and the key terms listed at the end of the chapter.
- Use the key at the back of the text to **correct** your answers.
- *Restudy* pages that correspond to any questions you answered incorrectly or material you feel uncertain about.

1. Aggregate planning is concerned with determining the quantity and timing of production in the:
   a) short term
   b) intermediate term
   c) long term
   d) all of the above

2. Aggregate planning deals with a number of constraints. These typically are:
   a) job assignments, job ordering, dispatching, and overtime help
   b) part-time help, weekly scheduling, and SKU production scheduling
   c) subcontracting, employment levels, inventory levels, and capacity
   d) capital investment, expansion or contracting capacity, and R&D
   e) facility location, production budgeting, overtime, and R&D

3. Aggregate planning may require:
   a) back ordering
   b) influencing demand
   c) counterseasonal product mixing
   d) subcontracting
   e) all of the above

4. An aggregate planning model is the:
   a) transportation method
   b) linear decision rule
   c) management coefficients model
   d) graphic method
   e) all of the above

5. The critical element in aggregate planning for most services is:
   a) capital investment
   b) labor flexibility

c) inventory management
d) subcontracting
e) all of the above

6. Which of the following aggregate planning strategies requires employing relatively unskilled personnel to be most effective?
   a) varying production rates through overtime or idle time
   b) using part-time workers
   c) back ordering during high-demand periods
   d) subcontracting

7. Which of the following aggregate planning strategies is likely to have the least impact on quality in the service industry?
   a) using part-time workers
   b) changing inventory level
   c) subcontracting
   d) varying production rates through overtime or idle time

8. Managers typically do not use sophisticated planning models because:
   a) these models do not provide information pertinent to the decision at hand
   b) they view these models as overly complex and do not fully understand them
   c) research has demonstrated that such models seldom work well
   d) the time periods addressed by such models are too long

9. Level scheduling usually results in _____ than other strategies.
   a) higher costs
   b) better quality
   c) more subcontracting
   d) more employee turnover

10. Yield management requires that management deals with:
    a) multiple pricing structures
    b) changes in demand
    c) forecasts of use
    d) forecasts of duration of use
    e) all of the above

Active Model Exercise

This active model contains a 6-month aggregate planning problem using a leveling strategy. You can use the scrollbars to adjust the base level of daily production during the month, the amount of daily overtime, and the amount of subcontracting. Note that the formulas are set up such that subcontracting is chosen before overtime since in the example the subcontracting cost per unit is less than the overtime cost per unit.

Questions

1. Each worker makes five units per day. If the number of workers is reduced from 10 to 9, dropping the daily capacity, what happens to the cost?

2. What regular time level minimizes the total cost?

3. How low can the regular daily capacity get before overtime will be required?

4. How low can the regular daily capacity get before there will not be enough capacity to meet the demand?

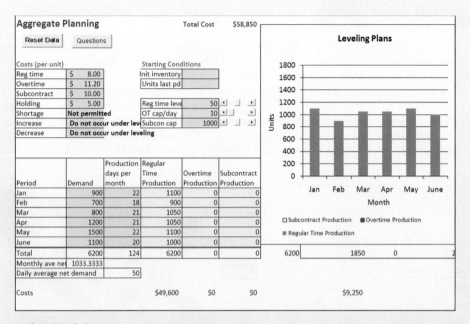

Aggregate Planning   Total Cost $58,850

Period	Demand	Production days per month	Regular Time Production	Overtime Production	Subcontract Production
Jan	900	22	1100	0	0
Feb	700	18	900	0	0
Mar	800	21	1050	0	0
Apr	1200	21	1050	0	0
May	1500	22	1100	0	0
June	1100	20	1000	0	0
Total	6200	124	6200	0	0
Monthly ave net	1033.3333				
Daily average net demand		50			

Costs $49,600 $0 $0 $9,250

▲ **Active Model 13.1** **Analysis of Aggregate Plan 1 Using the Roofing Manufacturer Data in Example 2**

Discussion Questions

1. Define aggregate planning.
2. Explain what the term *aggregate* in "aggregate planning" means.
3. List the strategic objectives of aggregate planning. Which one of these is most often addressed by the quantitative techniques of aggregate planning? Which one of these is generally the most important?
4. Define chase strategy.
5. What is a pure strategy? Provide a few examples.
6. What is level scheduling? What is the basic philosophy underlying it?
7. Define mixed strategy. Why would a firm use a mixed strategy instead of a simple pure strategy?

8. What are the advantages and disadvantages of varying the size of the workforce to meet demand requirements each period?
9. Why are mathematical models not more widely used in aggregate planning?
10. How does aggregate planning in service differ from aggregate planning in manufacturing?
11. What is the relationship between the aggregate plan and the master production schedule?
12. Why are graphical aggregate planning methods useful?
13. What are major limitations of using the transportation method for aggregate planning?
14. How does yield management impact an aggregate plan?

Ethical Dilemma

Airline passengers today stand in numerous lines, are crowded into small seats on mostly full airplanes, and often spend time on taxiways because of air-traffic problems or lack of open gates. But what gripes travelers almost as much as these annoyances is finding out that the person sitting next to them paid a much lower fare than they did for their seat. This concept of "yield management" or "revenue management" results in ticket pricing that can range from free to thousands of dollars on the same plane. Figure 13.8

illustrates what passengers recently paid for various seats on an 11:35 A.M. flight from Minneapolis to Anaheim, California, on an Airbus A320.

Make the case for, and then against, this pricing system. Does the general public seem to accept yield management? What would happen if you overheard the person in front of you in line getting a better room rate at a Hilton Hotel? How do customers manipulate the airline systems to get better fares?

Sales	Fare	Seats
First class	$817	1
Full fare	792	4
Corporate discount	491	5
21-day advance	273	20
Deep discounts	190	33
Frequent flyer program	0	7
Connections	—	53
Empty	—	27

▲ **Figure 13.8**   Yield Management Seat Costs on a Typical Flight

Problems*

• **13.1** Prepare a graph of the monthly forecasts and average forecasted demand for Industrial Air Corp., a manufacturer of a variety of large air conditioners for commercial applications.

Month	Production Days	Demand Forecast
January	22	1,000
February	18	1,100
March	22	1,200
April	21	1,300
May	22	1,350
June	21	1,350
July	21	1,300
August	22	1,200
September	21	1,100
October	22	1,100
November	20	1,050
December	20	900

•• **13.2** a) Develop another plan for the Mexican roofing manufacturer described in Examples 1 to 4 (pages 534–537) and Solved Problem 13.1 (page 548). For this plan, plan 5, the firm wishes to maintain a constant workforce of six, using subcontracting to meet remaining demand. Is this plan preferable?

b) The same roofing manufacturer in Examples 1 to 4 and Solved Problem 13.1 has yet a sixth plan. A constant workforce of seven is selected, with the remainder of demand filled by subcontracting. Is this better than plans 1–5? **Px**

••• **13.3** The president of Hill Enterprises, Terri Hill, projects the firm's aggregate demand requirements over the next 8 months as follows:

Jan.	1,400	May	2,200
Feb.	1,600	June	2,200
Mar.	1,800	July	1,800
Apr.	1,800	Aug.	1,400

Her operations manager is considering a new plan, which begins in January with 200 units on hand and ends with zero inventory. Stockout cost of lost sales is $100 per unit. Inventory holding cost is $20 per unit per month. Ignore any idle-time costs. The plan is called plan A.

*Note: **Px** means the problem may be solved with POM for Windows and/or Excel OM.

Plan A: Vary the workforce level to execute a "chase" strategy by producing the quantity demanded in the *prior* month. The December demand and rate of production are both 1,600 units per month. The cost of hiring additional workers is $5,000 per 100 units. The cost of laying off workers is $7,500 per 100 units. Evaluate this plan. **Px**

•• **13.4** Using the information in Problem 13.3, develop plan B. Produce at a constant rate of 1,400 units per month, which will meet minimum demands. Then use subcontracting, with additional units at a premium price of $75 per unit. Evaluate this plan by computing the costs for January through August. **Px**

•• **13.5** Hill is now considering plan C. Beginning inventory, stockout costs, and holding costs are provided in Problem 13.3:
a) Plan C: Keep a stable workforce by maintaining a constant production rate equal to the average requirements and allow varying inventory levels.
b) Plot the demand with a graph that also shows average requirements. Conduct your analysis for January through August. **Px**

••• **13.6** Hill's operations manager (see Problems 13.3 through 13.5) is also considering two mixed strategies for January–August:
a) Plan D: Keep the current workforce stable at producing 1,600 units per month. Permit a maximum of 20% overtime at an additional cost of $50 per unit. A warehouse now constrains the maximum allowable inventory on hand to 400 units or less.
b) Plan E: Keep the current workforce, which is producing 1,600 units per month, and subcontract to meet the rest of the demand. Evaluate plans D and E. **Px**

••• **13.7** Michael Carrigg, Inc., is a DVD manufacturer in need of an aggregate plan for July through December. The company has gathered the following data:

Costs	
Holding cost	$8/DVD/month
Subcontracting	$80/DVD
Regular-time labor	$12/hour
Overtime labor	$18/hour for hours above 8 hours/worker/day
Hiring cost	$40/worker
Layoff cost	$80/worker

Demand	
July	400
Aug.	500
Sept.	550
Oct.	700
Nov.	800
Dec.	700

Other Data	
Current workforce (June)	8 people
Labor-hours/DVD	4 hours
Workdays/month	20 days
Beginning inventory	150 DVDs*
Ending inventory	0 DVDs

*Note that there is no holding cost for June.

What will each of the two following strategies cost?
a) Vary the workforce so that production meets demand. Carrigg had eight workers on board in June.
b) Vary overtime only and use a constant workforce of eight. **Px**

•• **13.8** You manage a consulting firm down the street from Michael Carrigg, Inc., and to get your foot in the door, you have told Mr. Carrigg (see Problem 13.7) that you can do a better job at aggregate planning than his current staff. He said, "Fine. You do that, and you have a 1-year contract." You now have to make good on your boast using the data in Problem 13.7. If you develop a plan with back orders, which Mr. Carrigg doesn't like, be sure to include a $16-per-DVD-per-month cost.

••• **13.9** Mary Rhodes, operations manager at Kansas Furniture, has received the following estimates of demand requirements:

July	Aug.	Sept.	Oct.	Nov.	Dec.
1,000	1,200	1,400	1,800	1,800	1,600

Assuming stockout costs for lost sales of $100 per unit, inventory carrying costs of $25 per unit per month, and zero beginning and ending inventory, evaluate these two plans on an *incremental* cost basis:
• Plan A: Produce at a steady rate (equal to minimum requirements) of 1,000 units per month and subcontract additional units at a $60 per unit premium cost.
• Plan B: Vary the workforce, which performs at a current production level of 1,300 units per month. The cost of hiring additional workers is $3,000 per 100 units produced. The cost of layoffs is $6,000 per 100 units cut back. **Px**

••• **13.10** Mary Rhodes (see Problem 13.9) is considering two more mixed strategies. Using the data in Problem 13.9, compare plans C and D with plans A and B and make a recommendation.
• Plan C: Keep the current workforce steady at a level producing 1,300 units per month. Subcontract the remainder to meet demand. Assume that 300 units remaining from June are available in July.
• Plan D: Keep the current workforce at a level capable of producing 1,300 units per month. Permit a maximum of 20% overtime at a premium of $40 per unit. Assume that warehouse

limitations permit no more than a 180-unit carryover from month to month. This plan means that any time inventories reach 180, the plant is kept idle. Idle time per unit is $60. Any additional needs are subcontracted at a cost of $60 per incremental unit.

••• **13.11** Liz Perry Health and Beauty Products has developed a new shampoo and you need to develop its aggregate schedule. The cost accounting department has supplied you the cost relevant to the aggregate plan and the marketing department has provided a four-quarter forecast. All are shown as follows:

Quarter	Forecast
1	1,400
2	1,200
3	1,500
4	1,300

Costs	
Previous quarter's output	1,500 units
Beginning inventory	0 units
Stockout cost for back orders	$50 per unit
Inventory holding cost	$10 per unit for every unit held at the end of the quarter
Hiring workers	$40 per unit
Layoff workers	$80 per unit
Unit cost	$30 per unit
Overtime	$15 extra per unit
Subcontracting	Not available

Your job is to develop an aggregate plan for the next four quarters.
a) First, try a chase plan by hiring and layoffs (to meet the forecast) as necessary.
b) Then try a plan that holds employment steady.
c) Which is the more economical plan for Liz Perry Health and Beauty Products? **Px**

••• **13.12** Missouri's Soda Pop, Inc., has a new fruit drink for which it has high hopes. Steve Allen, the production planner, has assembled the following cost data and demand forecast:

Quarter	Forecast
1	1,800
2	1,100
3	1,600
4	900

Costs/Other Data
Previous quarter's output = 1,300 cases
Beginning inventory = 0 cases
Stockout cost = $150 per case
Inventory holding cost = $40 per case at end of quarter
Hiring employees = $40 per case
Terminating employees = $80 per case
Subcontracting cost = $60 per case
Unit cost on regular time = $30 per case
Overtime cost = $15 extra per case
Capacity on regular time = 1,800 cases per quarter

Steve's job is to develop an aggregate plan. The three initial options he wants to evaluate are:
• Plan A: a chase strategy that hires and fires personnel as necessary to meet the forecast.
• Plan B: a level strategy.
• Plan C: a level strategy that produces 1,200 cases per quarter and meets the forecasted demand with inventory and subcontracting.
a) Which strategy is the lowest-cost plan?
b) If you are Steve's boss, the VP for operations, which plan do you implement and why? **Px**

•• **13.13** Josie Gall's firm has developed the following supply, demand, cost, and inventory data. Allocate production capacity to meet demand at a minimum cost using the transportation method. What is the cost? Assume that the initial inventory has no holding cost in the first period and backorders are not permitted.

Supply Available

Period	Regular Time	Overtime	Subcontract	Demand Forecast
1	30	10	5	40
2	35	12	5	50
3	30	10	5	40

Initial inventory	20 units
Regular-time cost per unit	$100
Overtime cost per unit	$150
Subcontract cost per unit	$200
Carrying cost per unit per month	$ 4 **Px**

•• **13.14** Haifa Instruments, an Israeli producer of portable kidney dialysis units and other medical products, develops a 4-month aggregate plan. Demand and capacity (in units) are forecast as follows:

Capacity Source	Month 1	Month 2	Month 3	Month 4
Labor				
Regular time	235	255	290	300
Overtime	20	24	26	24
Subcontract	12	15	15	17
Demand	255	294	321	301

The cost of producing each dialysis unit is $985 on regular time, $1,310 on overtime, and $1,500 on a subcontract. Inventory carrying cost is $100 per unit per month. There is to be no beginning or ending inventory in stock and backorders are not permitted. Set up a production plan that minimizes cost using the transportation method. **Px**

•• **13.15** The production planning period for flat-screen monitors at Georgia's Fernandez Electronics, Inc., is 4 months. Cost data are as follows:

Regular-time cost per monitor	$ 70
Overtime cost per monitor	$110
Subcontract cost per monitor	$120
Carrying cost per monitor per month	$ 4

For each of the next 4 months, capacity and demand for flat-screen monitors are as follows:

	Period			
	Month 1	**Month 2**	**Month 3ª**	**Month 4**
Demand	2,000	2,500	1,500	2,100
Capacity				
Regular time	1,500	1,600	750	1,600
Overtime	400	400	200	400
Subcontract	600	600	600	600

ªFactory closes for 2 weeks of vacation.

Fernandez Electronics expects to enter the planning period with 500 monitors in stock. Back ordering is not permitted (meaning, for example, that monitors produced in the second month cannot be used in the first month). Develop a production plan that minimizes costs using the transportation method. **Px**

••• **13.16** A large Omaha feed mill, B. Swart Processing, prepares its 6-month aggregate plan by forecasting demand for 50-pound bags of cattle feed as follows: January, 1,000 bags; February, 1,200; March, 1,250; April, 1,450; May, 1,400; and June, 1,400. The feed mill plans to begin the new year with no inventory left over from the previous year and backorders are not permitted. It projects that capacity (during regular hours) for producing bags of feed will remain constant at 800 until the end of April, and then increase to 1,100 bags per month when a planned expansion is completed on May 1. Overtime capacity is set at 300 bags per month until the expansion, at which time it will increase to 400 bags per month. A friendly competitor in Sioux City, Iowa, is also available as a backup source to meet demand—but can provide only 500 bags total during the 6-month period. Develop a 6-month production plan for the feed mill using the transportation method.

Cost data are as follows:

Regular-time cost per bag (until April 30)	$12.00
Regular-time cost per bag (after May 1)	$11.00
Overtime cost per bag (during entire period)	$16.00
Cost of outside purchase per bag	$18.50
Carrying cost per bag per month	$ 1.00 **Px**

•• **13.17** Lon Min has developed a specialized airtight vacuum bag to extend the freshness of seafood shipped to restaurants. He has put together the following demand cost data:

Quarter	Forecast (units)	Regular Time	Over-time	Sub-contract
1	500	400	80	100
2	750	400	80	100
3	900	800	160	100
4	450	400	80	100

Initial inventory = 250 units
Regular time cost = $1.00/unit
Overtime cost = $1.50/unit
Subcontracting cost = $2.00/unit
Carrying cost = $0.20/unit/quarter
Back-order cost = $0.50/unit/quarter

Min decides that the initial inventory of 250 units will incur the 20¢/unit cost from each prior quarter (unlike the situation in most companies, where a 0 unit cost is assigned).

a) Find the optimal plan using the transportation method.
b) What is the cost of the plan?
c) Does any regular time capacity go unused? If so, how much in which periods?
d) What is the extent of back ordering in units and dollars? **Px**

••• **13.18** José Martinez of El Paso has developed polished stainless steel parts for his tortilla machine that makes it more of a "showpiece" for display in Mexican restaurants. He needs to develop a 5-month aggregate plan. His forecast of capacity and demand follows:

	Month				
	1	**2**	**3**	**4**	**5**
Demand	150	160	130	200	210
Capacity					
Regular	150	150	150	150	150
Overtime	20	20	10	10	10

Subcontracting: 100 units available over the 5-month period
Beginning inventory: 0 units
Ending inventory required: 20 units

Costs	
Regular-time cost per unit	$100
Overtime cost per unit	$125
Subcontract cost per unit	$135
Inventory cost per unit per month	$ 3

Assume that back orders are not permitted. Using the transportation method, what is the total cost of the optimal plan? **Px**

•••• **13.19** Chris Fisher, owner of an Ohio firm that manufactures display cabinets, develops an 8-month aggregate plan. Demand and capacity (in units) are forecast as follows:

Capacity Source (units)	Jan.	Feb.	Mar.	Apr.	May	June	July	Aug.
Regular time	235	255	290	300	300	290	300	290
Overtime	20	24	26	24	30	28	30	30
Subcontract	12	16	15	17	17	19	19	20
Demand	255	294	321	301	330	320	345	340

The cost of producing each unit is $1,000 on regular time, $1,300 on overtime, and $1,800 on a subcontract. Inventory carrying cost is $200 per unit per month. There is no beginning or ending inventory in stock, and no back orders are permitted from period to period.

a) Set up a production plan that minimizes cost by producing exactly what the demand is each month. Let the workforce vary by using regular time first, then overtime, and then subcontracting. This plan allows no backorders or inventory. What is this plan's cost?

b) Through better planning, regular-time production can be set at exactly the same amount, 275 units, per month. Does this alter the solution?

c) If overtime costs rise from $1,300 to $1,400, will your answer to part (a) change? What if overtime costs then fall to $1,200? **Px**

••• **13.20** Forrester and Cohen is a small accounting firm, managed by Joseph Cohen since the retirement in 2005 of his partner Brad Forrester. Cohen and his 3 CPAs can together bill 640 hours per month. When Cohen or another accountant bills more than 160 hours per month, he or she gets an additional "overtime" pay of $62.50 for each of the extra hours: This is above and beyond the $5,000 salary each draws during the month. (Cohen draws the same base pay as his employees.) Cohen strongly discourages any CPA from working (billing) more than 240 hours in any given month. The demand for billable hours for the firm over the next 6 months is estimated below:

Month	Estimate of Billable Hours
Jan.	600
Feb.	500
Mar.	1,000
Apr.	1,200
May	650
June	590

Cohen has an agreement with his former partner that Brad Forrester will help out during the busy tax season, if needed, for an hourly fee of $125. Cohen will not even consider laying off one of his colleagues in the case of a slow economy. He could, however, hire another CPA at the same salary, as business dictates.

a) Develop an aggregate plan for the 6-month period.

b) Compute the cost of Cohen's plan of using overtime and Forrester.

c) Should the firm remain as is, with a total of 4 CPAs?

•• **13.21** Refer to the CPA firm in Problem 13.20. In planning for next year, Cohen estimates that billable hours will increase by 10% in each of the 6 months. He therefore proceeds to hire a fifth CPA. The same regular time, overtime, and outside consultant (i.e., Forrester) costs still apply.

a) Develop the new aggregate plan and compute its costs.

b) Comment on the staffing level with five accountants. Was it a good decision to hire the additional accountant?

•• **13.22** Southeastern Airlines's daily flight from Atlanta to Charlotte uses a Boeing 737, with all-coach seating for 120 people. In the past, the airline has priced every seat at $140 for the one-way flight. An average of 80 passengers are on each flight. The variable cost of a filled seat is $25. Katie Morgan, the new operations manager, has decided to try a yield revenue approach, with seats priced at $80 for early bookings and at $190 for bookings within 1 week of the flight. She estimates that the airline will sell 65 seats at the lower price and 35 at the higher price. Variable cost will not change. Which approach is preferable to Ms. Morgan?

Case Studies

Southwestern University: (G)*

With the rising demands of a successful football program, the campus police chief at Southwestern University, John Swearingen, wants to develop a 2-year plan that involves a request for additional resources.

The SWU department currently has 26 sworn officers. The size of the force has not changed over the past 15 years, but the following changes have prompted the chief to seek more resources:

• The size of the athletic program, especially football, has increased.
• The college has expanded geographically, with some new research facilities and laboratories now miles away from the main campus.
• Traffic and parking problems have increased.
• More portable, expensive computers with high theft potential are dispersed across the campus.
• Alcohol and drug problems have increased.
• The size of the surrounding community has doubled.
• The police need to spend more time on education and prevention programs.

The college is located in Stephenville, Texas, a small town about 30 miles southwest of the Dallas/Forth Worth metroplex. During the summer months, the student population is around 5,000. This number swells to 20,000 during fall and spring semesters. Thus demand

for police and other services is significantly lower during the summer months. Demand for police services also varies by:

• Time of day (peak time is between 10 P.M. and 2 A.M.).
• Day of the week (weekends are the busiest).
• Weekend of the year (on football weekends, 50,000 extra people come to campus).
• Special events (check-in, checkout, commencement).

Football weekends are especially difficult to staff. Extra police services are typically needed from 8 A.M. to 5 P.M. on five football Saturdays. All 26 officers are called in to work double shifts. More than 40 law enforcement officers from surrounding locations are paid to come in on their own time, and a dozen state police lend a hand free of charge (when available). Twenty-five students and local residents are paid to work traffic and parking. During the last academic year (a 9-month period), overtime payments to campus police officers totaled over $120,000.

Other relevant data include the following:

• The average starting salary for a police officer is $28,000.
• Work-study and part-time students and local residents who help with traffic and parking are paid $9.00 an hour.

- Overtime is paid to police officers who work over 40 hours a week at the rate of $18.00 an hour. Extra officers who are hired part time from outside agencies also earn $18.00 an hour.
- There seems to be an unlimited supply of officers who will work for the college when needed for special events.
- With days off, vacations, and average sick leave considered, it takes five persons to cover one 24-hour, 7-day-a-week position.

The schedule of officers during fall and spring semesters is:

	Weekdays	Weekend
First shift (7 A.M.–3 P.M.)	5	4
Second shift (3 P.M.–11 P.M.)	5	6
Third shift (11 P.M.–7 A.M.)	6	8

Staffing for football weekends and special events is *in addition to* the preceding schedule. Summer staffing is, on average, half that shown.

Swearingen thinks that his present staff is stretched to the limit. Fatigued officers are potential problems for the department and the community. In addition, neither time nor personnel has been set aside for crime prevention, safety, or health programs. Interactions of police officers with students, faculty, and staff are minimal and usually negative in nature. In light of these problems, the chief would like to request funding for four additional officers, two assigned to new programs and two to alleviate the overload on

his current staff. He would also like to begin limiting overtime to 10 hours per week for each officer.

Discussion Questions

1. Which variations in demand for police services should be considered in an aggregate plan for resources? Which variations can be accomplished with short-term scheduling adjustments?
2. Evaluate the current staffing plan. What does it cost? Are 26 officers sufficient to handle the normal workload?
3. What would be the additional cost of the chief's proposal? How would you suggest that he justify his request?
4. How much does it currently cost the college to provide police services for football games? What would be the pros and cons of completely subcontracting this work to outside law enforcement agencies?
5. Propose other alternatives.

*This integrated case study runs throughout the text. Other issues facing Southwestern's football expansion include: (A) managing the stadium project (Chapter 3); (B) forecasting game attendance (Chapter 4); (C) quality of facilities (Chapter 6); (D) break-even analysis for food services (Supplement 7 Web site); (E) where to locate the new stadium (Chapter 8 Web site); (F) inventory planning of football programs (Chapter 12 Web Site).

Source: Adapted from C. Haksever, B. Render, and R. Russell, *Service Management and Operations*, 2nd ed. (Upper Saddle River, NJ: Prentice Hall, 2000), 308–309. Reprinted by permission of Prentice Hall, Inc.

Andrew-Carter, Inc.

Andrew-Carter, Inc. (A-C), is a major Canadian producer and distributor of outdoor lighting fixtures. Its products are distributed throughout South and North America and have been in high demand for several years. The company operates three plants to manufacture fixtures and distribute them to five distribution centers (warehouses).

During the present global slowdown, A-C has seen a major drop in demand for its products, largely because the housing market has declined. Based on the forecast of interest rates, the head of operations feels that demand for housing and thus for A-C's products will remain depressed for the foreseeable future. A-C is considering closing one of its plants, as it is now operating with a forecast excess capacity of 34,000 units per week. The forecast weekly demands for the coming year are as follows:

Warehouse 1	9,000 units
Warehouse 2	13,000
Warehouse 3	11,000
Warehouse 4	15,000
Warehouse 5	8,000

Plant capacities, in units per week, are as follows:

Plant 1, regular time	27,000 units
Plant 1, on overtime	7,000
Plant 2, regular time	20,000
Plant 2, on overtime	5,000
Plant 3, regular time	25,000
Plant 3, on overtime	6,000

If A-C shuts down any plants, its weekly costs will change, because fixed costs will be lower for a nonoperating plant. Table 1 shows production costs at each plant, both variable at regular time and overtime, and fixed when operating and shut down. Table 2 shows distribution costs from each plant to each distribution center.

▼ **Table 1** Andrew-Carter, Inc., Variable Costs and Fixed Production Costs per Week

Plant	Variable Cost (per unit)	Fixed Cost per Week Operating	Fixed Cost per Week Not Operating
1, regular time	$2.80	$14,000	$6,000
1, overtime	3.52		
2, regular time	2.78	12,000	5,000
2, overtime	3.48		
3, regular time	2.72	15,000	7,500
3, overtime	3.42		

▼ **Table 2** Andrew-Carter, Inc., Distribution Costs per Unit

From Plants	To Distribution Centers W1	W2	W3	W4	W5
1	$.50	$.44	$.49	$.46	$.56
2	.40	.52	.50	.56	.57
3	.56	.53	.51	.54	.35

Discussion Questions

1. Evaluate the various configurations of operating and closed plants that will meet weekly demand. Determine which configuration minimizes total costs.
2. Discuss the implications of closing a plant.

Source: Reprinted by permission of Professor Michael Ballot, University of the Pacific, Stockton, CA.

Additional Case Studies

Internet Case Studies: Visit our Companion Web site at www.prenhall.com/heizer *for this free case study:*

- **Cornwell Glass:** Involves setting a production schedule for an auto glass producer.

Harvard has selected these Harvard Business School cases to accompany this chapter:

harvardbusinessonline.hbsp.harvard.edu

- **MacPherson Refrigeration Ltd.** (#93-D021): Students need to evaluate three aggregate production plans for the company's products.
- **Sport Obermeyer Ltd.** (#695-022): This Asian skiwear company has to match supply with demand for products with uncertain demand and a globally dispersed supply chain.
- **Chaircraft Corp.** (#689-082): Illustrates effective production planning in a multistage process affected by seasonal demand.

Bibliography

Chen, Fangruo. "Salesforce Initiative, Market Information, and Production/Inventory Planning." *Management Science* 51, no. 1 (January 2005): 60–75.

Fisher, M. L., J. H. Hammond, W. R. Obermeyer, and A. Raman. "Making Supply Meet Demand in an Uncertain World." *Harvard Business Review* 72, no. 3 (1994): 83–93.

Gunasekaran, A., and H. B. Marri. "Application of Aggregate Planning Models in Developing Countries." *International Journal of Computed Applications in Technology* 20, no. 4 (2004): 172.

Hopp, Wallace J., and Mark L. Spearman. *Factory Physics*, 3rd ed. New York: Irwin/McGraw-Hill (2008).

Hurtubise, S., and C. Olivier. "Planning Tools for Managing the Supply Chain." *Computers & Industrial Engineering* 46, no. 4 (June 2004): 763.

Kimes, S. E., and G. M. Thompson. "Restaurant Revenue Management at Chevy's." *Decision Sciences* 35, no. 3 (summer 2004): 371–393.

Metters, R., K. King-Metters, M. Pullman, and S. Walton. *Successful Service Operations Management.* 2nd ed. Mason, OH: Thompson-South-Western (2006).

Mukhopadhyay, S., S. Samaddar, and G. Colville. "Improving Revenue Management Decision Making for Airlines." *Decision Science* 38, no. 2 (May 2007): 309–327.

Plambeck, Erica L., and Terry A. Taylor. "Sell the Plant? The Impact of Contract Manufacturing on Innovation, Capacity, and Profitability." *Management Science* 51, no. 1 (January 2005): 133–150.

Ryan, D. M. "Optimization Earns Its Wings." *OR/MS Today* 27, no. 2 (2000): 26–30.

Sasser, W. E. "Match Supply and Demand in Service Industries." *Harvard Business Review* 54, no. 6 (November–December 1976): 133–140.

Silver, E. A., D. F. Pyke, and R. Peterson. *Inventory Management and Production Planning and Scheduling.* New York: Wiley (1998).

Vollmann, T. E., W. L. Berry, D. C. Whybark, and F. R. Jacobs. *Manufacturing Planning and Control for Supply Chain Management*, 5th ed. Burr Ridge, IL: Irwin (2005).

Internet Resource

APICS courses: **www.apics.org**

Material Requirements Planning (MRP) and ERP

Chapter Outline

Ten OM Strategy Decisions

Design of Goods and Services

Managing Quality

Process Strategy

Location Strategies

Layout Strategies

Human Resources

Supply Chain Management

Inventory Management
   Independent Demand
   Dependent Demand
   JIT and Lean Operations

Scheduling
   Aggregate
   Short-Term

Maintenance

Learning Objectives

When you complete this chapter you should be able to

1. Develop a product structure
2. Build a gross requirements plan
3. Build a net requirements plan
4. Determine lot sizes for lot-for-lot, EOQ, and PPB
5. Describe MRP II
6. Describe closed-loop MRP
7. Describe ERP

Global Company Profile: Wheeled Coach

MRP Provides a Competitive Advantage for Wheeled Coach

Wheeled Coach, headquartered in Winter Park, Florida, is the largest manufacturer of ambulances in the world. The $200 million firm is an international competitor that sells more than 25% of its vehicles to markets outside the U.S. Twelve major ambulance designs are produced on assembly lines (i.e., a repetitive process) at the Florida plant, using 18,000 different inventory items, of which 6,000 are manufactured and 12,000 purchased. Most of the product line is custom designed and

◀ *This cutaway of one ambulance interior indicates the complexity of the product, which for some rural locations may be the equivalent of a hospital emergency room in miniature. To complicate production, virtually every ambulance is custom-ordered. This customization necessitates precise orders, excellent bills of materials, exceptional inventory control from supplier to assembly, and an MRP system that works.*

▶ *Wheeled Coach uses work cells to feed the assembly line. It maintains a complete carpentry shop (to provide interior cabinetry), a paint shop (to prepare, paint, and detail each vehicle), an electrical shop (to provide for the complex electronics in a modern ambulance), an upholstery shop (to make interior seats and benches), and as shown here, a metal fabrication shop (to construct the shell of the ambulance).*

assembled to meet the specific and often unique requirements demanded by the ambulance's application and customer preferences.

This variety of products and the nature of the process demand good material requirements planning. Effective use of an MRP system requires accurate bills of material and inventory records. The Wheeled Coach system, which uses MAPICS DB software, provides daily updates and has reduced inventory by more than 30% in just 2 years.

Wheeled Coach insists that four key tasks be performed properly. First, the material plan must meet both the requirements of the master schedule and the capabilities of the production facility.

Second, the plan must be executed as designed. Third, inventory investment must be minimized through effective "time-phased" material deliveries, consignment inventories, and a constant review of purchase methods. Finally, excellent record integrity must be maintained. Record accuracy is recognized as a fundamental ingredient of Wheeled Coach's successful MRP program. Its cycle counters are charged with material audits that not only correct errors but also investigate and correct problems.

Wheeled Coach Industries uses MRP as the catalyst for low inventory, high quality, tight schedules, and accurate records. Wheeled Coach has found competitive advantage via MRP.

 On six parallel lines, ambulances move forward each day to the next workstation. The MRP system makes certain that just the materials needed at each station arrive overnight for assembly the next day.

Video 14.1

MRP at Wheeled Coach Ambulances

▶ *Here an employee is installing the wiring for an ambulance. There are an average of 15 miles of wire in a Wheeled Coach vehicle. This compares to 17 miles of wire in a sophisticated F-16 fighter jet.*

Wheeled Coach and many other firms have found important benefits in MRP. These benefits include (1) better response to customer orders as the result of improved adherence to schedules, (2) faster response to market changes, (3) improved utilization of facilities and labor, and (4) reduced inventory levels. Better response to customer orders and to the market wins orders and market share. Better utilization of facilities and labor yields higher productivity and return on investment. Less inventory frees up capital and floor space for other uses. These benefits are the result of a strategic decision to use a *dependent* inventory scheduling system. Demand for every component of an ambulance is dependent.

DEPENDENT DEMAND

Dependent demand means that the demand for one item is related to the demand for another item. Consider a Ford F-150 truck. Ford's demand for tires and radiators depends on the production of F-150's. Five tires and one radiator go into each finished F-150 truck. Demand for items is *dependent* when the relationship between the items can be determined. Therefore, once management receives an order or makes a forecast of the demand for the final product, quantities required for all components can be computed, because all components are dependent items. The Boeing Aircraft operations manager who schedules production of one plane per week, for example, knows the requirements down to the last rivet. For any product, all components of that product are dependent demand items. *More generally, for any item for which a schedule can be established, dependent techniques should be used.*

When the requirements of MRP are met, dependent models are preferable to the EOQ models described in Chapter 12.[1] Dependency exists for all component parts, subassemblies, and supplies once a master schedule is known. Dependent models are better not only for manufacturers and distributors but also for a wide variety of firms from restaurants to hospitals. The dependent technique used in a production environment is called **material requirements planning (MRP)**.

Because MRP provides such a clean structure for dependent demand, it has evolved as the basis for Enterprise Resource Planning (ERP). ERP is an information system for identifying and planning the enterprise-wide resources needed to take, make, ship, and account for customer orders. We will discuss ERP in the latter part of this chapter.

Material requirements planning (MRP)

A dependent demand technique that uses a bill-of-material, inventory, expected receipts, and a master production schedule to determine material requirements.

DEPENDENT INVENTORY MODEL REQUIREMENTS

Effective use of dependent inventory models requires that the operations manager know the following:

1. Master production schedule (what is to be made and when)
2. Specifications or bill of material (materials and parts required to make the product)
3. Inventory availability (what is in stock)
4. Purchase orders outstanding (what is on order, also called expected receipts)
5. Lead times (how long it takes to get various components)

We now discuss each of these requirements in the context of material requirements planning (MRP).

Master Production Schedule

Master production schedule (MPS)

A timetable that specifies what is to be made and when.

A **master production schedule (MPS)** specifies what is to be made (i.e., the number of finished products or items) and when. The schedule must be in accordance with a production plan. The production plan sets the overall level of output in broad terms (e.g., product families, standard hours, or dollar volume). The plan also includes a variety of inputs, including financial plans, customer demand, engineering capabilities, labor availability, inventory fluctuations, supplier performance, and other considerations. Each of these inputs contributes in its own way to the production plan, as shown in Figure 14.1.

As the planning process moves from the production plan to execution, each of the lower-level plans must be feasible. When one is not, feedback to the next higher level is used to make the

---

[1]The inventory models (EOQ) discussed in Chapter 12 assumed that the demand for one item was independent of the demand for another item. For example, EOQ assumes the demand for refrigerator parts is *independent* of the demand for refrigerators and that demand for parts is constant.

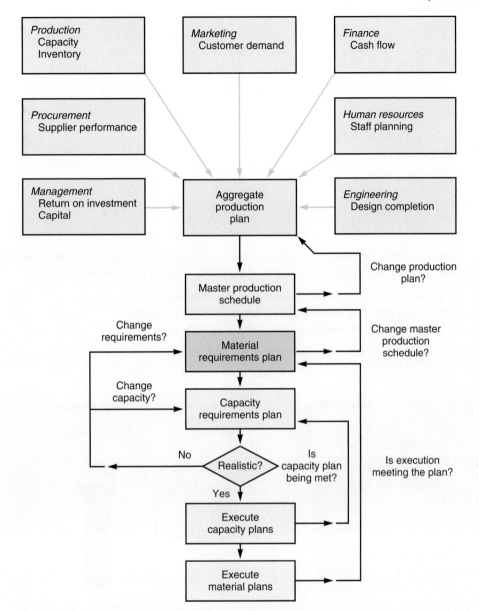

◄ **Figure 14.1**

The Planning Process

Regardless of the complexity of the planning process, the aggregate production plan and its derivative, the master production schedule, must be developed.

necessary adjustment. One of the major strengths of MRP is its ability to determine precisely the feasibility of a schedule within aggregate capacity constraints. This planning process can yield excellent results. The production plan sets the upper and lower bounds on the master production schedule. The result of this production planning process is the master production schedule.

The master production schedule tells us what is required to satisfy demand and meet the production plan. This schedule establishes what items to make and when: It *disaggregates* the aggregate production plan. While the *aggregate production plan* (as discussed in Chapter 13) is established in gross terms such as families of products or tons of steel, the *master production schedule* is established in terms of specific products. Figure 14.2 shows the master production schedules for three stereo models that flow from the aggregate production plan for a family of stereo amplifiers.

Managers must adhere to the schedule for a reasonable length of time (usually a major portion of the production cycle—the time it takes to produce a product). Many organizations establish a master production schedule and establish a policy of not changing ("fixing") the near-term portion of the plan. This near-term portion of the plan is then referred to as the "fixed," "firm," or "frozen" schedule. Wheeled Coach, the subject of the *Global Company Profile* for this chapter, fixes the last 14 days of its schedule. Only changes farther out, beyond the fixed schedule are permitted. The master production schedule is a "rolling" production schedule. For example, a fixed 7-week plan has an additional week added to it as each week is completed, so a 7-week fixed schedule is

The master production schedule is derived from the aggregate schedule.

▶ **Figure 14.2**

The Aggregate Production Plan Provides the Basis for Development of the Detailed Master Production Schedule

Months	January				February			
Aggregate Production Plan (Shows the total quantity of amplifiers)	1,500				1,200			
Weeks	1	2	3	4	5	6	7	8
Master Production Schedule (Shows the specific type and quantity of amplifier to be produced)								
240-watt amplifier	100		100		100		100	
150-watt amplifier		500		500		450		450
75-watt amplifier			300				100	

maintained. Note that the master production schedule is a statement of *what is to be produced*, not a forecast of demand. The master schedule can be expressed in any of the following terms:

1. A *customer order in a job shop* (make-to-order) company
2. *Modules in a repetitive* (assemble-to-order or forecast) company
3. An *end item in a continuous* (stock-to-forecast) company

This relationship of the master production schedule to the processes is shown in Figure 14.3.

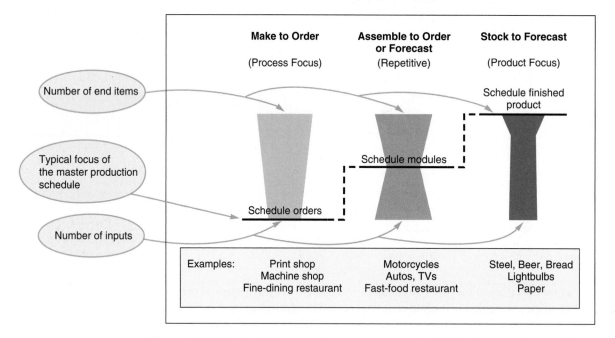

▲ **Figure 14.3**   Typical Focus of the Master Production Schedule in Three Process Strategies

A master production schedule for two of Nancy's Specialty Foods' products, crabmeat quiche and spinach quiche, might look like Table 14.1.

▶ **Table 14.1**

Master Production Schedule for Crabmeat Quiche and Spinach Quiche at Nancy's Specialty Foods

	Gross Requirements for Crabmeat Quiche									
Day	6	7	8	9	10	11	12	13	14	and so on
Amount	50		100	47	60		110	75		

	Gross Requirements for Spinach Quiche									
Day	7	8	9	10	11	12	13	14	15	16	and so on
Amount	100	200	150			60	75		100		

Bills of Material

Defining what goes into a product may seem simple, but it can be difficult in practice. As we noted in Chapter 5, to aid this process, manufactured items are defined via a bill of material. A **bill of material (BOM)** is a list of quantities of components, ingredients, and materials required to make a product. Individual drawings describe not only physical dimensions but also any special processing as well as the raw material from which each part is made. Nancy's Specialty Foods has a recipe for quiche, specifying ingredients and quantities, just as Wheeled Coach has a full set of drawings for an ambulance. Both are bills of material (although we call one a recipe, and they do vary somewhat in scope).

Because there is often a rush to get a new product to market, however, drawings and bills of material may be incomplete or even nonexistent. Moreover, complete drawings and BOMs (as well as other forms of specifications) often contain errors in dimensions, quantities, or countless other areas. When errors are identified, engineering change notices (ECNs) are created, further complicating the process. An *engineering change notice* is a change or correction to an engineering drawing or bill of material.

One way a bill of material defines a product is by providing a product structure. Example 1 shows how to develop the product structure and "explode" it to reveal the requirements for each component. A bill of material for item A in Example 1 consists of items B and C. Items above any level are called *parents*; items below any level are called *components* or *children*. By convention, the top level in a BOM is the 0 level.

Bill of material (BOM)
A listing of the components, their description, and the quantity of each required to make one unit of a product.

EXAMPLE 1

Developing a product structure and gross requirements

Speaker Kits, Inc., packages high-fidelity components for mail order. Components for the top-of-the-line speaker kit, "Awesome" (A), include 2 standard 12-inch speaker kits (Bs) and 3 speaker kits with amp-boosters (Cs).

Each B consists of 2 speakers (Ds) and 2 shipping boxes each with an installation kit (E). Each of the three 300-watt speaker kits (Cs) has 2 speaker boosters (Fs) and 2 installation kits (Es). Each speaker booster (F) includes 2 speakers (Ds) and 1 amp-booster (G). The total for each Awesome is 4 standard 12-inch speakers and twelve 12-inch speakers with the amp-booster. (Most purchasers require hearing aids within 3 years, and at least one court case is pending because of structural damage to a men's dormitory.) As we can see, the demand for B, C, D, E, F, and G is completely dependent on the master production schedule for A—the Awesome speaker kits.

Approach: Given the above information, we construct a product structure and "explode" the requirements.

Solution: This structure has four levels: 0, 1, 2, and 3. There are four parents: A, B, C, and F. Each parent item has at least one level below it. Items B, C, D, E, F, and G are components because each item has at least one level above it. In this structure, B, C, and F are both parents and components. The number in parentheses indicates how many units of that particular item are needed to make the item immediately above it. Thus, $B_{(2)}$ means that it takes two units of B for every unit of A, and $F_{(2)}$ means that it takes two units of F for every unit of C.

Learning Objective

1. Develop a product structure

**Excel Om Data File
Ch14Ex1.xls**

Once we have developed the product structure, we can determine the number of units of each item required to satisfy demand for a new order of 50 Awesome speaker kits. We "explode" the requirements as shown:

Part B:	$2 \times$ number of As =	$(2)(50) =$	100
Part C:	$3 \times$ number of As =	$(3)(50) =$	150
Part D:	$2 \times$ number of Bs + $2 \times$ number of Fs =	$(2)(100) + (2)(300) =$	800
Part E:	$2 \times$ number of Bs + $2 \times$ number of Cs =	$(2)(100) + (2)(150) =$	500
Part F:	$2 \times$ number of Cs =	$(2)(150) =$	300
Part G:	$1 \times$ number of Fs =	$(1)(300) =$	300

Insight: We now have a visual picture of the Awesome speaker kit requirements and knowledge of the quantities required. Thus, for 50 units of A, we will need 100 units of B, 150 units of C, 800 units of D, 500 units of E, 300 units of F, and 300 units of G.

Learning exercise: If there are 100 Fs in stock, how many Ds do you need? [Answer: 600.]

Related problems: 14.1, 14.3a, 14.13a, 14.25a

Bills of material not only specify requirements but also are useful for costing, and they can serve as a list of items to be issued to production or assembly personnel. When bills of material are used in this way, they are usually called *pick lists*.

Modular bills

Bills of material organized by major subassemblies or by product options.

Modular Bills   Bills of material may be organized around product modules (see Chapter 5). *Modules* are not final products to be sold but are components that can be produced and assembled into units. They are often major components of the final product or product options. Bills of material for modules are called **modular bills**. Bills of material are sometimes organized as modules (rather than as part of a final product) because production scheduling and production are often facilitated by organizing around relatively few modules rather than a multitude of final assemblies. For instance, a firm may make 138,000 different final products but may have only 40 modules that are mixed and matched to produce those 138,000 final products. The firm builds an aggregate production plan and prepares its master production schedule for the 40 modules, not the 138,000 configurations of the final product. This approach allows the MPS to be prepared for a reasonable number of items (the narrow portion of the middle graphic in Figure 14.3) and to postpone assembly. The 40 modules can then be configured for specific orders at final assembly.

Planning bills (or kits)

A material grouping created in order to assign an artificial parent to a bill of material; also called "pseudo" bills.

Phantom bills of material

Bills of material for components, usually assemblies, that exist only temporarily; they are never inventoried.

Planning Bills and Phantom Bills   Two other special kinds of bills of material are planning bills and phantom bills. **Planning bills** are created in order to assign an artificial parent to the bill of material. Such bills are used (1) when we want to group subassemblies so the number of items to be scheduled is reduced and (2) when we want to issue "kits" to the production department. For instance, it may not be efficient to issue inexpensive items such as washers and cotter pins with each of numerous subassemblies, so we call this a *kit* and generate a planning bill. The planning bill specifies the *kit* to be issued. Consequently, a planning bill may also be known as **kitted material**, or **kit**. **Phantom bills of material** are bills of material for components, usually subassemblies, that exist only temporarily. These components go directly into another assembly and are never inventoried. Therefore, components of phantom bills of material are coded to receive special treatment; lead times are zero, and they are handled as an integral part of their parent item. An example is a transmission shaft with gears and bearings assembly that is placed directly into a transmission.

Low-level coding

A number that identifies items at the lowest level at which they occur.

Low-Level Coding   Low-level coding of an item in a BOM is necessary when identical items exist at various levels in the BOM. **Low-level coding** means that the item is coded at the lowest level at which it occurs. For example, item D in Example 1 is coded at the lowest level at which

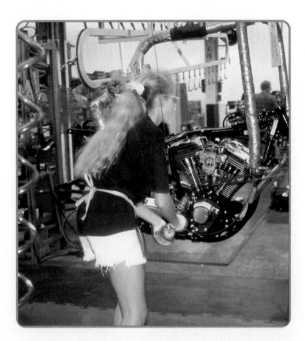

◀ *For manufacturers like Harley-Davidson, which produces a large number of end products from a relatively small number of options, modular bills of material provide an effective solution.*

it is used. Item D could be coded as part of B and occur at level 2. However, because D is also part of F, and F is level 2, item D becomes a level-3 item. Low-level coding is a convention to allow easy computing of the requirements of an item. When the BOM has thousands of items or when requirements are frequently recomputed, the ease and speed of computation become a major concern.

Low-level coding ensures that an item is always at the lowest level of usage.

Accurate Inventory Records

As we saw in Chapter 12, knowledge of what is in stock is the result of good inventory management. Good inventory management is an absolute necessity for an MRP system to work. If the firm has not achieved at least 99% record accuracy, then material requirements planning will not work.[2]

Purchase Orders Outstanding

Knowledge of outstanding orders should exist as a by-product of well-managed purchasing and inventory-control departments. When purchase orders are executed, records of those orders and their scheduled delivery dates must be available to production personnel. Only with good purchasing data can managers prepare good production plans and effectively execute an MRP system.

Lead Times for Components

Once managers determine when products are needed, they determine when to acquire them. The time required to acquire (that is, purchase, produce, or assemble) an item is known as **lead time**. Lead time for a manufactured item consists of *move*, *setup*, and *assembly* or *run times* for each component. For a purchased item, the lead time includes the time between recognition of need for an order and when it is available for production.

When the bill of material for Awesome speaker kits (As), in Example 1, is turned on its side and modified by adding lead times for each component (see Table 14.2), we then have a *time-phased product structure*. Time in this structure is shown on the horizontal axis of Figure 14.4 with item A due for completion in week 8. Each component is then offset to accommodate lead times.

Lead time

In purchasing systems, the time between recognition of the need for an order and receiving it; in production systems, it is the order, wait, move, queue, setup, and run times for each component.

[2]Record accuracy of 99% may sound good, but note that even when each component has an availability of 99% and a product has only seven components, the likelihood of a product being completed is only .932 (since $.99^7 = .932$).

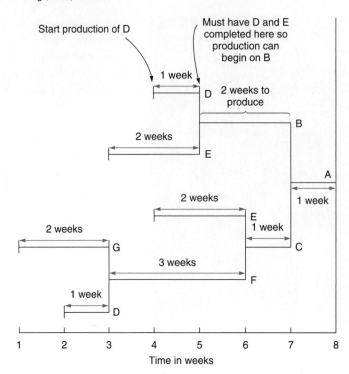

▼ **Table 14.2**

Lead Times for Awesome Speaker Kits (As)

Component	Lead Time
A	1 week
B	2 weeks
C	1 week
D	1 week
E	2 weeks
F	3 weeks
G	2 weeks

MRP STRUCTURE

Although most MRP systems are computerized, the MRP procedure is straightforward and can be done by hand. A master production schedule, a bill of material, inventory and purchase records, and lead times for each item are the ingredients of a material requirements planning system (see Figure 14.5).

Once these ingredients are available and accurate, the next step is to construct a gross material requirements plan. The **gross material requirements plan** is a schedule, as shown in Example 2. It combines a master production schedule (that requires one unit of A in week 8) and the time-phased schedule (Figure 14.4). It shows when an item must be ordered from suppliers if there is no inventory on hand or when the production of an item must be started to satisfy demand for the finished product by a particular date.

Gross material requirements plan

A schedule that shows the total demand for an item (prior to subtraction of on-hand inventory and scheduled receipts) and (1) when it must be ordered from suppliers, or (2) when production must be started to meet its demand by a particular date.

► **Figure 14.5**

Structure of the MRP System

MRP software programs are popular because many organizations face dependent demand situations.

EXAMPLE 2

Building a gross
requirements plan

Each Awesome speaker kit (item A of Example 1) requires all the items in the product structure for A. Lead times are shown in Table 14.2.

Approach: Using the information in Example 1 and Table 14.2, we construct the gross material requirements plan with a production schedule that will satisfy the demand of 50 units of A by week 8.

Solution: We prepare a schedule as shown in Table 14.3.

◀ **Table 14.3**

Gross Material Requirements Plan for 50 Awesome Speaker Kits (As)

			Week						
	1	**2**	**3**	**4**	**5**	**6**	**7**	**8**	**Lead Time**
A. Required date								50	
Order release date							50		1 week
B. Required date							100		
Order release date					100				2 weeks
C. Required date							150		
Order release date						150			1 week
E. Required date					200	300			
Order release date			200	300					2 weeks
F. Required date						300			
Order release date			300						3 weeks
D. Required date				600	200				
Order release date		600		200					1 week
G. Required date				300					
Order release date	300								2 weeks

You can interpret the gross material requirements shown in Table 14.3 as follows: If you want 50 units of A at week 8, you must start assembling A in week 7. Thus, in week 7, you will need 100 units of B and 150 units of C. These two items take 2 weeks and 1 week, respectively, to produce. Production of B, therefore, should start in week 5, and production of C should start in week 6 (lead time subtracted from the required date for these items). Working backward, we can perform the same computations for all of the other items. Because D and E are used in two different places in Awesome speaker kits, there are two entries in each data record.

Insight: The gross material requirements plan shows when production of each item should begin and end in order to have 50 units of A at week 8. Management now has an initial plan.

Learning exercise: If the lead time for G decreases from 2 weeks to 1 week, what is the new order release date for G? [Answer: 300 in week 2.]

Related problems: 14.2, 14.4, 14.6, 14.8b, 14.9, 14.10a, 14.11a, 14.13b, 14.25b

So far, we have considered *gross material requirements*, which assumes that there is no inventory on hand. When there is inventory on hand, we prepare a **net requirements plan**. When considering on-hand inventory, we must realize that many items in inventory contain subassemblies or parts. If the gross requirement for Awesome speaker kits (As) is 100 and there are 20 of those speakers on hand, the net requirement for Awesome speaker kits (As) is 80 (that is, 100 − 20). However, each Awesome speaker kit on hand contains 2 Bs. As a result, the requirement for Bs drops by 40 Bs (20 A kits on hand × 2 Bs per A). Therefore, if inventory is on hand for a parent item, the requirements for the parent item and all its components decrease because each Awesome kit contains the components for lower-level items. Example 3 shows how to create a net requirements plan.

Net material requirements
The result of adjusting gross requirements for inventory on hand and scheduled receipts.

EXAMPLE 3

Determining net requirements

Speaker Kits, Inc., developed a product structure from a bill of material in Example 1. Example 2 developed a gross requirements plan. Given the following on-hand inventory, Speaker Kits, Inc., now wants to construct a net requirements plan.

Active Model 14.1

Examples 1–3 are further illustrated in Active Model 14.1 on the CD-ROM and in the Exercise on pages 590–591.

Item	On Hand	Item	On Hand
A	10	E	10
B	15	F	5
C	20	G	0
D	10		

Approach: A net material requirements plan includes gross requirements, on-hand inventory, net requirements, planned order receipt, and planned order release for each item. We begin with A and work backward through the components.

Solution: Shown in the chart below is the net material requirements plan for product A.

Lot Size	Lead Time (weeks)	On Hand	Safety Stock	Allo-cated	Low-Level Code	Item Identi-fication		Week 1	2	3	4	5	6	7	8
Lot-for-Lot	1	10	—	—	0	A	Gross Requirements								50
							Scheduled Receipts								
							Projected On Hand 10	10	10	10	10	10	10	10	10
							Net Requirements								40
							Planned Order Receipts								40
							Planned Order Releases							40	
Lot-for-Lot	2	15	—	—	1	B	Gross Requirements							80[A]	
							Scheduled Receipts								
							Projected On Hand 15	15	15	15	15	15	15	15	
							Net Requirements							65	
							Planned Order Receipts							65	
							Planned Order Releases						65		
Lot-for-Lot	1	20	—	—	1	C	Gross Requirements							120[A]	
							Scheduled Receipts								
							Projected On Hand 20	20	20	20	20	20	20	20	
							Net Requirements							100	
							Planned Order Receipts							100	
							Planned Order Releases						100		
Lot-for-Lot	2	10	—	—	2	E	Gross Requirements						130[B]	200[C]	
							Scheduled Receipts								
							Projected On Hand 10	10	10	10	10	10			
							Net Requirements						120	200	
							Planned Order Receipts						120	200	
							Planned Order Releases				120	200			
Lot-for-Lot	3	5	—	—	2	F	Gross Requirements							200[C]	
							Scheduled Receipts								
							Projected On Hand 5	5	5	5	5	5	5		
							Net Requirements							195	
							Planned Order Receipts							195	
							Planned Order Releases					195			
Lot-for-Lot	1	10	—	—	3	D	Gross Requirements					390[F]	130[B]		
							Scheduled Receipts								
							Projected On Hand 10	10	10	10					
							Net Requirements					380	130		
							Planned Order Receipts					380	130		
							Planned Order Releases				380	130			
Lot-for-Lot	2	0	—	—	3	G	Gross Requirements					195[F]			
							Scheduled Receipts								
							Projected On Hand				0				
							Net Requirements					195			
							Planned Order Receipts					195			
							Planned Order Releases			195					

Net Material Requiremnts Plan for Product A *Note that the superscript is the source of the demand.*

Constructing a net requirements plan is similar to constructing a gross requirements plan. Starting with item A, we work backward to determine net requirements for all items. To do these computations, we refer to the product structure, on-hand inventory, and lead times. The gross requirement for A is 50 units in week 8. Ten items are on hand; therefore, the net requirements and the scheduled **planned order receipt** are both 40 items in week 8. Because of the 1-week lead time, the **planned order release** is 40 items in week 7 (see the arrow connecting the order receipt and order release). Referring to week 7 and the product structure in Example 1, we can see that 80 (2×40) items of B and 120 (3×40) items of C are required in week 7 to have a total for 50 items of A in week 8. The letter superscripted A to the right of the gross figure for items B and C was generated as a result of the demand for the parent, A. Performing the same type of analysis for B and C yields the net requirements for D, E, F, and G. Note the on-hand inventory in row E in week 6 is zero. It is zero because the on-hand inventory (10 units) was used to make B in week 5. By the same token, the inventory for D was used to make F in week 3.

Insight: Once a net requirement plan is completed, management knows the quantities needed, an ordering schedule, and a production schedule for each component.

Learning exercise: If the on-hand inventory quantity of component F is 95 rather than 5, how many units of G will need to be ordered in week 1? [Answer: 105 units.]

Related problems: 14.5, 14.7, 14.8c, 14.10b, 14.11b, 14.12, 14.13c, 14.14, 14.15, 14.16a, 14.25, 14.27

Planned order receipt
The quantity planned to be received at a future date.

Planned order release
The scheduled date for an order to be released.

Examples 2 and 3 considered only product A, the Awesome speaker kit, and its completion only in week 8. Fifty units of A were required in week 8. Normally, however, there is a demand for many products over time. For each product, management must prepare a master production schedule (as we saw earlier in Table 14.1). Scheduled production of each product is added to the master schedule and ultimately to the net material requirements plan. Figure 14.6 shows how several product schedules, including requirements for components sold directly, can contribute to one gross material requirements plan.

Most inventory systems also note the number of units in inventory that have been assigned to specific future production but not yet used or issued from the stockroom. Such items are often referred to as *allocated* items. Allocated items increase requirements and may then be included in an MRP planning sheet, as shown in Figure 14.7.

The allocated quantity has the effect of increasing the requirements (or, alternatively, reducing the quantity on hand). The logic, then, of a net requirements MRP is:

Learning Objective

3. Build a net requirements plan

$$\underbrace{\left[\left(\begin{array}{c}\text{Gross}\\\text{requirements}\end{array}\right)+\left(\text{Allocations}\right)\right]}_{\text{Total requirements}}-\underbrace{\left[\left(\begin{array}{c}\text{On}\\\text{hand}\end{array}\right)+\left(\begin{array}{c}\text{Scheduled}\\\text{receipts}\end{array}\right)\right]}_{\text{Available inventory}}=\begin{array}{c}\text{Net}\\\text{requirements}\end{array}$$

◀ **Figure 14.6**

Several Schedules Contributing to a Gross Requirements Schedule for B

One B is in each A, and one B is in each S; additionally, 10 Bs sold directly are scheduled in week 1, and 10 more that are sold directly are scheduled in week 2.

Lot Size	Lead Time	On Hand	Safety Stock	Allocated	Low-Level Code	Item ID		Period							
								1	2	3	4	5	6	7	8
Lot FoR Lot	1	0	0	10	0	Z	Gross Requirements								80̶ 90
							Scheduled Receipts								0
							Projected On Hand 0	0	0	0	0	0	0	0	0
							Net Requirements								90
							Planned Order Receipts								90
							Planned Order Releases							90	

▲ **Figure 14.7** Sample MRP Planning Sheet for Item Z

Safety Stock The continuing task of operations managers is to remove variability. This is the case in MRP systems as in other operations systems. Realistically, however, managers need to realize that bills of material and inventory records, like purchase and production quantities, as well as lead times, may not be perfect. This means that some consideration of safety stock may be prudent. Because of the significant domino effect of any change in requirements, safety stock should be minimized, with a goal of ultimate elimination. When safety stock is deemed absolutely necessary, the usual policy is to build it into the projected on-hand inventory of the MRP logic. Distortion can be minimized when safety stock is held at the finished goods level and at the purchased component or raw material level.

MRP MANAGEMENT

The material requirements plan is not static. And since MRP systems increasingly are integrated with just-in-time (JIT) techniques, we now discuss these two issues.

MRP Dynamics

Bills of material and material requirements plans are altered as changes in design, schedules, and production processes occur. Additionally, changes occur in material requirements whenever the master production schedule is modified. Regardless of the cause of any changes, the MRP model can be manipulated to reflect them. In this manner, an up-to-date requirements schedule is possible.

Due to the changes that occur in MRP data, it is not uncommon to recompute MRP requirements about once a week. Conveniently, a central strength of MRP is its timely and accurate *replanning* capability. However, many firms find they do not want to respond to minor scheduling or quantity changes even if they are aware of them. These frequent changes generate what is called **system nervousness** and can create havoc in purchasing and production departments if implemented. Consequently, OM personnel reduce such nervousness by evaluating the need and impact of changes prior to disseminating requests to other departments. Two tools are particularly helpful when trying to reduce MRP system nervousness.

The first is time fences. **Time fences** allow a segment of the master schedule to be designated as "not to be rescheduled." This segment of the master schedule is therefore not changed during the periodic regeneration of schedules. The second tool is pegging. **Pegging** means tracing upward in the BOM from the component to the parent item. By pegging upward, the production planner can determine the cause for the requirement and make a judgment about the necessity for a change in the schedule.

With MRP, the operations manager *can* react to the dynamics of the real world. How frequently the manager wishes to impose those changes on the firm requires professional judgment. Moreover, if the nervousness is caused by legitimate changes, then the proper response may be to investigate the production environment—not adjust via MRP.

MRP and JIT

MRP does not do detailed scheduling—it plans. MRP will tell you that a job needs to be completed on a certain week or day but does not tell you that Job X needs to run on Machine A at 10:30 A.M. and be completed by 11:30 A.M. so that Job X can then run on machine B. MRP is also

System nervousness
Frequent changes in an MRP system.

Time fences
A means for allowing a segment of the master schedule to be designated as "not to be rescheduled."

Pegging
In material requirements planning systems, tracing upward in the bill of material from the component to the parent item.

a planning technique with *fixed* lead times. Fixed lead times can be a limitation. For instance, the lead time to produce 50 units may vary substantially from the lead time to produce 5 units. These limitations complicate the marriage of MRP and just-in-time (JIT). What is needed is a way to make MRP more responsive to moving material rapidly in small batches. An MRP system combined with JIT can provide the best of both worlds. MRP provides the plan and an accurate picture of requirements; then JIT rapidly moves material in small batches, reducing work-in-process inventory. Let's look at four approaches for integrating MRP and JIT: finite capacity scheduling, small buckets, balanced flow, and supermarkets.

Finite Capacity Scheduling (FCS)   Most MRP software loads work into infinite size "buckets." The **buckets** are time units, usually one week. Traditionally, when work is to be done in a given week, MRP puts the work there without regard to capacity. Consequently, MRP is considered an *infinite* scheduling technique. Frequently, as you might suspect, this is not realistic. Finite capacity scheduling (FCS), which we discuss in Chapter 15, considers department and machine capacity, which is *finite*, hence the name. FCS provides the precise scheduling needed for rapid material movement. We are now witnessing a convergence of FCS and MRP. Sophisticated FCS systems modify the output from MRP systems to provide a finite schedule.

> **Buckets**
> Time units in a material requirements planning system.

Small Bucket Approach   MRP is an excellent tool for resource and scheduling management in process-focused facilities, that is, in job shops. Such facilities include machine shops, hospitals, and restaurants, where lead times are relatively stable and poor balance between work centers is expected. Schedules are often driven by work orders, and lot sizes are the exploded bill-of-material size. In these enterprises, MRP can be integrated with JIT through the following steps.

Step 1: Reduce MRP "buckets" from weekly to daily to perhaps hourly. Buckets are time units in an MRP system. Although the examples in this chapter have used weekly *time buckets*, many firms now use daily or even fraction-of-a-day time buckets. Some systems use a **bucketless system** in which all time-phased data have dates attached rather than defined time periods or buckets.

Step 2: The planned receipts that are part of a firm's planned orders in an MRP system are communicated to the work areas for production purposes and used to sequence production.

Step 3: Inventory is moved through the plant on a JIT basis.

Step 4: As products are completed, they are moved into inventory (typically finished-goods inventory) in the normal way. Receipt of these products into inventory reduces the quantities required for subsequent planned orders in the MRP system.

Step 5: A system known as *back flush* is used to reduce inventory balances. **Back flushing** uses the bill of material to deduct component quantities from inventory as each unit is completed.

> **Bucketless system**
> Time-phased data are referenced using dated records rather than defined time periods, or buckets.

> **Back flush**
> A system to reduce inventory balances by deducting everything in the bill of material on completion of the unit.

The focus in these facilities becomes one of maintaining schedules. Nissan achieves success with this approach by computer communication links to suppliers. These schedules are confirmed, updated, or changed every 15 to 20 minutes. Suppliers provide deliveries 4 to 16 times per day. Master schedule performance is 99% on time, as measured every hour. On-time delivery from suppliers is 99.9% and for manufactured piece parts, 99.5%.

Balanced Flow Approach   MRP supports the planning and scheduling necessary for repetitive operations, such as the assembly lines at Harley-Davidson, Whirlpool, and a thousand other places. In these environments, the planning portion of MRP is combined with JIT execution. The JIT portion uses kanbans, visual signals, and reliable suppliers to pull the material through the facility. In these systems, execution is achieved by maintaining a carefully balanced flow of material to assembly areas with small lot sizes.

Supermarket   Another technique that joins MRP and JIT is the use of a "supermarket." In many firms, subassemblies, their components, and hardware items are common to a variety of products. In such cases, releasing orders for these common items with traditional lead-time offset, as is done in an MRP system, is not necessary. The subassemblies, components, and hardware items can be maintained in a common area, sometimes called a **supermarket**, adjacent to the production areas where they are used. Items in the supermarket are replenished by a JIT/kanban system.

> **Supermarket**
> An inventory area that holds common items that are replenished by a kanban system.

LOT-SIZING TECHNIQUES

An MRP system is an excellent way to determine production schedules and net requirements. However, whenever we have a net requirement, a decision must be made about *how much* to order. This decision is called a **lot-sizing decision**. There are a variety of ways to determine lot sizes in an MRP system; commercial MRP software usually includes the choice of several lot-sizing techniques. We now review a few of them.

Lot-sizing decision

The process of, or techniques used in, determining lot size.

Lot-for-lot

A lot-sizing technique that generates exactly what is required to meet the plan.

Lot-for-Lot In Example 3, we used a lot-sizing technique known as **lot-for-lot**, which produced exactly what was required. This decision is consistent with the objective of an MRP system, which is to meet the requirements of *dependent* demand. Thus, an MRP system should produce units only as needed, with no safety stock and no anticipation of further orders. When frequent orders are economical and just-in-time inventory techniques implemented, lot-for-lot can be very efficient. However, when setup costs are significant or management has been unable to implement JIT, lot-for-lot can be expensive. Example 4 uses the lot-for-lot criteria and determines cost for 10 weeks of demand.

<table>
<tr><td>

EXAMPLE 4

Lot sizing with lot-for-lot

Learning Objective

4. Determine lot sizes for lot-for-lot, EOQ, and PPB

</td><td>

Speaker Kits, Inc., wants to compute its ordering and carrying cost of inventory on lot-for-lot criteria.

Approach: With lot-for-lot, we order material only as it is needed. Once we have the cost of ordering (setting up), the cost of holding each unit for a given time period, and the production schedule, we can assign orders to our net requirements plan.

Solution: Speaker Kits has determined that, for the 12-inch speaker unit, setup cost is $100 and holding cost is $1 per period. The production schedule, as reflected in net requirements for assemblies, is as follows:

MRP Lot Sizing: Lot-for-Lot Technique*

		1	2	3	4	5	6	7	8	9	10
Gross requirements		35	30	40	0	10	40	30	0	30	55
Scheduled receipts											
Projected on hand	35	35	0	0	0	0	0	0	0	0	0
Net requirements		0	30	40	0	10	40	30	0	30	55
Planned order receipts			30	40		10	40	30		30	55
Planned order releases		30	40		10	40	30		30	55	

*Holding costs = $1/unit/week; setup cost = $100; gross requirements average per week = 27; lead time = 1 week.

The lot-sizing solution using the lot-for-lot technique is shown in the table. The holding cost is zero as there is never any inventory; but seven separate setups (one associated with each order) yield a total cost of $700.

Insight: When supply is reliable and frequent orders are inexpensive, but holding cost or obsolescence is high, lot-for-lot ordering can be very efficient.

Learning exercise: What is the impact on total cost if holding cost is $2 per period rather than $1? [Answer: Total holding cost remains zero, as no units are held from one period to the next with lot-for-lot.]

Related problems: 14.17, 14.20, 14.21, 14.22

</td></tr>
</table>

MRP is preferable when demand is dependent. Statistical techniques such as EOQ may be preferable when demand is independent.

Economic Order Quantity As discussed in Chapter 12, EOQ can be used as a lot-sizing technique. But as we indicated there, EOQ is preferable when *relatively constant* independent demand exists, not when we *know* the demand. EOQ is a statistical technique using averages (such as average demand for a year), whereas the MRP procedure assumes *known* (dependent) demand reflected in a master production schedule. Operations managers should take advantage of demand information when it is known, rather than assuming a constant demand. EOQ is examined in Example 5.

◀ *This Nissan line in Smyrna, Tennessee, has little inventory because Nissan schedules to a razor's edge. At Nissan, MRP helps reduce inventory to world-class standards. World-class automobile assembly requires that purchased parts have a turnover of slightly more than once a day and that overall turnover approaches 150 times per year.*

EXAMPLE 5

Lot sizing with EOQ

With a setup cost of $100 and a holding cost per week of $1, Speaker Kits, Inc., wants to examine its cost with lot sizes based on an EOQ criteria.

Approach: Using the same cost and production schedule as in Example 4, we determine net requirements and EOQ lot sizes.

Solution: Ten-week usage equals a gross requirement of 270 units; therefore, weekly usage equals 27, and 52 weeks (annual usage) equals 1,404 units. From Chapter 12, the EOQ model is:

$$Q^* = \sqrt{\frac{2DS}{H}}$$

where D = annual usage = 1,404
S = setup cost = $100
H = holding (carrying) cost, on an annual basis per unit
= $1 × 52 weeks = $52

$$Q^* = 73 \text{ units}$$

MRP Lot Sizing: EOQ Technique*

		1	2	3	4	5	6	7	8	9	10
Gross requirements		35	30	40	0	10	40	30	0	30	55
Scheduled receipts											
Projected on hand	35	35	0	43	3	3	66	26	69	69	39
Net requirements		0	30	0	0	7	0	4	0	0	16
Planned order receipts			73			73		73			73
Planned order releases		73			73		73			73	

*Holding costs = $1/unit/week; setup cost = $100; gross requirements average per week = 27; lead time = 1 week.

$$\text{Setups} = 1,404/73 = 19 \text{ per year}$$
$$\text{Setup cost} = 19 × \$100 = \$1,900$$
$$\text{Holding cost} = \frac{73}{2} × (\$1 × 52 \text{ weeks}) = \$1,898$$
$$\text{Setup cost} + \text{Holding cost} = \$1,900 + 1,898 = \$3,798$$

The EOQ solution yields a computed 10-week cost of $730 [$3,798 × (10 weeks/52 weeks) = $730].

Insight: EOQ can be an effective lot-sizing technique when demand is relatively constant. However, notice that actual holding cost will vary from the computed $730, depending on the rate of actual usage. From the preceding table, we can see that in our 10-week example, costs really are $400 for four setups, plus a holding cost of 318 units at $1 per week for a total of $718. Because usage was not constant, the actual computed cost was in fact less than the theoretical EOQ ($730), but more than the lot-for-lot rule ($700). If any stockouts had occurred, these costs too would need to be added to our actual EOQ cost of $718.

Learning exercise: What is the impact on total cost if holding cost is $2 per period rather than $1? [Answer: The EOQ quantity becomes 52, the theoretical annual total cost becomes $5,404, and the 10-week cost is $1,039 ($5,404 × (10/52)).]

Related problems: 14.18, 14.20, 14.21, 14.22

Part period balancing (PPB)
An inventory ordering technique that balances setup and holding costs by changing the lot size to reflect requirements of the next lot size in the future.

Economic part period (EPP)
A period of time when the ratio of setup cost to holding cost is equal.

Part Period Balancing **Part period balancing (PPB)** is a more dynamic approach to balance setup and holding cost.[3] PPB uses additional information by changing the lot size to reflect requirements of the next lot size in the future. PPB attempts to balance setup and holding cost for known demands. Part period balancing develops an **economic part period (EPP)**, which is the ratio of setup cost to holding cost. For our Speaker Kits example, EPP = $100/$1 = 100 units. Therefore, holding 100 units for one period would cost $100, exactly the cost of one setup. Similarly, holding 50 units for two periods also costs $100 (2 periods × $1 × 50 units). PPB merely adds requirements until the number of part periods approximates the EPP—in this case, 100. Example 6 shows the application of part period balancing.

EXAMPLE 6

Lot sizing with part period balancing

Speaker Kits, Inc., wants to compute the costs associated with lot sizing using part period balancing. It will use a setup cost of $100 and a $1 holding cost.

Approach: Using the same costs and production schedule as Examples 3 and 4, we develop a format that helps us compute the PPB quantity and apply that to our net requirements plan.

Solution: The procedure for computing the order releases of 80, 100, and 55 is shown in the following PPB calculation. In the second table, we apply the PPB order quantities to the net requirements plan.

PPB Calculations

Periods Combined	Trial Lot Size (cumulative net requirements)	Part Periods		Costs		
				Setup	Holding	Total
2	30	0	40 units held for 1 period = $40			
2, 3	70	40 = 40 × 1	10 units held for 3 periods = $30			
2, 3, 4	70	40				
2, 3, 4, 5	80	70 = 40 × 1 + 10 × 3		100 +	70	= 170
2, 3, 4, 5, 6	120	230 = 40 × 1 + 10 × 3 + 40 × 4				
(Therefore, combine periods 2 through 5; 70 is as close to our EPP of 100 as we are going to get.)						
6	40	0				
6, 7	70	30 = 30 × 1				
6, 7, 8	70	30 = 30 × 1 + 0 × 2				
6, 7, 8, 9	100	120 = 30 × 1 + 30 × 3		100 +	120	= 220
(Therefore, combine periods 6 through 9; 120 is as close to our EPP of 100 as we are going to get.)						
10	55	0		100 +	0	= 100
				300 +	190	= 490

---

[3] J. J. DeMatteis, "An Economic Lot-Sizing Technique: The Part-Period Algorithms," *IBM Systems Journal* 7 (1968): 30–38.

MRP Lot Sizing: PPB Technique*

		1	2	3	4	5	6	7	8	9	10
Gross requirements		35	30	40	0	10	40	30	0	30	55
Scheduled receipts											
Projected on hand	35	35	0	50	10	10	0	60	30	30	0
Net requirements		0	30	0	0	0	40	0	0	0	55
Planned order receipts			80				100				55
Planned order releases		80				100				55	

*Holding costs = $1/unit/week; setup cost = $100; gross requirements average per week = 27; lead time = 1 week.

EPP is 100 (setup cost divided by holding cost = $100/$1). The first lot is to cover periods 1, 2, 3, 4, and 5 and is 80.

The total costs are $490, with setup costs totaling $300 and holding costs totaling $190.

Insight: Both the EOQ and PPB approaches to lot sizing balance holding cost and ordering cost. But PPB places an order each time holding cost equals ordering cost, while EOQ takes a longer averaging approach.

Learning exercise: What is the impact on total cost if holding cost is $2 per period rather than $1? [Answer: With higher holding costs, reorder points become more frequent, with orders now being placed for 70 units in period 1, 50 in period 4, 60 in period 6, and 55 in period 9.]

Related problems: 14.19, 14.20, 14.21, 14.22

Wagner-Whitin Algorithm   The **Wagner-Whitin procedure** is a dynamic programming model that adds some complexity to the lot-size computation. It assumes a finite time horizon beyond which there are no additional net requirements. It does, however, provide good results.[4]

Wagner-Whitin procedure
A technique for lot-size computation that assumes a finite time horizon beyond which there are no additional net requirements to arrive at an ordering strategy.

Lot-Sizing Summary   In the three Speaker Kits lot-sizing examples, we found the following costs:

Lot-for-lot	$700
EOQ	$730
Part period balancing	$490

These examples should not, however, lead operations personnel to hasty conclusions about the preferred lot-sizing technique. In theory, new lot sizes should be computed whenever there is a schedule or lot-size change anywhere in the MRP hierarchy. However, in practice, such changes cause the instability and system nervousness referred to earlier in this chapter. Consequently, such frequent changes are not made. This means that all lot sizes are wrong because the production system cannot respond to frequent changes.

In general, the lot-for-lot approach should be used whenever low-cost deliveries can be achieved. Lot-for-lot is the goal. Lots can be modified as necessary for scrap allowances, process constraints (for example, a heat-treating process may require a lot of a given size), or raw material purchase lots (for example, a truckload of chemicals may be available in only one lot size). However, caution should be exercised prior to any modification of lot size because the modification can cause substantial distortion of actual requirements at lower levels in the MRP hierarchy. When setup costs are significant and demand is reasonably smooth, part period balancing (PPB), Wagner-Whitin, or even EOQ should provide satisfactory results. Too much concern with lot sizing yields false accuracy because of MRP dynamics. A correct lot size can be determined only after the fact, based on what actually happened in terms of requirements.

---

[4]We leave discussion of the algorithm to mathematical programming texts. The Wagner-Whitin algorithm yields a cost of $455 for the data in Examples 4, 5, and 6.

▶ *Many MRP programs, such as* Resource Manager for Excel *and* DB, *are commercially available.* Resource Manager's *initial menu screen is shown here.*

A demo program is available for student use at **www.usersolutions.com**.

EXTENSIONS OF MRP

In this section, we review three extensions of MRP.

Material Requirements Planning II (MRP II)

Material requirements planning II (MRP II)

A system that allows, with MRP in place, inventory data to be augmented by other resource variables; in this case, MRP becomes *material resource planning*.

Material requirements planning II is an extremely powerful technique. Once a firm has MRP in place, inventory data can be augmented by labor-hours, by material cost (rather than material quantity), by capital cost, or by virtually any other resource. When MRP is used this way, it is usually referred to as **MRP II**, and *resource* is usually substituted for *requirements*. MRP then stands for material *resource* planning.

For instance, so far in our discussion of MRP, we have scheduled units (quantities). However, each of these units requires resources in addition to its components. Those additional resources include labor-hours, machine-hours, and accounts payable (cash). Each of these resources can be used in an MRP format just as we used quantities. Table 14.4 shows how to determine the labor-hours, machine-hours, and cash that a sample master production schedule will require in each period. These requirements are then compared with the respective capacity (that is, labor-hours, machine-hours, cash, etc.), so operations managers can make schedules that will work.

To aid the functioning of MRP II, most MRP II computer programs are tied into other computer files that provide data to the MRP system or receive data from the MRP system. Purchasing, production scheduling, capacity planning, and warehouse management are a few examples of this data integration.

Learning Objective

5. Describe MRP II

▶ **Table 14.4**

Material Resource Planning (MRP II)

By utilizing the logic of MRP, resources such as labor, machine-hours, and cost can be accurately determined and scheduled. Weekly demand for labor, machine-hours, and payables for 100 units are shown.

			Week		
	5	**6**	**7**	**8**
A. Units (lead time 1 week)				100
Labor: 10 hours each				1,000
Machine: 2 hours each				200
Payable: $0 each				$ 0
B. Units (lead time 2 weeks, 2 each required)			200	
Labor: 10 hours each			2,000	
Machine: 2 hours each			400	
Payable: Raw material at $5 each			$1,000	
C. Units (lead time 4 weeks, 3 each required)	300			
Labor: 2 hours each	600			
Machine: 1 hour each	300			
Payable: Raw material at $10 each	$3,000			

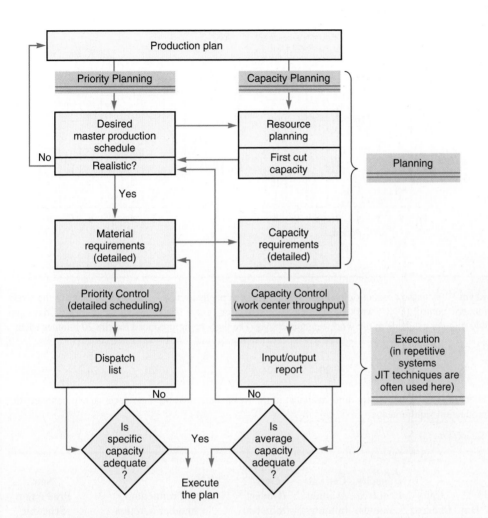

◀ **Figure 14.8**

Closed-Loop Material Requirements Planning

Source: Adapted from *Capacity Planning and Control Study Guide* (Alexandria, VA: American Production and Inventory Control Society). Reprinted by permission.

Learning Objective

6. Describe closed-loop MRP

Closed-Loop MRP

Closed-loop material requirements planning implies an MRP system that provides feedback to scheduling from the inventory control system. Specifically, a **closed-loop MRP system** provides information to the capacity plan, master production schedule, and ultimately to the production plan (as shown in Figure 14.8). Virtually all commercial MRP systems are closed-loop.

Capacity Planning

In keeping with the definition of closed-loop MRP, feedback about workload is obtained from each work center. **Load reports** show the resource requirements in a work center for all work currently assigned to the work center, all work planned, and expected orders. Figure 14.9(a) shows that the initial load in the milling center exceeds capacity in weeks 4 and 6. Closed-loop MRP systems allow production planners to move the work between time periods to smooth the load or at least bring it within capacity. (This is the "capacity planning" side of Figure 14.8.) The closed-loop MRP system can then reschedule all items in the net requirements plan (see Figure 14.9[b]).

Tactics for smoothing the load and minimizing the impact of changed lead time include the following:

1. *Overlapping,* which reduces the lead time, sends pieces to the second operation before the entire lot is completed on the first operation.
2. *Operations splitting* sends the lot to two different machines for the same operation. This involves an additional setup, but results in shorter throughput times, because only part of the lot is processed on each machine.
3. *Order,* or, *lot splitting* involves breaking up the order and running part of it ahead of schedule.

Example 7 shows a brief detailed capacity scheduling example using order splitting to improve utilization.

Closed-loop MRP system
A system that provides feedback to the capacity plan, master production schedule, and production plan so planning can be kept valid at all times.

Load report
A report for showing the resource requirements in a work center for all work currently assigned there as well as all planned and expected orders.

▶ **Figure 14.9**

(a) Initial Resource Requirements Profile for a Milling Center
(b) Smoothed Resource Requirements Profile for a Milling Center

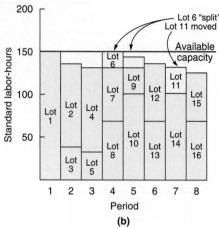

EXAMPLE 7

Order splitting

Kevin Watson, the production planner at Wiz Products, needs to develop a capacity plan for the direct numeric control (DNC) work cell. He has the production orders shown below for the next 5 days and 440 minutes available in the work center each day. The parts being produced require 20 minutes each.

Day	1	2	3	4	5
Orders	20	24	23	20	24

Approach: Compute the time available in the work center and the time necessary to complete the production requirements.

Solution:

Day	Units Ordered	Capacity Required (minutes)	Capacity Available (minutes)	Utilization: Over/ (Under) (minutes)	Production Planner's Action	New Production Schedule
1	20	400	440	(40)		22
2	24	480	440	40	Split order: move 2 units to day 1	22
3	23	460	440	20	Split order: move 1 unit to day 4	22
4	20	400	440	(40)		22
5	24	480	440	40	Split order: move 1 unit to day 4 and 1 unit to day 6 or request overtime.	22
	111					

Insight: By splitting the order, the production planner is able to utilize capacity more effectively and still meet the order requirements.

Learning exercise: If the units ordered for day 5 increase to 26, what are the production planner's options? [Answer: In addition to moving 1 unit to day 4, move the 3 units of production to day 6, or request overtime.]

Related problems: 14.23, 14.24

When the workload consistently exceeds work-center capacity, the tactics just discussed are not adequate. This may mean adding capacity. Options include adding capacity via personnel, machinery, overtime, or subcontracting.

MRP IN SERVICES

The demand for many services or service items is classified as dependent demand when it is directly related to or derived from the demand for other services. Such services often require product-structure trees, bills-of-material and labor, and scheduling. MRP can make a major contribution to operational performance in such services. Examples from restaurants, hospitals, and hotels follow.

Restaurants   In restaurants, ingredients and side dishes (bread, vegetables, and condiments) are typically meal components. These components are dependent on the demand for meals. The meal is an end item in the master schedule. Figure 14.10 shows (a) a product-structure tree and (b) a bill of material for veal picante, a top-selling entrée in a New Orleans restaurant. Note that the various components of veal picante (that is, veal, sauce, and linguini) are prepared by different kitchen personnel (see part [a] of Figure 14.10). These preparations also require different amounts of time to complete. Figure 14.10(c) shows a bill-of-labor for the veal dish. It lists the operations to be performed, the order of operations, and the labor requirements for each operation (types of labor and labor-hours).

Hospitals   MRP is also applied in hospitals, especially when dealing with surgeries that require known equipment, materials, and supplies. Houston's Park Plaza Hospital and many hospital suppliers, for example, use the technique to improve the scheduling and management of expensive surgical inventory.

Hotels   Marriott develops a bill-of-material (BOM) and a bill-of-labor when it renovates each of its hotel rooms. Marriott managers explode the BOM to compute requirements for materials, furniture, and decorations. MRP then provides net requirements and a schedule for use by purchasing and contractors.

Distribution Resource Planning (DRP)

When dependent techniques are used in the supply chain, they are called distribution resource planning (DRP). **Distribution resource planning (DRP)** is a time-phased stock-replenishment plan for all levels of the supply chain.

Distribution resource planning (DRP)
A time-phased stock-replenishment plan for all levels of a distribution network.

(a) PRODUCT STRUCTURE TREE

(b) BILL OF MATERIALS

Part Number	Description	Quantity	Unit of Measure	Unit Cost
10001	Veal picante	1	Serving	—
20002	Cooked linguini	1	Serving	—
20003	Prepared veal and sauce	1	Serving	—
20004	Spinach	0.1	Bag	0.94
30004	Uncooked linguini	0.5	Pound	—
30005	Veal	1	Serving	2.15
30006	Sauce	1	Serving	0.80

(c) BILL OF LABOR FOR VEAL PICANTE

Work Center	Operation	Labor Type	Labor-Hours Setup Time	Labor-Hours Run Time
1	Assemble dish	Chef	.0069	.0041
2	Cook linguini	Helper one	.0005	.0022
3	Cook veal and sauce	Assistant chef	.0125	.0500

◀ **Figure 14.10**

Product Structure Tree, Bill-of-Material, and Bill-of-Labor for Veal Picante

Source: Adapted from John G. Wacker, "Effective Planning and Cost Control for Restaurants," *Production and Inventory Management* (1st quarter 1985): 60. Reprinted by permission of American Production and Inventory Control Society.

DRP procedures and logic are analogous to MRP. With DRP, expected demand becomes gross requirements. Net requirements are determined by allocating available inventory to gross requirements. The DRP procedure starts with the forecast at the retail level (or the most distant point of the distribution network being supplied). All other levels are computed. As is the case with MRP, inventory is then reviewed with an aim to satisfying demand. So that stock will arrive when it is needed, net requirements are offset by the necessary lead time. A planned order release quantity becomes the gross requirement at the next level down the distribution chain.

DRP *pulls* inventory through the system. Pulls are initiated when the top or retail level orders more stock. Allocations are made to the top level from available inventory and production after being adjusted to obtain shipping economies. Effective use of DRP requires an integrated information system to rapidly convey planned order releases from one level to the next. The goal of the DRP system is small and frequent replenishment within the bounds of economical ordering and shipping.[5]

ENTERPRISE RESOURCE PLANNING (ERP)

Enterprise resource planning (ERP)

An information system for identifying and planning the enterprise-wide resources needed to take, make, ship, and account for customer orders.

Advances in MRP II systems that tie customers and suppliers to MRP II have led to the development of enterprise resource planning (ERP) systems. **Enterprise resource planning (ERP)** is software that allows companies to (1) automate and integrate many of their business processes, (2) share a common database and business practices throughout the enterprise, and (3) produce information in real time. A schematic showing some of these relationships for a manufacturing firm appears in Figure 14.11.

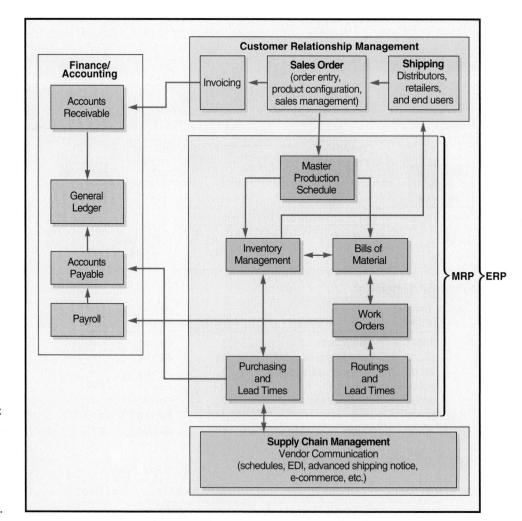

▶ **Figure 14.11**

MRP and ERP Information Flows, Showing Customer Relationship Management (CRM), Supply Chain Management (SCM), and Finance/Accounting

Other functions such as human resources are often also included in ERP systems.

---

[5]For an expanded discussion of time-phased stock-replenishment plans, see the section "Opportunities in an Integrated Supply Chain" in Chapter 11 of this text.

The objective of an ERP system is to coordinate a firm's whole business, from supplier evaluation to customer invoicing. This objective is seldom achieved, but ERP systems are evolving as umbrella systems that tie together a variety of specialized systems. This is accomplished by using a centralized database to assist the flow of information among business functions. Exactly what is tied together, and how, varies on a case-by-case basis. In addition to the traditional components of MRP, ERP systems usually provide financial and human resource (HR) management information. ERP systems also include:

Learning Objective

7. Describe ERP

- *Supply chain management (SCM)* software to support sophisticated vendor communication, e-commerce, and those activities necessary for efficient warehousing and logistics. The idea is to tie operations (MRP) to procurement, to materials management, and to suppliers, providing the tools necessary for effective management of all four areas.
- *Customer relationship management (CRM)* software for the incoming side of the business. CRM is designed to aid analysis of sales, target the most profitable customers, and manage the sales force.

Besides these five modules (MRP, finance, HR, SCM, and CRM), many other options are usually available from vendors of ERP software. These vendors have built modules to provide a variety of "solution" packages that are mixed and matched to individual company needs. Indeed, the trick to these large database and integrated ERP systems is to develop interfaces that allow file access to the databases. SAP, a large ERP vendor, has developed about a thousand *business application-programming interfaces* (BAPIs) to access its database. Similarly, other ERP vendors have designed the systems to facilitate integration with third-party software. The demand for interfaces to ERP systems is so large that a new software industry has developed to write the interfaces. This new category of programs is sometimes called *middleware* or *enterprise application integration* (EAI) software. These interfaces allow the expansion of ERP systems so they can integrate with other systems, such as warehouse management, logistics exchanges, electronic catalogs, quality management, and product life cycle management. It is this potential for integration with other systems, including the rich supply of third-party software offerings, that makes ERP so enticing.

In addition to data integration, ERP software promises reduced transaction costs and fast, accurate information. A strategic emphasis on just-in-time systems and supply chain integration drives the desire for enterprise-wide software. The *OM in Action* box "Managing Benetton with ERP Software," provides an example of how ERP software helps integrate company operations.

OM in Action   Managing Benetton with ERP Software

Thanks to ERP, the Italian sportswear company Benetton can probably claim to have the world's fastest factory and the most efficient distribution in the garment industry. Located in Ponzano, Italy, Benetton makes and ships 50 million pieces of clothing each year. That is 30,000 boxes every day—boxes that must be filled with exactly the items ordered going to the correct store of the 5,000 Benetton outlets in 60 countries. This highly automated distribution center uses only 19 people. Without ERP, hundreds of people would be needed.

Here is how ERP software works:

1. *Ordering:* A salesperson in the south Boston store finds that she is running out of a best-selling blue sweater. Using a laptop PC, her local Benetton sales agent taps into the ERP sales module.
2. *Availability:* ERP's inventory software simultaneously forwards the order to the mainframe in Italy and finds that half the order can be filled immediately from the Italian warehouse. The rest will be manufactured and shipped in 4 weeks.

3. *Production:* Because the blue sweater was originally created by computer-aided design (CAD), ERP manufacturing software passes the specifications to a knitting machine. The knitting machine makes the sweaters.
4. *Warehousing:* The blue sweaters are boxed with a radio frequency ID (RFID) tag addressed to the Boston store and placed in one of the 300,000 slots in the Italian warehouse. A robot flies by, reading RFID tags, picks out any and all boxes ready for the Boston store, and loads them for shipment.
5. *Order tracking:* The Boston salesperson logs onto the ERP system through the Internet and sees that the sweater (and other items) are completed and being shipped.
6. *Planning:* Based on data from ERP's forecasting and financial modules, Benetton's chief buyer decides that blue sweaters are in high demand and quite profitable. She decides to add three new hues.

Sources: The Wall Street Journal (April 10, 2007): B1; *Frontline Solutions* (April 2003): 54; and *MIT Sloan Management Review* (fall 2001): 46–53.

In an ERP system, data are entered only once into a common, complete, and consistent database shared by all applications. For example, when a Nike salesperson enters an order into his ERP system for 20,000 pairs of sneakers for Foot Locker, the data are instantly available on the manufacturing floor. Production crews start filling the order if it is not in stock, accounting prints Foot Locker's invoice, and shipping notifies the Foot Locker of the future delivery date. The salesperson, or even the customer, can check the progress of the order at any point. This is all accomplished using the same data and common applications. To reach this consistency, however, the data fields must be defined identically across the entire enterprise. In Nike's case, this means integrating operations at production sites from Vietnam to China to Mexico, at business units across the globe, in many currencies, and with reports in a variety of languages.

Each ERP vendor produces unique products. The major vendors, SAP AG (a German firm), BEA (Canada), SSAGlobal, American Software, PeopleSoft/Oracle, CMS Software (all of the U.S.), sell software or modules designed for specific industries (a set of SAP's modules is shown in Figure 14.12). However, companies must determine if their way of doing business will fit the standard ERP module. If they determine that the product will not fit the standard ERP product, they can change the way they do business to accommodate the software. But such a change can have an adverse impact on their business process, reducing a competitive advantage. Alternatively, ERP software can be customized to meet their specific process requirements. Although the vendors build the software to keep the customization process simple, many companies spend up to five times the cost of the software to customize it. In addition to the expense, the major downside of customization is that when ERP vendors provide an upgrade or enhancement to the software, the customized part of the code must be rewritten to fit into the new version. ERP programs cost from a minimum of $300,000 for a small company to hundreds of millions of dollars for global giants like General Motors and Coca-Cola. It is easy to see, then, that ERP systems

▼ **Figure 14.12**   SAP's Modules for ERP

Cash to Cash
Covers all financial related activity:

Accounts receivable	General ledger	Cash management
Accounts payable	Treasury	Asset management

Promote to Deliver
Covers front-end customer-oriented activities:

Marketing

Quote and order processing

Transportation

Documentation and labeling

After sales service

Warranty and guarantees

Design to Manufacture
Covers internal production activities:

Design engineering	Shop floor reporting
Production engineering	Contract/project management
Plant maintenance	Subcontractor management

Recruit to Retire
Covers all HR- and payroll-oriented activity:

Time and attendance	Payroll
Travel and expenses	

Procure to Pay
Covers sourcing activities:

Vendor sourcing

Purchase requisitioning

Purchase ordering

Purchase contracts

Inbound logistics

Supplier invoicing/matching

Supplier payment/settlement

Supplier performance

Dock to Dispatch
Covers internal inventory management:

Warehousing	Forecasting	Physical inventory
Distribution planning	Replenishment planning	Material handling

Source: www.sap.com.

OM in Action   There Is Nothing Easy about ERP

In 2000, the Switzerland-based consumer food giant Nestlé SA signed a $200 million contract with SAP for an ERP system. To this $200 million, Nestlé added $80 million for consulting and maintenance. And this was in addition to $500 million for hardware and software as part of a data center overhaul. Jeri Dunn, CIO of Nestlé USA, counsels that successful implementation is dependent on changing business processes and achieving universal "buy-in." Then, and only then, can an organization focus on installing the software. With many autonomous divisions and 200 operating companies and subsidiaries in 80 countries, the challenge of changing the processes and obtaining buy-in was substantial.

Standardizing processes is difficult, fraught with dead ends and costly mistakes. Nestlé had 28 points of customer order entry, multiple purchasing systems, and no idea how much volume was being done with a particular vendor; every factory did purchasing on its own with its own specifications. Nestlé USA was paying 29 different prices for vanilla—to the same vendor!

The newly established common databases and business processes led to consistent data and more trustworthy demand forecasts for the many Nestlé products. Nestlé now forecasts down to the level of the distribution center. This improved forecasting allows the company to reduce inventory and the related transportation expenses that occur when too much of a product is sent to one place while there is a shortage in another. The supply chain improvements accounted for much of Nestlé's $325 million in savings.

ERP projects are notorious for taking a long time and a lot of money, and this one was no exception, but after 3 years, the last modules of Nestlé's system were installed—and Nestlé thinks this installation is a success.

Sources: Materials Management and Distribution (March 2003): 27; *Businessline* (March 12, 2004): 1; and *CIO* (May 15, 2002): 62–70.

are expensive, full of hidden issues, and time consuming to install. As the *OM in Action* box "There Is Nothing Easy about ERP" notes, Nestlé, too, found nothing easy about ERP.

Advantages and Disadvantages of ERP Systems

We have alluded to some of the pluses and minuses of ERP. Here is a more complete list of both.

Advantages:
1. Provides integration of the supply chain, production, and administrative process.
2. Creates commonality of databases.
3. Can incorporate improved, reengineered, "best processes."
4. Increases communication and collaboration among business units and sites.
5. Has a software database that is off-the-shelf coding.
6. May provide a strategic advantage over competitors.

Disadvantages:
1. Is very expensive to purchase, and even more costly to customize.
2. Implementation may require major changes in the company and its processes.
3. Is so complex that many companies cannot adjust to it.
4. Involves an ongoing process for implementation, which may never be completed.
5. Expertise in ERP is limited, with staffing an ongoing problem.

ERP in the Service Sector

ERP vendors have developed a series of service modules for such markets as health care, government, retail stores, and financial services. Springer-Miller Systems, for example, has created an ERP package for the hotel market with software that handles all front- and back-office functions. This system integrates tasks such as maintaining guest histories, booking room and dinner reservations, scheduling golf tee times, and managing multiple properties in a chain. PeopleSoft/Oracle combines ERP with supply chain management to coordinate airline meal preparation. In the grocery industry, these supply chain systems are known as *efficient consumer response* (ECR) systems. As is the case in manufacturing, **efficient consumer response** systems tie sales to buying, to inventory, to logistics, and to production.

Efficient consumer response (ECR)
Supply chain management systems in the grocery industry that tie sales to buying, to inventory, to logistics, and to production.

Summary

Material requirements planning (MRP) is the preferred way to schedule production and inventory when demand is dependent. For MRP to work, management must have a master schedule, precise requirements for all components, accurate inventory and purchasing records, and accurate lead times.

Production should often be lot-for-lot in an MRP system. When properly implemented, MRP can contribute in a major way to reduction in inventory while improving customer-service levels. MRP techniques allow the operations manager to schedule and replenish stock on a "need-to-order" basis rather than simply a "time-to-order" basis.

The continuing development of MRP systems has led to the integration of production data with a variety of other activities, including the supply chain and sales. As a result, we now have integrated database-oriented enterprise resource planning (ERP) systems. These expensive and difficult-to-install ERP systems, when successful, support strategies of differentiation, response, and cost leadership.

Key Terms

Material requirements planning (MRP) (p. 562)
Master production schedule (MPS) (p. 562)
Bill of material (BOM) (p. 565)
Modular bills (p. 566)
Planning bills (or kits) (p. 566)
Phantom bills of material (p. 566)
Low-level coding (p. 566)
Lead time (p. 567)
Gross material requirements plan (p. 568)
Net material requirements (p. 569)

Planned order receipt (p. 571)
Planned order release (p. 571)
System nervousness (p. 572)
Time fences (p. 572)
Pegging (p. 572)
Buckets (p. 573)
Bucketless system (p. 573)
Back flush (p. 573)
Supermarket (p. 573)
Lot-sizing decision (p. 574)
Lot-for-lot (p. 574)

Part period balancing (PPB) (p. 576)
Economic part period (EPP) (p. 576)
Wagner-Whitin procedure (p. 577)
Material requirements planning II (MRP II) (p. 578)
Closed-loop MRP system (p. 579)
Load report (p. 579)
Distribution resource planning (DRP) (p. 581)
Enterprise resource planning (ERP) (p. 582)
Efficient consumer response (ECR) (p. 585)

Using Software to Solve MRP Problems

There are many commercial MRP software packages, for companies of all sizes. MRP software for small and medium-size companies includes User Solutions, Inc., a demo of which is available at **www.usersolutions.com**, and MAX, from Exact Software North America, Inc. Software for larger systems is available from SAP, CMS, BEA, Oracle, i2 Technologies, and many others. The Excel OM software that accompanies this text includes an MRP module, as does POM for Windows. The use of both is explained in the following sections.

✖ Using Excel OM

Using Excel OM's MRP module requires the careful entry of several pieces of data. The initial MRP screen is where we enter (1) the total number of occurrences of items in the BOM (including the top item), (2) what we want the BOM items to be called (i.e., Item no., Part), (3) total number of periods to be scheduled, and (4) what we want the periods called (i.e., days, weeks).

Excel OM's second MRP screen provides the data entry for an indented bill of material. Here we enter (1) the name of each item in the BOM, (2) the quantity of that item in the assembly, and (3) the correct indent (i.e., parent/child relationship) for each item. The indentations are critical as they provide the logic for the BOM explosion. The indentations should follow the logic of the product structure tree with indents for each assembly item in that assembly.

Excel OM's third MRP screen repeats the indented BOM and provides the standard MRP tableau for entries. This is shown in Program 14.1 using the data from Examples 1, 2, and 3.

▐P Using POM for Windows

The POM for Windows MRP module can also solve Examples 1 to 3. Up to 18 periods can be analyzed. Here are the inputs required:

1. *Item names:* The item names are entered in the left column. The same item name will appear in more than one row if the item is used by two parent items. Each item must follow its parents.
2. *Item level:* The level in the indented BOM must be given here. The item *cannot* be placed at a level more than one below the item immediately above.
3. *Lead-time:* The lead time for an item is entered here. The default is 1 week.
4. *Number per parent:* The number of units of this subassembly needed for its parent is entered here. The default is 1.
5. *On hand:* List current inventory on hand once, even if the subassembly is listed twice.

The data in columns A, B, C, D (down to row 15) are entered on the second screen and automatically transferred here.

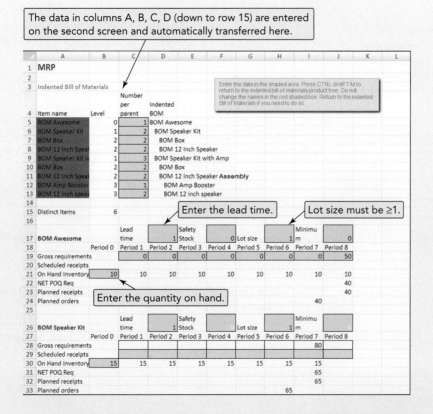

6. *Lot size:* The lot size can be specified here. A 0 or 1 will perform lot-for-lot ordering. If another number is placed here, then all orders for that item will be in integer multiples of that number.

7. *Demands:* The demands are entered in the end item row in the period in which the items are demanded.

8. *Scheduled receipts:* If units are scheduled to be received in the future, they should be listed in the appropriate time period (column) and item (row). (An entry here in level 1 is a demand; all other levels are receipts.)

Further details regarding POM for Windows are seen in Appendix IV.

Solved Problems

Virtual Office Hours help is available on Student DVD.

Solved Problem 14.1

Determine the low-level coding and the quantity of each component necessary to produce 10 units of an assembly we will call Alpha. The product structure and quantities of each component needed for each assembly are noted in parenthesis.

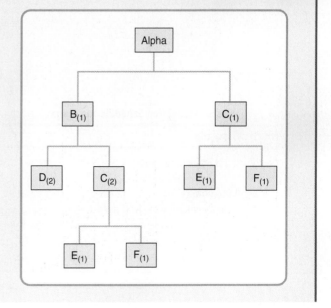

solution

Redraw the product structure with low-level coding. Then multiply down the structure until the requirements of each branch are determined. Then add across the structure until the total for each is determined.

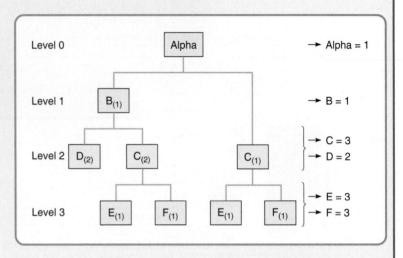

Es required for left branch:

$$(1_{alpha} \times 1_B \times 2_C \times 1_E) = 2$$

and Es required for right branch:

$$(1_{alpha} \times 1_C \times 1_E) = \frac{1}{3} \text{ Es required in total}$$

Then "explode" the requirement by multiplying each by 10, as shown in the following table:

Level	Item	Quantity per Unit	Total Requirements for 10 Alpha
0	Alpha	1	10
1	B	1	10
2	C	3	30
2	D	2	20
3	E	3	30
3	F	3	30

Solved Problem 14.2

Using the product structure for Alpha in Solved Problem 14.1, and the following lead times, quantity on hand, and master production schedule, prepare a net MRP table for Alphas.

Item	Lead Time	Qty On Hand
Alpha	1	10
B	2	20
C	3	0
D	1	100
E	1	10
F	1	50

Master Production Schedule for Alpha

Period	6	7	8	9	10	11	12	13
Gross requirements			50			50		100

solution

See the chart on the next page.

Net Material Requirements Planning Sheet for Alpha

The letter in parentheses (A) is the source of the demand.

Period (week, day)

Lot Size	Lead Time (# of Periods)	On Hand	Safety Stock	Allocated	Low-Level Code	Item ID		PoH	1	2	3	4	5	6	7	8	9	10	11	12	13
Lot-for-Lot	1	10	—	—	0	Alpha (A)	Gross Requirements									50			50		100
							Scheduled Receipts														
							Projected On Hand	10													
							Net Requirements									40			50		100
							Planned Order Receipts									40			50		100
							Planned Order Releases								40			50		100	
Lot-for-Lot	2	20	—	—	1	B	Gross Requirements								40(A)			50(A)		100(A)	
							Scheduled Receipts														
							Projected On Hand	20													
							Net Requirements								20			50		100	
							Planned Order Receipts								20			50		100	
							Planned Order Releases						20			50		100			
Lot-for-Lot	3	0	—	—	2	C	Gross Requirements						40(B)		40(A)	100(B)		200(B) + 50(A)		100(A)	
							Scheduled Receipts														
							Projected On Hand	0													
							Net Requirements						40		40	100		250		100	
							Planned Order Receipts						40		40	100		250		100	
							Planned Order Releases			40		40	100		250		100				
Lot-for-Lot	1	100	—	—	2	D	Gross Requirements						40(B)			100(B)		200(B)			
							Scheduled Receipts														
							Projected On Hand	100					60								
							Net Requirements						0			40		200			
							Planned Order Receipts									40		200			
							Planned Order Releases								40		200				
Lot-for-Lot	1	10	—	—	3	E	Gross Requirements			40(C)		40(C)	100(C)		250(C)		100(C)				
							Scheduled Receipts														
							Projected On Hand	10		10											
							Net Requirements			30		40	100		250		100				
							Planned Order Receipts			30		40	100		250		100				
							Planned Order Releases		30		40	100		250		100					
Lot-for-Lot	1	50	—	—	3	F	Gross Requirements			40(C)		40(C)	100(C)		250(C)		100(C)				
							Scheduled Receipts														
							Projected On Hand	50		0		10					—				
							Net Requirements			0		30	100		250		100				
							Planned Order Receipts					30	100		250		100				
							Planned Order Releases			30		100		250		100					

Self-Test

- **Before taking the self-test**, refer to the learning objectives listed at the beginning of the chapter and the key terms listed at the end of the chapter.
- Use the key at the back of the text to **correct** your answers.
- **Restudy** pages that correspond to any questions you answered incorrectly or material you feel uncertain about.

1. The list of quantities of components, ingredients, and materials required to produce a product is the:
   a) bill-of-material
   b) engineering change notice
   c) purchase order
   d) all of the above

2. _____ allows a segment of the master schedule to be designated as "not to be rescheduled."
   a) Regenerative MRP
   b) System nervousness
   c) Pegging
   d) DRP
   e) None of the above

3. A lot-sizing procedure that assumes a finite time horizon beyond which there are no additional net requirements is:
   a) Wagner-Whitin algorithm
   b) part period balancing
   c) economic order quantity
   d) all of the above

4. Breaking up the order and running part of it ahead of schedule is known as:
   a) overlapping
   b) operations splitting
   c) order, or lot, splitting
   d) pegging

5. In a product structure diagram:
   a) parents are found only at the top level of the diagram
   b) parents are found at every level in the diagram
   c) children are found at every level of the diagram except the top level
   d) all items in the diagrams are both parents and children
   e) all of the above are true

6. The difference between a gross material requirements plan (gross MRP) and a net materials requirements plan (net MRP) is:
   a) the gross MRP may not be computerized, but the net MRP must be computerized
   b) the gross MRP includes consideration of the inventory on hand, whereas the net MRP doesn't include the inventory consideration
   c) the net MRP includes consideration of the inventory on hand, whereas the gross MRP doesn't include the inventory consideration
   d) the gross MRP doesn't take taxes into account, whereas the net MRP includes the tax considerations
   e) the net MRP is only an estimate, whereas the gross MRP is used for actual production scheduling

7. To effectively use dependent inventory models, the operations manager needs to know:
   a) the master production schedule (which tells what is to be made and when)
   b) the specifications or bill-of-material (which tells how to make the product)
   c) the purchase orders outstanding (which tell what is on order)
   d) the lead times (or how long it takes to get various components)
   e) all of the above

8. A phantom bill-of-material is a bill-of-material developed for:
   a) a final product for which production is to be discontinued
   b) a subassembly that exists only temporarily
   c) a module that is a major component of a final product
   d) the purpose of grouping subassemblies when we wish to issue "kits" for later use

9. When a bill-of-material is used in order to assign an artificial parent to a bill-of-material, it is usually called a:
   a) modular bill-of-material
   b) pick list
   c) phantom bill-of-material
   d) planning bill-of-material

Active Model Exercise

We use Active Model 14.1 to demonstrate the effects of lot sizes (multiples) and minimum lot sizes.

Questions

1. Suppose that item B must be ordered in multiples of dozens. Which items are affected by this change?

2. Suppose that the minimum order quantity for item C is 200 units. Which items are affected by this change?

Order Releases

[Reset Data] [Questions]

Master Production Schedule

	Week							
	1	2	3	4	5	6	7	8
Item A	0	0	0	0	0	0	0	50

Item Master File

	Lead time	On hand	Lot size multiple	Minimum lot size
A	1	10	1	0
B	2	15	1	0
C	1	20	1	0
D	1	10	1	0
E	2	10	1	0
F	3	5	1	0
G	2	0	1	0

Planned Order Releases

	Week							
	1	2	3	4	5	6	7	8
A							40	
B					65			
C						100		
D		380		130				
E			120	200				
F			195					
G	195							

◀ **Active Model 14.1**

An Analysis of the MRP Model Used by Speaker Kits, Inc., in Examples 1–3

Internet and Student CD-ROM/DVD Exercises

Visit our Companion Web site or use your student CD-ROM/DVD to help with material in this chapter.

 On Our Companion Web Site, www.prenhall.com/heizer
- Self-Study Quizzes
- Practice Problems
- Virtual Company Tour
- Internet Cases
- PowerPoint Lecture

 On Your Student CD-ROM
- Practice Problems
- Active Model Exercise
- Excel OM
- Excel OM Example Data File
- POM for Windows

 On Your Student DVD
- Video Clip and Video Case
- Virtual Office Hours for Solved Problems

Discussion Questions

1. What is the difference between a *gross* requirements plan and a *net* requirements plan?
2. Once a material requirements plan (MRP) has been established, what other managerial applications might be found for the technique?
3. What are the similarities between MRP and DRP?
4. How does MRP II differ from MRP?
5. Which is the best lot-sizing policy for manufacturing organizations?
6. What impact does ignoring carrying cost in the allocation of stock in a DRP system have on lot sizes?
7. MRP is more than an inventory system; what additional capabilities does MRP possess?
8. What are the options for the production planner who has: (a) scheduled more than capacity in a work center next week? (b) a consistent lack of capacity in that work center?
9. Master schedules are expressed in three different ways depending on whether the process is continuous, a job shop, or repetitive. What are these three ways?
10. What functions of the firm affect an MRP system? How?
11. What is the rationale for (a) a phantom bill of material, (b) a planning bill of material, and (c) a pseudo bill of material?

12. Identify five specific requirements of an effective MRP system.
13. What are the typical benefits of ERP?
14. What are the distinctions between MRP, DRP, and ERP?
15. As an approach to inventory management, how does MRP differ from the approach taken in Chapter 12, dealing with economic order quantities (EOQ)?
16. What are the disadvantages of ERP?
17. Use the Web or other sources to:
    (a) Find stories that highlight the advantages of an ERP system.
    (b) Find stories that highlight the difficulties of purchasing, installing, or failure of an ERP system.
18. Use the Web or other sources to identify what an ERP vendor (SAP, PeopleSoft/Oracle, American Software, etc.) includes in these software modules:
    (a) Customer relationship management.
    (b) Supply chain management.
    (c) Product life cycle management.
19. The very structure of MRP systems suggests fixed lead times. However, many firms have moved toward JIT and kanban techniques. What are the techniques, issues, and impact of adding JIT inventory and purchasing techniques to an organization that has MRP?

Ethical Dilemma

For many months your prospective ERP customer has been analyzing the hundreds of assumptions built into the $800,000 ERP software you are selling. So far, you have knocked yourself out to try to make this sale. If the sale goes through, you will reach your yearly quota and get a nice bonus. On the other hand, loss of this sale may mean you start looking for other employment.

The accounting, human resource, supply chain, and marketing teams put together by the client have reviewed the specifications and finally recommended purchase of the software. However, as you

looked over their shoulders and helped them through the evaluation process, you began to realize that their purchasing procedures—with much of the purchasing being done at hundreds of regional stores—were not a good fit for the software. At the very least, the customizing will add $250,000 to the implementation and training cost. The team is not aware of the issue, and you know that the necessary $250,000 is not in the budget.

What do you do?

Problems*

•   **14.1**   You have developed the following simple product structure of items needed for your gift bag for a rush party for prospective pledges in your organization. You forecast 200 attendees. Assume that there is no inventory on hand of any of the items. Explode the bill of material. (Subscripts indicate the number of units required.)

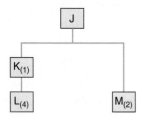

••   **14.2**   You are expected to have the gift bags in Problem 14.1 ready at 5 P.M.. However, you need to personalize the items (monogrammed pens, note pads, literature from the printer, etc.). The lead time is 1 hour to assemble 200 Js once the other items are prepared. The other items will take a while as well. Given the volunteers you have, the other time estimates are item K (2 hours), item L (1 hour), and item M (4 hours). Develop a time-phased assembly plan to prepare the gift bags.

••   **14.3**   The demand for subassembly S is 100 units in week 7. Each unit of S requires 1 unit of T and 2 units of U. Each unit of T requires 1 unit of V, 2 units of W, and 1 unit of X. Finally, each unit of U requires 2 units of Y and 3 units of Z. One firm manufactures all items. It takes 2 weeks to make S, 1 week to make T, 2 weeks to make U, 2 weeks to make V, 3 weeks to make W, 1 week to make X, 2 weeks to make Y, and 1 week to make Z.
a) Construct a product structure. Identify all levels, parents, and components.
b) Prepare a time-phased product structure.

••   **14.4**   Using the information in Problem 14.3, construct a gross material requirements plan. **P✗**

••   **14.5**   Using the information in Problem 14.3, construct a net material requirements plan using the following on-hand inventory.

Item	On-Hand Inventory	Item	On-Hand Inventory
S	20	W	30
T	20	X	25
U	40	Y	240
V	30	Z	40 **P✗**

••   **14.6**   Refer again to Problems 14.3 and 14.4. In addition to 100 units of S, there is also a demand for 20 units of U, which is a component of S. The 20 units of U are needed for maintenance purposes. These units are needed in week 6. Modify the *gross material requirements plan* to reflect this change. **P✗**

••   **14.7**   Refer again to Problems 14.3 and 14.5. In addition to 100 units of S, there is also a demand for 20 units of U, which is a component of S. The 20 units of U are needed for maintenance purposes. These units are needed in week 6. Modify the *net material requirements plan* to reflect this change. **P✗**

••   **14.8**   As the production planner for Adams-Ebert Products, Inc., you have been given a bill of material for a bracket that is made up of a base, two springs, and four clamps. The base is assembled from one clamp and two housings. Each clamp has one handle and one casting. Each housing has two bearings and one shaft. There is no inventory on hand.
a) Design a product structure noting the quantities for each item and show the low-level coding.
b) Determine the gross quantities needed of each item if you are to assemble 50 brackets.
c) Compute the net quantities needed if there are 25 of the base and 100 of the clamp in stock. **P✗**

••   **14.9**   Your boss at Adams-Ebert Products, Inc., has just provided you with the schedule and lead times for the bracket in Problem 14.8. The unit is to be prepared in week 10. The lead times for the components are bracket (1 week), base (1 week), spring (1 week), clamp (1 week), housing (2 weeks), handle (1 week), casting (3 weeks), bearing (1 week), and shaft (1 week).
a) Prepare the time-phased product structure for the bracket.
b) In what week do you need to start the castings? **P✗**

•••**14.10**   a) Given the product structure and master production schedule (Figure 14.14 on the next page), develop a gross requirements plan for all items.
b) Given the preceding product structure, master production schedule, and inventory status (Figure 14.14), develop a net materials requirements (planned order release) for all items. **P✗**

*Note: **P✗** means the problem may be solved with POM for Windows and/or Excel OM. Many of the exercises in this chapter (14.1 through 14.16 and 14.23 through 14.27) can be done on *Resource Manager for Excel*, a commercial system made available by User Solutions, Inc. Access to a trial version of the software and a set of notes for the user is available at **www.usersolutions.com**.

Lot Size	Lead Time (# of periods)	On Hand	Safety Stock	Allo-cated	Low-Level Code	Item ID		Period (week, day)							
								1	2	3	4	5	6	7	8
						Gross Requirements									
						Scheduled Receipts									
						Projected On Hand									
						Net Requirements									
						Planned Order Receipts									
						Planned Order Releases									
						Gross Requirements									
						Scheduled Receipts									
						Projected On Hand									
						Net Requirements									
						Planned Order Receipts									
						Planned Order Releases									
						Gross Requirements									
						Scheduled Receipts									
						Projected On Hand									
						Net Requirements									
						Planned Order Receipts									
						Planned Order Releases									
						Gross Requirements									
						Scheduled Receipts									
						Projected On Hand									
						Net Requirements									
						Planned Order Receipts									
						Planned Order Releases									
						Gross Requirements									
						Scheduled Receipts									
						Projected On Hand									
						Net Requirements									
						Planned Order Receipts									
						Planned Order Releases									

▲ **Figure 14.13   MRP Form for Homework Problems in Chapter 14**

For several problems in this chapter, a copy of this form may be helpful.

••• **14.11** Given the following product structure, master production schedule, and inventory status (Figure 14.15 on page 594) and assuming the requirements for each BOM item is 1: (a) develop a gross requirements plan for Item C; (b) develop a net requirements plan for Item C. **Px**

•••• **14.12** Based on the following data (see Figure 14.15), complete a net material requirements schedule for:

a) All items (10 schedules in all), assuming the requirement for each BOM item is 1.

b) All 10 items, assuming the requirement for all items is 1, except B, C, and F, which require *2 each.* **Px**

••• **14.13** Electro Fans has just received an order for one thousand 20-inch fans due week 7. Each fan consists of a housing assembly, two grills, a fan assembly, and an electrical unit. The housing assembly consists of a frame, two supports, and a handle. The fan assembly consists of a hub and five blades. The electrical unit consists of a motor, a switch, and a knob. The

▼ **Figure 14.14   Information for Problem 14.10**

Master Production Schedule for X1

PERIOD	7	8	9	10	11	12
Gross requirements		50		20		100

ITEM	LEAD TIME	ON HAND		ITEM	LEAD TIME	ON HAND
X1	1	50		C	1	0
B1	2	20		D	1	0
B2	2	20		E	3	10
A1	1	5				

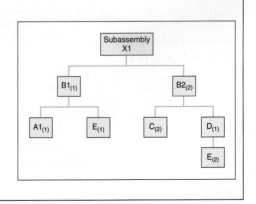

▶ **Figure 14.15**

Information for Problems 14.11 and 14.12

Period			8	9	10	11	12
Gross requirements: A			100		50		150
Gross requirements: H				100		50	

Item	On Hand	Lead Time	Item	On Hand	Lead Time
A	0	1	F	75	2
B	100	2	G	75	1
C	50	2	H	0	1
D	50	1	J	100	2
E	75	2	K	100	2

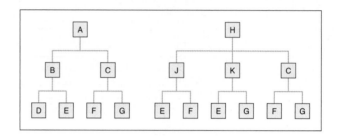

following table gives lead times, on-hand inventory, and scheduled receipts.

a) Construct a product structure.
b) Construct a time-phased product structure.
c) Prepare a net material requirements plan. **Px**

Data Table for Problem 14.13

Component	Lead Time	On Hand Inventory	Lot Size	Scheduled Receipt
20″ Fan	1	100	—	
Housing	1	100	—	
Frame	2	—	—	
Supports (2)	1	50	100	
Handle	1	400	500	
Grills (2)	2	200	500	
Fan Assembly	3	150	—	
Hub	1	—	—	
Blades (5)	2	—	100	
Electrical Unit	1	—	—	
Motor	1	—	—	
Switch	1	20	12	
Knob	1	—	25	200 knobs in week 2

••• **14.14** A part structure, lead time (weeks), and on-hand quantities for product A are shown in Figure 14.16. From the information shown, generate

a) An indented bill of material for product A (see Figure 5.9 in Chapter 5 as an example of a BOM).
b) Net requirements for each part to produce 10 As in week 8 using lot-for-lot. **Px**

••• **14.15** You are product planner for product A (in Problem 14.14 and Figure 14.16). The field service manager, Al Trostel, has just called and told you that the requirements for B and F should each be increased by 10 units for his repair requirements in the field.

a) Prepare a list showing the quantity of each part required to produce the requirements for the service manager *and* the production request of 10.
b) Prepare a net requirement plan by date for the new requirements (for both production and field service), assuming that the field service manager wants his 10 units of B and F in week 6 and the 10 production units in week 8. **Px**

••• **14.16** You have just been notified via fax that the lead time for component G of product A (Problem 14.15 and Figure 14.16) has been increased to 4 weeks.

▶ **Figure 14.16**

Information for Problems 14.14, 14.15 and 14.16

PART	INVENTORY ON HAND
A	0
B	2
C	10
D	5
E	4
F	5
G	1
H	10

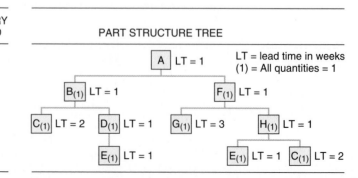

a) Which items have changed and why?

b) What are the implications for the production plan?

c) As production planner, what can you do? **Px**

Data Table for Problems 14.17 through 14.19*

Period	1	2	3	4	5	6	7	8	9	10	11	12
Gross requirements	30		40		30	70	20		10	80		50

*Holding cost = $2.50/unit/week; setup cost = $150; lead time = 1 week; beginning inventory = 40.

• • • **14.17** Develop a lot-for-lot solution and calculate total relevant costs for the data in the preceding table. **Px**

• • • **14.18** Develop an EOQ solution and calculate total relevant costs for the data in the preceding table. Stockout costs equal $10 per unit. **Px**

• • • **14.19** Develop a PPB solution and calculate total relevant costs for the data in the preceding table. **Px**

• • • **14.20** Using the gross requirements schedule in Examples 4, 5, and 6 in the text, prepare an alternative ordering system that always orders 100 units the week prior to a shortage (a fixed order quantity of 100) with the same costs as in the example (setup at $100 each, holding at $1 per unit per period). What is the cost of this ordering system? **Px**

• • • **14.21** Using the gross requirements schedule in Examples 4, 5, and 6 in the text, prepare an alternative ordering system that orders every 3 weeks for 3 weeks ahead (a periodic order quantity). Use the same costs as in the example (setup at $100 each, holding at $1 per unit per period). What is the cost of this ordering system? **Px**

• • • **14.22** Using the gross requirements schedule in Examples 4, 5, and 6 in the text, prepare an alternative ordering system of your own design that uses the same cost as in the example (setup at $100 each, holding at $1 per unit per period). Can you do better than the costs shown in the text? What is the cost of your ordering system? **Px**

• • • **14.23** Katherine Hepburn, Inc., has received the following orders:

Period	1	2	3	4	5	6	7	8	9	10
Order size	0	40	30	40	10	70	40	10	30	60

The entire fabrication for these units is scheduled on one machine. There are 2,250 usable minutes in a week, and each unit will take 65 minutes to complete. Develop a capacity plan, using lot splitting, for the 10-week time period.

• • • **14.24** David Jurman, Ltd., has received the following orders:

Period	1	2	3	4	5	6	7	8	9	10
Order size	60	30	10	40	70	10	40	30	40	0

The entire fabrication for these units is scheduled on one machine. There are 2,250 usable minutes in a week, and each unit will take 65 minutes to complete. Develop a capacity plan, using lot splitting, for the 10-week time period.

• • **14.25** Heather Adams, production manager for a Colorado exercise equipment manufacturer, needs to schedule an order for 50 UltimaSteppers, which are to be shipped in week 8. Subscripts indicate quantity required for each parent. Assume lot-for-lot ordering. Below is information about the steppers:

Item	Lead Time	On-Hand Inventory	Components
Stepper	2	20	$A_{(1)}$, $B_{(3)}$, $C_{(2)}$
A	1	10	$D_{(1)}$, $F_{(2)}$
B	2	30	$E_{(1)}$, $F_{(3)}$
C	3	10	$D_{(2)}$, $E_{(3)}$
D	1	15	
E	2	5	
F	2	20	

a) Develop a product structure for Heather.

b) Develop a time-phased structure.

c) Develop a net material requirements plan for F. **Px**

• • • • **14.26** You are scheduling production of your popular Rustic Coffee Table. The table requires a top, four legs, $\frac{1}{8}$ gallon of stain, $\frac{1}{16}$ gallon of glue, 2 short braces between the legs and 2 long braces between the legs, and a brass cap that goes on the bottom of each leg. You have 100 gallons of glue in inventory, but none of the other components. All items except the brass caps, stain, and glue are ordered on a lot-for-lot basis. The caps are purchased in quantities of 1,000, stain and glue by the gallon. Lead time is 1 day for each item. Schedule the order releases necessary to produce 640 coffee tables on days 5 and 6, and 128 on days 7 and 8. **Px**

• • • • **14.27** Using the data for the coffee table in Problem 14.26, build a labor schedule when the labor standard for each top is 2 labor hours; each leg including brass cap installation requires $\frac{1}{4}$ hour, as does each cross brace. Base assembly requires 1 labor-hour, and final assembly requires 2 labor-hours. What is the total number of labor-hours required each day, and how many employees are needed each day at 8 hours per day?

Case Studies

Ikon's Attempt at ERP

Ikon Office Solutions is the world's largest independent office technology company, with revenues approaching $5 billion and operations in the U.S., Canada, Mexico, the United Kingdom, France, Germany, and Denmark. Ikon is pursing a growth strategy to move from what was more than 80 individually operating copier dealers to an integrated solutions company. Its goal is to provide total office technology solutions, ranging from copiers, digital printers, and document management services to systems integration, training, and other network technology services. The company has rapidly expanded its service capability with an aggressive acquisition effort that has included technology services and document management companies.

Given these objectives, the company seemed to need ERP software. A few years ago, it began a pilot project in the Northern California district to assess the possibility of using SAP's enterprise software applications companywide. Chief Information Officer David Gadra, who joined Ikon about a month after the pilot system was turned on, however, decided not to roll it out. Ikon will take a $25 million write-off on the cost of the pilot.

"There were a number of factors that made us decide this project was more challenging than beneficial for us," says Gadra. "When we added everything up—human factors, functionality gaps, and costs incurred—we decided our environment is ill defined for SAP." Instead, Ikon is bringing all 13 of its regional operations onto a home-grown application system.

"I don't blame the consultants or SAP," he says. "We made errors on our side in estimating the amount of business change we'd have to make as part of this implementation."

The vast majority of the $25 million loss represents consultant fees; less than 10% went to pay for the software itself. At any given point in the project, Ikon was paying 40 to 50 outside consultants $300 an hour.

Ikon budgeted $12 million to get the system running. That cost came in at over $14 million, including $8 million paid to IBM for consulting.

A major reason the company decided to drop SAP was its conclusion that the software didn't sufficiently address the needs of a service company like Ikon, as opposed to those of manufacturers. For example, SAP didn't have an adequate feature for tracking service calls. Ikon also had great difficulty assembling an internal team of SAP experts. Ikon's costs were high because the firm relied heavily on consultants.

"I am extremely disappointed by Ikon's announcement," says SAP America president Jeremy Coote, describing Ikon's earlier pilot as on time and "extremely successful." Coote calls Ikon's decision to scrap the project "an example of what happens when you don't sell at the corporate level" as well as the divisional level. A newer version of SAP is to include a service management module.

Discussion Questions

1. What are the information needs at Ikon and what alternatives does Ikon have to meet these needs?
2. What are the advantages and disadvantages of ERP software in meeting these needs?
3. What risks did the company take in selecting SAP software for evaluation?
4. Why did Ikon cancel the SAP project?

Sources: Ikon Annual Reports; *Information Week* (April 1997): 25; and J. R. Gordon and S. R. Gordon, *Information Systems: A Management Approach*, 3rd ed. (New York: Wiley, 2003).

MRP at Wheeled Coach

Video Case

Wheeled Coach, the world's largest manufacturer of ambulances, builds thousands of different and constantly changing configurations of its products. The custom nature of its business means lots of options and special designs—and a potential scheduling and inventory nightmare. Wheeled Coach addressed such problems, and succeeded in solving a lot of them, with an MRP system (described in the *Global Company Profile* that opens this chapter). As with most MRP installations, however, solving one set of problems uncovers a new set.

One of the new issues that had to be addressed by plant manager Lynn Whalen was newly discovered excess inventory. Managers discovered a substantial amount of inventory that was not called for in any finished products. Excess inventory was evident because of the new level of inventory accuracy required by the MRP system. The other reason was a new series of inventory reports generated by the IBM MAPICS MRP system purchased by Wheeled Coach. One of those reports indicates where items are used and is known as the "Where Used" report. Interestingly, many inventory items were not called out on bills-of-material (BOMs) for any current products. In some cases, the reason some parts were in the stockroom remained a mystery.

The discovery of this excess inventory led to renewed efforts to ensure that the BOMs were accurate. With substantial work, BOM accuracy increased and the number of engineering change notices

(ECNs) decreased. Similarly, purchase-order accuracy, with regard to both part numbers and quantities ordered, was improved. Additionally, receiving department and stockroom accuracy went up, all helping to maintain schedule, costs, and ultimately, shipping dates and quality.

Eventually, Lynn Whalen concluded that the residual amounts of excess inventory were the result, at least in part, of rapid changes in ambulance design and technology. Another source was customer changes made after specifications had been determined and materials ordered. This latter excess occurs because, even though Wheeled Coach's own throughput time is only 17 days, many of the items that it purchases require much longer lead times.

Discussion Questions*

1. Why is accurate inventory such an important issue at Wheeled Coach?
2. Why does Wheeled Coach have excess inventory, and what kind of a plan would you suggest for dealing with it?
3. Be specific in your suggestions for reducing inventory and how to implement them.

*You may wish to view this case on your DVD before answering the questions.

Additional Case Studies

Internet Case Study: Visit our Companion Web site at www.prenhall.com/heizer *for this free case study:*

- **Auto Parts, Inc.:** Distributor of automobile replacement parts has major MRP problems.

Harvard has selected these Harvard Business School cases to accompany this chapter:

harvardbusinessonline.hbsp.harvard.edu

- **Digital Equipment Corp.: The Endpoint Model** (#688-059): Describes implementation of an MRP II system to reduce cycle time of orders.
- **Tektronix, Inc.: Global ERP Implementation** (#699-043): Examines Tektronix's implementation of an ERP system in its three global business divisions.
- **Vardelay Industries, Inc.** (#697-037): Discusses ERP and related issues of process reengineering, standardization, and change management.
- **Moore Medical Corp.** (#601-142): Examines Moore's ERP investment and further investment in additional modules.

Bibliography

Anussornnitisarn, P., and S. F. Nof. "e-Work: The Challenge of the Next Generation ERP Systems." *Production Planning & Control* 14, no. 8 (December 2003): 753–765.

Bell, Steve. "Time Fence Secrets." *APICS* 16, no. 4 (April 2006): 44–48.

Bolander, Steven F., and Sam G. Taylor. "Scheduling Techniques: A Comparison of Logic." *Production and Inventory Management Journal* 41, no. 1 (1st quarter 2000): 1–5.

Crandall, Richard E. "The Epic Life of ERP." *APICS* 16, no. 2 (February 2006): 17–19.

Gattiker, Thomas F. "Anatomy of an ERP Implementation Gone Awry." *Production and Inventory Management* 43, nos. 3–4 (3rd/4th quarter 2002): 96–105.

Kanet, J., and V. Sridharan. "The Value of Using Scheduling Information in Planning Material Requirements." *Decision Sciences* 29, no. 2 (spring 1998): 479–498.

Koh, S. C. L., and S. M. Saad. "Managing Uncertainty in ERP-controlled Manufacturing Environments." *International Journal of Production Economics* 101, no. 1 (May 2006): 109.

Krupp, James A. G. "Integrating Kanban and MRP to Reduce Lead Time." *Production and Inventory Management Journal* 43, nos. 3–4 (3rd/4th quarter 2002): 78–82.

Lawrence, Barry F., Daniel F. Jennings, and Brian E. Reynolds. *ERP in Distribution.* Florence, KY: Thomson South-Western, (2005).

Moncrief, Stephen. "Push and Pull." *APICS—The Performance Advantage* (June 2003): 46–51.

Norris, G. *E-Business & ERP.* New York: Wiley (2005).

Olson, D. L. *Managerial Issues of Enterprise Resource Planning.* New York: McGraw-Hill (2004).

Segerstedt, A. "Master Production Scheduling and a Comparison of MRP and Cover-Time Planning." *International Journal of Production Research* 44, no. 18–19 (September 2006): 3585.

Summer, M. *Enterprise Resource Planning.* Upper Saddle River, NJ: Prentice Hall (2005).

Wacker, John G., and Malcolm Miller. "Configure-to-Order Planning Bills of Material: Simplifying a Complex Product Structure for Manufacturing Planning and Control." *Production and Inventory Management Journal* 41, no. 2 (2nd quarter 2000): 21–26.

Wagner, H. M., and T. M. Whitin. "Dynamic Version of the Economic Lot Size Model." *Management Science* 5, no. 1 (1958): 89–96.

Internet Resources

American Software: **www.amsoftware.com**
APICS magazine online edition:
   www.apics.org/resources/magazine
Armstrong Management Group: **www.armstrongmg.com**
Business Research in Information and Technology: **www.brint.com**
CMS Software, Inc.: **www.cmssoftware.com**

i2 Technologies: **www.i2.com**
Intelligent Enterprise Software: **www.iqms.com**
Oracle/Peoplesoft: **www.oracle.com**
SAP America: **www.sap.com**
Software evaluation: **www.technologyevaluation.com**
SSA Global: **www.ssaglobal.com**

Short-Term Scheduling

Chapter Outline

Ten OM Strategy Decisions

Design of Goods and Services

Managing Quality

Process Strategy

Location Strategies

Layout Strategies

Human Resources

Supply Chain Management

Inventory Management

Scheduling
  Aggregate
  Short-Term

Maintenance

Learning Objectives

When you complete this chapter you should be able to

1. Explain the relationship between short-term scheduling, capacity planning, aggregate planning, and a master schedule

2. Draw Gantt loading and scheduling charts

3. Apply the assignment method for loading jobs

4. Name and describe each of the priority sequencing rules

5. Use Johnson's rule

6. Define finite capacity scheduling

7. List the steps in the theory of constraints

8. Use the cyclical scheduling technique

Scheduling Airplanes When Weather Is the Enemy

Operations managers at airlines learn to expect the unexpected. Events that require rapid rescheduling are a regular part of life. Throughout the ordeals of tornadoes, ice storms, and snowstorms, airlines across the globe struggle to cope with delays, cancellations, and furious passengers. The inevitable changes to the schedule often create a ripple effect that impacts passengers at dozens of airports in the network. Close to 10% of Delta Air Lines's flights are disrupted in a typical year, half because of weather; the cost is $440 million in lost revenue, overtime pay, and food and lodging vouchers.

4 A.M.	10 A.M.	1:30 P.M.	5 P.M.	10 P.M.
FORECAST: Rain with a chance of light snow for Atlanta.	FORECAST: Freezing rain after 5 P.M.	FORECAST: Rain changing to snow.	FORECAST: Less snow than expected.	FORECAST: Snow tapering off.
ACTION: Discuss status of planes and possible need for cancellations.	ACTION: Ready deicing trucks; develop plans to cancel 50% to 80% of flights after 6 P.M.	ACTION: Cancel half the flights from 6 P.M. to 10 A.M.; notify passengers and reroute planes.	ACTION: Continue calling passengers and arrange alternate flights.	ACTION: Find hotels for 1,600 passengers stranded by the storm.

▲ *Here is what Delta officials had to do one December day when a storm bore down on Atlanta.*

▼ *To improve flight rescheduling efforts, Delta employees monitor giant screens that display meteorological charts, weather patterns, and maps of Delta flights at its Operations Control Center in Atlanta.*

Weather-related disruptions can create major scheduling and expensive snow removal issues for airlines (left), just as they create major inconveniences for passengers (right).

▶ *In an effort to maintain schedules, Delta Air Lines uses elaborate equipment as shown here for ice removal.*

Now Delta is taking the sting out of the scheduling nightmares that come from weather-related problems with its $33-million high-tech nerve center adjacent to the Hartsfield-Jackson Atlanta International Airport. From computers to telecommunications systems to deicers, Delta's Operations Control Center more quickly notifies customers of schedule changes, reroutes flights, and gets jets into the air. The Operations Control Center's job is to keep flights flowing as smoothly as possible in spite of the disruptions.

With earlier access to information, the center's staff of 18 pores over streams of data transmitted by computers and adjusts to changes quickly. Using mathematical scheduling models described in this chapter, Delta decides on schedule and route changes. This means coordinating incoming and outgoing aircraft, ensuring that the right crews are on hand, rescheduling connections to coordinate arrival times, and making sure information gets to passengers as soon as possible.

Delta's software, called the Inconvenienced Passenger Rebooking System, notifies passengers of cancellations or delays, and even books them onto rival airlines if necessary. With 150,000 passengers flying into and out of Atlanta every day, Delta estimates its scheduling efforts save $35 million a year.

THE STRATEGIC IMPORTANCE OF SHORT-TERM SCHEDULING

Delta Air Lines doesn't schedule just its 625 aircraft every day. It also schedules over 10,000 pilots and flight attendants to accommodate passengers who wish to reach their destinations. This schedule, based on huge computer programs, plays a major role in satisfying customers. Delta finds competitive advantage with its flexibility for last-minute adjustments to demand and weather disruptions.

Manufacturing firms also make schedules that match production to customer demands. Lockheed Martin's Dallas plant schedules machines, tools, and people to make aircraft parts. Lockheed's mainframe computer downloads schedules for parts production into a flexible machining system (FMS) in which a manager makes the final scheduling decision. The FMS allows parts of many sizes or shapes to be made, in any order. This scheduling versatility results in parts produced on a just-in-time basis, with low setup times, little work-in-process, and high machine utilization. Efficient scheduling is how companies like Lockheed Martin meet due dates promised to customers and face time-based competition.

The strategic importance of scheduling is clear:

- Effective scheduling means faster movement of goods and services through a facility. This means greater use of assets and hence greater capacity per dollar invested, which, in turn, *lowers cost*.
- Added capacity, faster throughput, and the related flexibility mean better customer service through *faster delivery*.
- Good scheduling also contributes to realistic commitments and hence *dependable delivery*.

SCHEDULING ISSUES

Learning Objective

1. Explain the relationship between short-term scheduling, capacity planning, aggregate planning, and a master schedule

Scheduling deals with the timing of operations. The types of scheduling decisions made in five organizations—a hospital, a college, a manufacturer, a restaurant, and an airline—are shown in Table 15.1. As you can see from Figure 15.1, a sequence of decisions affects scheduling. Schedule decisions begin with *capacity* planning, which involves *total facility and equipment resources available* (discussed in Chapter 7 and its Supplement). Capacity plans are usually annual or quarterly as new equipment and facilities are purchased or discarded. Aggregate planning (Chapter 13) makes decisions regarding the use of facilities, inventory, people, and outside contractors. Aggregate plans are typically monthly, and *resources are allocated in terms of an aggregate measure such as total units, tons, or shop hours*. However, the master schedule breaks down the aggregate plan and develops a *schedule for specific products or product lines for each week*.

▶ **Table 15.1**

Scheduling Decisions

Video 15.1
Scheduling at Hard Rock

Organization	Managers Must Schedule the Following
Arnold Palmer Hospital	Operating room use Patient admissions Nursing, security, maintenance staffs Outpatient treatments
University of Missouri	Classrooms and audiovisual equipment Student and instructor schedules Graduate and undergraduate courses
Lockheed Martin factory	Production of goods Purchases of materials Workers
Hard Rock Cafe	Chef, waiters, bartenders Delivery of fresh foods Entertainers Opening of dining areas
Delta Air Lines	Maintenance of aircraft Departure timetables Flight crews, catering, gate, and ticketing personnel

Capacity Planning
(Long term; years)
Changes in Facilities
Changes in Equipment
See Chapter 7 and Supplement 7

Capacity Plan for New Facilities
Adjust capacity to the demand suggested by strategic plan

Aggregate Planning
(Intermediate term; quarterly or monthly)
Facility utilization
Personnel changes
Subcontracting
See Chapter 13

Aggregate Production Plan for All Bikes
(Determine personnel or subcontracting necessary to
match aggregate demand to existing facilities/capacity)

Month	1	2
Bike Production	800	850

Master Schedule
(Intermediate term; weekly)
Material requirements planning
Disaggregate the aggregate plan
See Chapters 13 and 14

Master Production Schedule for Bike Models
(Determine weekly capacity schedule)

	Month 1				Month 2			
Week	1	2	3	4	5	6	7	8
Model 22		200		200		200		200
Model 24	100		100		150		100	
Model 26	100		100		100		100	

Short Term Scheduling
(Short term; days, hours, minutes)
Work center loading
Job sequencing/dispatching
See this chapter

Work Assigned to Specific Personnel and Work Centers
Make finite capacity schedule by matching specific
tasks to specific people and machines

Assemble
Model 22 in
work center 6

▲ **Figure 15.1** The Relationship between Capacity Planning, Aggregate Planning, Master Schedule,
and Short-Term Scheduling

Short-term schedules then translate capacity decisions, aggregate (intermediate) planning, and master schedules into job sequences and *specific assignments of personnel, materials, and machinery*. In this chapter, we describe the narrow issue of scheduling goods and services in the *short run* (that is, matching daily or hourly requirements to specific personnel and equipment).

The objective of scheduling is to allocate and prioritize demand (generated by either forecasts or customer orders) to available facilities. Two significant factors in achieving this allocation and prioritizing are (1) the type of scheduling, forward or backward, and (2) the criteria for priorities. We discuss these two topics next.

Forward and Backward Scheduling

Scheduling involves assigning due dates to specific jobs, but many jobs compete simultaneously for the same resources. To help address the difficulties inherent in scheduling, we can categorize scheduling techniques as (1) forward scheduling and (2) backward scheduling.

Forward scheduling starts the schedule as soon as the job requirements are known. Forward scheduling is used in a variety of organizations such as hospitals, clinics, fine-dining restaurants, and machine tool manufacturers. In these facilities, jobs are performed to customer order, and delivery is often requested as soon as possible. Forward scheduling is usually designed to produce a schedule that can be accomplished even if it means not meeting the due date. In many instances, forward scheduling causes a buildup of work-in-process inventory.

Forward scheduling
Scheduling that begins the schedule as soon as the requirements are known.

▶ *U.S. Steel maintains its world-class operation by automating the scheduling of people, machines, and tools through its cold-reduction-mill control room. Computerized scheduling software helps managers monitor production.*

Backward scheduling

Scheduling that begins with the due date and schedules the final operation first and the other job steps in reverse order.

Backward scheduling begins with the due date, scheduling the *final* operation first. Steps in the job are then scheduled, one at a time, in reverse order. By subtracting the lead time for each item, the start time is obtained. However, the resources necessary to accomplish the schedule may not exist. Backward scheduling is used in many manufacturing environments, as well as service environments such as catering a banquet or scheduling surgery. In practice, a combination of forward and backward scheduling is often used to find a reasonable trade-off between what can be achieved and customer due dates.

Machine breakdowns, absenteeism, quality problems, shortages, and other factors further complicate scheduling. (See the *OM in Action* box "Scheduling Workers Who Fall Asleep Is a Killer—Literally.") Consequently, assignment of a date does not ensure that the work will be performed according to the schedule. Many specialized techniques have been developed to aid in preparing reliable schedules.

OM in Action   Scheduling Workers Who Fall Asleep Is a Killer—Literally

The accidents at the nuclear plants at Three Mile Island, Pennsylvania, and Chernobyl, Russia, and the disaster at Bhopal, India, all had one thing in common: they occurred between midnight and 4:00 A.M. These facilities had other problems, but the need for sleep simply results in unreliable workplace performance. In some cases, unable to cope with a constantly changing work schedule, workers just plain fall asleep.

The same is true for pilots. Their inconsistent schedules often force them to snooze in the cockpit to get enough sleep. The Dassault Falcon 20 that was destroyed on impact in Greenland in 2001 crashed at 4:43 A.M. and was piloted by a crew that may have been awake for 22 hours at the time of the accident. Similarly, the captain and first officer of the DC-8 that crashed on approach at Guantanamo Bay, Cuba, in 1993 had been awake for 23.5 and 19 hours, respectively. One FedEx pilot recently complained of falling asleep while taxiing to take off.

Millions of people work in industries that maintain round-the-clock schedules. In interviews, employees from graveyard shifts report tales of seeing sleeping assembly-line workers fall off their stools, batches of defective parts sliding past dozing inspectors, and exhausted forklift operators crashing into walls. Virtually all shift workers are sleep deprived. And the National Highway Traffic Safety Administration indicates that drowsiness may be a factor in as many as 100,000 crashes annually.

Scheduling is a major problem in firms with 24/7 shifts, but some managers are taking steps to deal with schedule-related sleep problems among workers. Motorola, Dow Chemical, Detroit Edison, Pennzoil, and Exxon, for instance, all give workers several days off between shift changes.

It is possible for operations managers to make shift work less dangerous with shifts that do not exceed 12 hours, that encourage 8 hours of sleep each day, and that have extended time off between shift changes. As more is learned about the economic toll of non-daytime schedules and changing schedules, companies are learning to improve scheduling.

Sources: Air Safety Week (March 22, 2004): 1; *Safety and Health* (January 2004): 14; and *Knight-Ridder Tribune News* (April 9, 2006): 1.

Scheduling Criteria

The correct scheduling technique depends on the volume of orders, the nature of operations, and the overall complexity of jobs, as well as the importance placed on each of four criteria. These four criteria are:

1. *Minimize completion time:* This criterion is evaluated by determining the average completion time per job.
2. *Maximize utilization:* This is evaluated by determining the percent of the time the facility is utilized.
3. *Minimize work-in-process (WIP) inventory:* This is evaluated by determining the average number of jobs in the system. The relationship between the number of jobs in the system and WIP inventory will be high. Therefore, the fewer the number of jobs that are in the system, the lower the inventory.
4. *Minimize customer waiting time:* This is evaluated by determining the average number of late days.

These four criteria are used in this chapter, as they are in industry, to evaluate scheduling performance. Additionally, good scheduling approaches should be simple, clear, easily understood, easy to carry out, flexible, and realistic.

Table 15.2 provides an overview of different processes and approaches to scheduling.

We now examine scheduling in process-focused facilities, in repetitive facilities, and in the service sector.

SCHEDULING PROCESS-FOCUSED FACILITIES

Process-focused facilities (also known as *intermittent* or *job-shop facilities*),[1] as we see in Table 15.2, are high-variety, low-volume systems commonly found in manufacturing and service organizations. These are production systems in which products are made to order. Items made under this system usually differ considerably in terms of materials used, order of processing, processing requirements, time of processing, and setup requirements. Because of these differences,

◄ **Table 15.2**

Different Processes Suggest Different Approaches to Scheduling

- **Process-focused facilities (job shops)** The scheduling focus is on generating a forward-looking schedule that is initially achieved with MRP due dates and refined with the finite capacity scheduling techniques discussed in this chapter. These facilities include most of the production in the world. Examples include foundries, machine shops, cabinet shops, print shops, many restaurants, and the fashion industry.

- **Work cells (focused facilities that process families of similar components)** The scheduling focus is on generating a forward-looking schedule. MRP generates due dates, and subsequent detail scheduling/dispatching is done at the work cell with kanbans and priority rules. Examples include work cells at ambulance manufacturer Wheeled Coach, aircraft engine rebuilder Standard Aero, and greeting-card maker Hallmark.

- **Repetitive facilities (assembly lines)** The scheduling focus is on generating a forward-looking schedule that is achieved by balancing the line with traditional assembly-line techniques as presented in Chapter 9. Pull techniques, such as JIT and kanban (discussed in Chapter 16), signal component scheduling to support the assembly line. Repetitive facilities include assembly lines for a wide variety of products from autos to home appliances and computers. These scheduling problems are challenging but typically occur only when the process is new or when products or models change.

- **Product-focused facilities (continuous)** These facilities produce very high volume and limited-variety products such as paper on huge machines at International Paper, beer in a brewery at Anheuser-Busch, or rolled steel in a Nucor plant. Scheduling generates a forward-looking schedule that can meet a reasonably stable demand with the existing fixed capacity. Capacity in such facilities is usually limited by long-term capital investment. The capacity of the facility is usually known, as is the setup and run time for the limited range of products. This makes scheduling rather straightforward.

---

[1]Much of the literature on scheduling is about manufacturing; therefore, the traditional term *job-shop scheduling* is often used.

scheduling can be complex. To run a facility in a balanced and efficient manner, the manager needs a production planning and control system. This system should:

1. Schedule incoming orders without violating capacity constraints of individual work centers.
2. Check the availability of tools and materials before releasing an order to a department.
3. Establish due dates for each job and check progress against need dates and order lead times.
4. Check work in progress as jobs move through the shop.
5. Provide feedback on plant and production activities.
6. Provide work efficiency statistics and monitor operator times for payroll and labor distribution analyses.

Whether the scheduling system is manual or automated, it must be accurate and relevant. This means it requires a production database with both planning and control files.[2] Three types of planning files are:

1. An *item master file*, which contains information about each component the firm produces or purchases.
2. A *routing file*, which indicates each component's flow through the shop.
3. A *work-center master file*, which contains information about the work center, such as capacity and efficiency.

Control files track the actual progress made against the plan for each work order.

LOADING JOBS

Loading

The assigning of jobs to work or processing centers.

Loading means the assignment of jobs to work or processing centers. Operations managers assign jobs to work centers so that costs, idle time, or completion times are kept to a minimum. Loading work centers takes two forms.[3] One is oriented to capacity; the second is related to assigning specific jobs to work centers.

First, we examine loading from the perspective of capacity via a technique known as *input–output* control. Then, we present two approaches used for loading: *Gantt charts* and the *assignment method* of linear programming.

Input–Output Control

Many firms have difficulty scheduling (that is, achieving effective throughput) because they overload the production processes. This often occurs because they do not know actual performance in the work centers. Effective scheduling depends on matching the schedule to performance. Lack of knowledge about capacity and performance causes reduced throughput.

Input–output control

A system that allows operations personnel to manage facility work flows by tracking work added to a work center and its work completed.

Input–output control is a technique that allows operations personnel to manage facility work flows. If the work is arriving faster than it is being processed, the facility is overloaded, and a backlog develops. Overloading causes crowding in the facility, leading to inefficiencies and quality problems. If the work is arriving at a slower rate than jobs are being performed, the facility is underloaded, and the work center may run out of work. Underloading the facility results in idle capacity and wasted resources. Example 1 shows the use of input–output controls.

EXAMPLE 1

Input–output control

DNC Machining, Inc., manufactures driveway security fences and gates from small to large. It wants to develop an input–output control report for the aluminum machining work center for 5 weeks (weeks 6/6 through 7/4). The planned input is 280 standard hours per week. The actual input is close to this figure, varying between 250 and 285. Output is scheduled at 320 standard hours, which is the assumed capacity. A backlog of 300 hours exists in the work center.

Approach: DNC uses schedule information to create Figure 15.2, which monitors the workload-capacity relationship at the work center.

[2]For an expanded discussion, see *APICS Study Aid—Detailed Scheduling and Planning* (Alexandria, VA: American Production and Inventory Control Society).

[3]Note that this discussion can apply to facilities that might be called a "shop" in a manufacturing firm, a "unit" in a hospital, or a "department" in an office or a large kitchen.

solution: The deviations between scheduled input and actual output are shown in Figure 15.2. Actual output (270 hours) is substantially less than planned. Therefore, neither the input plan nor the output plan is being achieved.

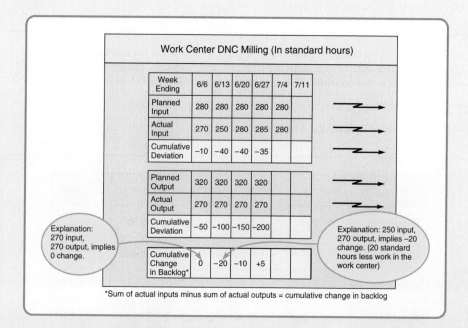

◄ **Figure 15.2**

Input–Output Control

Insight: The backlog of work in this work center has actually increased by 5 hours by week 6/27. This increases work-in-process inventory, complicating the scheduling task and indicating the need for manager action.

Learning exercise: If actual output for the week of 6/27 was 275 (instead of 270), what changes? [Answer: Output cumulative deviation now is –195, and cumulative change in backlog is 0.]

Related problem: 15.21

Input–output control can be maintained by a system of **ConWIP cards,** which control the amount of work in a work center. ConWIP is an acronym for *constant work-in-process.* The ConWIP card travels with a job (or batch) through the work center. When the job is finished, the card is released and returned to the initial workstation, authorizing the entry of a new batch into the work center. The ConWIP card effectively limits the amount of work in the work center, controls lead time, and monitors the backlog.

The options available to operations personnel to manage facility work flow include the following:

1. Correcting performances
2. Increasing capacity
3. Increasing or reducing input to the work center by (a) routing work to or from other work centers, (b) increasing or decreasing subcontracting, (c) producing less (or producing more)

Producing less is not a popular solution, but the advantages can be substantial. First, customer-service levels may improve because units may be produced on time. Second, efficiency may actually improve because there is less work in process cluttering the work center and adding to overhead costs. Third, quality may improve because less work-in-process hides fewer problems.

Gantt Charts

Gantt charts are visual aids that are useful in loading and scheduling. The name is derived from Henry Gantt, who developed them in the late 1800s. The charts show the use of resources, such as work centers and labor.

When used in *loading*, Gantt charts show the loading and idle times of several departments, machines, or facilities. They display the relative workloads in the system so that the manager

ConWIP cards

Cards that control the amount of work in a work center, aiding input–output control.

Gantt charts

Planning charts used to schedule resources and allocate time.

knows what adjustments are appropriate. For example, when one work center becomes over-loaded, employees from a low-load center can be transferred temporarily to increase the work-force. Or if waiting jobs can be processed at different work centers, some jobs at high-load centers can be transferred to low-load centers. Versatile equipment may also be transferred among centers. Example 2 illustrates a simple Gantt load chart.

EXAMPLE 2

Gantt load chart

A New Orleans washing machine manufacturer accepts special orders for machines to be used in such unique facilities as submarines, hospitals, and large industrial laundries. The production of each machine requires varying tasks and durations. The company wants to build a load chart for the week of March 8.

Approach: The Gantt chart is selected as the appropriate graphical tool.

Solution: Figure 15.3 shows the completed Gantt chart.

▶ **Figure 15.3**

Gantt Load Chart for the Week of March 8

Work Center \ Day	Monday	Tuesday	Wednesday	Thursday	Friday
Metalworks	Job 349	✕	← Job 350		→
Mechanical		← Job 349	→	Job 408	
Electronics	Job 408			Job 349	
Painting	← Job 295	→	Job 408	✕	Job 349

Processing   Unscheduled   ✕ Center not available (e.g., maintenance time, repairs, shortages)

Insight: The four work centers process several jobs during the week. This particular chart indicates that the metalworks and painting centers are completely loaded for the entire week. The mechanical and electronic centers have some idle time scattered during the week. We also note that the metalworks center is unavailable on Tuesday, and the painting center is unavailable on Thursday, perhaps for preventive maintenance.

Learning exercise: What impact results from the electronics work center closing on Tuesday for preventive maintenance? [Answer: none.]

Related problem: 15.1b

Learning Objective

2. Draw Gantt loading and scheduling charts

The Gantt *load chart* has a major limitation: It does not account for production variability such as unexpected breakdowns or human errors that require reworking a job. Consequently, the chart must also be updated regularly to account for new jobs and revised time estimates.

A Gantt *schedule chart* is used to monitor jobs in progress.[4] It indicates which jobs are on schedule and which are ahead of or behind schedule. In practice, many versions of the chart are found. The schedule chart in Example 3 places jobs in progress on the vertical axis and time on the horizontal axis.

EXAMPLE 3

Gantt scheduling chart

First Printing in Winter Park, Florida, wants to use a Gantt chart to show the scheduling of three orders, jobs A, B, and C.

Approach: In Figure 15.4, each pair of brackets on the time axis denotes the estimated starting and finishing of a job enclosed within it. The solid bars reflect the actual status or progress of the job. We are just finishing day 5.

---

[4]Gantt charts are also used for project scheduling, as noted in Chapter 3, "Project Management."

Solution:

Insight: Figure 15.4 illustrates that job A is about a half-day behind schedule at the end of day 5. Job B was completed after equipment maintenance. We also see that job C is ahead of schedule.

Learning exercise: Redraw the Gantt chart to show that job A is a half-day *ahead* of schedule. [Answer: The purple bar now extends all the way to the end of the activity.]

Related problems: 15.1a, 15.2

Assignment Method

The **assignment method** involves assigning tasks or jobs to resources. Examples include assigning jobs to machines, contracts to bidders, people to projects, and salespeople to territories. The objective is most often to minimize total costs or time required to perform the tasks at hand. One important characteristic of assignment problems is that only one job (or worker) is assigned to one machine (or project).

Assignment method
A special class of linear programming models that involves assigning tasks or jobs to resources.

Each assignment problem uses a table. The numbers in the table will be the costs or times associated with each particular assignment. For example, if First Printing has three available typesetters (A, B, and C) and three new jobs to be completed, its table might appear as follows. The dollar entries represent the firm's estimate of what it will cost for each job to be completed by each typesetter.

	Typesetter		
Job	A	B	C
R-34	$11	$14	$ 6
S-66	$ 8	$10	$11
T-50	$ 9	$12	$ 7

The assignment method involves adding and subtracting appropriate numbers in the table to find the lowest *opportunity cost*[5] for each assignment. There are four steps to follow:

Learning Objective

3. Apply the assignment method for loading jobs

1. Subtract the smallest number in each row from every number in that row and then, from the resulting matrix, subtract the smallest number in each column from every number in that column. This step has the effect of reducing the numbers in the table until a series of zeros, meaning *zero opportunity costs*, appear. Even though the numbers change, this reduced problem is equivalent to the original one, and the same solution will be optimal.

[5]Opportunity costs are those profits foregone or not obtained.

2. Draw the minimum number of vertical and horizontal straight lines necessary to cover all zeros in the table. If the number of lines equals either the number of rows or the number of columns in the table, then we can make an optimal assignment (see step 4). If the number of lines is less than the number of rows or columns, we proceed to step 3.

3. Subtract the smallest number not covered by a line from every other uncovered number. Add the same number to any number(s) lying at the intersection of any two lines. Do not change the value of the numbers that are covered by only one line. Return to step 2 and continue until an optimal assignment is possible.

4. Optimal assignments will always be at zero locations in the table. One systematic way of making a valid assignment is first to select a row or column that contains only one zero square. We can make an assignment to that square and then draw lines through its row and column. From the uncovered rows and columns, we choose another row or column in which there is only one zero square. We make that assignment and continue the procedure until we have assigned each person or machine to one task.

Example 4 shows how to use the assignment method.

EXAMPLE 4

Assignment method

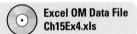

Excel OM Data File
Ch15Ex4.xls

First Printing and Copy Center wants to find the minimum total cost assignment of 3 jobs to 3 typesetters.

Approach: The cost table shown earlier in this section is repeated here, and steps 1 through 4 are applied.

TYPESETTER / JOB	A	B	C
R-34	$11	$14	$ 6
S-66	$ 8	$10	$11
T-50	$ 9	$12	$ 7

Solution:

Step 1a: Using the previous table, subtract the smallest number in each row from every number in the row. The result is shown in the table on the left.

TYPESETTER / JOB	A	B	C
R-34	5	8	0
S-66	0	2	3
T-50	2	5	0

TYPESETTER / JOB	A	B	C
R-34	5	6	0
S-66	0	0	3
T-50	2	3	0

Step 1b: Using the above left table, subtract the smallest number in each column from every number in the column. The result is shown in the table on the right.

Step 2: Draw the minimum number of vertical and horizontal straight lines needed to cover all zeros. Because two lines suffice, the solution is not optimal.

TYPESETTER / JOB	A	B	C
R-34	5	6	0
S-66	0	0	3
T-50	②	3	0

Smallest uncovered number

Step 3:   Subtract the smallest uncovered number (2 in this table) from every other uncovered number and add it to numbers at the intersection of two lines.

TYPESETTER \ JOB	A	B	C
R-34	3	4	0
S-66	0	0	5
T-50	0	1	0

Return to step 2. Cover the zeros with straight lines again.

TYPESETTER \ JOB	A	B	C
R-34	3	4	0
S-66	0	0	
T-50	0	1	0

Because three lines are necessary, an optimal assignment can be made (see step 4 on page 610). Assign R-34 to person C, S-66 to person B, and T-50 to person A. Referring to the original cost table, we see that:

$$\text{Minimum cost} = \$6 + \$10 + \$9 = \$25$$

Insight: If we had assigned S-66 to typesetter A, we could not assign T-50 to a zero location.

Learning exercise: If it costs $10 for Typesetter C to complete Job R-34 (instead of $6), how does the solution change? [Answer: R-34 to A, S-66 to B, T-50 to C: cost = $28.]

Related problems: 15.3, 15.4, 15.5, 15.6, 15.7, 15.8, 15.9

Some assignment problems entail *maximizing* profit, effectiveness, or payoff of an assignment of people to tasks or of jobs to machines. It is easy to obtain an equivalent minimization problem by converting every number in the table to an *opportunity loss*. To convert a maximizing problem to an equivalent minimization problem, we create a minimizing table by subtracting every number in the original payoff table from the largest single number in that table. We then proceed to step 1 of the four-step assignment method. It turns out that minimizing the opportunity loss produces the same assignment solution as the original maximization problem.

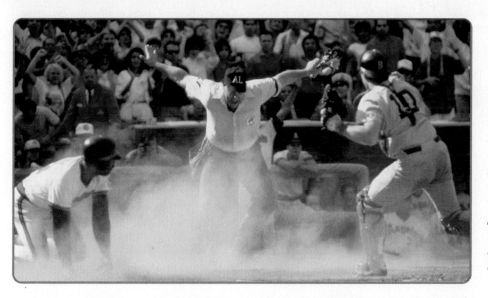

◄ *The problem of scheduling major league baseball umpiring crews from one series of games to the next is complicated by many restrictions on travel, ranging from coast-to-coast time changes, airline flight schedules, and night games running late. The league strives to achieve these two conflicting objectives: (1) balance crew assignments relatively evenly among all teams over the course of a season and (2) minimize travel costs. Using the assignment problem formulation, the time it takes the league to generate a schedule has been significantly decreased, and the quality of the schedule has improved.*

Sequencing
Determining the order in which jobs should be done at each work center.

Priority rules
Rules used to determine the sequence of jobs in process-oriented facilities.

First come, first served (FCFS)
Jobs are completed in the order they arrived.

Shortest processing time (SPT)
Jobs with the shortest processing times are assigned first.

Earliest due date (EDD)
Earliest due date jobs are performed first.

Longest processing time (LPT)
Jobs with the longest processing time are completed first.

SEQUENCING JOBS

Scheduling provides a basis for assigning jobs to work centers. *Loading* is a capacity-control technique that highlights overloads and underloads. **Sequencing** (also referred to as dispatching) specifies the order in which jobs should be done at each center. For example, suppose that 10 patients are assigned to a medical clinic for treatment. In what order should they be treated? Should the first patient to be served be the one who arrived first or the one who needs emergency treatment? Sequencing methods provide such detailed information. These methods are referred to as priority rules for sequencing or dispatching jobs to work centers.

Priority Rules for Dispatching Jobs

Priority rules provide guidelines for the sequence in which jobs should be worked. The rules are especially applicable for process-focused facilities such as clinics, print shops, and manufacturing job shops. We will examine a few of the most popular priority rules. Priority rules try to minimize completion time, number of jobs in the system, and job lateness while maximizing facility utilization.

The most popular priority rules are:

- **FCFS: first come, first served.** The first job to arrive at a work center is processed first.
- **SPT: shortest processing time.** The shortest jobs are handled first and completed.
- **EDD: earliest due date.** The job with the earliest due date is selected first.
- **LPT: longest processing time.** The longer, bigger jobs are often very important and are selected first.

Example 5 compares these rules.

EXAMPLE 5

Priority rules for dispatching

Five architectural rendering jobs are waiting to be assigned at Avanti Sethi Architects. Their work (processing) times and due dates are given in the following table. The firm wants to determine the sequence of processing according to (1) FCFS, (2) SPT, (3) EDD, and (4) LPT rules. Jobs were assigned a letter in the order they arrived.

JOB	JOB WORK (PROCESSING) TIME (DAYS)	JOB DUE DATE (DAYS)
A	6	8
B	2	6
C	8	18
D	3	15
E	9	23

Approach: Each of the four priority rules is examined in turn. Four measures of effectiveness can be computed for each rule and then compared to see which rule is best for the company.

Solution:

1. The *FCFS* sequence shown in the next table is simply A-B-C-D-E. The "flow time" in the system for this sequence measures the time each job spends waiting plus time being processed. Job B, for example, waits 6 days while job A is being processed, then takes 2 more days of operation time itself; so it will be completed in 8 days—which is 2 days later than its due date.

JOB SEQUENCE	JOB WORK (PROCESSING) TIME	FLOW TIME	JOB DUE DATE	JOB LATENESS
A	6	6	8	0
B	2	8	6	2
C	8	16	18	0
D	3	19	15	4
E	9	28	23	5
	28	77		11

Active Model 15.1

Example 5 is further illustrated in Active Model 15.1 on the CD-ROM and in the Exercise on page 630.

The first-come, first-served rule results in the following measures of effectiveness:

a. Average completion time $= \dfrac{\text{Sum of total flow time}}{\text{Number of jobs}}$

$= \dfrac{77 \text{ days}}{5} = 15.4 \text{ days}$

b. Utilization $= \dfrac{\text{Total job work (processing) time}}{\text{Sum of total flow time}}$

$= \dfrac{28}{77} = 36.4\%$

c. Average number of jobs in the system $= \dfrac{\text{Sum of total flow time}}{\text{Total job work (processing) time}}$

$= \dfrac{77 \text{ days}}{28 \text{ days}} = 2.75 \text{ jobs}$

d. Average job lateness $= \dfrac{\text{Total late days}}{\text{Number of jobs}} = \dfrac{11}{5} = 2.2 \text{ days}$

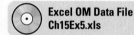

Excel OM Data File
Ch15Ex5.xls

2. The *SPT* rule shown in the next table results in the sequence B–D–A–C–E. Orders are sequenced according to processing time, with the highest priority given to the shortest job.

JOB SEQUENCE	JOB WORK (PROCESSING) TIME	FLOW TIME	JOB DUE DATE	JOB LATENESS
B	2	2	6	0
D	3	5	15	0
A	6	11	8	3
C	8	19	18	1
E	9	28	23	5
	28	65		9

Measurements of effectiveness for SPT are:

a. Average completion time $= \dfrac{65}{5} = 13 \text{ days}$

b. Utilization $= \dfrac{28}{65} = 43.1\%$

c. Average number of jobs in the system $= \dfrac{65}{28} = 2.32 \text{ jobs}$

d. Average job lateness $= \dfrac{9}{5} = 1.8 \text{ days}$

3. The *EDD* rule shown in the next table gives the sequence B–A–D–C–E. Note that jobs are ordered by earliest due date first.

Learning Objective

4. Name and describe each of the priority sequencing rules

JOB SEQUENCE	JOB WORK (PROCESSING) TIME	FLOW TIME	JOB DUE DATE	JOB LATENESS
B	2	2	6	0
A	6	8	8	0
D	3	11	15	0
C	8	19	18	1
E	9	28	23	5
	28	68		6

Measurements of effectiveness for EDD are:

a. Average completion time $= \dfrac{68}{5} = 13.6$ days

b. Utilization $= \dfrac{28}{68} = 41.2\%$

c. Average number of jobs in the system $= \dfrac{68}{28} = 2.43$ jobs

d. Average job lateness $= \dfrac{6}{5} = 1.2$ days

4. The *LPT* rule shown in the next table results in the order E–C–A–D–B.

JOB SEQUENCE	JOB WORK (PROCESSING) TIME	FLOW TIME	JOB DUE DATE	JOB LATENESS
E	9	9	23	0
C	8	17	18	0
A	6	23	8	15
D	3	26	15	11
B	2	28	6	22
	28	103		48

Measures of effectiveness for LPT are:

a. Average completion time $= \dfrac{103}{5} = 20.6$ days

b. Utilization $= \dfrac{28}{103} = 27.2\%$

c. Average number of jobs in the system $= \dfrac{103}{28} = 3.68$ jobs

d. Average job lateness $= \dfrac{48}{5} = 9.6$ days

The results of these four rules are summarized in the following table:

RULE	AVERAGE COMPLETION TIME (DAYS)	UTILIZATION (%)	AVERAGE NUMBER OF JOBS IN SYSTEM	AVERAGE LATENESS (DAYS)
FCFS	15.4	36.4	2.75	2.2
SPT	13.0	43.1	2.32	1.8
EDD	13.6	41.2	2.43	1.2
LPT	20.6	27.2	3.68	9.6

Insight: LPT is the least effective measurement for sequencing for the Avanti Sethi firm. SPT is superior in 3 measures, and EDD is superior in the fourth (average lateness).

Learning exercise: If job A takes 7 days (instead of 6), how do the 4 measures of effectiveness change under the FCFS rule? [Answer: 16.4 days, 35.4%, 2.83 jobs, 2.8 days late.]

Related problems: 15.10, 15.12a–d, 15.13, 15.14

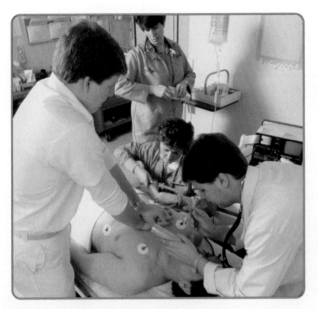

◀ *Your doctor may use a first-come, first-served priority rule satisfactorily. However, such a rule may be less than optimal for this emergency room. What priority rule might be best, and why? What priority rule is often used on the TV programs* Grey's Anatomy *and* E.R.*?*

The results in Example 5 are typically true in the real world also. No one sequencing rule always excels on all criteria. Experience indicates the following:

1. Shortest processing time is generally the best technique for minimizing job flow and minimizing the average number of jobs in the system. Its chief disadvantage is that long-duration jobs may be continuously pushed back in priority in favor of short-duration jobs. Customers may view this dimly, and a periodic adjustment for longer jobs must be made.
2. First come, first served does not score well on most criteria (but neither does it score particularly poorly). It has the advantage, however, of appearing fair to customers, which is important in service systems.
3. Earliest due date minimizes maximum tardiness, which may be necessary for jobs that have a very heavy penalty after a certain date. In general, EDD works well when lateness is an issue.

> *The results of a dispatching rule change depending on how full the facility is.*

Critical Ratio

Another type of sequencing rule is the critical ratio. The **critical ratio (CR)** is an index number computed by dividing the time remaining until due date by the work time remaining. As opposed to the priority rules, critical ratio is dynamic and easily updated. It tends to perform better than FCFS, SPT, EDD, or LPT on the average job-lateness criterion.

> **Critical ratio (CR)**
> A sequencing rule that is an index number computed by dividing the time remaining until due date by the work time remaining.

The critical ratio gives priority to jobs that must be done to keep shipping on schedule. A job with a low critical ratio (less than 1.0) is one that is falling behind schedule. If CR is exactly 1.0, the job is on schedule. A CR greater than 1.0 means the job is ahead of schedule and has some slack.

The formula for critical ratio is:

$$CR = \frac{\text{Time remaining}}{\text{Workdays remaining}} = \frac{\text{Due date} - \text{Today's date}}{\text{Work (lead) time remaining}}$$

Example 6 shows how to use the critical ratio.

EXAMPLE 6

Critical ratio

Today is day 25 on Zyco Medical Testing Laboratories' production schedule. Three jobs are on order, as indicated here:

Job	Due Date	Workdays Remaining
A	30	4
B	28	5
C	27	2

Approach: Zyco wants to compute the critical ratios, using the formula for CR.

Solution:

Job	Critical Ratio	Priority Order
A	$(30 - 25)/4 = 1.25$	3
B	$(28 - 25)/5 = .60$	1
C	$(27 - 25)/2 = 1.00$	2

Insight: Job B has a critical ratio of less than 1, meaning it will be late unless expedited. Thus, it has the highest priority. Job C is on time and job A has some slack. Once job B has been completed, we would recompute the critical ratios for jobs A and C to determine whether their priorities have changed.

Learning exercise: Today is day 24 (a day earlier) on Zyco's schedule. Recompute the CRs and determine the priorities. [Answer: 1.5, 0.8, 1.5; B is still number 1, but now jobs A and C are tied for second.]

Related problems: 15.11, 15.12e, 15.16

In most production scheduling systems, the critical-ratio rule can help do the following:

1. Determine the status of a specific job.
2. Establish relative priority among jobs on a common basis.
3. Relate both stock and make-to-order jobs on a common basis.
4. Adjust priorities (and revise schedules) automatically for changes in both demand and job progress.
5. Dynamically track job progress.

Sequencing *N* Jobs on Two Machines: Johnson's Rule

The next step in complexity is the case in which *N* jobs (where *N* is 2 or more) must go through two different machines or work centers in the same order. This is called the *N*/2 problem.

Johnson's rule
An approach that minimizes processing time for sequencing a group of jobs through two work centers while minimizing total idle time in the work centers.

Johnson's rule can be used to minimize the processing time for sequencing a group of jobs through two work centers. It also minimizes total idle time on the machines. *Johnson's rule* involves four steps:

1. All jobs are to be listed, and the time that each requires on a machine is to be shown.
2. Select the job with the shortest activity time. If the shortest time lies with the first machine, the job is scheduled first. If the shortest time lies with the second machine, schedule the job last. Ties in activity times can be broken arbitrarily.
3. Once a job is scheduled, eliminate it.
4. Apply steps 2 and 3 to the remaining jobs, working toward the center of the sequence.

Example 7 shows how to apply Johnson's rule.

EXAMPLE 7

Johnson's rule

Five specialty jobs at a La Crosse, Wisconsin, tool and die shop must be processed through two work centers (drill press and lathe). The time for processing each job follows:

Work (processing) Time for Jobs (hours)

Job	Work Center 1 (drill press)	Work Center 2 (lathe)
A	5	2
B	3	6
C	8	4
D	10	7
E	7	12

The owner, Niranjan Pati, wants to set the sequence to minimize his total processing time for the five jobs.

Approach: Pati applies the four steps of Johnson's rule.

Solution:

1. The job with the shortest processing time is A, in work center 2 (with a time of 2 hours). Because it is at the second center, schedule A last. Eliminate it from consideration.

				A

2. Job B has the next shortest time (3 hours). Because that time is at the first work center, we schedule it first and eliminate it from consideration.

B				A

Learning Objective

5. Use Johnson's rule

3. The next shortest time is job C (4 hours) on the second machine. Therefore, it is placed as late as possible.

B			C	A

4. There is a tie (at 7 hours) for the shortest remaining job. We can place E, which was on the first work center, first. Then D is placed in the last sequencing position.

B	E	D	C	A

The sequential times are:

Work center 1	3	7	10	8	5
Work center 2	6	12	7	4	2

The time-phased flow of this job sequence is best illustrated graphically:

Thus, the five jobs are completed in 35 hours.

Insight: The second work center will wait 3 hours for its first job, and it will also wait 1 hour after completing job B.

Learning exercise: If job C takes 8 hours in work center 2 (instead of 4 hours), what sequence is best? [Answer: B–E–C–D–A.]

Related problems: 15.15, 15.17, 15.18

Limitations of Rule-Based Dispatching Systems

The scheduling techniques just discussed are rule-based techniques, but rule-based systems have a number of limitations. Among these are the following:

1. Scheduling is dynamic; therefore, rules need to be revised to adjust to changes in orders, process, equipment, product mix, and so forth.
2. Rules do not look upstream or downstream; idle resources and bottleneck resources in other departments may not be recognized.
3. Rules do not look beyond due dates. For instance, two orders may have the same due date. One order involves restocking a distributor and the other is a custom order that will shut down the customer's factory if not completed. Both may have the same due date, but clearly the custom order is more important.

Despite these limitations, schedulers often use sequencing rules such as SPT, EDD, or critical ratio. They apply these methods at each work center and then modify the sequence to deal with a multitude of real-world variables. They may do this manually or with finite capacity scheduling software.

> *Scheduling can be complex and still yield poor results—not a very fruitful combination. Even with sophisticated rules, good scheduling is very difficult.*

FINITE CAPACITY SCHEDULING (FCS)

Finite capacity scheduling (FCS)

Computerized short-term scheduling that overcomes the disadvantage of rule-based systems by providing the user with graphical interactive computing.

Short-term scheduling is also called finite capacity scheduling.[6] **Finite capacity scheduling (FCS)** overcomes the disadvantages of systems based exclusively on rules by providing the scheduler with interactive computing and graphic output. In dynamic scheduling environments such as job shops (with a high variety, low volume, and shared resources) we expect changes—but changes disrupt schedules. Therefore, operations managers are moving toward FCS systems that allow virtually instantaneous change by the operator. Improvements in communication on the shop floor are also enhancing the accuracy and speed of information necessary for effective control in job shops. Computer-controlled machines can monitor events and collect information in near real-time. This means the scheduler can make schedule changes based on up-to-the-minute information. These schedules are often displayed in Gantt chart form. In addition to

▶ *This Lekin finite capacity scheduling software presents a schedule of the five jobs and the two work centers shown in Example 7 (pages 616–617) in Gantt chart form. The software is capable of using a variety of priority rules, several shop types, up to 50 jobs, 20 work centers, and 100 machines to generate a schedule. The Lekin software is on your CD and can solve many of the problems at the end of this chapter.*

[6]Finite capacity scheduling (FCS) systems go by a number of names, including finite scheduling and advance planning systems (APS). The name manufacturing execution systems (MES) may also be used, but this name tends to suggest an emphasis on the reporting system from shop operations back to the scheduling activity. See O. Gusikhim and G. Rossi, "Well-Connected: MES Data Integration in the Automobile Supply Chain," *APICS: The Performance Advantage* (February 2005): 32–35.

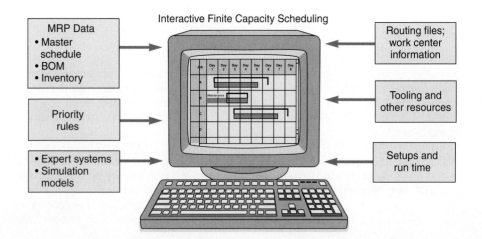

Finite Capacity Scheduling Systems Combine MRP and Shop Floor Production Data to Generate a Gantt Chart That Can Be Manipulated by the User on a Computer Screen

including priority rule options, many of the current FCS systems also combine an "expert system" or simulation techniques and allow the scheduler to assign costs to various options. The scheduler has the flexibility to handle any situation, including order, labor, or machine changes.

The initial data for finite scheduling systems is often the output from an MRP system. The output from MRP systems is traditionally in weekly "buckets" that have no capacity constraint. These systems just tell the planner when the material is needed, ignoring the capacity issue. Because *infinite*-size buckets are unrealistic and inadequate for detail scheduling, MRP data require refinement. MRP output is combined with routing files, due dates, capacity of work centers, tooling, and other resource availability to provide the data needed for effective FCS. These are the same data needed in any manual system, but FCS software formalizes them, speeds analysis, and makes changes easier. The combining of MRP and FCS data, priority rules, models to assist analysis, and Gantt chart output is shown in Figure 15.5.

Finite capacity scheduling allows delivery requirements to be based on today's conditions and today's orders, not according to some predefined rule. The scheduler determines what constitutes a "good" schedule. FCS software packages such as Lekin, ProPlanner, Preactor, Asprova, and Jobplan are currently used at over 60% of U.S. plants.

> **Learning Objective**
>
> 6. Define finite capacity scheduling

THEORY OF CONSTRAINTS

Throughput, an important concept in operations, is the number of units processed through the facility and sold. Throughput is a critical difference between the successful and the unsuccessful enterprise. This has led to a focus on constraints, popularized by the book *The Goal: A Process of Ongoing Improvement* by Eliyahu Goldratt and Jeff Cox.[7] The **theory of constraints (TOC)** is a body of knowledge that deals with anything that limits an organization's ability to achieve its goals. Constraints can be physical (such as process or personnel availability, raw materials, or supplies) or nonphysical (such as procedures, morale, and training). Recognizing and managing these limitations through a five-step process is the basis of the theory of constraints:

> **Theory of constraints (TOC)**
>
> A body of knowledge that deals with anything that limits an organization's ability to achieve its goals.

Step 1: Identify the constraints.
Step 2: Develop a plan for overcoming the identified constraints.
Step 3: Focus resources on accomplishing step 2.
Step 4: Reduce the effects of the constraints by off-loading work or by expanding capability. Make sure that the constraints are recognized by all those who can have impact on them.
Step 5: Once one set of constraints is overcome, go back to step 1 and identify new constraints.

The *OM in Action* box "Banking and the Theory of Constraints (TOC)" illustrates these five steps and shows that TOC is used in services as well as manufacturing.

> **Learning Objective**
>
> 7. List the steps in the theory of constraints

[7]Eliyahu M. Goldratt and Jeff Cox, *The Goal: A Process of Ongoing Improvement* (Croton-on-Hudson, NY: North River Press, 1986). For more discussion of the constraints, see J. Davies, V. J. Mabin, and S. J. Balderstone, "The Theory of Constraints," *Omega* 33, no. 6 (December 2005): 506; and I. Ehie and C. Sheu, "Integrating Six Sigma and Theory of Constraints for Continuous Improvement," *Journal of Manufacturing Technology and Management* 16, no. 5/6 (2005): 542–553.

OM in Action Banking and the Theory of Constraints (TOC)

When a midwestern U.S. bank identified its weakest link as the mortgage department, with a home-loan processing time of over a month, it turned to the principles of TOC to reduce the average loan time. A cross-functional mortgage improvement team of eight people employed the five steps outlined in the text. Using flowcharting, the team discovered that it was taking too long to (1) conduct property appraisals and surveys and (2) verify applicant employment. So the first step of TOC was to identify these two constraints.

The second step in TOC was to develop a plan to reduce the time taken for employment verification and for conducting appraisals and surveys. The team learned that it could reduce employment verification to 2 weeks by having the loan officer request the last 2 years of W-2 forms and the last month's pay stub. It found similar solutions to reducing survey/appraisal time.

As a third step, it had personnel refocus their resources so the two constraints could be performed at a higher level of efficiency. The result was decreased operating expense and inventory (money, in this banking example) and increased throughput.

The fourth TOC step required that employees support the earlier steps by focusing on the two time constraints. The bank also placed a higher priority on verification so that constraint could be overcome.

Finally, the bank began to look for new constraints once the first ones were overcome. Like all continuing improvement efforts, the process starts over before complacency sets in.

Sources: Decision Support Systems (March 2001): 451–468; *The Banker's Magazine* (January–February 1997): 53–59; and *Bank Systems and Technology* (September 1999): S10.

Bottlenecks

Bottleneck

An operation that limits output in the production sequence.

Bottleneck work centers are constraints that limit the output of production. Bottlenecks have less capacity than the preceding or following work centers. They constrain throughput. Bottlenecks are a common occurrence because even well-designed systems are seldom balanced for very long. Changing products, product mixes, and volumes often create multiple and shifting bottlenecks. Consequently, bottleneck work centers occur in nearly all process-focused facilities, from hospitals and restaurants to factories. Successful operations managers deal with bottlenecks by ensuring that the bottleneck stays busy, increasing the bottleneck's capacity, rerouting work, changing lot size, changing work sequence, or accepting idleness at other workstations.

Several techniques for dealing with the bottleneck are:

- Increasing capacity of the constraint. This may require a capital investment or more people and may take a while to implement.
- Ensuring that well-trained and cross-trained employees are available to ensure full operation and maintenance of the work center causing the constraint.
- Developing alternative routings, processing procedures, or subcontractors.
- Moving inspections and tests to a position just before the bottleneck. This approach has the advantage of rejecting any potential defects before they enter the bottleneck.
- Scheduling throughput to match the capacity of the bottleneck. This may mean scheduling less work at the work centers supplying the bottleneck.

As an example, Arnold Palmer Hospital's constraint in delivery of babies was hospital bed availability. This bottleneck's *long-term* solution was to add capacity via a 4-year construction project (see the video case studies in Chapter 3 and Supplement 7). Because the *immediate* constraint could not be handled by scheduling babies—they operate on their own schedule—the hospital staff developed a new process to help reduce the bottleneck. The solution: If a woman ready for discharge could not be picked up prior to 5 P.M., staffers drove the woman and her baby home themselves. Not only did this free up a bed for the next patient, it created good will as well.

Drum, Buffer, Rope

Drum, buffer, rope is another idea from the theory of constraints. In this context, the *drum* is the beat of the system. It provides the schedule—the pace of production. The *buffer* is the resource, usually inventory, necessary to keep the constraint(s) operating at capacity. And the *rope* provides the synchronization necessary to pull the units through the system. The rope can be thought of as kanban signals.

SCHEDULING REPETITIVE FACILITIES

The scheduling goals defined at the beginning of this chapter are also appropriate for repetitive production. You may recall from Chapter 7 that repetitive producers make standard products from modules. The usual approach is to develop a forward-looking schedule on a balanced assembly line. (Refer to Table 15.2 on page 605).

Repetitive producers want to satisfy customer demands, lower inventory investment, and reduce the batch (or lot) size, with existing equipment and processes. A technique to move toward these goals is to use a level-material-use schedule. **Level material use** means frequent, high-quality, small lot sizes that contribute to just-in-time production. This is exactly what world-class producers such as Harley-Davidson, John Deere, and Johnson Controls do. The advantages of level material use are:

Level material use
The use of frequent, high-quality, small lot sizes that contribute to just-in-time production.

1. Lower inventory levels, which releases capital for other uses
2. Faster product throughput (that is, shorter lead times)
3. Improved component quality and hence improved product quality
4. Reduced floor-space requirements
5. Improved communication among employees because they are closer together (which can result in improved teamwork and *esprit de corps*)
6. Smoother production process because large lots have not "hidden" the problems

Suppose a repetitive producer runs large monthly batches: With a level-material-use schedule, management would move toward shortening this monthly cycle to a weekly, daily, or even hourly cycle.

One way to develop a level-material-use schedule is to first determine the minimum lot size that will keep the production process moving. This is illustrated in the next chapter, "JIT and Lean Operations."

SCHEDULING SERVICES

Scheduling service systems differs from scheduling manufacturing systems in several ways:

- In manufacturing, the scheduling emphasis is on machines and materials; in services, it is on staffing levels.
- Inventories can help smooth demand for manufacturers, but many service systems do not maintain inventories.
- Services are labor-intensive, and the demand for this labor can be highly variable.
- Legal considerations, such as wage and hour laws and union contracts that limit hours worked per shift, week, or month, constrain scheduling decisions.
- Because services usually schedule people rather than material, behavioral, social, seniority, and status issues complicate scheduling.

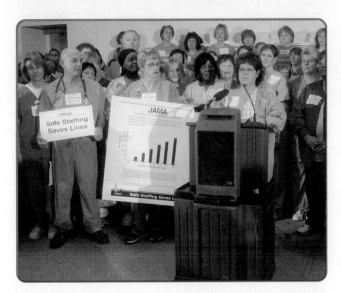

◄ *Good scheduling in the health care industry can help keep nurses happy and costs contained. Here, nurses in Boston protest nurse-staffing levels in Massachusetts hospitals. Shortages of qualified nurses is a chronic problem.*

The following examples note the complexity of scheduling services.

Hospitals   A hospital is an example of a service facility that may use a scheduling system every bit as complex as one found in a job shop. Hospitals seldom use a machine shop priority system such as first come, first served (FCFS) for treating emergency patients. However, they do schedule products (such as surgeries) just like a factory, and capacities must meet wide variations in demand.

Banks   Cross training of the workforce in a bank allows loan officers and other managers to provide short-term help for tellers if there is a surge in demand. Banks also employ part-time personnel to provide a variable capacity.

Retail Stores   Scheduling optimization systems, such as Workbrain, Cybershift, and Kronos, are used at retailers including Wal-Mart, Payless Shoe stores, Target, and Radio Shack. These systems track individual store sales, transactions, units sold, and customer traffic in 15-minute increments to create work schedules. Wal-Mart's 1.3 million and Target's 350,000 employees used to take thousands of managers' hours to schedule; now staffing is drawn up nationwide in a few hours, and customer checkout experience has improved dramatically.

Airlines   Airlines face two constraints when scheduling flight crews: (1) a complex set of FAA work-time limitations and (2) union contracts that guarantee crew pay for some number of hours each day or each trip. Airline planners must build crew schedules that meet or exceed crews' pay guarantees. Planners must also make efficient use of their other expensive resource: aircraft. These schedules are typically built using linear programming models. The *OM in Action* box

OM in Action   Scheduling Aircraft Turnaround

Airlines that face increasingly difficult financial futures have recently discovered the importance of efficient scheduling of ground turnaround activities for flights. For some low-cost, point-to-point carriers like Southwest Airlines, scheduling turnarounds in 20 minutes has been standard policy for years. Yet for others, like Continental, United, and US Airways, the approach is new. This figure illustrates how US Airways deals with speedier schedules. Now its planes average seven trips a day, instead of six, meaning the carrier can sell tens of thousands more seats a day.

▶ *US Airways is cutting the turnaround time on commercial flights from the current 45 minutes to 20 minutes for Boeing 737s. To the right is a list of procedures that must be completed before the flight can depart:*

1 Ticket agent takes flight plan to pilot, who loads information into aircraft computer. About 130 passengers disembark from the plane.

2 Workers clean trash cans, seat pockets, lavatories, etc.

3 Catering personnel board plane and replenish supply of drinks and ice.

4 A fuel truck loads up to 5,300 gallons of fuel into aircraft's wings.

5 Baggage crews unload up to 4,000 pounds of luggage and 2,000 pounds of freight. "Runners" rush the luggage to baggage claim area in terminal.

6 Ramp agents, who help park aircraft upon arrival, "push" plane back away from gate.

Sources: US Airways, Boeing, *Knight-Ridder Business Tribune News* (October 6, 2004): 1; and *Aviation Week & Space Technology* (January 29, 2001): 50.

OM in Action Scheduling for Peaks by Swapping Employees

When calls to Choice Hotel International's reservation line surged after a recent ad campaign, Choice V.P. Don Brockwell found his call center short-staffed. So he quickly arranged to add 20 agents per shift—but not by hiring or calling a temp service. Instead, the additional workers were employees of 1-800-Flowers.com. Choice and Flowers's unusual deal helps both reduce reliance on outsourcers. It also bolsters recruiting and retention because call center workers have more varied work and are less subject to a seasonal business cycle.

The deal works in part because Choice's high season is mid-May through early October, while Flowers's call volume increases between October and May, with surges at Christmas, Valentine's Day, and Mother's Day. The companies typically lend each other as many as 100 employ-

ees, for weeks at a time, in the three call centers they share. But some workers might even change assignments in the middle of a shift. Most employees like the variety. "When you sit down and sell hotel rooms for 8 hours a day, selling flowers is a nice break," says Rick Hilliner, a former teacher, now at the Grand Junction, Colorado, center.

Sources: The Wall Street Journal (April 10, 2006): B3; and *Call Center Magazine* (March 2005): 18–24.

"Scheduling Aircraft Turnaround" details how very short-term schedules (20 minutes) can help an airline become more efficient.

24/7 Operations   Emergency hot lines, police/fire departments, telephone operations, and mail-order businesses (such as L.L. Bean) schedule employees 24 hours a day, 7 days a week. To allow management flexibility in staffing, sometimes part-time workers can be employed. This provides both benefits (in using odd shift lengths or matching anticipated workloads) and difficulties (from the large number of possible alternatives in terms of days off, lunch hour times, rest periods, starting times). Most companies use computerized scheduling systems to cope with these complexities.[8] The *OM in Action* box "Scheduling for Peaks by Swapping Employees" provides yet another example of flexibility in scheduling.

Scheduling Service Employees with Cyclical Scheduling

A number of techniques and algorithms exist for scheduling service-sector employees such as police officers, nurses, restaurant staff, tellers, and retail sales clerks. Managers, trying to set a timely and efficient schedule that keeps personnel happy, can spend substantial time each month developing employee schedules. Such schedules often consider a fairly long planning period (say, 6 weeks). One approach that is workable yet simple is *cyclical scheduling*.

Cyclical Scheduling   Cyclical scheduling with inconsistent staffing needs is often the case in services such as restaurants and police work. Here the objective focuses on developing a schedule with the minimum number of workers.[9] In these cases, each employee is assigned to a shift and has time off. Let's look at Example 8.

[8]See A. Kevin, "Scheduling to Balance Firm and Worker Needs," *Canadian HR Reporter* 18, no. 8 (October 24, 2005): 8.
[9]See Vinh Quan, "Retail Labor Scheduling," *OR/MS Today*, 31, no. 6 (December 2004): 32–35; or G. Laporte, "The Art and Science of Designing Rotating Schedules," *Journal of the Operational Research Society*, 50, no. 10 (1999): 1011–1017.

EXAMPLE 8

Cyclical scheduling

Hospital administrator Doris Laughlin wants to staff the oncology ward using a standard 5-day work-week with two consecutive days off, but also wants to minimize the staff. However, as in most hospitals, she faces an inconsistent demand. Weekends have low usage. Doctors tend to work early in the week, and patients peak on Wednesday, then taper off.

Approach: Doris must first establish staffing requirements. Then the following 5-step process is applied.

Solution:

1. Determine the necessary daily staffing requirements. Doris has done this:

Day	Monday	Tuesday	Wednesday	Thursday	Friday	Saturday	Sunday
Staff required	5	5	6	5	4	3	3

2. Identify the two consecutive days that have the *lowest total requirement* and circle these. Assign these two days off to the first employee. In this case, the first employee has Saturday and Sunday off because 3 plus 3 is the *lowest sum* of any 2 days. In the case of a tie, choose the days with the lowest adjacent requirement. If there are more than one, make an arbitrary decision.

3. We now have an employee working each of the uncircled days; therefore, make a new row for the next employee by subtracting 1 from the first row (because one day has been worked)—except for the circled days (which represent the days not worked) and any day that has a zero. That is, do not subtract from a circled day or a day that has a value of zero.

4. In the new row, identify the two consecutive days that have the lowest total requirement and circle them. Assign the next employee to the remaining days.

5. Repeat the process (steps 3 and 4) until all staffing requirements are met.

	MONDAY	TUESDAY	WEDNESDAY	THURSDAY	FRIDAY	SATURDAY	SUNDAY
Employee 1	5	5	6	5	4	③	③
Employee 2	4	4	5	4	3	③	③
Employee 3	3	3	4	3	②	③	3
Employee 4	2	2	3	②	②	3	2
Employee 5	①	①	2	2	2	2	1
Employee 6	1	1	1	1	1	①	⓪
Employee 7						1	
Capacity (measured in number of employees)	5	5	6	5	4	3	3
Excess capacity	0	0	0	0	0	1	0

Doris needs six full-time employees to meet the staffing needs and one employee to work Saturday.

Notice that capacity (number of employees) equals requirements, provided an employee works overtime on Saturday, or a part-time employee is hired for Saturday.

Insight: Doris has implemented an efficient scheduling system that accommodates 2 consecutive days off for every employee.

Learning exercise: If Doris meets the staffing requirement for Saturday with a full-time employee, how does she schedule that employee? [Answer: That employee can have any 2 days off, except Saturday, and capacity will exceed requirements by 1 person each day the employee works (except Saturday).]

Related problems: 15.19, 15.20

Using the approach in Example 8, Colorado General Hospital saved an average of 10 to 15 hours a month and found these added advantages: (1) no computer was needed, (2) the nurses were happy with the schedule, (3) the cycles could be changed seasonally to accommodate avid skiers, and (4) recruiting was easier because of predictability and flexibility. This approach yields an optimum, although there may be multiple optimal solutions.

Other cyclical scheduling techniques have been developed to aid service scheduling. Some approaches use linear programming: This is how Hard Rock Cafe schedules its services (see the Video Case Study at the end of this chapter). There is a natural bias in scheduling to use tools that are understood and yield solutions that are accepted.

Summary

Scheduling involves the timing of operations to achieve the efficient movement of units through a system. This chapter addressed the issues of short-term scheduling in process-focused, repetitive, and service environments. We saw that process-focused facilities are production systems in which products are made to order and that scheduling tasks in them can become complex. Several aspects and approaches to scheduling, loading, and sequencing of jobs were introduced. These ranged from Gantt charts and the assignment method of scheduling to a series of priority rules, the critical-ratio rule, Johnson's rule for sequencing, and finite capacity scheduling. We also examined the theory of constraints and the concept of bottlenecks.

Service systems generally differ from manufacturing systems. This leads to the use of first-come, first-served rules and appointment and reservation systems, as well as to heuristics and linear programming approaches for matching capacity to demand in service environments.

Key Terms

Forward scheduling *(p. 603)*
Backward scheduling *(p. 604)*
Loading *(p. 606)*
Input–output control *(p. 606)*
ConWIP Cards *(p. 607)*
Gantt charts *(p. 607)*
Assignment method *(p. 609)*

Sequencing *(p. 612)*
Priority rules *(p. 612)*
First come, first served (FCFS) *(p. 612)*
Shortest processing time (SPT) *(p. 612)*
Earliest due date (EDD) *(p. 612)*
Longest processing time (LPT) *(p. 612)*
Critical ratio (CR) *(p. 615)*

Johnson's rule *(p. 616)*
Finite capacity scheduling (FCS) *(p. 618)*
Theory of constraints (TOC) *(p. 619)*
Bottleneck *(p. 620)*
Level material use *(p. 621)*

Using Software for Short-Term Scheduling

In addition to the commercial software we noted in this chapter, short-term scheduling problems can be solved with the Excel OM software that comes on the text's CD. POM for Windows also includes a scheduling module. The use of each of these programs is explained next.

✗ Using Excel OM

Excel OM has two modules that help solve short-term scheduling problems: Assignment and Job Shop Scheduling. The Assignment module is illustrated in Programs 15.1 and 15.2. The input screen, using the Example 4 data, appears first, as Program 15.1. Once the data are all entered, we choose the Tools command, followed by the Solver command. Excel's Solver uses linear programming to optimize assignment problems. The constraints are also shown in Program 15.1. We then select the Solve command and the solution appears in Program 15.2.

Excel OM's Job Shop Scheduling module is illustrated in Program 15.3. Program 15.3 uses Example 5's data. Because jobs are listed in the sequence in which they arrived (see column A), the results are for the FCFS rule. Program 15.3 also shows some of the formulas (columns F, G, H, I, J) used in the calculations.

To solve with the SPT rule, we need four intermediate steps: (1) Select (that is, highlight) the data in columns A, B, C for all jobs; (2) invoke the Data command; (3) invoke the Sort command; and (4) sort by Time (column B) in *ascending* order. To solve for EDD, step 4 changes to sort by Due Date (column D) in *ascending* order. Finally, for an LPT solution, step 4 becomes sort by Due Date (column D) in *descending* order.

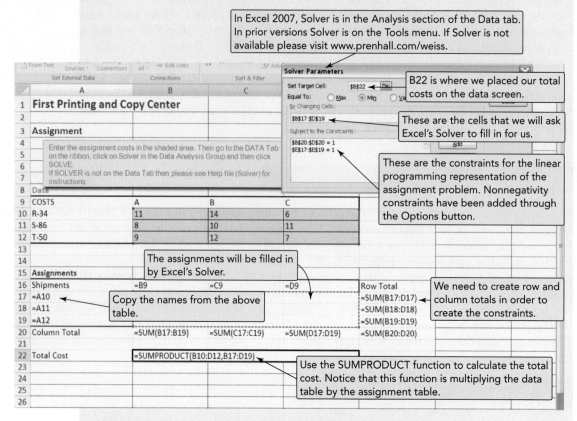

In Excel 2007, Solver is in the Analysis section of the Data tab. In prior versions Solver is on the Tools menu. If Solver is not available please visit www.prenhall.com/weiss.

B22 is where we placed our total costs on the data screen.

These are the cells that we will ask Excel's Solver to fill in for us.

These are the constraints for the linear programming representation of the assignment problem. Nonnegativity constraints have been added through the Options button.

The assignments will be filled in by Excel's Solver.

Copy the names from the above table.

We need to create row and column totals in order to create the constraints.

Use the SUMPRODUCT function to calculate the total cost. Notice that this function is multiplying the data table by the assignment table.

▲ **Program 15.1** Excel OM's Assignment Module Using Example 4's Data

After entering the problem data in the yellow area, select Tools, then Solver.

▼ **Program 15.2** Excel OM Output Screen for Assignment Problem Described in Program 15.1

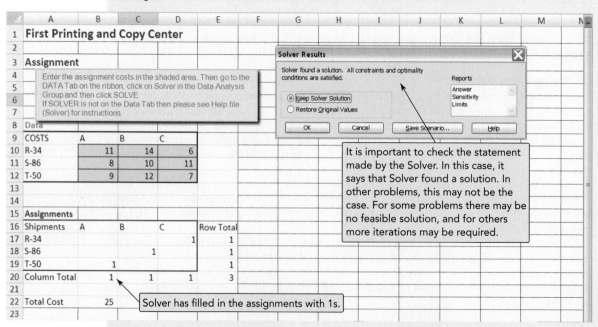

It is important to check the statement made by the Solver. In this case, it says that Solver found a solution. In other problems, this may not be the case. For some problems there may be no feasible solution, and for others more iterations may be required.

Solver has filled in the assignments with 1s.

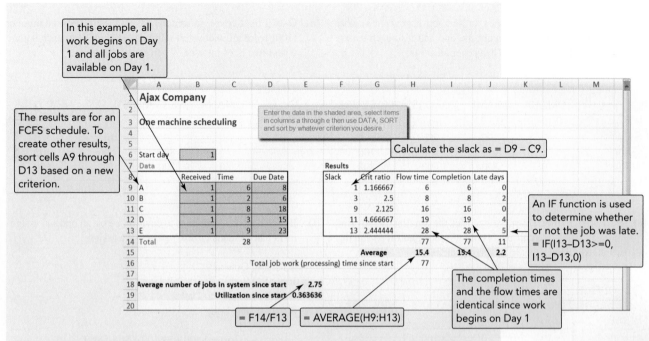

▲ **Program 15.3**   Excel OM's Job Shop Scheduling Module Applied to Example 5's Data

P Using POM For Windows

POM for Windows can handle both categories of scheduling problems we see in this chapter. Its Assignment module is used to solve the traditional one-to-one assignment problem of people to tasks, machines to jobs, and so on. Its Job Shop Scheduling module can solve a one- or two-machine job-shop problem. Available priority rules include SPT, FCFS, EDD, and LPT. Each can be examined in turn once the data are all entered. Refer to Appendix IV for specifics regarding POM for Windows.

Solved Problems

Virtual Office Hours help is available on Student DVD.

Solved Problem 15.1

King Finance Corporation, headquartered in New York, wants to assign three recently hired college graduates, Julie Jones, Al Smith, and Pat Wilson, to regional offices. However, the firm also has an opening in New York and would send one of the three there if it were more economical than a move to Omaha, Dallas, or Miami. It will cost $1,000 to relocate Jones to New York, $800 to relocate Smith there, and $1,500 to move Wilson. What is the optimal assignment of personnel to offices?

OFFICE HIREE	OMAHA	MIAMI	DALLAS
Jones	$800	$1,100	$1,200
Smith	$500	$1,600	$1,300
Wilson	$500	$1,000	$2,300

Solution

(a) The cost table has a fourth column to represent New York. To "balance" the problem, we add a "dummy" row (person) with a zero relocation cost to each city.

(b) Subtract the smallest number in each row and cover all zeros (column subtraction of each column's zero will give the same numbers and therefore is not necessary):

OFFICE HIREE	OMAHA	MIAMI	DALLAS	NEW YORK
Jones	$800	$1,100	$1,200	$1,000
Smith	$500	$1,600	$1,300	$ 800
Wilson	$500	$1,000	$2,300	$1,500
Dummy	0	0	0	0

OFFICE HIREE	OMAHA	MIAMI	DALLAS	NEW YORK
Jones	0̸	300	400	200
Smith	0̸	1,100	800	300
Wilson	0̸	500	1,800	1,000
Dummy	0̸	0̸	0̸	0̸

(c) Only 2 lines cover, so subtract the smallest uncovered number (200) from all uncovered numbers, and add it to each square where two lines intersect. Then cover all zeros:

OFFICE / HIREE	OMAHA	MIAMI	DALLAS	NEW YORK
Jones	0̸	100	200	0̸
Smith	0̸	900	600	100̸
Wilson	0̸	300	1,600	800̸
Dummy	2̶0̶0̶	0	0	0̸

(d) Only 3 lines cover, so subtract the smallest uncovered number (100) from all uncovered numbers, and add it to each square where two lines intersect. Then cover all zeros:

OFFICE / HIREE	OMAHA	MIAMI	DALLAS	NEW YORK
Jones	0̶	0̶	100	0̶
Smith	0̸	800	500	100
Wilson	0̸	200	1,500	800
Dummy	3̶0̶0̶	0̶	0̶	100̶

(e) Still only 3 lines cover, so subtract the smallest uncovered number (100) from all uncovered numbers, add it to squares where two lines intersect, and cover all zeros:

OFFICE / HIREE	OMAHA	MIAMI	DALLAS	NEW YORK
Jones	1̶0̶0̶	0̸	1̶0̶0̶	0̸
Smith	0̶	700	400	0̸
Wilson	0̶	100	1,400	700̸
Dummy	4̶0̶0̶	0̸	0̸	100̸

(f) Because it takes four lines to cover all zeros, an optimal assignment can be made at zero squares. We assign:

Wilson to Omaha
Jones to Miami
Dummy (no one) to Dallas
Smith to New York

$$Cost = \$500 + \$1,100 + \$0 + \$800$$
$$= \$2,400$$

Solved Problem 15.2

A defense contractor in Dallas has six jobs awaiting processing. Processing time and due dates are given in the table. Assume that jobs arrive in the order shown. Set the processing sequence according to FCFS and evaluate.

JOB	JOB PROCESSING TIME (DAYS)	JOB DUE DATE (DAYS)
A	6	22
B	12	14
C	14	30
D	2	18
E	10	25
F	4	34

Solution

FCFS has the sequence A–B–C–D–E–F.

JOB SEQUENCE	JOB PROCESSING TIME	FLOW TIME	DUE DATE	JOB LATENESS
A	6	6	22	0
B	12	18	14	4
C	14	32	30	2
D	2	34	18	16
E	10	44	25	19
F	4	48	34	14
	48	182		55

1. Average completion time = 182/6 = 30.33 days
2. Average number of jobs in system = 182/48 = 3.79 jobs
3. Average job lateness = 55/6 = 9.16 days
4. Utilization = 48/182 = 26.4%

Solved Problem 15.3

The Dallas firm in Solved Problem 15.2 also wants to consider job sequencing by the SPT priority rule. Apply SPT to the same data and provide a recommendation.

solution

SPT has the sequence D–F–A–E–B–C.

JOB SEQUENCE	JOB PROCESSING TIME	FLOW TIME	DUE DATE	JOB LATENESS
D	2	2	18	0
F	4	6	34	0
A	6	12	22	0
E	10	22	25	0
B	12	34	14	20
C	14	48	30	18
	48	124		38

1. Average completion time = 124/6 = 20.67 days
2. Average number of jobs in system = 124/48 = 2.58 jobs
3. Average job lateness = 38/6 = 6.33 days
4. Utilization = 48/124 = 38.7%

SPT is superior to FCFS in this case on all four measures. If we were to also analyze EDD, we would, however, find its average job lateness to be lowest at 5.5 days. SPT is a good recommendation. SPT's major disadvantage is that it makes long jobs wait, sometimes for a long time.

Solved Problem 15.4

Use Johnson's rule to find the optimum sequence for processing the jobs shown through two work centers. Times at each center are in hours.

JOB	WORK CENTER 1	WORK CENTER 2
A	6	12
B	3	7
C	18	9
D	15	14
E	16	8
F	10	15

solution

B	A	F	D	C	E

The sequential times are:

Work center 1	3	6	10	15	18	16
Work center 2	7	12	15	14	9	8

Solved Problem 15.5

Illustrate the throughput time and idle time at the two work centers
in Solved Problem 15.4 by constructing a time-phased chart.

solution

Active Model Exercise

This exercise, found on your CD-ROM, allows you to evaluate changes to input data in the job-shop sequencing model.

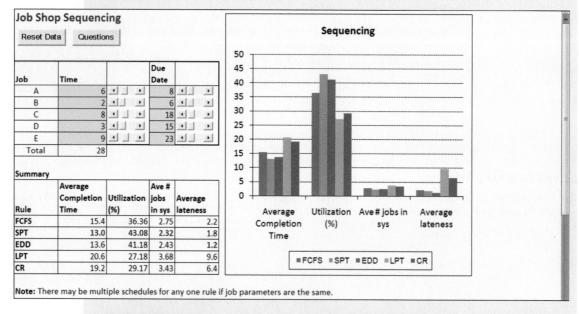

▲ **Active Model 15.1**   An Analysis of the Sequencing of Jobs Using the Example 5 Data of the Architectural Firm

Questions

1. Which schedule (rule) minimizes the average completion time, maximizes the utilization, and minimizes the average number of jobs in the system for this example?

2. Use the scrollbar to change the processing time for job C and use the scrollbar to modify the due date for job C. Does the same rule always minimize the average completion time?

3. Which schedule (rule) minimizes the average lateness for this example?

4. Use the scrollbar to change the due date for job C. Does the same rule always minimize the average lateness?

Self-Test

- ***Before taking the self-test***, *refer to the learning objectives listed at the beginning of the chapter and the key terms listed at the end of the chapter.*
- *Use the key at the back of the text to* **correct** *your answers.*
- ***Restudy*** *pages that correspond to any questions you answered incorrectly or material you feel uncertain about.*

1. A visual aid used in loading and scheduling jobs is:
   a) a Gantt chart
   b) a planning file
   c) a bottleneck
   d) a drum, buffer, rope
   e) a level material chart

2. Shop loading:
   a) means the assignment of dates to specific jobs or operations steps
   b) is typically managed using an assembly chart
   c) means the assignment of jobs to work or processing centers
   d) is oriented toward the management of work-in-process inventories
   e) solves the bottleneck problem

3. The most popular priority rules include:
   a) FCFS
   b) EDD
   c) SPT
   d) all of the above

4. Which of the following dispatch rules tends to maximize the number of jobs completed on time?
   a) FCFS: first come, first served
   b) EDD: earliest due date

   c) SPT: shortest processing time
   d) LPT: longest processing time

5. Which of the following dispatch rules tends to minimize the average number of jobs in the system?
   a) FCFS: first come, first served
   b) EDD: earliest due date
   c) SPT: shortest processing time
   d) LPT: longest processing time
   e) CR: critical ratio

6. Of the following dispatching rules, which is considered to be dynamic?
   a) FCFS: first come, first served
   b) CR: critical ratio
   c) SPT: shortest processing time
   d) EDD: earliest due date
   e) LPT: longest processing time

7. The chief disadvantage of the shortest processing time dispatch rule is that _____.

8. The theory of constraints pays special attention to:
   a) the nature of the individual in charge of scheduling
   b) the number of part-time employees
   c) bottleneck operations
   d) jobs with the most rewarding operations
   e) all of the above

Internet and Student CD-ROM/DVD Exercises

Visit our Companion Web site or use your student CD-ROM/DVD to help with material in this chapter.

 On Our Companion Web Site, www.prenhall.com/heizer
- Internet Case
- Self-Study Quizzes
- Practice Problems
- Virtual Company Tour
- PowerPoint Lecture

On Your Student CD-ROM
- Practice Problems
- Active Model Exercise
- Excel OM
- Excel OM Example Data Files
- Lekin Scheduling Software
- POM for Windows

On Your Student DVD
- Video Clip and Video Case
- Virtual Office Hours for Solved Problems

Discussion Questions

1. What is the overall objective of scheduling?
2. List the four criteria for determining the effectiveness of a *scheduling* decision. How do these criteria relate to the four criteria for *sequencing* decisions?
3. Describe what is meant by "loading" work centers. What are the two ways work centers can be loaded? What are two techniques used in loading?
4. Name five priority sequencing rules. Explain how each works to assign jobs.

5. What are the advantages and disadvantages of the shortest processing time (SPT) rule?
6. What is a due date?
7. Explain the terms *flow time* and *lateness*.
8. Which shop-floor scheduling rule would you prefer to apply if you were the leader of the only team of experts charged with defusing several time bombs scattered throughout your building? You can see the bombs; they are of different types. You can tell how long each one will take to defuse. Discuss.

9. When is Johnson's rule best applied in job-shop scheduling?
10. State the four effectiveness measures for dispatching rules.
11. What are the steps of the assignment method of linear programming?
12. State the five-step process that serves as the basis of the theory of constraints.
13. What are the advantages of level material flow?
14. What are the techniques available to operations managers to deal with a bottleneck operation? Which of these does not increase throughput?
15. What is input–output control?

Ethical Dilemma

Scheduling people to work second and third shifts (evening and "graveyard") is a problem in almost every 24-hour company. The *OM in Action* box "Scheduling Workers Who Fall Asleep Is a Killer—Literally," on page 604 describes potentially dangerous issues on the night shift at FedEx and a nuclear power plant. Perhaps even more significantly, ergonomic data indicate the body does not respond well to significant shifts in its natural circadian rhythm of sleep. There are also significant long-run health issues with frequent changes in work and sleep cycles.

Consider yourself the manager of a nonunion steel mill that must operate 24-hour days, and where the physical demands are such that

8-hour days are preferable to 10- or 12-hour days. Your empowered employees have decided that they want to work weekly rotating shifts. That is, they want a repeating work cycle of 1 week, 7 A.M. to 3 P.M., followed by a second week from 3 P.M. to 11 P.M., and the third week from 11 P.M. to 7 A.M. You are sure this is not a good idea in terms of both productivity and the long-term health of the employees. If you do not accept their decision, you undermine the work empowerment program, generate a morale issue, and perhaps, more significantly, generate few more votes for a union. What is the ethical position and what do you do?

Problems*

•• **15.1** Ron Satterfield's excavation company uses both Gantt scheduling charts and Gantt load charts.

a) Today, which is the end of day 7, Ron is reviewing the Gantt chart depicting these schedules:
   - Job #151 was scheduled to begin on day 3 and to take 6 days. As of now, it is 1 day ahead of schedule.
   - Job #177 was scheduled to begin on day 1 and take 4 days. It is currently on time.
   - Job #179 was scheduled to start on day 7 and take 2 days. It actually got started on day 6 and is progressing according to plan.
   - Job #211 was scheduled to begin on day 5, but missing equipment delayed it until day 6. It is progressing as expected and should take 3 days.
   - Job #215 was scheduled to begin on day 4 and take 5 days. It got started on time but has since fallen behind 2 days.

Draw the Gantt scheduling chart for the activities above.

b) Ron now wants to use a Gantt load chart to see how much work is scheduled in each of his three work teams: Able, Baker, and Charlie. Five jobs constitute the current work load for these three work teams: Job #250, requiring 48 hours and #275 requiring 32 hours for Work Team Able; Jobs #210, and #280 requiring 16 and 24 hours, respectively, for Team Baker; and Job #225, requiring 40 hours, for Team Charlie.

Prepare the Gantt load chart for these activities.

•• **15.2** First Printing and Copy Center has 4 more jobs to be scheduled, in addition to those shown in Example 3 in the chapter. Production scheduling personnel are reviewing the Gantt chart at the end of day 4.
   - Job D was scheduled to begin early on day 2 and to end on the middle of day 9. As of now (the review point after day 4), it is 2 days ahead of schedule.
   - Job E should begin on day 1 and end on day 3. It was on time.

   - Job F was to begin on day 3, but maintenance forced a delay of $1\frac{1}{2}$ days. The job should now take 5 full days. It is now on schedule.
   - Job G is a day behind schedule. It started at the beginning of day 2 and should require 6 days to complete.

Develop a Gantt schedule chart for First Printing and Copy Center.

• **15.3** The Orange Top Cab Company has a taxi waiting at each of four cabstands in Evanston, Illinois. Four customers have called and requested service. The distances, in miles, from the waiting taxis to the customers are given in the following table. Find the optimal assignment of taxis to customers so as to minimize total driving distances to the customers.

Cab Site	Customer			
	A	**B**	**C**	**D**
Stand 1	7	3	4	8
Stand 2	5	4	6	5
Stand 3	6	7	9	6
Stand 4	8	6	7	4 **Px**

• **15.4** Molly Riggs's medical testing company wishes to assign a set of jobs to a set of machines. The following table provides the production data of each machine when performing the specific job:

Job	Machine			
	A	**B**	**C**	**D**
1	7	9	8	10
2	10	9	7	6
3	11	5	9	6
4	9	11	5	8

a) Determine the assignment of jobs to machines that will *maximize* total production.

b) What is the total production of your assignments? **Px**

*Note: **Px** means the problem may be solved with POM for Windows and/or Excel OM.

• **15.5** The Johnny Ho Manufacturing Company in Columbus, Ohio, is putting out four new electronic components. Each of Ho's four plants has the capacity to add one more product to its current line of electronic parts. The unit-manufacturing costs for producing the different parts at the four plants are shown in the accompanying table. How should Ho assign the new products to the plants to minimize manufacturing costs?

Electronic Component	Plant			
	1	**2**	**3**	**4**
C53	$0.10	$0.12	$0.13	$0.11
C81	0.05	0.06	0.04	0.08
D5	0.32	0.40	0.31	0.30
D44	0.17	0.14	0.19	0.15 **Px**

• **15.6** Claire Consultants has been entrusted with the task of evaluating a business plan that has been divided into four sections—marketing, finance, operations and human resources. Chris, Steve, Juana, and Rebecca form the evaluation team. Each of them has expertise in a certain field and tends to finish that section faster. The estimated times taken by each team member for each section have been outlined in the table below. Further information states that each of these individuals is paid $60/hour.
a) Assign each member to a different section such that Claire Consultants's overall cost is minimized.
b) What is the total cost of these assignments?

Times Taken by Team Members for Different Sections (minutes)

	Marketing	Finance	Operations	HR
Chris	80	120	125	140
Steve	20	115	145	160
Juana	40	100	85	45
Rebecca	65	35	25	75 **Px**

•• **15.7** The Akron Police Department has five detective squads available for assignment to five open crime cases. The chief of detectives, Paul Kuzdrall, wishes to assign the squads so that the total time to conclude the cases is minimized. The average number

of days, based on past performance, for each squad to complete each case is as follows:

Squad	Case				
	A	**B**	**C**	**D**	**E**
1	14	7	3	7	27
2	20	7	12	6	30
3	10	3	4	5	21
4	8	12	7	12	21
5	13	25	24	26	8

Each squad is composed of different types of specialists, and whereas one squad may be very effective in certain types of cases, it may be almost useless in others.
a) Solve the problem by using the assignment method.
b) Assign the squads to the above cases, but with the constraint that squad 5 cannot work on case E because of a conflict. **Px**

• **15.8** Tigers Sports Club has to select 4 separate co-ed doubles teams to participate in an inter-club table tennis tournament. The pre-selection results in the selection of a group of 4 men—Raul, Jack, Gray, and Ajay—and 4 women—Barbara, Dona, Stella, and Jackie. Now, the task ahead lies in pairing these men and women in the best fashion. The table below shows a matrix that has been designed for this purpose, indicating how each of the men complements the game of each of the women. A higher score indicates a higher degree of compatibility in the games of the two individuals concerned. Find the best pairs.

Game Compatibility Matrix

	Barbara	Dona	Stella	Jackie
Raul	30	20	10	40
Jack	70	10	60	70
Gray	40	20	50	40
Ajay	60	70	30	90 **Px**

••• **15.9** James Gross, chairman of the College of Oshkosh's business department, needs to assign professors to courses next semester. As a criterion for judging who should teach each course, Professor Gross reviews the past 2 years' teaching evaluations (which were filled out by students). Since each of the four professors taught each of the four courses at one time or another during the 2-year period, Gross is able to record a course rating for each instructor. These ratings are shown in the following table.
a) Find the assignment of professors to courses to maximize the overall teaching rating.
b) Assign the professors to the courses with the exception that Professor Fisher cannot teach Statistics.

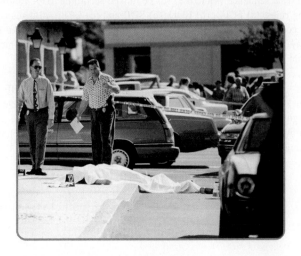

Professor	Course			
	Statistics	Management	Finance	Economics
W. W. Fisher	90	65	95	40
D. Golhar	70	60	80	75
Z. Hug	85	40	80	60
N. K. Rustagi	55	80	65	55 **Px**

•• **15.10** The following jobs are waiting to be processed at the same machine center. Jobs are logged as they arrive:

Job	Due Date	Duration (days)
A	313	8
B	312	16
C	325	40
D	314	5
E	314	3

In what sequence would the jobs be ranked according to the following decision rules: (a) FCFS, (b) EDD, (c) SPT, and (d) LPT? All dates are specified as manufacturing planning calendar days. Assume that all jobs arrive on day 275. Which decision is best and why? **Px**

• **15.11** The following 5 overhaul jobs are waiting to be processed at Avianic's Engine Repair Inc. These jobs were logged as they arrived. All dates are specified as planning calendar days. Assume that all jobs arrived on day 180; today's date is 200.

Job	Due Date	Duration (days)
103	214	10
205	223	7
309	217	11
412	219	5
517	217	15

Using the critical ratio scheduling rule, in what sequence would the jobs be processed? **Px**

•• **15.12** An Alabama lumberyard has four jobs on order, as shown in the following table. Today is day 205 on the yard's schedule. In what sequence would the jobs be ranked according to the following decision rules:
a) FCFS
b) SPT
c) LPT
d) EDD
e) Critical ratio
Which is best and why? Which has the minimum lateness?

Job	Due Date	Remaining Time (days)
A	212	6
B	209	3
C	208	3
D	210	8

Px

•• **15.13** The following jobs are waiting to be processed at Rick Carlson's machine center. Carlson's machine center has a relatively long backlog and sets fresh schedules every 2 weeks, which do not disturb earlier schedules. Below are the jobs received during the previous 2 weeks. They are ready to be scheduled today, which is day 241 (day 241 is a work day). Job names refer to names of clients and contract numbers.

Job	Date Job Received	Production Days Needed	Date Job Due
BR-02	228	15	300
CX-01	225	25	270
DE-06	230	35	320
RG-05	235	40	360
SY-11	231	30	310

a) Complete the table below. (Show your supporting calculations.)
b) Which dispatching rule has the best score for flow time?
c) Which dispatching rule has the best score for utilization?
d) Which dispatching rule has the best score for lateness?
e) Which dispatching rule would you select? Support your decision.

Dispatching Rule	Job Sequence	Flow Time	Utilization	Average Number of Jobs	Average Lateness
EDD					
SPT					
LPT					
FCFS					

•• **15.14** The following jobs are waiting to be processed at Julie Morel's machine center:

Job	Date Order Received	Production Days Needed	Date Order Due
A	110	20	180
B	120	30	200
C	122	10	175
D	125	16	230
E	130	18	210

In what sequence would the jobs be ranked according to the following rules: (a) FCFS, (b) EDD, (c) SPT, and (d) LPT? All dates are according to shop calendar days. Today on the planning calendar is day 130, and none of the jobs have been started or scheduled. Which rule is best? **Px**

•• **15.15** Sunny Park Tailors has been asked to make three different types of wedding suits for separate customers. The table below highlights the time taken in hours for (1) cutting and sewing and (2) delivery of each of the suits. Which schedule finishes sooner: First-come, first-served (123) or a schedule using Johnson's rule?

Times Taken for Different Activities (hours)

Suit	Cut and Sew	Deliver
1	4	2
2	7	7
3	6	5

Px

•• **15.16** The following jobs are waiting to be processed at Jeremy LaMontagne's machine center. Today is day 250.

Job	Date Job Received	Production Days Needed	Date Job Due
1	215	30	260
2	220	20	290
3	225	40	300
4	240	50	320
5	250	20	340

Using the critical ratio scheduling rule, in what sequence would the jobs be processed? **Px**

••• **15.17** The following set of seven jobs is to be processed through two work centers at George Heinrich's printing company. The sequence is first printing, then binding. Processing time at each of the work centers is shown in the following table:

Job	Printing (hours)	Binding (hours)
T	15	3
U	7	9
V	4	10
W	7	6
X	10	9
Y	4	5
Z	7	8

a) What is the optimal sequence for these jobs to be scheduled?
b) Chart these jobs through the two work centers.
c) What is the total length of time of this optimal solution?
d) What is the idle time in the binding shop, given the optimal solution? **Px**

••• **15.18** Six jobs are to be processed through a two-step operation. The first operation involves sanding, and the second involves painting. Processing times are as follows:

Job	Operation 1 (hours)	Operation 2 (hours)
A	10	5
B	7	4
C	5	7
D	3	8
E	2	6
F	4	3

Determine a sequence that will minimize the total completion time for these jobs. Illustrate graphically. **Px**

•• **15.19** Jesse's Barber Shop at O'Hare Airport is open 7 days a week but has fluctuating demand. Jesse is interested in treating his barbers as well as he can with steady work and preferably 5 days of work with two consecutive days off. His analysis of his staffing needs resulted in the following plan. Schedule Jesse's staff with the minimum number of barbers.

	Day						
	Mon.	Tue.	Wed.	Thu.	Fri.	Sat.	Sun.
Barbers needed	6	5	5	5	6	4	3

•• **15.20** Given the following demand for waiters and waitresses at Pentico's Bar and Grill, determine the minimum wait staff needed with a policy of 2 consecutive days off.

	Day						
	Mon.	Tue.	Wed.	Thu.	Fri.	Sat.	Sun.
Wait staff needed	3	4	4	5	6	7	4

•• **15.21** Lifang Wu owns an automated machine shop that makes precision auto parts. He has just compiled an input–output report for the grinding work center. Complete this report and analyze the results.

Input–Output Report

Period	1	2	3	4	Total
Planned input	80	80	100	100	
Actual input	85	85	85	85	
Deviation					
Planned output	90	90	90	90	
Actual output	85	85	80	80	
Deviation					
Initial backlog: 30					

Case Studies

Old Oregon Wood Store

In 2007, George Brown started the Old Oregon Wood Store to manufacture Old Oregon tables. Each table is carefully constructed by hand using the highest-quality oak. Old Oregon tables can support more than 500 pounds, and since the start of the Old Oregon Wood Store, not one table has been returned because of faulty workman-

ship or structural problems. In addition to being rugged, each table is beautifully finished using a urethane varnish that George developed over 20 years of working with wood-finishing materials.

The manufacturing process consists of four steps: preparation, assembly, finishing, and packaging. Each step is performed by one

▶ **Figure 15.6**

Manufacturing Time in Minutes

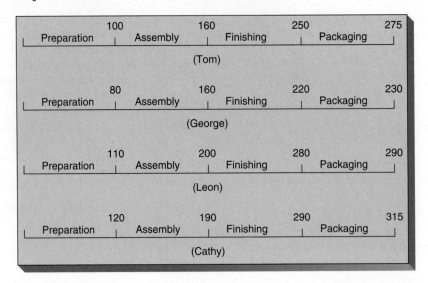

person. In addition to overseeing the entire operation, George does all of the finishing. Tom Surowski performs the preparation step, which involves cutting and forming the basic components of the tables. Leon Davis is in charge of the assembly, and Cathy Stark performs the packaging.

Although each person is responsible for only one step in the manufacturing process, everyone can perform any one of the steps. It is George's policy that occasionally everyone should complete several tables on his or her own without any help or assistance. A small competition is used to see who can complete an entire table in the least amount of time. George maintains average total and intermediate completion times. The data are shown in Figure 15.6.

It takes Cathy longer than the other employees to construct an Old Oregon table. In addition to being slower than the other employees, Cathy is also unhappy about her current responsibility of packaging, which leaves her idle most of the day. Her first preference is finishing, and her second preference is preparation.

In addition to quality, George is concerned with costs and efficiency. When one of the employees misses a day, it causes major scheduling problems. In some cases, George assigns another employee overtime to complete the necessary work. At other times, George simply waits until the employee returns to work to complete his or her step in the manufacturing process. Both solutions cause

problems. Overtime is expensive, and waiting causes delays and sometimes stops the entire manufacturing process.

To overcome some of these problems, Randy Lane was hired. Randy's major duties are to perform miscellaneous jobs and to help out if one of the employees is absent. George has given Randy training in all phases of the manufacturing process, and he is pleased with the speed at which Randy has been able to learn how to completely assembly Old Oregon tables. Randy's average total and intermediate completion times are given in Figure 15.7.

Discussion Questions

1. What is the fastest way to manufacture Old Oregon tables using the original crew? How many could be made per day?
2. Would production rates and quantities change significantly if George would allow Randy to perform one of the four functions and make one of the original crew the backup person?
3. What is the fastest time to manufacture a table with the original crew if Cathy is moved to either preparation or finishing?
4. Whoever performs the packaging function is severely underutilized. Can you find a better way of utilizing the four- or five-person crew than either giving each a single job or allowing each to manufacture an entire table? How many tables could be manufactured per day with this scheme?

▶ **Figure 15.7**

Randy's Completion Times in Minutes

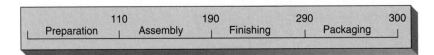

Scheduling at Hard Rock Cafe

Video Case

Whether it's scheduling nurses at Mayo Clinic, pilots at Southwest Airlines, classrooms at UCLA, or servers at a Hard Rock Cafe, it's clear that good scheduling is important. Proper schedules use an organization's assets (1) more effectively, by serving customers promptly, and (2) more efficiently, by lowering costs.

Hard Rock Cafe at Universal Studios, Orlando, is the world's largest restaurant, with 1,100 seats on two main levels. With typical turnover of employees in the restaurant industry at 80% to 100% per

year, Hard Rock General Manager Ken Hoffman takes scheduling very seriously. Hoffman wants his 160 servers to be effective, but he also wants to treat them fairly. He has done so with scheduling software and flexibility that has increased productivity while contributing to turnover that is half the industry average. His goal is to find the fine balance that gives employees financially productive daily work shifts while setting the schedule tight enough so as to not overstaff between lunch and dinner.

The weekly schedule begins with a sales forecast. "First, we examine last year's sales at the cafe for the same day of the week," says Hoffman. "Then we adjust our forecast for this year based on a variety of closely watched factors. For example, we call the Orlando Convention Bureau every week to see what major groups will be in town. Then we send two researchers out to check on the occupancy of nearby hotels. We watch closely to see what concerts are scheduled at Hard Rock Live—the 3,000-seat concert stage next door. From the forecast, we calculate how many people we need to have on duty each day for the kitchen, the bar, as hosts, and for table service."

Once Hard Rock determines the number of staff needed, servers submit request forms, which are fed into the software's linear programming mathematical model. Individuals are given priority rankings from 1 to 9 based on their seniority and how important

they are to fill each day's schedule. Schedules are then posted by day and by workstation. Trades are handled between employees, who understand the value of each specific shift and station.

Hard Rock employees like the system, as does the general manager, since sales per labor-hour are rising and turnover is dropping.

Discussion Questions*

1. Name and justify several factors that Hoffman could use in forecasting weekly sales.
2. What can be done to lower turnover in large restaurants?
3. Why is seniority important in scheduling servers?
4. How does the schedule impact on productivity?

*You may wish to view this case on your DVD before answering the questions.

Additional Case Studies

Internet case study: Visit our Companion Web site at www.prenhall.com/heizer for this free case study:

- **Payroll Planning, Inc.:** Describes setting a schedule for handling the accounting for dozens of client firms.

Harvard has selected these Harvard Business School cases to accompany this chapter:

harvardbusinessonline.hbsp.harvard.edu

- **The Patient Care Delivery Model at Massachusetts General Hospital** (#699-154): Examines the implementation of a new patient care delivery model.
- **Southern Pulp and Paper** (#696-103): Describes a paper mill whose poorly scheduled paper machines are a bottleneck in the operation.

Bibliography

Abbink, Erwin, et al. "Reinventing Crew Scheduling at Netherlands Railways." *Interfaces* 35, no. 5 (September–October 2005): 393–401.

Bard, Jonathan F. "Staff Scheduling in High Volume Service Facilities with Downgrading." *IIE Transactions* 36 (2004): 985–997.

Bolander, Steven F., and Sam G. Taylor. "Scheduling Techniques: A Comparison of Logic." *Production and Inventory Management Journal* (1st quarter 2000): 1–5.

Cayirli, Tugba, and Emre Veral. "Outpatient Scheduling in Health Care: A Review of Literature." *Production and Operations Management* 12, no. 4 (winter 2003): 519–549.

Chapman, Stephen. *Fundamentals of Production Planning and Control.* Upper Saddle River, NJ: Prentice Hall (2006).

Davis, Darwin J., and Vincent A. Mabert. "Order Dispatching and Labor Assignment in Cellular Manufacturing Systems." *Decision Sciences* 31, no. 4 (fall 2000): 745–771.

Haksever, C., B. Render, and R. Russell. *Service Management and Operations*, 2nd ed. Upper Saddle River, NJ: Prentice Hall (2000).

Leung, Joseph Y. T. *Handbook of Scheduling: Algorithms, Models, and Performance Analysis.* Boca Raton, FL: Chapman & Hall/CRC Press (2004).

Levinson, William A. *Beyond the Theory of Constraints.* New York: Productivity Press, 2007.

Mabin, V. S., and S. J. Balderstone. "The Performance of the Theory of Constraints Methodology: Analysis and Discussion of Successful TOC Applications." *International Journal of Operations and Production Management*, 23, no. 5–6 (2003): 508–596.

Mondschein, S. V., and G. Y. Weintraub. "Appointment Policies in Service Operations." *Production and Operations Management* 12, no. 2 (summer 2003): 266–286.

Morton, Thomas E., and David W. Pentico. *Heuristic Scheduling Systems.* New York: Wiley (1993).

Pinedo, M. *Scheduling: Theory, Algorithms, and Systems*, 2nd ed. Upper Saddle River, N.J.: Prentice Hall (2002).

Plenert, Gerhard, and Bill Kirchmier. *Finite Capacity Scheduling.* New York: Wiley (2000).

Render, B., R. M. Stair, and M. Hanna. *Quantitative Analysis for Management*, 9th ed. Upper Saddle River, NJ: Prentice Hall (2006).

Schaefers, J., R. Aggoune, F. Becker, and R. Fabbri. "TOC Based Planning and Scheduling Model." *International Journal of Operations and Production Management* 42, no. 13 (July 2004): 2639.

Wright, P. D., K. M. Bretthauer, and M. J. Côté. "Reexamining the Nurse Scheduling Problem." *Decision Sciences* 37, no. 1 (February 2006): 39–70.

Internet Resources

CMS Software: **www.cmssoftware.com**
Finite scheduling software: **www.asprova.com**
GE Fanuc Automation: **www.gefanuc.com**

ILOG Model Development: **www.ilog.com**
MDSI, Shop Floor Communication: **www.mdsi2.com**
Production Scheduling: **www.production-scheduling.com**

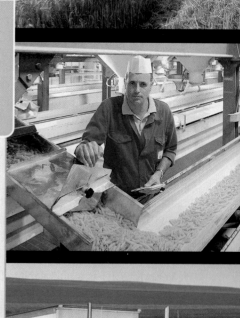

CHAPTER 16

JIT and Lean Operations

Chapter Outline

Ten OM Strategy Decisions

Design of Goods and Services

Managing Quality

Process Strategy

Location Strategies

Layout Strategies

Human Resources

Supply Chain Management

Inventory Management
    Independent Demand
    Dependent Demand
    JIT and Lean Operations

Scheduling

Maintenance

Learning Objectives

When you complete this chapter you should be able to

1. Define just-in-time, TPS,
   and lean operations
2. Define the seven wastes and the 5Ss
3. Explain JIT partnerships
4. Determine optimal setup time
5. Define kanban
6. Compute the required number
   of kanbans
7. Explain the principles of the
   Toyota Production System

Global Company Profile:
Toyota Motor Corporation

Achieving Competitive Advantage with Lean Operations at Toyota Motor Corporation

Toyota Motor Corporation, with annual sales of over 9 million cars and trucks, is the largest vehicle manufacturer in the world. Two techniques, just-in-time (JIT) and the Toyota Production System (TPS), have been instrumental in this post-WWII growth. Toyota, with a wide range of vehicles, competes head-to-head with successful long-established companies in Europe and the U.S. Taiichi Ohno, a former vice president of Toyota, created the basic framework for the world's most discussed systems for improving productivity, JIT and TPS. These two concepts provide much of the foundation for lean operations:

- Central to JIT is a philosophy of continued problem solving. In practice, JIT means making only what is needed, when it is needed. JIT provides an excellent vehicle for finding and eliminating problems because problems are easy to find in a system that has no slack. When excess inventory is eliminated, quality, layout, scheduling, and supplier issues become immediately evident—as does excess production.

- Central to TPS is a continuing effort to create and produce products under ideal conditions. Ideal conditions exist only when facilities, machines, and people are brought together, adding value without waste. Waste undermines productivity by diverting resources to excess inventory, unnecessary processing, and poor quality. Respect for people, extensive training, cross-training, and standard work practices of empowered employees focusing on driving out waste are fundamental to TPS.

Toyota's latest implementation of TPS and JIT are present at its new San Antonio plant,

Railway lines bring in engines from a Toyota plant in Alabama, axles from a supplier in Arkansas, and ship out finished trucks.

Tundras go from main assembly complex to test track or to staging area where they are shipped by truck or rail.

Toyota Logistics Services coordinates the shipment of finished Tundras by truck or rail.

Completed trucks exit here

Main assembly complex
Tundras are built here.

Land available for Toyota expansion

Supplier buildings surround main assembly complex.

Reception entrance

Large supplier sites for future expansion.

1 **Metalsa**
Truck frames

2 **Kautex**
Fuel tanks

3 **Tenneco Automotive**
Exhaust systems

4 **Curtis-Maruyasu America Inc.**
Tubing

5 **Millenium Steel Service Texas LLC**
Steel processing

6 **Green Metals Inc.**
Scrap steel recycling

7 **Avanzar Interior Technologies**
Seats and interior parts

8 **Toyotetsu Texas**
Stamped parts

9 **Futaba Industrial Texas Corp.**
Stamped Parts

10 **Toyoda-Gosei Texas LLC**
Interior/exterior parts

11 **Reyes-Amtex**
Interior parts

12 **Vutex Inc.**
Assembly services

13 **Takumi Stamping Texas Inc.**
Stamped Parts

14 **MetoKote**
E-coater

14 Suppliers outside the main plant

Outside: Toyota has a 2,000-acre site with 14 of the 21 onsite suppliers, adjacent rail lines, and near-by interstate highway. The site provides expansion space for both Toyota and for its suppliers — and provides an environment for Just-in-time.

Assembly Components
placed in cab for easy access rather than on shelves adjacent to the assembly line.

Andon
problem display board that communicates abnormalities.

Pull System
units produced only when more production is needed.

Kanban
signal that indicates production of small batches of components.

Respect for People
employees treated as knowledge workers.

Empowered Employees
can stop production, ideas solicited, quality circles, etc.

KAIZEN AREA

Kaizen Area
an area where suggestions are tested and evaluated.

Level Schedules
models mixed on production lines to meet customer orders.

Minimal machines
Proprietary machines designed for specific Toyota applications.

Reception entrance

JIT
parts and supplies delivered just as needed in the quantity needed.

Jidoka
machines with built-in devices for monitoring performance and making judgements.

Standard Work Practices
rigorous, agreed upon, documented procedures for production.

1. **AGC Automotive Americas**
Glass assemblies

2. **ARK Inc.**
Industrial waste management, recycling

3. **HERO Assemblers LLP**
Assembly of tire onto wheel

4. **HERO Logistics LLP**
Logistics

5. **PPG Industries Inc.**
Glass assemblies

6. **Reyes Automotive Group**
Interior/exterior parts

7. **Tokai Rika**
Functional parts

7 Suppliers inside the main plant

Inside: Toyota's San Antonio plant has about 2 million interior sq. ft., providing facilities for 7 of the 21 onsite suppliers, and capacity to build 200,000 pick-up trucks annually. But most importantly, inside, Toyota practices the world-class Toyota Production System.

the largest Toyota land site for an automobile assembly plant in the U.S. Interestingly, despite its annual production of 200,000 Tundra pick-up trucks, the building itself is one of the smallest in the industry. Modern automobiles have 30,000 parts, but at Toyota, independent suppliers combine many of these parts into sub-assemblies. Twenty-one of these suppliers are on site at the San

Antonio facility and transfer components to the assembly line on a JIT basis.

Operations such as these taking place in the new San Antonio plant are why Toyota continues to perform near the top in quality and maintain the lowest labor-hour assembly time in the industry. JIT, TPS, and lean operations work—and they provide a competitive advantage at Toyota Motor Corporation.

As shown in the *Global Company Profile*, the Toyota Production System (TPS) contributes to a world-class operation at Toyota Motor Corporation. In this chapter, we discuss JIT, TPS, and lean operations as approaches to continuing improvement that drive out waste and lead to world-class organizations.

JUST-IN-TIME, THE TOYOTA PRODUCTION SYSTEM, AND LEAN OPERATIONS

Just-in-time (JIT)
Continuous and forced problem solving via a focus on throughput and reduced inventory.

Toyota Production System (TPS)
Focus on continuous improvement, respect for people, and standard work practices.

Lean operations
Eliminates waste through a focus on exactly what the customer wants.

Just-in-time (JIT) is an approach of continuous and forced problem solving via a focus on throughput and reduced inventory. The **Toyota Production System (TPS)**, with its emphasis on continuous improvement, respect for people, and standard work practices, is particularly suited for assembly lines. **Lean operations** supplies the customer with exactly what the customer wants when the customer wants it, without waste, through continuous improvement. Lean operations are driven by workflow initiated by the "pull" of the customer's order. When implemented as a comprehensive manufacturing strategy, JIT, TPS, and lean systems sustain competitive advantage and result in increased overall returns.[1]

If there is any distinction between JIT, TPS, and lean operations, it is that:

- JIT emphasizes forced problem solving.
- TPS emphasizes employee learning and empowerment in an assembly-line environment.
- Lean operations emphasize understanding the customer.

However, in practice, there is little difference, and the terms are often used interchangeably. Leading organizations use the approaches and techniques that make sense for them. In this chapter, we use the term *lean operations* to encompass all of the related approaches and techniques.

Regardless of the label put on operations improvement, good production systems require that managers address three issues that are pervasive and fundamental to operations management: eliminate waste, remove variability, and speed throughput. We first introduce these three issues and then discuss the major attributes of JIT, TPS, and lean operations. Finally, we look at lean operations applied to services.

Eliminate Waste

Traditional producers have limited goals—accepting, for instance, the production of some defective parts and inventory. Lean producers set their sights on perfection; no bad parts, no inventory, only value-added activities, and no waste. Any activity that does not add value in the eyes of the customer is a waste. The customer defines product value. If the customer does not want to pay for it, it is a waste. Taiichi Ohno, noted for his work on the Toyota Production System, identified seven categories of waste. These categories have become popular in lean organizations and cover many of the ways organizations waste or lose money. Ohno's **seven wastes** are:

- *Overproduction:* Producing more than the customer orders or producing early (before it is demanded) is waste. Inventory of any kind is usually a waste.
- *Queues:* Idle time, storage, and waiting are wastes (they add no value).
- *Transportation:* Moving material between plants or between work centers and handling more than once is waste.
- *Inventory:* Unnecessary raw material, work-in-process (WIP), finished goods, and excess operating supplies add no value and are wastes.
- *Motion:* Movement of equipment or people that adds no value is waste.
- *Overprocessing:* Work performed on the product that adds no value is waste.
- *Defective product:* Returns, warranty claims, rework, and scrap are a waste.

Seven wastes
Overproduction
Queues
Transportation
Inventory
Motion
Overprocessing
Defective product

A broader perspective—one that goes beyond immediate production—suggests that other resources, such as energy, water, and air, are often wasted but should not be. Efficient, ethical, socially responsible production minimizes inputs and maximizes outputs, wasting nothing.

---

[1]Research suggests that the more JIT is comprehensive in breadth and depth, the greater overall returns will be. See Rosemary R. Fullerton and Cheryl S. McWatters, "The Production Performance Benefits from JIT Implementation," *Journal of Operations Management* 19, no. 1 (January 2001): 81–96.

For over a century, managers have used "housekeeping" for a neat, orderly, and efficient workplace and as a means of reducing waste. Operations managers have embellished "housekeeping" to include a checklist—now known as the 5Ss.[2] The Japanese developed the initial 5Ss. Not only are the 5Ss a good checklist for lean operations, they also provide an easy vehicle with which to assist the culture change that is often necessary to bring about lean operations. The **5Ss** follow:

- *Sort/segregate:* Keep what is needed and remove everything else from the work area; when in doubt, throw it out. Identify non-value items and remove them. Getting rid of these items makes space available and usually improves work flow.
- *Simplify/straighten:* Arrange and use methods analysis tools (see Chapter 7 and Chapter 10) to improve work flow and reduce wasted motion. Consider long-run and short-run ergonomic issues. Label and display for easy use only what is needed in the immediate work area. For examples of visual displays see Chapter 10, Figure 10.8.
- *Shine/sweep:* Clean daily; eliminate all forms of dirt, contamination, and clutter from the work area.
- *Standardize:* Remove variations from the process by developing standard operating procedures and checklists; good standards make the abnormal obvious. Standardize equipment and tooling so that cross-training time and cost are reduced. Train and retrain the work team so that when deviations occur, they are readily apparent to all.
- *Sustain/self-discipline:* Review periodically to recognize efforts and to motivate to sustain progress. Use visuals wherever possible to communicate and sustain progress.

U.S. managers often add two additional Ss that contribute to establishing and maintaining a lean workplace:

- *Safety:* Build good safety practices into the above five activities.
- *Support/maintenance:* Reduce variability, unplanned downtime, and costs. Integrate daily shine tasks with preventive maintenance.

The Ss provide a vehicle for continuous improvement with which all employees can identify. Operations managers need think only of the examples set by a well-run hospital emergency room or the spit-and-polish of a fire department for a benchmark. Offices and retail stores, as well as manufacturers, have also successfully used the 5Ss in their respective efforts to eliminate waste and move to lean operations.[3] Operations managers reduce waste any way possible so assets are released for other, more productive, purposes.

Remove Variability

Managers seek to remove variability caused by both internal and external factors. **Variability** is any deviation from the optimum process that delivers perfect product on time, every time. Variability is a polite word for problems. The less variability in a system, the less waste in the system. Most variability is caused by tolerating waste or by poor management. Among the many sources of variability are:

- Incomplete or inaccurate drawings or specifications
- Poor production processes that allow employees and suppliers to produce improper quantities or late or non-conforming units
- Unknown customer demands

Both JIT and inventory reduction are effective tools for identifying causes of variability. The precise timing of JIT makes variability evident, just as inventory hides variability. The removal of variability allows managers to move good materials on schedule and add value at each step of the production process.

5Ss
A lean production checklist:
Sort
Simplify
Shine
Standardize
Sustain

Variability
Any deviation from the optimum process that delivers perfect product on time, every time.

---

[2]The term 5S comes from the Japanese words seiri (*sort* and clear out), seiton (*straighten* and configure), seiso (*scrub* and cleanup), seiketsu (maintain *sanitation* and cleanliness of self and workplace), and shitsuke (*self-discipline and standardization* of these practices).

[3]Jeff Arnold and Christy Bures, "Revisiting a Retail Challenge," *Industrial Engineer* 35, no. 12 (December 2003): 38–41; and Lea A. P. Tonkin, "Elgin Sweeper Company Employees Clear a Path Toward Lean Operations with Their Lean Enterprise System," *Target* 20, no. 2 (2004): 46–52.

Improve Throughput

Throughput

The time required to move orders through the production process, from receipt to delivery.

Throughput is a measure (in units or time) that it takes to move an order from receipt to delivery. Each minute products remain on the books, costs accumulate and competitive advantage is lost. The time that an order is in the shop is called **manufacturing cycle time**. This is the time between the arrival of raw materials and the shipping of finished product. For example, phone-system manufacturer Northern Telecom now has materials pulled directly from qualified suppliers to the assembly line. This effort has reduced a segment of Northern's manufacturing cycle time from 3 weeks to just 4 hours, the incoming inspection staff from 47 to 24, and problems on the shop floor caused by defective materials by 97%. Driving down manufacturing cycle time can make a major improvement in throughput.

Manufacturing cycle time

The time between the arrival of raw materials and the shipping of finished products.

Pull system

A concept that results in material being produced only when requested and moved to where it is needed just as it is needed.

A technique for increasing throughput is a pull system. A **pull system** *pulls a* unit to where it is needed just as it is needed. Pull systems are a standard tool of JIT systems. Pull systems use signals to request production and delivery from supplying stations to stations that have production capacity available. The pull concept is used both within the immediate production process and with suppliers. By *pulling* material through the system in very small lots—just as it is needed—waste and inventory are removed. As inventory is removed, problems become evident, and continuous improvement is emphasized. Removing the cushion of inventory also reduces both investment in inventory and manufacturing cycle time. A push system dumps orders on the next downstream workstation, regardless of timeliness and resource availability. Push systems are the antithesis of JIT. Pulling material through a production process as it is needed rather than in a "push" mode typically lowers cost and improves schedule performance, enhancing customer satisfaction.

JUST-IN-TIME (JIT)

With its forced problem solving via a focus on rapid throughput and reduced inventory, JIT provides a powerful strategy for improving operations. With JIT, materials arrive *where* they are needed only *when* they are needed. When good units do not arrive just as needed, a "problem" has been identified. By driving out waste and delay in this manner, JIT reduces costs associated with excess inventory, cuts variability and waste, and improves throughput. JIT is a key ingredient of lean operations and is particularly helpful in supporting strategies of rapid response and low cost. Every moment material is held, an activity that adds value should be occurring. Consequently, as Figure 16.1 suggests, JIT often yields a competitive advantage.

Effective JIT requires a meaningful buyer–supplier partnership.

▶ *Many services have adopted JIT techniques as a normal part of their business. Restaurants like Olive Garden and Red Lobster expect and receive JIT deliveries. Both buyer and supplier expect fresh, high-quality produce delivered without fail just when it is needed. The system doesn't work any other way.*

JIT TECHNIQUES:

Suppliers:	Few vendors; Supportive supplier relationships; Quality deliveries on time, directly to work areas.
Layout:	Work-cells; Group technology; Flexible machinery; Organized workplace; Reduced space for inventory.
Inventory:	Small lot sizes; Low setup time; Specialized parts bins
Scheduling:	Zero deviation from schedules; Level schedules; Suppliers informed of schedules; Kanban techniques
Preventive maintenance:	Scheduled; Daily routine; Operator involvement
Quality production:	Statistical process control; Quality suppliers; Quality within the firm
Employee empowerment:	Empowered and cross-trained employees; Training support; Few job classifications to ensure flexibility of employees
Commitment:	Support of management, employees, and suppliers

WHICH RESULTS IN:

Rapid throughput frees assets

Quality improvement reduces waste

Cost reduction adds pricing flexibility

Variability reduction

Rework reduction

WHICH WINS ORDERS BY:

Faster response to the customer at lower cost and higher quality—

A Competitive Advantage

◄ **Figure 16.1**

JIT Contributes to Competitive Advantage

JIT Partnerships

A **JIT partnership** exists when a supplier and a purchaser work together with open communication and a goal of removing waste and driving down costs. Close relationships and trust are critical to the success of JIT. Figure 16.2 shows the characteristics of JIT partnerships. Some specific goals of JIT partnerships are:

- *Removal of unnecessary activities*, such as receiving, incoming inspection, and paperwork related to bidding, invoicing, and payment.
- *Removal of in-plant inventory* by delivery in small lots directly to the using department as needed.
- *Removal of in-transit inventory* by encouraging suppliers to locate nearby and provide frequent small shipments. The shorter the flow of material in the resource pipeline, the less inventory. Inventory can also be reduced through a technique known as *consignment*. **Consignment inventory** (see the *OM in Action* box "Lean Production at Cessna Aircraft"), a variation of vendor-managed inventory (Chapter 11), means the supplier maintains the title to the inventory until it is used. For instance, an assembly plant may find a hardware supplier that is willing to locate its warehouse where the user currently has its stockroom. In this manner, when hardware is needed, it is no farther than the stockroom, and the supplier can ship to other, perhaps smaller, purchasers from the "stockroom."
- *Obtain improved quality and reliability* through long-term commitments, communication, and cooperation.

JIT partnerships

Partnerships of suppliers and purchasers that remove waste and drive down costs for mutual benefits.

Consignment inventory

An arrangement in which the supplier maintains title to the inventory until it is used.

Leading organizations view suppliers as extensions of their own organizations and expect suppliers to be fully committed to improvement. Such relationships require a high degree of respect by both supplier and purchaser. Supplier concerns can be significant; Harley-Davidson, for example, initially had difficulty implementing JIT because supplier issues outweighed the perceived benefits.

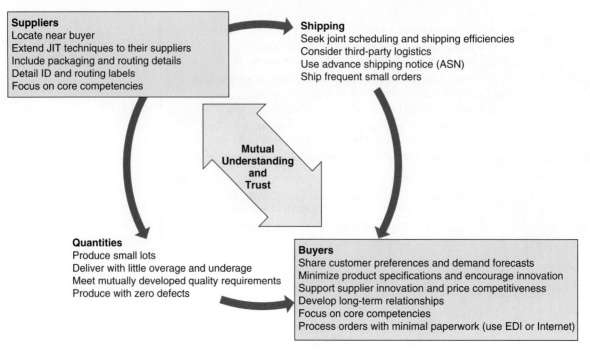

Suppliers
Locate near buyer
Extend JIT techniques to their suppliers
Include packaging and routing details
Detail ID and routing labels
Focus on core competencies

Shipping
Seek joint scheduling and shipping efficiencies
Consider third-party logistics
Use advance shipping notice (ASN)
Ship frequent small orders

**Mutual
Understanding
and
Trust**

Quantities
Produce small lots
Deliver with little overage and underage
Meet mutually developed quality requirements
Produce with zero defects

Buyers
Share customer preferences and demand forecasts
Minimize product specifications and encourage innovation
Support supplier innovation and price competitiveness
Develop long-term relationships
Focus on core competencies
Process orders with minimal paperwork (use EDI or Internet)

▲ **Figure 16.2** **Characteristics of JIT Partnerships**

Concerns of Suppliers

Successful JIT partnerships require that supplier concerns be addressed. These concerns include:

1. *Diversification:* Suppliers may not want to tie themselves to long-term contracts with one customer. The suppliers' perception is that they reduce their risk if they have a variety of customers.
2. *Scheduling:* Many suppliers have little faith in the purchaser's ability to produce orders to a smooth, coordinated schedule.
3. *Changes:* Engineering or specification changes can play havoc with JIT because of inadequate lead time for suppliers to implement the necessary changes.
4. *Quality:* Capital budgets, processes, or technology may limit quality.
5. *Lot sizes:* Suppliers may see frequent delivery in small lots as a way to transfer buyer's holding costs to suppliers.

OM in Action   **Lean Production at Cessna Aircraft**

When Cessna Aircraft opened its new plant in Independence, Kansas, it saw the opportunity to switch from a craftwork mentality producing small single-engine planes to a lean manufacturing system. In doing so, Cessna adopted three lean practices.

First, Cessna set up consignment- and vendor-managed inventories with several of its suppliers. Blanket purchase orders allow Honeywell, for example, to maintain a 30-day supply of avionic parts onsite. Other vendors were encouraged to use a nearby warehouse to keep parts that could then be delivered daily to the production line.

Second, Cessna managers committed to cross-training, in which team members learn the duties of other team members and can shift across assembly lines as needed. To develop these technical skills, Cessna brought in 60 retired assembly-line workers to mentor and teach new employees. Employees were taught to work as a team and to assume responsibility for their team's quality.

Third, the company used group technology and manufacturing cells to move away from a batch process that resulted in large inventories and unsold planes. Now, Cessna pulls product through its plant only when a specific order is placed.

These commitments to manufacturing efficiency are part of the lean operations that has made Cessna the world's largest manufacturer of single-engine aircraft.

Sources: **www.cessna.com** (2007); *Strategic Finance* (November 2002): 32; *Purchasing* (September 4, 2003): 25–30; and *Fortune* (May 1, 2000): 1222B.

JIT LAYOUT

JIT layouts reduce another kind of waste—movement. The movement of material on a factory floor (or paper in an office) does not add value. Consequently, managers want flexible layouts that reduce the movement of both people and material. JIT layouts place material directly in the location where needed. For instance, an assembly line should be designed with delivery points next to the line so material need not be delivered first to a receiving department and then moved again. This is what VF Corporation's Wrangler Division in Greensboro, North Carolina, did; denim is now delivered directly to the line. Toyota has gone one step farther and places hardware and components in the chassis of each vehicle moving down the assembly line. This is not only convenient, but it allows Toyota to save space and opens areas adjacent to the assembly line previously occupied by shelves. When a layout reduces distance, firms often save labor and space and may have the added bonus of eliminating potential areas for accumulation of unwanted inventory. Table 16.1 provides a list of layout tactics.

Distance Reduction

Reducing distance is a major contribution of work cells, work centers, and focused factories (see Chapter 9). The days of long production lines and huge economic lots, with goods passing through monumental, single-operation machines, are gone. Now firms use work cells, often arranged in a U shape, containing several machines performing different operations. These work cells are often based on group technology codes (as discussed in Chapter 5). Group technology codes help identify components with similar characteristics so we can group them into families. Once families are identified, work cells are built for them. The result can be thought of as a small product-oriented facility where the "product" is actually a group of similar products—a family of products. The cells produce one good unit at a time, and ideally they produce the units *only* after a customer orders them.

Increased Flexibility

Modern work cells are designed so they can be easily rearranged to adapt to changes in volume, product improvements, or even new designs. Almost nothing in these new departments is bolted down. This same concept of layout flexibility applies to office environments. Not only is most office furniture and equipment movable, but so are office walls, computer connections, and telecommunications. Equipment is modular. Layout flexibility aids the changes that result from product *and* process improvements that are inevitable with a philosophy of continuous improvement.

Impact on Employees

Employees working together are cross trained so they can bring flexibility and efficiency to the work cell. JIT layouts allow employees to work together so they can tell each other about problems and opportunities for improvement. When layouts provide for sequential operations, feedback can be immediate. Defects are waste. When workers produce units one at a time, they test each product or component at each subsequent production stage. Machines in work cells with self-testing poka-yoke functions detect defects and stop automatically when they occur. Before JIT, defective products were replaced from inventory. Because surplus inventory is not kept in JIT facilities, there are no such buffers. Getting it right the first time is critical.

Reduced Space and Inventory

Because JIT layouts reduce travel distance, they also reduce inventory by removing space for inventory. When there is little space, inventory must be moved in very small lots or even single units. Units are always moving because there is no storage. For instance, each month Security Pacific Corporation's focused facility sorts 7 million checks, processes 5 million statements, and mails 190,000 customer statements. With a JIT layout, mail processing time has been reduced by 33%, salary costs by tens of thousands of dollars per year, floor space by 50%, and in-process waiting lines by 75% to 90%. Storage, including shelves and drawers, has been removed.

▼ **Table 16.1**

JIT Layout Tactics

Build work cells for families of products

Include a large number of operations in a small area

Minimize distance

Design little space for inventory

Improve employee communication

Use poka-yoke devices

Build flexible or movable equipment

Cross-train workers to add flexibility

In a JIT system, each worker inspects the arriving part, knowing that the part must be good before it goes on to the next "customer."

Just-in-time tactics are being incorporated in manufacturing to improve quality, drive down inventory investment, and reduce other costs. However, JIT is also established practice in restaurants, where customers expect it, and a necessity in the produce business, where there is little choice. Pacific Pre-Cut Produce, a $14 million fruit and vegetable processing company in Tracy, California, holds inventory to zero. Buyers are in action in the wee hours of the morning. At 6 A.M., produce production crews show up. Orders for very specific cuts and mixtures of fruit and vegetable salads and stir-fry ingredients for supermarkets, restaurants, and institutional kitchens pour in from 8 A.M. until 4 P.M. Shipping begins at 10 P.M. and continues until the last order is filled and loaded at 5 A.M. the next morning. Inventories are once again zero, and things are relatively quiet for an hour or so; then the routine starts again. Pacific Pre-Cut Produce has accomplished a complete cycle of purchase, manufacture, and shipping in about 24 hours.

VP Bob Borzone calls the process the ultimate in mass customization. "We buy everything as a bulk commodity, then slice and dice it to fit the exact requirements of the end user. There are 20 different stir-fry mixes. Some customers want the snow peas clipped on both ends, some just on one. Some want only red bell peppers in the mix, some only yellow. You tailor the product to the customer's requirements. You're trying to satisfy the need of a lot of end users, and each restaurant and retailer wants to look different."

Sources: Supermarket News (September 27, 2004): 31; *Inbound Logistics* (August 1997): 26–32; and *Progressive Grocer* (January 1998): 51–56.

JIT INVENTORY

Inventories in production and distribution systems often exist "just in case" something goes wrong. That is, they are used just in case some variation from the production plan occurs. The "extra" inventory is then used to cover variations or problems. Effective inventory tactics require "just in time," not "just in case." **Just-in-time inventory** is the minimum inventory necessary to keep a perfect system running. With just-in-time inventory, the exact amount of goods arrives at the moment it is needed, not a minute before or a minute after. The *OM in Action* box "Let's Try Zero Inventory" suggests that it can be done. Some useful JIT inventory tactics are shown in Table 16.2 and discussed in more detail in the following sections.

Just-in-time inventory

The minimum inventory necessary to keep a perfect system running.

Reduce Variability

The idea behind JIT is to eliminate inventory that hides variability in the production system. This concept is illustrated in Figure 16.3, which shows a lake full of rocks. The water in the lake represents inventory flow, and the rocks represent problems such as late deliveries, machine breakdowns, and poor personnel performance. The water level in the lake hides variability and problems. Because inventory hides problems, they are hard to find.

▶ **Figure 16.3**

Inventory Has Two Costs, One for Holding the Inventory and One for the Problems It Hides— Just as Water in a Lake Hides the Rocks

 Video 16.1

Sailing through the Problems of Excess Inventory

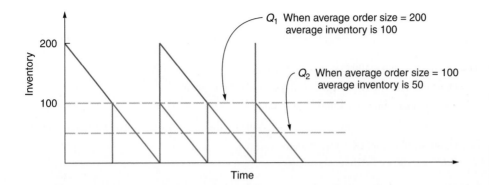

◀ **Figure 16.4**

Frequent Orders Reduce Average Inventory

A lower order size increases the number of orders and total ordering cost but reduces average inventory and total holding cost.

Reduce Inventory

Operations managers move toward JIT by first removing inventory. Reducing inventory uncovers the "rocks" in Figure 16.3(a) that represent the variability and problems currently being tolerated. With reduced inventory, management chips away at the exposed problems until the lake is clear. After the lake is clear, managers make additional cuts in inventory and continue to chip away at the next level of exposed problems (see Figure 16.3[b]). Ultimately, there will be virtually no inventory and no problems (variability).

Dell estimates that the rapid changes in technology costs $\frac{1}{2}\%$ to 2% of its inventory's value *each week*. Shigeo Shingo, co-developer of the Toyota JIT system, says, "Inventory is evil." He is not far from the truth. If inventory itself is not evil, it hides evil at great cost.

"Inventory is evil."
Shigeo Shingo

Reduce Lot Sizes

Just-in-time has also come to mean elimination of waste by reducing investment in inventory. The key to JIT is producing good product in small lot sizes. Reducing the size of batches can be a major help in reducing inventory and inventory costs. As we saw in Chapter 12, when inventory usage is constant, the average inventory level is the sum of the maximum inventory plus the minimum inventory divided by 2. Figure 16.4 shows that lowering the order size increases the number of orders but drops inventory levels.

Ideally, in a JIT environment, order size is one and single units are being pulled from one adjacent process to another. More realistically, analysis of the process, transportation time, and containers used for transport are considered when determining lot size. Such analysis typically results in a small lot size but a lot size larger than one. Once a lot size has been determined, the EOQ production order quantity model can be modified to determine the desired setup time. We saw in Chapter 12 that the production order quantity model takes the form:

$$Q^* = \sqrt{\frac{2DS}{H[1-(d/p)]}} \qquad (16\text{-}1)$$

where D = Annual demand
        S = Setup cost
        H = Holding cost
        d = Daily demand
        p = Daily production

Example 1 shows how to determine the desired setup time.

▼ **Table 16.2**

JIT Inventory Tactics

Use a pull system to move inventory
Reduce lot size
Develop just-in-time delivery systems with suppliers
Deliver directly to the point of use
Perform to schedule
Reduce setup time
Use group technology

EXAMPLE 1

Determining optimal setup time

Crate Furniture, Inc., a firm that produces rustic furniture, desires to move toward a reduced lot size. Crate Furniture's production analyst, Aleda Roth, determined that a 2-hour production cycle would be acceptable between two departments. Further, she concluded that a setup time that would accommodate the 2-hour cycle time should be achieved.

Approach: Roth developed the following data and procedure to determine optimum setup time analytically:

D = Annual demand = 400,000 units

d = Daily demand = 400,000 per 250 days = 1,600 units per day

p = Daily production rate = 4,000 units per day

Q = EOQ desired = 400 (which is the 2-hour demand; that is, 1,600 per day per four 2-hour periods)

H = Holding cost = $20 per unit per year

S = Setup cost (to be determined)

Solution: Roth determines that the cost, on an hourly basis, of setting up equipment is $30. Further, she computes that the setup cost per setup should be:

$$Q = \sqrt{\frac{2DS}{H(1-d/p)}}$$

$$Q^2 = \frac{2DS}{H(1-d/p)}$$

$$S = \frac{(Q^2)(H)(1-d/p)}{2D}$$

$$S = \frac{(400)^2(20)(1-1,600/4,000)}{2(400,000)}$$

$$= \frac{(3,200,000)(0.6)}{800,000} = \$2.40$$

Setup time = $2.40/(hourly labor rate)

= $2.40/($30 per hour)

= 0.08 hour, or 4.8 minutes

Learning Objective

4. Determine optimal set-up time

Insight: Now, rather than produce components in large lots, Crate Furniture can produce in a 2-hour cycle with the advantage of an inventory turnover of four *per day*.

Learning exercise: If labor cost goes to $40 per hour, what should be the setup time? [Answer: .06 hour, or 3.6 minutes.]

Related problems: 16.8, 16.9, 16.10

Only two changes need to be made for small-lot material flow to work. First, material handling and work flow need to be improved. With short production cycles, there can be very little wait time. Improving material handling is usually easy and straightforward. The second change is more challenging, and that is a radical reduction in setup times. We discuss setup reduction next.

Reduce Setup Costs

Both inventory and the cost of holding it go down as the inventory-reorder quantity and the maximum inventory level drop. However, because inventory requires incurring an ordering or setup cost that must be applied to the units produced, managers tend to purchase (or produce) large orders. With large orders, each unit purchased or ordered absorbs only a small part of the setup cost. Consequently, the way to drive down lot sizes *and* reduce average inventory is to reduce setup cost, which in turn lowers the optimum order size.

Reduced lot sizes must be accompanied by reduced setup times; otherwise, the setup cost is assigned to fewer units.

The effect of reduced setup costs on total cost and lot size is shown in Figure 16.5. Moreover, smaller lot sizes hide fewer problems. In many environments, setup cost is highly correlated with setup time. In a manufacturing facility, setups usually require a substantial amount of preparation. Much of the preparation required by a setup can be done prior to shutting down the machine or process. Setup times can be reduced substantially, as shown in Figure 16.6. For instance, in Kodak's Guadalajara, Mexico, plant a team reduced the setup time to change a bearing from 12 hours to 6 minutes![4] This is the kind of progress that is typical of world-class manufacturers.

[4]Frank Carguello and Marty Levin, "Excellence at Work in Guadalajara, Mexico, Operation," *Target* 15, no. 3 (3rd quarter 1999): 51–53.

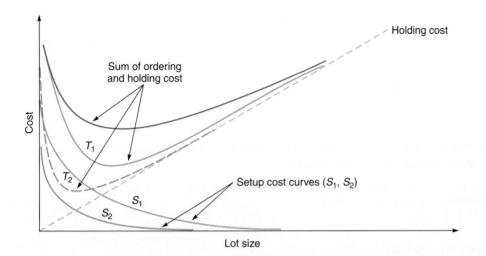

More frequent orders require reducing setup costs; otherwise, inventory costs will rise. As the setup costs are lowered (from S_1 to S_2), inventory costs also fall (from T_1 to T_2).

Just as setup costs can be reduced at a machine in a factory, setup time can also be reduced during the process of getting the order ready. It does little good to drive down factory setup time from hours to minutes if orders are going to take 2 weeks to process or "set up" in the office. This is exactly what happens in organizations that forget that JIT concepts have applications in offices as well as in the factory. Reducing setup time (and cost) is an excellent way to reduce inventory investment and to improve productivity.

JIT SCHEDULING

Effective schedules, communicated both within the organization and to outside suppliers, support JIT. Better scheduling also improves the ability to meet customer orders, drives down inventory by allowing smaller lot sizes, and reduces work-in-process. For instance, Ford Motor Company now ties some suppliers to its final assembly schedule. Ford communicates its schedules to bumper manufacturer Polycon Industries from the Ford Oakville production control system. The scheduling system describes the style and color of the bumper needed for each vehicle moving down the final assembly line. The scheduling system transmits the information to portable terminals carried by Polycon warehouse personnel who load the bumpers onto conveyors leading to the loading dock. The bumpers are then trucked 50 miles to the Ford plant. Total time is 4 hours. Table 16.3 suggests several items that can contribute to achieving these goals, but two techniques (in addition to communicating schedules) are paramount. They are *level schedules* and *kanban*.

▼ **Table 16.3**

JIT Scheduling Tactics

Communicate schedules to suppliers
Make level schedules
Freeze part of the schedule
Perform to schedule
Seek one-piece-make and one-piece-move
Eliminate waste
Produce in small lots
Use kanbans
Make each operation produce a perfect part

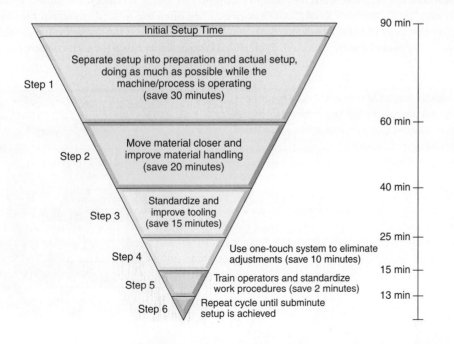

◀ **Figure 16.6**

Steps for Reducing Setup Times

Reduced setup times are a major JIT component.

JIT Level Material-Use Approach

AA BBB C AA BBB C AA BBB C AA BBB C AA BBB C AA BBB C AA BBB C AA BBB C

Large-Lot Approach

AAAAAA BBBBBBBBB CCC AAAAAA BBBBBBBBB CCC AAAAAA BBBBBBBBB CCC

Time

▲ **Figure 16.7**   Scheduling Small Lots of Parts A, B, and C Increases Flexibility to Meet Customer Demand and Reduces Inventory

The JIT approach to scheduling produces just as many of each model per time period as the large-lot approach, provided that setup times are lowered.

Level Schedules

Level schedules

Scheduling products so that each day's production meets the demand for that day.

Level schedules process frequent small batches rather than a few large batches. Because this technique schedules many small lots that are always changing, it has on occasion been called "jelly bean" scheduling. Figure 16.7 contrasts a traditional large-lot approach using large batches with a JIT level schedule using many small batches. The operations manager's task is to make and move small lots so the level schedule is economical. This requires success with the issues discussed in this chapter that allow small lots. As lots get smaller, the constraints may change and become increasingly challenging. At some point, processing a unit or two may not be feasible. The constraint may be the way units are sold and shipped (four to a carton), or an expensive paint changeover (on an automobile assembly line), or the proper number of units in a sterilizer (for a food-canning line).

The scheduler may find that *freezing* the portion of the schedule closest to due dates allows the production system to function and the schedule to be met. Freezing means not allowing changes to be part of the schedule. Operations managers expect the schedule to be achieved with no deviations from the schedule.

Kanban

Kanban

The Japanese word for *card*, which has come to mean "signal"; a kanban system moves parts through production via a "pull" from a signal.

One way to achieve small lot sizes is to move inventory through the shop only as needed rather than *pushing* it on to the next workstation whether or not the personnel there are ready for it. As noted earlier, when inventory is moved only as needed, it is referred to as a *pull* system, and the ideal lot size is one. The Japanese call this system *kanban*. Kanbans allow arrivals at a work center to match (or nearly match) the processing time.

Kanban is a Japanese word for *card*. In their effort to reduce inventory, the Japanese use systems that "pull" inventory through work centers. They often use a "card" to signal the need for another container of material—hence the name *kanban*. *The card is the authorization for the next container of material to be produced.* Typically, a kanban signal exists for each container of items

▶ *A kanban need not be as formal as signal lights or empty carts. The cook in a fast-food restaurant knows that when six cars are in line, eight meat patties and six orders of french fries should be cooking.*

Diagram of Outbound Stockpoint with Warning-Signal Marker

Signal marker hanging on post for part Z405 shows that production should start for that part. The post is located so that workers in normal locations can easily see it.

Signal marker on stack of boxes.

Part numbers mark location of specific part.

to be obtained. An order for the container is then initiated by each kanban and "pulled" from the producing department or supplier. A sequence of kanbans "pulls" the material through the plant.

The system has been modified in many facilities so that even though it is called a *kanban*, the card itself does not exist. In some cases, an empty position on the floor is sufficient indication that the next container is needed. In other cases, some sort of signal, such as a flag or rag (Figure 16.8) alerts that it is time for the next container.

When there is visual contact between producer and user, the process works like this:

1. The user removes a standard-size container of parts from a small storage area, as shown in Figure 16.8.
2. The signal at the storage area is seen by the producing department as authorization to replenish the using department or storage area. Because there is an optimum lot size, the producing department may make several containers at a time.

Figure 16.9 shows how a kanban works, pulling units as needed from production. This system is similar to the resupply that occurs in your neighborhood supermarket: The customer buys; the stock clerk observes the shelf or receives notice from the end-of-day sales list and restocks. When the limited supply, if any, in the store's storage is depleted, a "pull" signal is sent to the warehouse, distributor, or manufacturer for resupply, usually that night. The complicating factor in a manufacturing firm is the time needed for actual manufacturing (production) to take place.

Learning Objective

5. Define kanban

▲ **Figure 16.9** **Kanban Signals "Pull" Material Through the Production Process**

As a customer "pulls" an order from finished goods, a signal (card) is sent to the final assembly area. The final assembly area produces and resupplies finished goods. When final assembly needs components, it sends a signal to its suppliers, a subassembly area and a work cell. These areas supply final assembly. The work cell, in turn, sends a signal to the raw material supplier, and the subassembly area notifies the work cell and purchased parts supplier of a requirement.

▶ *Kanban containers at Harley-Davidson are specially made for individual parts, and many feature padding to protect the finish. These containers serve an important role in inventory reduction: Because they are the only place inventory is stored, they serve as a signal to supply new parts to the line. After all the pieces have been removed, the container is returned to its originating cell, signaling the worker there to build more.*

 Video 16.2

JIT at Harley-Davidson

Several additional points regarding kanbans may be helpful:

- When the producer and user are not in visual contact, a card can be used; otherwise, a light or flag or empty spot on the floor may be adequate.
- Because a pull station may require several resupply components, several kanban pull techniques can be used for different products at the same pull station.
- Usually, each card controls a specific quantity or parts, although multiple card systems are used if the producing work cell produces several components or if the lot size is different from the move size.
- In an MRP system (see Chapter 14), the schedule can be thought of as a "build" authorization and the kanban as a type of "pull" system that initiates the actual production.
- The kanban cards provide a direct control (limit) on the amount of work-in-process between cells.
- If there is an immediate storage area, a two-card system may be used—one card circulates between user and storage area, and the other circulates between the storage area and the producing area.

Determining the Number of Kanban Cards or Containers   The number of kanban cards, or containers, in a JIT system sets the amount of authorized inventory. To determine the number of containers moving back and forth between the using area and the producing areas, management first sets the size of each container. This is done by computing the lot size, using a model such as the production order quantity model (discussed in Chapter 12 and shown again on page 649 in Equation [16-1]). Setting the number of containers involves knowing (1) lead time needed to produce a container of parts and (2) the amount of safety stock needed to account for variability or uncertainty in the system. The number of kanban cards is computed as follows:

$$\text{Number of kanbans (containers)} = \frac{\text{Demand during lead time} + \text{Safety stock}}{\text{Size of container}}$$

Example 2 illustrates how to calculate the number of kanbans needed.

EXAMPLE 2

Determining the number of kanban containers

Hobbs Bakery produces short runs of cakes that are shipped to grocery stores. The owner, Ken Hobbs, wants to try to reduce inventory by changing to a kanban system. He has developed the following data and asked you to finish the project.

$$\text{Daily demand} = 500 \text{ cakes}$$

$$\text{Production lead time} = \text{Wait time} + \text{Material handling time} + \text{Processing time} = 2 \text{ days}$$

$$\text{Safety stock} = \tfrac{1}{2} \text{ day}$$

$$\text{Container size (determined on a production order size EOQ basis)} = 250 \text{ cakes}$$

Approach: Having determined that the EOQ size is 250, we then determine the number of kanbans (containers) needed.

Solution: Demand during lead time (= Lead time × Daily demand = 2 days × 500 cakes =) 1,000

Safety stock = 250

$$\text{Number of kanbans (containers) needed} =$$
$$\frac{\text{Demand during lead time} + \text{Safety stock}}{\text{Container size}} = \frac{1,000 + 250}{250} = 5$$

Insight: Once the reorder point is hit, five containers should be released.

Learning exercise: If lead time drops to 1 day, how many containers are needed? [Answer: 3.]

Related problems: 16.1, 16.2, 16.3, 16.4, 16.5, 16.6

Learning Objective

6. Compute the required number of kanbans

Advantages of Kanban   Containers are typically very small, usually a matter of a few hours' worth of production. Such a system requires tight schedules. Small quantities must be produced several times a day. The process must run smoothly with little variability in quality of lead time because any shortage has an almost immediate impact on the entire system. Kanban places added emphasis on meeting schedules, reducing the time and cost required by setups, and economical material handling.

Whether it is called kanban or something else, the advantages of small inventory and *pulling* material through the plant only when needed are significant. For instance, small batches allow only a very limited amount of faulty or delayed material. Problems are immediately evident. Numerous aspects of inventory are bad; only one aspect—availability—is good. Among the bad aspects are poor quality, obsolescence, damage, occupied space, committed assets, increased insurance, increased material handling, and increased accidents. Kanban systems put downward pressure on all these negative aspects of inventory.

In-plant kanban systems often use standardized, reusable containers that protect the specific quantities to be moved. Such containers are also desirable in the supply chain. Standardized containers reduce weight and disposal costs, generate less wasted space in trailers, and require less labor to pack, unpack, and prepare items.

The manufacturing inventory to sales ratio continues to drop, thanks in large part to JIT.

JIT QUALITY

The relationship between JIT and quality is a strong one. They are related in three ways. First, JIT cuts the cost of obtaining good quality. This saving occurs because scrap, rework, inventory investment, and damage costs are buried in inventory. JIT forces down inventory; therefore, fewer bad units are produced and fewer units must be reworked. In short, whereas inventory *hides* bad quality, JIT immediately *exposes* it.

◄ *The New United Motor Manufacturing (NUMMI) plant in Fremont, California, is a joint venture between Toyota and General Motors and builds cars for both companies. The plant was, of course, designed as a Toyota Production System (TPS), using just-in-time (JIT). Management even moved a water tower to ensure that new loading docks would facilitate JIT arrivals and JIT movement of parts within the plant. This plant, like most JIT facilities, also empowers employees so they can stop the entire production line by pulling the overhead cord if any quality problems are spotted.*

Learning Objective

7. Explain the principles of
the Toyota Production System

Second, JIT improves quality. As JIT shrinks queues and lead time, it keeps evidence of errors fresh and limits the number of potential sources of error. In effect, JIT creates an early warning system for quality problems so that fewer bad units are produced and feedback is immediate. This advantage can accrue both within the firm and with goods received from outside vendors.

Finally, better quality means fewer buffers are needed and, therefore, a better, easier-to-employ JIT system can exist. Often the purpose of keeping inventory is to protect against unreliable quality. If consistent quality exists, JIT allows firms to reduce all costs associated with inventory. Table 16.4 suggests some requirements for quality in a JIT environment.

TOYOTA PRODUCTION SYSTEM

Toyota Motor's Eiji Toyoda and Taiichi Ohno are given credit for the Toyota Production System (TPS) (see the *Global Company Profile* that opens this chapter). Three core components of TPS are continuous improvement, respect for people, and standard work practice.

Continuous Improvement

Continuous improvement under TPS means building an organizational culture and instilling in its people a value system stressing that processes can be improved—indeed, that improvement is an integral part of every employee's job. Instilling these values begins at recruiting and continues through extensive and continuing training. One of the reasons continuous improvement works at Toyota, we should note, is because of another core value at Toyota, Toyota's respect for people.

Respect for People

At Toyota, people are recruited, trained, and treated as knowledge workers. Aided by aggressive cross-training and few job classifications, TPS engages the mental as well as physical capacities of employees in the challenging task of improving operations. Employees are empowered. They are empowered to make improvements. They are empowered to stop machines and processes when quality problems exist. Indeed, empowered employees are a necessary part of TPS. This means that those tasks that have traditionally been assigned to staff are moved to employees. Toyota recognizes that employees know more about their jobs than anyone else. TPS respects employees by giving them the opportunity to enrich both their jobs and their lives.

Standard Work Practice

Standard work practice at Toyota includes these underlying principles:

- Work is completely specified as to content, sequence, timing, and outcome.
- Internal and external customer–supplier connections are direct, specifying personnel, methods, timing, and quantity.
- Product and service flows are to be simple and direct. Goods and services are directed to a specific person or machine.
- Improvements in the system must be made in accordance with the "scientific method," at the lowest possible level in the organization.[5]

TPS requires that activities, connections, and flows include built-in tests to automatically signal problems. Any gap between what is expected and what occurs becomes immediately evident. The education and training of Toyota's employees and the responsiveness of the system to problems make the seemingly rigid system flexible and adaptable to changing circumstances. The result is ongoing improvements in reliability, flexibility, safety, and efficiency.

---

[5]Adopted from Steven J. Spear, "Learning to Lead at Toyota," *Harvard Business Review* 82, no. 5 (May 2004): 78–86; Steven Spear and H. Kent Bowen, "Decoding the DNA of the Toyota Production System," *Harvard Business Review* 77, no. 5 (September–October 1999): 97–106.

LEAN OPERATIONS

Lean production can be thought of as the end result of a well-run OM function. While JIT and TPS tend to have an *internal* focus, lean production begins *externally* with a focus on the customer. Understanding what the customer wants and ensuring customer input and feedback are starting points for lean production. Lean operations means identifying customer value by analyzing all the activities required to produce the product and then optimizing the entire process from the customer's perspective. The manager identifies what creates value for the customer and what does not.

Building a Lean Organization

The transition to lean production is difficult. Building an organizational culture where learning, empowerment, and continuous improvement are the norm is a challenge. However, organizations that focus on JIT, quality, and employee empowerment are often lean producers. Such firms drive out activities that do not add value in the eyes of the customer: they include leaders like United Parcel Service, Harley-Davidson, and, of course, Toyota. Even traditionally craft-oriented organizations such as Louis Vuitton (see the *OM in Action* box) find improved productivity with lean operations. Lean operations adopt a philosophy of minimizing waste by striving for perfection through continuous learning, creativity, and teamwork. They tend to share the following attributes:

- *Use JIT techniques* to eliminate virtually all inventory.
- *Build systems that help employees* produce a perfect part every time.
- *Reduce space requirements* by minimizing travel distance.
- *Develop partnerships with suppliers*, helping them to understand the needs of the ultimate customer.
- *Educate suppliers* to accept responsibility for satisfying end customer needs.
- *Eliminate all but value-added activities.* Material handling, inspection, inventory, and rework are the likely targets because these do not add value to the product.
- *Develop employees* by constantly improving job design, training, employee commitment, teamwork, and empowerment.
- *Make jobs challenging*, pushing responsibility to the lowest level possible.
- *Build worker flexibility* through cross-training and reducing job classifications.

Success requires the full commitment and involvement of managers, employees, and suppliers. The rewards that lean producers reap are spectacular. Lean producers often become benchmark performers.

OM in Action   Going Lean at Louis Vuitton

LVMH Moet Hennessy Louis Vuitton is the world's largest luxury-goods company. Its Louis Vuitton unit, responsible for half of the company's profit, makes very upscale handbags and enjoys a rich markup on sales of about $5 billion. The return-on-investment is excellent, but sales could be even better: the firm often can't match production with the sales pace of a successful new product. In the high fashion business that is all about speed-to-market, this is bad news; a massive overhaul was in order.

Changes on the factory floor were key to the overhaul. The traditional approach to manufacturing at Louis Vuitton was batch production: craftsmen, working on partially completed handbags, performed specialized tasks such as cutting, gluing, sewing, and assembly. Carts moved batches of semi-finished handbags on to the next workstation. It took 20 to 30 workers 8 days to make a handbag. And defects were high. Lean manufacturing looked like the way to go.

Craftsmen were retrained to do multiple tasks in small U-shaped work cells. Each work cell now contains 6 to 12

cross-trained workers and the necessary sewing machines and work tables. Consistent with one-piece flow, the work is passed through the cell from worker to worker. The system reduces inventory and allows workers to detect flaws earlier. Rework under the old system was sometimes as high as 50% and internal losses as high as 4%. Returns are down by two-thirds. The system has not only improved productivity and quality, it also allows Louis Vuitton to respond to the market faster—with daily scheduling as opposed to weekly scheduling.

Sources: The Wall Street Journal (October 9, 2006): A1, A15 and (January 31, 2006): A1, A13.

LEAN OPERATIONS IN SERVICES

The features of lean operations apply to services just as they do in other sectors. Here are some examples applied to suppliers, layout, inventory, and scheduling in the service sector.

Suppliers   As we have noted, virtually every restaurant deals with its suppliers on a JIT basis. Those that do not are usually unsuccessful. The waste is too evident—food spoils and customers complain or get sick.

Layouts   Lean layouts are required in restaurant kitchens, where cold food must be served cold and hot food hot. McDonald's, for example, has reconfigured its kitchen layout at great expense to drive seconds out of the production process, thereby speeding delivery to customers. With the new process, McDonald's can produce made-to-order hamburgers in 45 seconds. Layouts also make a difference in airline baggage claim, where customers expect their bags just-in-time.

Inventory   Stockbrokers drive inventory down to nearly zero every day. Most sell and buy orders occur on an immediate basis because an unexecuted sell or buy order is not acceptable to most clients. A broker may be in serious trouble if left holding an unexecuted trade. Similarly, McDonald's reduces inventory waste by maintaining a finished-goods inventory of only 10 minutes; after that, it is thrown away. Hospitals, such as Arnold Palmer (described in this chapter's Video Case Study), manage JIT inventory and low safety stocks for many items. Even critical supplies such as pharmaceuticals may be held to low levels by developing community networks as backup systems. In this manner, if one pharmacy runs out of a needed drug, another member of the network can supply it until the next day's shipment arrives.

Scheduling   At airline ticket counters, the focus of the system is customer demand, but rather than being satisfied by inventory availability, demand is satisfied by personnel. Through elaborate scheduling, ticket counter personnel show up just-in-time to cover peaks in customer demand. In other words, rather than "things" inventoried, personnel are scheduled. At a salon, the focus is only slightly different: the *customer* is scheduled to assure prompt service. At McDonald's and Wal-Mart, scheduling of personnel is down to 15-minute increments, based on precise forecasting of demand. Additionally, at McDonald's, production is done in small lots to ensure that fresh, hot hamburgers are delivered just-in-time. In short, both personnel and production are scheduled to meet specific demand. Notice that in all three of these lean organizations— the airline ticket counter, the salon, and McDonald's—scheduling is a key ingredient. Excellent forecasts drive those schedules. Those forecasts may be very elaborate, with seasonal, daily, and even hourly components in the case of the airline ticket counter (holiday sales, flight time, etc.), seasonal and weekly components at the salon (holidays and Fridays create special problems), or down to a few minutes at McDonald's.

Lean hospitals have suppliers bring ready-to-use supplies directly to storage areas, nurses' stations, and operating rooms. Only a 24-hour reserve is maintained.

Video 16.3

JIT at Arnold Palmer Hospital

▶ *Lean operations take on an unusual form in an operating room. McKesson-General, Baxter International, and many other hospital suppliers provide surgical supplies for hospitals on a JIT basis. (1) They deliver prepackaged surgical supplies based on hospital operating schedules, and (2) the surgical packages themselves are prepared so supplies are available in the sequence in which they will be used during surgery.*

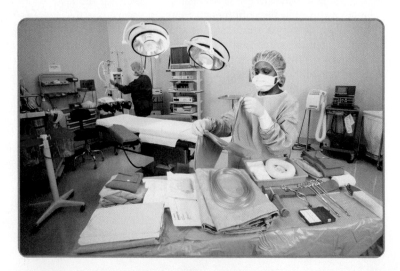

To deliver goods and services to customers under continuously changing demand, suppliers need to be reliable, inventories lean, cycle times short, and schedules nimble. A lean focus engages and empowers employees to create and deliver the customer's perception of value, eliminating whatever does not contribute to this goal. Lean operations are currently being developed with great success in many firms, regardless of their products. Lean techniques are widely used in both goods-producing and service-producing firms; they just look different.

Summary

JIT, TPS, and lean operations are philosophies of continuous improvement. Lean operations focus on customer desires, TPS focuses on respect for people and standard work practices, and JIT focuses on driving out waste by reducing inventory. But all three approaches reduce waste in the production process. And because waste is found in anything that does not add value, organizations that implement these techniques are adding value more efficiently than other firms. The expectation of these systems is that empowered employees work with committed management to build systems that respond to customers with ever-lower cost and higher quality.

Key Terms

Just-in-time (JIT) *(p. 642)*
Toyota Production System (TPS) *(p. 642)*
Lean operations *(p. 642)*
Seven wastes *(p. 642)*
5Ss *(p. 643)*

Variability *(p. 643)*
Throughput *(p. 644)*
Manufacturing cycle time *(p. 644)*
Pull system *(p. 644)*
JIT partnerships *(p. 645)*

Consignment inventory *(p. 645)*
Just-in-time inventory *(p. 648)*
Level schedules *(p. 652)*
Kanban *(p. 652)*

Solved Problem

 Virtual Office Hours help is available on Student DVD.

Solved Problem 16.1

Krupp Refrigeration, Inc., is trying to reduce inventory and wants you to install a kanban system for compressors on one of its assembly lines. Determine the size of the kanban and the number of kanbans (containers) needed.

Setup cost = \$10

Annual holding cost per compressor = \$100

Daily production = 200 compressors

Annual usage = 25,000 (50 weeks × 5 days each
                          × daily usage of 100 compressors)

Lead time = 3 days

Safety stock = $\frac{1}{2}$ day's production of compressors

Solution

First, we must determine kanban container size. To do this, we determine the production order quantity (see discussion in Chapter 12 or Equation [16-1]), which determines the kanban size:

$$Q_p = \sqrt{\frac{2DS}{H\left(1-\dfrac{d}{p}\right)}} = \sqrt{\frac{2(25,000)(10)}{H\left(1-\dfrac{d}{p}\right)}} = \sqrt{\frac{500,000}{100\left(1-\dfrac{100}{200}\right)}} = \sqrt{\frac{500,000}{50}}$$

$$= \sqrt{10,000} = 100 \text{ compressors. So the production order size and the size of the kanban container} = 100.$$

Then we determine the number of kanbans:

Demand during lead time = 300 (= 3 days × daily usage of 100)

Safety stock = 100 (= $\frac{1}{2}$ day's production × 200)

$$\text{Number of kanbans} = \frac{\text{Demand during lead time} + \text{Safety stock}}{\text{Size of container}}$$

$$= \frac{300 + 100}{100} = \frac{400}{100} = 4 \text{ containers}$$

Self-Test

- ***Before taking the self-test,*** *refer to the learning objectives listed at the beginning of the chapter and the key terms listed at the end of the chapter.*
- *Use the key at the back of the text to* ***correct*** *your answers.*
- ***Restudy*** *pages that correspond to any questions you answered incorrectly or material you feel uncertain about.*

1. Continuous improvement and forced problem solving is a reasonable definition of:
   a) lean operations
   b) expedited management
   c) the 5Ss of housekeeping
   d) just-in-time
   e) Toyota Production System

2. Supplying the customer needs without waste best describes:
   a) lean operations
   b) expedited management
   c) the 5Ss of housekeeping
   d) just-in-time
   e) Toyota Production System

3. Employee empowerment and standard work practices best describes:
   a) lean operations
   b) expedited management
   c) the 5Ss of housekeeping
   d) just-in-time
   e) Toyota Production System

4. Taiichi Ohno's seven wastes are _____, _____, _____, _____, _____, _____, and _____.

5. The 5Ss for lean production are _____, _____, _____, _____, and _____.

6. A "pull" system:
   a) dumps orders on the next downstream workstation
   b) defines the time between arrival and shipping
   c) is the time it takes to move an order from receipt to delivery
   d) produces material only when requested
   e) all of the above

7. Concerns of suppliers when moving to JIT include:
   a) small lots may seem economically prohibitive
   b) realistic quality demands
   c) changes without adequate lead time
   d) erratic schedules
   e) all of the above

8. TPS's standard work practices include:
   a) completely specified work
   b) "pull" systems
   c) level scheduling
   d) kanbans
   e) JIT techniques

9. Lean producers remove waste by:
   a) focusing on inventory reduction
   b) using JIT techniques
   c) reducing space requirements
   d) developing partnerships with suppliers
   e) all of the above

10. Manufacturing cycle time is:
    a) time to push an order through a facility
    b) time from order receipt to delivery
    c) time between arrival of raw material and shipping of finished product
    d) time between placing an order with a supplier and receipt

Internet and Student CD-ROM/DVD Exercises

Visit our Companion Web site or use your student CD-ROM/DVD to help with material in this chapter.

 On Our Companion Web Site,
  www.prenhall.com/heizer
- Self-Study Quizzes
- Practice Problems
- Virtual Company Tour
- PowerPoint Lecture

 On Your Student CD-ROM
- Practice Problems
- Excel OM
- POM for Windows

 On Your Student DVD
- Video Clips and Video Case
- Virtual Office Hours for Solved Problem

Discussion Questions

1. What is JIT?
2. What is a lean producer?
3. What is TPS?
4. What is level scheduling?
5. JIT attempts to remove delays, which do not add value. How then does JIT cope with weather and its impact on crop harvest and transportation times?

6. What are three ways in which JIT and quality are related?
7. How does TPS contribute to competitive advantage?
8. What are the characteristics of just-in-time partnerships with respect to suppliers?
9. Discuss how the Japanese word for *card* has application in the study of JIT.

10. Standardized, reusable containers have fairly obvious benefits for shipping. What is the purpose of these devices within the plant?

11. Does lean production work in the service sector? Provide an illustration.

12. Which lean techniques work in both the manufacturing *and* service sectors?

Ethical Dilemma

In this lean operations world, in an effort to lower handling costs, speed delivery, and reduce inventory, retailers are forcing their suppliers to do more and more in the way of preparing their merchandise for their cross-docking warehouses, shipment to specific stores, and shelf presentation. Your company, a small manufacturer of aquarium decorations, is in a tough position. First, Mega-Mart wanted you to develop bar-code technology, then special packaging, then small individual shipments bar coded for each store (this way when the merchandise hits the warehouse it is cross-docked immediately to the correct truck and store and is ready for shelf placement). And now Mega-Mart wants you to develop RFID—immediately. Mega-Mart has made it clear that suppliers that cannot keep up with the technology will be dropped.

Earlier, when you didn't have the expertise for bar codes, you had to borrow money and hire an outside firm to do the development, purchase the technology, and train your shipping clerk. Then, meeting the special packaging requirement drove you into negative income for several months, resulting in a loss for last year. Now it appears that the RFID request is impossible. Your business, under the best of conditions, is marginally profitable, and the bank may not be willing to bail you out again. Over the years, Mega-Mart has slowly become your major customer and without them, you are probably out of business. What are the ethical issues and what do you do?

Problems*

• **16.1** Leblanc Electronics, Inc., in Nashville, produces short runs of custom airwave scanners for the defense industry. You have been asked by the owner, Larry Leblanc, to reduce inventory by introducing a kanban system. After several hours of analysis, you develop the following data for scanner connectors used in one work cell. How many kanbans do you need for this connector?

Daily demand	1,000 connectors
Lead time	2 days
Safety stock	$\frac{1}{2}$ day
Kanban size	500 connectors

• **16.2** Chip Gillikin's company wants to establish kanbans to feed a newly established work cell. The following data have been provided. How many kanbans are needed?

Daily demand	250 units
Production lead time	$\frac{1}{2}$ day
Safety stock	$\frac{1}{4}$ day
Kanban size	50 units

•• **16.3** Chris Millikan Manufacturing, Inc., is moving to kanbans to support its telephone switching-board assembly lines. Determine the size of the kanban for subassemblies and the number of kanbans needed.

Setup cost = $30

Annual holding
            cost = $120 per subassembly

Daily production = 20 subassemblies

Annual usage = 2,500 (50 weeks × 5 days each
                            × daily usage of 10 subassemblies)

Lead time = 16 days

Safety stock = 4 days' production of subassemblies.

Note: means the problem may be solved with POM for Windows and/or Excel OM.

•• **16.4** Maggie Moylan Motorcycle Corp. uses kanbans to support its transmission assembly line. Determine the size of the kanban for the mainshaft assembly and the number of kanbans needed.

Setup cost = $20

Annual holding cost
of mainshaft assembly = $250 per unit

Daily production = 300 mainshafts

Annual usage = 20,000 (= 50 weeks × 5 days each
                            × daily usage of 80 mainshafts)

Lead time = 3 days

Safety stock = $\frac{1}{2}$ day's production of mainshafts

• **16.5** Discount-Mart, a major East Coast retailer, wants to determine the economic order quantity (see Chapter 12 for EOQ formulas) for its halogen lamps. It currently buys all halogen lamps from Specialty Lighting Manufacturers, in Atlanta. Annual demand is 2,000 lamps, ordering cost per order is $30, carrying cost per lamp is $12.

a) What is the EOQ?

b) What are the total annual costs of holding and ordering (managing) this inventory?

c) How many orders should Discount-Mart place with Specialty Lighting per year? **Px**

••• **16.6** Discount-Mart (see Problem 16.5), as part of its new JIT program, has signed a long-term contract with Specialty Lighting and will place orders electronically for its halogen lamps. Ordering costs will drop to $.50 per order, but Discount-Mart also reassessed its carrying costs and raised them to $20 per lamp.

a) What is the new economic order quantity?

b) How many orders will now be placed?

c) What is the total annual cost of managing the inventory with this policy? **Px**

•• **16.7** How do your answers to Problems 16.5 and 16.6 provide insight into a JIT purchasing strategy?

••• **16.8** Bill Penny has a repetitive manufacturing plant producing trailer hitches in Arlington, Texas. The plant has an average inventory turnover of only 12 times per year. He has therefore determined that he will reduce his component lot sizes. He has developed the following data for one component, the safety chain clip:

$$\text{Annual demand} = 31,200 \text{ units}$$
$$\text{Daily demand} = 120 \text{ units}$$
$$\text{Daily production (in 8 hours)} = 960 \text{ units}$$
$$\text{Desired lot size (1 hour of production)} = 120 \text{ units}$$
$$\text{Holding cost per unit per year} = \$12$$
$$\text{Setup labor cost per hour} = \$20$$

How many minutes of setup time should he have his plant manager aim for regarding this component?

••• **16.9** Given the following information about a product, at Phyllis Simon's firm, what is the appropriate setup time?

$$\text{Annual demand} = 39,000 \text{ units}$$
$$\text{Daily demand} = 150 \text{ units}$$
$$\text{Daily production} = 1,000 \text{ units}$$
$$\text{Desired lot size} = 150 \text{ units}$$
$$\text{Holding cost per unit per year} = \$10$$
$$\text{Setup labor cost per hour} = \$40$$

••• **16.10** Rick Wing has a repetitive manufacturing plant producing automobile steering wheels. Use the following data to prepare for a reduced lot size. The firm uses a work year of 305 days.

Annual demand for steering wheels	30,500
Daily demand	100
Daily production (8 hours)	800
Desired lot size (2 hours of production)	200
Holding cost per unit per year	$10

a) What is the setup cost, based on the desired lot size?

b) What is the setup time, based on $40 per hour setup labor?

Case Studies

Mutual Insurance Company of Iowa

Mutual Insurance Company of Iowa (MICI) has a major insurance office facility located in Des Moines, Iowa. The Des Moines office is responsible for processing all of MICI's insurance claims for the entire nation. The company's sales have experienced rapid growth during the last year, and as expected, record levels in claims followed. Over 2,500 forms for claims a day are now flowing into the office for processing. Unfortunately, fewer than 2,500 forms a day are flowing out. The total time to process a claim, from the time it arrives to the time a check is mailed, has increased from 10 days to 10 weeks. As a result, some customers are threatening legal action. Sally Cook, the manager of Claims Processing, is particularly distressed, as she knows that a claim seldom requires more than 3 hours of actual work. Under the current administrative procedures, human resources limitations, and facility constraints, there appear to be no easy fixes for the problem. But clearly, something must be done, as the workload has overwhelmed the existing system.

MICI management wants aggressive, but economical, action taken to fix the problem. Ms. Cook has decided to try a JIT approach to claim processing. With support from her bosses, and as a temporary fix, Cook has brought in part-time personnel from MICI sales divisions across the country to help. They are to work down the claims backlog while a new JIT system is installed.

Meanwhile, Claims Processing managers and employees are to be trained in JIT principles. With JIT principles firmly in mind, managers will redesign jobs to move responsibilities for quality control activities to each employee, holding them responsible for quality work and any necessary corrections. Cook will also initiate worker-training programs that explain the entire claim processing flow, as well as provide comprehensive training on each step in the process. Data-entry skills will also be taught to both employees and managers in an effort to fix responsibility for data accuracy on the processor rather than on data entry clerks. Additionally, cross training will be emphasized to enable workers within departments to process a variety of customer claim applications in their entirety.

Cook and her supervisors are also reexamining the insurance and claim forms currently in use. They want to see if standardization of forms will cut processing time, reduce data-entry time, and cut work-in-process.

They hope the changes will also save training time. Making changes in work methods and worker skills leads logically to a need for change in the layout of the Claims Processing Department. This potential change represents a major move from the departmental layout of the past, and will be a costly step. To help ensure the successful implementation of this phase of the changeover, Cook estab-

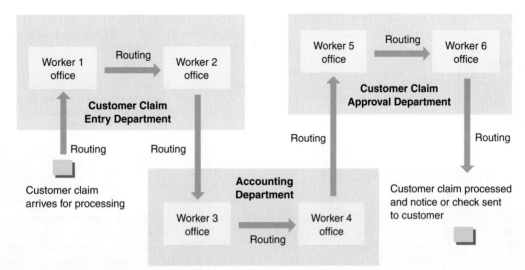

▲ **Figure 16.10** Claims Processing Department Layout

lished a team made up of supervisors, employees, and an outside office layout consultant. She also had the team visit the Kawasaki motorcycle plant in Lincoln, Nebraska, to observe their use of work cells to aid JIT.

The team concluded that a change in the office facilities was necessary to successfully implement and integrate JIT concepts at MICI. The team believes it should revise the layout of the operation and work methods to bring them in line with "group technology cell" layouts. An example of the current departmental layout and claim processing flow pattern is presented in Figure 16.10. As can be seen in this figure, customer claims arrive for processing at the facility and flow through a series of offices and departments to eventually complete the claim process. Although the arrangement of the offices and workers in Figure 16.10 is typical, the entire facility actually operates 20 additional flows, each consisting of the same three departments. However, not all of the 20 flows are configured the same. The number of employees, for example, varies depending on the claim form requirements (larger claims have to be approved by more people). So while all forms must pass through the same three departments (Customer

Claim Entry, Accounting, and Customer Claim Approval), the number of workers for each claim may vary from two to four. For this reason, the MICI facility currently maintains a staff of over 180 office workers just to process and route claims. All these people work for Ms. Cook.

Discussion Questions

1. Identify the attributes you would expect the Claims Processing Department at MICI to have once the new JIT system is in place.
2. What will the restructured cell layout for claim processing in Figure 16.10 look like? Draw it.
3. What assumptions are you making about personnel and equipment in the new group technology cell layout?
4. How will the new JIT oriented system benefit the MICI operation? Explain.

Source: Adapted from Marc J. Schniederjans, *Topics in Just-in-Time Management*, pp. 283–285. Reprinted by permission of Prentice Hall, Inc., Upper Saddle River, NJ.

JIT after the Fire

World-renowned Toyota Motor Corporation has a worldwide presence, with Toyota's investment in North America alone exceeding $13 billion in 11 manufacturing plants. Toyota is at the forefront of lean firms and a showcase of JIT. Executives from all over the world make the journey to Toyota to see how JIT works.

But early one Saturday morning in February, a fire roared through the huge Aisin Seiki plant in Kariya, Japan. The fire incinerated the main source of crucial brake valves that Toyota buys from Aisin and uses in most of its cars. Aisin has long been a supplier of the critical brake-fluid-proportioning valves (P-valves), supplying 99% of Toyota's requirement for the valve. About 80% of Aisin's total output goes to Toyota. As the smoke cleared, the extent of the disaster was clear—most of the 506 special machines used to manufacture the P-valves were useless. A few might be repaired in 2 weeks, but most would need to be replaced—and the

lead time was 6 weeks. Both Aisin and Toyota had been operating at full capacity.

Consistent with JIT practices, Toyota maintained only a 4-hour supply of the valve. And there were few of the valves in the closely knit network that constituted Toyota's supply chain. Depending on a single source and holding little inventory is a risk, but it also keeps Toyota lean and its costs low. The Toyota plants in Japan build 14,000 cars a day. Without that valve, production would come to a rapid halt. Moreover, Toyota production managers were dismayed to find they needed 200 variations of the P-valve.

Consistent with the *keiretsu* networks that are typical of Japan's manufacturing sector, Toyota holds 23% of Aisin's stock, and Aisin's president is Kanshiro Toyoda of the Toyoda family that founded the automaker. Kosuke Ikebuchi, a Toyota senior managing director, was tracked down at 8 A.M. at a golf course clubhouse and given the bad news.

Discussion Questions

1. If you are Mr. Ikebuchi, what do you do?
2. What does this experience tell you (and Aisin and Toyota) about just-in-time?

3. If you had been in charge of Chrysler's JIT supplies the morning of September 11, 2001, what actions would you have taken?

Sources: Case is based on material in: *The Wall Street Journal* (July 20, 2007): B1, (May 8, 1997): A1, A5 and (September 24, 2001): B1, B4; and *Harvard Business Review* (September–October 1999): 97–106.

JIT at Arnold Palmer Hospital

Video Case

Orlando's Arnold Palmer Hospital, founded in 1989, specializes in treatment of women and children and is renowned for its high-quality rankings (top 10% of 2000 benchmarked hospitals), its labor and delivery volume (more than 13,000 births per year, and growing), and its neonatal intensive care unit (one of the highest survival rates in the nation). But quality medical practices and high patient satisfaction require costly inventory—some $30 million per year and thousands of SKUs.* With pressure on medical care to manage and reduce costs, Arnold Palmer Hospital has turned toward controlling its inventory with just-in-time (JIT) techniques.

Within the hospital, for example, drugs are now distributed at nursing workstations via dispensing machines (almost like vending machines) that electronically track patient usage and post the related charge to each patient. The dispensing stations are refilled each night, based on patient demand and prescriptions written by doctors.

To address JIT issues externally, Arnold Palmer Hospital turned toward a major distribution partner, McKesson General Medical, which as a first-tier supplier provides the hospital with about one quarter of all its medical/surgical inventory. McKesson supplies sponges, basins, towels, mayo stand covers, syringes, and hundreds of other medical/surgical items. To ensure coordinated daily delivery of inventory purchased from McKesson, an account executive has been assigned to the hospital on a full-time basis, as well as two other individuals who address customer service and product issues. The result has been a drop in Central Supply average daily inventory from $400,000 to $114,000 since JIT.

JIT success has also been achieved in the area of *custom surgical packs*. Custom surgical packs are the sterile coverings, disposable plastic trays, gauze, and the like, specialized to each type of surgical procedure. Arnold Palmer Hospital uses 10 different custom packs for various surgical procedures. "Over 50,000 packs are used each year, for a total cost of about $1.5 million," says George DeLong, head of Supply Chain Management.

The packs are not only delivered in a JIT manner but packed that way as well. That is, they are packed in the reverse order they are used so each item comes out of the pack in the sequence it is needed. The packs are bulky, expensive, and must remain sterile. Reducing

the inventory and handling while maintaining an assured sterile supply for scheduled surgeries presents a challenge to hospitals.

Here is how the supply chain works: Custom packs are *assembled* by a packing company with *components supplied* primarily from manufacturers selected by the hospital, and *delivered* by McKesson from its local warehouse. Arnold Palmer Hospital works with its own surgical staff (through the Medical Economics Outcome Committee) to identify and standardize the custom packs to reduce the number of custom pack SKUs. With this integrated system, pack safety stock inventory has been cut to one day.

The procedure to drive the custom surgical pack JIT system begins with a "pull" from the doctor's daily surgical schedule. Then, Arnold Palmer Hospital initiates an electronic order to McKesson between 1:00 and 2:00 P.M. daily. At 4:00 A.M. the next morning McKesson delivers the packs. Hospital personnel arrive at 7:00 A.M. and stock the shelves for scheduled surgeries. McKesson then reorders from the packing company, which in turn "pulls" necessary inventory for the quantity of packs needed from the manufacturers.

Arnold Palmer Hospital's JIT system reduces inventory investment, expensive traditional ordering, and bulky storage, and supports quality with a sterile delivery.

Discussion Questions**

1. What do you recommend be done when an error is found in a pack as it is opened for an operation?
2. How might the procedure for custom surgical packs described here be improved?
3. When discussing JIT in services, the text notes that suppliers, layout, inventory, and scheduling are all used. Provide an example of each of these at Arnold Palmer Hospital.
4. When a doctor proposes a new surgical procedure, how do you recommend the SKU for a new custom pack be entered into the hospital's supply chain system?

*SKU = stock keeping unit

**You may wish to view this video case on your student DVD before answering these questions.

Additional Case Studies

Harvard has selected these Harvard Business School cases to accompany this text:

harvardbusinessonline.hbsp.harvard.edu

- **Johnson Controls Automotive Systems Group: The Georgetown, Kentucky, Plant** (#693-086): Examines the challenge of JIT with growing variation and a change from JIT delivery to JIT assembly.
- **Injex Industries** (#697-003): Examines supplier concerns as Injex provides components to a single, demanding customer on a JIT basis.

Bibliography

Ahls, Bill. "Advanced Memory and Lean Change," *IIE Solutions* 33, no. 1 (January 2001): 40–42.

Bacheldor, Beth, and Laurie Sullivan. "Never Too Lean." *Information Week* 985 (April 19, 2004): 36–42.

Bruun, Peter, and Robert N. Mefford. "Lean Production and the Internet." *International Journal of Production Economics* 89, no. 3 (June 18, 2004): 247.

Burke, Robert, and Gregg Messel. "From Simulation to Implementation: Cardinal Health's Lean Journey." *Target: Innovation at Work* 19, no. 2 (2nd quarter 2003): 27–32.

Hall, Robert W. "'Lean' and the Toyota Production System." *Target* 20, no. 3 (3rd issue 2004): 22–27.

Keyte, Beau, and Drew Locher. *The Complete Lean Enterprise.* University Park, IL: Productivity Press, 2004.

King, Andrew A., and Michael J. Lenox. "Lean and Green? An Empirical Examination of the Relationship Between Lean Production and Environmental Performance." *Production and Operations Management* 10, no. 3 (fall 2001): 244–256.

Klassen, Robert D. "Just-in-Time Manufacturing and Pollution Prevention Generate Mutual Benefits in the Furniture Industry." *Interfaces* 30, no. 3 (May–June 2000): 95–106.

Morgan, James M., and Jeffrey K. Liker. *The Toyota Product Development System.* New York: Productivity Press, 2007.

Parks, Charles M. "The Bare Necessities of Lean." *Industrial Engineer* 35, no. 8 (August 2003): 39.

Schonberger, Richard J. "Lean Extended." *Industrial Engineer* (December 2005): 26–31.

van Veen-Dirks, Paula. "Management Control and the Production Environment." *International Journal of Production Economics* 93 (January 8, 2005): 263.

Womack, James P., and Daniel T. Jones. "Lean Consumption." *Harvard Business Review* (March 2005): 58–68.

Womack, James P., and Daniel T. Jones. *Lean Solutions: How Companies and Customers Can Create Value and Wealth Together.* New York: The Free Press, 2005.

Internet Resources

Business Open Learning Archive: **www.bola.biz/index.html**

Gemba Research: **www.gemba.com**

Kanban—and the environment:
www.epa.gov/lean/thinking/kanban.htm

Kanban—explanation:
www.graphicproducts.com/tutorials/kanban/

Manufacturing Engineering: **www.mfgeng.com**

Mid-America Manufacturing Technology Center:
www.mamtc.com

Toyota Motor Corp.:
www.toyota.co.jp/en/vision/production_system

CHAPTER 17

Maintenance and Reliability

Chapter Outline

Ten OM Strategy Decisions

Design of Goods and Services

Managing Quality

Process Strategy

Location Strategies

Layout Strategies

Human Resources

Supply Chain Management

Inventory Management

Scheduling

Maintenance

Learning Objectives

When you complete this chapter you should be able to

1. Describe how to improve system reliability
2. Determine system reliability
3. Determine mean time between failures (MTBF)
4. Distinguish between preventive and breakdown maintenance
5. Describe how to improve maintenance
6. Compare preventive and breakdown maintenance costs

Global Company Profile: Orlando Utilities Commission

Maintenance Provides a Competitive Advantage for Orlando Utilities Commission

The Orlando Utilities Commission (OUC) owns and operates power plants that supply power to two central Florida counties. Every year, OUC takes each one of its power-generating units off-line for 1 to 3 weeks to perform maintenance work.

Additionally, each unit is also taken off-line every 3 years for a complete overhaul and turbine generator inspection. Overhauls are scheduled for spring and fall, when the weather is mildest and demand for power is low. These overhauls last from 6 to 8 weeks.

Units at OUC's Stanton Energy Center require that maintenance personnel perform approximately 12,000 repair and preventive maintenance tasks a year. To accomplish these tasks efficiently, many of these jobs are scheduled daily via a computerized

maintenance management program. The computer generates preventive maintenance work orders and lists of required materials.

Every day that a plant is down for maintenance costs OUC about $110,000 extra for the replacement cost of power that must be generated elsewhere. However, these costs pale beside the costs associated with a forced outage. An unexpected outage could cost OUC an additional $350,000 to $600,000 each day!

Scheduled overhauls are not easy; each one has 1,800 distinct tasks and requires 72,000 labor-hours. But the value of preventive maintenance was illustrated by the first overhaul of a new turbine generator. Workers discovered a cracked rotor blade, which could have destroyed a $27 million piece of

▲ *The Stanton Energy Center in Orlando.*

◄ Two employees are on scaffolding near the top of Stanton Energy Center's 23-story high boiler, checking and repairing super heaters.

▲ This inspector is examining a low-pressure section of turbine. The tips of these turbine blades will travel at supersonic speeds of 1,300 miles per hour when the plant is in operation. A crack in one of the blades can cause catastrophic failure.

◄ Maintenance of capital-intensive facilities requires good planning to minimize downtime. Here, turbine overhaul is under way. Organizing the thousands of parts and pieces necessary for a shutdown is a major effort.

equipment. To find such cracks, which are invisible to the naked eye, metals are examined by dye tests, X-rays, and ultrasound.

At OUC, preventive maintenance is worth its weight in gold. As a result, OUC's electric distribution system has been ranked number one in the Southeast U.S. by PA Consulting Group— a leading consulting firm. Effective maintenance provides a competitive advantage for the Orlando Utilities Commission.

669

THE STRATEGIC IMPORTANCE OF MAINTENANCE AND RELIABILITY

Managers at Orlando Utilities Commision, and every other organization, must avoid the undesirable results of equipment failure. The results of failure can be disruptive, inconvenient, wasteful, and expensive in dollars and even in lives. Machine and product failures can have far-reaching effects on an organization's operation, reputation, and profitability. In complex, highly mechanized plants, an out-of-tolerance process or a machine breakdown may result in idle employees and facilities, loss of customers and goodwill, and profits turning into losses. In an office, the failure of a generator, an air-conditioning system, or a computer may halt operations. A good maintenance and reliability strategy protects both a firm's performance and its investment.

The objective of maintenance and reliability is to maintain the capability of the system. Good maintenance removes variability. Systems must be designed and maintained to reach expected performance and quality standards. **Maintenance** includes all activities involved in keeping a system's equipment in working order. **Reliability** is the probability that a machine part or product will function properly for a specified time under stated conditions.

Two firms that recognize the strategic importance of dedicated maintenance are Walt Disney Company and United Parcel Service. Disney World, in Florida, is intolerant of failures or breakdowns. Disney's reputation makes it not only one of the most popular vacation destinations in the world but also a mecca for benchmarking teams that want to study its maintenance and reliability practices.

Likewise, UPS's famed maintenance strategy keeps its delivery vehicles operating and looking as good as new for 20 years or more. The UPS program involves dedicated drivers who operate the same truck every day and dedicated mechanics who maintain the same group of vehicles. Drivers and mechanics are both responsible for the performance of a vehicle and stay closely in touch with each other.

The interdependency of operator, machine, and mechanic is a hallmark of successful maintenance and reliability. As Figure 17.1 illustrates, it is not only good maintenance and reliability procedures that make Disney and UPS successful, but the involvement of their employees as well.

In this chapter, we examine four important tactics for improving the reliability and maintenance not only of products and equipment but also of the systems that produce them. The four tactics are organized around reliability and maintenance.

The reliability tactics are:

1. Improving individual components
2. Providing redundancy

The maintenance tactics are

1. Implementing or improving preventive maintenance
2. Increasing repair capabilities or speed

Maintenance

All activities involved in keeping a system's equipment in working order.

Reliability

The probability that a machine part or product will function properly for a specified time under stated conditions.

▶ **Figure 17.1**

Good Maintenance and Reliability Strategy Requires Employee Involvement and Good Procedures

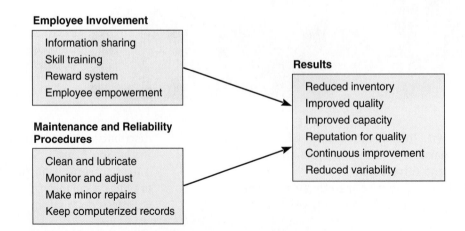

Variability corrupts processes and creates waste. The operations manager must drive out variability: Designing for reliability and managing for maintenance are crucial ingredients for doing so.

RELIABILITY

Systems are composed of a series of individual interrelated components, each performing a specific job. If any *one* component fails to perform, for whatever reason, the overall system (for example, an airplane or machine) can fail. First, we discuss improving individual components, and then we discuss providing redundancy.

Improving Individual Components

Because failures do occur in the real world, understanding their occurrence is an important reliability concept. We now examine the impact of failure in a series. Figure 17.2 shows that as the number of components in a *series* increases, the reliability of the whole system declines very quickly. A system of $n = 50$ interacting parts, each of which has a 99.5% reliability, has an overall reliability of 78%. If the system or machine has 100 interacting parts, each with an individual reliability of 99.5%, the overall reliability will be only about 60%!

To measure reliability in a system in which each individual part or component may have its own unique rate of reliability, we cannot use the reliability curve in Figure 17.2. However, the method of computing system reliability (R_s) is simple. It consists of finding the product of individual reliabilities as follows:

$$R_s = R_1 \times R_2 \times R_3 \times \ldots \times R_n \tag{17-1}$$

where R_1 = reliability of component 1
       R_2 = reliability of component 2

and so on.

Equation (17-1) assumes that the reliability of an individual component does not depend on the reliability of other components (that is, each component is independent). Additionally, in this equation as in most reliability discussions, reliabilities are presented as *probabilities*. Thus, a .90 reliability means that the unit will perform as intended 90% of the time. It also means that it will fail $1 - .90 = .10 = 10\%$ of the time. We can use this method to evaluate the reliability of a service or a product, such as the one we examine in Example 1.

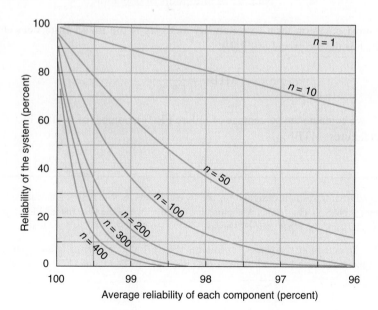

◄ **Figure 17.2**

Overall System Reliability as a Function of Number of *n* Components (Each with the Same Reliability) and Component Reliability with Components in a Series

EXAMPLE 1

Reliability in a series

The National Bank of Greeley, Colorado, processes loan applications through three clerks set up in series, with reliabilities of .90, .80, and .99. It wants to find the system reliability.

Approach: Apply Equation (17-1) to solve for R_s.

Solution: The reliability of the loan process is:

$$R_s = R_1 \times R_2 \times R_3 = (.90)(.80)(.99) = .713, \text{ or } 71.3\%$$

Insight: Because each clerk in the series is less than perfect, the error probabilities are cumulative and the resulting reliability for this series is .713, which is less than any one clerk.

Learning exercise: If the lowest-performing clerk (.80) is replaced by a clerk performing at .95 reliability, what is the new expected reliability? [Answer: .846.]

Related problems: 17.1, 17.2, 17.5, 17.11

⊙ **Active Model 17.1**

Example 1 is further illustrated in Active Model 17.1 on your CD-ROM.

Component reliability is often a design or specification issue for which engineering design personnel may be responsible. However, supply chain personnel may be able to improve components of systems by staying abreast of suppliers' products and research efforts. Supply chain personnel can also contribute directly to the evaluation of supplier performance.

The basic unit of measure for reliability is the *product failure rate* (FR). Firms producing high-technology equipment often provide failure-rate data on their products. As shown in Equations (17-2) and (17-3), the failure rate measures the percent of failures among the total number of products tested, FR(%), or a number of failures during a period of time, FR(*N*):

$$\text{FR}(\%) = \frac{\text{Number of failures}}{\text{Number of units tested}} \times 100\% \tag{17-2}$$

$$\text{FR}(N) = \frac{\text{Number of failures}}{\text{Number of unit-hours of operation time}} \tag{17-3}$$

Mean time between failures (MTBF)
The expected time between a repair and the next failure of a component, machine, process, or product.

Perhaps the most common term in reliability analysis is the **mean time between failures (MTBF)**, which is the reciprocal of FR(*N*):

$$\text{MTBF} = \frac{1}{\text{FR}(N)} \tag{17-4}$$

In Example 2, we compute the percentage of failure FR(%), number of failures FR(*N*), and mean time between failures (MTBF).

EXAMPLE 2

Determining mean time between failures

Twenty air-conditioning systems designed for use by astronauts in NASA space shuttles were operated for 1,000 hours at NASA's Huntsville, Alabama, test facility. Two of the systems failed during the test—one after 200 hours and the other after 600 hours.

Approach: To determine the percent of failures [FR(%)], the number of failures per unit of time [FR(N)], and the mean time between failures (MTBF), we use Equations (17-2), (17-3), and (17-4), respectively.

Solution: Percent of failures:

$$FR(\%) = \frac{\text{Number of failures}}{\text{Number of units tested}} = \frac{2}{20}(100\%) = 10\%$$

Number of failures per operating hour:

$$FR(N) = \frac{\text{Number of failures}}{\text{Operating time}}$$

where

$$\text{Total time} = (1{,}000 \text{ hr})(20 \text{ units})$$
$$= 20{,}000 \text{ unit-hour}$$

$$\text{Nonoperating time} = 800 \text{ hr for 1st failure} + 400 \text{ hr for 2nd failure}$$
$$= 1{,}200 \text{ unit-hour}$$

$$\text{Operating time} = \text{Total time} - \text{Nonoperating time}$$
$$FR(N) = \frac{2}{20{,}000 - 1{,}200} = \frac{2}{18{,}800}$$

$$= .000106 \text{ failure/unit-hour}$$

Because $\text{MTBF} = \dfrac{1}{FR(N)}$

$$\text{MTBF} = \frac{1}{.000106} = 9{,}434 \text{ hr}$$

Learning Objective

3. Determine mean time between failure (MTBF)

If the typical space shuttle trip lasts 6 days, NASA may be interested in the failure rate per trip:

$$\text{Failure rate} = (\text{Failures/unit-hr})(24 \text{ hr/day})(6 \text{ days/trip})$$
$$= (.000106)(24)(6)$$
$$= .0153 \text{ failure/trip}$$

Insight: Mean time between failures (MTBF) is the standard means of stating reliability.

Learning exercise: If non-operating time drops to 800, what is the new MTBF? [Answer: 9,606 hrs.]

Related problems: 17.6, 17.7

If the failure rate recorded in Example 2 is too high, NASA will have to either increase the reliability of individual components, and thus of the system, or install several backup air-conditioning units on each space shuttle. Backup units provide redundancy.

Providing Redundancy

To increase the reliability of systems, **redundancy** is added. The technique here is to "back up" components with additional components. This is known as putting units in parallel and is a standard operations management tactic, as noted in the *OM in Action* box "Tomcat F-14 Pilots Love Redundancy." Redundancy is provided to ensure that if one component fails, the system has recourse to another. For instance, say that reliability of a component is .80 and we back it up with another component with reliability of .80. The resulting reliability is the probability of the first component working plus the probability of the backup (or parallel) component working multiplied by the probability of needing the backup component $(1 - .8 = .2)$. Therefore:

Redundancy
The use of components in parallel to raise reliability.

$$\begin{pmatrix} \text{Probability} \\ \text{of first} \\ \text{component} \\ \text{working} \end{pmatrix} + \left[\begin{pmatrix} \text{Probability} \\ \text{of second} \\ \text{component} \\ \text{working} \end{pmatrix} \times \begin{pmatrix} \text{Probability} \\ \text{of needing} \\ \text{second} \\ \text{component} \end{pmatrix} \right] =$$

$$(.8) \quad + \quad [(.8) \quad \times \quad (1 - .8)] \quad = .8 + .16 = .96$$

OM in Action   Tomcat F-14 Pilots Love Redundancy

In a world that accepts software with bugs and computer systems that crash, it is worth remembering that some computer systems operate without fail. Where are these systems? They are in fighter jets, the space shuttle, nuclear power plants, and flood-control systems. These systems are all extraordinarily reliable, even though they depend heavily on software. Such systems are all about redundancy—they have their own software and their own processors—and use most of their cycles to perform internal quality checks.

The Tomcat F-14's variable-wing geometry allows it to fly very fast and to slow down quickly when landing on an aircraft carrier. The calculations to determine the correct wing position as air speed changes are determined by software and dedicated processors. The processors run in tandem so multiple calculations verify outgoing signals.

Only 10% of the F-14's software is used to fly the plane; 40% is used to do automatic testing and verification; the remaining 50% is redundancy. Highly reliable systems work because the design includes self-checking and redundancy. These redundant systems find potential problems and correct them before a failure can occur. If you are a Tomcat F-14 pilot, you love redundancy.

Source: Information.com (April 1, 2002): 34.

Example 3 shows how redundancy can improve the reliability of the loan process presented in Example 1.

EXAMPLE 3

Reliability with a parallel process

Active Model 17.2

Example 3 is further illustrated in Active Model 17.2 on the CD-ROM.

The National Bank is disturbed that its loan-application process has a reliability of only .713 (see Example 1) and would like to improve this situation.

Approach: The bank decides to provide redundancy for the two least reliable clerks.

Solution: This procedure results in the following system:

$$R_1 \qquad R_2 \qquad R_3$$
$$0.90 \qquad 0.80$$
$$\downarrow \qquad \downarrow$$

$$0.90 \rightarrow 0.80 \rightarrow 0.99 = [.9 + .9(1 - .9] \times [.8 + .8(1 - .8)] \times .99$$
$$= [.9 + (.9)(.1)] \times [.8 + (.8)(.2)] \times .99$$
$$= .99 \times .96 \times .99 = .94$$

Insight: By providing redundancy for two clerks, National Bank has increased reliability of the loan process from .713 to .94.

Learning exercise: What happens when the bank replaces both R_2 clerks with one new clerk who has a reliability of .90. [Answer: $R_s = .88$.]

Related problems: 17.8, 17.9, 17.10, 17.12, 17.13, 17.14, 17.16, 17.18

Learning Objective

4. Distinguish between preventive and breakdown maintenance

Preventive maintenance
A plan that involves routine inspections, servicing, and keeping facilities in good repair to prevent failure.

Breakdown maintenance
Remedial maintenance that occurs when equipment fails and must be repaired on an emergency or priority basis.

MAINTENANCE

There are two types of maintenance: preventive maintenance and breakdown maintenance. **Preventive maintenance** involves performing routine inspections and servicing and keeping facilities in good repair. These activities are intended to build a system that will find potential failures and make changes or repairs that will prevent failure. Preventive maintenance is much more than just keeping machinery and equipment running. It also involves designing technical and human systems that will keep the productive process working within tolerance; it allows the system to perform. The emphasis of preventive maintenance is on understanding the process and keeping it working without interruption. **Breakdown maintenance** occurs when equipment fails and must be repaired on an emergency or priority basis.

Implementing Preventive Maintenance

Preventive maintenance implies that we can determine when a system needs service or will need repair. Therefore, to perform preventive maintenance, we must know when a system requires service or when it is likely to fail. Failures occur at different rates during the life of a product. A high initial failure rate, known as **infant mortality**, may exist for many products.[1] This is why many electronic firms "burn in" their products prior to shipment: That is to say, they execute a variety of tests (such as a full wash cycle at Whirlpool) to detect "startup" problems prior to shipment. Firms may also provide 90-day warranties. We should note that many infant mortality failures are not product failures per se, but rather failure due to improper use. This fact points up the importance in many industries of operations management's building an after-sales service system that includes installing and training.

Once the product, machine, or process "settles in," a study can be made of the MTBF (mean time between failure) distribution. Such distributions often follow a normal curve. When these distributions exhibit small standard deviations, then we know we have a candidate for preventive maintenance, even if the maintenance is expensive.[2]

Once our firm has a candidate for preventive maintenance, we want to determine *when* preventive maintenance is economical. Typically, the more expensive the maintenance, the narrower must be the MTBF distribution (that is, have a small standard deviation). Additionally, if the process is no more expensive to repair when it breaks down than the cost of preventive maintenance, perhaps we should let the process break down and then do the repair. However, the consequence of the breakdown must be fully considered. Even some relatively minor breakdowns have catastrophic consequences. (See the *OM in Action* box "Preventive Maintenance Saves Lives" on the next page). At the other extreme, preventive maintenance costs may be so incidental that preventive maintenance is appropriate even if the MTBF distribution is rather flat (that is, it has a large standard deviation). In any event, consistent with job enrichment practices, machine operators must be held responsible for preventive maintenance of their own equipment and tools.

With good reporting techniques, firms can maintain records of individual processes, machines, or equipment. Such records can provide a profile of both the kinds of maintenance required and the timing of maintenance needed. Maintaining equipment history is an important part of a preventive maintenance system, as is a record of the time and cost to make the repair. Such records can also provide information about the family of equipment and suppliers.

Reliability and maintenance are of such importance that most systems are now computerized. Figure 17.3 shows the major components of such a system with files to be maintained on the left and reports generated on the right.

Both Boeing and General Motors are pursuing competitive advantage via their reliability and maintenance information systems. Boeing can now monitor the health of an airplane in flight and relay relevant information in real time to the ground, providing a head start on reliability and maintenance issues. Similarly, General Motors, with its On Star wireless satellite service,

Infant mortality
The failure rate early in the life of a product or process.

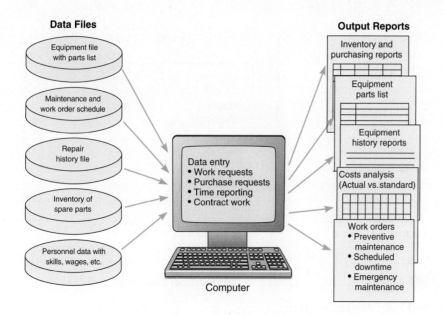

◀ **Figure 17.3**

A Computerized Maintenance System

---

[1]Infant mortality failures often follow a negative exponential distribution.
[2]See, for example, J. Michael Brock, John R. Michael, and David Morganstein, "Using Statistical Thinking to Solve Maintenance Problems," *Quality Progress* (May 1989): 55–60.

Flight 5481's trip was short. It lasted 70 seconds. The flight left the Charlotte Airport, bound for Greenville/Spartanburg, but seconds after lift-off, the nose of the aircraft pitched upward, the plane rolled, and, moments later, slammed into the corner of a maintenance facility at the airport. The Beech 1900D commuter plane carried 21 people to their death. The following are selected comments from the final moments of the flight:

8:47:02—Co-pilot Jonathan Gibbs: "Wuh."
8:47:03—Capt. Katie Leslie: "Help me. . . . You got it?"
8:47:05—Gibbs: "Oh (expletive). Push down."
8:47:12—Leslie: "Push the nose down."
8:47:14—Leslie: "Oh my God."
8:47:16—Leslie (calling to controllers): "We have an emergency for Air Midwest fifty-four eighty-one."
8:47:18—Faint voice from passenger area: "Daddy."
8:47:26—Leslie: "Oh my God, ahh."
8:47:26—Gibbs: "Uh, uh, God, ahh (expletive)."
8:47:28 End of recording

The National Transportation Safety Board's focus in this situation is a preventive maintenance error made two days prior to the crash. The mechanic and a supervisor skipped at least 12 steps required in the maintenance of the tension of the pitch-control cables during the *Detail 6* check that include the pitch of the control cable tension. Data show that the control column position changed during the maintenance and the plane lost about two-thirds down-elevator capability. Investigators believe that the aircraft would have been flyable with fully functioning controls had it been given proper preventive maintenance. Maintenance can improve quality, reduce costs, and win orders. It can also be a matter of life and death.

Sources: Aviation Week and Space Technology (May 26, 2003): 52; *USA Today* (May 21, 2003): 8A; and *The Wall Street Journal* (May 21, 2003): D3 and (May 20, 2003): D1, D3.

alerts car owners to 1,600 possible diagnostic failures, such as faulty airbags sensor or even the need for an oil change. For GM, the service provides immediate data that its engineers can use to jump on quality issues before customers even notice a problem. This has saved the firm an estimated $100 million in warranty costs by catching problems early.[3]

Figure 17.4(a) shows a traditional view of the relationship between preventive maintenance and breakdown maintenance. In this view, operations managers consider a *balance* between the two costs. Allocating more resources to preventive maintenance will reduce the number of breakdowns. At some point, however, the decrease in breakdown maintenance costs may be less than the increase in preventive maintenance costs. At this point, the total cost curve begins to rise. Beyond this optimal point, the firm will be better off waiting for breakdowns to occur and repairing them when they do.

▲ **Figure 17.4** **Maintenance Costs**

[3]"Big Mechanic Is Watching," *Forbes* (June 5, 2006): 48.

Unfortunately, cost curves such as in Figure 17.4(a) seldom consider the *full costs of a breakdown*. Many costs are ignored because they are not *directly* related to the immediate breakdown. For instance, the cost of inventory maintained to compensate for downtime is not typically considered. Moreover, downtime can have a devastating effect on morale: Employees may begin to believe that performance to standard and maintaining equipment are not important. Finally, downtime adversely affects delivery schedules, destroying customer relations and future sales. When the full impact of breakdowns is considered, Figure 17.4(b) may be a better representation of maintenance costs. In Figure 17.4(b), total costs are at a minimum when the system does not break down.

Assuming that all potential costs associated with downtime have been identified, the operations staff can compute the optimal level of maintenance activity on a theoretical basis. Such analysis, of course, also requires accurate historical data on maintenance costs, breakdown probabilities, and repair times. Example 4 shows how to compare preventive and breakdown maintenance costs to select the least expensive maintenance policy.

EXAMPLE 4

Comparing preventive and breakdown maintenance costs

Farlen & Halikman is a CPA firm specializing in payroll preparation. The firm has been successful in automating much of its work, using high-speed printers for check processing and report preparation. The computerized approach, however, has problems. Over the past 20 months, the printers have broken down at the rate indicated in the following table:

Number of Breakdowns	Number of Months That Breakdowns Occurred
0	2
1	8
2	6
3	4
	Total: 20

Each time the printers break down, Farlen & Halikman estimates that it loses an average of $300 in production time and service expenses. One alternative is to purchase a service contract for preventive maintenance. Even if Farlen & Halikman contracts for preventive maintenance, there will still be breakdowns, *averaging* one breakdown per month. The price for this service is $150 per month.

Approach: To determine if the CPA firm should follow a "run until breakdown" policy or contract for preventive maintenance, we follow a 4-step process:

Step 1: Compute the *expected number* of breakdowns (based on past history) if the firm continues as is, without the service contract.

Step 2: Compute the expected breakdown cost per month with no preventive maintenance contract.

Step 3: Compute the cost of preventive maintenance.

Step 4: Compare the two options and select the one that will cost less.

Learning Objective

6. Compare preventive and breakdown maintenance costs

Solution:

Step 1:

Number of Breakdowns	Frequency	Number of Breakdowns	Frequency
0	2/20 = .1	2	6/20 = 0.3
1	8/20 = .4	3	4/20 = 0.2

$$\begin{pmatrix} \text{Expected number} \\ \text{of breakdowns} \end{pmatrix} = \sum \left[\begin{pmatrix} \text{Number of} \\ \text{breakdowns} \end{pmatrix} \times \begin{pmatrix} \text{Corresponding} \\ \text{frequency} \end{pmatrix} \right]$$

$$= (0)(.1) + (1)(.4) + (2)(.3) + (3)(.2)$$

$$= 0 + .4 + .6 + .6$$

$$= 1.6 \text{ breakdowns/month}$$

Step 2:

$$\text{Expected breakdown cost} = \begin{pmatrix} \text{Expected number} \\ \text{of breakdowns} \end{pmatrix} \times \begin{pmatrix} \text{Cost per} \\ \text{breakdown} \end{pmatrix}$$

$$= (1.6)(\$300)$$

$$= \$480/\text{month}$$

Step 3:

$$\begin{pmatrix} \text{Preventive} \\ \text{maintenance cost} \end{pmatrix} = \begin{pmatrix} \text{Cost of expected} \\ \text{breakdowns if service} \\ \text{contract signed} \end{pmatrix} + \begin{pmatrix} \text{Cost of} \\ \text{service contract} \end{pmatrix}$$

$$= (1 \text{ breakdown/month})(\$300) + \$150/\text{month}$$

$$= \$450/\text{month}$$

Step 4: Because it is less expensive overall to hire a maintenance service firm ($450) than to not do so ($480), Farlen & Halikman should hire the service firm.

Insight: Determining the expected number of breakdowns for each option is crucial to making a good decision. This typically requires good maintenance records.

Learning exercise: What is the best decision if the preventive maintenance contract cost increases to $195 per month? [Answer: At $495 (= $300 + $195) per month, "run until breakdown" becomes less expensive (assuming that all costs are included in the $300 per breakdown cost).]

Related problems: 17.3, 17.4, 17.17

Using variations of the technique shown in Example 4, operations managers can examine maintenance policies.

Increasing Repair Capabilities

Because reliability and preventive maintenance are seldom perfect, most firms opt for some level of repair capability. Enlarging or improving repair facilities can get the system back in operation faster. A good maintenance facility should have these six features:

1. Well-trained personnel
2. Adequate resources
3. Ability to establish a repair plan and priorities[4]
4. Ability and authority to do material planning
5. Ability to identify the cause of breakdowns
6. Ability to design ways to extend MTBF

However, not all repairs can be done in the firm's facility. Managers must, therefore, decide where repairs are to be performed. Figure 17.5 shows some of the options and how they rate in terms of speed, cost, and competence. Consistent with the advantages of employee empowerment, a strong case can be made for employees' maintaining their own equipment. This approach, however, may also be the weakest link in the repair chain because not every employee can be trained in all aspects of equipment repair. Moving to the right in Figure 17.5 may improve the competence of the repair work, but it also increases cost, as it may entail expensive offsite repair with corresponding increases in replacement time and shipping.

▶ **Figure 17.5**

The Operations Manager Must Determine How Maintenance Will Be Performed

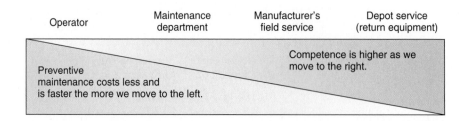

[4]You may recall from our discussion of network planning in Chapter 3 that DuPont developed the critical path method (CPM) to improve the scheduling of maintenance projects.

However, preventive maintenance policies and techniques must include an emphasis on employees accepting responsibility for the maintenance they are capable of doing. Employee maintenance may be only of the "clean, check, and observe" variety, but if each operator performs those activities within his or her capability, the manager has made a step toward both employee empowerment and maintaining system performance.

TOTAL PRODUCTIVE MAINTENANCE

Many firms have moved to bring total quality management concepts to the practice of preventive maintenance with an approach known as **total productive maintenance (TPM)**. It involves the concept of reducing variability through employee involvement and excellent maintenance records. In addition, total productive maintenance includes:

- Designing machines that are reliable, easy to operate, and easy to maintain
- Emphasizing total cost of ownership when purchasing machines, so that service and maintenance are included in the cost
- Developing preventive maintenance plans that utilize the best practices of operators, maintenance departments, and depot service
- Training workers to operate and maintain their own machines

High utilization of facilities, tight scheduling, low inventory, and consistent quality demand reliability.[5] Total productive maintenance is the key to reducing variability and improving reliability.

Total productive maintenance (TPM)
Combines total quality management with a strategic view of maintenance from process and equipment design to preventive maintenance.

TECHNIQUES FOR ENHANCING MAINTENANCE

Two other OM techniques have proven beneficial to effective maintenance: simulation and expert systems.

Simulation Because of the complexity of some maintenance decisions, computer simulation is a good tool for evaluating the impact of various policies. For instance, operations personnel can decide whether to add more staff by determining the trade-offs between machine downtime costs and the costs of additional labor.[6] Management can also simulate the replacement of parts that have not yet failed as a way of preventing future breakdowns. Simulation via physical models can also be useful. For example, a physical model can vibrate an airplane to simulate thousands of hours of flight time to evaluate maintenance needs.

Expert Systems OM managers use expert systems (that is, computer programs that mimic human logic) to assist staff in isolating and repairing various faults in machinery and equipment. For instance, General Electric's DELTA system asks a series of detailed questions that aid the user in identifying a problem. DuPont uses expert systems to monitor equipment and to train repair personnel.

Summary

Operations managers focus on design improvements and backup components to improve reliability. Reliability improvements also can be obtained through the use of preventive maintenance and excellent repair facilities.

Some firms use automated sensors and other controls to warn when production machinery is about to fail or is becoming damaged by heat, vibration, or fluid leaks. The goal of such procedures is not only to avoid failures but also to perform preventive maintenance before machines are damaged.

Finally, many firms give employees a sense of "ownership" of their equipment. When workers repair or do preventive maintenance on their own machines, breakdowns are less common. Well-trained and empowered employees ensure reliable systems through preventive maintenance. In turn, reliable, well-maintained equipment not only provides higher utilization but also improves quality and performance to schedule. Top firms build and maintain systems so that customers can count on products and services that are produced to specifications and on time.

[5]This conclusion is supported by a number of studies; see, for example, Kathleen E. McKone, Roger G. Schroeder, and Kristy O. Cua, "The Impact of Total Productive Maintenance Practices on Manufacturing Performance," *Journal of Operations Management* 19, no. 1 (January 2001): 39–58.
[6]Christian Striffler, Walton Hancock, and Ron Turkett, "Maintenance Staffs: Size Them Right," *IIE Solutions* 32, no. 12 (December 2000): 33–38.

Key Terms

Maintenance *(p. 670)*
Reliability *(p. 670)*
Mean time between failures (MTBF) *(p. 672)*

Redundancy *(p. 673)*
Preventive maintenance *(p. 674)*
Breakdown maintenance *(p. 674)*

Infant mortality *(p. 675)*
Total productive maintenance (TPM)
 (p. 679)

Using Software to Solve Reliability Problems

 Excel OM and POM for Windows may be used to solve reliability problems. The reliability modules allows us to enter (1) number of systems (components) in the series (1 through 10); (2) number of backup, or parallel, components (1 through 12); and (3) component reliability for both series and parallel data.

Solved Problems

Virtual Office Hours help is available on Student DVD.

Solved Problem 17.1

The semiconductor used in the Sullivan Wrist Calculator has five circuits, each of which has its own reliability rate. Component 1 has a reliability of .90; component 2, .95; component 3, .98; component 4, .90; and component 5, .99. What is the reliability of one semiconductor?

Solution

Semiconductor reliability, $R_s = R_1 \times R_2 \times R_3 \times R_4 \times R_5$

$$= (.90)(.95)(.98)(.90)(.99)$$

$$= .7466$$

Solved Problem 17.2

A recent engineering change at Sullivan Wrist Calculator places a backup component in each of the two least reliable transistor circuits. The new circuits will look like the following:

What is the reliability of the new system?

Solution

$$\text{Reliability} = [.9 + (1-.9) \times .9] \times .95 \times .98 \times [.9 + (1-.9) \times .9] \times .99$$

$$= [.9 + .09] \times .95 \times .98 \times [.9 + .09] \times .99$$

$$= .99 \times .95 \times .98 \times .99 \times .99$$

$$= .903$$

Internet and Student CD-ROM/DVD Exercises

Visit our Companion Web site or use your student CD-ROM/DVD to help with material in this chapter.

 On Our Companion Web Site,
www.prenhall.com/heizer
- Self-Study Quizzes
- Practice Problems
- Virtual Company Tour
- Internet Case
- PowerPoint Lecture

On Your Student CD-ROM
- Practice Problems
- Active Model Exercise
- POM for Windows

On Your Student DVD
- Virtual Office Hours for Solved Problems

Self-Test

- **Before taking the self-test**, *refer to the learning objectives listed at the beginning of the supplement and the key terms listed at the end of the supplement.*
- *Use the key at the back of the text to* ***correct*** *your answers.*
- ***Restudy*** *pages that correspond to any questions you answered incorrectly or material you feel uncertain about.*

1. The appropriate maintenance policy is developed by balancing preventive maintenance costs, and breakdown maintenance costs. The problem is that:
   a) preventive maintenance costs are very difficult to identify
   b) full breakdown costs are seldom considered
   c) preventive maintenance should be performed, regardless of the cost
   d) breakdown maintenance must be performed, regardless of the cost

2. The objective of maintenance and reliability is to:
   a) increase the mean time between failures (MTBF)
   b) be tolerant of failures or breakdowns
   c) maintain the capability of the system
   d) improve individual components by providing redundancy
   e) improve product design

3. Maintenance can be improved by:
   a) enlarging repair crews
   b) increasing repair capabilities
   c) providing more inventory of replacement items
   d) all of the above

4. Maintenance data files typically include:
   a) equipment file, work order requests, time reporting
   b) cost analysis, contract work, time reporting
   c) repair history, equipment file, personnel skills data
   d) work requests, history reports, purchasing reports
   e) time reporting, actual vs. standard costs, and parts lists

5. The process that is intended to find potential failures and make changes or repairs is known as:
   a) breakdown maintenance
   b) failure maintenance
   c) preventive maintenance
   d) all of the above

6. Undesirable results of system failure and downtime include:
   a) not producing within quality standards
   b) not producing adequate volume
   c) excessive costs
   d) reduced system performance
   e) all of the above

7. Infant mortality:
   a) is a very rare phenomenon in the life of products
   b) is generally found from the MTBF (mean time between failure) rate
   c) is often due to improper use
   d) may be eliminated by breakdown maintenance
   e) is none of the above

Discussion Questions

1. What is the objective of maintenance and reliability?
2. How does one identify a candidate for preventive maintenance?
3. Explain the notion of "infant mortality" in the context of product reliability.
4. Why is simulation often an appropriate technique for maintenance problems?
5. What is the trade-off between operator-performed maintenance versus supplier-performed maintenance?
6. How can a manager evaluate the effectiveness of the maintenance function?
7. How does machine design contribute to either increasing or alleviating the maintenance problem?
8. What roles can information technology play in the maintenance function?
9. During an argument as to the merits of preventive maintenance at Windsor Printers, the company owner asked, "Why fix it before it breaks?" How would you, as the director of maintenance, respond?
10. Will preventive maintenance eliminate *all* breakdowns?

Ethical Dilemma

When a McDonnell Douglas DC-10 crashed over Iowa, a subsequent investigation suggested that the plane's hydraulic systems did not provide enough protection. The DC-10 had three separate hydraulic systems, all of which failed when an engine exploded. The engine threw off shreds of metal that severed two of the lines, and the third line required power from the demolished engine that was no longer available. The DC-10, unlike other commercial jets, had no shutoff valves that might have stemmed the flow of hydraulic fluid. Lockheed's similar L-1011 trijet had four hydraulic systems. A McDonnell Douglas VP said at the time, "You can always be extreme and not have a practical airplane. You can be perfectly safe and never get off the ground." Discuss the pros and cons of McDonnell's position. How might you design a reliability experiment? What has since happened to the McDonnell Douglas Corporation?

Problems*

• **17.1** The Beta II computer's electronic processing unit contains 50 components in series. The average reliability of each component is 99.0%. Using Figure 17.2, determine the overall reliability of the processing unit.

• **17.2** A testing process at Boeing Aircraft has 400 components in series. The average reliability of each component is 99.5%. Use Figure 17.2 to find the overall reliability of the whole testing process.

• **17.3** What are the *expected* number of yearly breakdowns for the power generator at Orlando Utilities that has exhibited the following data over the past 20 years?

Number of breakdowns	0	1	2	3	4	5	6
Number of years in which breakdown occurred		2	2	5	4	5	2	0	**Px**

• **17.4** Each breakdown of a graphic plotter table at Airbus Industries costs $50. Find the expected daily breakdown cost, given the following data:

Number of breakdowns	0	1	2	3	4
Daily breakdown probability	.1	.2	.4	.2	.1	**Px**

•• **17.5** A new aircraft control system is being designed that must be 98% reliable. This system consists of three components in series. If all three of the components are to have the same level of reliability, what level of reliability is required? **Px**

•• **17.6** Robert Klassan Manufacturing, a medical equipment manufacturer, subjected 100 heart pacemakers to 5,000 hours of testing. Halfway through the testing, 5 pacemakers failed. What was the failure rate in terms of the following:
a) Percent of failures?
b) Number of failures per unit-hour?
c) Number of failures per unit-year?
d) If 1,100 people receive pacemaker implants, how many units can we expect to fail during the following 1 year?

•• **17.7** A manufacturer of disk drives for notebook computers wants a MTBF of at least 50,000 hours. Recent test results for 10 units were one failure at 10,000 hrs, another at 25,000 hrs, and two more at 45,000 hrs. The remaining units were still running at 60,000 hours. Determine the following:
a) Percent of failures.
b) Number of failures per unit-hour
c) MTBF at this point in the testing

•• **17.8** What is the reliability of the following production process? $R_1 = 0.95$, $R_2 = 0.90$, $R_3 = 0.98$.

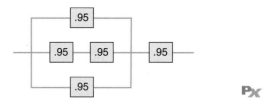

•• **17.9** What is the reliability that bank loans will be processed accurately if each of the 5 clerks shown in the chart has the reliability shown?

•• **17.10** Merrill Kim Sharp has a system composed of three components in parallel. The components have the following reliabilities:

$$R_1 = 0.90, \qquad R_2 = 0.95, \qquad R_3 = 0.85$$

What is the reliability of the system? (*Hint:* See Example 3.) **Px**

• **17.11** A medical control system has three components in series with individual reliabilities (R_1, R_2, R_3) as shown:

What is the reliability of the system? **Px**

•• **17.12** a) What is the reliability of the system shown?

b) How much did reliability improve if the medical control system shown in Problem 17.11 changed to the redundant parallel system shown here? **Px**

••• **17.13** Assume that for cardiac bypass surgery, 85% of patients survive the surgery, 95% survive the recovery period after surgery, 80% are able to make the lifestyle changes needed to extend their survival to 1 year or more, and only 10% of those who do not make the lifestyle changes survive more than a year. What is the likelihood that a given patient will survive more than a year? **Px**

•• **17.14** Elizabeth Irwin's design team has proposed the following system with component reliabilities as indicated:

What is the reliability of the system? **Px**

•• **17.15** The maintenance department at Mechanical Dynamics has presented you with the following failure curve. What does it suggest?

•• **17.16** Rick Wing, salesperson for Wave Soldering Systems, Inc. (WSSI), has provided you with a proposal for improving the temperature control on your present machine. The machine uses a hot-air knife to cleanly remove excess solder from printed circuit boards; this is a great concept, but the hot-air temperature control lacks reliability. According to Wing, engineers at WSSI have improved the reliability of the critical temperature controls. The new system still has the four sensitive integrated circuits controlling the temperature, but the new machine has a backup for each. The four integrated circuits have reliabilities of .90, .92, .94, and .96. The four backup circuits all have a reliability of .90.
a) What is the reliability of the new temperature controller?
b) If you pay a premium, Wing says he can improve all four of the backup units to .93. What is the reliability of this option? **Px**

••• **17.17** The fire department has a number of failures with its oxygen masks and is evaluating the possibility of outsourcing preventive maintenance to the manufacturer. Because of the risk associated with a failure, the cost of each failure is estimated at $2,000. The current maintenance policy (with station employees performing maintenance) has yielded the following history:

Number of breakdowns	0	1	2	3	4	5
Number of years in which breakdowns occurred		4	3	1	5	5	0

This manufacturer will guarantee repairs on any and all failures as part of a service contract. The cost of this service is $5,000 per year.

a) What is the expected number of breakdowns per year with station employees performing maintenance?
b) What is the cost of the current maintenance policy?
c) What is the more economical policy?

••• **17.18** As VP for operations at Brian Normoyle Engineering, you must decide which product design, A or B, has the higher reliability. B is designed with backup units for components R_3 and R_4. What is the reliability of each design?

•••• **17.19** A typical retail transaction consists of several smaller steps, which can be considered components subject to failure. A list of such components might include:

Component	Description	Definition of Failure
1	Find product in proper size, color, etc.	Can't find product
2	Enter cashier line	No lines open; lines too long; line experiencing difficulty
3	Scan product UPC for name, price, etc.	Won't scan; item not on file; scans incorrect name or price
4	Calculate purchase total	Wrong weight; wrong extension; wrong data entry; wrong tax
5	Make payment	Customer lacks cash; check not acceptable; credit card refused
6	Make change	Makes change incorrectly
7	Bag merchandise	Damages merchandise while bagging; bag splits
8	Conclude transaction and exit	No receipt; unfriendly, rude, or aloof clerk

Let the eight probabilities of success be .92, .94, .99, .99, .98, .97, .95, and .96. What is the reliability of the system, that is, the probability that there will be a satisfied customer? If you were the store manager, what do you think should be an acceptable value for this probability? Which components would be good candidates for backup, which for redesign?

Case Study

Worldwide Chemical Company

Jack Smith wiped the perspiration from his face. It was another scorching-hot summer day, and one of the four process refrigeration units was down. The units were critical to the operation of Worldwide Chemical Company's Fibers Plant, which produces synthetic fibers and polymer flake for a global market.

Before long, Al Henson, the day-shift production superintendent, was on the intercom, shouting his familiar proclamation that "heads would roll" if the unit was not back on-line within the hour. However, Jack Smith, the maintenance superintendent, had heard it all before—nothing ever happened as a result of Henson's temper tantrums. "Serves him right," he thought. "Henson is uncooperative when we want to perform scheduled maintenance, so it doesn't get done and equipment goes down."

At that moment, however, Henson was genuinely furious over the impact that the breakdown would have on his process yield figures. Meeting with plant manager Beth Conner, he was charging that all the maintenance department did was "sit around" and play cards like firemen waiting for an alarm to send them to a three-alarm blaze across town. The "fix-it" approach to maintenance was costing the plant throughput that was vital to meeting standard costs and avoiding serious variances. Foreign competitors were delivering high-quality fibers in less time and at lower prices. Conner had already been called on the carpet at corporate headquarters over output levels that were significantly below the budgeted numbers. The business cycle contained predictable seasonal variations. That meant building inventories that would be carried for months, tying up scarce capital, a characteristic of most continuous processes. Monthly shipments would look bad. Year-to-date shipments would look even worse because of machine breakdowns and lost output to date. Conner knew that something had to be done to develop machine reliability. Capacity on demand was needed to respond to growing foreign competition. Unreliable production equipment was jeopardizing the company's TQM effort by causing process variations that affected both first-quality product yields and on-time deliveries, but no one seemed to have the answer to the problem of machine breakdowns.

The maintenance department operated much like a fire department, rushing to a breakdown with a swarm of mechanics, some who disassembled the machine while others pored over wiring schematics and still others hunted for spare parts in the maintenance warehouse. Eventually, they would have the machine back up, though sometimes only after working through the night to get the production line going again. Maintenance had always been done this way. However, with new competitors, machine reliability had suddenly become a major barrier to competing successfully.

Rumors of a plant closing were beginning to circulate and morale was suffering, making good performance that much more difficult. Beth Conner knew she needed solutions if the plant had any chance of survival.

Discussion Questions

1. Can Smith and Hensen do anything to improve performance?
2. Is there an alternative to the current operations approach of the maintenance department?
3. How could production make up for lost output resulting from scheduled maintenance?
4. How could maintenance mechanics be better utilized?
5. Is there any way to know when a machine breakdown is probable?

Source: Patrick Owings, under the supervision of Professor Marilyn M. Helms, University of Tennessee at Chattanooga.

Additional Case Studies

Internet case study: Visit our Companion Web site at www.prenhall.com/heizer for this free case study:

- **Cartak's Department Store:** Requires the evaluation of the impact of an additional invoice verifier.

Harvard has selected these Harvard Business School cases to accompany this chapter:

harvardbusinessonline.hbsp.harvard.edu

- **The Dana-Farber Cancer Institute** (#699-025): Examines organizational and process characteristics that may have contributed to a medical error.
- **Workplace Safety at Alcoa (A)** (#692-042): Looks at the challenge facing the manager of a large aluminum manufacturing plant in its drive for improved safety.
- **A Brush with AIDS (A)** (#394-058): Examines the ethical dilemma when needles penetrate container walls.

Bibliography

Blank, Ronald. *The Basics of Reliability*. University Park, IL: Productivity Press, 2004.

Condra, Lloyd W. *Reliability Improvement with Design of Experiments*, 2nd ed. New York: Marcel Dekker, 2001.

Cua, K. O., K. E. McKone, and R. G. Schroeder. "Relationships between Implementation of TQM, JIT, and TPM and Manufacturing Performance." *Journal of Operations Management* 19, no. 6 (November 2001): 675–694.

Finigen, Tim, and Jim Humphries. "Maintenance Gets Lean." *IE Industrial Systems* 38, no. 10 (October 2006): 26–31.

Keizers, J. M., J. W. M. Bertrand, and J. Wessels. "Diagnosing Order Planning Performance at a Navy Maintenance and Repair Organization, Using Logistic Regression." *Production and Operations Management* 12, no. 4 (winter 2003): 445–463.

Sova, Roger, and Lea A. P. Tonkin. "Total Productive Maintenance at Crown International." *Target: Innovation at Work* 19, no. 1 (1st quarter 2003): 41–44.

Weil, Marty. "Beyond Preventive Maintenance." *APICS* 16, no. 4 (April 2006): 40–43.

Westerkamp, Thomas A. "Plan for Maintenance Productivity." *IIE Solutions* 33, no. 8 (August 2001): 36–41.

Internet Resources

Alion System Reliability Analysis Center: **rac.alionscience.com**
Center for System Reliability: **reliability.sandia.gov**
Reliability Engineering: **www.enre.umd.edu**

Society for Maintenance and Reliability Professionals:
www.smrp.org
Society of Reliability Engineers: **www.sre.org**

QUANTITATIVE MODULE

A

Decision-Making Tools

Module Outline

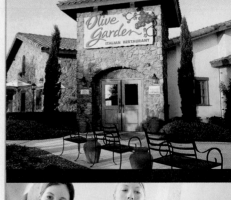

Learning Objectives

When you complete this module you should be able to

1. Create a simple decision tree
2. Build a decision table
3. Explain when to use each of the three types of decision-making environments
4. Calculate an expected monetary value (EMV)

5. Compute the expected value of perfect information (EVPI)
6. Evaluate the nodes in a decision tree
7. Create a decision tree with sequential decisions

▲ *The wildcatter's decision was a tough one. Which of his new Kentucky lease areas—Blair East or Blair West— should he drill for oil? A wrong decision in this type of wildcat oil drilling could mean the difference between success and bankruptcy. Talk about decision making under uncertainty and pressure! But using a decision tree, Tomco Oil President Thomas E. Blair identified 74 different options, each with its own potential net profit. What had begun as an overwhelming number of geological, engineering, economic, and political factors now became much clearer. Says Blair, "Decision tree analysis provided us with a systematic way of planning these decisions and clearer insight into the numerous and varied financial outcomes that are possible."*[1]

> *"The business executive is by profession a decision maker. Uncertainty is his opponent. Overcoming it is his mission."*
>
> *John McDonald*

Operations managers are decision makers. To achieve the goals of their organizations, managers must understand how decisions are made and know which decision-making tools to use. To a great extent, the success or failure of both people and companies depends on the quality of their decisions. Bill Gates, who developed the DOS and Windows operating systems, became chairman of the most powerful software firm in the world (Microsoft) and a billionaire. In contrast, the Firestone manager who headed the team that designed the flawed tires that caused so many accidents with Ford Explorers in the late 1990s is not working there anymore.

THE DECISION PROCESS IN OPERATIONS

What makes the difference between a good decision and a bad decision? A "good" decision— one that uses analytic decision making—is based on logic and considers all available data and possible alternatives. It also follows these six steps:

1. Clearly define the problem and the factors that influence it.
2. Develop specific and measurable objectives.
3. Develop a model—that is, a relationship between objectives and variables (which are measurable quantities).
4. Evaluate each alternative solution based on its merits and drawbacks.
5. Select the best alternative.
6. Implement the decision and set a timetable for completion.

Throughout this book, we have introduced a broad range of mathematical models and tools to help operations managers make better decisions. Effective operations depend on careful decision making. Fortunately, there are a whole variety of analytic tools to help make these decisions.

---

[1]J. Hosseini, "Decision Analysis and Its Application in the Choice between Two Wildcat Ventures," *Interfaces* 16, no. 2. Reprinted by permission, INFORMS, 901 Elkridge Landing Road, Suite 400, Linthicum, Maryland 21090 USA.

This module introduces two of them—decision tables and decision trees. They are used in a wide number of OM situations, ranging from new-product analysis (Chapter 5), to capacity planning (Supplement 7), to location planning (Chapter 8), to scheduling (Chapter 15), and to maintenance planning (Chapter 17).

FUNDAMENTALS OF DECISION MAKING

Regardless of the complexity of a decision or the sophistication of the technique used to analyze it, all decision makers are faced with alternatives and "states of nature." The following notation will be used in this module:

1. Terms:
    a. *Alternative*—A course of action or strategy that may be chosen by a decision maker (e.g., not carrying an umbrella tomorrow).
    b. *State of nature*—An occurrence or a situation over which the decision maker has little or no control (e.g., tomorrow's weather).
2. Symbols used in a decision tree:
    a. ☐—decision node from which one of several alternatives may be selected.
    b. ◯—a state-of-nature node out of which one state of nature will occur.

To present a manager's decision alternatives, we can develop *decision trees* using the above symbols. When constructing a decision tree, we must be sure that all alternatives and states of nature are in their correct and logical places and that we include *all* possible alternatives and states of nature.

> "Management means, in the last analysis, the substitution of thought for brawn and muscle, of knowledge for folklore and tradition, and of cooperation for force."
>
> *Peter Drucker*

EXAMPLE A1

A simple decision tree

Getz Products Company is investigating the possibility of producing and marketing backyard storage sheds. Undertaking this project would require the construction of either a large or a small manufacturing plant. The market for the product produced—storage sheds—could be either favorable or unfavorable. Getz, of course, has the option of not developing the new product line at all.

Approach: Getz decides to build a decision tree.

Solution: Figure A.1 illustrates Getz's decision tree.

◀ **Figure A.1**

Getz Products Decision Tree

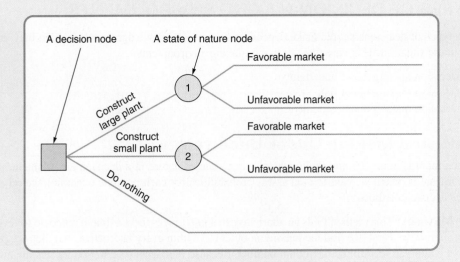

Learning Objective

1. Create a simple decision tree

Insight: We never want to overlook the option of "doing nothing" in a decision tree as that is usually a possible decision.

Learning exercise: Getz now considers constructing a medium-sized plant as a fourth option. Redraw the tree in Figure A.1 to accommodate this. [Answer: Your tree will have a new node and branches between "Construct large plant" and "Construct small plant."]

Related problems: A.2e, A.8b, A.14a, A.15a, A.17a, A.18

DECISION TABLES

Decision table

A tabular means of analyzing decision alternatives and states of nature.

We may also develop a decision or payoff table to help Getz Products define its alternatives. For any alternative and a particular state of nature, there is a *consequence* or *outcome*, which is usually expressed as a monetary value. This is called a *conditional value*. Note that all of the alternatives in Example A2 are listed down the left side of the table, that states of nature (outcomes) are listed across the top, and that conditional values (payoffs) are in the body of the **decision table**.

EXAMPLE A2

A decision table

Learning Objective

2. Build a decision table

▶ **Table A.1**

Decision Table with Conditional Values for Getz Products

Getz Products now wishes to organize the following information into a table. With a favorable market, a large facility will give Getz Products a net profit of $200,000. If the market is unfavorable, a $180,000 net loss will occur. A small plant will result in a net profit of $100,000 in a favorable market, but a net loss of $20,000 will be encountered if the market is unfavorable.

Approach: These numbers become conditional values in the decision table. We list alternatives in the left column and states of nature across the top of the table.

Solution: The completed table is shown in Table A.1.

	States of Nature	
Alternatives	**Favorable Market**	**Unfavorable Market**
Construct large plant	$200,000	−$180,000
Construct small plant	$100,000	−$ 20,000
Do nothing	$ 0	$ 0

Insight: The toughest part of decision tables is getting the data to analyze.

Learning exercise: In Examples A3 and A4, we see how to use tables to make decisions.

TYPES OF DECISION-MAKING ENVIRONMENTS

The types of decisions people make depend on how much knowledge or information they have about the situation. There are three decision-making environments:

- Decision making under uncertainty
- Decision making under risk
- Decision making under certainty

Learning Objective

3. Explain when to use each of the three types of decision-making environments

Decision Making Under Uncertainty

When there is complete *uncertainty* as to which state of nature in a decision environment may occur (that is, when we cannot even assess probabilities for each possible outcome), we rely on three decision methods:

Maximax

A criterion that finds an alternative that maximizes the maximum outcome.

Maximin

A criterion that finds an alternative that maximizes the minimum outcome.

Equally likely

A criterion that assigns equal probability to each state of nature.

1. **Maximax:** This method finds an alternative that *max*imizes the *max*imum outcome for every alternative. First, we find the maximum outcome within every alternative, and then we pick the alternative with the maximum number. Because this decision criterion locates the alternative with the *highest* possible *gain*, it has been called an "optimistic" decision criterion.
2. **Maximin:** This method finds the alternative that *max*imizes the *min*imum outcome for every alternative. First, we find the minimum outcome within every alternative, and then we pick the alternative with the maximum number. Because this decision criterion locates the alternative that has the *least* possible *loss*, it has been called a "pessimistic" decision criterion.
3. **Equally likely:** This method finds the alternative with the highest average outcome. First, we calculate the average outcome for every alternative, which is the sum of all outcomes divided by the number of outcomes. We then pick the alternative with the maximum number. The equally likely approach assumes that each state of nature is equally likely to occur.

Getz Products Company would like to apply each of these three approaches now.

Approach: Given Getz's decision table of Example A2, he determines the maximax, maximin, and equally likely decision criteria.

Solution: Table A.2 provides the solution.

◀ **Table A.2**

Decision Table for Decision Making under Uncertainty

Alternatives	States of Nature		Maximum in Row	Minimum in Row	Row Average
	Favorable Market	**Unfavorable Market**			
Construct large plant	$200,000	–$180,000	$200,000 ◀	–$180,000	$10,000
Construct small plant	$100,000	–$ 20,000	$100,000	–$ 20,000	$40,000 ◀
Do nothing	$ 0	$ 0	$ 0	$ 0 ◀	$ 0
			Maximax ┘	Maximin	Equally ┘ likely

1. The maximax choice is to construct a large plant. This is the *maximum* of the *maximum* number within each row, or alternative.
2. The maximin choice is to do nothing. This is the *maximum* of the *min*imum number within each row, or alternative.
3. The equally likely choice is to construct a small plant. This is the maximum of the average outcome of each alternative. This approach assumes that all outcomes for any alternative are *equally likely*.

Insight: There are optimistic decision makers ("maximax") and pessimistic ones ("maximin"). Maximax and maximin present best case–worst case planning scenarios.

Learning exercise: Getz reestimates the outcome for constructing a large plant when the market is favorable and raises it to $250,000. What numbers change in Table A.2? Do the decisions change? [Answer: The maximax is now $250,000, and the row average is $35,000 for large plant. No decision changes.]

Related problems: A.1, A.2b–d, A.4, A.6

Decision Making Under Risk

Decision making under risk, a more common occurrence, relies on probabilities. Several possible states of nature may occur, each with an assumed probability. The states of nature must be mutually exclusive and collectively exhaustive and their probabilities must sum to 1.[2] Given a decision table with conditional values and probability assessments for all states of nature, we can determine the **expected monetary value (EMV)** for each alternative. This figure represents the expected value or *mean* return for each alternative *if we could repeat the decision a large number of times.*

The EMV for an alternative is the sum of all possible payoffs from the alternative, each weighted by the probability of that payoff occurring:

Expected monetary value (EMV)
The expected payout or value of a variable that has different possible states of nature, each with an associated probability.

Learning Objective

4. Calculate an expected monetary value (EMV)

$$EMV \text{ (Alternative } i) = \text{(Payoff of 1st state of nature)}$$
$$\times \text{(Probability of 1st state of nature)}$$
$$+ \text{(Payoff of 2nd state of nature)}$$
$$\times \text{(Probability of 2nd state of nature)}$$
$$+ \cdots + \text{(Payoff of last state of nature)}$$
$$\times \text{(Probability of last state of nature)}$$

Example A4 illustrates how to compute the maximum EMV.

[2]To review these and other statistical terms, refer to the CD-ROM Tutorial 1, "Statistical Review for Managers."

EXAMPLE A4

Expected monetary value

▶ **Table A.3**

Decision Table for Getz Products

Excel OM Data File ModAEx4.xls

Getz would like to find the EMV for each alternative.

Approach: Getz Products' operations manager believes that the probability of a favorable market is exactly the same as that of an unfavorable market; that is, each state of nature has a .50 chance of occurring. He can now determine the EMV for each alternative (see Table A.3):

	States of Nature	
Alternatives	**Favorable Market**	**Unfavorable Market**
Construct large plant (A_1)	$200,000	−$180,000
Construct small plant (A_2)	$100,000	−$ 20,000
Do nothing (A_3)	$ 0	$ 0
Probabilities	.50	.50

Solution:

1. $\text{EMV}(A_1) = (.5)(\$200,000) + (.5)(-\$180,000) = \$10,000$
2. $\text{EMV}(A_2) = (.5)(\$100,000) + (.5)(-\$20,000) = \$40,000$
3. $\text{EMV}(A_3) = (.5)(\$0) + (.5)(\$0) = \$0$

Insight: The maximum EMV is seen in alternative A_2. Thus, according to the EMV decision criterion, Getz would build the small facility.

Learning exercise: What happens to the three EMVs if Getz increases the conditional value on the "large plant/favorable market" result to $250,000? [Answer: $\text{EMV}(A_1) = \$35,000$. No change in decision.]

Related problems: A.2e, A.3a, A.5a, A.7a, A.8, A.9a, A.10, A.11, A.12, A.14a,b, A.16a, A.22

Decision Making Under Certainty

Now suppose that the Getz operations manager has been approached by a marketing research firm that proposes to help him make the decision about whether to build the plant to produce storage sheds. The marketing researchers claim that their technical analysis will tell Getz with certainty whether the market is favorable for the proposed product. In other words, it will change Getz's environment from one of decision making *under risk* to one of decision making *under certainty*. This information could prevent Getz from making a very expensive mistake. The marketing research firm would charge Getz $65,000 for the information. What would you recommend? Should the operations manager hire the firm to make the study? Even if the information from the study is perfectly accurate, is it worth $65,000? What might it be worth? Although some of these questions are difficult to answer, determining the value of such *perfect information* can be very useful. It places an upper bound on what you would be willing to spend on information, such as that being sold by a marketing consultant. This is the concept of the expected value of perfect information (EVPI), which we now introduce.

Expected Value of Perfect Information (EVPI)

If a manager were able to determine which state of nature would occur, then he or she would know which decision to make. Once a manager knows which decision to make, the payoff increases because the payoff is now a certainty, not a probability. Because the payoff will increase with knowledge of which state of nature will occur, this knowledge has value. Therefore, we now look at how to determine the value of this information. We call this difference between the payoff under perfect information and the payoff under risk the **expected value of perfect information (EVPI)**.

$$\text{EVPI} = \text{Expected value with perfect information} - \text{Maximum EMV}$$

To find the EVPI, we must first compute the **expected value *with* perfect information (EVwPI)**, which is the expected (average) return if we have perfect information before a decision has to be

EVPI places an upper limit on what you should pay for information.

Expected value of perfect information (EVPI)

The difference between the payoff under perfect information and the payoff under risk.

Expected value with perfect information (EVwPI)

The expected (average) return if perfect information is available.

made. To calculate this value, we choose the best alternative for each state of nature and multiply its payoff times the probability of occurrence of that state of nature:

Expected value with
perfect information (EVwPI) = (Best outcome or consequence for 1st state of nature)
$\times$ (Probability of 1st state of nature)

+ (Best outcome for 2nd state of nature)
$\times$ (Probability of 2nd state of nature)

+ $\cdots$ + (Best outcome for last state of nature)
$\times$ (Probability of last state of nature)

In Example A5 we use the data and decision table from Example A4 to examine the expected value of perfect information.

Learning Objective

5. Compute the expected value of perfect information (EVPI)

EXAMPLE A5

Expected value of perfect information

The Getz operations manager would like to calculate the maximum that he would pay for information—that is, the expected value of perfect information, or EVPI.

Approach: Referring back to Table A.3, he follows a two-stage process. First, the expected value *with* perfect information (EVwPI) is computed. Then, using this information, EVPI is calculated.

Solution:
1. The best outcome for the state of nature "favorable market" is "build a large facility" with a payoff of $200,000. The best outcome for the state of nature "unfavorable market" is "do nothing" with a payoff of $0. Expected value *with* perfect information = ($200,000)(0.50) + ($0)(0.50) = $100,000. Thus, if we had perfect information, we would expect (on the average) $100,000 if the decision could be repeated many times.
2. The maximum EMV is $40,000 for A_2, which is the expected outcome without perfect information. Thus:

$$EVPI = EVwPI - Maximum\ EMV$$
$$= \$100,000 - \$40,000 = \$60,000$$

Insight: The *most* Getz should be willing to pay for perfect information is $60,000. This conclusion, of course, is again based on the assumption that the probability of each state of nature is 0.50.

Learning exercise: How does the EVPI change if the "large plant/favorable market" conditional value is $250,000? [Answer: EVPI = $85,000.]

Related problems: A.3b, A.5b, A.7, A.9, A.14, A.16

DECISION TREES

Decisions that lend themselves to display in a decision table also lend themselves to display in a decision tree. We will therefore analyze some decisions using decision trees. Although the use of a decision table is convenient in problems having one set of decisions and one set of states of nature, many problems include *sequential* decisions and states of nature. When there are two or more sequential decisions, and later decisions are based on the outcome of prior ones, the decision tree approach becomes appropriate. A **decision tree** is a graphic display of the decision process that indicates decision alternatives, states of nature and their respective probabilities, and payoffs for each combination of decision alternative and state of nature.

Expected monetary value (EMV) is the most commonly used criterion for decision tree analysis. One of the first steps in such analysis is to graph the decision tree and to specify the monetary consequences of all outcomes for a particular problem.

Analyzing problems with *decision trees* involves five steps:

1. Define the problem.
2. Structure or draw the decision tree.
3. Assign probabilities to the states of nature.
4. Estimate payoffs for each possible combination of decision alternatives and states of nature.
5. Solve the problem by computing the expected monetary values (EMV) for each state-of-nature node. This is done by working *backward*—that is, by starting at the right of the tree and working back to decision nodes on the left.

Decision tree
A graphical means of analyzing decision alternatives and states of nature.

▶ *Decision tree software permits users to solve decision-analysis problems with flexibility, power, and ease. Programs such as DPL, Tree Plan, and Supertree allow decision problems to be analyzed with less effort and in greater depth than ever before. Full-color presentations of the options open to managers always have impact. In this photo, wildcat drilling options are explored with DPL software.*

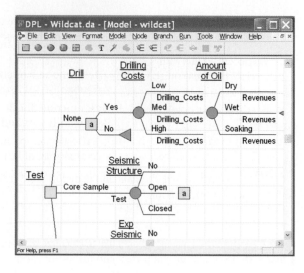

EXAMPLE A6

Solving a tree for EMV

Getz wants to develop a completed and solved decision tree.

Approach: The payoffs are placed at the right-hand side of each of the tree's branches (see Figure A.2). The probabilities (first used by Getz in Example A4) are placed in parentheses next to each state of nature. The expected monetary values for each state-of-nature node are then calculated and placed by their respective nodes. The EMV of the first node is $10,000. This represents the branch from the decision node to "construct a large plant." The EMV for node 2, to "construct a small plant," is $40,000. The option of "doing nothing" has, of course, a payoff of $0.

Solution: The branch leaving the decision node leading to the state-of-nature node with the highest EMV will be chosen. In Getz's case, a small plant should be built.

▶ **Figure A.2**

Completed and Solved Decision Tree for Getz Products

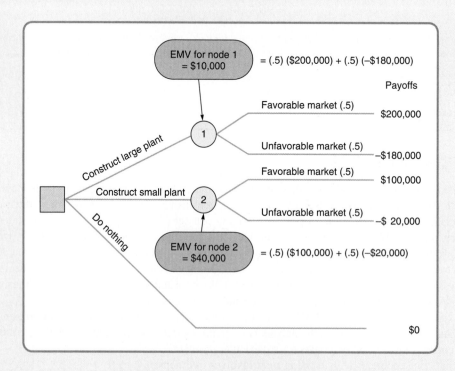

Insight: This graphical approach is an excellent way for managers to understand all the options in making a major decision. Visual models are often preferred over tables.

Learning exercise: Correct Figure A.2 to reflect a $250,000 payoff for "construct large plant/favorable market." [Answer: Change one payoff and recompute the EMV for node 1.]

Related problems: A.2e, A.8b, A.14a,b, A.17, A.18

A More Complex Decision Tree

When a *sequence* of decisions must be made, decision trees are much more powerful tools than are decision tables. Let's say that Getz Products has two decisions to make, with the second decision dependent on the outcome of the first. Before deciding about building a new plant, Getz has the option of conducting its own marketing research survey, at a cost of $10,000. The information from this survey could help it decide whether to build a large plant, to build a small plant, or not to build at all. Getz recognizes that although such a survey will not provide it with *perfect* information, it may be extremely helpful.

Getz's new decision tree is represented in Figure A.3 of Example A7. Take a careful look at this more complex tree. Note that *all possible outcomes and alternatives* are included in their logical sequence. This procedure is one of the strengths of using decision trees. The manager is forced to examine all possible outcomes, including unfavorable ones. He or she is also forced to make decisions in a logical, sequential manner.

> *There is a widespread use of decision trees beyond just OM decision making.*

Getz Products wishes to develop the new tree for this sequential decision.

Approach: Examining the tree in Figure A.3, we see that Getz's first decision point is whether to conduct the $10,000 market survey. If it chooses not to do the study (the lower part of the tree), it can either build a large plant, a small plant, or no plant. This is Getz's second decision point. If the decision is to build, the market will be either favorable (.50 probability) or unfavorable (also .50 probability). The payoffs for each of the possible consequences are listed along the right-hand side. As a matter of fact, this lower portion of Getz's tree is *identical* to the simpler decision tree shown in Figure A.2.

EXAMPLE A7

A decision tree with sequential decisions

◀ **Figure A.3**

Getz Products Decision Tree with Probabilities and EMVs Shown

The short parallel lines mean "prune" that branch, as it is less favorable than another available option and may be dropped.

Learning Objective

7. Create a decision tree with sequential decisions

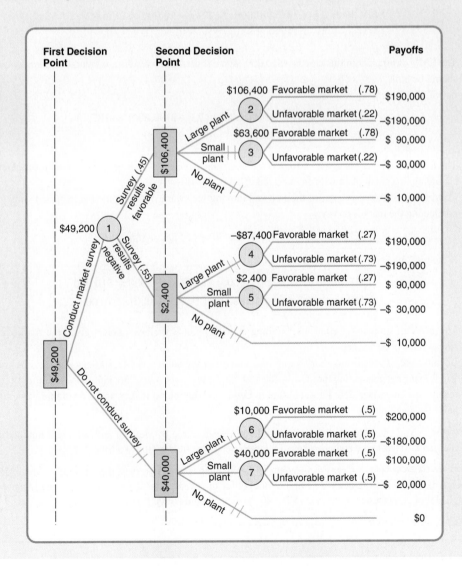

Solution: The upper part of Figure A.3 reflects the decision to conduct the market survey. State-of-nature node number 1 has 2 branches coming out of it. Let us say there is a 45% chance that the survey results will indicate a favorable market for the storage sheds. We also note that the probability is .55 that the survey results will be negative.

The rest of the probabilities shown in parentheses in Figure A.3 are all *conditional* probabilities. For example, .78 is the probability of a favorable market for the sheds given a favorable result from the market survey. Of course, you would expect to find a high probability of a favorable market given that the research indicated that the market was good. Don't forget, though: There is a chance that Getz's $10,000 market survey did not result in perfect or even reliable information. Any market research study is subject to error. In this case, there remains a 22% chance that the market for sheds will be unfavorable given positive survey results.

Likewise, we note that there is a 27% chance that the market for sheds will be favorable given negative survey results. The probability is much higher, .73, that the market will actually be unfavorable given a negative survey.

Finally, when we look to the payoff column in Figure A.3, we see that $10,000—the cost of the marketing study—has been subtracted from each of the top 10 tree branches. Thus, a large plant constructed in a favorable market would normally net a $200,000 profit. Yet because the market study was conducted, this figure is reduced by $10,000. In the unfavorable case, the loss of $180,000 would increase to $190,000. Similarly, conducting the survey and building *no plant* now results in a −$10,000 payoff.

With all probabilities and payoffs specified, we can start calculating the expected monetary value of each branch. We begin at the end or right-hand side of the decision tree and work back toward the origin. When we finish, the best decision will be known.

1. Given favorable survey results:

$$EMV \text{ (node 2)} = (.78)(\$190,000) + (.22)(-\$190,000) = \$106,400$$
$$EMV \text{ (node 3)} = (.78)(\$90,000) + (.22)(-\$30,000) = \$63,600$$

The EMV of no plant in this case is −$10,000. Thus, if the survey results are favorable, a large plant should be built.

2. Given negative survey results:

$$EMV \text{ (node 4)} = (.27)(\$190,000) + (.73)(-\$190,000) = -\$87,400$$
$$EMV \text{ (node 5)} = (.27)(\$90,000) + (.73)(-\$30,000) = \$2,400$$

The EMV of no plant is again −$10,000 for this branch. Thus, given a negative survey result, Getz should build a small plant with an expected value of $2,400.

3. Continuing on the upper part of the tree and moving backward, we compute the expected value of conducting the market survey:

$$EMV(\text{node 1}) = (.45)(\$106,400) + (.55)(\$2,400) = \$49,200$$

4. If the market survey is *not* conducted:

$$EMV \text{ (node 6)} = (.50)(\$200,000) + (.50)(-\$180,000) = \$10,000$$
$$EMV \text{ (node 7)} = (.50)(\$100,000) + (.50)(-\$20,000) = \$40,000$$

The EMV of no plant is $0. Thus, building a small plant is the best choice, given the marketing research is not performed.

5. Because the expected monetary value of conducting the survey is $49,200—versus an EMV of $40,000 for not conducting the study—the best choice is to *seek marketing information*. If the survey results are favorable, Getz Products should build the large plant; if they are unfavorable, it should build the small plant.

Insight: You can reduce complexity in a large decision tree by viewing and solving a number of smaller trees—start at the end branches of a large one. Take one decision at a time.

Learning exercise: Getz estimates that if he conducts a market survey, there is really only a 35% chance the results will indicate a favorable market for the sheds. How does the tree change? [Answer: The EMV of conducting the survey = $38,800, so Getz should not do it now.]

Related problems: A.13, A.18, A.19, A.20, A.21, A.23

Using Decision Trees in Ethical Decision Making

Decision trees can also be a useful tool to aid ethical corporate decision making. The decision tree illustrated in Example A8, developed by Harvard Professor Constance Bagley, provides guidance as to how managers can both maximize shareholder value and behave ethically. The tree can be applied to any action a company contemplates, whether it is expanding operations in a developing country or reducing a workforce at home.

Ethical decision making

Smithson Corp. is opening a plant in Malaysia, a country with much less stringent environmental laws than the U.S., its home nation. Smithson can save $18 million in building the manufacturing facility—and boost its profits—if it does not install pollution-control equipment that is mandated in the U.S. but not in Malaysia. But Smithson also calculates that pollutants emitted from the plant, if unscrubbed, could damage the local fishing industry. This could cause a loss of millions of dollars in income as well as create health problems for local inhabitants.

Approach: Smithson decides to build a decision tree to model the problem.

Solution: Figure A.4 outlines the choices management can consider. For example, if in management's best judgment the harm to the Malaysian community by building the plant will be greater than the loss in company returns, the response to the question "Is it ethical?" will be no.

Now, say Smithson proposes building a somewhat different plant, one *with* pollution controls, despite a negative impact on company returns. That decision takes us to the branch "Is it ethical *not* to take action?" If the answer (for whatever reason) is no, the decision tree suggests proceeding with the plant but notifying the Smithson Board, shareholders, and others about its impact.

◄ **Figure A.4**

Smithson's Decision Tree for Ethical Dilemma

Source: Modified from Constance E. Bagley, "The Ethical Leader's Decision Tree," *Harvard Business Review* (January–February 2003): 18–19.

Insight: This tree allows managers to view the options graphically. This is a good way to start the process.

Ethical decisions can be quite complex: What happens, for example, if a company builds a polluting plant overseas, but this allows the company to sell a life-saving drug at a lower cost around the world? Does a decision tree deal with all possible ethical dilemmas? No—but it does provide managers with a framework for examining those choices.

Summary

This module examines two of the most widely used decision techniques—decision tables and decision trees. These techniques are especially useful for making decisions under risk. Many decisions in research and development, plant and equipment, and even new buildings and structures can be ana- lyzed with these decision models. Problems in inventory con- trol, aggregate planning, maintenance, scheduling, and pro- duction control are just a few other decision table and deci- sion tree applications.

Key Terms

Decision table *(p. 688)*
Maximax *(p. 688)*
Maximin *(p. 688)*
Equally likely *(p. 688)*

Expected monetary value (EMV) *(p. 689)*
Expected value of perfect information
  (EVPI) *(p. 690)*

Expected value with perfect information
  (EVwPI) *(p. 690)*
Decision tree *(p. 691)*

Using Software for Decision Models

Analyzing decision tables is straightforward with Excel, Excel OM, and POM for Windows. When deci- sion trees are involved, Excel OM or commercial packages such as DPL, Tree Plan, and Supertree pro- vide flexibility, power, and ease. POM for Windows will also analyze trees but does not have graphic capabilities.

✕ Using Excel OM

Excel OM allows decision makers to evaluate decisions quickly and to perform sensitivity analysis on the results. Program A.1 uses the Getz data to illustrate input, output, and selected formulas needed to compute the EMV and EVPI values.

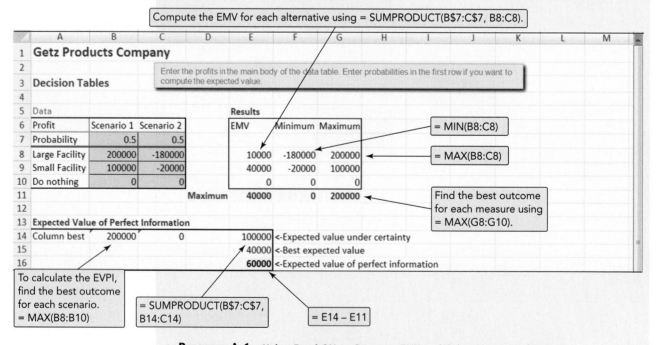

▲ **Program A.1   Using Excel OM to Compute EMV and Other Measures for Getz**

Program A.2 uses Excel OM to create the decision tree for Getz Products shown earlier in Example A6. The tool to create the tree is seen in the window on the right.

▲ **Program A.2**   **Getz Products' Decision Tree Using Excel OM**

Using POM for Windows

POM for Windows can be used to calculate all of the information described in the decision tables and decision trees in this module. For details on how to use this software, please refer to Appendix IV.

Self-Test

- *Before taking the self-test*, *refer to the learning objectives at the beginning of the module, the notes in the margins, and the glossary at the end of the module.*
- *Use the key at the back of the book to **correct** your answers.*
- *Restudy pages that correspond to any questions you answered incorrectly or material you feel uncertain about.*

1. In decision theory terminology, a course of action or a strategy that may be chosen by a decision maker is called a(n):
   a) payoff
   b) alternative
   c) state of nature
   d) all of the above

2. In decision theory, probabilities are associated with:
   a) payoffs
   b) alternatives
   c) states of nature
   d) all of the above

3. If probabilities are available to the decision maker, then the decision-making environment is called:
   a) certainty
   b) uncertainty
   c) risk
   d) none of the above

4. Which of the following is a decision-making criterion that is used for decision making under risk?
   a) expected monetary value criterion
   b) pessimistic (maximin) criterion

   c) optimistic (maximax) criterion
   d) equally likely criterion

5. The most that a person should pay for perfect information is:
   a) the EVPI
   b) the maximum EMV minus the minimum EMV
   c) the minimum EMV
   d) the maximum EMV

6. A decision tree is preferable to a decision table when:
   a) a number of sequential decisions are to be made
   b) probabilities are available
   c) the maximax criterion is used
   d) the objective is to maximize regret

7. On a decision tree, at each state-of-nature node:
   a) the alternative with the greatest EMV is selected
   b) an EMV is calculated
   c) all probabilities are added together
   d) the branch with the highest probability is selected

8. On a decision tree, once the tree has been drawn and the payoffs and probabilities have been placed on the tree, the analysis (computing EMVs and selecting the best alternative):
   a) is done by working backward (starting on the right and moving to the left)
   b) is done by working forward (starting on the left and moving to the right)
   c) is done by starting at the top of the tree and moving down
   d) is done by starting at the bottom of the tree and moving up

Solved Problems

 Virtual Office Hours help is available on Student DVD.

Solved Problem A.1

Stella Yan Hua is considering the possibility of opening a small dress shop on Fairbanks Avenue, a few blocks from the university. She has located a good mall that attracts students. Her options are to open a small shop, a medium-sized shop, or no shop at all. The market for a dress shop can be good, average, or bad. The probabilities for these three possibilities are .2 for a good market, .5 for an average market, and .3 for a bad market. The net profit or loss for the medium-sized or small shops for the various market conditions are given in the following table. Building no shop at all yields no loss and no gain. What do you recommend?

	States of Nature		
Alternatives	**Good Market ($)**	**Average Market ($)**	**Bad Market ($)**
Small shop	75,000	25,000	−40,000
Medium-sized shop	100,000	35,000	−60,000
No shop	0	0	0
Probabilities	.20	.50	.30

solution

The problem can be solved by computing the expected monetary value (EMV) for each alternative:

$$\text{EMV (Small shop)} = (.2)(\$75,000) + (.5)(\$25,000) + (.3)(-\$40,000) = \$15,500$$

$$\text{EMV (Medium-sized shop)} = (.2)(\$100,000) + (.5)(\$35,000) + (.3)(-\$60,000) = \$19,500$$

$$\text{EMV (No shop)} = (.2)(\$0) + (.5)(\$0) + (.3)(\$0) = \$0$$

As you can see, the best decision is to build the medium-sized shop. The EMV for this alternative is $19,500.

Solved Problem A.2

T.S. Amer's Ski Shop in Nevada has a 100-day season. T.S. has established the probability of various store traffic, based on historical records of skiing condition, as indicated in the table to the right. T.S. has four merchandising plans, each focusing on a popular name brand. Each plan yields a daily net profit as noted in the table. He also has a meteorologist friend, who for a small fee, will accurately tell tomorrow's weather so T.S. can implement one of his four merchandising plans.
a)   What is the expected monetary value (EMV) under risk?
b)   What is the expected value with perfect information (EVwPI)?
c)   What is the expected value of perfect information (EVPI)?

Decision Alternatives (merchandising plan focusing on:)	Traffic in Store Because of Ski Conditions (states of nature)			
	1	**2**	**3**	**4**
Patagonia	$40	92	20	48
North Face	50	84	10	52
Cloud Veil	35	80	40	64
Columbia	45	72	10	60
Probabilities	.20	.25	.30	.25

solution

a)   The highest expected monetary value under risk is:

$$\text{EMV (Patagonia)} = .20(40) + .25(92) + .30(20) + .25(48) = \$49$$

$$\text{EMV (North Face)} = .20(50) + .25(84) + .30(10) + .25(52) = \$47$$

$$\text{EMV (Cloud Veil)} = .20(35) + .25(80) + .30(40) + .25(64) = \$55$$

$$\text{EMV (Columbia)} = .20(45) + .25(72) + .30(10) + .25(60) = \$45$$

So the maximum EMV = $55

b)   The expected value with perfect information is:

$$\text{EVwPI} = .20(50) + .25(92) + .30(40) + .25(64)$$

$$= 10 + 23 + 12 + 16 = \$61$$

c)   The expected value of perfect information is:

$$\text{EVPI} = \text{EVwPI} - \text{Maximum EMV} = 61 - 55 = \$6$$

Solved Problem A.3

Daily demand for cases of Tidy Bowl cleaner at Ravinder Nath's Supermarket has always been 5, 6, or 7 cases. Develop a decision tree that illustrates her decision alternatives as to whether to stock 5, 6, or 7 cases.

Solution

The decision tree is shown in Figure A.5.

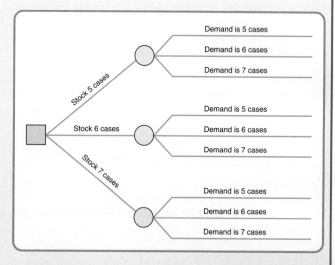

▲ **Figure A.5**   **Demand at Ravinder Nath's Supermarket**

Internet and Student CD-ROM/DVD Exercises

Visit our Companion Web site or use your student CD-ROM/DVD to help with this material in this module.

 On Our Companion Web Site,
www.prenhall.com/heizer
- Self-Study Quizzes
- Practice Problems
- Internet Case
- PowerPoint Lecture

 On Your Student CD-ROM
- Practice Problems
- Excel OM
- Excel OM Example Data File
- POM for Windows

 On Your Student DVD
- Virtual Office Hours for Solved Problems

Discussion Questions

1. Identify the six steps in the decision process.
2. Give an example of a good decision you made that resulted in a bad outcome. Also give an example of a bad decision you made that had a good outcome. Why was each decision good or bad?
3. What is the *equally likely* decision model?
4. Discuss the differences between decision making under certainty, under risk, and under uncertainty.
5. What is a decision tree?
6. Explain how decision trees might be used in several of the 10 OM decisions.
7. What is the expected value of perfect information?
8. What is the expected value *with* perfect information?
9. Identify the five steps in analyzing a problem using a decision tree.
10. Why are the maximax and maximin strategies considered to be optimistic and pessimistic, respectively?
11. The expected value criterion is considered to be the rational criterion on which to base a decision. Is this true? Is it rational to consider risk?
12. When are decision trees most useful?

Problems*

•   **A.1**   Given the following conditional value table, determine the appropriate decision under uncertainty using:
a) Maximax.
b) Maximin.
c) Equally likely.

*Note: **PX** means the problem may be solved with POM for Windows and/or Excel OM.

	States of Nature		
Alternatives	**Very Favorable Market**	**Average Market**	**Unfavorable Market**
Build new plant	$350,000	$240,000	−$300,000
Subcontract	$180,000	$ 90,000	−$ 20,000
Overtime	$110,000	$ 60,000	−$ 10,000
Do nothing	$ 0	$ 0	$ 0 **PX**

••• **A.2** Even though independent gasoline stations have been having a difficult time, Susan Helms has been thinking about starting her own independent gasoline station. Susan's problem is to decide how large her station should be. The annual returns will depend on both the size of her station and a number of marketing factors related to the oil industry and demand for gasoline. After a careful analysis, Susan developed the following table:

Size of First Station	Good Market ($)	Fair Market ($)	Poor Market ($)
Small	50,000	20,000	−10,000
Medium	80,000	30,000	−20,000
Large	100,000	30,000	−40,000
Very large	300,000	25,000	−160,000

For example, if Susan constructs a small station and the market is good, she will realize a profit of $50,000.
a) Develop a decision table for this decision, like the one illustrated in Table A.2 earlier.
b) What is the maximax decision?
c) What is the maximin decision?
d) What is the equally likely decision?
e) Develop a decision tree. Assume each outcome is equally likely, then find the highest EMV. **Px**

• **A.3** Clay Whybark, a soft-drink vendor at Hard Rock Cafe's annual Rockfest, created a table of conditional values for the various alternatives (stocking decision) and states of nature (size of crowd):

Alternatives	States of Nature (demand)		
	Big	Average	Small
Large stock	$22,000	$12,000	−$2,000
Average stock	$14,000	$10,000	$6,000
Small stock	$ 9,000	$ 8,000	$4,000

The probabilities associated with the states of nature are 0.3 for a big demand, 0.5 for an average demand, and 0.2 for a small demand.
a) Determine the alternative that provides Clay Whybark the greatest expected monetary value (EMV).
b) Compute the expected value of perfect information (EVPI). **Px**

•• **A.4** Raymond Jacobs owns a health and fitness center, the Muscle-Up, in Ashland. He is considering adding more floor space to meet increasing demand. He will either add no floor space (N), a moderate area of floor space (M), a large area of floor space (L), or an area of floor space that doubles the size of the facility (D). Demand will either stay fixed, increase slightly, or increase greatly. The following are the changes in Muscle-Up's annual profits under each combination of expansion level and demand change level:

Demand Change	Expansion Level			
	N	M	L	D
Fixed	$ 0	−$4,000	−$10,000	−$50,000
Slight Increase	$2,000	$8,000	$ 6,000	$ 4,000
Major Increase	$3,000	$9,000	$20,000	$40,000

Raymond is risk averse and wishes to use the maximin criterion.
a) What are his decision alternatives and what are the states of nature?
b) What should he do? **Px**

• **A.5** Howard Weiss, Inc., is considering building a sensitive new airport scanning device. His managers believe that there is a probability of 0.4 that the ATR Co. will come out with a competitive product. If Weiss adds an assembly line for the product and ATR Co.

does not follow with a competitive product, Weiss's expected profit is $40,000; if Weiss adds an assembly line and ATR follows suit, Weiss still expects $10,000 profit. If Weiss adds a new plant addition and ATR does not produce a competitive product, Weiss expects a profit of $600,000; if ATR does compete for this market, Weiss expects a loss of $100,000.
a) Determine the EMV of each decision.
b) Compute the expected value of perfect information. **Px**

•• **A.6** Deborah Watson's factory is considering three approaches for meeting an expected increase in demand. These three approaches are increasing capacity, using overtime, and buying more equipment. Demand will increase either slightly (S), moderately (M), or greatly (G). The profits for each approach under each possible scenario are as follows:

Approach	Demand Scenario		
	S	M	G
Increasing Capacity	$700,000	$700,000	$ 700,000
Using Overtime	$500,000	$600,000	$1,000,000
Buying Equipment	$600,000	$800,000	$ 800,000

Since the goal is to maximize, and Deborah is risk-neutral, she decides to use the *equally likely* decision criterion to make the decision as to which approach to use. According to this criterion, which approach should be used?

• **A.7** The following payoff table provides profits based on various possible decision alternatives and various levels of demand at Amber Gardner's software firm:

	Demand	
	Low	High
Alternative 1	$10,000	$30,000
Alternative 2	$ 5,000	$40,000
Alternative 3	−$ 2,000	$50,000

The probability of low demand is 0.4, whereas the probability of high demand is 0.6.
a) What is the highest possible expected monetary value?
b) What is the expected value *with* perfect information (EVwPI)?
c) Calculate the expected value of perfect information for this situation. **Px**

• **A.8** Leah Johnson, director of Legal Services of Brookline, wants to increase capacity to provide free legal advice but must decide whether to do so by hiring another full-time lawyer or by using part-time lawyers. The table below shows the expected *costs* of the two options for three possible demand levels:

Alternatives	States of Nature		
	Low Demand	Medium Demand	High Demand
Hire full-time	$300	$500	$ 700
Hire part-time	$ 0	$350	$1,000
Probabilities	.2	.5	.3

a) Using expected value, what should Ms. Johnson do?
b) Draw an appropriate decision tree showing payoffs and probabilities. **Px**

•• **A.9** Chung Manufacturing is considering the introduction of a family of new products. Long-term demand for the product group is somewhat predictable, so the manufacturer must be concerned with the risk of choosing a process that is inappropriate. Chen Chung is VP of operations. He can choose among batch manufacturing or custom manufacturing, or he can invest in group technology. Chen won't be able to forecast demand accurately until after he makes the process choice. Demand will be classified into four compartments: poor, fair, good, and excellent. The table below indicates the payoffs (profits) associated with each process/demand combination, as well as the probabilities of each long-term demand level:

	Poor	Fair	Good	Excellent
Probability	.1	.4	.3	.2
Batch	–$ 200,000	$1,000,000	$1,200,000	$1,300,000
Custom	$ 100,000	$ 300,000	$ 700,000	$ 800,000
Group technology	–$1,000,000	–$ 500,000	$ 500,000	$2,000,000

a) Based on expected value, what choice offers the greatest gain?
b) What would Chen Chung be willing to pay for a forecast that would accurately determine the level of demand in the future? **PX**

•• **A.10** Consider the following decision table, which Dinesh Dave has developed for Appalacian Enterprises:

Decision Alternatives	Probability:	States of Nature		
		.40 Low	.20 Medium	.40 High
A		$40	$100	$60
B		$85	$ 60	$70
C		$60	$ 70	$70
D		$65	$ 75	$70
E		$70	$ 65	$80

Which decision alternative maximizes the expected value of the payoff? **PX**

•• **A.11** The University of Dallas bookstore stocks textbooks in preparation for sales each semester. It normally relies on departmental forecasts and preregistration records to determine how many copies of a text are needed. Preregistration shows 90 operations management students enrolled, but bookstore manager Curtis Ketterman has second thoughts, based on his intuition and some historical evidence. Curtis believes that the distribution of sales may range from 70 to 90 units, according to the following probability model:

Demand	70	75	80	85	90
Probability	.15	.30	.30	.20	.05

This textbook costs the bookstore $82 and sells for $112. Any unsold copies can be returned to the publisher, less a restocking fee and shipping, for a net refund of $36.
a) Construct the table of conditional profits.
b) How many copies should the bookstore stock to achieve highest expected value? **PX**

•• **A.12** Palmer Cheese Company is a small manufacturer of several different cheese products. One product is a cheese spread sold to retail outlets. Susan Palmer must decide how many cases of cheese spread to manufacture each month. The probability that demand will be 6 cases is .1, for 7 cases it is .3, for 8 cases it is .5, and for 9 cases it is .1. The cost of every case is $45, and the price Susan gets for each case is $95. Unfortunately, any cases not sold by the end of the month are of no value as a result of spoilage. How many cases should Susan manufacture each month? **PX**

••• **A.13** Ronald Lau, chief engineer at South Dakota Electronics, has to decide whether to build a new state-of-the-art processing facility. If the new facility works, the company could realize a profit of $200,000. If it fails, South Dakota Electronics could lose $180,000. At this time, Lau estimates a 60% chance that the new process will fail.

The other option is to build a pilot plant and then decide whether to build a complete facility. The pilot plant would cost $10,000 to build. Lau estimates a 50-50 chance that the pilot plant will work. If the pilot plant works, there is a 90% probability that the complete plant, if it is built, will also work. If the pilot plant does not work, there is only a 20% chance that the complete project (if it is constructed) will work. Lau faces a dilemma. Should he build the plant? Should he build the pilot project and then make a decision? Help Lau by analyzing this problem. **PX**

•• **A.14** Karen Villagomez, president of Wright Industries, is considering whether to build a manufacturing plant in the Ozarks. Her decision is summarized in the following table:

Alternatives	Favorable Market	Unfavorable Market
Build large plant	$400,000	–$300,000
Build small plant	$ 80,000	–$ 10,000
Don't build	$ 0	$ 0
Market probabilities	0.4	0.6

a) Construct a decision tree.
b) Determine the best strategy using expected monetary value (EMV).
c) What is the expected value of perfect information (EVPI)? **PX**

•• **A.15** Deborah Kellogg buys Breathalyzer test sets for the Denver Police Department. The quality of the test sets from her two suppliers is indicated in the following table:

Percent Defective	Probability for Loomba Technology	Probability for Stewart-Douglas Enterprises
1	.70	.30
3	.20	.30
5	.10	.40

For example, the probability of getting a batch of tests that are 1% defective from Loomba Technology is .70. Because Kellogg orders 10,000 tests per order, this would mean that there is a .7 probability of getting 100 defective tests out of the 10,000 tests if Loomba

Technology is used to fill the order. A defective Breathalyzer test set can be repaired for $0.50. Although the quality of the test sets of the second supplier, Stewart-Douglas Enterprises, is lower, it will sell an order of 10,000 test sets for $37 less than Loomba.

a) Develop a decision tree.

b) Which supplier should Kellogg use? **Px**

•• **A.16** Deborah Hollwager, a concessionaire for the Des Moines ballpark, has developed a table of conditional values for the various alternatives (stocking decision) and states of nature (size of crowd):

	States of Nature (size of crowd)		
Alternatives	**Large**	**Average**	**Small**
Large inventory	$20,000	$10,000	–$2,000
Average inventory	$15,000	$12,000	$6,000
Small inventory	$ 9,000	$ 6,000	$5,000

If the probabilities associated with the states of nature are 0.3 for a large crowd, 0.5 for an average crowd, and 0.2 for a small crowd, determine:

a) The alternative that provides the greatest expected monetary value (EMV).

b) The expected value of perfect information (EVPI). **Px**

• **A.17** Joseph Biggs owns his own sno-cone business and lives 30 miles from a California beach resort. The sale of sno-cones is highly dependent on his location and on the weather. At the resort, his profit will be $120 per day in fair weather, $10 per day in bad weather. At home, his profit will be $70 in fair weather and $55 in bad weather. Assume that on any particular day, the weather service suggests a 40% chance of foul weather.

a) Construct Joseph's decision tree.

b) What decision is recommended by the expected value criterion? **Px**

•• **A.18** Kenneth Boyer is considering opening a bicycle shop in north Chicago. Boyer enjoys biking, but this is to be a business endeavor from which he expects to make a living. He can open a small shop, a large shop, or no shop at all. Because there will be a 5-year lease on the building that Boyer is thinking about using, he wants to make sure he makes the correct decision. Boyer is also thinking about hiring his old marketing professor to conduct a marketing research study to see if there is a market for his services. The results of such a study could be either favorable or unfavorable. Develop a decision tree for Boyer. **Px**

••• **A.19** F. J. Brewerton Retailers, Inc., must decide whether to build a small or a large facility at a new location in south Texas. Demand at the location will either be low or high, with probabilities 0.4 and 0.6, respectively. If Brewerton builds a small facility and demand proves to be high, he then has the option of expanding the facility. If a small facility is built and demand proves to be high, and then the retailer expands the facility, the payoff is $270,000. If a small facility is built and demand proves to be high, but Brewerton then decides not to expand the facility, the payoff is $223,000.

If a small facility is built and demand proves to be low, then there is no option to expand and the payoff is $200,000. If a large facility is built and demand proves to be low, Brewerton then has the option of stimulating demand through local advertising. If he does not exercise this option, then the payoff is $40,000. If he does exercise the advertising option, then the response to advertising will either be modest or sizable, with probabilities of 0.3 and 0.7, respectively. If the response is modest, the payoff is $20,000. If it is sizable, the pay-

off is $220,000. Finally, if a large facility is built and demand proves to be high, then no advertising is needed and the payoff is $800,000.

a) What should Brewerton do to maximize his expected payoff?

b) What is the value of this expected payoff?

••• **A.20** Dick Holliday is not sure what he should do. He can build either a large video rental section or a small one in his drugstore. He can also gather additional information or simply do nothing. If he gathers additional information, the results could suggest either a favorable or an unfavorable market, but it would cost him $3,000 to gather the information. Holliday believes that there is a 50–50 chance that the information will be favorable. If the rental market is favorable, Holliday will earn $15,000 with a large section or $5,000 with a small. With an unfavorable video-rental market, however, Holliday could lose $20,000 with a large section or $10,000 with a small section. Without gathering additional information, Holliday estimates that the probability of a favorable rental market is .7. A favorable report from the study would increase the probability of a favorable rental market to .9. Furthermore, an unfavorable report from the additional information would decrease the probability of a favorable rental market to .4. Of course, Holliday could ignore these numbers and do nothing. What is your advice to Holliday?

•••• **A.21** Jeff Kaufmann's machine shop sells a variety of machines for job shops. A customer wants to purchase a model XPO2 drilling machine from Jeff's store. The model XPO2 sells for $180,000, but Jeff is out of XPO2s. The customer says he will wait for Jeff to get a model XPO2 in stock. Jeff knows that there is a wholesale market for XPO2s from which he can purchase an XPO2. Jeff can buy an XPO2 today for $150,000, or he can wait a day and buy an XPO2 (if one is available) tomorrow for $125,000. If at least one XPO2 is still available tomorrow, Jeff can wait until the day after tomorrow and buy an XPO2 (if one is still available) for $110,000.

There is an 0.40 probability that there will be no model XPO2s available tomorrow. If there are model XPO2s available tomorrow, there is a 0.70 probability that by the day after tomorrow, there will be no model XPO2s available in the wholesale market. Three days from now, it is certain that no model XPO2s will be available on the wholesale market. What is the maximum expected profit that Jeff can achieve? What should Jeff do?

•••• **A.22** The city of Segovia is contemplating building a second airport to relieve congestion at the main airport and is considering two potential sites, X and Y. Hard Rock Hotels would like to purchase land to build a hotel at the new airport. The value of land has been rising in anticipation and is expected to skyrocket once the city decides between sites X and Y. Consequently, Hard Rock would like to purchase land now. Hard Rock will sell the land if the city chooses not to locate the airport nearby. Hard Rock has four choices: (1) buy land at X, (2) buy land at Y, (3) buy land at both X and Y, or (4) do nothing. Hard Rock has collected the following data (which are in millions of euros):

	Site X	Site Y
Current purchase price	27	15
Profits if airport and hotel built at this site	45	30
Sale price if airport not built at this site	9	6

Hard Rock determines there is a 45% chance the airport will be built at X (hence, a 55% chance it will be built at Y).

a) Set up the decision table.

b) What should Hard Rock decide to do to maximize total net profit? **Px**

···· A.23 Louisiana is busy designing new lottery scratch-off games. In the latest game, Bayou Boondoggle, the player is instructed to scratch off one spot: A, B, or C. A can reveal "Loser, " "Win \$1," or "Win \$50." B can reveal "Loser" or "Take a Second Chance." C can reveal "Loser" or "Win \$500." On the second chance, the player is instructed to scratch off D or E. D can reveal "Loser" or "Win \$1." E can reveal "Loser" or "Win \$10." The probabilities at A are .9, .09, and .01. The probabilities at B are .8 and .2. The probabilities at C are .999 and .001. The probabilities at D are .5 and .5. Finally, the probabilities at E are .95 and .05. Draw the decision tree that represents this scenario. Use proper symbols and label all branches clearly. Calculate the expected value of this game. **Px**

Case Studies

Tom Tucker's Liver Transplant

Tom Tucker, a robust 50-year-old executive living in the northern suburbs of St. Paul, has been diagnosed by a University of Minnesota internist as having a decaying liver. Although he is otherwise healthy, Tucker's liver problem could prove fatal if left untreated.

Firm research data are not yet available to predict the likelihood of survival for a man of Tucker's age and condition without surgery. However, based on her own experience and recent medical journal articles, the internist tells him that if he elects to avoid surgical treatment of the liver problem, chances of survival will be approximately as follows: only a 60% chance of living 1 year, a 20% chance of surviving for 2 years, a 10% chance for 5 years, and

a 10% chance of living to age 58. She places his probability of survival beyond age 58 without a liver transplant to be extremely low.

The transplant operation, however, is a serious surgical procedure. Five percent of patients die during the operation or its recovery stage, with an additional 45% dying during the first year. Twenty percent survive for 5 years, 13% survive for 10 years, and 8%, 5%, and 4% survive, respectively, for 15, 20, and 25 years.

Discussion Questions

1. Do you think that Tucker should select the transplant operation?
2. What other factors might be considered?

Ski Right Corp.

After retiring as a physician, Bob Guthrie became an avid downhill skier on the steep slopes of the Utah Rocky Mountains. As an amateur inventor, Bob was always looking for something new. With the recent deaths of several celebrity skiers, Bob knew he could use his creative mind to make skiing safer and his bank account larger. He knew that many deaths on the slopes were caused by head injuries. Although ski helmets have been on the market for some time, most skiers consider them boring and basically ugly. As a physician, Bob knew that some type of new ski helmet was the answer.

Bob's biggest challenge was to invent a helmet that was attractive, safe, and fun to wear. Multiple colors and using the latest fashion designs would be musts. After years of skiing, Bob knew that many skiers believe that how you look on the slopes is more important than how you ski. His helmets would have to look good and fit in with current fashion trends. But attractive helmets were not enough. Bob had to make the helmets fun and useful. The name of the new ski helmet, Ski Right, was sure to be a winner. If Bob could come up with a good idea, he believed that there was a 20% chance that the market for the Ski Right helmet would be excellent. The chance of a good market should be 40%. Bob also knew that the market for his helmet could be only average (30% chance) or even poor (10% chance).

The idea of how to make ski helmets fun and useful came to Bob on a gondola ride to the top of a mountain. A busy executive on the gondola ride was on his cell phone trying to complete a complicated merger. When the executive got off the gondola, he dropped the phone and it was crushed by the gondola mechanism. Bob decided that his new ski helmet would have a built-in cell phone and an AM/FM stereo radio. All the electronics could be operated by a control pad worn on a skier's arm or leg.

Bob decided to try a small pilot project for Ski Right. He enjoyed being retired and didn't want a failure to cause him to go back to work. After some research, Bob found Progressive Products (PP). The company was willing to be a partner in developing the Ski Right and sharing any profits. If the market was excellent, Bob would net \$5,000 per month. With a good market, Bob would net \$2,000. An average market would result in a loss of \$2,000, and a poor market would mean Bob would be out \$5,000 per month.

Another option for Bob was to have Leadville Barts (LB) make the helmet. The company had extensive experience in making bicycle helmets. Progressive would then take the helmets made by Leadville Barts and do the rest. Bob had a greater risk. He estimated that he could lose \$10,000 per month in a poor market or \$4,000 in an average market. A good market for Ski Right would result in \$6,000 profit for Bob, and an excellent market would mean a \$12,000 profit per month.

A third option for Bob was to use TalRad (TR), a radio company in Tallahassee, Florida. TalRad had extensive experience in making military radios. TalRad could also make the helmets, and Progressive Products could do the rest of production and distribution. Again, Bob would be taking on greater risk. A poor market would mean a \$15,000 loss per month, and an average market would mean a \$10,000 loss. A good market would result in a net profit of \$7,000 for Bob. An excellent market would return \$13,000 per month.

Bob could also have Celestial Cellular (CC) develop the cell phones. Thus, another option was to have Celestial make the phones and have Progressive do the rest of the production and distribution. Because the cell phone was the most expensive component of the helmet, Bob could lose \$30,000 per month in a poor market. He could lose \$20,000 in an average market. If the market was good or excellent, Bob would see a net profit of $10,000 or $30,000 per month, respectively.

Bob's final option was to forget about Progressive Products entirely. He could use Leadville Barts to make the helmets, Celestial Cellular to make the phones, and TalRad to make the AM/FM stereo radios. Bob could then hire some friends to assemble everything and market the finished Ski Right helmets. With this final alternative, Bob could realize a net profit of $55,000 a month in an excellent market. Even if the market was just good, Bob would net $20,000. An average market, however, would mean a loss of $35,000. If the market was poor Bob would lose $60,000 per month.

Discussion Questions

1. What do you recommend?
2. Compute the expected value of perfect information.
3. Was Bob completely logical in how he approached this decision problem?

Source: B. Render, R. M. Stair, and M. Hanna, *Quantitative Analysis for Management*, 10th ed. Upper Saddle River, N.J.: Prentice Hall (2009). Reprinted by permission of Prentice Hall, Inc.

Additional Case Study

See our Companion Web site at **www.prenhall.com/heizer** *for this additional free case study:*

- **Arctic, Inc.:** A refrigeration company has several major options with regard to capacity and expansion.

Bibliography

Balakrishnan, R., B. Render, and R. M. Stair, Jr. *Managerial Decision Modeling with Spreadsheets*, 2nd ed. Upper Saddle River, NJ: Prentice Hall (2007).

Collin, Ian. "Scale Management and Risk Assessment for Deepwater Developments." *World Oil* 224, no. 5 (May 2003): 62.

Hammond, J. S., R. L. Kenney, and H. Raiffa. "The Hidden Traps in Decision Making." 76, no. 5 *Harvard Business Review* (September–October 1998): 47–60.

Keefer, Donald L. "Balancing Drug Safety and Efficacy for a Go/No-Go Decision." *Interfaces* 34, no. 2 (March–April 2004): 113–116.

Lin, H. "Decision Theory and Analysis." *Futurics* 28, no. 1–2 (2004): 27–47.

Miller, C. C., and R. D. Ireland. "Intuition in Strategic Decision Making." *Academy of Management Executive* 19, no. 1 (February 2005): 19.

Raiffa, H., and R. Schlaifer. *Applied Statistical Decision Theory*. New York: Wiley (2000).

Render, B., R. M. Stair Jr., and M. Hanna. *Quantitative Analysis for Management*, 10th ed. Upper Saddle River, NJ: Prentice Hall (2009).

QUANTITATIVE MODULE B

Linear Programming

Module Outline

Learning Objectives

When you complete this module you should be able to

1. Formulate linear programming models, including an objective function and constraints
2. Graphically solve an LP problem with the iso-profit line method
3. Graphically solve an LP problem with the corner-point method
4. Interpret sensitivity analysis and shadow prices
5. Construct and solve a minimization problem
6. Formulate production-mix, diet, and labor scheduling problems

705

▶ *The storm front closed in quickly on Chicago's O'Hare Airport, shutting it down without warning. The heavy thunderstorms, lightning, and poor visibility sent American Airlines passengers and ground crew scurrying. Because American Airlines uses linear programming (LP) to schedule flights, hotels, crews, and refueling, LP has a direct impact on profitability. If American gets a major weather disruption at one of its hubs, a lot of flights may get canceled, which means a lot of crews and airplanes in the wrong places. LP is the tool that helps airlines such as American unsnarl and cope with this weather mess.*

Many operations management decisions involve trying to make the most effective use of an organization's resources. Resources typically include machinery (such as planes, in the case of an airline), labor (such as pilots), money, time, and raw materials (such as jet fuel). These resources may be used to produce products (such as machines, furniture, food, or clothing) or services (such as airline schedules, advertising policies, or investment decisions). **Linear programming (LP)** is a widely used mathematical technique designed to help operations managers plan and make the decisions necessary to allocate resources.

A few examples of problems in which LP has been successfully applied in operations management are:

1. Scheduling school buses to *minimize* the total distance traveled when carrying students
2. Allocating police patrol units to high crime areas to *minimize* response time to 911 calls
3. Scheduling tellers at banks so that needs are met during each hour of the day while *minimizing* the total cost of labor
4. Selecting the product mix in a factory to make best use of machine- and labor-hours available while *maximizing* the firm's profit
5. Picking blends of raw materials in feed mills to produce finished feed combinations at *minimum* cost
6. Determining the distribution system that will *minimize* total shipping cost from several warehouses to various market locations
7. Developing a production schedule that will satisfy future demands for a firm's product and at the same time *minimize* total production and inventory costs
8. Allocating space for a tenant mix in a new shopping mall so as to *maximize* revenues to the leasing company (see the *OM in Action* box "Using LP to Select Tenants in a Shopping Mall").

Linear programming (LP)
A mathematical technique designed to help operations managers plan and make decisions relative to the trade-offs necessary to allocate resources.

REQUIREMENTS OF A LINEAR PROGRAMMING PROBLEM

All LP problems have four properties in common:

1. LP problems seek to *maximize* or *minimize* some quantity (usually profit or cost). We refer to this property as the **objective function** of an LP problem. The major objective of a typical firm is to maximize dollar profits in the long run. In the case of a trucking or airline distribution system, the objective might be to minimize shipping costs.
2. The presence of restrictions, or **constraints**, limits the degree to which we can pursue our objective. For example, deciding how many units of each product in a firm's product line to manufacture is restricted by available labor and machinery. We want, therefore, to maximize or minimize a quantity (the objective function) subject to limited resources (the constraints).

Objective function
A mathematical expression in linear programming that maximizes or minimizes some quantity (often profit or cost, but any goal may be used).

Constraints
Restrictions that limit the degree to which a manager can pursue an objective.

OM in Action   Using LP to Select Tenants in a Shopping Mall

Homart Development Company is one of the largest shopping-center developers in the U.S. When starting a new center, Homart produces a tentative floor plan, or "footprint," for the mall. This plan outlines sizes, shapes, and spaces for large department stores. Leasing agreements are reached with the two or three major department stores that will become anchor stores in the mall. The anchor stores are able to negotiate highly favorable occupancy agreements. Homart's profits come primarily from the rent paid by the nonanchor tenants—the smaller stores that lease space along the aisles of the mall. The decision as to allocating space to potential tenants is, therefore, crucial to the success of the investment.

The tenant mix describes the desired stores in the mall by their size, general location, and type of merchandise or service provided. For example, the mix might specify two small jewelry stores in a central section of the mall and a medium-size shoe store and a large restaurant in one of the side aisles. In the past, Homart developed a plan for tenant mix using "rules of thumb" developed over years of experience in mall development.

Now, to improve its bottom line in an increasingly competitive marketplace, Homart treats the tenant-mix problem as an LP model. First, the model assumes that tenants can be classified into categories according to the type of merchandise or service they provide. Second, the model assumes that for each store type, store sizes can be estimated by distinct category. For example, a small jewelry store is said to contain about 700 square feet and a large one about 2,200 square feet. The tenant-mix model is a powerful tool for enhancing Homart's mall planning and leasing activities.

Sources: Chain Store Age (March 2000): 191–192; *Business World* (March 18, 2002): 1; and *Interfaces* (March–April 1988): 1–9.

3. There must be *alternative courses of action* to choose from. For example, if a company produces three different products, management may use LP to decide how to allocate among them its limited production resources (of labor, machinery, and so on). If there were no alternatives to select from, we would not need LP.
4. The objective and constraints in linear programming problems must be expressed in terms of *linear equations* or inequalities.

FORMULATING LINEAR PROGRAMMING PROBLEMS

One of the most common linear programming applications is the *product-mix problem*. Two or more products are usually produced using limited resources. The company would like to determine how many units of each product it should produce to maximize overall profit given its limited resources. Let's look at an example.

Shader Electronics Example

The Shader Electronics Company produces two products: (1) the Shader x-pod, a portable music player, and (2) the Shader BlueBerry, an internet-connected color telephone. The production process for each product is similar in that both require a certain number of hours of electronic work and a certain number of labor-hours in the assembly department. Each x-pod takes 4 hours of electronic work and 2 hours in the assembly shop. Each BlueBerry requires 3 hours in electronics and 1 hour in assembly. During the current production period, 240 hours of electronic time are available, and 100 hours of assembly department time are available. Each x-pod sold yields a profit of $7; each BlueBerry produced may be sold for a $5 profit.

Shader's problem is to determine the best possible combination of x-pods and BlueBerrys to manufacture to reach the maximum profit. This product-mix situation can be formulated as a linear programming problem.

We begin by summarizing the information needed to formulate and solve this problem (see Table B.1). Further, let's introduce some simple notation for use in the objective function and constraints. Let:

$$X_1 = \text{number of x-pods to be produced}$$
$$X_2 = \text{number of BlueBerrys to be produced}$$

Active Model B.1

This example is further illustrated in Active Model B.1 on the CD-ROM and in the Exercise on page 725.

We name the decision variables X_1 and X_2 here but point out that any notation (e.g., x-p and B) would be fine as well.

► **Table B.1**

**Shader Electronics
Company Problem Data**

Department	Hours Required to Produce One Unit		Available Hours This Week
	x-pods (X_1)	BlueBerrys (X_2)	
Electronic	4	3	240
Assembly	2	1	100
Profit per unit	$7	$5	

Now we can create the LP *objective function* in terms of X_1 and X_2:

$$\text{Maximize profit} = \$7X_1 + \$5X_2$$

Our next step is to develop mathematical relationships to describe the two constraints in this problem. One general relationship is that the amount of a resource used is to be less than or equal to ($\leq$) the amount of resource *available*.

First constraint: Electronic time used is $\leq$ Electronic time available.

$$4X_1 + 3X_2 \leq 240 \text{ (hours of electronic time)}$$

Second constraint: Assembly time used is $\leq$ Assembly time available.

$$2X_1 + 1X_2 \leq 100 \text{ (hours of assembly time)}$$

Both these constraints represent production capacity restrictions and, of course, affect the total profit. For example, Shader Electronics cannot produce 70 x-pods during the production period because if $X_1 = 70$, both constraints will be violated. It also cannot make $X_1 = 50$ x-pods and $X_2 = 10$ BlueBerrys. This constraint brings out another important aspect of linear programming; that is, certain interactions will exist between variables. The more units of one product that a firm produces, the fewer it can make of other products.

GRAPHICAL SOLUTION TO A LINEAR PROGRAMMING PROBLEM

The easiest way to solve a small LP problem such as that of the Shader Electronics Company is the **graphical solution approach**. The graphical procedure can be used only when there are two **decision variables** (such as number of x-pods to produce, X_1, and number of BlueBerrys to produce, X_2). When there are more than two variables, it is *not* possible to plot the solution on a two-dimensional graph; we then must turn to more complex approaches described later in this module.

Graphical Representation of Constraints

To find the optimal solution to a linear programming problem, we must first identify a set, or region, of feasible solutions. The first step in doing so is to plot the problem's constraints on a graph.

The variable X_1 (x-pods, in our example) is usually plotted as the horizontal axis of the graph, and the variable X_2 (BlueBerrys) is plotted as the vertical axis. The complete problem may be restated as:

$$\text{Maximize profit} = \$7X_1 + \$5X_2$$

Subject to the constraints:

$$4X_1 + 3X_2 \leq 240 \text{ (electronics constraint)}$$
$$2X_1 + 1X_2 \leq 100 \text{ (assembly constraint)}$$
$$X_1 \geq 0 \text{ (number of x-pods produced is greater than or equal to 0)}$$
$$X_2 \geq 0 \text{ (number of BlueBerrys produced is greater than or equal to 0)}$$

The first step in graphing the constraints of the problem is to convert the constraint *inequalities* into *equalities* (or equations).

Constraint A: $4X_1 + 3X_2 = 240$
Constraint B: $2X_1 + 1X_2 = 100$

The equation for constraint A is plotted in Figure B.1 and for constraint B in Figure B.2.

Learning Objective

1. Formulate linear programming models, including an objective function and constraints

Graphical solution approach
A means of plotting a solution to a two-variable problem on a graph.

Decision variables
Choices available to a decision maker.

These last two constraints are also called the nonnegativity constraints.

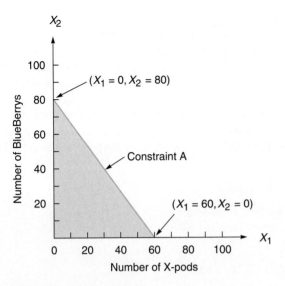

▲ **Figure B.1   Constraint A**

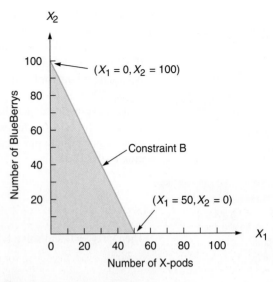

▲ **Figure B.2   Constraint B**

To plot the line in Figure B.1, all we need to do is to find the points at which the line $4X_1 + 3X_2 = 240$ intersects the X_1 and X_2 axes. When $X_1 = 0$ (the location where the line touches the X_2 axis), it implies that $3X_2 = 240$ and that $X_2 = 80$. Likewise, when $X_2 = 0$, we see that $4X_1 = 240$ and that $X_1 = 60$. Thus, constraint A is bounded by the line running from $(X_1 = 0, X_2 = 80)$ to $(X_1 = 60, X_2 = 0)$. The shaded area represents all points that satisfy the original *inequality*.

Constraint B is illustrated similarly in Figure B.2. When $X_1 = 0$, then $X_2 = 100$; and when $X_2 = 0$, then $X_1 = 50$. Constraint B, then, is bounded by the line between $(X_1 = 0, X_2 = 100)$ and $(X_1 = 50, X_2 = 0)$. The shaded area represents the original inequality.

Figure B.3 shows both constraints together. The shaded region is the part that satisfies both restrictions. The shaded region in Figure B.3 is called the *area of feasible solutions*, or simply the **feasible region**. This region must satisfy *all* conditions specified by the program's constraints and is thus the region where all constraints overlap. Any point in the region would be a *feasible solution* to the Shader Electronics Company problem. Any point outside the shaded area would represent an *infeasible solution*. Hence, it would be feasible to manufacture 30 x-pods and 20 BlueBerrys $(X_1 = 30, X_2 = 20)$, but it would violate the constraints to produce 70 x-pods and 40 BlueBerrys. This can be seen by plotting these points on the graph of Figure B.3.

Feasible region
The set of all feasible combinations of decision variables.

Iso-Profit Line Solution Method

Now that the feasible region has been graphed, we can proceed to find the *optimal* solution to the problem. The optimal solution is the point lying in the feasible region that produces the highest profit.

◀ **Figure B.3**

Feasible Solution Region for the Shader Electronics Company Problem

Iso-profit line method

An approach to solving a linear programming maximization problem graphically.

Once the feasible region has been established, several approaches can be taken in solving for the optimal solution. The speediest one to apply is called the **iso-profit line method**.[1]

We start by letting profits equal some arbitrary but small dollar amount. For the Shader Electronics problem, we may choose a profit of $210. This is a profit level that can easily be obtained without violating either of the two constraints. The objective function can be written as $210 = 7X_1 + 5X_2$.

This expression is just the equation of a line; we call it an *iso-profit line*. It represents all combinations (of X_1, X_2) that will yield a total profit of $210. To plot the profit line, we proceed exactly as we did to plot a constraint line. First, let $X_1 = 0$ and solve for the point at which the line crosses the X_2 axis:

$$\$210 = \$7(0) + \$5X_2$$
$$X_2 = 42 \text{ BlueBerrys}$$

Then let $X_2 = 0$ and solve for X_1:

$$\$210 = \$7X_1 + \$5(0)$$
$$X_1 = 30 \text{ x-pods}$$

We can now connect these two points with a straight line. This profit line is illustrated in Figure B.4. All points on the line represent feasible solutions that produce a profit of $210.

We see, however, that the iso-profit line for $210 does not produce the highest possible profit to the firm. In Figure B.5, we try graphing three more lines, each yielding a higher profit. The middle equation, $280 = $7X_1 + $5X_2$, was plotted in the same fashion as the lower line. When $X_1 = 0$:

$$\$280 = \$7(0) + 5X_2$$
$$X_2 = 56 \text{ BlueBerrys}$$

When $X_2 = 0$:

$$\$280 = \$7X_1 + \$5(0)$$
$$X_1 = 40 \text{ x-pods}$$

Again, any combination of x-pods (X_1) and BlueBerrys (X_2) on this iso-profit line will produce a total profit of $280.

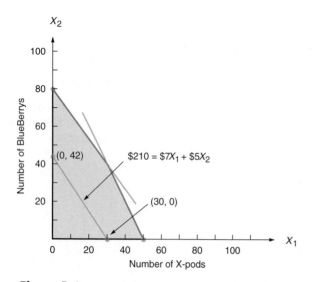

▲ **Figure B.4**   A Profit Line of $210 Plotted for the Shader Electronics Company

▲ **Figure B.5**   Four Iso-Profit Lines Plotted for the Shader Electronics Company

Note that the third line generates a profit of $350, even more of an improvement. The farther we move from the 0 origin, the higher our profit will be. Another important point to note is that these iso-profit lines are parallel. We now have two clues as to how to find the optimal solution to the original problem. We can draw a series of parallel profit lines (by carefully moving our ruler in a plane parallel to the first profit line). The highest profit line that still touches some point of the feasible region will pinpoint the optimal solution. Notice that the fourth line ($420) is too high to count because it does not touch the feasible region.

The highest possible iso-profit line is illustrated in Figure B.6. It touches the tip of the feasible region at the corner point ($X_1 = 30$, $X_2 = 40$) and yields a profit of $410.

Corner-Point Solution Method

A second approach to solving linear programming problems employs the **corner-point method**. This technique is simpler in concept than the iso-profit line approach, but it involves looking at the profit at every corner point of the feasible region.

The mathematical theory behind linear programming states that an optimal solution to any problem (that is, the values of X_1, X_2 that yield the maximum profit) will lie at a *corner point*, or *extreme point*, of the feasible region. Hence, it is necessary to find only the values of the variables at each corner; the maximum profit or optimal solution will lie at one (or more) of them.

Once again we can see (in Figure B.7) that the feasible region for the Shader Electronics Company problem is a four-sided polygon with four corner, or extreme, points. These points are

Corner-point method

A method for solving graphical linear programming problems.

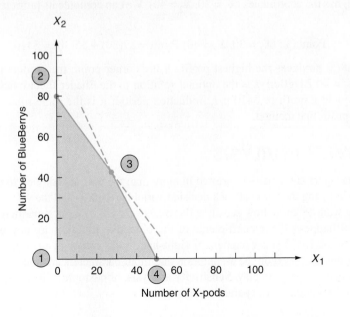

Learning Objective

3. Graphically solve an LP problem with the corner-point method

labeled ①, ②, ③ and ④ on the graph. To find the (X_1, X_2) values producing the maximum profit, we find out what the coordinates of each corner point are, then determine and compare their profit levels:

Point ①:	$(X_1 = 0, X_2 = 0)$	Profit $\$7(0) + \$5(0) = \$0$
Point ②:	$(X_1 = 0, X_2 = 80)$	Profit $\$7(0) + \$5(80) = \$400$
Point ④:	$(X_1 = 50, X_2 = 0)$	Profit $\$7(50) + \$5(0) = \$350$

We skipped corner point ③ momentarily because to find its coordinates *accurately*, we will have to solve for the intersection of the two constraint lines. As you may recall from algebra, we can apply the method of *simultaneous equations* to the two constraint equations:

$$4X_1 + 3X_2 = 240 \quad \text{(electronics time)}$$
$$2X_1 + 1X_2 = 100 \quad \text{(assembly time)}$$

To solve these equations simultaneously, we multiply the second equation by –2:

$$-2(2X_1 + 1X_2 = 100) = -4X_1 - 2X_2 = -200$$

and then add it to the first equation:

$$
\begin{aligned}
+4X_1 + 3X_2 &= 240 \\
-4X_1 - 2X_2 &= -200 \\
\hline
+ 1X_2 &= 40
\end{aligned}
$$

or:

$$X_2 = 40$$

Doing this has enabled us to eliminate one variable, X_1, and to solve for X_2. We can now substitute 40 for X_2 in either of the original equations and solve for X_1. Let us use the first equation. When $X_2 = 40$, then:

$$4X_1 + 3(40) = 240$$
$$4X_1 + 120 = 240$$

or:

$$4X_1 = 120$$
$$X_1 = 30$$

Although the values for X_1 and X_2 are integers for Shader Electronics, this will not always be the case.

Thus, point ③ has the coordinates $(X_1 = 30, X_2 = 40)$. We can compute its profit level to complete the analysis:

$$\text{Point ③: } (X_1 = 30, X_2 = 40) \text{ Profit} = \$7(30) + \$5(40) = \$410$$

Because point ③ produces the highest profit of any corner point, the product mix of $X_1 = 30$ x-pods and $X_2 = 40$ BlueBerrys is the optimal solution to the Shader Electronics problem. This solution will yield a profit of $410 per production period; it is the same solution we obtained using the iso-profit line method.

SENSITIVITY ANALYSIS

Parameter
Numerical value that is given in a model.

Sensitivity analysis
An analysis that projects how much a solution may change if there are changes in the variables or input data.

Operations managers are usually interested in more than the optimal solution to an LP problem. In addition to knowing the value of each decision variable (the X_is) and the value of the objective function, they want to know how sensitive these answers are to input **parameter** changes. For example, what happens if the coefficients of the objective function are not exact, or if they change by 10% or 15%? What happens if right-hand-side values of the constraints change? Because solutions are based on the assumption that input parameters are constant, the subject of sensitivity analysis comes into play. **Sensitivity analysis**, or postoptimality analysis, is the study of how sensitive solutions are to parameter changes.

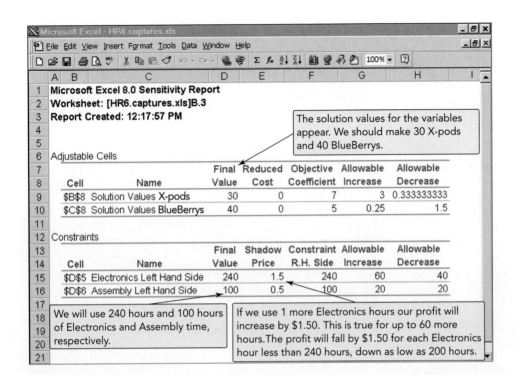

There are two approaches to determining just how sensitive an optimal solution is to changes. The first is simply a trial-and-error approach. This approach usually involves resolving the entire problem, preferably by computer, each time one input data item or parameter is changed. It can take a long time to test a series of possible changes in this way.

The approach we prefer is the analytic postoptimality method. After an LP problem has been solved, we determine a range of changes in problem parameters that will not affect the optimal solution or change the variables in the solution. This is done without resolving the whole problem. LP software, such as Excel's Solver or POM for Windows, has this capability. Let us examine several scenarios relating to the Shader Electronics example.

Program B.1 is part of the Excel Solver computer-generated output available to help a decision maker know whether a solution is relatively insensitive to reasonable changes in one or more of the parameters of the problem. (The complete computer run for these data, including input and full output, is illustrated in Programs B.2 and B.3 later in this module.)

Sensitivity Report

The Excel *Sensitivity Report* for the Shader Electronics example in Program B.1 has two distinct components: (1) a table titled Adjustable Cells and (2) a table titled Constraints. These tables permit us to answer several what-if questions regarding the problem solution.

It is important to note that while using the information in the sensitivity report to answer what-if questions, we assume that we are considering a change to only a *single* input data value. That is, the sensitivity information does not always apply to simultaneous changes in several input data values.

The *Adjustable Cells* table presents information regarding the impact of changes to the objective function coefficients (i.e., the unit profits of $7 and $5) on the optimal solution. The *Constraints* table presents information related to the impact of changes in constraint right-hand-side (RHS) values (i.e., the 240 hours and 100 hours) on the optimal solution. Although different LP software packages may format and present these tables differently, the programs all provide essentially the same information.

*The Sensitivity Report
has two parts: Adjustable
Cells and Constraints.*

*We are analyzing only
one change at a time.*

Changes in the Resources or Right-Hand-Side Values

The right-hand-side values of the constraints often represent resources available to the firm. The resources could be labor-hours or machine time or perhaps money or production materials available. In the Shader Electronics example, the two resources are hours available of electronics time and hours of assembly time. If additional hours were available, a higher total profit could be realized. How much should the company be willing to pay for additional hours? Is it profitable to

(a)

Changed assembly constraint from $2X_1 + 1X_2 = 100$ to $2X_1 + 1X_2 = 110$

Corner point ③ is still optimal, but values at this point are now $X_1 = 45$, $X_2 = 20$, with a profit = $415.

Electronics constraint is unchanged

(b)

Changed assembly constraint from $2X_1 + 1X_2 = 100$ to $2X_1 + 1X_2 = 90$

Corner point ③ is still optimal, but values at this point are now $X_1 = 15$, $X_2 = 60$, with a profit = $405.

Electronics constraint is unchanged

▲ **Figure B.8** Shader Electronics Sensitivity Analysis on Right-Hand-Side (RHS) Resources

If the size of the feasible region increases, the optimal objective function value could improve.

have some additional electronics hours? Should we be willing to pay for more assembly time? Sensitivity analysis about these resources will help us answer these questions.

If the right-hand side of a constraint is changed, the feasible region will change (unless the constraint is redundant), and often the optimal solution will change. In the Shader example, there were 100 hours of assembly time available each week and the maximum possible profit was $410. If the available assembly hours are *increased* to 110 hours, the new optimal solution seen in Figure B.8(a) is (45,20) and the profit is $415. Thus, the extra 10 hours of time resulted in an increase in profit of $5 or $0.50 per hour. If the hours are *decreased* to 90 hours as shown in Figure B.8(b), the new optimal solution is (15,60) and the profit is $405. Thus, reducing the hours by 10 results in a decrease in profit of $5 or $0.50 per hour. This $0.50 per hour change in profit that resulted from a change in the hours available is called the shadow price, or **dual** value. The **shadow price** for a constraint is the improvement in the objective function value that results from a one-unit increase in the right-hand side of the constraint.

Shadow price (or **dual**)
The value of one additional unit of a scarce resource in LP.

Validity Range for the Shadow Price Given that Shader Electronics' profit increases by $0.50 for each additional hour of assembly time, does it mean that Shader can do this indefinitely, essentially earning infinite profit? Clearly, this is illogical. How far can Shader increase its assembly time availability and still earn an extra $0.50 profit per hour? That is, for what level of increase in the RHS value of the assembly time constraint is the shadow price of $0.50 valid?

The shadow price is valid only as long as the change in the RHS is within the Allowable Increase and Allowable Decrease values.

The shadow price of $0.50 is valid as long as the available assembly time stays in a range within which all current corner points continue to exist. The information to compute the upper and lower limits of this range is given by the entries labeled Allowable Increase and Allowable Decrease in the *Sensitivity Report* in Program B.1. In Shader's case, these values show that the shadow price of $0.50 for assembly time availability is valid for an increase of up to 20 hours from the current value and a decrease of up to 20 hours. That is, the available assembly time can range from a low of 80 (= 100 − 20) to a high of 120 (= 100 +20) for the shadow price of $0.50 to be valid. Note that the allowable decrease implies that for each hour of assembly time that Shader loses (up to 20 hours), its profit decreases by $0.50.

Changes in the Objective Function Coefficient

Let us now focus on the information provided in Program B.1 titled Adjustable Cells. Each row in the Adjustable Cells table contains information regarding a decision variable (i.e., x-pods or BlueBerrys) in the LP model.

Allowable Ranges for Objective Function Coefficients   As the unit profit contribution of either product changes, the slope of the iso-profit lines we saw earlier in Figure B.5 changes. The size of the feasible region, however, remains the same. That is, the locations of the corner points do not change.

The limits to which the profit coefficient of x-pods or BlueBerrys can be changed without affecting the optimality of the current solution is revealed by the values in the Allowable Increase and Allowable Decrease columns of the *Sensitivity Report* in Program B.1. The allowable increase in the objective function coefficient for BlueBerrys is only $0.25. In contrast, the allowable decrease is $1.50. Hence, if the unit profit of BlueBerrys drops to $4 (i.e., a decrease of $1 from the current value of $5), it is still optimal to produce 30 x-pods and 40 BlueBerrys. The total profit will drop to $370 (from $410) because each BlueBerry now yields less profit (of $1 per unit). However, if the unit profit drops below $3.50 per BlueBerry (i.e., a decrease of more than $1.50 from the current $5 profit), the current solution is no longer optimal. The LP problem will then have to be resolved using Solver, or other software, to find the new optimal corner point.

> *There is an allowable decrease and an allowable increase for each objective function coefficient over which the current optimal solution remains optimal.*

> *A new corner point becomes optimal if an objective function coefficient is decreased or increased too much.*

SOLVING MINIMIZATION PROBLEMS

Many linear programming problems involve *minimizing* an objective such as cost instead of maximizing a profit function. A restaurant, for example, may wish to develop a work schedule to meet staffing needs while minimizing the total number of employees. Also, a manufacturer may seek to distribute its products from several factories to its many regional warehouses in such a way as to minimize total shipping costs.

Minimization problems can be solved graphically by first setting up the feasible solution region and then using either the corner-point method or an **iso-cost** line approach (which is analogous to the iso-profit approach in maximization problems) to find the values of X_1 and X_2 that yield the minimum cost.

Example B1 shows how to solve a minimization problem.

Learning Objective

5. Construct and solve a minimization problem

Iso-cost

An approach to solving a linear programming minimization problem graphically.

Cohen Chemicals, Inc., produces two types of photo-developing fluids. The first, a black-and-white picture chemical, costs Cohen $2,500 per ton to produce. The second, a color photo chemical, costs $3,000 per ton.

Based on an analysis of current inventory levels and outstanding orders, Cohen's production manager has specified that at least 30 tons of the black-and-white chemical and at least 20 tons of the color chemical must be produced during the next month. In addition, the manager notes that an existing inventory of a highly perishable raw material needed in both chemicals must be used within 30 days. To avoid wasting the expensive raw material, Cohen must produce a total of at least 60 tons of the photo chemicals in the next month.

Approach: Formulate this information as a minimization LP problem.

Let:

$$X_1 = \text{number of tons of black-and-white picture chemical produced}$$
$$X_2 = \text{number of tons of color picture chemical produced}$$
$$\text{Objective: Minimize cost} = \$2,500X_1 + \$3,000X_2$$

Subject to:

$$X_1 \geq 30 \text{ tons of black-and-white chemical}$$
$$X_2 \geq 20 \text{ tons of color chemical}$$
$$X_1 + X_2 \geq 60 \text{ tons total}$$
$$X_1, X_2 \geq 0 \text{ nonnegativity requirements}$$

EXAMPLE B1

A minimization problem with two variables

▶ **Figure B.9**

Cohen Chemicals'
Feasible Region

Solution: To solve the Cohen Chemicals problem graphically, we construct the problem's feasible region, shown in Figure B.9.

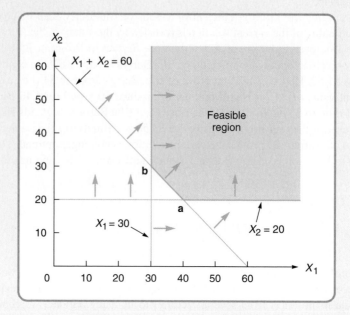

Minimization problems are often unbounded outward (that is, on the right side and on the top), but this characteristic causes no problem in solving them. As long as they are bounded inward (on the left side and the bottom), we can establish corner points. The optimal solution will lie at one of the corners.

In this case, there are only two corner points, **a** and **b**, in Figure B.9. It is easy to determine that at point **a**, $X_1 = 40$ and $X_2 = 20$, and that at point **b**, $X_1 = 30$ and $X_2 = 30$. The optimal solution is found at the point yielding the lowest total cost.

Thus:

$$\text{Total cost at } \mathbf{a} = 2{,}500X_1 + 3{,}000X_2$$
$$= 2{,}500(40) + 3{,}000(20)$$
$$= \$160{,}000$$
$$\text{Total cost at } \mathbf{b} = 2{,}500X_1 + 3{,}000X_2$$
$$= 2{,}500(30) + 3{,}000(30)$$
$$= \$165{,}000$$

The lowest cost to Cohen Chemicals is at point **a**. Hence the operations manager should produce 40 tons of the black-and-white chemical and 20 tons of the color chemical.

Insight: The area is either not bounded to the right or above in a minimization problem (as it is in a maximization problem).

Learning exercise: Cohen's second constraint is recomputed and should be $X_2 \geq 15$. Does anything change in the answer? [Answer: Now $X_1 = 45$, $X_2 = 15$, and Total cost = \$157,500.]

Related problems: B.3, B.5, B.6, B.11, B.12, B.22, B.24

LINEAR PROGRAMMING APPLICATIONS

Learning Objective

6. Formulate production-mix, diet, and labor scheduling problems

The foregoing examples each contained just two variables (X_1 and X_2). Most real-world problems contain many more variables, however. Let's use the principles already developed to formulate a few more-complex problems. The practice you will get by "paraphrasing" the following LP situations should help develop your skills for applying linear programming to other common operations situations.

It has been said that an airline seat is the most perishable commodity in the world. Each time an airliner takes off with an empty seat, a revenue opportunity is lost forever. For Continental, Delta, and other major airlines, which each fly thousands of flight legs per day on hundreds of planes, the schedule is their very heartbeat. These schedules, all developed with massive LP models (Delta's program has 40,000 constraints and 60,000 variables), assign aircraft to specific routes and assign pilots and flight attendants to each of these aircraft.

One flight leg for Continental might consist of a Boeing 777 assigned to fly at 7:05 A.M. from Houston to Chicago to arrive at 9:15 A.M. Continental's problem, like that of Delta and every other competitor, is to match planes such as 737s, 767s, or 777s to flight legs such as Houston-Chicago and to fill seats with paying passengers. And when schedule disruptions occur due to a hurricane (like Katrina in 2005), mechanical problems, or crew unavailability, planes and people are often in the wrong place.

That is why Continental runs its *Crew Solver* and *OptSolver* systems and Delta runs its *ColdStart* model every day. These LP models include constraints such as aircraft availability, maintenance needs, crew training requirements, arrival/departure needs, and so on. The airlines' objectives are to minimize a combination of operating costs and lost passenger revenue, called "spill costs."

The savings from LP have been about $100 million per year at Continental and $300 million per year at the larger Delta Air Lines.

Sources: Interfaces (July–August 2004): 253–271, (January–February 2003): 5–22, and (September–October 1999): 123–131.

Production-Mix Example

Example B2 involves another *production-mix* decision. Limited resources must be allocated among various products that a firm produces. The firm's overall objective is to manufacture the selected products in such quantities as to maximize total profits.

Failsafe Electronics Corporation primarily manufactures four highly technical products, which it supplies to aerospace firms that hold NASA contracts. Each of the products must pass through the following departments before they are shipped: wiring, drilling, assembly, and inspection. The time requirements in each department (in hours) for each unit produced and its corresponding profit value are summarized in this table:

Product	Department				Unit Profit
	Wiring	**Drilling**	**Assembly**	**Inspection**	
XJ201	.5	3	2	.5	$ 9
XM897	1.5	1	4	1.0	$12
TR29	1.5	2	1	.5	$15
BR788	1.0	3	2	.5	$11

The production time available in each department each month and the minimum monthly production requirement to fulfill contracts are as follows:

Department	Capacity (hours)	Product	Minimum Production Level
Wiring	1,500	XJ201	150
Drilling	2,350	XM897	100
Assembly	2,600	TR29	200
Inspection	1,200	BR788	400

Approach: Formulate this production-mix situation as an LP problem. The production manager first specifies production levels for each product for the coming month. He lets:

$$X_1 = \text{number of units of XJ201 produced}$$

$$X_2 = \text{number of units of XM897 produced}$$

$$X_3 = \text{number of units of TR29 produced}$$

$$X_4 = \text{number of units of BR788 produced}$$

Solution: The LP formulation is:

Objective: Maximize profit = $9X_1 + 12X_2 + 15X_3 + 11X_4$

subject to:

$$.5X_1 + 1.5X_2 + 1.5X_3 + 1X_4 \leq 1,500 \text{ hours of wiring available}$$
$$3X_1 + 1X_2 + 2X_3 + 3X_4 \leq 2,350 \text{ hours of drilling available}$$
$$2X_1 + 4X_2 + 1X_3 + 2X_4 \leq 2,600 \text{ hours of assembly available}$$
$$.5X_1 + 1X_2 + .5X_3 + .5X_4 \leq 1,200 \text{ hours of inspection}$$
$$X_1 \geq 150 \text{ units of XJ201}$$
$$X_2 \geq 100 \text{ units of XM897}$$
$$X_3 \geq 200 \text{ units of TR29}$$
$$X_4 \geq 400 \text{ units of BR788}$$
$$X_1, X_2, X_3, X_4 \geq 0$$

Insight: There can be numerous constraints in an LP problem. The constraint right-hand sides may be in different units, but the objective function uses one common unit—dollars of profit, in this case. Because there are more than two decision variables, this problem is not solved graphically.

Learning exercise: Solve this LP problem as formulated. What is the solution? [Answer: $X_1 = 150$, $X_2 = 300$, $X_3 = 200$, $X_4 = 400$.]

Related problems: B.7, B.8, B.10, B.19, B.20, B.21, B.23, B.28, B.29

Diet Problem Example

Example B3 illustrates the *diet problem*, which was originally used by hospitals to determine the most economical diet for patients. Known in agricultural applications as the *feed-mix problem*, the diet problem involves specifying a food or feed ingredient combination that will satisfy stated nutritional requirements at a minimum cost level.

EXAMPLE B3

A diet problem

The Feed 'N Ship feedlot fattens cattle for local farmers and ships them to meat markets in Kansas City and Omaha. The owners of the feedlot seek to determine the amounts of cattle feed to buy to satisfy minimum nutritional standards and, at the same time, minimize total feed costs.

Each grain stock contains different amounts of four nutritional ingredients: A, B, C, and D. Here are the ingredient contents of each grain, in *ounces per pound of grain*:

Ingredient	Feed		
	Stock X	Stock Y	Stock Z
A	3 oz	2 oz	4 oz
B	2 oz	3 oz	1 oz
C	1 oz	0 oz	2 oz
D	6 oz	8 oz	4 oz

The cost per pound of grains X, Y, and Z is $0.02, $0.04, and $0.025, respectively. The minimum requirement per cow per month is 64 ounces of ingredient A, 80 ounces of ingredient B, 16 ounces of ingredient C, and 128 ounces of ingredient D.

The feedlot faces one additional restriction—it can obtain only 500 pounds of stock Z per month from the feed supplier, regardless of its need. Because there are usually 100 cows at the Feed 'N Ship feedlot at any given time, this constraint limits the amount of stock Z for use in the feed of each cow to no more than 5 pounds, or 80 ounces, per month.

Approach: Formulate this as a minimization LP problem.

Let: X_1 = number of pounds of stock X purchased per cow each month

X_2 = number of pounds of stock Y purchased per cow each month

X_3 = number of pounds of stock Z purchased per cow each month

Solution:

$$\text{Objective:} \qquad \text{Minimize cost} = .02X_1 + .04X_2 + .025X_3$$

$$\text{subject to: Ingredient A requirement:} \quad 3X_1 + \quad 2X_2 + \quad 4X_3 \geq 64$$

$$\text{Ingredient B requirement:} \quad 2X_1 + \quad 3X_2 + \quad 1X_3 \geq 80$$

$$\text{Ingredient C requirement:} \quad 1X_1 + \quad 0X_2 + \quad 2X_3 \geq 16$$

$$\text{Ingredient D requirement:} \quad 6X_1 + \quad 8X_2 + \quad 4X_3 \geq 128$$

$$\text{Stock Z limitation:} \qquad\qquad\qquad X_3 \leq 80$$

$$X_1, X_2, X_3 \geq 0$$

The cheapest solution is to purchase 40 pounds of grain X_1, at a cost of \$0.80 per cow.

Insight: Because the cost per pound of stock X is so low, the optimal solution excludes grains Y and Z.

Learning exercise: The cost of a pound of stock X just increased by 50%. Does this affect the solution? [Answer: Yes, when the cost per pound of grain X is \$0.03, $X_1 = 16$ pounds, $X_2 = 16$ pounds, $X_3 = 0$, and cost = \$1.12 per cow.]

Related problems: B.6, B.30

Labor Scheduling Example

Labor scheduling problems address staffing needs over a specific time period. They are especially useful when managers have some flexibility in assigning workers to jobs that require overlapping or interchangeable talents. Large banks and hospitals frequently use LP to tackle their labor scheduling. Example B4 describes how one bank uses LP to schedule tellers.

EXAMPLE B4

Scheduling bank tellers

Arlington Bank of Commerce and Industry is a busy bank that has requirements for between 10 and 18 tellers depending on the time of day. Lunchtime, from noon to 2 P.M., is usually heaviest. The table below indicates the workers needed at various hours that the bank is open.

Time Period	Number of Tellers Required	Time Period	Number of Tellers Required
9 A.M.–10 A.M.	10	1 P.M.–2 P.M.	18
10 A.M.–11 A.M.	12	2 P.M.–3 P.M.	17
11 A.M.–Noon	14	3 P.M.–4 P.M.	15
Noon–1 P.M.	16	4 P.M.–5 P.M.	10

The bank now employs 12 full-time tellers, but many people are on its roster of available part-time employees. A part-time employee must put in exactly 4 hours per day but can start anytime between 9 A.M. and 1 P.M. Part-timers are a fairly inexpensive labor pool because no retirement or lunch benefits are provided them. Full-timers, on the other hand, work from 9 A.M. to 5 P.M. but are allowed 1 hour for lunch. (Half the full-timers eat at 11 A.M., the other half at noon.) Full-timers thus provide 35 hours per week of productive labor time.

By corporate policy, the bank limits part-time hours to a maximum of 50% of the day's total requirement.

Part-timers earn \$6 per hour (or \$24 per day) on average, whereas full-timers earn \$75 per day in salary and benefits on average.

Approach: The bank would like to set a schedule, using LP, that would minimize its total manpower costs. It will release 1 or more of its full-time tellers if it is profitable to do so.

We can let:

$$F = \text{full-time tellers}$$

$$P_1 = \text{part-timers starting at 9 A.M. (leaving at 1 P.M.)}$$

$$P_2 = \text{part-timers starting at 10 A.M. (leaving at 2 P.M.)}$$

$$P_3 = \text{part-timers starting at 11 A.M. (leaving at 3 P.M.)}$$

$$P_4 = \text{part-timers starting at noon (leaving at 4 P.M.)}$$

$$P_5 = \text{part-timers starting at 1 P.M. (leaving at 5 P.M.)}$$

Solution: Objective function:

$$\text{Minimize total daily manpower cost} = \$75F + \$24(P_1 + P_2 + P_3 + P_4 + P_5)$$

Constraints: For each hour, the available labor-hours must be at least equal to the required labor-hours:

$$F + P_1 \geq 10 \quad \text{(9 A.M. to 10 A.M. needs)}$$
$$F + P_1 + P_2 \geq 12 \quad \text{(10 A.M. to 11 A.M. needs)}$$
$$\tfrac{1}{2}F + P_1 + P_2 + P_3 \geq 14 \quad \text{(11 A.M. to noon needs)}$$
$$\tfrac{1}{2}F + P_1 + P_2 + P_3 + P_4 \geq 16 \quad \text{(noon to 1 P.M. needs)}$$
$$F + P_2 + P_3 + P_4 + P_5 \geq 18 \quad \text{(1 P.M to 2 P.M. needs)}$$
$$F + P_3 + P_4 + P_5 \geq 17 \quad \text{(2 P.M to 3 P.M. needs)}$$
$$F + P_4 + P_5 \geq 15 \quad \text{(3 P.M to 4 P.M. needs)}$$
$$F + P_5 \geq 10 \quad \text{(4 P.M to 5 P.M. needs)}$$

Only 12 full-time tellers are available, so:

$$F \leq 12$$

Part-time worker-hours cannot exceed 50% of total hours required each day, which is the sum of the tellers needed each hour:

$$4(P_1 + P_2 + P_3 + P_4 + P_5) \leq .50(10 + 12 + 14 + 16 + 18 + 17 + 15 + 10)$$

or:

$$4P_1 + 4P_2 + 4P_3 + 4P_4 + 4P_5 \leq 0.50(112)$$
$$F, P_1, P_2, P_3, P_4, P_5 \geq 0$$

There are two alternative optimal schedules that Arlington Bank can follow. The first is to employ only 10 full-time tellers ($F = 10$) and to start 7 part-timers at 10 A.M. ($P_2 = 7$), 2 part-timers at 11 A.M. and noon ($P_3 = 2$ and $P_4 = 2$), and 3 part-timers at 1 P.M. ($P_5 = 3$). No part-timers would begin at 9 A.M.

The second solution also employs 10 full-time tellers, but starts 6 part-timers at 9 A.M. ($P_1 = 6$), 1 part-timer at 10 A.M. ($P_2 = 1$), 2 part-timers at 11 A.M. and noon ($P_3 = 2$ and $P_4 = 2$), and 3 part-timers at 1 P.M. ($P_5 = 3$). The cost of either of these two policies is $1,086 per day.

Insight: It is not unusual for multiple optimal solutions to exist in large LP problems. In this case, it gives management the option of selecting, at the same cost, between schedules. To find an alternate optimal solution, you may have to enter the constraints in a different sequence.

Learning exercise: The bank decides to give part-time employees a raise to $7 per hour. Does the solution change? [Answer: Yes, cost = $1,142, $F = 10$, $P_1 = 6$, $P_2 = 1$, $P_3 = 2$, $P_4 = 5$, $P_5 = 0$.]

Related problem: B.18

THE SIMPLEX METHOD OF LP

Simplex method

An algorithm for solving linear programming problems of all sizes.

Most real-world linear programming problems have more than two variables and thus are too complex for graphical solution. A procedure called the **simplex method** may be used to find the optimal solution to such problems. The simplex method is actually an algorithm (or a set of instructions) with which we examine corner points in a methodical fashion until we arrive at the best solution—highest profit or lowest cost. Computer programs (such as Excel OM and POM for Windows) and Excel spreadsheets are available to solve linear programming problems via the simplex method.

For details regarding the algebraic steps of the simplex algorithm, see Tutorial 3 on the CD-ROM that accompanies this book, or refer to a management science textbook.[2]

[2]See, for example, Barry Render, Ralph M. Stair, and Michael Hanna, *Quantitative Analysis for Management*, 9th ed. (Upper Saddle River, NJ: Prentice Hall, 2006): Chapters 7–9; or Raju Balakrishnan, Barry Render, and Ralph M. Stair, *Managerial Decision Modeling with Spreadsheets*, 2nd ed. (Upper Saddle River, NJ: Prentice Hall, 2007): Chapters 2–4.

Summary

This module introduces a special kind of model, linear programming. LP has proven to be especially useful when trying to make the most effective use of an organization's resources.

The first step in dealing with LP models is problem formulation, which involves identifying and creating an objective function and constraints. The second step is to solve the problem. If there are only two decision variables, the problem can be solved graphically, using the corner-point method or the iso-profit/iso-cost line method. With either approach, we first identify the feasible region, then find the corner point yielding the greatest profit or least cost. LP is used in a wide variety of business applications, as the examples and homework problems in this module reveal.

Key Terms

Linear programming (LP) *(p. 706)*
Objective function *(p. 706)*
Constraints *(p. 706)*
Graphical solution approach *(p. 708)*
Decision variables *(p. 708)*

Feasible region *(p. 709)*
Iso-profit line method *(p. 710)*
Corner-point method *(p. 711)*
Parameter *(p. 712)*
Sensitivity analysis *(p. 712)*

Shadow price (or dual) *(p. 714)*
Iso-cost *(p. 715)*
Simplex method *(p. 720)*

Using Software to Solve LP Problems

All LP problems can also be solved with the simplex method, using software such as Excel OM and POM for Windows or Excel. This approach produces valuable economic information such as the shadow price, or dual, and provides complete sensitivity analysis on other inputs to the problems. Excel uses Solver, which requires that you enter your own constraints. Excel OM and POM for Windows require only that demand data, supply data, and shipping costs be entered. In the following section we illustrate how to create an Excel spreadsheet for LP problems.

✖ Using Excel Spreadsheets

Excel offers the ability to analyze linear programming problems using built-in problem-solving tools. Excel's tool is named Solver. Solver is limited to 200 changing cells (variables), each with 2 boundary constraints and up to 100 additional constraints. These capabilities make Solver suitable for the solution of complex, real-world problems.

We use Excel to set up the Shader Electronics problem in Program B.2. The objective and constraints are repeated here:

Objective function: Maximize profit =
$$\$7(\text{No. of x-pods}) + \$5(\text{No. of BlueBerrys})$$

$$\text{Subject to:} \quad 4(\text{x-pods}) + 3(\text{BlueBerrys}) \leq 240$$

$$2(\text{x-pods}) + 1(\text{BlueBerry}) \leq 100$$

◄ Program B.2

Using Excel to Formulate the Shader Electronics Problem

		Computations	
Value	**Cell**	**Excel Formula**	**Action**
Left Hand Side	D4	=SUMPRODUCT($B$8:$C$8,B4:C4)	Copy to D5:D6
Slack	G5	=F5-D5	Copy to G6
			Select Tools, Solver
			Set Solver parameters as displayed
			Press Solve

The Excel screen in Program B.3 shows Solver's solution to the Shader Electronics Company problem. Note that the optimal solution is now shown in the *changing cells* (cells B8 and C8, which served as the variables). The Reports selection performs more extensive analysis of the solution and its environment. Excel's sensitivity analysis capability was illustrated earlier in Program B.1.

▶ **Program B.3**

Excel Solution to Shader Electronics LP Problem

Using Excel OM and POM for Windows

Excel OM and POM for Windows can handle relatively large LP problems. As output, the software provides optimal values for the variables, optimal profit or cost, and sensitivity analysis. In addition, POM for Windows provides graphical output for problems with only two variables.

Solved Problems

Solved Problem B.1

Smith's, a Niagara, New York clothing manufacturer that produces men's shirts and pajamas, has two primary resources available: sewing-machine time (in the sewing department) and cutting-machine time (in the cutting department). Over the next month, owner Barbara Smith can schedule up to 280 hours of work on sewing machines and up to 450 hours of work on cutting machines. Each shirt produced requires 1.00 hour of sewing time and 1.50

hours of cutting time. Producing each pair of pajamas requires .75 hour of sewing time and 2 hours of cutting time.

To express the LP constraints for this problem mathematically, we let:

$$X_1 = \text{number of shirts produced}$$
$$X_2 = \text{number of pajamas produced}$$

Solution

First constraint: $1X_1 + .75X_2 \leq 280$ hours of sewing-machine time available—our first scarce resource

Second constraint: $1.5X_1 + \textcircled{2}X_2 \leq 450$ hours of cutting-machine time available—our second scarce resource

Note: This means that each pair of pajamas takes 2 hours of the cutting resource.

Smith's accounting department analyzes cost and sales figures and states that each shirt produced will yield a $4 contribution to profit and that each pair of pajamas will yield a $3 contribution to profit. This information can be used to create the LP *objective function* for this problem:

Objective function: maximize total contribution to profit = $4X_1 + $3X_2

Solved Problem B.2

We want to solve the following LP problem for Kevin Caskey Wholesale Inc. using the corner-point method:

$$\text{Objective: Maximize profit} = \$9X_1 + \$7X_2$$

$$\text{Constraints:}\quad 2X_1 + 1X_2 \le 40$$

$$X_1 + 3X_2 \le 30$$

$$X_1, X_2 \ge 0$$

solution

Figure B.10 illustrates these constraints:

Corner-point **a**: $(X_1 = 0, X_2 = 0)$ Profit = 0

Corner-point **b**: $(X_1 = 0, X_2 = 10)$ Profit $= 9(0) + 7(10) = \$70$

Corner-point **d**: $(X_1 = 20, X_2 = 0)$ Profit $= 9(20) + 7(0) = \$180$

Corner-point **c** is obtained by solving equations $2X_1 + 1X_2 = 40$ and $X_1 + 3X_2 = 30$ simultaneously. Multiply the second equation by -2 and add it to the first.

$$2X_1 + 1X_2 = \ \ 40$$
$$\underline{-2X_1 + 6X_2 = -60}$$
$$-5X_2 = -20$$

Thus $X_2 = 4$.

And $X_1 + 3(4) = 30$ or $X_1 + 12 = 30$ or $X_1 = 18$

Corner-point **c**: $(X_1 = 18, X_2 = 4)$ Profit $= 9(18) + 7(4) = \$190$

Hence the optimal solution is:

$$(x_1 = 18, x_2 = 4)\qquad \text{Profit} = \$190$$

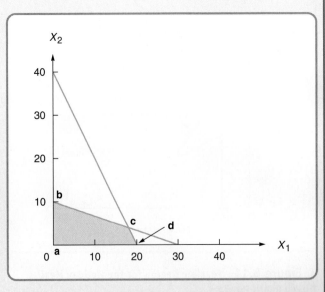

▲ **Figure B.10** K. Caskey Wholesale, Inc.'s Feasible Region

Solved Problem B.3

Holiday Meal Turkey Ranch is considering buying two different types of turkey feed. Each feed contains, in varying proportions, some or all of the three nutritional ingredients essential for fattening turkeys. Brand Y feed costs the ranch $.02 per pound. Brand Z costs $.03 per pound. The rancher would like to determine the lowest-cost diet that meets the minimum monthly intake requirement for each nutritional ingredient.

The following table contains relevant information about the composition of brand Y and brand Z feeds, as well as the minimum monthly requirement for each nutritional ingredient per turkey.

	Composition of Each Pound of Feed		
Ingredient	**Brand Y Feed**	**Brand Z Feed**	**Minimum Monthly Requirement**
A	5 oz	10 oz	90 oz
B	4 oz	3 oz	48 oz
C	.5 oz	0	1.5 oz
Cost/lb	$.02	$.03	

solution

If we let:

X_1 = number of pounds of brand Y feed purchased

X_2 = number of pounds of brand Z feed purchased

then we may proceed to formulate this linear programming problem as follows:

$$\text{Objective: Minimize cost (in cents)} = 2X_1 + 3X_2$$

subject to these constraints:

$$5X_1 + 10X_2 \ge 90 \text{ oz} \qquad (\textit{ingredient A constraint})$$
$$4X_1 + 3X_2 \ge 48 \text{ oz} \qquad (\textit{ingredient B constraint})$$
$$\tfrac{1}{2}X_1 \ge 1\tfrac{1}{2} \text{ oz} \qquad (\textit{ingredient C constraint})$$

Figure B.11 illustrates these constraints.

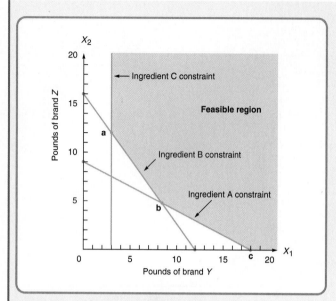

The iso-cost line approach may be used to solve LP minimization problems such as that of the Holiday Meal Turkey Ranch. As with iso-profit lines, we need not compute the cost at each corner point, but instead draw a series of parallel cost lines. The last cost point to touch the feasible region provides us with the optimal solution corner.

For example, we start in Figure B.12 by drawing a 54¢ cost line, namely, $54 = 2X_1 + 3X_2$. Obviously, there are many points in the feasible region that would yield a lower total cost. We proceed to move our iso-cost line toward the lower left, in a plane parallel to the 54¢ solution line. The last point we touch while still in contact with the feasible region is the same as corner point **b** of Figure B.11. It has the coordinates $(X_1 = 8.4, X_2 = 4.8)$ and an associated cost of 31.2 cents.

▲ **Figure B.11**   **Feasible Region for the Holiday Meal Turkey Ranch Problem**

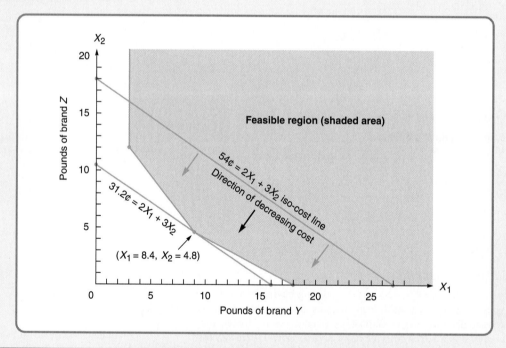

► **Figure B.12**

Graphical Solution to the Holiday Meal Turkey Ranch Problem Using the Iso-Cost Line

Note that the last line parallel to the 54¢ iso-cost line that touches the feasible region indicates the optimal corner point.

Active Model Exercise

This Active Model describes the Shader Electronics example maximization problem, which has two less-than-or-equal-to constraints. You can use the scrollbars to change any of the eight numbers in the example or to move the iso-profit line.

Questions

1. By how much does the profit on x-pods need to rise to make it the only product manufactured?
2. By how much does the profit on x-pods need to fall to stop manufacturing it?
3. What happens to the profit as the number of assembly hours available increases by 1 hour at a time? For how many hours is this true?
4. What happens if we can reduce the electronics time for BlueBerrys to 2.5 hours?

LP Graph

Reset Data   Questions

	x-pods	BlueBerrys		
Profit	7	5		
Electronic hrs	4	3	<	240
Assembly hrs	2	1	<	100

Optimal profit = $ 410.00
Produce   30 x-pods
and   40 BlueBerrys

Isoprofit value $ 410.00

Linear Program

Electronic hrs ——— Assembly hrs ———
Isoprofit Line ········

◀ **Active Model B.1**

**Analysis of the Shader
Electronics Example Data**

Self-Test

- ***Before taking the self-test,*** *refer to the learning objectives listed
  at the beginning of the module and the key terms listed at the end
  of the module.*
- *Use the key at the back of the text to **correct** your answers.*
- ***Restudy*** *pages that correspond to any questions you answered
  incorrectly or material you feel uncertain about.*

1. When using a graphical solution procedure, the region bounded
by the set of constraints is called the:
a) solution
b) feasible region
c) infeasible region
d) maximum profit region
e) iso region

2. Using the *graphical solution procedure* to solve a maximization
problem requires that we:
a) move the iso-profit line up until it no longer intersects with
any constraint equation
b) move the iso-profit line down until it no longer intersects
with any constraint equation
c) apply the method of simultaneous equations to solve for the
intersections of constraints
d) find the value of the objective function at the origin

3. Which of the following is *not* a property of all linear programming problems?
a) the presence of restrictions
b) optimization of some objective
c) a computer program
d) alternate courses of action to choose from
e) usage of only linear equations and inequalities

4. A feasible solution to a linear programming problem:
a) must satisfy all of the problem's constraints simultaneously
b) need not satisfy all of the constraints, only some of them
c) must be a corner point of the feasible region
d) must give the maximum possible profit

5. Consider the following linear programming problem:

$$\text{Maximize} \quad 12X + 10Y$$
$$\text{Subject to:} \quad 4X + 3Y \leq 480$$
$$2X + 3Y \leq 360$$
$$X, Y \geq 0$$

The maximum possible value for the objective function is:
a) 1,600   d) 1,440
b) 1,520   e) 0
c) 1,800

6. Consider the following linear programming problem:

$$\text{Maximize} \quad 12X + 10Y$$
$$\text{Subject to:} \quad 4X + 3Y \leq 480$$
$$2X + 3Y \leq 360$$
$$X, Y \geq 0$$

Which of the following points (X, Y) is *not* feasible?
a) (0, 100)   d) (20, 90)
b) (100, 10)   e) (0, 70)
c) (70, 70)

7. Consider the following linear programming problem:

$$\text{Maximize} \quad 4X + 10Y$$
$$\text{Subject to:} \quad 3X + 4Y \leq 480$$
$$4X + 2Y \leq 360$$
$$X, Y \geq 0$$

The feasible corner points are (48, 84), (0, 120), (0, 0), (90, 0).
What is the maximum possible value for the objective function?
a) 1,032   d) 1,600
b) 1,200   e) 840
c) 360

Internet And Student CD-ROM/DVD Exercises

Visit our Companion Web site or use your student CD-ROM/DVD to help with material in this module.

 On Our Companion Web Site,
www.prenhall.com/heizer
- Self-Study Quizzes
- Practice Problems
- Internet Case
- PowerPoint Lecture

 On Your Student CD-ROM
- Practice Problems
- Active Model Exercise
- POM for Windows

On Your Student DVD
- Virtual Office Hours for Solved Problems

Discussion Questions

1. List at least four applications of linear programming problems.
2. What is a "corner point"? Explain why solutions to linear programming problems focus on corner points.
3. Define the feasible region of a graphical LP problem. What is a feasible solution?
4. Each linear programming problem that has a feasible region has an infinite number of solutions. Explain.
5. Under what circumstances is the objective function more important than the constraints in a linear programming model?
6. Under what circumstances are the constraints more important than the objective function in a linear programming model?
7. Why is the diet problem, in practice, applicable for animals but not for people?
8. How many feasible solutions are there in a linear program? Which ones do we need to examine to find the optimal solution?

9. Define shadow price (or dual).
10. Explain how to use the iso-cost line in a graphical minimization problem.
11. Compare how the corner-point and iso-profit line methods work for solving graphical problems.
12. Where a constraint crosses the vertical or horizontal axis, the quantity is fairly obvious. How does one go about finding the quantity coordinates where two constraints cross, not at an axis?
13. Suppose a linear programming (maximation) problem has been solved and that the optimal value of the objective function is $300. Suppose an additonal constraint is added to this problem. Explain how this might affect each of the following:
    (a) The feasible region.
    (b) The optimal value of the objective function.

Problems*

• **B.1** Solve the following linear programming problem graphically:

$$\text{Maximize} \quad Z = 4X + 6Y$$
$$\text{Subject to:} \quad X + 2Y \leq 8$$
$$5X + 4Y \leq 20$$
$$X, Y \geq 0 \quad \text{P}\times$$

• **B.2** Solve the following linear programming problem graphically:

$$\text{Maximize} \quad Z = X + 10Y$$
$$\text{Subject to:} \quad 4X + 3Y \leq 36$$
$$2X + 4Y \leq 40$$
$$Y \geq 3$$
$$X, Y \geq 0 \quad \text{P}\times$$

• **B.3** Solve the following linear program graphically:

$$\text{Minimize} \quad Z = X_1 + X_2$$
$$8X_1 + 16X_2 \geq 64$$
$$X_1 \geq 0$$
$$X_2 \geq -2 \quad \text{P}\times$$

*Note: **P**✕ means the problem may be solved with POM for Windows and/or Excel or Excel OM.*

•• **B.4** Consider the following linear programming problem:

$$\text{Maximize} \quad Z = 30X_1 + 10X_2$$
$$\text{Subject to:} \quad 3X_1 + X_2 \leq 300$$
$$X_1 + X_2 \leq 200$$
$$X \leq 100$$
$$X_2 \geq 50$$
$$X_1 - X_2 \leq 0$$
$$X_1, X_2 \geq 0$$

a) Solve the problem graphically.
b) Is there more than one optimal solution? Explain. **P**✕

• **B.5** Solve the following LP problem graphically:

$$\text{Minimize} \quad Z = 24X + 15Y$$
$$\text{Subject to:} \quad 7X + 11Y \geq 77$$
$$16X + 4Y \geq 80$$
$$X, Y \geq 0 \quad \text{P}\times$$

•• **B.6** Ed Silver Dog Food Company wishes to introduce a new brand of dog biscuits composed of chicken- and liver-flavored biscuits that meet certain nutritional requirements. The liver-flavored biscuits contain 1 unit of nutrient A and 2 units of nutrient B; the chicken-flavored biscuits contain 1 unit of nutrient A and 4 units of nutrient B. According to federal requirements, there must be at least 40 units of nutrient A and 60 units of nutrient B in a package of the new mix. In addition, the company has decided that there can be no more than 15 liver-flavored biscuits in a package. If it costs 1¢ to make 1 liver-flavored biscuit and 2¢ to make 1 chicken-flavored, what is the optimal product mix for a package of the biscuits to minimize the firm's cost?

a) Formulate this as a linear programming problem.

b) Solve this problem graphically, giving the optimal values of all variables.

c) What is the total cost of a package of dog biscuits using the optimal mix? **Px**

•   **B.7** The Electrocomp Corporation manufactures two electrical products: air conditioners and large fans. The assembly process for each is similar in that both require a certain amount of wiring and drilling. Each air conditioner takes 3 hours of wiring and 2 hours of drilling. Each fan must go through 2 hours of wiring and 1 hour of drilling. During the next production period, 240 hours of wiring time are available and up to 140 hours of drilling time may be used. Each air conditioner sold yields a profit of $25. Each fan assembled may be sold for a $15 profit.

Formulate and solve this LP production-mix situation, and find the best combination of air conditioners and fans that yields the highest profit. **Px**

•   **B.8** The Lauren Shur Tub Company manufactures two lines of bathtubs, called model A and model B. Every tub requires blending a certain amount of steel and zinc; the company has available a total of 25,000 lb of steel and 6,000 lb of zinc. Each model A bathtub requires a mixture of 125 lb of steel and 20 lb of zinc, and each yields a profit of $90. Each model B tub requires 100 lb of steel and 30 lb of zinc and can be sold for a profit of $70.

Find by graphical linear programming the best production mix of bathtubs. **Px**

••   **B.9** Spitzfire, Inc., manufactures specialty cars and trucks. It has just opened a new factory where the C1 car and the T1 truck can both be manufactured. To make either vehicle, processing in the assembly shop and in the paint shop are required. It takes 1/40 of a day and 1/60 of a day to paint a truck of type T1 and a car of type C1 in the paint shop, respectively. It takes 1/50 of a day to assemble either type of vehicle in the assembly shop.

A T1 truck and a C1 car yield profits of $300 and $220, respectively, per vehicle sold.

a) Define the objective function and constraint equations.

b) Graph the feasible region.

c) What is a maximum-profit daily production plan at the new factory?

d) How much profit will such a plan yield, assuming whatever is produced is sold. **Px**

•   **B.10** MSA Computer Corporation manufactures two models of minicomputers, the Alpha 4 and the Beta 5. The firm employs 5 technicians, working 160 hours each per month, on its assembly line. Management insists that full employment (that is, *all* 160 hours of time) be maintained for each worker during next month's operations. It requires 20 labor-hours to assemble each Alpha 4 computer and 25 labor-hours to assemble each Beta 5 model. MSA wants to see at least 10 Alpha 4s and at least 15 Beta 5s produced during the production period. Alpha 4s generate a $1,200 profit per unit, and Betas yield $1,800 each.

Determine the most profitable number of each model of minicomputer to produce during the coming month. **Px**

•   **B.11** The Sweet Smell Fertilizer Company markets bags of manure labeled "not less than 60 lb dry weight." The packaged manure is a combination of compost and sewage wastes. To provide good-quality fertilizer, each bag should contain at least 30 lb of compost but no more than 40 lb of sewage. Each pound of compost costs Sweet Smell 5¢ and each pound of sewage costs 4¢. Use a graphical LP method to determine the least-cost blend of compost and sewage in each bag. **Px**

•   **B.12** Consider Faud Shatara's following linear programming formulation:

$$\text{Minimize cost} = \$1X_1 + \$2X_2$$
$$\text{Subject to:} \quad X_1 + 3X_2 \geq 90$$
$$8X_1 + 2X_2 \geq 160$$
$$3X_1 + 2X_2 \geq 120$$
$$X_2 \leq 70$$

a) Graphically illustrate the feasible region to indicate to Faud which corner point produces the optimal solution.

b) What is the cost of this solution? **Px**

•   **B.13** The LP relationships that follow were formulated by Jeffrey Rummel at the Connecticut Chemical Company. Which ones are invalid for use in a linear programming problem, and why?

$$\text{Maximize} = 6X_1 + \frac{1}{2}X_1X_2 + 5X_3$$
$$\text{Subject to:} \quad 4X_1X_2 + 2X_3 \leq 70$$
$$7.9X_1 - 4X_2 \geq 15.6$$
$$3X_1 + 3X_2 + 3X_3 \geq 21$$
$$19X_2 - \frac{1}{3}X_3 = 17$$
$$-X_1 - X_2 + 4X_3 = 5$$
$$4X_1 + 2X_2 + 3\sqrt{X_3} \leq 80$$

••   **B.14** Kalyan Singhal Corp. makes three products, and it has three machines available as resources as given in the following LP problem:

$$\text{Maximize contribution} = 4X_1 + 4X_2 + 7X_3$$
$$\text{Subject to:} \quad 1X_1 + 7X_2 + 4X_3 \leq 100 \text{ (hours on machine 1)}$$
$$2X_1 + 1X_2 + 7X_3 \leq 110 \text{ (hours on machine 2)}$$
$$8X_1 + 4X_2 + 1X_3 \leq 100 \text{ (hours on machine 3)}$$

a) Determine the optimal solution using LP software.

b) Is there unused time available on any of the machines with the optimal solution?

c) What would it be worth to the firm to make an additional hour of time available on the third machine?

d) How much would the firm's profit increase if an extra 10 hours of time were made available on the second machine at no extra cost? **Px**

••   **B.15** Consider the following LP problem developed at Jeff Spencer's San Antonio optical scanning firm:

$$\text{Maximize profit} = \$1X_1 + \$1X_2$$
$$\text{Subject to:} \quad 2X_1 + 1X_2 \leq 100$$
$$1X_1 + 2X_2 \leq 100$$

a) What is the optimal solution to this problem? Solve it graphically.

b) If a technical breakthrough occurred that raised the profit per unit of X_1 to \$3, would this affect the optimal solution?

c) Instead of an increase in the profit coefficient X_1, to \$3, suppose that profit was overestimated and should only have been \$1.25. Does this change the optimal solution? **Px**

••• **B.16** The Arden County, Maryland, superintendent of education is responsible for assigning students to the three high schools in his county. He recognizes the need to bus a certain number of students, for several sectors, A–E, of the county are beyond walking distance to a school. The superintendent partitions the county into five geographic sectors as he attempts to establish a plan that will minimize the total number of student miles traveled by bus. He also recognizes that if a student happens to live in a certain sector and is assigned to the high school in that sector, there is no need to bus him because he can walk to school. The three schools are located in sectors B, C, and E.

The accompanying table reflects the number of high-school-age students living in each sector and the distance in miles from each sector to each school:

| | *Distance to School* | | | |
Sector	School in Sector B	School in Sector C	School in Sector E	Number of Students
A	5	8	6	700
B	0	4	12	500
C	4	0	7	100
D	7	2	5	800
E	12	7	0	400
				2,500

Each high school has a capacity of 900 students.

a) Set up the objective function and constraints of this problem using linear programming so that the total number of student miles traveled by bus is minimized.

b) Solve the problem. **Px**

•• **B.17** The National Credit Union has \$250,000 available to invest in a 12-month commitment. The money can be placed in Treasury notes yielding an 8% return or in municipal bonds at an average rate of return of 9%. Credit union regulations require diversification to the extent that at least 50% of the investment be placed in Treasury notes. Because of defaults in such municipalities as Cleveland and New York, it is decided that no more than 40% of the investment be placed in bonds. How much should the National Credit Union invest in each security so as to maximize its return on investment? **Px**

•• **B.18** Boston's famous Limoges Restaurant is open 24 hours a day. Servers report for duty at 3 A.M., 7 A.M., 11 A.M., 3 P.M., 7 P.M., or 11 P.M., and each works an 8-hour shift. The following table shows the minimum number of workers needed during the 6 periods into which the day is divided:

Period	Time	Number of Servers Required
1	3 A.M.–7 A.M.	3
2	7 A.M.–11 A.M.	12
3	11 A.M.–3 P.M.	16
4	3 P.M.–7 P.M.	9
5	7 P.M.–11 P.M.	11
6	11 P.M.–3 A.M.	4

Owner Michelle Limoges' scheduling problem is to determine how many servers should report for work at the start of each time period in order to minimize the total staff required for one day's operation. (*Hint:* Let X_i equal the number of servers beginning work in time period i, where $i = 1, 2, 3, 4, 5, 6$.) **Px**

• **B.19** A craftsman named Chuck Synovec builds two kinds of birdhouses, one for wrens and a second for bluebirds. Each wren birdhouse takes 4 hours of labor and 4 units of lumber. Each bluebird house requires 2 hours of labor and 12 units of lumber. The craftsman has available 60 hours of labor and 120 units of lumber. Wren houses yield a profit of \$6 each and bluebird houses yield a profit of \$15 each.

a) Write out the objective and constraints.

b) Solve graphically. **Px**

•• **B.20** Each coffee table produced by Robert West Designers nets the firm a profit of \$9. Each bookcase yields a \$12 profit. West's firm is small and its resources limited. During any given production period (of 1 week), 10 gallons of varnish and 12 lengths of high-quality redwood are available. Each coffee table requires approximately 1 gallon of varnish and 1 length of redwood. Each bookcase takes 1 gallon of varnish and 2 lengths of wood.

Formulate West's production-mix decision as a linear programming problem, and solve. How many tables and bookcases should be produced each week? What will the maximum profit be? **Px**

•• **B.21** Par, Inc., produces a standard golf bag and a deluxe golf bag on a weekly basis. Each golf bag requires time for cutting and dyeing and time for sewing and finishing, as shown in the following table:

| | *Hours Required per Bag* | |
Product	Cutting and Dyeing	Sewing and Finishing
Standard Bag	1/2	1
Deluxe Bag	1	2/3

The profits per bag and weekly hours available for cutting and dyeing and for sewing and finishing are as follows:

Product	Profit per Unit (\$)
Standard bag	10
Deluxe bag	8

Activity	Weekly Hours Available
Cutting and dyeing	300
Sewing and finishing	360

Par Inc., will sell whatever quantities it produces of these two products.

a) Find the mix of standard and deluxe golf bags to produce per week that maximizes weekly profit from these activities.

b) What is the value of the profit? **Px**

• **B.22** Solve the following linear programming problem graphically:

$$\text{Minimize cost} = 4X_1 + 5X_2$$

$$\text{Subject to:} \quad X_1 + 2X_2 \geq 80$$

$$3X_1 + X_2 \geq 75$$

$$X_1, X_2 \geq 0 \quad \textbf{Px}$$

•• **B.23** Thompson Distributors packages and distributes industrial supplies. A standard shipment can be packaged in a class A container, a class K container, or a class T container. A single class A container yields a profit of $9; a class K container, a profit of $7; and a class T container, a profit of $15. Each shipment prepared requires a certain amount of packing material and a certain amount of time.

Resources Needed per Standard Shipment

Class of Container	Packing Material (pounds)	Packing Time (hours)
A	2	2
K	1	6
T	3	4

Total amount of resource available each week	130 pounds	240 hours

Jason Thompson, head of the firm, must decide the optimal number of each class of container to pack each week. He is bound by the previously mentioned resource restrictions but also decides that he must keep his 6 full-time packers employed all 240 hours (6 workers × 40 hours) each week.

Formulate and solve this problem using LP software. **Px**

•• **B.24** How many corner points are there in the feasible region of the following problem?

$$\text{Minimize } Z = X - Y$$

$$\text{Subject to:} \quad X \leq 4$$

$$-X \leq 2$$

$$X + 2Y \leq 6$$

$$-X + 2Y \leq 8$$

$$Y \geq 0$$

(*Note:* X values can be negative in this problem.)

•• **B.25** The Denver advertising agency promoting the new Breem dishwashing detergent wants to get the best exposure possible for the product within the $100,000 advertising budget ceiling placed on it. To do so, the agency needs to decide how much of the budget to spend on

each of its two most effective media: (1) television spots during the afternoon hours and (2) large ads in the city's Sunday newspaper. Each television spot costs $3,000; each Sunday newspaper ad costs $1,250. The expected exposure, based on industry ratings, is 35,000 viewers for each TV commercial and 20,000 readers for each newspaper advertisement. The agency director, Deborah Kellogg, knows from experience that it is important to use both media in order to reach the broadest spectrum of potential Breem customers. She decides that at least 5 but no more than 25 television spots should be ordered, and that at least 10 newspaper ads should be contracted. How many times should each of the two media be used to obtain maximum exposure while staying within the budget? Use the graphical method to solve. **Px**

••• **B.26** Libby Temple Manufacturing has three factories (1, 2, and 3) and three warehouses (A, B, and C). The following table shows the shipping costs between each factory and warehouse, the factory manufacturing capabilities (in thousands), and the warehouse capacities (in thousands). Management would like to keep the warehouses filled to capacity in order to generate demand.

a) Write the objective function and the constraint in equations. Let X_{1A} = 1,000s of units shipped from factory 1 to warehouse A, and so on.

b) Solve by computer.

To / From	Warehouse A	Warehouse B	Warehouse C	Production Capability
Factory 1	$ 6	$ 5	$ 3	6
Factory 2	$ 8	$10	$ 8	8
Factory 3	$11	$14	$18	10
Capacity	7	12	5	**Px**

•••• **B.27** A fertilizer manufacturer has to fulfill supply contracts to its two main customers (650 tons to Customer A and 800 tons to Customer B). It can meet this demand by shipping existing inventory from any of its three warehouses. Warehouse 1 (W1) has 400 tons of inventory onhand, Warehouse 2 (W2) has 500 tons, and Warehouse 3 (W3) has 600 tons. The company would like to arrange the shipping for the lowest cost possible, where the per-ton transit costs are as follows:

	W1	W3	W3
Customer A	$7.50	$6.25	$6.50
Customer B	6.75	7.00	8.00

a) Explain what each of the six decision variables (V) is: (*Hint:* Look at the Solver report on the next page.)

V1: _____

V2: _____

V3: _____

V4: _____

V5: _____

V6: _____

b) Write out the objective function in terms of the variables (V1, V2, etc.) and the objective coefficients.

c) Aside from nonnegativity of the variables, what are the five constraints? Write a short description for each constraint, and write out the formula (and circle the type of equality/inequality).

	Description	Variables and Coefficients	What Type?	RHS
C1:	_____	Formula: _____	(=> | = | =<)	_____
C2:	_____	Formula: _____	(=> | = | =<)	_____
C3:	_____	Formula: _____	(=> | = | =<)	_____
C4:	_____	Formula: _____	(=> | = | =<)	_____
C5:	_____	Formula: _____	(=> | = | =<	_____

After you formulate and enter the linear program for Problem B.27 in Excel, the Solver gives you the following sensitivity report:

Adjustable Cells

Cell	Name	Final Value	Reduced Cost	Objective Coefficient	Allowable Increase	Allowable Decrease
$B$6	V1	0	1.5	7.5	1E+30	1.5
$C$6	V2	100	0	6.25	0.25	0.75
$D$6	V3	550	0	6.5	0.75	0.25
$E$6	V4	400	0	6.75	0.5	1E+30
$F$6	V5	400	0	7	0.75	0.5
$G$6	V6	0	0.75	8	1E+30	0.75

Constraints

Cell	Name	Final Value	Shadow Price	Constraint R.H. Side	Allowable Increase	Allowable Decrease
$H$7	C1	650	6.5	650	50	550
$H$8	C2	800	7.25	800	50	400
$H$9	C3	400	−0.5	400	400	50
$H$10	C4	500	−0.25	500	550	50
$H$11	C5	550	0	600	1E+30	50

d) How many of the constraints are binding?

e) How much slack/surplus is there with the nonbinding constraint(s)?

f) What is the range of optimality on variable V3?

g) If we could ship 10 tons less to Customer A, how much money *might* we be able to save? If we could chose to short *either* Customer A or Customer B by 10 tons, which would we prefer to short? Why? ✖

•••• **B.28** New Orleans's Mt. Sinai Hospital is a large, private, 600-bed facility complete with laboratories, operating rooms, and X-ray equipment. In seeking to increase revenues, Mt. Sinai's administration has decided to make a 90-bed addition on a portion of adjacent land currently used for staff parking. The administrators feel that the labs, operating rooms, and X-ray department are not being fully utilized at present and do not need to be expanded to handle additional patients. The addition of 90 beds, however, involves deciding how many beds should be allocated to the medical staff (for medical patients) and how many to the surgical staff (for surgical patients).

The hospital's accounting and medical records departments have provided the following pertinent information. The average hospital stay for a medical patient is 8 days, and the average medical patient generates $2,280 in revenues. The average surgical patient is in the hospital 5 days and generates $1,515 in revenues. The laboratory is capable of handling 15,000 tests per year more than it *was* handling. The average medical patient requires 3.1 lab tests, the average surgical patient 2.6 lab tests. Furthermore, the average medical patient uses 1 X-ray, the average surgical patient 2 X-rays. If the hospital were expanded by 90 beds, the X-ray department could handle up to 7,000 X-rays without significant additional cost. Finally, the administration estimates that up to 2,800 additional operations could be performed in existing operating-room facilities. Medical patients, of course, require no surgery, whereas each surgical patient generally has one surgery performed.

Formulate this problem so as to determine how many medical beds and how many surgical beds should be added to maximize revenues. Assume that the hospital is open 365 days per year. **Px**

•••• **B.29** Charles Watts Electronics manufactures the following six peripheral devices used in computers especially designed for jet fighter planes: internal modems, external modems, graphics circuit boards, jump drives, hard disk drives, and memory expansion boards. Each of these technical products requires time, in minutes, on three types of electronic testing equipment as shown in the following table:

	Internal Modem	External Modem	Circuit Board	Jump Drives	Hard Drives	Memory Boards
Test device 1	7	3	12	6	18	17
Test device 2	2	5	3	2	15	17
Test device 3	5	1	3	2	9	2

The first two test devices are available 120 hours per week. The third (device 3) requires more preventive maintenance and may be used only 100 hours each week. The market for all six computer components is vast, and Watts Electronics believes that it can sell as many units of each product as it can manufacture. The table that follows summarizes the revenues and material costs for each product:

Device	Revenue per Unit Sold ($)	Material Cost per Unit ($)
Internal modem	200	35
External modem	120	25
Graphics circuit board	180	40
Jump drive	130	45
Hard disk drive	430	170
Memory expansion board	260	60

In addition, variable labor costs are $15 per hour for test device 1, $12 per hour for test device 2, and $18 per hour for test device 3. Watts Electronics wants to maximize its profits.

a) Formulate this problem as an LP model.

b) Solve the problem by computer. What is the best product mix?

c) What is the value of an additional minute of time per week on test device 1? test device 2? test device 3? Should Watts Electronics add more test device time? If so, on which equipment? **Px**

•••• **B.30** You have just been hired as a planner for the municipal school system, and your first assignment is to redesign the subsidized lunch program. In particular, you are to formulate the least expensive lunch menu that will still meet all state and federal nutritional guidelines.

The guidelines are as follows: A meal must be between 500 and 800 calories. It must contain at least 200 calories of protein, at least 200 calories of carbohydrates, and no more than 400 calories of fat. It also needs to have at least 200 calories of a food classified as a fruit or vegetable.

Here is the list of the foods you can consider as possible menu items, with contract-determined prices and nutritional information. Note that all percentages sum to 100% per food—as all calories are protein, carbohydrate, or fat calories. For example, a serving of applesauce has 100 calories, all of which are carbohydrate, and it counts as a fruit/veg food. You are allowed to use fractional servings, such as 2.25 servings of turkey breast and a 0.33 portion of salad. Cost and nutritional attributes scale likewise: e.g., a 0.33 portion of salad cost $.30 and has 33 calories.

Food	Cost/Serving	Calories/Serving	% protein	% carbs	% fat	Fruit/Veg
Applesauce	$0.30	100	0%	100%	0%	Y
Canned corn	$0.40	150	20%	80%	0%	Y
Fried chicken	$0.90	250	55%	5%	40%	N
French fries	$0.20	400	5%	35%	60%	N
Mac and cheese	$0.50	430	20%	30%	50%	N
Turkey breast	$1.50	300	67%	0%	33%	N
Garden salad	$0.90	100	15%	40%	45%	Y

Formulate and solve as a linear problem. Print out your formulation in Excel showing the objective function coefficients and constraint matrix in standard form.

- Display, on a separate page, the full *Answer Report* as generated by Excel Solver.

- Highlight *and label as* Z the objective value for the optimal solution on the Answer Report.
- Highlight the nonzero decision variables for the optimal solution on the Answer Report.
- Display, on a separate page, the full *Sensitivity Report* as generated by Excel Solver. ✗

Case Study

Golding Landscaping and Plants, Inc.

Kenneth and Patricia Golding spent a career as a husband-and-wife real estate investment partnership in Washington, DC. When they finally retired to a 25-acre farm in northern Virginia's Fairfax County, they became ardent amateur gardeners. Kenneth planted shrubs and fruit trees, and Patricia spent her hours potting all sizes of plants. When the volume of shrubs and plants reached the point that the Goldings began to think of their hobby in a serious vein, they built a greenhouse adjacent to their home and installed heating and watering systems.

By 2005, the Goldings realized their retirement from real estate had really only led to a second career—in the plant and shrub business—and they filed for a Virginia business license. Within a matter of months, they asked their attorney to file incorporation documents and formed the firm Golding Landscaping and Plants, Inc.

Early in the new business's existence, Kenneth Golding recognized the need for a high-quality commercial fertilizer that he could blend himself, both for sale and for his own nursery. His goal was to keep his costs to a minimum while producing a top-notch product that was especially suited to the northern Virginia climate.

Working with chemists at George Mason University, Golding blended "Golding-Grow." It consists of four chemical compounds, C-30, C-92, D-21, and E-11. The cost per pound for each compound is indicated in the following table:

Chemical Compound	Cost per Pound
C-30	$.12
C-92	.09
D-21	.11
E-11	.04

The specifications for Golding-Grow are established as:

a. Chemical E-11 must constitute at least 15% of the blend.
b. C-92 and C-30 must together constitute at least 45% of the blend.
c. D-21 and C-92 can together constitute no more than 30% of the blend.
d. Golding-Grow is packaged and sold in 50-lb bags.

Discussion Questions

1. Formulate an LP problem to determine what blend of the four chemicals will allow Golding to minimize the cost of a 50-lb bag of the fertilizer.
2. Solve to find the best solution.

Additional Case Study

See our Companion Web site at **www.prenhall.com/heizer** *for this additional internet case study:*

• **Chase Manhattan Bank:** This scheduling case involves finding the optimal number of full-time versus part-time employees at a bank.

Bibliography

Bard, J. F. "Staff Scheduling in High Volume Services with Downgrading." *IIE Transactions* 36 (October 2004): 985.

Begley, S. "Did You Hear About the Salesman Who Travelled Better?" *OR/MS Today* 31 (January 2004): 20.

Brown, G., R. F. Dell, and A. M. Newman. "Optimizing Military Capital Planning." *Interfaces* 34, no. 6 (November–December 2004): 415–425.

Chakravarti, N. "Tea Company Steeped in OR." *OR/MS Today* 27 (April 2000): 32–34.

daSilva, C. G., et al. "An Interactive Decision Support System for an Aggregate Planning Production Model." *Omega* 34 (April 2006): 167.

Desroisers, Jacques. "Air Transat Uses ALTITUDE to Manage Its Aircraft Routing, Crew Pairing, and Work Assignment." *Interfaces* 30 (March–April 2000): 41–53.

Le Blanc, Larry J., et al. "Nu-Kote's Spreadsheet Linear Programming Models for Optimizing Transportation." *Interfaces* 34 (March–April 2004): 139–146.

Lyon, Peter, R. John Milne, Robert Orzell, and Robert Rice. "Matching Assets with Demand in Supply Chain Management at IBM Microelectronics." *Interfaces* 31 (January 2001): 108–124.

Martin, C. H. "Ohio University's College of Business Uses Integer Programming to Schedule Classes." *Interfaces* 34 (November–December 2004): 460–465.

Neureuther, B. D., G. G. Polak, and N. R. Sanders. "A Hierarchical Production Plan for a Make-to-order Steel Fabrication Plant." *Production Planning & Control* 15 (April 2004): 324.

Peeteis, M., and Z. Degraeve. "An LP Based Lower Bound for the Simple Assembly Line Balancing Problem." *European Journal of Operational Research* 168 (February 2006): 716.

Render, B., R. M. Stair, and Michael Hanna. *Quantitative Analysis for Management*, 9th ed. Upper Saddle River, NJ: Prentice Hall (2006).

Render, B., R. M. Stair, and R. Balakrishman. *Managerial Decision Modeling with Spreadsheets*, 2nd ed. Upper Saddle River, NJ: Prentice Hall (2007).

Sodhi, M. S., and S. Norri. "A Fast and Optimal Modeling Approach Applied to Crew Rostering at London Underground." *Annals of OR* 127 (March 2004): 259.

Taylor, Bernard. *Introduction to Management Science*, 9th ed. Upper Saddle River, NJ: Prentice Hall (2008).

van den Briel, M. H. L., et. al. "America West Airlines Develops Efficient Boarding Strategies." *Interfaces* 35, no. 3 (May–June 2005): 191–201.

Yu, G., et al. "Optimizing Pilot Planning and Training for Continental Airlines." *Interfaces* 34 (July–August 2004): 253–271.

QUANTITATIVE MODULE C

Transportation Models

Module Outline

Learning Objectives

When you complete this module you should be able to

1. Develop an initial solution to a transportation model with the northwest-corner and intuitive lowest-cost methods

2. Solve a problem with the stepping-stone method

3. Balance a transportation problem

4. Solve a problem with degeneracy

▲ *The problem facing rental companies like Avis, Hertz, and National is cross-country travel. Lots of it. Cars rented in New York end up in Chicago, cars from L.A. come to Philadelphia, and cars from Boston come to Miami. The scene is repeated in over 100 cities around the U.S. As a result, there are too many cars in some cities and too few in others. Operations managers have to decide how many of these rentals should be trucked (by costly auto carriers) from each city with excess capacity to each city that needs more rentals. The process requires quick action for the most economical routing; so rental car companies turn to transportation modeling.*

Because location of a new factory, warehouse, or distribution center is a strategic issue with substantial cost implications, most companies consider and evaluate several locations. With a wide variety of objective and subjective factors to be considered, rational decisions are aided by a number of techniques. One of those techniques is transportation modeling.

The transportation models described in this module prove useful when considering alternative facility locations *within the framework of an existing distribution system*. Each new potential plant, warehouse, or distribution center will require a different allocation of shipments, depending on its own production and shipping costs and the costs of each existing facility. The choice of a new location depends on which will yield the minimum cost *for the entire system*.

TRANSPORTATION MODELING

Transportation modeling

An iterative procedure for solving problems that involves minimizing the cost of shipping products from a series of sources to a series of destinations.

Transportation modeling finds the least-cost means of shipping supplies from several origins to several destinations. *Origin points* (or *sources*) can be factories, warehouses, car rental agencies like Avis, or any other points from which goods are shipped. *Destinations* are any points that receive goods. To use the transportation model, we need to know the following:

1. The origin points and the capacity or supply per period at each.
2. The destination points and the demand per period at each.
3. The cost of shipping one unit from each origin to each destination.

The transportation model is actually a class of the linear programming models discussed in Quantitative Module B. As it is for linear programming, software is available to solve transportation problems. To fully use such programs, though, you need to understand the assumptions that underlie the model. To illustrate one transportation problem, in this module we look at a company called Arizona Plumbing, which makes, among other products, a full line of bathtubs. In our example, the firm must decide which of its factories should supply which of its

To From	Albuquerque	Boston	Cleveland
Des Moines	$5	$4	$3
Evansville	$8	$4	$3
Fort Lauderdale	$9	$7	$5

warehouses. Relevant data for Arizona Plumbing are presented in Table C.1 and Figure C.1. Table C.1 shows, for example, that it costs Arizona Plumbing $5 to ship one bathtub from its Des Moines factory to its Albuquerque warehouse, $4 to Boston, and $3 to Cleveland. Likewise, we see in Figure C.1 that the 300 units required by Arizona Plumbing's Albuquerque warehouse may be shipped in various combinations from its Des Moines, Evansville, and Fort Lauderdale factories.

The first step in the modeling process is to set up a *transportation matrix*. Its purpose is to summarize all relevant data and to keep track of algorithm computations. Using the information displayed in Figure C.1 and Table C.1, we can construct a transportation matrix as shown in Figure C.2.

To From	Albuquerque	Boston	Cleveland	Factory capacity
Des Moines	$5	$4	$3	100
Evansville	$8	$4	$3	300
Fort Lauderdale	$9	$7	$5	300
Warehouse requirement	300	200	200	700

Des Moines capacity constraint

Cell representing a possible source-to-destination shipping assignment (Evansville to Cleveland)

Cost of shipping 1 unit from Fort Lauderdale factory to Boston warehouse

Cleveland warehouse demand

Total demand and total supply

Northwest-corner rule

A procedure in the transportation model where one starts at the upper-left-hand cell of a table (the northwest corner) and systematically allocates units to shipping routes.

DEVELOPING AN INITIAL SOLUTION

Once the data are arranged in tabular form, we must establish an initial feasible solution to the problem. A number of different methods have been developed for this step. We now discuss two of them, the northwest-corner rule and the intuitive lowest-cost method.

The Northwest-Corner Rule

The **northwest-corner rule** requires that we start in the upper-left-hand cell (or northwest corner) of the table and allocate units to shipping routes as follows:

1. Exhaust the supply (factory capacity) of each row (e.g., Des Moines: 100) before moving down to the next row.
2. Exhaust the (warehouse) requirements of each column (e.g., Albuquerque: 300) before moving to the next column on the right.
3. Check to ensure that all supplies and demands are met.

Example C1 applies the northwest-corner rule to our Arizona Plumbing problem.

EXAMPLE C1

The northwest-corner rule

Arizona Plumbing wants to use the northwest-corner rule to find an initial solution to its problem.

Approach: Follow the 3 steps listed above. See Figure C.3.

Solution: To make the initial solution, these five assignments are made:

1. Assign 100 tubs from Des Moines to Albuquerque (exhausting Des Moines's supply).
2. Assign 200 tubs from Evansville to Albuquerque (exhausting Albuquerque's demand).
3. Assign 100 tubs from Evansville to Boston (exhausting Evansville's supply).
4. Assign 100 tubs from Fort Lauderdale to Boston (exhausting Boston's demand).
5. Assign 200 tubs from Fort Lauderdale to Cleveland (exhausting Cleveland's demand and Fort Lauderdale's supply).

▶ **Figure C.3**

Northwest-Corner Solution to Arizona Plumbing Problem

From \ To	(A) Albuquerque	(B) Boston	(C) Cleveland	Factory capacity
(D) Des Moines	$5 100	$4	$3	100
(E) Evansville	$8 200	$4 100	$3	300
(F) Fort Lauderdale	$9	$7 (100)	$5 200	300
Warehouse requirement	300	200	200	700

Means that the firm is shipping 100 bathtubs from Fort Lauderdale to Boston

The total cost of this shipping assignment is $4,200 (see Table C.2).

▶ **Table C.2**

Computed Shipping Cost

Route				
From	**To**	**Tubs Shipped**	**Cost per Unit**	**Total Cost**
D	A	100	$5	$ 500
E	A	200	8	1,600
E	B	100	4	400
F	B	100	7	700
F	C	200	5	$1,000
				Total: $4,200

Insights: The solution given is feasible because it satisfies all demand and supply constraints. The northwest-corner rule is easy to use, but it totally ignores costs, and therefore should only be considered as a starting position.

Learning exercise: Does the shipping assignment change if the cost from Des Moines to Albuquerque increase from $5 per unit to $10 per unit? Does the total cost change? [Answer: The assignment is the same, but cost = $4,700.]

Related problems: C.1a, C.3a, C.9, C.11, C.12

The Intuitive Lowest-Cost Method

The **intuitive method** makes initial allocations based on lowest cost. This straightforward approach uses the following steps:

1. Identify the cell with the lowest cost. Break any ties for the lowest cost arbitrarily.
2. Allocate as many units as possible to that cell without exceeding the supply or demand. Then cross out that row or column (or both) that is exhausted by this assignment.
3. Find the cell with the lowest cost from the remaining (not crossed out) cells.
4. Repeat steps 2 and 3 until all units have been allocated.

Intuitive method
A cost-based approach to finding an initial solution to a transportation problem.

> Arizona Plumbing now wants to apply the intuitive lowest-cost approach.
>
> *Approach:* Apply the 4 steps listed above to the data in Figure C.2.
>
> *Solution:* When the firm uses the intuitive approach on the data (rather than the northwest-corner rule) for its starting position, it obtains the solution seen in Figure C.4.
>
> The total cost of this approach = $3(100) + $3(100) + $4(200) + $9(300) = $4,100.
> (D to C)   (E to C)   (E to B)   (F to A)

EXAMPLE C2

The intuitive lowest-cost approach

▲ **Figure C.4** **Intuitive Lowest-Cost Solution to Arizona Plumbing Problem**

Insight: This method's name is appropriate as most people find it intuitively correct to include costs when making an initial assignment.

Learning exercise: If the cost per unit from Des Moines to Cleveland is not $3, but rather $6, does this initial solution change? [Answer: Yes, now D–B = 100, D–C = 0, E–B = 100, E–C = 200, F–A = 300. Others unchanged at zero. Total cost stays the same.]

Related problems: C.1b, C.2, C.3b

While the likelihood of a minimum-cost solution *does* improve with the intuitive method, we would have been fortunate if the intuitive solution yielded the minimum cost. In this case, as in the northwest-corner solution, it did not. Because the northwest-corner and the intuitive lowest-cost approaches are meant only to provide us with a starting point, we often will have to employ an additional procedure to reach an *optimal* solution.

THE STEPPING-STONE METHOD

Stepping-stone method

An iterative technique for moving from an initial feasible solution to an optimal solution in the transportation method.

The **stepping-stone method** will help us move from an initial feasible solution to an optimal solution. It is used to evaluate the cost effectiveness of shipping goods via transportation routes not currently in the solution. When applying it, we test each unused cell, or square, in the transportation table by asking: What would happen to total shipping costs if one unit of the product (for example, one bathtub) was tentatively shipped on an unused route? We conduct the test as follows:

Learning Objective

2. Solve a problem with the stepping-stone method

1. Select any unused square to evaluate.
2. Beginning at this square, trace a closed path back to the original square via squares that are currently being used (only horizontal and vertical moves are permissible). You may, however, step over either an empty or an occupied square.
3. Beginning with a plus (+) sign at the unused square, place alternating minus signs and plus signs on each corner square of the closed path just traced.
4. Calculate an improvement index by first adding the unit-cost figures found in each square containing a plus sign and then by subtracting the unit costs in each square containing a minus sign.
5. Repeat steps 1 through 4 until you have calculated an improvement index for all unused squares. If all indices computed are *greater than or equal to zero*, you have reached an optimal solution. If not, the current solution can be improved further to decrease total shipping costs.

Example C3 illustrates how to use the stepping-stone method to move toward an optimal solution. We begin with the northwest-corner initial solution developed in Example 1.

EXAMPLE C3

Checking unused routes with stepping stone

There is only one closed path that can be traced for each unused cell.

Arizona Plumbing wants to evaluate unused shipping routes.

Approach: Start with Example C1's Figure C.3 and follow the 5 steps listed above. As you can see, the four currently unassigned routes are Des Moines to Boston, Des Moines to Cleveland, Evansville to Cleveland, and Fort Lauderdale to Albuquerque.

Solution: **Steps 1 and 2.** Beginning with the Des Moines–Boston route, first trace a closed path *using only currently occupied squares* (see Figure C.5). Place alternating plus and minus signs in the corners of this path. In the upper left square, for example, we place a minus sign because we have *subtracted* 1 unit from the original 100. Note that we can use only squares currently used for shipping to turn the corners of the route we are tracing. Hence, the path Des Moines–Boston to Des Moines–Albuquerque to Fort Lauderdale–Albuquerque to Fort Lauderdale–Boston to Des Moines–Boston would not be acceptable because the Fort Lauderdale–Albuquerque square is empty. It turns out that *only one closed route exists for each empty square*. Once this one closed path is identified, we can begin assigning plus and minus signs to these squares in the path.

Step 3. How do we decide which squares get plus signs and which squares get minus signs? The answer is simple. Because we are testing the cost-effectiveness of the Des Moines–Boston shipping route, we try shipping 1 bathtub from Des Moines to Boston. This is 1 *more* unit than we *were* sending between the two cities, so place a plus sign in the box. However, if we ship 1 more unit than before from Des Moines to Boston, we end up sending 101 bathtubs out of the Des Moines factory. Because the Des Moines factory's capacity is only 100 units, we must ship 1 bathtub less from Des Moines to Albuquerque. This change prevents us from violating the capacity constraint.

To indicate that we have reduced the Des Moines–Albuquerque shipment, place a minus sign in its box. As you continue along the closed path, notice that we are no longer meeting our Albuquerque warehouse requirement for 300 units. In fact, if we reduce the Des Moines–Albuquerque shipment to 99 units, we must increase the Evansville–Albuquerque load by 1 unit, to 201 bathtubs. Therefore, place a plus sign in that box to indicate the increase. You may also observe that those squares in which we turn a corner (and only those squares) will have plus or minus signs.

Finally, note that if we assign 201 bathtubs to the Evansville–Albuquerque route, then we must reduce the Evansville–Boston route by 1 unit, to 99 bathtubs, to maintain the Evansville factory's capac-

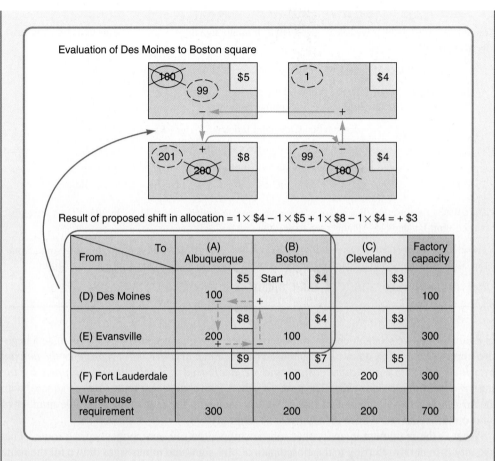

Evaluation of Des Moines to Boston square

Result of proposed shift in allocation = $1 \times \$4 - 1 \times \$5 + 1 \times \$8 - 1 \times \$4 = + \$3$

From \ To	(A) Albuquerque	(B) Boston	(C) Cleveland	Factory capacity
(D) Des Moines	$5 100_	Start $4 +	$3	100
(E) Evansville	$8 200 +	$4 100 -	$3	300
(F) Fort Lauderdale	$9	$7 100	$5 200	300
Warehouse requirement	300	200	200	700

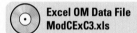

◀ **Figure C.5**

Stepping-Stone Evaluation of Alternative Routes for Arizona Plumbing

ity constraint of 300 units. To account for this reduction, we thus insert a minus sign in the Evansville–Boston box. By so doing we have balanced supply limitations among all four routes on the closed path.

Step 4. Compute an improvement index for the Des Moines–Boston route by adding unit costs in squares with plus signs and subtracting costs in squares with minus signs.

$$\text{Des Moines–Boston index} = \$4 - \$5 + \$8 - \$4 = +\$3$$

This means that for every bathtub shipped via the Des Moines–Boston route, total transportation costs will increase by $3 over their current level.

Let us now examine the unused Des Moines–Cleveland route, which is slightly more difficult to trace with a closed path (see Figure C.6). Again, notice that we turn each corner along the path only at squares on the existing route. Our path, for example, can go through the Evansville–Cleveland box but

◀ **Figure C.6**

Testing Des Moines to Cleveland

From \ To	(A) Albuquerque	(B) Boston	(C) Cleveland	Factory capacity
(D) Des Moines	$5 100_	$4	Start $3 +	100
(E) Evansville	$8 200+	$4 - 100	$3	300
(F) Fort Lauderdale	$9	$7 + 100	$5 - 200	300
Warehouse requirement	300	200	200	700

Because the cities in the tables are in random order, crossing an unoccupied cell is fine.

cannot turn a corner; thus we cannot place a plus or minus sign there. We may use occupied squares only as stepping-stones:

$$\text{Des Moines–Cleveland index} = \$3 - \$5 + \$8 - \$4 + \$7 - \$5 = +\$4$$

Again, opening this route fails to lower our total shipping costs.

Two other routes can be evaluated in a similar fashion:

$$\text{Evansville–Cleveland index} = \$3 - \$4 + \$7 - \$5 = +\$1$$
$$(\text{Closed path} = EC - EB + FB - FC)$$
$$\text{Fort Lauderdale–Albuquerque index} = \$9 - \$7 + 4 - \$8 = -\$2$$
$$(\text{Closed path} = FA - FB + EB - EA)$$

Insight: Because this last index is negative, we can realize cost savings by using the (currently unused) Fort Lauderdale–Albuquerque route.

Learning exercise: What would happen to total cost if Arizona used the shipping route from Des Moines to Cleveland? [Answer: Total cost of the current solution would increase by $400.]

Related problems: C.1c, C.3c, C.7, C.8, C.10, C.13, C.15, C.16, C.17

In Example C3, we see that a better solution is indeed possible because we can calculate a negative improvement index on one of our unused routes. *Each negative index represents the amount by which total transportation costs could be decreased if one unit was shipped by the source–destination combination.* The next step, then, is to choose that route (unused square) with the *largest* negative improvement index. We can then ship the maximum allowable number of units on that route and reduce the total cost accordingly.

What is the maximum quantity that can be shipped on our new money-saving route? That quantity is found by referring to the closed path of plus signs and minus signs drawn for the route and then selecting the *smallest number found in the squares containing minus signs.* To obtain a new solution, we add this number to all squares on the closed path with plus signs and subtract it from all squares on the path to which we have assigned minus signs.

One iteration of the stepping-stone method is now complete. Again, of course, we must test to see if the solution is optimal or whether we can make any further improvements. We do this by evaluating each unused square, as previously described. Example C4 continues our effort to help Arizona Plumbing arrive at a final solution.

EXAMPLE C4
Improvement indices

Arizona Plumbing wants to continue solving the problem.

Approach: Use the improvement indices calculated in Example C3. We found in Example C3 that the largest (and only) negative index is on the Fort Lauderdale–Albuquerque route (which is the route depicted in Figure C.7).

Solution: The maximum quantity that may be shipped on the newly opened route, Fort Lauderdale–Albuquerque (FA), is the smallest number found in squares containing minus signs—in this case, 100 units. Why 100 units? Because the total cost decreases by $2 per unit shipped, we know we would like to ship the maximum possible number of units. Previous stepping-stone calculations indicate that each unit shipped over the FA route results in an increase of 1 unit shipped from Evansville (E) to Boston (B) and a decrease of 1 unit in amounts shipped both from F to B (now 100 units) and from E to A (now 200 units). Hence, the maximum we can ship over the FA route is 100 units. This solution results in zero units being shipped from F to B. Now we take the following four steps:

1. Add 100 units (to the zero currently being shipped) on route FA.
2. Subtract 100 from route FB, leaving zero in that square (though still balancing the row total for F).
3. Add 100 to route EB, yielding 200.
4. Finally, subtract 100 from route EA, leaving 100 units shipped.

Note that the new numbers still produce the correct row and column totals as required. The new solution is shown in Figure C.8.

◀ **Figure C.7**

Transportation Table: Route FA

◀ **Figure C.8**

Solution at Next Iteration (Still Not Optimal)

Total shipping cost has been reduced by (100 units) × ($2 saved per unit) = $200 and is now $4,000. This cost figure, of course, can also be derived by multiplying the cost of shipping each unit by the number of units transported on its respective route, namely: 100($5) + 100($8) + 200($4) + 100($9) + 200($5) = $4,000.

Insight: Looking carefully at Figure C.8, however, you can see that it, too, is not yet optimal. Route EC (Evansville–Cleveland) has a negative cost improvement index of $–1. Closed path = EC – EA + FA – FC.

Learning exercise: Find the final solution for this route on your own. [Answer: Programs C.1 and C.2, at the end of this module, provide an Excel OM solution.]

Related problems: C.4, C.6, C.7, C.8, C.10, C.13, C.15, C.16, C.17

SPECIAL ISSUES IN MODELING

Demand Not Equal to Supply

A common situation in real-world problems is the case in which total demand is not equal to total supply. We can easily handle these so-called unbalanced problems with the solution procedures that we have just discussed by introducing **dummy sources** or **dummy destinations**. If total supply is greater than total demand, we make demand exactly equal the surplus by creating a dummy destination. Conversely, if total demand is greater than total supply, we introduce a dummy source (factory) with a supply equal to the excess of demand. Because these units will not in fact be shipped, we assign cost coefficients of zero to each square on the dummy location. In each case, then, the cost is zero. Example C5 demonstrates the use of a dummy destination.

Dummy sources

Artificial shipping source points created when total demand is greater than total supply to effect a supply equal to the excess of demand over supply.

Dummy destinations

Artificial destination points created when the total supply is greater than the total demand; they serve to equalize the total demand and supply.

EXAMPLE C5

Adjusting for unequal supply and demand with a dummy column

Arizona Plumbing decides to increase the production in its Des Moines factory from 100 tubs to 250 bathtubs. This increases supply over demand and creates an unbalanced problem.

Approach: To reformulate this unbalanced problem, we refer back to the data presented in Example C1 and present the new matrix in Figure C.9. First, we use the northwest-corner rule to find the initial feasible solution. Then, once the problem is balanced, we can proceed to the solution in the normal way.

Solution: Total cost = 250($5) + 50($8) + 200($4) + 50($3) + 150($5) + 150(0) = $3,350

▶ **Figure C.9**

Northwest-Corner Rule with Dummy

 Excel OM Data File ModCExC5.xls

From \ To	(A) Albuquerque	(B) Boston	(C) Cleveland	Dummy	Factory capacity
(D) Des Moines	$5 \ 250	$4	$3	0	250
(E) Evansville	$8 \ 50	$4 \ 200	$3 \ 50	0	300
(F) Fort Lauderdale	$9	$7	$5 \ 150	0 \ 150	300
Warehouse requirement	300	200	200	150	850

New Des Moines capacity

Insight: Excel OM and POM for Windows software automatically perform the balance for you. But if you are solving by hand, be careful to decide first whether a dummy row (source) or a dummy column (destination) is needed.

Learning exercise: Arizona instead increases Des Moines's capacity to 350 tubs. Does the initial northwest-corner solution change? [Answer: Yes, now D–A = 300, D–B = 50, E–B = 150, E–C = 150, F–C = 50, F–Dummy = 250. Cost = $3,000.]

Related problems: C.5, C.9, C.14

Learning Objective

3. Balance a transportation problem

Degeneracy

To apply the stepping-stone method to a transportation problem, we must observe a rule about the number of shipping routes being used: *The number of occupied squares in any solution (initial or later) must be equal to the number of rows in the table plus the number of columns minus 1.* Solutions that do not satisfy this rule are called *degenerate*.

Degeneracy

An occurrence in transportation models in which too few squares or shipping routes are being used, so that tracing a closed path for each unused square becomes impossible.

Degeneracy occurs when too few squares or shipping routes are being used. As a result, it becomes impossible to trace a closed path for one or more unused squares. The Arizona Plumbing problem we just examined was not degenerate, as it had 5 assigned routes (3 rows or factories + 3 columns or warehouses − 1).

To handle degenerate problems, we must artificially create an occupied cell: That is, we place a zero or a *very* small amount (representing a fake shipment) in one of the unused squares and *then treat that square as if it were occupied.* Remember that the chosen square must be in such a position as to allow all stepping-stone paths to be closed. We illustrate this procedure in Example C6.

EXAMPLE C6

Dealing with dengeneracy

Martin Shipping Company has three warehouses from which it supplies its three major retail customers in San Jose. Martin's shipping costs, warehouse supplies, and customer demands are presented in the transportation table in Figure C.10. It wants to make an initial shipping assignment.

◀ **Figure C.10**

Martin's Northwest-Corner Rule

From \ To	Customer 1	Customer 2	Customer 3	Warehouse supply
Warehouse 1	$8 100	$2	$6	100
Warehouse 2	$10 0	$9 100	$9 20	120
Warehouse 3	$7	$10	$7 80	80
Customer demand	100	100	100	300

Excel OM Data File ModCExC6.xls

Approach: To make the initial shipping assignments in that table, we apply the northwest-corner rule.

Solution: The initial solution is degenerate because it violates the rule that the number of used squares must equal the number of rows plus the number of columns minus 1. To correct the problem, we may place a zero in the unused square that permits evaluation of all empty cells. Some experimenting may be needed because not every cell will allow tracing a closed path for the remaining cells. Also, we want to avoid placing the 0 in a cell that has a negative sign in a closed path. No reallocation will be possible if we do this.

For this example, we try the empty square that represents the shipping route from Warehouse 2 to Customer 1. Now we can close all stepping-stone paths and compute improvement indices.

Insight: We must always check the unused squares in a transportation solution to make sure the *Number of rows + Number of columns − 1* = Number of occupied squares.

Learning exercises: Explain why the "zero" cannot be placed in the Warehouse 3-Customer 1 square. [Answer: The route from Warehouse1-Customer 2 cannot be closed now.] Why did this problem become degenerate? [Answer: Our first assignment, 100 units to the Warehouse 1-Customer 1 cell, fully met both the first row and first columns needs in one cell.]

Related problems: C.11, C.12

Learning Objective

4. Solve a problem with degeneracy

Summary

The transportation model, a form of linear programming, is used to help find the least-cost solutions to systemwide shipping problems. The northwest-corner method (which begins in the upper-left corner of the transportation table) or the intuitive lowest-cost method may be used for finding an initial feasible solution. The stepping-stone algorithm is then used for finding optimal solutions. Unbalanced problems are those in which the total demand and total supply are not equal. Degeneracy refers to the case in which the number of rows + the number of columns − 1 is not equal to the number of occupied squares. The transportation model approach is one of the four location models described earlier in Chapter 8. Additional solution techniques are presented on your CD in Tutorial 4.

Key Terms

Transportation modeling *(p. 734)*
Northwest-corner rule *(p. 736)*
Intuitive method *(p. 737)*

Stepping-stone method *(p. 738)*
Dummy sources *(p. 741)*

Dummy destinations *(p. 741)*
Degeneracy *(p. 742)*

Using Software to Solve Transportation Problems

Excel, Excel OM, and POM for Windows may all be used to solve transportation problems. Excel uses Solver, which requires that you enter your own constraints. Excel OM also uses Solver but is prestructured so that you need enter only the actual data. POM for Windows similarly requires that only demand data, supply data, and shipping costs be entered.

✕ Using Excel OM

Excel OM's Transportation module uses Excel's built-in Solver routine to find optimal solutions to transportation problems. Program C.1 illustrates the input data (from Arizona Plumbing) and total-cost formulas. To reach an optimal solution, we must go to Excel's *Tools* bar, request *Solver*, then select *Solve*. In Excel 2007, *Solver* is in the *Analysis* section of the *Data* tab. The output appears in Program C.2.

In Excel 2007, Solver is in the Analysis section of the Data tab. In the prior Excel version Solver is on the Tools menu. If Solver is not available please visit www.prenhall.com/weiss.

Our target cell is the total cost cell (B21), which we wish to minimize by changing the shipment cells (B16 through D18). The constraints ensure that the number shipped is equal to the number demanded and that we don't ship more units than we have on hand.

Enter the origin and destination names, the shipping costs, and the total supply and demand figures.

Nonnegativity constaints have been added through the Options button

These are the cells in which Solver will place the shipments.

The total shipments to and from each location are calculated here.

The total cost is created here by multiplying the data table by the shipment table using the SUMPRODUCT function.

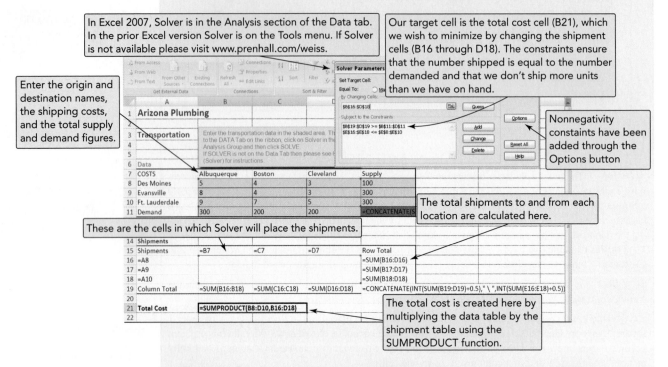

▲ **Program C.1** Excel OM Input Screen and Formulas, Using Arizona Plumbing Data

▼ **Program C.2** Output from Excel OM with Optimal Solution to Arizona Plumbing Problem

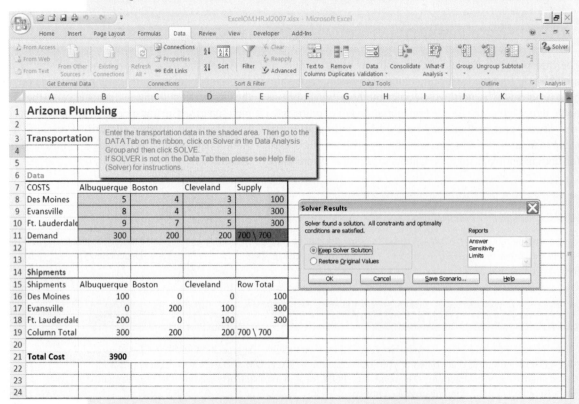

P Using POM for Windows

The POM for Windows Transportation module can solve both maximization and minimization problems by a variety of methods. Input data are the demand data, supply data, and unit shipping costs. See Appendix IV for further details.

Solved Problems

 Virtual Office Hours help on Student DVD.

Solved Problem C.1

Williams Auto Top Carriers currently maintains plants in Atlanta and Tulsa to supply auto top carriers to distribution centers in Los Angeles and New York. Because of expanding demand, Williams has decided to open a third plant and has narrowed the choice to one of two cities—New Orleans and Houston. Table C.3 provides perti-nent production and distribution costs as well as plant capacities and distribution demands.

Which of the new locations, in combination with the existing plants and distribution centers, yields a lower cost for the firm?

◀ **Table C.3**

Production Costs, Distribution Costs, Plant Capabilities, and Market Demands for Williams Auto Top Carriers

| | **To Distribution Centers** | | | |
| | Los | New | Normal | Unit |
From Plants	**Angeles**	**York**	**Production**	**Production Cost**
Existing plants				
Atlanta	$8	$5	600	$6
Tulsa	$4	$7	900	$5
Proposed locations				
New Orleans	$5	$6	500	$4 (anticipated)
Houston	$4	$6[a]	500	$3 (anticipated)
Forecast demand	800	1,200	2,000	

[a]Indicates distribution cost (shipping, handling, storage) will be $6 per carrier between Houston and New York.

Solution

To answer this question, we must solve two transportation problems, one for each combination. We will recommend the location that yields a lower total cost of distribution and production in combination with the existing system.

We begin by setting up a transportation table that represents the opening of a third plant in New Orleans (see Figure C.11). Then we use the northwest-corner method to find an initial solution. The total cost of this first solution is $23,600. Note that the cost of each individual "plant-to-distribution-center" route is found by adding the distribution costs (in the body of Table C.3) to the respective unit production costs (in the right-hand column of Table C.3). Thus, the total production-plus-shipping cost of one auto top carrier from Atlanta to Los Angeles is $14 ($8 for shipping plus $6 for production).

◀ **Figure C.11**

Initial Williams Transportation Table for New Orleans

From \ To	Los Angeles	New York	Production capacity
Atlanta	$14 — 600	$11	600
Tulsa	$9 — 200	$12 — 700	900
New Orleans	$9	$10 — 500	500
Demand	800	1,200	2,000

$$
\begin{aligned}
\text{Total cost} &= (600 \text{ units} \times \$14) + (200 \text{ units} \times \$9) \\
&\quad + (700 \text{ units} \times \$12) + (500 \text{ units} \times \$10) \\
&= \$8,400 + \$1,800 + \$8,400 + \$5,000 \\
&= \$23,600
\end{aligned}
$$

Is this initial solution (in Figure C.11) optimal? We can use the stepping-stone method to test it and compute improvement indices for unused routes:

Improvement index for Atlanta–New York route

$$
\begin{aligned}
&= +\$11 \text{ (Atlanta–New York)} - \$14 \text{ (Atlanta–Los Angeles)} \\
&\quad + \$9 \text{ (Tulsa–Los Angeles)} - \$12 \text{ (Tulsa–New York)} \\
&= -\$6
\end{aligned}
$$

Improvement index for New Orleans–Los Angeles route

$$
\begin{aligned}
&= +\$9 \text{ (New Orleans–Los Angeles)} \\
&\quad - \$10 \text{ (New Orleans–New York)} \\
&\quad + \$12 \text{ (Tulsa–New York)} \\
&\quad - \$9 \text{ (Tulsa–Los Angeles)} \\
&= \$2
\end{aligned}
$$

Because the firm can save \$6 for every unit shipped from Atlanta to New York, it will want to improve the initial solution and send as many units as possible (600, in this case) on this currently unused route (see Figure C.12). You may also want to confirm that the total cost is now \$20,000, a savings of \$3,600 over the initial solution.

Next, we must test the two unused routes to see if their improvement indices are also negative numbers:

Index for Atlanta–Los Angeles

$$
= \$14 - \$11 + \$12 - \$9 = \$6
$$

Index for New Orleans–Los Angeles

$$
= \$9 - \$10 + \$12 - \$9 = \$2
$$

Because both indices are greater than zero, we have already reached our optimal solution for the New Orleans location. If Williams elects to open the New Orleans plant, the firm's total production and distribution cost will be \$20,000.

This analysis, however, provides only half the answer to Williams's problem. The same procedure must still be followed to determine the minimum cost if the new plant is built in Houston. Determining this cost is left as a homework problem. You can help provide complete information and recommend a solution by solving Problem C.8 (on p. 749).

▶ **Figure C.12**

Improved Transportation Table for Williams

From \ To	Los Angeles	New York	Production capacity
Atlanta	$14	$11 600	600
Tulsa	$9 800	$12 100	900
New Orleans	$9	$10 500	500
Demand	800	1,200	2,000

Solved Problem C.2

In Solved Problem C.1, we examined the Williams Auto Top Carriers problem by using a transportation table. An alternative approach is to structure the same decision analysis using linear programming (LP), which we explained in detail in Quantitative Module B.

Solution

Using the data in Figure C.11 (p. 745), we write the objective function and constraints as follows:

$$
\text{Minimize total cost} = \$14X_{\text{Atl,LA}} + \$11X_{\text{Atl,NY}} + \$9X_{\text{Tul,LA}} + \$12X_{\text{Tul,NY}} + \$9X_{\text{NO,LA}} + \$10X_{\text{NO,NY}}
$$

$$
\begin{aligned}
\text{Subject to:} \quad & X_{\text{Atl,LA}} + X_{\text{Atl,NY}} && \leq 600 && \text{(production capacity at Atlanta)} \\
& X_{\text{Tul,LA}} + X_{\text{Tul,NY}} && \leq 900 && \text{(production capacity at Tulsa)} \\
& X_{\text{NO,LA}} + X_{\text{NO,NY}} && \leq 500 && \text{(production capacity at New Orleans)} \\
& X_{\text{Atl,LA}} + X_{\text{Tul,LA}} + X_{\text{NO,LA}} && \geq 800 && \text{(Los Angeles demand constraint)} \\
& X_{\text{Atl,NY}} + X_{\text{Tul,NY}} + X_{\text{NO,NY}} && \geq 1200 && \text{(New York demand constraint)}
\end{aligned}
$$

Self-Test

- ***Before taking the self-test***, *refer to the learning objectives at the beginning of the module and the key terms listed at the end of the module.*
- *Use the key at the back of the text to **correct** your answers.*
- ***Restudy*** *pages that correspond to any questions you answered incorrectly or material you feel uncertain about.*

1. With the transportation technique, the initial solution can be generated in any fashion one chooses. The only restriction is that:
  a) the solution be optimal
  b) one uses the northwest-corner method
  c) the edge constraints for supply and demand are satisfied
  d) the solution not be degenerate
  e) all of the above

2. The purpose of the stepping-stone method is to:
  a) develop the initial solution to a transportation problem
  b) identify the relevant costs in a transportation problem
  c) determine whether a given solution is feasible or not
  d) assist one in moving from an initial feasible solution to the optimal solution
  e) overcome the problem of degeneracy

3. The purpose of a *dummy source* or a *dummy destination* in a transportation problem is to:
  a) provide a means of representing a dummy problem
  b) obtain a balance between total supply and total demand
  c) prevent the solution from becoming degenerate
  d) make certain that the total cost does not exceed some specified figure
  e) change a problem from maximization to minimization

4. In a transportation problem, what indicates that the minimum cost solution has been found?
  a) all improvement indices are negative or zero

  b) all improvement indices are positive or zero
  c) all improvement indices are equal to zero
  d) all cells in the dummy row are empty

5. If the number of filled cells in a transportation table does not equal the number of rows plus the number of columns minus 1, the problem is said to be:
  a) unbalanced
  b) degenerate
  c) optimal
  d) a maximization problem
  e) a minimization problem

6. If a solution to a transportation problem is degenerate, then:
  a) it will be impossible to evaluate all empty cells without removing the degeneracy
  b) a dummy row or column must be added
  c) there will be more than one optimal solution
  d) the problem has no feasible solution
  e) increase the cost of each cell by 1

7. In solving a facility location problem in which there are two possible locations being considered, the transportation algorithm may be used. In doing this:
  a) two rows (sources) would be added to the existing rows and the enlarged problem would be solved
  b) two separate transportation problems would be solved
  c) costs of zero would be used for each of the new facilities
  d) the stepping-stone method must be used to evaluate the empty cells
  e) a dummy row must be added

Internet and Student CD-ROM/DVD Exercises

Visit our Companion Web site or use your student CD-ROM/DVD to help with material in this module.

 On Our Companion Web site, www.prenhall.com/heizer
- Self-Study Quizzes
- Practice Problems
- Internet Case
- PowerPoint Lecture

 On Your Student CD-ROM
- Practice Problems
- Excel OM
- Excel OM Example Data Files
- POM for Windows

 On Your Student DVD
- Virtual Office Hours for Solved Problems

Discussion Questions

1. What are the three information needs of the transportation model?
2. What are the steps in the intuitive lowest-cost method?
3. Identify the three "steps" in the northwest-corner rule.
4. How do you know when an optimal solution has been reached?
5. Which starting technique generally gives a better initial solution, and why?

6. The more sources and destinations there are for a transportation problem, the smaller the percentage of all cells that will be used in the optimal solution. Explain.
7. All of the transportation examples appear to apply to long distances. Is it possible for the transportation model to apply on a much smaller scale, for example, within the departments of a

store or the offices of a building? Discuss; create an example or prove the application impossible.

8. Develop a *northeast*-corner rule and explain how it would work. Set up an initial solution for the Arizona Plumbing problem analyzed in Example C1.

9. What is meant by an unbalanced transportation problem, and how would you balance it?

10. How many occupied cells must all solutions use?

11. Explain the significance of a negative improvement index in a transportation-minimizing problem.

12. How can the transportation method address production costs in addition to transportation costs?

13. Explain what is meant by the term *degeneracy* within the context of transportation modeling.

Problems*

• **C.1** Find an initial solution to the following transportation problem.

From	To			Supply
	Los Angeles	Calgary	Panama City	
Mexico City	$ 6	$18	$ 8	100
Detroit	$17	$13	$19	60
Ottawa	$20	$10	$24	40
Demand	50	80	70	

a) Use the northwest-corner method. What is its total cost?

b) Use the intuitive lowest-cost approach. What is its total cost?

c) Using the stepping-stone method, find the optimal solution. Compute the total cost. **Px**

• **C.2** Consider the transportation table below. Unit costs for each shipping route are in dollars. What is the total cost of the basic feasible solution that the intuitive least cost method would find for this problem? **Px**

Destination

Source	A	B	C	D	E	Supply
1	12	8	5	10	4	18
2	6	11	3	7	9	14
Demand	6	8	12	4	2	

• **C.3** a) Use the northwest-corner method to find an initial feasible solution to the following problem. What must you do before beginning the solution steps?

b) Use the intuitive lowest-cost approach to find an initial feasible solution. Is this approach better than the northwest-corner method?

c) Find the optimal solution using the stepping-stone method.

From	To			Supply
	A	B	C	
X	$10	$18	$12	100
Y	$17	$13	$ 9	50
Z	$20	$18	$14	75
Demand	50	80	70	

Px

Note: **Px** means the problem may be solved with POM for Windows and/or Excel OM.

• **C.4** Consider the transportation table below. The solution displayed was obtained by performing some iterations of the transportation method on this problem. What is the total cost of the shipping plan that would be obtained by performing *one more iteration* of the stepping stone method on this problem?

Destination

Source	Denver	Yuma	Miami	Supply
Houston	$2 10	$8	$1	10
St. Louis	$4 10	$5 10	$6	20
Chicago	$6	$3 10	$2 20	30
Demand	20	20	20	

•• **C.5** Tharp Air Conditioning manufactures room air conditioners at plants in Houston, Phoenix, and Memphis. These are sent to regional distributors in Dallas, Atlanta, and Denver. The shipping costs vary, and the company would like to find the least-cost way to meet the demands at each of the distribution centers. Dallas needs to receive 800 air conditioners per month, Atlanta needs 600, and Denver needs 200. Houston has 850 air conditioners available each month, Phoenix has 650, and Memphis has 300. The shipping cost per unit from Houston to Dallas is $8, to Atlanta $12, and to Denver $10. The cost per unit from Phoenix to Dallas is $10, to Atlanta $14, and to Denver $9. The cost per unit from Memphis to Dallas is $11, to Atlanta $8, and to Denver $12. How many units should owner Devorah Tharp ship from each plant to each regional distribution center? What is the total transportation cost? (Note that a "dummy" destination is needed to balance the problem.) **Px**

•• **C.6** The following table is the result of one or more iterations:

a) Complete the next iteration using the stepping-stone method.

b) Calculate the "total cost" incurred if your results were to be accepted as the final solution. **Px**

From \ To	1	2	3	Capacity
A	30 40	30	5 10	50
B	10	10 30	10	30
C	20	10 30	25 45	75
Demand	40	60	55	155

•• **C.7** The three blood banks in Franklin County are coordinated through a central office that facilitates blood delivery to four hospitals in the region. The cost to ship a standard container of blood from each

bank to each hospital is shown in the table below. Also given are the biweekly number of containers available at each bank and the biweekly number of containers of blood needed at each hospital. How many shipments should be made biweekly from each blood bank to each hospital so that total shipment costs are minimized?

	To				
From	Hosp. 1	Hosp. 2	Hosp. 3	Hosp. 4	Supply
Bank 1	$ 8	$ 9	$11	$16	50
Bank 2	$12	$ 7	$ 5	$ 8	80
Bank 3	$14	$10	$ 6	$ 7	120
Demand	90	70	40	50	250	**Px**

•• **C.8** In Solved Problem C.1 (page 746), Williams Auto Top Carriers proposed opening a new plant in either New Orleans or Houston. Management found that the total system cost (of production plus distribution) would be $20,000 for the New Orleans site. What would be the total cost if Williams opened a plant in Houston? At which of the two proposed locations (New Orleans or Houston) should Williams open the new facility? **Px**

•• **C.9** For the following William Gehrlein Corp. data, find the starting solution and initial cost using the northwest-corner method. What must you do to balance this problem?

	To				
From	W	X	Y	Z	Supply
A	$132	$116	$250	$110	220
B	$220	$230	$180	$178	300
C	$152	$173	$196	$164	435
Demand	160	120	200	230		**Px**

•• **C.10** The Tara Tripp Clothing Group owns factories in three towns (W, Y, and Z), which distribute to three Walsh retail dress shops in three other cities (A, B, and C). The following table summarizes factory availabilities, projected store demands, and unit shipping costs:

Walsh Clothing Group

From \ To	Dress Shop A	Dress Shop B	Dress Shop C	Factory availability
Factory W	$4	$3	$3	35
Factory Y	$6	$7	$6	50
Factory Z	$8	$2	$5	50
Store demand	30	65	40	135

a) Complete the analysis, determining the optimal solution for shipping at the Tripp Clothing Group.
b) How do you know if it is optimal or not? **Px**

•• **C.11** Consider the following transportation problem at Frank Timoney Enterprises in Clifton Park, NY.

	To			
From	Destination A	Destination B	Destination C	Supply
Source 1	$8	$9	$4	72
Source 2	$5	$6	$8	38
Source 3	$7	$9	$6	46
Source 4	$5	$3	$7	19
Demand	110	34	31	175

a) Find an initial solution using the northwest-corner rule. What special condition exists?
b) Explain how you will proceed to solve the problem.
c) What is the optimal solution? **Px**

•• **C.12** Lawson Mill Works (LMW) ships pre-cut lumber to three building-supply houses from mills in Mountpelier, Nixon, and Oak Ridge. Determine the best shipment schedule for LMW from the data provided by James Lawson, the traffic manager at LMW. Use the northwest-corner starting procedure and the stepping-stone method. Refer to the following table. (*Note:* You may face a degenerate solution in one of your iterations.) **Px**

Lawson Mill Works

From \ To	Supply House 1	Supply House 2	Supply House 3	Mill capacity (in tons)
Mountpelier	$3	$3	$2	25
Nixon	$4	$2	$3	40
Oak Ridge	$3	$2	$3	30
Supply house demand (in tons)	30	30	35	95

••• **C.13** Captain Cabell Corp. manufacturers fishing equipment. Currently, the company has a plant in Los Angeles and a plant in New Orleans. David Cabell, the firm's owner, is deciding where to build a new plant—Philadelphia or Seattle. Use the following table to find the total shipping costs for each potential site. Which should Cabell select?

	Warehouse			
Plant	Pittsburgh	St. Louis	Denver	Capacity
Los Angeles	$100	$75	$50	150
New Orleans	$ 80	$60	$90	225
Philadelphia	$ 40	$50	$90	350
Seattle	$110	$70	$30	350
Demand	200	100	400	

•• **C.14** Susan Helms Manufacturing Co. has hired you to evaluate its shipping costs. The following table shows present demand, capacity, and freight costs between each factory and each warehouse. Find the shipping pattern with the lowest cost. **Px**

Susan Helms Manufacturing Data

From \ To	Warehouse 1	Warehouse 2	Warehouse 3	Warehouse 4	Plant capacity
Factory 1	4	7	10	12	2,000
Factory 2	7	5	8	11	2,500
Factory 3	9	8	6	9	2,200
Warehouse demand	1,000	2,000	2,000	1,200	6,700 / 6,200

•• **C.15** Drew Rosen Corp. is considering adding a fourth plant to its three existing facilities in Decatur, Minneapolis, and Carbondale. Both St. Louis and East St. Louis are being considered. Evaluating only the transportation costs per unit as shown in the table, decide which site is best.

	From Existing Plants			
To	Decatur	Minneapolis	Carbondale	Demand
Blue Earth	$20	$17	$21	250
Ciro	$25	$27	$20	200
Des Moines	$22	$25	$22	350
Capacity	300	200	150	

	From Proposed Plants	
To	East St. Louis	St. Louis
Blue Earth	$29	$27
Ciro	$30	$28
Des Moines	$30	$31
Capacity	150	150

•• **C.16** Using the data from Problem C.15 and the unit production costs in the following table, show which locations yield the lowest cost.

Location	Production Costs ($)
Decatur	$50
Minneapolis	60
Carbondale	70
East St. Louis	40
St. Louis	50

•••• **C.17** Dalton Pharmaceuticals enjoys a dominant position in the southeast U.S. with over 800 discount retail outlets. These stores are served by twice-weekly deliveries from Dalton's 16 warehouses, which are in turn supplied daily by 7 factories that manufacture about 70% of all of the chain's products.

It is clear to Marilyn Helms, VP operations, that an additional warehouse is desperately needed to handle growth and backlogs. Three cities, Mobile, Tampa, and Huntsville, are under final consideration. The following table illustrates the current and proposed factory/warehouse capacities/demands and shipping costs per average box of supplies.

a) Based on shipping costs only, which city should be selected for the new warehouse?

b) One study shows that Ocala's capacity can increase to 500 boxes per day. Would this affect your decision in part (a)?

c) Because of a new intrastate shipping agreement, rates for shipping from each factory in Florida to each warehouse in Florida drop by $1 per carton. How does this factor affect your answer to parts (a) and (b)?

Table for Problem C.17

	Warehouse								
Factory	Atlanta, GA	New Orleans, LA	Jackson MS	Birmingham, AL	Montgomery, AL	Raleigh, NC	Ashville, NC	Columbia, SC	Capacity (cartons per day)
Valdosta, GA	$3	$5	$4	$3	$4	$6	$8	$8	350
Ocala, FL	4	6	5	5	6	7	6	7	300
Augusta, GA	1	4	3	2	2	6	7	8	400
Stuart, FL	3	5	2	6	6	5	5	6	200
Biloxi, MS	4	1	4	3	3	8	9	10	600
Starkville, MS	3	3	1	2	2	6	5	6	400
Durham, NC	4	8	8	7	7	2	2	2	500
Requirements (cartons/day)	150	250	50	150	100	200	150	300	

(table continued)

Table for Problem C.17 (cont'd)

	Warehouse					Alternatives			
Factory	Orlando, FL	Miami, FL	Jacksonville, FL	Wilmington, NC	Charlotte, NC	Mobile, AL	Tampa, FL	Huntsville, AL	Capacity (cartons (per day)
Valdosta, GA	$9	$10	$8	$8	$11	$4	$6	$3	350
Ocala, FL	2	3	2	6	7	5	2	5	300
Augusta, GA	7	9	6	8	9	3	5	2	400
Stuart, FL	2	2	3	5	5	6	3	5	200
Biloxi, MS	7	13	9	8	8	2	6	3	600
Starkville, MS	6	8	7	7	8	3	6	2	400
Durham, NC	6	8	5	1	2	8	7	8	500
Requirements (cartons/day)	250	300	300	100	150	300	300	300	

Case Study

Custom Vans, Inc.

Custom Vans, Inc., specializes in converting standard vans into campers. Depending on the amount of work and customizing to be done, the customizing can cost less than $1,000 to more than $5,000. In less than 4 years, Tony Rizzo was able to expand his small operation in Gary, Indiana, to other major outlets in Chicago, Milwaukee, Minneapolis, and Detroit.

Innovation was the major factor in Tony's success in converting a small van shop into one of the largest and most profitable custom van operations in the Midwest. Tony seemed to have a special ability to design and develop unique features and devices that were always in high demand by van owners. An example was Shower-Rific, which was developed by Tony only 6 months after Custom Vans, Inc., was started. These small showers were completely self-contained, and they could be placed in almost any type of van and in a number of different locations within a van. Shower-Rific was made of fiberglass, and contained towel racks, built-in soap and shampoo holders, and a unique plastic door. Each Shower-Rific took 2 gallons of fiberglass and 3 hours of labor to manufacture.

Most of the Shower-Rifics were manufactured in Gary in the same warehouse where Custom Vans, Inc., was founded. The manufacturing plant in Gary could produce 300 Shower-Rifics in a month, but this capacity never seemed to be enough. Custom Van shops in all locations were complaining about not getting enough Shower-Rifics, and because Minneapolis was farther away from Gary than the other locations, Tony was always inclined to ship Shower-Rifics to the other locations before Minneapolis. This infuriated the manager of Custom Vans at Minneapolis, and after many heated discussions, Tony decided to start another manufacturing plant for Shower-Rifics at Fort Wayne, Indiana. The manufacturing plant at Fort Wayne could produce 150 Shower-Rifics per month.

The manufacturing plant at Fort Wayne was still not able to meet current demand for Shower-Rifics, and Tony knew that the demand for his unique camper shower would grow rapidly in the next year. After consulting with his lawyer and banker, Tony concluded that he should open two new manufacturing plants as soon as possible. Each plant would have the same capacity as the Fort Wayne manufacturing plant. An initial investigation into possible manufacturing locations was made, and Tony decided that the two new plants should be located in Detroit, Michigan; Rockford, Illinois; or Madison, Wisconsin. Tony knew that selecting the best location for the two new manufacturing plants would be difficult. Transportation costs and demands for the various locations would be important considerations.

The Chicago shop was managed by Bill Burch. This shop was one of the first established by Tony, and it continued to outperform the other locations. The manufacturing plant at Gary was supplying 200 Shower-Rifics each month, although Bill knew that the demand for the showers in Chicago was 300 units. The transportation cost per unit from Gary was $10, and although the transportation cost from Fort Wayne was double that amount, Bill was always pleading with Tony to get an additional 50 units from the Fort Wayne manufacturer. The two additional manufacturing plants would certainly be able to supply Bill with the additional 100 showers he needed. The transportation costs would, of course, vary, depending on which two locations Tony picked. The transportation cost per shower would be $30 from Detroit, $5 from Rockford, and $10 from Madison.

Wilma Jackson, manager of the Custom Van shop in Milwaukee, was the most upset about not getting an adequate supply of showers. She had a demand for 100 units, and at the present time, she was only getting half of this demand from the Fort Wayne manufacturing plant. She could not understand why Tony didn't ship her all 100 units from Gary. The transportation cost per unit from Gary was only $20, while the transportation cost from Fort Wayne was $30. Wilma was hoping that Tony would select Madison for one of the manufacturing locations. She would be able to get all the showers needed, and the transportation cost per unit would only be $5. If not in Madison, a new plant in Rockford would be able to supply her total needs, but the transportation cost per unit would be twice as much as it would be from Madison. Because the transportation cost per unit from Detroit would be $40, Wilma speculated that even if Detroit became one of the new plants, she would not be getting any units from Detroit.

Custom Vans, Inc., of Minneapolis was managed by Tom Poanski. He was getting 100 showers from the Gary plant. Demand was 150 units. Tom faced the highest transportation costs of all locations. The transportation cost from Gary was $40 per unit. It would cost $10 more if showers were sent from the Fort Wayne location. Tom was hoping that Detroit would not be one of the new plants, as the transportation cost would be $60 per unit. Rockford and Madison would have a cost of $30 and $25, respectively, to ship one shower to Minneapolis.

The Detroit shop's position was similar to Milwaukee's—only getting half of the demand each month. The 100 units that Detroit did receive came directly from the Fort Wayne plant. The transportation cost was only $15 per unit from Fort Wayne, while it was $25 from Gary. Dick Lopez, manager of Custom Vans, Inc., of Detroit, placed the probability of having one of the new plants in Detroit fairly high. The factory would be located across town, and the transportation cost would be only $5 per unit. He could get 150 showers from the new plant in Detroit and the other 50 showers from Fort Wayne. Even if Detroit was not selected, the other two locations were not intolerable. Rockford had a transportation cost per unit of $35, and Madison had a transportation cost of $40.

Tony pondered the dilemma of locating the two new plants for several weeks before deciding to call a meeting of all the managers of the van shops. The decision was complicated, but the objective was clear—to minimize total costs. The meeting was held in Gary, and everyone was present except Wilma.

Tony: Thank you for coming. As you know, I have decided to open two new plants at Rockford, Madison, or Detroit. The two locations, of course, will change our shipping practices, and I sincerely hope that they will supply you with the Shower-Rifics that you have been wanting. I know you could have sold more units, and I want you to know that I am sorry for this situation.

Dick: Tony, I have given this situation a lot of consideration, and I feel strongly that at least one of the new plants should be located in Detroit. As you know, I am now only getting half of the showers that I need. My brother, Leon, is very interested in running the plant, and I know he would do a good job.

Tom: Dick, I am sure that Leon could do a good job, and I know how difficult it has been since the recent layoffs by the auto industry. Nevertheless, we should be considering total costs and not personalities. I believe that the new plants should be located in Madison and Rockford. I am farther away from the other plants than any other shop, and these locations would significantly reduce transportation costs.

Dick: That may be true, but there are other factors. Detroit has one of the largest suppliers of fiberglass, and I have checked prices. A new plant in Detroit would be able to purchase fiberglass for $2 per gallon less than any of the other existing or proposed plants.

Tom: At Madison, we have an excellent labor force. This is due primarily to the large number of students attending the University of Wisconsin. These students are hard workers, and they will work for $1 less per hour than the other locations that we are considering.

Bill: Calm down, you two. It is obvious that we will not be able to satisfy everyone in locating the new plants. Therefore, I would like to suggest that we vote on the two best locations.

Tony: I don't think that voting would be a good idea. Wilma was not able to attend, and we should be looking at all of these factors together in some type of logical fashion.

Discussion Question

Where would you locate the two new plants? Why?

Source: From *Managerial Decision Modeling with Spreadsheets* by R. Balakrishnan, B. Render, and R. M. Stair. 2nd ed. Copyright © 2007. Reprinted by permission of Prentice Hall, Inc., Upper Saddle River, NJ.

Additional Case Study

Visit our Companion Web site at **www.prenhall.com/heizer** *for this free internet case study:*

• **Consolidated Bottling (B):** This case involves determining where to add bottling capacity.

Bibliography

Balakrishnan, R., Render, B., and R. M. Stair. *Managerial Decision Modeling with Spreadsheets*, 2nd. ed. Upper Saddle River, NJ: Prentice Hall (2007).

Drezner, Z. *Facility Location: A Survey of Applications and Methods.* Secaucus, NJ: Springer-Verlag (1995).

Haksever, C., B. Render, and R. Russell. *Service Management and Operations*, 2nd ed. Upper Saddle River, NJ: Prentice Hall (2000).

Koksalan, M., and H. Sural. "Efes Beverage Group Makes Location and Distribution Decisions for Its Malt Plants." *Interfaces* 29 (March–April 1999): 89–103.

Ping, J., and K. F. Chu. "A Dual-Matrix Approach to the Transportation Problem." *Asia–Pacific Journal of Operations Research* 19 (May 2002): 35–46.

Render, B., R. M. Stair, and M. Hanna. *Quantitative Analysis for Management*, 10th ed. Upper Saddle River, NJ: Prentice Hall (2009).

Schmenner, R. W. "Look Beyond the Obvious in Plant Location." *Harvard Business Review* 57, no. 1 (January–February 1979): 126–132.

Taylor, B. *Introduction to Management Science*, 9th ed., Upper Saddle River, NJ: Prentice Hall (2008).

QUANTITATIVE MODULE D

Waiting-Line Models

Module Outline

Learning Objectives

When you complete this module you should be able to

1. Describe the characteristics of arrivals, waiting lines, and service systems
2. Apply the single-channel queuing model equations
3. Conduct a cost analysis for a waiting line
4. Apply the multiple-channel queuing model formulas
5. Apply the constant-service-time model equations
6. Perform a limited-population model analysis

▶ *Paris's EuroDisney, Tokyo's Disney Japan, and the U.S.'s Disney World and Disneyland all have one feature in common—long lines and seemingly endless waits. However, Disney is one of the world's leading companies in the scientific analysis of queuing theory. It analyzes queuing behaviors and can predict which rides will draw what length crowds. To keep visitors happy, Disney makes lines appear to be constantly moving forward, entertains people while they wait, and posts signs telling visitors how many minutes until they reach each ride.*

Queuing theory
A body of knowledge about waiting lines.

Waiting line (queue)
Items or people in a line awaiting service.

The body of knowledge about waiting lines, often called **queuing theory**, is an important part of operations and a valuable tool for the operations manager. **Waiting lines** are a common situation—they may, for example, take the form of cars waiting for repair at a Midas Muffler Shop, copying jobs waiting to be completed at a Kinko's print shop, or vacationers waiting to enter the Space Mountain ride at Disney. Table D.1 lists just a few OM uses of waiting-line models.

Waiting-line models are useful in both manufacturing and service areas. Analysis of queues in terms of waiting-line length, average waiting time, and other factors helps us to understand service systems (such as bank teller stations), maintenance activities (that might repair broken machinery), and shop-floor control activities. Indeed, patients waiting in a doctor's office and broken drill presses waiting in a repair facility have a lot in common from an OM perspective. Both use human and equipment resources to restore valuable production assets (people and machines) to good condition.

CHARACTERISTICS OF A WAITING-LINE SYSTEM

In this section, we take a look at the three parts of a waiting-line, or queuing, system (as shown in Figure D.1):

1. *Arrivals or inputs to the system:* These have characteristics such as population size, behavior, and a statistical distribution.
2. *Queue discipline, or the waiting line itself:* Characteristics of the queue include whether it is limited or unlimited in length and the discipline of people or items in it.
3. *The service facility:* Its characteristics include its design and the statistical distribution of service times.

We now examine each of these three parts.

▶ **Table D.1**

Common Queuing Situations

Situation	Arrivals in Queue	Service Process
Supermarket	Grocery shoppers	Checkout clerks at cash register
Highway toll booth	Automobiles	Collection of tolls at booth
Doctor's office	Patients	Treatment by doctors and nurses
Computer system	Programs to be run	Computer processes jobs
Telephone company	Callers	Switching equipment forwards calls
Bank	Customers	Transactions handled by teller
Machine maintenance	Broken machines	Repair people fix machines
Harbor	Ships and barges	Dock workers load and unload

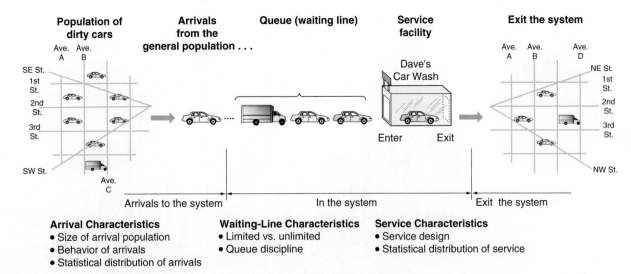

▲ **Figure D.1** **Three Parts of a Waiting Line, or Queuing System, at Dave's Car Wash**

Arrival Characteristics

The input source that generates arrivals or customers for a service system has three major characteristics:

1. *Size* of the arrival population
2. *Behavior* of arrivals
3. *Pattern* of arrivals (statistical distribution)

Size of the Arrival (Source) Population   Population sizes are considered either unlimited (essentially infinite) or limited (finite). When the number of customers or arrivals on hand at any given moment is just a small portion of all potential arrivals, the arrival population is considered **unlimited**, or **infinite**. Examples of unlimited populations include cars arriving at a big-city car wash, shoppers arriving at a supermarket, and students arriving to register for classes at a large university. Most queuing models assume such an infinite arrival population. An example of a **limited**, or **finite**, population is found in a copying shop that has, say, eight copying machines. Each of the copiers is a potential "customer" that may break down and require service.

Pattern of Arrivals at the System   Customers arrive at a service facility either according to some known schedule (for example, one patient every 15 minutes or one student every half hour) or else they arrive *randomly*. Arrivals are considered random when they are independent of one another and their occurrence cannot be predicted exactly. Frequently in queuing problems, the number of arrivals per unit of time can be estimated by a probability distribution known as the **Poisson distribution**.[1] For any given arrival time (such as 2 customers per hour or 4 trucks per minute), a discrete Poisson distribution can be established by using the formula:

$$P(x) = \frac{e^{-\lambda}\lambda^x}{x!} \quad \text{for } x = 0, 1, 2, 3, 4\ldots \tag{D-1}$$

where $P(x)$ = probability of x arrivals
   x = number of arrivals per unit of time
   λ = average arrival rate
   e = 2.7183 (which is the base of the natural logarithms)

With the help of the table in Appendix II, which gives the value of $e^{-\lambda}$ for use in the Poisson distribution, these values are easy to compute. Figure D.2 illustrates the Poisson distribution for $\lambda = 2$ and $\lambda = 4$. This means that if the average arrival rate is $\lambda = 2$ customers per hour, the probability of

Unlimited, or infinite, population
A queue in which a virtually unlimited number of people or items could request the services, or in which the number of customers or arrivals on hand at any given moment is a very small portion of potential arrivals.

Limited, or finite, population
A queue in which there are only a limited number of potential users of the service.

Poisson distribution
A discrete probability distribution that often describes the arrival rate in queuing theory.

---

[1]When the arrival rates follow a Poisson process with mean arrival rate, λ, the time between arrivals follows a negative exponential distribution with mean time between arrivals of $1/\lambda$. The negative exponential distribution, then, is also representative of a Poisson process but describes the time between arrivals and specifies that these time intervals are completely random.

▶ **Figure D.2**

Two Examples of the Poisson Distribution for Arrival Times

▶ **Figure D.2**

Two Examples of the Poisson Distribution for Arrival Times

0 customers arriving in any random hour is about 13%, probability of 1 customer is about 27%, 2 customers about 27%, 3 customers about 18%, 4 customers about 9%, and so on. The chances that 9 or more will arrive are virtually nil. Arrivals, of course, are not always Poisson distributed (they may follow some other distribution). Patterns, therefore, should be examined to make certain that they are well approximated by Poisson before that distribution is applied.

Behavior of Arrivals   Most queuing models assume that an arriving customer is a patient customer. Patient customers are people or machines that wait in the queue until they are served and do not switch between lines. Unfortunately, life is complicated by the fact that people have been known to balk or to renege. Customers who *balk* refuse to join the waiting line because it is too long to suit their needs or interests. *Reneging* customers are those who enter the queue but then become impatient and leave without completing their transaction. Actually, both of these situations just serve to highlight the need for queuing theory and waiting-line analysis.

> *"The other line always moves faster."*
>
> Etorre's Observation

> *"If you change lines, the one you just left will start to move faster than the one you are now in."*
>
> O'Brien's Variation

Waiting-Line Characteristics

The waiting line itself is the second component of a queuing system. The length of a line can be either limited or unlimited. A queue is *limited* when it cannot, either by law or because of physical restrictions, increase to an infinite length. A small barbershop, for example, will have only a limited number of waiting chairs. Queuing models are treated in this module under an assumption of *unlimited* queue length. A queue is *unlimited* when its size is unrestricted, as in the case of the toll booth serving arriving automobiles.

A second waiting-line characteristic deals with *queue discipline*. This refers to the rule by which customers in the line are to receive service. Most systems use a queue discipline known as the **first-in, first-out (FIFO) rule**. In a hospital emergency room or an express checkout line at a supermarket, however, various assigned priorities may preempt FIFO. Patients who are critically injured will move ahead in treatment priority over patients with broken fingers or noses. Shoppers with fewer than 10 items may be allowed to enter the express checkout queue (but are *then* treated as first-come, first-served). Computer-programming runs also operate under priority scheduling. In most large companies, when computer-produced paychecks are due on a specific date, the payroll program gets highest priority.[2]

First-in, first-out (FIFO) rule
A queue discipline in which the first customers in line receive the first service.

Service Characteristics

The third part of any queuing system are the service characteristics. Two basic properties are important: (1) design of the service system and (2) the distribution of service times.

---

[2]The term *FIFS* (first-in, first-served) is often used in place of FIFO. Another discipline, LIFS (last-in, first-served) also called last-in, first-out (LIFO), is common when material is stacked or piled so that the items on top are used first.

Basic Queuing System Designs Service systems are usually classified in terms of their number of channels (for example, number of servers) and number of phases (for example, number of service stops that must be made). A **single-channel queuing system**, with one server, is typified by the drive-in bank with only one open teller. If, on the other hand, the bank has several tellers on duty, with each customer waiting in one common line for the first available teller, then we would have a **multiple-channel queuing system**. Most banks today are multichannel service systems, as are most large barbershops, airline ticket counters, and post offices.

In a **single-phase system**, the customer receives service from only one station and then exits the system. A fast-food restaurant in which the person who takes your order also brings your food and takes your money is a single-phase system. So is a driver's license agency in which the person taking your application also grades your test and collects your license fee. However, say the restaurant requires you to place your order at one station, pay at a second, and pick up your food at a third. In this case, it is a **multiphase system**. Likewise, if the driver's license agency is large or busy, you will probably have to wait in one line to complete your application (the first service stop), queue again to have your test graded, and finally go to a third counter to pay your fee. To help you relate the concepts of channels and phases, Figure D.3 presents four possible channel configurations.

Single-channel queuing system
A service system with one line and one server.

Multiple-channel queuing system
A service system with one waiting line but with several servers.

Single-phase system
A system in which the customer receives service from only one station and then exits the system.

Multiphase system
A system in which the customer receives services from several stations before exiting the system.

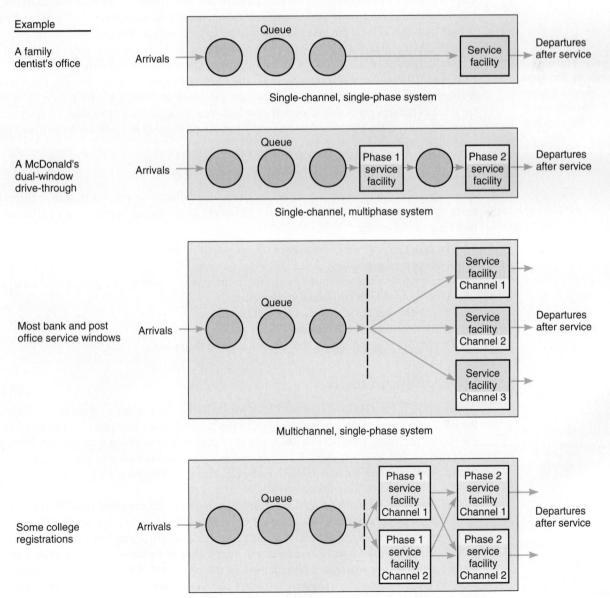

▲ **Figure D.3** Basic Queuing System Designs

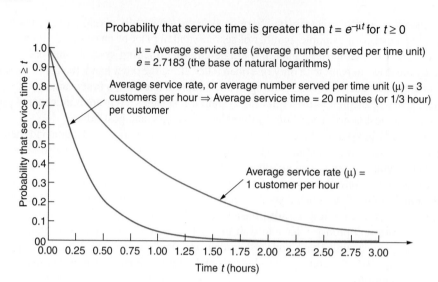

Probability that service time is greater than $t = e^{-\mu t}$ for $t \geq 0$

μ = Average service rate (average number served per time unit)
e = 2.7183 (the base of natural logarithms)

Average service rate, or average number served per time unit (μ) = 3
customers per hour $\Rightarrow$ Average service time = 20 minutes (or 1/3 hour)
per customer

Average service rate (μ) =
1 customer per hour

*Although Poisson
and exponential
distributions are
commonly used to
describe arrival rates
and service times,
normal and Erlang
distributions, or others,
may be more valid in
certain cases.*

**Negative exponential
probability distribution**

A continuous probability
distribution often used to
describe the service time
in a queuing system.

Service Time Distribution   Service patterns are like arrival patterns in that they may be either constant or random. If service time is constant, it takes the same amount of time to take care of each customer. This is the case in a machine-performed service operation such as an automatic car wash. More often, service times are randomly distributed. In many cases, we can assume that random service times are described by the **negative exponential probability distribution**.

Figure D.4 shows that if *service times* follow a negative exponential distribution, the probability of any very long service time is low. For example, when an average service time is 20 minutes (or three customers per hour), seldom if ever will a customer require more than 1.5 hours in the service facility. If the mean service time is 1 hour, the probability of spending more than 3 hours in service is quite low.

Measuring a Queue's Performance

Queuing models help managers make decisions that balance service costs with waiting-line costs. Queuing analysis can obtain many measures of a waiting-line system's performance, including the following:

1. Average time that each customer or object spends in the queue.
2. Average queue length.
3. Average time that each customer spends in the system (waiting time plus service time).
4. Average number of customers in the system.
5. Probability that the service facility will be idle.
6. Utilization factor for the system.
7. Probability of a specific number of customers in the system.

QUEUING COSTS

As described in the *OM in Action* box "Free Movie Tickets if You Aren't Seen in 30 Minutes at the ER," operations managers must recognize the trade-off that takes place between two costs: the cost of providing good service and the cost of customer or machine waiting time. Managers want queues that are short enough so that customers do not become unhappy and either leave without buying or buy but never return. However, managers may be willing to allow some waiting if it is balanced by a significant savings in service costs.

One means of evaluating a service facility is to look at total expected cost. Total cost is the sum of expected service costs plus expected waiting costs.

As you can see in Figure D.5, service costs increase as a firm attempts to raise its level of service. Managers in *some* service centers can vary capacity by having standby personnel and machines that they can assign to specific service stations to prevent or shorten excessively long lines. In grocery stores, for example, managers and stock clerks can open extra checkout counters. In banks and airport check-in points, part-time workers may be called in to help. As the level of service improves (that is, speeds up), however, the cost of time spent waiting in lines decreases. (Refer again to Figure D.5.) Waiting cost may reflect lost productivity of workers

*What does the long wait
in the typical doctor's
office tell you about the
doctor's perception of
your cost of waiting?*

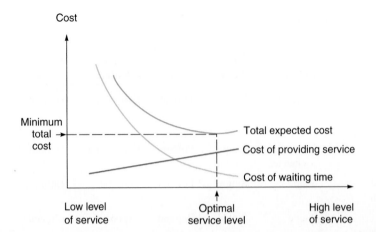

◀ **Figure D.5**

The Trade-off between Waiting Costs and Service Costs

Different organizations place different values on their customers' time, don't they?

while tools or machines await repairs or may simply be an estimate of the cost of customers lost because of poor service and long queues. In some service systems (for example, an emergency ambulance service), the cost of long waiting lines may be intolerably high.

THE VARIETY OF QUEUING MODELS

A wide variety of queuing models may be applied in operations management. We will introduce you to four of the most widely used models. These are outlined in Table D.2, and examples of each follow in the next few sections. More complex models are described in queuing theory textbooks[3] or can be developed through the use of simulation (the topic of module F). Note that all four queuing models listed in Table D.2 have three characteristics in common. They all assume:

Visit a bank or a drive-through restaurant and time arrivals to see what kind of distribution (Poisson or other) they might reflect.

1. Poisson distribution arrivals
2. FIFO discipline
3. A single-service phase

In addition, they all describe service systems that operate under steady, ongoing conditions. This means that arrival and service rates remain stable during the analysis.

OM in Action   Free Movie Tickets if You Aren't Seen in 30 Minutes at the ER

Other hospitals smirked when Dearborn, Michigan's Oakwood Healthcare rolled out an emergency room (ER) guarantee that promised a written apology and movie tickets to patients not seen by a doctor within 30 minutes. Even employees cringed at what sounded like a cheap marketing ploy.

But if you have visited an ER lately and watched some patients wait for hours on end—the *official* average wait is 47 minutes, according to a national hospital group—you can understand why Oakwood's patient satisfaction levels have soared. The 30-minute guarantee was a huge success, and all four of Oakwood Healthcare's hospitals have now rolled it out. Fewer than 1% of last year's 191,000 ER patients asked for free tickets.

"We're down to 17 minutes on average," says Corrine Victor, the ER administrator. Soon, she claims, "we'll start offering a 15-minute guarantee." Oakwood's CEO even extended the ER guarantee to on-time surgery, 45-minute meal service orders, and other custom room services. "Medicine is a service business," says Larry Alexander, the

head of an ER in Sanford, Florida. "And people are in the mindset of the fast-food industry."

How did Oakwood make good on its promise to shorten the ER queue? It first studied queuing theory, then reengineered its billing, records, and lab operations to drive down service time. Then, to improve service capability, Oakwood upgraded its technical staff. Finally, it replaced its ER physicians with a crew willing to work longer hours.

Sources: The Wall Street Journal (July 3, 2002); D1; and Crain's Detroit Business (March 4, 2002): 1.

[3]See, for example, N. U. Prabhu, *Foundations of Queuing Theory*, Kluwer Academic Publishers (1997).

▼ **Table D.2** Queuing Models Described in This Chapter

Model	Name (technical name in parentheses)	Example	Number of Channels	Number of Phases	Arrival Rate Pattern	Service Time Pattern	Population Size	Queue Discipline
A	Single-channel system (M/M/1)	Information counter at department store	Single	Single	Poisson	Exponential	Unlimited	FIFO
B	Multichannel (M/M/S)	Airline ticket counter	Multi-channel	Single	Poisson	Exponential	Unlimited	FIFO
C	Constant service (M/D/1)	Automated car wash	Single	Single	Poisson	Constant	Unlimited	FIFO
D	Limited population (finite population)	Shop with only a dozen machines that might break	Single	Single	Poisson	Exponential	Limited	FIFO

Model A (M/M/1): Single-Channel Queuing Model with Poisson Arrivals and Exponential Service Times

The most common case of queuing problems involves the *single-channel*, or single-server, waiting line. In this situation, arrivals form a single line to be serviced by a single station (see Figure D.3 on p. 757). We assume that the following conditions exist in this type of system:

What is the impact of equal service and arrival rates?

1. Arrivals are served on a first-in, first-out (FIFO) basis, and every arrival waits to be served, regardless of the length of the line or queue.
2. Arrivals are independent of preceding arrivals, but the average number of arrivals (*arrival rate*) does not change over time.
3. Arrivals are described by a Poisson probability distribution and come from an infinite (or very, very large) population.
4. Service times vary from one customer to the next and are independent of one another, but their average rate is known.
5. Service times occur according to the negative exponential probability distribution.
6. The service rate is faster than the arrival rate.

When these conditions are met, the series of equations shown in Table D.3 can be developed. Examples D1 and D2 illustrate how Model A (which in technical journals is known as the M/M/1 model) may be used.[4]

▶ *The giant Moscow McDonald's boosts 900 seats, 800 workers, and $80 million in annual sales (vs. less than $2 million in a U.S. outlet). Americans would balk at the average waiting time of 45 minutes, but Russians are used to such long lines. McDonald's represents good service in Moscow.*

[4]In queuing notation, the first letter refers to the arrivals (where M stands for Poisson distribution); the second letter refers to service (where M is again a Poisson distribution, which is the same as an exponential rate for service—and a D is a constant service rate); the third symbol refers to the number of servers. So an M/D/1 system (our Model C) has Poisson arrivals, constant service, and one server.

λ = mean number of arrivals per time period

μ = mean number of people or items served per time period

L_s = average number of units (customers) in the system (waiting and being served)

$$= \frac{\lambda}{\mu - \lambda}$$

W_s = average time a unit spends in the system (waiting time plus service time)

$$= \frac{1}{\mu - \lambda}$$

L_q = average number of units waiting in the queue

$$= \frac{\lambda^2}{\mu(\mu - \lambda)}$$

W_q = average time a unit spends waiting in the queue

$$= \frac{\lambda}{\mu(\mu - \lambda)} = \frac{L_q}{\lambda}$$

ρ = utilization factor for the system

$$= \frac{\lambda}{\mu}$$

P_0 = probability of 0 units in the system (that is, the service unit is idle)

$$= 1 - \frac{\lambda}{\mu}$$

$P_{n>k}$ = probability of more than k units in the system, where n is the number of units in the system

$$= \left(\frac{\lambda}{\mu}\right)^{k+1}$$

Tom Jones, the mechanic at Golden Muffler Shop, is able to install new mufflers at an average rate of 3 per hour (or about 1 every 20 minutes), according to a negative exponential distribution. Customers seeking this service arrive at the shop on the average of 2 per hour, following a Poisson distribution. They are served on a first-in, first-out basis and come from a very large (almost infinite) population of possible buyers.

We would like to obtain the operating characteristics of Golden Muffler's queuing system.

Approach: This is a single-channel (M/M/1) system and we apply the formulas in Table D.3.

Solution:

λ = 2 cars arriving per hour

μ = 3 cars serviced per hour

$$L_s = \frac{\lambda}{\mu - \lambda} = \frac{2}{3-2} = \frac{2}{1}$$

= 2 cars in the system, on average

$$W_s = \frac{1}{\mu - \lambda} = \frac{1}{3-2} = 1$$

= 1-hour average time in the system

$$L_q = \frac{\lambda^2}{\mu(\mu - \lambda)} = \frac{2^2}{3(3-2)} = \frac{4}{3(1)} = \frac{4}{3}$$

= 1.33 cars waiting in line, on average

$$W_q = \frac{\lambda}{\mu(\mu - \lambda)} = \frac{2}{3(3-2)} = \frac{2}{3} \text{ hour}$$

= 40-minute average waiting time per car

$$\rho = \frac{\lambda}{\mu} = \frac{2}{3}$$

= 66.6% of time mechanic is busy

$$P_0 = 1 - \frac{\lambda}{\mu} = 1 - \frac{2}{3}$$

= .33 probability there are 0 cars in the system

EXAMPLE D1

A single-channel queue

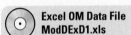
Excel OM Data File ModDExD1.xls

Active Model D.1

Example D1 is further illustrated in Active Model D.1 on your CD-ROM.

Probability of More Than k Cars in the System

k	$P_{n>k} = (2/3)^{k+1}$
0	.667 ← Note that this is equal to $1 - P_0 = 1 - .33 = .667$.
1	.444
2	.296
3	.198 ← Implies that there is a 19.8% chance that more than 3 cars are in the system.
4	.132
5	.088
6	.058
7	.039

Insight: Recognize that arrival and service times are converted to the same rate. For example, a service time of 20 minutes is stated as an average *rate* of 3 mufflers *per hour*. It's also important to differentiate between time in the *queue* and time in the *system*.

Learning exercise: If $\mu = 4$ cars/hour instead of the current 3 arrivals, what are the new values of L_s, W_s, L_q, W_q, ρ and P_0? [Answer: 1 car, 30 min., .5 cars, 15 min., 50%, .50.]

Related problems: D.1, D.2, D.3, D.4, D.6, D.7, D.8, D.9a–e, D.10, D.11a–c, D.12a–d.

Once we have computed the operating characteristics of a queuing system, it is often important to do an economic analysis of their impact. Although the waiting-line model described above is valuable in predicting potential waiting times, queue lengths, idle times, and so on, it does not identify optimal decisions or consider cost factors. As we saw earlier, the solution to a queuing problem may require management to make a trade-off between the increased cost of providing better service and the decreased waiting costs derived from providing that service.

Example D2 examines the costs involved in Example D1.

EXAMPLE D2

Economic analysis of example D1

Learning Objective

3. Conduct a cost analysis for a waiting line

Golden Muffler Shop's owner is interested in cost factors as well as the queuing parameters computed in Example D1. He estimates that the cost of customer waiting time, in terms of customer dissatisfaction and lost goodwill, is $10 per hour spent *waiting* in line. Jones, the mechanic, is paid $7 per hour.

Approach: First compute the average daily customer waiting time, then the daily salary for Jones, and finally the total expected cost.

Solution: Because the average car has a $\frac{2}{3}$-hour wait (W_q) and because there are approximately 16 cars serviced per day (2 arrivals per hour times 8 working hours per day), the total number of hours that customers spend waiting each day for mufflers to be installed is:

$$\frac{2}{3}(16) = \frac{32}{3} = 10\frac{2}{3}\text{ hour}$$

Hence, in this case:

$$\text{Customer waiting-time cost} = \$10\left(10\frac{2}{3}\right) = \$106.67\text{ per day}$$

The only other major cost that Golden's owner can identify in the queuing situation is the salary of Jones, the mechanic, who earns $7 per hour, or $56 per day. Thus:

$$\text{Total expected costs} = \$106.67 + \$56$$
$$= \$162.67\text{ per day}$$

This approach will be useful in Solved Problem D.2 on page 776.

Insight: L_q and W_q are the two most important queuing parameters when it comes to cost analysis. Calculating customer wait times, we note, is based on average time waiting in the queue (W_q) times the number of arrivals per hour (λ) times the number of hours per day. This is because this example is set on a daily basis. This is the same as using L_q, since $L_q = W_q \lambda$.

Learning exercise: If the customer waiting time is actually $20 per hour and Jones gets a salary increase to $10 per hour, what are the total daily expected costs? [Answer: $293.34.]

Related problems: D.12e–f, D.13, D.22, D.23, D.24

◀ **Table D.4**

Queuing Formulas for Model B: Multichannel System, Also Called M/M/S

M = number of channels open
λ = average arrival rate
μ = average service rate at each channel

The probability that there are zero people or units in the system is:

$$P_0 = \cfrac{1}{\left[\displaystyle\sum_{n=0}^{M-1} \frac{1}{n!}\left(\frac{\lambda}{\mu}\right)^n\right] + \frac{1}{M!}\left(\frac{\lambda}{\mu}\right)^M \frac{M\mu}{M\mu - \lambda}} \quad \text{for } M\mu > \lambda$$

The average number of people or units in the system is:

$$L_s = \frac{\lambda\mu(\lambda/\mu)^M}{(M-1)!(M\mu - \lambda)^2} P_0 + \frac{\lambda}{\mu}$$

The average time a unit spends in the waiting line and being serviced (namely, in the system) is:

$$W_s = \frac{\mu(\lambda/\mu)^M}{(M-1)!(M\mu - \lambda)^2} P_0 + \frac{1}{\mu} = \frac{L_s}{\lambda}$$

The average number of people or units in line waiting for service is:

$$L_q = L_s - \frac{\lambda}{\mu}$$

The average time a person or unit spends in the queue waiting for service is:

$$W_q = W_s - \frac{1}{\mu} = \frac{L_q}{\lambda}$$

Model B (M/M/S): Multiple-Channel Queuing Model

Now let's turn to a multiple-channel queuing system in which two or more servers or channels are available to handle arriving customers. We still assume that customers awaiting service form one single line and then proceed to the first available server. Multichannel, single-phase waiting lines are found in many banks today: A common line is formed, and the customer at the head of the line proceeds to the first free teller. (Refer to Figure D.3 on p. 757 for a typical multichannel configuration.)

The multiple-channel system presented in Example D3 again assumes that arrivals follow a Poisson probability distribution and that service times are exponentially distributed. Service is first-come, first-served, and all servers are assumed to perform at the same rate. Other assumptions listed earlier for the single-channel model also apply.

The queuing equations for Model B (which also has the technical name M/M/S) are shown in Table D.4. These equations are obviously more complex than those used in the single-channel model; yet they are used in exactly the same fashion and provide the same type of information as the simpler model. (*Note:* The POM for Windows and Excel OM software described later in this chapter can prove very useful in solving multiple-channel, as well as other, queuing problems.)

Learning Objective

4. Apply the multiple-channel queuing model formulas

EXAMPLE D3

A multiple-channel queue

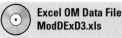

Excel OM Data File ModDExD3.xls

The Golden Muffler Shop has decided to open a second garage bay and hire a second mechanic to handle installations. Customers, who arrive at the rate of about $\lambda = 2$ per hour, will wait in a single line until 1 of the 2 mechanics is free. Each mechanic installs mufflers at the rate of about $\mu = 3$ per hour.

The company wants to find out how this system compares with the old single-channel waiting-line system.

Approach: Compute several operating characteristics for the $M = 2$ channel system, using the equations in Table D.4, and compare the results with those found in Example D1.

Solution:

$$P_0 = \cfrac{1}{\left[\displaystyle\sum_{n=0}^{1}\frac{1}{n!}\left(\frac{2}{3}\right)^n\right] + \frac{1}{2!}\left(\frac{2}{3}\right)^2 \cfrac{2(3)}{2(3)-2}}$$

$$= \cfrac{1}{1 + \frac{2}{3} + \frac{1}{2}\left(\frac{4}{9}\right)\left(\frac{6}{6-2}\right)} = \cfrac{1}{1 + \frac{2}{3} + \frac{1}{3}} = \frac{1}{2}$$

$$= .5 \text{ probability of zero cars in the system}$$

Then:

$$L_s = \frac{(2)(3)(2/3)^2}{1![2(3)-2]^2}\left(\frac{1}{2}\right) + \frac{2}{3} = \frac{8/3}{16}\left(\frac{1}{2}\right) + \frac{2}{3} = \frac{3}{4}$$

$$= .75 \text{ average number of cars in the system}$$

$$W_s = \frac{L_s}{\lambda} = \frac{3/4}{2} = \frac{3}{8} \text{ hour}$$

$$= 22.5 \text{ minutes average time a car spends in the system}$$

$$L_q = L_s - \frac{\lambda}{\mu} = \frac{3}{4} - \frac{2}{3} = \frac{9}{12} - \frac{8}{12} = \frac{1}{12}$$

$$= .083 \text{ average number of cars in the queue (waiting)}$$

$$W_q = \frac{L_q}{\lambda} = \frac{.083}{2} = .0415 \text{ hour}$$

$$= 2.5 \text{ minutes average time a car spends in the queue (waiting)}$$

Insight: It is very interesting to see the big differences in service performance when an additional server is added.

Learning exercise: If $\mu = 4$ per hour, instead of $\mu = 3$, what are the new values for P_0, L_s, W_s, L_q, and W_q? [Answers: 0.6, .53 cars, 16 min, .033 cars, 1 min.]

Related problems: D.9f, D.11d, D.15, D.20

 Active Model D.2

Examples D2 and D3 are further illustrated in Active Model D.2 on the CD-ROM and in the Exercise on page 774.

We can summarize the characteristics of the 2-channel model in Example D3 and compare them to those of the single-channel model in Example D1 as follows:

	Single Channel	**Two Channels**
P_0	.33	.5
L_s	2 cars	.75 car
W_s	60 minutes	22.5 minutes
L_q	1.33 cars	.083 car
W_q	40 minutes	2.5 minutes

The increased service has a dramatic effect on almost all characteristics. For instance, note that the time spent waiting in line drops from 40 minutes to only 2.5 minutes.

Use of Waiting Line Tables Imagine the work a manager would face in dealing with $M = 3$, 4, or 5 channel waiting line models if a computer was not readily available. The arithmetic becomes increasingly troublesome. Fortunately, much of the burden of manually examining multiple channel queues can be avoided by using Table D.5. This table, the result of hundreds of computations, represents the relationship between three things: (1) a ratio we call ρ ([rho] which is simple to find—it's just λ/μ), (2) number of service channels open, and (3) the average number of customers in the queue, L_q (which is what we'd like to find). For any combination of utilization rate (ρ) and $M = 1, 2, 3, 4,$ or 5 open service channels, you can quickly look in the body of the table to read off the appropriate value for L_q.

◄ **Table D.5**

Values of L_q for $M = 1$–5
Service Channels and
Selected Values of
$\rho = \lambda/\mu$

			Poisson Arrivals, Exponential Service Times		
			Number of Service Channels, M		
ρ	1	2	3	4	5
.10	.0111				
.15	.0264	.0008			
.20	.0500	.0020			
.25	.0833	.0039			
.30	.1285	.0069			
.35	.1884	.0110			
.40	.2666	.0166			
.45	.3681	.0239	.0019		
.50	.5000	.0333	.0030		
.55	.6722	.0449	.0043		
.60	.9000	.0593	.0061		
.65	1.2071	.0767	.0084		
.70	1.6333	.0976	.0112		
.75	2.2500	.1227	.0147		
.80	3.2000	.1523	.0189		
.85	4.8166	.1873	.0239	.0031	
.90	8.1000	.2285	.0300	.0041	
.95	18.0500	.2767	.0371	.0053	
1.0		.3333	.0454	.0067	
1.2		.6748	.0904	.0158	
1.4		1.3449	.1778	.0324	.0059
1.6		2.8444	.3128	.0604	.0121
1.8		7.6734	.5320	.1051	.0227
2.0			.8888	.1739	.0398
2.2			1.4907	.2770	.0659
2.4			2.1261	.4305	.1047
2.6			4.9322	.6581	.1609
2.8			12.2724	1.0000	.2411
3.0				1.5282	.3541
3.2				2.3856	.5128
3.4				3.9060	.7365
3.6				7.0893	1.0550
3.8				16.9366	1.5184
4.0					2.2164
4.2					3.3269
4.4					5.2675
4.6					9.2885
4.8					21.6384

> "Queuing theory has
> shown that the death
> toll from a terrorist
> anthrax attack on
> Washington, D.C., could
> be cut by 90% by flying
> in 8,500 more doctors
> and nurses to reduce
> hospital waiting lines."
>
> *Fortune, September 4, 2006*

Example D4 illustrates the use of Table D.5.

EXAMPLE D4

Use of waiting line tables

Alaska National Bank is trying to decide how many drive-in teller windows to open on a busy Saturday. CEO Ted Eschenbach estimates that customers arrive at a rate of about $\lambda = 18$ per hour, and that each teller can service about $\mu = 20$ customers per hour.

Approach: Ted decides to use Table D.5 to compute L_q and W_q.

Solution: The ratio is $\rho = \lambda/\mu = \frac{18}{20} = .90$. Turning to the table, under $\rho = .90$, Ted sees that if only $M = 1$ service window is open, the average number of customers in line will be 8.1. If two windows are open, L_q drops to .2285 customers, to .03 for $M = 3$ tellers, and to .0041 for $M = 4$ tellers. Adding more open windows at this point will result in an average queue length of 0.

It is also a simple matter to compute the average waiting time in the queue, W_q, since $W_q = L_q/\lambda$. When one channel is open, $W_q = 8.1$ customers/(18 customers per hour) = .45 hours = 27 minutes waiting time; when two tellers are open, $W_q = .2285$ customers/(18 customers per hour) = .0127 hours $\cong \frac{3}{4}$ minute; and so on.

Insight: If a computer is not readily available, Table D.5 makes it easy to find L_q and to then compute W_q. Table D.5 is especially handy to compare L_q for different numbers of servers (M).

Learning exercise: The number of customers arriving on a Thursday afternoon at Alaska National is 15/hour. The service rate is still 20 customers/hour. How many people are in the queue if there are 1, 2, or 3 servers? [Answer: 2.25, .1227, .0147.]

Related problem: D.5

► *Long check-in lines such as at Los Angeles International (LAX) are a common airport sight. This is an M/M/S model—passengers wait in a single queue for one of several agents. Based on arrival rates that differ by the fraction of an hour, the airlines staff the counters with fewer or more servers.*

You might also wish to check the calculations in Example D3 against tabled values just to practice the use of Table D.5. You may need to interpolate if your exact ρ value is not found in the first column. Other common operating characteristics besides L_q are published in tabular form in queuing theory textbooks.

Model C (M/D/1): Constant-Service-Time Model

Some service systems have constant, instead of exponentially distributed, service times. When customers or equipment are processed according to a fixed cycle, as in the case of an automatic car wash or an amusement park ride, constant service times are appropriate. Because constant rates are certain, the values for L_q, W_q, L_s, and W_s are always less than they would be in Model A, which has variable service rates. As a matter of fact, both the average queue length and the average waiting time in the queue are halved with Model C. Constant-service-model formulas are given in Table D.6. Model C also has the technical name M/D/1 in the literature of queuing theory.

Learning Objective

5. Apply the constant-service-time model equations

► **Table D.6**

Queuing Formulas for Model C: Constant Service, Also Called M/D/1

Average length of queue: $L_q = \dfrac{\lambda^2}{2\mu(\mu - \lambda)}$

Average waiting time in queue: $W_q = \dfrac{\lambda}{2\mu(\mu - \lambda)}$

Average number of customers in system: $L_s = L_q + \dfrac{\lambda}{\mu}$

Average time in system: $W_s = W_q + \dfrac{1}{\mu}$

Example D5 gives a constant-service-time analysis.

EXAMPLE D5

A constant-service model

Excel OM Data File ModDExD5.xls

Active Model D.3

Example D5 is further illustrated in Active Model D.3 on your CD-ROM.

Inman Recycling, Inc., collects and compacts aluminum cans and glass bottles in Reston, Louisiana. Its truck drivers currently wait an average of 15 minutes before emptying their loads for recycling. The cost of driver and truck time while they are in queues is valued at $60 per hour. A new automated compactor can be purchased to process truckloads at a *constant* rate of 12 trucks per hour (that is, 5 minutes per truck). Trucks arrive according to a Poisson distribution at an average rate of 8 per hour. If the new compactor is put in use, the cost will be amortized at a rate of $3 per truck unloaded.

Approach: CEO Tony Inman hires a summer college intern to conduct an analysis to evaluate the costs versus benefits of the purchase. The intern uses the equation for W_q in Table D.6.

Solution: Current waiting cost/trip = (1/4 hr waiting now)($60/hr cost) = $15/trip

New system: $\lambda = 8$ trucks/hr arriving $\mu = 12$ trucks/hr served

Average waiting time in queue = $W_q = \dfrac{\lambda}{2\mu(\mu-\lambda)} = \dfrac{8}{2(12)(12-8)} = \dfrac{1}{12}$ hr

Waiting cost/trip with new compactor = (1/12 hr wait)($60/hr cost)   = $5/trip

Savings with new equipment = $15(current system) − $5(new system) = $10/trip

Cost of new equipment amortized: = $3/trip

Net savings: $7/trip

Insight: Constant service times, usually attained through automation, help control the variability inherent in service systems. This can lower average queue length and average waiting time. Note the 2 in the denominator of the equations for L_q and W_q in Table D.6.

Learning exercise: With the new constant-service-time system, what are the average waiting time in the queue, average number of trucks in the system, and average waiting time in the system? [Answer: 0.0833 hours, 1.33, 0.1667 hours.]

Related problems: D.14, D.16, D.21

Model D: Limited-Population Model

When there is a limited population of potential customers for a service facility, we must consider a different queuing model. This model would be used, for example, if we were considering equipment repairs in a factory that has 5 machines, if we were in charge of maintenance for a fleet of 10 commuter airplanes, or if we ran a hospital ward that has 20 beds. The limited-population model allows any number of repair people (servers) to be considered.

This model differs from the three earlier queuing models because there is now a *dependent* relationship between the length of the queue and the arrival rate. Let's illustrate the extreme situation: If your factory had five machines and all were broken and awaiting repair, the arrival rate would drop to zero. In general, then, as the *waiting line* becomes longer in the limited population model, the *arrival rate* of customers or machines drops.

Table D.7 displays the queuing formulas for the limited-population model. Note that they employ a different notation than Models A, B, and C. To simplify what can become time-consuming calculations, finite queuing tables have been developed that determine D and F. D represents the probability that a machine needing repair will have to wait in line. F is a waiting-time efficiency factor. D and F are needed to compute most of the other finite model formulas.

A small part of the published finite queuing tables is illustrated in this section. Table D.8 (on page 769) provides data for a population of $N = 5$.[5]

Learning Objective

6. Perform a limited-population model analysis

[5]Limited, or finite, queuing tables are available to handle arrival populations of up to 250. Although there is no definite number that we can use as a dividing point between limited and unlimited populations, the general rule of thumb is this: If the number in the queue is a significant proportion of the arrival population, use a limited population queuing model. For a complete set of *N*-values, see L. G. Peck and R. N. Hazelwood, *Finite Queuing Tables* (New York: Wiley, 1958).

► **Table D.7**

Queuing Formulas and Notation for Model D: Limited-Population Formulas

Service factor: $X = \dfrac{T}{T+U}$ Average number running: $J = NF(1-X)$

Average number waiting: $L = N(1-F)$ Average number being serviced: $H = FNX$

Average waiting time: $W = \dfrac{L(T+U)}{N-L} = \dfrac{T(1-F)}{XF}$ Number of population: $N = J + L + H$

Notation

D = probability that a unit will have to wait in queue N = number of potential customers
F = efficiency factor T = average service time
H = average number of units being served U = average time between unit service requirements
J = average number of units not in queue or in W = average time a unit waits in line
  service bay X = service factor
L = average number of units waiting for service
M = number of service channels

Source: L. G. Peck and R. N. Hazelwood, *Finite Queuing Tables* (New York: Wiley, 1958).

To use Table D.8, we follow four steps:

1. Compute X (the service factor), where $X = T/(T + U)$.
2. Find the value of X in the table and then find the line for M (where M is the number of service channels).
3. Note the corresponding values for D and F.
4. Compute L, W, J, H, or whichever are needed to measure the service system's performance.

Example D6 illustrates these steps.

EXAMPLE D6

A limited-population model

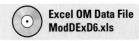
Excel OM Data File ModDExD6.xls

Past records indicate that each of the 5 laser computer printers at the U.S. Department of Energy, in Washington, DC, needs repair after about 20 hours of use. Breakdowns have been determined to be Poisson distributed. The one technician on duty can service a printer in an average of 2 hours, following an exponential distribution. Printer downtime costs $120 per hour. Technicians are paid $25 per hour. Should the DOE hire a second technician?

Approach: Assuming the second technician can also repair a printer in an average of 2 hours, we can use Table D.8 (because there are $N = 5$ machines in this limited population) to compare the costs of 1 versus 2 technicians.

Solution:

1. First, we note that $T = 2$ hours and $U = 20$ hours.

2. Then, $X = \dfrac{T}{T+U} = \dfrac{2}{2+20} = \dfrac{2}{22} = .091$ (close to .090 [to use for determining D and F]).

3. For $M = 1$ server, $D = .350$ and $F = .960$.

4. For $M = 2$ servers, $D = .044$ and $F = .998$.

5. The average number of printers *working* is $J = NF(1-X)$.
   For $M = 1$, this is $J = (5)(.960)(1 - .091) = 4.36$.
   For $M = 2$, it is $J = (5)(.998)(1 - .091) = 4.54$.

6. The cost analysis follows:

Number of Technicians	Average Number Printers Down ($N - J$)	Average Cost/Hr for Downtime ($N - J$)($120/hr)	Cost/Hr. for Technicians (at $25/hr)	Total Cost/hr
1	.64	$76.80	$25.00	$101.80
2	.46	$55.20	$50.00	$105.20

Insight: This analysis suggests that having only one technician on duty will save a few dollars per hour ($105.20 − $101.80 = $3.40). This may seem like a small amount, but it adds up to over $7,000 per year.

Learning exercise: DOE has just replaced its printers with a new model that seems to break down after about 18 hours of use. Recompute the costs. [Answer: For $M = 1$, $F = .95$, $J = 4.275$, and total cost/hr = $112.00. For $M = 2$, $F = .997$, $J = 4.487$, and total cost/hr = $111.56.]

Related problems: D.17, D.18, D.19

▼ Table D.8 Finite Queuing Tables for a Population of *N* = 5*

X	M	D	F	X	M	D	F	X	M	D	F	X	M	D	F	X	M	D	F
.012	1	.048	.999		1	.404	.945		1	.689	.801	.330	4	.012	.999		3	.359	.927
.019	1	.076	.998	.110	2	.065	.996	.210	3	.032	.998		3	.112	.986	.520	2	.779	.728
.025	1	.100	.997		1	.421	.939		2	.211	.973		2	.442	.904		1	.988	.384
.030	1	.120	.996	.115	2	.071	.995		1	.713	.783		1	.902	.583	.540	4	.085	.989
.034	1	.135	.995		1	.439	.933	.220	3	.036	.997	.340	4	.013	.999		3	.392	.917
.036	1	.143	.994	.120	2	.076	.995		2	.229	.969		3	.121	.985		2	.806	.708
.040	1	.159	.993		1	.456	.927		1	.735	.765		2	.462	.896		1	.991	.370
.042	1	.167	.992	.125	2	.082	.994	.230	3	.041	.997		1	.911	.569	.560	4	.098	.986
.044	1	.175	.991		1	.473	.920		2	.247	.965	.360	4	.017	.998		3	.426	.906
.046	1	.183	.990	.130	2	.089	.933		1	.756	.747		3	.141	.981		2	.831	.689
.050	1	.198	.989		1	.489	.914	.240	3	.046	.996		2	.501	.880		1	.993	.357
.052	1	.206	.988	.135	2	.095	.993		2	.265	.960		1	.927	.542	.580	4	.113	.984
.054	1	.214	.987		1	.505	.907		1	.775	.730	.380	4	.021	.998		3	.461	.895
.056	2	.018	.999	.140	2	.102	.992	.250	3	.052	.995		3	.163	.976		2	.854	.670
	1	.222	.985		1	.521	.900		2	.284	.955		2	.540	.863		1	.994	.345
.058	2	.019	.999	.145	3	.011	.999		1	.794	.712		1	.941	.516	.600	4	.130	.981
	1	.229	.984		2	.109	.991	.260	3	.058	.994	.400	4	.026	.977		3	.497	.883
.060	2	.020	.999		1	.537	.892		2	.303	.950		3	.186	.972		2	.875	.652
	1	.237	.983	.150	3	.012	.999		1	.811	.695		2	.579	.845		1	.996	.333
.062	2	.022	.999		2	.115	.990	.270	3	.064	.994		1	.952	.493	.650	4	.179	.972
	1	.245	.982		1	.553	.885		2	.323	.944	.420	4	.031	.997		3	.588	.850
.064	2	.023	.999	.155	3	.013	.999		1	.827	.677		3	.211	.966		2	.918	.608
	1	.253	.981		2	.123	.989	.280	3	.071	.993		2	.616	.826		1	.998	.308
.066	2	.024	.999		1	.568	.877		2	.342	.938		1	.961	.471	.700	4	.240	.960
	1	.260	.979	.160	3	.015	.999		1	.842	.661	.440	4	.037	.996		3	.678	.815
.068	2	.026	.999		2	.130	.988	.290	4	.007	.999		3	.238	.960		2	.950	.568
	1	.268	.978		1	.582	.869		3	.079	.992		2	.652	.807		1	.999	.286
.070	2	.027	.999	.165	3	.016	.999		2	.362	.932		1	.969	.451	.750	4	.316	.944
	1	.275	.977		2	.137	.987		1	.856	.644	.460	4	.045	.995		3	.763	.777
.075	2	.031	.999		1	.597	.861	.300	4	.008	.999		3	.266	.953		2	.972	.532
	1	.294	.973	.170	3	.017	.999		3	.086	.990		2	.686	.787	.800	4	.410	.924
.080	2	.035	.998		2	.145	.985		2	.382	.926		1	.975	.432		3	.841	.739
	1	.313	.969		1	.611	.853		1	.869	.628	.480	4	.053	.994		2	.987	.500
.085	2	.040	.998	.180	3	.021	.999	.310	4	.009	.999		3	.296	.945	.850	4	.522	.900
	1	.332	.965		2	.161	.983		3	.094	.989		2	.719	.767		3	.907	.702
.090	2	.044	.998		1	.638	.836		2	.402	.919		1	.980	.415		2	.995	.470
	1	.350	.960	.190	3	.024	.998		1	.881	.613	.500	4	.063	.992	.900	4	.656	.871
.095	2	.049	.997		2	.117	.980	.320	4	.010	.999		3	.327	.936		3	.957	.666
	1	.368	.955		1	.665	.819		3	.103	.988		2	.750	.748		2	.998	.444
.100	2	.054	.997	.200	3	.028	.998		2	.422	.912		1	.985	.399	.950	4	.815	.838
	1	.386	.950	.200	2	.194	.976		1	.892	.597	.520	4	.073	.991		3	.989	.631
.105	2	.059	.997																

*See notation in Table D.7.

▶ *This isn't Disney World, where waits are made tolerable—or even fun— via amusements and entertainment. This long line of frustrated customers is the Chicago office of the Consulate of Mexico, where immigrants apply for ID cards that are considered legal documents. How could the principles in this module be used to improve this queuing system?*

OTHER QUEUING APPROACHES

Many practical waiting-line problems that occur in service systems have characteristics like those of the four mathematical models already described. Often, however, *variations* of these specific cases are present in an analysis. Service times in an automobile repair shop, for example, tend to follow the normal probability distribution instead of the exponential. A college registration system in which seniors have first choice of courses and hours over other students is an example of a first-come, first-served model with a preemptive priority queue discipline. A physical examination for military recruits is an example of a multiphase system, one that differs from the single-phase models discussed earlier in this module. A recruit first lines up to have blood drawn at one station, then waits for an eye exam at the next station, talks to a psychiatrist at the third, and is examined by a doctor for medical problems at the fourth. At each phase, the recruit must enter another queue and wait his or her turn. Many models, some very complex, have been developed to deal with situations such as these. One of these is described in the *OM in Action* box "L.L. Bean Turns to Queuing Theory."

OM in Action   L.L. Bean Turns to Queuing Theory

L.L. Bean faced severe problems. It was the peak selling season, and the service level for incoming calls was simply unacceptable. Widely known as a high-quality outdoor goods retailer, about 65% of L.L. Bean's sales volume is generated through telephone orders via its toll-free service centers located in Maine.

Here is how bad the situation was: During certain periods, 80% of the calls received a busy signal, and those who did not often had to wait up to 10 minutes before speaking with a sales agent. L.L. Bean estimated it lost $10 million in profit because of the way it allocated telemarketing resources. Keeping customers waiting "in line" (on the phone) was costing $25,000 per day. On exceptionally busy days, the total orders lost because of queuing problems approached $500,000 in gross revenues.

Developing queuing models similar to those presented here, L.L. Bean was able to set the number of phone lines and the number of agents to have on duty for each half hour of every day of the season. Within a year, use of the model resulted in 24% more calls answered, 17% more orders taken, and 16% more revenues. The new system also meant 81% fewer abandoned callers and an 84% faster answering time. The percent of callers spending less than 20 seconds in the queue increased from 25% to 77%. Needless to say, queuing theory changed the way L.L. Bean thought about telecommunications.

Sources: Human Resource Management International Digest (November– December 2002): 4–9; and Interfaces (January/February 1991): 75–91 and (March/April 1993): 14–20.

Summary

Queues are an important part of the world of operations management. In this module, we describe several common queuing systems and present mathematical models for analyzing them.

The most widely used queuing models include Model A, the basic single-channel, single-phase system with Poisson arrivals and exponential service times; Model B, the multichannel equivalent of Model A; Model C, a constant-service-rate model; and Model D, a limited-population system. All four models allow for Poisson arrivals, first-in, first-out service, and a single-service phase. Typical operating characteristics we examine include average time spent waiting in the queue and system, average number of customers in the queue and system, idle time, and utilization rate.

A variety of queuing models exists for which all the assumptions of the traditional models need not be met. In these cases, we use more complex mathematical models or turn to a technique called *simulation*. The application of simulation to problems of queuing systems is addressed in Quantitative Module F.

Key Terms

Queuing theory *(p. 754)*
Waiting line (queue) *(p. 754)*
Unlimited, or infinite, population *(p. 755)*
Limited, or finite, population *(p. 755)*

Poisson distribution *(p. 755)*
First-in, first-out (FIFO) rule *(p. 756)*
Single-channel queuing system *(p. 757)*
Multiple-channel queuing system *(p. 757)*

Single-phase system *(p. 757)*
Multiphase system *(p. 757)*
Negative exponential probability
  distribution *(p. 758)*

Using Software to Solve Queuing Problems

Both Excel OM and POM for Windows may be used to analyze all but the last two homework problems in this module.

✗ Using Excel OM

Excel OM's Waiting-Line program handles all four of the models developed in this module. Program D.1 illustrates our first model, the M/M/1 system, using the data from Example D1.

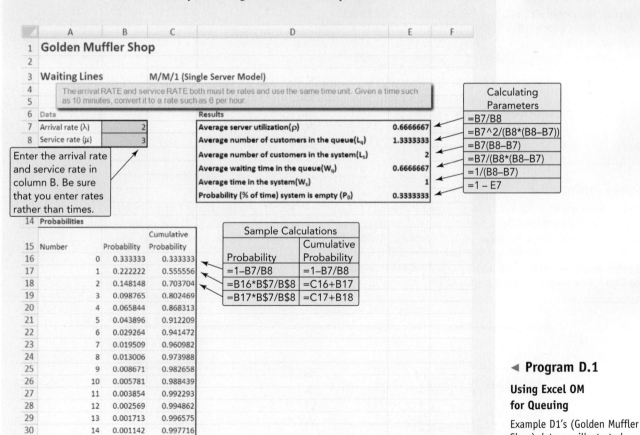

◄ **Program D.1**

Using Excel OM for Queuing

Example D1's (Golden Muffler Shop) data are illustrated in the M/M/1 model.

P Using POM For Windows

There are several POM for Windows queuing models from which to select in that program's Waiting-Line module. The program can include an economic analysis of cost data, and, as an option, you may display probabilities of various numbers of people/items in the system. See Appendix IV for further details.

Solved Problems

 Virtual Office Hours help is available on Student DVD.

Solved Problem D.1

Sid Das Brick Distributors currently employs 1 worker whose job is to load bricks on outgoing company trucks. An average of 24 trucks per day, or 3 per hour, arrive at the loading platform, according to a Poisson distribution. The worker loads them at a rate of 4 trucks per hour, following approximately the exponential distribution in his service times.

Das believes that adding an additional brick loader will substantially improve the firm's productivity. He estimates that a two-person crew loading each truck will double the loading rate (μ) from 4 trucks per hour to 8 trucks per hour. Analyze the effect on the queue of such a change and compare the results to those achieved with one worker. What is the probability that there will be more than 3 trucks either being loaded or waiting?

Solution

	Number of Brick Loaders	
	1	**2**
Truck arrival rate (λ)	3/hr	3/hr
Loading rate (μ)	4/hr	8/hr
Average number in system (L_s)	3 trucks	.6 truck
Average time in system (W_s)	1 hr	.2 hr
Average number in queue (L_q)	2.25 trucks	.225 truck
Average time in queue (W_q)	.75 hr	.075 hr
Utilization rate (ρ)	.75	.375
Probability system empty (P_0)	.25	.625

Probability of More Than k Trucks in System

	Probability $n > k$	
k	**One Loader**	**Two Loaders**
0	.75	.375
1	.56	.141
2	.42	.053
3	.32	.020

These results indicate that when only one loader is employed, the average truck must wait three quarters of an hour before it is loaded. Furthermore, there is an average of 2.25 trucks waiting in line to be loaded. This situation may be unacceptable to management. Note also the decline in queue size after the addition of a second loader.

Solved Problem D.2

Truck drivers working for Sid Das (see Solved Problem D.1) earn an average of $10 per hour. Brick loaders receive about $6 per hour. Truck drivers waiting *in the queue or at the loading platform* are drawing a salary but are productively idle and unable to generate revenue during that time. What would be the *hourly* cost savings to the firm if it employed 2 loaders instead of 1?

Referring to the data in Solved Problem D.1, we note that the average number of trucks *in the system* is 3 when there is only 1 loader and 6 when there are 2 loaders.

Solution

	Number of Loaders	
	1	**2**
Truck driver idle time costs [(Average number of trucks) × (Hourly rate)] = (3)($10) = $30		$ 6 = (.6)($10)
Loading costs	6	12 = (2)($6)
Total expected cost per hour	$36	$18

The firm will save $18 per hour by adding another loader.

Solved Problem D.3

Sid Das is considering building a second platform or gate to speed the process of loading trucks. This system, he thinks, will be even more efficient than simply hiring another loader to help out on the first platform (as in Solved Problem D.1).

Assume that the worker at each platform will be able to load 4 trucks per hour each and that trucks will continue to arrive at the rate of 3 per hour. Then apply the appropriate equations to find the waiting line's new operating conditions. Is this new approach indeed speedier than the other two that Das has considered?

solution

$$P_0 = \cfrac{1}{\left[\displaystyle\sum_{n=0}^{1} \frac{1}{n!}\left(\frac{3}{4}\right)^n\right] + \frac{1}{2!}\left(\frac{3}{4}\right)^2 \frac{2(4)}{2(4)-3}}$$

$$= \cfrac{1}{1 + \frac{3}{4} + \frac{1}{2}\left(\frac{3}{4}\right)^2 \left(\frac{8}{8-3}\right)} = .4545$$

$$L_s = \frac{3(4)(3/4)^2}{(1)!(8-3)^2}(.4545) + \frac{3}{4} = .873$$

$$W_s = \frac{.873}{3} = .291 \text{ hr}$$

$$L_q = .873 - 3/4 = .123$$

$$W_q = \frac{.123}{3} = .041 \text{ hr}$$

Looking back at Solved Problem D.1, we see that although length of the *queue* and average time in the queue are lowest when a second platform is open, the average number of trucks in the *system* and average time spent waiting in the system are smallest when two workers are employed at a *single* platform. Thus, we would probably recommend not building a second platform.

Solved Problem D.4

St. Elsewhere Hospital's cardiac care unit (CCU) has 5 beds, which are virtually always occupied by patients who have just undergone major heart surgery. Two registered nurses are on duty in the CCU in each of the three 8-hour shifts. About every 2 hours (following a Poisson distribution), one of the patients requires a nurse's attention. The nurse will then spend an average of 30 minutes (exponen-

tially distributed) assisting the patient and updating medical records regarding the problem and care provided.

Because immediate service is critical to the 5 patients, two important questions are: What is the average number of patients being attended by the nurses? What is the average time that a patient spends waiting for one of the nurses to arrive?

solution

$$N = 5 \text{ patients}$$

$$M = 2 \text{ nurses}$$

$$T = 30 \text{ minutes}$$

$$U = 120 \text{ minutes}$$

$$X = \frac{T}{T+U} = \frac{30}{30+120} = .20$$

From Table D.8 (p. 769), with $X = .20$ and $M = 2$, we see that:

$$F = .976$$

$$H = \text{average number being attended to} = FNX$$

$$= (.976)(5)(.20) = .98 \approx 1 \text{ patient at any given time}$$

$$W = \text{average waiting time for a nurse} = \frac{T(1-F)}{XF}$$

$$= \frac{30(1-.976)}{(.20)(.976)} = 3.69 \text{ minutes}$$

Self-Test

1. Most systems use the queue discipline known as:
   - a) last-in, first-out (LIFO)
   - b) first-in, first-out (FIFO)
   - c) balking customers first
   - d) exponential smoothing
   - e) self-serve

2. Which of the following is *not* an assumption in common queuing mathematical models?
   - a) arrivals come from an infinite, or very large population
   - b) arrivals are Poisson distributed
   - c) arrivals are treated on a first-in, first-out basis and do not balk or renege
   - d) service times follow the exponential distribution
   - e) the average arrival rate is faster than the average service rate

3. Which of the following is *not* a key operating characteristic for a queuing system?
   - a) utilization rate
   - b) percent idle time
   - c) average time spent waiting in the system and in the queue
   - d) average number of customers in the system and in the queue
   - e) average number of customers who renege

4. Three parts of a queuing system are:
   - a) the inputs, the queue, and the service facility
   - b) the calling population, the utilization, and the service facility
   - c) the arrival system, the waiting line, and the service facility
   - d) all of the above

5. A company has one computer technician who is responsible for repairs on the company's 20 computers. As a computer breaks, the technician is called to make the repair. If the repairperson is busy, the machine must wait to be repaired. This is an example of:
   - a) a multichannel system
   - b) a finite population system
   - c) a constant service rate system
   - d) a multiphase system
   - e) all of the above

6. If everything else remains the same, including the mean arrival rate and service rate, except that the service time becomes constant instead of exponential:
   - a) the average queue length will be halved
   - b) the average waiting time will be doubled
   - c) the average queue length will increase
   - d) we cannot tell from the information provided

7. Customers enter the waiting line at a cafeteria's only cash register on a first-come, first-served basis. The arrival rate follows a Poisson distribution, while service times follow an exponential distribution. If the average number of arrivals is six per minute and the average service rate of a single server is ten per minute, what is the average number of customers in the system?
   - a) 0.6
   - b) 0.9
   - c) 1.5
   - d) .25
   - e) 1.0

Active Model Exercise

In this active model example, we can examine the relationship between arrival and service rates, and costs and the number of servers. The first two inputs to the model are arrival and service rates in customers per hour. The average time between arrivals and service time is also displayed, but do not change these two numbers, which are shaded in pink.

Questions

1. What number of mechanics yields the lowest total daily cost? What is the minimum total daily cost?

2. Use the scrollbar on the arrival rate. What would the arrival rate need to be to require a third mechanic?

3. Use the scrollbar on the goodwill cost and determine the range of goodwill costs for which you would have exactly 1 mechanic. Two mechanics?

4. How high would the wage rate need to be to make 1 mechanic the least costly option?

5. If a second mechanic is added, is it less costly to have the 2 mechanics working separately or to have the 2 mechanics work as a single team with a service rate that is twice as fast?

Multiple Server System with Costs

Reset Data   Questions

Arrival rate (l)	2
(Average time between arrivals)	30 minutes
Service rate (m)	3
(Average service time)	20 minutes

Cost Analysis

Wages ($/hr)	$ 7.00
Loss of goodwill for time waiting ($/hr)	$ 10.00
Hours per day	8

Multiple Server Cost Model

■ Daily goodwill costs ■ Daily wages

▲ **Active Model D.2** **An Analysis of the Golden Muffler Shop (Examples D2–D3) with Cost as a Variable**

Internet and Student CD-ROM/DVD Exercises

Visit our Companion Web site or use your student CD-ROM/DVD to help with material in this module.

 On Our Companion Web Site, www.prenhall.com/heizer
- Self-Study Quizzes
- Practice Problems
- Internet Case
- PowerPoint Lecture

 On Your Student CD-ROM
- Practice Problems
- Active Model Exercises
- Excel OM
- Excel OM Example Data Files
- POM for Windows

 On Your Student DVD
- Virtual Office Hours for Solved Problems

Discussion Questions

1. Name the three parts of a typical queuing system.
2. When designing a waiting line system, what "qualitative" concerns need to be considered?
3. Name the three factors that govern the structure of "arrivals" in a queuing system.
4. State the seven common measures of queuing system performance.
5. State the assumptions of the "basic" single-channel queuing model (Model A or M/M/1).
6. Is it good or bad to operate a supermarket bakery system on a strict first-come, first-served basis? Why?
7. Describe what is meant by the waiting-line terms *balk* and *renege*. Provide an example of each.
8. Which is larger, W_s or W_q? Explain.
9. Briefly describe three situations in which the first-in, first-out (FIFO) discipline rule is not applicable in queuing analysis.
10. Describe the behavior of a waiting line where $\lambda > \mu$. Use both analysis and intuition.
11. Discuss the likely outcome of a waiting line system where $\mu > \lambda$, but only by a tiny amount. (For example, $\mu = 4.1$, $\lambda = 4$).

12. Provide examples of four situations in which there is a limited, or finite, waiting line.
13. What are the components of the following queuing systems? Draw and explain the configuration of each.
    (a) Barbershop.
    (b) Car wash.
    (c) Laundromat.
    (d) Small grocery store.
14. Do doctors' offices generally have random arrival rates for patients? Are service times random? Under what circumstances might service times be constant?
15. What happens if two single-channel systems have the same mean arrival and service rates, but the service time is constant in one and exponential in the other?
16. What dollar value do you place on yourself per hour that you spend waiting in lines? What value do your classmates place on themselves? Why do the values differ?

Problems*

• **D.1** Customers arrive at Paul Harrold's Styling Shop at a rate of 3 per hour, distributed in a Poisson fashion. Paul can perform haircuts at a rate of 5 per hour, distributed exponentially.
a) Find the average number of customers waiting for haircuts.
b) Find the average number of customers in the shop.
c) Find the average time a customer waits until it is his or her turn.
d) Find the average time a customer spends in the shop.
e) Find the percentage of time that Paul is busy. **Px**

• **D.2** There is only one copying machine in the student lounge of the business school. Students arrive at the rate of $\lambda = 40$ per hour (according to a Poisson distribution). Copying takes an average of 40 seconds, or $\mu = 90$ per hour (according to an exponential distribution). Compute the following:
a) The percentage of time that the machine is used.
b) The average length of the queue.
c) The average number of students in the system.
d) The average time spent waiting in the queue.
e) The average time in the system. **Px**

• **D.3** Glen Schmidt owns and manages a chili-dog and soft-drink stand near the Georgeville campus. While Glen can service 30 customers per hour on the average (μ), he gets only 20 customers per hour (λ). Because Glen could wait on 50% more customers than actually visit his stand, it doesn't make sense to him that he should have any waiting lines.

Glen hires you to examine the situation and to determine some characteristics of his queue. After looking into the problem, you find it follows the six conditions for a single-channel waiting line (as seen in Model A). What are your findings? **Px**

• **D.4** Sam Certo, a Longwood vet, is running a rabies vaccination clinic for dogs at the local grade school. Sam can "shoot" a dog every 3 minutes. It is estimated that the dogs will arrive independently and randomly throughout the day at a rate of one dog every 6 minutes according to a Poisson distribution. Also assume that Sam's shooting times are exponentially distributed. Compute the following:
a) The probability that Sam is idle.
b) The proportion of the time that Sam is busy.
c) The average number of dogs being vaccinated and waiting to be vaccinated.
d) The average number of dogs waiting to be vaccinated.
e) The average time a dog waits before getting vaccinated.
f) The average amount of time a dog spends waiting in line and being vaccinated. **Px**

•• **D.5** The pharmacist at Arnold Palmer Hospital, Saad Alwan, receives 12 requests for prescriptions each hour, Poisson distributed. It takes him a mean time of 4 minutes to fill each, following a negative exponential distribution. Use the waiting line table, Table D.5 and $W_q = \dfrac{L_q}{\lambda}$, to answer these questions.
a) What is the average number of prescriptions in the queue?
b) How long will the average prescription spend in the queue?
c) Alwan decides to hire a second pharmacist, Ajay Aggerwal, whom he went to school with and who operates at the same speed in filling prescriptions. How will the answers to parts a and b change? **Px**

• **D.6** Calls arrive at James Hamann's hotel switchboard at a rate of 2 per minute. The average time to handle each is 20 seconds. There is only one switchboard operator at the current time. The Poisson and exponential distributions appear to be relevant in this situation.
a) What is the probability that the operator is busy?
b) What is the average time that a caller must wait before reaching the operator?
c) What is the average number of calls waiting to be answered? **Px**

•• **D.7** Automobiles arrive at the drive-through window at the downtown Urbana, Illinois, post office at the rate of 4 every 10 minutes. The average service time is 2 minutes. The Poisson distribution is appropriate for the arrival rate and service times are exponentially distributed.
a) What is the average time a car is in the system?
b) What is the average number of cars in the system?
c) What is the average number of cars waiting to receive service?
d) What is the average time a car is in the queue?
e) What is the probability that there are no cars at the window?
f) What percentage of the time is the postal clerk busy?
g) What is the probability that there are exactly 2 cars in the system? **Px**

• **D.8** Missouri's Stephen Allen Electronics Corporation retains a service crew to repair machine breakdowns that occur on an average of $\lambda = 3$ per 8-hour workday (approximately Poisson in nature). The crew can service an average of $\mu = 8$ machines per workday, with a repair time distribution that resembles the exponential distribution.
a) What is the utilization rate of this service system?
b) What is the average downtime for a broken machine?
c) How many machines are waiting to be serviced at any given time?
d) What is the probability that more than one machine is in the system? the probability that more than two are broken and waiting to be repaired or being serviced? more than three? more than four? **Px**

•• **D.9** Zimmerman's Bank is the only bank in the small town of St. Thomas. On a typical Friday, an average of 10 customers per hour arrive at the bank to transact business. There is one teller at the bank, and the average time required to transact business is 4 minutes. It is assumed that service times may be described by the exponential distribution. A single line would be used, and the customer at the front of the line would go to the first available bank teller. If a single teller is used, find:
a) The average time in the line.
b) The average number in the line.
c) The average time in the system.
d) The average number in the system.
e) The probability that the bank is empty.
f) Zimmerman is considering adding a second teller (who would work at the same rate as the first) to reduce the waiting time for customers. She assumes that this will cut the waiting time in half. If a second teller is added, find the new answers to parts (a) to (e). **Px**

•• **D.10** Susan Slotnick manages a Cleveland, Ohio, movie theater complex called Cinema I, II, III, and IV. Each of the four auditoriums plays a different film; the schedule staggers starting times

Note: **Px** means the problem may be solved with POM for Windows and/or Excel OM.

to avoid the large crowds that would occur if all four movies started at the same time. The theater has a single ticket booth and a cashier who can maintain an average service rate of 280 patrons per hour. Service times are assumed to follow an exponential distribution. Arrivals on a normally active day are Poisson distributed and average 210 per hour.

To determine the efficiency of the current ticket operation, Susan wishes to examine several queue-operating characteristics.

a) Find the average number of moviegoers waiting in line to purchase a ticket.

b) What percentage of the time is the cashier busy?

c) What is the average time that a customer spends in the system?

d) What is the average time spent waiting in line to get to the ticket window?

e) What is the probability that there are more than two people in the system? More than three people? More than four? **Px**

•• **D.11** Bill Youngdahl has been collecting data at the TU student grill. He has found that, between 5:00 P.M. and 7:00 P.M., students arrive at the grill at a rate of 25 per hour (Poisson distributed) and service time takes an average of 2 minutes (exponential distribution). There is only 1 server, who can work on only 1 order at a time.

a) What is the average number of students in line?

b) What is the average time a student is in the grill area?

c) Suppose that a second server can be added to team up with the first (and, in effect, act as one faster server). This would reduce the average service time to 90 seconds. How would this affect the average time a student is in the grill area?

d) Suppose a second server is added and the 2 servers act independently, with *each* taking an average of 2 minutes. What would be the average time a student is in the system? **Px**

••• **D.12** The wheat harvesting season in the American Midwest is short, and farmers deliver their truckloads of wheat to a giant central storage bin within a 2-week span. Because of this, wheat-filled trucks waiting to unload and return to the fields have been known to back up for a block at the receiving bin. The central bin is owned cooperatively, and it is to every farmer's benefit to make the unloading/storage process as efficient as possible. The cost of grain deterioration caused by unloading delays and the cost of truck rental and idle driver time are significant concerns to the cooperative members. Although farmers have difficulty quantify-

ing crop damage, it is easy to assign a waiting and unloading cost for truck and driver of $18 per hour. During the 2-week harvest season, the storage bin is open and operated 16 hours per day, 7 days per week, and can unload 35 trucks per hour according to an exponential distribution. Full trucks arrive all day long (during the hours the bin is open) at a rate of about 30 per hour, following a Poisson pattern.

To help the cooperative get a handle on the problem of lost time while trucks are waiting in line or unloading at the bin, find the following:

a) The average number of trucks in the unloading system.

b) The average time per truck in the system.

c) The utilization rate for the bin area.

d) The probability that there are more than three trucks in the system at any given time.

e) The total daily cost to the farmers of having their trucks tied up in the unloading process.

f) As mentioned, the cooperative uses the storage bin heavily only 2 weeks per year. Farmers estimate that enlarging the bin would cut unloading costs by 50% next year. It will cost $9,000 to do so during the off-season. Would it be worth the expense to enlarge the storage area? **Px**

••• **D.13** Radovilsky's Department Store in Haywood, California, maintains a successful catalog sales department in which a clerk takes orders by telephone. If the clerk is occupied on one line, incoming phone calls to the catalog department are answered automatically by a recording machine and asked to wait. As soon as the clerk is free, the party who has waited the longest is transferred and serviced first. Calls come in at a rate of about 12 per hour. The clerk can take an order in an average of 4 minutes. Calls tend to follow a Poisson distribution, and service times tend to be exponential.

The cost of the clerk is $10 per hour, but because of lost goodwill and sales, Radovilsky's loses about $25 per hour of customer time spent waiting for the clerk to take an order.

a) What is the average time that catalog customers must wait before their calls are transferred to the order clerk?

b) What is the average number of callers waiting to place an order?

c) Radovilsky's is considering adding a second clerk to take calls. The store's cost would be the same $10 per hour. Should it hire another clerk? Explain your decision. **Px**

• **D.14** Karen Brown's Coffee Shop decides to install an automatic coffee vending machine outside one of its stores to reduce the number of people standing in line inside. Karen charges $3.50 per cup. However, it takes too long for people to make change. The service time is a constant 3 minutes, and the arrival rate is 15 per hour (Poisson distributed).

a) What is the average wait in line?

b) What is the average number of people in line?

c) Karen raises the price to $5 per cup and takes 60 seconds off the service time. However, because the coffee is now so expensive, the arrival rate drops to 10 per hour. Now what are the average wait time and the average number of people in the queue (waiting)? **Px**

••• **D.15** The typical subway station in Washington, DC, has six turnstiles, each of which can be controlled by the station manager to be used for either entrance or exit control—but never for both. The manager must decide at different times of the day how many turnstiles to use for entering passengers and how many to use for exiting passengers.

At the George Washington University (GWU) Station, passengers enter the station at a rate of about 84 per minute between the hours of 7 A.M. and 9 A.M. Passengers exiting trains at the stop reach the exit turnstile area at a rate of about 48 per minute during the same morning rush hours. Each turnstile can allow an average of 30 passengers per minute to enter or exit. Arrival and service times have been thought to follow Poisson and exponential distributions, respectively. Assume riders form a common queue at both entry and exit turnstile areas and proceed to the first empty turnstile.

The GWU station manager, Ernie Forman, does not want the average passenger at his station to have to wait in a turnstile line for more than 6 seconds, nor does he want more than 8 people in any queue at any average time.

a) How many turnstiles should be opened in each direction every morning?

b) Discuss the assumptions underlying the solution of this problem using queuing theory. **PX**

•• **D.16** Yvette Freeman's Car Wash takes a constant time of 4.5 minutes in its automated car wash cycle. Autos arrive following a Poisson distribution at the rate of 10 per hour. Yvette wants to know:

a) The average waiting time in line.

b) The average length of the line. **PX**

••• **D.17** Debra Bishop's cabinet-making shop, in Des Moines, has five tools that automate the drilling of holes for the installation of hinges. These machines need setting up for each order of cabinets. The orders appear to follow the Poisson distribution, averaging 3 per 8-hour day. There is a single technician for setting these machines. Her service times are exponential, averaging 2 hours each.

a) What is the service factor for this system?

b) What is the average number of these machines in service?

c) What impact on machines in service would there be if a second technician were available? **PX**

••• **D.18** Two technicians, working separately, monitor a group of 5 computers that run an automated manufacturing facility. It takes an average of 15 minutes (exponentially distributed) to adjust a computer that develops a problem. Computers run for an average of 85 minutes (Poisson distributed) without requiring adjustments. Determine the following:

a) The average number of computers waiting for adjustment.

b) The average number being adjusted.

c) The average number of computers not in working order. **PX**

••• **D.19** One mechanic services 5 drilling machines for a steel plate manufacturer. Machines break down on an average of once every 6 working days, and breakdowns tend to follow a Poisson distribution. The mechanic can handle an average of one repair job per day. Repairs follow an exponential distribution.

a) On the average, how many machines are waiting for service?

b) On the average, how many drills are in running order?

c) How much would waiting time be reduced if a second mechanic were hired? **PX**

••• **D.20** Richard Insinga, the administrator at an Onienta Hospital emergency room faces the problem of providing treatment for patients who arrive at different rates during the day. There are 4 doctors available to treat patients when needed. If not needed, they can be assigned other responsibilities (such as doing lab tests, reports, X-ray diagnoses) or else rescheduled to work at other hours.

It is important to provide quick and responsive treatment, and Rchard feels that, on the average, patients should not have to sit in the waiting area for more than 5 minutes before being seen by a doctor. Patients are treated on a first-come, first-served basis and see the first available doctor after waiting in the queue. The arrival pattern for a typical day is as follows:

Time	Arrival Rate
9 A.M.–3 P.M.	6 patients/hour
3 P.M.–8 P.M.	4 patients/hour
8 P.M.–midnight	12 patients/hour

Arrivals follow a Poisson distribution, and treatment times, 12 minutes on the average, follow the exponential pattern.

How many doctors should be on duty during each period to maintain the level of patient care expected? **PX**

••• **D.21** The Ponchatrain Bridge is a 16-mile toll bridge that crosses Lake Ponchatrain in New Orleans. Currently, there are 7 toll booths, each staffed by an employee. Since Hurricane Katrina, the Port Authority has been considering replacing the employees with machines. Many factors must be considered because the employees are unionized. However, one of the Port Authority's concerns is the effect that replacing the employees with machines will have on the times that drivers spend in the system. Customers arrive to any one toll booth at a rate of 10 per minute. In the exact change lanes with employees, the service time is essentially constant at 5 seconds for each driver. With machines, the average service time would still be 5 seconds, but it would be exponential rather than constant, because it takes time for the coins to rattle around in the machine. Contrast the two systems for a single lane. **PX**

••• **D.22** The registration area at a large convention of building contractors is taking place in Las Vegas. There are 200 people arriving per hour (Poisson distributed), and the cost of their waiting time in the queue is valued at $100 per person per hour. The Las Vegas Convention Bureau provides servers to register guests at a fee of $15 per person per hour. It takes about one minute to register an attendee (exponentially distributed). A single waiting line, with multiple servers, is set up.

a) What is the minimum number of servers for this system?

b) What is the optimal number of servers for this system?

c) What is the cost for the system, per hour, at the optimum number of servers?

d) What is the server utilization rate with the minimum number of servers? **PX**

•• **D.23** Refer to Problem D.22. A new registration manager, Lisa Houts, is hired who initiates a program to entertain the people in line with a juggler whom she pays $15/hour. This reduces the waiting costs to $50 per hour.

a) What is the optimal number of servers?

b) What is the cost for the system, per hour, at the optimal service level?

•••• **D.24** The Chattanooga Furniture store gets an average of 50 customers per shift. Marilyn Helms, the manager, wants to calculate whether she should hire 1, 2, 3, or 4 salespeople. She has determined that average waiting times will be 7 minutes with one salesperson, 4 minutes with two salespeople, 3 minutes with three salespeople, and 2 minutes with four salespeople. She has estimated the cost per minute that customers wait at $1. The cost per salesperson per shift (including fringe benefits) is $70.

How many salespeople should be hired?

Case Studies

New England Foundry

For more than 75 years, New England Foundry, Inc. (NEFI), has manufactured wood stoves for home use. In recent years, with increasing energy prices, president George Mathison has seen sales triple. This dramatic increase has made it difficult for George to maintain quality in all his wood stoves and related products.

Unlike other companies manufacturing wood stoves, NEFI is in the business of making *only* stoves and stove-related products. Its major products are the Warmglo I, the Warmglo II, the Warmglo III, and the Warmglo IV. The Warmglo I is the smallest wood stove, with a heat output of 30,000 BTUs, and the Warmglo IV is the largest, with a heat output of 60,000 BTUs.

The Warmglo III outsold all other models by a wide margin. Its heat output and available accessories were ideal for the typical home. The Warmglo III also had a number of other outstanding features that made it one of the most attractive and heat-efficient stoves on the market. These features, along with the accessories, resulted in expanding sales and prompted George to build a new factory to manufacture the Warmglo III model. An overview diagram of the factory is shown in Figure D.6.

The new foundry used the latest equipment, including a new Disamatic that helped in manufacturing stove parts. Regardless of new equipment or procedures, casting operations have remained basically unchanged for hundreds of years. To begin with, a wooden pattern is made for every cast-iron piece in the stove. The wooden pattern is an exact duplicate of the cast-iron piece that is to be manufactured. All NEFI patterns are made by Precision Patterns, Inc. and are stored in the pattern shop and maintenance room. Next, a specially formulated sand is molded around the wooden pattern. There can be two or more sand molds for each pattern. The sand is mixed and the molds are made in the molding room. When the wooden pattern is removed, the resulting sand molds form a negative image of the desired casting. Next, molds are transported to the casting room, where molten iron is poured into them and allowed to cool. When the iron has solidified, molds are moved into the cleaning, grinding, and preparation room, where they are dumped into large vibrators that shake most of the sand from the casting. The rough castings are then subjected to both sandblasting to remove the rest of the sand and grinding to finish some of their surfaces. Castings are then painted with a special heat-resistant paint, assembled into workable stoves, and inspected for manufacturing defects that may have gone undetected. Finally, finished stoves are moved

▲ **Figure D.7** **Overview of Factory after Changes**

to storage and shipping, where they are packaged and transported to the appropriate locations.

At present, the pattern shop and the maintenance department are located in the same room. One large counter is used by both maintenance personnel, who store tools and parts (which are mainly used by the casting department); and sand molders, who need various patterns for the molding operation. Pete Nawler and Bob Dillman, who work behind the counter, can service a total of 10 people per hour (about 5 per hour each). On the average, 4 people from casting and 3 from molding arrive at the counter each hour. People from molding and casting departments arrive randomly, and to be served, they form a single line.

Pete and Bob have always had a policy of first come, first served. Because of the location of the pattern shop and maintenance department, it takes an average of 3 minutes for an individual from the casting department to walk to the pattern and maintenance room, and it takes about 1 minute for an individual to walk from the molding department to the pattern and maintenance room.

After observing the operation of the pattern shop and maintenance room for several weeks, George decided to make some changes to the factory layout. An overview of these changes appears in Figure D.7.

Separating the maintenance shop from the pattern shop would have a number of advantages. It would take people from the casting department only 1 minute instead of 3 to get to the new maintenance room. The time from molding to the pattern shop would be unchanged. Using motion and time studies, George was also able to determine that improving the layout of the maintenance room would allow Bob to serve 6 people from the casting department per hour; improving the layout of the pattern department would allow Pete to serve 7 people from the molding shop per hour.

Discussion Questions

1. How much time would the new layout save?
2. If casting personnel were paid $9.50 per hour and molding personnel were paid $11.75 per hour, how much could be saved per hour with the new factory layout?
3. Should George have made the change in layout?

Source: From *Quantitative Analysis for Management,* 9th ed., by B. Render, R. Stair, and M. Hanna, pp. 602–604. Copyright © 2006. Reprinted by permission of Prentice Hall, Inc., Upper Saddle River, NJ.

▲ **Figure D.6** **Overview of Factory**

The Winter Park Hotel

Donna Shader, manager of the Winter Park Hotel, is considering how to restructure the front desk to reach an optimum level of staff efficiency and guest service. At present, the hotel has five clerks on duty, each with a separate waiting line, during peak check-in time of 3:00 P.M. to 5:00 P.M. Observation of arrivals during this period shows that an average of 90 guests arrive each hour (although there is no upward limit on the number that could arrive at any given time). It takes an average of 3 minutes for the front-desk clerk to register each guest.

Ms. Shader is considering three plans for improving guest service by reducing the length of time that guests spend waiting in line. The first proposal would designate one employee as a quick-service clerk for guests registering under corporate accounts, a market segment that fills about 30% of all occupied rooms. Because corporate guests are preregistered, their registration takes just 2 minutes. With these guests separated from the rest of the clientele, the average time for registering a typical guest would climb to 3.4 minutes. Under this plan, noncorporate guests would choose any of the remaining four lines.

The second plan is to implement a single-line system. All guests could form a single waiting line to be served by whichever of five clerks became available. This option would require sufficient lobby space for what could be a substantial queue.

The use of an automatic teller machine (ATM) for check-ins is the basis of the third proposal. This ATM would provide about the same service rate as would a clerk. Because initial use of this technology might be minimal, Shader estimates that 20% of customers, primarily frequent guests, would be willing to use the machines. (This might be a conservative estimate if guests perceive direct benefits from using the ATM, as bank customers do. Citibank reports that some 95% of its Manhattan customers use its ATMs.) Ms. Shader would set up a single queue for customers who prefer human check-in clerks. This line would be served by the five clerks, although Shader is hopeful that the ATM will allow a reduction to four.

Discussion Questions

1. Determine the average amount of time that a guest spends checking in. How would this change under each of the stated options?
2. Which option do you recommend?

Source: From *Quantitative Analysis for Management*, 9th ed., by B. Render, R. Stair, and M. Hanna, p. 604. Copyright © 2006. Reprinted by permission of Prentice Hall, Inc., Upper Saddle River, NJ.

Additional Case Study

See our Companion Web site at www.prenhall.com/heizer for this additional free internet case study:

- **Pantry Shopper:** The case requires the redesign of a checkout system for a supermarket.

Bibliography

Cabral, F. B. "The Slow Server Problem for Uninformed Customers." *Queuing Systems* 50, no. 4 (August 2005): 353.

Dasgupta, Ani, and Ghosh, Madhubani. "Including Performance in a Queue via Prices: The Case of a Riverine Port." *Management Science* 46, no. 11 (November 2000): 1466–1484.

Joy, M., and S. Jones. "Transient Probabilities for Queues with Applications to Hospital Waiting Line Management." *Health Care Management Science* 8, no. 3 (August 2005): 231.

Prabhu, N. U. *Foundations of Queuing Theory*. Dordecht, Netherlands: Kluwer Academic Publishers (1997).

Ramaswami, V., et al. "Ensuring Access to Emergency Services in the Presence of Long Internet Dial-Up Calls." *Interfaces* 35, no. 5 (September–October 2005): 411–425.

Render, B., R. M. Stair, and R. Balakrishnan. *Managerial Decision Modeling with Spreadsheets*, 2nd ed. Upper Saddle River, NJ: Prentice Hall (2007).

Render, B., R. M. Stair, and M. Hanna. *Quantitative Analysis for Management*, 9th ed. Upper Saddle River, NJ: Prentice Hall (2006).

Ryan, Sarah M. "Stochastic Models in Queuing Theory Review." *Journal of the American Statistical Association* 100 (March 2005): 350.

Windmeijer, F., H. Gravelle, and P. Hoonhout. "Waiting Lists, Waiting Times and Admissions." *Health Economics* 14, no. 9 (September 2005): 971.

QUANTITATIVE MODULE E

Learning Curves

Module Outline

Learning Objectives

When you complete this module you should be able to

1. Define learning curve
2. Use the arithmetic concept to estimate times
3. Compute learning curve effects with the logarithmic and learning-curve coefficient approaches
4. Describe the strategic implications of learning curves

781

▶ *Medical procedures such as heart surgery follow a learning curve. Research indicates that the death rate from heart transplants drops at a 79% learning curve, a learning rate not unlike that in many industrial settings. It appears that as doctors and medical teams improve with experience, so do your odds as a patient. If the death rate is halved every three operations, practice may indeed make perfect.*

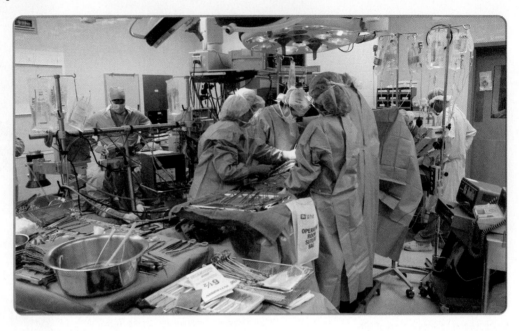

Learning curves

The premise that people and organizations get better at their tasks as the tasks are repeated; sometimes called experience curves.

Most organizations learn and improve over time. As firms and employees perform a task over and over, they learn how to perform more efficiently. This means that task times and costs decrease.

Learning curves are based on the premise that people and organizations become better at their tasks as the tasks are repeated. A learning curve graph (illustrated in Figure E.1) displays labor-hours per unit versus the number of units produced. From it we see that the time needed to produce a unit decreases, usually following a negative exponential curve, as the person or company produces more units. In other words, *it takes less time to complete each additional unit a firm produces*. However, we also see in Figure E.1 that the time *savings* in completing each subsequent unit *decreases*. These are the major attributes of the learning curve.

Learning curves were first applied to industry in a report by T. P. Wright of Curtis-Wright Corp. in 1936.[1] Wright described how direct labor costs of making a particular airplane decreased with learning, a theory since confirmed by other aircraft manufacturers. Regardless of the time needed to produce the first plane, learning curves are found to apply to various categories of air frames (e.g., jet fighters versus passenger planes versus bombers). Learning curves have since been applied not only to labor but also to a wide variety of other costs, including material and purchased components. The power of the learning curve is so significant that it plays a major role in many strategic decisions related to employment levels, costs, capacity, and pricing.

▶ **Figure E.1**

The Learning-Curve Effect States That Time per Repetition Decreases as the Number of Repetitions Increases

[1]T. P. Wright, "Factors Affecting the Cost of Airplanes," *Journal of the Aeronautical Sciences* (February 1936).

The learning curve is based on a *doubling* of production: That is, when production doubles, the decrease in time per unit affects the rate of the learning curve. So, if the learning curve is an 80% rate, the second unit takes 80% of the time of the first unit, the fourth unit takes 80% of the time of the second unit, the eighth unit takes 80% of the time of the fourth unit, and so forth. This principle is shown as:

$$T \times L^n = \text{Time required for the } n\text{th unit} \tag{E-1}$$

where T = unit cost or unit time of the first unit
         L = learning curve rate
         n = number of times T is doubled

If the first unit of a particular product took 10 labor-hours, and if a 70% learning curve is present, the hours the fourth unit will take require doubling twice—from 1 to 2 to 4. Therefore, the formula is

$$\text{Hours required for unit } 4 = 10 \times (.7)^2 = 4.9 \text{ hours}$$

LEARNING CURVES IN SERVICES AND MANUFACTURING

Different organizations—indeed, different products—have different learning curves. The rate of learning varies depending on the quality of management and the potential of the process and product. *Any change in process, product, or personnel disrupts the learning curve.* Therefore, caution should be exercised in assuming that a learning curve is continuing and permanent.

As you can see in Table E.1, industry learning curves vary widely. The lower the number (say 70% compared to 90%), the steeper the slope and the faster the drop in costs. By tradition, learning curves are defined in terms of the *complements* of their improvement rates. For example, a 70% learning curve implies a 30% decrease in time each time the number of repetitions is doubled. A 90% curve means there is a corresponding 10% rate of improvement.

Stable, standardized products and processes tend to have costs that decline more steeply than others. Between 1920 and 1955, for instance, the steel industry was able to reduce labor-hours per unit to 79% each time cumulative production doubled.

Learning curves have application in services as well as industry. As was noted in the caption for the opening photograph, 1-year death rates of heart transplant patients at Temple University Hospital follow a 79% learning curve. The results of that hospital's 3-year study of 62 patients receiving transplants found that every three operations resulted in a halving of the 1-year death rate. As more hospitals face pressure from both insurance companies and the government to enter fixed-price negotiations for their services, their ability to learn from experience becomes

> **Learning Objective**
>
> 1. Define learning curve

> *Try testing the learning-curve effect on some activity you may be performing. For example, if you need to assemble four bookshelves, time your work on each and note the rate of improvement.*

◀ **Table E.1**

Examples of Learning-Curve Effects

Example	Improving Parameter	Cumulative Parameter	Learning-Curve Slope (%)
1. Model-T Ford production	Price	Units produced	86
2. Aircraft assembly	Direct labor-hours per unit	Units produced	80
3. Equipment maintenance at GE	Average time to replace a group of parts	Number of replacements	76
4. Steel production	Production worker labor-hours per unit produced	Units produced	79
5. Integrated circuits	Average price per unit	Units produced	72[a]
6. Handheld calculator	Average factory selling price	Units produced	74
7. Disk memory drives	Average price per bit	Number of bits	76
8. Heart transplants	1-year death rates	Transplants completed	79

[a]Constant dollars.

Sources: James A. Cunningham, "Using the Learning Curve as a Management Tool," *IEEE Spectrum* (June 1980): 45. © 1980 IEEE; and Davis B. Smith and Jan L. Larsson, "The Impact of Learning on Cost: The Case of Heart Transplantation." *Hospital and Health Services Administration* (spring 1989): 85–97.

increasingly critical. In addition to having applications in both services and industry, learning curves are useful for a variety of purposes. These include:

1. Internal: Labor forecasting, scheduling, establishing costs and budgets.
2. External: Supply chain negotiations (see the SMT case study at the end of this module).
3. Strategic: Evaluation of company and industry performance, including costs and pricing.

APPLYING THE LEARNING CURVE

A mathematical relationship enables us to express the time required to produce a certain unit. This relationship is a function of how many units have been produced before the unit in question and how long it took to produce them. Although this procedure determines how long it takes to produce a given unit, the consequences of this analysis are more far reaching. Costs drop and efficiency goes up for individual firms and the industry. Therefore, severe problems in scheduling occur if operations are not adjusted for implications of the learning curve. For instance, if learning-curve improvement is not considered when scheduling, the result may be labor and productive facilities being idle a portion of the time. Furthermore, firms may refuse additional work because they do not consider the improvement in their own efficiency that results from learning. From a supply chain perspective, our interest is in negotiating what our suppliers' costs should be for further production of units based on the size of an order. The foregoing are only a few of the ramifications of the effect of learning curves.

With this in mind, let us look at three ways to approach the mathematics of learning curves: arithmetic analysis, logarithmic analysis, and learning-curve coefficients.

Arithmetic Approach

The arithmetic approach is the simplest approach to learning-curve problems. As we noted at the beginning of this module, each time that production doubles, labor per unit declines by a constant factor, known as the learning rate. So, if we know that the learning rate is 80% and that the first unit produced took 100 hours, the hours required to produce the 2nd, 4th, 8th, and 16th units are as follows:

Nth Unit Produced	Hours for Nth Unit
1	100.0
2	$80.0 = (.8 \times 100)$
4	$64.0 = (.8 \times 80)$
8	$51.2 = (.8 \times 64)$
16	$41.0 = (.8 \times 51.2)$

As long as we wish to find the hours required to produce N units and N is one of the doubled values, then this approach works. Arithmetic analysis does not tell us how many hours will be needed to produce other units. For this flexibility, we must turn to the logarithmic approach.

▼ **Table E.2**   Learning Curve Values of b

Logarithmic Approach

The logarithmic approach allows us to determine labor for *any* unit, T_N, by the formula:

$$T_N = T_1(N^b) \tag{E-2}$$

Learning Rate (%)	b
70	−.515
75	−.415
80	−.322
85	−.234
90	−.152

where
T_N = time for the Nth unit
T_1 = hours to produce the first unit
b = (log of the learning rate)/(log 2) = slope of the learning curve

Some of the values for b are presented in Table E.2. Example E1 shows how this formula works.

EXAMPLE E1

Using logs to compute learning curves

The learning rate for a typical CPA to conduct a dental practice audit is 80%. Greg Lattier, a new graduate of Lee College, completed his first audit in 100 hours. If the dental offices he audits are about the same, how long should he take to finish his third job?

Approach: We will use the logarathmic approach in Equation (E-2).

Solution:
$$T_N = T_1(N^b)$$
$$T_3 = (100 \text{ hours})(3^b)$$
$$= (100)(3^{\log .8/\log 2})$$
$$= (100)(3^{-.322}) = 70.2 \text{ labor-hours}$$

Insight: Greg improved quickly from his first to his third audit. An 80% rate means that from just the first to second jobs, his time decreased by 20%.

Learning exercise: If Greg's learning rate was only 90%, how long would the third audit take? [Answer: 84.621 hours.]

Related problems: E.1, E.2, E.9, E.10, E.11, E.16

Learning Objective

3. Compute learning curve effects with the logarithmic and learning-curve coefficient approaches

The logarithmic approach allows us to determine the hours required for *any* unit produced, but there *is* a simpler method.

Learning-Curve Coefficient Approach

The learning-curve coefficient technique is embodied in Table E.3 and the following equation:

$$T_N = T_1 C \qquad \text{(E-3)}$$

where T_N = number of labor-hours required to produce the Nth unit
T_1 = number of labor-hours required to produce the first unit
C = learning-curve coefficient found in Table E.3

The learning-curve coefficient, C, depends on both the learning rate (70%, 75%, 80%, and so on) and the unit number of interest.

▼ **Table E.3**   Learning-Curve Coefficients, Where Coefficient, $C = N^{(\log \text{ of learning rate}/\log 2)}$

Unit Number (N)	70% Unit Time	70% Total Time	75% Unit Time	75% Total Time	80% Unit Time	80% Total Time	85% Unit Time	85% Total Time	90% Unit Time	90% Total Time
1	1.000	1.000	1.000	1.000	1.000	1.000	1.000	1.000	1.000	1.000
2	.700	1.700	.750	1.750	.800	1.800	.850	1.850	.900	1.900
3	.568	2.268	.634	2.384	.702	2.502	.773	2.623	.846	2.746
4	.490	2.758	.562	2.946	.640	3.142	.723	3.345	.810	3.556
5	.437	3.195	.513	3.459	.596	3.738	.686	4.031	.783	4.339
6	.398	3.593	.475	3.934	.562	4.299	.657	4.688	.762	5.101
7	.367	3.960	.446	4.380	.534	4.834	.634	5.322	.744	5.845
8	.343	4.303	.422	4.802	.512	5.346	.614	5.936	.729	6.574
9	.323	4.626	.402	5.204	.493	5.839	.597	6.533	.716	7.290
10	.306	4.932	.385	5.589	.477	6.315	.583	7.116	.705	7.994
11	.291	5.223	.370	5.958	.462	6.777	.570	7.686	.695	8.689
12	.278	5.501	.357	6.315	.449	7.227	.558	8.244	.685	9.374
13	.267	5.769	.345	6.660	.438	7.665	.548	8.792	.677	10.052
14	.257	6.026	.334	6.994	.428	8.092	.539	9.331	.670	10.721
15	.248	6.274	.325	7.319	.418	8.511	.530	9.861	.663	11.384
16	.240	6.514	.316	7.635	.410	8.920	.522	10.383	.656	12.040
17	.233	6.747	.309	7.944	.402	9.322	.515	10.898	.650	12.690
18	.226	6.973	.301	8.245	.394	9.716	.508	11.405	.644	13.334
19	.220	7.192	.295	8.540	.388	10.104	.501	11.907	.639	13.974
20	.214	7.407	.288	8.828	.381	10.485	.495	12.402	.634	14.608
25	.191	8.404	.263	10.191	.355	12.309	.470	14.801	.613	17.713
30	.174	9.305	.244	11.446	.335	14.020	.450	17.091	.596	20.727
35	.160	10.133	.229	12.618	.318	15.643	.434	19.294	.583	23.666
40	.150	10.902	.216	13.723	.305	17.193	.421	21.425	.571	26.543
45	.141	11.625	.206	14.773	.294	18.684	.410	23.500	.561	29.366
50	.134	12.307	.197	15.776	.284	20.122	.400	25.513	.552	32.142

Example E2 uses the preceding equation and Table E.3 to calculate learning-curve effects.

EXAMPLE E2

Using learning-curve coefficients

Excel OM Data File ModEExE2.xls

Active Model E.1

Examples E2 and E3 are further illustrated in Active Model E.1 on the CD-ROM and in the Exercise on page 790.

It took a Korean shipyard 125,000 labor-hours to produce the first of several tugboats that you expect to purchase for your shipping company, Great Lakes, Inc. Boats 2 and 3 have been produced by the Koreans with a learning factor of 85%. At $40 per hour, what should you, as purchasing agent, expect to pay for the fourth unit?

Approach: First, search Table E.3 for the fourth unit and a learning rate of 85%. The learning-curve coefficient, C, is .723.

Solution: To produce the fourth unit, then, takes:

$$T_N = T_1 C$$
$$T_4 = (125,000 \text{ hours})(.723)$$
$$= 90,375 \text{ hours}$$

To find the cost, multiply by $40:

$$90,375 \text{ hours} \times \$40 \text{ per hour} = \$3,615,000$$

Insight: The learning-curve coefficient approach is very easy to apply. If we had not factored learning into our cost estimates, the price would have been 125,000 hours × $40 per hour (same as the first boat) = $6,000,000.

Learning exercise: If the learning factor improved to 80%, how would the cost change? [Answer: It would drop to $3,200,000.]

Related problems: E.1, E.2, E.3a, E.5a,c, E.6a,b, E.9, E.10, E.11, E.14, E.16, E.22

Table E.3 also shows *cumulative values*. These allow us to compute the total number of hours needed to complete a specified number of units. Again, the computation is straightforward. Just multiply the table coefficient value times the time required for the first unit. Example E3 illustrates this concept.

EXAMPLE E3

Using cumulative coefficients

Example E2 computed the time to complete the fourth tugboat that Great Lakes plans to buy. How long will *all four* boats require?

Approach: We look at the "total time" column in Table E.3 and find that the cumulative coefficient for 4 boats with an 85% learning factor is 3.345.

Solution: The time required is:

$$T_N = T_1 C$$
$$T_4 = (125,000)(3.345) = 418,125 \text{ hours in total for all 4 boats}$$

Insight: For an illustration of how Excel OM can be used to solve Examples E2 and E3, see Program E.1 at the end of this module.

Learning exercise: What is the value of T_4 if the learning factor is 80% instead of 85%? [Answer: 392,750 hours.]

Related problems: E.3b, E.4, E.5b,c, E.6c, E.7, E.15, E.19, E.20a

Using Table E.3 requires that we know how long it takes to complete the first unit. Yet, what happens if our most recent or most reliable information available pertains to some other unit? The answer is that we must use these data to find a revised estimate for the first unit and then apply the table coefficient to that number. Example E4 illustrates this concept.

Great Lakes, Inc., believes that unusual circumstances in producing the first boat (see Example E2) imply that the time estimate of 125,000 hours is not as valid a base as the time required to produce the third boat. Boat number 3 was completed in 100,000 hours. It wants to solve for the revised estimate for boat number 1.

Approach: We return to Table E.3, with a unit value of $N = 3$ and a learning-curve coefficient of $C = .773$ in the 85% column.

Solution: To find the revised estimate, divide the actual time for boat number 3, 100,000 hours, by $C = .773$:

$$\frac{100,000}{.773} = 129,366 \text{ hours}$$

So, 129,366 hours is the new (revised) estimate for boat 1.

Insight: Any change in product, process, or personnel will change the learning curve. The new estimate for boat 1 suggests that related cost and volume estimates need to be revised.

Learning exercise: Boat 4 was just completed in 90,000 hours. Great Lakes thinks the 85% learning rate is valid but isn't sure about the 125,000 hours for the first boat. Find a revised estimate for boat 1. [Answer: 124,481, suggesting that boat 1's time was fairly accurate after all.]

Related problems: E.8, E.12, E.13, E.17, E.18, E.20b, E.21, E.23

STRATEGIC IMPLICATIONS OF LEARNING CURVES

So far, we have shown how operations managers can forecast labor-hour requirements for a product. We have also shown how purchasing agents can determine a supplier's cost, knowledge that can help in price negotiations. Another important application of learning curves concerns strategic planning.

An example of a company cost line and industry price line are so labeled in Figure E.2. These learning curves are straight because both scales are log scales. When the *rate* of change is constant, a log-log graph yields a straight line. If an organization believes its cost line to be the "company cost" line, and the industry price is indicated by the dashed horizontal line, then the company must have costs at the points below the dashed line (for example, point *a* or *b*) or else operate at a loss (point *c*).

Lower costs are not automatic; they must be managed down. When a firm's strategy is to pursue a curve steeper than the industry average (the company cost line in Figure E.2), it does this by:

1. Following an aggressive pricing policy
2. Focusing on continuing cost reduction and productivity improvement
3. Building on shared experience
4. Keeping capacity growing ahead of demand

◀ **Figure E.2**

Industry Learning Curve for Price Compared with Company Learning Curve for Cost

Note: Both the vertical and horizontal axes of this figure are log scales. This is known as a log-log graph.

Costs may drop as a firm pursues the learning curve, but volume must increase for the learning curve to exist. Moreover, managers must understand competitors before embarking on a learning-curve strategy. Weak competitors are undercapitalized, stuck with high costs, or do not understand the logic of learning curves. However, strong and dangerous competitors control their costs, have solid financial positions for the large investments needed, and have a track record of using an aggressive learning-curve strategy. Taking on such a competitor in a price war may help only the consumer.

LIMITATIONS OF LEARNING CURVES

Before using learning curves, some cautions are in order:

- Because learning curves differ from company to company, as well as industry to industry, estimates for each organization should be developed rather than applying someone else's.
- Learning curves are often based on the time necessary to complete the early units; therefore, those times must be accurate. As current information becomes available, reevaluation is appropriate.
- Any changes in personnel, design, or procedure can be expected to alter the learning curve, causing the curve to spike up for a short time, even if it is going to drop in the long run.
- While workers and process may improve, the same learning curves do not always apply to indirect labor and material.
- The culture of the workplace, as well as resource availability and changes in the process, may alter the learning curve. For instance, as a project nears its end, worker interest and effort may drop, curtailing progress down the curve.

Summary

The learning curve is a powerful tool for the operations manager. This tool can assist operations managers in determining future cost standards for items produced as well as purchased. In addition, the learning curve can provide understanding about company and industry performance. We saw three approaches to learning curves: arithmetic analysis, logarithmic analysis, and learning-curve coefficients found in tables. Software can also help analyze learning curves.

Key Term

Learning curves (p. 782)

Using Software for Learning Curves

Excel, Excel OM, and POM for Windows may all be used in analyzing learning curves. You can use the ideas in the following section on Excel OM to build your own Excel spreadsheet if you wish.

X Using Excel OM

Program E.1 shows how Excel OM develops a spreadsheet for learning-curve calculations. The input data come from Examples E2 and E3. In cell B7, we enter the unit number for the base unit (which does not have to be 1), and in B8 we enter the time for this unit.

P Using POM for Windows

The POM for Windows Learning Curve module computes the length of time that future units will take, given the time required for the base unit and the learning rate (expressed as a number between 0 and 1). As an option, if the times required for the first and Nth units are already known, the learning *rate* can be computed. See Appendix IV for further details.

These are used for computations. Do not touch these cells. In cell B11, the time for the first unit is computed, allowing us to use initial units other than unit 1. In cell B12, the power to be raised to is computed, making the formulas in the rest of column B much simpler.

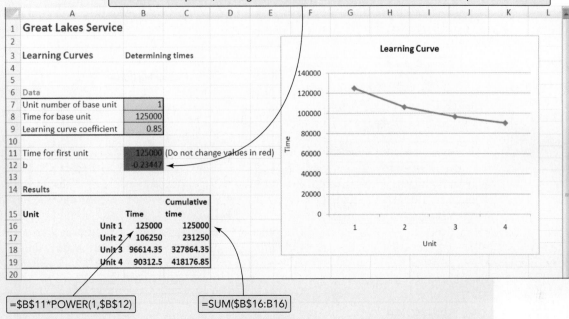

=$B$11*POWER(1,$B$12)

=SUM($B$16:B16)

▲ **Program E.1**   **Excel OM's Learning-Curve Module, Using Data from Examples E2 and E3**

Solved Problems

 Virtual Office Hours help is available on Student DVD.

Solved Problem E.1

Digicomp produces a new telephone system with built-in TV screens. Its learning rate is 80%.

a)   If the first one took 56 hours, how long will it take Digicomp to make the eleventh system?

b)   How long will the first 11 systems take in total?

c)   As a purchasing agent, you expect to buy units 12 through 15 of the new phone system. What would be your expected cost for the units if Digicomp charges $30 for each labor-hour?

solution — from Table E.3, coefficient for 80% unit time

(a) $T_N = T_1 C$

$T_{11} = (56 \text{ hours})(.462) = 25.9 \text{ hours}$

(b)   Total time for the first 11 units = (56 hours)(6.777) = 379.5 hours

from Table E.3, coefficient for 80% total time

(c)   To find the time for units 12 through 15, we take the total cumulative time for units 1 to 15 and subtract the total time for units 1 to 11, which was computed in part (b). Total time for the first 15 units = (56 hours)(8.511) = 476.6 hours. So, the time for units 12 through 15 is 476.6 − 379.5 = 97.1 hours. (This figure could also be confirmed by computing the times for units 12, 13, 14, and 15 separately using the unit-time column and then adding them.) Expected cost for units 12 through 15 = (97.1 hours) ($30 per hour) = $2,913.

Solved Problem E.2

If the first time you performed a job took 60 minutes, how long will the eighth job take if you are on an 80% learning curve?

solution

Three doublings from 1 to 2 to 4 to 8 implies $.8^3$. Therefore, we have:

$$60 \times (.8)^3 = 60 \times .512 = 30.72 \text{ minutes}$$

or, using Table E.3, we have $C = .512$. Therefore:

$$60 \times .512 = 30.72 \text{ minutes}$$

Active Model Exercise

This active model, found on your CD-ROM, allows you to evaluate important elements in the learning curve model described in Examples E2 and E3. You may change any input parameter in a green colored cell.

▶ **Active Model E.1**

Great Lakes, Inc. Learning Curve Analysis of Boats, Using Example E2 and E3 Data

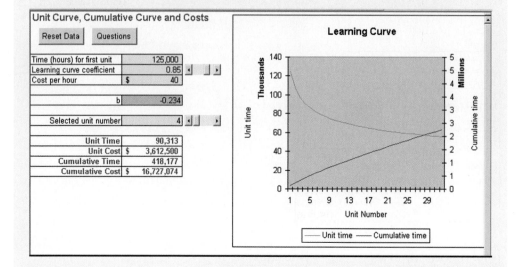

Questions

1. If the learning is not as good as expected and rises to 90%, how much will the fourth boat cost?

2. What should the learning-curve rate to keep the total cost of the first 4 boats below $16,000,000?

3. How many boats need to be produced before the cost of the next boat is at or below $4,000,000?

4. How many boats need to be produced before the *average* cost of each boat is below $4,000,000?

Self-Test

- *Before taking the self-test*, refer to the learning objectives listed at the beginning of the module.
- *Use the key at the back of the text to **correct** your answers.*
- **Restudy** *pages that correspond to any questions you answered incorrectly or material you feel uncertain about.*

1. A learning curve describes:
   a) the rate at which an organization acquires new information
   b) the amount of production time per unit as the total number of units produced increases
   c) the decrease in production time per unit as the total number of units produced increases
   d) the increase in number of units produced per unit time as the total number of units produced increases

2. Limitations of the learning-curve approach include:
   a) learning curves are only valid when considering relatively simple production processes
   b) learning curves are only valid when the total number of units produced is relatively small

   c) learning curves must be redeveloped whenever the product or production process is modified
   d) learning curves are only applicable when considering a highly automated production process
   e) all of the above

3. Another name for the learning curve is:
   a) a production curve
   b) an experience curve
   c) an exponential curve
   d) all of the above

4. Learning curves have different rates because of:
   a) industry technology
   b) changes in product
   c) the amount of shared experience
   d) change in personnel
   e) all of the above

5. Applications of learning curves include _____, _____, _____, _____, and _____.

Internet and Student CD-ROM/DVD Exercises

Visit our Companion Web site or use your student CD-ROM/DVD to help with material in this module.

 On Our Companion Web Site,
   www.prenhall.com/heizer
- Self-Study Quizzes
- Practice Problems
- Internet Exercises
- PowerPoint Lecture

On Your Student CD-ROM
- Practice Problems
- Active Mode Exercises
- Excel OM
- Excel OM Example Data Files
- POM for Windows

 On Your Student DVD
- Virtual Office Hours for Solved
   Problems

Discussion Questions

1. What are some of the limitations of learning curves?
2. Identify three applications of the learning curve.
3. What are the approaches to solving learning-curve problems?
4. Refer to Example E2. What are the implications for Great Lakes, Inc., if the engineering department wants to change the engine in the third and subsequent tugboats that the firm purchases?

5. Why isn't the learning-curve concept as applicable in a high-volume assembly line as it is in most other human activities?
6. What are the elements that can disrupt the learning curve?
7. Explain the concept of the "doubling" effect in learning curves.
8. What techniques can a firm use to move to a steeper learning curve?

Problems*

• **E.1** Amand Heinl, an IRS auditor, took 45 minutes to process her first tax return. The IRS uses an 85% learning curve. How long will the:
a) 2nd return take?
b) 4th return take?
c) 8th return take? **Px**

• **E.2** Seton Hall Trucking Co. just hired Sally Kissel to verify daily invoices and accounts payable. She took 9 hours and 23 minutes to complete her task on the first day. Prior employees in this job have tended to follow a 90% learning curve. How long will the task take at the end of:
a) the 2nd day?
b) the 4th day?
c) the 8th day?
d) the 16th day? **Px**

• **E.3** If Professor Tacy Quinn takes 15 minutes to grade the first exam and follows an 80% learning curve, how long will it take her:
a) to grade the 25th exam?
b) to grade the first 10 exams? **Px**

• **E.4** If it took 563 minutes to complete a hospital's first cornea transplant, and the hospital uses a 90% learning rate, what is the cumulative time to complete:
a) the first 3 transplants?
b) the first 6 transplants?
c) the first 8 transplants?
d) the first 16 transplants? **Px**

•• **E.5** Beth Zion Hospital has received initial certification from the state of California to become a center for liver transplants. The hospital, however, must complete its first 18 transplants under

Note: **Px** means the problem may be solved with POM for Windows and/or Excel OM.

great scrutiny and at no cost to the patients. The very first transplant, just completed, required 30 hours. On the basis of research at the hospital, Beth Zion estimates that it will have an 80% learning curve. Estimate the time it will take to complete:
a) the 5th liver transplant.
b) all of the first 5 transplants.
c) the 18th transplant.
d) all 18 transplants. **Px**

•• **E.6** Refer to Problem E.5. Beth Zion Hospital has just been informed that only the first 10 transplants must be performed at the hospital's expense. The cost per hour of surgery is estimated to be $5,000. Again, the learning rate is 80% and the first surgery took 30 hours.
a) How long will the 10th surgery take?
b) How much will the 10th surgery cost?
c) How much will all 10 cost the hospital? **Px**

• **E.7** Manceville Air has just produced the first unit of a large industrial compressor that incorporated new technology in the control circuits and a new internal venting system. The first unit took 112 hours of labor to manufacture. The company knows from past experience that this labor content will decrease significantly as more units are produced. In reviewing past production data, it appears that the company has experienced a 90% learning curve when producing similar designs. The company is interested in estimating the total time to complete the next 7 units. Your job as the production cost estimator is to prepare the estimate. **Px**

• **E.8** John Howard, a student at the University of South Alabama, bought 6 bookcases for his dorm room. Each required unpacking of parts and assembly, which included some nailing and bolting. John completed the first bookcase in 5 hours and the second in 4 hours.
a) What is his learning rate?
b) Assuming the same rate continues, how long will the 3rd bookcase take?
c) The 4th, 5th, and 6th cases?
d) All 6 cases? **Px**

•• **E.9** Professor Mary Beth Marrs took 6 hours to prepare the first lecture in a new course. Traditionally, she has experienced a 90% learning factor. How much time should it take her to prepare the 15th lecture? **Px**

• **E.10** The first vending machine that Michael Vest, Inc., assembled took 80 labor-hours. Estimate how long the fourth machine will require for each of the following learning rates:
a) 95%
b) 87%
c) 72% **Px**

• **E.11** Kara-Smith Systems is installing networks for Advantage Insurance. The first installation took 46 labor-hours to complete. Estimate how long the 4th and the 8th installations will take for each of the following learning rates:
a) 92%
b) 84%
c) 77% **Px**

••• **E.12** Baltimore Assessment Center screens and trains employees for a computer assembly firm in Towson, Maryland. The progress of all trainees is tracked and those not showing the proper progress are moved to less demanding programs. By the tenth repetition trainees must be able to complete the assembly task in 1 hour or less. Torri Olson-Alves has just spent 5 hours on the fourth unit and 4 hours completing her eighth unit, while another trainee, Julie Burgmeier, took 4 hours on the third and 3 hours on the sixth unit. Should you encourage either or both of the trainees to continue? Why? **Px**

•• **E.13** The better students at Baltimore Assessment Center (see Problem E.12) have an 80% learning curve and can do a task in 20 minutes after just six times. You would like to weed out the weak students sooner and decide to evaluate them after the third unit. How long should the third unit take? **Px**

•• **E.14** Wanda Fennell, the purchasing agent for Northeast Airlines, is interested in determining what she can expect to pay for airplane number 4 if the third plane took 20,000 hours to produce. What would Fennell expect to pay for plane number 5? number 6? Use an 85% learning curve and a $40-per-hour labor charge. **Px**

•• **E.15** Using the data from Problem E.14, how long will it take to complete the twelfth plane? The fifteenth plane? How long will it

take to complete planes 12 through 15 inclusive? At $40 per hour, what can Fennell, as purchasing agent, expect to pay for all 4 planes? **Px**

•• **E.16** Dynamic RAM Corp. produces semiconductors and has a learning curve of .7. The price per bit is 100 millicents when the volume is $.7 \times 10^{12}$ bits. What is the expected price at 1.4×10^{12} bits? What is the expected price at 89.6×10^{12} bits? **Px**

•• **E.17** Central Power owns 25 small power generating plants. It has contracted with Genco Services to overhaul the power turbines of each of the plants. The number of hours that Genco billed Central to complete the third turbine was 460. Central pays Genco $60 per hour for its services. As the maintenance manager for Central, you are trying to estimate the cost of overhauling the fourth turbine. How much would you expect to pay for the overhaul of number 5 and number 6? All the turbines are similar and an 80% learning curve is appropriate. **Px**

•• **E.18** It takes 28,718 hours to produce the eighth locomotive at a large French manufacturing firm. If the learning factor is 80%, how long does it take to produce the 10th locomotive? **Px**

•• **E.19** Eric Krassow's firm is about to bid on a new radar system. Although the product uses new technology, Krassow believes that a learning rate of 75% is appropriate. The first unit is expected to take 700 hours, and the contract is for 40 units.
a) What is the total amount of hours to build the 40 units?
b) What is the average time to build each of the 40 units?
c) Assume that a worker works 2,080 hours per year. How many workers should be assigned to this contract to complete it in a year? **Px**

••• **E.20** As the estimator for Arup Mukherjee Enterprises, your job is to prepare an estimate for a potential customer service contract. The contract is for the service of diesel locomotive cylinder heads. The shop has done some of these in the past on a sporadic basis. The time required to service each cylinder head has been exactly 4 hours, and similar work has been accomplished at an 85% learning curve. The customer wants you to quote the total time in batches of 12 and 20.
a) Prepare the quote.
b) After preparing the quote, you find a labor ticket for this customer for five locomotive cylinder heads. From the notations on the labor ticket, you conclude that the fifth unit took 2.5 hours. What do you conclude about the learning curve and your quote? **Px**

•• **E.21** Sara Bredbenner and Blake DeYoung are teammates at a discount store; their new job is assembling swing sets for customers. Assembly of a swing set has a learning rate of 90%. They forgot to time their effort on the first swing set, but spent 4 hours on the second set. They have 6 more sets to do. Determine approximately how much time will be (was) required for:
a) the 1st unit.
b) the 8th unit.
c) all 8 units. **Px**

•• **E.22** Kelly-Lambing, Inc., a builder of government-contracted small ships, has a steady work force of 10 very skilled craftspeople. These workers can supply 2,500 labor-hours each per year. Kelly-Lambing is about to undertake a new contract, building a new style of boat. The first boat is expected to take 6,000 hours to complete. The firm thinks that 90% is the expected learning rate.

a) What is the firm's "capacity" to make these boats—that is, how many units can the firm make in 1 year?

b) If the operations manager can increase the learning rate to 85% instead of 90%, how many units can the firm make?

• • • **E.23** The service times for a new data entry clerk have been measured and sequentially recorded as shown below.

Report	Time (minutes)
1	66
2	56
3	53
4	48
5	47
6	45
7	44
8	41

a) What is the learning curve rate, based on this information?

b) Using an 85% learning curve rate and the above times, estimate the length of time the clerk will take to complete the 48th report. **Px**

• • **E.24** If the first unit of a production run takes 1 hour and the firm is on an 80% learning curve, how long will unit 100 take? (*Hint:* Apply the coefficient in Table E.3 twice.) **Px**

• • • • **E.25** Using the accompanying log-log graph, answer the following questions:

a) What are the implications for management if it has forecast its cost on the optimum line?

b) What could be causing the fluctuations above the optimum line?

c) If management forecast the 10th unit on the optimum line, what was that forecast in hours?

d) If management built the 10th unit as indicated by the actual line, how many hours did it take?

Case Study

SMT's Negotiation with IBM

SMT and one other, much larger company were asked by IBM to bid on 80 more units of a particular computer product. The RFQ (request for quote) asked that the overall bid be broken down to show the hourly rate, the parts and materials component in the price, and any charges for subcontracted services. SMT quoted $1.62 million and supplied the cost breakdown as requested. The second company submitted only one total figure, $5 million, with no cost breakdown. The decision was made to negotiate with SMT.

The IBM negotiating team included two purchasing managers and two cost engineers. One cost engineer had developed manufacturing cost estimates for every component, working from engineering drawings and cost-data books that he had built up from previous experience and that contained time factors, both setup and run times, for a large variety of operations. He estimated materials costs by working both from data supplied by the IBM corporate purchasing staff and from purchasing journals. He visited SMT facilities to see the tooling available so that he would know what processes were being used. He assumed that there would be perfect conditions and trained operators, and he developed cost estimates for the 158th unit (previous orders were for 25, 15, and 38 units). He added 5% for scrap-and-flow loss; 2% for the use of temporary tools, jigs, and fixtures; 5% for quality control; and 9% for purchasing burden. Then, using an 85% learning curve, he backed up his costs to get an estimate for the first unit. He next checked the data on hours and materials for the 25, 15, and 38 units already made and found that his estimate for the first unit was within 4% of actual cost. His check, however, had indicated a 90% learning-curve effect on hours per unit.

In the negotiations, SMT was represented by one of the two owners of the business, two engineers, and one cost estimator. The sessions opened with a discussion of learning curves. The IBM cost estimator demonstrated that SMT had in fact been operating on a 90% learning curve. But, he argued, it should be possible to move to an 85% curve, given the longer runs, reduced setup time, and increased continuity of workers on the job that would be possible with an order for 80 units. The owner agreed with this analysis and was willing to reduce his price by 4%.

However, as each operation in the manufacturing process was discussed, it became clear that some IBM cost estimates were too low because certain crating and shipping expenses had been overlooked. These oversights were minor, however, and in the following discussions, the two parties arrived at a common understanding of specifications and reached agreements on the costs of each manufacturing operation.

At this point, SMT representatives expressed great concern about the possibility of inflation in material costs. The IBM negotiators volunteered to include a form of price escalation in the contract, as previously agreed among themselves. IBM representatives suggested that if overall material costs changed by more than 10%, the price could be adjusted accordingly. However, if one party took the initiative to have the price revised, the other could require an analysis of *all* parts and materials invoices in arriving at the new price.

Another concern of the SMT representatives was that a large amount of overtime and subcontracting would be required to meet IBM's specified delivery schedule. IBM negotiators thought that a relaxation in the delivery schedule might be possible if a price

(continued)

concession could be obtained. In response, the SMT team offered a 5% discount, and this was accepted. As a result of these negotiations, the SMT price was reduced almost 20% below its original bid price.

In a subsequent meeting called to negotiate the prices of certain pipes to be used in the system, it became apparent to an IBM cost estimator that SMT representatives had seriously underestimated their costs. He pointed out this apparent error because he could not understand why SMT had quoted such a low figure. He wanted to be sure that SMT was using the correct manufacturing process. In any case, if SMT estimators had made a mistake, it should be noted. It was IBM's policy to seek a fair price both for itself and for its suppliers. IBM procurement managers believed that if a vendor was losing money on a job, there would be a tendency to cut corners. In addition, the IBM negotiator felt that by pointing out the error, he generated some goodwill that would help in future sessions.

Discussion Questions

1. What are the advantages and disadvantages to IBM and SMT from this approach?
2. How does SMT's proposed learning rate compare with that of other industries?
3. What are the limitations of the learning curve in this case?

Source: Adapted from E. Raymond Corey, *Procurement Management: Strategy, Organization, and Decision Making* (New York: Van Nostrand Reinhold).

Bibliography

Abernathy, W. J., and K. Wayne. "Limits of the Learning Curve." *Harvard Business Review* 52 (September–October 1974): 109–119.

Bailey, C. D., and E. N. McIntyre. "Using Parameter Prediction Models to Forecast Post-interruption Learning." *IIE Transactions* 35 (December 2003): 1077.

Camm, J. "A Note on Learning Curve Parameters." *Decision Sciences* (summer 1985): 325–327.

Couto, J. P., and J. C. Teixeira. "Using Linear Model for Learning Curve Effect on Highrise Floor Construction." *Construction Management & Economics* 23 (May 2005): 355.

Hall, G., and S. Howell. "The Experience Curve from the Economist's Perspective." *Strategic Management Journal* (July–September 1985): 197–210.

Lapré, Michael A., Amit Shankar Mukherjee, and Luk N. Van Wassenhove. "Behind the Learning Curve: Linking Learning Activities to Waste Reduction." *Management Science* 46, no. 5 (May 2000): 597–611.

McDonald, A., and L. Schrattenholzer. "Learning Curves and Technology Assessment." *International Journal of Technology Management* 23 (2002): 718.

Smith, J., *Learning Curve for Cost Control*. Norcross, GA: Industrial Engineering and Management Press, Institute of Industrial Engineers. (1998).

Smunt, T. L., and C. A. Watts. "Improving Operations Planning with Learning Curves." *Journal of Operations Management* 21 (January 2003): 93.

Weston, M. *Learning Curves*. New York: Crown Publishing (2000).

QUANTITATIVE MODULE F

Simulation

Module Outline

Learning Objectives

When you complete this module you should be able to

1. List the advantages and
   disadvantages of modeling
   with simulation
2. Perform the five steps in a
   Monte Carlo simulation
3. Simulate a queuing problem
4. Simulate an inventory problem
5. Use Excel spreadsheets to create
   a simulation

▲ *When Bay Medical Center faced severe overcrowding at its outpatient clinic, it turned to computer simulation to try to reduce bottlenecks and improve patient flow. A simulation language called Micro Saint analyzed current data relating to patient service times between clinic rooms. By simulating different numbers of doctors and staff, simulating the use of another clinic for overflow, and simulating a redesign of the existing clinic, Bay Medical Center was able to make decisions based on an understanding of both costs and benefits. This resulted in better patient service at lower cost.*

Source: Micro Analysis and Design Simulation Software, Inc., Boulder, CO.

There are many kinds of simulations, and although this module stresses Monte Carlo simulations, you should be aware of "physical" simulations (such as a wind tunnel model) as well.

Simulation
The attempt to duplicate the features, appearance, and characteristics of a real system, usually via a computerized model.

Simulation models abound in our world. The city of Atlanta, for example, uses them to control traffic. Europe's Airbus Industries uses them to test the aerodynamics of proposed jets. The U.S. Army simulates war games on computers. Business students use management gaming to simulate realistic business competition. And thousands of organizations like Bay Medical Center develop simulation models to help make operations decisions.

Most of the large companies in the world use simulation models. Table F.1 lists just a few areas in which simulation is now being applied.

WHAT IS SIMULATION?

Simulation is the attempt to duplicate the features, appearance, and characteristics of a real system. In this module, we will show how to simulate part of an operations management system by building a mathematical model that comes as close as possible to representing the reality of the system. The model will then be used to estimate the effects of various actions. The idea behind simulation is threefold:

1. To imitate a real-world situation mathematically
2. Then to study its properties and operating characteristics
3. Finally to draw conclusions and make action decisions based on the results of the simulation

In this way, a real-life system need not be touched until the advantages and disadvantages of a major policy decision are first measured on the model.

To use simulation, an OM manager should:

1. Define the problem.
2. Introduce the important variables associated with the problem.
3. Construct a numerical model.

▶ **Table F.1**

Some Applications of Simulation

Ambulance location and dispatching	Bus scheduling
Assembly-line balancing	Design of library operations
Parking lot and harbor design	Taxi, truck, and railroad dispatching
Distribution system design	Production facility scheduling
Scheduling aircraft	Plant layout
Labor-hiring decisions	Capital investments
Personnel scheduling	Production scheduling
Traffic-light timing	Sales forecasting
Voting pattern prediction	Inventory planning and control

4. Set up possible courses of action for testing by specifying values of variables.
5. Run the experiment.
6. Consider the results (possibly modifying the model or changing data inputs).
7. Decide what course of action to take.

These steps are illustrated in Figure F.1.

The problems tackled by simulation may range from very simple to extremely complex, from bank-teller lines to an analysis of the U.S. economy. Although small simulations can be conducted by hand, effective use of the technique requires a computer. Large-scale models, simulating perhaps years of business decisions, are virtually all handled by computer.

In this module, we examine the basic principles of simulation and then tackle some problems in the areas of waiting-line analysis and inventory control. Why do we use simulation in these areas when mathematical models described in other chapters can solve similar problems? The answer is that simulation provides an alternative approach for problems that are very complex mathematically. It can handle, for example, inventory problems in which demand or lead time is not constant.

ADVANTAGES AND DISADVANTAGES OF SIMULATION

Simulation is a tool that has become widely accepted by managers for several reasons. The main *advantages* of simulation are as follows:

1. Simulation is relatively straightforward and flexible.
2. It can be used to analyze large and complex real-world situations that cannot be solved by conventional operations management models.
3. Real-world complications can be included that most OM models cannot permit. For example, simulation can use *any* probability distribution the user defines; it does not require standard distributions.
4. "Time compression" is possible. The effects of OM policies over many months or years can be obtained by computer simulation in a short time.
5. Simulation allows what-if? types of questions. Managers like to know in advance what options will be most attractive. With a computerized model, a manager can try out several policy decisions within a matter of minutes.
6. Simulations do not interfere with real-world systems. It may be too disruptive, for example, to experiment physically with new policies or ideas in a hospital or manufacturing plant.
7. Simulation can study the interactive effects of individual components or variables in order to determine which ones are important.

The main *disadvantages* of simulation are as follows:

1. Good simulation models can be very expensive; they may take many months to develop.
2. It is a trial-and-error approach that may produce different solutions in repeated runs. It does not generate optimal solutions to problems (as does linear programming).
3. Managers must generate all of the conditions and constraints for solutions that they want to examine. The simulation model does not produce answers without adequate, realistic input.
4. Each simulation model is unique. Its solutions and inferences are not usually transferable to other problems.

MONTE CARLO SIMULATION

When a system contains elements that exhibit *chance* in their behavior, the **Monte Carlo method** of simulation may be applied. The basis of Monte Carlo simulation is experimentation on chance (or *probabilistic*) elements by means of random sampling.

The technique breaks down into five simple steps:

1. Setting up a probability distribution for important variables.
2. Building a cumulative probability distribution for each variable.
3. Establishing an interval of random numbers for each variable.
4. Generating random numbers.
5. Actually simulating a series of trials.

Let's examine these steps in turn.

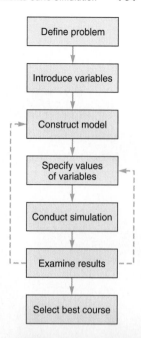

▲ **Figure F.1**

The Process of Simulation

Define problem → Introduce variables → Construct model → Specify values of variables → Conduct simulation → Examine results → Select best course

Learning Objective

1. List the advantages and disadvantages of modeling with simulation

Monte Carlo method

A simulation technique that uses random elements when chance exists in their behavior.

Learning Objective

2. Perform the five steps in a Monte Carlo simulation

▶ Computer simulation models have been developed to address a variety of productivity issues at fast-food restaurants such as Burger King. In one, the ideal distance between the drive-through order station and the pickup window was simulated. For example, because a longer distance reduced waiting time, 12 to 13 additional customers could be served per hour— a benefit of about $20,000 in extra sales per restaurant per year. In another simulation, a second drive-through window was considered. This model predicted a sales increase of 15%.

Step 1. Establishing Probability Distributions. The basic idea in the Monte Carlo simulation is to generate values for the variables making up the model under study. In real-world systems, a lot of variables are probabilistic in nature. To name just a few: inventory demand; lead time for orders to arrive; times between machine breakdowns; times between customer arrivals at a service facility; service times; times required to complete project activities; and number of employees absent from work each day.

One common way to establish a *probability distribution* for a given variable is to examine historical outcomes. We can find the probability, or relative frequency, for each possible outcome of a variable by dividing the frequency of observation by the total number of observations. Here's an example.

The daily demand for radial tires at Barry's Auto Tire over the past 200 days is shown in columns 1 and 2 of Table F.2. Assuming that past arrival rates will hold in the future, we can convert this demand to a probability distribution by dividing each demand frequency by the total demand, 200. The results are shown in column 3.

Step 2. Building a Cumulative Probability Distribution for Each Variable. The conversion from a regular probability distribution, such as in column 3 of Table F.2, to a **cumulative probability distribution** is an easy job. In column 4, we see that the cumulative probability for each level of demand is the sum of the number in the probability column (column 3) added to the previous cumulative probability.

Step 3. Setting Random-Number Intervals. Once we have established a cumulative probability distribution for each variable in the simulation, we must assign a set of numbers to represent each possible value or outcome. These are referred to as **random-number intervals**. Basically, a **random number** is a series of digits (say, two digits from 01, 02, . . . , 98, 99, 00) that have been selected by a totally random process—a process in which each random number has an equal chance of being selected.

If, for example, there is a 5% chance that demand for Barry's radial tires will be 0 units per day, then we will want 5% of the random numbers available to correspond to a demand of 0 units. If a total of 100 two-digit numbers is used in the simulation, we could assign a demand of 0 units to the first 5 random numbers: 01, 02, 03, 04, and 05.[1] Then a simulated demand for 0 units

Cumulative probability distribution
The accumulation of individual probabilities of a distribution.

Random-number intervals
A set of numbers to represent each possible value or outcome in a computer simulation.

Random number
A series of digits that have been selected by a totally random process.

▶ **Table F.2**

Demand for Barry's Auto Tire

To establish a probability distribution for tires, we assume that historical demand is a good indicator of future outcomes.

(1) Demand for Tires	(2) Frequency	(3) Probability of Occurrence	(4) Cumulative Probability
0	10	10/200 = .05	.05
1	20	20/200 = .10	.15
2	40	40/200 = .20	.35
3	60	60/200 = .30	.65
4	40	40/200 = .20	.85
5	30	30/200 = .15	1.00
	200 days	200/200 = 1.00	

[1]Alternatively, we could have assigned the random numbers 00, 01, 02, 03, and 04 to represent a demand of 0 units. The 2 digits 00 can be thought of as either 0 or 100. As long as 5 numbers out of 100 are assigned to the 0 demand, it does not make any difference which 5 they are.

Daily Demand	Probability	Cumulative Probability	Interval of Random Numbers
0	.05	.05	01 through 05
1	.10	.15	06 through 15
2	.20	.35	16 through 35
3	.30	.65	36 through 65
4	.20	.85	66 through 85
5	.15	1.00	86 through 00

would be created every time one of the numbers 01 to 05 was drawn. If there is also a 10% chance that demand for the same product will be 1 unit per day, we could let the next 10 random numbers (06, 07, 08, 09, 10, 11, 12, 13, 14, and 15) represent that demand—and so on for other demand levels.

Similarly, we can see in Table F.3 that the length of each interval on the right corresponds to the probability of 1 of each of the possible daily demands. Thus, in assigning random numbers to the daily demand for 3 radial tires, the range of the random-number interval (36 through 65) corresponds *exactly* to the probability (or proportion) of that outcome. A daily demand for 3 radial tires occurs 30% of the time. All of the 30 random numbers greater than 35 up to and including 65 are assigned to that event.

Step 4. Generating Random Numbers. Random numbers may be generated for simulation problems in two ways. If the problem is large and the process under study involves many simulation trials, computer programs are available to generate the needed random numbers. If the simulation is being done by hand, the numbers may be selected from a table of random digits.

Step 5. Simulating the Experiment. We may simulate outcomes of an experiment by simply selecting random numbers from Table F.4. Beginning anywhere in the table, we note the interval in Table F.3 into which each number falls. For example, if the random number chosen is 81 and the interval 66 through 85 represents a daily demand for 4 tires, then we select a demand of 4 tires. Example F1 carries the simulation further.

> *You may start random number intervals at either 01 or 00, but the text starts at 01 so that the top of each range is the cumulative probability.*

▼ **Table F.4**   **Table of Random Numbers**

52	06	50	88	53	30	10	47	99	37	66	91	35	32	00	84	57	07
37	63	28	02	74	35	24	03	29	60	74	85	90	73	59	55	17	60
82	57	68	28	05	94	03	11	27	79	90	87	92	41	09	25	36	77
69	02	36	49	71	99	32	10	75	21	95	90	94	38	97	71	72	49
98	94	90	36	06	78	23	67	89	85	29	21	25	73	69	34	85	76
96	52	62	87	49	56	59	23	78	71	72	90	57	01	98	57	31	95
33	69	27	21	11	60	95	89	68	48	17	89	34	09	93	50	44	51
50	33	50	95	13	44	34	62	64	39	55	29	30	64	49	44	30	16
88	32	18	50	62	57	34	56	62	31	15	40	90	34	51	95	26	14
90	30	36	24	69	82	51	74	30	35	36	85	01	55	92	64	09	85
50	48	61	18	85	23	08	54	17	12	80	69	24	84	92	16	49	59
27	88	21	62	69	64	48	31	12	73	02	68	00	16	16	46	13	85
45	14	46	32	13	49	66	62	74	41	86	98	92	98	84	54	33	40
81	02	01	78	82	74	97	37	45	31	94	99	42	49	27	64	89	42
66	83	14	74	27	76	03	33	11	97	59	81	72	00	64	61	13	52
74	05	81	82	93	09	96	33	52	78	13	06	28	30	94	23	37	39
30	34	87	01	74	11	46	82	59	94	25	34	32	23	17	01	58	73
59	55	72	33	62	13	74	68	22	44	42	09	32	46	71	79	45	89
67	09	80	98	99	25	77	50	03	32	36	63	65	75	94	19	95	88
60	77	46	63	71	69	44	22	03	85	14	48	69	13	30	50	33	24
60	08	19	29	36	72	30	27	50	64	85	72	75	29	87	05	75	01
80	45	86	99	02	34	87	08	86	84	49	76	24	08	01	86	29	11
53	84	49	63	26	65	72	84	85	63	26	02	75	26	92	62	40	67
69	84	12	94	51	36	17	02	15	29	16	52	56	43	26	22	08	62
37	77	13	10	02	18	31	19	32	85	31	94	81	43	31	58	33	51

Source: Reprinted from *A Million Random Digits with 100,000 Normal Deviates*, Rand (New York: The Free Press, 1995). Used by permission.

EXAMPLE F1

Simulating demand

Barry's Auto Tire wants to simulate 10 days of demand for radial tires.

Approach: Earlier, we went through steps 1 and 2 in the Monte Carlo method (in Table F.2) and step 3 (in Table F.3). Now we need to generate random numbers (step 4) and simulate demand (step 5).

Solution: We select the random numbers needed from Table F.4, starting in the upper-left-hand corner and continuing down the first column and record the corresponding daily demand:

Day Number	Random Number	Simulated Daily Demand
1	52	3
2	37	3
3	82	4
4	69	4
5	98	5
6	96	5
7	33	2
8	50	3
9	88	5
10	90	5

39 Total 10-day demand

39/10 = 3.9 = tires average daily demand

Insight: It is interesting to note that the average demand of 3.9 tires in this 10-day simulation differs substantially from the *expected* daily demand, which we may calculate from the data in Table F.3:

$$\text{Expected demand} = \sum_{i=1}^{5} (\text{probability of } i \text{ units}) \times (\text{demand of } i \text{ units})$$

$$= (.05)(0) + (.10)(1) + (.20)(2) + (.30)(3) + (.20)(4) + (.15)(5)$$

$$= 0 + .1 + .4 + .9 + .8 + .75$$

$$= 2.95 \text{ tires}$$

However, if this simulation was repeated hundreds or thousands of times, the average *simulated* demand would be nearly the same as the *expected* demand.

Learning exercise: Resimulate the 10 days, this time with random numbers from column 2 of Table F.4. What is the average daily demand? [Answer: 2.5.]

Related problems: F.1, F.2, F.3, F.4, F.5, F.7, F.9, F.10, F.14, F.20

Naturally, it would be risky to draw any hard and fast conclusions about the operation of a firm from only a short simulation like Example F1. Seldom would anyone actually want to go to the effort of simulating such a simple model containing only one variable. Simulating by hand does, however, demonstrate the important principles involved and may be useful in small-scale studies.

OM in Action   Simulating Taco Bell's Restaurant Operation

Determining how many employees to schedule each 15 minutes to perform each function in a Taco Bell restaurant is a complex and vexing problem. So Taco Bell, the $6-billion giant with 7,000 U.S. and foreign locations, decided to build a simulation model. It selected MODSIM as its software to develop a new labor-management system called LMS.

To develop and use a simulation model, Taco Bell had to collect a substantial amount of data. Almost everything that takes place in a restaurant, from customer arrival patterns to the time it takes to wrap a taco, had to be translated into reliable, accurate data. Just as an example, analysts had to conduct time studies and data analysis for every task that is part of preparing every item on the menu. To the researcher's surprise, the hours devoted to collecting data greatly exceeded those needed to actually build the LMS model.

Inputs to LMS include staffing, such as number of people and positions. Outputs are performance measures, such as mean time in the system, mean time at the counter, people utilization, and equipment utilization. The model paid off. More than $53 million in labor costs were saved in LMS's first 4 years of use.

Sources: Nation's Restaurant News (August 15, 2005): 68–69; *OR/MS Today* (June 2000): 30 and J. Heuter and W. Swart *Interfaces* 28, (January–February 1998): 75–91.

SIMULATION OF A QUEUING PROBLEM

An important use of simulation is in the analysis of waiting-line problems. As we saw in Module D, the assumptions required for solving queuing problems are quite restrictive. For most realistic queuing systems, simulation may be the only approach available.

Example F2 illustrates the use of simulation for a large unloading dock and its associated queue. Arrivals of barges at the dock are not Poisson-distributed, and unloading rates (service times) are not exponential or constant. As such, the mathematical waiting-line models of Module D cannot be used.

Learning Objective

3. Simulate a queuing problem

Following long trips down the Mississippi River from industrial midwestern cities, fully loaded barges arrive at night in New Orleans. Barges are unloaded on a first-in, first-out basis. Any barges not unloaded on the day of arrival must wait until the following day. However, tying up barges in dock is an expensive proposition, and the superintendent cannot ignore the angry phone calls from barge owners reminding him that "time is money!" He decides that before going to the Port of New Orleans controller to request additional unloading crews, he should conduct a simulation study of arrivals, unloadings, and delays. A 100-day simulation would be ideal, but for purposes of illustration, the superintendent can begin with a shorter 15-day analysis.

Approach: Follow the 5 steps in Monte Carlo simulation: (1) establish probability distributions for the important variables (i.e., barge arrivals and barge unloadings); (2 and 3) create cumulative distributions and random number intervals for each variable; (4) draw random numbers from Table F.4; and (5) simulate the experiment.

Solution: The number of barges docking on any given night ranges from 0 to 5. The probability of 0, 1, 2, 3, 4, and 5 arrivals is displayed in Table F.5. In the same table, we establish cumulative probabilities and corresponding random-number intervals for each possible value.

EXAMPLE F2

A barge-unloading simulation with two variables

Number of Arrivals	Probability	Cumulative Probability	Random-Number Interval
0	.13	.13	01 through 13
1	.17	.30	14 through 30
2	.15	.45	31 through 45
3	.25	.70	46 through 70
4	.20	.90	71 through 90
5	.10	1.00	91 through 00
	1.00		

◀ **Table F.5**

Overnight Barge Arrival Rates and Random-Number Intervals

The dock superintendent believes that the number of barges unloaded also tends to vary from day to day. In Table F.6, the superintendent provides information from which we can create a probability distribution for the variable *daily unloading rate*. As we just did for the arrival variable, we can set up an interval of random numbers for the unloading rates.

Daily Unloading Rates	Probability	Cumulative Probability	Random-Number Interval
1	.05	.05	01 through 05
2	.15	.20	06 through 20
3	.50	.70	21 through 70
4	.20	.90	71 through 90
5	.10	1.00	91 through 00
	1.00		

◀ **Table F.6**

Unloading Rates and Random-Number Intervals

The relation between random-number intervals and cumulative probability is that the top end of each interval is equal to the cumulative probability percentage.

Random numbers are drawn from the top row of Table F.4 to generate daily arrival rates. To create daily unloading rates, they are drawn from the second row of Table F.4. Table F.7 shows the day-to-day port simulation.

▶ **Table F.7**

Queuing Simulation of Port of New Orleans Barge Unloadings

(1) Day	(2) Number Delayed from Previous Day	(3) Random Number	(4) Number of Nightly Arrivals	(5) Total to Be Unloaded	(6) Random Number	(7) Number Unloaded
1	⊖ [a]	52	3	3	37	3
2	0	06	0	0	63	⓪ [b]
3	0	50	3	3	28	3
4	0	88	4	4	02	1
5	3	53	3	6	74	4
6	2	30	1	3	35	3
7	0	10	0	0	24	⓪ [c]
8	0	47	3	3	03	1
9	2	99	5	7	29	3
10	4	37	2	6	60	3
11	3	66	3	6	74	4
12	2	91	5	7	85	4
13	3	35	2	5	90	4
14	1	32	2	3	73	③ [d]
15	0	00	5	5	59	3
	20 Total delays		41 Total arrivals			39 Total unloadings

[a]We can begin with no delays from the previous day. In a long simulation, even if we started with five overnight delays, that initial condition would be averaged out.

[b]Three barges could have been unloaded on day 2. Yet because there were no arrivals and no backlog existed, zero unloadings took place.

[c]The same situation as noted in footnote b takes place.

[d]This time, 4 barges could have been unloaded, but because only 3 were in queue, the number unloaded is recorded as 3.

Insight: The superintendent will likely be interested in at least three useful and important pieces of information:

$$\left(\begin{array}{c}\text{Average number of barges}\\\text{delayed to the next day}\end{array}\right) = \frac{20 \text{ delays}}{15 \text{ days}}$$

$$= 1.33 \text{ barges delayed per day}$$

$$\text{Average number of nightly arrivals} = \frac{41 \text{ arrivals}}{15 \text{ days}}$$

$$= 2.73 \text{ arrivals per night}$$

$$\text{Average number of barges unloaded each day} = \frac{39 \text{ unloadings}}{15 \text{ days}}$$

$$= 2.60 \text{ unloadings per day}$$

The simulation in Table F.7 by itself provides interesting data, but these three averages are management information to help make decisions.

Learning exercise: If the random numbers for day 15 were 03 and 93 (instead of 00 and 59), how would these 3 averages change? [Answer: They would be 1.33 (unchanged), 2.4, and 2.4.]

Related problems: F.6, F.8, F.15, F.19, F.21

When the data from Example F2 are analyzed in terms of delay costs, idle labor costs, and the cost of hiring extra unloading crew, the dock superintendent and port controller can make a better staffing decision. They may even choose to resimulate the process assuming different unloading rates that correspond to increased crew sizes. Although simulation cannot guarantee an optimal solution to problems such as this, it can be helpful in recreating a process and identifying good decision alternatives.

SIMULATION AND INVENTORY ANALYSIS

In Chapter 12, we introduced inventory models. The commonly used EOQ models are based on the assumption that both product demand and reorder lead time are known, constant values. In most real-world inventory situations, though, demand and lead time are variables, so accurate analysis becomes extremely difficult to handle by any means other than simulation.

Learning Objective

4. Simulate an inventory problem

In this section, we present an inventory problem with two decision variables and two probabilistic components. The owner of the hardware store in Example F3 would like to establish *order quantity* and *reorder point* decisions for a particular product that has probabilistic (uncertain) daily demand and reorder lead time. He wants to make a series of simulation runs, trying out various order quantities and reorder points, to minimize his total inventory cost for the item. Inventory costs in this case will include ordering, holding, and stockout costs.

EXAMPLE F3

An inventory simulation with two variables

Simkin's Hardware Store, in Reno, sells the Ace model electric drill. Daily demand for this particular product is relatively low but subject to some variability. Lead times tend to be variable as well. Mark Simkin wants to develop a simulation to test an inventory policy of ordering 10 drills, with a reorder point of 5. In other words, every time the on-hand inventory level at the end of the day is 5 or less, Simkin will call his supplier that evening and place an order for 10 more drills. Simkin notes that if the lead time is 1 day, the order will not arrive the next morning but rather at the beginning of the following workday.

Approach: Simkin wants to follow the 5 steps in the Monte Carlo simulation process.

Solution: Over the past 300 days, Simkin has observed the sales shown in column 2 of Table F.8. He converts this historical frequency into a probability distribution for the variable daily demand (column 3). A cumulative probability distribution is formed in column 4 of Table F.8. Finally, Simkin establishes an interval of random numbers to represent each possible daily demand (column 5).

(1) Demand for Ace Drill	(2) Frequency	(3) Probability	(4) Cumulative Probability	(5) Interval of Random Numbers
0	15	.05	.05	01 through 05
1	30	.10	.15	06 through 15
2	60	.20	.35	16 through 35
3	120	.40	.75	36 through 75
4	45	.15	.90	76 through 90
5	30	.10	1.00	91 through 00
	300 days	1.00		

◄ **Table F.8**

Probabilities and Random-Number Intervals for Daily Ace Drill Demand

When Simkin places an order to replenish his inventory of drills, there is a delivery lag of from 1 to 3 days. This means that lead time may also be considered a probabilistic variable. The number of days that it took to receive the past 50 orders is presented in Table F.9. In a fashion similar to the creation of the demand variable, Simkin establishes a probability distribution for the lead time variable (column 3 of Table F.9), computes the cumulative distribution (column 4), and assigns random-number intervals for each possible time (column 5).

(1) Lead Time (days)	(2) Frequency	(3) Probability	(4) Cumulative Probability	(5) Random-Number Interval
1	10	.20	.20	01 through 20
2	25	.50	.70	21 through 70
3	15	.30	1.00	71 through 00
	50 orders	1.00		

◄ **Table F.9**

Probabilities and Random-Number Intervals for Reorder Lead Time

The entire process is simulated in Table F.10 for a 10-day period. We assume that beginning inventory (column 3) is 10 units on day 1. We took the random numbers (column 4) from column 2 of Table F.4.

▶ **Table F.10**

Simkin Hardware's First Inventory Simulation. Order Quantity = 10 Units; Reorder Point = 5 units

(1) Day	(2) Units Received	(3) Beginning Inventory	(4) Random Number	(5) Demand	(6) Ending Inventory	(7) Lost Sales	(8) Order?	(9) Random Number	(10) Lead Time
1		10	06	1	9	0	No		
2	0	9	63	3	6	0	No		
3	0	6	57	3	③ a	0	Yes	⑩ b	1
4	0	3	㉙④ c	5	0	2	Ⓝo d		
5	⑩ e	10	52	3	7	0	No		
6	0	7	69	3	4	0	Yes	33	2
7	0	4	32	2	2	0	No		
8	0	2	30	2	0	0	No		
9	⑩ f	10	48	3	7	0	No		
10	0	7	88	4	3	0	Yes	14	1
					Totals: 41	2			

[a]This is the first time inventory dropped to the reorder point of five drills. Because no prior order was outstanding, an order is placed.

[b]The random number 02 is generated to represent the first lead time. It was drawn from column 2 of Table F.4 as the next number in the list being used. A separate column could have been used from which to draw lead-time random numbers if we had wanted to do so, but in this example, we did not do so.

[c]Again, notice that the random digits 02 were used for lead time (see footnote b). So the next number in the column is 94.

[d]No order is placed on day 4 because there is an order outstanding from the previous day that has not yet arrived.

[e]The lead time for the first order placed is 1 day, but as noted in the text, an order does not arrive the next morning but rather the beginning of the following day. Thus, the first order arrives at the start of day 5.

[f]This is the arrival of the order placed at the close of business on day 6. Fortunately for Simkin, no lost sales occurred during the 2-day lead time before the order arrived.

Table F.10 was filled in by proceeding 1 day (or line) at a time, working from left to right. It is a four-step process:

1. Begin each simulated day by checking to see whether any ordered inventory has just arrived. If it has, increase current inventory by the quantity ordered (10 units, in this case).
2. Generate a daily demand from the demand probability distribution for the selected random number.
3. Compute: Ending inventory = Beginning inventory minus Demand. If on-hand inventory is insufficient to meet the day's demand, satisfy as much demand as possible and note the number of lost sales.
4. Determine whether the day's ending inventory has reached the reorder point (5 units). If it has, and if there are no outstanding orders, place an order. Lead time for a new order is simulated for the selected random number corresponding to the distribution in Table F.9.

Insights: Simkin's inventory simulation yields some interesting results. The average daily ending inventory is:

$$\text{Average ending inventory} = \frac{41 \text{ total units}}{10 \text{ days}} = 4.1 \text{ units/day}$$

We also note the average lost sales and number of orders placed per day:

$$\text{Average lost sales} = \frac{2 \text{ sales lost}}{10 \text{ days}} = .2 \text{ units/day}$$

$$\text{Average number of orders placed} = \frac{3 \text{ orders}}{10 \text{ days}} = .3 \text{ orders/day}$$

Learning exercise: How would these 3 averages change if the random numbers for day 10 were 04 and 93 instead of 88 and 14? [Answer: 4.5, .2 (no change), and .2.]

Related problems: F.11, F.16a

Example F4 shows how these data can be useful in studying the inventory costs of the policy being simulated.

Simkin wants to put a cost on the ordering policy simulated in Example F3.

Approach: Simkin estimates that the cost of placing each order for Ace drills is $10, the holding cost per drill held at the end of each day is $.50, and the cost of each lost sale is $8. This information enables us to compute the total daily inventory cost.

Solution: Here are the three cost components:

$$\text{Daily order cost} = (\text{Cost of placing 1 order})$$
$$\times (\text{Number of orders placed per day})$$
$$= \$10 \text{ per order} \times .3 \text{ order per day} = \$3$$

$$\text{Daily holding cost} = (\text{Cost of holding 1 unit for 1 day})$$
$$\times (\text{Average ending inventory})$$
$$= 50\cent \text{ per unit per day} \times 4.1 \text{ units per day} = \$2.05$$

$$\text{Daily stockout cost} = (\text{Cost per lost sale})$$
$$\times (\text{Average number of lost sales per day})$$
$$= \$8 \text{ per lost sale} \times .2 \text{ lost sales per day} = \$1.60$$

$$\text{Total daily inventory cost} = \text{Daily order cost} + \text{Daily holding cost}$$
$$+ \text{Daily stockout cost} = \$6.65$$

Insights: This cost will help Simkin decide if the Q = 10, ROP = 5 order policy is a good one.

Learning exercise: If the cost of placing an order is really $20 (instead of $10), what is the correct total daily inventory cost? [Answer: $9.65.]

Related problems: F.12, F.13, F.16b, F.17, F.18

Now that we have worked through Examples F3 and F4, we want to emphasize something very important: This simulation should be extended many more days before we draw any conclusions as to the cost of the order policy being tested. If a hand simulation is being conducted, 100 days would provide a better representation. If a computer is doing the calculations, 1,000 days would be helpful in reaching accurate cost estimates. (Moreover, remember that even with a 1,000-day simulation, the generated distribution should be compared with the desired distribution to ensure valid results.)

OM in Action   Simulating Jackson Memorial Hospital's Operating Rooms

Miami's Jackson Memorial Hospital, Florida's largest with 1,576 inpatient beds, is also one of the U.S.'s finest. In 1996, it received the highest accreditation score of any public-sector hospital in the country. Jackson's operations management team is constantly seeking ways of increasing hospital efficiency, and the construction of new operating rooms (ORs) prompted the development of a simulation of the existing 31 ORs.

The OR section of the hospital includes a patient holding area and a patient recovery area, both of which were experiencing problems owing to ineffective scheduling of OR services. A simulation study, modeled using the ARENA software package, sought to maximize use of OR rooms and staff. Inputs to the model included (1) the amount of time a patient waits in the holding area, (2) the specific process the patient undergoes, (3) the staff schedule, (4) room availability, and (5) time of day.

The first hurdle that the management team had to deal with at Jackson was the vast number of records to review to extract the information necessary for the simulation model. The second hurdle was the quality of the data. A thorough analysis of the records determined which were good and which had to be discarded. In the end, Jackson's carefully screened databases led to a good set of data inputs for the model. The simulation model then successfully developed five measures of performance: (1) number of procedures a day, (2) average case time, (3) staff utilization, (4) room utilization, and (5) average waiting time in the holding area.

Sources: Knight Ridder Tribune Business Service (May 3, 2004): 1. M. A. Centeno et al., "Challenges of Simulating Hospital Facilities," *Proceedings of the 12th Annual Conference of the Production and Operations Management Society.* (March 2001).

The cost of simulating a frontal car crash at Ford was $60,000 in 1985. By 1998, the event could be simulated for $200. It now costs under $10 and takes just minutes.

Let us say that Simkin *does* complete a 1,000-day simulation of the policy from Example F3 (order quantity = 10 drills, reorder point = 5 drills). Does this complete his analysis? The answer is no—this is just the beginning! Simkin must now compare *this* potential strategy with other possibilities. For example, what about order quantity = 10, reorder point = 4? Or order quantity = 12, reorder point = 6? Or order quantity = 14, reorder point = 5? Perhaps every combination of values—of order quantity from 6 to 20 drills and reorder points from 3 to 10—should be simulated. After simulating all reasonable combinations of order quantities and reorder points, Simkin would likely select the pair yielding the lowest total inventory cost. Problem F.12 later in this module gives you a chance to help Simkin begin this series of comparisons.

Summary

Simulation involves building mathematical models that attempt to act like real operating systems. In this way, a real-world situation can be studied without imposing on the actual system. Although simulation models can be developed manually, simulation by computer is generally more desirable. The Monte Carlo approach uses random numbers to represent variables, such as inventory demand or people waiting in line, which are then simulated in a series of trials. Simulation is widely used as an operations tool because its advantages usually outweigh its disadvantages.

Key Terms

Simulation *(p. 796)*
Monte Carlo method *(p. 797)*
Cumulative probability distribution *(p. 798)*
Random-number intervals *(p. 798)*
Random number *(p. 798)*

Using Software in Simulation

Computers are critical in simulating complex tasks. They can generate random numbers, simulate thousands of time periods in a matter of seconds or minutes, and provide management with reports that improve decision making. A computer approach is almost a necessity in order to draw valid conclusions from a simulation.

Computer programming languages can help the simulation process. *General-purpose languages*, such as BASIC or C++, constitute one approach. *Special-purpose simulation languages*, such as GPSS and SIMSCRIPT, have a few advantages: (1) they require less programming time for large simulations, (2) they are usually more efficient and easier to check for errors, and (3) random-number generators are already built in as subroutines.

Commercial, easy-to-use prewritten simulation programs are also available. Some are generalized to handle a wide variety of situations ranging from queuing to inventory. These include programs such as Extend, Modsim, Witness, MAP/1, Enterprise Dynamics, Simfactory, ProModel, Micro Saint, and ARENA. The *OM in Action* box on page 805, "Simulating Jackson Memorial Hospital's Operating Rooms," described one application of ARENA software.

Spreadsheet software such as Excel can also be used to develop simulations quickly and easily. Such packages have built-in random-number generators and develop outputs through "data-fill" table commands.

Learning Objective

5. Use Excel spreadsheets to create a simulation

✗ Using Excel Spreadsheets

The ability to generate random numbers and then "look up" these numbers in a table to associate them with a specific event makes spreadsheets excellent tools for conducting simulations. Program F.1 illustrates an Excel simulation for Example F1.

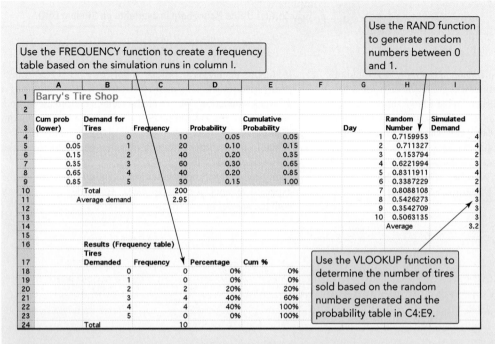

▲ **Program F.1** Using Excel to Simulate Tire Demand for Barry's Auto Tire Shop

The output shows a simulated average of 3.2 tires per day (in cell I14).

Notice that the cumulative probabilities are calculated in column E of Program F.1. This procedure reduces the chance of error and is useful in larger simulations involving more levels of demand.

The =VLOOKUP function in column I looks up the random number (generated in column H) in the leftmost column of the defined lookup table ($A$4:$B$9). The =VLOOKUP function moves downward through this column until it finds a cell that is bigger than the random number. It then goes to the previous row and gets the value from column B of the table.

In column H, for example, the first random number shown is .716. Excel looked down the left-hand column of the lookup table ($A$4:$B$9) of Program F.1 until it found .85. From the previous row it retrieved the value in column B which is 4. Pressing the F9 function key recalculates the random numbers and the simulation.

Value	Cell	Excel Formula	Action
Cumulative probability	A4	=0	
Cumulative probability	A5	=A4+D4	Copy to A6:A9
Random Number	H4	=RAND()	Copy to H5:H13
Demand	I4	=VLOOKUP(H4,$A$4:$B$9,2,TRUE)	Copy to I5:I13
Average	I14	=AVERAGE(I4:I13)	
Frequency	C18	=FREQUENCY($I$4:$I$13,$B$18:$B$23)	Array copy to C19:C23
Total	C24	=SUM(C18:C23)	
Percentage	D18	=C18/$C$24	Copy to D19:D23
Average simulated demand	D25	=SUMPRODUCT(B18:B23,D18:D23)	
Cumulative Percentage	E18	=D18	
Cumulative Percentage	E19	=E18+D19	Copy to E20:E23
			Press the F9 Key to simulate

Using POM for Windows and Excel OM

POM for Windows and Excel OM are capable of handling any simulation that contains only one random variable, such as Example F1. For further details, please refer to Appendix IV.

Solved Problem F.1

Higgins Plumbing and Heating maintains a stock of 30-gallon hot-water heaters that it sells to homeowners and installs for them. Owner Jerry Higgins likes the idea of having a large supply on hand to meet any customer demand. However, he also recognizes that it is expensive to do so. He examines hot-water heater sales over the past 50 weeks and notes the following:

Hot-Water Heater Sales per Week	Number of Weeks This Number Was Sold
4	6
5	5
6	9
7	12
8	8
9	7
10	3
	50 weeks total data

a) If Higgins maintains a constant supply of 8 hot-water heaters in any given week, how many times will he stockout during a 20-week simulation? We use random numbers from the seventh column of Table F.4 (on p. 799), beginning with the random digit 10.

b) What is the average number of sales per week over the 20-week period?

c) Using an analytic nonsimulation technique, determine the expected number of sales per week. How does this compare with the answer in part (b)?

Solution

Heater Sales	Probability	Random-Number Intervals
4	.12	01 through 12
5	.10	13 through 22
6	.18	23 through 40
7	.24	41 through 64
8	.16	65 through 80
9	.14	81 through 94
10	.06	95 through 00
	1.00	

(a)

Week	Random Number	Simulated Sales	Week	Random Number	Simulated Sales
1	10	4	11	08	4
2	24	6	12	48	7
3	03	4	13	66	8
4	32	6	14	97	10
5	23	6	15	03	4
6	59	7	16	96	10
7	95	10	17	46	7
8	34	6	18	74	8
9	34	6	19	77	8
10	51	7	20	44	7

With a supply of 8 heaters, Higgins will stock out three times during the 20-week period (in weeks 7, 14, and 16).

(b) Average sales by simulation = total sales/20 weeks = 135/20 = 6.75 per week

(c) Using expected values, we obtain:

$$E \text{ (sales)} = .12(4 \text{ heaters}) + .10(5)$$

$$+ .18(6) + .24(7) + .16(8)$$

$$+ .14(9) + .06(10) = 6.88 \text{ heaters}$$

With a longer simulation, these two approaches will lead to even closer values.

Solved Problem F.2

Random numbers may be used to simulate continuous distributions. As a simple example, assume that fixed cost equals $300, profit contribution equals $10 per item sold, and you expect an equally likely chance of 0 to 99 units to be sold. That is, profit equals −$300 + $10X, where X is the number sold. The mean amount you expect to sell is 49.5 units.

a) Calculate the expected value.

b) Simulate the sale of 5 items, using the following double-digit random numbers:

   37   77   13   10   85

c) Calculate the expected value of part (b) and compare with the results of part (a).

solution

(a) Expected value $= -300 + 10(49.5) = \$195$

(b) $-300 + \$10(37) = \$70$

   $-300 + \$10(77) = \$470$

   $-300 + \$10(13) = -\$170$

   $-300 + \$10(10) = -\$200$

   $-300 + \$10(85) = \$550$

(c) The mean of these simulated sales is $144. If the sample size were larger, we would expect the two values to be closer.

Self-Test

- **Before taking the self-test**, *refer to the learning objectives listed at the beginnning of the module and the key terms listed at the end of the module.*
- *Use the key at the back of the text to* **correct** *your answers.*
- **Restudy** *pages that correspond to any questions you answered incorrectly or material you feel uncertain about.*

1. The seven steps an operations manager should perform when using simulation to analyze a problem are

   _____, _____, _____, _____, _____, _____, and _____

2. The five steps required to implement the Monte Carlo simulation technique are

   _____, _____, _____, _____, and _____

3. When simulating the Monte Carlo experiment, the average simulated demand over the long run should approximate the:
   a) real demand
   b) expected demand
   c) sampled demand
   d) daily demand

4. The idea behind simulation is:
   a) to imitate a real-world situation
   b) to study the properties and operating characteristics of a real-world situation
   c) to draw conclusions and make action decisions based upon simulation results
   d) all of the above

5. Using simulation for a queuing problem:
   a) would be rare in a realistic situation
   b) is an unreasonable alternative if the arrival rate is not Poisson distributed but can be plotted on a curve
   c) would be appropriate if the service time was not exponential or constant
   d) all of the above

6. When assigning random numbers in Monte Carlo simulation:
   a) it is important to develop a cumulative probability distribution
   b) it is not important to assign the exact range of random number interval as the probability
   c) it is important to assign the particular appropriate random numbers
   d) all of the above

7. In a Monte Carlo simulation, a variable that we might want to simulate is:
   a) lead time for inventory orders to arrive
   b) times between machine breakdowns
   c) time between arrivals at a service facility
   d) number of employees absent from work each day
   e) all of the above

8. Use the following random numbers to simulate *yes* and *no* answers to 10 questions by starting in the first row and letting:
   a) the double-digit number 00–49 represent *yes* and 50–99 represent *no*
   b) the double-digit even numbers represent *yes* and the odd numbers represent *no*

   Random Numbers: 52   06   50   88   53   30   10   47
   99   37

Internet and Student CD-ROM/DVD Exercises

Visit our Companion Web site or use your student CD-ROM/DVD to help with material in this module.

 On Our Companion Web site,
   www.prenhall.com/heizer
- Self-Study Quizzes
- Practice Problems
- Internet Case
- PowerPoint Lectures

 On Your Student CD-ROM
- Practice Problems
- POM for Windows

 On Your Student DVD
- Virtual Office Hours for Solved Problems

Discussion Questions

1. State, in order, the seven steps an operations manager should perform when using simulation to analyze a problem.
2. List the advantages of simulation.
3. List the disadvantages of simulation.
4. Explain the difference between *simulated* average demand and *expected* average demand.
5. What is the role of random numbers in a Monte Carlo simulation?
6. Why might the results of a simulation differ each time you make a run?
7. What is Monte Carlo simulation? What principles underlie its use, and what steps are followed in applying it?
8. List six ways that simulation can be used in business.
9. Why is simulation such a widely used technique?

10. What are the advantages of special-purpose simulation languages?
11. In the simulation of an order policy for drills at Simkin's hardware (Example F3, pp. 803–804), would the results (of Table F.10) change significantly if a longer period were simulated? Why is the 10-day simulation valid or invalid?
12. Why is a computer necessary in conducting a real-world simulation?
13. Why might a manager be forced to use simulation instead of an analytical model in dealing with a problem of:
    (a) inventory order policy?
    (b) ships docking in a port to unload?
    (c) bank-teller service windows?
    (d) the U.S. economy?

Problems*

The problems that follow involve simulations that can be done by hand. However, to obtain accurate and meaningful results, long periods must be simulated. This task is usually handled by a computer. If you are able to program some of the problems in Excel or a computer language with which you are familiar, we suggest you try to do so. If not, the hand simulations will still help you understand the simulation process.

• **F.1**   The daily demand for tuna sandwiches at a Roosevelt University cafeteria vending machine is either 8, 9, 10, or 11, with probabilities 0.4, 0.3, 0.2, or 0.1, respectively. Assume the following random numbers have been generated: 09, 55, 73, 67, 53, 59, 04, 23, 88, and 84. Using these numbers, generate daily sandwich sales for 10 days. **Px**

• **F.2**   The number of machine breakdowns per day at Kristen Hodge's factory is either 0, 1, or 2, with probabilities 0.5, 0.3, or 0.2, respectively. The following random numbers have been generated: 13, 14, 02, 18, 31, 19, 32, 85, 31, and 94. Use these numbers to generate the number of breakdowns for 10 consecutive days. What proportion of these days had at least 1 breakdown? **Px**

• **F.3**   The table below shows the partial results of a Monte Carlo simulation. Assume that the simulation began at 8:00 A.M. and there is only one server.

Customer Number	Arrival Time	Service Time
1	8:01	6
2	8:06	7
3	8:09	8
4	8:15	6
5	8:20	6

a) When does service begin for customer number 3?
b) When will customer number 5 leave?
c) What is the average waiting time in line?
d) What is the average time in the system?

• **F.4**   Barbara Flynn sells papers at a newspaper stand for $.35. The papers cost her $.25, giving her a $.10 profit on each one she sells. From past experience Barbara knows that:
a) 20% of the time she sells 100 papers.
b) 20% of the time she sells 150 papers.
c) 30% of the time she sells 200 papers.
d) 30% of the time she sells 250 papers.
Assuming that Barbara believes the cost of a lost sale to be $.05 and any unsold papers cost her $.25, simulate her profit outlook over 5 days if she orders 200 papers for each of the 5 days. Use the following random numbers: 52, 06, 50, 88, and 53. **Px**

•• **F.5**   Children's Hospital is studying the number of emergency surgery kits that it uses on weekends. Over the last 40 weekends the number of kits used is as follows:

Number of Kits	Frequency
4	4
5	6
6	10
7	12
8	8

The following random numbers have been generated: 11, 52, 59, 22, 03, 03, 50, 86, 85, 15, 32, 47. Simulate 12 nights of emergency kit usage. What is the average number of kits used during these 12 nights? **Px**

• **F.6**   Susan Sherer's grocery store has noted the following figures with regard to the number of people who arrive at the store's three checkout stands and the time it takes to check them out:

Arrivals/Minute	Frequency
0	.3
1	.5
2	.2

Service Time (minute)	Frequency
1	.1
2	.3
3	.4
4	.2

*Note: **Px** means the problem may be solved with POM for Windows and/or Excel OM or Excel.

Simulate the utilization of the three checkout stands over 5 minutes, using the following random numbers: 07, 60, 77, 49, 76, 95, 51, 16, and 14. Record the results at the end of the 5-minute period. Start at time = 0. **Px**

• **F.7** A warehouse manager at Mary Beth Marrs Corp. needs to simulate the demand placed on a product that does not fit standard models. The concept being measured is "demand during lead time," where both lead time and daily demand are variable. The historical record for this product, along with the cumulative distribution, appear in the table. Random numbers have been generated to simulate the next 5 order cycles; they are 91, 45, 37, 65, and 51. What are the five demand values? What is their average?

Demand During Lead Time	Probability	Cumulative Probability
100	.01	.01
120	.15	.16
140	.30	.46
160	.15	.61
180	.04	.65
200	.10	.75
220	.25	1.00 **Px**

•• **F.8** The time between arrivals at the drive-through window of Barry Harmon's fast-food restaurant follows the distribution given in the table. The service-time distribution is also given. Use the random numbers provided to simulate the activity of the first 4 arrivals. Assume that the window opens at 11:00 A.M. and that the first arrival occurs afterward, based on the first interarrival time generated.

Time between Arrivals	Probability	Service Time	Probability
1	.2	1	.3
2	.3	2	.5
3	.3	3	.2
4	.2		

Random numbers for arrivals: 14, 74, 27, 03
Random numbers for service times: 88, 32, 36, 24
At what time does the fourth customer leave the system? **Px**

• **F.9** Phantom Controls monitors and repairs control circuit boxes on elevators installed in multistory buildings in downtown Chicago. The company has the contract for 108 buildings. When a box malfunctions, Phantom installs a new one and rebuilds the failed unit in its repair facility in Gary, Indiana. The data for failed boxes over the last 2 years is shown in the following table:

Number of Failed Boxes per Month	Probability
0	.10
1	.14
2	.26
3	.20
4	.18
5	.12

Simulate 2 years (24 months) of operation for Phantom and determine the average number of failed boxes per month from the simulation. Was it common to have fewer than 7 failures over 3 months of operation? (Start your simulation at the top of the 10th column of Table F.4 on page 799, RN = 37, and go down in the table.) **Px**

• **F.10** The number of cars arriving at Terry Haugen's Car Wash during the last 200 hours of operation is observed to be the following:

Number of Cars Arriving	Frequency
3 or fewer	0
4	20
5	30
6	50
7	60
8	40
9 or more	0
	200

a) Set up a probability and cumulative-probability distribution for the variable of car arrivals.
b) Establish random-number intervals for the variable.
c) Simulate 15 hours of car arrivals and compute the average number of arrivals per hour. Select the random numbers needed from column 1, Table F.4, beginning with the digits 52. **Px**

•• **F.11** Leonard Presby's newsstand uses naive forecasting to order tomorrow's papers. The number of newspapers ordered corresponds to the previous day's demands. Today's demand for papers was 22. Presby buys the newspapers for $.20 and sells them for $.50. Whenever there is unsatisfied demand, Presby estimates the lost goodwill cost at $.10. Complete the accompanying table, and answer the questions that follow.

Demand	Probability
21	.25
22	.15
23	.10
24	.20
25	.30

Day	Papers Ordered	Random Number	Demand	Revenue	Cost	Goodwill Cost	Net Profit
1	22	37					
2		19					
3		52					
4		8					
5		22					
6		61					

a) What is the demand on day 3?
b) What is the total net profit at the end of the 6 days?
c) What is the lost goodwill on day 6?
d) What is the net profit on day 2?
e) How many papers has Presby ordered for day 5? **Px**

•• **F.12** Simkin's Hardware simulated an inventory-ordering policy for Ace electric drills that involved an order quantity of 10 drills, with a reorder point of 5. This first attempt to develop a cost-effective ordering strategy was illustrated in Table F.10 of Example F3 (on p. 804). The brief simulation resulted in a total daily inventory cost of $6.65 in Example F4.

Simkin would now like to compare this strategy to one in which he orders 12 drills, with a reorder point of 6. Conduct a 10-day simulation (using random numbers from the right hand column of Table F.4, starting with 07, and using a beginning inventory = 12). Discuss the cost implications. **Px**

•• **F.13** Every home football game for the last 8 years at Eastern State University has been sold out. The revenues from ticket sales are significant, but the sale of food, beverages, and souvenirs has contributed greatly to the overall profitability of the football program. One particular souvenir is the football program for each game. The number of programs sold at each game is described by the probability distribution given in the table:

Number of Programs Sold	Probability
2,300	0.15
2,400	0.22
2,500	0.24
2,600	0.21
2,700	0.18

Each program costs $.80 to produce and sells for $2.00. Any programs that are not sold are donated to a recycling center and do not produce any revenue.

a) Simulate the sales of programs at 10 football games. Use the last column in the random-number table (Table F.4 on p. 799) and begin at the top of the column.

b) If the university decided to print 2,500 programs for each game, what would the average profits be for the 10 games that were simulated?

c) If the university decided to print 2,600 programs for each game, what would the average profits be for the 10 games that were simulated? **Px**

•   **F.14** Refer to the data in Solved Problem F.1, on page 808, which deals with Higgins Plumbing and Heating. Higgins has now collected 100 weeks of data and finds the following distribution for sales:

Hot-Water Heater Sales per Week	Number of Weeks This Number Was Sold	Hot-Water Heater Sales per Week	Number of Weeks This Number Was Sold
3	2	8	12
4	9	9	12
5	10	10	10
6	15	11	5
7	25		100

a) Assuming Higgins maintains a constant supply of 8 heaters, simulate the number of stockouts incurred over a 20-week period (using the seventh column of Table F.4).

b) Conduct this 20-week simulation two more times and compare your answers with those in part (a). Did they change significantly? Why or why not?

c) What is the new expected number of sales per week? **Px**

•••   **F.15** Taboo Tattoo and Tanning has two tanning beds. One bed serves the company's regular members exclusively. The second bed serves strictly walk-in customers (those without appointments) on a first-come, first-served basis. Gary Clendenen, the store manager, has noticed on several occasions during the busy 5 hours of the day (2:00 P.M. until 7:00 P.M.) that potential walk-in customers will most often walk away from the store if they see one person already waiting for the second bed. He wonders if capturing this lost demand would justify adding a third bed. Leasing and maintaining a tanning bed costs Taboo $600 per month. The price paid per customer varies according to the time in the bed, but Gary has calculated the average net income for every 10 minutes of tanning time to be $2. A study of the pattern of arrivals during the busy hours and the time spent tanning has revealed the following:

Time between Arrivals (minutes)	Probability	Time in Tanning Bed (minutes)	Probability
5	0.30	10	0.20
10	0.25	15	0.30
15	0.20	20	0.40
20	0.15	25	0.10
25	0.10		

a) Simulate 4 hours of operation (arrivals over 4 hours). Use the 14th column of Table F.4 (p. 799) for arrival times and the 8th column for tanning times. Assume there is one person who has just entered the bed at 2:00 P.M. for a 20-minute tan. Indicate which customers balk at waiting for the bed to become available. How many customers were lost over the 4 hours?

b) If the store is open an average of 24 days a month, will capturing all lost sales justify adding a new tanning bed? **Px**

•••   **F.16** Erin Davis owns and operates one of the largest Mercedes-Benz auto dealerships in Nebraska. In the past 36 months, her sales have ranged from a low of 6 new cars to a high of 12 new cars, as reflected in the following table:

Sales of New Cars/Month	Frequency
6	3
7	4
8	6
9	12
10	9
11	1
12	1
	36 months

Davis believes that sales will continue during the next 24 months at about the same historical rates, and that delivery times will also continue to follow the following pace (stated in probability form):

Delivery Time (months)	Probability
1	.44
2	.33
3	.16
4	.07
	1.00

Davis' current policy is to order 14 cars at a time (two full truckloads, with 7 autos on each truck), and to place a new order whenever the stock on hand reaches 12 autos.

a) What are the results of this policy when simulated over the next 2 years?

b) Davis establishes the following relevant costs: (1) carrying cost per Mercedes per month is $600; (2) cost of a lost sale averages $4,350; and (3) cost of placing an order is $570. What is the total inventory cost of this policy? **Px**

•• **F.17** Dumoor Appliance Center sells and services several brands of major appliances. Past sales for a particular model of refrigerator have resulted in the following probability distribution for demand:

Demand per week	0	1	2	3	4
Probability	0.20	0.40	0.20	0.15	0.05

The lead-time in weeks is described by the following distribution:

Lead time (weeks)	1	2	3
Probability	0.15	0.35	0.50

Based on cost considerations as well as storage space, the company has decided to order 10 of these each time an order is placed. The holding cost is $1 per week for each unit that is left in inventory at the end of the week. The stockout cost has been set at $40 per stockout. The company has decided to place an order whenever there are only two refrigerators left at the end of the week. Simulate 10 weeks of operation for Dumoor Appliance, assuming that there are currently 5 units in inventory. Determine what the weekly stockout cost and weekly holding cost would be for the problem. Use the random numbers in the first column of Table F.4 for demand and the second column for lead time. **Px**

•• **F.18** Repeat the simulation in Problem F.17, assuming that the reorder point is 4 units rather than 2. Compare the costs for these two situations. Again use the same random numbers as in Problem F.17. **Px**

••• **F.19** Johnny's Dynamo Dogs has a drive-through line. Customers arriving at this line during the busy hours (11:00 A.M. to 1:00 P.M.) either order items à la carte or on a value-meal basis. Currently 25% of meals are sold as value meals at an average contribution margin of $2.25. The à la carte meals earn $3.00 per meal but take longer to prepare and this slows the line. The following are the interarrival times that were recorded over the last 3 weeks of operation.

Interarrival Times for 500 Observations	
Time between Arrivals (minutes)	**Number of Occurrences**
1	100
2	150
3	125
4	100
5	25

In addition, the following service times for à la carte and value meals were recorded:

Customer Service Times for 500 Orders of Each Type			
Service Time (minutes)	**A la carte**	**Service Time (minutes)**	**Value Meals**
1	50	1	100
2	125	2	175
3	175	3	125
4	150	4	100

John Cottrell ("Johnny") has observed that because of street traffic the store loses all the potential customers who arrive when 4 cars are in the drive-through line (i.e., the line never exceeds four customers).

a) Simulate a 1-hour time period for the current mix of a la carte and value-meal orders. To start, assume two cars are in the line, each with 2-minute service times. Determine the number of meals served, the income from those meals, and the number of missed sales because customers go elsewhere.

b) Johnny is contemplating a reduction of $0.25 in the prices of value meals. He believes that this will increase the percentage of meals that are value meals from 25% to 40%. This will result in faster service times and fewer lost sales. Using simulation, determine if this change will be financially beneficial. Assume that the benefits will be available for 2 hours a day over a 20-day month. **Px**

••• **F.20** General Hospital in Richmond, Virginia, has an emergency room that is divided into six departments: (1) an initial exam station to treat minor problems or to make a diagnosis; (2) an X-ray department; (3) an operating room; (4) a cast-fitting room; (5) an observation room (for recovery and general observation before final diagnosis or release); and (6) an outprocessing department (where clerks check out patients and arrange for payment or insurance forms).

The probabilities that a patient will go from one department to another are presented in the following table:

From	To	Probability
Initial exam at emergency room entrance	X-ray department	.45
	Operating room	.15
	Observation room	.10
	Outprocessing clerk	.30
X-ray department	Operating room	.10
	Cast-fitting room	.25
	Observation room	.35
	Outprocessing clerk	.30
Operating room	Cast-fitting room	.25
	Observation room	.70
	Outprocessing clerk	.05
Cast-fitting room	Observation room	.55
	X-ray department	.05
	Outprocessing clerk	.40
Observation room	Operating room	.15
	X-ray department	.15
	Outprocessing clerk	.70

a) Simulate the trail followed by 10 emergency room patients. Proceed, one patient at a time, from each one's entry at the initial exam station until he or she leaves through outprocessing. You should be aware that a patient can enter the same department more than once.

b) Using your simulation data, determine the chances that a patient enters the X-ray department twice. **Px**

•••• F.21 Management of First Syracuse Bank is concerned over a loss of customers at its main office. One proposed solution calls for adding one or more drive-through teller stations so that customers can get quick service without parking. President David Pentico thinks the bank should risk only the cost of installing one drive-through. He is informed by his staff that the cost (amortized over a 20-year period) of building a drive-through is $12,000 per year. It also costs $16,000 per year in wages and benefits to staff each new teller window.

The director of management analysis, Marilyn Hart, believes that the following two factors encourage the immediate construction of two drive-through stations. According to a recent article in *Banking Research* magazine, customers who wait in long lines for drive-through teller service will cost banks an average of $1 per minute in lost goodwill. Also, although adding a second drive-through will cost an additional $16,000 in staffing, amortized construction costs can be cut to a total of $20,000 per year if two drive-throughs are installed simultaneously, instead of one at a time. To complete her analysis, Hart collected 1 month's worth of arrival and service rates at a competing bank. These data follow:

Interarrival Times for 1,000 Observations	
Time between Arrivals (minutes)	Number of Occurrences
1	200
2	250
3	300
4	150
5	100

Customer Service Time for 1,000 Customers	
Service Time (minutes)	Number of Occurrences
1	100
2	150
3	350
4	150
5	150
6	100

a) Simulate a 1-hour time period, from 1:00 P.M. to 2:00 P.M., for a single-teller drive-through.
b) Simulate a 1-hour time period, from 1:00 P.M. to 2:00 P.M., for a two-teller system.
c) Conduct a cost analysis of the two options. Assume that the bank is open 7 hours per day and 200 days per year. **Px**

•••• F.22 The Alfredo Fragrance Company produces only one product, a perfume called Hint of Elegance. Hint of Elegance consists of two secret ingredients blended into an exclusive fragrance that is marketed in Zurich. An economic expression referred to as the Cobb-Douglas function describes the production of Hint of Elegance, as follows:

$$X = \sqrt{(\text{Ingredient 1})(\text{Ingredient 2})}$$

where X is the amount of perfume produced.

The company operates at a level where ingredient 1 is set daily at 25 units and ingredient 2 at 36 units. Although the price Alfredo pays for ingredient 1 is fixed at $50 per unit, the cost of ingredient 2 and the selling price for the final perfume are both probabilistic. The sales price for Hint of Elegance follows this distribution:

Sales Price ($)	Probability
300	.2
350	.5
400	.3

The cost for ingredient 2 is as follows:

Ingredient 2 Cost ($)	Probability
35	.1
40	.6
45	.3

a) What is the profit equation for Alfredo Fragrance Company?
b) What is the expected profit to the firm?
c) Simulate the firm's profit for a period of 9 days, using these random numbers from Table F.4's top row: 52, 06, 50, 88, 53, 30, 10, 47, 99 for sales price, and 37, 66, 91, 35, 32, 00, 84, 57, 07 for ingredient 2 cost.
d) What is the expected daily profit as simulated in part (c)? **Px**

Case Study

Alabama Airlines' Call Center

Alabama Airlines opened its doors in December 2001 as a commuter service with its headquarters and hub located in Birmingham. The airline was started and managed by two former pilots, David Douglas and George Devenney. It acquired a fleet of 12 used prop-jet planes and the airport gates vacated by Delta Airlines' 2001 downsizing due to terrorist attacks.

With business growing quickly, Douglas turned his attention to Alabama Air's "800" reservations system. Between midnight and 6:00 A.M., only one telephone reservations agent had been on duty. The time between incoming calls during this period is distributed as shown in Table 1. Carefully observing and timing the agent,

▼ **Table 1 Incoming Call Distribution**

Time between Calls (minutes)	Probability
1	.11
2	.21
3	.22
4	.20
5	.16
6	.10

Douglas estimated that the time required to process passenger inquiries is distributed as shown in Table 2.

All customers calling Alabama Air go "on hold" and are served in the order of the calls received unless the reservations agent is available for immediate service. Douglas is deciding whether a second agent should be on duty to cope with customer demand. To maintain customer satisfaction, Alabama Air wants a customer to be "on hold" for no more than 3 to 4 minutes; it also wants to maintain a "high" operator utilization.

Furthermore, the airline is planning a new TV advertising campaign. As a result, it expects an increase in "800" line phone inquiries. Based on similar campaigns in the past, the incoming call distribution from midnight to 6:00 A.M. is expected to be

▼ **Table 2**   Service-Time Distribution

Time to Process Customer Inquiries (minutes)	Probability
1	.20
2	.19
3	.18
4	.17
5	.13
6	.10
7	.03

▼ **Table 3**   Incoming Call Distribution

Time between Calls (minutes)	Probability
1	.22
2	.25
3	.19
4	.15
5	.12
6	.07

as shown in Table 3. (The same service-time distribution will apply.)

Discussion Questions

1. Given the original call distribution, what would you advise Alabama Air to do for the current reservation system? Create a simulation model to investigate the scenario. Describe the model carefully and justify the duration of the simulation, assumptions, and measures of performance.

2. What are your recommendations regarding operator utilization and customer satisfaction if the airline proceeds with the advertising campaign?

Source: Professor Zbigniew H. Przasnyski, Loyola Marymount University. Reprinted by permission.

Additional Case Study

See our Companion Web site at **www.prenhall.com/heizer** *for this additional free internet case study:*

- **Saigon Transport:** This Vietnamese shipping company is trying to determine the ideal truck fleet size

Bibliography

Al-Zubaidi, H., and D. Tyler. "A Simulation Model of Quick Response Replenishment of Seasonal Clothing." *International Journal of Retail and Distribution Management* 32 (2004): 320.

Balakrishnan, R., B. Render, and R. M. Stair. *Managerial Decision Modeling with Spreadsheets,* 2nd ed. Upper Saddle River, NJ: Prentice Hall (2007).

Banks, J., J. S. Carson, B. L. Nelson, and D. M. Nicol. *Discrete-Event System Simulation,* 4th ed. Upper Saddle River, NJ: Prentice Hall (2005).

Gavirneni, S., D. J. Morrice, and P. Mullarkey. "Simulation Helps Maxager Shorten Its Sales." *Interfaces* 2 (March–April, 2004): 87–96.

Harrell, C. R., B. K. Ghosh, and R. O. Bowden. *Simulation Using Promodel.* 2nd ed. New York: McGraw-Hill (2004).

Kelton, W. D. *Simulation With Arena,* 4th ed. New York: McGraw-Hill (2007).

Law, A. *Simulation Modeling and Analysis,* 4th ed. New York: McGraw-Hill (2007).

Leemis, Larry, and Stephen Park. *Discrete Event Simulation* Upper Saddle River, NJ: Prentice Hall (2006).

Render, B., R. M. Stair, and M. Hanna. *Quantitative Analysis for Management,* 10th ed. Upper Saddle River, NJ: Prentice Hall (2009).

Robinson, S. *Simulation: The Practice of Model Development and Use.* New York: Wiley (2004).

Saltzman, Robert M., and Vijay Mehrotra. "A Call Center Uses Simulation to Drive Strategic Change." *Interfaces* 31, no. 3 (May–June 2001): 87–101.

Swain, J. J. "Software Survey: 'Gaming' Reality." *OR/MS Today* 32, no. 6 (December 2005): 44–55.

Thompson, G. M., and R. Verma. "Computer Simulation in Hospitality Teaching, Practice and Research." *Cornell Hotel and Restaurant Administration Quarterly* 44 (April 2003): 85.

van den Briel, M. H., et al. "America West Airlines Develops Efficient Boarding Strategies." *Interfaces* Vol 35, 3 (May–June 2005): 191–204.

APPENDICES

APPENDIX I   NORMAL CURVE AREAS

1.55
Standard Deviations

Area is
.93943

0   1.55
Mean   Z

To find the area under the normal curve, you can apply either Table I.1 or Table I.2. In Table I.1, you must know how many standard deviations that point is to the right of the mean. Then, the area under the normal curve can be read directly from the normal table. For example, the total area under the normal curve for a point that is 1.55 standard deviations to the right of the mean is .93943.

TABLE I.1

z	.00	.01	.02	.03	.04	.05	.06	.07	.08	.09
.0	.50000	.50399	.50798	.51197	.51595	.51994	.52392	.52790	.53188	.53586
.1	.53983	.54380	.54776	.55172	.55567	.55962	.56356	.56749	.57142	.57535
.2	.57926	.58317	.58706	.59095	.59483	.59871	.60257	.60642	.61026	.61409
.3	.61791	.62172	.62552	.62930	.63307	.63683	.64058	.64431	.64803	.65173
.4	.65542	.65910	.66276	.66640	.67003	.67364	.67724	.68082	.68439	.68793
.5	.69146	.69497	.69847	.70194	.70540	.70884	.71226	.71566	.71904	.72240
.6	.72575	.72907	.73237	.73565	.73891	.74215	.74537	.74857	.75175	.75490
.7	.75804	.76115	.76424	.76730	.77035	.77337	.77637	.77935	.78230	.78524
.8	.78814	.79103	.79389	.79673	.79955	.80234	.80511	.80785	.81057	.81327
.9	.81594	.81859	.82121	.82381	.82639	.82894	.83147	.83398	.83646	.83891
1.0	.84134	.84375	.84614	.84849	.85083	.85314	.85543	.85769	.85993	.86214
1.1	.86433	.86650	.86864	.87076	.87286	.87493	.87698	.87900	.88100	.88298
1.2	.88493	.88686	.88877	.89065	.89251	.89435	.89617	.89796	.89973	.90147
1.3	.90320	.90490	.90658	.90824	.90988	.91149	.91309	.91466	.91621	.91774
1.4	.91924	.92073	.92220	.92364	.92507	.92647	.92785	.92922	.93056	.93189
1.5	.93319	.93448	.93574	.93699	.93822	.93943	.94062	.94179	.94295	.94408
1.6	.94520	.94630	.94738	.94845	.94950	.95053	.95154	.95254	.95352	.95449
1.7	.95543	.95637	.95728	.95818	.95907	.95994	.96080	.96164	.96246	.96327
1.8	.96407	.96485	.96562	.96638	.96712	.96784	.96856	.96926	.96995	.97062
1.9	.97128	.97193	.97257	.97320	.97381	.97441	.97500	.97558	.97615	.97670
2.0	.97725	.97784	.97831	.97882	.97932	.97982	.98030	.98077	.98124	.98169
2.1	.98214	.98257	.98300	.98341	.98382	.98422	.98461	.98500	.98537	.98574
2.2	.98610	.98645	.98679	.98713	.98745	.98778	.98809	.98840	.98870	.98899
2.3	.98928	.98956	.98983	.99010	.99036	.99061	.99086	.99111	.99134	.99158
2.4	.99180	.99202	.99224	.99245	.99266	.99286	.99305	.99324	.99343	.99361
2.5	.99379	.99396	.99413	.99430	.99446	.99461	.99477	.99492	.99506	.99520
2.6	.99534	.99547	.99560	.99573	.99585	.99598	.99609	.99621	.99632	.99643
2.7	.99653	.99664	.99674	.99683	.99693	.99702	.99711	.99720	.99728	.99736
2.8	.99744	.99752	.99760	.99767	.99774	.99781	.99788	.99795	.99801	.99807
2.9	.99813	.99819	.99825	.99831	.99836	.99841	.99846	.99851	.99856	.99861
3.0	.99865	.99869	.99874	.99878	.99882	.99886	.99899	.99893	.99896	.99900
3.1	.99903	.99906	.99910	.99913	.99916	.99918	.99921	.99924	.99926	.99929
3.2	.99931	.99934	.99936	.99938	.99940	.99942	.99944	.99946	.99948	.99950
3.3	.99952	.99953	.99955	.99957	.99958	.99960	.99961	.99962	.99964	.99965
3.4	.99966	.99968	.99969	.99970	.99971	.99972	.99973	.99974	.99975	.99976
3.5	.99977	.99978	.99978	.99979	.99980	.99981	.99981	.99982	.99983	.99983
3.6	.99984	.99985	.99985	.99986	.99986	.99987	.99987	.99988	.99988	.99989
3.7	.99989	.99990	.99990	.99990	.99991	.99991	.99992	.99992	.99992	.99992
3.8	.99993	.99993	.99993	.99994	.99994	.99994	.99994	.99995	.99995	.99995
3.9	.99995	.99995	.99996	.99996	.99996	.99996	.99996	.99996	.99997	.99997

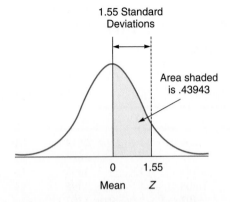

As an alternative to Table I.1, the numbers in Table I.2 represent the proportion of the total area away from the mean, μ, to one side. For example, the area between the mean and a point that is 1.55 standard deviations to its right is .43943.

					TABLE I.2					
z	.00	.01	.02	.03	.04	.05	.06	.07	.08	.09
0.0	.00000	.00399	.00798	.01197	.01595	.01994	.02392	.02790	.03188	.03586
0.1	.03983	.04380	.04776	.05172	.05567	.05962	.06356	.06749	.07142	.07535
0.2	.07926	.08317	.08706	.09095	.09483	.09871	.10257	.10642	.11026	.11409
0.3	.11791	.12172	.12552	.12930	.13307	.13683	.14058	.14431	.14803	.15173
0.4	.15542	.15910	.16276	.16640	.17003	.17364	.17724	.18082	.18439	.18793
0.5	.19146	.19497	.19847	.20194	.20540	.20884	.21226	.21566	.21904	.22240
0.6	.22575	.22907	.23237	.23565	.23891	.24215	.24537	.24857	.25175	.25490
0.7	.25804	.26115	.26424	.26730	.27035	.27337	.27637	.27935	.28230	.28524
0.8	.28814	.29103	.29389	.29673	.29955	.30234	.30511	.30785	.31057	.31327
0.9	.31594	.31859	.32121	.32381	.32639	.32894	.33147	.33398	.33646	.33891
1.0	.34134	.34375	.34614	.34850	.35083	.35314	.35543	.35769	.35993	.36214
1.1	.36433	.36650	.36864	.37076	.37286	.37493	.37698	.37900	.38100	.38298
1.2	.38493	.38686	.38877	.39065	.39251	.39435	.39617	.39796	.39973	.40147
1.3	.40320	.40490	.40658	.40824	.40988	.41149	.41309	.41466	.41621	.41174
1.4	.41924	.42073	.42220	.42364	.42507	.42647	.42786	.42922	.43056	.43189
1.5	.43319	.43448	.43574	.43699	.43822	.43943	.44062	.44179	.44295	.44408
1.6	.44520	.44630	.44738	.44845	.44950	.45053	.45154	.45254	.45352	.45449
1.7	.45543	.45637	.45728	.45818	.45907	.45994	.46080	.46164	.46246	.46327
1.8	.46407	.46485	.46562	.46638	.46712	.46784	.46856	.46926	.46995	.47062
1.9	.47128	.47193	.47257	.47320	.47381	.47441	.47500	.47558	.47615	.47670
2.0	.47725	.47778	.47831	.47882	.47932	.47982	.48030	.48077	.48124	.48169
2.1	.48214	.48257	.48300	.48341	.48382	.48422	.48461	.48500	.48537	.48574
2.2	.48610	.48645	.48679	.48713	.48745	.48778	.48809	.48840	.48870	.48899
2.3	.48928	.48956	.48983	.49010	.49036	.49061	.49086	.49111	.49134	.49158
2.4	.49180	.49202	.49224	.49245	.49266	.49286	.49305	.49324	.49343	.49361
2.5	.49379	.49396	.49413	.49430	.49446	.49461	.49477	.49492	.49506	.49520
2.6	.49534	.49547	.49560	.49573	.49585	.49598	.49609	.49621	.49632	.49643
2.7	.49653	.49664	.49674	.49683	.49693	.49702	.49711	.49720	.49728	.49736
2.8	.49744	.49752	.49760	.49767	.49774	.49781	.49788	.49795	.49801	.49807
2.9	.49813	.49819	.49825	.49831	.49836	.49841	.49846	.49851	.49856	.49861
3.0	.49865	.49869	.49874	.49878	.49882	.49886	.49889	.49893	.49897	.49900
3.1	.49903	.49906	.49910	.49913	.49916	.49918	.49921	.49924	.49926	.49929

APPENDIX II   VALUES OF $e^{-\lambda}$ FOR USE IN THE POISSON DISTRIBUTION

VALUES OF $e^{-\lambda}$

λ	$e^{-\lambda}$	λ	$e^{-\lambda}$	λ	$e^{-\lambda}$	λ	$e^{-\lambda}$
.0	1.0000	1.6	.2019	3.1	.0450	4.6	.0101
.1	.9048	1.7	.1827	3.2	.0408	4.7	.0091
.2	.8187	1.8	.1653	3.3	.0369	4.8	.0082
.3	.7408	1.9	.1496	3.4	.0334	4.9	.0074
.4	.6703	2.0	.1353	3.5	.0302	5.0	.0067
.5	.6065	2.1	.1225	3.6	.0273	5.1	.0061
.6	.5488	2.2	.1108	3.7	.0247	5.2	.0055
.7	.4966	2.3	.1003	3.8	.0224	5.3	.0050
.8	.4493	2.4	.0907	3.9	.0202	5.4	.0045
.9	.4066	2.5	.0821	4.0	.0183	5.5	.0041
1.0	.3679	2.6	.0743	4.1	.0166	5.6	.0037
1.1	.3329	2.7	.0672	4.2	.0150	5.7	.0033
1.2	.3012	2.8	.0608	4.3	.0136	5.8	.0030
1.3	.2725	2.9	.0550	4.4	.0123	5.9	.0027
1.4	.2466	3.0	.0498	4.5	.0111	6.0	.0025
1.5	.2231						

APPENDIX III   TABLE OF RANDOM NUMBERS

52	06	50	88	53	30	10	47	99	37	66	91	35	32	00	84	57	07
37	63	28	02	74	35	24	03	29	60	74	85	90	73	59	55	17	60
82	57	68	28	05	94	03	11	27	79	90	87	92	41	09	25	36	77
69	02	36	49	71	99	32	10	75	21	95	90	94	38	97	71	72	49
98	94	90	36	06	78	23	67	89	85	29	21	25	73	69	34	85	76
96	52	62	87	49	56	59	23	78	71	72	90	57	01	98	57	31	95
33	69	27	21	11	60	95	89	68	48	17	89	34	09	93	50	44	51
50	33	50	95	13	44	34	62	64	39	55	29	30	64	49	44	30	16
88	32	18	50	62	57	34	56	62	31	15	40	90	34	51	95	26	14
90	30	36	24	69	82	51	74	30	35	36	85	01	55	92	64	09	85
50	48	61	18	85	23	08	54	17	12	80	69	24	84	92	16	49	59
27	88	21	62	69	64	48	31	12	73	02	68	00	16	16	46	13	85
45	14	46	32	13	49	66	62	74	41	86	98	92	98	84	54	33	40
81	02	01	78	82	74	97	37	45	31	94	99	42	49	27	64	89	42
66	83	14	74	27	76	03	33	11	97	59	81	72	00	64	61	13	52
74	05	81	82	93	09	96	33	52	78	13	06	28	30	94	23	37	39
30	34	87	01	74	11	46	82	59	94	25	34	32	23	17	01	58	73
59	55	72	33	62	13	74	68	22	44	42	09	32	46	71	79	45	89
67	09	80	98	99	25	77	50	03	32	36	63	65	75	94	19	95	88
60	77	46	63	71	69	44	22	03	85	14	48	69	13	30	50	33	24
60	08	19	29	36	72	30	27	50	64	85	72	75	29	87	05	75	01
80	45	86	99	02	34	87	08	86	84	49	76	24	08	01	86	29	11
53	84	49	63	26	65	72	84	85	63	26	02	75	26	92	62	40	67
69	84	12	94	51	36	17	02	15	29	16	52	56	43	26	22	08	62
37	77	13	10	02	18	31	19	32	85	31	94	81	43	31	58	33	51

Source: Excerpted from *A Million Random Digits with 100,000 Normal Deviates*, The Free Press (1955): 7, with permission of the RAND Corporation.

APPENDIX IV   USING EXCEL OM AND POM FOR WINDOWS

Two approaches to computer-aided decision making are provided with this text: **Excel OM** and **POM** (Production and Operations Management) **for Windows**. These are the two most user-friendly software packages available to help you learn and understand operations management. Both programs can be used either to solve homework problems identified with a computer logo or to check answers you have developed by hand. Both software packages use the standard Windows interface and run on any IBM-compatible PC operating Windows XP or better.

EXCEL OM

Excel OM has also been designed to help you to better learn and understand both OM and Excel. Even though the software contains 24 modules and more than 50 submodules, the screens for every module are consistent and easy to use. Modules can be accessed through either of two menus that are added to Excel. The Heizer menu lists the modules in *chapter* order as illustrated for Excel 2007 in Program IV.1a. The Excel OM menu lists the modules in alphabetical order, as illustrated for earlier versions of Excel in Program IV.1b. This software is provided on the CD-ROM that is included in the back of this text at no cost to purchasers of this textbook. Excel 2000 or better must be on your PC.

To install Excel OM, insert the CD-ROM. The CD should start automatically. If not, click on the file named Start that is on the CD. After the web page opens, click on the Software option on the left hand side, click on Excel OM (version 3) and follow the instructions. Default values have been assigned in the setup program, but you may change them if you like. The default folder into which the program will be installed is named C:\ProgramFiles\ExcelOM3, and the default name

▼ **Program IV.1a   Excel OM Modules Menu in Add-Ins Tab in Excel 2007**

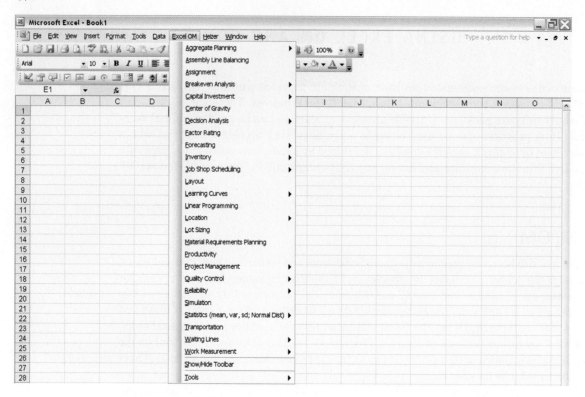

▲ **Program IV.1b**   Excel OM Modules Menu in Main Excel Menu for Versions of Excel Prior to Excel 2007

for the program group placed in the START menu is Excel OM 3. Generally speaking, it is simply necessary to click NEXT each time the installation asks a question.

Starting the Program   To start Excel OM, double-click on the Excel OM 3 shortcut placed on the desktop during installation. Alternatively, you may click on START, PROGRAMS, EXCEL OM 3. In Excel 2007 the Excel OM menu will appear in the Add-Ins tab of the Excel 2007 ribbon as displayed in Program IV.1a, while in earlier versions of Excel the Excel OM menu will appear in the main menu of Excel as displayed in Program IV.1b.

If you have Excel 2007 and do not see an Add-Ins Tab on the Ribbon or do not see Excel OM 3 on this tab as displayed in Program IV.1a, then your Excel 2007 security settings need to be revised to enable Excel OM 3. Please consult the Excel 2007 instructions on the CD-ROM or consult the support site, **www.prenhall.com/weiss**.

Excel OM serves two purposes in the learning process. First, it can simply help you solve homework problems. You enter the appropriate data, and the program provides numerical solutions. POM for Windows operates on the same principle. However, Excel OM allows for a second approach; that is, noting the Excel *formulas* used to develop solutions and modifying them to deal with a wider variety of problems. This "open" approach enables you to observe, understand, and even change the formulas underlying the Excel calculations, hopefully conveying Excel's power as an OM analysis tool.

POM FOR WINDOWS

POM for Windows is decision support software that is also offered free on every student CD. Program IV.2 shows a list of 24 OM modules on the CD that will be installed on your hard drive. Once you follow the standard setup instructions, a POM for Windows program icon will be

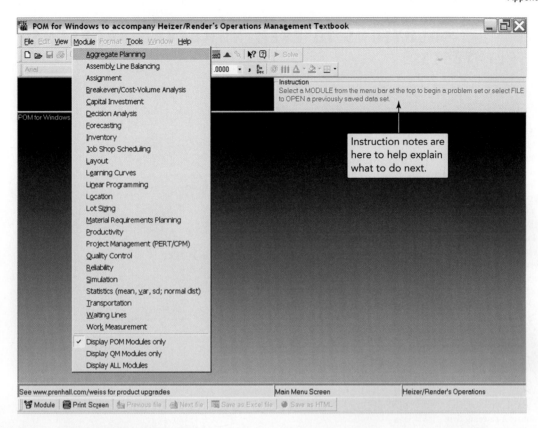

▲ **Program IV.2** **POM for Windows Module List**

added to your start menu and desktop. The program may be accessed by double-clicking on the icon. Updates to POM for Windows are available on the Internet through the Prentice Hall download library, found at **http://www.prenhall.com/weiss**.

APPENDIX V SOLUTIONS TO EVEN-NUMBERED PROBLEMS AND SELF-TESTS

Chapter 1

1.2 2 valves/hr.

1.4 Varies by site and source.

1.6 Productivity of labor: 9.3%
Productivity of resin: 11.1%
Productivity of capital: −10.0%
Productivity of energy: 6.1%

1.8 **(a)** .0096 rugs/labor-dollar
(b) .00787 rugs/dollar

1.10 Productivity of capital dropped; labor and energy productivity increased.

1.12 Before: 25 boxes/hr.
After: 27.08 boxes/hr.
Increase: 8.3%

1.14 **(a)** .293 loaves/dollar
(b) .359 loaves/dollar
(c) Labor change: 0%; Investment change: 22.5%

1.16 220 hours per laborer; 66,000 labor hours

Chapter 2

2.2 Cost leadership: Sodexho
Response: a catering firm
Differentiation: a fine-dining restaurant

2.4 The first few:
Arrow; Bidermann International, France
Braun; Procter & Gamble, U.S.
Lotus Autos; Proton, Malaysia
Firestone; Bridgestone, Japan
Godiva; Campbell Soup, U.S.

2.6 Some general thoughts to get you going:
(a) Energy costs change the cost structure of airlines.
(b) Environmental constraints force changes in process technology (paint manufacturing and application) and product design (autos).

2.8 Look at current ranking at **www.weforum.org**.

Chapter 3

3.2 Here are some detailed activities for the first two activities for Mefford's WBS:
1.11 Set initial goals for fundraising.
1.12 Set strategy, including identifying sources and solicitation place.
1.13 Raise the funds.
1.21 Identify voters' concerns.
1.22 Analyze competitor's voting record.
1.23 Establish position on issues.

3.4

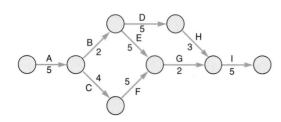

A–C–F–G–I is critical path; 21 days.
This is an AOA network.

3.6 **(a)**

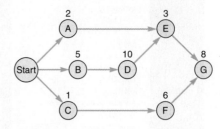

(b) B–D–E–G
(c) 26 days
(d)

Activity	Slack
A	13
B	0
C	11
D	0
E	0
F	11
G	0

3.8

3.10

3.12 **(a)**

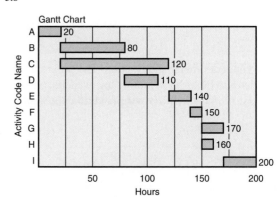

(b) A–B–E–G–I, is critical path.

(c) 34

3.14 (a)

A, 5.83, 0.69	G, 2.17, 0.25
B, 3.67, 0.11	H, 6.00, 1.00
C, 2.00, 0.11	I, 11.00, 0.11
D, 7.00, 0.11	J, 16.33, 1.00
E, 4.00, 0.44	K, 7.33, 1.78
F, 10.00, 1.78	

(b) C.P. is C–D–E–F–H–K. Time = 36.33 days.

(c) Slacks are 7.17, 5.33, 0, 0, 0, 0, 2.83, 0, 2.83, 18, and 0, respectively, for A through K.

(d) $P = .946$

3.16 Crash C to 3 weeks at $200 total for one week. Now both paths are critical. Not worth it to crash further.

3.18 Critical path currently is C–E for 12 days. $1,100 to crash by 4 days. Watch for parallel critical paths as you crash.

3.20 (a) 16 (A–D–G)

(b) $12,300

(c) D; 1 wk. for $75

(d) 7 wk.; $1,600

3.22 (a) A–C–E–H–I–K–M–N; 50 days

(b) 82.1%

(c) 58 days

3.24 (a) .0228

(b) .3085

(c) .8413

(d) .9772

(e) 24 mo.

3.26 (a)

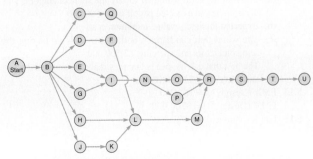

(b) Critical path is A–B–J–K–L–M–R–S–T–U for 18 days.

(c) i No, transmissions and drivetrains are not on the critical path.

ii No, halving engine-building time will reduce the critical path by only 1 day.

iii No, it is not on the critical path.

(d) Reallocating workers not involved with critical-path activities to activities along the critical path will reduce the critical path length.

Chapter 4

4.2 (a) None obvious.

(b) 7, 7.67, 9, 10, 11, 11, 11.33, 11, 9

(c) 6.4, 7.8, 11, 9.6, 10.9, 12.2, 10.5, 10.6, 8.4

(d) The 3-yr. moving average.

4.4 (a) 41.6

(b) 42.3

(c) Banking industry's seasonality.

4.6 (b) Naive = 23; 3-mo. moving = 21.33; 6-mo. weighted = 20.6; trend = 20.67

(c) Trend projection.

4.8 (a) 91.3

(b) 89

(c) MAD = 2.7

(d) MSE = 13.35

(e) MAPE = 2.99%

4.10 (a) 4.67, 5.00, 6.33, 7.67, 8.33, 8.00, 9.33, 11.67, 13.7

(b) 4.50, 5.00, 7.25, 7.75, 8.00, 8.25, 10.00, 12.25, 14.0

(c) Forecasts are about the same.

4.12 72

4.14 Method 1: MAD = .5; MSE = .085

Method 2: MAD = .51; MSE = .0721

4.16 $y = 421 + 33.6x$. When $x = 6$, $y = 622.8$.

4.18 49

4.20 $\alpha = .1$, $\beta = .8$, August forecast = $71,303; MSE = 12.7 for $\beta = .8$ vs. MSE = 18.87 for $\beta = .2$ in Problem 4.19.

4.22 Confirm that you match the numbers in Table 4.1.

4.24 (a) Observations do not form a straight line but do cluster about one.

(b) $y = .676 + 1.03x$

(c) 10 drums

(d) $r^2 = .68$; $r = .825$

4.26 270, 390, 189, 351 for fall, winter, spring, and summer, respectively.

4.28 Index is 0.709, winter; 1.037, spring; 1.553, summer; 0.700, fall.

4.30 (a) 337

(b) 380

(c) 423

4.32 (a) $y = 50 + 18x$

(b) $410

4.34 (a) 28

(b) 43

(c) 58

4.36 (a) $452.50

(b) Request is higher than predicted, so seek additional documentation.

(c) Include other variables (such as a destination cost index) to try to increase r and r^2.

4.38 (a) $y = -.158 + .1308x$

(b) 2.719

(c) $r = .966$; $r^2 = .934$

4.40 $131.2 \to 72.7$ patients; $90.6 \to 50.6$ patients

4.42 (a) They need more data and must be able to address seasonal *and* trend factors.

(b) Try to create your own naive model because seasonality is strong.

(c) Compute and graph your forecast.

4.44 Trend adjustment does not appear to give any significant improvement.

4.46 (a) $y = 1.03 + .0034x$, $r^2 = .479$

(b) For $x = 350$; $Y = 2.22$

(c) For $x = 800$; $Y = 3.75$

(Some rounding may occur, depending on software.)

4.48 (a) Sales (y) = $-9.349 + .1121$ (contracts)

(b) $r = .8963$; $S_{xy} = 1.3408$

Chapter 5

5.2 House-of-quality for a lunch:

5.4 Individual answer. Build a house-of-quality similar to the one shown in Problem 5.2, entering the *wants* on the left and entering the *hows* at the top.

5.6 An assembly chart for the eye-glasses is shown below:

5.8 Assembly chart for a table lamp:

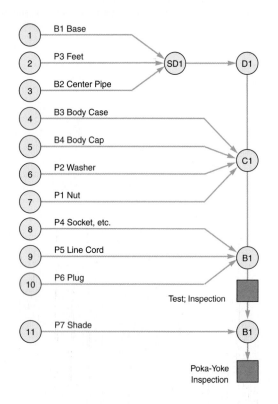

5.10 *Possible strategies:*

Notebook computer (growth phase):
Increase capacity and improve balance of production system.
Attempt to make production facilities more efficient.

Palm-held computer (introductory phase):
Increase R&D to better define required product characteristics.
Modify and improve production process.
Develop supplier and distribution systems.

Hand calculator (decline phase):
Concentrate on production and distribution cost reduction.

5.12 EMV of Proceed = $49,500,000
EMV of Do Value Analysis = $55,025,000
Therefore, do value analysis.

5.14

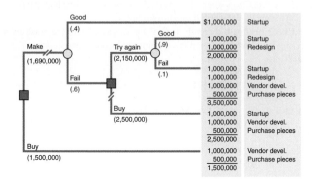

(a) The best decision would be to buy the semiconductors. This decision has an expected payoff of $1,500,000.

(b) Expected monetary value, minimum cost.

(c) The worst that can happen is that Ritz ends up buying the semiconductors and spending $3,500,000.
The best that can happen is that they make the semiconductors and spend only $1,000,000.

5.16 EMV (Design A) = $875,000
EMV (Design B) = $700,000

5.18 Use K1 with EMV = $27,500

Chapter 6

6.2 Individual answer, in the style of Figure 6.6(b).

6.4 Individual answer, in the style of Figure 6.6(f).

6.6 Partial flowchart for planning a party:

6.8 See figure on next page.

6.10 Individual answer, in the style of Figure 6.7 in the chapter.

6.12 Pareto chart, in the style of Example 1 with parking/drives most frequent, pool second, etc.

6.14 See figure on next page.
Materials: 4, 12, 14; Methods: 3, 7, 15, 16; Manpower: 1, 5, 6, 11; Machines: 2, 8, 9, 10, 13.

6.16 **(a)** A scatter diagram in the style of Figure 6.6(b) that shows a strong positive relationship between shipments and defects

(b) A scatter diagram in the style of Figure 6.6(b) that shows a mild relationship between shipments and turnover

(c) A Pareto chart in the style of Figure 6.6(d) that shows frequency of each type of defect

(d) A fishbone chart in the style of Figure 6.6(c) with the 4 *M*s showing possible causes of increasing defects in shipments

▼ *Figure for problem 6.8.*

Fish-Bone Chart for Dissatisfied Airline Customer

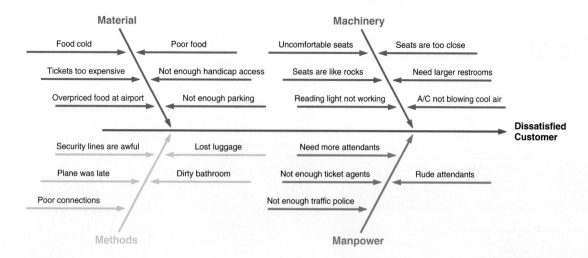

▼ *Figure for problem 6.14.*

Chapter 6 Supplement

S6.2 $\text{UCL}_{\bar{x}} = 52.31$
$\text{LCL}_{\bar{x}} = 47.69$
S6.4 $\text{UCL}_{\bar{x}} = 440$ calories
$\text{LCL}_{\bar{x}} = 400$ calories
S6.6 $\text{UCL}_{\bar{x}} = 3.728$
$\text{LCL}_{\bar{x}} = 2.236$
$\text{UCL}_R = 2.336$
$\text{LCL}_R = 0.0$
The process is in control.
S6.8   **(a)** $\text{UCL}_{\bar{x}} = 16.08$
$\text{LCL}_{\bar{x}} = 15.92$
S6.10 **(a)** 1.36, 0.61
(b) Using $\sigma_{\bar{x}}$, $\text{UCL}_{\bar{x}} = 11.83$, and $\text{LCL}_{\bar{x}} = 8.17$.
Using A_2, $\text{UCL}_{\bar{x}} = 11.90$, and $\text{LCL}_{\bar{x}} = 8.10$.
(c) $\text{UCL}_R = 6.98$; $\text{LCL}_R = 0$
(d) Yes
S6.12 $\text{UCL}_R = 6.058$; $\text{LCL}_R = 0.442$
Averages are increasing.

S6.14

UCL	LCL
.062	0
.099	0
.132	0
.161	0
.190	.01

S6.16 $\text{UCL}_p = .0313$; $\text{LCL}_p = 0$
S6.18 $\text{UCL}_p = 0.077$; $\text{LCL}_p = 0.003$
S6.20 **(a)** $\text{UCL}_p = .0581$
$\text{LCL}_p = 0$
S6.22 **(a)** c-chart
(b) $\text{UCL}_c = 13.3$
$\text{LCL}_c = 0$
(c) in control
(d) not in control

S6.24 $\mathrm{UCL}_c = 26.063$
$\mathrm{LCL}_c = 3.137$

S6.26 $C_p = 1.0$. The process is barely capable.

S6.28 $C_{pk} = 1.125$. Process *is* centered and will produce within tolerance.

S6.30 $C_{pk} = .166$

S6.32 AOQ = 2.2%

S6.34 (a) $\mathrm{UCL}_{\bar{x}} = 61.131$, $\mathrm{LCL}_{\bar{x}} = 38.421$, $\mathrm{UCL}_R = 41.62$, $\mathrm{LCL}_R = 0$
    (b) Yes, the process is in control for both $\bar{x}$- and R-charts.
    (c) They support West's claim. But variance from the mean needs to be reduced and controlled.

Chapter 7

7.2

7.4

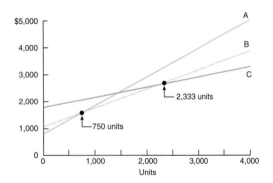

7.6 GPE is best below 100,000.
FMS is best between 100,000 and 300,000.
DM is best over 300,000.

7.8 Optimal process will change at 100,000 and 300,000.

7.10 (a)

    (b) Plan c
    (c) Plan b

7.12 Rent HP software since projected volume of 80 is above the crossover point of 75.

7.14 (a) Intermittent
    (b) $200,000

Chapter 7 Supplement

S7.2 69.2%

S7.4 88.9%

S7.6 81 chairs

S7.8 Design = 88,920
Fabrication = 160,680
Finishing = 65,520

S7.10 5.17 (or 6) bays

S7.12 (a) 6,250 units
    (b) 7,000 units

S7.14 $x = 10,000$

S7.16 (a) 12,500 units
    (b) $100,000
    (c) $350,000

S7.18 $\mathrm{BEP}_x = 25,000$

S7.20 Present equipment = $1,000 profit
New equipment = 0 profit

S7.22 (a) 50,000 bags
    (b) $125,000
    (c) 60,000 bags
    (d) $150,000
    (e) $7,500
    (f) 0.0
    (g) Indifferent at 75,000.
    (h) Manual process below 75,000.
        Mechanized process above 75,000.

S7.24 $\mathrm{BEP}_\$ = \$7,584.83$ per mo.
Daily meals = 9

S7.26 (a) $986.19
    (b) 140.9 servings

S7.28 Large line payoff = $100,000
Small line payoff = $66,666

S7.30 NPV = $20,360

S7.32 NPV = $1,764

S7.34 (a) Purchase two large ovens.
    (b) Equal quality, equal capacity.
    (c) Payments are made at end of each time period. And future interest rates are known.

S7.36 (a) $77,750
    (b) Yes, NPV = $2,274

Chapter 8

8.2 China, $1.44

8.4 India is $.05 less than elsewhere.

8.6 Atlanta = 53; Charlotte = 60; select Charlotte.

8.8 Hyde Park, with 54.5 points.

8.10 Location C, with a total *weighted* score of 1,530.

8.12 (a) Great Britain, at 36; (b) Great Britain is now 31; Holland is 30.

8.14 Italy is highest.

8.16 (a) Site 1 up to 125, site 2 from 125 to 233, site 3 above 233
    (b) Site 2

8.18 Above 10,000 cars, site C is lowest cost

8.20 (5.15, 7.31)

8.22 (a) (6.23, 6.08); (b) safety, etc.

8.24 (a) Site C is best, with a score of 374
    (b) For all positive values of W_7 such that $W_7 \leq 14$

Chapter 9

9.2 (a) $23,400
    (b) $20,600
    (c) $22,000
    (d) Plan B

9.4 Benders to area 1; Materials to 2; Welders to 3; Drills to 4; Grinder to 5; and Lathes to 6; Trips × Distance = 13,000 ft.

9.6 Layout #1, distance = 600 with areas fixed
Layout #2, distance = 602 with areas fixed

9.8 Layout #4, distance = 609
Layout #5, distance = 478

9.10 **(a)** 1.68 minutes
  (b) 4.76 ≈ 5
  (c) cleaning
9.12 **(b)** Cycle time = 9.6 min.; **(e)** There are 15 idle hours per day; **(f)** 8 workstations with 76.6% efficiency is possible.
9.14 **(a)**

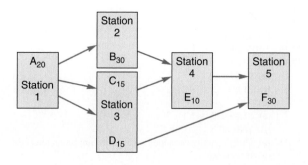

  (b) cycle time = 30 sec./unit
  (c) 4 stations = *theoertical* minimum, but 5 are needed
  (d) Station 1–Task A; 2–B; 3–C, D; 4–E; 5–F
  (e) Total idle = 30 sec.
  (f) E = 80% with 5 stations; E = 66.6% with 6 stations
9.16 **(a, b)** Cycle time = 6.67 min./unit. Multiple solutions with 5 stations. Here is a sample: A, F, G to station 1; B, C to station 2; D, E to station 3; H to station 4; and I, J to station 5. **(d)** Idle time = 5 min./cycle.
9.18 **(a)** Minimum no. of workstations = 2.6 (or 3).
  (b) Efficiency = 86.7%.
  (c) Cycle time = 6.67 min./unit with 400 min./day; minimum no. of workstations = 1.95 (or 2).
9.20 Minimum (theoretical) = 4 stations. Efficiency = 93.3% with 5 stations and 6 min. cycle time. Several assignments with 5 are possible.
9.22 **(a)** Theoretical min. no. workstations = 5
  (b) There are several possibilities. For example; Station 1–Task A; 2–C; 3–B and F; 4–D and G; 5–E, H, and I; 6–J. Or 1–A; 2–C; 3–B and F; 4–D and G; 5–E, H and I; 6–J.
  (c) $n = 6$
  (d) E = .7611

Chapter 10

10.2

Time	Operator	Time	Machine	Time
	Prepare Mill			
1	Load Mill	1	Idle	1
2		2		2
3	Idle	3	Mill Operating (Cutting Material)	3
4		4		4
5	Unload Mill	5	Idle	5
6		6		6

10.4 The first 10 steps of 10.4(a) are shown below. The remaining 10 steps are similar.

OPERATIONS CHART		SUMMARY						
PROCESS: CHANGE ERASER		SYMBOL		PRESENT			DIFF.	
ANALYST: _____				LH	RH	LH	RH	LH	RH
DATE: _____		○ OPERATIONS		1	8				
SHEET: 1 of 2		⇨ TRANSPORTS		3	8				
METHOD: PRESENT PROPOSED		□ INSPECTIONS		1					
REMARKS:		D DELAYS		15	4				
		▽ STORAGE							
		TOTALS		20	20				

LEFT HAND	DIST.	SYMBOL	SYMBOL	DIST.	RIGHT HAND
1 Reach for pencil		⇨	D		Idle
2 Grasp pencil		○	D		Idle
3 Move to work area		⇨	⇨		Move to pencil top
4 Hold pencil		D	○		Grasp pencil top
5 Hold pencil		D	○		Remove pencil top
6 Hold pencil		D	⇨		Set top aside
7 Hold pencil		D	⇨		Reach for old eraser
8 Hold pencil		D	○		Grasp old eraser
9 Hold pencil		D	○		Remove old eraser
10 Hold pencil		D	⇨		Set aside old eraser

10.6 Individual solution.
10.8

Process Chart				Summary		
Charted by *H. Molano*				○ Operation		*2*
				⇨ Transport		*3*
Date _____ Sheet *1* of *1*				□ Inspect		
Problem *Pit crew jack man*				D Delay		*2*
				▽ Store		
				Vert. Dist.		
				Hor. Dist.		
				Time (seconds)		*12.5*

Distance (feet)	Time (seconds)	Chart Symbols	Process Description
15	2.0	○⇨□D▽	Move to right side of car
	2.0	○⇨□D▽	Raise car
	1.0	○⇨□D▽	Wait for tire exchange to finish
10	1.8	○⇨□D▽	Move to left side of car
	2.0	○⇨□D▽	Raise car
	1.2	○⇨□D▽	Wait for tire exchange to finish
5	2.5	○⇨□D▽	Move back over wall from left side

10.10 The first portion of the activity chart is shown below.

ACTIVITY CHART						
	OPERATOR #1		OPERATOR #2		OPERATIONS: Wash and Dry Dishes	
	TIME	%	TIME	%	EQUIPMENT: Sink, Drip Rack, Towels, Soap	
WORK	11.75	84	11.75	84	OPERATOR: _____	
IDLE	2.25	16	2.25	16	STUDY NO.: 1 ANALYST: HSM	

SUBJECT				DATE		
PRESENT PROPOSED DEPT. HOUSECLEANING				SHEET 1 OF 1 CHART BY Hank		
	TIME	Operator #1	TIME	Operator #2	TIME	
		Fill sink w/dishes		Idle		
		Fill sink w/soap/water		Idle		
		Wash dishes (2 min.)		Idle		
		Fill sink w/dishes (1 min.)		Rinse (1 min.)		
				Dry dishes (3 min.)		

10.12 The first portion of the process chart is shown below.

PROCESS CHART		
Present Method ☐		
Proposed Method ☒		
SUBJECT CHARTED ___Printing and Copying Document___	DATE _____	
	CHART BY. __HSM__	
	CHART NO. __1__	
DEPARTMENT _____Clerical_____	SHEET NO. _1_ OF _1_	

DIST. IN FEET	TIME IN MINS.	CHART SYMBOLS	PROCESS DESCRIPTION
	0.25	○⇨☐D▽	Click on Print Command
50	0.25	○⇨☐D▽	Move to Printer
	0.50	○⇨☐D▽	Wait for Printer
	0.10	○⇨☐D▽	Read Error Message
100	0.50	○⇨☐D▽	Move to Supply Room
	0.25	○⇨☐D▽	Locate Correct Paper

Chapter 10 Supplement

S10.2 9.35 sec.
S10.4 (a) 11 sec.
 (b) 9.33 sec.
S10.6 55 sec.
S10.8 2.8 min.
S10.10 6.183 min.
S10.12 11.1 min.
S10.14 Standard time = 5.40 min.
S10.16 (a) Normal time = 3.083 min.
 (b) Standard time = 3.85 min.
S10.18 $n = 426$
S10.20 (a) 45.36, 13.75, 3.6, 15.09
 (b) 91.53 min.
 (c) 96 samples
S10.22 (a) 47.6 min.
 (b) 75 samples
S10.24 $n = 347$
S10.26 73.8%
S10.28 6.55 sec.
S10.30 (a) 240 min.
 (b) 150 hr.
 (c) Clean 8 rooms; refresh 16 rooms; 38 housekeepers
 (d) 50 employees

Chapter 11

11.2 Donna Inc, 8.2; Kay Corp., 9.8
11.4 Individual responses. Issues might include: academics, location, financial support, size, facilities, etc.
11.6 (a) $3.13
 (b) $7.69
11.8 (a) Option a is most economical.
 (b) The customer requirements may demand a faster schedule.
11.10 (a) Go with faster subcontractor.
 (b) Internal production or testing may require a faster schedule.
11.12 (a) Weeks of supply = 3.85
 (b) % of assets in inventory = 11.63%
 (c) Turnover = 13.5
 (d) No, but note they are in different industries
11.14 (a) Last year = 10.4
 (b) This year = 9.67
 (c) Yes

Chapter 11 Supplement

S11.2 Canada, 1.7
S11.4 Mexico, 3.3
S11.6 Moscow Bell, 7.1
S11.8 Insource, $X = 750,000$ units, which is less than expected demand

Chapter 12

12.2 A items are G2 and F3; B items are A2, C7, and D1; all others are C.
12.4 108 items
12.6 600 units
12.8 (a) 80 units
 (b) 73 units
12.10 2,100 units
12.12 (a) 189.74 units
 (b) 94.87
 (c) 31.62
 (d) 7.91
 (e) $1,897.30
 (f) $601,897
12.14 (a) Order quantity variations have limited impact on total cost.
 (b) EOQ = 50
12.16 (a) 671 units
 (b) 18.63
 (c) 559 = max. inventory
 (d) 16.7%
 (e) $1,117.90
12.18 (a) 1,217 units
 (b) 1,095 = max. inventory
 (c) 8.22 production runs
 (d) $657.30
12.20 (a) EOQ = 200, total cost = $1,446,380
 (b) EOQ = 200, total cost = $1,445,880
12.22 (a) 16,971 units
 (b) $530.33
 (c) $530.33
 (d) $56,250
 (e) $57,310.66
12.24 (a) EOQ = 410
 (b) Vendor Allen has slightly lower cost.
 (c) Optimal order quantity = 1,000 @ total cost of $128,920
12.26 (a) EOQ (1) = 336; EOQ (2) = 335
 (b) Order 1,200 from Vendor 2.
 (c) At 1,200 lb., total cost = $161,275.
 (d) Storage space and perishability.
12.28 (a) Z = 1.88
 (b) Safety stock = $Z\sigma = 1.88(5) = 9.4$ drives
 (c) ROP = 59.4 drives
12.30 100 kilos of safety stock
12.32 (a) 2,291 towels
 (b) 291 towels
12.34 ROP = 1,718 cigars
12.36 EOQ = 442
12.38 (a) Q = 400 lbs
 (b) $600
 (c) $600
 (d) ROP = 369.99
 (e) 69.99
 (f) $209.97
 (g) Safety stock = 61.61

Chapter 13

13.2 (a) $54,560 = total cost
 (b) $53,320 = total cost
 No, plan 2 is better than either of these.
13.4 Cost = $214,000 for plan B
13.6 (a) Plan D, $122,000; (b) plan E is $129,000

13.8 Each answer you develop will differ.

13.10 **(a)** Plan C, $92,000; **(b)** plan D, $82,300, assuming initial inventory = 0

13.12 **(a)** Cost is $314,000.
  (b) Cost is $329,000 (but an alternative approach yields $259,500).
  (c) Cost is $222,000.
  (d) Plan C.
  (e) Plan C, with lowest cost and steady employment.

13.14 $1,186,810

13.16 $100,750

13.18 $90,850

13.20 **(a, b)** Cost using O.T. and Forrester = $198,125.
  (c) A case could be made for either position.

13.22 Current model = $9,200 in sales; proposed model yields $9,350, which is only slightly better.

Chapter 14

14.2 The time-phased plan for the gift bags is:

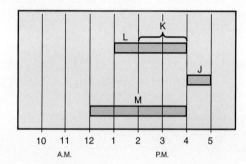

Someone should start on item M by noon.

14.4 Gross material requirements plan:

Item		Week 1	2	3	4	5	6	7	8	Lead Time (wk.)
S	Gross req.							100		
	Order release				100					2
T	Gross req.					100				
	Order release				100					1
U	Gross req.						200			
	Order release			200						2
V	Gross req.					100				
	Order release		100							2
W	Gross req.						200			
	Order release	200								3
X	Gross req.					100				
	Order release			100						1
Y	Gross req.			400						
	Order release	400								2
Z	Gross req.				600					
	Order release		600							1

14.6 Gross material requirements plan, modified to include the 20 units of U required for maintenance purposes:

Item		Week 1	2	3	4	5	6	7	8	Lead Time (wk.)
S	Gross req.							100		
	Order release					100				2
T	Gross req.						100			
	Order release					100				1
U	Gross req.						200	20		
	Order release				200	20				2
V	Gross req.						100			
	Order release			100						2
W	Gross req.						200			
	Order release		200							3
X	Gross req.						100			
	Order release				100					1
Y	Gross req.					400	40			
	Order release			400	40					2
Z	Gross req.					600	60			
	Order release			600	60					1

14.8 **(a)**

(b) For 50 brackets, the gross requirements are for 50 bases, 100 springs, 250 clamps, 250 handles, 250 castings, 100 housings, 200 bearings, and 100 shafts.

(c) For 50 brackets, net requirements are 25 bases, 100 springs, 125 clamps, 125 handles, 125 castings, 50 housings, 100 bearings, and 50 shafts.

14.10 **(a)** Gross material requirements plan for the first three items:

Item		Week 1	2	3	4	5	6	7	8	9	10	11	12
X1	Gross req.								50		20		100
	Order release							50		20		100	
B1	Gross req.								50		20		100
	Order release						50		20		100		
B2	Gross req.								100		40		200
	Order release							100		40		200	

(b) The net materials requirement plan for the first two items:

Level: 0 Item: X1	Parent: Lead Time:		Quantity: Lot Size: L4L									
Week No.	**1**	**2**	**3**	**4**	**5**	**6**	**7**	**8**	**9**	**10**	**11**	**12**
Gross Requirement								50		20		100
Scheduled Receipt												
On-Hand Inventory								50		0		0
Net Requirement								0		20		100
Planned Order Receipt										20		100
Planned Order Release									20		100	

Level: 1 Item: B1	Parent: X1 Lead Time: 2		Quantity: 1X Lot Size: L4L									
Week No.	**1**	**2**	**3**	**4**	**5**	**6**	**7**	**8**	**9**	**10**	**11**	**12**
Gross Requirement									20		100	
Scheduled Receipt												
On-Hand Inventory									20		0	
Net Requirement									0		100	
Planned Order Receipt											100	
Planned Order Release								100				

14.12 **(a)** Net material requirements schedule (only items A and H are shown):

		Week										
	1	**2**	**3**	**4**	**5**	**6**	**7**	**8**	**9**	**10**	**11**	**12**
A Gross required								100		50		150
On hand								0		0		0
Net required								100		50		150
Order receipt								100		50		150
Order release						100		50		150		
H Gross required								100		50		
On hand								0		0		
Net required								100		50		
Order receipt								100		50		
Order release						100		50				

(b) Net material requirements schedule (only items B and C are shown; schedule for items A and H remains the same as in part a.)

		Week											
	1 2 3 4 5	**6**	**7**	**8**	**9**	**10**	**11**	**12**	**13**				
B Gross Requirements			200		100		300						
Scheduled Receipts													
Projected On Hand	100			100		0		0					
Net Requirements				100		100		300					
Planned Order Receipts				100		100		300					
Planned Order Releases		100		100		300							
C Gross Requirements			200	200	100	100	300						
Scheduled Receipts													
Projected On Hand	50			50									
Net Requirements			150	200	100	100	300						
Planned Order Receipts			150	200	100	100	300						
Planned Order Releases		150	200	100	100	300							

14.14 **(a)**

Level	Description	Qty
0	A	1
1	B	1
2	C	1
2	D	1
3	E	1
1	F	1
2	G	1
2	H	1
3	E	1
3	C	1

Note: with low-level coding, "C" would be a level-3 code.

(b) Solution for Items A, B, F (on next page):

14.14 (b)

Lot Size	Lead Time	On Hand	Safety Stock	Allocated	Low-Level Code	Item ID		1	2	3	4	5	6	7	8
Lot for Lot	1	0	—	—	1	A	Gross Requirement								10
							Scheduled Receipt								
							Projected On Hand								0
							Net Requirement								10
							Planned Receipt								10
							Planned Release							10	
Lot for Lot	1	2	—	—	1	B	Gross Requirement							10	
							Scheduled Receipt								
							Projected On Hand	2	2	2	2	2	2	2	0
							Net Requirement							8	
							Planned Receipt							8	
							Planned Release						8		
Lot for Lot	1	5	—	—	1	F	Gross Requirement							10	
							Scheduled Receipt								
							Projected On Hand	5	5	5	5	5	5	5	0
							Net Requirement							5	
							Planned Receipt							5	
							Planned Release						5		

14.16 (a) Only item G changes.

(b) Component F and 4 units of A will be delayed one week.

(c) Options include: delaying 4 units of A for 1 week; asking supplier of G to expedite production.

14.18 EOQ = 57; Total cost = $1,630

14.20 $650

14.22 $455

14.24 Selection for first 5 weeks:

Week	Units	Capacity Required (time)	Capacity Available (time)	Over/(Under)	Production Scheduler's Action
1	60	3,900	2,250	1650	Lot split. Move 300 minutes (4.3 units) to week 2 and 1,350 minutes to week 3.
2	30	1,950	2,250	(300)	
3	10	650	2,250	(1,600)	
4	40	2,600	2,250	350	Lot split. Move 250 minutes to week 3. Operations split. Move 100 minutes to another machine, overtime, or subcontract.
5	70	4,550	2,250	2,300	Lot split. Move 1,600 minutes to week 6. Overlap operations to get product out door. Operations split. Move 700 minutes to another machine, overtime, or subcontract.

14.26 Here are the order releases for the table and the top:

Lot Size	Lead Time (# of periods)	On Hand	Safety Stock	Allocated	Low-Level Code	Item ID		1	2	3	4	5	6	7	8
Lot for Lot	1	—	—	—	0	Table	Gross Requirements					640	640	128	128
							Scheduled Receipts								
							Projected on Hand								
							Net Requirements					640	640	128	128
							Planned Order Receipts					640	640	128	128
							Planned Order Releases				640	640	128	128	
Lot for Lot	1	—	—	—	1	Top	Gross Requirements				640	640	128	128	
							Scheduled Receipts								
							Projected on Hand								
							Net Requirements				640	640	128	128	
							Planned Order Receipts				640	640	128	128	
							Planned Order Releases			640	640	128	128		

Chapter 15

15.2

Job	Day 1	Day 2	Day 3	Day 4	Day 5	Day 6	Day 7	Day 8	Day 9
D									
E									
F									
G									

Now

15.4 **(a)** 1–D, 2–A, 3–C, 4–B
 (b) 40
15.6 Chris–Finance, Steve–Marketing, Juana–H.R., Rebecca–Operations, $210
15.8 Ajay–Jackie, Jack–Barbara, Gray–Stella, Raul–Dona, 230.
15.10 **(a)** A, B, C, D, E
 (b) B, A, D, E, C
 (c) E, D, A, B, C
 (d) C, B, A, D, E
 SPT is best.
15.12 **(a)** A, B, C, D
 (b) B, C, A, D
 (c) D, A, C, B
 (d) C, B, D, A
 (e) D, C, A, B
 SPT is best on all measures.
15.14 **(a)** A, B, C, D, E
 (b) C, A, B, E, D
 (c) C, D, E, A, B
 (d) B, A, E, D, C
 EDD, then FCFS are best on lateness; SPT on other two measures.
15.16 1, 3, 4, 2, 5
15.18 E, D, C, A, B, F
15.20 7 employees needed; 6 have two consecutive days off. The 7th works only 3 days/week.

Chapter 16

16.2 3.75, or 4 kanbans
16.4 Size of kanban = 66; number of kanbans = 5.9, or 6
16.6 **(a)** EOQ = 10 lamps
 (b) 200 orders/yr.
 (c) $200
16.8 7.26 min.
16.10 **(a)** Setup cost = $5.74
 (b) Setup time = 8.61 min.

Chapter 17

17.2 From Figure 17.2, about 13% overall reliability.
17.4 Expected daily breakdowns = 2.0
 Expected cost = $100 daily
17.6 **(a)** 5.0%
 (b) .00001026 failures/unit-hr.
 (c) .08985
 (d) 98.83
17.8 R_s = .9941
17.10 R_p = .99925
17.12 **(a)** R_p = .984

 (b) Increase by 11.1%.
17.14 R = .7918
17.16 **(a)** .972
 (b) .980
17.18 System B is slightly higher, at .9397.

Quantitative Module A

A.2 **(a)**

Size of First Station	Good Market ($)	Fair Market ($)	Poor Market ($)	EV Under Equally Likely
Small	50,000	20,000	−10,000	20,000
Medium	80,000	30,000	−20,000	30,000
Large	100,000	30,000	−40,000	30,000
Very large	300,000	25,000	−160,000	55,000

 (b) Maximax: Build a very large station.
 (c) Maximin: Build a small station.
 (d) Equally likely: Build a very large station.
 (e)

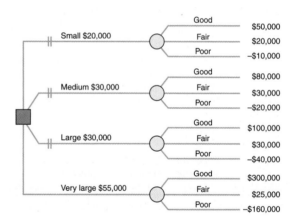

A.4 **(a)** Alternatives: N, M, L, D. States of nature: Fixed, Slight Increase, Major Increase
 (b) Use maximin criterion. No floor space (*N*).
A.6 Buying equipment at $733,333
A.8 **(a)** E(cost full-time) = $520
 E(cost part-timers) = $475
A.10 Alternative B; 74
A.12 8 cases; EMV = $352.50
A.14 **(a)**

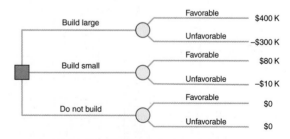

 (b) Small plant with EMV = $26,000
 (c) EVPI = $134,000

A.16 (a) Max EMV = $11,700

(b) EVPI = $13,200 − $11,700 = $1,500

A.18

A.20 No information and build large; $4,500.

A.22 (b) EMV(Y) = 4.2, which is best

Quantitative Module B

B.2 Profit = $100 at X = 0, Y = 10

B.4 (b) Yes; P = $3,000 at (75, 75) and (50, 150)

B.6 (a) Min $X_1 + 2X_2$

$X_1 + X_2 \geq 40$

$2X_1 + 4X_2 \geq 60$

$x_1 \leq 15$

(b) Cost = $.65 at (15, 25)

(c) 65¢

B.8 $x_1 = 200, x_2 = 0$, profit = $18,000

B.10 10 Alpha 4s, 24 Beta 5s, profit = $55,200

B.12 (a) $x_1 = 25.71, x_2 = 21.43$

(b) Cost = $68.57

B.14 (a) $x_1 = 7.95, x_2 = 5.95, x_3 = 12.6, P = \$143.76$

(b) No unused time

(c) 26¢

(d) $7.86

B.16 (a) Let X_{ij} = number of students bused from sector i to school j.

Objective: minimize total travel miles =

$$5X_{AB} + 8X_{AC} + 6X_{AE}$$
$$+ \; 0X_{BB} + 4X_{BC} + 12X_{BE}$$
$$+ \; 4X_{CB} + 0X_{CC} + 7X_{CE}$$
$$+ \; 7X_{DB} + 2X_{DC} + 5X_{DE}$$
$$+ 12X_{EB} + 7X_{EC} + 0X_{EE}$$

Subject to:

$X_{AB} + X_{AC} + X_{AE} = 700$ (number of students in sector A)

$X_{BB} + X_{BC} + X_{BE} = 500$ (number students in sector B)

$X_{CB} + X_{CC} + X_{CE} = 100$ (number of students in sector C)

$X_{DB} + X_{DC} + X_{DE} = 800$ (number of students in sector D)

$X_{EB} + X_{EC} + X_{EE} = 400$ (number of students in sector E)

$X_{AB} + X_{BB} + X_{CB} + X_{DB} + X_{EB} \leq 900$ (school B capacity)

$X_{AC} + X_{BC} + X_{CC} + X_{DC} + X_{EC} \leq 900$ (school C capacity)

$X_{AE} + X_{BE} + X_{CE} + X_{DE} + X_{EE} \leq 900$ (school E capacity)

(b) Solution: $X_{AB} = 400$

$X_{AE} = 300$

$X_{BB} = 500$

$X_{CC} = 100$

$X_{DC} = 800$

$X_{EE} = 400$

Distance = 5,400 "student miles"

B.18 Hire 30 workers; three solutions are feasible; two of these are:

16 begin at 7 A.M.

9 begin at 3 P.M.

2 begin at 7 P.M.

3 begin at 11 P.M.

An alternate optimum is:

3 begin at 3 A.M.

9 begin at 7 A.M.

7 begin at 11 A.M.

2 begin at 3 P.M.

9 begin at 7 P.M.

0 begin at 11 P.M.

B.20 Max $P = 9x_1 + 12x_2$

Subject to:

$x_1 + x_2 \leq 10$

$x_1 + 2x_2 \leq 12$

$x_1 = 8, x_2 = 2$; profit = $96

B.22 $x_1 = 14, x_2 = 33$, cost = 221

B.24 5 corner points

B.26 (a) Minimize = $6X_{1A} + 5X_{1B} + 3X_{1C} + 8X_{2A} + 10X_{2B} + 8X_{2C} + 11X_{3A} + 14X_{3B} + 18X_{3C}$

Subject to:

$X_{1A} + X_{2A} + X_{3A} = 7$

$X_{1B} + X_{2B} + X_{3B} = 12$

$X_{1C} + X_{2C} + X_{3C} = 5$

$X_{1A} + X_{1B} + X_{1C} \leq 6$

$X_{2A} + X_{2B} + X_{2C} \leq 8$

$X_{3A} + X_{3B} + X_{3C} \leq 10$

(b) Minimum cost = $219,000

B.28 One approach results in 2,790 medical patients and 2,104 surgical patients, with a revenue of $9,551,659 per year (which can change slightly with rounding). This yields 61 medical beds and 29 surgical beds.

B.30 Apple sauce = 0, Canned corn = 1.33, Fried chicken = 0.46, French fries = 0, Mac & Cheese = 1.13, Turkey = 0, Garden salad = 0, Cost = $1.51.

Quantitative Module C

C.2 $208

C.4 $170

C.6 (a) A–1, 10; B–1, 30; C–2, 60; A–3, 40; C–3, 15

(b) $1,775

C.8 Houston, $19,500

C.10 Total cost = $505

C.12 Initial cost = $260

Improved solution = $255

Final solution = $230

C.14 F1–W1, 1,000; F1–W4, 500; F2–W2, 2,000; F2–W3, 500; F3–W3, 1,500; F3–W4, 700; cost = $39,300

C.16 $60,900 with East St. Louis; $62,250 with St. Louis

Quantitative Module D

D.2 (a) 44%

(b) .36 people

(c) .8 people

(d) .53 min.

(e) 1.2 min.

D.4 (a) .5
(b) .5
(c) 1
(d) .5
(e) .05 hr.
(f) .1 hr.

D.6 (a) .667
(b) .667 min.
(c) 1.33

D.8 (a) .375
(b) 1.6 hr. (or .2 days)
(c) .225
(d) 0.141, 0.053, 0.020, 0.007

D.10 (a) 2.25
(b) .75
(c) .857 min. (.014 hr.)
(d) .64 min. (.011 hr.)
(e) 42%, 32%, 24%

D.12 (a) 6 trucks
(b) 12 min.
(c) .857
(d) .54
(e) $1,728/day
(f) Yes, save $3,096 in the first year.

D.14 (a) .075 hrs (4.5 min.)
(b) 1.125 people
(c) .0083 hrs (0.5 min.), 0.083 people

D.16 (a) .113 hr. = 6.8 min.
(b) 1.13 cars

D.18 (a) .05
(b) .743
(c) .793

D.20 3, 2, 4 MDs, respectively

D.22 (a) 4 servers
(b) 6 servers
(c) $109
(d) 83.33%

D.24 2 salespeople ($340)

Quantitative Module E

E.2 (a) 507 min.
(b) 456 min.
(c) 410 min.
(d) 369 min.

E.4 (a) 1,546 min.
(b) 2,872 min.
(c) 3,701 min.
(d) 6,779 min.

E.6 (a) 14.31 hr.
(b) $71,550
(c) $947,250

E.8 (a) 80%
(b) 3.51
(c) 3.2, 2.98, 2.81
(d) 21.5

E.10 (a) 72.2 hr.
(b) 60.55 hr.
(c) 41.47 hr.

E.12 Torri will take 3.67 hr. and Julie 2.43 hr. Neither trainee will reach 1 hr. by the 10th unit.

E.14 $748,240 for fourth, $709,960 for fifth, $679,960 for sixth

E.16 (a) 70 millicents/bit
(b) 8.2 millicents/bit

E.18 26,755 hr.

E.20 (a) 32.98 hr., 49.61 hr.
(b) Initial quote is high.

E.22 (a) Four boats can be completed.
(b) Five boats can be completed.

E.24 .227 hours

Quantitative Module F

F.2 0, 0, 0, 0, 0, 0, 0, 2, 0, 2

F.4 Profits = 20, −15, 20, 17.50, 20; average equals 12.50.

F.6 At the end of 5 min., two checkouts are still busy and one is available.

F.8

Arrivals	Arrival Time	Service Time	Departure Time
1	11:01	3	11:04
2	11:04	2	11:06
3	11:06	2	11:08
4	11:07	1	11:09

F.10 (a, b)

No. Cars	Prob.	Cum. Prob.	R.N. Interval
3 or fewer	0	0	—
4	.10	.10	01 through 10
5	.15	.25	11 through 25
6	.25	.50	26 through 50
7	.30	.80	51 through 80
8	.20	1.00	81 through 00
9 or more	0	—	—

(c) Average no. arrivals/hr. = 105/15 = 7 cars

F.12 Each simulation will differ. Using random numbers from right-hand column of the random number table, reading top to bottom, in the order used, results in a $9.20 cost. This is greater than the $6.65 in Example F3.

F.14 (a) 5 times
(b) 6.95 times; yes
(c) 7.16 heaters

F.16 (a) Expected average demand is about 8.75, average lead time is 1.86, average end inventory = 6.50, average lost sales = 4.04. Values and costs will vary with different sets of random numbers.
(b) $520,110, or $21,671 per month

F.18 Total stockout cost = $80; total holding cost = $40; so total cost = $120 with ROP = 4 vs. total cost = $223 with ROP = 2 in Problem F.17. Weekly costs are found by dividing by 10.

F.20 Here are the random-number intervals for the first two departments. Random number intervals correspond to probability of occurrence.

From	To	R.N. Interval
Initial exam	X-ray	01 through 45
	OR	46 through 60
	Observ.	61 through 70
	Out	71 through 00

From	To	R.N. Interval
X-ray	OR	01 through 10
	Cast	11 through 35
	Observ.	36 through 70
	Out	71 through 00

Each simulation will produce different results. Some will indeed show a person entering X-ray twice.

F.22 (a) Profit = 30 (sales price) − $1,250 − 36 (ingredient 2 cost)
(b) Expected profit = $7,924/day
(d) Expected profit from simulation = $7,770/day

CD Tutorial 1

T1.2 5.45; 4.06

T1.4 (a) .2743; (b) .5

T1.6 .1587; .2347; .1587

T1.8 (a) .0548;
(b) .6554;
(c) .6554;
(d) .2119

CD Tutorial 2

T2.2 (selected values)

Fraction Defective	Mean of Poisson	P(x ≤ 1)
.01	.05	.999
.05	.25	.974
.10	.50	.910
.30	1.50	.558
.60	3.00	.199
1.00	5.00	.040

T2.4 The plan meets neither the producer's nor the consumer's requirement.

CD Tutorial 3

T3.2 (a) $x_1 + 4x_2 + s_1 = 24$
$x_1 + 2x_2 + s_2 = 16$
(b) See the steps in the tutorial.
(c) Second tableau:

c_j	Mix	x_1	x_2	s_1	s_2	Qty.
9	x_2	.25	1	.25	0	6
0	s_2	.50	0	−.50	1	4
	z_j	2.25	9	2.25	0	54
	$c_j − z_j$	.75	0	−2.25	0	

(d) $x_1 = 8$, $x_2 = 4$, Profit = $60

T3.4 Basis for 1st tableau:
$A_1 = 80$
$A_2 = 75$

Basis for 2nd tableau:
$A_1 = 55$
$x_1 = 25$

Basis for 3rd tableau:
$x_1 = 14$
$x_2 = 33$

Cost = 221 at optimal solution

T3.6 (a) x_1
(b) A_1

CD Tutorial 4

T4.2 Cost = $980; 1–A = 20; 1–B = 50; 2–C = 20; 2–Dummy = 30; 3–A = 20; 3–C = 40

T4.4 Total = 3,100 mi.; Morgantown–Coaltown = 35; Youngstown–Coal Valley = 30; Youngstown–Coaltown = 5; Youngstown–Coal Junction = 25; Pittsburgh–Coaltown = 5; Pittsburgh–Coalsburg = 20

T4.6 (a) Using VAM, cost = 635; A–Y = 35; A–Z = 20; B–W = 10; B–X = 20; B–Y = 15; C–W = 30.
(b) Using MODI, cost is also 635 (i.e., initial solution was optimal). An *alternative* optimal solution is A–X = 20; A–Y = 15; A–Z = 20; B–W = 10; B–Y = 35; C–W = 30.

CD Tutorial 5

T5.2 (a) $I_{13} = 12$
(b) $I_{35} = 7$
(c) $I_{51} = 4$

T5.4 (a) Tour: 1–2–4–5–7–6–8–3–1; 37.9 mi.
(b) Tour: 4–5–7–1–2–3–6–8–4; 39.1 mi.

T5.6 Vehicle 1: Tour 1–2–4–3–5–1 = $134
Vehicle 2: Tour 1–6–10–9–8–7–1 = $188

T5.8 The cost matrix is shown below:

	1	2	3	4	5	6	7	8
1	—	107.26	118.11	113.20	116.50	123.50	111.88	111.88
2		—	113.53	111.88	118.10	125.30	116.50	118.10
3			—	110.56	118.70	120.50	119.90	124.90
4				—	109.90	119.10	111.88	117.90
5					—	111.88	106.60	118.50
6						—	111.88	123.50
7							—	113.20
8								—

Self-Tests

Chapter 1

1. d; **2.** b; **3.** c; **4.** a; **5.** c; **6.** a; **7.** d, **8.** a.

Chapter 2

1. d; **2.** a; **3.** d; **4.** d; **5.** a; **6.** d; **7.** c; **8.** differentiation, cost, response.

Chapter 3

1. a; **2.** c; **3.** a; **4.** d; **5.** d; **6.** b; **7.** c; **8.** a; **9.** d; **10.** b.

Chapter 4

1. d; **2.** d; **3.** b; **4.** d; **5.** a; **6.** a; **7.** simple regression has only one independent variable; **8.** exponential smoothing is a weighted moving average model in which all prior values are weighted with a set of exponentially declining weight; **9.** spot relationships between two variables.

Chapter 5

1. d; **2.** a; **3.** e; **4.** a; **5.** b; **6.** d; **7.** a list of products in descending order of their individual dollar contribution to the firm; **8.** they all have a finite life; **9.** engineering drawings and BOMs.

Chapter 6

1. c; **2.** d; **3.** continuous improvement; Six Sigma; Taguchi concepts; empowerment; benchmarking; JIT; TQM tools; **4.** environmental procedures; **5.** check sheets, scatter diagrams, cause-and-effect diagrams, Pareto charts, flowcharts, histograms, SPC charts; **6.** f; **7.** a; **8.** inspected.

Supplement 6

1. a; **2.** a; **3.** a; **4.** b; **5.** 2 std. dev.; **6.** $\bar{x}$-chart and R-chart; **7.** producer's risk, AQL; **8.** b.

Chapter 7

1. d; **2.** d; **3.** e; **4.** a; **5.** b; **6.** e; **7.** e; **8.** e.

Supplement 7

1. e; **2.** c; **3.** a; **4.** b; **5.** c; **6.** e; **7.** c; **8.** b.

Chapter 8

1. a; **2.** c; **3.** b; **4.** d; **5.** a; **6.** factor rating, break-even, center-of-gravity, transportation; **7.** d; **8.** e.

Chapter 9

1. b; **2.** a; **3.** b; **4.** e; **5.** b; **6.** fixed, process, product, retail, warehouse, office; **7.** family of products, stable forecast (demand), volume; **8.** adequate volume, stable demand, standardized product; adequate/quality supplies.

Chapter 10

1. d; **2.** e; **3.** d; **4.** a; **5.** c; **6.** b; **7.** c; **8.** c; **9.** a.

Supplement 10

1. b; **2.** c; **3.** e; **4.** c; **5.** c; **6.** c; **7.** e.

Chapter 11

1. d; **2.** requesting/pulling rather than pushing orders through the supply chain; **3.** d; **4.** b; **5.** d; **6.** c; **7.** b; **8.** to build a chain of suppliers that focuses on maximizing value to the ultimate customer; **9.** d; **10.** e.

Supplement 11

1. c; **2.** e; **3.** b; **4.** e; **5.** b; **6.** a; **7.** c; **8.** a.

Chapter 12

1. d; **2.** c; **3.** e; **4.** e; **5.** c; **6.** b; **7.** b; **8.** b; **9.** d.

Chapter 13

1. b; **2.** c; **3.** e; **4.** e; **5.** b; **6.** b; **7.** a; **8.** b; **9.** b; **10.** e.

Chapter 14

1. a; **2.** e; **3.** a; **4.** c; **5.** c; **6.** c; **7.** e; **8.** b; **9.** d.

Chapter 15

1. a; **2.** c; **3.** d; **4.** b; **5.** c; **6.** b; **7.** longer jobs keep getting pushed back; **8.** c.

Chapter 16

1. d; **2.** a; **3.** e; **4.** overproduction, queues, transportation, inventory, motion, overprocessing, defective product; **5.** sort; simplify; shine; standardize; sustain; **6.** d; **7.** e; **8.** a; **9.** e; **10.** c.

Chapter 17

1. b; **2.** b; **3.** d; **4.** c; **5.** c; **6.** e; **7.** c.

Module A

1. b; **2.** c; **3.** c; **4.** a; **5.** a; **6.** a; **7.** b; **8.** a.

Module B

1. b; **2.** a; **3.** c; **4.** a; **5.** b; **6.** c; **7.** b.

Module C

1. c; **2.** d; **3.** b; **4.** b; **5.** b; **6.** a; **7.** b.

Module D

1. b; **2.** e; **3.** e; **4.** c; **5.** b; **6.** a; **7.** d.

Module E

1. b; **2.** e; **3.** b; **4.** e; **5.** *internal* (manpower forecasting, production scheduling, cost/budget estimation), *external* (purchasing negotiations), *strategic* (cost analysis).

Module F

1. a. Define the problem; b. Introduce the important variables associated with the problem; c. Construct a numerical model; d. Set up possible courses of action for testing; e. Run the experiment; f. Consider the results; g. Decide what course of action to take. **2.** a. Set up a probability distribution for each of the important variables; b. Build a cumulative probability distribution for each of the important variables; c. Establish an interval of random numbers for each variable; d. Generate sets of random numbers; e. Actually simulate a set of trials; **3.** b; **4.** d; **5.** c; **6.** a; **7.** e; **8.** a. no yes no no no yes yes yes no yes; b. yes yes yes yes no yes yes no no no

Note: Page numbers beginning with a T are on the CD-ROM Tutorial chapters.

I1

Note: Page numbers beginning with a T are on the CD-ROM Tutorial chapters.

I5

PHOTO CREDITS

CHAPTER 1: p. 2: Hard Rock Café, p. 3: Hard Rock Café, p. 9: Henry Ford Museum & Greenfield Village, 15: Marc Asnin, CORBIS-NY, p. 18 (left): TEK Image/Photo Researchers, Inc., p. 18 (right): John McLean, Photo Researchers, Inc., p. 19: Siemens AG, p. 24: Andreas Buck/Das Fotoarchiv, Peter Arnold, Inc.

CHAPTER 2: p. 28: Boeing Commercial Airplane Group, p. 29: Boeing Commercial Airplane Group, p. 31: Neal Peters Collection, p. 33: Kraipit Phanvut, SIPA Press, p. 38: AP Wide World Photos, p. 45: **www.HondaNews.com**, p. 49 (left): Komatsu Ltd., p. 49 (right): Louis Psihoyos, Science Faction Images.

CHAPTER 3: p. 56 (top): QA Photos Ltd., p. 56 (bottom): Bechtel Corporation, Inc., p. 57 (top): Bill Pogue/Getty Images Inc.—Stone Allstock, p. 57 (middle): Thomas Hartwell, U.S. Agency for International Development (USAID), p. 57 (bottom): Joe Cavaretta, AP Wide World Photos, p. 62 (top): Jeff Topping/Getty Images, p. 62 (bottom left): Jonathan Bailey Associates, p. 62 (bottom right): Pia Gandolfo, Jonathan Bailey Associates, p. 66: Mai/Mai, Getty Images/Time Life Pictures, p. 73: Hard Rock Café, p. 75: Paul Chesley, Getty Images Inc.—Stone Allstock, p. 82: Stew Milne, AP Wide World Photos, p. 86: David Young-Wolff, PhotoEdit Inc., p. 97 (top left): Markus Diohy, Peter Arnold Inc., p. 97 (bottom right): Paramount/Dreamworks, Picture Desk, Inc./Kobal Collection.

CHAPTER 4: p. 104 (top): Jeff Greenberg, PhotoEdit, Inc., p. 104 (bottom): Kelly-Mooney Photography, Corbis/Bettmann, p. 105 (top): Peter Cosgrove, AP Wide World Photos, p. 105 (middle): Kevin Fleming, CORBIS-NY, p. 105 (bottom): Joe Raedle, Getty Images, p. 111: Fred Prouser, Corbis/Reuters America LLC, p. 124: Yamaha Motor Corp., USA, p. 131: ICI Paints, p. 137: Anton Vengo, Superstock, Inc., p. 146: Jim Olive, Peter Arnold, Inc., p. 149: Alan Copson, **Photolibrary.com**.

CHAPTER 5: p. 156: Regal Marine Industries, Inc., p. 157: Regal Marine Industries, Inc., p. 159 (left): John Acurso, John Acurso, Inc., p. 159 (middle): Viseon, Inc., p. 159 (right): Dutch Boy Paints/Sherwin Williams, p. 162: Chris Corsmeier, Chris Corsmeier Photography, p. 168 (left): Maximilian Stock, LTD, Phototake NYC, p. 168 (middle): Silicon Graphics, p. 168 (bottom): Maximilian Stock, LTD, Phototake NYC, p. 169: 3D Systems, p. 170: Adam Opel AG, p. 171: BMW of North America, LLC, p. 172 (left): Digital Vision, Getty Images/Digital Vision, p. 172 (right): Eugene Hoshiko, AP Wide World Photos, p. 178 (left): J.R. Simplot Company, p. 178 (right): David R. Frazier, David R. Frazier Photolibrary, Inc., p. 181: Tom Lyle, The Stock Shop, Inc./Mediachrome, p. 188: Maximilian Stock LTD, PhotoTake NYC.

CHAPTER 6: p. 192: Jonathan Bailey Associates, p. 193 (top): Cardinal Health Supply Technologies, p. 193 (middle): Jonathan Bailey Associates, p. 193 (bottom): Jonathan Bailey Associates, p. 196: Koichi Kamoshida/Liaison, Getty Images, p. 197: Tim Boyle, Getty Images, Inc.—Liasion, p. 201: TRW Automobile, General Manley Ford, p. 209: Ralf-Finn Hestoft, Corbis/SABA Press Photos, Inc., p. 211: Ann States Photography; p. 216: Bill Aron, PhotoEdit Inc.

SUPPLEMENT 6: p. 222: P.L. Vidor, BetzDearborn, Inc., p. 230: Donna McWilliam, AP Wide World Photos, p. 230: Richard Pasley Photography, p. 233: Charles O'Rear, CORBIS—NY, p. 237: Georgia Institute of Technology, p. 239: Roger Tully, Getty Images Inc.-Stone Allstock, p. 246: Corbis Digital Stock.

CHAPTER 7: p. 254 (bottom left): Federal Reserve Bank of Dallas, p. 254 (top right): Dell Inc., p. 255 (top right): Dell, Inc., p. 255 (bottom left): Greg Smith, Corbis/Bettmann, p. 262: Louis Psihoyos, Science Faction, p. 272 (left): NYT Graphics, New York Times Agency, p. 272 (right): Tony Freeman, PhotoEdit Inc., p. 274: Gensym Corporation, p. 276 (top): **Photos.com**, p. 276 (top right): Getty Images Inc.—Stone Allstock, p. 276 (middle): Patrick Barta, Corbis-NY, p. 276 (left middle): Ron Sully, Omnica Corporation, p. 276 (middle bottom): Garry Gay, Creative Eye/**MIRA.com**, p. 276 (bottom right): Jim Green, Dorling Kindersley Media Library, p. 276 (bottom left): Diamond Phoenix Corporation, p. 277 (right): Kruell/laif, Redux Pictures, p. 277 (left): Orlando Sentinel Communication, The Orlando Sentinel, p. 282: Robert Michael, CORBIS-NY.

SUPPLEMENT 7: p. 288: John Garrett, Getty Images, Inc.—Stone Allstock, p. 291: Chitose Suzuki, AP Wide World Photos, p. 294 (top): Lester Lefkowitz, Corbis—NY, p. 294 (bottom): Charles Thatcher, C. Thatcher, Inc., p. 297: James Schnepf Photography, Inc., p. 299: Jack Kenner, International Paper Company, p. 302 (right): Michelangelo Gisone, AP Wide World Photos, p. 302 (left): Bob Krist, Corbis/Bettmann, p. 309: Corbis Digital Stock.

CHAPTER 8: p. 316 (top): Chris Sorensen Photography, p. 316 (bottom): AP Wide World Photos, p. 317 (top): Jon Riley/Southern Stock, Jupiter Images—FoodPix—Creatas—Brand X—Banana Stock—PictureQuest, p. 317 (middle): Matt York, AP Wide World Photos, p. 317 (bottom): Shi Li/shzq, ImagineChina.com, p. 321: Allen Tannenbaum, p. 329 (right): Jay Heizer, p. 329 (left): Monica Lewis, True Bethel Baptist Church, p. 331: MapInfo Corporation, p. 337: Carl D. Walsh, Aurora & Quanta Productions, Inc., p. 340: David Buffington, Getty Images, Inc.—Photodisc.

CHAPTER 9: p. 346: Rick Wiliking, Corbis/Reuters America LLC, p. 347: Callie Lipkin Photography, Inc., p. 347 (top): Nany Siesel, New York Times Agency, p. 349: Chuck Keeler, Getty Images, Inc.—Stone Allstock, p. 352 (top): Wal Mart; p. 352 (bottom): Hard Rock Café, p. 353: Fabian Bimmer, AP Wide World Photos, p. 354: Chris Usher, Chris Usher Photography & Associates, Inc., p. 355 (top left): Michael Grecco, Stock Boston, p. 355 (bottom left): Dick Blume, The Image Works, p. 355 (bottom right): Corbis/Reuters America LLC, p. 361: UGS, p. 366: Boeing Commercial Airplane Group, p. 370: Cary Wolinsky, Jupiter Images—Foodpix-Cretas-Brand X-Banana Stock-Picture Quest, p. 383: Jonathan Bailey Associates.

CHAPTER 10: p. 388: John Raoux, The Orlando Sentinel, p. 396 (left): Pam Francis, Southwest Airlines, Co., p. 396 (right): Southwest Airlines, p. 397: Andy Freeberg Photography, p. 398 (left): Infogrip, Inc., p. 398 (middle): SafeType, Inc., p. 398 (right): DataHand Systems, Inc., p. 399 (left): Chad Ehlers, The Stock Connection, p. 399 (right): NUFEA, Boeing Commercial Airlines, p. 406: Lynn Goldsmith, Corbis/Bettmann.

SUPPLEMENT 10: p. 412: AP Wide World Photos, p. 413: Henry Horenstein, p. 416: Choice Hotels International Inc., p. 417: Laubrass, Inc., p. 418: F. Hoffmann, The Image Works, p. 420: Jonathan Bailey Associates, p. 427: Comstock Royalty Free Division.

CHAPTER 11: p. 432: Jay Heizer, p. 433: Jay Heizer, p. 434 (left): Bill Stormont, CORBIS-NY, p. 434 (middle top): Susan Van Etten, PhotoEdit Inc., p. 434 (middle bottom): David de Lossy, Ghislain & Marie, Getty Images Inc.—Image Bank, p. 434 (middle second from top): Getty Images/Digital Vision, p. 434 (middle right): Michael Newman, PhotoEdit Inc., p. 434 (right top): Jose Manuel Ribeiro, REUTERS, CORBIS—NY, p. 434 (right middle): Peter Byron, PhotoEdit Inc., p. 434 (bottom right): Richard Levine, Alamy Images, p. 436: Goodman, Jackson & Perkins, p. 446: Ariba, p. 449: South Carolina State Ports Authority, p. 450: Francesco Broli, p. 451: Federal Express Corporation, p. 452: Boeing Commercial Airplane Group, p. 458: Thomas Raupach, Peter Arnold Inc.

SUPPLEMENT 11: p. 464: Michael Abramson, Woodfin Camp & Associates, p. 465: Keith Dannemiller, Alamy Images, p. 469: Sherwin Crasto, CORBIS/REUTERS America LLC, p. 471 (left): HHi Corporation, p. 471 (right): Timothy Hursley/The Arkansas Office, Inc., p. 472: A. Ramey, PhotoEdit Inc.

CHAPTER 12: p. 482 (middle): David Burnett, Contact Press Images, Inc., p. 482 (top): Marilyn Newton, p. 482 (bottom): David Burnett, Contact Press Images, Inc., p. 483 (top): David Burnett, Contact Press Images, Inc., p. 483 (bottom): Contact Press Images, Inc., p. 487: Deere & Company, p. 488: McKesson Corporation, p. 489: Jens Meyer, AP Wide World Photos, p. 494: AP Wide World Photos, p. 499: Anthony Labbe Photography.

CHAPTER 13: p. 526: Anheuser-Busch Companies, Inc., p. 527 (top and middle): Anheuser-Busch Companies, Inc., p. 527 (bottom): Michael Newman, PhotoEdit, Inc. p. 529: Briggs & Stratton Power Products Marketing, p. 531 (right bottom): Getty Images—Stockbyte, p. 531 (top right): OAS (National Organization for Automotive Safety & Victim's Aid), p. 531 (left bottom): Ron Sherman, Creative Eye/MIRA.com, p. 531 (second down on right): Mark Richards, PhotoEdit Inc., p. 531 (third down on right): Michael Newman, PhotoEdit Inc., p. 531 (top left): Vario Images GmbH & Co. KG, Alamy Images, p. 532: John Deere & Company, p. 541: Greg Foster, Gregory Foster, Inc., p. 553: Corbis Royalty Free, p. 555: Fernando Sanchez.

CHAPTER 14: p. 560 (top): Collins Industries, Inc., p. 560 (bottom): Wheeled Coach Industries, Incorporated, p. 561 (top left): Wheeled Coach Industries, Incorporated, p. 561 (right bottom): Collins Industries, Inc., p. 567: Dave Bartruff, Stock Boston, p. 575: John Russell, AP Wide World Photos, p. 578: User Solutions, Inc.

LICENSE AGREEMENT AND LIMITED WARRANTY

READ THIS LICENSE CAREFULLY BEFORE USING THIS PACKAGE. BY USING THIS PACKAGE, YOU ARE AGREEING TO THE TERMS AND CONDITIONS OF THIS LICENSE. IF YOU DO NOT AGREE, DO NOT USE THE PACKAGE. PROMPTLY RETURN THE UNUSED PACKAGE AND ALL ACCOMPANYING ITEMS TO THE PLACE YOU OBTAINED IT. **THESE TERMS APPLY TO ALL LICENSED SOFTWARE ON THE DISK EXCEPT THAT THE TERMS FOR USE OF ANY SHAREWARE OR FREEWARE ON THE DISKETTES ARE AS SET FORTH IN THE ELECTRONIC LICENSE LOCATED ON THE DISK:**

1. GRANT OF LICENSE and OWNERSHIP: The enclosed computer programs and data ("Software") are licensed, not sold, to you by Prentice-Hall, Inc. ("We" or the "Company") in consideration of your purchase or adoption of the accompanying Company textbooks and/or other materials, and your agreement to these terms. We reserve any rights not granted to you. You own only the disk(s) but we and/or licensors own the Software itself. This license allows individuals who have purchased the accompanying Company textbook to use and display their copy of the Software on a single computer (i.e., with a single CPU) at a single location for academic use only, so long as you comply with the terms of this Agreement. You may make one copy for back up, or transfer your copy to another CPU, provided that the Software is usable on only one computer. This license allows instructors at educational institutions [only] who have adopted the accompanying Company textbook to install, use and display the enclosed copy of the Software on individual computers in the computer lab designated for use by any students of a course requiring the accompanying Company textbook and only for as long as such textbook is a required text for such course, at a single campus or branch or geographic location of an educational institution, for academic use only, so long as you comply with the terms of this Agreement.

2. RESTRICTIONS: You may not transfer or distribute the Software or documentation to anyone else. You may not copy the documentation or the Software. You may not reverse engineer, disassemble, decompile, modify, adapt, translate, or create derivative works based on the Software or the Documentation. You may be held legally responsible for any copying or copyright infringement which is caused by your failure to abide by the terms of these restrictions.

3. TERMINATION: This license is effective until terminated. This license will terminate automatically without notice from the Company if you fail to comply with any provisions or limitations of this license. Upon termination, you shall destroy the Documentation and all copies of the Software. All provisions of this Agreement as to limitation and disclaimer of warranties, limitation of liability, remedies or damages, and our ownership rights shall survive termination.

4. LIMITED WARRANTY AND DISCLAIMER OF WARRANTY: Company warrants that for a period of 60 days from the date you purchase this Software (or purchase or adopt the accompanying textbook), the Software, when properly installed and used in accordance with the Documentation, will operate in substantial conformity with the description of the Software set forth in the Documentation, and that for a period of 30 days the disk(s) on which the Software is delivered shall be free from defects in materials and workmanship under normal use. The Company does not warrant that the Software will meet your requirements or that the operation of the Software will be uninterrupted or error-free. Your only remedy and the Company's only obligation under these limited warranties is, at the Company's option, return of the disk for a refund of any amounts paid for it by you or replacement of the disk. THIS LIMITED WARRANTY IS THE ONLY WARRANTY PROVIDED BY THE COMPANY AND ITS LICENSORS, AND THE COMPANY AND ITS LICENSORS DISCLAIM ALL OTHER WARRANTIES, EXPRESS OR IMPLIED, INCLUDING WITHOUT LIMITATION, THE IMPLIED WARRANTIES OF MERCHANTABILITY AND FITNESS FOR A PARTICULAR PURPOSE. THE COMPANY DOES NOT WARRANT, GUARANTEE OR MAKE ANY REPRESENTATION REGARDING THE ACCURACY, RELIABILITY, CURRENTNESS, USE, OR RESULTS OF USE, OF THE SOFTWARE.

5. LIMITATION OF REMEDIES AND DAMAGES: IN NO EVENT, SHALL THE COMPANY OR ITS EMPLOYEES, AGENTS, LICENSORS, OR CONTRACTORS BE LIABLE FOR ANY INCIDENTAL, INDIRECT, SPECIAL, OR CONSEQUENTIAL DAMAGES ARISING OUT OF OR IN CONNECTION WITH THIS LICENSE OR THE SOFTWARE, INCLUDING FOR LOSS OF USE, LOSS OF DATA, LOSS OF INCOME OR PROFIT, OR OTHER LOSSES, SUSTAINED AS A RESULT OF INJURY TO ANY PERSON, OR LOSS OF OR DAMAGE TO PROPERTY, OR CLAIMS OF THIRD PARTIES, EVEN IF THE COMPANY OR AN AUTHORIZED REPRESENTATIVE OF THE COMPANY HAS BEEN ADVISED OF THE POSSIBILITY OF SUCH DAMAGES. IN NO EVENT SHALL THE LIABILITY OF THE COMPANY FOR DAMAGES WITH RESPECT TO THE SOFTWARE EXCEED THE AMOUNTS ACTUALLY PAID BY YOU, IF ANY, FOR THE SOFTWARE OR THE ACCOMPANYING TEXTBOOK. SOME JURISDICTIONS DO NOT ALLOW THE LIMITATION OF LIABILITY IN CERTAIN CIRCUMSTANCES, THE ABOVE LIMITATIONS MAY NOT ALWAYS APPLY.

6. GENERAL: THIS AGREEMENT SHALL BE CONSTRUED IN ACCORDANCE WITH THE LAWS OF THE UNITED STATES OF AMERICA AND THE STATE OF NEW YORK, APPLICABLE TO CONTRACTS MADE IN NEW YORK, AND SHALL BENEFIT THE COMPANY, ITS AFFILIATES AND ASSIGNEES. This Agreement is the complete and exclusive statement of the agreement between you and the Company and supersedes all proposals, prior agreements, oral or written, and any other communications between you and the company or any of its representatives relating to the subject matter. If you are a U.S. Government user, this Software is licensed with "restricted rights" as set forth in subparagraphs (a)-(d) of the Commercial Computer-Restricted Rights clause at FAR 52.227-19 or in subparagraphs (c)(1)(ii) of the Rights in Technical Data and Computer Software clause at DFARS 252.227-7013, and similar clauses, as applicable.

Should you have any questions concerning this agreement or if you wish to contact the Company for any reason, please contact in writing: Director, Media Production

Pearson Education

1 Lake Street

Upper Saddle River, NJ 07458